Official Rules of Sports & Games 1995-96

Official Rules of Sports & Games 1995-96

Edited by Tony Pocock

HAMLYN

First published in 1949 by Nicholas Kaye Ltd
Nineteenth edition 1995 by Hamlyn
an imprint of Reed Consumer Books Limited
Michelin House, 81 Fulham Road,
London SW3 6RB
and Auckland, Melbourne, Singapore and Toronto

ISBN 0 600 58702 9

A catalogue record for this book is available
from the British Library

Phototypeset by Wilmaset Ltd, Birkenhead, Wirral
Printed in Great Britain
by Mackays of Chatham

Contents

Introduction

Now in its nineteenth edition, the *Official Rules of Sports and Games* remains the premier reference book for all engaged in sport and sports administration in schools, universities and colleges of further education. Sport continues to enlarge its frontiers to a quite remarkable extent. Popular spectator sports, such as football and rugby, are attracting ever-increasing numbers of spectators and many of the so-called 'minority sports', such as korfball, handball and volleyball, are now played at a serious competitive level. There has also been an increased interest in American sports – with softball fast becoming one of the most popular participation sports in this country.

The frequency with which most sports and games change their rules makes compiling and editing a book such as this extremely hazardous. But the reader of this new edition can be confident that it is as up to date as possible at the time of going to press and will continue to give essential information on the thirty-one sports it covers.

I must acknowledge with thanks the help given me by Ros Sanderson throughout the compilation of this new edition and the generous co-operation of the following associations. Without their permission, always readily given, to reproduce their copyright Rules and Laws, publication would not have been possible.

London, 1995 Tony Pocock

Grand National Archery Society, National Agricultural Centre, Stoneleigh, Kenilworth CV8 2LG; Football Association, 16 Lancaster Gate, London W2 3LW; British Athletic Federation, 225A Bristol Road, Edgbaston, Birmingham B5 7UB; International Badminton Federation, 4 Manor Park, Mackenzie Way, Cheltenham, Gloucestershire GL51 9TX; British Baseball Federation, 66 Belvedere Road, Hessle, N. Humberside HU13 9JJ; International Basketball Federation, PO Box 70 06 07, D-81306 München, Germany; English Bowling Association, Lyndhurn Road, Worthing BN11 2AZ; Amateur Boxing Association of England, Crystal Palace National Sports Centre, London SE19 2BB; British American Football Association, 567 King's Road, Stretford, Manchester M32 8JQ; British American Football Referees' Association, c/o Dr J. Briggs, Dept of Computer Science, University of

York YO1 5DD; Marylebone Cricket Club, Lord's Cricket Ground, London NW8 8QN; British Crown Green Bowling Association, 14 Leighton Avenue, Maghull, Liverpool L31 0AH; English Curling Association, Little Wethers, Sandy Lane, Northwood HA6 3HA; Royal and Ancient Golf Club of St Andrews, Fife KY16 9JD; British Handball Association, 40 Newchurch Road, Rawtenstall, Rossendale BB4 7QX; Hockey Association, Norfolk House, 102 Saxon Gate West, Milton Keynes MK9 2EP; British Ice Hockey Association, Second Floor Suite, 517 Christchurch Road, Boscombe, Bournemouth BH1 4AG; British Korfball Association, PO Box 179, Maidstone ME14 1LU; English Lacrosse Union, Winton House, Winton Road, Bowdon, Altrincham WA14 2PB; All-England Women's Lacrosse Association, 4 Western Court, Bromley Street, Birmingham B9 4AN; All-England Netball Association, Netball House, 9 Paynes Park, Hitchin SG5 1EH; Tennis and Rackets Association, The Queen's Club, Palliser Road, West Kensington, London W14 9EQ; National Rounders Association, 3 Denehurst Avenue, Nottingham NG8 5DA; Rugby Football League, 180 Chapeltown Road, Leeds LS7 4HT; Rugby Football Union, Rugby Road, Twickenham TW1 1DZ; British Softball Federation, 81 The Dome, Dome Way, Redhill RH1 1DJ; Squash Rackets Association, PO Box 1106, London W3 0ZD; English Table Tennis Association, Third Floor, Queensbury House, Havelock Road, Hastings TN34 1HF; Lawn Tennis Association, The Queen's Club, West Kensington, London W14 9EG; English Volleyball Association, 27 South Road, West Bridgford, Nottingham NG2 7AG; Amateur Swimming Association, Harold Fern House, Derby Square, Loughborough LE11 0AL.

THE RULES OF

Archery

Archery

Grand National Archery Society (GNAS) Laws

3. The shooting regulations as prescribed in its Rules of Shooting shall be accepted as governing the relevant branches of the sport of archery throughout the area under the Society's jurisdiction. The Rules of Shooting are the responsibility of the National Council.

4. No Regional Society, County Association, archery club or similar organisation recognised by the Society shall include in its Constitution or Shooting Regulations any provisions which conflict with those of the Society. A copy of each County Association's and Regional Society's Constitution shall be deposited with the National Council.

12. All members, affiliated clubs, associated organisations, associations, county associations and regional societies shall accept the jurisdiction of the Society and shall conform to such conditions, shooting rules and regulations as may be determined from time to time.

14. (*a*) No archer other than a member of the Society or one whose national society is affiliated to the Federation Internationale de Tir a l'Arc may compete or officiate at any of the Society's meetings or at any meeting of a Regional Society or a County Association or at a Club or Association affiliated to a Regional Society. This clause does not apply to Ladies Paramount.

(*b*) No archer other than a British National of the United Kingdom may be the holder of a British National Championship or of any of the challenge trophies offered at the British National Target Championship meetings and the Grand National Archery meeting.

(*c*) A professional archer may not hold a Championship title or challenge trophy nor may he receive any prize in connection with any tournament organised by or held under the auspices of the Grand National Archery Society or any affiliated body unless specifically offered for competition for professional archers only, not shooting in competition with amateurs.

A professional archer is one who uses his skill in shooting with the bow and arrow as a means of making his living.

Declaration of professionalism or reinstatement of amateur status shall be dealt with by the National Council at its discretion. (NB For purposes of international competition the attention of members is drawn to the Rules of Amateur Status laid down from time to time by the Federation Internationale de Tir a l'Arc.)

22. (b) (i) No archer may compete for the Championship titles of, nor shoot for, more than one Region or County during an affiliation year.

(ii) A member of an Associated Club shall shoot for the Region and County to which the club through which he pays his Society affiliation fee is affiliated.

(iii) An Individual Member, and members of Associated Organisations shall, through the Honorary Secretaries of the appropriate Region and County, notify the GNAS Secretary not later than 1st October in any year of the Region and County for which he wishes to shoot.

(iv) If, since payment of his Society affiliation fee, an archer changes his club because of a change in his private residence, and the new club is situated in a different Region or County, he may, by notifying the Society's Secretary and the Regional or County Secretaries concerned, shoot for his new Region or County, always providing that paragraph (i) above shall apply.

(v) Within the United Kingdom an archer may belong to, and shoot for, more than one club in any one given discipline in any one affiliation year; but the club through which the archer's Society affiliation fee is paid shall be the 'first claim' club. Only by agreement with that club may an archer represent another club at any Club or Inter-Club event.

The disciplines being Outdoor Target, Indoor Target, Field, Flight, Clout and Popinjay Archery.

The archer may only represent the 'first claim' club at County, Regional or National events.

Amateur Status

An amateur in archery practises the sport in any one or more of the various disciplines as a leisure pursuit.

1. He shall observe the rules of the IOC, his International Federation and his National Federation.

2. Direct financial assistance other than that approved by NOC and NAA to individual archers is not permitted.

3. Full details of amateur status and the IOC Eligibility Code, etc. are to be found in FITA Constitution and Rules.

Juniors – All Disciplines
1. A junior is under 18 years of age.
2. When junior archers are shooting individually or in groups they must be supervised by a GNAS affiliated adult member.

1. TARGET ARCHERY – Senior and Junior
A. OUTDOOR

100. Target Faces
  (*a*) The diameters of the standard faces are 122cm and 80cm.

  (*b*) (i) The 122cm face is composed of a circle in the centre of 24.4cm diameter ringed by four concentric bands the breadth of each, measured radially, being 12.2cm.

  (ii) The 80cm face is composed of a circle in the centre of 16cm diameter ringed by four concentric bands the breadth of each, measured radially, being 8cm.

  (*c*) The colours of both target faces are, from centre outwards, gold, red, blue, black and white.

  (*d*) The 122cm face when used for 10 zone scoring and the 80cm face have each colour zone divided into two zones of equal width by a line not exceeding 2mm in width. Such dividing lines shall be entirely within the higher scoring zone.

  (*e*) (i) Except between black/white and black/blue dividing lines between colours may be used. Such dividing lines shall not exceed 2mm in width and shall be entirely within the higher scoring zone.

  (ii) The line marking the outermost edge of the white shall not exceed 2mm in width and shall be entirely within the scoring zone.

  (*f*) The centre of the gold is termed the 'pinhole' and shall be marked with a small cross (x) the lines of which shall not exceed 2mm in width.

  (*g*) Tolerances (plus/minus) on target faces are permitted as follows:–

122cm – 3mm on the diameter of each scoring zone.

  80cm – 2mm on the diameter of each scoring zone.

(Reference FITA Constitution and Rules.)

101. Range Layout
  (*a*) The targets shall be set up at one end of the ground. They shall be inclined at an angle of about 15 degrees, with the pinholes 130cm (4ft 3in) ± 5cm above the ground. The height of the pinhole on a line of faces shall at all times look straight.

(*b*) Minimum spacing of target centres shall be:
Archers shooting singly or in pairs   2.5m (8ft 2in)
Archers shooting in threes   3.66m (12ft)

(*c*) Each target boss shall be securely anchored so that it cannot blow off its stand. Likewise stands shall be anchored to prevent them from blowing over.

(*d*) All targets shall be clearly numbered. At tournaments where FITA rules do not apply, flags to indicate wind direction may, at the tournament organiser's discretion, be placed above the centre of each target. Such flags shall be of a colour easily visible and shall be placed above the centre of each target in such a manner that no part of the flag can obscure any part of the target or boss. Flags shall not be more than 30cm and not less than 25cm in any direction. Alternatively, a wind indicator flag may be placed at each end of the target line.

(*e*) The shooting line (over which the archers shall take up their shooting positions) shall be measured from points vertically below the pinholes. Tolerances on such measurements shall be as follows:–
METRIC   – up to and including 50m – ± 15cm
                – above 50m   – ± 30cm
IMPERIAL – up to and including 50 yd– ± 6in
                – above 50 yd   – ± 12in

(*f*) Shooting marks, consisting of discs or other flat markers, shall be positioned opposite the targets at the appropriate distances. The shooting marks are to bear the numbers of the target opposite which they are placed.

(*g*) Lines at right angles to the shooting line and extending from the shooting line to the target line making lanes containing one, two or three bosses may be laid down.

(*h*) A waiting line shall be placed at least five yards behind the shooting line.

(*j*) On grounds where the public have right of access an area shall be roped off to indicate that no one can pass behind the targets within 50 yards of them. Where an efficient backstop netting, a bank or other similar device (not a hedge or penetrable fence) high enough for the top of the stop as seen from the shooting line to be at least as far above the top of the target as the gold is below the top of the target, then this distance may be reduced to 25 yards. The area to be roped shall extend from the ends of the 'safety line' so that no one can pass within 20 yards of the ends of the target line, 10 yards of the shooting line and 15 yards behind the shooting line.

(*k*) All tents and other shelters shall be placed at least 10 yards behind the shooting line, maintaining adequate room for free passage of competitors and officials between the waiting line and the spectator line.

(*l*) Trade and refreshment areas shall be at least 25 yards behind the shooting line.

102. Equipment

Four types of bow are recognised.

(*a*) Bows and their accessories which conform in all respects to the following:

(i) A bow of any type may be used provided it subscribes to the accepted principle and meaning of the word bow as used in Target Archery; e.g. an article consisting of a handle (grip), riser and two flexible limbs each ending in a tip with a string nock.

The bow is braced for use by a single bowstring attached directly between the two string nocks only and, in operation, is held in one hand by its handle (grip) while the fingers of the other hand draw, hold back and release the string.

(ii) A bowstring may be made up of any number of strands of the material chosen for the purpose, with a centre serving to accommodate the drawing fingers, a nocking point to which may be added serving(s) to fit the arrow nock as necessary, and to locate this point one or two nock locators may be positioned and in each of the two ends of the bowstring a loop to be placed in the string nocks of the bow when braced.

In addition, one attachment is permitted on the string to serve as nose or lip mark.

The serving on the string must not end within the archer's vision at full draw. A bowstring must not in any way offer aid in aiming through 'peephole', marking or any other means.

(iii) (1) An arrowrest, which can be adjustable, any movable pressure button, pressure point or arrowplate and draw check indicator (audible and/or visual) may all be used on the bow provided they are not electric or electronic and do not offer an additional aid in aiming.

(2) The pressure point shall be placed no further than 4cm back (inside) from the throat of the handle (pivot point) of the bow.

(iv) A bowsight, bowmark or a point of aim on the ground for aiming is permitted, but at no time may more than one such device be used.

(1) A bowsight as attached to the bow for the purpose of aiming may allow for windage adjustment as well as elevation setting but shall not incorporate a prism or lens or other magnifying device, levelling or electric devices nor shall it provide for more than one sighting point. An attachment to which the bowsight is fixed is permitted.

(2) A bowmark is a single mark made on the bow for the purpose of aiming. Such mark may be made in pencil, tape or any other suitable marking material.

A plate or tape with distance markings may be mounted on the bow as a guide but must not in any way offer any additional aid.

(3) A point of aim on the ground is a marker placed in the shooting lane between the shooting line and the target. Such marker may not exceed a diameter of 7.5cm and must not protrude above the ground more than 15cm.

(v) Stabilisers and torque flight compensators on the bow are permitted provided they do not:

(1) Serve as a string guide.

(2) Touch anything but the bow.

(3) Represent any obstacle to other archers as far as place on the shooting line is concerned.

(vi) Arrows of any type may be used provided they subscribe to the accepted principle and meaning of the word arrow as used in Target Archery, and that such arrows do not cause undue damage to target faces and buttresses.

An arrow consists of a shaft with head (point), nock, fletching and, if desired, cresting and/or numbers. The arrows of each archer shall be marked with the archer's name, initials or insignia and all arrows used for the same end of 3 or 6 arrows shall carry the same pattern and colour(s) of fletching, nocks and cresting, if any.

Any captive arrow device is to be treated as though the arrow was non-captive.

(vii) Finger protection in the form of finger stalls or tips, gloves, shooting tab or tape (plaster) to draw, hold back and release the string is permitted, provided they are smooth and with no device to help to hold and/or release the string.

A separator between the fingers to prevent pinching the arrow may be used.

On the bow hand an ordinary glove, mitten or similar may be worn.

(viii) Field glasses, telescopes and other visual aids may be used for spotting arrows.

Ordinary spectacles as necessary or shooting spectacles provided they are fitted with the same lenses normally worn by the archer, and sun glasses, may be worn.

None may be fitted with microhole lenses, glasses or similar nor marked in any way which can assist in aiming.

(ix) Accessories are permitted such as bracers, dress shield, bowsling, belt or ground quiver, tassel and foot markers not protruding above the ground more than one centimetre.

(*b*) Crossbows which conform to the Rules and Conditions stated in Part V.

(*c*) Compound and other bows and their accessories which do not meet the requirements of para. 102a above.

(*d*) Traditional Longbows which conform to conditions specified in Part VI.

103. Separate Styles and Conditions

(*a*) Bows conforming to 102a.

(i) Free Style: As 102a.

(ii) Barebow:

(1) As 102a(i) and the bow must be free from any protrusions, marks or blemishes or laminated pieces which could be used in aiming. The inside of the upper limb shall be without trade marks.

(2) As 102a(ii) except that there shall be no attachments to the string to act as a nose or lip mark or other marks to aid finger position selection.

(3) As 102(a)(iii) except that no draw check indicator may be used nor overdraw facility as defined in 102(a)(iii)(2).

(4) The bow must be bare; therefore sights and mounted stabilisers as defined in 102(a)(iv) and 102(a)(v) cannot be used.

(iii) Traditional: As 203(*c*)

For target archery record purposes this style will be treated as Barebow style.

(*b*) Crossbows (see Part V).

(*c*) Bows conforming to 102(*c*).

(i) Unlimited – the bow must be free and held in the hand. The peak draw weight must not exceed 60 lbs. No shoot-through type of riser is permitted. The pressure point shall be placed no further than 6 cm back (inside) from the throat of the handle (pivot point) of the bow. There is no restriction as to accessories except that any sight, levelling device or draw check indicator must not be electric or electronic.

(ii) Limited – the bow must be free and held in the hand and the string must be drawn, held back and released by the fingers of the other hand. The peak draw weight must not exceed 60 lbs. No shoot-through type of riser is permitted. Restriction on pressure point is as defined in 102(*a*)(iii)(2). A level, peepsight and pressure button are permitted but a scope is not allowed. A cable guard may be fitted, a multipin sight is permitted.

Any sight, levelling device or draw check indicator must not be electric or electronic.

(iii) Bowhunter: As 203(*g*).

For target archery record and classification purposes this style will be treated as Limited style.

(*d*) Bows which are recognised in 102(*b*) and 102(*c*) *may not be used in direct competition* with bows recognised in 102(*a*) except that archers using bows as recognised in 102(*c*) may compete for the GNAS Handicap Improvement Medal under the conditions defined in

801(*e*)(iii). The allocation of any separate prize, medal, trophy or other award shall be a matter for each individual tournament organiser. Classification, handicap or other distinction shall remain the sole prerogative of the Grand National Archery Society.

104. Shooting

(*a*) Shooting, except in the case of permanently or semi-permanently disabled archers, shall be from an unsupported standing position, placing one foot on each side of the shooting line.

(*b*) (i) The order in which archers shall shoot at their respective targets shall be the order in which they appear on the target list and the drawing up of the target list shall be a matter for arrangement by the tournament organisers. Unless otherwise directed, No. 3 on each target shall be the Target Captain, and No. 4 the Lieutenant. The Captain shall be responsible for the orderly conduct of shooting in accordance with the Rules of Shooting.

(ii) The order of shooting in all Tournaments of Record Status shall rotate. For other tournaments, including Club Target Days, rotation shall be optional.

(*c*) (i) For all GNAS rounds, the two longest distances of the Metric rounds and the long Metric Rounds, six arrows shall be shot at an end. Each archer shall shoot three arrows and immediately retire and, when all on a target have shot, shall shoot three more. If an archer persists in shooting more than three arrows consecutively he may be disqualified by the Judge.

(ii) For the two shortest distances of the Metric rounds and the Short Metric Rounds, three arrows shall be shot at an end. If an archer persists in shooting more than three arrows consecutively he may be disqualified by the Judge.

(*d*) In the event of an archer shooting more than the specified number of arrows at an end the archer shall be penalised by losing the value of his best arrow(s) in the target, and such arrow(s) shall not be measured for a Gold prize.

(*e*) An arrow shall be deemed not to have been shot, if the archer can touch it with his bow without moving his feet from their normal position in relation to the shooting line. In which case another arrow may be shot in its place. If another arrow is not available he may only retrieve his misnocked arrow with the Judge's permission.

(*f*) If for any cause an archer is not prepared to shoot before all have shot, such archer shall lose the benefit of that end.

(*g*) Archers arriving late shall not be allowed to make up any ends that they have missed.

(*h*) Archers shall retire from the shooting line as soon as their last arrow has been shot except that an archer may remain on the shooting line to keep company with another archer still shooting.

(*j*) Two and a half minutes shall be the maximum time for an archer to shoot three arrows, the time to start from when the archer steps on to the shooting line. In the event of an equipment failure during a timed end a Judge may allow extra time for the correction of such failure and for the archer to shoot any remaining arrows.

Should an item of equipment other than the arrow be projected beyond the shooting line, the Judge may call 'Fast' at the conclusion of that end to permit retrieval of the item, the failure to be rectified and the archer allowed to shoot any remaining arrows before the field advances to score.

(*k*) Whilst an archer is on the shooting line, he shall receive no information by word or otherwise from anyone except the Judge or Field Captain(s).

(*l*) At any meeting no practice is allowed on the ground the same day, except that six arrows may be shot as sighters before the beginning of each day's shooting, but only after competitors have come under the Judge's orders at the Assembly. Such sighters shall not be recorded.

(*m*) If for any reason an archer is alone on a target he must notify the Judge who shall arrange for him to be transferred to another target or another archer to be transferred to join him.

(*n*) The maximum number of archers on a target shall be six.

105. Control of Shooting

(*a*) The Lady Paramount shall be the supreme arbitrator on all matters connected with the tournament at which she officiates.

(*b*) At all times, whenever shooting takes place, it must be under the control of a Field Captain.

At larger meetings a Judge shall be appointed to take charge of the shooting. Field Captains, to whom the Judge may delegate his authority, may be appointed as necessary. If a Field Captain has not been appointed previously, the Judge may appoint any experienced archer to act in this capacity.

At tournaments the Judge and Field Captains shall be non-shooting.

(*c*) The Judge shall be in sole control of the shooting and shall resolve all disputes (subject to the supreme authority of the Lady Paramount) in accordance with the Rules of Shooting.

(*d*) The Judge shall give the signal for assembly 15 minutes before the time appointed for shooting, and shall give the signal to start shooting. The Judge shall indicate when each end is completed, and no archer shall advance from the shooting line before receiving the signal.

(*e*) The Judge shall be responsible for deciding the value of all doubtful arrows when called by a Target Captain.

If an arrow or target face has been touched beforehand, other than by the Judge, the arrow shall be ineligible for the higher value.

(*f*) The Judge shall be responsible for measuring arrows for the purpose of Gold prizes.

(*g*) The Judge shall be empowered to disqualify any archer if he observes any breach of the Shooting Rules or has any such breach reported to him by the Field Captain or by a Target Captain.

(*h*) The Judge may exchange, if shooting is being delayed by two slow archers on the same target, one of the slow archers with a quicker one from another target.

(*j*) The Judge may order the replacement of a faulty target, or may move the archers to another one.

(*k*) The Judge, in consultation with the Secretary or Organiser, shall be responsible for deciding the duration of intervals for meals, refreshments or suspension of shooting due to weather conditions, accidents or like occurrences – and further, make any other arrangement as needed in each case.

(*l*) The Judge shall exercise control over the use of loudspeakers and photographers and the presence of other spectators so that the comfort and concentration of competitors is not disturbed. Spectators shall not go up to targets except with the permission of the Judge.

(*m*) At FITA Star Tournaments and World Record Status Tournaments there shall be an initial equipment inspection. At other FITA Round Tournaments an archer's equipment shall be liable to inspection at any time.

(*n*) No archer may draw his bow, with or without an arrow, except when standing on the shooting line. If an arrow is used, the archer shall aim towards the targets but only after being satisfied that the field is clear both in front of and behind the targets. If an archer, while drawing his bow with an arrow before the shooting starts or during breaks between distances, looses an arrow, intentionally or otherwise, such an arrow shall count as part of the next end of scoring arrows to be shot. The scorer shall make a note to this effect on the archer's scoresheet and enter the values of all hits for that end (3 or 6 arrows as the case may be), but the highest scoring arrow will be forfeited. This also applies to sighter arrows shot before or after the signal indicating the $2\frac{1}{2}$ minutes allowed to shoot an end of three arrows. Such action must be initialled by a Judge and the archer concerned.

(*p*) Archers, other than those actually shooting or moving to and from the shooting line, shall remain behind the waiting line.

(*q*) Any necessary interpretation of these rules or any decision on an occurrence not covered in these rules shall be made by the Judge.

106. Scoring

(*a*) The scoring points for hits on the target face for GNAS Rounds are: Gold 9, Red 7, Blue 5, Black 3, White 1.

The scoring points for hits on the target face for Metric Rounds are: Inner Gold 10, Outer Gold 9, Inner Red 8, Outer Red 7, Inner Blue 6, Outer Blue 5, Inner Black 4, Outer Black 3, Inner White 2, Outer White 1.

The value shall be determined by the position of the arrow shaft.

(*b*) Archers shall identify their arrows by pointing at the nocks. Neither the arrow nor the target face shall be touched until the final decision as to the score has been given and any such interference with the target or arrow shall disqualify the archer from scoring the higher value.

At record status tournaments it will be mandatory to adopt a system of scoring which prevents any archer being the sole recorder of their own score. Approved systems of scoring to achieve this are included in Part 1 of Appendix G. At all other events, including club target days, the approved systems in Part 1 of Appendix G are recommended, and it is mandatory to use at least the system shown in Part 2 of Appendix G. All scores must be recorded in a permanent blue or black medium i.e. not pencil or erasable ball-point. Misses are to be recorded as a cross (X).

(*c*) If an arrow touches two colours or any dividing line it shall be scored as being of that of the higher value.

(*d*) If any doubt or dispute shall arise it shall be decided by the Target Captain subject to appeal to the Judge.

(*e*) Any alteration to the recorded score must be initialled by the Judge in a different coloured ink prior to the withdrawal of the arrow from the target.

No arrows shall be withdrawn from the target (without the express direction of the Captain) until all the archers' scores have been entered on the score sheet and the Captain is satisfied that they are correctly entered.

(*f*) If an arrow is observed to rebound from a target, the archer concerned shall draw the attention of the Judge to the fact after having shot his sixth arrow (or third if shooting in ends of 3 only) by retiring two paces from the shooting line and holding his bow above his head.

Upon the Judge satisfying himself that the claim is justified, the archer shall be permitted to shoot another arrow separately in the same end after all archers on that target have completed their normal shooting, such arrow to be numbered or preferably marked by the Judge.

To prevent frivolous rebound claims, the archer is to be warned individually that if six original arrows were shot not including a rebound, then his highest scoring arrow may, at the discretion of the Judge on repetition of a false claim, be deducted from that end's score. The Judge shall take part in that competitor's scoring to ensure that only the correct number of arrows are scored, and that the rebound was not caused by striking another arrow already in the target. An arrow passing through a boss cannot be scored.

(g) An arrow passing through the target face but remaining in the boss shall be withdrawn by the Captain or Lieutenant and shall be inserted from the back in the same place and at the assumed angle of original penetration until the pile is visible in the target face, when the score shall be determined.

(h) An arrow hitting and remaining embedded in another arrow shall be scored the same as the arrow struck.

(j) An arrow in the target, which has or may have been deflected by another arrow already in the target, shall be scored according to the position of its shaft in the target face.

(k) An arrow on the ground believed to have hit and rebounded from another arrow shall be scored the value of the struck arrow, if the latter is found in the target with its nock damaged in a compatible manner.

(l) If an arrow fails to enter the boss and is hanging in the target face, it shall be pushed in by the Judge or shall be removed and the Judge will ensure that the appropriate score is recorded when scoring takes place.

(m) The FITA Rule that rebounds shall only be scored if arrow holes on the target face are marked applies to all FITA/Metric Rounds shot including those shot at Club Target Days, intercounty matches, etc. (see 108(e)).

(n) An archer may delegate another archer on the same target to record his score and pick up his arrows.

(p) An incapacitated archer may nominate an assistant, who shall be under the control and discipline of the Judge, to record his score and pick up his arrows.

(q) In the event of a tie for a score prize the winner shall be the one of those who tie who has the greatest number of hits. Should this result in a tie the prize shall be awarded to the archer among those who tie who has the greatest number of Golds. Should this number also be the same the archers shall be declared joint winners. Where the prize is for (i) most hits, or (ii) most Golds, ties shall be resolved on the above principle in the following order (i) highest score, most Golds, (ii) highest score, most hits.

(r) When a shoot (other than the annual Grand National Archery Meeting and the UK National Target Championship) is abandoned due to adverse weather conditions, the placings and prizes shall be awarded on the cumulative score at the conclusion of the last full end shot by the competitors, by instruction of the Judge.

107. Dress Regulation

(a) At all tournaments with National Record Status (including FITA Star tournaments) members of the Society shooting and officiating are required to wear the accepted dress of the Society.

(b) (i) Ladies are required to wear a dress or skirt or trousers or shorts with suitable top (not strapless or beachwear).

(ii) Gentlemen are required to wear trousers or shorts with long or short sleeved shirts.

(iii) Sweaters/cardigans/blazers may be worn.

(iv) Each garment shall be plain dark green or white. There is no objection to wearing green and white garments together.

(v) Waterproof clothing worn only during inclement weather is not subject to these regulations, but both white and green waterproofs are available and are recommended.

(c) Footwear must be worn at all times during the tournament.

(d) Advertising material must not be carried or worn except in conformity with FITA rules. The name/emblem of an archer's Country, Regional or County Association or Club may be worn on the uniform or shooting clothes.

(e) Any archer not conforming to the above regulations shall be requested by the Judge and Organiser to leave the shooting line and will not be permitted to shoot.

(f) At National tournaments where there is a Home Nations team competition incorporated, nominated members of the teams will be permitted to wear the dress of their home Nation (i.e. England, Wales, Scotland or N. Ireland) as approved by their organisation.

108. Recognised Rounds for Record, Handicap and Classification Purposes.

(a) The following rounds are recognised by the Society:

(i) Dozens of arrows at each distance

(b) Rounds for National Records Purposes:

(i) The following table allows archers to establish which of the rounds in Tables 108(a)(i) and (ii) may be shot for record purposes.

(ii) Single round records may be claimed for all rounds specified in Tables 108(a)(i) and (ii) subject to restrictions given in 108(b)(i).

(iii) Double round records may be claimed for rounds marked ★ in Tables 108(a)(i) and (ii) subject to restrictions given in 108(b)(i).

(iv) Distance records may be claimed when shot during the following complete rounds subject to restrictions given in 108(b)(i): FITA (Gentlemen), FITA (Ladies), Metrics I, II, III and IV.

(v) See Part VII for regulations governing record claims.

(c) Rounds for Handicap and Classification Purposes:

TARGET – OUTDOOR
Dozens of arrows at each distance

Outdoor – GNAS ROUNDS (5 Zone Scoring)

See 108 (b) (i)	See 108 (b) (iii)	Round	122 cm FACE						
			100Y	80Y	60Y	50Y	40Y	30Y	20Y
A	★	York	6	4	2				
A	★	Hereford		6	4	2			
C	★	Bristol I		6	4	2			
D	★	Bristol II			6	4	2		
E	★	Bristol III				6	4	2	
F	★	Bistol IV					6	4	2
A		St. George	3	3	3				
A		Albion		3	3	3			
A		Windsor			3	3	3		
D		Short Windsor				3	3	3	
E		Junior Windsor					3	3	3
A		New Western	4	4					
A		Long Western		4	4				
A		Western			4	4			
D		Short Western				4	4		
E		Junior Western					4	4	
F		Short Junior Western						4	4
A	★	American			$2\frac{1}{2}$	$2\frac{1}{2}$	$2\frac{1}{2}$		
E		St. Nicholas					4	3	
A		New National	4	2					
A		Long National		4	2				
A		National			4	2			
D		Short National				4	2		
E		Junior National					4	2	
F		Short Junior National						4	2

TARGET – OUTDOOR
Dozens of arrows at each distance

Outdoor – GNAS ROUNDS (5 Zone Scoring)

See 108 (b) (i)	See 108 (b) (iii)	Round	122 cm FACE								
			100Y	80Y	60Y	50Y	40Y	30Y	20Y	15Y	10Y
A		New Warwick	2	2							
A		Long Warwick		2	2						
A		Warwick			2	2					
D		Short Warwick				2	2				
E		Junior Warwick					2	2			
F		Short Junior Warwick						2	2		
—		Bristol V							6	4	2

TARGET – OUTDOOR

Dozens of arrows at each distance

Outdoor – METRIC ROUNDS (10 Zone Scoring)

Round	122cm FACE								80cm FACE						See 108(b)(iii)	See 108(b)(i)
	90m	70m	60m	50m	40m	30m	20m	15m	50m	40m	30m	20m	10m	5m		
Metric V							3	3					3	3		—
Long Metric V							3	3								—
Short Metric V													3	3		—
Half FITA (Gentlemen)	1½	1½							1½		1½					—
Half FITA (Ladies)/Half Metric I		1½	1½						1½		1½					—
Half Metric II			1½	1½						1½	1½					—
Half Metric III				1½	1½						1½	1½				—
Half Metric IV					1½	1½						1½	1½			—
Half Metric V						1½	1½						1½	1½		—
FITA Standard Bow				3		3										—

	Group Letters as shown in Tables 108(a)(i) and (ii)					
	A	B	C	D	E	F
Gentlemen	●					
Ladies	●	●				
Junior Gentlemen U-18	●	●	●			
Junior Gentlemen U-16	●	●	●	●		
Junior Gentlemen U-14	●	●	●	●	●	
Junior Gentlemen U-12	●	●	●	●	●	●
Junior Ladies U-18	●	●	●	●		
Junior Ladies U-16	●	●	●	●	●	
Junior Ladies U-13	●	●	●	●	●	●

(i) All rounds in Tables 108(a)(i) and (ii) may be shot by any archer irrespective of age.

(ii) See GNAS Handicap and Classification Tables for regulations governing the Handicap and Classification schemes.

(iii) See Part VIII for regulations governing the GNAS Handicap Improvement Medal.

(d) In every round the longer or longest distance is shot first and the shorter or shortest distance last.

(e) (i) When FITA/Metric rounds as stated in Table 108(a)(ii) are shot, FITA Rules apply subject to minimum standards given in 108(e)(ii).

(ii) Minimum standards (at the organiser's discretion a higher standard of control may be adopted):

(1) Club Target Days and Non-Record Status Tournaments: Arrow holes need not be marked in which case rebounds will not score. FITA Time Control need not be applied.

(2) Tournaments with UK Record Status: Arrow holes shall be marked. If Visual Time Control is not available then Time Control must be applied in the following manner:

Two audible signals for archers in the first detail to take their positions on the shooting line.

After 20 seconds one audible signal for shooting to commence.

After 2½ minutes (or earlier if shooting line is clear) 2 audible signals indicate that the archers remaining on the shooting line shall retire and the next detail take their place.

After 20 seconds one audible signal for the second detail to commence shooting.

And so continue until both details have shot their two ends (or one depending on the distances being shot) when 3 audible signals shall indicate that archers are to move forward to score and collect arrows. If at any time a competitor indicates a rebound then shooting is interrupted strictly in accordance with the procedure set out in FITA Constitution and Rules.

(3) FITA Star Tournaments Visual Time Control shall be adopted as set out in FITA Constitution and Rules. Automatic timing devices need not be incorporated into any adequately designed light system. Rebounds shall be scored (FITA Constitution and Rules).

(4) FITA Star Tournaments with World Record Status: FITA requires conditions as near to World Championships standards as can reasonably be attained. Visual Time Control shall be used.

(f) (i) A FITA Round may be shot in one day or over two consecutive days under FITA Rules.

(ii) All other Rounds to be shot in one day. (Except in accordance with Rule for Championship of more than one day's duration.)

109. Other Rounds

(a) Local Rounds – In addition to rounds specified in Tables 108(a)(i)(ii)(iii) & (iv) any local round made up of other numbers of arrows at specified distances may be used in Clubs and Tournaments.

(b) All local rounds must be shot in all respects to the Rules of Shooting. They are not recognised for GNAS Record, Classification or Handicap purposes.

110. Club Events

(a) Target Day

(i) A Target Day is any day and time appointed under the Rules of the Club and previously announced to the members.

(ii) There is no statutory limit to the number of officially appointed Target Days in any one week.

(iii) All scores made must be entered in the Club Record Book.

(iv) Target Days should commence punctually at the announced time.

(v) All shooting shall be in accordance with GNAS Rules of Shooting.

(vi) On any Club Target Day there shall be a minimum of two archers shooting, not necessarily on the same target, each recording the other's scores in order that these scores may be recognised. An archer shooting alone may claim his score provided that it has been recorded throughout by a non-shooting archer.

(b) Open Meeting

An Open Meeting is an event run as a competition open to all members of GNAS and FITA affiliated members, with all the necessary organisation, advertising of the event, judging, etc., run under GNAS Rules of Shooting.

111. Six Gold Badge

(*a*) There are four types of badge; a senior and junior badge for archers shooting bows as recognised in 102(*a*) and a senior and junior badge for archers shooting bows as recognised in 102(*c*).

(*b*) The award, which is for six consecutive arrows shot during the competition at one end into the gold zone, is open to members of the Society. For the purpose of the six gold badge only on FITA rounds the 9 and 10 scoring rings will be treated as golds.

(*c*) The shortest distances at which the badge may be gained are:
Gentlemen – 80yd (70m)   Ladies – 60yd (60m)

(*d*) The six gold end must be made at a meeting organised by the Society or any of its associated bodies or in competition at an associated club Target Day, under GNAS Rules of Shooting.

(*e*) (i) Claims for the award must be submitted to the GNAS Secretary on the appropriate claim form.

(ii) If the six gold end is made at a tournament the tournament organiser must sign.

(iii) If the six gold end is made at an associated club Target Day the Club Secretary must sign.

(*f*) An archer is entitled to only one senior six gold badge for each type of bow, but holders of the junior badge(s) are also entitled to claim and hold a senior badge for each type of bow.

112. FITA Star Badge

The award is open to Members of the Society according to qualifications and applications as laid down in FITA Rules. Claims for the award must be submitted to the GNAS Secretary on the appropriate form.

113. GNAS Arrow Award for Juniors

GNAS has instituted the 'GNAS Arrow Awards' scheme for Juniors. The scheme, which commenced on 1.1.89, and details on how the awards can be claimed, are given below.

(*a*) The Arrow Awards are open to juniors of the Society under 16 years of age and are in the form of Red, Blue and Black badges.

(*b*) The Award may be claimed only once in each age group and archers may shoot for an Award in age groups above, but not below, their own. Archers submitting valid claims for Awards higher than their

Qualifying rounds and scores for GNAS

Arrow Awards for Juniors

	Gentlemen FITA	Ladies FITA / Metric I	Metric II	Metric III	Metric IV	York	Hereford / Bristol I	Bristol II	Bristol III	Bristol IV
RED AWARD Junior Gentlemen U/16:										
H/C 43 Recurve	998	1077	1152	—	—	819	988	1110	—	—
41 Compound Limited	1033	1107	1177	—	—	859	1019	1133	—	—
37 Compound Unlimited	1097	1162	1223	—	—	934	1075	1174	—	—
RED AWARD Junior Ladies U/16:										
H/C 53 Recurve	797	892	996	1130	—	603	802	968	1069	—
51 Compound Limited	840	933	1031	1156	—	647	843	1001	1095	—
47 Compound Unlimited	923	1009	1096	1205	—	735	919	1059	1141	—
BLUE AWARD Junior Gentlemen U/14:										
H/C 55 Recurve	753	849	957	1101	—	560	760	934	1042	—
53 Compound Limited	797	892	996	1130	—	603	802	968	1069	—
49 Compound Unlimited	882	972	1065	1181	—	691	882	1031	1119	—
BLACK AWARD Junior Ladies U/13 and Junior Gentlemen U/12:										
H/C 69 Recurve	451	526	638	840	1051	292	456	640	792	950
H/C 67 Compound Limited	491	571	687	883	1084	325	498	685	883	983
63 Compound Unlimited	576	664	783	965	1141	396	584	774	911	1044

age group may also claim the lower awards down to their age group, providing they have not been gained previously.

(c) (i) The table opposite indicates the qualifying rounds and scores for separate bows/styles in each age group, for the relevant colour badge.

(ii) Number of Rounds: Four in a calendar year, including at least one FITA/Metric round. One round must be shot at an open tournament; the remainder may be shot at any associated club target day when a minimum of two archers are shooting together including, or under the supervision of a senior member.

(d) Claims for the Award shall be made on the appropriate claim form obtainable from GNAS office by sending a s.a.e. (club secretaries may hold stocks of these forms). The form must be returned to the office fully completed by providing the information requested on the form, and signed by the archer and his/her Club Records Officer or Secretary.

114. GNAS 'Compound Wheel' Awards

Archers shooting Compound Bows at FITA Star Tournaments and National Compound Championships when a FITA round is shot can claim GNAS Compound Wheel awards.

(a) The colours of the awards are:–
1000–White, 1100–Black,
1200–Blue, 1300–Red

(b) Claims for the award shall be made on the appropriate claim form obtainable from GNAS office.

115. Rose Awards

(a) These awards are open to all members of GNAS shooting at record status Rose York/Hereford tournaments for which the organiser has paid a Rose levy. Roses will be awarded free.

(b) Gentlemen/Junior Gentlemen must shoot the York round. Ladies/Junior Ladies must shoot the Hereford round.

(c) The colours of the awards are:
800 – White, 900 – Black, 1000 – Blue,
1100 – Red, 1200 – Yellow

(d) Claims for the award shall be made on the appropriate claim form which, together with the results sheet, must be submitted to the GNAS Office by the tournament organiser within 28 days of the event.

B. INDOOR

120. GNAS Rules of Shooting for Target Archery – Outdoor shall apply except as enumerated in the following paragraphs.

121. Target Faces

(a) The diameters of the standard faces are 40cm, 60cm and 80cm.

(b) (i) The 40cm face is composed of a circle in the centre of 8cm diameter ringed by four concentric bands the breadth of each, measured radially, being 4cm.

(ii) The 60cm face is composed of a circle in the centre of 12cm diameter ringed by four concentric bands the breadth of each, measured radially, being 6cm.

(iii) The 80cm face is as defined in Rule 100.

(c) Colours: see 100(c).

(d) The 40cm and 60cm faces have each colour zone divided into two zones of equal width by a line not exceeding 2mm in width. Such dividing lines shall be entirely within the higher scoring zone.

(e) Dividing lines: See 100(e)(i) and (ii).

(f) Pinhole: See 100(f).

(g) Tolerance (plus/minus) on the 40cm and 60cm faces is 1mm on the diameter of each scoring zone.

122. Range Layout

(a) The targets may be set up at any angle between vertical and 15° but a line of targets shall be set up at the same angle.

(b) The height of the pinholes shall be 130cm (4ft 3in) above the ground except if the 40cm target faces are in two lines, one above the other, when the height of the pinholes shall be 100cm and 160cm above the ground. The tolerance on heights shall not exceed ±2cm. The height of the pinholes on a line of faces shall at all times look straight.

(c) Target centres shall be placed so as to allow archers to stand at a minimum of 0.91m (3ft) intervals while shooting.

(d) The shooting line (over which archers shall take up their shooting positions) shall be measured from points vertically below the 'pinholes'. If targets are in two lines, one above the other and at an angle, the measurement shall be taken from points vertically below halfway between the two pinholes. The tolerance on measurements shall be as follows: Metric ±10cm, Imperial ±4in.

(e) A waiting line shall be placed five yards behind the shooting line. If space does not permit, a waiting line may be omitted.

123. Recognised Rounds for Record, Handicap and Classification For bows as defined 102(a) and 102(c)

(a) The following rounds are recognised by the Society:

(b) Rounds for National Record Purposes

(i)

		INDOOR ROUNDS (10 Zone Scoring)	
●	●	FITA 18m	5 doz at 18m – 40cm face
●		FITA 25m – Freestyle	5 doz at 25m – 60cm face
	●	FITA 25m – Compound	5 doz at 25m – 40cm face
●		Combined FITA – Freestyle	5 doz at 25m – 60cm face & 5 doz at 18m – 40cm face
	●	Combined FITA – Compound	5 doz at 25m – 40cm face & 5 doz at 18m – 40cm face
	●	Double FITA 25m – Compound	5 doz at 25m – 40cm face shot twice
●	●	Bray I	2½ doz at 18m – 40cm face
●		Bray II – Freestyle	2½ doz at 25m – 60cm face
	●	Bray II – Compound	2½ doz at 25m – 40cm face
●	●	★Portsmouth	5 doz at 20yd – 60cm face
●	●	Stafford	6 doz at 30m – 80cm face

(ii)

		INDOOR ROUNDS – SPECIALS	
●	●	★Worcester	5 doz at 20yd – 40.64cm (16 in) special face scoring 5,4,3,2,1 outwards from centre white
●	●	Vegas	5 doz at 18m – special face scoring 10,9,8,7,6 outwards from inner gold

(i) Single round records may be claimed for any round stated in Tables 123(*a*)(i) and (ii).
(ii) Double round records may be claimed for rounds marked ★ in Tables 123(*a*)(i) and (ii).

(iii) See part VII for regulations governing record claims.

(c) Rounds for Handicap and Classification Purposes

(i) All rounds in Tables 123(a)(i) and (ii) may be shot.

(ii) See GNAS Handicap and Classification Tables for regulations governing the Handicap and Classification schemes.

124. Local Rounds

In addition to rounds specified in 123(a)(i) and (ii), any 'local' round made up of other numbers of arrows at specified distances may be used in clubs and tournaments provided the Rules of Shooting are adhered to in all respects and subject to their non-recognition by the GNAS for Record, Classification or Handicap purposes.

125. Regulations for the Stafford and Portsmouth Rounds

(a) The general Rules of Target Archery – Indoor shall apply.

(b) An end shall consist of three arrows.

(c) One end of sighter arrows shall be shot.

(d) The scoring points on the target, reading from inner gold to outer white, are 10, 9, 8, 7, 6, 5, 4, 3, 2, 1.

126. Regulations for the Bray I and Bray II Rounds

(a) The general Rules of Target Archery – Indoor shall apply.

(b) An end shall consist of three arrows.

(c) Two ends of sighter arrows shall be shot.

(d) The scoring points on the target, reading from inner gold to outer white, are 10, 9, 8, 7, 6, 5, 4, 3, 2, 1.

127. Regulations for the FITA 18m, FITA 25m and Combined FITA Rounds

(a) When these rounds are shot FITA Rules apply subject to minimum standards given in 127(a)(i).

(i) Minimum standards (at the organiser's discretion a higher standard of control may be adopted).

(1) Club Target Days and Non-Record Status Tournaments: arrow holes need not be marked, in which case rebounds will not score. FITA Time Control need not be applied.

(2) Tournaments with UK Record Status: arrow holes shall be marked. If Visual Time Control is not available then Time Control must be applied in the following manner:

Two audible signals for archers in the first detail to take their positions on the shooting line.

After 20 seconds one audible signal for shooting to commence.

After 2½ minutes (or earlier if shooting line is clear) 2 audible signals indicate that the archers remaining on the shooting line shall retire and the next detail take their place.

After 20 seconds one audible signal for the second detail to commence shooting.

And so continue until both details have shot their two ends (or one depending on the distances being shot) when 3 audible signals shall indicate that archers are to move forward to score and collect arrows.

If at any time a competitor indicates a rebound then shooting is interrupted strictly in accordance with the procedure set out in FITA Constitution and Rules.

(3) Tournaments with World Record Status: FITA requires conditions as near to World Championships standards as can reasonably be attained. Visual Time Control shall be used.

128. Regulations for the Worcester Round

(a) The general Rules of Target Archery – Indoor shall apply except as enumerated in the following paragraphs.

(b) **Target Faces**

(i) The target face used shall be circular 40.64cm (16in) in diameter. This target face is composed as follows:

A circle in the centre 8.13cm (3in) diameter ringed by four concentric bands, the breadth of each measured radially being 4.064cm (1.6in). The centre circle shall be coloured white and the four concentric bands black. The concentric bands shall be divided by white lines. Each of the white dividing lines shall be of no greater width than 1mm (0.04in). Such dividing lines shall be entirely within the higher scoring zone.

(ii) Tolerances on target faces are permitted as follows: 2mm (0.08in) on each zone and 2mm (0.08in) on full 40.64cm (16in) diameter.

(c) **Shooting**

(i) 104(b)(ii) (rotation) will not apply to this round.

(ii) Five arrows shall be shot at an end. Each archer will shoot his five arrows before retiring from the shooting line.

(iii) One end of sighter arrows shall be shot.

(iv) In the event of an archer shooting more than five arrows at an end the archer shall be penalised by losing the value of his arrow(s) in the target.

(v) The maximum number of archers on a target boss shall be four.

(vi) Five minutes shall be the maximum time for an archer to shoot an end, the time to start from when the archer steps on to the shooting line.

(d) **Scoring**

The scoring points for hits on the target face are: 5, 4, 3, 2, 1, reading from the centre white circle.

(*e*) **Recognised Round**
 (i) The Round shall consist of 12 ends (60 arrows).
(ii) The distance to be shot is 20 yards.
(iii) Each boss shall hold four target faces.
(iv) Target faces shall be arranged thus:

      1   2
      3   4

 (v) Two archers of a group shall shoot five arrows when the second group shall then shoot their five arrows.
(vi) The first group of two archers shall shoot at the higher targets; the second group at the lower targets.
(vii) When all archers have shot 30 arrows those who have been shooting at the lower targets shall change to the higher targets and those who have been shooting at the higher targets shall shoot at the lower targets, thus:

those who have been shooting on targets 1 and 2 shall shoot the remaining 30 arrows on targets 3 and 4 retaining their same shooting positions.

129. Regulations for the Vegas Round
 (*a*) The general Rules of Target Archery – Indoor shall apply except as enumerated in the following paragraphs.
 (*b*) **Target Faces**
The target face is composed as follows:
Three separate 5-zone centres equal in size and colour to the innermost scoring zones of the 40cm FITA Indoor target face as defined in 121. The gold of each centre shall be arranged in triangular form and each shall be numbered. Centre number 1 shall be in the lower left corner, centre number 2 at the apex of the triangle and centre number 3 shall be in the lower right corner. The 'pinholes' of the golds shall be 21.3cm apart.
 (*c*) **Range Layout**
Each boss shall hold four faces.
 (*d*) **Shooting**
 (i) 104(*b*)(ii) (rotation) shall not apply.
 (ii) The first groups of two archers shall shoot at the higher targets and the second group at the lower targets. When all archers have shot 30 arrows those who have been shooting at the lower targets shall change to the higher targets and those who have been shooting at the higher targets shall shoot at the lower targets.
(iii) Each archer shall shoot in ends of three arrows.
(iv) Two ends of sighter arrows shall be shot.
 (v) Arrows shall be numbered and shall be shot in ascending numerical sequence, one arrow at each target centre in the order 1, 2 and 3.

(e) **Scoring**
  (i) The scoring points for hits on the target, reading from the inner Gold to the Blue, are 10, 9, 8, 7, 6.
  (ii) An arrow not shot in the order prescribed in Rule 129(*d*)(v) or an arrow striking a target centre other than that at which it should have been shot in the order so prescribed shall be scored a miss.

II. FIELD ARCHERY – Senior and Junior

200. Regulations
  (*a*) GNAS Rules of Shooting 102, 103, 201–206 shall apply to GNAS recognised rounds and any other traditional or local rounds run under the GNAS Rules of Shooting.
  (*b*) FITA Constitution & Rules, Part V(*c*), shall apply generally to the FITA recognised rounds, i.e. the Hunter and the Field (with exceptions as listed) and to the FITA Combination Round. (See under 201, 206(*b*).)
  (*c*) There shall be an initial tackle inspection at the All-British & Open Field Archery Championships. At other events, tackle is liable to inspection at any time during the shoot, but judges will inspect any equipment offered to them before the shoot begins. Any tackle found at any time thereafter in contravention of the rules will entail disqualification.
  (*d*) There shall be separate classes and styles for Ladies, Gentlemen and Juniors (see 203, 204).

201. New FITA Field Rules (1989)
FITA Arrowhead Rounds (24 unmarked plus 24 marked)
These are only shot when formally applied for as FITA Award Events, in which case FITA Field Rules (1989) apply in their entirety (except as provided for under (*f*) below) under the control of an international or National Field Judge.
New FITA Rounds, whether 24 unmarked, 24 marked, combined (24 u/m + 24m/d) or combination (12 u/m + 12 m/d) are shot according to FITA Field Rules (1989) with the following exceptions:–
  (*a*) Control may be in the hands of an international, National or Regional Field Judge (if Record Status is applied for).
  (*b*) Initial tackle inspection may be replaced by spot checks on the course.
  (*c*) Arrowholes need not be marked, for the GNAS bouncer/pass-through rule will apply (see 202*k*).

(*d*) Target numbers may be in any readily visible colours and may be displayed at the shooting posts rather than at the targets.

(*e*) (i) GNAS Limited class and U/15 Unlimited class shoot from red posts.

(ii) GNAS Bowhunter, Traditional, Traditional Long-bow and all Juniors under 15 (in any class other than U/L under 15) shoot from blue posts.

(iii) Special posts may be set for under 12s, in which case no records shall be available to them.

(*f*) When an official Arrowhead Round is shot for the All-British National Field Championships the above relaxations, (*e*)(i) & (ii), apply but only those archers conforming to FITA regulations can claim FITA Arrowhead awards.

(*g*) FITA ARROWHEAD AWARDS – The award is open to Members of the Society according to qualifications and applications as laid down in FITA Rules. Claims for the award must be submitted to the GNAS Field Records Officer on the appropriate form.

ARROWHEAD AWARDS ALL DIVISIONS

	Award	Gents	Ladies
1	Green	390	320
2	Brown	450	380
3	Grey	510	440
4	Black	570	500
5	White	630	560

202. General Field Archery Rules

(*a*) Judges shall be appointed, one of whom shall be the Chairman in charge of the event.

(*b*) The duties of the Chairman and other Judges shall be:

(i) to ensure that adequate safety precautions have been observed in the layout of the course and practice area.

(ii) to address the assembled competitors before the shoot commences on safety precautions and any other appropriate matter, including method of starting the event, the starting points of each group, etc.

(iii) to ensure that all competitors are conversant with the rules of the competition and the method of scoring.

(iv) to resolve disputes or queries that may arise in interpretation of the rules or other matters.

(*c*) Each shooting group shall consist of not more than six and not less than three archers, one of whom shall be designated Target Captain and two others as scorers.

(*d*) The Target Captain shall be responsible for the orderly conduct of shooting within the group, and have the ultimate responsibility for scoring the arrows.

(*e*) Each scorer shall be supplied with and complete a separate set of score cards for the shooting group and the duties of scorers shall be as follows:

(i) to write down the score of each competitor in the group.

(ii) to complete the score card at the end of the shooting.

(iii) to ensure that the cards are returned without delay to the Scores Commission.

(*f*) The score cards shall be signed by the scorer at the end of shooting, and by the archer as an acceptance of the final score.

(*g*) Should the two cards not agree, then the lower score shall be taken as the result.

(*h*) The use of binoculars and other visual aids is not permitted in GNAS Field Archery and FITA Unmarked Rounds.

(*j*) The archer's more forward foot must be in contact with and behind the shooting post while shooting, except in the GNAS Hunter, the Field and the Combination Rounds, the Stamp Unmarked, the Stamp Marked, the Stamp Combination, the New FITA Rounds and the Arrowhead Round when the archer shall stand with both feet behind the relevant shooting line, which is an imaginary line parallel to the target through the shooting post.

(*k*) If, in competitions where the arrow holes have not been marked, an arrow is observed to rebound from, or is believed to have passed through, the target butt, a Judge shall check it, and if it appears that the arrow has rebounded or passed through, then another arrow may be shot at that target from the same position from which the rebounding or passing-through arrow was shot.

(*l*) An arrow shall be deemed not to have been shot, if the archer can touch it with his bow without moving his feet from his shooting position, in which case another arrow may be shot in its place.

(*m*) Archers waiting their turn to shoot shall stand well back behind the archers who are shooting.

(*n*) An archer raising the bow towards a target on unmarked distances may not thereafter alter the sight before he has shot an arrow from that post or forfeited the shot.

(*o*) Timing. In Hunter, Field, Combination and FITA rounds, whether marked or unmarked, an archer is allowed 5 minutes overall where 4 shots are taken from one post, and 4 minutes overall where 3 shots are taken from one post. On walk-ups the archer is allowed $1\frac{1}{2}$ minutes per arrow.

203. Shooting Styles

(*a*) **Freestyle** – Archers using equipment that conforms to 102(*a*).

(*b*) **Barebow** – Archers using equipment that conforms to 103(*a*)(ii).

(*c*) (i) *Traditional* – Archers using equipment as for Barebow above, but the arrow shafts shall be made of wood and may comprise a metallic pile and a plastic nock. Furthermore, they must adhere to one anchor point and to one finger-position on the string throughout a tournament. An arrowrest is permitted, but may not be adjustable; a pressure button is not permitted.

(ii) *Traditional Longbow* – Archers using equipment as defined in 601 except that the bow must be bare; therefore marks on bow limb or rubber bands are not allowed, neither is a 'kisser' allowed on the string. Archers must adhere to one anchor point and to one finger-position on the string throughout a tournament.

(*d*) **Crossbow** – Archers using equipment as defined in 501.

(*e*) **Compound Unlimited** – Archers using equipment as defined in 103(*c*)(i).

(*f*) **Compound Limited** – Archers using equipment as defined in 103(*c*)(ii). Multipin sights are permitted.

(*g*) **Compound Bowhunter** – Archers using equipment generally as in Barebow above. No marking or attachment may appear on the bow or the string which might be used as an aid to aiming. A cable-guard, pressure button and an adjustable arrow rest and plate are permitted. Only one stabiliser no longer than 30.5cm (12in) overall may be fitted. No release aid or overdraw may be used.

Note 1: In the above Compound styles, no bow may be used that has a peak weight over 60lbs, or incorporates electric or electronic releases or sights, has an overdraw greater than 6cm inside the bow (4cm for Limited, none for Bowhunter), or uses a shoot-through riser.

Note 2: In all the above styles, the following exceptions to Target Archery practices apply:

(i) No artificial points of aim are permitted.

(ii) Arrows must be numbered by means of distinctive bands at least 3mm in width and approximately 3mm apart.

(iii) No notes or memoranda may be used which might assist in improving scores.

(iv) No aids for estimating distances are allowed.

204. Juniors (General)

(*a*) Junior archers are those under 18 years of age. They are placed in three categories of age-groups. The date of birth must fall before the (first) day of the tournament.

> Juniors (15/17)
> Juniors (12/14)
> Juniors (under 12)

(*b*) There is nothing to prevent a Junior choosing to shoot in a higher age-group than his age would warrant provided that he complies with the regulations appertaining to that group.

(*c*) Where Juniors under 15 years of age shoot in a group containing archers above this age, the Juniors shall shoot last.

205. Target Faces

There are 5 types of face in use:

(*a*) (i) New FITA 5 zone face as described in FITA Rules (1989) scoring 5, 4, 3, 2 & 1. (These must be used for Arrowhead and New FITA Rounds.)

(ii) For the GNAS STAMP ROUND the FITA 5 zone face shall be used. These need not be the FITA licensed faces.

(*b*) GNAS Hunter & Field. There are four faces for GNAS Hunter and Field: 60cm, 45cm, 30cm and 15cm diameters.

All four faces consist of an outer ring, an inner ring, and a centre spot. The lines between the scoring zones to be invisible from the post, but an exception may be made for the 30 cm and the 15 cm faces as the distances are so short.

The dimensions of the faces are:

Diameters of	Outer Ring Face	Inner Ring Face	Centre Spot
	60cm	30cm	10cm
	45cm	22.5cm	7.5cm
	30cm	15cm	5cm
	15cm	7.5cm	2.5cm

Scoring values

The centre spot	5 points	
The inner ring	4 points	
The outer ring	3 points	

Hunter Round Faces

The outer ring and the inner ring shall be black, and the centre spot shall be white.

The background on which the face is printed shall be the same colour as the outer ring.

Field Round Faces

The outer ring and the centre spot shall be black, and the inner ring shall be white. The background on which the face is printed shall be the same colour as the outer ring.

Animal Picture Faces Animal pictures bearing the Hunter Round faces and the Field Round faces respectively, may also be used, but the inner ring shall be inside the animal's contour. The lines of the face need only be outlined but the centre spot shall be in a contrasting colour to be plainly visible.

(c) Forester Round Faces

The target faces shall be of animal or bird design, and shall have inscribed on them an outer circle of fixed diameter, an inner circle of half that diameter, and a spot of one sixth that diameter.

Thus:		
24in Face	12in Inner Circle	4in Spot
18in Face	9in Inner Circle	3in Spot
12in Face	6in Inner Circle	2in Spot
6in Face	3in Inner Circle	1in Spot

(d) Big Game Round Faces

The target faces shall be of animal or bird design, with the scoring area divided into two parts. The high-scoring area is the smaller area, situated in the 'heart/lung' region of the animal, and is known as the 'kill' zone. The low-scoring area is the remainder of the animal within the marked perimeter, and is known as the 'wound' zone.

Targets are classed into groups one, two, three and four, according to size.

Group 1. 40in × 28in – Bear, deer, moose, elk, caribou.

Group 2. 28in × 22in – Antelope, small deer, wolf, mountain lion.

Group 3. 22in × 14in – Coyote, javelina, turkey, fox, goose, wildcat, pheasant.

Group 4. 14in × 11in – Turtle, duck, grouse, crow, skunk, jackrabbit, wood-chuck.

Any animal or bird consistent in size with a particular group may be used.

(e) National Animal Round Faces

The target faces shall be of an animal or bird design, and shall have described upon them a circle of either 30, 22.5, 15, or 7.5cm diameter according to the size of the animal picture and in the heart/lung region. The higher scoring area (the kill zone) shall be within the circle and the remainder of the animal shall be the lower scoring area (the wound zone).

Swedish Big Game Round faces fulfil the requirements set out above and shall be used at National Record Status events.

206. Field Rounds in GNAS

For Target Faces refer to 205.

Courses should be laid out in such a way as to provide safety, maximum interest and variety, and to make best use of available terrain. Direction indicators should be placed as necessary to ensure safety.

(a) FITA ROUNDS (according to FITA Rules (1989)).

New FITA Rounds (as above, with GNAS relaxations. See 201.)

(*b*) GNAS HUNTER, FIELD & COMBINATION

For full details, including rules of shooting, refer to FITA Constitution & Rules (1985) Part V(C), but in particular the following apply:

(i) Two posts are to be placed side by side at every position where two archers are expected to shoot together, which is the standard procedure.

(ii) Arrows shall be shot in ascending numerical order.

(iii) *60cm and 45cm Faces* After two archers have shot they will be allowed to go forward to score and withdraw their arrows, either at the request of the next detail or on their own volition.

30cm Faces Four faces shall be placed in the form of a square. Every shooting position shall have two posts placed side by side.

Archers shooting from the left post shall shoot their first two arrows at the top left face, and the remaining two arrows at the lower left face; archers shooting from the right post shall shoot similarly at the top and lower right faces. After the first two archers have shot they will be allowed to go forward to score and withdraw their arrows, either at the request from the next detail or on their own volition.

15cm Faces Sixteen faces shall be placed in four vertical columns (1, 2, 3 and 4 from the left) of four faces (A, B, C and D from the top). Every shooting position to have two posts placed side by side. Archers shooting in the first detail shall shoot one arrow at each of the faces in column 1 starting at face A and then B, C and D from the appropriate posts; archers shooting from the right post in the first detail shall shoot their arrows in a similar manner at the faces in column 3.

The archers in the second detail shall shoot their arrows in a similar manner from the left post at faces in column 2, and from the right post at faces in column 4.

When more than four archers are in the shooting group then the fifth archer shall shoot from the left-hand post and the sixth from the right-hand post, in a similar manner, after the first four archers have scored and drawn their arrows.

(iv) No archer shall relate to another archer the target distances on unmarked distances during the tournament.

(v) On walk-up targets, a time limit shall be allowed of $1\frac{1}{2}$ minutes per arrow; on fixed position shots an archer is allowed 5 minutes for 4 arrows overall. The timing begins when the archer takes his position at the post, which he shall do as soon as it becomes available.

A Judge, having observed an archer exceed the time limit, shall caution him by a signed note on the score card, indicating the time of the warning. At the second warning, and any subsequent warnings, during that tournament, the highest scoring arrow at the target where the warning is given, shall be annulled.

GNAS Hunter Round   Shot on Hunter faces.

The Hunter Round consists of 28 targets with one arrow from each of four different posts for each target. The Round may be shot Marked or Unmarked.

Four targets with 15cm faces placed between 5 and 15 metres.

Eight targets with 30cm faces placed between 10 and 30 metres.

Ten targets with a 45cm face placed between 20 and 40 metres.

Six targets with a 60cm face placed between 30 and 50 metres.

Tolerance on distances shall not exceed ±1.0%

Total number of arrows, 112.

Scoring 5, 4, 3 for spot, inner and outer respectively.

Maximum possible score, 560.

Juniors

Juniors (15/17) shoot from the same posts as adults in all cases.

Juniors (12/14) shoot two arrows from each of the two nearest shooting posts at single-faced targets, which will be either 45cm or 60cm faces.

Juniors (under 12) shoot all four shots from the front post on *all targets*. Organisers *may* provide suitably placed extra forward posts for under 12s at their discretion. In this case no under 12 records can be claimed and a statement to this effect must appear on entry forms for Record Status Tournaments.

GNAS Field Round   Shot on FITA Field faces.

The Field Round consists of 28 Targets with four arrows at each Target. Distances are marked.

Twice at each of 15, 20, 25 and 30 metres at 30cm faces	32 arrows
Twice at each of 35, 40 and 45 metres at a 45cm face	24 arrows
Twice at each of 50, 55 and 60 metres at a 60cm face	24 arrows
Twice 6, 8, 10 and 12 metres at 15cm faces	8 arrows
Twice 15, 20, 25 and 30 metres at 30cm faces	8 arrows
Twice 30, 35, 40 and 45 metres at a 45cm face	8 arrows
Twice 45, 50, 55 and 60 metres at a 60cm face	8 arrows

Tolerance on distances shall not exceed ±1.0%.

Total number of arrows, 112.

Scoring 5, 4, 3 for spot, inner and outer respectively.

Maximum possible score, 560.

Juniors

Juniors (15/17) shoot from the same posts as adults in all cases.

Juniors (12/14) shoot all four shots from the front post on 60cm walk-up target; and have a forward post provided 15 metres in advance of the Adult posts on the fixed position targets at 60, 55, 50 and 45 metres. (Note that this latter target is a 45cm face.)

Juniors (under 12) shoot the same privilege shots as Juniors (12/14), and in addition, shoot from the front post at ALL walk-up targets.

Organisers *may* provide suitably placed extra forward posts for under 12s at their discretion. In this case no under-12 records can be claimed and a statement to this effect must appear on entry forms for Record Status Tournaments.

GNAS Combination Round

The Combination Round shall consist of one unit (14 targets representing a correct half of those shot in the full round) of Unmarked Hunter Targets and one unit of Marked FITA Field Targets laid out consecutively. Where both units are shot over the same course, the Hunter unit shall be shot first. The use of binoculars or the carrying of them is not permitted during the shooting of the Hunter unit.

This Combination Round is a GNAS Round and is not recognised as such by FITA.

Total number of arrows, 112.

Scoring 5, 4, 3 for spot, inner and outer respectively.

Maximum possible score, 560.

Juniors

The rules regarding shooting posts for Juniors in the Hunter and Field Rounds apply to the appropriate unit in this Round.

(c) Foresters Round

Shot on Foresters faces. Distances may be marked or unmarked.

The Round consists of 28 targets (or two units)

The standard unit shall consist of the following 14 shots:

Three 24in faces at a distance of up to 70 yards.

Four 18in faces at a distance of up to 50 yards.

Four 12in faces at a distance of up to 40 yards.

Three 6in faces at a distance of up to 20 yards.

Shooting Rules: At a 24in target, four arrows are shot, one from each of four posts. At an 18in target, three arrows are shot, one from each of three posts. At a 12in target, two arrows are shot, one from each of two posts. At a 6in target, only one arrow is shot from one post. Multi-post shots may be equidistant from the target or 'walk-away' or 'walk-up'.

Scoring   Aiming spot – 15 points
           Inner Circle   – 10 points
           Outer Circle – 5 points

Total number of arrows – 70 arrows

Maximum possible score – 1050 points

Juniors

Juniors (15/17) shoot from the same posts as Adults in all cases.

Juniors (12/14) shoot from the same posts as Adults at the 6in and 12in faces. They shoot two arrows from the middle distance post and one arrow from the front post at 18in faces. They shoot two arrows from each of the two nearest posts at the 24in faces.

Juniors (under 12) shoot all arrows from the front post at all targets.

(d) Four-Shot Foresters Round

Shot on Foresters faces. Distances shall not be marked.

The Round consists of 28 targets (or two units), with four walk-up shots on each target.

Distribution of faces, as in Foresters Round.

Scoring as in Foresters Round.

Total number of arrows, 112.

Maximum possible score, 1680 points.

Juniors

Juniors (15/17) shoot from the same posts as Adults in all cases.

Juniors (12/14) shoot two arrows from each of the two nearest shooting posts at the targets showing 18in and 24in faces.

Juniors (under 12) shoot all arrows from the front post at all targets.

(e) The Big Game Round

Shot on Big Game faces, the Big Game Round consists of 28 targets (or two units) marked or unmarked.

The standard unit is made up of the following 14 targets at the suggested ranges:

Three group 1 targets at a distance of 70 to 40 yards.

Three group 2 targets at a distance of 50 to 30 yards.

Four group 3 targets at a distance of 40 to 20 yards

Four group 4 targets at a distance of 30 to 10 yards.

Shooting Rules: Three shots are permitted at each target, one from each of the three posts, each successive post being closer to the target than the previous one.

Arrows shall be identifiable as to order of shooting. The archer shall stop shooting as soon as a hit is considered to have been made.

Scoring: The score is decided by the position of the arrow in the target (i.e. in the 'kill' or 'wound' zone) and the number of arrows shot.

	Kill	Wound
1st arrow score	20	16
2nd arrow score	14	10
3rd arrow score	8	4

Only the score of the first 'scoring' arrow counts.

Maximum possible score, 560.

Juniors

Juniors (15/17) shoot from the same posts as Adults in all cases.

Juniors (12/14) shoot two arrows from the middle distance post and one from the front post until a hit is scored.

Juniors (under 12) shoot up to three arrows from the front post until a hit is scored.

(f) The National Animal Round

Shot on Animal faces conforming to the specifications given in 205.

The National Animal Round is shot over 32 targets (or two units) not marked. When two units are shot, the targets shall be mixed so that the units are not consecutive.

The course shall be laid out so that each unit shall consist of the following targets set within the prescribed range. Organisers are required to provide a good variety of shots.

Number of faces	Kill zone diameter	Distance Range
4	30cm	55–30 metres
4	22.5cm	45–20 metres
4	15cm	35–10 metres
4	7.5cm	20–5 metres

Shooting: Two arrows shall be shot at each target, one from each of two posts set within the prescribed range.

Scoring: Kill zone   – 10 points

Wound zone – 5 points

Total number of arrows in a Round, 64

Maximum possible score, 640.

Juniors

Juniors (15/17) shoot from the same posts as Adults in all cases.

Juniors (12/14) shoot both arrows from the nearest shooting post at the 30cm kill zone faces.

Juniors (under 12) shoot both arrows at the 30cm kill zone and the 22.5 kill zone diameter faces from a single privilege post set at an appropriate distance.

(g) The Stamp Round, Unmarked, Marked and Combination

For target faces refer to 205(a).

For full details including rules of shooting, refer to 206(b) with the following amendments.

Face sizes are the only alterations:–

For 60cm read 80cm

For 45cm read 60cm

For 30cm read 40cm

For 15cm read 20cm

The unmarked Stamp round uses the same distances as the GNAS Hunter Round.

The marked Stamp round uses the same distances as the GNAS Field Round.

III. FLIGHT SHOOTING – Senior and Junior

300. Basis
(a) The three classes for which competitions may take place are:
   A. Target Bows
   B. Flight Bows
   C. Free-style.
Ladies, Gentlemen and Juniors may compete equally in each class.
   (b) The classes may be subdivided into bow weights, as follows:
   1 – 16kg (35lb)
   2 – 23kg (50lb)
   3 – Unlimited.
Except for the target bow and unlimited classes flight bows shall be weighed as follows:
   (i) Bows shall be weighed just prior to commencement of shooting. Weight of bow, length of arrow, and the class for which this combination is eligible, shall be recorded on a label affixed to the face of the bow.
   (ii) The weight of the bow shall be taken at two inches less than the length of the longest arrow, and again at one inch less than the length of this arrow. The difference in these weights shall be added to the last weight of the bow at full draw.
   Weighing bows at full draw is optional with the competitor. When an overdraw device is used and permits a draw in excess of one inch from the back of the bow, this excess shall be considered a portion of the arrow length for bow weighing purposes.
   (c) For classes A and B only hand bows may be used and the bow must be held in the unsupported hand.
   (d) If competitions for both Target and Flight Bows are being held on the same occasion, all shooting with Target Bows must be completed first.
   (e) The use of Class A and B equipment by one archer to compete in each class at the same flight event is permitted.

301. Range Layout
(a) The Range Line, at right angles to the shooting line shall be clearly marked at 150 yards then at 50 yard intervals to at least 50 yards beyond the existing longest distance shot in the UK.

(*b*) Red warning flags shall be placed at each side of the range at 75 yards from the line of distance markers at a distance of 150 yards from the shooting line.

302. Equipment
(*a*) A Target Bow is any bow with which the user has shot at least two standard Target or Field Rounds. In the event of a breakage, a similar bow may be used as replacement.

(*b*) Any type of bow, other than a crossbow, may be entered for Classes B and C.

(*c*) In the Target Bow class competitors must use their own length standard target arrows and normal tab or shooting glove.

(*d*) In Classes B and C any type of arrow may be used.

(*e*) Sipurs are not permitted in Class A.

(*f*) Mechanical releases, inter-moving drawing and/or release aides are prohibited.

The following may be used in Classes B and C:

Six-gold ring, flipper or strap (single or double), block sipur, and angle measuring device.

(*g*) In the event of a breakage a substitute bow or limb may be used providing it is checked for conforming to its class. In the event of this not being done the archer will automatically be transferred to the unlimited class.

303. Shooting
(*a*) Competitors should be at least six feet apart, and must not advance their leading foot over the shooting line.

(*b*) Each competitor may have one assistant or adviser, who must keep at least one yard behind the shooting line.

(*c*) (i) At least four ends, each of three arrows, will be shot.

(ii) After all classes have shot the first end competitors and officials will go forward. Competitors will stand by their furthest arrow. A marker with a label attached bearing the name of the competitor and class will then be placed at the pile end of the furthest arrow in each class.

(iii) Arrows will then be withdrawn.

(iv) Succeeding ends will then be shot and markers adjusted where necessary.

(*d*) A Flight event may be shot on the same day and at the same venue as a Clout event without contravening rule 104(*l*).

304. Control of Shooting
There shall be a Range Captain in charge who will act as Referee and Judge. His decision shall be final. He will also be responsible for the

safety of the spectators, who must at all times, when shooting is in progress, be not less than 10 yards behind the shooting line.

305. Measurements

Measurement of distances shall be made with a steel tape along the range line. The distances shot shall be measured to that point on the range line at which a line at right angles to the range line passes the point where the arrow enters the ground. If the arrow is lying on the ground the line should pass through the pile end of the arrow.

IV. CLOUT SHOOTING – Senior and Junior

400. Regulations

GNAS Rules of Shooting for Target Archery – Outdoor shall apply except as enumerated in the following paragraphs.

The organisers shall take all reasonable steps to ensure that there be no risk occasioned to people, animals or property from arrows that miss the target area by overshot or to either side (NB a distance of 75 yards from the Clout centre to the boundary of any land to which the public has access is deemed reasonable).

401. Targets

The centre of the target shall be marked by a brightly coloured distinctive flag 12in square, set as close as practicable to ground level on a smooth vertical stick. The stick should not project above the flag.

402. Shooting

(*a*) Shooting may be either 'two way' or 'one way'.

(*b*) Six sighter arrows shall be shot in each direction when shooting two ways.

(*c*) The organiser, after considering general safety, archers' comfort and the duties of scorers, shall use his discretion as to the number of archers allocated to each target.

(*d*) A Clout event may be shot on the same day and at the same venue as a Flight event without contravening Rule 104(*l*).

403. Scoring

(*a*) Scores shall be determined according to the distance of arrows at point of entry in ground from centre of flag stick.

> Within a radius of 18 inches – 5 points
> 3 feet – 4 points
> 6 feet – 3 points
> 9 feet – 2 points
> 12 feet – 1 point

Arrows which have hit and remain embedded in the Clout shall score 5 provided they are not embedded in a lower scoring ring whereupon they shall score according to the ring in which they are embedded.

(*b*)   Rings of the above radii may be marked on the ground, the lines drawn being wholly within each circle.

(*c*)   Where it is not practical to draw lines on the ground, scores shall be determined with a non-stretch cord or tape looped round the centre stick and clearly marked to measure the various radii. .

Where this method of measuring is used an area should be marked on the ground (conveniently a square or circle) which will contain the whole of the Clout scoring zone and which for all purposes included in (*d*) be termed the Target Area. The scorer should allow adequate time for all archers shooting to determine the position of the arrows in the said area before carrying out the following procedure. The scorer shall carry the taut cord round at ground level and one assistant scorer following the cord at each 'colour' shall withdraw and carry all arrows from the 'colour' for which he is responsible. An arrow lying loose on the ground shall be scored in accordance with the position of its point. The arrows shall then be placed in distinct groups on or stuck into the ground at the appropriate section of the scoring cord and competitors will call their scores in the usual manner, picking up their arrows as they do so.

(*d*)   No person other than the appointed scorers shall enter the target area until all arrows have been withdrawn and placed in their respective scoring groups. An arrow withdrawn by any other than an appointed scorer shall not be scored.

404. Round

(*a*)   A Clout Round consists of 36 arrows.

(*b*)   At Record Status Tournaments the distances given below must be shot. There is nothing to prevent a junior holding a record in a round of a higher age group.

At other meetings the distance to be shot shall be determined by the organisers but would normally be as given.

Gentlemen	–	9 score yards
Ladies	–	7 score yards
Junior Gentlemen:		
Under 18 years	–	7 score yards
Under 16 years	–	6 score yards
Under 14 years	–	5 score yards
Under 12 years	–	4 score yards
Junior Ladies:		
Under 18 years	–	6 score yards

Under 16 years – 5 score yards
Under 13 years – 4 score yards

405. Six Clout Badge

(a) A six clout badge is for six clouts in one end shot during competition and is open to all members of the society shooting bows recognised in 102(a), 102(c) and 102(d) at the minimum distances in Rule 404(b)

(b) The six clout end must be at a meeting organised by the Society or any of its associated bodies, Regional or County Societies, under GNAS Rules of Shooting.

(c) Claims must be submitted to the GNAS Office on the six gold claim form signed by the tournament organiser.

V. CROSSBOW ARCHERY

500. Regulations

GNAS Rules of Shooting for Target Archery – Outdoors shall apply except as enumerated in the following paragraphs.

(a) Crossbowmen shall shoot on separate targets from other archers and not compete with them.

(b) No person less than 12 years of age may shoot or manipulate a crossbow.

501. Equipment

(a) A crossbow stock and mechanism may be made from any material. No mechanical aids or rests are permitted. Prods may be made of any other material except metal. The length measured along the curves shall not exceed 36 inches.

(b) The draw-length shall be measured from the back of the prod to the string latch. Draw-weight shall not exceed 1280lb/in with a maximum draw of 18 inches. (To determine the lb/in multiply the draw-length by the draw-weight.) The draw-weight shall be marked on the prod, e.g. 70lb @ 18in.

(c) A string may be made of any non-metallic material.

(d) Bolts may be made of any material and of such design as not to cause unreasonable damage to the target. Bolt length is minimum 12 inches, maximum 15 inches. Three fletchings, feather or plastic, shall be fitted.

(e) Telescopic or magnifying sights are not allowed.

(f) Stirrups attached to the stock or ground are permitted, provided that Rule 501(b) is complied with.

(g) Pistol crossbows are not permitted.

502. Recognised Rounds

(*a*) Windsor Round shot on a 60cm FITA face scoring 9, 7, 5, 3, 1. The Championship Round shall be a Double Windsor.

(*b*) American Round shot on a 60cm FITA face scoring 10, 9, 8, 7, 6, 5, 4, 3, 2, 1.

(*c*) Western Round shot on an 80cm FITA face scoring 10, 9, 8, 7, 6, 5, 4, 3, 2, 1.

(*d*) Any recognised GNAS or FITA Round.

503. Field Archery

(*a*) Current Field Archery Rules shall apply with those exceptions detailed in 500(*a*) and (*b*).

(*b*) Targets shall be fixed below skyline.

(*c*) Field Rounds as recognised by GNAS or FITA shall be shot.

504. The Crossbow and the Law

When travelling on public transport or walking in a public thoroughfare it is essential that the prod be removed and the stock and prod be carried in a case or cover.

505. Safety Rules

If shooting is interrupted for any reason, crossbows shall be lowered immediately so that they are directed at the ground immediately in front of the shooting line and the bolt removed. A crossbow may *not* be drawn or cocked except on the shooting line and in the direction of the targets.

PART VI. TRADITIONAL LONGBOW – Senior and Junior

600. Regulations

GNAS Rules of Shooting for Target Archery – Outdoor shall apply except as enumerated in the following paragraphs.

601. Equipment

(*a*) The bow shall be the traditional longbow made from wood, with stacked belly, and nocks. For a 24in–26in arrow, not less than 5ft in length; and for a 27in or longer arrow, not less than 5ft 6in in length, this being measured between the string nocks. At no point shall the depth of the bow – measured from back to belly – be less than $\frac{5}{8}$ (five eighths) of the width of the bow at the same section.

Bows of bamboo, constructed in conformity with the above, shall be permitted. Strings may be of either natural or manmade substance, and may, if desired, embody a 'kisser' at any point as required, to facilitate a consistent draw position. The use of extended 'platform' tabs for this purpose is not encouraged.

(b) Marks on the bow limb, or rubber bands of no more than ⅛in in depth and thickness, are permitted; but sights as such shall not be allowed. The bow shall carry no support for the arrow.

(c) Arrows shall have wooden steles (shafts), shall be fitted with feather fletchings, and may have either horn-reinforced, self or applied nocks. Piles shall be flush fitting. Shouldered Field piles, whilst permitted, should be avoided because of excess damage to targets. Broadhead, edged, bodkin, silver-spoon and other large diameter piles shall not be permitted.

Every archer is expected to have and to shoot arrows properly marked, so that there shall be no difficulty in claiming them.

(d) Artificial points of aim on the ground are permitted, but such shall not exceed a height of 6in from the ground, or 3in in diameter; nor shall they impede any other archer. Binoculars and telescopes shall not be used.

VII. RECORDS
All Disciplines – Senior and Junior

700. National Record

A National Record may be established and submitted to National Council for ratification at:

(a) Any tournament organised by FITA, FITA Members or GNAS.

(b) Any tournament which has been granted Record Status by National Council. Applications (all disciplines) to hold a Record Status Tournament must be received by the GNAS Office at least six calendar months prior to the date of the tournament. It shall be a condition that such tournaments, except for Inter-Regional and Inter-County tournaments, shall be open to all GNAS members shooting bows as recognised in rules 102(a) and 102(c).

701. Submission of Claims

Claims for National Records shall be submitted to the GNAS Secretary on the appropriate form except for National Championships and UK Masters Tournament when the Secretary will submit claims to National Council.

The claim forms must be completed prior to the dispersal of the Meeting at which the record has been made. One copy shall be handed to the archer and one copy retained by the Tournament Organiser. Both copies must be sent to the Secretary within 28 days of the date on which the record was made.

The claim form sent by the tournament organiser shall be accompanied by the original score sheet (or a photocopy), signed as in 106(*b*), and the results sheet as circulated.

702. Target Archery

(*a*) World Records may be established for the FITA Round and each distance of the FITA Round according to qualifications laid down in FITA Rules.

Claims for World Records shall be submitted to the GNAS Secretary supported by the necessary documents for onward transmissions to FITA for ratification.

(*b*) National Records may be claimed for rounds, either single, double or distance, as defined in rules 108 and 123, when shot at recognised Record Status tournaments. Where a double round is shot on the one day the second round will not be accepted for a single round record.

(*c*) Initial National Records in compound classes will only be ratified if the scores submitted exceed 75% of the existing freestyle record for the round.

(*d*) Initial National Records in long-bow class will only be ratified if scores submitted exceed 40% of the existing freestyle record for the round.

(*e*) Initial National Records in crossbow class will only be ratified if scores submitted for recognised rounds given in Rules 502(*a*), (*b*) & (*c*) together with light and clout rounds exceed 60% of the freestyle record for the same named rounds as at 11.7.92.

703. Field Archery

(*a*) Record Rounds are restricted to National Animal, Unmarked Hunter, Marked Field and FITA Combination Rounds.

(*b*) National Records are to be maintained for all classes and styles in Field Archery. But initial claims for records in Compound classes will only be entertained if the scores submitted exceed 75% of the corresponding record scores for the conventional recurve bow class or style.

(*c*) National Records may be claimed by and granted to Junior Field archers (both under 12 and under 15 years of age) if the round shot was that appropriate to the age of the claimant, or if the claimant has shot a more difficult round than his age demanded. No Junior may hold a National Record for a round for a higher age group unless he has shot to the conditions appropriate to that age-group, and has stated his intentions to the organiser in advance.

(*d*) Records will not be kept for Juniors (under 12) class in respect of the National Animal Round.

704. Flight Shooting

(*a*) National Records may be claimed in all classes at a recognised Record Status tournament. The measurements must be checked and witnessed by the Range Captain and one other responsible person. In addition the Range Captain must certify that the ground over which the shot was made was reasonably flat and level.

(*b*) A new record may be established when the measurement is at least one yard longer than the existing record.

705. Clout Shooting

(*a*) National Records may be claimed for both single and double rounds shot 'one way' and 'two way' at distances stated in 404(*b*). Where a double round is shot on a single day the second round will not be accepted for a single round record.

(*b*) Initial National Records in Compound classes will only be ratified if the scores submitted exceed 75% of the existing freestyle record.

VIII. HANDICAP AND CLASSIFICATION SCHEMES
This section is given in GNAS Rules of Shooting.

IX. OTHER FORMS OF ARCHERY

900. Popinjay Shooting

Set-up for Popinjay

(*a*) The full complement of a Popinjay 'roost' shall consist of:
One Cock Bird
Four Hens
Minimum of twenty-four Chicks.

(*b*) Body size of all birds shall be 1½in long, ¾in diameter – only the plumage shall differ:
– that of the Cock Bird being most resplendent and 10in–12in high.
– that of the Hen Birds being shorter 6in–8in high and less colourful.
– that of the Chicks being shortest 3in–4in high.

(*c*) The Chicks shall be perched on spikes 6in long, not less than 4in apart, in three rows, the vertical height between rows being not less than 3 feet. The Hen Birds shall be perched on spikes 18in above the top row and shall be spaced not less than 8in apart.

The Cock Bird shall be perched on a central spike not less than 30in above the top row.

(*d*) The perches may be attached to, or hauled up a mast or wall to a height of 90 feet (measured to the Cock Bird).

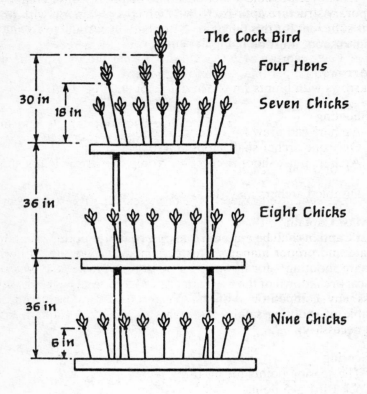

The Cock Bird

Four Hens

Seven Chicks

30 in

18 in

36 in

Eight Chicks

36 in

6 in

Nine Chicks

Typical Popinjay 'roost' showing minimum complement.

Arrangements must be made to ensure that when in position the perches are firmly held against movement by wind.

(*e*) All obstructions on and within the framework of perches must be softened with rubber or sponge rubber (or similar resilient material) to lessen the risk of arrow breakage.

(*f*) No hard and fast shooting position is dictated, although it should be pointed out to all competitors that a near vertical, close to mast attitude will offer a better target to the archer, inasmuch as a greater number of birds will be in line of the arrow flight path.

(*g*) Each and every part of the Popinjay Mast and Framework of

Perches must be made to be safe from breakage and/or dislodgement by arrow or the elements.

(*h*) Whenever possible a shelter should be provided for competitors; a temporary structure approx. 7ft 6in high covered on top with ½in wire mesh is sufficient for this purpose. If no shelter is available competitors waiting to shoot must be made to wait outside the arrow fall-out area.

901. Arrows
Only arrows with blunts ¾in to 1in diameter shall be used.

902. Shooting
(*a*) Archers will draw for order of shooting.

(*b*) Only one archer shall shoot at a time.

(*c*) Archers must shoot in rotation – only one arrow being shot per end.

(*d*) Disabled archers may shoot with the aid of a prop.

903. Mast Captain
A Mast Captain shall be appointed to ensure that shooting is conducted in a safe and proper manner. This person shall have the authority to terminate shooting – for instance in the event of inclement weather or technical breakdown of the mast apparatus – and shall have authority to dismiss any competitor shooting dangerously or considered to be incapable of shooting safely. Assistants to the Mast Captain may be found necessary.

904. Scoring
(*a*) The scoring points for hits are:

Cock Bird   – 5 points
Hen Bird   – 3 points
Chick   – 1 point

(*b*) Birds must be struck with the arrow and be dislodged and fall to the ground to score.

905. Round
Results may be determined by time limit or by a declared number of arrows.

906. Regulations for Tournaments
Popinjay Tournament Schedules shall bear the following information:

(*a*) Whether competition is determined by time limit or by number of arrows shot per person.

(*b*) Maximum number of archers that will be accepted.

Note: The GNAS Insurance Scheme does not cover for risks attendant on the erection and dismantling of Popinjay Masts.

920. Archery Golf
Regulations

(*a*) Only one bow shall be used throughout a round. In case of breakage it may be replaced.

(*b*) Any arrows may be used.

(*c*) The archer shall 'hole out' by hitting a white cardboard disc 4in in diameter, placed on the ground at least one yard within the edge of the green level with the hole.

(*d*) An arrow landing off the fairway or in a bunker shall incur one extra stroke.

(*e*) The archer must stand immediately behind where his arrow lands to shoot the next arrow.

(*f*) A lost arrow incurs the normal penalty (as in golf) for stroke play but loses the hole in match play.

(*g*) The winner of the previous 'hole' takes the first shot for the next hole.

(*h*) The current Golf Rules and local Course Regulations shall apply in all cases not covered by the foregoing rules.

940. Archery Darts
Regulations

GNAS Rules of Shooting for Target Archery shall apply except as enumerated in the following paragraphs:

Target Faces

Archery Darts Faces 76.2cm (2ft 6in) in diameter shall be used.

General Rules

(*a*) The targets shall be set up so that the centre of the Bull is at the centre of a 122cm minimum diameter boss 130cm from the ground.

(*b*) The minimum shooting distance shall be 13.7m (15yd).

(*c*) An End shall consist of three arrows unless a game is finished in less.

(*d*) The order of starting shall be determined by the toss of a coin.

(*e*) Each match must start and finish on a Double (the narrow outer ring). The inner ring counts treble; the inner Bull counts 50; and the outer Bull 25.

(*f*) A practice end of three arrows must be shot at the Bull.

(*g*) The value of an arrow shall be determined by the position of the greater part of the shaft.

(*h*) Scoring shall be by the subtraction method, so that the score required for the completion of each game is always shown.

(*j*) If the score required to complete the game is exceeded in the course of an End, then that End ceases, and no account is taken of the score obtained during that End.

Note: Local variations may be used.

APPENDIX A

Etiquette

A Good Archer:

Does not talk in a loud voice whilst others are shooting.

Does not talk to another competitor who obviously prefers to be silent.

Does not make any exclamation on the shooting line which might disconcert a neighbour in the act of shooting.

Does not go behind the target to retrieve his arrows before his score has been recorded.

Does not walk up and down the shooting line comparing scores.

Does not touch anyone else's equipment without permission.

Does not leave litter.

When calling scores does so in groups of three, for example '7–7–5' pause '5–5–3'.

If he breaks another's arrow through his own carelessness, pays for it in cash on the spot.

Thanks the Target Captain at the end of each round for work on his behalf.

APPENDIX B
Public Liability Insurance
APPENDIX C
Minimum Standard of the Judge for Tournaments
APPENDIX D
Metric Conversion Table
APPENDIX E
Rules of Shooting for Visually-Handicapped Archers
APPENDIX F
Drug Control Procedures
APPENDIX G
Approved Scoring System

Reprinted by permission of the Grand National Archery Society. A number of the Rules have here been abbreviated, and Appendixes B to G omitted, for reasons of space. Copies of the complete senior and junior Rules and Regulations and of the FITA Constitution and Rules can be obtained from the Society.

THE LAWS OF
Association Football

The Field of Play

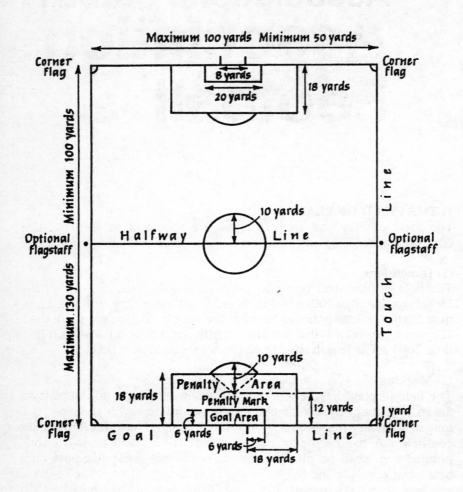

Association Football

1. THE FIELD OF PLAY

The Field of Play and appurtenances are shown in the plan on the opposite page.

(1) Dimensions

The field of play shall be rectangular, its length being not more than 130yd nor less than 100yd and its breadth not more than 100yd nor less than 50yd. (In International Matches the length shall be not more than 120yd nor less than 110yd and the breadth not more than 80yd nor less than 70yd.) The length shall in all cases exceed the breadth.

(2) Marking

The field of play shall be marked with distinctive lines, not more than 5in in width, not by a **V**-shaped rut, in accordance with the plan, the longer boundary lines being called the touch-lines and the shorter the goal-lines. A flag on a post not less than 5ft high and having a non-pointed top, shall be placed at each corner; a similar flag-post may be placed opposite the halfway-line on each side of the field of play, not less than 1yd outside the touch-line. A half-way line shall be marked out across the field of play. The centre of the field of play shall be indicated by a suitable mark and a circle with a 10yd radius shall be marked round it.

(3) The Goal-Area

At each end of the field of play two lines shall be drawn at right angles to the goal-line, 6yd from each goal-post. These shall extend into the field of play for a distance of 6yd and shall be joined by a line drawn parallel with the goal-line. Each of the spaces enclosed by these lines and the goal-line shall be called the goal-area.

(4) The Penalty-Area

At each end of the field of play two lines shall be drawn at right angles to the goal-line, 18yd from each goal-post. These shall extend into the field of play for a distance of 18yd and shall be joined by a line drawn parallel with the goal-line. Each of the spaces enclosed by these lines and the goal-line shall be called a penalty-area. A suitable mark shall be made within each penalty-area, 12yd from the mid-point of the goal-line, measured along an undrawn line at right angles thereto. These shall be the penalty-kick marks. From each penalty-kick mark an arc of a circle, having a radius of 10yd, shall be drawn outside the penalty-area.

(5) The Corner-Area

From each corner-flag post a quarter circle, having a radius of 1yd, shall be drawn inside the field of play.

(6) The Goals

The goals shall be placed on the centre of each goal-line and shall consist of two upright posts, equidistant from the corner-flags and 8yd apart (inside measurement), joined by a horizontal cross-bar, the lower edge of which shall be 8ft from the ground. The width and depth of the goal-posts and the width and depth of the cross-bars shall not exceed 5in (12cm). The goal-posts and the cross-bars shall have the same width.

   Nets may be attached to the posts, cross-bars and ground behind the goals. They should be appropriately supported and be so placed as to allow the goalkeeper ample room.

INTERNATIONAL BOARD DECISIONS

(1) In International Matches the dimensions of the field of play shall be: maximum 110m × 75m; minimum 100m × 64m.

(2) National Associations must adhere strictly to these dimensions. Each National Association organising an International Match must advise the Visiting Association, before the match, of the place and the dimensions of the field of play.

(3) The Board has approved this table for the Laws of the Game:

Table of Metric Equivalents

130yd	..	.. 120m	12yd ..	.. 11m
120yd	..	.. 110m	10yd ..	.. 9.15m
110yd	..	.. 100m	8yd ..	.. 7.32m
100yd	..	.. 90m	6yd ..	.. 5.50m
80yd	..	.. 75m	1yd ..	.. 1m
70yd	..	.. 64m	8ft ..	.. 2.44m
50yd	..	.. 45m	5ft ..	.. 1.50m
18yd	..	.. 16.50m	28in ..	.. 0.71m

27in	..	..	0.68m
9in	..	..	0.22m
5in	..	..	0.12m
$\frac{1}{2}$in	..	..	12.7mm
$\frac{3}{8}$in	..	..	10mm

14oz = 396g
16oz = 453g
8.5lb/sq in = 600g/cm^2
15.6lb/sq in = 1,100g/cm^2

(4) The goal-line shall be marked the same width as the depth of the goal-posts and the cross-bar so that the goal-line and the goal-posts will conform to the same interior and exterior edges.

(5) The 6yd (for the outline of the goal-area) and the 18yd (for the outline of the penalty-area), which have to be measured along the goal-line, must start from the inner sides of the goal-posts.

(6) The space within the inside areas of the field of play includes the width of the lines marking these areas.

(7) All Associations shall provide standard equipment, particularly in International Matches, when the Laws of the Game must be complied with in every respect and especially with regard to the size of the ball and other equipment which must conform to the regulations. All cases of failure to provide standard equipment must be reported to FIFA.

(8) In a match played under the rules of a competition, if the cross-bar becomes displaced or broken play shall be stopped and the match abandoned unless the cross-bar has been repaired and replaced in position or a new one provided without such being a danger to the players. A rope is not considered to be a satisfactory substitute for a cross-bar.

In a friendly match, by mutual consent, play may be resumed without the cross-bar provided it has been removed and no longer constitutes a danger to the players. In these circumstances, a rope may be used as a substitute for a cross-bar. If a rope is not used and the ball crosses the goal-line at a point which in the opinion of the Referee is below where the cross-bar should have been he shall award a goal.

The game shall be restarted by the Referee dropping the ball at the place where it was when play was stopped, unless it was within the goal-area at that time, in which case it shall be dropped on that part of the goal-area line which runs parallel to the goal-line, at the point nearest to where the ball was when play was stopped.

(9) National Associations may specify such maximum and minimum dimensions for the cross-bars and goal-posts, within the limits laid down in Law 1, as they consider appropriate.

(10) Goal-posts and cross-bars must be made of wood, metal or other approved material as decided from time to time by the International FA Board. They may be square, rectangular, round, half round, or elliptical in shape. Goal-posts and cross-bars made of other materials and in other shapes are not permitted. The goal-posts must be of white colour.

(11) 'Curtain-raisers' to International Matches should only be played following agreement on the day of the match, and taking into account the condition of the field of play, between representatives of the two Associations and the Referee (of the International Match).

(12) National Associations, particularly in International Matches, should restrict the number of photographers around the field of play, have a line ('photographers' line') marked behind the goal-lines at least 2m from the corner-flag going through a point at least 3.5 m behind the intersection of the goal-line with the line marking the goal-area to a point situated at least 6m behind the goal-posts, prohibit photographers from passing over these lines and forbid the use of artificial lighting in the form of 'flash-lights'.

Advice to Referees: Visit the ground in good time before a match to see that everything is in order. If through bad weather or negligence the state of the ground is such that it may endanger the players, refuse to sanction play. If the lines are not properly marked see that, if time allows, it is done before the match.

Examine the goal-nets before every match, ensure that they are properly pegged down and that they are intact.

2. THE BALL

The ball shall be spherical; the outer casing shall be of leather or other approved materials. No material shall be used in its construction which might prove dangerous to the players. The circumference of the ball shall not be more than 28in nor less than 27in. The weight of the ball at the start of the game shall not be more than 16oz nor less than 14oz. The pressure shall be equal to 0.6–1.1 atmosphere (= 600–1,100 g/cm^2) at sea level. The ball shall not be changed during the game unless authorised by the Referee.

INTERNATIONAL BOARD DECISIONS

(1) The ball used in any match shall be considered the property of the Association or Club on whose ground the match is played, and at the close of play it must be returned to the Referee.

(2) The International Board, from time to time, shall decide what constitutes approved materials. Any approved material shall be certified as such by the International Board.

(3) The board has approved these equivalents of the weights specified in the Law:

14 to 16 ounces = 396 to 453 grammes.

(4) If the ball bursts or becomes deflated during the course of a match, the game shall be stopped and restarted by dropping the new ball at the

place where the first ball became defective, unless it was within the goal-area at that time, in which case it shall be dropped on that part of the goal-area line which runs parallel to the goal-line, at the point nearest to where the ball was when play was stopped.

(5) If this happens during a stoppage of the game (place-kick, goal-kick, corner-kick, free-kick, penalty-kick or throw-in) the game shall be restarted accordingly.

3. NUMBER OF PLAYERS

(1) A match shall be played by two teams, each consisting of not more than 11 players, one of whom shall be the goalkeeper.

(2) Substitutes may be used in any match played under the rules of an official competition under the jurisdiction of FIFA, Confederations or National Associations, subject to the following conditions:

(*a*) That the authority of the International Association(s) or National Association(s) concerned has been obtained;

(*b*) That, subject to the restriction contained in the following paragraphs (*c*) and (*d*), the rules of a competition shall state how many, if any, substitutes may be designated and how many of those designated may be used;

(*c*) That a team shall not be permitted to use more than two substitutes in any match who must be chosen from not more than five players whose names may (subject to the rules of the competition) be required to be given to the Referee prior to the commencement of the match.

(*d*) Notwithstanding the limitation imposed in (*c*), a team may also use a third substitute provided that he is designated as a substitute goalkeeper, who may be used to replace only the goalkeeper.

If, however, the goalkeeper is ordered off, the designated subtitute goalkeeper may subsequently replace another player of the same team and play as goalkeeper.

(3) Substitutes may be used in any other match provided that the two teams concerned reach agreement on a maximum number, not exceeding five, and that the terms of such agreement are intimated to the Referee, before the match. If the Referee is not informed, or if the teams fail to reach agreement, no more than 2 substitutes shall be permitted. In all cases the substitutes must be chosen from not more than five players whose names may be required to be given to the Referee prior to the commencement of the match.

(4) Any of the other players may change places with the goalkeeper, provided that the Referee is informed before the change is made, and provided also that the change is made during a stoppage in the game.

(5) When a goalkeeper or any other player is to be replaced by a substitute, the following conditions shall be observed:

(*a*) The Referee shall be informed of the proposed substitution, before it is made;

(*b*) The substitute shall not enter the field of play until the player he is replacing has left, and then only after having received a signal from the Referee;

(*c*) He shall enter the field during a stoppage in the game, and at the halfway-line;

(*d*) A player who has been replaced shall not take any further part in the game;

(*e*) A substitute shall be subject to the authority and jurisdiction of the Referee whether called upon to play or not;

(*f*) The substitution is completed when the substitute enters the field of play, from which moment he becomes a player and the player whom he is replacing ceases to be a player.

Punishment: (*a*) Play shall not be stopped for an infringement of paragraph 4. The players concerned shall be cautioned immediately the ball goes out of play.

(*b*) If a substitute enters the field of play without the authority of the Referee, play shall be stopped. The substitute shall be cautioned and removed from the field or sent off according to the circumstances. The game shall be restarted by the Referee dropping the ball at the place where it was when he stopped play, unless it was within the goal-area at that time, in which case it shall be dropped on that part of the goal area line which runs parallel to the goal-line, at the point nearest to where the ball was when play was stopped.

(*c*) For any other infringement of this Law, the player concerned shall be cautioned, and if the game is stopped by the Referee to administer the caution, it shall be restarted by an indirect free-kick, to be taken by a player of the opposing team, from the place where the ball was when play was stopped, subject to the over-riding conditions imposed in Law 13.

(*d*) If a Competition's rules require the names of substitutes to be given to the Referee, prior to the commencement of the match, then failure to do so will mean that no substitutes can be permitted.

INTERNATIONAL BOARD DECISIONS

(1) The minimum number of players in a team is left to the discretion of National Associations.

(2) The Board is of the opinion that a match should not be considered valid if there are fewer than 7 players in either of the teams.

(3) A player who has been ordered off before play begins may only be replaced by one of the named substitutes. The kick-off must not be delayed to allow the substitute to join his team.

A player who has been ordered off after play has started may not be replaced. A named substitute who has been ordered off, either before or after play has started, may not be replaced. (This decision only relates to players who are ordered off under Law 12. It does not apply to players who have infringed Law 4.)

4. PLAYERS' EQUIPMENT

(1) (*a*) The basic compulsory equipment of a player shall consist of a jersey or shirt, shorts, stockings, shinguards and footwear.

(*b*) A player shall not wear anything which is dangerous to another player.

(2) Shinguards, which must be covered entirely by the stockings, shall be made of a suitable material (rubber, plastic, polyurethane or similar substance) and shall afford a reasonable degree of protection.

(3) The goalkeeper shall wear colours which distinguish him from the other players and from the Referee.

Punishment: For any infringement of this Law, the player at fault shall be instructed to leave the field of play by the Referee, to adjust his equipment or obtain any missing equipment, when the ball next ceases to be in play, unless by then the player has already corrected his equipment. Play shall not be stopped immediately for an infringement of this Law. A player who is instructed to leave the field to adjust his equipment or obtain missing equipment shall not return without first reporting to the Referee, who shall satisfy himself that the player's equipment is in order. The player shall only re-enter the game at a moment when the ball has ceased to be in play.

INTERNATIONAL BOARD DECISIONS

(1) In International Matches, International Competitions, International Club Competitions and friendly matches between clubs of different National Associations, the Referee, prior to the start of the game, shall inspect the players' equipment, and prevent any player whose equipment does not conform to the requirements of this Law from playing until such time as it does comply.

The rules of any competition may include a similar provision.

(2) If the Referee finds that a player is wearing articles not permitted by the Laws and which may constitute a danger to other players, he shall order him to take them off. If he fails to carry out the Referee's instruction, the player shall not take part in the match.

(3) A player who has been prevented from taking part in the game or a player who has been sent off the field for infringing Law 4 must report to the Referee during a stoppage of the game and may not enter or re-enter the field of play unless and until the Referee has satisfied himself that the player is no longer infringing Law 4.

(4) A player who has been prevented from taking part in a game or who has been sent off because of an infringement of Law 4, and who enters or re-enters the field of play to join or rejoin his team in breach of the conditions of Law 12 (*j*), shall be cautioned.

If the Referee stops the game to administer the caution, the game shall be restarted by an indirect free-kick, taken by a player of the opposing side, from the place where the ball was when the Referee stopped the game, subject to the over-riding conditions in Law 13.

Advice to Referees: If asked to do so, examine the players' footwear or other equipment before the match or during the interval. If you have any reason for doubt you may require to examine a player's footwear etc. at any time.

For infringement of this Law there is no need to wait for any appeal; note the offence, which need not be reported.

5. REFEREES

A Referee shall be appointed to officiate in each game. His authority and the exercise of the powers granted to him by the Laws of the Game commence as soon as he enters the field of play.

His power of penalising shall extend to offences committed when play has been temporarily suspended, or when the ball is out of play. His decisions on points of fact connected with the play shall be final, so far as the result of the game is concerned.

He shall:

(*a*) Enforce the Laws.

(*b*) Refrain from penalising in cases where he is satisfied that, by doing so, he would be giving an advantage to the offending team.

(*c*) Keep a record of the game; act as timekeeper and allow the full or agreed time, adding thereto all time lost through accident or other cause.

(*d*) Have discretionary power to stop the game for any infringement of the Laws and to suspend or terminate the game whenever, by reason of the elements, interference by spectators, or other cause, he deems such stoppage necessary. In such a case he shall submit a detailed report to the competent authority, within the stipulated time, and in accordance with the provisions set up by the National Association under whose jurisdiction the match was played.

(*e*) From the time he enters the field of play, caution and show a yellow card to any player guilty of misconduct or ungentlemanly behaviour. In such cases the Referee shall send the name of the offender to the competent authority, within the stipulated time,* and in accord-

*In England, within two days, Sunday not included.

ance with the provisions set up by the National Association under whose jurisdiction the match was played.

(*f*) Allow no person other than the players and Linesmen to enter the field of play without his permission.

(*g*) Stop the game if, in his opinion, a player has been seriously injured; have the player removed as soon as possible from the field of play, and immediately resume the game. If a player is slightly injured the game shall not be stopped until the ball has ceased to be in play. A player who is able to go to the touch- or goal-line for attention of any kind shall not be treated on the field of play.

(*h*) Send off the field of play and show a red card to any player who, in his opinion, is guilty of violent conduct, serious foul play, the use of foul or abusive language, or who persists in misconduct after having received a caution.

(*i*) Signal for recommencement of the game after all stoppages.

(*j*) Decide that the ball provided for a match meets with the requirements of Law 2.

INTERNATIONAL BOARD DECISIONS

(1) Referees in International Matches shall wear a blazer or blouse the colour of which is distinctive from the colours worn by the contesting teams.

(2) Referees for International Matches will be selected from a neutral country unless the countries concerned agree to appoint their own officials.

(3) The Referee must be chosen from the official list of International Referees. This need not apply to Amateur and Youth International matches.

(4) The Referee shall report to the appropriate authority misconduct or any misdemeanour on the part of spectators, officials, players, named substitutes or other persons which take place either on the field of play or in its vicinity at any time prior to, during, or after the match in question so that appropriate action can be taken by the authority concerned.

(5) Linesmen are assistants of the Referee. In no case shall the Referee consider the intervention of a Linesman if he himself has seen the incident and, from his position on the field, is better able to judge. With this reserve, and the Linesmen neutral, the Referee can consider the intervention and if the information of the Linesman applies to that phase of the game immediately before the scoring of a goal, the Referee may act thereon and cancel the goal.

(6) The Referee, however, can only reverse his first decision so long as the game has not been restarted.

(7) If the Referee has decided to apply the advantage clause and to let the game proceed, he cannot revoke his decision if the presumed advantage has not been realised, even though he has not, by any gesture, indicated his decision. This does not exempt the offending player from being dealt with by the Referee.

(8) The Laws of the Game are intended to provide that games should be played with as little interference as possible, and in this view it is the duty of Referees to penalise only deliberate breaches of the Law. Constant whistling for trifling and doubtful breaches produces bad feeling and loss of temper on the part of the players and spoils the pleasure of spectators.

(9) By paragraph (*d*) of Law 5 the Referee is empowered to terminate a match in the event of grave disorder, but he has no power or right to decide, in such event, that either team is disqualified and thereby the loser of the match. He must send a detailed report to the proper authority who alone has the power to deal further with this matter.

(10) If a player commits two infringements of a different nature at the same time, the Referee shall punish the more serious offence.

(11) It is the duty of the Referee to act upon the information of neutral Linesmen with regard to incidents that do not come under the personal notice of the Referee.

(12) The Referee shall not allow any person to enter the field until play has stopped, and only then, if he has given him a signal to do so.

(13) The coach may convey tactical instructions to players during the match.

The coach and other officials, however, must remain within the confines of the technical area, where such an area is provided, and they must conduct themselves, at all times, in a responsible manner.

(14) In tournaments or competitions where a fourth official is appointed, his role and duties shall be in accordance with the guide-lines approved by the International Football Association Board.

Advice to Referees: To referee in such a way that you will win the respect of players and spectators:–

(*a*) Learn to understand every Law.

(*b*) Be absolutely fair and impartial in every decision.

(*c*) Keep physically fit and in good training.

When considering the suspension or abandonment of a match on account of adverse or deteriorating weather conditions, only make a decision after very careful consideration of all relevant factors.

When cautioning a player, state he is being cautioned and inquire his name, and that if he persists in misconduct after having received a caution, he will be ordered off the field. The Referee will only show the yellow card after this procedure has been completed.

If a player is to be sent off for a second cautionable offence in a match, the Referee is required to show first the yellow card and immediately afterwards the red card (thus making it obvious that the player is being sent off because of a second cautionable offence and not because of an offence requiring immediate expulsion). For a single offence requiring an immediate expulsion, only the red card is shown after the standard procedure.

Note the procedure if a player is cautioned; a Referee who fails to report misconduct which came under his notice may be suspended, if it is proved to the satisfaction of the Council that the case of misconduct should have been further investigated.

Compare watches with the Linesmen, both before the game and at half-time.

Do not trust to memory alone in keeping a record of the game; note the time of start and the time at which, if no time has to be allowed for stoppages, half-time and the end of the game will fall due. Note also the goals as they are scored.

The application of the provisions of 5 (g) should be strictly observed. Referees should be concerned about the welfare of players in their application of this section and are reminded of the need for a rapid assessment and to stop play when a serious injury and/or head injury occurs; they must be vigilant and err on the side of caution in such cases. Care needs to be exercised before a seriously injured player is removed from the field of play – continue to err on the side of safety – and accept the advice of those who are medically qualified or claim to have such similar skills.

Registered Referees are not permitted to officiate in unsanctioned matches or competitions.

6. LINESMEN

Two Linesmen shall be appointed whose duty (subject to the decision of the Referee) shall be to indicate:

(a) When the ball is out of play;
(b) Which side is entitled to a corner-kick, goal-kick or throw-in;
(c) When a substitution is desired.

They shall also assist the Referee to control the game in accordance with the Laws. In the event of undue interference or improper conduct by a Linesman, the Referee shall dispense with his services and arrange for a substitute to be appointed. (The matter shall be reported by the Referee to the competent authority.) The Linesmen should be equipped with flags by the Club on whose ground the match is played.

INTERNATIONAL BOARD DECISIONS

(1) Linesmen where neutral shall draw the Referee's attention to any breach of the Laws of the Game of which they become aware if they

consider that the Referee may not have seen it, but the Referee shall always be the judge of the decision to be taken.

(2) In International 'A' Matches, National Associations should appoint neutral Linesmen from the International List.

(3) In International Matches, Linesmen's flags shall be of a vivid colour – bright reds and yellows. Such flags are recommended for use in all other matches.

(4) A Linesman may be subject to disciplinary action only upon a report of the Referee for unjustified interference or insufficient assistance.

Advice to Referees: To prevent being touched by the ball or interfering with play, Linesmen should, as far as possible, keep out of the field of play.

7. DURATION OF THE GAME

The duration of the game shall be two equal periods of 45 minutes, unless otherwise mutually agreed upon subject to the following:

(*a*) Allowance shall be made in either period for all time lost through substitution, the transport from the field of injured players, time-wasting or other cause, the amount of which shall be a matter for the discretion of the Referee.

(*b*) Time shall be extended to permit of a penalty-kick being taken at or after the expiration of the normal period in either half.

At half-time the interval shall not exceed 5 minutes, except by the consent of the Referee.

INTERNATIONAL BOARD DECISIONS

(1) If a match has been stopped by the Referee, before the completion of the time specified in the Rules, for any reason stated in Law 5, it must be replayed in full unless the rules of the competition concerned provide for the result of the match at the time of such stoppage to stand.

(2) Players have a right to an interval at half-time.

Advice to Referees: A Referee has no power to set aside the Rules of Cup and other Competitions where the time to be played is specified. It is essential that Referees are aware of precise details of Competition Rules, e.g. number of substitutions, method of deciding the outcome of drawn matches.

Normal period means 90 minutes, or if a shorter period is mutually agreed upon and is permissible under the Rules of the Competition, the period should be divided in equal halves.

8. THE START OF PLAY

(*a*) *At the beginning of the game* choice of ends and the kick-off shall be decided by the toss of a coin. The team winning the toss shall have the option of choice of ends or the kick-off.

The Referee having given a signal, the game shall be started by a player taking a place-kick (i.e. a kick at the ball while it is stationary on the ground in the centre of the field of play) into his opponents' half of the field of play. Every player shall be in his own half of the field and every player of the team opposing that of the kicker shall remain not less than 10yd from the ball until it is kicked-off; it shall not be deemed in play until it has travelled the distance of its own circumference. The kicker shall not play the ball a second time until it has been played or touched by another player.

(*b*) *After a goal has been scored* the game shall be restarted in like manner by a player of the team losing the goal.

(*c*) *After half-time*: When restarting after half-time, ends shall be changed and the kick-off shall be taken by a player of the opposite team to that of the player who started the game.

Punishment. For any infringement of this Law, the kick-off shall be retaken, except in the case of the kicker playing the ball again before it has been touched or played by another player; for this offence, an indirect free-kick shall be taken by a player of the opposing team from the place where the infringement occurred, subject to the over-riding conditions imposed in Law 13.

A goal shall not be scored direct from a kick-off.

(*d*) *After any other temporary suspension*: When restarting the game after a temporary suspension of play from any cause not mentioned elsewhere in these Laws, provided that immediately prior to the suspension the ball has not passed over the touch- or goal-lines, the Referee shall drop the ball at the place where it was when play was suspended, unless it was within the goal-area at that time, in which case it shall be dropped on that part of the goal-area line which runs parallel to the goal-line, at the point nearest to where the ball was when play was stopped. It shall be deemed in play when it has touched the ground; if, however, it goes over the touch- or goal-lines after it has been dropped by the Referee, but before it is touched by a player, the Referee shall again drop it. A player shall not play the ball until it has touched the ground. If this section of the Law is not complied with the Referee shall again drop the ball.

INTERNATIONAL BOARD DECISIONS

(1) If, when the Referee drops the ball, a player infringes any of the Laws before the ball has touched the ground, the player concerned shall be cautioned or sent off the field according to the seriousness of the offence, but a free-kick cannot be awarded to the opposing team

because the ball was not in play at the time of the offence. The ball shall therefore be again dropped by the Referee.

(2) Kicking-off by persons other than the players competing in a match is prohibited.

Advice to Referees: Note which side kick off; the kick must be taken by a player competing in the match.

When extra time is necessary, play shall be restarted according to 8(*a*). The interval between the end of the normal period of play and the start of the extra period shall be under the jurisdiction of the Referee.

9. BALL IN AND OUT OF PLAY
The ball is out of play:

(*a*) When it has wholly crossed the goal-line or touch-line, whether on the ground or in the air.

(*b*) When the game has been stopped by the Referee.

The ball is in play at all other times from the start of the match to the finish, including:

(*a*) If it rebounds from a goal-post, cross-bar or corner-flag post into the field of play.

(*b*) If it rebounds off either the Referee or Linesmen when they are in the field of play.

(*c*) In the event of a supposed infringement of the Laws, until a decision is given.

INTERNATIONAL BOARD DECISIONS
(1) The lines belong to the areas of which they are the boundaries. In consequence, the touch-lines and the goal-lines belong to the field of play.

10. METHOD OF SCORING
Except as otherwise provided by these Laws, a goal is scored when the whole of the ball has passed over the goal-line, between the goal-posts and under the cross-bar, provided it has not been thrown, carried or intentionally propelled by hand or arm, by a player of the attacking side, except in the case of a goalkeeper, who is within his own penalty-area.

The team scoring the greater number of goals during the game shall be the winner; if no goals or an equal number of goals are scored the game shall be termed a 'draw'.

INTERNATIONAL BOARD DECISIONS
(1) Law 10 defines the only method according to which a match is won or drawn; no variation whatsoever can be authorised.

(2) A goal cannot in any case be allowed if the ball has been prevented by some outside agency from passing over the goal-line. If this happens in the normal course of play, other than at the taking of a penalty-kick, the game must be stopped and restarted by the Referee dropping the ball at the place where the ball came into contact with the interference, unless it was within the goal-area at that time, in which case it shall be dropped on that part of the goal-area line which runs parallel to the goal-line, at the point nearest to where the ball was when play was stopped.

(3) If, when the ball is going into goal, a spectator enters the field before it passes wholly over the goal-line, and tries to prevent a score, a goal shall be allowed if the ball goes into goal, unless the spectator has made contact with the ball or has interfered with play, in which case the Referee shall stop the game and restart it by dropping the ball at the place where the contact or interference occurred, unless it was within the goal-area at that time, in which case it shall be dropped on that part of the goal-area line which runs parallel to the goal-line, at the point nearest to where the ball was when play was stopped.

11. OFF-SIDE

(1) A player is in an off-side position if he is nearer to his opponents' goal-line than the ball, unless:

(a) He is in his own half of the field of play; or

(b) He is not nearer to his opponents' goal-line than at least two of his opponents.

(2) A player shall only be declared off-side and penalised for being in an off-side position, if, at the moment the ball touches, or is played by, one of his team, he is, in the opinion of the Referee:

(a) Interfering with play or with an opponent; or

(b) Seeking to gain an advantage by being in that position.

(3) A player shall not be declared off-side by the Referee:

(a) Merely because of his being in an off-side position; or

(b) If he receives the ball, direct, from a goal-kick, a corner-kick, or a throw-in.

(4) If a player is declared off-side, the Referee shall award an indirect free-kick, which shall be taken by a player of the opposing team from the place where the infringement occurred, unless the offence is committed by a player in his opponents' goal-area, in which case, the free-kick shall be taken from any point within the goal-area.

INTERNATIONAL BOARD DECISIONS

(1) Off-side shall not be judged at the moment the player in question receives the ball, but at the moment when the ball is passed to him by one of his own side. A player who is not in an off-side position when one

of his colleagues passes the ball to him, or takes a free-kick, does not therefore become off-side if he goes forward during the flight of the ball. (2) A player who is level with the second last opponent or with the last two opponents is not in an off-side position.

12. FOULS AND MISCONDUCT

A player who intentionally commits any of the following nine offences:

(*a*) Kicks or attempts to kick an opponent;

(*b*) Trips an opponent, i.e. throwing or attempting to throw him by the use of the legs or by stooping in front of or behind him;

(*c*) Jumps at an opponent;

(*d*) Charges an opponent in a violent or dangerous manner;

(*e*) Charges an opponent from behind unless the latter be obstructing;

(*f*) Strikes or attempts to strike an opponent or spits at him;

(*g*) Holds an opponent;

(*h*) Pushes an opponent;

(*i*) Handles the ball, i.e. carries, strikes or propels the ball with his hand or arm (this does not apply to the goalkeeper within his own penalty-area);

shall be penalised by the award of a *direct free-kick* to be taken by the opposing side from the place where the offence occurred, unless the offence is committed by a player in his opponents' goal-area, in which case the free-kick shall be taken from any point within the goal-area.

Should a player of the defending side intentionally commit one of the above nine offences within the penalty-area he shall be penalised by a *penalty-kick*.

A penalty-kick can be awarded irrespective of the position of the ball, if in play, at the time an offence within the penalty-area is committed.

A player committing any of the five following offences:

1. Playing in a manner considered by the Referee to be dangerous, e.g. attempting to kick the ball while held by the goalkeeper;

2. Charging fairly, i.e. with the shoulder, when the ball is not within playing distance of the players concerned and they are definitely not trying to play it;

3. When not playing the ball, intentionally obstructing an opponent, i.e. running between the opponent and the ball, or interposing the body so as to form an obstacle to an opponent;

4. Charging the goalkeeper except when he:

(*a*) Is holding the ball;

(*b*) Is obstructing an opponent;

(*c*) Has passed outside his goal-area;

5. When playing as goalkeeper and within his own penalty-area:

(*a*) From the moment he takes control of the ball with his hands, he takes more than 4 steps in any direction whilst holding, bouncing or throwing the ball in the air and catching it again without releasing it into play; or

(*b*) having released the ball into play before, during or after the 4 steps, he touches it again with his hands, before it has been touched or played by another player of the same team outside the penalty-area, or by a player of the opposing team either inside or outside of the penalty-area; or

(*c*) touches the ball with his hands after it has been deliberately kicked to him by a team-mate, or

(*d*) indulges in tactics which, in the opinion of the Referee, are designed merely to hold up the game and thus waste time and so give an unfair advantage to his own team,

shall be penalised by the award of an *indirect free-kick* to be taken by the opposing side from the place where the infringement occurred, subject to the over-riding conditions imposed in Law 13.

A player shall be *cautioned* and shown the yellow card if:

(*j*) He enters or re-enters the field of play to join or rejoin his team after the game has commenced, or leaves the field of play during the progress of the game (except through accident) without, in either case, first having received a signal from the Referee showing him that he may do so. If the Referee stops the game to administer the caution it shall be restarted by an indirect free-kick taken by a player of the opposing team from the place where the ball was when the Referee stopped the game, subject to the over-riding conditions imposed in Law 13. If, however, the offending player has committed a more serious offence he shall be penalised according to that section of the Law he infringed;

(*k*) He persistently infringes the Laws of the Game.

(*l*) He shows, by word or action, dissent from any decision given by the Referee;

(*m*) He is guilty of ungentlemanly conduct.

For any of these last three offences, in addition to the caution, an *indirect free-kick* shall be awarded to the opposing side from the place where the offence occurred, subject to the over-riding conditions imposed in Law 13, unless a more serious infringement of the Laws of the Game was committed.

A player shall be sent off the field of play and shown the red card if in the opinion of the Referee, he:

(*n*) Is guilty of violent conduct;

(*o*) Is guilty of serious foul play;

(*p*) Uses foul or abusive language;

(*q*) Is guilty of a second cautionable offence after having received a caution.

If play is stopped by reason of a player being ordered from the field for an offence without a separate breach of the Law having been committed, the game shall be resumed by an *indirect free-kick* awarded to the opposing side from the place where the infringement occurred, subject to the over-riding conditions imposed in Law 13.

INTERNATIONAL BOARD DECISIONS

(1) If the goalkeeper either intentionally strikes an opponent by throwing the ball vigorously at him, or pushes him with the ball while holding it, the Referee shall award a penalty-kick, if the offence took place within the penalty-area.

(2) If a player deliberately turns his back to an opponent when he is about to be tackled, he may be charged but not in a dangerous manner.

(3) In case of body-contact in the goal-area between an attacking player and the opposing goalkeeper not in possession of the ball, the Referee, as sole judge of intention, shall stop the game if, in his opinion, the action of the attacking player was intentional, and award an indirect free-kick.

(4) If a player leans on the shoulders of another player of his own team in order to head the ball, the Referee shall stop the game, caution the player for ungentlemanly conduct and award an indirect free-kick to the opposing side.

(5) A player's obligation when joining or rejoining his team after the start of the match to 'report to the Referee' must be interpreted as meaning to 'draw the attention of the Referee from the touch-line'. The signal from the Referee shall be made by a definite gesture which makes the player understand that he may come into the field of play; it is not necessary for the Referee to wait until the game is stopped (this does not apply in respect of an infringement of Law 4), but the Referee is the sole judge of the moment in which he gives his signal of acknowledgement.

(6) The letter and spirit of Law 12 do not oblige the Referee to stop a game to administer a caution. He may, if he chooses, apply the advantage. If he does apply the advantage, he shall caution the player when play stops.

(7) If a player covers up the ball without touching it in an endeavour not to have it played by an opponent, he obstructs but does not infringe Law 12, paragraph 3, because he is already in possession of the ball and covers it for tactical reasons whilst the ball remains within playing distance. In fact, he is actually playing the ball and does not commit an infringement; in this case, the player may be charged because he is in fact playing the ball.

(8) If a player intentionally stretches his arms to obstruct an opponent

and steps from one side to the other, moving his arms up and down to delay his opponent, forcing him to change course, but does not make 'bodily contact' the Referee shall caution the player for ungentlemanly conduct and award an indirect free-kick.

(9) If a player intentionally obstructs the opposing goalkeeper, in an attempt to prevent him from putting the ball into play in accordance with Law 12, 5(a), the Referee shall award an indirect free-kick.

(10) If after a Referee has awarded a free-kick a player protests violently by using abusive or foul language and is sent off the field, the free-kick should not be taken until the player has left the field.

(11) Any player, whether he is within or outside the field of play, whose conduct is ungentlemanly or violent, whether or not it is directed towards an opponent, a colleague, the Referee, a Linesman or other person, or who uses foul or abusive language, is guilty of an offence, and shall be dealt with according to the nature of the offence committed.

(12) If in the opinion of the Referee a goalkeeper intentionally lies on the ball longer than is necessary, he shall be penalised for ungentlemanly conduct and:

(a) Be cautioned, and an indirect free-kick awarded to the opposing team;

(b) In case of repetition of the offence, be sent off the field.

(13) The offence of spitting at officials or other persons, or similar unseemly behaviour, shall be considered as violent conduct within the meaning of section (n) of Law 12.

(14) If, when a Referee is about to caution a player, and before he has done so, the player commits another offence which merits a caution, the player shall be sent off the field of play.

(15) If, in the opinion of the Referee, a player who is moving toward his opponents' goal with an obvious opportunity to score a goal is intentionally impeded by an opponent, through unlawful means, i.e. an offence punishable by a free-kick (or a penalty-kick), thus denying the attacking player's team the aforesaid goal-scoring opportunity, the offending player shall be sent off the field of play for serious foul play in accordance with Law 12(o).

(16) If, in the opinion of the Referee, a player, other than the goalkeeper within his own penalty-area, denies his opponents a goal, or an obvious goal-scoring opportunity, by intentionally handling the ball, he shall be sent off the field of play for serious foul play in accordance with Law 12(o).

(17) The International FA Board is of the opinion that a goalkeeper, in the circumstances described in Law 12, 5(a), will be considered to be in control of the ball when he takes possession of the ball by touching it with any part of his hands or arms. Possession of the ball would include the goalkeeper intentionally parrying the ball, but would not include the

circumstances where, in the opinion of the Referee, the ball rebounds accidentally from the goalkeeper, for example after he has made a save. (18) Subject to the terms of Law 12, a player may pass the ball to his own goalkeeper using his head or chest or knee, etc. If, however, in the opinion of the Referee, a player uses a deliberate trick in order to circumvent article 5(c) of Law 12, the player will be guilty of ungentlemanly conduct and will be punished accordingly under the terms of Law 12; that is to say, the player will be cautioned and shown the yellow card and an indirect free-kick will be awarded to the opposing team from the place where the player committed the offence.

In such circumstances, it is irrelevant whether the goalkeeper subsequently touches the ball with his hands or not. The offence is committed by the player in attempting to circumvent both the text and the spirit of Law 12.

Advice to Referees: A thorough knowledge of this Law is absolutely essential, but its correct application depends on the Referee's ability to make up his mind whether or not a player's offending action is intentional/deliberate.

Jumping at an opponent and not jumping for the ball is a foul; there is no such thing as accidental jumping at an opponent.

Although an opponent is entitled to make a fair charge on the goalkeeper when he is holding the ball in his hands, it is not then permissible for an opponent to attempt to kick the ball.

13. FREE-KICK

Free-kicks shall be classified under two headings:

'Direct' (from which a goal can be scored direct against the *offending side*), and 'Indirect' (from which a goal cannot be scored unless the ball has been played or touched by a player other than the kicker before passing through the goal).

When a player is taking a direct or an indirect free-kick inside his own penalty-area, all of the opposing players shall be at least 10yd (9.15m) from the ball and shall remain outside the penalty-area until the ball has been kicked out of the area. The ball shall be in play immediately it has travelled the distance of its own circumference and is beyond the penalty-area. The goalkeeper shall not receive the ball into his hands, in order that he may thereafter kick it into play. If the ball is not kicked direct into play, beyond the penalty-area, the kick shall be retaken.

When a player is taking a direct or an indirect free-kick outside his own penalty-area, all of the opposing players shall be at least 10yd from the ball, until it is in play, unless they are standing on their own goal-line, between the goal-posts. The ball shall be in play when it has travelled the distance of its own circumference.

If a player of the opposing side encroaches into the penalty-area, or within 10yd of the ball, as the case may be, before a free-kick is taken, the Referee shall delay the taking of the kick until the Law is complied with.

The ball must be stationary when a free-kick is taken, and the kicker shall not play the ball a second time, until it has been touched or played by another player.

Notwithstanding any other reference in these Laws to the point from which a free-kick is to be taken:

1. Any free-kick awarded to the defending team, within its own goal-area, may be taken from any other point within the goal-area.

2. Any indirect free-kick awarded to the attacking team within its opponents' goal-area shall be taken from the part of the goal-area line which runs parallel to the goal-line, at the point nearest to where the offence was committed.

Punishment. If the kicker, after taking the free-kick, plays the ball a second time before it has been touched or played by another player, an indirect free-kick shall be taken by a player of the opposing team from the spot where the infringement occurred, unless the offence is committed by a player in his opponents' goal-area, in which case the free-kick shall be taken from the point anywhere within that half of the goal-area in which the offence occurred.

INTERNATIONAL BOARD DECISIONS

(1) In order to distinguish between a direct and an indirect free-kick, the Referee, when he awards an indirect free-kick, shall indicate accordingly by raising an arm above his head. He shall keep his arm in that position until the kick has been taken and retain the signal until the ball has been played or touched by another player or goes out of play.

(2) Players who do not retire to the proper distance when a free-kick is taken must be cautioned and on any repetition be ordered off. It is particularly requested of Referees that attempts to delay the taking of a free-kick by encroaching should be treated as serious misconduct.

(3) If, when a free-kick is being taken, any of the players dance about or gesticulate in a way calculated to distract their opponents, it shall be deemed ungentlemanly conduct for which the offender(s) shall be cautioned.

Advice to Referees: If a player kicks the ball directly into his own goal from a direct or indirect free-kick, the Referee should award a corner-kick provided that in the case of a free-kick inside the penalty-area the ball had first been kicked into play. In this context any free-kick incorrectly taken from inside the penalty-area must be retaken. When a player kicks the ball directly into his opponents' goal from an indirect free-kick, the Referee should award a goal-kick to the opponents.

14. PENALTY-KICK

A penalty-kick shall be taken from the penalty-mark and, when it is being taken, all players, with the exception of the player taking the kick, properly identified, and the opposing goalkeeper, shall be within the field of play but outside the penalty-area, and at least 10yd from the penalty-mark. The opposing goalkeeper must stand (without moving his feet) on his own goal-line, between the goal-posts, until the ball is kicked. The player taking the kick must kick the ball forward; he shall not play the ball a second time until it has been touched or played by another player. The ball shall be deemed in play directly it is kicked, i.e. when it has travelled the distance of its circumference. A goal may be scored direct from a penalty-kick. When a penalty-kick is being taken during the normal course of play, or when time has been extended at half-time or full-time to allow a penalty-kick to be taken or retaken, a goal shall not be nullified if, before passing between the posts and under the cross-bar, the ball touches either or both of the goal-posts, or the cross-bar, or the goalkeeper, or any combination of these agencies, providing that no other infringement has occurred.

Punishment: For any infringement of this Law:

(*a*) By the defending team, the kick shall be retaken if a goal has not resulted;

(*b*) By the attacking team, other than by the player taking the kick, if a goal is scored the goal shall be disallowed and the kick retaken;

(*c*) By the player taking the penalty-kick, committed after the ball is in play, a player of the opposing team shall take an indirect free-kick from the spot where the infringement occurred, subject to the over-riding conditions imposed in Law 13.

INTERNATIONAL BOARD DECISIONS

(1) When the Referee has awarded a penalty-kick, he shall not signal for it to be taken until the players have taken up position in accordance with the Law.

(2) (*a*) If, after the kick has been taken, the ball is stopped in its course towards goal, by an outside agent, the kick shall be retaken.

(*b*) If, after the kick has been taken, the ball rebounds into play, from the goalkeeper, the cross-bar or a goal-post, and is then stopped in its course by an outside agent, the Referee shall stop play and restart it by dropping the ball at the place where it came into contact with the outside agent, unless it was within the goal-area at that time, in which case it shall be dropped on that part of the goal-area line which runs parallel to the goal-line, at the point nearest to where the ball was when play was stopped.

(3) (*a*) If, after having given the signal for a penalty-kick to be taken, the Referee sees that the goalkeeper is not in his right place on the goal-

line, he shall, nevertheless, allow the kick to proceed. It shall be retaken, if a goal is not scored.

(*b*) If, after the Referee has given the signal for the penalty-kick to be taken, and before the ball has been kicked, the goalkeeper moves his feet, the Referee shall, nevertheless, allow the kick to proceed. It shall be retaken, if a goal is not scored.

(*c*) If, after the Referee has given the signal for a penalty-kick to be taken, and before the ball is in play, a player of the defending team encroaches into the penalty-area, or within 10yd of the penalty-mark, the Referee shall, nevertheless, allow the kick to proceed. It shall be retaken, if a goal is not scored.

The player concerned shall be cautioned.

(4) (*a*) If, when a penalty-kick is being taken, the player taking the kick is guilty of ungentlemanly conduct, the kick, if already taken, shall be retaken, if a goal is scored.

The player concerned shall be cautioned.

(*b*) If, after the Referee has given the signal for a penalty-kick to be taken, and before the ball is in play, a colleague of the player taking the kick encroaches into the penalty-area or within 10yd of the penalty-mark, the Referee shall, nevertheless, allow the kick to proceed. If a goal is scored, it shall be disallowed, and the kick retaken.

The player concerned shall be cautioned.

(*c*) If, in the circumstances described in the foregoing paragraph, the ball rebounds into play from the goalkeeper, the cross-bar or a goal-post, and a goal has not been scored, the Referee shall stop the game, caution the player and award an indirect free-kick to the opposing team from the place where the infringement occurred, subject to the over-riding conditions imposed in Law 13.

(5) (*a*) If, after the Referee has given the signal for a penalty-kick to be taken, and before the ball is in play, the goalkeeper moves from his position on the goal-line, or moves his feet, and a colleague of the kicker encroaches into the penalty-area or within 10yd of the penalty-mark, the kick, if taken, shall be retaken.

The colleague of the kicker shall be cautioned.

(*b*) If, after the Referee has given the signal for a penalty-kick to be taken, and before the ball is in play, a player of each team encroaches into the penalty-area, or within 10yd of the penalty-mark, the kick, if taken, shall be retaken.

The players concerned shall be cautioned.

(6) When a match is extended, at half-time or full-time, to allow a penalty-kick to be taken or retaken, the extension shall last until the moment that the penalty-kick has been completed, i.e. until the Referee has decided whether or not a goal is scored, and the game shall terminate immediately the Referee has made his decision.

After the player taking the penalty-kick has put the ball into play, no player other than the defending goalkeeper may play or touch the ball before the kick is completed.

(7) When a penalty-kick is being taken in extended time:

(*a*) The provisions of all the foregoing paragraphs, except paragraphs 2(*b*) and 4(*c*) shall apply in the usual way; and

(*b*) In the circumstances described in paragraphs 2(*b*) and 4(*c*) the game shall terminate immediately the ball rebounds from the goal-keeper, the cross-bar or the goal-post.

Advice to Referees: If the original offence was sufficiently serious to justify the offender being sent from the field of play, the penalty-kick alone is not sufficient punishment. If the ball hits a goal-post or the cross-bar and rebounds into play, the player taking the penalty-kick must not play it again until it has been touched by another player.

15. THROW-IN

When the whole of the ball passes over the touch-line, either on the ground or in the air, it shall be thrown in from the point where it crossed the line, in any direction, by a player of the team opposite to that of the player who last touched it. The thrower at the moment of delivering the ball must face the field of play and part of each foot shall be either on the touch-line or on the ground outside the touch-line. The thrower shall use both hands and shall deliver the ball from behind and over his head. The ball shall be in play immediately it enters the field of play, but the thrower shall not again play the ball until it has been touched or played by another player. A goal shall not be scored direct from a throw-in.

Punishment: (*a*) If the ball is improperly thrown in, the throw-in shall be taken by a player of the opposing team.

(*b*) If the thrower plays the ball a second time before it has been touched or played by another player, an indirect free-kick shall be taken by a player of the opposing team from the place where the infringement occurred, subject to the over-riding conditions imposed in Law 13.

INTERNATIONAL BOARD DECISIONS

(1) If a player taking a throw-in plays the ball a second time by handling it within the field of play before it has been touched or played by another player, the Referee shall award a direct free-kick.

(2) A player taking a throw-in must face the field of play with some part of his body.

(3) If, when a throw-in is being taken, any of the opposing players dance about or gesticulate in a way calculated to distract or impede the thrower, it shall be deemed ungentlemanly conduct, for which the offender(s) shall be cautioned.

(4) A throw-in taken from any position other than the point where the ball passed over the touch-line shall be considered to have been improperly thrown in.

Advice to Referees: When a ball is thrown by a player directly from a throw-in into his opponents' goal, the Referee should award a goal-kick. If, however, a player throws the ball directly into his own goal, the Referee should award a corner-kick.

16. GOAL-KICK

When the whole of the ball passes over the goal-line, excluding that portion between the goal-posts, either in the air or on the ground, having last been played by one of the attacking team, it shall be kicked direct into play beyond the penalty-area, from any point within the goal-area by a player of the defending team. A goalkeeper shall not receive the ball into his hands from a goal-kick in order that he may thereafter kick it into play. If the ball is not kicked beyond the penalty-area, i.e. direct into play, the kick shall be retaken. The kicker shall not play the ball a second time until it has touched or been played by another player. A goal shall not be scored direct from such a kick. Players of the team opposing that of the player taking the goal-kick shall remain outside the penalty-area until the ball has been kicked out of the penalty-area.

Punishment: If a player taking a goal-kick plays the ball a second time after it has passed beyond the penalty-area, but before it has touched or been played by another player, an indirect free-kick shall be awarded to the opposing team, to be taken from the place where the infringement occurred, subject to the over-riding conditions imposed in Law 13.

INTERNATIONAL BOARD DECISIONS

(1) When a goal-kick has been taken and the player who has kicked the ball touches it again before it has left the penalty-area, the kick has not been taken in accordance with the Law and must be retaken.

Advice to Referees: Before giving the signal for the kick, make sure that the player and the ball are correctly positioned.

17. CORNER-KICK

When the whole of the ball passes over the goal-line, excluding that portion between the goal-posts, either in the air or on the ground, having last been played by one of the defending team, a member of the attacking team shall take a corner-kick, i.e. the whole of the ball shall be placed within the quarter circle at the nearest corner-flag post, which must not be moved, and it shall be kicked from that position.

A goal may be scored direct from such a kick. Players of the team opposing that of the player taking the corner-kick shall not approach within 10yd of the ball until it is in play, i.e. it has travelled the distance of its own circumference, nor shall the kicker play the ball a second-time until it has been touched or played by another player.

Punishment: (*a*) If the player who takes the kick plays the ball a second time before it has been touched or played by another player, the Referee shall award an indirect free-kick to the opposing team, to be taken from the place where the infringement occurred, subject to the over-riding conditions imposed in Law 13.

(*b*) For any other infringement the kick shall be retaken.

Advice to Referees: If a player, before taking a corner-kick, removes the corner flag-post, order it to be replaced before giving the signal for the corner-kick to be taken.

Reprinted by permission of the Football Association. For reasons of space a number of appendixes, including procedures to be adopted by the Referee and Linesmen in given circumstances, a check-list for Referees, signals by the Referee and Linesmen and a number of helpful diagrams have been omitted. These are all included in the Laws of Association Football 1994–95, *obtainable from the Football Association.*

Athletics

Athletics

NOTES

Attention is drawn to the fact that in the Rules the words 'must', 'shall' and 'should' are frequently used. The variation in phrase is intentional. When the word 'must' or 'shall' is used the Rule is compulsory. Where 'should' is employed, while the Federation hopes that the Rule will be complied with, strict compliance is not essential. The Rules for Competition cover indoor as well as outdoor competition. The attention of Promoters and Officials is drawn to Appendix A which sets out the principal requirements and modifications for indoor competitions.

The following terms used throughout the Rules have the following meanings:

Terms	Definitions
British Athletic Federation ('The Federation')	The Member Federation of the IAAF responsible for athletics in the United Kingdom of Great Britain and Northern Ireland
National Association	AA of Wales, AAA of England, Northern Ireland AAF, Scottish Athletics Federation
Regional Association	Midland AA, North of England AA, South of England AA, and such other Associations as may be formed by the Federation from time to time
District	A Scottish District, a District of the North of England AA or similar geographical subdivisions of a 'Region'

Club

having a separate Committee for
administration purposes
Affiliated Club, Business House Club,
University, College, School, Services
Unit, or Pre-Service Unit

The Council of the Federation is responsible for the interpretation of
Federation Rules.

GENERAL RULES

1. ELIGIBILITY TO COMPETE
All competitions held under the Rules of the British Athletic Federation
(BAF) are confined to amateurs under the following definitions (herein-
after termed amateurs under BAF rules).

1. Definition of Amateur
An amateur is a person who abides by the eligibility rules of the
Federation.

2. Restriction of Competition to Amateurs
Competition under Federation Rules is restricted to amateur athletes
who are under the jurisdiction of a Member of the IAAF and who are
eligible under the rules laid down by the BAF.

3. Ineligibility to Compete
The following persons are ineligible to take part in competitions under
Federation Rules:
Any persons who:

(*a*) have taken part in any competition in which any of the competitors in any of the events were to their knowledge ineligible to compete
under Federation Rules.
Note: This does not apply to any athletics meeting which is solely
restricted to the Veteran age group.

(*b*) are ineligible to compete in competitions under the jurisdiction of
any national governing body of amateur athletics affiliated to the IAAF.

(*c*) take part in any athletics meeting which is not sanctioned by the
Federation or one of its Member Associations.

(*d*) take part in any competition outside the United Kingdom of
Great Britain and Northern Ireland which is not sanctioned, recognised
or certified by the Member Association of the IAAF.

(*e*) have competed, or are competing in any sport for pecuniary reward, other than as permitted by IAAF Rules which have been accepted by the Federation.

(*f*) are suspended or banned for a doping offence under Rule 24 (15) or (16), or by the Governing Body of any other Sport.

(*g*) ask for, or receive, directly or indirectly, any monetary consideration, reward or employment for becoming, or continuing as a member of a Club or any other athletic organisation.

(*h*) use the services of an Athletes' Representative other than one approved under Rule 11.

(*i*) have been suspended or banned for being in breach of Rules 16 or 17 (Advertising and Sponsorship or Clothing).

(*j*) have committed any acts or made any statements either verbally or in writing, or have been responsible for any breaches of the Rules, or other conduct which, in the opinion of the Council of the Federation, is considered to be insulting, improper or likely to bring the sport and/or the Federation into disrepute.

Unless the period of ineligibility is stated in the relevant Rule or Regulation of the IAAF or the Federation, those ineligible under this Rule shall be deemed ineligible for a period set down in guidelines produced by the Council of the Federation or, in the absence of such guidelines, for such period as that Council shall decide.

4. Eligibility

An athlete does not cease to be an amateur under Federation Rules:

(*a*) by the receipt of fees or expenses for acting as an official in any other sport.

(*b*) by achieving a performance of merit in a competition and becoming eligible for a training grant or subvention donated by a sponsor or organiser. All monies awarded will be administered in a manner approved by the Federation.

Any promoter wishing to award training grants or subventions must obtain clearance, in advance, from the Federation (see Rule 12).

(*c*) by accepting assistance in the form of equipment and services for training and competition, subject to the control of the Federation. Such assistance may include the following items:
  (i) Sports equipment and clothing
  (ii) Insurance cover for accidents, illness, disability and personal property
  (iii) Cost of medical treatment and physiotherapy
  (iv) Cost of coaching
  (v) Cost of accommodation, food, transport, education and professional training.

2. CLUBS
Athletics is organised within the following disciplines:
- (*a*) Track and Field
- (*b*) Race Walking
- (*c*) Road Running
- (*d*) Cross Country
- (*e*) Fell and Hill Running
- (*f*) Tug-of-War

Each Club must be affiliated to the Regional or National Association in whose geographical area of responsibility the Club's headquarters are located.

3. CLUB MEMBERSHIP

4. FIRST CLAIM STATUS

5. HARDSHIP EXEMPTION

6. COMPETITION CONDITIONS

7. AGE GROUPS
(1) The Competition Year for all athletic activities shall extend from 1st October to 30th September in the following year.

Note: For events which begin within one Competition Year but have a final or subsequent round falling in the first month of the following Competition Year, eligibility to compete in that final or subsequent round will be the same as that for the initial stage of the event or competition.

(2) The operative date for determining membership of age groups for all athletes under the age of 17 shall be for Track and Field and Race Walking, midnight on 31st August/1st September at the end of the Competition Year, and for all other disciplines, midnight on 31st December/1st January within the Competition Year.

(3) The Age Groups for all athletic activities shall be:
   (i) Under 13 Boys and Girls
Competition shall be confined to boys or girls who are aged 11 on the day of competition and under 13 on the operative date for the relevant discipline noted in (2) above.
   (ii) Under 15 Boys and Girls
Competition shall be confined to boys or girls who are aged 13 or 14 on the operative date for the relevant discipline listed in (2) above.

(iii) Under 17 Men and Women
Competition shall be confined to men or women who are aged 15 or 16 on the operative date for the relevant discipline listed in (2) above.
(iv) Junior Men and Women
Competition shall be confined to men or women as defined in Rules 107 (Track and Field), 207 (Road Running) and 507 (Cross Country).
(v) Senior Men and Women
A Senior is a competitor who is at least 20 years of age at midnight on the date as defined in Rules 107 (Track and Field), 207 (Road Running) and 507 (Cross Country).
(vi) Veteran Men and Women
(*a*) Events for men shall be confined to competitors who are at least 40 years of age on the date of the competition.
(*b*) Events for women shall be confined to competitors who are at least 35 years of age on the date of the competition.

8. TEAM EVENTS

9. COUNTY QUALIFICATIONS (ENGLAND)

10. REGIONAL AND DISTRICT CHAMPIONSHIP QUALIFICATIONS

11. ATHLETES' REPRESENTATIVES

12. PERMISSION TO PROMOTE

13. PERMISSION TO TELEVISE

14. ENTRIES

15. PROGRAMME AND PUBLISHED MATTER

16. ADVERTISING AND SPONSORSHIP

17. CLOTHING

(1) In all events competitors must wear at least vest and shorts (or equivalent clothing) which are clean and so designed and worn as not to be objectionable, even if wet.

(2) When competing in any Team or Relay competition competitors shall wear the registered colours of the team they are representing, unless the Referee has given permission for a change to be made.

Note: Clubs are permitted to have two sets of colours registered at any one time. In Team or Relay Races all competitors should wear registered vests of the same design.

(3) In individual County, District, Regional or National Championships athletes must wear the vest of their first-claim affiliated Club, or their County, Regional or National vest. The Club concerned must be the one which in terms of Rule 2 (6) caters for that particular discipline of athletics.

Note: In exceptional circumstances the Referee may grant permission for an alternative vest to be worn.

(4) Except as is allowed for in Rule 16, competitors are not allowed to take into an arena or course any form of advertising material, nor to display on their person any such advertising other than:

(*a*) the accepted name of their affiliated Club in lettering which should not exceed 4cm in height. In the case of County or Regional vests the lettering indicating the name shall not exceed 6cm in height.

(*b*) a single Trade Mark of the manufacturer or supplier of the clothing they are wearing, which must not exceed 20 sq cm with a maximum height of 4cm.

(5) Alternative vests complying with (1) above suitable for longer distance races may be worn after approval by the Federation in addition to colours nominated in (2).

18. NUMBER CARDS

(1) Competitors shall be supplied with and wear during competition a distinctive number card corresponding with their number in the programme or start list. No competitor shall be allowed to take part in any competiton without wearing the appropriate number card(s) and such card(s) must not be cut, folded or otherwise concealed or mutilated in any way.

(2) Organisations which have contracts with commercial sponsors for the addition of lettering on number cards to be worn at meetings are not to allow this lettering to exceed 4cm in height and 15cm in width or 48 sq cm in area. The sponsor's name may appear either above or below the number.

(3) Organisers must ensure that the same style of number card is issued to, and worn by, all competitors taking part in the meeting.

19. BETTING
All betting is strictly prohibited.

20. CHALLENGE CUPS

21. ASSISTANCE

(1) No athlete shall receive advice or similar assistance during the progress of an event or competition. 'Assistance' means any direct help conveyed by any means including any technical device.

(2) 'Assistance' is also to be interpreted as including pacing by persons not participating in a race unless assisting a blind or partially sighted runner.

(3) For the purpose of this Rule the following shall not be considered as assistance:

(*a*) a medical examination during the progress of an event by medical personnel solely to determine whether an athlete is fit enough to continue in the competition.

(*b*) verbal or other communication, without the use of any technical device, from an individual who is not in the competition area.

(*c*) the use of heart monitors in races in excess of 10,000m.

(4) Athletes receiving assistance as defined above are liable to be disqualified.

22. MISCONDUCT

(1) Any individual athlete or official of an affiliated Club making a false entry for competition shall be dealt with by the appropriate Member Association of the Federation for misconduct.

(2) Any competitor (or other person) interfering or attempting to interfere with the decision of an event official, or indulging in unfair practices or misbehaviour, including the use of offensive or abusive language shall, at the discretion of the Referee, be disqualified from the competition and, if deemed necessary, reported to the appropriate Member Association of the Federation for further action. Performances achieved prior to disqualification shall stand.

(3) Athletes or officials who shall knowingly conduct themselves in a manner which, in the opinion of the Council of the Federation, may bring discredit to the sport of athletics, shall be deemed to have committed an offence against the Federation, for which they shall be liable to suspension.

23. PROTESTS

(1) Any protest or objection against the qualification to compete, or the statements in the entry form of another competitor or Club shall be made to the Referee or to the Member Association as appropriate, in the manner prescribed in (2) below. When practicable such protest or

objection should be made before the date of the competition, or normally within 14 days of the date of the competition.

(2) Every protest or objection lodged under (1) shall be accompanied by a deposit of £10 and shall be made in writing and be signed by the individual objector or by an authorised official. If, upon investigation, the protest or objection shall appear to have been made on no reasonable grounds, the deposit shall be forfeited to the appropriate Association.

(3) The Referee may decide the protest or objection made under (1) on the ground, but if the decision is objected to at the time, the Referee shall be required to refer the matter to the appropriate Member Association. Any protest or objection referred in this manner shall be decided within one month of receipt by that Member Association.

(4) In the event of a protest or objection being lodged against a successful competitor, team or Club, the prize or prizes shall be withheld until the protest or objection shall have been finally disposed of in a manner provided for in this Rule. If within a period of three months from the date of the competition the protest or objection shall be sustained the prize or prizes shall be awarded as if the competitor, team or Club objected to had not taken part in the competition.

(5) Any competitor, team or Club may appeal against the decision of the Member Association. Notice of Appeal must be sent to the Federation within 14 days of receipt of such decision and must be accompanied by a further deposit of £50, which will be refundable at the discretion of the Federation. The appeal will be determined in accordance with the procedures established by the Federation.

(6) Without prejudice to the foregoing, where any dispute exists between any person and another person, or between any person and a National or Regional Association or the Federation, any party to such dispute may refer the matter for resolution in accordance with the Appeal Procedure established by the Federation.

24. DOPING

(1) Doping in or out of competition is strictly forbidden and is an offence.

(2) The Federation is responsible for the co-ordination and disciplinary procedures of all doping related matters. It is responsible for the supervision of testing both in and out of competition. All such testing is operated and co-ordinated by the relevant Sports Council Doping Control Unit, or the IAAF. All other doping matters are delegated to its Drug Advisory Committee.

(3) To be eligible for participation in athletic competitions held under Federation and IAAF Rules all athletes must make themselves available for testing when required.

(4) Athletes who may be considered for selection for Great Britain and Northern Ireland teams at international competitions will be placed on the 'out of competition register' and must notify the Federation with details of their contact address and any subsequent changes of address (e.g. at college, or university, whilst training abroad, whilst on holiday and so on) of more than five days duration. All athletes on the 'out of competition register' will be notified of their inclusion by the Federation.

(5) The offence of doping takes place when:

(a) a prohibited substance is found to be present within an athlete's body tissue or fluids; or

(b) an athlete takes advantage of a prohibited technique; or

(c) an athlete admits having used or taken advantage of a prohibited substance or a prohibited technique; or

(d) an athlete fails or refuses to submit to doping control and produce a sample after having been requested to do so by an authorised official; or

(e) a person assists or incites others, or admits having assisted or incited others to use prohibited substances or prohibited techniques; or

(f) an athlete on the 'out of competition register' fails to notify the Federation of a change of address of more than five days duration and consequently is not available at the notified address when requested to undertake a test, without an explanation acceptable to the Drug Advisory Committee.

(6) 'Prohibited substances' shall have the same meaning as in the IAAF 'Rules and Procedural Guidelines for Doping Control'.

Note: A copy of the list current at the time of publication is included in the BAF handbook. This list may be added to or amended by the IAAF Doping Commission from time-to-time.

(7) The expression 'prohibited substance' shall include a metabolite of a prohibited substance.

(8) It is the duty of all athletes to ensure that no substances enter their body tissues or fluids which are prohibited under these Rules. Athletes are warned that they are responsible for all and any substance detected in samples given by them.

(9) An athlete may request the Doping Commission of the IAAF to grant prior exemption to allow the taking of a prohibited substance. Such exemption will only be granted in cases of clear and compelling clinical need. Use of such a substance in accordance with the prior exemption obtained before the sample is taken will not be considered an offence of doping. The athlete must produce to the Independent Sampling Officer written proof of exemption when the sample is taken and the test form must be endorsed accordingly.

(10) The expression 'prohibited technique' shall include:

(*a*) blood infusion ('blood doping')

(*b*) use of substances and/or methods, which alter the integrity and validity of urine samples used in doping control.

(11) An admission may be made either verbally, in a verifiable manner or in writing. For the purpose of these rules, a statement is not to be regarded as an admission where it is made more than six years after the facts to which it relates.

(12) An athlete who is requested to submit to doping control by an authorised official must do so whether such a request is made during or outside competition. Failure to submit to doping control and produce a sample will be a doping offence and the sanctions regarding eligibility set out below shall apply. The athlete will be deemed to be ineligible as if a positive result under (15) below had been obtained.

(13) Anti-doping tests shall be carried out under the auspices of the relevant Sports Council, or the IAAF, by Independent Sampling Officers unless otherwise required by the BAF.

Note: See BAF handbook for Rules and Procedures relating to testing.

(14) The Federation Drug Advisory Committee will deal with any offences under its Doping Procedures. Under these procedures disciplinary proceedings will take place in three stages:

(*a*) suspension (An athlete shall be suspended from the time that the Drug Advisory Committee considers that there is evidence that a doping offence may have taken place and written notice to that effect has been sent to the athlete concerned);

(*b*) hearing;

(*c*) decision on eligibility.

(15) Where an athlete has committed one of the following doping offences in or out of competition

(*a*) The finding in an athlete's body tissue or fluids of a prohibiting substance.

(*b*) The use of, or taking advantage of, prohibited techniques.

(*c*) Admitting having taken advantage of, or having used, a prohibited substance.

(*d*) Admitting having taken advantage of, or having used, a prohibited technique.

(*e*) Refusal to submit to doping control and produce a sample.

(*f*) Assisting or inciting others to use prohibited substances or prohibited techniques or admitting having assisted or incited others.

(*g*) The failure to notify the Federation of a change of address as required in (4) above and consequently not being available at his/her notified address when requested to undertake an out of competition test, without an explanation acceptable to the Drug Advisory Committee.

he/she shall be declared ineligible to take part in any athletic event within the United Kingdom or abroad:

   (i) for a first offence – for a minimum of four years from the date of the provision of the sample or of the sanctionable offence, together with any additional period necessary to include a subsequent equivalent competition to that in which the athlete was disqualified.

   (ii) for a second offence – for life from the date of the provision of the sample or of the sanctionable offence.

(16) Where an athlete has committed one of the following doping offences:

(*a*) The finding in an athlete's body tissue or fluids of a prohibited substance.

(*b*) Admitting having taken advantage of, or having used, a prohibited substance.

he/she shall be declared ineligible to take part in any athletic event within the United Kingdom or abroad:

   (i) For the first offence – for three months from the date of the provision of the sample.

   (ii) For the second offence – two years from the date of the provision of the sample.

   (iii) For a third offence – for life from the date of the provision of the sample.

(17) Where substances are detected in an athlete's body tissue or fluids which fall within Part 1 and Part 2 of Schedule 1 of the IAAF 'Procedural Guidelines for Doping Control', the sample shall be regarded as falling primarily within Part 1 for the purposes of determining the appropriate period of ineligibility.

(18) Persons other than athletes who assist or incite others, or admit to having assisted or incited others, to use a prohibited substance or prohibited technique shall be subject to appropriate sanctions imposed by the Federation.

(19) Where athletes have been declared ineligible under (15)(i), (16)(i) or (16)(ii) above and wish to resume competing after their period of ineligibility has expired they must have made themselves available for out of competition testing throughout that period of ineligibility.

(20) If the results of any testing carried out under (19) above on an athlete during the period of ineligibility prove positive, this will constitute a separate doping offence and the athlete will be subject to a further sanction as appropriate.

(21) Only in exceptional circumstances may an athlete apply to the Federation for reinstatement before the full period of ineligibility has expired.

(22) A departure or departures from the procedures set out in the Rules and Procedures Concerning Doping Control shall not invalidate the finding that a prohibited substance was present in a sample, or that a prohibited technique had been used, unless this departure(s) was such as to cast real doubt on the reliability of such a finding.

TRACK AND FIELD COMPETITION RULES

The General Rules 1–24 apply to all Track and Field Competitions.

100. TEAM EVENTS
(1) Rule 8 applies.

101. ENTRIES
(1) Rule 14 applies.

102. FOOTWEAR
(1) Competitors may compete in bare feet or with footwear on one or both feet. The purpose of the shoes for competition is to give protection and stability to the feet and a firm grip on the ground. Such shoes, however, must not be so constructed as to give the competitor any additional assistance, and no spring or device of any kind may be incorporated in the shoes. A shoe strap over the instep is permitted.

(2) The sole and the heel of the shoes shall be so constructed as to provide for the use of up to 11 spikes. Any number of spikes up to 11 may be used, but the number of spike positions shall not exceed 11.

(3) When a competition is conducted on a synthetic surface that part of each spike which projects from the sole or the heel must not exceed 9 mm, except in the High Jump and the Javelin events where it must not exceed 12mm. These spikes shall have a maximum diameter of 4mm. For non-synthetic surfaces the maximum length of spike shall be 25mm and the maximum diameter 4mm.

(4) The sole and/or heel may have grooves, ridges, indentations or protuberances provided these features are constructed of the same or similar material to the basic sole itself.

(5) In the High Jump the sole shall have a maximum thickness of 13mm and the heel shall have a maximum thickness of 19mm. In all other events shoes may be of any thickness.

(6) Competitors may not use any appliance, either inside or outside the shoes which will have the effect of increasing the thickness of the sole above the permitted maximum or which can give the wearer any advantage which would not be obtained from the type of shoes described in the previous paragraphs.

103. NUMBERS

(1) Rule 18 applies.

(2) Competitors should be supplied with two number cards to be displayed visibly, one on the breast and the other on the back. Competitors in the High Jump and Pole Vault may wear their number card on the breast or on the back only. Where photo-finish equipment is in use the meeting organisers may require competitors to wear additional numbers of the adhesive type on the side of their shorts facing the camera(s).

(3) In Field Events where competitors wish to take their trials wearing their tracksuit, they must wear their number card(s) on the outside of their tracksuit (or other covering).

104. PROTESTS

(1) Rule 23 applies.

107. COMPETITIONS CONFINED TO PARTICULAR AGE GROUPS

TRACK EVENTS

108. TRACK MEASUREMENTS

(1) Tracks should be level. For record purposes the maximum allowance for lateral inclination of tracks shall not exceed 1:100, and in the running direction 1:1000 downwards; any inclination shall be uniform.

(2) The inner edge of all tracks must be distinctly marked, cinder and other permanent tracks preferably by a raised border of concrete or other suitable material, 5cm ± 1.25cm in height and at least 5cm in width. Where it is not possible to have a raised border the inner edge shall be marked with a white line or white tape 5cm in width. All other lanes shall be marked with a white line 5cm in width.

(3) For championship events (whether National, Regional or County), or for any record to be accepted, the inside edge of the track must have a raised border, or be adequately flagged or coned to prevent any competitor running on the line itself. The flags shall be placed on the line at an angle of 60 degrees with the ground, pointing away from the track, at intervals of 5m.

(4) It is recommended that the direction of running be left hand inside.

(5) In all races where lanes are used the width of each lane shall be not less than 1.22m and not more than 1.25m. The lanes shall be measured for width from the outside edge of one marking line to the outside edge of the next line working outwards from the inner border of the track.

(6) (*a*) The track must be measured 30cm outwards from the track side of the inner edge if there is a raised border. If there is no raised border the track must be measured 20cm outwards from the track side of the inner edge.

(*b*) In measuring lanes for distance the inner lane shall be measured as stated in paragraph (*a*) and the outer lanes 20cm outwards from their respective inner borders.

(7) Races up to 110 metres must be run on a straight course in lanes so as to allow a separate course for each competitor.

(8) Individual races up to and including 400 metres should be run in lanes, with a separate lane for each competitor.

(9) Races over 400 metres and up to and including 800 metres may be run in lanes as far as the end of the first bend.
Note: The starting lines will be the same as for 200 metres plus the following distances:

Lane 1 + zero	Lane 5 + 0.145m
Lane 2 + 0.007m	Lane 6 + 0.224m
Lane 3 + 0.034m	Lane 7 + 0.325m
Lane 4 + 0.079m	Lane 8 + 0.444m

(10) In all races run wholly or partly in lanes the start shall be so staggered that the distance from start to finish shall be the same for each competitor.

109. STATIONS

(1) In all races stations for competitors shall be drawn. In straight sprint races the competitor drawing No. 1 shall take the station on the left facing the winning post, the competitor drawing No. 2 the next station and so on.

(2) In races on a circular track, the competitor drawing No. 1 shall take the station nearest the centre of the ground, the competitor drawing No. 2 the next station and so on.

Note: It is recommended that when a curved starting line is being used the inside lane is left unoccupied.

(3) It is recommended that a limit be placed on the number of competitors in races. In general the number should not be so great as to create possible danger or unfairness to any competitor, and if at the beginning of any race the number of competitors appears to the Referee to be excessive, dangerous or unfair, he or she shall have the power to order that the competitors be divided into such heats as he or she in his or her sole discretion considers necessary, and the event shall be run off accordingly.

Note: WAAA: For guidance, where races are started from a curved line the number of competitors in each heat should not normally exceed:

800m	10 where there are 6 lanes
	12 where there are 8 lanes
1500m	12 where there are 6 lanes
	14 where there are 8 lanes
3000m	14 where there are 6 lanes
	18 where there are 8 lanes

(4) In competitions where the composition of heats is printed in the programme, competitors shall not be allowed to compete in any heat other than that in which their name appears; but the Referee, whose decision shall be final, shall have power, if he or she is of the opinion that it would be just and reasonable, to permit a departure from the rule.

110. STARTING BLOCKS

(1) The use of starting blocks is permitted in races up to and including 400 metres, including the first leg of a relay race, provided such leg does not exceed 400 metres.

(2) Their use is optional.

(3) Athletes may use their own starting blocks, but such starting blocks must be approved by the Starter.

Note: On all-weather tracks the organisers may insist that only starting blocks provided by them shall be used.

(4) The following rules apply to the construction and use of starting blocks:

(*a*) They must be constructed entirely of rigid materials

(*b*) They may be adjustable but must be without springs or other devices to give artificial aid to the runner

(*c*) They must be fixed to the track by a number of pins or spikes, arranged to cause minimum possible damage to the track surface. The arrangement must permit the starting blocks to be quickly and easily removed, and the anchorage must permit no movement during the actual start (*d*) When in position on the track, no part of the starting block must overlap the starting line or extend beyond the lane for that athlete.

(5) When starting blocks are being used both hands must be in contact with the ground when the athlete is in the 'set' position.

111. THE START

(1) The start of a race shall be denoted by a line 5cm in width at right angles to the inner edge of the track. The distance of the race shall be measured from the edge of the starting line further from the finish, to the edge of the finish line nearer to the start.

(2) In all races not run in lanes the starting line shall be curved so that wherever it occurs on the track all the runners can cover the same distance in the race.

(3) All questions concerning the start shall be in the absolute discretion of the Starter, whose decision shall be final.

(4) Start Recallers should be appointed at National and Regional Championships from within the appointed team of Starters. They may also be appointed at other meetings.

(5) Competitors must be placed in their respective stations by Marksmen (Starter's Assistants). Marksmen shall assemble competitors 3m behind the starting line (or in the case of races run entirely or partly in lanes, behind each starting line) and, once so placed, shall signal to the Starter that all is ready.

If in the opinion of the Starter an athlete has failed to comply within a reasonable time with the instructions of the Marksmen to prepare to come to the assembly line, then it may be considered a false start.

(6) Competitors must not touch the start line or the ground in front of it with their hands or feet when on their mark.

(7) All races (except Time Handicaps) shall be started by the report of a revolver or other similar apparatus and a start shall be made to the actual report. The revolver or similar apparatus shall be fired upwards into the air and it is essential that it should give a satisfactory flash which can be clearly seen by the Timekeepers. The time shall be taken from the flash.

(8) (*a*) The Starter shall first receive a signal from the Chief Marksman that all competitors are ready.

(*b*) After the Starter has ascertained that the Timekeepers are ready, he shall give the competitors the following commands:

- (i) For competitors running a distance up to and including 400m: 'On your marks', 'Set', and when all the competitors are set, i.e. motionless on their mark, the revolver shall be fired.
- (ii) For competitors running or walking a distance greater than 400m: the command shall be 'On your marks', after which the competitors shall approach the start line without touching it, and

assume a steady position. Competitors must not touch the ground with their hands. When the steady position has been achieved by all the competitors the revolver shall be fired.

(9) On the command 'On your marks' (for distances greater than 400m) or 'Set' (for distances up to and including 400m) all competitors shall at once and without delay assume their full and final Set position. Failure to comply with either command after a reasonable time shall constitute a false start.

(10) After the 'On your marks' command competitors must assume a position whereby both hands and at least one knee are in contact with the ground when a crouch start is being used.

(11) If, for any reason, the Starter has to speak to any of the competitors after the command 'On your marks' and before the revolver is fired, or if the concentration of any competitor or the Starter is disturbed before the revolver is fired, he or she shall order all competitors to stand up and the Marksmen shall place them on the assembly lines again.

(12) If a competitor after the command 'On your marks' disturbs the other competitors in the race through sound or otherwise, it may be considered a false start.

(13) If a competitor commences a starting motion after assuming a full and final set position, and before the report of the gun, it shall be considered a false start.

(14) Any competitor making a false start must be warned. If a competitor is responsible for two false starts, or three in the case of a Combined Event (Pentathlon, Heptathlon, Octathlon or Decathlon) that athlete shall be disqualified.

(15) If in the opinion of the Starter, or the Start Recaller, the start was not fair, the competitors must be recalled with a second shot. If the Starter decides that the unfair start was due to one or more competitors 'beating the gun', it shall be considered a false start and the Starter must warn the offender or offenders, who shall be disqualified if they continue to offend after one such warning, or two in the case of a Combined Event.

Note: In practice, when one or more competitors 'beat the gun' others are inclined to follow and, strictly speaking, any competitor who does so has beaten the gun. The Starter should warn only such competitor or competitors who in his or her opinion were responsible for beating the gun. This may result in more than one competitor being warned. If the unfair start is not due to any competitor no warning shall be given.

112. THE RACE

(1) In all races run in lanes competitors should keep in their allotted lane from start to finish. If the Referee is satisfied, on the report of a

Judge or Umpire, or otherwise, that a competitor has deliberately run out of lane, the Referee shall disqualify that competitor, but if the Referee considers that such action was unintentional, he or she may, at his or her discretion, disqualify if of the opinion that a material advantage was gained thereby. (The table below may be used for guidance in determining the advantage gained.) This Rule shall also apply to any portion of a race run in lanes.

Note: When an Umpire observes that an athlete has run out of his or her lane, it is recommended that the Umpire marks the track where the infringement took place.

Track 400 metres Stride 2.30m	Advantage Gained by Encroaching *t* cm on Inside of Lane			
Number of Strides	t = 50mm	t = 100mm	t = 150mm	t = 300mm
	mm	mm	mm	mm
1	4	7	11	22
2	7	14	22	44
3	11	22	33	66
4	14	29	44	88
5	18	36	54	109
6	22	44	65	131
7	25	51	76	153
8	29	58	87	175
9	33	65	98	197
10	36	72	109	219

This table shows, mathematically, the theoretical advantage gained by taking from 1 to 10 strides inside the inner border of a lane. The distances are shown in millimetres, e.g. four strides 150mm inside gives an advantage of 44mm.

(2) Any competitor jostling, running or walking across, or obstructing another competitor so as to impede his or her progress shall be liable to disqualification.

(3) A competitor after voluntarily leaving the track or course shall not be allowed to continue in the race.

(4) The start of the final lap shall be signalled, usually by ringing a bell. In races longer than 1500m a lap scorer(s) shall be appointed by the Referee, who shall keep a record of the laps covered by each competitor.

(5) The Referee shall have the power to order a race to be re-held when he or she considers it just and reasonable to do so. If in any heat a competitor is disqualified the Referee shall have the power to permit any competitor affected by the act resulting in the disqualification to compete in a subsequent round of the event.

(6) No person except an official Timekeeper or other person appointed to do so by the Chief Timekeeper shall:

(*a*) indicate intermediate times to competitors;

(*b*) give times to be announced over the public address system.

(7) No attendant shall accompany any competitors on their mark.

(8) No competitor shall receive any advice or similar assistance during the progress of a race. 'Assistance' means direct help or advice conveyed by any means, and pacing in running events by persons not participating in the race. Athletes receiving such assistance and advice are liable to be disqualified (see Rule 21).

(9) In races of 200m or less the wind velocity should be measured and recorded whenever possible, and this is essential in the case of a record claim. The gauge should be set up parallel to the track, 50m from the finish line, not more than 2m from the edge of the track adjacent to lane 1, and at a height of approximately 1.22m.

(10) The periods for which the wind component should be measured are:

All distances up to and including 100m	10sec.
100m Hurdles and 110m Hurdles	13sec.
200m, commencing as the runners enter the straight	10sec.

See also Rule 141 (14) and (19).

(11) The wind gauge shall be read in metres per second, rounded to the next higher tenth of a metre per second in the positive direction. (For example: a reading of +2.03 m/sec. shall be recorded as +2.1 m/sec.; a reading of −2.03 m/sec. shall be recorded as −2.0 m/sec.)

113. THE FINISH

(1) The finish shall be a line 5cm in width drawn across the track at right angles to the inner edge.

(2) Two white posts shall denote the extremities of the finish line and shall be placed at least 30cm from the edge of the track. The finish posts shall be of rigid construction of about 1.4m in height, 80mm in width and 20mm in thickness.

(3) The competitors shall be placed in the order in which any part of the body, i.e. the torso (as distinguished from head, neck, arms, hands, feet and legs), reaches the vertical plane of the edge of the finish line nearer to the start.

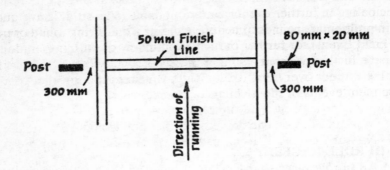

Diagram of Finish Posts

114. TIES

(1) In the event of a tie in any heat which affects the qualification of competitors to compete in the next round or final, where practicable, the tying competitors shall all qualify, failing which they shall compete again to decide the qualifiers.

(2) In the case of a tie for first place in any final, the Referee is empowered to decide whether it is practicable to arrange for the competitors so tying to compete again. If the Referee decides that it is not, the result shall stand. Ties in other placings shall remain.

115. QUALIFICATION FROM PRELIMINARY HEATS

(1) In the preliminary rounds of races, at least the winner, and preferably the winner and second, should qualify for the next round or final. Any other competitors to qualify shall be decided either according to their places or according to their times. Where any qualifying position is decided by time only one system of timing may be applied in determining times.

(2) The following minimum times must be allowed between the last heat of the round and the first heat of the subsequent round or final.

	Minimum minutes rest
Up to 100m	20
Over 100m and up to 200m	40
Over 200m and up to 400m	60
Over 400m and up to 800m	80
Over 800m	100

(3) In any athletics meeting competitors shall be excluded from participating in further events, including relays, when they have qualified in preliminary rounds or heats (including a qualifying round or pool in a Field Event) for further participation in any event but then do not compete further without giving a valid reason to the Referee. If a meeting extends over more than one day the exclusion shall apply to all subsequent events of the meeting.

116. HURDLE RACES

(1) All hurdle races shall be run in lanes and competitors shall run only in their own lane throughout.

(2) A hurdle shall consist of two uprights, or standards, supporting a rectangular frame or gate and should have a level top rail.

(3) The total weight of the hurdle shall be not less than 10kg.

(4) The extreme width of the hurdle shall be 1.2m and the extreme length of the base shall be 70cm. The top bar shall be 70mm in width and should be between 10mm and 25mm thick. The top bar should be striped in black and white, or in some other contrasting colours in such a manner that the lighter stripes appear at the end of the hurdle and that they shall be at least 225mm in width.

(5) The hurdle shall be made of wood or metal and shall consist of two bases and two uprights supporting the rectangular frame reinforced by one or more cross-bars, the uprights to be fixed at the extreme end of each base.

(6) The hurdle may be adjustable in height but should be rigidly fastened at the required height for each event.

(7) The hurdles shall be so placed on the track that the ends carrying the uprights shall be farthest from, with the counter-weights nearest to, the starting line.

(8) The hurdle shall be of such design that a force of at least 3.6kg applied to the centre of the top of the cross-bar is required to overturn it. Where an adjustable hurdle is used the counter-weights must be adjustable to the effect that in every position relating to the height of the hurdle the force required to overturn the hurdle when adjusted shall be at least 3.6kg and not more than 4kg.

Note: To check the resisting force of hurdles, a simple spring balance should be used by the application of a pulling force to the centre of the top of the cross-bar. Alternatively, use a cord with a hook, applied to the centre of the top of the cross-bar. Take the cord along over a pulley fixed conveniently and load the other end of the cord with the appropriate weights.

(9) The force required to overturn hurdles for Under-17 Men and Women and younger age groups shall be at least 2.7kg and not more than 3kg.

(10) Where hurdles are used which overturn with less force than the minimum specified in (8) or (9) above as appropriate, the competitors shall be informed that an athlete knocking down three or more hurdles, or any part of three or more hurdles, shall be disqualified.

(11) Where hurdles comply with (8) or (9) above, as appropriate, knocking down any number of hurdles shall not disqualify, nor shall it disentitle a competitor from claiming a record.

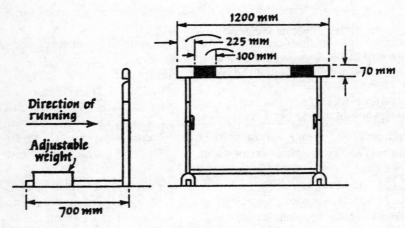

(adjustable weight may be inside or outside base)

Example of Approved Hurdle

(12) Competitors who trail a foot or leg below the plane of the top of the bar of the hurdle at the instant of clearance, or negotiate any hurdle not in their lane, or in the opinion of the Referee deliberately knock down any hurdle by hand or foot shall be disqualified.

(13) Specifications for particular hurdle events are:

Distance of race	Height of hurdle	Distance to 1st flight	Distance between flights	Distance to finish	Number of hurdles	Standard Track Marking Colour
MEN'S EVENTS						
Seniors (3.6kg Toppling Weight)						
110m	106.7cm	13.72m	9.14m	14.02m	10	Blue
400m	91.4cm	45m	35m	40m	10	Green
Juniors (3.6kg Toppling Weight)						
110m	99.0cm	13.72m	9.14m	14.02m	10	Blue
200m	76.2cm	18.29m	18.29m	17.1m	10	Purple
400m	91.4cm	45m	35m	40m	10	Green
Under-17 (2.7kg Toppling Weight)						
100m	91.4cm	13m	8.5m	10.5m	10	Yellow
400m	84.0cm	45m	35m	40m	10	Green
Under-15 (2.7kg Toppling Weight)						
80m	84.0cm	12m	8m	12m	8	Black
Under-13 (2.7kg Toppling Weight)						
80m	76.2cm	12m	8m	12m	8	Black
75m	76.2cm	11.5m	7.5m	11m	8	Orange
WOMEN'S EVENTS						
Seniors and Juniors (3.6kg Toppling Weight)						
100m	84.0cm	13m	8.5m	10.5m	10	Yellow
400m	76.2cm	45m	35m	40m	10	Green
Under-17 (2.7kg Toppling Weight)						
80m	76.2cm	12m	8m	12m	8	Black
100m	76.2cm	13m	8.5m	10.5m	10	Yellow
200m	76.2cm	16m	19m	13m	10	White
300m	76.2cm	50m	35m	40m	7	Green
Under-15 (2.7kg Toppling Weight)						
75m	76.2cm	11.5m	7.5m	11m	8	Orange
Under-13 (2.7kg Toppling Weight)						
70m	68.5cm	11m	7m	10m	8	Pink

Specifications for Veterans' Events are given in full in the BAF's Rules for Competition.

(14) Under-15 Girls may compete in Under-17 Women 80m hurdles competition but they may not compete in more than one hurdle age group in the course of the meeting.

(15) Specifications for Indoor Hurdle events are:

Distance of race	Height of hurdle	Distance to 1st flight	Distance between flights	Distance to finish	Number of hurdles	Toppling weight
MEN'S EVENTS						
Seniors						
50m	106.7cm	13.72m	9.14m	8.86m	4	3.6kg
60m	106.7cm	13.72m	9.14m	9.72m	5	3.6kg
Juniors						
60m	99.0cm	13.72m	9.14m	9.72m	5	3.6kg
Under 17						
60m	91.4cm	13m	8.5m	13m	5	2.7kg
Under 15 Boys						
60m	84.0cm	12m	8m	16m	5	2.7kg
Under 13 Boys						
60m	76.2cm	11.5m	7.5m	18.5m	5	2.7kg
WOMEN'S EVENTS						
Seniors and Juniors						
50m	84.0cm	13m	8.5m	11.5m	4	3.6kg
60m	84.0cm	13m	8.5m	13m	5	3.6kg
Under 17						
60m	76.2cm	12m	8m	16m	5	2.7kg
Under 15 Girls						
60m	76.2cm	11.5m	7.5m	18.5m	5	2.7kg
Under 13 Girls						
60m	68.5cm	11m	7m	21m	5	2.7kg

Note: In each case there shall be a tolerance of 3mm above and below the standard height to allow for variation in manufacture.

117. STEEPLECHASE RACES
Only Senior, Junior and Under-17 Men and Senior Women are allowed to contest any steeplechase event.

(1) The hurdle may be made of heavy timber or of metal with a bar of heavy timber. In either case it must be constructed in such a way that it may not be easily overturned.

(2) The hurdle shall be 91.4cm in height and should be at least 3.96m in total width. The section of the top bar of the hurdle should be 12.7cm square.

(3) The weight of each hurdle should be between 80kg and 100kg.

(4) The hurdle shall be placed on the track so that about 30cm of the top bar, measured from the inside edge of the track, will be inside the field (i.e. the top bar will overlap the track edge).

(5) The top bar should be striped in black and white or in some other contrasting colours in such a manner that the white stripes appear at the end of each hurdle, and the stripes should be at least 30cm wide.

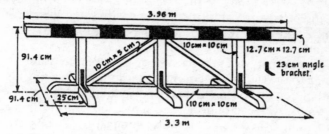

Specifications of Approved Heavy Timber Hurdle

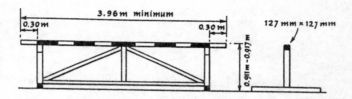

Specifications of Approved Hurdle with Metal Base

Note: In the case of all hurdle heights there shall be a tolerance of 3mm above and below the height of 91.4cm to allow for variation in manufacture.

(6) The hurdle at the water jump must be firmly fixed and be 91.4cm in height, 3.66m in total width, whilst the section of the top bar should be 12.7cm square.

(7) The water jump shall be 3.6m in width and length, the water being 70cm in depth at the hurdle end, remaining at this depth for a distance of 30cm and then sloping to the level of the track at the farther end.

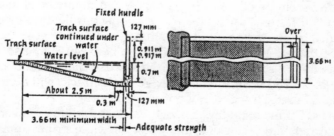

Steeplechase Water Jump – simplified diagrams

To ensure safe landing of the competitors, the bottom of the water jump should be covered at the further end with suitable material, at least 3.66m wide and 2.5m long, the thickness of which should not exceed approximately 25mm.

(8) Every competitor must go over or through the water. A competitor jumping to the right or left of the water jump, or trailing his or her leg or foot alongside any obstacle shall be disqualified. The competitor may jump or vault over each hurdle and may place a foot or feet on each hurdle, including the one at the water jump.

(9) The standard events are:

Distance of Race	Age Group	Number of Hurdles	Number of Water Jumps	Distance from start to first hurdle
3000 metres	Senior Men	28	7	257.8m
2000 metres	Junior Men	18	5	203.8m
1500 metres	Under-17 Men	13	3	255.8m

Note: Owing to the water jump having to be constructed on the arena inside or outside the track, thereby shortening or lengthening the normal distance of the lap, it is not possible to lay down any rule specifying the exact length of the lap or to state precisely the position of the water jump.

It should be borne in mind that there must be enough distance from the starting line to the first hurdle to prevent competitors from overcrowding and there should be approximately 62.2m from the last hurdle to the finish line.

The water jump should be, where possible, the fourth jump in each lap. If necessary, the finish line should be moved to another part of the track.

The following measurements are given as a guide and any adjustments necessary should be made by lengthening or shortening the distance at the starting point of the race. It is assumed that a lap of 400m has been shortened by 6m by constructing the water jump inside the track.

(10) 3000 Metres

Distance from starting point to commencement of 1st lap, to be run without jumps	242.0m
Distance from commencement of 1st lap to 1st hurdle	15.8m
From 1st to 2nd hurdle	79.0m
From 2nd to 3rd hurdle	79.0m
From 3rd hurdle to water jump	79.0m
From water jump to 4th hurdle	79.0m

From 4th hurdle to finishing line

$$\begin{array}{r} 62.2\text{m} \\ \hline 7 \text{ laps of } 394\text{m} = 2758.0\text{m} \\ \text{plus} \qquad 242.0\text{m} \\ \hline 3000.0\text{m} \end{array}$$

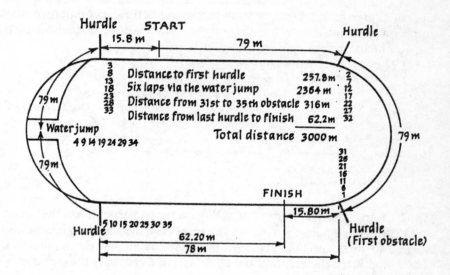

(11) 2000 Metres

(If the course is laid out with a lap of 394m.)

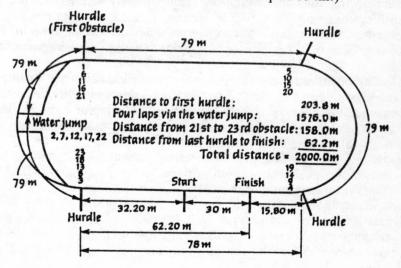

(12) 1500 Metres
(If the course is laid out with a lap of 394m.)

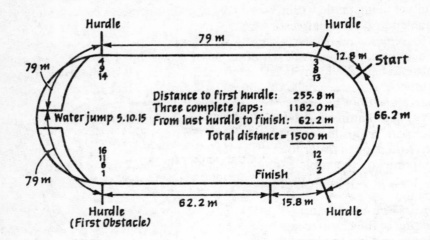

Distance to first hurdle: 255.8 m
Three complete laps: 1182.0 m
From last hurdle to finish: 62.2 m
Total distance = 1500 m

118. RELAY RACES

(1) Lines shall be drawn across the track to mark the distance of the stages and to denote the scratch line. Lines shall also be drawn 10m before and after the scratch line to denote the take-over zone. These lines are to be included in the zonal measurements.

(2) Except for the first runner, where the stage to be run does not exceed 200 metres, the outgoing runners may commence their run not more than 10m outside the take-over zone; where the stage exceeds 200 metres the outgoing runners must commence their run within the take-over zone. Additional lines in a different colour from that used for the take-over zone markings should be drawn to indicate the additional 10m zone at all change-over points.

(3) The positions of the teams at the start of the race shall be drawn and shall be retained at each take-over zone, except that, in races where lanes are not used or have ceased to operate, waiting runners can move to an inner position on the track as incoming team-mates arrive, provided this can be done without fouling.

(4) When relay races up to and including 400 metres are contested on a circular track each team should, if possible, have a separate lane and each lane must be the full distance.

(5) Where the first section of a relay race is 200 metres or 400 metres, the first 400 metres section(s) should, if possible, be run in lanes with staggered starts. Alternatively, where the first section of a relay is 400 metres, lanes shall cease to operate at the beginning of the back straight on either the first or second lap.

(6) In events where the first lap only is run in lanes, competitors after leaving the take-over zone are free to take up any position on the track.

(7) In sprint relay races up and down a track the take-over is by touch, contact being made within a clearly defined area of 1m beyond, and at each end of, the relay distance.

(8) When a relay race is being run in lanes competitors may place one check mark on the track within their own lane but may not place, or cause to be placed, any marking object on or alongside the track. On a synthetic surface, chalk or similar substances which leave indelible marks must not be used.

(9) The baton must be carried in the hand throughout the race. If dropped, it must be recovered by the athlete who dropped it, who may leave the lane in order to retrieve the baton. Provided this procedure is adopted, no other athlete is impeded, and by so doing the distance of the race is not lessened, dropping the baton shall not result in disqualification.

(10) The baton must be passed only within the take-over zone. The passing of the baton commences when it is first touched by the receiving runner and is completed the moment it is in the hands of the receiving runner only. Within the take-over zone it is only the position of the baton which is decisive, and not the position of the body or limbs of the competitors.

Note: To assist the judges, it is recommended that the batons be of distinctive colours.

(11) Competitors after handing over the baton should remain in their lanes or zone until the course is clear to avoid obstruction to other competitors. Should any competitor wilfully impede a member of another team by running out of position or lane at the finish of a stage that competitor is liable to cause the disqualification of his or her own team.

(12) Assistance by pushing off or by any other methods will cause disqualification.

(13) On completion of the final leg the baton is to be handed to an official by the last runner. It is not to be dropped or thrown from the hand. Failure to comply with this instruction may lead to disqualification.

(14) Once a team has competed in the preliminary round(s) of an event the composition of the team must not be altered for any subsequent round or final, except in the case of injury or illness where the Referee is satisfied, on medical or other evidence, that a competitor is unfit to compete in a subsequent round, when permission may be given for the substitution of another competitor.

(15) It is permissible for the order of running to be changed between heats and succeeding round or final without reference to the Referee.

(16) No competitor may run two sections for a team.

(17) The relay baton shall be a smooth hollow tube circular in section made of any rigid material in one piece, the length of which shall not be more than 30cm or less than 28cm. The circumference shall be 12–13cm and the weight shall not be less than 50g.

119. TIMEKEEPING

Note: Manually operated electronic timers have generally superseded conventional watches. In the following Rule the terms 'timer' and 'watch' are used to distinguish between these two types.

General Conditions

(1) The Timekeepers must be in line with the finish. Wherever possible Timekeepers should be on the outside of the track and at least 5m from the outside lane. In order that they all have a good view of the finish line, and of the Starter, an elevated position should be provided.

(2) The time of an athlete shall be taken from the flash from the Starter's pistol or other device to the moment when the body of that competitor (i.e. the torso, as distinguished from the head, neck, hands, arms, feet or legs) reaches the vertical plane of the edge of the finish line nearer to the start (See Rule 32).

(3) It is desirable, wherever possible, to record lap times and the leader's number in races of 800m and over, and, in addition, times at each 1000m in races of 3000m and over. Such information is essential in the case of a record claim.

(4) No person except an official Timekeeper or other person appointed to do so by the Chief Timekeeper shall:

(*a*) Indicate intermediate times to competitors.

(*b*) Give times to be announced over the public address system.

Manually Operated Timing

(5) Timekeepers should use:

(*a*) Quartz crystal-controlled electronic timers.

Alternatively, or additionally, they may use:

(*b*) Conventional watches with dials and hands which have obtained certificates from a nationally recognised standardising organisation stating that the requirements of the NPL Test Leaflet TH42C have been met. Such a certificate should be renewed every three years.

(6) Quartz crystal-controlled electronic timers may be used for hand timing in all races.

(7) Conventional watches with dials and hands may be used for timing races up to and including 3000m.

(8) For all hand timed races on the track the times shall be returned to 0.1 second by Timekeepers using manually operated electronic timers, or conventional stop watches. Timings in 1/100th seconds not ending in zero shall be rounded up to the next longer 1/10th second e.g. 10.10s shall be returned as 10.1s but 10.11s shall be returned as 10.2s.

(9) For races contested partly or wholly outside the stadium timings will be returned to the next longer full second.

(10) Each Timekeeper shall time independently and declare the recorded time to the Chief Timekeeper immediately. The Chief Timekeeper may inspect the readings to verify the times and must do so if a record claim is involved.

(11) Unless satisfied that a mistake has been made the Chief Timekeeper shall declare the time in accordance with the following conditions:

(*a*) When three Timekeepers are timing one placing and two agree but one disagrees the time shown by the two agreeing shall be the official time

(*b*) If all the Timekeepers disagree the middle time shall be the official time

(*c*) If, for any reason, only two times are taken the longer shall be the official time

(*d*) If the hand of an analogue display stops between the dial divisions the time read from it shall be to the longer of the two readings.

(12) In the event of a record claim the time shall be taken by three Graded Timekeepers each of whom should be Grade 1 or 2. They shall show their timings to the Chief Timekeeper and certify these times on the appropriate Record Application Form.

Fully Automated Timing

(13) A fully automated timing device approved by the Federation may be used for timing all races. To be approved, such a device will require a certificate of accuracy from a nationally recognised standardising organisation showing an error of less than 0.001% (3.6 milliseconds per nominal hour) at 20°C and at its operating nominal voltage. The timing device must start within 2 milliseconds (0.002s) of the report and flash from the pistol or other starting device.

(14) A videotape system may also be used, provided:

(*a*) it is started automatically by the Starter's gun;

(*b*) it uses a videotape camera aligned with the finish line and videotape that produces at least 50 frames per second;

(*c*) it incorporates a timing device that generates a reading to 1/100th of a second. When a frame by frame videotape based system is used, the official time for each competitor shall be read from the time of the frame when the competitor is positioned exactly at, or immediately after, the finish line.

(*d*) it is able to produce a printed picture which shows
(i) the time of each runner, and
(ii) whether or not the timing device has been started automatically by the Starter's gun.

(*e*) it carries a certificate of accuracy from a nationally recognised standardising organisation within the parameters laid down in (13) above.

(15) Where a videotape system is being used the Chief Photo-finish Judge shall consider the frames immediately before and after the finish line. If there is any change of position between the two frames, a dead heat shall be declared between the two athletes whose positions have changed.

Note: A photo-finish system based on a combination of video CCD (Charge Coupled Device) camera with a minimum of 100 lines per second, a computer and an appropriate electronic timing device can be used, provided this system is calibrated by a nationally recognised standardising organisation. In all fully automatic and video-based systems, the picture production and the time system must be synchronised.

(16) Times shall be read from the photo-finish picture as follows:

(*a*) For events up to and including 10,000m unless the time recorded is an exact 1/100th of a second, it shall be read and recorded to the next longer 1/100th of a second.

(*b*) For events longer than 10000m and held entirely on the track times shall be returned to the next longer 1/10th of a second.

(*c*) For events held partly or entirely outside the stadium the time shall be returned to the next longer full second.

These times shall be the official times unless the Chief Photo-finish Judge deems that an error has occurred when the Chief Timekeeper shall provide manual times in accordance with (11) above.

(17) A timing device which operates automatically at either the start or the finish, but not at both, shall be considered to produce neither manual nor fully automatic times and shall not therefore be used to obtain official times.

(18) In the event of a record claim the Chief Photo-finish Judge shall sign the Record Application Form and attach a copy of the photo-finish print. No details of the manually recorded times are required on the Form.

FIELD EVENTS

120. GENERAL CONDITIONS

(1) A draw shall be made to decide the order in which competitors shall take their trials and this order should be printed in the programme. The Judges shall have the power to alter this order. Competitors cannot hold over any of their trials to a subsequent round, except in the High Jump and Pole Vault.

(2) If competitors are entered in both a track event and a field event or in more than one field event taking place simultaneously, the Judges may allow them to take their trials in an order different from that decided upon prior to the start of the competition.

(3) In throwing or jumping for distance no competitor is allowed to have more than one trial recorded in any one round of the competition.

(4) Competitors who unreasonably delay making a trial in a field event render themselves liable to having that trial disallowed and recorded as a fault, and for a second delay at any time during the competition to disqualification from taking any further trials, but any performances previous to the disqualification shall stand for inclusion in the final result of the competition.

(5) It is a matter for the Referee to decide, having regard to all the circumstances, what is an unreasonable delay. The following times should not normally be exceeded:

(a) in the High Jump, Long Jump, Triple Jump, Shot, Discus, Hammer and Javelin – one and a half minutes.

(b) in the Pole Vault – two minutes, the time beginning as soon as the uprights have been adjusted to the satisfaction of the competitor.

(c) The period between two consecutive trials by the same athlete should never be less than 4 minutes for Pole Vault and 3 minutes for other field events.

Note: The time normally allowed for a trial shall be considered as part of this period.

(d) when three or fewer competitors remain in the competition the time in the High Jump should be extended from one and a half minutes to three minutes and in the Pole Vault from two minutes to four minutes.

Note: This does not apply for Combined Events Competitions.

Note: If the time allowed elapses once the competitor has started a trial, that trial should not for that reason be disallowed.

(6) If in the opinion of the Referee the conditions warrant it, that official shall have power to change the place of the competition in any field event. Such a change should be made only after a round is completed.

(7) If for any reason a competitor is hampered in a trial in a field event, the Referee shall have power to award a substitute trial.

(8) Where in any of the field events the Organisers or the Referee consider it advantageous a qualifying round shall be held prior to the competition proper.

(*a*) All competitors who reach the prescribed standard in the qualifying round or pool shall compete in the competition proper. If less than the prescribed number of competitors reach the qualifying standard then the leading athletes up to that prescribed number shall take part in the competition proper; where necessary Rules 121(7), 126(3) or 130(3) shall be used to decide the qualifiers. If a tie for the final place in the competition remains after these Rules have been applied, all those competitors so tying shall be included in the competition proper.

(*b*) In each qualifying round each competitor shall be allowed three trials (High Jump and Pole Vault excepted) but the performance accomplished shall not be considered part of the competition proper. Once competitors have reached the qualifying standard they shall not take any more trials.

(9) If qualifying rounds or pools are held the order for taking trials in the competition proper shall be determined by a fresh draw.

When in accordance with the Rules the best competitors are allowed three more trials, they shall take their trials in the same order as was drawn for the first three rounds.

(10) In any athletics meeting competitors shall be excluded from participating in further events, including relays, when they have qualified in preliminary rounds (including qualifying rounds or pools in field events) or heats for further participation in any event but then do not compete further without giving a valid reason to the Referee. If a meeting extends over more than one day the exclusion shall apply to all subsequent events of the meeting.

Note: This is not to be read as infringing the rights of competitors qualified under Rules 126(1)(*b*) or 130(1)(*b*) from opting out of one or more of their additional trials since they have already qualified for inclusion in the final result.

(11) Once a competition has begun competitors are not permitted to use runways or take-off areas for practice or warm up purposes nor are they permitted to use throwing sites for practice trials, with or without implements.

VERTICAL JUMPS (HIGH JUMP AND POLE VAULT)

121. GENERAL CONDITIONS

(1) Unless such details are specified in the programme, the Judge shall decide the height at which the competition shall start, and the different heights to which the bar will be raised at the end of each round. The competitors shall be informed of the details before the competition begins.

(2) Competitors may commence jumping/vaulting at any of the heights above the minimum height and may jump/vault at their own discretion at any subsequent height. Three consecutive failures, regardless of the height at which any such failure occurs, disqualify from further participation, except in the case of a jump-off of a first place tie.
Note: The effect of this Rule is that competitors may forego their second and third jumps/vaults at a particular height (after failing once or twice) and still jump/vault at a subsequent height. If competitors forgo a trial at a certain height, they may not make any subsequent attempt at that height except in the resolution of a tie.

(3) Even after all the other competitors have failed, a competitor is entitled to continue until he or she has forfeited the right to compete further, and the best jump/vault shall be recorded as the winning height.

(4) After the competitor has won the competition the height or heights to which the bar is raised shall be decided after the Judge or Referee in charge of the event has consulted the wishes of the competitor.
Note: This does not apply for Combined Events Competitions where the increases in height shall be uniformly 3cm in the High Jump and 10cm in the Pole Vault throughout the competition.

(5) All measurements shall be made perpendicularly from the ground to the upper side of the cross-bar where it is lowest. A steel tape should be used. Alternatively a scientific apparatus which has a certificate of accuracy from a nationally recognised standardising organisation may be used. Any measurement of a new height shall be made before competitors attempt that height. In the case of a record claim the officials must check the measurement after the height has been cleared.
Note: Judges shall ensure, before commencing the competition, that the under-side and front of the cross-bar are distinguishable, and that the bar is always replaced in a similar manner.

(6) (*a*) The height shall be recorded to the nearest 1cm below the height measured if that distance is not a whole centimetre.

(*b*) Unless there is only one competitor remaining the bar shall not be raised by less than 2cm in the High Jump or 5cm in the Pole Vault after each round.

(7) Ties

Ties shall be decided as follows:

(*a*) The competitor with the lowest number of jumps/vaults at the height *at which the tie occurs* shall be awarded the higher place.

(*b*) If the tie still remains, the competitor with the lowest total of failures throughout the competition up to and including the height last cleared shall be awarded the higher place.

Example: High Jump

	1.67m	1.72m	1.75m	1.77m	1.80m	1.82m	1.85m	Total Failures	Position
Jones	—	xo	o	xo	—	xxo	All	4	2=
Smith	o	o	o	x—	xo	xxo	failed	4	2=
Brown	o	o	x—	o	xxo	xxo	three	5	4
Black	o	—	—	xxo	xxo	xo	times	5	1

Jones, Smith, Brown and Black all cleared 1.82m and failed at 1.85m
o = cleared   x = failed   — = did not jump

(*c*) if the tie still remains:

(i) If it concerns first place, the competitors tying shall have one more jump/vault at the lowest height at which any of them finally failed, and if no decision is reached the bar shall be lowered or raised 2cm for the High Jump and 5cm for the Pole Vault. They shall then attempt one jump/vault at each height until one competitor clears a height and the remaining competitor(s) fail at the same height. Competitors so tying must jump/vault on each occasion when resolving the tie.

(ii) If it concerns any other place, the competitors shall be awarded the same place in the competition.

Example:

	1.75m	1.80m	1.83m	1.86m	1.88m	Total Failures	Jump off 1.86m	1.84m	1.86m	Position
Green	o	xo	xo	xxx		2	x	o	x	2
Johnson	—	xo	xo	—	xxx	2	x	o	o	1
Baker	—	xxo	xo	xxx		3				3

o = cleared   x = failed   — = did not jump

Note: All competitors shall be credited with the best of all their jumps/vaults, including those taken in a jump-off of a first place tie.

122. HIGH JUMP

(1) Rules 120 and 121 apply.

(2) The uprights or posts shall not be moved during the competition unless the Referee considers the take-off or landing area has become unsuitable. Such a change shall be made only after a round has been completed.

(3) Competitors may place marks to assist them in their run-up and take-off. Where the competition takes place on a synthetic surface, chalk or similar substances which leave indelible marks must not be used.

(4) The distance of the run-up is unlimited.

(5) Competitors fail if they:

(*a*) In the course of a jump dislodge the bar so that it falls from the pegs; or

(*b*) Take-off from both feet; or

(*c*) Touch the ground, including the landing area, beyond the plane of the uprights either between or outside the uprights with any part of the body, without first clearing the bar, unless in the opinion of the Judge no advantage is gained.

123. HIGH JUMP SPECIFICATIONS

(1) Any style or kind of uprights or posts may be used provided they are rigid. Uprights should be sufficiently tall so as to exceed the maximum height to which the bar can be raised by at least 10cm.

(2) The distance between the uprights should not be less than 4.0m or more than 4.04m.

(3) The cross-bar shall be of any suitable material.

(*a*) It shall be of uniform thickness, and should be circular with square ends provided it has a uniform section throughout, the diameter shall be at least 29mm but not more than 31mm.

(*b*) The ends of a circular bar shall be constructed in such a way that one flat or concave surface of 29–35mm × 150–200mm is obtained.

(*c*) The front of the bar should be painted. The length of the cross-bar should not be less than 3.98m and not more than 4.02m. The maximum weight of the cross-bar shall be 2kg.

(*d*) Those parts of the bar which rest on the supports shall be smooth; they may not be covered with any material which has the effect of increasing friction between them and the supports.

(4) Each peg supporting the cross-bar shall be flat and rectangular, 4cm wide and extending 6cm from the uprights *in the direction of the opposite upright*. The supports must be firmly fixed to the uprights and be without any kind of spring. The supports may not be covered with rubber or with any other material which has the effect of increasing the

friction between the surface of the cross-bar and the supports. The ends of the cross-bar shall rest on the pegs in such a manner that it easily falls to the ground, either forwards or backwards, if touched by the competitor.

There shall be a space of at least 1cm between the ends of the cross-bar and the uprights.

(5) The ground round the take-off should be level but a maximum inclination of 1:250 in the direction of the centre of the cross-bar is permitted in the case of a synthetic take-off area.

(6) The minimum length of the runway shall be 15m but 25m is desirable if conditions permit.

(7) The landing area should measure not less than 5m long (that is at the take-off side) by 3m wide.

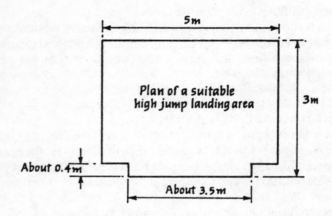

Note: The uprights and landing areas shall be so designed that there is a clearance of at least 10cm between them when in use to avoid displacement of the cross-bar through movement of the landing area causing contact with the uprights.

124. POLE VAULT

(1) Rules 120 and 121 apply.

(2) No marks may be placed on the runways, but a competitor may place marks alongside the runway.

(3) The distance of the run-up is unlimited.

(4) Competitors may have the uprights moved in either direction, but not more than 40cm in the direction of the runway, and not more than 80cm to the landing area from the prolongation of the inside edge of the top of the box.

Note: A white line 1cm wide may be drawn at right angles to the axis of the runway at the level of the inside edge of the top of the box. This line should be prolonged as far as the outside edge of the uprights.

(5) The take-off for the pole shall be from a wooden or metal box. A competitor is permitted to place sand in the box when it is his turn to vault.

(6) A competitor fails if he:

(a) In the course of a vault dislodges the bar so that it falls from the pegs; or

(b) Touches the ground, including the landing area beyond the vertical plane of the upper part of the box with any part of his body or with the pole, without first clearing the bar; or

(c) At the moment he makes a vault, or after leaving the ground, places his lower hand above the upper one, or moves the upper hand higher up on the pole.

(7) No one should touch the pole unless it is falling away from the bar or uprights; if it is so touched and the Referee or Judge is of the opinion it would have dislodged the bar so that it fell from the pegs the vault shall be recorded as a failure.

(8) Competitors may use their own poles. No competitor shall be allowed to use another's pole except with the consent of the owner.

(9) The pole may be of any material or combination of materials and any length or diameter, but the basic surface must be smooth. The pole may have a binding of not more than two layers of adhesive tape of uniform thickness and with a smooth surface. The poles shall have no other assistance or device, except that the lower end of the pole may have protective layers of tape for a distance of approximately 30cm

(10) The use of tape on the hands or fingers shall not be allowed except in the case of need to cover an open cut. The use of a forearm cover to prevent injury shall be allowed. Competitors are permitted to use an adhesive substance on their hands or on the pole, in order to obtain a better grip.

(11) If in making an attempt the competitor's pole is broken it shall not be counted as a failure.

(12) Under-15 and Under-13 girls are not permitted to compete in Pole Vault events.

125. POLE VAULT SPECIFICATIONS

(1) Any style or kind of uprights or posts may be used provided they are rigid.

(2) The distance between the uprights, or between extension arms where such are used, should be not less than 4.30cm or more than 4.37m wide.

(3) The cross-bar shall be of any suitable material.

(*a*) It shall be of uniform thickness, and should be circular with square ends provided it has a uniform section throughout, the diameter shall be at least 29mm but not more than 31mm.

(*b*) The ends of a circular bar shall be constructed in such a way that one flat or concave surface of 29–35mm × 150–200mm is obtained.

(*c*) The front of the bar should be painted. The length of the cross-bar should be not less than 4.48m and not more than 4.52m. The maximum weight of the cross-bar shall be 2.25kg.

(*d*) Those parts of the bar which rest on the supports shall be smooth. They may not be covered with rubber or any other material which has the effect of increasing friction between them and the supports.

(4) The pegs supporting the cross-bar shall extend horizontally not more than 7.5cm from the face of the uprights *on the side further from the runway* and must be without notches or indentations of any kind. The pegs must be of uniform thickness throughout and not more than 13mm in diameter. The pegs may not be covered with any material which has the effect of increasing the friction with the ends of the bar.

(5) As an alternative to (4) above, the pegs supporting the cross-bar may be placed upon extension arms 38cm in length permanently fixed to the uprights, thus allowing the uprights to be placed wider apart without increasing the length of the cross-bar.

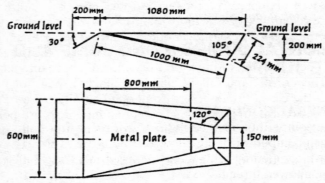

(6) The box in which to plant the pole may be of wood or metal and shall be 1m in length, 60cm in width at the front end, tapering to 15cm in width at the bottom of the stopboard, where it shall be 20cm in depth. The front edge of the box must be level with the runway and firmly fixed to the ground. If the box is constructed of wood, the bottom shall be lined with 2.5mm sheet metal for a distance of 80cm from the front of the box.

(7) The length of the runway is unlimited. The runway should be level and its minimum length shall be 40m but 45m is desirable if conditions permit. For record purposes the maximum allowance for lateral incli-nation of the runway must not exceed 1:100 and in the running direction

of 1:1000 downwards. The minimum width of the runway shall be 1.22m.

(8) The landing area should measure not less than 5m by 5m, excluding the two protection pads on either side of the box.

Note: The contours of the bed around the edges of the box should allow for the bending of the lower part of the pole in the direction of the bed. This can be achieved if the bed maintains the angles produced by the box, i.e. 105° between the base and the front edge of the box, and 120° between the base and the sides of the box.

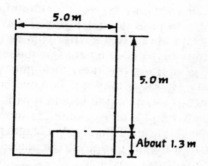

Plan of a suitable landing area

HORIZONTAL JUMPS (LONG JUMP AND TRIPLE JUMP)

126. GENERAL CONDITIONS
(1) The competition may be decided in either of the following ways:

(*a*) Each competitor being allowed from three to six trials; or

(*b*) Each competitor being allowed three trials and the three to eight best being allowed three more trials (see Rule 120(9)). In the event of a tie for the final place(s), any competitor so tying shall be allowed the three additional trials.

(Tying means, in this connection, achieving the same distance and Rule 126(3) should not, therefore, be applied.)

To qualify for these further trials the athlete must have achieved a valid performance. The competition conditions must be explained to the competitors before the event begins.

(2) Competitors shall be credited with the best of all their trials, including jumps taken in resolving a first-place tie.

(3) In the case of a tie, the second-best performance of the competitors tying shall determine the result. If the tie remains, the third-best

jump will be decisive and so on. If the tie still remains and it concerns first place, the competitors so tying shall have such additional extra trials as is required to determine the tie; if the tie concerns any other place, the competitors shall be awarded the same place in the competition.

(4) The take-off shall be from a board the edge of which nearer to the landing area shall be called the 'take-off line'. If a competitor takes off before reaching the board, it shall not for that reason be counted as a failure.

(5) The distance of the run is unlimited.

(6) No marks shall be placed on the runway, but a competitor may place marks alongside the runway. No competitor may place, or cause to be placed, any mark beyond the 'take-off line'.

(7) It shall be counted as a failure if any competitor:

(a) Touches the ground beyond the take-off line or take-off line extended with any part of the body, whether running up without jumping or in the act of jumping.

(b) Takes off from outside either end of the board, whether beyond or behind the take-off line extended.

(c) In the course of landing, touches the ground outside the landing area nearer to the take-off line than the break in the sand to which the measurement of the jump would have been made.

(d) After a completed jump, walks back through the landing area.

(e) Employs any form of somersaulting.

(8) The measurement of the jump shall be made at right angles from the nearest break in the ground in the landing area made by any part of the body of the competitor to the take-off-line. Only valid trials shall be measured.

(9) The height shall be recorded to the nearest 1cm below the height measured if that distance is not a whole centimetre.

(10) If calibrated measuring equipment is used its accuracy must be checked with a steel or fibre-glass tape; otherwise a steel or fibre-glass tape should be used and the part of the tape showing the distance jumped must be held at the take-off line. Alternatively a scientific apparatus, which has a certificate of accuracy from a nationally recognised standardising organisation may be used.

(11) Whenever possible wind velocity should be measured and recorded.

(a) The gauge should be set up at 20m from the take-off line, not more than 2m from the edge of the runway and at a height of approximately 1.22m.

(b) The velocity shall be measured for a period of 5 seconds from the time a competitor passes a mark placed 40m (Long Jump) or 35m (Triple Jump) from the take-off line. If a competitor runs less than 40m or 35m as the case may be, the reading shall be taken from the time the athlete commences the run.

(c) The wind gauge shall be read in metres per second, rounded to the next higher tenth of a metre per second in the positive direction. (For example, a reading of +2.03m/sec. shall be recorded as +2.1m/sec.; a reading of −2.03m/sec. shall be recorded as −2.0m/sec.) (see also Rules 141.14 and 142.19.)

127. GENERAL SPECIFICATIONS

(1) A take-off board shall be rigidly fixed in the ground, flush therewith. It shall be made of wood 1.21–1.23m long, 19.8–20.2cm wide and maximum 10cm deep, and painted white.

(2) The runway should be level. The length of the runway is unlimited but its minimum length shall be 40m but 45m is desirable if conditions permit.

(3) The minimum width of the runway shall be 1.22m.

(4) For record purposes the maximum allowance for lateral inclination of the runway must not exceed 1:100 and in running direction 1:1000 downwards.

(5) In order that jumps can be measured accurately the sand in the landing area should be moistened before the competition.

(6) The surface of the sand in the landing area should be level with the top of the take-off board.

(7) Immediately beyond the the take-off line there shall be placed a board of plasticine or other suitable material for recording the athlete's footprint in the case of a foot fault. The specifications for the plasticine indicator board are as follows:

(a) The board shall be rigid, 98–102mm wide and 1.21–1.22m long, covered with plasticine or other suitable material on the top surface

(b) The surface shall rise from the level of the take-off board at an angle of 30° in the direction of running to a maximum height above the take-off board of 7mm

(c) The board shall be mounted in a recess or shelf in the runway, on the side of the take-off board nearer the landing area. When mounted in this recess, the whole assembly must be sufficiently rigid to accept the full force of the athlete's foot

(d) The surface of the board beneath the plasticine shall be of a material in which the spikes of an athlete's shoe will grip and not skid. Note: The layer of plasticine can be smoothed off by means of a roller or suitably shaped scraper for the purposes of removing the footprints of the competitors.

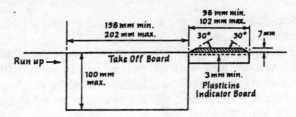

No Jump Indicator for Long Jump and Triple Jump

(8) If it is not possible to install an Indicator Board as specified in (7), soft earth or damp sand should be sprinkled to a height of 7mm above the level of the take-off board over a width of 10cm beyond the edge of the board nearer to the landing area. At the take-off line the sand should be raised at an angle of 30° to the height of 7mm.

(9) The landing area should have a minimum width of 2.75m, a maximum width of 3m, and be at least 9m long. It should, if possible, be so placed that the middle of the runway, if extended, would coincide with the middle of the landing area.

Note: When the axis of the runway is not in line with the centre of the landing area this shall be achieved by placing a tape which shall delimit a landing area which has the same width on either side of the central axis of the runway prolonged.

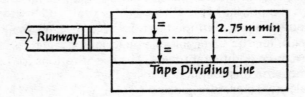

Centralised Long Jump/Triple Jump Landing Area

128. LONG JUMP

(1) Rules 120, 126 and 127 apply.

(2) A space of at least 1m but no more than 3m, of a similar surface to the runway, should be left between the take-off board and the landing area.

(3) The distance between the take-off board and the end of the landing area should be at least 10m.

129. TRIPLE JUMP

(1) Rules 120, 126 and 127 apply.

(2) The hop shall be made so that competitors shall first land upon the same foot with which they shall have taken off, in the step they shall land on the other foot, from which subsequently the jump is performed. It shall not be considered a failure if competitors, during the step phase, touch the ground with the 'sleeping' leg.

(3) The ground between the take-off board and the landing area must be level.

(4) The distance between the take-off board and the landing area should be 13m or 11m for Senior competition, 9m for Junior competition, and as appropriate for Women's competition, but it must be appreciated that suitable distances will vary according to the standard of the competition.

(5) Under-15 and Under-13 girls are not permitted to compete in Triple Jump events.

THROWING EVENTS

130. GENERAL CONDITIONS

(1) The competition may be decided in either of the following ways:

(a) Each competitor being allowed from three to six trials; or

(b) Each competitor being allowed three trials and the three to eight best competitors being allowed three more trials (see Rule 120.9). In the event of a tie for the final place(s), any competitor so tying shall be allowed the three additional trials.

(Tying means in this connection achieving the same distance and Rule 130.3 should not, therefore, be applied.)

To qualify for these further trials the athlete must have achieved a valid performance. The competition conditions must be explained to the competitors before the event begins.

(2) Competitors shall be credited with the best of all their trials, including throws taken in resolving a first place tie.

(3) In the case of a tie, the second-best performance of the competitors tying shall determine the result. If the tie remains, the third-best throw will be decisive and so on. If the tie remains and it concerns first place, the competitors so tying shall have such additional extra trials as is required to determine the tie. If the tie concerns any other place, the competitors shall be awarded the same place in the competition.

(4) No competitor may place, or cause to be placed, any mark within the throwing sector.

(5) Competitors shall use only those implements provided for general use. Subject to any regulations laid down by the Promoting Body, competitors who wish to use their own implements must submit them to the Referee for approval. No competitor shall be allowed to use another's implement without the prior permission of the owner.

(6) No device of any kind (e.g. the taping of the fingers) which in any way assists a competitor when making a throw shall be allowed, except in throwing the Hammer where the taping of individual fingers is permitted.

Note: The use of tape to cover injuries to the hand will be allowed only if the Referee is satisfied on medical or other evidence that the tape is necessary. The use of tape on the wrist will be allowed.

(7) In order to obtain a better grip, competitors are permitted to use an adhesive substance on their hands only.

(8) In order to protect the spine from injury a competitor may wear a belt of leather or some other suitable material.

(9) When markers are used to indicate the best throw of each competitor and to show record distances they shall be placed on a line or tape outside the sector lines.

Note: The outer ends of the sector lines should be marked with flags.

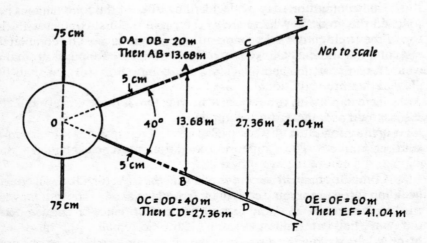

Note: The 40° sector may be laid out accurately and conveniently by making the distance between two points on the inside edge of the sector lines 20m from the centre of the circle exactly 13.68m apart.

131. PUTTING THE SHOT

(1) Rules 120 and 130 apply.

(2) *In order to avoid accidents throwing sectors must be roped off at a height of approximately 1m and at a minimum distance of 2m outside the sector lines. Alternatively, the central throwing area must be roped off as a unit at a height of 1m.*

(3) Competitors must be given instructions that implements must be thrown during practice only from the circle. Implements must be returned by *hand* during practice or competition and must not be thrown back to the starting area. The Referee or other appropriate official shall disqualify from competing in the event any athletes who wilfully disobey the above instructions after having their attention drawn to them.

(4) No practice trials shall be allowed after a competition has begun.

(5) Gloves may not be worn.

(6) Competitors must not spray or spread any substance on the surface of a throwing circle nor on their shoes.

(7) A competitor must commence the throw from a stationary position within the circle.

(8) It shall be a foul throw if the competitor, after stepping into the circle and starting to make the throw, touches with any part of the body the ground outside the circle, the top of the stop-board or the top of the circle rim. A competitor is allowed to touch the inside of the iron band or stop-board.

(9) The competitor must not leave the circle until the implement has touched the ground. When leaving the circle the first contact with the top of the circle rim or the ground outside the circle must be completely behind the white line which is drawn outside the circle, the rear edge of which runs theoretically through the centre of the circle.

Note: To comply with this requirement a competitor's first step on leaving the circle must be wholly in the area marked 'A'.

(10) Provided that in the course of a trial the foregoing Rules have not been infringed, a competitor may interrupt a trial once started, may lay the implement down, may leave the circle, before returning to a stationary position and beginning a fresh trial.

Note: When leaving the circle the competitor must step out as required in 9. All the moves permitted by this paragraph shall be included in the maximum time normally allowed for a trial as given in Rule 120.5.

(11) The shot shall be put from the shoulder with one hand only. At the time the competitor takes a stance in the ring to commence a put, the shot shall touch or be in close contact with the chin and the hand shall

not be dropped below this position during the act of putting. The shot must not be brought behind the line of the shoulders.

(12) In making a put the competitors may rest their feet against but not on top of the stop-board.

(13) A foul throw or letting go of the implement in an attempt shall be reckoned as a trial.

(14) For a valid put the shot must fall completely within the inner edges of lines marking a sector of 40° set out on the ground so that the radii lines cross at the centre of the circle (see diagram below Rule 130.9.)

(15) All measurements must be made from the nearer edge of the first mark made in the ground by the implement to the inner edge of the circle rim along a line drawn from the mark to the centre of the circle.

(16) All measurements should be made immediately after each put. A steel or fibre-glass tape should be used for measurement, and that part of the tape showing the distance put must be held by the official at the circle. Alternatively, approved datum measurement equipment may be used, as may a scientific apparatus which has a certificate of accuracy from a nationally recognised standardising organisation.

(17) The distance shall be recorded to the nearest 1cm below the distance measured if that distance is not a whole centimetre.

132. PUTTING THE SHOT SPECIFICATIONS

(1) The circle shall be measured from the inside. The surface should be of concrete, asphalt or some other firm but not slippery material. The surface should be lightly stippled when being laid to give a rough but not ribbed surface.

(2) The surface of the inside of the circle should be level and 20mm ± 6mm lower than the upper edge of the ring which should be level with the ground outside.

(3) Circle Rings.

Construction – The rim shall be made of band iron, steel, or other suitable material and be painted white.

Measurements – (Metal) – The inside diameter of the circle shall measure 2.135m maximum, and the rim of the circle shall be at least 6mm thick.

(Wood) – The inside diameter of the circle shall measure 2.135m maximum, and the rim of the circle shall be 7.5cm thick. A tolerance of ±5mm is permitted for the inside diameter of a circle.

(4) A white line 5cm wide shall be drawn from the top of the circle, extending for at least 75cm on either side of the circle, the theoretical extension of this line across the circle dividing it into front and rear halves with the rear edge passing through the centre of the circle.

(5) A portable circle meeting with the specifications above is permissible.

(6) A curved stop-board of wood painted white, 1.21–1.23m long on the inside, 11.2–11.4cm wide and 9.8–10.2cm high in relation to the level of the inside of the circle shall be fixed in the middle of the circumference of the front half of the circle. The board shall curve so that the inside edge coincides with the inner edge of the circle and shall be fixed firmly to the ground.

(7) The shot shall be of solid iron, brass or any metal not softer than brass, or a shell of such metal filled with lead or some other material.

(8) The shot shall be spherical in shape, its surface shall have no roughness and the finish shall be smooth. It shall conform to the following specifications.

MEN	SENIORS		JUNIORS	
	Minimum	Maximum	Minimum	Maximum
Weight	7.26kg		6.25kg	
Diameter	110mm	130mm	106mm	126mm
	UNDER-17		UNDER-15	
Weight	5kg		4kg	
Diameter	101mm	118mm	95mm	110mm
	UNDER-13			
Weight	3.25kg			
Diameter	90mm	105mm		
WOMEN	SENIORS AND JUNIORS		UNDER-17	
	Minimum	Maximum	Minimum	Maximum
Weight	4kg		4kg	
Diameter	95mm	110mm	95mm	110mm
	UNDER-15		UNDER-13	
Weight	3.25kg		2.72kg	
Diameter	90mm	105mm	85mm	95mm

Note: It is recommended that implements issued for competition should exceed the specified weights by at least 5gr.

In these Rules 'smooth' implies a normal cast or turned surface which may or may not have been coated with a fine powder, sand blasted, sprayed or painted – such surfaces are 'orthodox'. Any surface which has been roughened by ribbing, grooving, knurling and so on, is not 'smooth'. No unorthodox surface is permitted.

VETERANS	MEN 40–49		MEN 50–59	
	Minimum	Maximum	Minimum	Maximum
Weight	7.26kg		6kg	
Diameter	110mm	130mm		
	MEN 60–69		MEN 70 AND OVER	
Weight	5kg		4kg	
Diameter	101mm	118mm	95mm	110mm
	WOMEN 35–49		WOMEN 50 AND OVER	
Weight	4kg		3kg	
Diameter	95mm	110mm		

133. THROWING THE HAMMER

(1) Rules 120 and 130 apply.

(2) *In order to avoid accidents throwing sectors must be roped off at a height of approximately 1m and to make a 60° safety sector inside which the hammer throwing sector is centrally placed. Alternatively, the central throwing area must be roped off as a unit at a height of 1m.*

Note: Referees are reminded of the need to ensure that discus, hammer and javelin competitions (including warm-up for these events) are not held at the same time within the central throwing area when the standard of any of the competitors is likely to create possible danger to the officials operating within and alongside the respective sectors of these events.

(3) Competitors must be given instructions that implements must be thrown during practice only from the circle. Implements must be returned by *hand* during practice or competition and must not be thrown back to the starting area. The Referee or other appropriate official shall disqualify from competing in the event any athlete who wilfully disobeys the above instructions after having his or her attention drawn to them.

(4) No practice trials shall be allowed after a competition has begun.

(5) All throws shall be made from a cage (see Rule 137).

(6) Gloves may be worn. The gloves must be smooth on back and front, and the tip of the fingers, other than the thumb, must be exposed.

(7) A competitor must not spray or spread any substance on the surface of a throwing circle nor on his shoes.

(8) A competitor must commence the throw from a stationary position within the circle; he may adopt any position he chooses.

(9) It shall be a foul throw if the competitor, after he has stepped into

the circle and started to make the throw, touches with any part of his body the ground outside the circle, or the top of the circle rim. A competitor is allowed to touch the inside of the iron band.

(10) The competitor must not leave the circle until the hammer has touched the ground. When leaving the circle the first contact with the top of the circle rim or the ground outside the circle must be completely behind the white line which is drawn outside the circle, the rear edge of which runs theoretically through the centre of the circle.

Note: To comply with this rule a competitor's first step on leaving the circle must be wholly in the area marked 'A'.

(11) The competitor in his starting position prior to the preliminary swings or turns is allowed to put the head of the hammer on the ground inside or outside the circle.

(12) It shall not be considered a foul throw if the head of the hammer touches the ground when the competitor makes the preliminary swings or turns, but if, having so touched the ground, he stops throwing so as to begin a trial again, this shall count as a failure.

(13) Provided that in the course of the trial the foregoing Rules have not been infringed, a competitor may interrupt a trial once started, may lay the hammer down, may leave the circle before returning to a stationary position and beginning a fresh trial.
Note: If a hammer first hits the cage and then lands within the sector, the throw shall not, for that reason, be considered invalid.

When leaving the circle the competitor must step out as required in (10) above. All the moves permitted by this paragraph shall be included in the maximum time normally allowed for a trial as given in Rule 120(5).

(14) If the hammer breaks during a throw or while in the air, it shall not be counted as a throw, provided it was made in accordance with the Rules. If the competitor thereby loses his balance and commits a foul, it shall not count against him.

(15) A foul throw or letting go of the hammer in an attempt shall be reckoned as a trial.

(16) For a valid throw the hammer head must fall completely within the inner edges of lines marking a sector of 40° set out on the ground so that the radii lines cross at the centre of the circle.
Note: The 40° sector may be laid out accurately and conveniently by

making the distance between two points on the inside edge of the sector line 40m from the centre of the circle exactly 27.36m apart (see diagram below Rule 128.9). The outer ends of the sector lines should be marked with flags.

(17) All measurements must be made from the nearer edge of the mark first made in the ground by the head of the hammer to the inner edge of the circle along a line drawn from the mark to the centre of the circle.

(18) A steel or fibre-glass tape should be used for measurement, and that part of the tape showing the distance thrown must be held by the official at the circle. Alternatively, approved datum measurement equipment may be used, as may a scientific apparatus which has obtained a certificate of accuracy from a nationally recognised standardising organisation.

(19) The distance shall be recorded in even centimetre units to the nearest unit below the distance measured if that distance is not a whole even centimetre.

134. THROWING THE HAMMER SPECIFICATIONS
This rule is given in full in BAF's Rules for Competition.

135. THROWING THE DISCUS
(1) Rules 120 and 130 apply.

(2) *In order to avoid accidents throwing sectors must be roped off at a height of approximately 1m and to make a 60° safety sector inside which the discus throwing sector is centrally placed.*

Note: Referees are reminded of the need to ensure that discus, hammer and javelin competitions (including warm-up for these events) are not held at the same time within the central throwing area when the standard of any of the competitors is likely to create possible danger to the officials operating within and alongside the respective sectors of these events.

(3) Competitors must be given instructions that implements must be thrown during practice only from the circle. Implements must be returned by *hand* during practice or competition and must not be thrown back to the starting area. The Referee or other appropriate official shall disqualify from competing in the event any athletes who wilfully disobey the above instructions after having their attention drawn to them.

(4) No practice trials shall be allowed after a competition has begun.

(5) All throws shall be made from a cage (see Rule 137).

(6) Gloves may not be worn.

(7) Competitors must not spray or spread any substance on the surface of a throwing circle nor on their shoes.

(8) Competitors must commence the throw from a stationary position within the circle; they may adopt any position they choose.

(9) It shall be a foul throw if the competitor, after stepping into the circle and starting to make the throw, touches with any part of the body the ground outside the circle, or the top of the circle rim. A competitor is allowed to touch the inside of the iron band.

(10) The competitor must not leave the circle until the discus has touched the ground. When leaving the circle the first contact with the top of the circle rim or the ground outside the circle must be completely behind the white line which is drawn outside the circle, the rear edge of which runs theoretically through the centre of the circle.

Note: To comply with this rule a competitor's first step on leaving the circle must be wholly in the area marked 'A'.

(11) Provided that in the course of a trial the foregoing Rules have not been infringed, a competitor may interrupt a trial once started, may lay down the discus, may leave the circle before returning to a stationary position and beginning a fresh trial.

Note: When leaving the circle the competitor must step out as required above. All the moves permitted by this paragraph shall be included in the maximum time normally allowed for a trial as given in Rule 120.5.

(12) A foul throw or letting go of the discus in an attempt shall be reckoned as a trial. If a discus breaks during a fair throw it shall not be counted as a trial.

(13) For a valid throw the discus must fall completely within the inner edges of lines marking a sector of 40° set out on the ground so that the radii lines cross at the centre of the circle.

Note: If the discus first hits the cage and then lands within the sector, the throw shall not, for that reason, be considered invalid.

Note: The 40° sector may be laid out accurately and conveniently by making the distance between two points on the inside edge of the sector lines 40m from the centre of the circle exactly 27.36m apart (see diagram below Rule 130.9). The outer ends of the sector lines should be marked with flags.

(14) All measurements must be made from the nearer edge of the mark first made in the ground by the discus to the inner edge of the circle along a line drawn from the mark to the centre of the circle.

(15) A steel tape should be used for measurement, and that part of the tape showing the distance thrown must be held by the official at the circle. Alternatively, approved datum measurement equipment may be used, as may a scientific apparatus which has obtained a certificate of accuracy from a nationally recognised standardising organisation.

(16) The distance shall be recorded in even centimetre units to the nearest unit below the distance measured if that distance is not a whole even centimetre.

136. THROWING THE DISCUS SPECIFICATIONS
This rule is given in full in BAF's Rules for Competition.

137. CAGES FOR HAMMER AND DISCUS
Hammer Throwing Cage
(1) All hammer throws shall be made from an enclosure or cage to ensure the safety of spectators, officials and competitors.
Specifications are given in the BAF's Rules for Competition.

138. THROWING THE JAVELIN
(1) Rules 120 and 130 apply.
(2) *In order to avoid accidents a safety sector covering the landing area must be roped off at a height approximately 1m and at a minimum distance of 2m outside the sector lines. Alternatively, the central throwing area must be roped off as a unit at a height of 1m.*
Note: Referees are reminded of the need to ensure that discus, hammer and javelin competitions (including warm-up for these events) are not held at the same time within the central throwing area when the standard of any of the competitors is likely to create possible danger to the officials operating within and alongside the respective sectors of these events.

(3) Competitors must be given instructions that implements must be thrown during practice only from the arc. Implements must be returned by *hand* during practice or competition and must not be thrown back to the starting area. The Referee or other appropriate official shall disqualify from competing in the event any athletes who wilfully disobey the above instructions after having their attention drawn to them.

(4) No practice throws shall be allowed after the competition has begun.

(5) Gloves may not be worn.

(6) The javelin must be held in one hand only, and at the grip, so that the little (or fourth) finger is nearest to the point.

(7) No marks shall be placed on the runway but the competitors may place marks at the side of the runway.

(8) In the course of running up to throw a competitor may not cross either of the parallel lines forming the runway.

(9) The javelin shall be thrown over the shoulder or upper part of the throwing arm, and must not be slung or hurled.

(10) At no time after preparing to throw, and until the javelin has been discharged into the air, may the competitor turn completely round so that the back is towards the throwing arc.

(11) Non-orthodox styles are not permitted.

(12) It is a foul throw if the competitor steps on or beyond the arc or extended scratch line on the ground marked 'N' on the diagram below.

(13) A throw shall be valid only if the tip of the metal head strikes the ground before any other part of the javelin.

(14) A competitor shall not leave the runway until the javelin has touched the ground. The competitor shall then, from a standing position, leave the runway from behind the arc and the lines drawn from the extremities of the arc at right angles to the parallel lines which define the runway.

(15) A foul throw or letting go of the javelin in an attempt shall be reckoned as a trial. If a javelin breaks during a fair throw it shall not be counted as a trial.

(16) The arc must be clearly marked on the ground by chalk or otherwise, and all measurements must be made from the nearer edge of the mark first made in the ground by the tip of the metal head of the javelin to the inside edge of the javelin arc along a line from the point of the fall to the centre of the circle of which the arc is a part.

(17) For a valid throw the javelin must land so that the point from which the measurement is to be made is within the inner edges of lines marking the sector set out on the ground by extending the lines from the centre of the circle of which the arc is a part, through the points at which the arc joins the lines marking the runway.

(18) A steel tape should be used for measurement, and the part of the tape showing the distance thrown must be held by the official at the arc. Alternatively, approved datum measurement equipment may be used, as may a scientific apparatus which has obtained a certificate of accuracy from a nationally recognised standardising organisation.

(19) The distance shall be recorded in even centimetre units to the nearest unit below the distance measured if that distance is not a whole even centimetre.

(20)

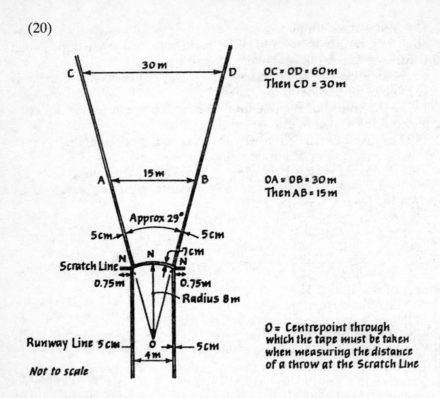

OC = OD = 60m
Then CD = 30m

OA = OB = 30m
Then AB = 15m

O = Centrepoint through
which the tape must be taken
when measuring the distance
of a throw at the Scratch Line

Not to scale

139. THROWING THE JAVELIN SPECIFICATIONS
This rule is given in full in BAF Rules for Competition.

140. COMBINED EVENTS
(1) The Outdoor Pentathlon (Senior Men) consists of five events which shall be held on one day in the following order: Long Jump, Throwing the Javelin, 200 metres. Throwing the Discus and 1500 metres.

The Indoor Pentathlon (Men) consists of five events which shall be held on one day in the following order: 60 metres Hurdles, Long Jump, Putting the Shot, High Jump, 1000 metres.

(2) The Outdoor Pentathlon (Senior Women) consists of five events which shall be held on one day, or on two consecutive days in the following order: First day – 100 metres Hurdles, Putting the Shot, High Jump. Second day – Long Jump, 800 metres.

Note: If practicable, there should be at least a 30-minute break between events. If the Pentathlon (Women) is held on one day, the competition shall be split into two sessions with a break of one hour between each session.

The Indoor Pentathlon (Women) consists of five events and shall be held on one day in the following order: 60 metres Hurdles, High Jump, Putting the Shot, Long Jump, 800 metres.

(3) The Outdoor Heptathlon (Women) consists of seven events which shall be held on two consecutive days in the following order: First day: 100 metres Hurdles, High Jump, Putting the Shot, 200 metres. Second day: Long Jump, Throwing the Javelin, 800 metres.

Note: This event is restricted to Under-17, Junior and Senior competition only. Rest periods between events shall be as for Pentathlon (Women) in (2) above. No claim for a record will be considered if the order of events differs from that above.

(4) For Under-17 Women's Pentathlon and Heptathlon Senior scoring tables should be used but with the 80 metres Hurdles (76.2cm).

Pentathlon (Under-15 Girls) consists of five events which should be held in the following order: Long Jump, 75 metres Hurdles (76.2cm) (using 80 metres Hurdles table and adding one second to the time), Putting the Shot (3.25kg shot to be used but scored as for 4kg shot), (Break of one hour), High Jump, 800 metres.

(5) The Indoor Heptathlon (Men) consists of seven events which shall be held over two consecutive days in the following order: First day – 60 metres, Long Jump, Putting the Shot, High Jump. Second day – 60 metres Hurdles, Pole Vault, 1000 metres.

(6) The Decathlon (Men) consists of ten events which shall be held on two consecutive days in the following order: First day – 100 metres, Long Jump, Putting the Shot, High Jump, 400 metres. Second day – 110 metres Hurdles, Throwing the Discus, Pole Vault, Throwing the Javelin, 1500 metres.

At the discretion of the organisers, it is permissible, where circumstances make it desirable, to decide all the events on the same day. If all the events are decided on the same day it is permissible to vary the order. No claim for a record will be considered if the order of events differs from that set out above.

(7) The Combined Events Referee shall have jurisdiction over the conduct of the combined events competition. However, the Track and Field Referees, where appointed, shall retain jurisdiction over the individual events within the competition.

(8) In all Combined competitions three trials only are allowed in the Long Jump and in each Throwing Event.

(9) In track events run entirely in lanes, at least four competitors should start in each group whenever possible. In other track events at least five competitors should start in each group, and one such group should consist of those competitors occupying the leading positions prior to the final event.

(10) The time of each competitor should be taken by three Time-

keepers independently. Where fully automatic timing is in operation, times shall be given to 1/100th of a second and scored by using the appropriate tables to 1/100th second. Only one system of timing may be applied throughout each event. For record purposes, however, electrical times shall be applied regardless of whether such times are available for other competitors in the event.

(11) In the running and hurdles events competitors shall be disqualified in any event in which they have been responsible for three false starts.

(12) Where the hurdles used do not comply with Rule 116.8 or 116.9 a competitor knocking down three or parts of three or more hurdles shall score no points in that event.

(13) In High Jump and Pole Vault, Rules 120(5)(c) and 121(4) do not apply to a Combined Events competition. Heights will be increased uniformly throughout the competition by 3cm in the High Jump and 10cm in the Pole Vault.

(14) Any athlete failing to take part in any of the events shall not be allowed to take part in any subsequent event in that competition but shall be considered to have abandoned the competition. That athlete shall not figure in the final classification.

(15) The winner shall be the competitor who has obtained the highest number of points in the five, seven, eight or ten events as the case may be, awarded on a basis of the IAAF Combined Events Scoring Tables, modified where necessary as indicated above.

(16) In the event of a tie, the winner shall be the competitor who has received the highest points in a majority of events. If this does not resolve the tie, the winner shall be the competitor who has scored the highest number of points in any one of the events. This procedure shall apply to ties for any place in the competition.

(17) In UK National Under-20 Championships competitors shall use Senior throwing implements and run in hurdle races as laid down for Senior competition in Rule 116. All other Championships shall use Specifications for throwing events and hurdles as laid down for the Junior age group.

141. RULES FOR RECORDS
This rule is given in full in BAF Rules for Competition.

RULES FOR ULTRA-DISTANCE TRACK EVENTS, ROAD RUNNING, TEAM RACES, ROAD RELAYS, RACE WALKING, CROSS COUNTRY AND FELL & HILL RUNNING
These are given in full in the BAF Handbook.

Appendix A
Indoor competitions – code of practice

A1 Events
Competitions may be held at such race distances and in such field events as are appropriate to the size of track and other facilities available. Hammer, discus and javelin are considered unsuitable for indoor competition.

A2 Tracks and Measurements
Tracks for indoor meetings should comply with Rule 108 with the following amendments:

(*a*) Banking of bends is permitted

(*b*) Races up to and including 60m must be run on a straight course in lanes, and it is recommended that races up to and including 200m should be run in lanes. In 400m races the first two complete bends on a track of 200m or less should be run in lanes, and a 'break' line shall be marked on the track in a distinctive colour

(*c*) Hurdle events are as specified in Rule 116.15

(*d*) 2000m Steeplechase shall be run over 19 barriers, one barrier on the first lap and 2 thereafter. The exact location of the barriers will be determined by local conditions, banking etc, but normally will be about 15m from the end of the home straight and 15m from the end of the back straight. There will be no hurdle at the end of the home straight on the first lap. Water jumps are not considered practical

(*e*) In events run in lanes or partly in lanes there shall be only one competitor per lane.

A3 Field Events
(*a*) **High Jump** Owing to the common use of banked tracks, a slope is acceptable in the approach run insofar as the banking forms part of the approach, but not less than the final 5m of an approach shall be on level ground. No competitor may use any other form of banking device or ramp.

(*b*) **Long Jump, Triple Jump and Pole Vault** In the long jump, triple jump and pole vault competitors may start their approach on the banking of the oval track provided that the last 40m is on the level runway.

(*c*) **Shot**

   (i) It is essential for safety reasons that a stopping device is provided at the end of the putting area

(ii) Specifications for the indoor shot are the same as outdoor, but special plastic or rubber cased shots are permissible, which shall be spherical in shape with a smooth surface.

(iii) The circle may be portable or permanent. If the circle is portable it shall not vary from the level of the landing area by more than ±3cm.

(iv) The sector shall be 40° and shall be extended as far as the limitations of space allow.

(v) Fibre boards may be used in the landing area to facilitate marking of the landing of the shot.

A4 Combined Events
The Combined Events are as specified in Rule 140.

A5 Records
The IAAF and the Federation now recognise Records for Indoor Competitions but for Senior Competitions only. Claims for records should be made in accordance with Rule 141.

A6 General Guidance
Indoor areas are invariably much smaller than outdoor ones and it is vital that every effort is made to keep the centre of the track clear, particularly the space between timekeepers or judges and the finish line. Similarly, the area at the start must be kept clear of persons and equipment. Warming-up on the track must be forbidden.

Photo-finish equipment should preferably be sited above the timekeepers' stand.

APPENDIX B
RULES AND PROCEDURES CONCERNING DOPING CONTROL

APPENDIX C
DOPING CONTROL PROHIBITED SUBSTANCES

APPENDIX D
PERMISSION TO TELEVISE – PROCEDURAL GUIDELINES

APPENDIX E
OFFICIALS

APPENDIX F
TIMEKEEPERS – CODE OF PRACTICE

APPENDIX G
SPECIFIC RULES RELATING TO TRADITIONAL SCOTTISH HEAVY EVENTS

APPENDIX H
ROAD WALKING RULES FOR CHAMPIONSHIPS

APPENDIX I
SAFETY REQUIREMENTS FOR FELL RACES
Appendixes B to I are given in full in BAF Rules for Competitions.

Reprinted by permission of the BAF. Some of the Rules and many of the appendixes for example, Rules 20 and 107 as well as appendixes B and C, have been abbreviated or omitted for reasons of space. Copies of the current edition of the BAF Handbook, containing the complete BAF Rules for Competitions and all appendixes are available from the Federation.

Badminton

Badminton

1. Court

1.1 The court shall be a rectangle and laid out as in the diagram on page 149 (except in the case provided for in Law 1.5) and to the measurements there shown, defined by lines 40mm wide.

1.2 The lines shall be easily distinguishable and preferably be coloured white or yellow.

1.3.1 To show the zone in which a shuttle of correct pace lands when tested (Law 4.4), an additional four marks 40mm by 40mm may be made inside each side-line for singles of the right service court, 530mm and 990mm from the back boundary line.

1.3.2 In making these marks, their width shall be within the measurement given, i.e. the marks will be from 530mm to 570mm and from 950mm to 990mm from the outside of the back boundary line.

1.4 All lines form part of the area which they define.

1.5 Where space does not permit the marking out of a court for doubles, a court may be marked out for singles only as shown in the diagram on page 151. The back boundary lines become also the long service lines, and the posts, or the strips of material representing them (Law 2.2), shall be placed on the side-lines.

2. Posts

2.1 The posts shall be 1.55m in height from the surface of the court. They shall be sufficiently firm to remain vertical and keep the net strained as provided in Law 3, and shall be placed on the doubles side-lines as shown in Diagram A.

2.2 Where it is not practicable to have posts on the side-lines, some method must be used to indicate the position of the side-lines where they pass under the net, e.g. by the use of thin posts or strips of material 40mm wide, fixed to the side-lines and rising vertically to the net cord.

2.3 On a court marked for doubles, the posts or strips of material representing the posts shall be placed on the side-lines for doubles, irrespective of whether singles or doubles is being played.

3. Net

3.1 The net shall be made of fine cord of dark colour and even thickness with a mesh not less than 15mm and not more than 20mm.

3.2 The net shall be 760mm in depth.

3.3 The top of the net shall be edged with a 75mm white tape doubled over a cord or cable running through the tape. This tape must rest upon the cord or cable.

3.4 The cord or cable shall be of sufficient size and weight to be firmly stretched flush with the top of the posts.

3.5 The top of the net from the surface of the court shall be 1.524m at the centre of the court and 1.55m over the side-lines for doubles.

3.6 There shall be no gaps between the ends of the net and the posts. If necessary, the full depth of the net should be tied at the ends.

4. Shuttle

Principles

The shuttle may be made from natural and/or synthetic materials. Whatever material the shuttle is made from, the flight characteristics, generally, should be similar to those produced by a natural feathered shuttle with a cork base covered by a thin layer of leather. Having regard to the Principles:

4.1 *General Design*

4.1.1 The shuttle shall have 16 feathers fixed in the base.

4.1.2 The feathers can have a variable length from 64mm to 70mm, but in each shuttle they shall be the same length when measured from the tip of the top of the base.

4.1.3 The tips of the feathers shall form a circle with a diameter from 58mm to 68mm.

4.1.4 The feathers shall be fastened firmly with thread or other suitable material.

4.1.5 The base shall be:

25mm to 28mm in diameter.

Rounded on the bottom.

4.2 *Weight*

The shuttle shall weigh from 4.74g to 5.50g.

4.3 *Non-feathered Shuttle*

4.3.1 The skirt, or simulation of feathers in synthetic materials, replaces natural feathers.

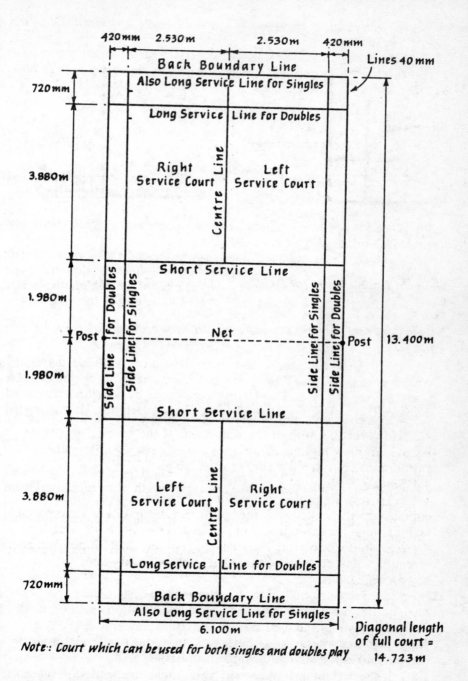

420mm   2.530m   2.530m   420mm

Lines 40mm

Back Boundary Line
Also Long Service Line for Singles

720mm

Long Service   Line For Doubles

Right
Service Court

Centre Line

Left
Service Court

3.880m

Short Service Line

1.980m

Side Line For Doubles

Side Line for Singles

Side Line for Singles

Side Line for Doubles

Post

Net

Post   13.400m

1.980m

Short Service Line

Left
Service Court

Centre Line

Right
Service Court

3.880m

Long Service   Line for Doubles

720mm

Back Boundary Line
Also Long Service Line for Singles

6.100m

Diagonal length
of full court =
14.723m

Note: Court which can be used for both singles and doubles play

**Optional testing marks are shown on page 150

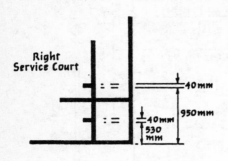

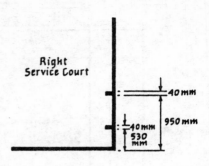

Optional Testing Marks for Doubles Court
(See Law 1.3)
NB measurement of marks 40mm by 40mm

Optional Testing Marks for Singles Court
(See Law 1.3)
NB measurements of marks 40mm by 40mm

4.3.2 The base is described in Law 4.1.5.

4.3.3 Measurements and weight shall be as in Laws 4.1.2, 4.1.3 and 4.2. However, because of the difference of the specific gravity and behaviour of synthetic materials in comparison with feathers, a variation of up to ten per cent is acceptable.

4.4 *Shuttle Testing*

4.4.1 To test a shuttle, use a full underhand stroke which makes contact with the shuttle over the back boundary line. The shuttle shall be hit at an upward angle and in a direction parallel to the side lines.

4.4.2 A shuttle of correct pace will land not less than 530mm and not more than 990mm short of the other back boundary line.

4.5 *Modifications*

Subject to there being no variation in the general design, pace and flight of the shuttle, modifications in the above specifications may be made with the approval of the National Organisation concerned:

4.5.1 In places where atmospheric conditions due to either altitude or climate makes the standard shuttle unsuitable; or

4.5.2 If special circumstances exist which make it otherwise necessary in the interests of the game.

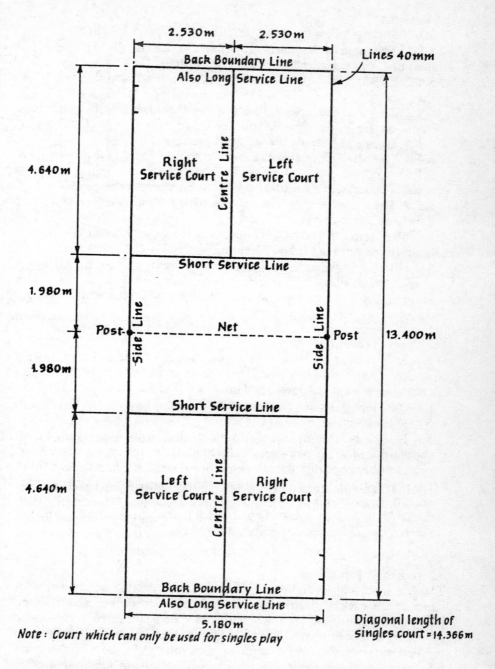

Note: *Court which can only be used for singles play*

**Optional testing marks are shown on the previous page*

5. Racket

5.1 The parts of a racket are described in Laws 5.1.1. to 5.1.7.

5.1.1 The main racket parts are called the handle, the stringed area, the head, the shaft, the throat and the frame.

5.1.2 The handle is the part of the racket intended to be gripped by the player.

5.1.3 The stringed area is the part of the racket with which it is intended the player hits the shuttle.

5.1.4 The head bounds the stringed area.

5.1.5 The shaft connects the handle to the head (subject to Law 5.1.6).

5.1.6 The throat (if present) connects the shaft to the head.

5.1.7 The frame is the name given to the head, throat, shaft and handle taken together.

5.2 The frame of the racket, including the handle, shall not exceed 680mm in overall length and 230mm in overall width.

5.3.1 The stringed area shall be flat and consist of a pattern of crossed strings either alternately interlaced or bonded where they cross. The stringing pattern shall be generally uniform and, in particular, not less dense in the centre than in any other area.

5.3.2 The stringed area shall not exceed 280mm in overall length and 220mm in overall width.

5.3.3. However, the strings may extend into an area which otherwise would be the throat, provided that the width of the extended stringed area does not exceed 35mm and provided that the overall length of the stringed area does not then exceed 330mm.

5.4 *The racket*:

5.4.1 Shall be free of attached objects and protrusions, other than those utilised solely and specifically to limit or prevent wear and tear, or vibration, or to distribute weight, or to secure the handle by cord to the player's hand, and which are reasonable in size and placement for such purposes; and

5.4.2 Shall be free of any device which makes it possible for a player to change materially the shape of the racket.

6. Approved Equipment

The International Badminton Federation shall rule on any question of whether any racket, shuttle or equipment or any prototypes used in the playing of Badminton complies with the specifications or is otherwise approved or not approved for play. Such ruling may be undertaken on the Federation's initiative or upon application by any party with a bona fide interest therein including any player, equipment manufacturer or National Organisation or member thereof.

7. Players

7.1 'Player' applies to all those taking part in a match.

7.2 The game shall be played, in the case of doubles, by two players a side, or in the case of singles, by one player a side.

7.3 The side having the right to serve shall be called the serving side, and the opposing side shall be called the receiving side.

8. Toss

8.1 Before commencing play, the opposing sides shall toss and the side winning the toss shall exercise the choice in either Law 8.1.1 or Law 8.1.2.

8.1.1 To serve or receive first.

8.1.2 To start play at one end of the court or the other.

8.2 The side losing the toss shall then exercise the remaining choice.

9. Scoring

9.1 The opposing sides shall play the best of three games unless otherwise arranged.

9.2 Only the serving side can add a point to its score.

9.3 In doubles and Men's singles a game is won by the first side to score 15 points, except as provided in Law 9.6.

9.4 In Ladies' singles a game is won by the first side to score 11 points, except as provided in Law 9.6.

9.5.1 If the score becomes 13-all or 14-all (9-all or 10-all in Ladies' singles), the side which first scored 13 or 14 (9 or 10) shall have the choice of 'setting' or 'not setting' the game (Law 9.6).

9.5.2 This choice can only be made when the score is first reached and must be made before the next service is delivered.

9.5.3 The relevant side (Law 9.5.1) is given the opportunity to set at 14-all (10-all in Ladies' singles) despite any previous decision not to set by that side or the opposing side at 13-all (9-all in Ladies' singles).

9.6 If the game has been set, the score is called 'Love-all' and the side first scoring the set number of points (Law 9.6.1 to 9.6.4) wins the game.

9.6.1 13-all setting to 5 points

9.6.2 14-all setting to 3 points

9.6.3 9-all setting to 3 points

9.6.4 10-all setting to 2 points

9.7 The side winning a game serves first in the next game.

10. Change of Ends

10.1 Players shall change ends:

10.1.1 At the end of the first game;

10.1.2 Prior to the beginning of the third game (if any); and

10.1.3 In the third game, or in one-game match, when the leading score reaches:
– 6 in a game of 11 points
– 8 in a game of 15 points
10.2 When players omit to change ends as indicated by Law 10.1, they shall do so immediately the mistake is discovered and the existing score shall stand.

11. Service

11.1 In a correct service:

11.1.1 Neither side shall cause undue delay to the delivery of the service;

11.1.2 The server and receiver shall stand within diagonally opposite service courts without touching the boundary lines of these service courts; some part of both feet of the server and receiver must remain in contact with the surface of the court in a stationary position until the service is delivered (Law 11.4);

11.1.3 The server's racket shall initially hit the base of the shuttle while the whole of the shuttle is below the server's waist;

11.1.4 The shaft of the server's racket at the instant of hitting the shuttle shall be pointing in a downward direction to such an extent that the whole of the head of the racket is discernibly below the whole of the server's hand holding the racket;

11.1.5 The movement of the server's racket must continue forwards after the start of the service (Law 11.2) until the service is delivered; and

11.1.6 The flight of the shuttle shall be upwards from the server's racket to pass over the net, so that, if not intercepted, it falls in the receiver's service court.

11.2 Once the players have taken their positions, the first forward movement of the server's racket head is the start of the service.

11.3 The server shall not serve before the receiver is ready, but the receiver shall be considered to have been ready if a return of service is attempted.

11.4 The service is delivered when, once started (Law 11.2), the shuttle is hit by the server's racket or the shuttle lands on the floor.

11.5 In doubles, the partners may take up any positions which do not unsight the opposing server or receiver.

12. Singles

12.1 The players shall serve from, and receive in, their respective right service courts when the server has not scored or has scored an even number of points in that game.

12.2 The player shall serve from, and receive in, their respective left service courts when the server has scored an odd number of points in that game.

12.3 If a game is set, the total points scored by the server in that game shall be used to apply Laws 12.1 and 12.2.

12.4 The shuttle is hit alternately by the server and the receiver until a 'fault' is made or the shuttle ceases to be in play.

12.5.1 If the receiver makes a 'fault' or the shuttle ceases to be in play because it touches the surface of the court inside the receiver's court, the server scores a point. The server then serves again from the alternate service court.

12.5.2 If the server makes a 'fault' or the shuttle ceases to be in play because it touches the surface of the court inside the server's court, the server loses the right to continue serving, and the receiver then becomes the server, with no point scored by either player.

13. Doubles

13.1 At the start of a game, and each time a side gains the right to serve, the service shall be delivered from the right service court.

13.2 Only the receiver shall return the service: should the shuttle touch or be hit by the receiver's partner, the serving side scores a point.

13.3.1 After the service is returned, the shuttle is hit by either player of the serving side and then by either player of the receiving side, and so on, until the shuttle ceases to be in play.

13.3.2 After the service is returned, a player may hit the shuttle from any position on that player's side of the net.

13.4.1 If the receiving side makes a 'fault' or the shuttle ceases to be in play because it touches the surface of the court inside the receiving side's court, the serving side scores a point, and the server serves again.

13.4.2 If the serving side makes a 'fault' or the shuttle ceases to be in play because it touches the surface of the court inside the serving side's court, the server loses the right to continue serving, with no point scored by either side.

13.5.1 The player who serves at the start of any game shall serve from, or receive in, the right service court when that player's side has not scored or has scored an even number of points in that game, and the left service court otherwise.

13.5.2 The player who receives at the start of any game shall receive in, or serve from, the right service court when that player's side has not scored or has scored an even number of points in that game, and the left service court otherwise.

13.5.3 The reverse pattern applies to the partners.

13.5.4 If a game is set, the total points scored by a side in that game shall be used to apply Laws 13.5.1 to 13.5.3.

13.6 Service in any turn of serving shall be delivered from alternate service courts, except as provided in Laws 14 and 16.

13.7 The right to serve passes consecutively from the initial server in any game to the initial receiver in that game, and then consecutively from that player to that player's partner and then to one of the opponents and then the opponent's partner, and so on.

13.8 No player shall serve out of turn, receive out of turn, or receive two consecutive services in the same game, except as provided in Laws 14 and 16.

13.9 Either player of the winning side may serve first in the next game and either player of the losing side may receive.

14. Service-Court Errors

14.1 A service-court error has been made when a player:

14.1.1 Has served out of turn;

14.1.2 Has served from the wrong service court; or

14.1.3 Standing in the wrong service court, was prepared to receive the service and it has been delivered.

14.2 When a service-court error has been made, then:

14.2.1 If the error is discovered before the next service is delivered, it is a 'let' unless only one side was at fault and lost the rally, in which case the error shall not be corrected.

14.2.2 If the error is not discovered before the next service is delivered, the error shall not be corrected.

14.3 If there is a 'let' because of a service court error, the rally is replayed and the error corrected.

14.4 If a service-court error is not to be corrected, play in that game shall proceed without changing the players' new service courts (nor, when relevant, the new order of serving).

15. Faults

It is a 'fault':

15.1 If a service is not correct (Law 11.1).

15.2 If the server, in attempting to serve, misses the shuttle.

15.3 If, on service, the shuttle is caught on the net and remains suspended on top or, on service, after passing over the net is caught in the net.

15.4 If in play, the shuttle:

15.4.1 Lands outside the boundaries of the court;

15.4.2 Passes through or under the net;

15.4.3 Fails to pass the net;

15.4.4 Touches the roof, ceiling, or side walls;

15.4.5 Touches the person or dress of a player; or

15.4.6 Touches any other object or person outside the immediate surroundings of the court;

(*Where necessary, on account of the structure of the building, the local badminton authority may, subject to the right of veto of its National Organisation, make by-laws dealing with cases in which a shuttle touches an obstruction.*)

15.5 If when in play, the initial point of contact with the shuttle is not on the striker's side of the net. (The striker may, however, follow the shuttle over the net with the racket in the course of a stroke.)

15.6 If, when the shuttle is in play, a player:

15.6.1 Touches the net or its supports with racket, person or dress;

15.6.2 Invades an opponent's court with racket or person in any degree except as permitted in Law 15.5; or

15.6.3 Invades an opponent's court under the net with racket or person such that an opponent is obstructed or distracted;

15.6.4 Obstructs an opponent, i.e. prevents an opponent from making a legal stroke where the shuttle is followed over the net.

15.7 If, in play, a player deliberately distracts an opponent by any action such as shouting or making gestures.

15.8 If, in play, the shuttle:

15.8.1 Be caught and held on the racket and then slung during the execution of a stroke:

15.8.2 Be hit twice in succession by the same player with two strokes:

15.8.3 Be hit by a player and the player's partner successively; or

15.8.4 Touches a player's racket and continues towards the back of that player's court.

15.9 If a player is guilty of flagrant, repeated or persistent offences under Law 18.

16. Lets

'Let' is called by the Umpire, or by a player (if there is no Umpire) to halt play.

16.1 A 'let' may be given for any unforeseen or accidental occurrence.

16.2 If a shuttle is caught on the net and remains suspended on top, or after passing over the net is caught in the net, it is a 'let' except during service.

16.3 If during service, the receiver and server are both faulted at the same time, it shall be a 'let'.

16.4 If the server serves before the receiver is ready, it shall be a 'let'.

16.5 If during play, the shuttle disintegrates and the base completely separates from the rest of the shuttle, it shall be a 'let'.

16.6 If a Line Judge is unsighted and the Umpire is unable to make a decision, it shall be a 'let'.

16.7 When a 'let' occurs, the play since the last service shall not count, and the player who served shall serve again, except when Law 14 is applicable.

17. Shuttle not in Play
A shuttle is not in play when:

17.1 It strikes the net and remains attached there or suspended on top;

17.2 It strikes the net or post and starts to fall towards the surface of the court on the striker's side of the net;

17.3 It hits the surface of the court; or

17.4 A 'fault' or 'let' has occurred.

18. Continuous Play, Misconduct, Penalties
18.1 Play shall be continuous from the first service until the match is concluded, except as allowed in Laws 18.2 and 18.3.

18.2 An interval not exceeding 5 minutes is allowed between the second and third games of all matches in all of the following situations:

18.2.1 In international competitive events;

18.2.2 In IBF sanctioned events; and

18.2.3 In all other matches (unless the National Organisation has previously published a decision not to allow such an interval). (Note: Badminton Association of England Limited has resolved that except in international events there will be no interval of 5 minutes between the second and third games of matches in England unless prior approval of Badminton Association of England Limited has been obtained.)

18.3 When necessitated by circumstances not within the control of the players, the Umpire may suspend play for such a period as the Umpire may consider necessary. If play be suspended, the existing score shall stand and play be resumed from that point.

18.4 Under no circumstances shall play be suspended to enable a player to recover his strength or wind, or to receive instruction or advice.

18.5.1 Except in the intervals provided in Laws 18.2 and 18.3, no player shall be permitted to receive advice during a match.

18.5.2 Except during the interval described in Law 18.2, no player shall leave the court during a match without the Umpire's consent.

18.6 The Umpire shall be sole judge of any suspension of play.

18.7 A player shall not:

18.7.1 Deliberately cause suspension of play;

18.7.2 Deliberately interfere with the speed of the shuttle;

18.7.3 Behave in an offensive manner; or

18.7.4 Be guilty of misconduct not otherwise covered by the Laws of Badminton.

18.8 The Umpire shall administer any breach of Law 18.4, 18.5, or 18.7 by:

18.8.1 Issuing a warning to the offending side;

18.8.2 Faulting the offending side, if previously warned; or

18.8.3 In cases of flagrant offence or persistent offences, faulting the offending side and reporting the offending side immediately to the Referee, who shall have the power to disqualify.

18.9 Where a Referee has not been appointed, the responsible official shall have the power to disqualify.

19. Officials and Appeals

19.1 The Referee is in overall charge of the tournament or event of which a match forms part.

19.2 The Umpire, where appointed, is in charge of the match, the court and its immediate surrounds. The Umpire shall report to the Referee. In the absence of a Referee, the Umpire shall report instead to the responsible official.

19.3 The Service Judge shall call service faults made by the server should they occur (Law 11).

19.4 A Line Judge shall indicate whether a shuttle is 'in' or 'out'. An Umpire shall:

19.5 Uphold and enforce the Laws of Badminton, and especially call a 'fault' or 'let' should either occur, without appeal being made by the players;

19.6 Give a decision on any appeal regarding a point of dispute, if made before the next service is delivered;

19.7 Ensure players and spectators are kept informed of the progress of the match;

19.8 Appoint or remove Line Judges or a Service Judge in consultation with the Referee;

19.9 Not overrule the decisions of Line Judges and the Service Judge on points of fact;

19.10.1 Where another court official is not appointed, arrange for their duties to be carried out;

19.10.2 Where an appointed official is unsighted, carry out the official's duties or play a 'let';

19.11 Decide upon any suspension of play;

19.12 Record and report to the Referee all matters in relation to Law 18; and

19.13 Take to the Referee all unsatisfied appeals on questions of Law only. (Such appeals must be made before the next service is delivered, or, if at the end of a game, before the side that appeals has left the court.)

APPENDIX 1
Imperial Measurements

APPENDIX 2
Handicap Matches

APPENDIX 3
Games of Other than 11 or 15 Points

APPENDIX 4
Vocabulary

APPENDIX 5
Badminton for Disabled People

RECOMMENDATIONS TO COURT OFFICIALS
1. Introduction
2. Officials and their Decisions
3. Recommendations to Umpires
4. General Advice on Umpiring
5. Instructions to Service Judges
6. Instructions to Line Judges

Reprinted by permission of the International Badminton Federation. Appendixes 1 to 5 and the Recommendations to Court Officials are given in full in the Laws of Badminton, available from the Federation.

Baseball

Baseball

1. Objectives of The Game

1.01 Baseball is a game between two teams of 9 players each, under direction of a manager, played on an enclosed field in accordance with these rules, under jurisdiction of one or more umpires.

1.02 The objective of each team is to win by scoring more runs than the opponent.

1.03 The winner of the game shall be that team which shall have scored, in accordance with these rules, the greater number of runs at the conclusion of a regulation game.

1.04 *The Playing Field.* The field shall be laid out according to the instructions below, supplemented by diagrams 1, 2 and 3 on pp. 165, 166 and 167.

The infield shall be a 90ft square. The outfield shall be the area between the two foul-lines formed by extending two sides of the square, as in diagram 1. The distance from home base to the nearest fence, stand or other obstruction on fair territory shall be 250ft or more. A distance of 320ft or more along the foul-lines, and 400ft or more to centre field is preferable. The infield shall be graded so that the base lines and home plate are level. The pitcher's plate shall be 10in above the level of home plate. The degree of slope from a point 6in in front of the pitcher's plate to a point 6ft towards home plate shall be 1in to 1ft and such degree of slope shall be uniform. The infield and outfield, including the boundary lines, are fair territory and all other area is foul territory.

It is desirable that the line from home base through the pitcher's plate to second base shall run east-northeast.

It is recommended that the distance from home base to the backstop, and from the base lines to the nearest fence, stand or other obstruction on foul territory shall be 60ft or more. See diagram 1.

When location of home base is determined, with a steel tape measure 127ft 3⅜in in desired direction to establish second base. From home base, measure 90ft towards first base; from second base, measure 90ft towards first base; the intersection of these lines establishes first base. From home base, measure 90ft towards third base; from second base, measure 90ft towards third base; the intersection of these lines establishes third base. The distance between first base and third base is 127ft 3⅜in. All measurements from home base shall be taken from the point where the first and third base-lines intersect.

The catcher's box, the batters' boxes, the coaches' boxes, the 3ft first base lines and the next batters' boxes shall be laid out as shown in Diagrams 1 and 2.

The foul-lines and all other playing lines indicated in the diagrams by solid black lines shall be marked with wet, unslaked lime, chalk or other white material.

The grass lines and dimensions shown on the diagrams are those used in many fields, but they are not mandatory and each club shall determine the size and shape of the grassed and bare areas of its playing field.

1.05 Home base shall be marked by a five-sided slab of whitened rubber. It shall be a 17in square with two of the corners removed so that one edge is 17in long, two adjacent sides are 8½in and the remaining two sides are 12in and set at an angle to make a point. It shall be set in the ground with the point at the intersection of the lines extending from home base to first base and to third base; with the 17in edge facing the pitcher's plate, and the two 12in edges coinciding with the first and third base lines. The top edges of home plate shall be bevelled and the base shall be fixed in the ground level with the ground surface.

1.06 First, second and third bases shall be marked by white canvas bags, securely attached to the ground as indicated in diagram 2. The first and third base bags shall be entirely within the infield. The second base bag shall be centred on second base. The bags shall be 15in square, not less than 3 nor more than 5in thick, and filled with soft material.

1.07 The pitcher's plate shall be a rectangular slab of whitened rubber, 24in by 6in. It shall be set in the ground as shown in diagrams 1 and 2, so that the distance between the pitcher's plate and home base (the rear point of home plate) shall be 60ft 6in.

Diagram 1

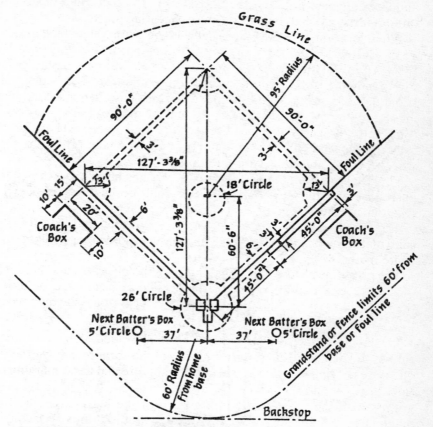

Grass Line

95' Radius

90'-0"

90'-0"

127'-3⅜"

18' Circle

Foul Line

Foul Line

3'

3'

13'

13'

10'   15'

20'

6'

127'-3⅜"

60'-6"

3'

3'

45'-0"

10'

Coach's Box

Coach's Box

3'

6'

6'

45'-0"

26' Circle

Next Batter's Box 5' Circle

Next Batter's Box 5' Circle

37'

37'

Grandstand or fence limits 60' from base or foul line

60' Radius From home base

Backstop

———— Base lines, Batter's box, Catcher's box, Foul line, Pitcher's Plate, Coach's box

—·— Base lines

——— Grass lines

Diagram 2

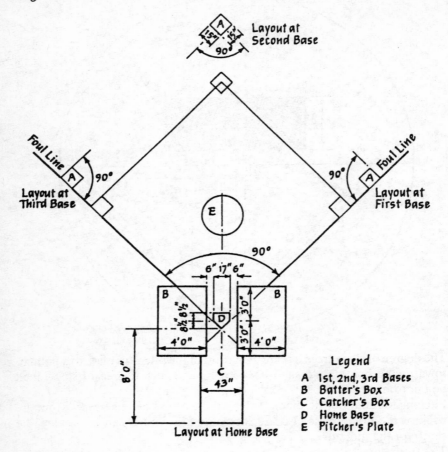

Layout at
Second Base

Foul Line

Layout at
Third Base

90°

90°

Foul Line

Layout at
First Base

90°

E

6" 17" 6"

B   B

8½" 8½"

30" 30"

30" 30"

4'0"   4'0"

D

8'0"

C

43"

Legend

A 1st, 2nd, 3rd Bases
B Batter's Box
C Catcher's Box
D Home Base
E Pitcher's Plate

Layout at Home Base

Diagram 3

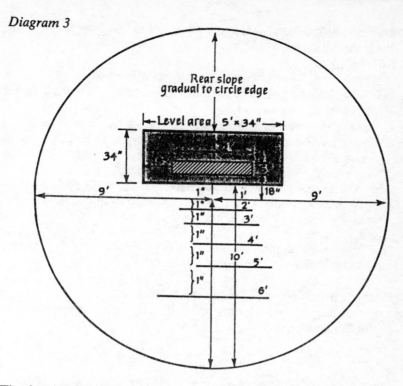

The degree of slope from a point 6″ in front of the pitcher's plate to a point 6′ towards the home plate shall be 1″ to 1′, and such degree of slope shall be uniform.

Pitching Mound – an 18″ diameter circle, the centre of which is 59′ from the back of the home plate. Locate the front edge of rubber 18″ behind the centre of the mound.

The front edge of rubber to the back point of home plate measures 60′6″. The slope starts 6″ from the front edge of rubber.

The slope shall be 6″ from starting point, 6″ in front of rubber to a point 6″ in front of rubber, and the slope shall be uniform.

The level area surrounding rubber should be 6″ in front of rubber, 18″ to each side and 22″ to the rear of rubber. Total level area should be 5′ × 34″.

1.08 The home club shall furnish players' benches, one each for the home and visiting teams. Such benches shall not be less than 25ft from the base lines. They shall be roofed and enclosed at the back and ends.

1.09 The ball shall be a sphere formed by yarn wound around a small core of cork, rubber or similar material, covered with two stripes of white horsehide or cowhide, tightly stitched together. It shall weigh not less than 5 nor more than $5\frac{1}{4}$oz and measure not less than 9 nor more than $9\frac{1}{4}$in in circumference.

1.10 (*a*) The bat shall be a smooth, round stick not more than $2\frac{3}{4}$in in diameter at the thickest part and not more than 42in in length. The bat shall be one piece of solid wood.

(*b*) Cupped bats. An indentation in the end of the bat up to 1in in depth is permitted and may be no wider than 2in and no less than 1in in diameter. The indentation must be curved with no foreign substance added.

(*c*) The bat handle, for not more than 18in from its end, may be covered or treated with any material or substance to improve the grip. Any such material or substance, which extends past the 18in limitation, shall cause the bat to be removed from the game.

(*d*) No coloured bat may be used in a professional game unless approved by the Rules Committee.

1.11 (*a*) (1) All players on a team shall wear uniforms identical in colour, trim and style, and all players' uniforms shall include minimal six-inch numbers on their backs.

Section 1.11 is given in full in the Official Baseball Rules.

1.12 The catcher may wear a leather mitt not more than 38in in circumference, nor more than $15\frac{1}{2}$in from top to bottom. Such limits shall include all lacing and any leather band or facing attached to the outer edge of the mitt. The space between the thumb section and the finger section of the mitt shall not exceed 6in at the top of the mitt and 4in at the base of thumb crotch. The web shall measure not more than 7in across the top or more than 6in from its top to the base of the thumb crotch. The web may be either a lacing or lacing through leather tunnels, or a centre piece of leather which may be an extension of the palm, connected to the mitt with lacing and constructed so that it will not exceed any of the above mentioned measurements.

1.13 The first baseman may wear a leather glove or mitt not more than 12in long from top to bottom and not more than 8in wide across the palm, measured from the base of the thumb crotch to the outer edge of the mitt. The space between the thumb section and the finger section of the mitt shall not exceed 4in at the top of the mitt and $3\frac{1}{2}$in at the base of the thumb crotch. The mitt shall be constructed so that this space is permanently fixed and cannot be enlarged, extended, widened, or deepened by the use of any materials or process whatever. The web of the mitt shall measure not more than 5in from its top to the base of the thumb crotch. The web may be either a lacing, lacing through leather tunnels, or a centre piece of leather which may be an extension of the palm connected to the mitt with lacing and constructed so that it will not exceed the above-mentioned measurements. The webbing shall not be constructed of wound or wrapped lacing or deepened to make a net type of trap. The glove may be of any weight.

1.14 Each fielder, other than the first baseman or catcher, may use or wear a leather glove.

Section 1.14 is given in full in the Official Baseball Rules.

1.15 (*a*) The pitcher's glove shall be uniform in colour, including all stitching, lacing and webbing. The pitcher's glove may not be white or grey.
  (*b*) No pitcher shall attach to his glove any foreign material of a colour different from the glove.

1.16 *Section 1.16, concerning the use of helmets, is given in full in the Official Baseball Rules.*

1.17 Playing equipment, including but not limited to the bases, pitchers' plate, baseball, bats, uniforms, catcher's mitts, first baseman's gloves, infielders' and outfielders' gloves and protective helmets, as detailed in the provisions of this rule, shall not contain any undue commercialisation of the product. Designations by the manufacturer on any such equipment must be in good taste as to the size and content of the manufacturer's logo or the brand name of the item. The provisions of this Section 1.17 shall apply to professional leagues only.

2. Definitions of Terms

All definitions in rule 2 are listed alphabetically.
Adjudged is a judgement decision by the umpire.
An *Appeal* is the act of a fielder in claiming violation of the rules by the offensive team.
A *Balk* is an illegal act by the pitcher with a runner or runners on base, entitling all runners to advance one base.
A *Ball* is a pitch which does not enter the strike zone in flight and is not struck at by the batter.
A *Base* is one of four points which must be touched by a runner in order to score a run; more usually applied to the canvas bags and the rubber plate which mark the base points.
A *Base Coach* is a team member in uniform who is stationed in the coach's box at first or third base to direct the batter and the runners.

A *Base on Balls* is an award of first base granted to a batter who, during his time at bat, receives four pitches outside the strike zone.

A *Batter* is an offensive player who takes his position in the batter's box.

Batter-Runner is a term that identifies the offensive player who has just finished his time at bat until he is put out or until the play on which he became a runner ends.

The *Batter's Box* is the area within which the batter shall stand during his time at bat.

The *Battery* is the pitcher and the catcher.

Bench or Dugout is the seating facilities reserved for players, substitutes and other team members in uniform when they are not actively engaged on the playing field.

A *Bunt* is a batted ball not swung at, but intentionally met with the bat and tapped slowly within the infield.

A *Called Game* is one in which, for any reason, the umpire-in-chief terminates play.

A *Catch* is the act of a fielder in getting secure possession in his hand or glove of a ball in flight and firmly holding it; providing he does not use his cap, protector, pocket or any other part of his uniform in getting possession. It is not a catch, however, if simultaneously or immediately following his contact with the ball, he collides with a player, or with a wall, or if he falls down, and as a result of such collision or falling, drops the ball. It is not a catch if a fielder touches a fly ball which then hits a member of the offensive team or an umpire and then is caught by another defensive player. If the fielder has made the catch and drops the ball while in the act of making a throw following the catch, the ball shall be adjudged to have been caught. In establishing the validity of the catch, the fielder shall hold the ball long enough to prove that he has complete control of the ball and that his release of the ball is voluntary and intentional.

The *Catcher* is the fielder who takes his position back of the home base.

The *Catcher's Box* is that area within which the catcher shall stand until the pitcher delivers the ball.

The *Club* is a person or group of persons responsible for assembling the team personnel, providing the playing field and required facilities, and representing the team in relations with the league.

A *Coach* is a team member in uniform appointed by the manager to perform such duties as the manager may designate, such as but not limited to acting as base coach.

A *Dead Ball* is a ball out of play because of a legally created temporary suspension of play.

The *Defence (or Defensive)* is the team, or any player of the team, in the field.

A *Double Header* is two regularly scheduled or rescheduled games, played in immediate succession.

A *Double Play* is a play by the defence in which two offensive players are put out as a result of continuing action, providing there is no error between put-outs.

(*a*) A force double play is one in which both put-outs are force plays.

(*b*) A reverse force double play is one in which the first out is a force play and the second out is made on runner for whom the force is removed by reason of the first out.

Dugout (see definition of bench).

A *Fair Ball* is a batted ball that settles on fair ground between home and first base, or between home and third base, or that is on or over fair territory when bounding to the outfield past first or third base, or that touches first, second or third base, or that first falls on fair territory on or beyond first base or third base, or that, while on or over fair territory, touches the person of an umpire or player, or that, while over fair territory, passes out of the playing field in flight.

Fair Territory is that part of the playing field within, and including the first base and third base lines, from home base to the bottom of the playing field fence and perpendicularly upwards. All foul-lines are positioned in fair territory.

A *Fielder* is any defensive player.

Fielder's Choice is the act of a fielder who handles a fair grounder and, instead of throwing to first base to put out the batter-runner, throws to another base in an attempt to put out a preceding runner.

A *Fly Ball* is a batted ball that goes high in the air in flight.

A *Force Play* is a play in which a runner legally loses his right to occupy a base by reason of the batter becoming a runner.

A *Forfeited Game* is a game declared ended by the umpire-in-chief in favour of the offended team by the score of 9 to 0, for violation of the rules.

A *Foul Ball* is a batted ball that settles on foul territory between home and first base, or between home and third base, or that bounds past first or third base on or over foul territory, or that first falls on foul territory, beyond first or third base, or that, while on or over foul territory, touches the person of an umpire or player, or any object foreign to the natural ground.

A foul fly shall be judged according to the relative position of the ball and the foul-line, including the foul-pole, and not as to whether the fielder is on foul or fair territory at the time he touches the ball.

Foul Territory is that part of the playing field outside the first and third base lines extended to the fence and perpendicularly upwards.

A *Foul Tip* is a batted ball that goes sharp and direct from the bat to the catcher's hands and is legally caught. It is not a foul tip unless caught and any foul tip that is caught is a strike, and the ball is in play. It is not a catch if it is a rebound, unless the ball has first touched the catcher's glove or hand.

A *Ground Ball* is a batted ball that rolls or bounces close to the ground.

The *Home Team* is the team on whose grounds the game is played, or if the game is played on neutral grounds, the home team shall be designated by mutual agreement.

Illegal (or Illegally) is contrary to these rules.

An *Illegal Pitch* is (1) A pitch delivered to the batter when the pitcher does not have his pivot foot in contact with the pitcher's plate; (2) A quick return pitch. An illegal pitch when runners are on base is a balk.

An *Infielder* is a fielder who occupies a position on the infield.

An *Infield Fly* is a fair fly ball (not including a line nor an attempted bunt) which can be caught by an infielder with ordinary effort, when first and second, or first, second and third bases are occupied, before two are out. The pitcher, catcher and any outfielder who stations himself in the infield on the play shall be considered infielders for the purpose of this rule.

When it seems apparent that a batted ball will be an infield fly, the umpire shall immediately declare 'infield fly' for the benefit of the runners. If the ball is near the base lines, the umpire shall declare 'infield fly, if fair'.

The ball is alive and runners may advance at the risk of the ball being caught, or retouch and advance after the ball has been touched, the same as on any fly ball. If the hit becomes a foul ball, it is treated the same as any foul.

If a declared infield fly is allowed to fall untouched to the ground, and bounces foul before passing first or third base, it is a foul ball. If a declared infield fly falls untouched to the ground outside the baseline, and bounces fair before passing first or third base, it is an infield fly.

In Flight describes a batted, thrown or pitched ball which has not yet touched the grounds or some object other than a fielder.

In Jeopardy is a term indicating that the ball is in play and an offensive player may be put out.

An *Inning* is that portion of a game within which the teams alternate on offence and defence and in which there are three put-outs for each team. Each team's time at bat is a half-inning.

Interference

(*a*) Offensive interference is an act by the team at bat which interferes with, obstructs, impedes, hinders or confuses any fielder attempting to make a play. If the umpire declares the batter, batter-runner, or a runner out for interference, all other runners shall return to the last base that was, in the judgement of the umpire, legally touched at the time of the interference, unless otherwise provided by these rules.

(*b*) Defensive interference is an act by a fielder which hinders or prevents a batter from hitting a pitch.

(*c*) Umpire's interference occurs (1) When an umpire hinders, impedes or prevents a catcher's throw attempting to prevent a stolen base, or (2) When a fair ball touches an umpire on fair territory before passing a fielder.

(*d*) Spectator interference occurs when a spectator reaches out of the stands, or goes on the playing field, and touches a live ball.

On any interference the ball is dead.

The *League* is a group of clubs whose teams play each other in a pre-arranged schedule under these rules for the league championship.

The *League President* shall enforce the official rules, resolve any disputes involving the rules, and determine any protested games. The league president may fine or suspend any player, coach, manager or umpire for violation of these rules, at his discretion.

Legal (or Legally) is in accordance with these rules.

A *Live Ball* is a ball which is in play.

A *Line Drive* is a batted ball that goes sharp and direct from the bat to a fielder without touching the ground.

The *Manager* is a person appointed by the club to be responsible for the team's actions on the field, and to represent the team in communications with the umpire and the opposing team. A player may be appointed to be manager.

An *Obstruction* is the act of a fielder who, while not in possession of the ball and not in the act of fielding the ball, impeded the progress of any runner.

Offence is the team, or any play of the team, at bat.

Official Scorer. See Rule 10.

An *Out* is one of the three required retirements of an offensive team during its time at bat.

An *Outfielder* is a fielder who occupies a position in the outfield, which is the area of the playing field most distant from home base.

Overslide (or Oversliding) is the act of an offensive player when his slide to a base, other than when advancing from home to first base, is with such momentum that he loses contact with the base.

A *Penalty* is the application of these rules following an illegal act.

The *Person* of a player or an umpire is any part of his body, his clothing or his equipment.

A *Pitch* is a ball delivered to the batter by the pitcher.

A *Pitcher* is the fielder designated to deliver the pitch to the batter.

The pitcher's *Pivot Foot* is that foot which is in contact with the pitcher's plate as he delivers the pitch.

'Play' is the umpire's order to start the game or to resume action following any dead ball.

A *Quick Return* pitch is one made with obvious intent to catch a batter off balance. It is an illegal pitch.

Regulation Game. See Rules 4.10 and 4.11.

A *Retouch* is the act of a runner in returning to a base as legally required.

A *Run (or Score)* is the score made by an offensive player who advances from batter to runner and touches first, second, third and home bases in that order.

A *Run-Down* is the act of the defence in an attempt to put out a runner between bases.

A *Runner* is an offensive player who is advancing toward, or touching, or returning to any base.

'*Safe*' is a declaration by the umpire that a runner is entitled to the base for which he was trying.

Set Position is one of the two legal pitching positions.

Squeeze Play is a term to designate a play when a team, with a runner on third base, attempts to score that runner by means of a bunt.

A *Strike* is a legal pitch when so called by the umpire, which:

    (*a*) Is struck at by the batter and missed;

    (*b*) Is not struck at, if any part of the ball passes through any part of the strike zone;

    (*c*) Is fouled by the batter when he has less than two strikes;

    (*d*) Is bunted foul;

    (*e*) Touches the batter as he strikes at it;

    (*f*) Touches the batter in flight in the strike zone; or

    (*g*) Becomes a foul tip.

The *Strike Zone* is that area over home plate the upper limit of which is a horizontal line at the midpoint between the top of the shoulders and the top of the uniform pants, and the lower level is a line at the top of the knees. The strike zone shall be determined from the batter's stance as the batter is prepared to swing at a pitched ball.

A *Suspended Game* is a called game which is to be completed at a later date.

A *Tag* is the action of a fielder in touching a base with his body while holding the ball securely and firmly in his hand or glove; or touching a runner with the ball, or with his hand or glove holding the ball, while holding the ball securely and firmly in his hand or glove.

A *Throw* is the act of propelling the ball with the hand and arm to a given objective and is to be distinguished, always, from the pitch.

A *Tie Game* is a regulation game which is called when each team has the same number of runs.

'*Time*' is the announcement by an umpire of a legal interruption of play, during which the ball is dead.

Touch. To touch a player or umpire is to touch any part of his body, his clothing or his equipment.

A *Triple Play* is a play by the defence in which three offensive players are put out as a result of continuous action, providing there is no error between put-outs.

A *Wild Pitch* is one so high, so low, or so wide of the plate that it cannot be handled with ordinary effort by the catcher.

Wind-Up Position is one of the two legal pitching positions.

3. Game Preliminaries

Section 3 is given in full in the Official Baseball Rules.

4. Starting and Ending a Game

4.01 Unless the home club shall have given previous notice that the game has been postponed or will be delayed in starting, the umpire, or umpires, shall enter the playing field 5 minutes before the hour set for the game to begin and proceed directly to home base where they shall be met by the managers of the opposing team.

In sequence:

(*a*) First, the home manager shall give his batting order to the umpire-in-chief, in duplicate.

(*b*) Next, the visiting manager shall give his batting order to the umpire-in-chief, in duplicate.

(*c*) The umpire-in-chief shall make certain that the original and copies of the respective batting orders are identical, and then tender a copy of each batting order to the opposing manager. The copy retained by the umpire shall be the official batting order. The tender of the batting order by the umpire shall establish the batting orders. Thereafter, no substitutions shall be made by either manager, except as provided in these rules.

(*d*) As soon as the home team's batting order is handed to the umpire-in-chief the umpires are in charge of the playing field and from that moment they shall have sole authority to determine when a game shall be called, suspended or resumed on account of weather or the condition of the playing field.

4.02 The players of the home team shall take their defensive positions, the first batter of the visiting team shall take his position in the batter's box, the umpire shall call 'Play' and the game shall start.

4.03 When the ball is put in play at the start of, or during a game, all fielders other than the catcher shall be on fair territory.

(*a*) The catcher shall station himself directly back of the plate. He may leave his position at any time to catch a pitch or make a play except that when the batter is being given an intentional base on balls, the

catcher must stand with both feet within the lines of the catcher's box until the ball leaves the pitcher's hand.
Penalty: Balk.

(*b*) The pitcher, while in the act of delivering the ball to the batter, shall take his legal position;

(*c*) Except for the pitcher and the catcher, any fielder may station himself anywhere in fair territory.

(*d*) Except for the batter, or a runner attempting to score, no offensive player shall cross the catcher's lines when the ball is in play.

4.04 The batting order shall be followed throughout the game unless a player is substituted for another. In that case the substitute shall take the place of the replaced player in the batting order.

4.05 (*a*) The offensive team shall station two base coaches on the field during its term at bat, one near first and one near third base.

(*b*) Base coaches shall be limited to two in number and shall (1) be in team uniform, and (2) remain within the coach's box at all times.
Penalty: The offending base coach shall be removed from the game, and shall leave the playing field.

4.06 (*a*) No manager, player, substitute, coach, trainer or batboy shall at any time, whether from the bench, the coach's box or on the playing field, or elsewhere:

(1) Incite, or try to incite, by word or sign a demonstration from spectators;

(2) Use language which will in any manner refer to or reflect upon opposing players, an umpire or any spectator;

(3) Call 'Time' or employ any other word or phrase or commit any other act while the ball is alive and in play for the obvious purpose of trying to make the pitcher commit a balk;

(4) Make intentional contact with the umpire in any manner.

(*b*) No fielder shall take a position that is in the batter's line of vision, and with deliberate unsportsmanlike intent, act in a manner to distract the batter.
Penalty: The offender shall be removed from the game, he shall leave the playing field, and, if a balk is made, it shall be nullified.

4.07 When a manager, player, coach or trainer is ejected from a game, he shall leave the field immediately and take no further part in that game. He shall remain in the club house or change to street clothes and either leave the park or take a seat in the grandstand well removed from the vicinity of his team's bench or bullpen.

4.08 When the occupants of a player's bench show violent disapproval of an umpire's decision the umpire shall first give warning that such disapproval shall cease.

Penalty: If such action continues the umpire shall order the offenders from the bench to the club house. If he is unable to detect the offender, or offenders, he may clear the bench of all substitute players. The manager of the offending team shall have the privilege of recalling to the playing field only those players needed for substitution in the game.

4.09 How a Team Scores

(*a*) One run shall be scored each time a runner legally advances and touches first, second, third and home base before three men are put out to end the inning. *Exception*: A run is not scored if the runner advances to home base during a play in which the third out is made (1) by the batter-runner before he touches first base; (2) by any runner being forced out; or (3) by a preceding runner who is declared out because he failed to touch one of the bases.

(*b*) When the winning run is scored in the last half-inning of a regulation game, or in the last half of an extra inning, as the results of a base on balls, hit batter or any other play with the bases full which forces the runner on third to advance, the umpire shall not declare the game ended until the runner forced to advance from third has touched home base and the batter-runner has touched first base.

Penalty: If the runner on third refuses to advance to the touch home base in a reasonable time, the umpire shall disallow the run, call out the offending player and order the game resumed. If, with two out, the batter-runner refuses to advance to and touch first base, the umpire shall disallow the run, call out the offending player, and order the game resumed. If, before two are out, the batter-runner refuses to advance to and touch first base, the run shall count, but the offending player shall be called out.

4.10 (*a*) A regulation game consists of nine innings, unless extended because of a tie score, or shortened (1) because the home team needs none of its half of the ninth inning or only a fraction of it, or (2) because the umpire calls the game.

Exception: National Association Leagues may adopt a rule providing that one or both games of a doubleheader shall be seven innings in length. In such games, any of these rules applying to the ninth innings shall apply to the seventh innings.

(*b*) If the score is tied after nine completed innings, play shall continue until (1) the visiting team has scored more total runs than the home team at the end of a completed inning, or (2) the home team scores the winning run in an uncompleted inning.

(c) If a game is called, it is a regulation game:

(1) If five innings have been completed;

(2) If the home team has scored more runs in four or four and a fraction half innings than the visiting team has scored in five completed half-innings;

(3) If the home team scores one or more runs in its half of the fifth inning to tie the scores.

(d) If each team has the same number of runs when the game ends, the umpire shall declare it a 'Tie Game'.

(e) If a game is called before it has become a regulation game, the umpire shall declare it 'No Game'.

(f) Rain checks will not be honoured for any regulation or suspended game which has progressed to or beyond a point of play described in 4.10 (c).

4.11 The score of a regulation game is the total number of runs scored by each team at the moment the game ends.

(a) The game ends when the visiting team completes its half of the ninth inning if the home team is ahead.

(b) The game ends when the ninth inning is completed, if the visiting team is ahead.

(c) If the home team scores the winning run in its half of the ninth inning (or its half of an extra inning after a tie), the game ends immediately when the winning run is scored. *Exception*: If the batter in a game hits a home run out of the playing field, the batter-runner and all runners on base are permitted to score, in accordance with the base-running rules, and the game ends when the batter-runner touches home plate.

Approved Ruling: The batter hits a home run out of the playing field to win the game in the last half of the ninth or an extra inning, but is called out for passing a preceding runner. The game ends immediately when the winning run is scored.

(d) A called game ends at the moment the umpire terminates play. *Exception*: If the game is called while an inning is in progress and before it is completed, the game becomes a *suspended* game in each of the following situations:

(1) The visiting team has scored one or more runs to tie the score and the home team has not scored.

(2) The visiting team has scored one or more runs to take the lead and the home team has not tied the score or retaken the lead. National Association Leagues may also adopt the following rules for suspended games in addition to 4.11 (d) (1) and (2) above. (If adopted by a National Association League, Rule 4.10 (c), (d) and (e) would not apply to their games.)

(3) The game has not become a regulation game (4½ innings with the home team ahead, or 5 innings with the visiting club ahead or tied).

(4) Any regulation game tied at the point play is stopped because of weather, curfew or other reason.

(5) If a game is suspended before it becomes a regulation game, and is continued prior to another regularly scheduled game, the regularly scheduled game will be limited to seven innings.

(6) If a game is suspended after it is a regulation game, and is continued prior to another regularly scheduled game, the regularly scheduled game will be a nine inning game.

Exception: The above sections (3), (4), (5) and (6) will not apply to the last scheduled game between the two teams during the championship season, or League Playoffs.

Any suspended game not completed prior to the last scheduled game between the two teams during the championship season, will become a called game.

4.12 Suspended Games

(*a*) A league shall adopt the following rules providing for completion at a future date of games terminated for any of the following reasons:

(1) A curfew imposed by law.

(2) A time limit permissible under league rules.

(3) Light failure or malfunction of a mechanical field device under control of the home club. (Mechanical field device shall include automatic tarpaulin or water removal equipment.)

(4) Darkness, when a law prevents the lights from being turned on.

(5) Weather, if the game is called while an inning is in progress, and before it is completed, and one of the following situations prevails:

    (i) The visiting team has scored one or more runs to tie the score, and the home team has not scored.

    (ii) The visiting team has scored one or more runs to take the lead, and the home team has not tied the score or retaken the lead.

(*b*) Such games shall be known as suspended games. No game called because of a curfew, weather, or a time limit shall be a suspended game unless it has progressed far enough for it to be a regulation game under the provisions of Rule 4.10. A game called under the provisions of Rule 4.12 (*a*), (3) or (4) shall be a suspended game at any time after it starts.

Note: Weather and similar conditions – 4.12 (*a*) (1–5) – shall take precedence in determining whether a called game shall be a suspended game. A game can only be considered a suspended game if stopped for any of the five reasons specified in Section (*a*). Any regulation game called due to weather with the score tied (unless the situation outlined in 4.12 (*a*) (5) (i) prevails) is a tie game and must be replayed in its entirety.

(*c*) A suspended game shall be resumed and completed as follows:

(1) Immediately preceding the next scheduled single game between the two clubs on the same grounds; or

(2) Immediately preceding the next scheduled doubleheader between the two clubs on the same grounds, if no single game remains on the schedule; or

(3) If suspended on the last scheduled date between the two clubs in that city, transferred and played on the grounds of the opposing club, if possible;

(i) Immediately preceding the next scheduled single game, or

(ii) Immediately preceding the next scheduled doubleheader, if no single game remains on the schedule.

(4) If a suspended game has not been resumed and completed on the last date scheduled for the two clubs, it shall be a called game.

(*d*) A suspended game shall be resumed at the exact point of suspension of the original game. The completion of a suspended game is a continuation of the original game. The lineup and batting order of both teams shall be exactly the same as the lineup and batting order at the moment of suspension, subject to the rules governing substitution. Any player may be replaced by a player who had not been in the game prior to the suspension. No player removed before the suspension may be returned to the lineup.

A player who was not with the club when the game was suspended may be used as a substitute, even if he has taken the place of a player no longer with the club who would not have been eligible because he had not been removed from the lineup before the game was suspended.

(*e*) Rain checks will not be honoured for any regulation or suspended game which has progressed to or beyond a point of play described in 4.10(*c*).

4.13 Rules Governing Doubleheaders

(*a*) (1) Only two championship games shall be played on one date. Completion of a suspended game shall not violate this rule.

(2) If two games are scheduled to be played for one admission on one date, the first game shall be the regularly scheduled game.

(*b*) After the start of the first game of a doubleheader, that game shall be completed before the second game of the doubleheader shall begin.

(*c*) The second game of a doubleheader shall start 20 minutes after the first game is completed, unless a longer interval (not to exceed 30 minutes) is declared by the umpire-in-chief and announced to the opposing managers at the end of the first game. *Exception*: If the league president has approved a request by the home club for a longer interval between games for some special event, the umpire-in-chief shall declare such longer interval and announce it to the opposing managers. The umpire-in-chief of the first game shall be the timekeeper controlling the interval between games.

(*d*) The umpire shall start the second game of a doubleheader, if at all possible, and play shall continue as long as ground conditions, local time restrictions, or weather permit.

(*e*) When a regularly scheduled doubleheader is delayed in starting for any cause, any game that is started is the first game of the doubleheader.

(*f*) When a rescheduled game is part of a doubleheader the rescheduled game shall be the second game, and the first game shall be the regularly scheduled game for that date.

4.14 The umpire-in-chief shall order the playing field lights turned on whenever in his opinion darkness makes further play in daylight hazardous.

4.15 A game may be forfeited to the opposing team when a team:

(*a*) Fails to appear upon the field, or being upon the field, refuses to start play within 5 minutes after the umpire has called 'Play' at the appointed hour for beginning the game, unless such delayed appearance is, in the umpire's judgement, unavoidable.

(*b*) Employs tactics palpably designed to delay or shorten the game.

(*c*) Refuses to continue play during a game unless the game has been terminated or suspended by the umpire.

(*d*) Fails to resume play, after suspension, within one minute after the umpire has called 'Play'.

(*e*) After warning by the umpire, wilfully and persistently violates any rules of the game.

(*f*) Fails to obey within a reasonable time the umpire's order for removal of a player from the game.

(*g*) Fails to appear for the second game of a doubleheader within 20 minutes after the close of the first game unless the umpire-in-chief of the first game shall have extended the time of the intermission.

4.16 A game shall be forfeited to the visiting team if, after it has been suspended, the order of the umpire to grounds-keepers respecting preparation for the field for resumption of play are not complied with.

4.17 A game shall be forfeited to the opposing team when a team is unable or refuses to place nine players on the field.

4.18 If the umpire declares a game forfeited, he shall transmit a written report to the league president within 24 hours thereafter, but failure of such transmittal shall not effect the forfeiture.

4.19 Protesting Games. Each league shall adopt rules governing the procedure for protesting a game, when a manager claims that an umpire's decision is in violation of these rules. No protest shall ever be permitted on judgement decisions by the umpire. In all protested games, the decision of the league president shall be final.

Even if it is held that the protested decision violated the rules, no replay of the game will be ordered unless in the opinion of the league president the violation adversely affected the protesting team's chances of winning the game.

5. Putting The Ball In Play.
Live Ball

5.01 At the time set for beginning the game the umpire shall call 'Play'.

5.02 After the umpire calls 'Play' the ball is live and in play and remains alive and in play until for legal cause, or at the umpire's call of 'Time' suspending play, the ball becomes dead. While the ball is dead no player may be put out, no bases may be run and no runs may be scored, except that runners may advance one or more bases as the results of acts which occurred while the ball was alive (such as, but not limited to, a balk, an overthrow, interference, or a home run or other fair ball hit out of the playing field). Should a ball come partially apart in a game, it is in play until the play is completed.

5.03 The pitcher shall deliver the pitch to the batter who may elect to strike the ball, or who may not offer at it, as he chooses.

5.04 The offensive team's objective is to have its batter become a runner, and its runners advance.

5.05 The defensive team's objective is to prevent offensive players from becoming runners, and to prevent their advance around the bases.

5.06 When a batter becomes a runner and touches all bases legally he shall score one run for his team.

5.07 When three offensive players are legally put out, that team takes the field and the opposing team becomes the offensive team.

5.08 If a thrown ball accidentally touches a base coach, or a pitched or thrown ball touches an umpire, the ball is alive and in play. However, if the coach interferes with a thrown ball, the runner is out.

5.09 The ball becomes dead and the runners advance one base, or return to their bases, without liability to put out, when:

(*a*) A pitched ball touches a batter, or his clothing, while in his legal batting position; runners, if forced, advance.

(*b*) The plate umpire interferes with the catcher's throw; runners may not advance.

Note: The interference shall be disregarded if the catcher's throw retires the runner.

(*c*) A balk is committed; runners advance (see Penalty 8.05).

(*d*) A ball is illegally batted; runners return.

(*e*) A foul ball is not caught; runners return. The umpire shall not put the ball in play until all runners have retouched their bases.

(*f*) A fair ball touches a runner or an umpire on fair territory before it touches an infielder, including the pitcher, or touches an umpire before it has passed an infielder other than the pitcher.

If a fair ball goes through, or by, an infielder, and touches a runner immediately back of him, or touches a runner after being deflected by an infielder, the ball is in play and the umpire shall not declare the runner out. In making such decision the umpire must be convinced that the ball passed through, or by, the infielder and that no other infielder had the chance to make a play on the ball; runners advance, if forced.

(*g*) A pitched ball lodges in the umpire's or catcher's mask or paraphernalia and remains out of play; runners advance one base.

(*h*) Any legal pitch touches a runner trying to score; runners advance.

5.10 The ball becomes dead when the umpire calls 'Time'. The umpire-in-chief shall call 'Time':

(*a*) When in his judgement weather, darkness or similar conditions make immediate further play impossible.

(*b*) When light failure makes it difficult or impossible for the umpires to follow the play.

Note: A league may adopt its own regulations governing games interrupted by light failure.

(*c*) When an accident incapacitates a player or an umpire.

(1) If an accident to a runner is such as to prevent him from proceeding to a base to which he is entitled, as on a home run hit out of the playing field, or an award of one or more bases, a substitute runner shall be permitted to complete the play.

(*d*) When a manager requests 'Time' for a substitution, or for a conference with one of his players.

(*e*) When the umpire wishes to examine the ball, to consult with either manager, or for any similar cause.

(*f*) When a fielder, after catching a fly ball, falls into a bench or stand, or falls across ropes into a crowd when spectators are on the field. As pertains to runners, the provisions of 7.04 (*c*) shall prevail.

If a fielder after making a catch steps into a bench, but does not fall, the ball is in play and runners may advance at their own peril.

(*g*) When an umpire orders a player or any other person removed from the playing field.

(*h*) Except in the cases stated in paragraphs (*b*) and (*c*) (1) of this rule, no umpire shall call 'Time' while a play is in progress.

5.11 After the ball is dead, play shall be resumed when the pitcher takes his place on the pitcher's plate with a new ball or the same ball in his possession and the plate umpire calls 'Play'. The plate umpire shall call 'Play' as soon as the pitcher takes his place on the plate with the ball in his possession.

6. The Batter
6.01 (*a*) Each play of the offensive team shall bat in the order that his name appears in his team's batting order.

(*b*) The first batter in each inning after the first inning shall be the player whose name follows that of the last player who legally completed his time at bat in the preceding inning.

6.02 (*a*) The batter shall take his position in the batter's box promptly when it is his time at bat.

(*b*) The batter shall not leave his position in the batter's box after the pitcher comes to Set Position, or starts his windup.
Penalty: If the pitcher pitches, the umpire shall call 'Ball' or 'Strike' as the case may be.

(*c*) If the batter refuses to take his position in the batter's box during his time at bat, the umpire shall order the pitcher to pitch, and shall call 'Strike' on each such pitch. The batter may take his proper position after any such pitch, and the regular ball and strike count shall continue, but if he does not take his proper position before three strikes are called, he shall be declared out.

6.03 The batter's legal position shall be with both feet within the batter's box.
Approved Ruling: The lines defining the box are within the batter's box.

6.04 A batter has legally completed his time at bat when he is put out or becomes a runner.

6.05 A batter is out when:

(*a*) His fair or foul fly ball (other than a foul tip) is legally caught by a fielder.

(*b*) A third strike is legally caught by the catcher.

(*c*) A third strike is not caught by the catcher when first base is occupied before two are out.

(*d*) He bunts foul on third strike.

(*e*) An infield fly is declared.

(*f*) He attempts to hit a third strike and the ball touches him.

(*g*) His fair ball touches him before touching a fielder.

(*h*) After hitting or bunting a fair ball, his bat hits the ball a second time in fair territory. The ball is dead and no runners may advance. If the batter-runner drops his bat and the ball rolls against the bat in fair territory and, in the umpire's judgement, there was no intention to interfere with the course of the ball, the ball is alive and in play.

(*i*) After hitting or bunting a foul ball, he intentionally deflects the course of the ball in any manner while running to first base. The ball is dead and no runners may advance.

(*j*) After a third strike or after he hits a fair ball, he or first base is tagged before he touches first base.

(*k*) In running the last half of the distance from home base to first base, while the ball is being fielded to first base, he runs outside (to the right of) the 3ft line, or inside (to the left of) the foul-line and, in the umpire's judgement, in so doing interferes with the fielder taking the throw at first base; except that he may run outside (to the right of) the 3ft line or inside (to the left of) the foul-line to avoid a fielder attempting to field a batted ball.

(*l*) An infielder intentionally drops a fair fly ball or line drive with first, first and second, first and third, or first, second and third base occupied before two are out. The ball is dead and runner or runners shall return to their original base or bases.

Approved Ruling: In this situation, the batter is not out if the infielder permits the ball to drop untouched to the ground, except when the Infield Fly Rule applies.

(*m*) A preceding runner shall, in the umpire's judgement, intentionally interfere with a fielder who is attempting to catch a thrown ball or to throw a ball in an attempt to complete any play.

(*n*) With two out, a runner on third base, and two strikes on the batter, the runner tries to steal home base on a legal pitch and the ball touches the runner in the batter's strike zone. The umpire shall call 'Strike Three', the batter is out and the run shall not count; before two are out, the umpire shall call 'Strike Three', the ball is dead, and the run counts.

6.06 A batter is out for illegal action when:

(*a*) He hits a ball with one or both feet on the ground entirely outside the batter's box.

(*b*) He steps from one batter's box to the other while the pitcher is in position ready to pitch.

(*c*) He interferes with the catcher's fielding or throwing by stepping out of the batter's box or making any other movement that hinders the catcher's play at home base. *Exception*: Batter is not out if any runner attempting to advance is put out, or if runner trying to score is called out for batter's interference.

(*d*) He uses or attempts to use a bat that, in the umpire's judgement, has been altered or tampered with in such a way to improve the distance factor or cause an unusual reaction on the baseball. This includes bats that are filled, flat-surfaced, nailed, hollowed, grooved or covered with a substance such as paraffin, wax, etc.

No advancement on the bases will be allowed and any out or outs made during a play shall stand.

In addition to being called out, the player shall be ejected from the game and may be subject to additional penalties as determined by his league president.

6.07 Batting out of Turn

(*a*) A batter shall be called out, on appeal, when he fails to bat in his proper turn, and another batter completes a time at bat in his place.

(1) The proper batter may take his place in the batter's box at any time before the improper batter becomes a runner or is put out, and any balls and strikes shall be counted in the proper batter's time at bat.

(*b*) When an improper batter becomes a runner or is put out, and the defensive team appeals to the umpire before the first pitch to the next batter of either team, or before any play or attempted play, the umpire shall (1) declare the proper batter out; and (2) nullify any advance or score made because of a ball batted by the improper batter or because of the improper batter's advance to first base on a hit, an error, a base on balls, a hit batter or otherwise.

Note: If a runner advances, while the improper batter is at bat, on a stolen base, balk, wild pitch or passed ball, such advance is legal.

(*c*) When an improper batter becomes a runner or is put out, and a pitch is made to the next batter of either team before an appeal is made, the improper batter thereby becomes the proper batter, and the results of his time at bat become legal.

(*d*) (1) When the proper batter is called out because he has failed to bat in turn, the next batter shall be the batter whose name follows that of the proper batter thus called out.

(2) When an improper batter becomes a proper batter because no appeal is made before the next pitch, the next batter shall be the batter whose name follows that of such legalised improper batter. The instant an improper batter's actions are legalised, the batting order picks up with the name following that of the legalised improper batter.

6.08 The batter becomes a runner and is entitled to first base without liability to be put out (provided he advances to and touches first base) when:

(*a*) Four 'balls' have been called by the umpire.

(*b*) He is touched by a pitched ball which he is not attempting to hit unless: (1) The ball is in the strike zone when it touches the batter; or (2) The batter makes no attempt to avoid being touched by the ball.

If the ball is in the strike zone when it touches the batter, it shall be called a strike, whether or not the batter tries to avoid the ball. If the ball is outside the strike zone when it touches the batter, it shall be called a ball if he makes no attempt to avoid being touched.

Approved Ruling: When the batter is touched by a pitched ball which does not entitle him to first base, the ball is dead and no runner may advance.

(*c*) The catcher or any fielder interferes with him. If a play follows the interference, the manager of the offence may advise the plate umpire that he elects to decline the interference penalty and accept the play. However, if the batter reaches first base on a hit, an error, a base on balls, a hit batsman, or otherwise, and all other runners advance at least one base, the play proceeds without reference to the interference.

(*d*) A fair ball touches an umpire or a runner on fair territory before touching a fielder.

If a fair ball touches an umpire after having passed a fielder other than the pitcher, or having touched a fielder, including the pitcher, the ball is in play.

6.09 The batter becomes a runner when:

(*a*) He hits a fair ball.

(*b*) The third strike called by the umpire is not caught, providing (1) first base is unoccupied, or (2) first base is occupied with two out.

(*c*) A fair ball, after having passed a fielder other than a pitcher, or after having been touched by a fielder, including the pitcher, shall touch an umpire or runner on fair territory.

(*d*) A fair ball passes over a fence or into the stands at a distance from homebase of 250ft or more. Such a hit entitles the batter to a home run when he shall have touched all bases legally. A fair fly ball that passes out of the playing field at a point less than 250ft from home base shall entitle the batter to advance to second base only.

(*e*) A fair ball, after touching the ground, bounds into the stands, or passes through, over or under a fence, or through or under a scoreboard, or through or under a shrubbery, or vines on the fence, in which case the batter and the runners shall be entitled to advance two bases.

(*f*) Any fair ball which, either before or after touching the ground, passes through or under a fence, or through or under a scoreboard, or through any opening in the fence or scoreboard, or through or under a shrubbery, or vines on the fence, or which sticks in a fence or scoreboard, in which case the batter and the runners shall be entitled to advance two bases.

(*g*) Any bounding fair ball is deflected by the fielder into the stands, or over or under a fence on fair or foul territory, in which case the batter and all runners shall be entitled to advance two bases.

(*h*) Any fair fly ball is deflected by the fielder into the stands, or over the fence into foul territory, in which case the batter shall be entitled to advance to second base; but if deflected into the stands or over the fence in fair territory, the batter shall be entitled to a home run. However, should such a fair fly be deflected at a point less than 250ft from home plate, the batter shall be entitled to two bases only.

6.10. *Section 6.10, concerning the Designated Hitter Rule, is given in full in the Official Baseball Rules.*

7. The Runner

7.01 A runner acquires the right to an unoccupied base when he touches it before he is out. He is then entitled to it until he is put out, or forced to vacate it for another runner legally entitled to that base.

If a runner legally acquires title to a base, and the pitcher assumes his pitching position, the runner may not then return to a previously occupied base.

7.02 In advancing, a runner shall touch first, second, third and home base in order. If forced to return, he shall retouch all bases in reverse order, unless the ball is dead under any provision of Rule 5.09. In such cases, the runner may go directly to his original base.

7.03 Two runners may not occupy a base, but if, while the ball is alive, two runners are touching a base, the following runner shall be out when tagged. The preceding runner is entitled to the base.

7.04 Each runner, other than the batter, may without liability to be put out, advance one base when:

(*a*) There is a balk.

(*b*) The batter's advance without liability to be put out forces the runner to vacate his base, or when the batter hits a fair ball that touches another runner or the umpire before such ball has been touched by, or has passed a fielder, if the runner is forced to advance.

(c) A fielder, after catching a fly ball, falls into a bench or stand, or falls across ropes into a crowd when spectators are on the field.

(d) While he is attempting to steal a base, the batter is interfered with by the catcher or any other fielder.

Note: When a runner is entitled to a base without liability to be put out, while the ball is in play, or under any rule in which the ball is in play after the runner reaches the base to which he is entitled, and the runner fails to touch the base to which he is entitled before attempting to advance to the next base, the runner shall forfeit his exemption from liability to be put out, and he may be put out by tagging the base or by tagging the runner before he returns to the missed base.

7.05 Each runner including the batter-runner may without liability to be put out, advance:

(a) To home base, scoring a run, if a fair ball goes out of the playing field and he touches all bases legally; or if a fair ball which, in the umpire's judgement, would have gone out of the playing field in flight, is deflected by the act of a fielder throwing his glove, cap or any article of his apparel.

(b) Three bases, if a fielder deliberately touches a fair ball with his cap, mask, or any part of his uniform detached from its proper place on his person. The ball is in play and the batter may advance to home base at his peril.

(c) Three bases, if a fielder deliberately throws his glove at and touches a fair ball. The ball is in play and the batter may advance to home base at his peril.

(d) Two bases, if a fielder deliberately touches a thrown ball with his cap, mask or any part of his uniform detached from its proper place on his person. The ball is in play.

(e) Two bases, if a fielder deliberately throws his glove at and touches a thrown ball. The ball is in play.

(f) Two bases, if a fair ball bounces or is deflected into the stands outside the first or third base lines; or if it goes through or under a field fence, or through or under a scoreboard, or through or under shrubbery or vines on the fence; or if it sticks in such fence, scoreboard, shrubbery or vines.

(g) Two bases when, with no spectators on the playing field, a thrown ball goes into the stands, or into a bench (whether or not the ball rebounds into the field), or over or under or through a field fence, or on a slanting part of the screen above the backstop, or remains in the meshes of a wire screen protecting spectators. The ball is dead. When such wild throw is the first play by an infielder, the umpire, in awarding such bases, shall be governed by the positions of the runners at the time the ball was pitched; in all other cases the umpire shall be governed by the position of the runners at the time the wild throw was made.

Approved Ruling: If all runners, including the batter-runner, have advanced at least one base when an infielder makes a wild throw on the first play after the pitch, the award shall be governed by the position of the runners when the wild throw was made.

(*h*) One base, if a ball, pitched to the batter, or thrown by the pitcher from his position on the pitcher's plate to a base to catch a runner, goes into a stand or bench, or over or through a field fence or backstop. The ball is dead.

Approved Ruling: When a wild pitch or passed ball goes through or by the catcher, or deflects off the catcher, and goes directly into the dugout, stands, above the break, or any area where the ball is dead, the awarding of bases shall be one base. One base shall also be awarded if the pitcher while in contact with the rubber throws to a base, and the throw goes directly into the stands or into any area where the ball is dead. If, however, the pitched or thrown ball goes through or by the catcher or through the fielder and remains on the playing field, and is subsequently kicked or deflected into the dugout, stands or other area where the ball is dead, the awarding of bases shall be two bases from position of runners at the time of the pitch or throw.

(*i*) One base, if the batter becomes a runner on Ball Four or Strike Three, when the pitch passes the catcher and lodges in the umpire's mask or paraphernalia.

If the batter becomes a runner on a wild pitch which entitles the runners to advance one base the batter-runner shall be entitled to first base only.

7.06 When obstruction occurs, the umpire shall call or signal 'Obstruction'.

(*a*) If a play is being made on the obstructed runner, or if the batter-runner is obstructed before he touches first base, the ball is dead and all runners shall advance, without liability to be put out, to the bases they would have reached, in the umpire's judgement, if there had been no obstruction. The obstructed runner shall be awarded at least one base beyond the base he had last legally touched before the obstruction. Any preceding runners, forced to advance by the award of bases as the penalty for obstruction, shall advance without liability to be put out.

(*b*) If no play is being made on the obstructed runner, the play shall proceed until no further action is possible. The umpire shall then call 'Time' and impose such penalties, if any, as in his judgement will nullify the act of obstruction.

7.07 If, with a runner positioned on third base and trying to score by means of a squeeze play or a steal, the catcher or any other fielder steps on, or in front of home base without possession of the ball, or touches the batter or his bat, the pitcher shall be charged with a balk, the batter shall be awarded first base on the interference of the fielder and the ball shall be dead.

7.08 Any runner is out when:

(*a*) (1) He runs more than 3ft away from a direct line between bases to avoid being tagged, unless his action is to avoid interference with a fielder fielding a batted ball; or (2) after touching first base, he leaves the baseline, obviously abandoning his effort to touch the next base.

Approved Ruling: When a batter becomes a runner on third strike not caught, and starts for his bench or position, he may advance to first base at any time before he enters the bench. To put him out, the defence must tag him or first base before he touches first base.

(*b*) He intentionally interferes with a thrown ball; or hinders a fielder attempting to make a play on a batted ball.

(*c*) He is tagged, when the ball is alive, while off his base. *Exception*: A batter-runner cannot be tagged out after overrunning or oversliding first base if he returns immediately to the base.

Approved Rulings: (1) If the impact of a runner breaks a base loose from its position, no play can be made on that runner at that base if he had reached the base safely. (2) If a base is dislodged from its position during a play, any following runner on the same play shall be considered as touching or occupying the base if, in the umpire's judgement, he touches or occupies the point marked by the dislodged bag.

(*d*) He fails to retouch his base after a fair or foul ball is legally caught before he, or his base, is tagged by a fielder. He shall not be called out for failure to retouch his base after the first following pitch, or any play or attempted play. This is an appeal play.

(*e*) He fails to reach the next base before a fielder tags him or the base, after he has been forced to advance by reason of the batter becoming a runner. However, if a following runner is put out on a force play, the force is removed and the runner must be tagged to be put out. The force is removed as soon as the runner touches the base to which he is forced to advance, and if he overslides or overruns the base, the runner must be tagged to be put out. However, if the forced runner, after touching the next base, retreats for any reason towards the base he had last occupied, the force play is reinstated, and he can again be put out if the defence tags the base to which he is forced.

(*f*) He is touched by a fair ball in fair territory before the ball has touched or passed an infielder. The ball is dead and no runner may score, nor runners advance, except runners forced to advance. *Exception*: If a runner is touching his base when touched by an infield fly, he is not out, although the batter is out.

If a runner is touched by an infield fly when he is not touching his base, both runner and batter are out.

(*g*) He attempts to score on a play in which the batter interferes with the play at home base before two are out. With two out, the interference puts the batter out and no score counts.

(*h*) He passes a preceding runner before such a runner is out.

(*i*) After he has acquired legal possession of a base, he runs the bases in reverse order for the purpose of confusing the defence or making a travesty of the game. The umpire shall immediately call 'Time' and declare the runner out.

(*j*) He fails to return at once to first base after overrunning or oversliding that base. If he attempts to run to second he is out when tagged. If, after overrunning or oversliding first base he starts toward the dugout, or toward his position, and fails to return to first base at once, he is out on appeal, when he or the base is tagged.

(*k*) In running or sliding for home base, he fails to touch home base and makes no attempt to return to the base, when a fielder holds the ball in his hand, while touching home base, and appeals to the umpire for the decision.

7.09 It is interference by a batter or runner when:

(*a*) After a third strike he hinders the catcher in his attempt to field the ball.

(*b*) After hitting or bunting a fair ball, his bat hits the ball a second time in fair territory. The ball is dead and no runners may advance. If the batter-runner drops his bat and the ball rolls against the bat in fair territory and, in the umpire's judgement, there was no intention to interfere with the course of the ball, the ball is alive and in play.

(*c*) He intentionally deflects the course of a foul ball in any manner.

(*d*) Before two are out and a runner on third base, the batter hinders a fielder in making a play at home base; the runner is out.

(*e*) Any member or members of the offensive team stand or gather round any base to which a runner is advancing, to confuse, hinder or add to the difficulty of the fielders. Such runner shall be declared out for the interference of his team-mate or team-mates.

(*f*) Any batter or runner who has just been put out hinders or impedes any following play being made on a runner. Such runner shall be declared out for the interference of his team-mate.

(*g*) If, in the judgement of the umpire, a base runner wilfully and deliberately interferes with a batted ball or a fielder in the act of fielding a batted ball with the obvious intent to break up a double play, the ball is dead. The umpire shall call the runner out for interference and also call out the batter-runner because of the action of his team-mate. In no event may bases be run or runs scored due to such action by a runner.

(*h*) If, in the judgement of the umpire, a batter-runner wilfully and deliberately interferes with a batted ball or a fielder in the act of fielding a batted ball, with the obvious intent to break up a double play, the ball is dead; the umpire shall call the batter-runner out for interference and shall also call out the runner who had advanced closest to the home plate regardless where the double play might have been possible. In no event shall bases be run because of such interference.

(*i*) In the judgement of the umpire, the base coach at third base, or first base, by touching or holding the runner, physically assists him in returning to or leaving third base or first base.

(*j*) With a runner on third base, the base coach leaves his box and acts in any manner to draw a throw by a fielder.

(*k*) In running the last half of the distance from home base to first base while the ball is being fielded to first base, he runs outside (to the right of) the 3ft line, or inside (to the left of) the foul-line and, in the umpire's judgement, interferes with the fielder taking the throw at first base, or attempting to field a batted ball.

(*l*) He fails to avoid a fielder who is attempting to field a batted ball, or intentionally interferes with a thrown ball, provided that if two or more fielders attempt to field a batted ball, and the runner comes in contact with one or more of them, the umpire shall determine which fielder is entitled to the benefit of this rule, and shall not declare the runner out for coming in contact with a fielder other than the one the umpire determines to be entitled to field such a ball.

(*m*) A fair ball touches him on fair territory before touching a fielder. If a fair ball goes through, or by, an infielder, and touches a runner immediately back of him, or touches the runner after having being deflected by a fielder, the umpire shall not declare the runner out for being touched by a batted ball. In making such decision the umpire must be convinced that the ball passed through, or by, the fielder, and that no other infielder had a chance to make a play on the ball. If, in the judgement of the umpire, the runner deliberately and intentionally kicks such a batted ball on which the infielder has missed a play, then the runner shall be called out for interference.

Penalty for interference: The runner is out and the ball is dead.

7.10 Any runner shall be called out, on appeal, when:

(*a*) After a fly ball is caught, he fails to retouch his original base before he or his original base is tagged.

(*b*) With the ball in play, while advancing or returning to a base, he fails to touch each base in order before he, or a missed base, is tagged.

Approved Rulings: (1) No runner may return to touch a missed base after a following runner has scored. (2) When the ball is dead, no runner may return to touch a missed base or one he has left after he has advanced to and touched a base beyond the missed base.

(*c*) He overruns or overslides first base and fails to return to the base immediately, and he or the base is tagged.

(*d*) He fails to touch home base and makes no attempt to return to that base, and home base is tagged.

Any appeal under this rule must be made before the next pitch, or any play or attempted play. If the violation occurs during a play which ends a half-inning, the appeal must be made before the defensive team leaves the field.

An appeal is not to be interpreted as a play or an attempted play.

Successive appeals may not be made on a runner at the same base. If the defensive team on its first appeal errs, a request for a second appeal on the same runner at the same base shall not be allowed by the umpire. (Intended meaning of the word 'err' is that the defensive team in making an appeal threw the ball out of play. For example, if the pitcher threw to first base to appeal and threw the ball into the stands, no second appeal would be allowed.)

Appeal plays may require an umpire to recognise an apparent 'fourth out'. If the third out is made during a play in which an appeal play is sustained on another runner, the appeal play decision takes precedence in determining the out. If there is more than one appeal during a play that ends a half-inning, the defence may elect to take the out that gives it the advantage. For the purpose of this rule, the defence team has 'left the field' when the pitcher and all infielders have left fair territory on their way to the bench or clubhouse.

7.11 The players, coaches or any member of an offensive team shall vacate any space (including both dugouts) needed by a fielder who is attempting to field a batted or thrown ball.
Penalty: Interference shall be called and the batter or runner on whom the play is being made shall be declared out.

7.12 Unless two are out, the status of a following runner is not affected by a preceding runner's failure to touch or retouch a base. If, upon appeal, the preceding runner is the third out, no runners following him shall score. If such third out is the result of a force play, neither preceding runners shall score.

8. The Pitcher
8.01 Legal pitching delivery. There are two legal pitching positions, the windup position and the set position, either may be used at any time.

Pitchers shall take signs from the catchers while standing on the rubber.

(*a*) *The Windup Position*. The pitcher shall stand facing the batter, his entire pivot foot on, or in front of and touching and not off the end of the pitcher's plate, and the other foot free. From this position any natural movement associated with his delivery of the ball to the batter commits him to the pitch without interruption or alteration. He shall not raise either foot from the ground, except that in his actual delivery of the ball to the batter, he may take one step backward, and one step forward with his free foot.

When a pitcher holds the ball with both hands in front of his body, with his entire pivot foot on, or in front of and touching but not off the end of the pitcher's plate, and his other foot free, he will be considered in the windup position.

(*b*) *The Set Position*. Set position shall be indicated by the pitcher when he stands facing the batter with his entire pivot foot on, or in front of, and in contact with, and not off the end of the pitcher's plate, and his other foot in front of the pitcher's plate, holding the ball in both hands in front of his body and coming to a complete stop. From such set position he may deliver the ball to the batter, throw to a base or step backward off the pitcher's plate with his pivot foot. Before assuming set position, the pitcher may elect to make any natural preliminary motion such as that known as 'the stretch'. But if he so elects, he shall come to set position before delivering the ball to the batter. After assuming set position, any natural motion associated with his delivery of the ball to the batter commits him to the pitch without alteration or interruption.

Preparatory to coming to a set position, the pitcher shall have one hand on his side; from this position he shall go to his set position as defined in Rule 8.01 (*b*) without interruption and in one continuous motion.

The whole width of the foot in contact with the rubber must be on the rubber. A pitcher cannot pitch from off the end of the rubber with just the side of his foot touching the rubber.

The pitcher, following his stretch, must (*a*) hold the ball in both hands in front of his body and (*b*) come to a complete stop. This must be enforced. Umpires should watch this closely. Pitchers are constantly attempting to 'beat the rule' in their efforts to hold runners on bases and in cases where the pitcher fails to make a complete 'stop' called for in the rules, the umpire should immediately call a 'Balk'.

(*c*) At any time during the pitcher's preliminary movement and until his natural pitching motion commits him to the pitch, he may throw to any base provided he steps toward such base before making the throw.

(*d*) If the pitcher makes an illegal pitch with the bases unoccupied, it shall be called a ball unless the batter reaches first base on a hit, an error, a base on balls, a hit batter or otherwise.

(*e*) If the pitcher removes his pivot foot from contact with the pitcher's plate by stepping backward with that foot, he thereby becomes an infielder and if he makes a wild throw from that position, it shall be considerd the same as a wild throw by any other fielder.

8.02 The pitcher shall not:

(*a*) (1) Bring his pitching hand in contact with his mouth or lips while in the 18ft circle surrounding the pitching rubber. *Exception*: Provided it is agreed by both managers, the umpire, prior to the start of the game played in cold weather, may permit the pitcher to blow on his hand.

Penalty: For violation of this part of this rule the umpire shall immediately call a ball. However, if the pitch is made and the batter reaches first base on a hit, an error, a hit batsman or otherwise, and no other runner is put out before advancing at least one base, the play shall proceed without reference to the violation. Repeated offenders shall be subject to a fine by the league president.

(2) Apply a foreign substance of any kind to the ball.

(3) Expectorate on the ball, either hand or his glove.

(4) Rub the ball on his glove, person or clothing.

(5) Deface the ball in any manner.

(6) Deliver what is called the 'shine' ball, 'spit' ball, 'mud' ball or 'emery' ball. The pitcher, of course, is allowed to rub the ball between his bare hands.

Penalty: For violation of any part of this rule 8.02 (*a*) (2–6) the umpire shall:

(*a*) Call the pitch a ball, warn the pitcher and have announced on the public address system the reason for the action.

(*b*) In the case of a second offence by the same pitcher in the same game, the pitcher shall be disqualified from the game.

(*c*) If a play follows the violation called by the umpire, the manager of the offence may advise the plate umpire that he elects to accept the play. Such election shall be made immediately at the end of the play. However, if the batter reaches first base on a hit, an error, a base on balls, a hit batsman, or otherwise, and no other runner is out before advancing at least one base, the play shall proceed without reference to the violation.

(*d*) Even though the offence elects to take the play, the violation shall be recognised and the penalties in (*a*) and (*b*) will still be in effect.

(*e*) The umpire shall be sole judge on whether any portion of this rule has been violated.

(*b*) Have on his person, or in his possession, any foreign substance. For such infraction of this section (*b*) the penalty shall be immediate ejection from the game.

(c) Intentionally delay the game by throwing the ball to players other than the catcher, when the batter is in position, except in an attempt to retire a runner.

Penalty: If, after warning by the umpire, such delaying action is repeated, the pitcher shall be removed from the game.

(d) Intentionally pitch at the batter. If in the umpire's judgement, such a violation occurs, the umpire may elect either to:

1. Expel the pitcher, or the manager and the pitcher, from the game; or

2. Warn the pitcher and the manager of both teams that another such pitch will result in the immediate expulsion of that pitcher (or a replacement) and the manager.

If, in the umpire's judgement, circumstances warrant, both teams may be officially 'warned' prior to the game or at any time during the game.

(League Presidents may take additional action under authority provided in Rule 9.05.)

To pitch at a batter's head is unsportsmanlike and highly dangerous. It should be – and is – condemned by everybody. Umpires should act without hesitation in enforcement of this rule.

8.03 When a pitcher takes his position at the beginning of each inning, or when he relieves another pitcher, he shall be permitted to pitch not to exceed eight preparatory pitches to his catcher during which play shall be suspended. A league by its own action may limit the number of preparatory pitches to less than eight preparatory pitches. Such preparatory pitches shall not consume more than one minute of time. If a sudden emergency causes a pitcher to be summoned into the game without any opportunity to warm up, the umpire-in-chief shall allow him as many pitches as the umpire deems necessary.

8.04 When the bases are unoccupied, the pitcher shall deliver the ball to the batter within 20 seconds after he receives the ball. Each time the pitcher delays the game by violating this rule, the umpire shall call 'Ball'.

The intent of this rule is to avoid unnecessary delays. The umpire shall insist that the catcher return the ball promptly to the pitcher, and that the pitcher take his position on the rubber promptly. Obvious delay by the pitcher should instantly be penalised by the umpire.

8.05 If there is a runner, or runners, it is a balk when:

(a) The pitcher, while touching his plate, makes any motion naturally associated with his pitch and fails to make such delivery. If a left-handed or right-handed pitcher swings his free foot past the back edge of the pitcher's rubber, he is required to pitch to the batter except to throw to second base on a pick-off play.

(*b*) The pitcher, while touching his plate, feints a throw to first base and fails to complete the throw.

(*c*) The pitcher, while touching his plate, fails to step directly toward a base before throwing to that base.

(*d*) The pitcher, while touching his plate, throws, or feints a throw to an unoccupied base, except for the purpose of making a play.

(*e*) The pitcher makes an illegal pitch. A quick pitch is an illegal pitch. Umpires will judge a quick pitch as one delivered before the batter is reasonably set in the batter's box. With runners on base the penalty is a balk; with no runners on base, it is a ball. The quick pitch is dangerous and should not be permitted.

(*f*) The pitcher delivers the ball to the batter while he is not facing the batter.

(*g*) The pitcher makes any motion naturally associated with his pitch while he is not touching the pitcher's plate.

(*h*) The pitcher unnecessarily delays the game.

(*i*) The pitcher, without having the ball, stands on or astride the pitcher's plate or while off the plate, he feints a pitch.

(*j*) The pitcher, after coming to a legal pitching position, removes one hand from the ball other than in an actual pitch, or in throwing to a base.

(*k*) The pitcher, while touching his plate, accidentally or intentionally drops the ball.

(*l*) The pitcher, while giving an intentional base on balls, pitches when the catcher is not in the catcher's box.

(*m*) The pitcher delivers the pitch from set position without coming to a stop.

Penalty: The ball is dead, and each runner shall advance one base without liability to be put out, unless the batter reaches first on a hit, an error, a base on balls, a hit batter, or otherwise, and all other runners advance at least one base, in which case the play proceeds without reference to the balk.

Approved Ruling: In cases where a pitcher balks and throws wild, either to a base or homeplate, a runner or runners may advance beyond the base to which he is entitled at his own risk.

Approved Ruling: A runner who misses the first base to which he is advancing and who is called out on appeal shall be considered as having advanced one base for the purpose of this rule.

Section 8.06, concerning the visit of the manager or coach to the pitcher, is given in full in the Official Baseball Rules.

9. The Umpire
9.01 (*a*) The league president shall appoint one or more umpires to officiate at each league championship game. The umpire shall be

responsible for the conduct of the game in accordance with these official rules and for maintaining discipline and order on the playing field during the game.

Rule 9 is given in full in the Official Baseball Rules.

Section 10.01 is given in full in the Official Baseball Rules.

10.02 The official score report prescribed by the league president shall make provisions for entering the information listed below, in a form convenient for the compilation of permanent statistical records:

(*a*) The following records for each batter and runner:

(1) Number of times he batted, except that no time at bat shall be charged against a player when:

 (i) He hits a sacrifice bunt or fly;

 (ii) He is awarded first base on four called balls;

(iii) He is hit by a pitched ball;

(iv) He is awarded first base because of interference or obstruction;

(2) Number of runs scored;

(3) Number of safe hits;

(4) Number of runs batted in;

(5) Two-base hits;

(6) Three-base hits;

(7) Home runs;

(8) Total bases on safe hits;

(9) Stolen bases;

(10) Sacrifice bunts;

(11) Sacrifice flies;

(12) Total number of bases on balls;

(13) Separate listing of any intentional bases on balls;

(14) Number of times hit by a pitched ball;

(15) Number of times awarded first base for interference or obstruction;

(16) Strikeouts.

(*b*) The following records for each fielder:

(1) Number of putouts;

(2) Number of assists;

(3) Number of errors;

(4) Number of double plays participated in;

(5) Number of triple plays participated in.

(*c*) The following records for each pitcher:

(1) Number of innings pitched;

(2) Total number of batters faced;

(3) Number of batters officially at bat against pitcher computed according to 10.02 (*a*) (1);

(4) Number of hits allowed;

(5) Number of runs allowed;

(6) Number of earned runs allowed;

(7) Number of home runs allowed;

(8) Number of sacrifice hits allowed;

(9) Number of sacrifice flies allowed;

(10) Total number of bases on balls allowed;

(11) Separate listing of any intentional bases on balls allowed;

(12) Number of batters hit by pitched balls;

(13) Number of strikeouts;

(14) Number of wild pitches;

(15) Number of balks.

(*d*) The following additional data:

(1) Name of the winning pitcher;

(2) Name of the losing pitcher;

(3) Names of the starting pitcher and the finishing pitcher for each team;

(4) Name of pitcher credited with save.

(*e*) Number of passed balls allowed by each catcher.

(*f*) Number of players participating in double plays and triple plays.

(*g*) Number of runners left on base by each team. This total shall include all runners who get on base by any means and who do not score and are not put out. Include in this total a batter-runner whose batted ball results in another runner being retired for the third out.

(*h*) Names of batters who hit home runs with bases full.

(*i*) Names of batters who ground into force double plays and reverse force double plays.

(*j*) Names of runners caught stealing.

(*k*) Number of outs when the winning run is scored, if the game is won in the last half-inning.

(*l*) The score by innings for each team.

(*m*) Names of umpires, listed in this order (1) plate umpire, (2) first base umpire, (3) second base umpire, (4) third base umpire.

(*n*) Time required to play the game, with delays for weather or light failure deducted.

The Official Baseball Rules have been reprinted by permission of the Commissioner of Baseball. The copyright in the Rules is owned and registered by the Commissioner of Baseball.

Sections 1.11, 1.16, 3, 6.10, 8.06, 9, 10.01 and sections 10.03–10.24 are given in full in the Official Baseball Rules, obtainable from the Administration Secretary of the British Baseball Federation.

Basketball

Full-size Regulation Court

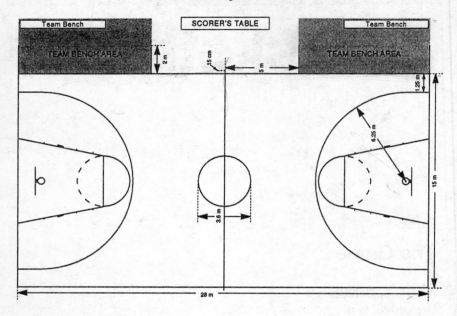

Regulation Free-throw Line

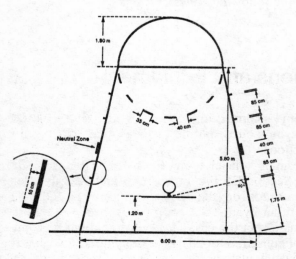

Basketball

RULE 1

The Game

Article 1. Definition

Basketball is played by two teams of five players each. The purpose of each team is to score into the opponents' basket and to prevent the other team from securing the ball or scoring. The ball may be passed, thrown, tapped, rolled or dribbled in any direction, subject to the restrictions laid down in the following Rules.

RULE 2

Dimensions and Equipment

Article 2. Court – Dimension

1. The playing court shall be a rectangular, flat, hard surface free from obstructions.

2. For the main official competitions of FIBA (see 'Official Game Procedures', Section E), the dimensions shall be 28m in length by 15m in width, measured from the inside edge of the boundary line.

3. For all other events, the appropriate entity of FIBA, such as the Zone Commission in the case of zone or continental competitions, or the National Federation for all domestic competitions, has the authority to approve existing playing courts with dimensions which fall within the following limits: minus 4m on the length and minus 2m on the width, provided that the variations are proportional to each other.

4. The height of the ceiling or the lowest obstruction shall be at least 7m.

5. The playing surface shall be uniformly and adequately lighted. The light units shall be placed where they will not hinder the vision of the players.

6. All new courts shall be constructed in accordance with the requirements specified for the main official competitions of FIBA, that is: 28m by 15m.

Article 3. Lines and Dimensions
The lines mentioned in this Article shall:
   1. Be drawn in the same colour,
   2. Be 0.05m (5cm) in width, and
   3. Be completely and perfectly visible.

A. Boundary Lines
1. The playing court shall be marked by lines as defined in Art. 2 which shall be, at every point, at least 2m from the spectators, advertising boards or any other obstruction.

2. The lines of the long sides of the court shall be termed the sidelines, those of the short sides, the endlines.

B. Centre Line
A centre line shall be drawn parallel to the endlines from the mid-points of the sidelines and shall extend 0.15m (15cm) beyond each sideline.

C. Free Throw Lines, Restricted Areas and Free Throw Lanes
1. A free throw line shall be drawn parallel to each endline. It shall have its further edge 5.80m from the inner edge of the endline and shall be 3.60m long. Its mid-point shall lie on the imaginary line joining the mid-points of the two endlines.

2. The restricted areas shall be the floor areas marked on the court limited by the endlines, the free throw lines and the lines which originate at the endlines, their outer edges being 3m from the mid-points of the endlines and terminating at the outer edge of the free throw lines.

If the inside of the restricted areas is painted, it must be of the same colour as that of the centre circle.

3. The free throw lanes are the restricted areas extended into the playing court by semicircles with a radius of 1.80m and their centres at the mid-points of the free throw lines. Similar semicircles shall be drawn with a broken line within the restricted areas.

4. Lane places along the free throw lanes to be used by players during free throws shall be marked as follows:

(*a*) The first line shall be marked 1.75m from the inside edge of the endline, measured along the line at the side of the free throw lane.

(*b*) The first lane place shall be 0.85m (85cm) in width and shall be limited by the beginning of the neutral zone.

(*c*) The neutral zone shall be 0.40m (40cm) in width and is a solid block marked in the same colour as the other lines.

(*d*) The second lane place shall be adjacent to the neutral zone and shall be 0.85m (85cm) in width.

(*e*) The third lane place, also 0.85m (85cm) in width, shall be marked adjacent to the lines limiting the second lane place.

(*f*) All lines used to mark these lane places shall be 0.10m (10cm) long and perpendicular to the outside of the lines which indicate the free throw lanes.

D. Centre Circle

The centre circle shall be marked in the centre of the court and shall have a radius of 1.80m measured to the outer edge of the circumference.

If the inside of the centre circle is painted, it must be of the same colour as that of the restricted areas.

E. Three-Point Field Goal Area

A team's three-point field goal area shall be the entire floor area of the playing court except for the area near its opponents' basket limited by and including:

1. Two parallel lines extending from the endline, 1.25m from the sidelines, and

2. An arc (semicircle) of 6.25m to the outer edge, which intersects the parallel lines.

3. The centre of the arc shall be taken from the point on the floor directly perpendicular to the exact centre of the opponents' basket. The distance of this point from the inside edge of the mid-point of the endline is 1.575m.

Note: Even if the court is less than 15m in width, the arc shall be drawn 6.25m from the centre of the basket.

F. Team Bench Areas

Team bench areas shall be marked as follows:

1. Outside the court on the same side as the scorer's table and the team benches (see diagram of full-size regulation court).

2. Each area shall be limited by a line extending from the endline, at least 2m in length, and by another line at least 2m in length, drawn 5m from the centre line and perpendicular to the sideline.

Comments

1. During the game, the only persons permitted to be in the team bench area are the Coach, the Assistant Coach, the substitutes and a maximum of five team followers with special responsibilities, e.g. manager, doctor, masseur, statistician, interpreter. No other person may sit within 5m of a team bench.

2. To be a team follower is a privilege, and this involves a responsibility. As a consequence, his behaviour comes under the jurisdiction of the officials.

3. When conditions warrant it, the Referee may reduce the number of team followers who are in the team bench area.

Article 4. Equipment

A. Backboards

1. The two backboards shall be made of suitable transparent material, made in one piece and having the same degree of rigidity as those made of hard wood 0.03m (3cm) thick.

They may also be of hard wood, 0.03m (3cm) thick and painted white.

2. The dimensions of the backboards shall be 1.80m horizontally and 1.05m vertically, with the lower edges 2.90m above the floor.

3. The appropriate entity of FIBA such as the Zone Commission in the case of Zone or continental competitions, or the National Federation for all domestic competitions, has the authority to also approve backboard dimensions of 1.80m horizontally and 1.20m vertically, with their lower edges 2.75m above the floor.

4. The front surface of the two backboards shall be flat and:

(*a*) All lines shall be drawn as follows:

(*i*) In white, if the backboard is transparent,

(*ii*) In black in all other cases,

(*iii*) 0.05m (5cm) in width.

(*b*) The borders shall be marked with a line as per a. above.

(*c*) A rectangle shall be drawn behind the ring on each backboard as follows:

(*i*) Outside dimensions of 0.59m (59cm) horizontally and 0.45m (45cm) vertically.

(*ii*) The top edge of the base of the rectangle shall be level with the top of the ring.

5. The backboards shall be firmly mounted as follows:

(*a*) At each end of the court at right angles to the floor, parallel to the endlines.

(*b*) Their centres shall lie in the perpendiculars erected at the points in the court 1.20m from the inner edge of the mid-point of each endline.

(*c*) The uprights supporting the backboards shall be at a distance of at least 2m from the outer edge of the endlines and shall be of a bright colour in contrast with the background in order that they will be clearly visible to the players.

6. The padding on both backboards shall be as follows:

(*a*) For the bottom and sides of the backboards, the padding shall cover the bottom surface of the board and the side surface to a distance of a minimum of 0.35m (35cm) from the bottom.

(*b*) The padding of the bottom edge of the backboard shall be of a minimum thickness of 0.05m (5cm).

(*c*) The front and back surface shall be covered to a minimum of 0.02m (2cm) from the bottom and the padding shall be of a minimum thickness of 0.02m (2cm).

7. The backboard supports shall be padded as follows:

(*a*) Any backboard support behind the backboard and at a height of less than 2.75m above the floor shall be padded on the bottom surface of the support to a distance of 1.20m from the face of the backboard.

The minimum thickness of the padding shall be 0.05m (5cm) and shall be of the same density as that of the padding on the backboards.

(*b*) All portable backboards must have the bases completely padded and to a minimum height of 2.15m on the court side surface.

The minimum thickness of the padding shall be 0.15m (15cm).

B. Baskets

The baskets shall be comprised of the rings and the nets.

1. The rings shall be constructed as follows:

(*a*) Solid iron, with a 0.45m (45cm) inside diameter, painted orange.

(*b*) The metal of the rings shall be of a minimum diameter of 0.017m (17mm) and of a maximum diameter of 0.020m (20mm) with the addition of small gauge loops on the under edge or similar device for attaching the nets.

(*c*) They shall be rigidly attached to the backboards (see Note below) and the top edge shall be positioned horizontally 3.05m above the floor, equidistant from the two vertical edges of the backboard.

Note: It is strongly recommended that the rings be fixed to the framework of the backboard in such a manner that no force, transmitted by the ring, is directly applied to the backboard.

(*d*) The nearest point of the inside edge of the ring shall be 0.15m (15cm) from the face of the backboard.

(*e*) Pressure-release rings may be used. They shall meet the following specifications:

(*i*) They shall have rebound characteristics identical to those of a non-movable ring. The pressure-release mechanism shall ensure these characteristics, as well as protect both ring and backboard. The design of the ring and its construction shall be such as to ensure player safety.

(*ii*) For those rings with a 'positive-lock' system, the pressure-release mechanism must not disengage until a static load of 105 kg has been applied to the top of the ring at the most distant point from the backboard.

(*iii*) When the pressure-release mechanism is released, the ring shall not rotate more than 30 degrees below the original horizontal position.

(*iv*) After release and with the load no longer applied, the ring shall return automatically and instantly to the original position.

2. The nets shall be of white cord suspended from the rings and constructed in order that they check the ball momentarily as it passes through the basket. They shall be not less than 0.40m (40cm) and not more than 0.45m (45cm) in length.

C. Ball – Material, Size and Weight

1. The ball shall be spherical and of an approved orange shade in colour.

2. It shall be made with an outer surface of leather, rubber or synthetic material.

3. It shall be not less than 0.749m (74.9cm) and not more than 0.780m (78cm) in circumference.

4. It shall weigh not less than 567gr nor more than 650gr.

5. It shall be inflated to an air pressure such that when it is dropped onto the playing surface from a height of about 1.80m measured from the bottom of the ball, it will rebound to a height, measured to the top of the ball, of not less than about 1.20m nor more than about 1.40m.

6. The width of the seams and/or channels of the ball shall not exceed 0.00635m (6.35mm).

7. The home team shall provide at least 2 used balls that meet the above specifications. The Referee shall be the sole judge of the legality of the balls.

As the game ball, should the above balls prove to be inadequate, he may select either a ball provided by the visiting team or one of the balls used by either team for the warm-up.

D. Technical Equipment

The following technical equipment shall be provided by the home team and shall be at the disposal of the officials and their assistants:

1. A Game Clock and a Stop-watch

(*a*) The Timekeeper shall be provided with a game clock and a stop-watch.

(*b*) The game clock shall be used for timing periods of play and the intervals between them and it shall be placed so that it is clearly visible to everyone involved with the game.

(*c*) The stop-watch shall be used for timing time-outs.

(*d*) If the main game clock is placed above the centre of the playing floor, there shall be a duplicate at each end of the playing floor at floor level. Each duplicate shall indicate both the score and the remaining time. These duplicates must be clearly visible to everyone involved with the game.

2. A 30-second device

(*a*) The device shall be operated by the 30-second operator for the administration of the 30-second Rule.

(*b*) The device shall be automatic, digital count-down type, indicating the time in seconds.

(*c*) It shall be constructed in such a way that:

1. When neither team is in control of the ball there is no display on the device.

2. When stopped for an out-of-bounds decision and no re-setting of the device is to take place, the device can subsequently be restarted from that time.

3. Signals

There shall be equipment for at least two separate signals with distinctly different and very loud sound as provided for in these Rules.

(*a*) One for the timekeeper (which shall sound automatically to indicate the end of a period, half and game) and the same one for the scorer (which shall be sounded manually only during a dead ball period to draw the attention of the officials that a time-out, a substitution, etc. has been requested), and

(*b*) One for the 30-second device operator which shall sound automatically to indicate the end of the 30-second period.

4. Scoreboard

There shall be a scoreboard clearly visible to everyone involved with the game, including spectators.

5. Scoresheet

The official scoresheet shall be the one approved by the International Basketball Federation and shall be filled in by the scorer before and during the game as provided for in these Rules.

6. Player Foul Markers

These shall be at the disposal of the scorer as follows:

(*a*) The markers shall be white with numbers of a minimum size of 0.20m (20cm) in length and 0.10m (10cm) in width.

(*b*) For games played in 2 × 20 minutes, they shall be numbered 1 to 5 (from 1 to 4 in black, with the number 5 in red).

(*c*) For games played in 4 × 12 minutes, they shall be numbered 1 to 6 (from 1 to 5 in black, with the number 6 in red).

7. Team Foul Markers

Two team foul markers shall be provided for the scorer as follows:

    (*a*) They shall be red, and

    (*b*) They shall be 0.20m (20cm) in width, 0.35m (35cm) in height, preferably triangular in shape and constructed in such a way that when positioned on the scorer's table they are clearly visible to everyone involved in the game.

Note: Electrical or electronic devices may be used, but they shall meet the specifications outlined above.

8. Team Fouls Indicator

There shall be a suitable device to indicate the number of team fouls. The device shall stop at the number of team fouls (8 for games of 2×20 minutes and 5 for games of 4×12 minutes) to indicate that a team has reached the Penalty status (Art. 58).

For the equipment to be used in Official Competitions of FIBA (*see* Official Game Procedures, Section E).

RULE 3

Officials and their Duties

Article 5. Officials and their Assistants

1. The officials shall be a Referee and an Umpire, who shall be assisted by a timekeeper, a scorer, an assistant scorer and a 30-second operator.

2. A technical commissioner may also be present. His duty during the game is primarily to supervise the work of the table officials and to assist the Referee and Umpire in the smooth functioning of the game.

3. The officials and their assistants shall conduct the game in accordance with the Rules and the official FIBA interpretations of the Rules as determined by the FIBA World Technical Commission.

4. It cannot be too strongly emphasised that the Referee and the Umpire of a given game should not be connected in any way with either of the organisations represented on the court.

5. The officials, their assistants or the technical commissioner have no authority to agree to changes to the Rules.

6. The uniform of the Referee and Umpire shall be:

    (*a*) grey shirt,

    (*b*) Long black trousers, and

    (*c*) black basketball shoes and black socks.

Article 6. Referee: Powers

1. The Referee shall inspect and approve all equipment to be used during the game.

2. He shall designate the official timepiece and recognise the time-keeper, the scorer, the assistant scorer and the 30-second operator.

3. He shall not permit any player to wear objects which are danger-ous to other players (*see* Art. 13.6).

4. He shall administer a jump ball at the centre circle to start the game.

5. If the officials disagree on whether or not a goal shall count, he shall make the final decision.

6. He shall have the power to stop a game when conditions warrant it. He shall also have the power to determine that a team shall forfeit the game if it refuses to play after being instructed to do so or if the team, by its actions, prevents the game from being played.

7. At the end of each half and of each extra period or at any time he feels it is necessary, he shall carefully examine the scoresheet, approve the score and confirm the time that remains to be played.

8. After any consultation with the technical commissioner and/or the table officials, he shall always make the final decision.

9. The Referee shall have the power to make decisions on any point not specifically covered by the rules.

Article 7. Officials: Time and Place for Decisions

1. The officials shall have powers to make decisions for infractions of the Rules committed either within or outside the boundary lines.

2. These powers shall start when they arrive on the court, which shall be twenty minutes before the game is scheduled to begin.

The Referee's approval and signing of the scoresheet at the end of the game terminates the connection of the officials with the game.

3. Penalties for fouls committed during intervals of play shall be administered as described in the appropriate Articles.

4. If, during the period between the end of playing time and the signing of the scoresheet, there is any unsportsmanlike behaviour by players, coaches, assistant coaches or team followers, the Referee must record on the scoresheet that an incident has occurred and ensure that a detailed report is submitted to the responsible authority which shall deal with the matter with appropriate severity.

5. Neither official shall have the authority to set aside or question the decisions made by the other within the limits of his respective duties as outlined in these Rules.

Comments

If, at the end of a game, there are doubts regarding the exact termination of playing time (example: the timekeeper fails to stop the game clock on a violation, a held ball or a foul), the officials shall:

1. Immediately consult each other to determine the exact time that remained to be played when:

(*a*) The ball was released on an attempt for a field goal, or

(*b*) The violation, the held ball or the foul occurred.

2. If further consultation proves necessary, the Referee should seek advice from the technical commissioner, if he is present, as well as from the table officials.

It is the Referee who shall make the final decision.

3. If an extra period is required as a result of free throw(s) taken following a foul committed simultaneously with or just prior to the end of the second half or an extra period, then all fouls that are committed after the signal to end playing time, but prior to the completion of the free throw(s), shall be considered to have occurred during an interval of play and penalised in accordance with the appropriate Article.

4. Should a protest be filed by one of the teams, the Referee shall immediately report the incident to the appropriate authority.

Article 8. Officials: Duties when an Infraction is Committed

Infraction: any foul or violation committed by a player or a coach.

1. When a violation is committed:

(*a*) The official shall blow his whistle and simultaneously give the appropriate signal to stop the clock, causing the ball to become dead.

(*b*) The above is followed by the appropriate sequence of signals as established in the 'Referee's Manual'.

(*c*) The ball is then awarded to an opponent for a throw-in according to Art. 31.

2. When a personal foul is committed:

(*a*) The official shall blow his whistle and simultaneously give the appropriate signal to stop the clock, causing the ball to become dead.

(*b*) He shall then indicate to the offender that a foul has been committed.

The offending player is required to acknowledge this by raising his hand in the air only if requested to do so by the official.

(*c*) The official shall then follow the procedure for reporting a foul to the scorer's table as established in the 'Referee's Manual'.

(*d*) When the foul has been acknowledged by the scorer, inscribed on the scoresheet and the foul marker raised, the officials shall resume the game according to the appropriate Article(s).

3. For an Unsportsmanlike, Disqualifying, Technical or Double foul, the official shall immediately give the appropriate signal for the type of foul.

Comments

1. The officials shall not blow their whistles after a successful free throw or a successful field goal.

2. After each foul or jump ball decision, the officials shall always exchange their positions on the court.

3. For all international games, if verbal communication is necessary to make a decision clear, it shall be conducted in English.

Article 9. Scorer and Assistant Scorer: Duties

A. 1. The scorer shall keep a record of the names and numbers of players who are to start the game and of all substitutes who enter the game.

When there is an infraction of the Rules pertaining to a submission of a line-up, substitutions or numbers of players, he shall notify the nearer official as soon as possible after the infraction is discovered.

2. He shall keep a chronological running summary of points scored and shall record the field goals and the free throws made.

3. He shall record the personal and technical fouls called on each player and shall notify the Referee immediately when the 5th foul (for games of 2 × 20 minutes) or the 6th foul (for games of 4 × 12 minutes) is called on any player.

Similarly, he shall record the technical fouls called on each coach and shall notify the Referee immediately when, according to Art. 53, Penalty B., a coach must leave the game.

4. He shall record the time-outs charged to each team and shall notify the coach through an official when he has taken the second time-out (for games of 2 × 20 minutes) or third time-out (for games of 4 × 12 minutes) in each half.

5. He shall signal to the officials when the timekeeper indicates to him that 50 seconds have elapsed from the start of the time-out.

6. He shall indicate the number of fouls committed by each player. Every time a player commits a foul, he shall raise, in a manner visible to both coaches, the marker with the number corresponding to the number of fouls committed by that player.

7. He shall use the team foul markers in the following manner:

(a) For games played in 2 × 20 minutes:
The moment the ball goes into play following the seventh (7th) player foul by a team in a half, a red marker shall be positioned on the scorer's table at the end nearer the bench of the team that has committed the seventh player foul.

(b) For games played in 4 × 12 minutes:
The moment the ball goes into play following the fourth (4th) player foul by a team in a period, a red marker shall be positioned on the scorer's table at the end nearer the bench of the team that has committed the fourth player foul.

8. He shall effect substitutions according to Art. 32.

9. The sounding of the scorer's signal does not stop the clock or the game, nor does it cause the ball to become dead.

The scorer should be careful to sound his signal only when the ball is dead and the game clock is stopped, and before the ball again goes into play.

B. The assistant scorer shall operate the scoreboard. His duties shall not counteract or conflict with those of the other table officials.

Article 10. Timekeeper: Duties

1. The timekeeper shall keep a record of playing time and time of stoppage as provided in these Rules.

2. The timekeeper shall note when each half is to start and shall notify the Referee more than three minutes before this time so that he may notify the teams, or cause them to be notified.

3. For a charged time-out, the timekeeper shall start a stop-watch and shall direct the scorer to signal when 50 seconds have elapsed after the start of the time-out.

4. The timekeeper shall indicate with a very loud signal the expiration of playing time in each half or a period.

5. If the timekeeper's signal fails to sound or it is not heard, the timekeeper shall use every possible means at his disposal to notify the Referee immediately.

6. The signal of the timekeeper causes the ball to become dead and the game clock to be stopped.

Article 11. 30-second Operator: Duties

The 30-second operator shall operate the 30-second device (clock) as provided in Art. 18 of these Rules.

RULE 4

Players, Substitutes and Coaches

Article 12. Teams

Each team shall consist of:

(*i*) Not more than ten (10) team members eligible to play, for games played in 2 × 20 minutes.

(*ii*) Not more than twelve (12) team members eligible to play, for games played in 4 × 12 minutes or for tournaments in which a team has to play more than three (3) games.

(*iii*) A coach and, if a team wishes, an assistant coach.

(*iv*) A captain, who shall be one of the team members eligible to play.

Article 13. Players and Substitutes

1. Five (5) players from each team shall be on the court during playing time and may be substituted in accordance with the provisions contained in these Rules.

2. A member of the team is a player when he is on the court and is entitled to play. Otherwise he is a substitute.

3. A substitute becomes a player when the official beckons him to enter the court and a player becomes a substitute when the official beckons that player's replacement onto the playing court.

4. The uniform of the players shall consist of:

(a) Shirts of the same single solid colour, front and back (striped shirts are not permitted).

1. Side inserts are permitted.

2. Side inserts shall be centred vertically below the armpit and shall be a maximum of 0.03m (3cm) on either side of the seam for a total of 0.06m (6cm) in width.

3. A trim around the neck or arm openings shall be no more than 0.03m (3cm) in width.

Male players must place (tuck) their shirts inside their playing shorts during a game.

(b) T-shirts may be worn under the shirts provided they are of the same single colour as the shirt.

(c) Shorts of the same single solid colour, front and back, but not necessarily the same colour as the shirts.

1. A trim is permitted.

2. A trim down the sides shall be a maximum of 0.03m (3cm) on either side of the seam for a total of 0.06m (6cm) in width.

3. A trim around the leg openings shall be no more than 0.03m (3cm) in width.

(d) Undergarments that extend below the shorts may be worn provided they are of the same single colour as the shorts.

5. Each player shall be numbered on the front and back of his shirt with plain numbers of a solid colour contrasting with the colour of the shirt.

The numbers shall be clearly visible and:

(a) Those on the back shall be at least 0.20m (20cm) high.

(b) Those on the front shall be at least 0.10m (10cm) high.

(c) The numbers shall be not less than 0.02m (2cm) wide.

(d) Teams shall use numbers from 4 to 15.

(e) Players on the same team shall not wear duplicate numbers.

Note: If a player changes his number during the game, he shall report the change to the scorer and to the Referee.

6. The Referee shall not permit any player to wear equipment that is dangerous to other players.

(*a*) The following are not permitted:

1. Finger, hand, wrist, elbow or forearm guards, casts or braces made of leather, plastic, pliable (soft) plastic, metal or any other hard substance, even if it is covered by soft padding.

2. Equipment that could cut or cause abrasions.

3. Head decorations, headwear and jewellery.

(*b*) The following are permitted:

(*i*) Shoulder, upper arm, thigh or lower leg protective equipment if the material is padded so as not to create a danger for other players.

(*ii*) Knee braces if they are properly covered.

(*iii*) Protector for a broken nose, even if it is made of hard material.

(*iv*) Eyeglasses, if they do not create a danger for other players.

(*v*) Headbands, maximum 0.05m (5cm) in width, made of non-abrasive, single colour cloth, pliable plastic or rubber.

7. All equipment used by players must be appropriate for basketball. Any equipment that is designed to increase a player's height or reach or in any other way give an unfair advantage, shall not be permitted.

8. Any other equipment not specifically mentioned in these Rules must first receive the approval of the FIBA World Technical Commission.

Comments

1. Provisions contained in this Article regarding size, colour and placement of numbers to be worn by team members eligible to play must be strictly respected. Numbers must be clearly visible and easily identifiable by officials and scorer.

2. Advertising, where permitted, shall not interfere with the visibility of the numbers on the front and back of shirts. Under no circumstances may the numbers on the shirts be reduced in size.

3. Teams must have a minimum of two sets of shirts, one light (preferably white) and the other dark in colour.

4. For all games:

(*a*) The first team named in the programme (home team) shall wear light-coloured shirts (preferably white), and

(*b*) The second team named in the programme (visitors) shall wear dark-coloured shirts.

(*c*) However, if the two teams involved agree, they may interchange the colours of the shirts.

5. For main FIBA competitions, players of the same team shall:

(*a*) Wear shoes which are all of the same colour or colours.

(*b*) Wear socks which are all of the same colour or colours.

Article 14. Captain: Duties and Powers

1. When necessary, the captain shall be the representative of his

team on the court. He may address an official to obtain essential information. This shall be done in a courteous manner and only when the ball is dead and the clock is stopped.

2. Before leaving the playing court for any valid reason, the captain shall inform the Referee of the number of the player who will replace him as captain during his absence.

Article 15. Coaches: Duties and Powers

1. At least 20 minutes before the game is scheduled to begin, each coach shall give the scorer a written list of the names and numbers of the team members who are to play in the game, as well as the names of the captain of the team, the coach and the assistant coach.

2. At least 10 minutes before the game, both coaches shall confirm their agreement with the names and numbers of their team members and the names of the coaches inscribed by signing the scoresheet. At the same time, they shall indicate the five players who are to start the game. The coach of Team 'A' will be the first to provide this information.

3. Only the coach or the assistant coach shall make the request for charged time-outs.

4. When a coach or assistant coach requires a substitution to be effected, the substitute must report to the scorer to make the request and must be ready to play immediately.

5. If there is an assistant coach his name must be inscribed on the scoresheet before the beginning of the game (his signature is not necessary). He shall assume the responsibilities of the coach if, for any reason, the coach is unable to continue.

6. The team captain may act as coach if the coach is unable to continue and there is no assistant coach inscribed on the scoresheet (or the latter is unable to continue). If the captain must leave the playing court for any valid reason, he may continue to act as coach. However, if he must leave following a disqualifying foul, or if he is unable to act as coach because of injury, his substitute as captain shall replace him as coach.

7. Only the coach whose name is inscribed on the scoresheet, is permitted to remain standing during the game.

Comments

1. A player who has been designated by the coach to start the game may be replaced in the event of an injury, provided that the Referee is satisfied that the injury is genuine.

2. Substitutes arriving late may play, provided that the coach had included them in the list of team members given to the scorer prior to the start of the game.

3. The coach (or the assistant coach) is the only representative of the team who may communicate with the table officials during the game. He may do so whenever the clock is stopped, the ball is dead and it is necessary to seek information concerning the score, time, scoreboard or number of fouls.

His contact with the table officials must be calm and courteous at all times. He must not interfere with the normal progress of the game.

RULE 5

Timing Regulations

Article 16. Playing Time
The game shall consist of:
1. Two (2) halves of twenty (20) minutes each, or
2. Four (4) periods (quarters) of twelve (12) minutes each with intervals of two (2) minutes between the first and second period and between the third and fourth period.
3. The half-time interval shall be either ten (10) or fifteen (15) minutes and:
   (*a*) The local organisers shall decide, but the decision must be made known to all concerned at the latest one day before the competition (tournament) is due to start.
   (*b*) For single games the decision must be made known before the beginning of the game.
4. The duration of a game shall be decided by the appropriate division of FIBA:
   (*a*) For world competitions: the Central Board of FIBA.
   (*b*) For zone or continental competitions: the zone or the continental highest authority.
   (*c*) For national or local competitions: the national or local organisation.

Article 17. Game Clock Operations
1. The game clock shall be started when:
   (*a*) During a jump ball, the ball is legally tapped by a player(s) after having reached its highest point on a toss.
   (*b*) After an unsuccessful free throw and the ball is to continue in play, the ball touches a player on the court.
   (*c*) After a throw-in from out-of-bounds, the ball touches a player on the court.

2. The game clock shall be stopped when:

(*a*) Time expires at the end of a half or a period.

(*b*) An official blows his whistle.

(*c*) The 30-second signal is sounded.

(*d*) A field goal is scored against a team which has requested a charged time-out according to Art. 19 B. 3.

Article 18. Thirty-second Rule

1. When a player gains control of a live ball on the court, a shot for goal must be attempted by his team within 30 seconds.

2. Failure of the team in control of the ball to shoot for goal within 30 seconds will be indicated by the sounding of the 30-second signal.

An infraction of this Article is a violation.

3. The 30-second device shall be operated as follows:

(*a*) The 30-second device shall be started as soon as a player gains control of a live ball on the court.

(*b*) The device shall be stopped as soon as team control is ended, (see Art. 28).

(*c*) The device shall be re-set to 30 seconds and re-started only when a new 30-second period begins as player control is next established on the court.

(*i*) If the game is stopped because of an action(s) by an opponent(s) of the team in control of the ball, a new 30-second period shall be awarded to the team in control of the ball.

(*ii*) The mere touching of the ball by an opponent does not start a new 30-second period if the same team remains in control of the ball.

(*d*) The 30-second device shall be stopped but not re-set when:

(*i*) The ball has gone out-of-bounds and the throw-in is to be taken by a player from the same team that was previously in control of the ball.

(*ii*) The officials have suspended play to protect an injured player of the team in control of the ball.

(*iii*) The game is stopped because of an action(s) by the team in control of the ball.

The 30-second operator shall re-start the device from the time it was stopped as soon as a player of the same team gains control of the ball on the court after the throw-in.

(*e*) For any other reason(s), a new 30-second period shall be awarded to the team in control of the ball, unless, in the judgement of the officials, the opponents have been placed at a disadvantage, in which case the officials shall not award a new 30-second period to the team in control of the ball.

Comments

If the 30-second device sounds in error while the ball is in the air on a shot for goal:

1. The field goal shall count if the ball enters the basket without being touched by a player of either team.

2. The ball becomes dead and a jump ball shall be called if the ball is legally touched by a player of either team, or it is clear that the shot will not be successful.

3. All restrictions related to Art. 44 will apply if the ball has the opportunity to enter the basket and it is touched before it contacts the ring.

Article 19. Charged Time-out

A. Description:

A time-out of one (1) minute's duration shall be charged to a team under the following provisions:

1. For games played in 2 × 20 minutes, two (2) charged time-outs may be granted to each team during each half of playing time and one (1) charged time-out for each extra period.

2. For games played in 4 × 12 minutes, three (3) charged time-outs may be granted to each team during each half (two periods) of playing time and one (1) charged time-out for each extra period.

3. If the team responsible for the time-out is ready to play before the end of the charged time-out, the Referee shall resume the game as soon as possible.

4. During the time-out, the players are permitted to leave the playing court and sit on the team bench.

B. Procedure:

1. A coach or assistant coach has the right to request a charged time-out. He shall do so by going in person to the scorer and asking clearly for a 'time-out', making the proper conventional sign with his hands.

2. The scorer shall indicate to the officials that a request for a charged time-out has been made by sounding his signal as soon as the ball is dead and the game clock is stopped.

(*a*) The request by the scorer to the official must be made before the ball again goes into play and,

(*b*) If the official is reporting a foul, after the official has terminated his communication with the scorer's table.

3. A coach or assistant coach may also be granted a charged time-out:

(*a*) If a field goal is scored by his opponents after a request from him for a time-out, and

(*b*) Provided that such request was made before the ball left the hand(s) of the shooter.

In this case, the timekeeper shall immediately stop the game clock. The scorer shall then sound his signal and indicate to the officials that a charged time-out has been requested.

C. Restrictions:

1. A charged time-out is not permitted from the moment the ball goes into play for the first or only free throw, until the ball becomes dead again after a clock running phase of the game, except:

(*a*) When a foul occurs between free throws.

In this case the free throws will be completed and the time-out taken before the ball goes into play for the new foul penalty.

(*b*) When a foul occurs before the ball goes into play following the last free throw.

In this case the time-out will be taken before the ball goes into play for the new foul penalty.

(*c*) A violation is called before the ball goes into play following the last free throw, the penalty for which is a jump ball or a throw-in.

2. No time-out is charged if:

(*a*) An injured player is ready to play immediately (approximately 15 seconds) without receiving treatment.

(*b*) An injured player is substituted as soon as possible.

(*c*) A player who has committed his 5th foul (6th foul in a game played in 4 × 12 minutes) or has been disqualified is replaced within 30 seconds.

(*d*) An official permits a delay.

3. Unused time-outs may not be carried over to the next half or extra period.

Comments

The following points, related to the administration of charged time-outs, are brought to the attention of coaches and scorers:

1. The time-out is charged to the coach of the team who was first to make a request, unless the time-out is granted following a field goal scored by the opponents and without a foul being called.

2. A team's request for a charged time-out may be withdrawn only before the scorer signals to the officials that a request for a charged time-out has been made.

Article 20. Injury to Players or Officials

A. Injury to a Player
1. In case of injury to players, the officials may stop the game.
2. If the ball is alive when an injury occurs, the officials shall withhold their whistles until the play has been completed, that is, the team in control of the ball has shot for goal, lost control of the ball, has withheld the ball from play, or the ball has become dead.

However, when necessary to protect an injured player, the officials may suspend play immediately.

3. (*a*) If the injured player cannot continue to play immediately (approximately 15 seconds) or, if he receives treatment, he must be substituted within one (1) minute or as soon as possible if the injury prevents his substitution within one (1) minute.

(*b*) However, an injured player who has received treatment or recovers within one (1) minute may remain in the game, but:

(*i*) His team shall be charged with a time-out, except in the case of the team having to continue with fewer than 5 players.

(*ii*) The team shall not receive the full 60 seconds as for a 'normal' time-out and the game shall be restarted as soon as possible.

4. An injured player cannot remain in the game and must be substituted if:

(*a*) His injury is such that he cannot continue to play within one (1) minute.

(*b*) His team does not have any charged time-outs left, except in the case of the team having to continue with fewer than 5 players.

5. If free throws have been awarded to the injured player, they must be attempted by his substitute. The substitute for the injured player may not be substituted until the next substitution opportunity for his team.

6. During the game, the official shall order any player who is bleeding or has an open wound, to leave the playing court and cause this player to be substituted. The player may return to the court only after the bleeding has stopped and the area affected or the open wound has been completely and securely covered.

B. Injury to an Official
If an official is injured or for any other reason cannot continue to perform his duties within 10 minutes of the incident, the game shall be resumed and the other official will officiate alone until the end of the game, unless there is the possibility of replacing the injured official by a qualified substitute official.

Article 21. Tied Score and Extra Periods
1. If the score is tied at the expiration of the second half (game played

in 2 × 20 minutes) or the fourth period (game played in 4 × 12 minutes), the game shall be continued with an extra period of five (5) minutes or with as many such periods of 5 minutes as are necessary to break the tie.

2. Before the first extra period the teams shall toss a coin to determine the basket at which they will shoot.

3. They shall change baskets at the beginning of each additional extra period.

4. An interval of 2 minutes shall be allowed before each extra period.

5. Each extra period shall be started by a jump ball at the centre circle.

RULE 6

Playing Regulations

Article 22. Decision of a Game
A game shall be decided by the scoring of the greater number of points during the playing time.

Article 23. Beginning of the Game
1. The game cannot begin if one of the teams is not on the court with five (5) players ready to play.

2. The game shall be started by a jump ball at the centre circle.

3. The game officially begins when the Referee, with the ball, steps into the centre circle to administer the jump ball.

4. Procedures 2 and 3 above shall be followed at the beginning of each period.

5. Teams shall change baskets for the second half of all games.

Article 24. Status of the Ball
1. The ball is in play (goes into play) when:

(*a*) An official with the ball enters the circle to administer a jump ball.

(*b*) An official enters the free throw lane with or without the ball to administer a free throw.

(*c*) The ball is at the disposal of a player for a throw-in from out-of-bounds.

2. The ball becomes alive when:

(*a*) During a jump ball, it is legally tapped by a jumper(s) after having reached its highest point.

(*b*) An official places it at the disposal of a free throw shooter.

(*c*) After a throw-in from out-of-bounds, it touches a player on the court.

3. The ball becomes dead when:

(*a*) Any goal is legally made.

(*b*) An official's whistle sounds while the ball is alive or in play.

(*c*) It is apparent that the ball will not go into the basket on a free throw for:

(*i*) A free throw which is to be followed by another free throw(s).

(*ii*) A free throw which is to be followed by a further penalty.

(*d*) The 30-second operator's signal is sounded while the ball is alive. (*Exception:* see Art. 18, Comments.)

(*e*) Time expires for a half or a period.

(*f*) The ball which is already in flight on a shot for goal is legally touched by a player of either team after time has expired for a half or a period, or after a foul has been called.

The provisions of Articles 33 and 44 still apply.

Exceptions:

The ball does not become dead and the field goal counts if it is made, when:

1. The ball is in flight on a free throw or a shot for a field goal when b, d or e (above) occurs.

2. An opponent commits a foul while the ball is still in the control of a player who is in the act of shooting for goal and who finishes his shot with a continuous motion which started before the foul occurred (*see* Art. 29).

This (exception 2 above) does not apply at the end of a half or a period or after the 30-second signal has sounded.

Article 25. Location of a Player and of an Official

1. The location of a player is determined by where he is touching the floor. While he is in the air from a leap, he retains the same status as where he last touched the floor. This includes the boundary lines, the centre line, the 3-point line, the free throw line and the lines delimiting the free throw lanes. (*Exception:* see Art. 31 D.)

2. The location of an official is determined in the same manner as that of a player.

When the ball touches an official, it is the same as touching the floor at the official's location.

Article 26. Jump Ball

1. A jump ball takes place when an official tosses the ball between two opposing players.

2. For a jump ball to be legal, the ball must be tapped with the hand(s) by one or both jumpers.

3. A jump ball shall take place at the nearest circle:

(*a*) When held ball is called, that is, when one or more players of opposing teams have one or both hands firmly on the ball so that neither player could gain possession without undue roughness.

If there are more than two players involved, the jump ball shall be between two opposing players of approximately the same height as designated by the official.

(*b*) If the ball goes out-of-bounds and:

1. It was last touched simultaneously by two opponents, or
2. The official is in doubt as to who last touched the ball, or
3. If the officials disagree,

the jump ball shall be between the two players involved.

(*c*) Whenever a live ball lodges on the basket support:
the jump ball shall be between any two opponents.

(*d*) Whenever penalties of the same gravity are cancelled according to Art. 59 and the result is a jump ball:
the jump ball shall be between any two opponents.

(*e*) Whenever the ball accidentally enters the basket from below:
the jump ball shall be between any two opponents.

4. The following conditions shall apply:

(*a*) During a jump ball the two jumpers shall stand with their feet inside that half of the circle which is nearer to their own baskets, with one foot near the centre of the line that is between them.

(*b*) The official shall then toss the ball upward (vertically) between the jumpers to a height greater than either of them can reach by jumping and such that it will drop between them.

(*c*) The ball must be legally tapped by one or both of the jumpers after it reaches its highest point.

(*d*) Neither jumper shall leave his position until the ball has been legally tapped.

(*e*) Neither jumper may catch the ball or touch it more than twice until it has touched one of the eight non-jumpers, the floor, the basket or the backboard.

Under this provision four taps are possible, two by each jumper.

(*f*) The other players shall remain outside the circle until the ball has been tapped.

(*g*) If the ball is not tapped by one or both of the jumpers or if it touches the floor without being tapped by at least one of the jumpers, the jump ball shall be retaken.

(*h*) Team mates may not occupy adjacent positions around the circle if an opponent desires one of the positions.

An infraction of conditions a, c, d, e and f is a violation.

Article 27. How the Ball is Played

1. In basketball, the ball is played with the hands. It is a violation to run with the ball, kick it or strike it with the fist.

2. Kicking the ball means striking it or blocking it with the knee, any part of the leg below the knee, or the foot.

Such action is a violation only when it is done deliberately.

3. To accidentally contact or touch the ball with the foot or leg is not a violation.

Article 28. Control of the Ball

1. A player is in control when:

(*a*) He is holding or dribbling a live ball.

(*b*) The ball is at his disposal for a throw-in during an out-of-bounds situation.

2. A team is in control when:

(*a*) A player of that team is in control.

(*b*) The ball is being passed between team mates.

3. Team control continues until:

(*a*) An opponent secures control.

(*b*) The ball becomes dead.

(*c*) The ball is no longer in contact with the hand(s) of the shooter on a shot for goal.

Article 29. Player in the Act of Shooting

Throw: to hold the ball in one or both hands and then project it through the air towards the basket.

Dunk: to force or attempt to force the ball downwards into the basket with one or both hands.

Tap: to strike the ball with the hand or hands towards the basket.

1. A player is in the act of shooting when, in the judgement of an official, he has started an attempt to score by throwing, dunking or tapping the ball towards the opponents' basket and the attempt continues until the ball has left the player's hand(s).

2. In the case of an airborne shooter, the act of shooting continues until the attempt is completed (the ball has left the hand(s) of the shooter) and both the player's feet return to the floor.

Team control, however, ends when the ball is released.

3. For a foul to be considered to have been committed on a player in the act of shooting, the foul must occur, in the judgement of the Official, after a player has started the continuous movement of his arm(s) in his attempt to shoot for goal.

Continuous movement:

(*a*) Begins when the ball comes to rest in the hand(s) of the player and the shooting motion, usually upward, has started.

(*b*) May include arm(s) and/or body movement used by the player in his attempt to shoot for goal.

If the criteria regarding continuous movement are as stated above, then the player is considered to be in the act of shooting.

Note: There is no relationship between the number of steps taken and the act of shooting.

4. The goal shall count if made, even if the ball has left the player's hand after the whistle has blown.

This provision (number 4) does not apply:

(*a*) At the end of a period (see Art. 33).

(*b*) When the 30-second signal sounds (see Art. 18).

5. The goal does not count if an entirely new effort (movement) is made after the whistle has blown.

6. A player who taps the ball towards the basket directly from a jump ball is not considered to be in the act of shooting.

Penalty

See Art. 47, Penalty 2.

Article 30. Goal – When Made and its Value

1. A goal is made when a live ball enters the basket from above and remains within or passes through.

2. A goal from the field is credited to the team attacking the basket into which the ball is thrown as follows:

(*a*) A goal from a free throw counts one (1) point.

(*b*) A goal from the field counts two (2) points.

(*c*) A goal from the 3-point field goal area counts three (3) points.

3. If a team scores a field goal accidentally in its own basket, the points shall be recorded as scored by the Captain of the opposing team.

4. If a team deliberately scores a field goal in its own basket, it is an infraction of the spirit of these Rules, and:

(*a*) No points shall be scored.

(*b*) A technical foul shall be charged to the coach of the team who committed the infraction.

(*c*) The game shall resume according to the appropriate Article.

5. If a player deliberately causes the ball to enter the basket from below, it is a violation.

Comment

A three (3) point field goal attempt changes its status and becomes a two

(2) point field goal after the ball has touched the ring and is legally touched by an offensive or a defensive player before it enters the basket.

Article 31. Throw-in

A. Following a field goal or a successful last free throw:

1. Any opponent of the team credited with the score shall be entitled to throw the ball in from any point out-of-bounds on or behind the endline at the end of the court where the goal was made.

This is also applicable after an official hands the ball to a player or places it at his disposal after a time-out or after any stoppage of play.

2. He may pass it to a team-mate on or behind the endline, but the five (5) second count (see C3. below) starts the instant the ball is at the disposal of the first player out-of-bounds.

3. The official should not handle the ball unless by doing so the game can be resumed more quickly.

4. Opponents of the player making the throw-in shall not touch the ball after it passes through the basket.

Allowances may be made for touching the ball accidentally or instinctively, but if the game is delayed by interfering with the ball, it is a technical foul.

Exception:
Following a free throw(s) for a technical or disqualifying foul charged against a coach and/or unsportsmanlike or disqualifying foul committed by a player, the ball shall be thrown in from out-of-bounds at mid-court, opposite the scorer's table, whether or not the last free throw was successful.

B. Following an infraction or for any stoppage of play and the game is to be resumed by a throw-in (except after a valid free throw or field goal):

1. The player who is to throw the ball in, shall stand out-of-bounds as designated by the official, at the place nearest the point of the infraction or where the play was stopped, except directly behind the backboard. (*Exception*: see Comment 1.)

2. An official must hand the ball directly to, or place it at the disposal of, the player making the throw-in.

3. The player who is to make the throw-in shall not take and complete more than one normal step laterally (approximately 1 metre) and in more than one direction from the place designated by the official before releasing the ball.

(*a*) Several small steps in one direction are permitted provided the distance covered is not more than one normal step.

(*b*) To move backwards and perpendicular to the line as far as the circumstances will allow is permitted.

C. A player making a throw-in shall not violate the following provisions:

1. Touch the ball in the court before it has touched another player.
2. Step on the court while releasing the ball.
3. Consume more than five (5) seconds before releasing the ball.
4. Throw the ball over the backboard to another player on the court.
5. Cause the ball to touch out-of-bounds, or to lodge on the basket support or to enter the basket before contacting a player on the court following the release of the ball for the throw-in.

D. Any other player may not have any part of his body over the boundary line before the ball has been thrown across the line.

An infraction of B3, C and D is a violation.

Penalty
The ball is awarded to the opponents for a throw-in at the point of the original throw-in.

Comments
1. If the ball enters the basket but the field goal or the free throw is not valid, then the subsequent throw-in shall be made from out-of-bounds at the free throw line extended.
2. An official may toss the ball to the player making the throw-in provided that:
(*a*) The official is not more than 3 or 4 metres from the player who is to make the throw-in.
(*b*) The player making the throw-in is at the correct place as indicated by the official.
(*c*) The team about to gain possession of the ball does not gain an advantage.
3. When the margin (area) free of obstructions of the out-of-bounds territory is less than two (2) metres, no player of either team shall be within one (1) metre of the player making the throw-in.

Article 32. Substitutions
1. Before entering the court, a substitute shall report to the scorer and must be ready to play immediately.
2. The substitute shall remain outside the boundary line until the official beckons him onto the court.
3. The scorer shall indicate that a request for a substitution has been made by sounding his signal as soon as:

(*a*) The ball becomes dead,

(*b*) The game clock is stopped, and

(*c*) The official has terminated his communication with the scorer's table when that official is reporting a foul.

The request by the Scorer to the Official must be made before the ball again goes into play.

4. Substitutions shall be completed as quickly as possible.

If, in the opinion of the official, there is an unreasonable delay, a time-out shall be charged against the offending team.

5. Substitutions are subject to the following conditions:

(*a*) Following a violation, only the team which is to make the throw-in may substitute.

In such a situation, the opponents may also substitute, provided the team making the throw-in has made a substitution.

(*b*) Only the player who was attempting a free throw(s) may be substituted provided that:

(*i*) Such substitution was requested before the ball went into play for the first or only free throw.

(*ii*) The last or only free throw was successful or

after the last or only free throw, the ball becomes and remains dead as a result of further foul penalties.

In this case (b) the opponents may then be granted one substitution provided the request was made before the ball goes into play for the last or only free throw.

(*c*) No substitutions are permitted between free throws.

This condition is valid until the next substitution opportunity.

(*d*) If a foul occurs during free throws, substitutions will be permitted only after the free throws for the earlier foul have been completed and before the ball goes into play for the new foul penalty.

(*e*) A player involved in a jump ball may not be substituted by another player.

(*f*) A player who has been substituted cannot re-enter the game and a substitute who has become a player cannot leave the game until a clock-running phase of the game has occurred. (*Exception*: Art. 61 3a.)

(*g*) If a substitution is requested during a charged time-out, the substitute must report to the scorer and be beckoned by the nearest official before entering the game.

(*h*) A substitution request may be cancelled prior to the scorer's signal being sounded.

Article 33. When a Period or a Game is Terminated

1. A period, a half or a game shall terminate at the sounding of the timekeeper's signal indicating the end of playing time.

2. When a foul is committed simultaneously with or just prior to the timekeeper's signal ending any half or any period, any eventual free throw(s) as a result of the foul shall be taken.

3. If there is doubt regarding the termination of a period, a half or a game, the procedure detailed in Art. 7, Comments, shall be followed.

Article 34. Game Lost by Forfeit

A team shall lose the game by forfeit if:

1. It refuses to play after being instructed to do so by the Referee.
2. By its actions it prevents the game from being played.
3. Fifteen (15) minutes after the starting time, the team is not present or is not able to field five (5) players.

Penalty

The game is awarded to the opponents and the score shall be twenty to zero (20 to 0). Further, the forfeiting team shall receive zero (0) points in the classification.

Comment

For a two-game (home and away) total points series, the team that forfeits in the first or in the second game shall lose the series by 'Forfeit'.

Article 35. Game Lost by Default

A team shall lose a game by default if, during the game, the number of players of that team on the court is less than two.

Penalty

If the team to which the game is awarded is ahead, the score at the time of the stoppage shall stand. If the team to which the game is awarded is not ahead, the score shall be recorded as two to zero (2 to 0) in its favour. Further, the defaulting team shall receive one (1) point in the classification.

Comment

For a two-game (home and away) total points series, the team that defaults in the first or in the second game shall lose the series by 'Default'.

RULE 7

Violations

Article 36. Violations

1. A violation is an infraction of the Rules.

2. The penalty is the loss of the ball by the team that committed the violation (*Exceptions*: Art. 44 and 60).

3. The ball is awarded to the opponents for a throw-in from out-of-bounds at the closest point to the infraction, except directly behind the backboard (*Exceptions*: Art. 31-Comments 1, 44 and 60.)

Article 37. Player Out-of-Bounds and Ball Out-of-Bounds

1. A player is out-of-bounds when any part of his body is in contact with the floor or any object other than a player on, above or outside the boundary lines.

2. The ball is out-of-bounds when it touches:

(*a*) A player or any other person who is out-of-bounds.

(*b*) The floor or any object on, above or outside a boundary line.

(*c*) The supports or the back of the backboards.

3. The ball is caused to go out-of-bounds by the last player to touch it or be touched by it before it goes out-of-bounds, even if the ball goes out-of-bounds by touching something other than a player.

An infraction of this Article is a violation.

Article 38. Dribbling Rule

1. A dribble starts when a player, having gained control of the ball, throws, taps or rolls it on the floor and touches it again before it touches another player.

2. The dribble is completed the instant the player touches the ball simultaneously with both hands or permits the ball to come to rest in one or both hands.

3. There is no limit to the number of steps a player may take when the ball is not in contact with his hand.

4. The following are not dribbles:

(*a*) Successive shots for goal.

(*b*) Accidentally losing and then regaining player control (fumble) at the beginning or at the end of a dribble.

(*c*) Attempts to gain control of the ball by tapping it from the vicinity of other players striving for it.

(*d*) Tapping the ball from the control of another player.

(*e*) Blocking a pass and recovering the ball.

(*f*) Tossing the ball from hand(s) to hand(s) and permitting it to come to rest before touching the floor, provided he does not commit a travelling violation (see Art. 39).

5. A player shall not dribble a second time after his first dribble has ended, unless it is after he has lost control because of:

(*a*) A shot for goal,

(*b*) A tap by an opponent, or

(*c*) A pass or fumble that has then touched or been touched by another player.

6. A player shall not throw the ball against a backboard and touch it again before it touches another player unless, in the opinion of the official, it was a shot.

An infraction of this Article is a violation.

Comment

There is no violation of this Article unless the player has control of a live ball.

Article 39. Travel Rule

A. Definitions

1. A pivot takes place when a player who is holding a live ball steps once or more than once in any direction with the same foot, while the other foot, called the 'pivot' foot, is kept at its point of contact with the floor.

2. Travelling or progressing with the ball (inside the playing court), is the moving of one or both feet in any direction while holding the ball in excess of the limits outlined in this Article.

B. Establishing a Pivot Foot

1. A player who catches the ball with both feet on the floor may use either foot as the pivot foot. The moment one foot is lifted, the other becomes the pivot foot.

2. A player who catches the ball while moving or dribbling may stop and establish a pivot foot as follows:

(*a*) If one foot is touching the floor:

1. That foot becomes the pivot foot as soon as the other foot touches the floor.

2. The player may jump off that foot and simultaneously land on both feet, then neither foot can be the pivot foot.

(*b*) If both feet are off the floor and the player:

1. Lands simultaneously on both feet, then either foot may be the pivot foot. The moment one foot is lifted, the other becomes the pivot foot.

2. Lands on one foot followed by the other foot, then the first foot to touch the floor is the pivot foot.

3. Lands on one foot, the player may jump off that foot and simultaneously land on both feet, then neither foot can be the pivot foot.

C. Progressing with the Ball

1. After having established a pivot foot:

(*a*) On a pass or a try for a field goal, the pivot foot may be lifted but may not be returned to the floor before the ball is released from the hand(s),

(*b*) To start a dribble, the pivot foot may not be lifted before the ball is released from the hand(s).

2. After coming to a stop when neither foot is the pivot foot:

(*a*) On a pass or a try for a field goal, one or both feet may be lifted but may not be returned to the floor before the ball is released from the hand(s).

(*b*) To start a dribble, neither foot may be lifted before the ball is released from the hand(s).

An infraction of this Article is a violation.

Comment

There is no violation of this Article unless the player has control of a live ball.

Article 40. Three-second Rule

1. While his team is in control of the ball, a player shall not remain for more than three (3) consecutive seconds in the opponents' restricted area.

2. The lines bounding the restricted area are part of the restricted area and a player touching one of these lines is in the area.

3. The 3-second restriction is in force in all out-of-bounds situations.

The count shall start at the moment the player making the throw-in is out-of-bounds and the ball is at his disposal (is in play).

4. The 3-second restriction does not apply:

(*a*) While the ball is in the air during a shot for goal.

(*b*) During a rebound.

(*c*) When the ball is dead.

5. Allowance must be made for a player who, having been in the restricted area for less than 3 seconds, dribbles in to shoot for goal.

An infraction of this Article is a violation.

Comment

There is no violation of this Article unless the team has control of the ball.

Article 41. Closely Guarded Player

A closely guarded player (within 1 normal step) who is holding the ball shall pass, shoot, roll or dribble the ball within five (5) seconds.

An infraction of this Article is a violation.

Article 42. Ten-second Rule

1. A team's front court consists of the opponents' basket, the inbounds part of the backboard and that part of the court limited by the endline behind the opponents' basket, the sidelines and the edge of the centre line nearer to the opponents' basket.

The other part of the court, including the centre line and that team's basket, including the inbounds part of the backboard, is the team's back court.

2. When a player gains control of a live ball in his back court, his team must, within ten (10) seconds, cause the ball to go into its front court.

3. The ball goes into a team's front court when it touches the front court or touches a player who has part of his body in contact with the front court.

An infraction of this Article is a violation.

Article 43. Ball Returned to the Back Court

1. A player whose team is in control of the ball which is in the front court may not cause the ball to go into his back court.

2. The ball is considered to have gone into the back court when a player of the team in control of the ball is:

(*a*) The last to touch the ball before it goes into the back court, and

(*b*) A player of that same team is the first to touch the ball after

1. It has touched the back court, or

2. If this player is in contact with the back court.

3. This restriction applies to all situations in a team's front court, including throw-ins from out-of-bounds.

4. It does not apply to throw-ins from the mid-point of a sideline in accordance with the Penalties in Article 49, 50 or 53.

An infraction of this Article is a violation.

Comment
A ball that is deflected into the back court by a defensive player may be recovered by either team.

Article 44. Interference with the Ball on Offence and Defence

During playing time:
1. An offensive or a defensive player may not touch the ball when it is in its downward flight and completely above the level of the ring during a shot for a field goal.
This restriction applies only until:
(*a*) The ball touches the ring.
(*b*) It is evident that it shall not touch the ring.
2. A defensive player shall not touch the ball or the basket while the ball is within the basket.
3. An offensive or a defensive player shall not touch the basket or the backboard while the ball is in contact with the ring during a shot for a field goal.

Penalty
A. The ball becomes dead when the violation is called by the official(s).
1. If the violation is by the offence:
No point can be scored and the ball is awarded to the opponents for a throw-in from out-of-bounds at the free throw line extended.
2. If the violation is by the defence:
The shooter is awarded two (2) points, or three (3) points if the field goal was attempted from the three-point field goal area.
The game is re-started from out-of-bounds behind the endline as though the shot for goal has been successful.
3. For interference with the ball on defence or offence during a free throw see Art. 60.

B. When a shot is taken near the end of playing time (for a period or a half) and the ball has left the player's hand and is in the air before time expired:
1. If the ball enters the basket directly, the goal shall count.
2. If the ball strikes the ring, rebounds and then enters the basket, the goal shall count.
3. If, after the ball has touched the ring, a player of either team touches the ball, the basket or the backboard, it is a violation.
(*a*) If a defensive player commits the violation, the goal shall count and either 2 or 3 points shall be awarded.

(*b*) If an offensive player commits the violation, the ball becomes dead and the goal, if scored, shall not count.

4. These provisions apply until it is evident that the shot will not be successful.

RULE 8

Personal Fouls

Article 45. Fouls

1. A foul is an infraction of the Rules when personal contact with an opponent or unsportsmanlike behaviour is involved.

2. It is charged against the offender and consequently penalised according to the provisions of the relevant Article of the Rules.

Article 46. Contact

1. Basketball is, theoretically, a no-contact game. Nevertheless, it is obvious that personal contact cannot be avoided entirely when 10 players are moving with great speed over a limited space.

2. If personal contact results from a 'bona fide' attempt to play the ball (normal basketball play) and such contact does not place the opponent who has been contacted at a disadvantage, the contact may be considered incidental and need not be penalised.

3. Contact from behind is not a normal basketball play. The player behind is usually responsible for the contact because of his unfavourable position in relation to the ball and his opponent.

Comments

The basic principles listed below must be followed when making a decision on personal contact:

1. It is the duty of each player to avoid contact in any possible way.

2. Any player is entitled, within the limits of the Rules, to a normal place on the floor which is not occupied by an opponent, provided he does not cause personal contact in taking up such a position.

3. If a contact foul occurs, the foul is caused by the player responsible for the contact.

Article 47. Personal Foul

1. A personal foul is a player foul which involves contact with an opposing player, whether the ball is alive, in play, or dead.

2. A player shall not block, hold, push, charge, trip, impede the progress of an opponent by extending his arm, shoulder, hip, knee, or

foot, nor by bending his body into other than a normal position, nor shall he use any rough tactics.

Definitions:

Blocking is personal contact which impedes the progress of an opponent.

Charging is personal contact, with or without the ball, by pushing or moving into an opponent's torso.

Guarding from the *rear* is personal contact with an opponent by a defensive player from behind the opponent. The mere fact that the defensive player is attempting to play the ball does not justify his making contact with an opponent.

Handchecking is the action by a defensive player in a guarding situation where the hand(s) are used to contact an opponent to either impede his progress or to assist the defensive player in guarding his opponent.

Holding is personal contact with an opponent that interferes with his freedom of movement. This contact (holding) can occur with any part of the body.

Illegal use of hands occurs when a player contacts an opponent with his hand(s) in an attempt to play the ball. If such contact is only with the opponent's hand while it is on the ball, it shall be considered incidental.

Pushing is personal contact with any part of the body that takes place when a player forcibly moves or attempts to move an opponent who has or does not have control of the ball.

Illegal screening is an attempt to illegally delay or prevent an opponent who does not control the ball from reaching a desired position on the playing court.

Penalty

A personal foul shall be charged to the offender in all cases. In addition:

1. If the foul is committed on a player who is NOT in the act of shooting:

(*a*) The game shall be resumed by a throw-in by the non-offending team from out-of-bounds nearest the place of the infraction.

(*b*) If the offending team was in the penalty, then Art. 58 will come into effect.

2. If the foul is committed on a player who IS in the act of shooting:

(*a*) If the goal is made, it shall count and one (1) free throw shall be awarded.

(*b*) If the shot for goal for 2 points is unsuccessful, two (2) free throws shall be awarded.

(c) If the shot for goal for 3 points is unsuccessful, three (3) free throws shall be awarded.

3. If a foul is committed by a player while his team is in control of the ball:

(a) The game shall be resumed by a throw-in by the non-offending team from out-of-bounds nearest the place of the infraction.

(b) *Exceptions*: see Articles 48, 49, 50, 52 and 53.

Comments
A. Principle of Verticality

1. On the basketball court, each player has the right to a position on the floor and the space (cylinder) above him.

2. This principle protects the space on the floor which he occupies and the space above him.

3. As soon as the player leaves his vertical position (cylinder) and body contact occurs with an opponent who had already established his own vertical position (cylinder), the player who left his vertical position (cylinder) is responsible for the contact.

(a) The defender must not be penalised for leaving the floor vertically (within his cylinder) or having his hands and arms extended above him and within the cylinder.

(b) The offensive player, whether on the floor or airborne, shall not cause contact with the defensive player or use his arms to create additional space for himself (clear-out).

B. Legal Guarding Position

1. A defensive player has established a legal guarding position when:
(a) He is facing his opponent, and
(b) He has both feet on the floor in a normal straddle position.
The distance between his feet in a normal straddle position is generally proportional to his height.

2. The legal guarding position extends vertically above him (cylinder). He may raise his arms above his head but he must maintain them in a vertical position inside the imaginary cylinder.

C. Guarding a Player who Controls the Ball

1. In guarding a player who controls (he is holding or dribbling) the ball, the elements of time and distance do no apply.

2. The player with the ball must expect to be guarded and must be prepared to stop or change his direction whenever an opponent takes a legal guarding position in front of him, even if this is done within a fraction of a second.

3. The guarding (defensive) player must establish a legal guarding position without causing body contact prior to taking his position.

4. Once the defensive player has established a legal guarding position, he must maintain this position (see number 5. below), that is, he may not extend his arms, shoulders, hips or legs to prevent the dribbler from passing by him.

5. When judging a block/charge – player with the ball situation, an official shall use the following principles:

(*a*) The defensive player must establish an initial legal guarding position by facing the player with the ball and having both feet on the floor.

(*b*) The defensive player may remain stationary or move laterally or backwards in order to maintain the guarding position.

In moving to maintain the guarding position, one or both feet may be off the floor for an instant, as long as the lateral or backwards movement is considered normal defensive movement.

(*c*) The defensive player must be on the spot first and contact must occur on the torso.

If the contact is on the torso, then the defensive player would be considered to have been on the spot first.

If the three items above are present, then the foul is caused by the player with the ball.

D. The Player who is in the Air

1. A player who has jumped in the air from a spot on the court has the right to land again on the same spot.

2. He has the right to land on another spot on the court, provided that:

(*a*) The landing spot is not already occupied by an opponent(s) at the time of the take-off.

(*b*) The direct path between the take-off and landing spot is not already occupied by an opponent(s).

3. If a player has taken-off and landed but his momentum causes him to contact an opponent who has taken a legal guarding position near the landing spot, then the jumper is responsible for the contact.

4. A player may not move into the path of an opponent after the latter has jumped into the air.

5. Moving under a player who is in the air and contact occurs, is always an unsportsmanlike foul and in certain cases it may be a disqualifying foul.

E. Guarding a Player who does Not Control the Ball

1. A player who does not control the ball is entitled to move freely on the court and take any position not already occupied by another player.

2. The elements of time and distance shall apply. This means that a defensive player cannot take a position:

(*a*) So near to an opponent in motion that the latter does not have sufficient distance to either stop or change his direction.

(*b*) So quickly in the path of a moving opponent that the latter does not have sufficient time or distance to either stop or change his direction.

The distance is directly proportional to the speed of the opponent, never less than 1 and never more than 2 steps.

If a player disregards the elements of time and distance in taking his position and body contact with an opponent occurs, he is responsible for the contact.

3. Once a defensive player has taken a legal guarding position, he may not prevent his opponent from passing him by extending his arms, shoulders, hips or legs in his path. He may, however, turn or place his arm(s) in front of and close to his body to avoid injury.

4. Once a defensive player has taken a legal guarding position:

(*a*) He may shift or move laterally or backwards in order to remain in the path of his opponent.

(*b*) He may move forward toward his opponent, however, if body contact occurs, he is responsible for it.

(*c*) He must respect the element of space, that is, the distance between himself and his opponent as per 2b above.

F. Screening – Legal and Illegal

1. Screening occurs when a player attempts to delay or prevent an opponent who does not control the ball from reaching a desired position on the court.

2. Legal screening takes place when the player who is screening an opponent is:

(*a*) Stationary (inside his cylinder) when contact occurs.

(*b*) Has both feet on the floor when contact occurs.

3. Illegal screening takes place when the player who is screening an opponent:

(*a*) Was moving when contact occurred.

(*b*) Did not give the appropriate distance in setting a screen outside the field of vision of a stationary opponent when contact occurred.

(*c*) Did not respect the elements of time and distance on an opponent in motion when contact occurred.

4. If the screen is set within the field of vision of a stationary opponent (frontal or lateral), a player may establish the screen as close to him, short of contact, as he desires.

5. If the screen is set outside the field of vision of a stationary opponent, the screener must permit the opponent to take 1 normal step toward the screen without making contact.

6. If the opponent is in motion, the elements of time and distance shall apply. The screener must leave enough space so that the player who is being screened is able to avoid the screen by stopping or changing direction.

The distance required is never less than 1 normal step but never more than 2 steps.

7. A player who is legally screened is responsible for any contact with the player who has set up the screen.

G. Blocking

1. A player who is attempting to screen is committing a blocking foul if contact occurs when he is moving and his opponent is stationary or retreating from him.

2. If a player disregards the ball, faces an opponent and shifts his position as the opponent shifts, he is primarily responsible for any contact that ensues, unless other factors are involved.

The expression 'unless other factors are involved' refers to deliberate pushing, charging or holding of the player who is being screened.

3. It is legal for a player to extend his arm(s) or elbow(s) in taking position on the floor, but they must be lowered (inside the cylinder) when an opponent attempts to go by. If a player fails to lower the arm(s) or elbow(s) and contact occurs, it is blocking or holding.

H. Touching Opponents with the Hands

1. The touching of an opponent with a hand or hands, in itself, is not necessarily an infraction. However, when the opponent is in the field of vision of a player, there is no justification in touching with the hands and such action could be considered illegal personal contact.

The officials must decide whether an advantage has been gained.

2. If the contact restricts in any way the freedom of movement of an opponent, such contact is a foul.

3. A dribbler may not use an extended forearm or hand to prevent an opponent from securing the ball. Situations of this nature can result in an advantage not intended by the Rules and could lead to increased contact between opponents.

I. Post Play

1. The principle of verticality also applies to post play.

The offensive player in the post position and the opponent guarding him must respect each other's vertical rights (cylinder).

2. The post player must not be allowed to shoulder or hip his opponent out of position, nor interfere with the latter's freedom of movement by the use of extended elbows or arms.

3. The defensive player must not be allowed to interfere with the post

player's freedom of movement by the illegal use of arms, knees or other parts of the body.

Article 48. Double Foul

A. A double foul is a situation in which two opposing players commit fouls against each other at approximately the same time.

Penalty

1. A personal foul shall be charged against each offending player.
2. No free throws shall be awarded.
3. The game shall be resumed by a jump ball at the nearest circle between the two players involved.
4. If a valid field goal is scored at the same time, the ball shall be put into play from the endline by the opponents of the team who scored.

B. When a double foul and another foul are committed at approximately the same time, after the fouls have been charged and the eventual penalty administered, the game shall be resumed as though the double foul had not occurred.

Article 49. Unsportsmanlike Foul

1. An unsportsmanlike foul is a personal foul on a player with or without the ball which, in the opinion of the official, was deliberately committed by a player against an opposing player.
2. The unsportsmanlike foul must be interpreted the same way at the beginning as well as near the end of the game, that is, throughout the whole game.
3. The official must judge only the action.
4. To judge whether a foul is unsportsmanlike, the officials must apply the following principles:

(*a*) If a player commits a foul while making a legitimate effort to play the ball (normal basketball play), it is not an unsportsmanlike foul.

(*b*) If, in the effort to play the ball, the player causes excessive contact (hard foul), then the contact shall be considered to be unsportsmanlike.

(*c*) Holding, hitting or pushing a player who is away from the ball is usually an unsportsmanlike foul.

5. A player who repeatedly commits unsportsmanlike fouls may be disqualified.

Penalty

1. An unsportsmanlike foul shall be charged to the offender.

2. Free throw(s) shall be awarded to the non-offending team, followed by possession of the ball.

3. The number of free throws to be awarded shall be as follows:

(*a*) If the foul is committed on a player not in the act of shooting, two (2) free throws.

(*b*) If the foul is committed on a player who is in the act of shooting, the goal, if made, shall count and in addition one (1) free throw.

(*c*) If the foul is committed on a player in the act of shooting who fails to score, two (2) or three (3) free throws, according to the place from where the shot for goal was attempted.

4. During the free throw(s), all other players shall remain behind the free throw line extended and behind the 3-point field goal line until the free throw(s) have been completed.

5. After the free throw(s), whether or not the last free throw is successful, the ball shall be thrown in by any player of the free throw shooter's team from out-of-bounds at mid-court on the sideline opposite the scorer's table.

6. The player taking the throw-in shall have one foot on either side of the extended centre line, and shall be entitled to pass the ball to a player at any point on the playing court.

Article 50. Disqualifying Foul

Any flagrantly unsportsmanlike infraction of Article 47, 49, 52 or 53 is a disqualifying foul.

Penalty

1. A disqualifying foul shall be charged to the offender.

2. He shall be disqualified and shall go to and remain in his team's dressing room for the duration of the game or, if he so chooses, he shall leave the building.

3. Free throw(s) shall be awarded to the non-offending team, followed by possession of the ball.

4. The number of free throws to be awarded shall be as follows:

(*a*) If the foul is committed on a player not in the act of shooting, two (2) free throws.

(*b*) If the foul is committed on a player who is in the act of shooting, the goal, if made, shall count and in addition one (1) free throw.

(*c*) If the foul is committed on a player in the act of shooting who fails to score, two (2) or three (3) free throws, according to the place from where the shot for goal was attempted.

5. During the free throw(s), all other players shall remain behind the free throw line extended and behind the 3-point field goal line until the free throw(s) have been completed.

6. After the free throw(s), whether or not the last free throw is

successful, the ball shall be thrown in by any player of the free throw shooter's team from out-of-bounds at mid-court on the sideline opposite the scorer's table.

7. The player taking the throw-in shall have one foot on either side of the extended centre line, and shall be entitled to pass the ball to a player at any point on the playing court.

RULE 9

Technical Fouls

Article 51. Rules of Conduct: Definition
1. The proper conduct of the game demands the full and loyal cooperation with the officials and their assistants on the part of members of both teams, including coaches, substitutes and team followers.

2. Both teams are entitled to do their best to secure victory, but this must be done in a spirit of sportsmanship and fair play.

3. Any deliberate or repeated infringement of this cooperation or of the spirit of this Rule, shall be considered as a technical foul and penalised as provided in the appropriate Article(s).

Comments
1. Whenever acts of violence occur between players, substitutes, coaches and team followers who are on the team's bench, the Officials shall take the necessary action to stop them.

2. Any of the above persons who are guilty of flagrant acts of aggression against opponents shall be promptly disqualified from the game. Further the officials must report the incident to the body responsible for the competition.

3. The public enforcement officers may enter the court only if requested to do so by the officials.

However, should spectators enter the court with the obvious intention of committing acts of violence, the public enforcement officers must immediately intervene to protect players and officials.

4. All other areas, including entrances, exits, hallways, dressing rooms, etc. come under the jurisdiction of the organisers and of the forces responsible for the maintenance of public order.

5. The decisions of the officials are final and cannot be disregarded or contested.

Article 52. Technical Foul by a Player
1. Technical fouls by a player are all player fouls which do not involve contact with an opponent.

2. A player shall not disregard admonitions by officials or use unsportsmanlike tactics such as:

(*a*) Disrespectfully addressing or contacting an official, the technical commissioner if he is present, the scorer, the assistant scorer, the timekeeper, the 30-second operator or the opponents.

(*b*) Using language or gestures likely to offend or to incite the spectators.

(*c*) Baiting an opponent or obstructing his vision by waving his hands near his eyes.

(*d*) Delaying the game by preventing the throw-in being taken promptly.

(*e*) Not raising his hand properly after being requested to do so by an official after a foul is called on him.

(*f*) Changing his playing number without reporting to the scorer and to the Referee.

(*g*) Entering the court as a substitute without reporting to the scorer and being beckoned by an official.

(*h*) Leaving the court to gain an unfair advantage.

(*i*) Violating Article 60–D, Penalty 3, *Note: 'Interference with the last or only free throw'*.

(*j*) Grasping the ring in such a way that the weight of the player is supported by the ring.

A player may grasp the ring if, in the judgement of the official, he is trying to prevent injury to himself or to another player.

3. Technical infractions which are obviously unintentional and have no effect on the game or are of an administrative character are not considered technical fouls, unless there is repetition of the same infraction after a warning by an official.

4. Technical infractions which are deliberate or unsportsmanlike or give the offender an unfair advantage, shall be penalised promptly with a technical foul.

Penalty

1. A technical foul shall be charged to the offender.
2. Two (2) free throws shall be awarded to the opponents.
3. The captain shall designate the free throw shooter.

Comments

1. For flagrant or persistent infraction of this Article, a player shall be disqualified, removed from the game and the same penalty as for a disqualifying foul shall be applied.

2. If the discovery of the technical foul is made after the ball is in play, the penalty shall be administered as if the foul had occurred at the time

of discovery. Whatever occurred in the interval between the foul and its discovery shall be valid.

3. An official may prevent technical fouls by warning players when they are about to commit a minor infraction, such as failing to report to the scorer.

It is good judgement for the official to forestall and, in some cases, overlook minor technical infractions which are obviously unintentional and have no effect on the game.

Article 53. Technical Foul by Coaches, Substitutes or Team Followers

1. The coaches, assistant coaches, substitutes, and team followers must stay within their team bench area, except:

(*a*) A coach, assistant coach or team follower may enter the playing court to attend to an injured player after receiving permission from an official to do so.

(*b*) A doctor may enter the court without permission from one of the officials if, in the doctor's judgement, the injured player is in danger and requires immediate attention.

(*c*) A substitute may request a substitution at the scorer's table.

(*d*) A coach or assistant coach may request a charged time-out.

(*e*) A coach or assistant coach may enter the court to address his team members, only during a charged time-out and provided he remains in the vicinity of his team bench area.

However, a coach may address his players during the game provided he remains within his team bench area.

(*f*) When the clock is stopped, a coach or assistant coach may seek information from the scorer's table concerning the score, time or number of fouls, courteously and without interfering with the normal progress of the game.

2. A coach, assistant coach, substitute or team follower shall not disrespectfully address the officials, the technical commissioner if he is present, the scorer, the assistant scorer, the timekeeper, the 30-second operator or the opponents.

3. Only the coach, whose name is inscribed on the scoresheet is permitted to remain standing during the game.

Penalty

A. 1. A technical foul shall be charged to the coach.

2. Two (2) free throws shall be awarded to the opponents, followed by possession of the ball.

3. The captain shall designate the free throw shooter.

4. During the free throws, all other players shall remain behind the free throw line extended and behind the 3-point field goal line until the free throws have been completed.

5. After the free throws, whether or not the last free throw is successful, the ball shall be thrown in by any player of the free throw shooter's team from out-of-bounds at mid-court on the sideline opposite the Scorer's table. (*Exception*: see Art. 54, Penalty 3 and Art. 59, 2d.)

6. The player taking the throw-in shall have one foot on either side of the extended centre line and be entitled to pass the ball to a player at any point on the playing court.

B. 1. A coach shall be disqualified and shall go to and remain in his team's dressing room for the duration of the game or, if he so chooses, shall leave the building when:

(*a*) He is charged with any flagrant infraction of this Article.

(*b*) He is charged with two (2) technical fouls as a result of personal unsportsmanlike behaviour.

(*c*) He is charged with three (3) technical fouls accumulated as a result of unsportsmanlike conduct by himself, the assistant coach, any substitute, or any team follower who is on the team bench.

Note: A foul by a player who has previously committed his 5th foul (during a game played in 2 × 20 minutes) or his 6th foul (during a game played in 4 × 12 minutes) is charged to the coach.

2. For any flagrant infraction of this Article, the assistant coach, any substitute or any team follower shall be disqualified and shall go to and remain in his team's dressing room for the duration of the game or, if he so chooses, shall leave the building.

3. A coach who has been disqualified shall be replaced by the assistant coach as inscribed on the scoresheet. If no assistant coach is inscribed on the scoresheet, he shall be replaced by the captain.

Article 54. Technical Foul during an Interval of Play

1. Technical fouls may be called during an interval of play.

2. An interval of play is:

(*a*) The period prior to the start of the game (approximately 20 minutes).

(*b*) The interval between any periods, the half-time interval and the interval prior to all extra periods.

(*c*) The interval of play ends the moment the official with the ball enters the centre circle to administer the jump ball; that is, the moment the ball is in play.

Penalty

1. If the technical foul is called against:

(*a*) A team member eligible to play, it is charged to the team member and the penalty shall be two (2) free throws.

It shall count as one of the team fouls.

(*b*) A coach, assistant coach or team follower, it is charged to the coach and the penalty shall be two (2) free throws.

It shall not count as one of the team fouls.

2. During the free throws all players, except the free throw shooter, shall be behind the free throw line extended and behind the 3-point line until all free throws have been completed.

3. After the free throws have been completed, the game shall be started or resumed with a jump ball in the centre circle.

4. If more than one technical foul is called, see Art. 59.

Comments

1. Physical actions of players, coaches and team followers which could lead to damage of playing equipment, such as grasping the ring and violent dunking, must not be permitted by the officials.

2. When behaviour of this nature is observed by the officials, the coach of the offending team shall be warned immediately.

3. Should the action(s) be repeated, a technical foul shall be called immediately on the individual involved.

Article 55. Fighting

1. Any bench personnel who leave the confines of the team bench area during a fight or during any situation which may lead to a fight, shall be disqualified from the game and shall go to and remain in his team's dressing room for the duration of the game or, if he so chooses, shall leave the building.

2. However, the coach (only) may leave the confines of the team bench area during a fight or during any situation which may lead to a fight in order to assist the officials to maintain or to restore order.

3. If a coach leaves the confines of the team bench area and does not assist (help) in maintaining or restoring order, he shall be disqualified and shall go to and remain in his team's dressing room for the duration of the game or, if he so chooses, shall leave the building.

For any incident of this nature:

1. A single technical foul shall be charged against the coach or coaches and the technical foul(s) shall be administered according to the appropriate Article.

2. (*a*) Every disqualifying foul shall be recorded as described in the Official Game Procedures: scoresheet 6c(8)

(*b*) The disqualifying foul(s) shall not be recorded as a team foul(s).

(*c*) The disqualifying foul(s) shall not be administered, that is, there shall be no free throws taken by either team as a result of the disqualifying foul(s) for leaving the team bench area.

RULE 10

General Provisions

Article 56. Basic Principle

1. Each Official has power to call fouls independently from the other, at any time during the game, whether the ball is in play, alive or dead.

2. Any number of fouls may be called against one or both teams. Irrespective of the penalty, a foul shall be inscribed on the Scoresheet against the offender for each foul.

Article 57. Five/Six Fouls by a Player

1. In a game played in 2 × 20 minutes, a player who has committed five (5) fouls, either personal or technical, shall be informed of the fact and he must automatically leave the game.

2. In a game played in 4 × 12 minutes, a player who has committed six (6) fouls, either personal or technical, shall be informed of the fact and he must automatically leave the game.

Article 58. Team Fouls – Penalty Rule

1. Games played in 2 × 20 minutes:

When a team has committed seven (7) player fouls, personal or technical, in a half (20 minutes):

(*a*) All subsequent player personal fouls shall be penalised by two (2) free throws, whereby the player against whom the foul was committed shall shoot two (2) free throws.

(*b*) If a penalty of greater severity is involved, the appropriate Article in these Rules will apply.

2. Games played in 4 × 12 minutes:

When a team has committed four (4) player fouls, personal or technical, in a period (12 minutes):

(*a*) All subsequent player personal fouls shall be penalised by two (2) free throws, whereby the player against whom the foul was committed shall shoot two (2) free throws.

(*b*) If a penalty of greater severity is involved, the appropriate Article in these Rules will apply.

3. In the event that the foul is committed by a player while his team is in control of the ball, Art. 47, Penalty 3 shall apply.

4. All team fouls committed in any extra period shall be considered to be part of the last half or period.

Comment

All team member fouls occurring during an interval of play are considered to be part of the half or period immediately following.

Article 59. Fouls in Special Situations

1. Situations other than those foreseen in these Rules may occur when:

(*a*) Fouls are committed at approximately the same time.

(*b*) Fouls are committed during the same stopped-clock period which follows a foul or a double foul.

2. In such situations, the following principles shall be applied:

(*a*) A foul shall be charged for each offence.

(*b*) (*i*) Fouls against both teams that involve the same penalties shall be used to cancel each other, that is, they shall not be penalised by awarding free throws or possession of the ball for a throw-in.

(*ii*) The game shall be re-started by a jump ball at the nearest circle unless a field goal has been scored, in which case the game shall be re-started by a throw-in from out-of-bounds on or behind the endline.

(*iii*) Once the ball has gone into play for the first or only free throw of a foul penalty, then that foul penalty can no longer be used for cancelling another foul penalty.

(*c*) (*i*) Fouls against both teams that do not involve the same penalties shall be penalised and administered according to the order in which they occurred.

(*ii*) If fouls are called against both teams at approximately the same time, the officials must determine the order in which the fouls occurred.

This does not apply to a double foul situation, the penalty for which shall be administered according to Art. 48.

(*d*) The right to possession of the ball for a throw-in as the result of a foul penalty shall be forfeited in the event that another foul(s) is called against either team before the ball goes into play for the throw-in or in the event that further penalties must be administered after cancellation according to this Article.

(*e*) The principles contained in this Article are also applicable during any interval of play.

Article 60. Free Throws

A free throw is an opportunity given to a player to score one (1) point, uncontested, from a position behind the free throw line and inside the semicircle.

A. When a personal foul is called and the penalty is the awarding of free throw(s):

1. The player against whom the foul was committed shall be designated by the official to attempt the free throw(s).

2. If there is a request for the player who has been fouled to be substituted, he must attempt the free throw(s) before leaving the game.

3. If the player designated to attempt the free throw(s) must leave the game because of injury or disqualification, his substitute must attempt the free throw(s). If no substitute is available, the free throw(s) shall be attempted by the captain or by any player designated by him.

B. When a technical foul is called, the free throws may be attempted by any player of the opposing team as designated by the captain.

C. The free throw shooter:
1. Shall take a position behind the free throw line and inside the semicircle.
2. May use any method to shoot for goal but he must shoot in such a way that the ball enters the basket from above or touches the ring before it is touched by a player.
3. Shall release the ball within five (5) seconds from the time it is placed at his disposal by one of the officials.
4. Shall not touch the free throw line or the playing court beyond the free throw line until the ball has touched the ring.
5. Shall not fake a free throw.
6. Shall not touch the ball while it is on its way to the basket.
7. Shall not touch the basket or the backboard while the ball is in contact with the ring during a free throw.
8. During any free throw which is to be followed by further free throw(s), he shall not touch the ball or the basket for as long as the ball has the opportunity to enter the basket.

An infraction of C is a violation.

Note: If a violation is committed by a free throw shooter, any other violation committed by any other player at the same time or immediately after, shall be disregarded.

Penalty
No point(s) can be scored. The ball shall be awarded to the opponents for a throw-in from out-of-bounds at the free throw line extended.

D. During the free throw(s):
1. (*a*) A maximum of five (5) players may occupy the free throw lane places which are considered to be one (1) metre in depth.
(*b*) The first lane place on either side of the restricted area may be occupied only by the opponents of the free throw shooter.
(*c*) Players who occupy lane places shall take up alternate positions.
(*d*) Players shall occupy only the lane places to which they are entitled.

2. The players in the lane places:

(*a*) Shall not occupy lane places to which they are not entitled.

(*b*) Shall not enter the restricted area, the neutral zone or leave the lane place until the ball has left the hand(s) of the free throw shooter.

(*c*) Shall not touch the ball while it is on its way to the basket until it touches the ring or it is evident that it will not touch it.

(*d*) Shall not touch the basket or the backboard while the ball is in contact with the ring during the free throw.

(*e*) During any free throw which is to be followed by further free throw(s), they shall not touch the ball, the basket or the backboard for as long as the ball has the opportunity to enter the basket.

(*f*) An opponent of the free throw shooter shall not:

1. Touch the ball or the basket while the ball is within the basket.
2. Disconcert the free throw shooter by his actions.

An infraction of D is a violation.

Penalty

1. If the free throw is successful and the violation of 1, 2a, 2b or 2f(2) is by:

(*a*) A team-mate of the free throw shooter

(*b*) An opponent of the free throw shooter

(*c*) Both teams

the violation is disregarded and the goal shall count.

2. If the free throw is not successful and the violation of 1, 2a, 2b or 2f(2) is by:

(*a*) A team-mate of the free throw shooter.

The ball shall be awarded to the opponents for a throw-in.

(*b*) An opponent of the free throw shooter.

A substitute free throw shall be awarded to the free throw shooter.

(*c*) Both teams.

The game shall be resumed by a jump ball at the free throw line.

3. If the violation of 2c, 2d, 2e or 2f(1) is by:

(*a*) A team-mate of the free throw shooter.

No points can be scored and the ball shall be awarded to the opponents for a throw-in.

(*b*) An opponent of the free throw shooter.

The free throw shall be considered successful and one (1) point awarded.

(*c*) Both teams.

No points can be scored and the game is resumed with a jump ball at the free throw line.

Note: If during the last or only free throw, an opponent of the free throw shooter touches the ball before it touches the ring (and it is clear that it would have touched the ring), the free throw shall be considered successful and a technical foul is charged against the player who committed the violation.

Comment
During the last or only free throw, the attempt changes its status and becomes a two (2) point field goal, after the ball has touched the ring and is legally touched by an offensive or defensive player before it enters the basket.

E. All players who are NOT in the free throw lane places:
1. Shall be behind the free throw line extended and behind the 3-point field goal line until such time as the ball strikes the ring or the free throw ends (see Art. 61, Comments).
2. Shall not disconcert the free throw shooter by their actions.

An infraction of E is a violation.

Penalty
See D above, Penalty.

F. During free throw(s) which are to be followed by further free throw(s) according to Art. 59 or by free throw(s) to be taken according to Art. 33 (2) or by a throw-in at mid-court on the sideline:
1. Players shall not occupy any of the lane places.
2. All players shall be behind the free throw line extended and behind the 3-point field goal line.
3. The players shall not disconcert the free throw shooter by their actions.

An infraction to F is a violation.

Penalty
1. See D above, Penalty.
2. If more than one free throw is taken, the awarding of the ball out-of-bounds or the jump ball penalties shall apply only to a violation during the last free throw.

Article 61. Correctable Error
1. Officials may correct an error if a Rule is inadvertently set aside and results in the following situations only:

(*a*) Awarding an unmerited free throw(s).
(*b*) Permitting a wrong player to attempt a free throw(s).
(*c*) Attempting a free throw(s) at the wrong basket.
(*d*) Failure to award a merited free throw(s).
(*e*) Erroneously counting or cancelling a score by the officials.

2. To be correctable, errors in items *a*, b, *c*, *d*, or *e* must be discovered by an official or his assistants before the ball becomes alive following the first dead ball after the clock has started following the error, that is:

Error occurs	– All errors *a* to *e* occur during a dead ball.
Ball in play	– Error is correctable.
Ball alive	– Error is correctable.
Clock starts or continues to run	– Error is correctable.
Dead ball	– Error is correctable.
Ball in play	– Error is correctable.
Ball alive	– Error is no longer correctable.

3. After an error has been discovered and it is still correctable:
(*a*) If the player involved in the correction of the error is on the bench after having been legally substituted (not for having been disqualified or having committed his 5th or 6th foul), he must re-enter the playing court to participate in the correction of the error (at this point he becomes a player).

Upon completion of the correction, he may remain in the game unless the coach asks for a legal substitution, in which case the player may leave the playing court.

(*b*) If the player has been substituted because he has committed his 5th or 6th foul or has been disqualified, his legal substitute must participate in the correction of the error.

4. If the error is an unmerited free throw(s), a wrong player attempting free throw(s) or attempting free throw(s) at the wrong basket:

(*a*) The free throw(s) attempted as a result of the error and all the activity accompanying it (see Comments below) shall be cancelled unless there are unsportsmanlike, disqualifying, or technical fouls.

(*b*) Other points scored, consumed time and additional activity, which may have occurred prior to the recognition of the error, shall not be cancelled.

(*c*) To cancel the free throw(s) and the activity accompanying it, the error must be discovered within the time limits explained in number 2 above.

5. An official may stop the game immediately upon discovering a

correctable error, as long as it does not place either team at a disadvantage.

6. After the correction of the error, the game shall be restarted at the point at which it was interrupted to correct the error.

The ball shall be awarded to the team entitled to the ball at the time the error was discovered.

7. Correctable errors (1*a-e*) cannot be corrected after the Referee has approved and signed the Scoresheet.

8. Any errors or mistakes of record-keeping by the scorer which involve the score, number of fouls or number of time-outs, may be corrected by the officials any time prior to the Referee's signing of the Scoresheet.

Comments

A free throw and the activity accompanying is considered to have ended when the ball:

1. Enters the basket directly from above and remains within or passes through the basket.

2. No longer has the possibility to enter the basket.

3. Is legally touched by a player of either team after it has touched the ring.

4. Touches the floor without being legally touched.

5. Becomes dead.

Reprinted by permission of the International Basketball Federation. For reasons of space, the long Appendix on Official Game Procedures and the FIBA Referee's Manual have been omitted. Copies of the Official Basketball Rules including those appendixes can be obtained from the Federation.

Bowls

Bowls

The references in these Laws to he, him or his do not imply male exclusivity but apply equally to both males and females.

DEFINITIONS

1. (*a*) 'Controlling Body' means the body having immediate control of the conditions under which a match is played. The order shall be:

  (i) The World Bowls Board;

  (ii) The National Bowling Authority;

  (iii) Divisions within National Authorities;

  (iv) The Club on whose Green the Match is played.

(*b*) 'Skip' means the Player, who, for the time being, is in charge of the head on behalf of the team.

(*c*) 'Team' means either a Four, Triples or a Pair.

(*d*) 'Side' means any agreed number of Teams, whose combined scores determine the results of the match.

(*e*) 'Four' means a team of four players whose positions in order of playing are named Lead, Second, Third, Skip.

(*f*) 'Bowl in Course' means a Bowl from the time of its delivery until it comes to rest.

(*g*) 'End' means the playing of the Jack and all the Bowls of all the opponents in the same direction on a rink.

(*h*) 'Head' means the Jack and such Bowls as have come to rest within the boundary of the rink and are not dead.

(*i*) 'Mat Line' means the edge of the Mat which is nearest to the front ditch. From the centre of the Mat Line all necessary measurements to Jack or Bowls shall be taken.

(*j*) 'Master Bowl' means a Bowl which has been approved by the WBB as having the minimum bias required, as well as in all other respects complying with the Laws of the Game and is engraved with the words 'Master Bowl'.

  (i) A Standard Bowl of the same bias as the Master Bowl shall be kept in the custody of each National Authority.

(ii) A Standard Bowl shall be provided for the use of each official Licensed Tester.

(*k*) 'Jack High' means that the nearest portion of the Bowl referred to is in line with and at the same distance from the Mat Line as the nearest portion of the Jack.

(*l*) 'Pace of Green' means the number of seconds taken by a bowl from the time of its delivery to the moment it comes to rest, approximately 90ft (27.43m) from the Mat line.

(*m*) 'Displaced' as applied to a Jack or Bowl means 'disturbed' by any agency that is not sanctioned by these laws.

(*n*) 'A set of Bowls' means four Bowls all of a matched set which are of the same manufacture and are of the same weight, colour, bias and where applicable serial number and engraving.

THE GREEN

2. The Green – Area and Surface
The green should form a square of not less than 120ft (36.58m) and not more than 132ft (40.23m) a side. It shall have a suitable natural playing surface which shall be level. It shall be provided with suitable boundaries in the form of a ditch and bank.

3. The Ditch
The green shall be surrounded by a ditch which shall have a holding surface not injurious to bowls and be free from obstacles. The ditch shall be not less than 8in (203mm) nor more than 15in (381mm) wide and it shall be not less than 2in (51mm) nor more than 8in (203mm) below the level of the green.

4. Banks
The banks shall be not less than 9in (229mm) above the level of the green, preferably upright, or alternatively at an angle of not more than 35° from the perpendicular. The surface of the face of the bank shall be non-injurious to bowls. No steps likely to interfere with play shall be cut in the banks.

5. Division of the Green
The green shall be divided into spaces called rinks, each not more than 19ft (5.79m) nor less than 18ft (5.48m) wide. They shall be numbered consecutively, the centre line of each rink being marked on the bank at each end by a wooden peg or other suitable device. The four corners of the rink shall be marked by pegs made of wood or other suitable material, painted white, and fixed to the face of the bank and flush

therewith, or alternatively fixed on the bank not more than 4in (102mm) back from the face thereof. The corner pegs shall be connected by a green thread drawn tightly along the surface of the green, with sufficient loose thread to reach the corresponding pegs on the face or surface of the bank, in order to define the boundary of the rink.

White pegs or discs shall be fixed on the side banks to indicate a clear distance of 76ft (23.16m) from the ditch on the line of play. Under no circumstances shall the boundary thread be lifted while the Bowl is in motion. The boundary pegs of an outside rink shall be placed at least 2ft (61cm) from the side ditch.

6. Permissible Variations of Laws 2 and 5

(a) National Associations may admit greens not longer than 132ft (40.23m) nor shorter than 99ft (30.17m) in the direction of play.

(b) For domestic play the green may be divided into Rinks not less than 14ft (4.27m) nor more than 19ft (5.79m) wide. National Authorities may dispense with the use of boundary threads.

(c) National Authorities may approve artificial surfaces for domestic play.

MAT, JACK, BOWLS, FOOTWEAR

7. Mat

The mat shall be of a definite size, namely 24in (61cm) long and 14in (35.6cm) wide.

8. Jack

The Jack shall be round and white or yellow in colour, with a diameter of not less than $2\frac{15}{32}$in (63mm) nor more than $2\frac{17}{32}$in (64mm), and not less than 8oz (227g), nor more than 10oz (283g) in weight.

9. Bowls

(a) (i) Bowls shall be made of wood, rubber or composition and shall be black or brown in colour, and each Bowl of the set shall bear the member's individual and distinguishing mark on each side. The provision relating to the distinguishing mark on each side of the Bowl need not apply other than in International Matches, World Bowls Championships and Commonwealth Games. Bowls made of wood (Lignum Vitae) shall have a maximum diameter of $5\frac{1}{4}$in (133.35mm) and a minimum diameter of $4\frac{5}{8}$in (117mm) and the weight shall not exceed 3lb 8oz (1.59kg). Loading of Bowls made of wood is strictly prohibited.

(ii) For all International and Commonwealth Games Matches a Bowl made of rubber or composition shall have a maximum diameter of 5⅛in (130mm) and a minimum diameter of 4⁹⁄₁₆in (116mm) and the weight shall not exceed 3lb 8oz (1.59kg).

Subject to Bowls bearing a current stamp of the Board, and/or a current stamp of a Member National Authority, and/or the current stamp of the BIBC and provided they comply with the Board's Laws, they may be used in all matches controlled by the Board, or by any Member National Authority.

Notwithstanding the aforegoing provisions, any Member National Authority may adopt a different scale of weights and sizes of Bowls to be used in matches under its own control – such bowls may not be validly used in International Matches. World Bowls Championships, Commonwealth Games, or other matches controlled by the Board if they differ from the Board's Laws, and unless stamped with a current stamp of the Board or any Member National Authority or the BIBC.

(iii) The controlling body may, at its discretion, supply and require players to temporarily affix an adhesive marking to their Bowls in any competition game. Any temporary marking under this Law shall be regarded as part of the Bowl for all purposes under these Laws.

(*b*) *Bias of Bowls*. The master bowl shall have a bias approved by the World Bowls Board. A Bowl shall have a bias not less than that of the master bowl and shall bear the imprint of the Stamp of the World Bowls Board, or that of its National Authority. National Authorities may adopt a standard which exceeds the bias of the Master Bowl. To ensure accuracy of bias and visibility of stamp, all bowls shall be re-tested and re-stamped at least once every ten years, or earlier if the date of the stamp is not clearly legible.

(*c*) *Bowls Failing Test*. If a Bowl in the hands of a Licensed Tester has been declared as not complying with Law 9(*b*), it shall be altered, if possible, so as to comply before being returned. The owner of the Bowls shall be responsible for the expense involved.

If the Bowls cannot be altered to comply with Law 9(*a*) and (*b*) any current official stamp appearing thereon shall be cancelled prior to their return. The stamp shall be cancelled by the Tester by stamping an X over any current official stamp.

Bowls submitted for testing must be in sets of four.

(*d*) *Objection to Bowls*

A challenge may be lodged by an opposing player and/or by the Official Umpire and/or the Controlling Body.

A challenge or any intimation thereof shall not be lodged with any opposing player during the progress of the Match.

A challenge may be lodged with the Umpire at any time during a

Match, provided the Umpire is not a Player in that or any other match of the same competition.

If a challenge be lodged it shall be made not later than 10 minutes after the completion of the final end in which the Bowl was used.

Once a challenge is lodged with the Umpire, it cannot be withdrawn.

The challenge shall be based on the grounds that the Bowl does not comply with one or more of the requirements set out in Law 9(a) and (b).

The Umpire shall request the user of the Bowl to surrender it to him for forwarding to the Controlling Body. If the owner of the challenged Bowl refuses to surrender it to the Umpire, the Match shall thereuponbe forfeited to the opponent. The user or owner, or both, may be disqualified from playing in any match controlled or permitted by the Controlling Body, providing that the Bowl remains untested by a Licensed Tester.

On receipt of the Bowls, the Umpire shall take immediate steps to hand them to the Secretary of the Controlling Body, who shall arrange for a table test to be made as soon as practicable, and in the presence of a representative of the Controlling Body.

If a table test be not readily available, and any delay would unduly interfere with the progress of the competition, then, should an approved green testing device be available, it may be used to make an immediate test on the green. If a green test be made, it shall be done by, or in the presence of, the Umpire over a distance of not less than 70ft (21.35m). The comparison shall be between the challenged Bowl and the standard WBB Test Bowl, or if it be not readily available then a Bowl bearing a current stamp, of similar size or nearly so, should be used.

The decision of the Umpire, as a result of the test, shall be final and binding for that match.

The result of the subsequent table test shall not invalidate the decision given by the Umpire on the green test.

If a challenged Bowl, after an official table test, be found to comply with all the requirements of Law 9(a) and (b), it shall be returned to the user or owner.

If the challenged Bowl be found not to comply with Law 9(a) **and** (b), the match in which it was played shall be forfeited to the opponent.

If a Bowl in the hands of a Licensed Tester has been declared as not complying with the Law 9(b), it shall be altered, if possible, so as to comply, before being returned. The owner of the Bowl shall be responsible for the expense involved.

If the Bowl cannot be altered to comply with Law 9(a) and (b), any current official stamp appearing thereon shall be cancelled prior to its return. The stamp shall be cancelled by the Tester by stamping an X over any current official stamp.

(*e*) *Alteration to Bias*. A player shall not alter, or cause to be altered, other than by an Official Bowl Tester, the bias of any Bowl bearing the imprint of the official stamp of the Board, under penalty of suspension from playing for a period to be determined by the Council of the National Authority of which his club is a member. Such suspension shall be subject to confirmation by the Board or a Committee thereof appointed for that purpose and shall be operative among all Authorities in membership with the Board.

10. Footwear

Players, Umpires and Markers shall wear white, brown or black smooth-soled, heel-less footwear while playing on the green or acting as Umpires or Markers.

ARRANGING A GAME

11. General Form and Duration

A game of Bowls shall be played on one rink or on several rinks. It shall consist of a specified number of shots or ends, or shall be played for any period of time as previously arranged. The ends of the game shall be played alternately in opposite directions excepting as provided in Laws 38, 42, 44, 46 and 47.

12. Selecting the Rinks for Play

When a match is to be played, the draw for the rinks to be played on shall be made by the Skips or their representatives.

In a match for a trophy or where competing Skips have previously been drawn, the draw to decide the numbers of the rinks to be played on shall be made by the visiting Skips or their representatives.

No player in a competition or match shall play on the same rink on the day of such competition or match before play commences, under penalty of disqualification.

This law shall not apply in the case of open Tournaments.

13. Play Arrangements

Games shall be organised in the following play arrangements:
   (*a*) As a single game.
   (*b*) As a team game.
   (*c*) As a sides game.
   (*d*) As a series of single games, team games, or side games.
   (*e*) As a special tournament of games.

14. A single game shall be played on one rink of a Green as a single-handed game by two contending players, each playing two, three or four Bowls singly and alternately.

15. (*a*) A Pairs game shall be played by two contending teams of two players called Lead and Skip according to the order in which they play, and who at each end shall play four Bowls, alternately, the Leads first, then the Skips similarly.

(For other than Internationals and Commonwealth Games, players in a pairs game may play two, three or four bowls each, as previously arranged by the controlling body.)

(*b*) A Pairs game shall be played by two contending teams of two players called Lead and Skip according to the order in which they play, and who at each end shall play four Bowls alternately in the following order: Lead 2 Bowls, Skip 2 Bowls then repeat this order of play.

16. A Triples game shall be played by two contending teams of three players, who shall play two or three Bowls singly and in turn, the Leads playing first.

17. A Fours game shall be played by two contending teams of four players, each member playing two Bowls singly and in turn.

18. A side game shall be played by two contending sides, each composed of an equal number of teams/players.

19. Games in series shall be arranged to be played on several and consecutive occasions, as:

(*a*) A series or sequence of games organised in the form of an eliminating competition, and arranged as Singles, Pairs, Triples or Fours.

(*b*) A series or sequence of side matches organised in the form of a league competition, or an eliminating competition, or of Inter-Association matches.

20. A special tournament of games

Single games and team games may also be arranged in group form as a special tournament of games in which the contestants play each other in turn; or they may play as paired-off teams of players on one or several greens in accordance with a common timetable, success being adjudged by the number of games won, or by the highest net score in shots in accordance with the regulations governing the tournament.

21. For International Matches, World Bowls Championships and Commonwealth Games in matches where played:

(i) Singles shall be 21 shots up (shots in excess of 25 shall not count), four Bowls each player, played alternately;

(ii) Pairs shall be 21 ends, four Bowls each player, played alternately;

(iii) Triples shall be 18 ends, three Bowls each player, played alternately;

(iv) Fours shall be 21 ends, two Bowls each player, played alternately; *Provided* that Pairs, Triples and Fours may be of a lesser number of ends, but in the case of Pairs and Fours there shall not be less than 18 ends, but in the case of Triples not less than 15 ends, subject in all cases to the express approval of the Board as represented by its most senior officer present. If there be no officer of the Board present at the time, the decision shall rest with the 'Controlling Body' as defined in Law 1. Any decision to curtail the number of ends to be played shall be made before the commencement of any game, and such decision shall only be made on the grounds of climatic conditions, inclement weather, or shortage of time to complete a programme.

22. Awards
Cancelled.

STARTING THE GAME
23. (*a*) **Trial Ends** Before start of play in any competition, match or game, or on the resumption of an unfinished competition, match or game on another day, not more than one trial end each way shall be played.

(*b*) **Tossing for Opening Play** The Captain in a side game or Skips in a team game shall toss to decide which side or team shall play first, but in all singles games the Opponents shall toss, the winner of the toss to have the option of decision. In the event of a tied (no score) or a dead end, the first to play in the tied end or dead end shall again play first.

In all ends subsequent to the first the winner of the preceding score end shall play first.

24. Placing the Mat
At the beginning of the first end the player to play first shall place the centre line of the mat lengthwise on the centre line of the rink, the front edge of the mat to be 6ft (1.84m) from the ditch. (Where groundsheets are in use they shall be placed with the back edge 6ft (1.84m) from the ditch. The mat at the first and every subsequent end shall be placed at the back edge of the sheet – the mat's front edge being 6ft (1.84m) from the ditch.)

25. The Mat and its Replacement
After play has commenced in any end the mat shall not be moved from its first position.

If the mat be displaced during the progress of an end it shall be replaced as nearly as is practicable in the same position.

If the mat be out of alignment with the centre line of the rink it may be straightened at any time during the end.

After the last Bowl in each end has come to rest in play, or has sooner become dead, the mat shall be lifted and placed wholly beyond the face of the rear bank. Should the mat be picked up by a player before the end has been completed, the opposing player shall have the right of replacing the mat in its original position.

26. The Mat and Jack in Subsequent Ends

(*a*) In all subsequent ends the front edge of the mat shall be not less than 6ft (1.84m) from the rear ditch and the front edge of the mat not less than 76ft (23.16m) from the front ditch and on the centre line of the rink of play.

(*b*) Should the Jack be improperly delivered under Law 30, the opposing player may then move the mat in the line of play, subject to Clause (*a*) above, and deliver the Jack, but shall not play first. Should the Jack be improperly delivered twice by each player in any end, it shall not be delivered again in that end but shall be centred so that the front of the Jack is a distance of 6ft (1.84m) from the opposite ditch, and the mat placed at the option of the first to play.

If, after the Jack is set at regulation length from the ditch (6ft or 1.84m), both players each having improperly delivered the Jack twice, the end is made dead, the winner of the preceding scoring end shall deliver the Jack when the end is played anew.

(*c*) No one shall be permitted to challenge the legality of the original position of the mat after the first to play has delivered the first Bowl.

27. Stance on Mat

A player shall take his stance on the mat and, at the moment of delivering the Jack or his bowl, shall have one foot remaining entirely within the confines of the mat. The foot may be either in contact with, or over, the mat. Failure to observe this Law constitutes foot-faulting.

28. Foot-faulting

Should a player infringe the Law of foot-faulting, the Umpire may, after having given a warning, have the Bowl stopped and declared dead. If the Bowl has disturbed the head, the opponents shall have the option of either resetting the head, leaving the head as altered, or declaring the end dead.

29. Delivering the Jack

The player to play first shall deliver the Jack. If the Jack in its original course comes to rest at a distance of less than 6ft (1.84m) from the opposite ditch, it shall be moved out to a mark at that distance so that the front of the Jack is 6ft (1.84m) from the front ditch, with the nearest portion of the Jack to the mat line being 6ft (1.84m) from the edge of the opposite ditch.

If the Jack during its original course be obstructed or deflected by a neutral object or neutral person, or by a Marker, Opponent, or member of the opposing team, it shall be re-delivered by the same player. If it be obstructed or deflected by a member of his own team, it shall be re-delivered by the Lead of the opposing team, who shall be entitled to reset the mat.

30. Jack Improperly Delivered

Should the Jack in any end be not delivered from a proper stance on the mat, or if it ends its original course in the ditch or outside the side boundary of the rink, or less than 70ft (21.35m) in a straight line of play from the front edge of the mat, it shall be returned and the opposing player shall deliver the Jack, but shall not play first.

The Jack shall be returned if it is improperly delivered, but the right of the player who first delivered the Jack in that end, to play the first Bowl of the end, shall not be affected.

No one shall be permitted to challenge the legality of the original length of the Jack after the first to play has delivered the first Bowl.

31. Variations to Laws 24, 26, 29 and 30

Notwithstanding anything contained in Laws 24, 26, 29 and 30, any National Authority may for domestic purposes, but not in any International Matches, World Bowls Championships or Commonwealth Games, vary any of the distances mentioned in these Laws.

MOVEMENT OF BOWLS

32. 'Live' Bowl

A Bowl which, in its original course on the Green, comes to rest within the boundaries of the rink, and not less than 45ft (13.71m) from the front edge of the mat, shall be accounted as a 'live' Bowl and shall be in play.

33. 'Touchers'

A Bowl which, in its original course on the green, touches the Jack, even though such Bowl passes into the ditch within the boundaries of the rink, shall be accounted as a 'live' Bowl, and shall be called a 'toucher'. If after having come to rest a Bowl falls over and touches the Jack before the next succeeding Bowl is delivered, or if in the case of the last Bowl of an end it falls and touches the Jack within the period of 30 seconds invoked under Law 53, such Bowl shall also be a 'toucher'. No Bowl shall be accounted a 'toucher' by playing on to, or by coming into contact with, the Jack while the Jack is in the ditch. If a 'toucher' in the ditch cannot be seen from the mat, its position may be marked by a white or coloured peg about 2in (51mm) broad placed upright on the top of the bank and immediately in line with the place where the 'toucher' rests.

34. Marking a 'toucher'

A 'toucher' shall be clearly marked with a chalk mark by a member of the player's team. If, in the opinion of either Skip, or Opponent in Singles, a 'toucher' or a wrongly chalked Bowl comes to rest in such a position that the act of making a chalk mark, or of erasing it, is likely to move the Bowl or to alter the head, the Bowl shall not be marked or have its mark erased but shall be 'indicated' as a 'toucher' or 'non-toucher' as the case may be. If a Bowl is not so marked or not so 'indicated' before the succeeding Bowl comes to rest, it ceases to be a 'toucher'. If both Skips or Opponents agree that any subsequent movement of the Bowl eliminates the necessity for continuation of the 'indicated' provision, the Bowl shall thereupon be marked or have the chalk mark erased as the case may be. Care should be taken to remove 'toucher' marks from all Bowls before they are played, but should a player fail to do so, and should the Bowl not become a 'toucher' in the end in play, the marks shall be removed by the opposing Skip or his deputy or Marker immediately the Bowl comes to rest, unless the Bowl is 'indicated' as a 'non-toucher' in circumstances governed by earlier provisions of this Law.

35. Movement of 'Touchers'

A 'toucher' in play in the ditch may be moved by the impact of a Jack in play or of another 'toucher' in play, and also by the impact of a 'non-toucher' which remains in play after the impact, and any movement of the 'toucher' by such incidents shall be valid. However, should the 'non-toucher' enter the ditch at any time after the impact, it shall be dead, and the 'toucher' shall be deemed to have been displaced by a dead Bowl, and provisions of Law 38(e) shall apply.

36. Bowl Accounted 'Dead'

(a) Without limiting the application of any other of these Laws, a bowl shall be accounted dead if:

(i) Not being a 'toucher', comes to rest in the ditch or rebounds on the playing surface of the rink after contact with the bank or with the Jack or a 'toucher' in the ditch; or

(ii) After completing its original course, or after being moved as a result of play, it comes to rest wholly outside the boundaries of the playing surface of the rink, or within 45ft (13.71m) of the front of the mat; or

(iii) In its original course, passes beyond a side boundary of the rink on a bias which would prevent its re-entering the rink. (A Bowl is not rendered 'dead' by a player carrying it whilst inspecting the head.)

(b) Skips or the Opponents in Singles shall agree on the question as to whether or not a Bowl is 'dead'. Any member of either team may request a decision from the Skips but no member shall remove any Bowl prior to agreement by the Skips. Once their attention has been drawn to the matter, the Skips by agreement must make a decision. If they cannot reach agreement, the Umpire must make an immediate decision.

37. Bowl Rebounding

Only 'touchers' rebounding from the face of the bank to the ditch or the rink shall remain in play.

38. Bowl Displacement

(a) Displacement by rebounding 'non-toucher' – bowl displaced by a 'non-toucher' rebounding from the bank shall be restored as near as possible to its original position, by a member of the opposing team or by the Marker.

(b) Displacement by participating player – if a Bowl, while in motion or at rest on the green, or a 'toucher' in the ditch, be interfered with or displaced by one of the players, the opposing Skip shall have the option of:

(i) Restoring the Bowl as near as possible to its original position;

(ii) Letting it remain where it rests;

(iii) Declaring the Bowl 'dead'; or

(iv) Declaring the end 'dead'.

(c) Displacement by a neutral object or neutral person (other than as provided in Clause (d) hereof):

(i) Of a bowl in its original course – if such a Bowl be displaced within the boundaries of the rink of play without having disturbed the head, it shall be replayed. If it be displaced and it has disturbed the head, the Skips, or the Opponents in Singles, shall reach agreement on the final position of the displaced Bowl and on the replacement of the head, otherwise the end shall be 'dead'.

These provisions shall also apply to a Bowl in its original course displaced outside the boundaries of the rink of play provided such a Bowl was running on a bias which would have enabled it to re-enter the rink.

(ii) Of a Bowl at rest, or in motion as a result of play after being at rest – if such a bowl be displaced, the Skips or Opponents in Singles, shall come to an agreement as to the position of the Bowl and of the replacement of any parts of the head disturbed by the displaced Bowl, otherwise the end shall be 'dead'.

(d) Displacement inadvertently produced – if a Bowl be moved at the time of its being marked or measured it shall be restored to its former position by an opponent. If such displacement is caused by a Marker or an Umpire, the Marker or Umpire shall replace the Bowl.

(e) Displacement by a 'dead' Bowl – if a 'toucher' in the ditch be displaced by a 'dead' Bowl from the rink of play, it shall be restored to its original position by a player of the opposite team or by the Marker.

39. 'Line bowls'

A Bowl shall not be accounted as outside the line unless it be entirely clear of it. This shall be ascertained by looking perpendicularly down upon the Bowl or by placing a square on the green.

MOVEMENT OF JACK

40. A 'live' Jack in the Ditch

A Jack moved by a Bowl in play into the front ditch within the boundaries of the rink shall be deemed to be 'live'. It may be moved by the impact of a 'toucher' in play and also by the impact of a 'non-toucher' which remains in play after the impact; any movement of the Jack by such incidents shall be valid. However, should the 'non-toucher' enter the ditch after impact, it shall be 'dead' and the Jack shall be deemed to have been 'displaced' by a 'dead' Bowl and the provisions of Law 48 shall apply. If the Jack in the ditch cannot be seen from the mat its position shall be marked by a 'white' peg about 2in (51mm) broad and not more than 4in (102mm) in height, placed upright on top of the bank and immediately in line from the place where the Jack rests.

41. A Jack Accounted 'Dead'

Should the Jack be driven by a Bowl in play and come to rest wholly beyond the boundary of the rink, i.e. over the bank or over the side boundary, or into any opening or inequality of any kind in the bank, or rebound to a distance less than 61ft (18.59m) in a direct line from the centre of the front edge of the mat to the Jack in its rebounded position, it shall be accounted 'dead'.

(National Associations have the option to vary the distance to which a Jack may rebound and still be playable for games other than International and Commonwealth Games.)

42. 'Dead' End

When the Jack is 'dead', the end shall be regarded as a 'dead' end and shall not be accounted as a played end, even though all the Bowls in that end have been played. All 'dead' ends shall be played anew in the same direction unless both Skips or Opponents in Singles agree to play in the opposite direction.

After a 'dead' end situation the right to deliver the Jack shall always return to the player who delivered the original Jack.

43. Playing to a Boundary Jack

The Jack, if driven to the side boundary of the rink and not wholly beyond its limits, may be played to on either hand and if necessary a Bowl may pass outside the side limits of the rink. A Bowl so played, which comes to rest within the boundaries of the rink, shall not be accounted 'dead'.

If the Jack be driven to the side boundary line and comes to rest partly within the limits of the rink, a Bowl played outside the limits of the rink and coming to rest entirely outside the boundary line, even though it has made contact with the Jack, shall be accounted 'dead' and shall be removed to the bank by a member of the player's team.

44. A Damaged Jack

In the event of a Jack being damaged, the Umpire shall decide if another Jack is necessary and, if so, the end shall be regarded as a 'dead' end and another Jack shall be substituted and the end shall be replayed anew.

45. A Rebounding Jack

If the Jack is driven against the face of the bank and rebounds on to the rink, or after being played into the ditch it be operated on by a 'toucher' so as to find its way on to the rink, it shall be played to in the same manner as if it had never left the rink.

46. Jack Displacement

(*a*) *By a player*: If the Jack be diverted from its course while in motion on the green, or displaced while at rest on the green, or in the ditch, by any one of the players, the opposing Skip shall have the Jack restored to its former position, or allow it to remain where it rests and play the end to a finish, or declare the end 'dead'.

(*b*) *Inadvertently produced*: If the Jack be moved at the time of measuring by a player it shall be restored to its former position by an opponent.

47. Jack Displaced by Non-player

(*a*) If the Jack, whether in motion or at rest on the rink, or in the ditch, be displaced by a Bowl from another rink, or by any object or by an individual not a member of the team, the two Skips shall decide as to its original position, and if they are unable to agree, the end shall be declared 'dead'.

(*b*) If a Jack be displaced by a Marker or Umpire, it shall be restored by him to its original position, of which he shall be the sole judge.

48. Jack Displaced by 'Non-toucher'

A Jack displaced in the rink of play by a 'non-toucher' rebounding from the bank shall be restored, or as near as possible, to its original position by a player of the opposing team, or by the Marker in a Singles game. Should a Jack, however, after having been played into the ditch, be displaced by a 'dead Bowl', it shall be restored to its marked position by a player of the opposing team or by the Marker.

FOURS PLAY

The basis of the game of bowls is fours play.

49. The Rink and Fours Play

(*a*) *Designation of players*: A team shall consist of four players, named respectively Lead, Second, Third and Skip, according to the order in which they play, each playing two Bowls.

(*b*) *Order of play*: The Leads shall play their two Bowls alternately, and so on, each pair of players in succession to the end. No one shall play until his opponent's Bowl shall have come to rest. Except under circumstances provided for in Law 63, the order of play shall not be changed after the first end has been played, under penalty of disqualification, such penalty involving the forfeiture of the match or game to the opposing team.

50. Possession of the Rink

Possession of the rink shall belong to the team whose Bowl is being played. The players in possession of the rink for the time being shall not be interfered with, annoyed, or have their attention distracted in any way by their opponents.

As soon as each Bowl shall have come to rest, possession of the rink shall be transferred to the other team, time being allowed for marking a 'toucher'.

51. Position of Players
Players of each team not in the act of playing or controlling play shall stand behind the Jack and away from the head or 3ft (92cm) behind the mat. As soon as the Bowl is delivered, the Skip or player directing, if in front of the Jack, shall retire behind it.

52. Players and their Duties
(a) *The Skip* shall have sole charge of his team and his instructions shall be observed by his players. With the opposing Skip he shall decide all disputed points, and when both agree their decision shall be final.

If both Skips cannot agree, the point in dispute shall be referred to and considered by an Umpire, whose decision shall be final.

A Skip may at any time delegate his powers and any of his duties to other members of his team, provided that such delegation is notified to the opposing Skip.

(b) *The Third*: The Third player may have deputed to him the duty of measuring any and all disputed shots.

(c) *The Second*: The Second player shall keep a record of all shots scored for and against his team and shall at all times retain possession of the score card whilst play is in progress. He shall see that the names of all players are entered on the score card, shall compare his record of the game with that of the opposing Second player as each end is declared, and at the close of the game shall hand his score card to his Skip.

(d) *The Lead*: The Lead shall place the mat, and shall deliver the Jack, ensuring that the Jack is properly centred before playing his first Bowl.

(e) In addition to the duties specified in the preceding clauses, any player may undertake such duties as may be assigned to him by the Skip in Clause 52(a) hereof.

RESULT OF END

53. 'The Shot'
A shot or shots shall be adjudged by the Bowl or Bowls nearer to the Jack than any Bowl played by the opposing player or players.

When the last Bowl has come to rest, 30 seconds shall elapse, if either team desires, before the shots are counted.

Neither Jack nor Bowls shall be moved until each Skip has agreed as to the number of shots, except in circumstances where a Bowl has to be moved to allow the measuring of another Bowl.

54. Measuring Conditions to be Observed

No measuring shall be allowed until the end has been completed.

All measurements shall be made to the nearest point of each object. If a Bowl requiring to be measured is resting on another Bowl which prevents its measurement, the best available means shall be taken to secure its position, whereupon the other Bowl shall be removed. The same course shall be followed where more than two Bowls are involved, or where, in the course of measuring, a single Bowl is in danger of falling or otherwise changing its position.

When it is necessary to measure to a Bowl or Jack in the ditch, and another Bowl or Jack on the green, and measurement shall be made with the ordinary flexible measure. Calipers may be used to determine the shot when the Bowls in question and the Jack are on the same plane.

55. 'Tie' – No Shot

When at the conclusion of play in any end the nearest Bowl of each team is touching the Jack, or is deemed to be equidistant from the Jack, there shall be no score recorded. The end shall be declared 'drawn' and shall be counted a played end.

56. Nothing in these Laws shall be deemed to make it mandatory for the last player to play his last Bowl in any end, but he shall declare to his Opponent or opposing Skip his intention to refrain from playing it before the commencement of determining the result of the end and this declaration shall be irrevocable.

GAME DECISIONS

57. In the case of a single game or a team game or a side game played on one occasion, or at any stage of an eliminating competition, the victory decision shall be awarded to the player, team or side of players producing at the end of the game the higher total score of shots, or in the case of a 'game of winning ends', a majority of winning ends.

58. Tournament Games and Games in Series

In the case of tournament games or games in series, the victory decisions shall be awarded to the player, team or side of players producing at the end of the tournament or series of contests either the largest number of winning games or the highest net score of shots in accordance with the regulations governing the tournament or series of games.

Points may be used to indicate game successes.

Where points are equal, the aggregate shots scored against each team (or side) shall be divided into the aggregate shots it has scored. The team (or side) with the highest result shall be declared the winner.

59. Playing to a Finish and Possible Drawn Games

If in an eliminating competition, consisting of a stated or agreed upon number of ends, it be found, when all the ends have been played, that the scores are equal, an extra end or ends shall be played until a decision has been reached.

The Captains or Skips shall toss and the winner shall have the right to decide who shall play first. The extra end shall be played from where the previous end was completed, and the mat shall be placed in accordance with Law 24.

DEFAULTS OF PLAYERS IN FOURS PLAY

60. Absentee Players in any Team or Side

(a) *In a single fours game*, for a trophy, prize or other competitive award, where a club is represented by only one Four, each member of such Four shall be a bona fide member of the club. Unless all four players appear and are ready to play at the end of the maximum waiting period of 30 minutes, or should they introduce an ineligible player, then that team shall forfeit the match to the opposing team.

(b) *In a domestic Fours game*: Where, in a domestic Fours game the number of players cannot be accommodated in full teams of four players, three players may play against three players, but shall suffer the deduction of one-fourth of the total score of each team.

A smaller number of players than six shall be excluded from that game.

(c) *In a side game*: If, within a period of 30 minutes from the time fixed for the game, a single player is absent from one or both teams in a side game, whether a friendly club match or a match for a trophy, prize or other award, the game shall proceed, but in the defaulting team, the number of Bowls shall be made up by the Lead and Second players playing three Bowls each, but one-fourth of the total shots scored by each 'four' playing three men shall be deducted from their score at the end of the game.

Fractions shall be taken into account.

(d) *In a side game*: Should such default take place where more Fours than one are concerned, or where a Four has been disqualified for some other infringement, and where the average score is to decide the contest, the scores of the non-defaulting Fours only shall be counted, but such average shall, as a penalty in the case of the defaulting side, be arrived at by dividing the aggregate score of that side by the number of Fours that should have been played and not, as in the case of the other side, by the number actually engaged in the game.

61. Play Irregularities

(*a*) *Playing out of turn*: When a player has played before his turn, the opposing Skip shall have the right to stop the Bowl in its course and it shall be played in its proper turn, but, in the event of the bowl so played having moved or displaced the Jack or a Bowl, the opposing Skip shall have the option of allowing the end to remain as it is after the Bowl so played has come to rest, or of having the end declared 'dead'.

(*b*) *Playing the wrong Bowl*: A Bowl played by mistake shall be replaced by the player's own Bowl.

(*c*) *Changing Bowls*: A player shall not be allowed to change his Bowls during the course of a game, or in a resumed game, unless they be objected to as provided in Law 9(*d*), or when a Bowl has been so damaged in the course of play as, in the opinion of the Umpire, to render the Bowl (or Bowls) unfit for play.

(*d*) *Omitting to play*:

(i) If the result of an end has been agreed upon, or the head has been touched in the agreed process of determining the result, then a player who forfeits or has omitted to play a Bowl, shall forfeit the right to play it.

(ii) A player who has neglected to play a Bowl in the proper sequence shall forfeit the right to play such Bowl, if a Bowl has been played by each team before such mistake was discovered.

(iii) If before the mistake is noticed, a Bowl has been delivered in the reversed order and the head has not been disturbed, the opponent shall then play two successive Bowls to restore the correct sequence. If the head has been disturbed, Law 61(*a*) shall apply.

62. Play Interruptions

(*a*) *Game stoppages*: When a game of any kind is stopped, either by mutual arrangement or by the Umpire, after appeal to him on account of darkness or the conditions of the weather, or any other valid reason, it shall be resumed with the scores as they were when the game stopped. An end commenced, but not completed, shall be declared null.

(*b*) *Substitutes in a resumed game*: If in a resumed game any one of the four original players be not available, one substitute shall be permitted as stated in Law 63 below. Players, however, shall not be transferred from one team to another.

INFLUENCES AFFECTING PLAY

63. Leaving the Green

If during the course of a side Fours, Triples or Pairs game a player has to leave the green owing to illness, or other reasonable cause, his place shall be filled by a substitute, if in the opinion of both Skips (or failing agreement by them, then in the opinion of the Controlling Body) such substitution is necessary. Should the player affected be a Skip, his duties and position in a Fours game shall be assumed by the Third player, and the substitute shall play either as Lead, Second or Third. In the case of Triples the substitute may play either as Lead or Second but not a Skip, and in the case of Pairs the substitute shall play as Lead only. Such substitute shall be a member of the club to which the team belongs. In domestic play National Authorities may decide the position of any substitute.

If during the course of a single-handed game a player has to leave the green owing to illness, or reasonable cause, the provisions of Law 62(*a*) shall be observed.

No player shall be allowed to delay the play by leaving the rink or team, unless with the consent of his opponent, and then only for a period not exceeding 10 minutes.

Contravention of this Law shall entitle the Opponent or opposing team to claim the game or match.

64. Objects on the Green

Under no circumstances, other than as provided in Laws 29, 33 and 40, shall any extraneous object to assist a player be placed on the green, or on the bank, or on the Jack, or on a Bowl, or elsewhere.

65. Unforeseen Incidents

If during the course of play the position of the Jack or Bowls be disturbed by wind, storm or by any neutral object, the end shall be declared 'dead', unless the Skips are agreed as to the replacement of Jack or Bowls.

DOMESTIC ARRANGEMENTS

66. In addition to any matters specifically mentioned in these Laws. National Authorities may, in circumstances dictated by climate or other local conditions, make such other regulations as are deemed necessary and desirable, but such regulations must be submitted to the WBB for approval. For this purpose the Board shall appoint a committee, to be known as the 'Laws Committee', with powers to grant approval or otherwise to any proposal, such decision being valid until the proposal is submitted to the Board for a final decision.

67. Local Arrangements

Constituent clubs of National Authorities shall also, in making their domestic arrangements, make such regulations as are deemed necessary to govern their club competitions, but such regulations shall comply with the Laws of the Game and be approved by the Council of their National Authority.

68. National Visiting Teams or Sides

No team or side of bowlers visiting overseas or the British Isles shall be recognised by the World Bowls Board unless it first be sanctioned and recommended by the National Authority to which its members are affiliated.

69. Contracting Out

No club or club management committee or any individual shall have the right or power to contract out of any of the Laws of the Game as laid down by the World Bowls Board.

REGULATING SINGLE-HANDED, PAIRS AND TRIPLES GAMES

70. The foregoing Laws, where applicable, shall also apply to Single-Handed, Pairs and Triples games.

SPECTATORS

71. Persons not engaged in the game shall be situated clear of and beyond the limits of the rink of play and clear of the verges. They shall neither by word nor act disturb or advise the players. This shall not apply to advice given by a Manager or in his absence his delegated deputy of a team or side.

Betting or gambling in connection with any game or games shall not be permitted or engaged in within the grounds of any constituent club.

DUTIES OF MARKER

72. (a) In the absence of the Umpire the Marker shall control the game in accordance with the WBB Basic Laws. He shall, before play commences, examine all Bowls for the imprint of the WBB stamp, or that of its National Authority, such imprint to be clearly visible, and shall ascertain by measurement the width of the rink of play (see note on Stamp Details below).

(b) He shall centre the Jack and shall place a full-length Jack 6ft (1.84m) from the ditch.

(c) He shall ensure that the Jack is not less than 70ft (21.35m) from the front edge of the mat, after it has been centred.

(d) He shall stand at one side of the rink, and to the rear of the Jack.

(e) He shall answer affirmatively or negatively a player's enquiry as to whether a Bowl is Jack high. If requested he shall indicate the distance of any Bowl from the Jack, or from any other Bowl, and also, if requested, indicate which Bowl he thinks is shot and/or the relative position of any other Bowl.

(f) Subject to contrary directions from either opponent under Law 34, he shall mark all 'touchers' immediately they come to rest, and remove chalk marks from 'non-touchers'. With the agreement of both opponents he shall remove all 'dead' Bowls from the green and the ditch. He shall mark the positions of the Jack and 'touchers' which are in the ditch (see Laws 33 and 40).

(*g*) He shall not move, or cause to be moved, either Jack or Bowls until each player has agreed to the number of shots.

(*h*) He shall measure carefully all doubtful shots when requested by either player. If unable to come to a decision satisfactory to the players, he shall call in an Umpire. If an official Umpire has not been appointed, the Marker shall select one. The decision of the Umpire shall be final.

(*i*) He shall enter the score at each end and shall intimate to the players the state of the game. When the game is finished, he shall see that the scorecard, containing the names of the players, is signed by the players, and disposed of in accordance with the rules of the competition.

DUTIES OF UMPIRE

73. An Umpire shall be appointed by the Controlling Body of the Association, Club or Tournament Management Committee. His duties shall be as follows:

(*a*) He shall examine all bowls for the imprint of the WBB stamp or that of its National Authority and ascertain by measurement the width of the rinks of play.

(*b*) He shall measure any shot or shots in dispute, and for this purpose shall use a suitable measure. His decision shall be final.

(*c*) He shall decide all questions as to the distance of the mat from the ditch and the Jack from the mat.

(*d*) He shall decide as to whether or not Jack and/or Bowls are in play.

(*e*) He shall enforce the Laws of the Game.

(*f*) In World Bowls Championships and Commonwealth Games the Umpire's decision shall be final in respect of any breach of a Law, except that, upon questions relating to the meaning of interpretation of any Law there shall be a right of appeal to the Controlling Body.

WORLD BOWLS BOARD BY-LAWS

Professional Bowler

All players are eligible for selection for Commonwealth Games except those whose principal source of income is derived from playing the Game of Bowls.

Stamping of Bowls

Manufacturers/Testers will be entitled to use the registered IBB/WBB stamp, to facilitate the imprint between the inner and outer rings of Bowls. Imprints on running surfaces should be avoided wherever possible.

Stamp Details

BIB – International Bowling Board.

A – Denotes code letter of Manufacturer/Tester.
Numerals – Denotes year of expiry.
R – Denotes that the stamp is a registered trade mark.

A new WBB stamp is being phased in gradually and all new and retested Bowls will then carry the new WBB stamp. The IBB stamp will remain valid until the expiry date of each Bowl.

Metric Equivalents

In connection with the manufacture of Bowls there is no objection to manufacturers using metric equivalents in lieu of the present figures, always provided that Law 9 of the Board's Laws is complied with. Furthermore, there is no objection to manufacturers indicating various sizes of Bowls by numerals, and the manufacturers will be entitled to use the following table if they so desire.

Size in inches	Size number	May be rounded off Metric (mm)
$4\frac{9}{16}$	00	116
$4\frac{5}{8}$	0	117
$4\frac{3}{4}$	1	121
$4\frac{13}{16}$	2	122
$4\frac{7}{8}$	3	124
$4\frac{15}{16}$	4	125
5	5	127
$5\frac{1}{16}$	6	129
$5\frac{1}{8}$	7	131

THE RULES OF

Boxing

Boxing

RULE 1

Ring

In all tournaments, the ring shall conform with the following requirements:

(*a*) The minimum size shall be 14ft (4.27m) square and the maximum size 20ft (6.10m) square, measured inside the line of the ropes. In senior Championships the minimum size of the ring must be 16ft (4.88m) square.

(*b*) The platform shall be safely constructed, level and free from any obstructing projections and shall extend for at least 18in (50cm) outside the line of the ropes. It shall be fitted with four corner posts which shall be well padded or otherwise so constructed as to prevent injury to the boxers.

(*c*) The floor shall be covered with felt, rubber or other suitable, ABA-approved material having the same quality of elasticity, not less than ½in (1.5cm) and not more than ¾in (1.9cm) thick over which canvas shall be stretched and secured in place. The felt, rubber or other approved material, and canvas shall cover the entire platform.

(*d*) There shall be three or four ropes of a thickness of (1.18in) 3cm minimum to (1.96in) 5cm maximum tightly drawn from the corner posts at equal intervals from (1ft 3.7in) 40cm to (4ft 3in) 1.30m high. The ropes shall be covered with a soft or smooth material.

The ropes shall be joined on each side, at equal intervals, by two pieces of close textured canvas (1½in) 3 to 4cm wide. The pieces must not slide along the rope.

(*e*) The ring shall be provided with suitable steps at opposite corners for the use of the contestants, officials and seconds.

(*f*) At all Dinner/Boxing Tournaments a minimum distance of 6ft 6in (2m) shall be clear of all tables, excluding those required for use by officials.

(*g*) The only persons authorised to enter the ring shall be a boxer, coach, Referee, MC and Medical Officer on the instruction of the Referee.

RULE 2

Gloves

(i) For boxers 67kg and below, all will wear 8oz.

(ii) All boxers over 67kg will wear 10oz.

(iii) During Championships weight allowance will be discounted when deciding the weight of gloves to be used.

(iv) In Club Tournaments, if one boxer is over 67kg both boxers will wear 10oz gloves.

RULE 3

(*a*) Headguards

At all tournaments properly fitted headguards must be worn.

In cases of the headguard becoming displaced, the following shall apply:

1st occasion:

The Referee shall instruct the second to re-fit the headguard.

2nd occasion:

The Referee shall take similar action, except that he shall warn the second that if the headguard becomes displaced a third time, the bout shall be stopped R.S.C. in the opponent's favour.

The Referee shall use his discretion as to the time allowed for replacement of the headguard on occasions 1 and 2.

(*b*) Bandages

A soft surgical bandage, not to exceed 8ft 4in (2.5m) in length and 2in (5cm) in width, or a bandage of the Velpeau type or crepe not to exceed 2m (6ft 6in) in length, may be worn on each hand. No other kind of bandage may be used. The use of any kind of tapes, rubber or adhesive plaster, as bandages, is strictly forbidden, but a single strap of adhesive 3in (7.5cm) long and 1in (2.5cm) wide must be used at the upper wrists to secure the bandages.

Juniors must not wear bandages on the hands in Championships or contests of 3 × 1½ minutes per round.

(*c*) **Number of Contests**

Junior boxers may box a maximum of 14 contests per season; senior boxers a maximum of 18 contests per season, excluding Championships and Internationals in both cases.

(*d*) **Three Day Rule**

There shall be 3 clear days between contests. During specific recognised Championships and Internationals the 3-day rule will not apply.

RULE 4

Dress

Competitors shall be dressed in accordance with the following:

(*a*) Competitors shall box in light boots or shoes (without spikes and without any heels), socks, shorts reaching at least half-way down the thigh, and a vest covering the chest and back. Where shorts and vests are of the same colour the belt line must be clearly indicated by marking of a distinctive colour.

Note: The belt is an imaginary line that runs from the navel to the top of the hips.

(*b*)(i) Gum shields must be worn. If the gum shield comes out accidentally it shall be washed and replaced. If it is deliberately ejected or removed one or two times the boxer shall be cautioned. A third offence will warrant a warning.

   (ii) The Referee shall exclude from competing any senior or junior (over 15) boxer who is not wearing a cup-protector or any boxer who is not clean and properly dressed.

   (iii) In the event of a boxer's glove or dress becoming undone during the bout, the Referee shall stop the contest and have it attended to.

(*c*) No other objects may be worn during the competition.

(*d*) The use of grease, vaseline or products likely to be harmful or objectionable to an opponent, on the face, arms or any other part of the body is forbidden.

(*e*) Beards are forbidden. Long hair is not permissible unless completely covered by the headguard. A fringe in front must not extend below the level of the eyebrows.

(*f*) Every Regional Association will arrange for their boxers to have an ME3, which must contain a record of the boxers' bouts, names of opponents and showing the result, how won or lost.

(*g*) Competitors must wear distinguishing colours, such as red or blue sashes round the waist.

RULE 5

Classified Boxing Weights
A.B.A. Championships at 12 weights shall be:

Light Fly:	Over 45kg and not exceeding 48kg.
Fly:	Over 48kg and not exceeding 51kg.
Bantam:	Over 51kg and not exceeding 54kg.
Feather:	Over 54kg and not exceeding 57kg.
Light:	Over 57kg and not exceeding 60kg.
Light Welter:	Over 60kg and not exceeding 63.5kg.
Welter:	Over 63.5kg and not exceeding 67kg.
Light Middle:	Over 67kg and not exceeding 71kg.
Middle:	Over 71kg and not exceeding 75kg.
Light Heavy:	Over 75kg and not exceeding 81kg.
Heavy:	Over 81kg and not exceeding 91kg.
Super Heavy:	Over 91kg.

The junior weights shall be:

Class A	**Class B**
Over 15 and under 16 years of age.	*Over 16 and under 17 years of age.*
Not under 39kg or over 42kg	Not under 39kg or over 42kg
Not under 42kg or over 45kg	Not under 42kg or over 45kg
Not under 45kg or over 48kg	Not under 45kg or over 48kg
Not under 48kg or over 51kg	Not under 48kg or over 51kg
Not under 51kg or over 54kg	Not under 51kg or over 54kg
Not under 54kg or over 57kg	Not under 54kg or over 57kg
Not under 57kg or over 60kg	Not under 57kg or over 60kg
Not under 60kg or over 63.5kg	Not under 60kg or over 63.5kg
Not under 63.5kg or over 67kg	Not under 63.5kg or over 67kg
Not under 67kg or over 71kg	Not under 67kg or over 71kg
	Not under 71kg or over 74kg
	Not under 74kg or over 77kg

RULE 6

Weigh-in
Senior competitors to weigh-in on the day of competition, stripped. Juniors to weigh-in in boxing shorts only.

RULE 7

Draws and Byes

The draw shall take place after the weigh-in and medical examination. In competitions where there are more than four competitors a sufficient number of byes shall be drawn in the first series to reduce the number of competitors in the second series to 4, 8, 16 or 32. Bouts shall be drawn first.

Competitors drawing a bye in the first series shall be the first to box in the second series. If there is an odd number of byes, the boxer who draws the last bye will compete in the second series against the winner of the first bout in the first series.

Where the number of byes is even the boxers drawing byes shall box the first bouts in the second series in the order in which they are drawn.

No competitor may receive a bye in the first series and a 'walk-over' in the second series or two consecutive 'walk-overs'. Should such a situation arise a fresh draw shall be made of the other boxers remaining in the series who have not received a bye or a walk-over in the preceding series. The first boxer to be drawn will meet the boxer who has benefited from a bye or walk-over in the preceding series, and the new draw shall then proceed in the normal way.

Table for Drawing Bouts and Byes

No. of Entries	Bouts	Byes
5	1	3
6	2	2
7	3	1
8	4	–
9	1	7

RULE 8

Duration of Rounds

The number and duration of rounds for senior contests shall be as follows:

Contests:

Between open-class boxers – 3 rounds of 3 minutes each.

Between an open-class boxer and an intermediate-class boxer – 3 rounds of 3 minutes each.

Between intermediate-class boxers – 3 rounds of 3 minutes each.

Open and intermediate-class boxers may be permitted to box 4 × 2 minute rounds, if both boxers and trainers are in agreement.

Between an intermediate-class boxer and a novice-class boxer – 3 rounds of 2 minutes each or 4 rounds of 2 minutes each, by agreement. Between novice-class boxers – 3 rounds of 2 minutes each or 4 rounds of 2 minutes each, by agreement.

In every case, there shall be an interval lasting one minute between the rounds.

In junior contests, the duration of bouts shall not exceed three rounds of $1\frac{1}{2}$ minutes each round for juniors under 15 years of age; three rounds of 2 minutes for juniors from 15 to 16 years of age and three rounds of 2 minutes for juniors from 16 to 17 years of age, with 1 minute intervals between the rounds in each case.

RULE 9

The Second
Each competitor is entitled to one second and one assistant second who shall be governed by the following rules:

(a) Only the second and assistant second shall mount the ring platform, but only the chief second can enter the ring. Both seconds may service the boxer.

(b) No advice, assistance or encouragement shall be given to the competitor by his second or assistant during the progress of the rounds.

(c) A second may retire his boxer, and may, when he considers his boxer to be in difficulty, throw the towel into the ring, except when the Referee is in course of counting.

(d) During the boxing, neither second nor assistant second shall remain on the platform of the ring. The second or assistant second shall, before a round begins, remove from the platform of the ring, seats, towels, buckets, etc.

(e) Any second, assistant second or official encouraging or inciting spectators by words or signs to advise or encourage a boxer during the progress of a round or infringing the rules in any other way may be warned or disqualified from acting as a second, assistant second or official for the remainder of the contest concerned. If a second, assistant second or official is disqualified from acting in that capacity by the Referee for a second time at the same tournament, he will be suspended from taking any further part in that tournament. This action shall be recorded on the OIC's Report Form.

(f) No stimulant of any kind other than water may be administered to a boxer immediately prior to or during a bout.

Seconds must wear white or plain grey trousers, and white vest or white shirt or a white sweater. Training shoes or boxing boots must be worn. Track suits and white jackets are permitted.

If a second or his assistant infringes the Rules he may be warned or disqualified. His boxer may also be cautioned, warned or disqualified by the Referee for offences that have been committed by the second or assistant second.

RULE 10

Dressing Rooms

Suitable dressing-room accommodation must be provided for competitors at all tournaments. Whenever possible, separate dressing-room accommodation should be provided for appointed officials.

RULE 11

The 'Break'

When a Referee orders the two competitors to 'break' both boxers must step back one pace before recommencing to box. A boxer shall not attempt to strike his opponent on the 'break'. A competitor breaking this Rule shall be liable to disqualification.

RULE 12

Control of Bouts: Referees, Judges and Timekeepers

All contests shall be controlled by a Referee, three judges and a timekeeper. The Referee shall officiate in the ring. When less than 3 judges are available the Referee shall complete a scoring paper.

Referees shall use a score pad or introduction slip to record the names and colours of the boxers. In all cases when a bout is terminated through injury or other cause, the Referee shall record the reason thereon and give it to the official-in-charge.

The timekeeper shall be seated at one side of the ring and the judges at the remaining three sides. The seats shall afford them a satisfactory view of the boxing and shall be apart from the spectators. The Referee shall be solely responsible for the control of the bout in accordance with the Rules and the three judges shall independently award points.

When the bell/gong sounds to indicate the end of the contest both boxers must return immediately to their own corners. The Referee shall ensure that this is obeyed.

The Referee shall be attired in white when officiating at tournaments.

RULE 13

Announcement of Decision and Disposal of Scoring Papers

(a) At the end of each bout where the stipulated number of rounds has been completed, the Referee shall collect and verify the judges' scoring papers and instruct the MC to announce the decision stating whether this is a unanimous or majority decision and the judges' scores shall be made known to the public. The Referee will raise the hand of the winner.

(b) If a bout be terminated in favour of one boxer, the Referee shall instruct the MC to announce the name of the winner and the reason for the stoppage, then collect the judges' scoring papers.

(c) both boxers be unable to continue boxing due to injury or simultaneous knock-out, the judges' scoring papers will be collected and the verdict awarded to the boxer who was leading on points when the bout was stopped. In such cases, should the bout be terminated during a round the judges shall award points as though it had been a completed round of boxing.

(d) If a boxer be disqualified the Referee shall instruct the MC to announce the reason for disqualification and the name of the winner. If both boxers be disqualified the Referee shall instruct the MC to announce the reason(s). The judges' scoring papers shall then be collected by the Referee.

(e) When there are only two judges the Referee shall first complete his scoring paper and then collect the judges' scoring papers. Should there be less than two judges the Referee alone shall officiate; on no account shall he officiate with only one judge.

(f) At the termination of each bout the Referee shall hand the scoring papers to the MC who will be responsible for giving them to the official-in-charge, unless other arrangements for their disposal have been made by the ABA or other appropriate Association.

RULE 14

The Referee

1. The Referee shall officiate in the ring. At all tournaments he shall be dressed in white trousers, white shirt and light shoes or boots without raised heels.

2. He shall:

(a) Check the gloves and dress.

(b) Prevent a boxer from receiving undue and unnecessary punishment.

(*c*) See that the Rules and fair play are strictly observed.

(*d*) At the end of the contest collect and check the papers of the three judges; after checking he shall hand these papers to the adjudicator, OIC or announcer.

The Referee shall not indicate the winner, by raising a boxer's hand or otherwise, until the announcement has been made.

3. (*a*) He shall use three words of command:

'Stop' when ordering the boxers to stop boxing.

'Box' when ordering them to continue.

'Break' when breaking a clinch, upon which command each boxer shall step back before continuing boxing.

(*b*) When the winner of a bout is announced the Referee shall raise the hand of the winning boxer.

4. He shall indicate to a boxer by suitable explanatory signs or gestures any infringement of the Rules. Such signs or gestures may be accompanied by verbal cautions or warnings.

5. *Powers of the Referee*

The Referee is empowered:

(*a*) To terminate a contest at any stage if he considers that it is too one-sided.

(*b*) To terminate a contest at any stage if one of the boxers has received any injury on account of which the Referee decides he should not continue.

(*c*) To terminate a contest at any stage if he considers the contestants are not in earnest. In such cases he may disqualify one or both contestants.

(*d*) To caution or administer a warning to a boxer against fouls or for any other reason in the interests of fair play, or to ensure compliance with the Rules.

(*e*) To disqualify a boxer who fails to comply immediately with his orders, or behaves towards him in an offensive or aggressive manner at any time.

(*f*) To disqualify a second or assistant who has infringed the Rules, and the boxer himself if the second or assistant does not comply with the Referee's orders.

(*g*) With or without previous warning to disqualify a contestant for committing a foul.

(*h*) In the event of a knock-down, to suspend a count, if a boxer deliberately fails to retire to a neutral corner or delays to do so.

(*i*) To interpret the Rules in so far as they are applicable or relevant to the actual contest or to decide and take action on any circumstance of the contest which is not covered by a Rule.

6. Should a boxer receive 3 counts in any one round or 4 during a contest, the Referee must terminate the contest.

7. (a) If a boxer infringes the Rules but does not merit disqualification for such infringement, the Referee shall stop the contest and shall issue a warning to the offender. As a preliminary to a warning the Referee shall order the boxers to stop. The warning shall be clearly given and in such a way that the boxer understands the reason and the purpose of the warning. The Referee shall signal with his hand to each of the judges that a warning has been given and shall clearly indicate to them the boxer whom he has warned.

After giving the warning, the Referee shall order the boxers to 'Box'. If a boxer is given three warnings in a contest, he shall be disqualified.

(b) A Referee may caution a boxer. A caution is in the nature of advice or admonishment given by the Referee to a boxer to check or prevent undesirable practices or the less serious infringements of the Rules. To do so he will not necessarily stop the contest but may avail of a suitable safe opportunity during a round to admonish a boxer for an infringement of the Rules.

8. *Medical Examination of Referees for International Tournaments*

A Referee, before officiating in any international tournament conducted under these Rules, shall undergo a medical examination as to his physical fitness for carrying out his duties in the ring. His vision shall be at least 6 dioptres in each eye.

The wearing of spectacles by a Referee during the progress of a bout is not permitted, but contact lenses are allowed.

RULE 15

Judges

(a) Each judge shall independently judge the merits of the two contestants and shall decide the winner according to the Rules.

(b) He shall not speak to a contestant, nor to another judge, nor to anyone else except the Referee during the contest, but may, if necessary, at the end of a round, bring to the notice of the Referee any incident which he (the Referee) may appear not to have noticed, such as the misconduct of a second, loose ropes etc.

(c) The number of points awarded to each competitor shall be entered by a judge on his scoring paper immediately after the end of each round.

(d) At the end of the bout a judge shall total the points, nominate a winner and sign his scoring paper, and the unanimous/majority verdict shall be made known to the public.

(*e*) He shall not leave his seat until the verdict has been announced to the public.

RULE 16

The Timekeeper
The main duty of the timekeeper is to regulate the number and duration of the rounds and the intervals between rounds.

(*a*) He shall be seated directly at the ringside.

(*b*) Five seconds before the commencement of each round he shall clear the ring by ordering 'seconds out'.

(*c*) He shall commence and end each round by striking the gong or bell.

(*d*) He shall announce the number of each round immediately prior to commencing it.

(*e*) He shall take off time for temporary stoppages, or when instructed to do so by the Referee.

(*f*) He shall regulate all periods of time and counts by a watch or clock.

(*g*) At a 'knock-down' he shall signal to the Referee with his hand the passing of the seconds while the Referee is counting.

(*h*) If at the end of any round a boxer is 'down' and the Referee is in the course of counting, the gong indicating the end of the round will not be sounded. The gong will be sounded only when the Referee gives the command 'Box' indicating the continuation of the contest.

The intervals between rounds shall be of a full minute's duration.

RULE 17

Decisions
Decisions shall be as follows:

(*a*) *Win on points*
At the end of a contest the boxer who has been awarded the decision by a majority of the judges shall be declared the winner. If both boxers are injured, or are knocked out simultaneously, and cannot continue the contest, the judges shall record the points gained by each boxer up to its termination, and the boxer who was leading on points up to the actual end of the contest shall be declared the winner.

(*b*) *Win by retirement*
If a boxer retires voluntarily owing to injury or other cause, or if he fails to resume boxing immediately after the rest between rounds, his opponent shall be declared the winner.

(*c*) *Win by Referee stopping contest*

(i) *Outclassed*: If a boxer in the opinion of the Referee is being outclassed, or is receiving excessive punishment, the bout shall be stopped and his opponent declared the winner.

(ii) *Injury*: If a boxer in the opinion of the Referee is unfit to continue because of injury or other physical reasons, the bout shall be stopped and his opponent declared the winner. The right to make this decision rests with the Referee, who may consult the doctor. Having consulted the doctor, the Referee must follow his advice. When a Referee calls a doctor into the ring to examine a boxer, only these two officials should be present. No seconds should be allowed into the ring, nor on the apron.

(*d*) *Win by disqualification*: If a boxer is disqualified his opponent shall be declared the winner. If both boxers are disqualified the decision shall be announced accordingly.

The decision of the judges or Referee, as the case may be, shall be final and without appeal.

The Referee shall have power to caution, warn, or disqualify without warning.

(*e*) *Win by knock-out*: If a boxer is 'down' and he fails to resume boxing within 10 seconds, his opponent shall be declared the winner by a knock-out.

(*f*) *No contest*: A bout may be terminated by the Referee inside the scheduled distance owing to a material happening outside the responsibility of the boxers, or the control of the Referee, such as the ring becoming damaged, the failure of the lighting supply, exceptional weather conditions etc. In such circumstances the bout shall be declared 'no contest' and the official-in-charge shall decide the necessary further action.

RULE 18

Awarding of Points

In awarding points the following directives shall be observed:

Directive 1 – Concerning hits

(*a*) During each round a judge shall assess the respective scores of each boxer according to the number of hits obtained by each. Each hit to have scoring value must, without being blocked or guarded, land directly with the knuckle part of the closed glove of either hand on any part of the front or sides of the head or body above the belt with force. Swings landing as described above are scoring hits.

(*b*) The value of hits scored in a rally of infighting shall be assessed at the end of such rally and shall be credited to the boxer who has had the better of the exchanges according to the degree of his superiority.

(*c*) Hits which are struck by a boxer:

(i) While infringing any of the rules; or

(ii) With the side, the heel, the inside of the glove or with the open glove other than the knuckle part of the closed glove; or,

(iii) Which land on the arms; or

(iv) Which merely connect, without the weight of the body or shoulder, are not scoring hits.

Directive 2 – Concerning fouls

(*a*) During each round a judge shall assess the seriousness of and shall impose a commensurate scoring penalty for any foul witnessed by him irrespective of whether the Referee has observed such foul or not.

(*b*) If the Referee warns one of the competitors, the judges may award a point to the other competitor. When a judge decides to award a point to a competitor for a foul committed by his opponent for which the latter has been warned by the Referee, he shall place a 'W' in the appropriate column against the points of the warned competitor to show that he has done so. If he decides not so to award a point he shall in the appropriate column place the letter 'X' against the points allotted for that round to the warned competitor.

(*c*) If a Judge observes a foul apparently unnoticed by the Referee, and imposes an appropriate penalty on the offending competitor, he shall indicate that he has done so by placing in the appropriate column the letter 'J' against the points of the offending competitor and indicating the reason why he has done so.

Directive 3 – Concerning the awarding of points

(*a*) 20 points shall be awarded for each round. No fraction of points may be given. At the end of each round the better (more skilful) boxer shall receive 20 points and his opponent proportionately less. When boxers are equal in merit, each shall receive 20 points.

(*b*) If at the end of a contest and having marked each round in accordance with Directives 1 and 2 a judge shall find that the boxers are equal in points he shall award the decision to the boxer:

(i) Who has done most of the leading off or who has shown the better style;

or if equal in that respect,

(ii) Who has shown the better defence (blocking, parrying, ducking, side-stepping etc.) by which the opponent's attacks have been made to miss.

A winner must be nominated.

(*c*) No extra points shall be awarded for a knock-down.

RULE 19

Fouls

The competitor who does not obey the instructions of the Referee, acts against the boxing Rules, boxes in any unsportsmanlike manner, or commits fouls, can at the discretion of the Referee be cautioned, warned or disqualified without warning. Only three warnings may be given to the same boxer in one contest. A third warning brings automatic disqualification.

Each boxer is responsible in the same way for his second.

A Referee may, without stopping a contest, caution a boxer at some safe opportunity.

If he intends to warn a boxer, he shall stop the contest, and will demonstrate the infringement. He will then point to the boxer and to each of the three judges.

The following are fouls:

(1) Holding or hitting below the belt, tripping, kicking and butting with foot or knee.

(2) Hits or blows with head, shoulder, forearm, elbow, throttling of the opponent, pressing with arm or elbow in opponent's face, pressing the head of the opponent back over the ropes.

(3) Hitting with open glove, the inside of the glove, wrist or side of the hand.

(4) Hits landing on the back of the opponent, and especially any blow on the back of the neck or head or kidneys.

(5) Pivot blows.

(6) Attack whilst holding onto the ropes or making any unfair use of the ropes.

(7) Lying on, wrestling and throwing in the clinch.

(8) An attack on an opponent who is down or who is in the act of rising.

(9) Holding.

(10) Holding and hitting or pulling and hitting.

(11) Holding, or locking, of the opponent's arm or head, or pushing an arm underneath the arm of the opponent.

(12) Ducking below the belt of the opponent in a manner dangerous to the opponent.

(13) Completely passive defence by means of double cover and intentionally falling to avoid a blow.

(14) Useless, aggressive, or offensive utterances during the round.

(15) Not stepping back when ordered to break.

(16) Attempting to strike an opponent immediately after the Referee has ordered 'Break' and before taking a step back.

(17) Assaulting or behaving in an aggressive manner towards a Referee at any time.

Or any other act the Referee may deem improper.

If a Referee has any reason to believe that a foul has been committed which he himself has not seen he may consult the judges.

RULE 20

Down

(1) A boxer is considered 'down':

(i) If he touches the floor with any part of his body other than his feet; or

(ii) If he hangs helplessly on the ropes; or

(iii) If he is outside or partly outside the ropes; or

(iv) If following a hard punch he has not fallen and is not lying on the ropes, but is in a distressed state and cannot, in the opinion of the Referee, continue the bout.

(2) In the case of a knock-down the Referee shall immediately begin to count the seconds. If a boxer is down his opponent must at once go to the corner indicated by the Referee. He may only continue against the opponent who is knocked down after the latter has got up and on the command 'Box' of the Referee. If the opponent should not go to the corner indicated, on the command of the Referee, the Referee shall stop counting until the opponent has done so. The counting shall then be continued where it has been interrupted.

(3) When a boxer is 'down' the Referee shall count aloud from 1 to 10 with intervals of a second between the numbers, and shall indicate each second with his hand in such a manner that the boxer who has been knocked down may be aware of the count. Before the number one is counted, an interval of one second must have elapsed from the time when the boxer has fallen to the floor, and the time of announcing 'one'.

(4) When a boxer is 'down' as the result of a blow the bout shall not be continued until the Referee has reached the count of 8, even if the boxer is ready to continue before then. After the Referee has said '10' the bout ends and shall be decided as a 'knock-out'.

(5) In the event of a boxer being 'down' at the end of a round the Referee shall continue to count. Should the Referee count up to 10, such a boxer shall be deemed to have lost the bout by a 'knock-out'. If the boxer is fit to resume boxing before the count of 10 is reached, the Referee shall immediately use the command 'Box'.

(6) If a boxer is 'down' as the result of a blow and the bout is continued after the count of 8 has been reached, but the boxer falls again

without having received a fresh blow, the Referee shall continue the counting from the count of 8 at which he had stopped.

(7) If both boxers go down at the same time, counting will be continued as long as one of them is still down. If both boxers remain down until '10' the bout will be stopped and the decision given in accordance with the points awarded up to the time of the knock-down.

(8) A boxer who fails to resume boxing immediately after the termination of the rest interval, or who, when knocked down by a blow, fails to resume within 10 seconds, shall lose the contest.

RULE 21

Procedure After Knock-outs and RSC (H)

(1) If a boxer is rendered unconscious, then only the Referee and the doctor summoned should remain in the ring, unless the doctor needs extra help.

(2) A boxer who has been knocked out during a contest or wherein the Referee has stopped the contest due to a boxer having received hard blows to the head, making him defenceless or incapable of continuing, shall be examined by a doctor immediately afterwards and accompanied to his home or suitable accommodation by one of the officials on duty at the event.

(3) A boxer who has been knocked out during a contest or wherein the Referee has stopped the contest due to a boxer having received hard blows to the head, making him defenceless or incapable of continuing shall not be permitted to take part in competitive boxing or sparring for a period of at least 28 clear days after he has been knocked out.

(4) A boxer who has been knocked out during a contest or wherein the Referee has stopped the contest due to a boxer having received hard blows to the head, making him defenceless or incapable of continuing twice in a period of 84 days shall not be permitted to take part in competitive boxing or sparring during a period of 84 days from the second knock-out or RSC (H).

(5) A boxer who has been knocked out during a contest or wherein the Referee has stopped the contest due to a boxer having received hard blows to the head, making him defenceless or incapable of continuing three times in a period of 12 months shall not be allowed to take part in competitive boxing or sparring for a period of one year from the third knock-out or RSC (H).

(6) The Referee will indicate to the OIC and judges to annotate the score card 'RSCH' when he has stopped the contest as a result of a boxer being unable to continue as a result of blows to the head.

RULE 22

Shaking of Hands
Before beginning and after a bout, boxers shall shake hands in a proper manner, as a sign of purely sporting and friendly rivalry in accordance with the boxing rules. The shaking of hands takes place before beginning the first round and after the announcing of the result.

Any further shaking of hands between the rounds is prohibited.

RULE 23

Legal Substances/Drug Abuse
All aspects of the control of drugs are laid down in the booklet entitled: 'Medical Regulations and Rules Procedures relating to Drugs Control'. Any boxer or official infringing shall be liable to disqualification or suspension by the ABA. Any boxer who refuses, after a bout, to undergo a medical test to ascertain if he has committed any breach of this rule shall be liable to disqualification or suspension.

RULE 24

Medical Aspects of Boxing
These are laid down in the 'Medical Aspects of Amateur Boxing', 2nd Edition, 1989.

RULE 25

Attendance of a Doctor
It is desirable that a qualified Doctor of Medicine; so approved, shall be in attendance throughout a tournament.

RULE 26

Failure to Resume a Bout
In all bouts, any competitor failing to resume sparring when time is called shall lose the bout.

RULE 27

Breach of these Rules
The breaking of any of these Rules by a competitor or his second shall render such competitor liable to disqualification.

RULE 28

Suspected Foul
If the Referee suspects a foul which he himself has not clearly seen, he shall consult the judges and give his decision accordingly.

RULE 29
Competition Secretaries shall be allowed to see boxers' records as listed on ME3 (Boxers Medical/Record Card) on request.

Reprinted by permission of the Amateur Boxing Association. Some of the rules have been abbreviated and some of the appendixes omitted for reasons of space. Copies of the Complete Rules of Boxing can be obtained from the Association.

British American Football

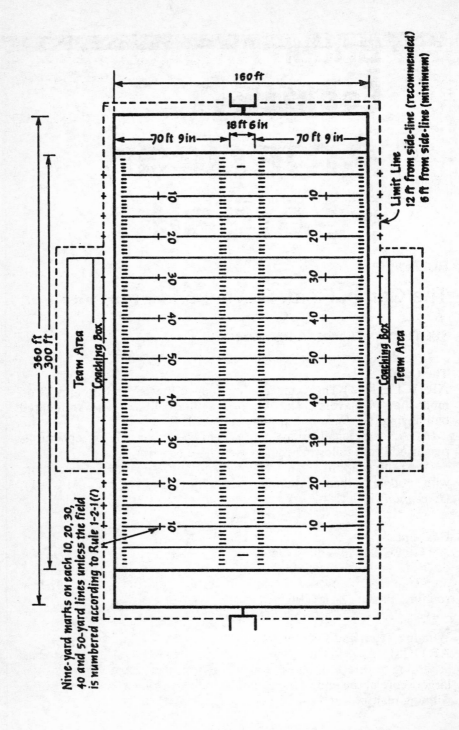

160 ft

18 ft 6 in

70 ft 9 in   70 ft 9 in

360 ft
300 ft

Team Area

Coaching Box

Coaching Box

Team Area

Limit Line
12 ft from side-line (recommended)
6 ft from side-line (minimum)

10   10
20   20
30   30
40   40
50   50
40   40
30   30
20   20
10   10

Nine-yard marks on each 10, 20, 30,
40 and 50-yard lines unless the field
is numbered according to Rule 1-2-1 (l)

British American Football

The Game, Field, Players and Equipment

SECTION 1. GENERAL PROVISIONS

The Game
ARTICLE 1. (*a*) The game shall be played between two teams of no more than 11 players each, on a rectangular field and with an inflated ball having the shape of a prolate spheroid.

(*b*) A team legally may play with fewer than 11 players but is penalised if the following requirements are not met:

1. At the snap, at least 7 men are on the offensive scrimmage line, with not less than 5 numbered 50-79 (Rules 2-21-2, 7-1-3-*b*-1). (*Exception*: Rule 1-4-2-*b*.)

Goal-lines
ARTICLE 2. Goal-lines, one for each team, shall be established at opposite ends of the field of play, and each team shall be allowed opportunities to advance the ball across the other team's goal-line by running, passing or kicking it.

Winning Team and Final Score
ARTICLE 3. (*a*) The teams shall be awarded points for scoring according to rule and, unless the game is forfeited, the team having the larger score at the end of the game, including extra periods, shall be the winning team.

(*b*) The game is ended and the score is final when the referee so declares (Rule 1-1-4-*b*).

(*c*) The score of a terminated-suspended game shall be the final score at the time of the suspension.

Supervision

ARTICLE 4. (*a*) The game shall be played under the supervision of either 4, 5, 6, or 7 officials: a referee, an umpire, a linesman, a line judge, a back judge, a field judge and a side judge. The use of a back judge, field judge and side judge is optional. The game may be played under the supervision of three officials under exceptional circumstances such as injury or delay in travel.

(*b*) The officials' jurisdiction begins 5 minutes before the scheduled kick-off and ends when, after the final period, the referee has left the field.

Team Captains

ARTICLE 5. (*a*) Each team shall designate to the referee one or more players as its field captain(s) and one player at a time shall speak for his team in all dealings with the officials. There shall be no more than four captains at the coin toss.

(*b*) A field captain's first announced choice of any options offered his team shall be irrevocable.

(*c*) Any player may request a team charged time-out.

Persons Subject to the Rules

ARTICLE 6. All players, substitutes, replaced players, coaches, trainers, cheerleaders in uniform, band members in uniform, mascots in uniform, commercial mascots and other persons affiliated with the teams are subject to the rules and shall be governed by the decisions of the officials. Affiliated persons are those authorised within the team area. The names of all persons subject to rules shall appear on a roster form which shall be given to the referee before kick-off. (*Exception*: cheerleaders, band members and mascots.)

Teams Subject to the Rules

ARTICLE 7. (*a*) Teams that are members of BAFA or affiliated leagues shall conduct all contests in Great Britain under the official football-playing rules of the Association. (*Exception*: games played under the auspices of an international organisation.)

(*b*) Teams not complying with football-playing rules that do not have a designated penalty are subject to league and/or BAFA sanctions.

SECTION 2. THE FIELD

Dimensions
ARTICLE 1. The field shall be a rectangular area with dimensions, lines, zones, goals and pylons as indicated and titled in the field diagram.

(*a*) Where it is not possible to fully mark the field as indicated:

1. The marking of the following lines is mandatory: side-lines, end-lines, goal-lines, yard-lines at 5-yard intervals, in-bounds-lines.

2. Where the size of the stadium does not permit a full-sized field to be marked, the end zones must be a minimum of 8 and a maximum of 13 yards in depth and equal in size. It is strongly recommended that the end zones be marked to the depth of 10 yards specified by rule, and that if necessary to accommodate this, the distance between the goal-lines should be reduced to 90 yards. The distance between the goal-lines should be a whole multiple of 10 yards. If the marked end zones are found to be less than 8 yards deep, the referee shall order the 5-yard line be used as the goal-line and the length of the field of play reduced accordingly.

3. The field of play shall be marked to a length of not less than 90 yards.

(*b*) All field dimension lines shown should be marked 4in in width with a white non-toxic material that is not injurious to the eyes or skin. (*Exception*: side-lines and end-lines may exceed 4in in width, and Rule 1-2-1-*h*.)

(*c*) Twenty-four-inch short yard-line extensions, 4in inside the side-lines and at the in-bounds lines, are recommended and all yard-lines shall be 4in from the side-lines (Rule 2-11-4). If for any reason it is not possible for all yard-line extensions to be marked, those at the in-bounds-lines should be marked first, followed by the side-line opposite the press box, followed by the press box side-line.

(*d*) A solid white area between the side-line and the coaching line is recommended.

(*e*) White field markings or contrasting decorative markings (e.g. logos, team names, emblems, event) are permissible in the end zones but shall not be closer than 4ft to any line.

(*f*) Contrasting colouring in the end zones may abut any line.

(*g*) Contrasting decorative material is permissible within the side-lines and between the goal-lines, but shall not obliterate yard-lines, goal-lines or side-lines.

(*h*) Goal-lines may be of one contrasting colour from the white lines.

(*i*) Advertising is permissible on the field, providing it meets the requirements of Rules 1-2-1-*e* and 1-2-1-*f*.

(*j*) White field yard-line numbers measuring 6ft in height and 4ft in width, with the tops of the numbers 9 yards from the side-lines are recommended.

(*k*) White directional arrows next to the field numbers (except the 50) indicating the direction toward the opponent's goal-line are permitted. The arrow is a triangle with an 18-in base and two sides that are 36in each.

(*l*) The two in-bounds-lines (hash marks) are 70ft 9in from the side-lines. In-bounds-lines and short yard-line extensions should measure 24in in length.

(*m*) Nine-yard marks, 12in in length every 10 yards, shall be located 9 yards from the side-lines. They are not required if the field is numbered according to Rule 1-2-1-*j*.

Marking Boundary Areas

ARTICLE 2. Measurements shall be from the inside edges of the boundary markings. The entire width of each goal-line shall be in the end zone.

Limit Lines and Coaching Lines

ARTICLE 3. (*a*) Limit lines should be marked with 12-in lines, at 24-in intervals, 12ft outside the side-lines and the end-lines, except in stadiums where the total field surface does not permit. In these stadiums, the limit lines shall not be less than 6ft from the side-lines and end-lines. Limit lines should be 4in in width and may be yellow. No person outside the team area shall be within the limit lines (see Rules 9-1-5-*a*, 9-2-1-*b*-1 and field diagram).

(*b*) The limit lines shall continue 6ft from the team area around the side and back of the team area, where the stadium permits.

(*c*) A coaching line shall be marked with a solid line 6ft outside the side-line between the 25-yard lines (Rule 9-1-5-*a*). It shall be marked between the 25-yard lines irrespective of the length of the field.

(*d*) A 4-in-by-4-in mark at each 5-yard line extended between the goal-lines as an extension of the coaching line for the yardage chain and down indicator's 6ft reference points is recommended.

Team Area

ARTICLE 4. (*a*) On each side of the field, a team area behind the limit line and between the 25-yard lines shall be marked for the exclusive use of substitutes, trainers and other persons affiliated to the team. The area between the coaching line and the limit line between the 25-yard lines should contain white diagonal lines or be marked distinctly for the use of coaches.

(*b*) The team area shall be limited to persons named on the team roster, including players in uniform and a maximum of 40 other individuals directly involved in the game. The 40 individuals not in uniform should wear special identification.

(c) Coaches are permitted in the area between the limit line and coaching line between the 25-yard lines. This area is the coaching box.

(d) Marking the team areas from the 25-yard lines is a game management requirement. They shall be marked between the 25-yard lines irrespective of the length of the field.

(e) In stadiums where the playing enclosure does not permit the team areas to be marked on both sides of the field, both teams may share a common side-line. In this case the team areas shall be marked on either side of midfield between the 5-yard line and the line 5 yards from midfield.

(f) No media personnel, including journalists, radio and television personnel or their equipment, shall be in the team area or coaching box, and no media personnel shall communicate in any way with persons in the team area or coaching box.

(g) Game management shall remove all persons not authorised by rule.

(h) Practice kicking nets are not permitted outside the team area. (*Exception*: in stadiums where playing enclosures are limited in size, nets, holders and kickers are permitted outside the team area) (Rule 9-2-1-b-1.)

Goals

ARTICLE 5. (a) Each goal shall consist of two uprights extending at least 20ft above the ground with a connecting horizontal cross-bar, the top of which is 10ft above the ground. The uprights and cross-bar should be white or yellow in colour. The inside of the uprights and cross-bar should be in the same vertical plane as the inside edge of the end-line.

1. The goal-posts shall be out-of-bounds.

2. Regardless of the position of the goal-posts, the size of the end zone or the distance between the goal-lines, the snap on a try play shall be made from any point on or behind Team B's 3-yard line (Rule 8-3-2-c).

(b) Above the cross-bar, the uprights should be white or yellow and 18ft 6in apart inside to inside.

(c) The designated white or yellow uprights and cross-bar shall be free of decorative material. (*Exception*: 4-in-by-42-in orange or red wind directional streamers at the top of the uprights are permitted.)

(d) The height of the cross-bar shall be measured from the top of each end of the cross-bar to the ground directly below.

(*e*) Goal-post(s) shall be padded with resilient material from the ground to a height of at least 6ft. 'Offset uprights' may be used.

(*f*) The following procedure will be adopted when one or both goals are missing or have been taken down and the original goals are not available for a try or field-goal attempt:

1. If a portable goal is available, it shall be erected or held in place at the request of Team A.

2. If a portable goal is not available but one goal is in place:

(*a*) On all scrimmage plays, Team B shall defend the end of the field where the goal is situated.

(*b*) On all free kick plays, Team A shall defend the end of the field where the goal is situated.

(*c*) After a change of possession, the teams will change ends if necessary so that Team B is defending the end where the goal is situated.

(*d*) There will be no change of ends at the end of the first or third periods (one minute time-out only). Captains will not have the option to select which goal-line to defend at the beginning of a half.

3. If no goals are available, the game may be played if both head coaches agree. In these circumstances no field goals shall be scored. Once stated, the coaches' decisions as to whether to start/continue shall be irrevocable. If one or both head coaches do not wish to play then the game shall be abandoned.

Pylons

ARTICLE 6. Soft flexible four-sided pylons 4in by 4in with an overall height of 18in, which may include a 2-in space between the bottom of the pylon and the ground, are recommended. They should be red or orange in colour and placed at the inside corners of the eight intersections of the side-lines with the goal-lines and end-lines. Pylons marking the intersections of the end-lines, goal-lines and side-lines which do not meet the requirements of this rule (for example, traffic cones) must be placed at least 6ft outside the side-line. Soccer corner-flag-style posts are prohibited.

Line-to-Gain and Down Indicators

ARTICLE 7. The official line-to-gain and down indicators shall be operated approximately 6ft outside the side-line opposite the press box, except in stadiums where the total playing enclosure does not permit.

(*a*) If a yardage chain is used, it shall join two rods not less than 5ft high, the rods' inside edges being exactly 10 yards apart when the chain is fully extended. It is recommended that the rods be 7ft high. Any other line-to-gain indicator that accurately measures the line to gain is permitted. Before the game, the linesman shall test and approve all line-to-gain indicators for accuracy and security.

(*b*) The down indicator shall be mounted on a rod not less then 5ft high. It is recommended that the rod be 6ft 6in high.

(*c*) An unofficial auxiliary line-to-gain indicator and an unofficial down indicator may be used 6ft outside the other side-line. These indicators shall conform to the same size requirements as the official indicators.

(*d*) Unofficial red or orange non-slip line-to-gain markers may be positioned off the side-lines on both sides of the field. Markers are rectangular, weighted material 10in by 32in. A triangle with an altitude of 5in is attached to the rectangle at the end toward the side-line.

(*e*) All line-to-gain and down-indicator rods shall have flat ends.

(*f*) Advertising and team or conference identification is permitted on the down and line-to-gain indicators. One manufacturer's logo or trademark is permitted on each indicator.

Markers and Obstructions

ARTICLE 8. All markers and obstructions within the playing enclosure shall be placed or constructed in such a manner as to avoid any possible hazard to players. This includes anything dangerous to anyone at the limit lines. The referee shall order removed any markers or obstructions constituting such a hazard. Yardage line markers must be placed at least 6ft outside the side-lines and should be collapsible and constructed in such a manner as to avoid any possible hazard to players. Markers which do not conform to this standard shall be removed.

Field Surface

ARTICLE 9. (*a*) No material or device shall be used to improve or degrade the playing surface or other conditions and give one player or team an advantage. (*Exception*: Rules 2-15-4-*a*, 2-15-4-*b* and 2-15-4-*c*.) *Penalty*: penalise under Rule 9-2-3-*c*.

(*b*) The referee may effect any improvement deemed necessary for proper game administration.

(*c*) The referee shall not allow the game to commence if there is any trip hazard in-bounds or within 6ft of the boundary lines. A trip hazard is defined to be any change of height of one in or more in the space of one in or less, with the exception of holes less than 2in in diameter.

(*d*) In stadia where discus circles or other objects present a different playing surface, it is strongly recommended that the field of play be shortened to avoid different surfaces in the field of play or end zones.

(*e*) The referee should make every effort to play the game at the place and time specified, and to make a report to the appropriate authority as soon as possible afterwards. However, if the markings and facilities available on a field are, in the judgement of the referee, so inadequate as to call into question the validity of the game or the safety of players, spectators or officials, then the game shall not proceed unless and until an improvement has been effected.

SECTION 3. THE BALL

Specifications
ARTICLE 1. The ball shall meet the following specifications:

(*a*) New or nearly new. (A nearly new ball is a ball that has not been altered and retains the properties and qualities of a new ball.)

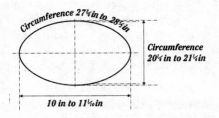

(*b*) Cover consisting of four panels of pebble-grained leather without corrugations other than seams.

(*c*) One set of eight-spaced lacings.

(*d*) Natural tan colour.

(*e*) Two 1in wide white stripes that are 3 to 3¼in from the end of the ball and located only on the two panels adjacent to the laces are optional.

(*f*) Conforms to maximum and minimum dimensions and shape indicated in the diagram:

Length 10in to 11.1in
Circumference 27¾in to 28½in
Circumference 20¾in to 21¼in

(*g*) Inflated to the pressure of 12.5 to 13.5 psi.

(*h*) Weight 14 to 15 ounces.

(*i*) The ball may not be altered. This includes the use of any ball-drying substance.

Administration and Enforcement
ARTICLE 2. (*a*) The referee shall test and be sole judge of no fewer than three and no more than six balls offered for play before and during the game. The referee may approve additional balls if warranted by conditions.

(*b*) Home management should provide a pressure pump and measuring device.

(*c*) The home team is responsible for providing legal balls and should notify the opponent of the type to be used.

(*d*) During the entire game, both teams shall use only balls that meet the required specifications and have been measured and tested according to rule.

(*e*) All balls to be used must be presented to the referee for testing 60 minutes prior to the start of the game.

1. The referee's first priority is to have three legal balls. If the home team does not provide at least three legal balls, the referee shall inform the away team and give them the opportunity to provide legal balls. If fewer than three legal balls are provided, the game will proceed with only the legal ball(s) being used. If no legal balls are provided, the referee shall select up to three balls which in his judgement are the best available.

2. When more than three legal balls are presented, the referee shall select the balls in best condition from those presented by both teams.

3. Where league regulations mandate the use of balls of a particular manufacture, and more than three legal balls are presented to the referee, the referee shall only select balls of another manufacture if there are fewer than three balls of the mandated manufacture.

(*f*) When the ball becomes dead nearer the side-lines than the hash mark, is unfit for play, is subject to measurement in a side zone or is inaccessible, a replacement ball shall be obtained from the ball-person.

(*g*) The referee or umpire shall determine the legality of each ball before it is put in play.

(*h*) The following procedures shall be used when measuring a ball:

1. All measurements shall be made after the ball is inflated to 13 psi.

2. The long circumference shall be measured around the ends of the ball but not over the laces.

3. The long diameter shall be measured with calipers from end to end but not in the nose indentation.

4. The short circumference shall be measured around the ball, over the valve, over the lace, but not over the cross lace.

(*i*) In wet conditions (or if the referee deems that conditions warrant it), teams must provide towels for the umpire and ball-persons to use to keep the ball dry. All towels should be white.

Marking Balls

ARTICLE 3. Marking a ball indicating a preference for any player or any situation is prohibited.

Penalty: Live-ball foul. Fifteen yards from the previous spot.

SECTION 4. PLAYERS AND PLAYING EQUIPMENT

Recommended Numbering
ARTICLE 1. It is strongly recommended that offensive players be numbered according to the following diagram:

80-99	70-79	60-69	50-59	60-69	70-79	80-99
End	Tackle	Guard	Centre	Guard	Tackle	End

1-49
Backs

Fullback   Halfback   Halfback   Quarterback   End
Tackle   Guard   Centre   Guard   Tackle   End

Players' Numbering
ARTICLE 2. (*a*) All players shall be numbered 1 through to 99. Any number preceded by zero (0) is illegal.

(*b*) On a scrimmage down, at least five offensive players on the scrimmage line shall be numbered 50 through to 79. (*Exception*: during a scrimmage kick formation, a player who initially is an exception to the 50-79 mandatory numbering remains an ineligible receiver during the down until a legal forward pass is touched by a Team B player. He must be positioned on the line of scrimmage and between the end players on the line of scrimmage.) A player remains an ineligible receiver and is an exception to the 50-79 mandatory numbering until the down is over, a time-out is charged to a team or the referee, or a period ends.

(*c*) No two players of the same team shall participate in the same down wearing identical numbers.

(*d*) Markings in the vicinity of the numbers are not permitted.
Penalty: Live-ball foul. Five yards from the previous spot.

(*e*) Numbers shall not be changed during play to deceive opponents.
Penalty: 15 yards from the previous spot. Flagrant offenders shall be disqualified.

Contrasting Colours
ARTICLE 3. (*a*) Players of opposing teams shall wear jerseys of contrasting colours. In the event of a clash, the visiting team shall wear white jerseys. Players of a team shall wear the same colour jerseys.

(*b*) A white jersey is one with only contrasting playing numbers, player's name, team, game, memorial insignia or the team or game's national flag attached. Team markings may be placed on the sleeves and/or shoulders. Jersey number colours shall be in sharp contrast to jersey colours.

Mandatory Equipment

ARTICLE 4. All players shall wear the following mandatory equipment, which shall be professionally manufactured and not altered to decrease protection:

(*a*) Soft knee pads at least 0.5in thick worn over the knees and covered by pants. No pads or protective equipment shall be worn outside the pants. Skateboard knee pads or any other type of pads worn outside the pants or jersey are prohibited. Bicep pads must be covered.

(*b*) Face masks and helmets with a secured four-point chin strap. If a chin strap is not secured, it is a violation. Officials should inform players when fewer than four snaps are secured without charging a time-out unless the player ignores the warning. Professionally manufactured eye-protectors or sun visors specifically designed for American football are permitted.

(*c*) Shoulder pads, hip pads with tailbone protector, thigh guards.

(*d*) An intra-oral yellow or any other readily visible coloured mouthpiece (not white) with FDA-approved base materials (FDCS) that covers all upper teeth.

(*e*) One jersey with sleeves that completely cover the shoulder pads that is not altered or designed to tear and conforms with Rule 1-4-4-*f*. Vests and/or a second jersey worn concurrently during the game are prohibited. Tee-shirts or other similar garments may be worn under shoulder pads.

(*f*) Clearly visible permanent Arabic block or Gothic numerals on one jersey at least 8 and 10in in height front and back, respectively, of a colour in distinct contrast with the jersey, and each player shall have the same colour numbers. A solid colour border is permitted. The individual bars must be approximately 1.5in wide. Identical numbers shall be worn on front and back of each player's jersey.

(*g*) Numbers on any part of the uniform shall correspond with the mandatory front and back numbers. (Memorial numbers are not legal.)
Note: If a player is not wearing mandatory equipment in compliance in all respects with Rule 1-4-4, the team shall be charged a time-out and the player shall not be permitted to play until he complies.
Violation: see Rules 3-3-6 and 3-4-2-*b*-2.
NOCSAE: All players shall wear helmets that carry a warning label regarding the risk of injury and a manufacturer's or reconditioner's certification indicating satisfaction of NOCSAE test standards. All such reconditioned helmets shall show recertification to indicate satisfaction with the NOCSAE test standard.

Illegal Equipment

ARTICLE 5. No player wearing illegal equipment shall be permitted to play. Any question as to the legality of a player's equipment shall be decided by the umpire. Illegal equipment includes the following:

(*a*) Equipment worn by a player, including artificial limbs, that would endanger other players.

(*b*) Hard, abrasive or unyielding substances on the hand, wrist, forearm or elbow of any player unless covered on all sides with closed-cell, slow-recovery foam padding no less than $\frac{1}{2}$in thick or an alternative material of the same minimum thickness and similar physical properties. Hard or unyielding substances are permitted, if covered, only to protect an injury. Hand and arm protectors (covered casts or splints) are permitted only to protect a fracture or dislocation.

(*c*) Thigh guards of any hard substances unless all surfaces are covered with material such as closed-cell vinyl foam that is at least $\frac{1}{4}$in thick on the outside surface and at least $\frac{3}{8}$in thick on the inside surface and the overlaps of the edges. Shin guards not covered on both sides and all edges with closed-cell, slow-recovery foam padding at least $\frac{1}{2}$in thick, or an alternative material of the same minimum thickness having similar physical properties. Therapeutic or preventive knee braces unless worn under the pants and entirely covered from direct external exposure.

(*d*) Projection of metal or other hard substance from a player's person or clothing. Rings, bracelets, earrings (except when covered by a helmet) and medallions worn outside the uniform are prohibited. Players should remove earrings and medallions and tuck long hair into the collar of their jersey. Pronged belt buckles must be taped to be legal.

(*e*) Shoe cleats – detachable:

1. More than $\frac{1}{2}$in in length (measured from tip of cleat to the shoe). (*Exception*: If attached to a $\frac{5}{32}$in or less raised platform wider than the base of the cleat and extended across the width of the shoe to within $\frac{1}{4}$in or less of the outer edges of the sole. A single toe cleat does not require a raised platform that extends across the width of the sole. The raised platform of the toe cleat is limited to $\frac{5}{32}$in or less. The $\frac{5}{32}$in or less is measured from the lowest point of the platform to the sole of the shoe.)

2. Made of any material liable to chip or fracture;

3. Without an effective locking device;

4. With concave sides;

5. Conical cleats with flat free ends not parallel with their bases or less than $\frac{3}{8}$in in diameter or with rounded free ends having arcs greater than $\frac{7}{16}$in;

6. Oblong cleats with free ends not parallel with bases or that measure less then $\frac{1}{4}$in by $\frac{3}{4}$in;

7. Circular or ring cleats without rounded edges and a wall less than $\frac{3}{16}$in thick;

8. Steel tipped cleats without steel equivalent to SAE 1070 hardener and drawn to Rockwell C scale 42-45.

(*f*) Shoe cleats – non-detachable:

1. More than ½in in length (measured from tip of cleat to sole of shoe);

2. Made of any material that burrs, chips or fractures;

3. With abrasive surfaces or cutting edges;

4. Made of any metallic material.

(*g*) Tape of any bandage on a hand, wrist, forearm or elbow unless used to protect an injury and specifically sanctioned by the umpire. Sanction for taping need not be obtained from the umpire for (i) light taping to protect an injury; (ii) one twist of tape to secure padding; and (iii) taping of adjacent fingers. Taping shall not be used for padding. All taping must be of adhesive material. Adhesive outer surfaces of any taping are prohibited.

(*h*) Helmets, jerseys or attachments that tend to conceal the ball by closely resembling it in colour.

(*i*) Adhesive material, grease or any other slippery substance applied to equipment or on a player's person, clothing or attachment that affects the ball or an opponent.

(*j*) Any face mask except those constructed of non-breakable material with rounded edges covered with resilient material designed to prevent chipping, burrs or an abrasiveness that would endanger players.

(*k*) Shoulder pads with the leading edge of the epaulet rounded with a radius more than half the thickness of the material used.

(*l*) Anything on the uniform other than a player's numbers, a player's name, memorial recognition, the team's national flag, or team, league or game identification, or authorised advertising material. No words, numbers or symbols are permitted on a player's person or tape except as listed above. (*Exception*: game information on a player's wrist or arm.)

(*m*) Gloves worn intentionally to closely resemble the opponent's jersey colour or not in conformance with Rule 1-4-5-*b*. Soccer goalkeeper's gloves are permitted provided that any abrasive material has been removed from the back of the hand.

(*n*) Jerseys that have been taped or tied in any manner. (*Exception*: the sleeves of the jersey may be taped.)

(*o*) Uniform attachments. (*Exception*: (1) one white towel without markings worn on the uniform and attached at the waist, with a maximum exposure of 4in by 12in; (2) hand warmers worn during inclement weather.)

(*p*) Rib pads and back protectors not totally covered.

Note: No player wearing illegal equipment shall be permitted to play.

If illegal equipment is discovered by an official, the team shall be charged a team time-out.

Violation: see Rules 3-3-6 and 3-4-2-*b*-2.

Exception: if equipment in Rule 1-4-5 becomes illegal through play, the player must leave the game until the illegal equipment is corrected but will not be charged a team time-out.

Mandatory and Illegal Equipment Enforcement
ARTICLE 6. Failure to wear mandatory equipment or the use of illegal equipment is enforced as follows:

(*a*) Each of the first three infractions for failure to wear mandatory equipment or wearing illegal equipment requires a charged time-out. The fourth infraction in a half requires a 5-yard penalty. The delay for the fourth time-out could be the first violation for not wearing mandatory equipment or wearing illegal equipment. The first three time-outs could have been taken by the team as charged team time-outs.

1. The time-outs are granted.

2. There is no offset for the first three violations when an opponent has fouled.

3. When time-outs are exhausted, the next violation is a dead-ball delay penalty at the succeeding spot.

4. A time-out is called, the offending team is indicated by the referee and the captain and coaches are notified through the officials nearest the side-lines.

(*b*) Officials should ascertain before the ready-for-play signal if players are not wearing mandatory equipment or are wearing illegal equipment. Only in an emergency shall the 25-second clock be interrupted.

(*c*) No jersey shall be changed on the field of play and such changes must be made in the team area of the player making the change. When it is determined that a jersey does not comply with Rule 1-4-4-*e* and/or 1-4-4-*f*, a team time-out will be charged to that team at the succeeding spot. If the team has expended its three time-outs, a delay will be charged under Rule 3-4-2-*b*-2. Players may change torn jerseys during team time-outs and return to play. A player may change a jersey and return during a delay penalty only if the game is not further delayed by that action.

(*d*) Tape shall not cover or partially cover a glove. Tape may be used to secure glove fasteners.

Coaches' Certification
ARTICLE 7. The head coach or his designated representative shall certify in writing to the umpire prior to the game that all players:

(*a*) Have been informed what equipment is mandatory by rule and what constitutes illegal equipment.

(*b*) Have been provided with the equipment mandated by rule.

(*c*) Have been instructed to wear and how to wear mandatory equipment during the game.

(*d*) Have been instructed to notify the coaching staff when equipment becomes illegal through play during the game.

Prohibited Signal Devices

ARTICLE 8. Players are prohibited from being equipped with any electronic, mechanical or other signal devices for the purpose of communicating with any source. (*Exception*: a medically prescribed hearing aid of the sound amplifier type for hearing-impaired players.) *Penalty:* 15 yards and disqualification of the player. Penalise as a dead-ball foul at the succeeding spot.

Prohibited Field Equipment

ARTICLE 9. (*a*) Television replay or monitor equipment is prohibited at the side-lines, press box or other locations within the playing enclosure for coaching or officiating purposes during the game.

(*b*) Motion pictures, any type of film, facsimile machines, video-tapes, photographs, writing-transmission machines and computers are prohibited for coaching purposes at any time during the game or between periods. Voice communication between the press box and team area is permitted. Where press-box space is not adequate, communication may originate from any area in the stands between the 25-yard lines extended to the top of the stadium.

(*c*) Media communicating equipment, including cameras, sound devices and microphones, is prohibited within the limit lines.

(*d*) Microphones, provided by home management, are recommended on referees. They may be used only on referees for penalty or other game announcements, if controlled by the referee, and shall not be open at other times. Microphones on other officials are prohibited. *Note*: If a radio microphone is provided, the referee shall use it providing it meets the following criteria:

1. it must have an on/off switch under the referee's control;
2. it must be of the clip-on variety;
3. the transmitter must be small enough to attach to a belt or fit in a pocket.

It shall be at the referee's discretion whether or not to use a microphone which does not meet the above criteria. Microphones and/or transmitters that cannot be carried by the referee are prohibited.

(*e*) Microphones attached to coaches for media transmission are prohibited during the game.

Coaches' Phones
ARTICLE 10. Coaches' phones and headsets are not subject to the rules before or during the game.

SECTION 5. MEDICAL PROVISION

Minimum Medical Requirements
ARTICLE 1. The minimum medical facilities during a game are:

(*a*) A qualified medical practitioner, nurse, paramedic, physiotherapist or first aider must be available.

(*b*) A first aid kit including a suitable (preferably inflatable) set of limb splints must be available.

(*c*) A stretcher must be available.

(*d*) An ambulance and crew must be available. An ambulance is defined to be a vehicle constructed and equipped for the purpose of carrying stretcher-bound patients to hospital.

(*e*) A telephone capable of use to summon the emergency services should be available.

Note: Available means inside or immediately outside the stadium. (*Exception*: an ambulance and its crew are defined to be available at a game even though they may be absent from the stadium in the act of transporting someone to hospital.)

Medical Requirement Administration
ARTICLE 2. (*a*) Game management is responsible for the provision of medical facilities that meet the requirements of Rule 1-5-1.

(*b*) The senior game management representative shall certify to the referee prior to the game that the medical requirement has been met.

(*c*) Game management shall inform the referee if at any stage during the game the medical requirement ceases to be met. The game will then be suspended (Rule 3-3-3-*b*).

RULE 2

Definitions

SECTION 1. APPROVED RULINGS AND OFFICIALS' SIGNALS
ARTICLE 1. (*a*) An Approved Ruling (AR) is an official decision on a given statement of facts. It serves to illustrate the spirit and application of the rules. If there is a conflict between the official rules and approved rulings, the rules take precedence.

(*b*) An official's signal [S] refers to the Official Football Signals 1 through to 47.

SECTION 2. THE BALL: LIVE, DEAD, LOOSE

Live Ball
ARTICLE 1. A live ball is a ball in play. A pass, kick or fumble that has not yet touched the ground is a live ball in flight.

Dead Ball
ARTICLE 2. A dead ball is a ball not in play.

Loose Ball
ARTICLE 3. A loose ball is a live ball not in player possession during:
   (*a*) A running play.
   (*b*) A scrimmage or free kick before possession is gained, regained or the ball is dead by rule.
   (*c*) The interval after a legal forward pass is touched and before it becomes complete, incomplete or intercepted (*Note*: This interval is during a forward pass play and the ball may be batted in any direction by a player eligible to touch it.)
   (*d*) All players are eligible to touch or recover a ball that is loose from a fumble or a backward pass, but eligibility to touch a ball loose from a kick is governed by kick rules (Rule 6) and eligibility to touch a forward pass is governed by pass rules (Rule 7).

When Ball is Ready for Play
ARTICLE 4. A dead ball is ready for play when the referee:
   (*a*) If time is in, sounds his whistle and signals ready for play.
   (*b*) If time is out, sounds his whistle and signals either 'start the clock' or 'ball ready for play'. (*Exception*: Rules 3-3-3-*f*-4-*c* and 3-3-3-*f*-4-*f*.)

In Possession
ARTICLE 5. 'In possession' is an abbreviation meaning the holding or controlling of a live ball or a ball to be free kicked.
   (*a*) A player is 'in possession' when he is holding or controlling the ball.
   (*b*) A team is 'in possession' when one of its players is 'in possession' or attempting to punt, drop kick or place kick, while a forward pass thrown by one of its players is in flight or was last in possession during a loose ball.

Belongs To

ARTICLE 6. 'Belongs to' as contrasted with 'in possession' denotes temporary custody of a dead ball. Legality of such custody is immaterial because the ball must next be put in play in accordance with rules governing the existing situation.

Catch, Interception, Recovery

ARTICLE 7. A catch is an act of establishing player possession of a live ball in flight.

(*a*) A catch of an opponent's fumble or pass is an interception.

(*b*) Securing player possession of a live ball after it strikes the ground is 'recovering it'.

(*c*) To catch, intercept or recover a ball, a player who leaves his feet to make a catch, interception or recovery must have the ball in his possession when he first returns to the ground in-bounds or is so held that the dead-ball provisions of Rule 4-1-3-*a* apply.

1. If one foot first lands in-bounds and the receiver has possession and control of the ball, it is a catch or interception even though a subsequent step or fall takes the receiver out-of-bounds.

2. Loss of ball simultaneously with returning to the ground is not a catch, interception or recovery.

(*d*) A catch by any kneeling or prone in-bounds player is a completion or interception (Rules 7-3-1, 7-3-2, 7-3-6 and 7-3-7).

(*e*) When in question, the catch, recovery or interception is not completed.

Simultaneous Catch or Recovery

ARTICLE 8. A simultaneous catch or recovery is a catch or recovery in which there is joint possession of a live ball by opposing players in-bounds.

SECTION 3. BLOCKING

Legal Block

ARTICLE 1. (*a*) Blocking is obstructing an opponent by contacting him with any part of the blocker's body.

(*b*) Pushing is blocking an opponent with open hands.

Below Waist

ARTICLE 2. (*a*) Blocking below the waist is the initial contact below the waist with any part of the blocker's body against an opponent other than the runner (Rule 9-1-2-*e*).

(*b*) Blocking below the waist applies to the original contact by a blocker against an opponent who has one or both feet on the ground. A blocker who makes contact above the waist and then slides below the waist has not blocked below the waist. If the blocker first contacts the opposing player's hands at the waist or above, it is a legal 'above the waist' block (Rule 9-1-2-*e*).

(*c*) The position of the ball at the snap (Rule 9-1-2-*e*) refers to an imaginary line through the ball parallel to the side-lines from end-line to end-line and is in effect until the ball crosses the neutral zone.

Chop Block

ARTICLE 3. A chop block is an illegal delayed block at the thigh or below against an opponent who is in contact with a team-mate of the blocker. A chop block is delayed if it occurs more than one second after a team-mate contacts the opponent. (*Exception*: the runner.) When in question, the contact is at the thigh or below.

Block in the Back

ARTICLE 4. (*a*) A block in the back is contact against an opponent occurring when the force of the initial contact is from behind and above the waist. (*Exception*: the runner.) When in question, the contact is below the waist (Rule 9-3-3-*c*).

(*b*) The position of the blocker's head or feet does not necessarily indicate the point of initial contact.

Frame (of the body)

ARTICLE 5. The frame of the opponent's body is at the shoulders or below other than the back (see exception to Rule 9-3-3-*a*-1-*c*).

SECTION 4. CLIPPING

ARTICLE 1. (*a*) Clipping is a block against an opponent occurring when the force of the initial contact is from behind and at or below the waist. (*Exception*: the runner.) (Rule 9-1-2-*d*.)

(*b*) The position of the blocker's head or feet does not necessarily indicate the point of initial contact.

SECTION 5. DELIBERATE DEAD-BALL ADVANCE

ARTICLE 1. Deliberately advancing is an attempt by the runner to advance the ball after any part of his person, other than a hand or foot, has touched the ground. (*Exception*: Rule 4-1-3-*b*.)

SECTION 6. DOWN AND BETWEEN DOWNS

ARTICLE 1. A down is a unit of the game that starts with a legal snap or legal free kick after the ball is ready for play and ends when the ball next becomes dead. Between downs is the interval during which the ball is dead.

SECTION 7. FAIR CATCH

Fair Catch
ARTICLE 1. (*a*) A fair catch of a scrimmage kick is a catch beyond the neutral zone by a player of Team B who has made a valid signal during a scrimmage kick that is untouched beyond the neutral zone.

(*b*) A fair catch of a free kick is a catch by a player of Team B who has made a valid signal during an untouched free kick.

(*c*) A valid, invalid or illegal fair catch signal deprives the receiving team of the opportunity to advance the ball and the ball is declared dead at the spot of the catch or recovery or at the spot of the foul if the catch precedes the signal.

(*d*) If the receiver shades his eyes from the sun, the ball is live and may be advanced.

Valid Signal
ARTICLE 2. A valid signal is a signal given by a player of Team B who has obviously signalled his intention by extending one hand only clearly above his head and waving the hand from side to side of the body more than once.

Illegal Signal
ARTICLE 3. (*a*) An illegal signal is a valid or invalid signal by a player of Team B beyond the neutral zone when a scrimmage kick is made and a fair catch is not permissible by rule.

(*b*) An illegal signal is a valid or invalid signal by a player of Team B when a free kick is made and a fair catch is not permissible by rule.

Invalid Signal
ARTICLE 4. An invalid signal is any signal by a player of Team B that does not meet the requirements of a valid signal.

SECTION 8. FORWARD, BEYOND AND FORWARD PROGRESS

Forward, Beyond
ARTICLE 1. Forward, beyond or in advance of, as related to either team, denotes direction towards the opponent's end-line. Converse terms are backward or behind.

Forward Progress

ARTICLE 2. Forward progress is a term indicating the end of advancement by the runner and applies to the position of the ball when it became dead by rule (Rules 4-1-3-*a*, 4-1-3-*b*, 4-2-1 and 4-2-4).

SECTION 9. FOUL AND VIOLATION

ARTICLE 1. A foul is a rule infraction for which a penalty is prescribed. A violation is a rule infraction for which no penalty is prescribed and that does not offset the penalty for a foul.

SECTION 10. FUMBLING, MUFFING, TOUCHING, BATTING OR BLOCKING A KICK

Fumble

ARTICLE 1. A fumble is any act other than passing, kicking or successful handing that results in loss of player possession.

Muff

ARTICLE 2. A muff is an unsuccessful attempt to catch or recover a ball that is touched in the attempt.

Batting

ARTICLE 3. Batting the ball is intentionally striking it or intentionally changing its direction with a hand or arm.

Touching

ARTICLE 4. Touching of a ball not in player possession denotes any contact with the ball. It may be intentional or unintentional, and it always precedes possession and control. When in question, a ball has not been touched on a kick or forward pass. (*Exception*: Rules 6-1-4 and 6-3-4.)

Blocking a Scrimmage Kick

ARTICLE 5. Blocking a scrimmage kick is touching the ball in or behind the neutral zone by an opponent of the kicker.

SECTION 11. LINES

Goal-lines

ARTICLE 1. Each goal-line is part of a vertical plane separating an end zone from the field of play when the ball is touched or is in player possession. The plane extends beyond the side-lines. A team's goal-line is that which it is defending.

Restraining Lines
ARTICLE 2. A restraining line is part of a vertical plane when a ball is touched or is in possession.

Yard-lines
ARTICLE 3. A yard-line is any line in the field of play parallel to the end-lines. A team's own yard-lines, marked or unmarked, are numbered consecutively from its own goal-line to the 50-yard line.

In-bounds Lines (Hash Marks)
ARTICLE 4. The two in-bounds lines are 70ft 9in from the side-lines. In-bounds lines and short yard-line extensions shall measure 24in in length.

Out-of-Bounds Lines
ARTICLE 5. The area enclosed by the side-lines and end-lines is 'in-bounds' and the area surrounding and including the side-lines and end-lines is 'out-of-bounds'.

Nine-Yard Marks
ARTICLE 6. Nine-yard marks, 12in in length every 10 yards, shall be located 9 yards from the side-lines. They are not required if the field is numbered according to Rule 1-2-1-*j*.

SECTION 12. HANDLING THE BALL
ARTICLE 1. (*a*) Handing the ball is transferring player possession from one team-mate to another without throwing, fumbling or kicking it.

(*b*) Except when permitted by rule, handing the ball forward to a team-mate is illegal.

(*c*) Loss of player possession by unsuccessful execution of attempted handing is a fumble. (*Exception*: the snap (Rule 2-23-1-*c*).)

(*d*) A backward handoff occurs when the runner releases the ball before it is beyond the yard-line where the runner is positioned.

SECTION 13. HUDDLE
ARTICLE 1. A huddle is two or more players grouped together before the snap or a free kick.

SECTION 14. HURDLING

ARTICLE 1. (*a*) Hurdling is an attempt by a player to jump with one or both feet or knees foremost over an opponent who is still on his feet.

(*b*) 'On his feet' means that no part of the opponent's body other than one or both feet is in contact with the ground.

(*c*) Hurdling an offensive player before the snap is a dead-ball foul. This includes offensive players in a three- or four-point stance.

SECTION 15. KICKS

Legal and Illegal Kicks

ARTICLE 1. Kicking the ball is intentionally striking the ball with the knee, lower leg or foot. When in question, a ball is accidentally kicked rather than intentionally kicked.

(*a*) A legal kick is a punt, drop kick or place kick, made according to the rules by a player of Team A before a change of team possession. Kicking the ball in any other manner is illegal.

(*b*) Any free kick or scrimmage kick continues to be a kick until it is caught or recovered by a player or becomes dead.

(*c*) A return kick is an illegal kick.

Punt

ARTICLE 2. A punt is a kick by a player who drops the ball and kicks it before it strikes the ground.

Drop Kick

ARTICLE 3. A drop kick is a kick by a player who drops the ball and kicks it as it touches the ground.

Place Kick

ARTICLE 4.

(*a*) A field goal place kick is a kick by a player of the team in possession while the ball is controlled on a tee or the ground by a team-mate.

(*b*) A free kick place kick is a kick by a player of the team in possession while the ball is positioned on a tee or the ground. It may be controlled by a team-mate.

(*c*) A tee is a device that elevates the ball for kicking purposes. It may not elevate the ball's lowest point more than 2in above the ground.

Free Kick

ARTICLE 5. A free kick is a kick by a player of the team in possession made under restrictions specified in Rules 6-1-1 and 6-1-2.

Kick-off
ARTICLE 6. A kick-off is a free kick that starts each half and follows each try or field goal. It must be a place kick or a drop kick.

Scrimmage Kick
ARTICLE 7. A scrimmage kick made in or behind the neutral zone is a legal kick by Team A during a scrimmage down before team possession changes. A scrimmage kick has crossed the neutral zone when it touches the ground, a player, an official or anything beyond the neutral zone.

Return Kick
ARTICLE 8. A return kick is a kick by a player of the team in possession after change of team possession during a down and is an illegal kick. It is a live-ball foul, and the ball becomes dead.

Field Goal Attempt
ARTICLE 9. A field goal attempt is any place kick or drop kick from scrimmage.

Scrimmage Kick Formation
ARTICLE 10. A scrimmage kick formation is a formation with at least one player 7 yards or more behind the neutral zone and no player in position to receive a hand-to-hand snap from between the snapper's legs.

SECTION 16. LOSS OF A DOWN
ARTICLE 1. 'Loss of a down' is an abbreviation meaning: 'loss of the right to repeat a down'.

SECTION 17. THE NEUTRAL ZONE
ARTICLE 1. The neutral zone is the space between the two lines of scrimmage extended to the side-lines and is the length of the ball. The neutral zone is established when the ball is ready for play and is resting on the ground with its long axis at right angles to the scrimmage line and parallel to the side-lines.

SECTION 18. ENCROACHMENT AND OFFSIDE

Encroachment
ARTICLE 1. (*a*) After the ready-for-play signal, encroachment occurs when an offensive player is in or beyond the neutral zone after the snapper touches or simulates touching the ball before the snap.

(*Exception*: when the ball is put in play, the snapper is not encroaching when he is in the neutral zone.)

(*b*) Encroachment occurs when a player of the kicking team is not behind his restraining line when the ball is legally free-kicked. (*Exception*: the kicker and holder are not encroaching when they are beyond their restraining line.)

Offside
ARTICLE 2. After the ready-for-play signal, offside occurs when a defensive player is in or beyond the neutral zone when the ball is legally snapped, contacts an opponent beyond the neutral zone before the ball is snapped, contacts the ball before it is snapped, or is not behind his restraining line when the ball is legally free-kicked.

SECTION 19. PASSES

Passing
ARTICLE 1. Passing the ball is throwing it. A pass continues to be a pass until it is caught, intercepted by a player or the ball becomes dead.

Forward and Backward Pass
ARTICLE 2. (*a*) A forward pass is determined by the point where the ball first strikes the ground, a player, an official or anything beyond the spot of the pass. All other passes are backward passes. When in question, it is a forward pass rather than a backward pass when thrown in or behind the neutral zone.

(*b*) When a Team A player is holding the ball to pass it forward toward the neutral zone, any intentional forward movement of his arm starts the forward pass. If a Team B player contacts the passer or ball after forward movement begins and the ball leaves the passer's hand, a forward pass is ruled regardless of where the ball strikes the ground or a player.

(*c*) When in question, the ball is passed and not fumbled during an attempted forward pass.

(*d*) A snap becomes a backward pass when the snapper releases the ball.

Crosses Neutral Zone
ARTICLE 3. (*a*) A legal forward pass has crossed the neutral zone when it first strikes the ground, a player, an official or anything beyond the neutral zone in-bounds. It has not crossed the neutral zone when it first

strikes the ground, a player, an official or anything in or behind the neutral zone in-bounds.

(*b*) A passer has crossed the neutral zone when any part of his body is beyond the neutral zone when the ball is released.

(*c*) A legal forward pass is beyond or behind the neutral zone where it crosses the side-line.

Catchable Forward Pass

ARTICLE 4. A catchable forward pass is an untouched legal forward pass beyond the neutral zone to an eligible Team A player who has a reasonable opportunity to catch the ball. When in question, a legal forward pass is catchable.

SECTION 20. PENALTY

ARTICLE 1. A penalty is a yardage loss imposed by rule against a team that has committed a foul and may include a loss of down, an automatic first down and disqualification. (*Exception*: Rule 7-3-4, penalty includes no yardage.)

SECTION 21. SCRIMMAGE

Scrimmage

ARTICLE 1. A scrimmage is the interplay of the two teams during a down in which play begins with a snap.

Scrimmage Line

ARTICLE 2. (*a*) The scrimmage-line for each team when the ball is ready for play is the yard line and its vertical plane that passes through the point of the ball nearest its own goal-line and extends to the side lines.

(*b*) A player of Team A is 'on his scrimmage-line' at the snap when he faces his opponents' goal-line with the line of his shoulders approximately parallel thereto and his head breaks the plane of the line drawn through the waistline of the snapper.

Backfield Line

ARTICLE 3. To be legally in the backfield, a Team A player's head must not break the plane of the line drawn through the rear-most part, other than the legs or feet, of the nearest Team A player (except the snapper) on the line of scrimmage.

SECTION 22. SHIFT

ARTICLE 1. A shift is a simultaneous change of position by two or more offensive players after the ball is ready for play for a scrimmage and before the next snap.

SECTION 23. SNAPPING THE BALL

ARTICLE 1. (*a*) Legally snapping the ball (a snap) is handing or passing it backward from its position on the ground with a quick and continuous motion of the hand or hands, the ball actually leaving the hand or hands in this motion.

(*b*) The snap starts when the ball is moved legally and ends when the ball leaves the snapper's hands.

(*c*) If, during any backward motion of a legal snap, the ball slips from the snapper's hand, it becomes a backward pass and is in play, provided the ball had been declared 'ready' (Rule 4-1-1).

(*d*) While resting on the ground and before the snap, the long axis of the ball must be at right angles to the scrimmage line (Rule 7-1-3-*a*-1).

(*e*) Unless moved in a backward direction, the movement of the ball does not start a legal snap. It is not a legal snap if the ball is first moved forward or lifted.

(*f*) If the ball is touched by Team B during a legal snap, the ball remains dead and Team B is penalised. If the ball is touched by Team B during an illegal snap, the ball remains dead and Team A is penalised.

(*g*) The snap need not be between the snapper's legs; but to be legal, it must be a quick and continuous backward motion.

(*h*) The ball must be snapped on or between the in-bounds-lines.

SECTION 24. SPEARING

ARTICLE 1. Spearing is the intentional use of the helmet in an attempt to punish an opponent.

SECTION 25. SPOTS

Enforcement Spot

ARTICLE 1. An enforcement spot is the point from which the penalty for a foul or violation is enforced.

Previous Spot

ARTICLE 2. The previous spot is the point from which the ball was last put in play.

Succeeding Spot
ARTICLE 3. The succeeding spot is the point at which the ball is next to be put in play. (*Exception*: Rule 10-2-2-g.)

Dead-Ball Spot
ARTICLE 4. The dead-ball spot is the point at which the ball became dead.

Spot of the Foul
ARTICLE 5. The spot of the foul is the point at which that foul occurs. If out-of-bounds between the goal-lines, it shall be the intersection of the nearer in-bounds-line and the yard-line extended through the spot of the foul. If out-of-bounds between the goal-line and the end-line or behind the end-line, the foul is in the end zone.

Out-of-Bounds Spot
ARTICLE 6. The out-of-bounds spot is the point at which, according to the rule, the ball becomes dead because of going or being declared out-of-bounds.

In-bounds Spot
ARTICLE 7. The in-bounds spot is the intersection of the nearer in-bounds line and the yard-line passing through the dead-ball spot, or the spot where the ball is left in a side zone by a penalty.

Spot Where Run Ends
ARTICLE 8. The spot where the run ends is at that point:
   (*a*) Where the ball is declared dead in player possession.
   (*b*) Where player possession is lost on a fumble.
   (*c*) Where a legal (or illegal) handing of the ball occurs.
   (*d*) From where an illegal forward pass is thrown.
   (*e*) From where a backward pass is thrown.
   (*f*) When an illegal scrimmage kick is made beyond the line of scrimmage.

Spot Where Kick Ends
ARTICLE 9. A scrimmage kick that crosses the neutral zone ends at the spot where possession is gained or regained or the ball is declared dead by rule.
   Exceptions:
   1. When a kick ends in Team B's end zone, the post-scrimmage kick enforcement spot is Team B's 20-yard line.
   2. An unsuccessful field goal attempt untouched by Team B beyond

the neutral zone – Basic enforcement spot: previous spot. If the previous spot is between Team B's 20-yard line and the goal-line, and the unsuccessful field-goal attempt is untouched by Team B beyond the neutral zone, the spot where the kick ends is the 20-yard line.

3. When Rule 6-3-11 is in effect, the post-scrimmage spot is the 20-yard line.

Basic Spot

ARTICLE 10. When 'basic spot' is stated in a penalty, fouls during a running play, a legal pass play or a legal kick play are penalised from the 'basic spot'. Fouls by the offensive team behind the 'basic spot' are enforced from the spot of the foul.

The following are the basic spots for enforcement on running plays, forward pass plays and legal kick plays:

(*a*) The basic spot on running plays when the run ends beyond the neutral zone is the spot where the related run ends, and fouls by the offensive team behind the basic spot are spot fouls (Rules 2-30-4 and 10-2-2-*c*-1).

(*b*) The basic spot on running plays when the run ends behind the neutral zone is the previous spot, and fouls by the offensive team behind the basic spot are spot fouls (Rules 2-30-4 and 10-2-2-*c*-2).

(*c*) The basic spot on running plays that occur when there is no neutral zone (interception run-backs, kick run-backs, fumble advances and so on) is the spot where the related run ends, and fouls by the offensive team behind the basic spot are spot fouls (Rules 2-30-4 and 10-2-2-*c*-3). (*Exception*: Rule 8-5-1.)

(*d*) The basic spot on legal forward pass plays is the previous spot, and fouls by the offensive team behind the basic spot are spot fouls (Rules 2-30-1 and 10-2-2-*d*).

Exceptions:

1. Defensive pass interference may be a spot foul.

2. Enforce roughing the passer on a completed forward pass from the end of the last run when it ends beyond the neutral zone and there is no change of team possession.

3. Enforce illegal touching from the previous spot.

(*e*) The basic spot on legal kick plays before a change of possession is the previous spot, and fouls by the offensive team behind the basic spot are spot fouls (Rules 2-30-2, 2-30-3 and 10-2-2-*e*). (*Exception*: Rule 9-1-3-*b* on scrimmage kicks.)

Post-scrimmage Kick Spot

ARTICLE 11. The post-scrimmage kick spot is the spot where the kick ends. Team B retains the ball after penalty enforcement from the post-scrimmage kick spot. Team B fouls behind the post-scrimmage kick spot are spot fouls (Rule 10-2-2-*e*-5).

Most Advantageous Spot
ARTICLE 12. The most advantageous spots are any enforcement spots the offended team chooses for the enforcement of live-ball fouls. They are the previous spot and the spot where the run or scrimmage kick ends (Rules 9-1-4-*a*, 9-2-2 and 10-2-1).

SECTION 26. TACKLING
ARTICLE 1. Tackling is grasping or encircling an opponent with a hand(s) or arm(s).

SECTION 27. TEAM AND PLAYER DESIGNATIONS

Teams A and B
ARTICLE 1. Team A is the team that is designated to put the ball in play and it retains that designation until the ball is next declared ready for play; Team B designates the opponents.

Offensive and Defensive Teams
ARTICLE 2. The offensive team is the team in possession, or the team to which the ball belongs; the defensive team in the opposing team.

Kicker
ARTICLE 3. The kicker is any player who punts, drop kicks or place kicks according to rule. He remains the kicker until he has had a reasonable time to regain his balance.

Lineman and Back
ARTICLE 4. (*a*) A lineman is any Team A player legally on his scrimmage-line when the ball is snapped. An ineligible pass receiver of Team A is 'on his scrimmage-line' at the snap when he faces his opponent's goal-line with the line of his shoulders parallel thereto and his head breaking the plane of the line drawn through the waistline of the snapper. An eligible pass receiver of Team A is 'on his scrimmage-line' at the snap when he faces his opponent's goal-line with the line of his shoulders approximately parallel thereto and his head breaking the plane of the line drawn through the waistline of the snapper. A Team A player also is a lineman when, after the ball is ready for play and the snapper touches or simulates touching the ball, his head breaks the

plane of the line drawn through the waistline of the snapper. (*Exception*: Rule 7-1-3-*b*-1.)

(*b*) A back is any Team A player whose head or body does not break the plane of the line drawn through the rear-most part, other than the legs or feet, of the nearest Team A player (except the snapper) on the line of scrimmage when the ball is snapped. A lineman becomes a back before the snap when he moves to a legal backfield position and stops.

Passer
ARTICLE 5. The passer is the player who throws a legal forward pass. He is a passer from the time he releases the ball until it is complete, incomplete, intercepted or he moves to participate in the play.

Player
ARTICLE 6. (*a*) A player is any one of the participants in the game who is not a substitute or a replaced player and is subject to the rules when in-bounds or out-of-bounds.

(*b*) An airborne player is a player not in contact with the ground.

Runner
ARTICLE 7. The runner is a player in possession of a live ball or simulating possession of a live ball. Rules 4-1-3-*a*, 4-1-3-*b* and 4-1-3-*n* apply only to a runner in possession of a live ball.

Snapper
ARTICLE 8. The snapper is the player who snaps the ball (Rule 7-1-3-*a*-1).

Substitute
ARTICLE 9. (*a*) A legal substitute is a replacement for a player or a player vacancy during the interval between downs.

(*b*) A legal incoming substitute becomes a player when he enters the field and communicates with a team-mate or an official, enters the huddle, is positioned in an offensive or defensive formation, or participates in a play.

Replaced Player
ARTICLE 10. A replaced player is one who participated during the previous down, has been replaced by a substitute and has left the field of play, including the end zones.

Player Vacancy
ARTICLE 11. A player vacancy occurs when a team has fewer than 11 players in the game.

Disqualified Player
ARTICLE 12. A disqualified player is one who is declared ineligible for further participation in the game.

Coach
ARTICLE 13. (*a*) A coach is a person subject to the rules who, while in the team area or coaching box observes the game and/or gives instructions to players and substitutes.

(*b*) A player/coach is regarded as being a coach when in the team area or coaching box and as a player or substitute otherwise.

(*c*) Each team shall designate a coach as its head coach, and so identify him on the roster form.

SECTION 28. TRIPPING
ARTICLE 1. Tripping is using the lower leg or foot to obstruct an opponent (except the runner) below the knees.

SECTION 29. TIMING DEVICES

Game Clock
ARTICLE 1. Any device under the direction of the appropriate judge used to time the game.

25-Second Clock
ARTICLE 2. Any device under the direction of the appropriate official to time the 25 seconds between the ready for play and the ball being put in play. The type of device is determined by the game management.

SECTION 30. PLAY CLASSIFICATION

Forward Pass Play
ARTICLE 1. A legal forward pass play is the interval between the snap and when a legal forward pass is complete, incomplete or intercepted.

Free Kick Play
ARTICLE 2. A free kick play is the interval from the time the ball is legally kicked until it comes into player possession or the ball is declared dead by rule.

Scrimmage Kick Play and Field Goal Play
ARTICLE 3. A scrimmage-kick play or field-goal play is the interval

between the snap and when a scrimmage kick comes into player possession or the ball is declared dead by rule.

Running Play
ARTICLE 4. A running play is any live-ball action other than that which occurs before player possession is re-established during a free kick play, a scrimmage kick play, or a legal forward pass play.

(*a*) A running play includes the spot where the run ends and the interval of any subsequent fumble or backward or illegal pass from the time the run ends until possession is gained, regained or the ball is declared dead by rule.

1. There may be more than one running play during a down if player possession is gained or regained beyond the neutral zone.

2. There may not be more than one running play behind the neutral zone if no change of team possession occurs, and the basic spot is the previous spot (Rule 10-2-2-*c*-2.)

(*b*) A run is that segment of a running play before player possession is lost.

Take-a-Knee Play
ARTICLE 5. (*a*) A take-a-knee play is any play from scrimmage where the Team A captain informs the referee that his team does not intend to advance the ball and the referee so informs the Team B captain and both head coaches.

(*b*) A series of take-a-knee plays continues until either

1. The Team A captain informs the referee that his team intends to advance the ball and the referee so informs the Team B captain and both head coaches.

2. A new series of downs is awarded to Team B.

3. A period ends.

(*c*) No change of team possession is possible on a take-a-knee play. (*Exception*: Rule 5-1-1-*c*).

SECTION 31. FIELD AREAS

The Field
ARTICLE 1. The field is the area within the limit lines and includes the limit lines and team areas and the space above it. (*Exception*: Enclosures over the field.)

Field-of-Play
ARTICLE 2. The field-of-play is the area within the boundary lines other than the end-zones.

End-Zones
ARTICLE 3. The end-zones are the 10-yard areas at both ends of the field between the end-lines and the goal-lines. The goal-lines and goal-line pylons are in the end-zone and a team's end-zone is the one they are defending.

Playing Surface
ARTICLE 4. The playing surface is the material or substance within the field.

Playing Enclosure
ARTICLE 5. The playing enclosure is that area bounded by the stadium, dome, stands, fences or other structures. (*Exception*: Scoreboards are not considered within the playing enclosure.)

SECTION 32. FIGHTING

Fighting and Incitement to Fight
ARTICLE 1. Fighting is any attempt by a player, coach or squad member in uniform to strike an opponent in a combative manner unrelated to football. Such acts include, but are not limited to:

(*a*) An attempt to strike an opponent with the head, arm(s), hand(s), leg(s) or foot (feet), whether or not there is contact.

(*b*) An unsportsmanlike act toward an opponent that causes the opponent to retaliate by fighting (Rule 9-5-1).

RULE 3

Periods, Time Factors and Substitutions

SECTION 1. START OF EACH PERIOD

First and Third Periods
ARTICLE 1. Each half shall start with a kick-off. Three minutes before the scheduled starting time, the referee shall toss a coin at midfield in the presence of no more than four field captains from each team and another game official, first designating the field captain of the visiting team to call the fall of the coin. The coin toss may take place earlier if national anthems are to be played or other ceremonies are to be performed.

During the coin toss, each team shall remain in its team area.
Penalty: Five yards from the succeeding spot.

(*a*) The winner of the toss shall choose one of the following options for the first or second half at the beginning of the half selected.

1. To designate which team shall kick off.

2. To designate which goal-line his team shall defend.

(*b*) The loser shall choose one of the above options for the half the winner of the toss did not select.

(*c*) The team not having the choice of options for a half shall exercise the option not chosen by the opponent.

(*d*) If the winner of the toss selects the second-half option, the referee shall use.

Second and Fourth Periods

ARTICLE 2. Between the first and second periods and also between the third and fourth periods, the teams shall defend opposite goal-lines.

(*a*) The ball shall be relocated at a spot corresponding exactly, in relation to goal-lines and side-lines, to its location at the end of the preceding period.

(*b*) Possession of the ball, the number of the down and the distance to be gained shall remain unchanged.

Extra periods

ARTICLE 3. If the scores are tied at the end of the fourth quarter, extra periods shall be played if the game is a playoff game and the game shall be continued until a team scores. Leagues may adopt regulations to play overtime if the scores are tied at the end of a regular season game. In that event, leagues may further adopt regulations that if the score is still tied at the end of the first extra period then the game shall be terminated and the result will stand as a tie.

The following is the procedure to be followed if overtime is to be played:

(*a*) Immediately after the conclusion of the fourth quarter, officials will instruct both teams to retire to their respective team areas. The officials will assemble at midfield and review the tie-breaker procedures.

(*b*) The officials will escort one captain from each team to the centre of the field for the coin toss, following the same procedure, and using the same signals, used for the pre-game toss.

(*c*) The referee will toss a coin and the visiting captain will call heads or tails while the coin is in the air. The winner of the toss shall be given the option of designating which team shall kick off or of designating which goal-line his team shall defend, and the loser shall have the remaining option. There is no option to defer.

(*d*) The intermission from the end of the fourth quarter to the start of the first extra period should not be longer than three minutes.

(*e*) In overtime, the team that scores first shall be declared the winner of the game, and the game shall be terminated upon any score. A score may be a touchdown, field goal, safety, a penalty that results in a safety, or a score awarded by the referee under Rule 9-1-4 for illegal interference or Rule 9-2-3 for an unfair act. If the score is a touchdown, no try will be attempted.

(*f*) Each extra period shall be of the same duration as the fourth quarter. The first extra period will start with a kick-off. At the end of each period the teams will change ends, following the procedure of Rule 3-1-2. (*Exception*: Regular season games terminated after the first period.) There will be a one-minute intermission between periods. There shall be no free kick after the one that begins the first extra period.

(*g*) A 2-minute warning shall be given in the extra period of a game which will be terminated after the first extra period.

(*h*) Each team is entitled to two charged time-outs during each extra period. Charged time-outs unused in any period cannot be carried forward for use in a subsequent period. Time-outs between periods shall be charged to the succeeding period.

(*i*) Disqualified players may not re-enter the game.

SECTION 2. PLAYING TIME AND INTERMISSIONS

Length of Periods and Intermissions
ARTICLE 1. The maximum total playing time in a game shall be 60 minutes, divided into four periods of 15 minutes each, with one-minute intermissions between the first and second periods (first half) and between the third and fourth periods (second half). (*Exception*: a one-minute intermission between the first and second and the third and fourth quarters may be extended for radio and television time-outs.) Leagues may adopt regulations to limit the playing time in a game to 48, 40 or 32 minutes, provided the four periods are of equal length.

(*a*) No period shall end until the ball is dead and the referee declares the period ended.

(*b*) The intermission between halves, which begins when the field is clear of all players and coaches, shall be 20 minutes.

Timing Adjustments
ARTICLE 2. Before the game starts, playing time and the intermission between halves may be shortened by the referee if he is of the opinion that darkness may interfere with the game. The four periods must be of equal length if the game is shortened before its start.

(*a*) Any time during the game, the playing time of any remaining period or periods and the intermission between halves may be shortened by mutual agreement of the opposing head coaches and the referee.

(*b*) Timing errors on the game clock may be corrected but shall be corrected only in the period in which they occur.

(*c*) Timing errors on a 25-second clock may be corrected by the referee. The 25-second clock shall start again.

(*d*) The 25-second clock is not started when the game clock is running with less than 25 seconds in a period.

(*e*) The game clock should not be stopped if the 25-second clock is started in conflict with Rule 3-2-2-*d*.

(*f*) Leagues may adopt regulations that at any time at or after the end of the second period, if the difference in the score exceeds a stipulated value, then the game shall be terminated. Such a value may not be less than 40 points.

Extension of Periods
ARTICLE 3. A period shall be extended until a down (other than a try), free from live-ball fouls not penalised as dead-ball fouls, has been played, when:

(*a*) A penalty is accepted for a live-ball foul(s) not penalised as a dead-ball foul that occurs during a down in which time expires.

(*b*) An inadvertent whistle is sounded during a down in which time expires.

(*c*) Offsetting fouls occur during a down in which time expires (Rule 8-3-2-*a*).

Timing Devices
ARTICLE 4. (*a*) Playing time shall be kept with a game clock that may be either a stop watch operated by an official, or a game clock operated by an assistant under the direction of the appropriate judge. The use of a game clock shall be determined by the game management.

(*b*) The 25 seconds between the ready for play and the ball being put in play shall be timed with a watch operated by the appropriate official or with 25-second clocks at each end of the playing enclosure operated by an assistant under the direction of the appropriate official. The use of a visual 25-second clock shall be determined by the game management.

(*c*) If a visual timing device becomes inoperative, both head coaches shall be notified by the referee immediately and both clocks shall be turned off.

When Clock Starts
ARTICLE 5. After a free kick, the game clock shall be started when the ball is touched legally in the field of play or crosses the goal-line after

being touched legally by Team B in its end zone. On a scrimmage down, the game clock shall be started when the ball is snapped legally or on prior signal by the referee. The clock shall not run during a try or during an extension of a period

(*a*) When the clock has been stopped, the referee shall declare the ball ready for play, and the clock shall start on the snap unless it was stopped because of one of the following situations:

1. When Team A is awarded a first down. (*Exception*: after a legal kick.)

2. For a referee's time-out for an injured player or official or an extended time-out for radio and television.

3. At the referee's discretion (Rule 3-4-2-*a* – an *exception* – and 3-4-3).

4. To complete a penalty.

5. For an inadvertent whistle. (*Exception*: during a legal kick.)

6. For a head coach's conference.

7. For a side-line warning.

8. For an illegal pass to conserve time.

9. For a measurement.

10. For a ball in an official's possession.

(*b*) If the clock was stopped for incidents 1 through 10, it shall be started on the ready for play.

(*c*) If incidents 1 through 10 occur in conjunction with any other situation that starts the clock on the snap, the clock will start on the snap.

(*d*) The clock stops at the end of a legal kick down and starts on the snap. (*Exception*: when the next play is a free kick or a try.)

When Clock Stops
ARTICLE 6. The game clock shall be stopped when each period ends. An official shall signal time-out when the rules provide for stopping the clock or when a time-out is charged to a team or to the referee. (*Exception*: Rule 3-3-2-*b*). Other officials should repeat time-out signals.

SECTION 3. TIME-OUTS

How Charged
ARTICLE 1. (*a*) The referee shall declare a time-out when he suspends play for any reason. Each time-out shall be charged to one of the teams or designated as a referee's time-out.

(*b*) When a team's time-outs are exhausted and it requests a time-out, the official should not acknowledge the request, interrupt the 25-second clock or stop the game clock.

(c) During a time-out, players shall not practise with a ball on the field of play. (*Exception*: during the half-time intermission.)

Time-out

ARTICLE 2. (a) An official shall declare a referee's time-out:
1. When there is a touchdown, field goal, touchback or safety.
2. When an injury time-out is allowed for one or more players or an official
3. When the clock is stopped to complete a penalty.
4. When a live ball goes out-of-bounds or is declared out-of-bounds.
5. When a forward pass becomes incomplete.
6. When Team A or Team B is awarded a first down.
7. When an inadvertent whistle is sounded.
8. When there is a possible first-down measurement.
9. When a delay is caused by both teams.
10. When a charged time-out is granted.
11. When there is a side-line warning.
12. When the ball becomes illegal.
13. When the ball is in possession of an official.
14. When there is a mandatory equipment (Rules 1-4-4) or an illegal equipment (Rule 1-4-5) violation.
15. When a legal kick down ends.
16. When a return kick is made.
17. When a scrimmage kick is made beyond the neutral zone.
18. When a false-start exception under Rule 7-1-3-*a*-5-*c* occurs.
19. When the 25-second clock is interrupted by circumstances beyond the control of either team.
(b) The referee only shall declare a time-out:
1. When a head coach's conference is requested.
2. When an unfair noise time-out is required.
3. When a radio or television time-out is allowed.
4. When a discretionary time-out is declared.

Referee's Discretionary Time-out

ARTICLE 3. (a) The referee may temporarily suspend the game when conditions warrant such action. The referee may declare and charge himself with a time-out for any contingency not elsewhere covered by the rules.

(b) When the game is stopped by actions of a person(s) not subject to the rules or for any other reasons not in the rules and cannot continue, the referee shall:

1. Suspend play and direct the players to their team areas.
2. Refer the problem to those responsible for the management of the game.
3. Resume the game when he determines conditions are satisfactory.

(c) If a game may not be resumed immediately after Rule 3-3-3-*a* and 3-3-3-*b* suspensions, it shall be terminated or resumed at a later time only by mutual consent of both teams.

(d) A suspended game, if resumed, will begin with the same time remaining and under the identical conditions of down, distance and field position.

(e) The game is a no-contest unless there is mutual consent of both teams to resume or terminate the game. (*Exception*: conference or league regulations.)

(f) The referee's discretionary time-out also applies to the following play situations:
1. When there is undue delay by officials in placing the ball for the next snap.
2. When there is a consultation with team captains.
3. When conditions warrant temporary suspension.
4. When the offensive team believes it is unable to communicate its signals to team-mates other than players positioned more than 7 yards from the middle lineman of the offensive formation because of crowd noise.

Administrative procedures for unfair noise (Rule 3-4-2-*b*-3):
(a) When the signal caller believes he is unable to communicate signals to team-mates because of crowd noise, he may raise his hands and look to the referee to request a legal delay.

(b) The referee may deny the request by pointing toward the defensive team's goal-line or may charge himself with a time-out and the offensive team may huddle.

(c) When the offensive team returns to the line of scrimmage, the game clock will start on the snap. The referee shall declare the ball ready for play by sounding his whistle with no hand signal. The 25-second clock is not in operation (Rule 3-4-2-*b*-3).

(d) Should the signal caller then, or later in the game, request a second legal delay by raising his hands and looking to the referee, the referee will again charge himself with a time-out if, in his opinion, the crowd noise makes it impossible to hear offensive signals.

(e) The referee then will request the defensive captain to ask the crowd for quiet. This signals the public address announcer to request co-operation and courtesy to the offensive team. The announcer will state that the defensive team will be charged a time-out, or penalised 5 yards if time-outs are exhausted, for the next crowd-noise infraction.

(*f*) When the offensive team returns to the line of scrimmage, the game clock will start on the snap. The referee shall declare the ball ready for play by sounding his whistle with no hand signal. The 25-second clock is not in operation (Rule 3-4-2-*b*-3).

(*g*) If the signal caller again during the game indicates by raising his hands and looking to the referee to request a legal crowd-noise delay and the referee agrees, a team time-out will be charged to the defensive team. If the defensive team has exhausted its allotment of time-outs, a 5-yard penalty is assessed.

(*h*) After this time-out or the penalty, the defensive team will be penalised 5 yards for each unsuccessful attempt to start a play. (*Violation*: Rules 3-3-6 and 3-4-2-*b*.)

Step 1 – Referee's time-out.

Step 2 – Referee's time-out plus captain's notification and public address announcement.

Step 3 – Time-out or 5-yard penalty if time-outs are exhausted.

Step 4 – 5-yard penalty for each additional infraction.

Charged Team Time-outs

ARTICLE 4. When time-outs are not exhausted, an official shall allow a charged team time-out when requested by any player when the ball is dead.

(*a*) Each team is entitled to three charged team time-outs during each half.

(*b*) After the ball is declared dead and before the snap, a legal substitute may request a time-out if he is between the 9-yard marks.

(*c*) A player who participated during the previous down may request a time-out between the time the ball is declared dead and the snap without being between the 9-yard marks.

(*d*) A player or incoming substitute may request a head coach's conference with the referee if the head coach believes a rule has been improperly enforced. If the rule enforcement is not changed, the coach's team will be charged a time-out, or a delay penalty if all time-outs have been used.

1. Only the referee may stop the clock for a coach's conference.

2. A request for a coach's conference must be made before the ball is snapped or free-kicked for the next play and before the end of the second or fourth period.

3. After a coach's conference, the full team time-out is granted if charged by the referee.

Injury Time-out

ARTICLE 5. (*a*) In the event of an injured player(s):

1. The referee may charge himself a time-out provided the player(s)

for whom the time-out is taken is removed from the game for at least one down.

2. The player(s) may remain in the game if his team is charged a time-out in the interval between downs or the period ends.

3. After a team's charged time-outs have been exhausted, the injured player(s) must leave for one down.

4. Whenever a participant suffers a laceration or wound where oozing or bleeding occurs, the player or game official shall go to the team area and be given appropriate medical treatment. He may not return to the game without approval of medical personnel.

(*b*) Any official may stop the clock for an injured player(s). When in question, the clock shall be stopped for an injured player.

(*c*) To curtail a possible time-gaining advantage by feigning injuries, attention is directed to the strongly worded statement in *The Football Code* concerning the feigning of any injury.

(*d*) An injury time-out may follow a charged team time-out.

(*e*) The referee may charge himself with a time-out for an injured official.

Violation Time-outs
ARTICLE 6. For noncompliance with Rules 1-4-4, 1-4-5, 3-3-3-*f*-4-*g* or 3-3-4-*d* during a down, a time-out shall be charged to a team at the succeeding spot (Rule 3-4-2-*b*).

Length of Time-outs
ARTICLE 7. (*a*) A charged team time-out requested by any player or a 2-minute warning time-out shall not exceed one minute 30 seconds. Other time-outs shall be no longer than the referee deems necessary to fulfil the purpose for which they are declared, including a radio or TV time-out, but any time-out may be extended by the referee for the benefit of an injured player.

(*b*) If during a charged team time-out or a 2-minute warning time-out both teams wish to resume play before the expiration of one minute, the referee will declare the ball ready for play.

(*c*) The length of a referee's time-outs depend on the circumstances of each time-out.

(*d*) The field captain must exercise his penalty option before he or a team-mate consults with his coach on a side-line during a time-out.

(*e*) The intermission after a safety, try or successful field goal shall be no more than one minute. It may be extended for radio or television.

Referee's Notification
ARTICLE 8. The referee shall notify both teams 30 seconds before a

charged team time-out or 2-minute warning time-out expires and 5 seconds later shall declare the ball ready for play:

(*a*) When a third time-out is charged to a team in either half, the referee shall notify the field captain and head coach of that team.

(*b*) When 2 minutes of playing time remain in each half (or when the ball becomes dead if alive at that time) the referee shall declare a referee's time-out and inform each field captain and head coach.

1. The clock starts on the snap after the 2-minute notification.

2. The referee shall signal the 2-minute warning to captains, coaches and spectators.

(*c*) If a visible game clock is not the official timing device during the last 2 minutes of each half, the referee or his representative shall notify each captain and head coach of the time remaining each time the clock is stopped by rule. Also, a representative may leave the team area along the limit line to relay timing information under these conditions.

SECTION 4. DELAYS

Delaying the Start of a Half

ARTICLE 1. (*a*) Each team shall have its players on the field for the opening play at the scheduled time for the beginning of each half. When both teams refuse to enter the field first for the start of either half, the home team must be the first to enter.

Penalty: 15 yards from the succeeding spot.

(*b*) The home management is responsible for clearing the field of play and end zones at the beginning of each half so the periods may start at the scheduled time. Bands, speeches, presentations, homecoming and similar activities are under the jurisdiction of home management and a prompt start of each half is mandatory.

Penalty: 10 yards from the succeeding spot.

(*Exception*: the referee may waive the penalty for circumstances beyond the control of the home management.)

Illegal Delay of the Game

ARTICLE 2. (*a*) The ball shall be declared ready for play consistently throughout the game by the referee when the officials are in position. Consuming more than 25 seconds to put the ball in play after it is declared ready for play is an illegal delay. (*Exception*: when the 25-second count is interrupted by circumstances beyond the control of either team, a new 25-second count shall be started and the game clock shall start on the snap. If the referee has positive knowledge of the elapsed time, he will reset and appropriately start the game clock.)

(*b*) Illegal delay also includes:

1. Deliberately advancing the ball after it is dead.
2. When a team has expended its three time-outs and commits a 1-4-4, 1-4-5, 3-3-3-*f*-4-*g* or 3-3-4-*d* rules infraction.
3. When a team is not ready to play after an intermission between periods (other than the half), after a score, after a radio/television/team time-out, or any time the referee orders the ball put in play.
4. Taking the ball off of the field of play or end zone.
Penalty: Five yards from the succeeding spot.

Unfair Game Clock Tactics
ARTICLE 3. The referee shall order the game clock started or stopped whenever, in his opinion, either team is trying to conserve or consume playing time by tactics obviously unfair. This includes starting the clock on the snap if the foul is by the team ahead in the score. The clock will start on the ready for play after an illegal forward or backward pass that conserves time for Team A.

SECTION 5. SUBSTITUTIONS

Substitution Procedures
ARTICLE 1. Any number of legal substitutes for either team may enter the game between periods, after a score or try, or during the interval between downs only for the purpose of replacing a player(s).

Legal Substitutions
ARTICLE 2. A legal substitute may replace a player or fill a player vacancy provided none of the following restrictions is violated:

(*a*) No incoming substitute or replaced player shall enter or leave the field of play or end zone while the ball is in play (live-ball foul).

(*b*) An incoming legal substitute must enter the field of play directly from his team area, and a substitute, player or replaced player leaving must depart at the side-line nearest his team area. A player who is replaced must immediately leave the field of play, including the end zones (dead-ball foul).

(*c*) Substitutes who become players must remain in the game for one play and replaced players must remain out of the game for one play except during the interval between periods, after a score, or when a time-out has been charged to a team, or to the referee (live-ball foul).

(*d*) One or more substitutes of the scrimmage-kicking team shall not delay for purposes of confusing the receiving team (live-ball foul).
Penalty: If ball is dead: 5 yards from the succeeding spot; otherwise, 5 yards from the previous spot.

RULE 4

Ball in Play, Dead Ball, Out of Bounds

SECTION 1. BALL IN PLAY – DEAD BALL

Dead Ball Becomes Alive
ARTICLE 1. After a dead ball has been declared ready for play, it becomes a live ball when it is legally snapped, or free kicked legally. A ball snapped or free kicked before the ready for play remains dead.

Live Ball Becomes Dead
ARTICLE 2. (*a*) A live ball becomes a dead ball as provided in the rules or when an official sounds his whistle (even though inadvertently), or otherwise declares the ball dead.

(*b*) If an official sounds his whistle inadvertently during a down:

1. When the ball is in player possession, then the team in possession may elect to put the ball in play where declared dead or replay the down.

2. When the ball is loose from a fumble, backward pass or illegal pass, then the team in possession may elect to put the ball in play where possession was lost or replay the down.

3. During a legal forward pass or a free or scrimmage kick, then the ball is returned to the previous spot and the down replayed.

4. After Team B gains possession on the try, then the try is over.

(*c*) If a foul occurs during any of the above downs, the penalty shall be administered as in any other play situation if not in conflict with other rules.

Ball Declared Dead
ARTICLE 3. A live ball becomes dead and an official shall sound his whistle or declare it dead:

(*a*) When it goes out-of-bounds other than a kick that scores a field goal after touching the uprights or crossbar, when a runner is out-of-bounds, or when a runner is so held that his forward progress is stopped. When in question, the ball is dead.

(*b*) When any part of the runner's body, except his hand or foot, touches the ground or when the runner is tackled or otherwise falls and loses possession of the ball as he contacts the ground with any part of his body, except his hand or foot. When in question, the ball is dead. (*Exception*: the ball remains alive when an offensive player has simulated a kick or is in position to kick the ball which is held for a place kick by a team-mate. The ball may be kicked, passed or advanced by rule.)

(c) When a touchdown, touchback, safety, field goal, or successful try occurs, or when Team A completes an illegal forward pass in Team B's end zone, or Team A completes a forward pass to an ineligible player in Team B's end zone.

(d) When during a try, a dead-ball rule applies.

(e) When a player of the kicking team catches or recovers any free kick or a scrimmage kick that has crossed the neutral zone.

(f) When a free kick, scrimmage kick or any other loose ball comes to rest and no player attempts to secure it.

(g) When a free kick or scrimmage kick (beyond the neutral zone) is caught or recovered by any player following a valid, invalid or illegal fair-catch signal.

(h) When a return kick or scrimmage kick beyond the neutral zone is made.

(i) When a forward pass strikes the ground.

(j) When a live ball not in player possession touches anything in-bounds other than a player, a player's equipment, an official, an official's equipment or the ground (inadvertent-whistle provisions apply). This includes any part of a goal that is in-bounds.

(k) When a simultaneous catch or recovery of a live ball occurs.

(l) When the ball becomes illegal while in play (inadvertent whistle provisions apply).

(m) When the ball is in possession of an official.

(n) When a runner simulates placing his knee on the ground.

(o) When a loose ball comes to rest and no player tries to secure it.

(p) When the ball is snapped on a take-a-knee play.

Ball Ready for Play
ARTICLE 4. No player shall put the ball in play until it is declared ready for play.
Penalty: dead-ball foul: 5 yards from the succeeding spot.

25-Second Count
ARTICLE 5. The ball shall be put into play within 25 seconds after it is declared ready for play, unless, during that interval, play is suspended. If play is suspended, the 25-second count will start again. (*Exception*: Unfair crowd-noise situations.)
Penalty: 5 yards.

SECTION 2. OUT-OF-BOUNDS

Player Out-of-Bounds
ARTICLE 1. (a) A player or an airborne player is out-of-bounds when

any part of his person touches anything, other than another player or game official, on or outside a boundary line.

(b) A player or an airborne player who touches a pylon is out-of-bounds behind the goal-line.

Held Ball Out-of-Bounds

ARTICLE 2. A ball in player possession is out-of-bounds when either the ball or any part of the runner touches the ground or anything else that is on or outside a boundary line except another player or game official.

Ball Out-of-Bounds

ARTICLE 3. (a) A ball not in player possession, other than a kick that scores a goal, is out-of-bounds when it touches the ground, a player or anything else that is on or outside a boundary line.

(b) A ball that touches a pylon is out-of-bounds behind the goal-line.

(c) If a live ball not in player possession crosses a boundary line and is then declared out-of-bounds, it is out-of-bounds at the crossing point.

Out-of-Bounds at Forward Point

ARTICLE 4. (a) If a live ball is declared out-of-bounds and the ball does not cross a boundary line, it is out-of-bounds at the ball's most forward point when it was declared dead.

(b) A touchdown may be scored if the ball is in-bounds and has broken the plane of the goal-line before or simultaneously with the runner's going out-of-bounds.

(c) A receiver who is in the opponent's end zone and contacting the ground is credited with a completion if he reaches over the side-line or end-line and catches a legal pass.

(d) The most forward point of the ball when declared out-of-bounds between the end-lines is the point of forward progress.

(e) When a runner dives or jumps toward the side-line and is airborne as he crosses the side-line, forward progress is determined by the position of the ball as it crosses the side-line.

RULE 5

Series of Downs, Line to Gain

SECTION 1. A SERIES: STARTED, BROKEN, RENEWED

When to Award Series

ARTICLE 1. (a) A series of four consecutive scrimmage downs shall be awarded to the team that is next to put the ball in play by a snap following a free kick, touchback, fair catch or change in team possession.

(*b*) A new series shall be awarded to Team A if it is in legal possession of the ball on or beyond its line to gain when it is declared dead.

(*c*) A new series shall be awarded to Team B if, after fourth down, Team A has failed to earn a first down.

(*d*) A new series shall be awarded to Team B if Team A's scrimmage kick goes out-of-bounds or comes to rest and no player attempts to secure it.

(*e*) A new series shall be awarded to the team in legal possession:

1. If a change of team possession occurs during the down.

2. If a player of Team B first touches a scrimmage kick that has crossed the neutral zone. (*Exception*: when a penalty for a foul by either team is accepted and the down is replayed or offsetting fouls are enforced and the down is replayed.)

3. If an accepted penalty awards the ball to the offended team.

4. If an accepted penalty mandates a first down.

(*f*) A new series shall be awarded to Team B whenever Team B, after a scrimmage kick, elects to take the ball at a spot of illegal touching. (*Exception*: when a penalty for a foul by either team is accepted and the down is replayed or offsetting fouls are enforced and the down is replayed.)

Line to Gain
ARTICLE 2. The line to gain for a series shall be established 10 yards in advance of the most forward point of the ball; but if this line is in the opponents' end zone, the goal-line becomes the line to gain.

Forward Progress
ARTICLE 3. (*a*) The most forward point of the ball when declared dead between the end-lines shall be the determining point in measuring distance gained or lost by either team during any down. The ball shall always be placed with its length axis parallel to the side-line before measuring. (*Exception*: when an airborne receiver completes a catch in-bounds after an opponent has driven him backward and the ball is declared dead at the spot of the catch, the forward progress is where the player received the ball.)

(*b*) Questionable distance for a first down should be measured without request. Unnecessary measurements to determine first downs shall not be granted.

(*c*) No request for a measurement shall be granted after the ball is declared ready for play.

Continuity of Downs Broken
ARTICLE 4. The continuity of a series of scrimmage downs is broken when:

(*a*) Team possession of the ball changes during a down.

(*b*) A player of Team B first touches a scrimmage kick that has crossed the neutral zone.

(*c*) A kick goes out-of-bounds.

(*d*) A kick comes to rest and no player attempts to secure it.

(*e*) At the end of a down, Team A has earned a first down. Any down may be repeated if so provided by the rules.

(*f*) After fourth down, Team A has failed to earn a first down.

(*g*) An accepted penalty mandates a first down.

(*h*) There is a score.

(*i*) The first half ends.

(*j*) A touchback is awarded to either team.

SECTION 2. DOWN AND POSSESSION AFTER A PENALTY

Foul During Free Kick
ARTICLE 1. When a scrimmage down follows the penalty for a foul committed during a free kick, the down and distance established by that penalty shall be first down with a new line or goal to gain. (*Exception*: live-ball foul penalised as dead-ball foul.)

Penalty Resulting in First Down
ARTICLE 2. It is a first down with a new line or goal to gain:

(*a*) After a penalty that leaves the ball in possession of Team A beyond its line to gain.

(*b*) When a penalty mandates a first down.

Foul Before Change of Team Possession
ARTICLE 3. After a distance penalty between the goal-lines, incurred during a scrimmage down and before any change of team possession during that down, the ball belongs to Team A and the down shall be repeated unless the penalty also involves loss of a down, mandates a first down, or leaves the ball on or beyond the line to gain. (*Exception*: Rules 10-2-2-*e*-5 and 10-2-2-*g*.) If the penalty involves loss of a down, the down shall count as one of the four in that series.

Foul After Change of Team Possession
ARTICLE 4. If a distance penalty is accepted for a foul incurred during a down after change of team possession, the ball belongs to the team in possession when the foul occurred. The down and distance established by any distance penalty incurred after change of team possession during

that down shall be first down with a new line or goal to gain. (*Exception*: live-ball fouls penalised as dead-ball fouls.) (Rule 10-2-2-*g*-1.)

Penalty Declined
ARTICLE 5. If a penalty is declined, the number of the next down shall be whatever it would have been if that foul had not occurred.

Foul Between Downs
ARTICLE 6. After a distance penalty incurred between downs, the number of the next down shall be the same as that established before the foul occurred unless enforcement for a foul by Team B leaves the ball on or beyond the line to gain or a penalty mandates a first down (Rules 9-1-1 and 9-1-2).

Foul Between Series
ARTICLE 7. The penalty for any dead-ball foul (including live-ball fouls penalised as dead-ball fouls and fouls after a free kick down) incurred after a series ends and before the next ready for play shall be enforced before the line to gain is established. The penalty for any dead-ball foul incurred after the ready for play shall be enforced after the line to gain is established.

Fouls by Both Teams
ARTICLE 8. If offsetting fouls occur during a down, that down shall be repeated. (*Exception*: Rule 10-1-4 *Exceptions*.)

Fouls During a Loose Ball
ARTICLE 9. Live-ball fouls not penalised as dead-ball fouls when the ball is loose shall be penalised from the basic or previous spot (Rules 10-2-2-*c*, 10-2-2-*d*, 10-2-2-*e* and 10-2-2-*f*).

Rules Decisions Final
ARTICLE 10. No rule decision may be changed after the ball is next legally snapped or legally free kicked.

RULE 6

Kicks

SECTION 1. FREE KICKS

Restraining Lines
ARTICLE 1. For any free-kick formation, the kicking team's restraining line shall be the yard-line through the most forward point from which the ball shall be kicked, and the receiving team's restraining line shall be

the yard-line 10 yards beyond that point. Unless relocated by a penalty, the kicking team's restraining line on a kick-off shall be 15 yards from the midfield line, regardless of the length of the field of play, and for a free kick after a safety, its 20-yard line.

Free-Kick Formation

ARTICLE 2. A ball from a free-kick formation must be kicked legally and from some point on Team A's restraining line and on or between the in-bounds lines. After the ball is ready for play and for any reason it falls from the tee, Team A shall not kick the ball and the official shall sound his whistle immediately. When the ball is kicked:

(*a*) All players of each team must be in-bounds.

(*b*) Each Team A player, except the holder and kicker of a place kick, must be behind the ball. After a safety, when a punt or drop kick is used, the ball shall be kicked within one yard behind the kicking team's restraining line.

(*c*) All Team B players must be behind their restraining line.

(*d*) All players of Team A must have been between the 9-yard marks after the ready for play signal.

(*e*) A Team A player who goes out-of-bounds during a free kick down may not return in-bounds during the down. (*Exception*: this does not apply to a Team A player who is blocked out-of-bounds and attempts to return in-bounds immediately.)

(*f*) No Team A player may block an opponent until Team A is eligible to touch a free-kicked ball.

Penalty: 5 yards from the previous spot (live-ball foul).

Free-Kick Recovery

ARTICLE 3. A Team A player may touch a free-kicked ball:

(*a*) After it touches a Team B player.

(*b*) After it breaks the plane of and remains beyond Team B's restraining line.

(*c*) After it touches any player, the ground or an official beyond Team B's restraining line.

Thereafter, all players of Team A become eligible to touch, recover or catch the kick. (*Exception*: Rule 6-1-2-*e*.) Illegal touching of a free kick is a violation that, when the ball becomes dead, gives the receiving team the privilege of taking the ball at the spot of the violation. However, if there are offsetting fouls, or a penalty, incurred by either team, before the ball becomes dead is enforced, this privilege is cancelled.

Forced Touching Disregarded

ARTICLE 4. (*a*) An in-bounds player blocked by an opponent into a free kick is not, while in-bounds, deemed to have touched the kick.

(*b*) An in-bounds player touched by a ball batted by an opponent is not deemed to have touched the ball.

Free Kick at Rest
ARTICLE 5. If a free kick comes to rest in-bounds and no player attempts to secure it, the ball becomes dead and belongs to receiving team at the dead-ball spot.

Free Kick Caught or Recovered
ARTICLE 6. (*a*) If a free kick is caught or recovered by a player of the receiving team, the ball continues in play. (*Exception*: Rules 4-1-3-*g*, 6-1-7, 6-5-1 and 6-5-2.) If caught or recovered by a player of the kicking team, the ball becomes dead.

(*b*) When opposing players, each eligible to touch the ball, simultaneously recover a rolling kick or catch a free kick, the simultaneous possession makes the ball dead. A kick declared dead in joint possession is awarded to the receiving team.

Touching Ground On or Behind Goal-lines
ARTICLE 7. The ball becomes dead and belongs to the team defending its goal-line when a free kick is untouched by Team B before touching the ground on or behind Team B's goal-line.

SECTION 2. FREE KICK OUT-OF-BOUNDS

Kicking Team
ARTICLE 1. A free kick out-of-bounds between the goal-lines, untouched in-bounds by a player of Team B, is a foul.
Penalty: Live-ball foul: 5 yards from the previous spot or the receiving team may put the ball in play 30 yards beyond Team A's restraining line at the in-bounds spot (touchback if this spot is in or beyond Team B's end zone).

Receiving Team
ARTICLE 2. When a free kick goes out-of-bounds between the goal-lines, the ball belongs to the receiving team at the in-bounds spot. When a free kick goes out-of-bounds behind the goal-line, the ball belongs to the team defending that goal-line.

SECTION 3. SCRIMMAGE KICKS

Behind the Neutral Zone
ARTICLE 1. (*a*) A scrimmage kick that fails to cross the neutral zone

continues in play. All players may catch or recover the ball behind the neutral zone and advance it.

(*b*) Blocking of a kick that occurs in the vicinity of the neutral zone is ruled as having occurred within or behind that zone.

Beyond the Neutral Zone

ARTICLE 2. (*a*) No in-bounds player of the kicking team shall touch a scrimmage kick that has crossed the neutral zone before it touches an opponent. Such illegal touching is a violation which, when the ball becomes dead, gives the receiving team the privilege of taking the ball at the spot of the violation.

(*b*) If a penalty incurred by either team before the ball becomes dead is enforced or there are offsetting fouls, the privilege is cancelled. (*Exception*: Rule 6-3-11 and Rule 8-4-2-*b*.)

(*c*) Illegal touching in Team A's end zone is ignored.

All Become Eligible

ARTICLE 3. When a scrimmage kick that has crossed the neutral zone touches a player of the receiving team who is in-bounds, any player may catch or recover the ball. (*Exception*: Rule 6-3-12.)

Forced Touching Disregarded

ARTICLE 4. (*a*) A player blocked by an opponent into a scrimmage kick that has crossed the neutral zone, shall not, while in-bounds, be deemed to have touched the kick.

(*b*) An in-bounds player touched by a ball batted by an opponent is not deemed to have touched the ball.

Catch or Recovery by Receiving Team

ARTICLE 5. If a scrimmage kick is caught or recovered by a player of the receiving team, the ball continues in play. (*Exception*: Rules 4-1-3-*g*, 6-3-9, 6-5-1 and 6-5-2.)

Catch or Recovery by Kicking Team

ARTICLE 6. (*a*) If a player of the kicking team catches or recovers a scrimmage kick that crossed the neutral zone, the ball becomes dead.

(*b*) When opposing players, each eligible to touch the ball, simultaneously recover a rolling kick or catch a scrimmage kick, this simultaneous possession makes the ball dead. A kick declared dead in joint possession of opposing players is awarded to the receiving team (Rules 2-2-8 and 4-1-3-*k*).

Out of Bounds Between Goal-lines or at Rest In-bounds

ARTICLE 7. If a scrimmage kick goes out-of-bounds between the goal-lines, or comes to rest in-bounds and no player attempts to secure it, the ball becomes dead and belongs to the receiving team at the dead-ball spot. (*Exception*: Rule 8-4-2-*b*.)

Out of Bounds Behind Goal-line
ARTICLE 8. If a scrimmage kick (other than one that scores a field goal) goes out-of-bounds behind a goal-line, the ball becomes dead and belongs to the team defending that goal-line (Rule 8-4-2-*b*).

Touching Ground On or Behind Goal-line
ARTICLE 9. The ball becomes dead and belongs to the team defending its goal-line when a scrimmage kick is untouched by Team B beyond the neutral zone before touching the ground on or behind Team B's goal-line (Rule 8-4-2-*b*.)

Legal and Illegal Kicks
ARTICLE 10. (*a*) A legal scrimmage kick is a punt, drop kick or place kick made according to rule.

(*b*) A return kick is an illegal kick and a live-ball foul that causes the ball to become dead.
Penalty: For a return kick (live-ball foul): 5 yards from the spot of the foul.

(*c*) A scrimmage kick beyond the neutral zone is a live-ball foul that causes the ball to become dead.
Penalty: For an illegal kick beyond the neutral zone (live-ball foul): 5 yards from the previous spot and loss of down.

(*d*) Any device or material used to mark the spot of a scrimmage place kick or elevate the ball makes the kick illegal.
Penalty: For an illegal kick (live-ball foul): 5 yards from the previous spot.

Loose Behind the Goal-line
ARTICLE 11. If a Team A player bats a scrimmage kick in Team B's end zone and it was untouched beyond the neutral zone by Team B, it is a violation. Team B may elect a touchback when the ball is declared dead.
Violation: Touchback. (*Exception*: Rule 8-4-2-*b*.)

Out-of-Bounds Player
ARTICLE 12. No Team A player who goes out-of-bounds during a scrimmage kick down may return in-bounds during the down. (*Exception*: this does not apply to a Team A player who is blocked out-of-bounds and attempts to return in-bounds immediately.)
Penalty: Live-ball foul: 5 yards from the previous spot.

SECTION 4. OPPORTUNITY TO CATCH A KICK

Interference with Opportunity
ARTICLE 1. A player of the receiving team within the boundary lines attempting to catch a kick and so located that he could have caught a free kick or a scrimmage kick that is beyond the neutral zone, must be given an unmolested opportunity to catch the kick

(a) No player of the kicking team may be within 2 yards of a player of the receiving team positioned to catch a free or scrimmage kick.

(b) This protection terminates when the kick touches the ground or is touched by any player of Team B beyond the neutral zone.

(c) If contact with a potential receiver is the result of a player being blocked by an opponent, it is not a foul.

(d) It is not a foul if a member of the kicking team is blocked by an opponent to within 2 yards of the receiver.

(e) It is a contact foul if the kicking team contacts the potential receiver before, or simultaneously with, his first touching of the ball. When in question, it is a contact foul.

Penalty: For foul between the goal-lines: receiving team's ball, first down, 15 yards beyond the spot of the foul for contact foul and 5 yards for noncontact foul. For foul behind goal-line: award touchback and penalise from succeeding spot. Flagrant offenders shall be disqualified.

SECTION 5. FAIR CATCH

Dead Where Caught
ARTICLE 1. (a) When a Team B player makes a fair catch, the ball becomes dead where caught and belongs to Team B at that spot.

(b) Rules pertaining to fair catch apply only when a scrimmage kick crosses the neutral zone or during free kicks.

(c) The purpose of the fair catch provision is to protect the receiver who, by his fair catch signal, agrees he or a team-mate will not advance after the catch.

(d) The ball shall be put in play by a snap by the receiving team at the spot of the catch if the ball is caught.

No Advance
ARTICLE 2. No Team B player shall carry a caught or recovered ball more than two steps in any direction following a valid, invalid or illegal fair catch signal by any Team B player.

Penalty: Dead-ball foul: 5 yards from the succeeding spot.

Illegal Signals
ARTICLE 3. (a) During a down in which a kick is made, no player of

Team B shall make any illegal fair catch signal during a free kick or beyond the neutral zone during a scrimmage kick. Any signal is illegal after a scrimmage kick is caught beyond the neutral zone or after it strikes the ground or after it touches another player beyond the neutral zone. A signal is illegal after a free kick is caught, strikes the ground or touches another player.

(*b*) A catch following an illegal signal is not a fair catch, and the ball is dead where caught. If the signal follows a catch, the ball is dead when the signal is first given.

(*c*) Fouls for illegal signals beyond the neutral zone apply only to Team B.

(*d*) An illegal signal beyond the neutral zone is possible only when the ball has crossed the neutral zone (Rule 2-15-7).

Penalty: Free kick: receiving team's ball 15 yards from the spot of the foul (Rule 10-2-2-*e*). Scrimmage kick: 15-yard penalty, post-scrimmage kick enforcement or basic spot enforcement (Rule 10-2-2-*e*-5).

Illegal Block

ARTICLE 4. A player of Team B who has made a valid, invalid or illegal signal for a fair catch and does not touch the ball shall not block or foul an opponent during that down.

Penalty: Free kick: receiving team's ball 15 yards from the spot of the foul (Rule 10-2-2-*e*). Scrimmage kick: 15-yard penalty, post-scrimmage kick enforcement or basic spot enforcement (Rule 10-2-2-*e*-5).

No Tackling

ARTICLE 5. No player of the kicking team shall tackle or block an opponent who has completed a fair catch. Only the player making a fair catch signal has this protection.

Penalty: Dead-ball foul: Receiving team's ball 15 yards from the succeeding spot.

RULE 7

Snapping and Passing the Ball

SECTION 1. THE SCRIMMAGE

Starting with a Snap

ARTICLE 1. The ball shall be put in play by a legal snap unless the rules provide for a legal free kick.

Penalty: Dead-ball foul: 5 yards. Penalise from the succeeding spot.

Not in a Side Zone
ARTICLE 2. The ball may not be snapped in a side zone. If the starting point for any scrimmage down is in a side zone, it shall be transferred to the in-bounds spot.

Offensive Team Requirements
ARTICLE 3. The offensive requirements for scrimmage are as follows:
  (*a*) Before the ball is snapped:
  1. (*a*) The snapper, after assuming his position for the succeeding snap and adjusting or simulating touching the ball, may not move to a different position.
  (*b*) The snapper may not lift the ball, move it beyond the neutral zone or simulate the start of a play.
  (*c*) The snapper may take his hands off the ball if it does not simulate the start of a play.
  (*d*) Infractions of *a*, *b* and *c* may be penalised whether or not the ball is snapped, and the penalty for any resultant offside or contact foul by an opponent shall be cancelled.
  2. (*a*) After the ball is ready for play and before the snap, each substitute of Team A shall have been between the 9-yard marks. Team A players who participated in the previous down shall have been between the 9-yard marks after the previous down and before the next snap.
  (*b*) After a team time-out, a 2-minute warning time-out, an injury time-out, a radio time-out, a television time-out or the end of a period, all Team A players shall have been between the 9-yard marks after the ready-for-play signal and before the snap.
  3. After the ball is ready for play, no player of the offensive team shall be in or beyond the neutral zone after the snapper touches or simulates touching the ball and before the snap. (*Exception*: (1) Substitutes and replaced players, and (2) offensive players in a scrimmage kick formation who, after the snapper touches the ball, point at opponents and break the neutral zone with their hand(s).)
  4. After the ball is ready for play, no offensive player shall contact an opponent or make a false start, which includes:
  (*a*) Feigning a charge.
  (*b*) A shift or movement that simulates the beginning of a play. This includes the snapper, who after assuming a position for the succeeding snap and touching or simulating touching the ball, moves to another position.
  (*c*) A lineman between the snapper and the player on the end of the line, after having placed a hand(s) on or near the ground, moves his hand(s), or makes any quick movement; or a lineman other than the snapper wearing a number 50-79, after having

placed a hand(s) on or near the ground, moves his hand(s), or makes any quick movement. (*Exception*: it is not a false start if any player on the line of scrimmage moves when threatened by a Team B player in the neutral zone. The threatened Team A player may not enter the neutral zone.)

(*d*) An offensive player between the snapper and the player on the end of the line, neither legally in the backfield nor legally on the line of scrimmage after having placed a hand(s) on or near the ground (below the knees), moves his hand(s) or makes any quick movement.

5. After the ball is ready for play, an official shall sound his whistle when:

(*a*) There is a false start.

(*b*) An offensive player is in or beyond the neutral zone after the snapper touches or simulates touching the ball.

(*c*) A Team A player moves when threatened by a Team B player in the neutral zone.

Note: An infraction of this rule may be penalised whether or not the ball is snapped and the penalty for any resultant offside or contact foul other than unsportsmanlike conduct or personal fouls by an opponent shall be cancelled.

(*b*) When the snap starts:

The offensive team must be in a formation that meets the following requirements:

1. At least 7 players on their scrimmage line, not less than 5 of whom shall be numbered 50 through 79. The remaining players must be either on their scrimmage line or behind their backfield line.

Exception:

(*a*) Rule 1-4-2-*b*.

(*b*) One player may be between his scrimmage line and his backfield line if in a position to receive a hand-to-hand snap from between the snapper's legs. When in such position, that player may receive the snap himself or it may go directly to any player legally in the backfield.

2. The player on each side of and next to the snapper may lock legs with the snapper, but any other lineman of the team on offence must have both feet outside the outside foot of the player next to him when the ball is snapped.

3. All players must be in-bounds and only the snapper may be encroaching on the neutral zone, but no part of his person may be beyond the neutral zone and his feet must be stationary behind the ball.

4. One player may be in motion, but not in motion toward his opponents' goal-line. A lineman may not be in motion at the snap.

Other players must be stationary in their positions without movement of the feet, body, head or arms.

Penalty: For fouls before the ball is snapped: 5 yards from the succeeding spot. For fouls when the ball is snapped: 5 yards from the previous spot.

Defensive Team Requirements

ARTICLE 4. The defensive team requirements are as follows:

(*a*) Before the snap starts:

1. After the ball is ready for play and until it is snapped, no player may touch the ball except when moved illegally as in Rule 7-1-3-*a*-1, nor may any player contact an opponent or in any other way interfere with him. An official shall sound his whistle immediately.

2. No player shall use words or signals that disconcert opponents when they are preparing to put the ball in play. No player may call defensive signals that simulate the sound or cadence of (or otherwise interfere with) offensive starting signals. An official shall sound his whistle immediately.

(*b*) When the snap starts:

1. No player may be in or beyond the neutral zone at the snap.

2. All players must be in-bounds.

Penalty: For fouls before the ball is snapped: 5 yards from the succeeding spot. For fouls when the ball is snapped: 5 yards from the previous spot.

Shift Plays

ARTICLE 5. (*a*) If a snap is preceded by a huddle or shift, all players of the offensive team must come to an absolute stop and remain stationary in their positions, without movement of the feet, body, head or arms, for at least one full second before the ball is snapped.

(*b*) It is not intended that Rule 7-1-3-*a* should prohibit smooth, rhythmical shifts if properly executed. A smooth, cadence shift or unhurried motion is not an infraction. However, it is the responsibility of an offensive player who moves before the snap to do so in a manner that in no way simulates the beginning of a play. After the ball is ready for play and all players are in scrimmage formation, no offensive player shall make a quick, jerky movement before the snap. Any such motion is an infraction of the rule. Although not intended to be all-inclusive, the following examples illustrate the type of movement prohibited before the snap:

1. A lineman moving his foot, shoulder, arm, body or head in a quick, jerky motion in any direction.

2. The snapper shifting or moving the ball, or moving his thumb or

fingers, or flexing elbows, jerking head or dipping shoulders or buttocks.

3. The quarterback 'chucking' hands at the snapper, flexing elbows under the snapper, jerking head or dropping shoulders quickly just before the snap.

4. A player starting in motion before the snap simulating receiving the ball by 'chucking' his hands toward the snapper or quarterback, or making any quick, jerky movement that simulates the beginning of a play.

Penalty: 5 yards from the previous spot; 5 yards from the succeeding spot for fouls before the ball is snapped.

Handing the Ball Forward
ARTICLE 6. No player may hand the ball forward except during a scrimmage down as follows:

(*a*) A Team A player who is behind his scrimmage line may hand the ball forward to a backfield team-mate who is also behind that line.

(*b*) A Team A player who is behind his scrimmage line may hand the ball forward to a team-mate who was on his scrimmage line when the ball was snapped, provided that team-mate left his line position by a movement of both feet that faced him toward his own end-line and was at least two yards behind his scrimmage line when he received the ball.

Penalty: 5 yards from the spot of the foul; also loss of a down if by Team A before team possession changes during a scrimmage down.

Planned Loose Ball
ARTICLE 7. A Team A player may not advance a planned loose ball in the vicinity of the snapper.

Penalty: 5 yards from the previous spot and loss of down.

SECTION 2. BACKWARD PASS AND FUMBLE

During Live Ball
ARTICLE 1. A runner may hand or pass the ball backward at any time, except to throw the ball intentionally out-of-bounds to conserve time.

Penalty: 5 yards from the spot of the foul; also loss of down if by Team A before team possession changes during a scrimmage down. (*Exception*: penalise 5 yards from the previous spot and loss of down if the foul, to conserve time, occurs beyond the neutral zone before a change of team possession.)

Caught or Recovered
ARTICLE 2. A backward pass or fumble may be caught or recovered by any in-bounds player.

(*a*) If caught or recovered by either team, the ball continues in play.

(*b*) If a backward pass or fumble is caught or recovered simultaneously by opposing players, the ball becomes dead and belongs to the team last in possession.

After the Ball is Snapped

ARTICLE 3. No offensive lineman may receive a hand-to-hand snap. *Penalty*: Live-ball foul: 5 yards from the previous spot.

Out-of-Bounds

ARTICLE 4. (*a*) When a backward pass goes out-of-bounds between the goal-lines, the ball belongs to the passing team at the out-of-bounds spot; if out-of-bounds behind a goal-line, it is a touchback or safety.

(*b*) When a fumble is out-of-bounds in advance of the spot of the fumble, the ball is returned to the fumbling team at the spot of the fumble. Fumbles out-of-bounds behind the spot of the fumble belong to the fumbling team at the out-of-bounds spot. (*Exception*: the ball belongs to the defending team at the spot of the fumble when the offensive team fumbles and the ball goes out-of-bounds in the opponent's end zone.)

At Rest

ARTICLE 5. When a backward pass or fumble comes to rest in-bounds and no player attempts to secure it, the ball becomes dead and belongs to the passing or fumbling team at the dead-ball spot.

SECTION 3. FORWARD PASS

Legal Forward Pass

ARTICLE 1. Team A may make one forward pass during each scrimmage down before team possession changes, provided the pass is thrown from a point in or behind the neutral zone.

Illegal Forward Pass

ARTICLE 2. A forward pass is illegal:

(*a*) If thrown by Team A when the passer is beyond the neutral zone.

(*b*) If thrown by Team B or if thrown by Team A after team possession has changed during the down.

(*c*) If it is the second forward pass by Team A during the same down.

(*d*) If intentionally thrown into an area not occupied by an eligible Team A player to save loss of yardage.

(*e*) If, to conserve time, the pass is not thrown immediately after the ball is first controlled after the snap.

(*f*) If thrown from behind the neutral zone after a runner in possession of the ball has gone beyond the neutral zone.

Penalty: 5 yards from the spot of the foul; also loss of a down if by Team A before team possession changes during a scrimmage down. (*Exception*: penalise 5 yards from the previous spot and loss of down if the foul, to conserve time, occurs beyond the neutral zone before a change of team possession.)

Eligibility to Touch Legal Pass

ARTICLE 3. Eligibility rules apply during a down when a legal forward pass is thrown. All Team B players are eligible to touch or catch a pass. When the ball is snapped, the following Team A players are eligible:

(*a*) Each player who is in an end position on his scrimmage line and who is wearing a number other than 50 through to 79.

(*b*) Each player who is legally in his backfield wearing a number other than 50 through to 79.

(*c*) A player wearing a number other than 50 through to 79, in position to receive a hand-to-hand snap from between the snapper's legs.

Eligibility Lost by Going Out-of-Bounds

ARTICLE 4. No eligible offensive player who goes out-of-bounds during a down shall touch a legal forward pass in the field of play or end zone until it has been touched by an opponent.

Exception: This does not apply to an eligible offensive player who attempts to return in-bounds immediately after being blocked out of bounds by an opponent.

Penalty: Loss of down at the previous spot.

Eligibility Regained

ARTICLE 5. When a Team B player touches a legal forward pass all players become eligible.

Completed Pass

ARTICLE 6. Any forward pass is completed when caught by a player of the passing team who is in-bounds, and the ball continues in play unless completed in the opponent's end zone or the pass has been caught simultaneously by opposing players. If a forward pass is caught simultaneously by opposing players in-bounds, the ball becomes dead and belongs to the passing team.

Incompleted Pass
ARTICLE 7.

(*a*) Any forward pass is incomplete when the pass touches the ground or is out-of-bounds by rule. It is also incomplete when a player jumps and receives the pass but first lands on or outside a boundary line unless his forward progress has been stopped in the field of play.

(*b*) When a legal forward pass is incomplete, the ball belongs to the passing team at the previous spot.

(*c*) When an illegal forward pass is incomplete, the ball belongs to the passing team at the spot of the pass. (*Exception*: if any illegal pass is thrown from the end zone, the offended team may accept a safety or decline the penalty and accept the result of the play.)

Illegal Contact and Pass Interference
ARTICLE 8. (*a*) During a down in which a legal forward pass crosses the neutral zone, illegal contact by Team A and Team B players is prohibited from the time the ball is snapped until it is touched by any player.

(*b*) Offensive pass interference by a Team A player beyond the neutral zone during a legal forward pass play in which a forward pass crosses the neutral zone is contact that interferes with a Team B eligible player. It is the responsibility of the offensive player to avoid the opponents. It is not offensive pass interference if it is the type that occurs:

1. When, after the snap, a Team A player immediately charges and contacts an opponent at a point not more than one yard beyond the neutral zone and does not continue the contact more than three yards beyond the neutral zone.
2. When two or more eligible players are making a simultaneous and bona fide attempt to reach, catch or bat the pass. Eligible players of either team have equal rights to the ball.
3. When the pass is in flight and two or more eligible players are in the area where they might receive or intercept the pass and an offensive player in that area impedes an opponent, and the pass is not catchable.

(*c*) Defensive pass interference is contact beyond the neutral zone by a Team B player whose intent to impede an eligible opponent is obvious and it could prevent the opponent the opportunity of receiving a catchable forward pass. When in question, a legal forward pass is catchable. Defensive pass interference occurs only after a forward pass is thrown. It is not defensive pass interference if it is the type that occurs:

1. When, after the snap, opposing players immediately charge and establish contact with opponents at a point that is within one yard beyond the neutral zone.

2. When two or more eligible players are making a simultaneous and bona fide attempt to reach, catch or bat the pass. Eligible players of either team have equal rights to the ball.

3. When a Team B player legally contacts an opponent before the pass is thrown.

Penalty: Pass interference by Team A: 15 yards from the previous spot. Pass interference by Team B: Team A's ball at the spot of the foul, first down, if the foul occurs less than 15 yards beyond the previous spot. If the foul occurs 15 or more yards beyond the previous spot, Team A's ball, first down, 15-yard penalty from the previous spot. When the ball is snapped between the Team B 17-yard line and the Team B 2-yard line and the spot of the foul is beyond the 2-yard line, the penalty shall place the ball at the 2-yard line, first down. No penalty enforced from outside the 2-yard line may place the ball inside the 2-yard line. (*Exception*: Rule 10-2-2-*g*-2.) If the previous spot was on or inside the two-yard line, first down halfway between the previous spot and the goal-line. (*Exception*: Rule 10-2-3 *Exception*.)

Contact Interference

ARTICLE 9. (*a*) Either Team A or Team B may legally interfere with opponents behind the neutral zone.

(*b*) Players of either team may legally interfere beyond the neutral zone after the pass has been touched.

(*c*) Defensive players may legally contact opponents who have crossed the neutral zone if the opponents are not in a position to receive a catchable forward pass.

1. Those infractions that occur during a down when a forward pass crosses the neutral zone are pass interference infractions only if the receiver had the opportunity to receive a catchable forward pass.

2. Those infractions that occur during a down when a forward pass does not cross the neutral zone are Rule 9-3-4 infractions and are penalised from the previous spot.

(*d*) Pass interference rules apply only during a down in which a legal forward pass crosses the neutral zone (Rules 2-19-3, 7-3-8).

(*e*) Contact by Team B with an eligible receiver involving unnecessary roughness that interferes with the reception of a catchable pass may be penalised either as pass interference or as a 15-yard personal foul enforced from the previous spot. Rule 7-3-8 is specific about contact during a pass. However if the interference involves an act that would ordinarily result in disqualification, the fouling player must leave the game.

(*f*) Physical contact is required to establish interference.

(*g*) Each player has territorial rights and incidental contact is ruled under 'attempt to reach the pass' in Rule 7-3-8. If opponents who are beyond the line collide while moving toward the pass, a foul by one or both players is indicated only if intent to impede the opponent is obvious. It is pass interference only if a catchable forward pass is involved.

(*h*) Pass interference rules do not apply after the pass has been touched anywhere in-bounds by an in-bounds player. If an opponent is fouled, the penalty is for the foul and not for the pass interference.

(*i*) After the pass has been touched, any player may execute a legal block during the remaining flight of the pass.

(*j*) Tackling or grasping a receiver or any other intentional contact before he touches the pass is evidence that the tackler is disregarding the ball and is therefore illegal.

(*k*) Tackling or running into a receiver when a forward pass is obviously underthrown or overthrown is disregarding the ball and is illegal. This is not pass interference but a violation of Rule 9-1-2-*f* and is penalised 15 yards from the previous spot plus a first down.

Ineligibles Downfield
ARTICLE 10. No originally ineligible player shall be or have been beyond the neutral zone until a legal forward pass that crosses the neutral zone has been thrown.
Exceptions:
1. When after the snap, a Team A player immediately charges and contacts an opponent at a point not more than one yard beyond the neutral zone and does not continue the contact more than 3 yards beyond the neutral zone.
2. When contact that has driven an opponent no more than 3 yards from the neutral zone is lost by a player who was ineligible at the snap, he must remain stationary at that spot until the pass is thrown.
Penalty: 5 yards from the previous spot.

Illegal Touching
ARTICLE 11. No originally ineligible player while in-bounds shall touch a legal forward pass until it has touched an opponent.
Penalty: 5 yards from the previous spot plus loss of a down.

RULE 8

Scoring

SECTION 1. VALUE OF SCORES

Scoring Plays
ARTICLE 1. The points value of scoring plays shall be:

Touchdown	6 points
Field-goal	3 points
Safety (points awarded to opponents)	2 points
Successful try touchdown	2 points
Successful try, field-goal or safety ..	1 point

Forfeited Games
ARTICLE 2. The score of a forfeited game shall be: Offended team 1 Opponent 0. If the offended team is ahead at the time of forfeit the score stands.

SECTION 2. TOUCHDOWN

How Scored
ARTICLE 1. A touchdown shall be scored when:

(*a*) A runner advancing from the field of play is legally in possession of a live ball when it penetrates the opponent's goal-line (plane).

(*b*) An eligible receiver catches a legal forward pass in the opponent's end zone.

(*c*) A fumble or backward pass is recovered, caught, intercepted, or awarded in the opponent's end zone

(*d*) A free kick is legally caught or recovered in the opponent's end zone.

(*e*) A scrimmage kick is legally caught or recovered in the opponent's end zone.

(*f*) The referee awards a touchdown under the provisions of Rule 9-1-4 penalty and Rule 9-2-3.

SECTION 3. TRY

How Scored
ARTICLE 1. The point or points shall be scored according to the point values in Rule 8-1-1 if the try results in what would be a touchdown, safety or field goal under rules governing play at other times.

Opportunity to Score
ARTICLE 2. A try is an opportunity for either team to score one or two points while the game clock is stopped and is a special interval in a game which, for purposes of penalty enforcement only, includes both a down and the 'ready' period that precedes it.

(*a*) The ball shall be put in play by the team that scored a 6-point touchdown. If a touchdown is scored during a down in which time expires, the winner of the game has been decided, and both head coaches agree to forgo the try, the period is not extended.

(*b*) The try, which is a scrimmage down, begins when the ball is ready for play.

(*c*) The snap may be from any point on or between the in-bounds lines on or behind the opponents' 3-yard line if the position of the ball is selected prior to the ready for play. The ball may be relocated following a charged time-out to either team unless preceded by a Team A foul or offsetting penalties (Rules 8-3-3-*a* and 8-3-3-*c*-1).

(*d*) The try ends when:
1. Either team scores.
2. If the ball is dead by rule.
3. An accepted penalty results in a score.
4. A Team A loss of a down penalty is accepted (Rule 8-3-3-*d*).

Fouls During a Try Before Team B Possession
ARTICLE 3.

(*a*) Offsetting fouls: the down shall be replayed if offsetting fouls occur. Any replay after offsetting penalties must be from the previous spot.

(*b*) Fouls by Team B on a try:
1. Team A shall have the option of declining the score and repeating the try after enforcement, or accepting the score with the enforcement only of any 15-yard penalty (including pass interference) from the spot of the next kick-off.
2. A replay after a penalty against Team B may be from any point on or between the in-bounds lines on the yard line where the penalty leaves the ball.

(*c*) Fouls by Team A on a try: after a foul by Team A on a successful try, the ball shall be put in play at the spot where the penalty leaves it.

(*d*) Penalties against Team A on a try, which include loss of down and yardage, nullify the score and yardage is not penalised on the succeeding kick-off. (*Note*: if Team B scores, any 15-yard penalty is assessed on the succeeding kick-off.)

(*e*) Dead-ball enforcement:
1. Fouls occurring after the ready for play and before the snap are penalised before the next snap.
2. Live-ball fouls penalised as dead-ball fouls occurring during the try down are penalised on the succeeding kick-off.

(*f*) Roughing or running into kicker or holder: roughing or running into the kicker or holder is a live-ball foul.

(g) Kick catch interference: The penalty for interference with a kick catch is enforced on the succeeding kick-off.

Fouls During a Try After Team B Possession
ARTICLE 4. (a) Distance penalties by either team are enforced on the succeeding kick-off.

(b) Scores by fouling teams are cancelled.

(c) If there are offsetting fouls, whether one or both occur after Team B possession, the down is not replayed.

Fouls After a Try
ARTICLE 5. Fouls after a try down and before the next kick-off are penalised on the succeeding kick-off.

Next Play
ARTICLE 6. After a try, the ball shall be put in play by a kick-off. The field captain of the team against which the 6-point touchdown was scored shall designate which team shall kick off.

SECTION 4. FIELD GOAL

How Scored
ARTICLE 1. (a) A field goal shall be scored for the kicking team if a drop kick or place kick passes over the cross-bar between the uprights of the receiving team's goal before it touches a player of the kicking team or the ground. The kick shall be a scrimmage kick but may not be a free kick.

(b) If a legal field goal attempt passes over the cross-bar between the uprights and is dead beyond the end-lines or is blown back but does not return over the cross-bar and is dead anywhere, it shall score a field goal. The entire goal, cross-bar, and uprights are treated as a line, not a plane, in determining forward progress of the ball.

Next Play
ARTICLE 2. (a) After a field goal is scored the ball shall be put in play by a kick-off. The field captain of the team scored against shall designate which team shall kick off.

(b) After an unsuccessful field goal attempt that crosses the neutral zone, the ball, untouched by Team B beyond the neutral zone, will next be put in play at the previous spot. If the previous spot was between Team B's 20-yard line and goal-line, the ball shall next be put in play at the 20-yard line. Otherwise, all rules pertaining to scrimmage kicks shall apply.

SECTION 5. SAFETY

How Scored
ARTICLE 1. It is a safety when:
(*a*) The ball becomes dead out-of-bounds behind a goal-line (except from an incompleted forward pass) or becomes dead in the possession of a player on, above, or behind his own goal-line, and the defending team is responsible for the ball being there. When in question, it is a touchback, not a safety.
(*b*) An accepted penalty for a foul leaves the ball on or behind the offending team's goal-line.
Exception: When a Team B player intercepts a forward pass, fumble or backward pass or catches a scrimmage or free kick between his 5-yard line and the goal-line and his original momentum carries him into the end zone, where the ball is declared dead in his team's possession or it goes out-of-bounds in the end zone, the ball belongs to Team B at the spot where the pass or fumble was intercepted or the kick was caught.

Kick After Safety
ARTICLE 2. After a safety is scored, the ball belongs to the defending team at its own 20-yard line, and that team shall put the ball in play on or between the in-bound lines by a free kick that may be a punt, drop kick or place kick.

SECTION 6. TOUCHBACK

When Declared
ARTICLE 1. It is a touchback when:
(*a*) The ball becomes dead out-of-bounds behind a goal-line (except from an incompleted forward pass) or becomes dead in the possession of a player on, above, or behind his own goal-line and the attacking team is responsible for the ball being there. (*Exception*: Rule 7-2-4-*b* exception.)
(*b*) A kick becomes dead by rule behind the defending team's goal-line, and the attacking team is responsible for the ball being there. (*Exception*: Rule 8-4-2-*b*.)
(*c*) A violation by the kicking team occurs in the receiving team's end zone.

Snap After a Touchback
ARTICLE 2. After a touchback is declared, the ball belongs to the defending team at its own 20-yard line, and that team shall put the ball in play on or between the in-bound lines by a snap. The snap shall be from midway between the in-bound lines on the 20-yard line, unless a

different position on or between the in-bound lines is selected before the ready for play. After the ready for play, the ball may be relocated after a charged team time-out, unless preceded by a Team A foul or offsetting penalties.

SECTION 7. RESPONSIBILITY AND IMPETUS

Responsibility
ARTICLE 1. The team responsible for the ball being out-of-bounds behind a goal-line or being dead in the possession of a player on or above or behind a goal-line is the team whose player carries the ball or imparts an impetus to it that forces it on, above or across the goal-line, or is responsible for a loose ball being on, above or behind the goal-line.

Initial Impetus
ARTICLE 2. (*a*) The impetus imparted by a player who kicks, passes, snaps or fumbles the ball shall be considered responsible for the ball's progress in any direction even though its course is deflected or reversed after striking the ground or after touching a player of either team.
   (*b*) Initial impetus is considered expended and the responsibility for the ball's progress is charged to a player:
   1. If he kicks a ball not in player possession or bats a loose ball after it strikes the ground. (*Exception*: the original impetus is not changed when a loose ball is batted or kicked in the end zone.)
   2. If the ball comes to rest and he gives it new impetus by any contact with it.
Exceptions:
   1. Rules 6-1-4-*a* and 6-3-4-*a*;
   2. The original impetus is not changed when a ball at rest in the end zone is moved when touched by a player.
   (*c*) A loose ball retains its original status when there is new impetus.

RULE 9

Conduct of Players and Others Subject to Rules

SECTION 1. PERSONAL AND INTERFERENCE FOULS

Flagrant Fouls
ARTICLE 1. Before the game, during the game and between periods, all flagrant fouls require disqualification. Team B disqualification fouls may require first downs if not in conflict with other rules.

Persons Subject to the Rules Restrictions

ARTICLE 2. No person subject to the rules shall commit a personal foul during the game or between the periods. Any act prohibited hereunder or any other act of unnecessary roughness is a personal foul.

(*a*) No person subject to the rules shall strike an opponent with the knee; strike an opponent's helmet (including the face mask), neck or face or any part of the body with an extended forearm, elbow, locked hands, palm, fist or the heel, back or side of the open hand, or gouge an opponent during the game or between the periods.

(*b*) No person subject to the rules shall strike an opponent with his foot or any part of his leg that is below the knee.

(*c*) There shall be no tripping. (*Exception*: the runner.)

(*d*) There shall be no clipping.

Exceptions:

1. When offensive players are on the line of scrimmage at the snap within a rectangular area centred on the middle lineman of the offensive formation and extending 5 yards laterally and 3 yards longitudinally in each direction, they may legally clip in the rectangular area.

(*a*) A player on the line of scrimmage within the legal clipping zone may not leave the zone and return and legally clip.

(*b*) The legal clipping zone exists until the ball is touched outside the legal clipping zone or the ball is outside the legal clipping zone after a fumble or muff from inside the clipping zone.

2. When a player turns his back on a potential blocker who has committed himself in intent and direction of movement.

3. When a player attempts to reach a runner or legally attempts to recover or catch a fumble, a muff, a backward pass, a kick or a touched forward pass, he may push an opponent at or below the waist.

4. When an eligible player behind the neutral zone pushes an opponent at or below the waist to get to a forward pass.

(*e*) Blocking below the waist is permitted except as follows:

1. Offensive players at the snap positioned more than 7 yards in any direction from the middle lineman of the offensive formation or in motion toward the ball at the snap are prohibited from blocking below the waist toward the ball until the ball has advanced beyond the neutral zone. The following formation sets are legal and the players are not restricted by Rule 9-1-2-*e* when blocking toward the ball:

(*a*) An offensive end positioned less than 2 yards from the legal clipping zone.

(*b*) A wingback positioned 1 yard to the outside of an end who is flexed no more than 1 yard from the legal clipping zone.

(*c*) A wingback positioned no more than 1 yard outside the legal clipping zone and inside an end who is 1 yard outside the wingback.

2. During a scrimmage down, defensive players are prohibited from blocking an eligible Team A receiver below the waist beyond the neutral zone unless attempting to get at the ball or runner. A Team A receiver remains eligible until a legal forward pass is no longer possible by rule.

3. During a down in which there is a free kick or scrimmage kick from a scrimmage kick formation, all players are prohibited from blocking below the waist except against the runner.

4. After any change of team possession all players are prohibited from blocking below the waist except against the runner.

5. A Team A player behind the neutral zone and in position to receive a backward pass shall not be blocked below the waist.

(*f*) No player shall tackle or run into a receiver when a forward pass to him is obviously not catchable. This is a personal foul and not pass interference.

(*g*) There shall be no piling on, falling on, or throwing the body on an opponent after the ball becomes dead.

(*h*) No opponent shall tackle or block the runner when he is clearly out-of-bounds or throw him to the ground after the ball becomes dead.

(*i*) There shall be no hurdling.

(*j*) No player shall run into or throw himself against an opponent obviously out of the play either before or after the ball is dead.

(*k*) No player shall continuously contact an opponent's helmet (including the face mask) with hand(s) or arm(s). (*Exception*: The runner.)

(*l*) No player intentionally shall use his helmet (including the face mask) to butt or ram an opponent.

(*m*) There shall be no spearing.

(*n*) No player shall intentionally strike a runner with the crown or the top of his helmet.

(*o*) No defensive player shall charge into a passer or throw him to the ground when it is obvious the ball has been thrown. This is roughing the passer, and the penalty is added to the end of the last run when it ends beyond the neutral zone and there is no change of team possession.

(*p*) There shall be no chop blocking.

(*q*) No defensive player, in an attempt to gain an advantage, may step, jump or stand on an opponent.

(*r*) No player shall charge into an opponent when a take-a-knee play has been notified.

Penalty: 15 yards from the basic spot and a first down for Team B fouls if the first down is not in conflict with other rules. Flagrant offenders shall be disqualified. All personal fouls occurring when a take-a-knee play has been notified require disqualification of offenders.

(s) No player shall grasp the face mask or any helmet opening of an opponent. The open hand may be legally used on the mask.

Penalty: Live-ball foul, basic spot. Defensive team: 5 yards for incidental grasping; 15 yards for twisting, turning or pulling, and first down for Team B fouls if not in conflict with other rules. Offensive team: 15 yards from the basic spot. All dead-ball fouls: 15 yards from the succeeding spot and a first down for a Team B foul if not in conflict with other rules. Flagrant offenders shall be disqualified. When in question, it is twisting, turning or pulling.

Roughing or Running into Kicker or Holder

ARTICLE 3. (a) When it is obvious that a scrimmage kick will be made, no opponent shall run into or rough the kicker, or holder of a place kick.

1. Roughing is a personal foul that endangers the kicker or holder.

2. Running into the kicker or holder is a foul that occurs when the kicker or holder are displaced from their kicking or holding positions but are not roughed.

3. Incidental contact with a kicker or holder is not a foul.

4. The kicker or holder must be protected from injury but contact that occurs when or after a scrimmage kick has been touched is not roughing or running into the kicker.

5. The kicker of a scrimmage kick loses protection as a kicker when he has had a reasonable time to regain his balance.

6. A defensive player blocked into the kicker or holder by a member of the kicking team is not exempt from running into or roughing the kicker fouls.

7. When a player, other than one who blocks a scrimmage kick, runs into or roughs the kicker or holder it is a foul.

8. When in question whether the foul is 'running into' or 'roughing', the foul is 'roughing'.

Penalty: 5 yards from the previous spot for running into the kicker or holder. 15 yards from the previous spot and also first down for roughing the kicker or holder. Flagrant offenders shall be disqualified.

(b) A kicker or holder simulating being roughed or run into by a defensive player commits an unsportsmanlike act.

Penalty: 15 yards from the previous spot.

(c) The kicker of a free kick may not be blocked until he has advanced 5 yards beyond his restraining line or the kick has touched a player, an official or the ground.

Penalty: 15 yards from the previous spot.

Illegal Interference

ARTICLE 4. (*a*) No substitute, coach, authorised attendant or any person subject to the rules other than a player or official, may interfere in any way with the ball or a player while the ball is in play.

Penalty: 15 yards from the enforcement spot most advantageous to the offended team. The referee may enforce any penalty he deems equitable including awarding a score.

(*b*) Participation by 12 or more players is illegal participation.

Penalty: 15 yards from the previous spot.

(*c*) No person not subject to the rules may interfere in any way with the ball or a player while the ball is in play.

(*d*) When anything other than persons subject to the rules and those not subject to the rules interferes in any way with a player or the ball in play, it is illegal interference.

Penalty: The referee may replay the down or take any action he deems equitable, including awarding a score.

(*e*) No player who is not on his team's roster form may participate.

1. A head coach may request a coach's conference with the referee if he believes an opposition player is not on the roster (Rule 3-3-4-*d*). If the player is on the roster, the coach's team will be charged a time-out, or a delay penalty if all time-outs have been used.

Penalty: Disqualification.

Game Administration Interference

ARTICLE 5. (*a*) While the ball is in play, coaches, substitutes and authorised attendants in the team area may not be between the side-lines and coaching line.

(*b*) The procedure for enforcement of Rule 9-1-5-*a* is as follows:

1. The head coach is informed by a game official that he is receiving a first or second warning because the area between the side-line and coaching line has been violated by coaches, players or persons authorised in the team area.

2. The official will record the time and period of each warning.

3. After a second warning, the official will notify the head coach that he has had two warnings and that the next infraction will result in a 5-yard penalty.

4. After a 5-yard penalty, the official will notify the head coach that he has had two warnings and a 5-yard penalty and will receive a 15-yard penalty for the next infraction.

5. An official shall stop the clock to give a side-line warning.

Penalty: 5 yards after two official warnings from a game official and 15 yards for each additional foul. Penalise as dead-ball fouls.

SECTION 2. NON-CONTACT FOULS

Unsportsmanlike Acts

ARTICLE 1. There shall be no unsportsmanlike conduct or any act that interferes with orderly game administration on the part of players, substitutes, coaches, authorised attendants or any other persons subject to the rules, before the game, during the game or between periods.

(*a*) Specifically prohibited acts and conduct include:

1. No player, substitute, coach or other person subject to the rules shall use obscene or vulgar language or gestures or engage in acts that provoke ill-will or are demeaning to an opponent, to game officials or to the image of the game, including:

    (*a*) Pointing the finger(s), hand(s), arm(s) or ball at an opponent.

    (*b*) Baiting or insulting an opponent verbally.

    (*c*) Inciting an opponent or spectators in any other way.

    (*d*) Any delayed, excessive or prolonged act by which a player attempts to focus attention upon himself.

    (*e*) Dissent with an official's decision.

2. No person subject to the rules, except players, officials and eligible substitutes, shall be on the field-of-play or end zones during any period without permission from the referee. If a player is injured, attendants may come in-bounds to attend him, but they must obtain recognition from an official.

3. After a score or any other play the player in possession must immediately return the ball to an official or leave it near the dead-ball spot. This prohibits:

    (*a*) Kicking or throwing the ball any distance that requires an official to retrieve it.

    (*b*) Throwing the ball out of the field.

    (*c*) Any other unsportsmanlike act or actions that delay the game.

Exception: spiking the ball or throwing it into the air to celebrate an apparent touchdown is permitted provided it does not cause undue delay.

4. No substitutes may enter the field-of-play or end zones for purposes other than replacing a player. This includes demonstrations after any play.

5. Persons subject to the rules, including bands, shall not create any noise that prohibits a team from hearing its signals.

6. No Team A player may attempt to advance the ball during a take-a-knee play.

Penalty: 15 yards from the succeeding spot. Penalise as a dead-ball foul. Flagrant offenders, if players or substitutes, shall be disqualified. Attempting to advance the ball during a take-a-knee play is a flagrant act and requires disqualification.

(*b*) Other prohibited acts include:

1. During the game, coaches, substitutes and authorised attendants in the team area shall not be on the field of play or outside the 25-yard lines without permission from the referee unless legally entering or leaving the field. (*Exception*: Rules 1-2-4-*h* and 3-3-8-*c*.)

2. No disqualified player shall enter the field-of-play.

3. No disqualified coach may enter the field-play or communicate with anyone who is within the field-play.

Penalty: 15 yards from the succeeding spot. Penalise as a dead-ball foul. Flagrant offenders, if players or substitutes, shall be disqualified.

Unfair Tactics

ARTICLE 2. (*a*) No player shall conceal the ball in or beneath his clothing or equipment or substitute any other article for the ball.

(*b*) No simulated replacements or substitutions may be used to confuse opponents. No tactic associated with substitutes or the substitution process may be used to confuse opponents.

(*c*) No equipment may be used to confuse opponents (Rule 1-4-2-*e*).

Penalty: 15 yards from the most advantageous spot to the offended team. Flagrant offenders shall be disqualified.

Unfair Acts

ARTICLE 3. The referee may enforce any penalty he considers equitable, including awarding a score:

(*a*) If a team refuses to play within 2 minutes after ordered to do so by the referee.

(*b*) If a team repeatedly commits fouls that can be penalised only by halving the distance to its goal-line. The referee shall, after one warning, forfeit the game to the opponents for Rules 9-2-3-*a* and 9-2-3-*b* infractions.

(*c*) If an obviously unfair act not specifically covered by the rules occurs during the game.

Contacting an Official

ARTICLE 4. Intentionally contacting a game official physically during the game by persons subject to the rules is a foul.

Penalty: Dead-ball foul: 15 yards and disqualification.

SECTION 3. BLOCKING, USE OF HAND AND ARM

Who May Block

ARTICLE 1. Players of either team may block opponents provided it is not forward pass interference, interference with opportunity to catch a kick, or a personal foul.

Interfering for or Helping the Runner
ARTICLE 2. (*a*) The runner or passer may use his hand or arm to ward off or push opponents.

(*b*) The runner shall not grasp a team-mate; and no other player of his team shall grasp, push, lift or charge into him to assist him in forward progress.

(*c*) Team-mates of the runner or passer may interfere for him by blocking but shall not use interlocked interference by grasping or encircling one another in any manner while contacting an opponent. *Penalty*: 5 yards from the basic spot.

Use of Hand or Arm by Offence
ARTICLE 3. (*a*) A team-mate of a runner or a passer legally may block with his shoulders, his hands, the outer surface of his arms or any other part of his body under the following provisions:
1. The hand(s) shall be:
   (*a*) In advance of the elbow.
   (*b*) Inside the frame of the opponent's body. (*Exception*: when the opponent turns his back to the blocker.)
   (*c*) At or below the shoulders of the blocker and the opponent. (*Exception*: when the opponent squats, ducks or submarines.)
2. The hand(s) shall be open with the palm(s) facing the frame of the opponent or closed or cupped with the palms not facing the opponent.
Penalty: 10 yards from the basic spot.

(*b*) Holding or illegal obstruction by a team-mate of the runner or passer applies to Rule 9-3-3-*a*:
1. The hand(s) and arm(s) shall not be used to grasp, pull or encircle in any way that illegally impedes or illegally obstructs an opponent.
2. The hand(s) and arm(s) shall not be used to hook, clamp or otherwise illegally impede or illegally obstruct an opponent.
Penalty: 10 yards from the basic spot.

(*c*) A block in the back is illegal.
Exceptions:
1. When offensive players are on the line of scrimmage at the snap within a rectangular area centred on the middle lineman of the offensive formation and extending 5 yards laterally and 3 yards longitudinally in each direction, they may legally block in the back in the rectangular area.
   (*a*) A player on the line of scrimmage within this blocking zone may not leave the zone and return and legally block in the back.

(*b*) The blocking zone exists until the ball is touched outside the zone or the ball is outside the zone after a fumble or muff from inside the zone.

2. When a player turns his back on a potential blocker who has committed himself in intent and direction of movement.

3. When a player attempts to reach a runner or legally attempts to recover or catch a fumble, a muff, a backward pass, a kick or a touched forward pass, he may push an opponent in the back above the waist.

4. When the opponent turns his back to the blocker under Rule 9-3-3-*a*-1-*b*.

5. When an eligible player behind the neutral zone pushes an opponent in the back above the waist to get to a forward pass.

Penalty: 10 yards from the basic spot.

(*d*) The following acts by a team-mate of the runner or passer are illegal:

1. The hand(s) and arm(s) shall not be used to deliver a blow.

2. During no block shall the hands be locked.

3. Continuous contact to an opponent's helmet (including the face mask) with hand(s) or arm(s) (Rule 9-1-2-*k*).

Penalty: 15 yards from the basic spot. Disqualification if flagrant.

(*e*) A player on the kicking team may:

1. During a scrimmage kick play, use his hand(s) and/or arm(s) to ward off an opponent attempting to block him when he is beyond the neutral zone.

2. During a free kick play, use his hand(s) and/or arm(s) to ward off an opponent who is attempting to block him.

3. During a scrimmage kick play or a free kick play, when he is eligible to touch the ball, legally use his hand(s) and/or arm(s) to push an opponent in an attempt to reach a loose ball.

(*f*) An eligible player of the passing team legally may use his hand(s) and/or arm(s) to ward off or push an opponent in an attempt to reach a loose ball after a legal forward pass has been touched by any player (Rules 7-3-5, 7-3-8, 7-3-9 and 7-3-11).

Use of Hands or Arms by Defence
ARTICLE 4.

(*a*) Defensive players may use hands and arms to push, pull, ward off or lift offensive players when attempting to reach the runner.

(*b*) Defensive players may not use hands and arms to tackle, hold or otherwise illegally obstruct an opponent other than a runner.

Penalty: 10 yards from the basic spot.

(*c*) Defensive players may use hands and arms to push, pull, ward off or lift offensive players obviously attempting to block them. Defensive players may ward off or legally block an eligible pass receiver until that player occupies the same yard line as the defender or until the opponent could not possibly block him. Continuous contact is illegal.

Penalty: 5, 10 or 15 yards from the basic spot.

(*d*) When no attempt is being made to get at the ball or the runner, defensive players must comply with Rules 9-3-3-*a*, 9-3-3-*b*, 9-3-3-*c* and 9-3-3-*d*.

Penalty: 5, 10 or 15 yards from the basic spot.

(*e*) When a legal forward pass crosses the neutral zone during a forward pass play and a contact foul that is not pass interference is committed, the enforcement spot is the previous spot. This includes Rule 9-3-4-*c*.

Penalty: 5, 10 or 15 yards from the basic spot, plus first down if the foul occurred against an eligible receiver.

(*f*) A defensive player legally may use his hand or arm to ward off or block an opponent in an attempt to reach a loose ball (Rule 9-1-2-*d* *Exceptions* 3 and 4 and Rule 9-3-3-*c* *Exceptions* 3 and 5):

1. During a backward pass, fumble or kick that he is eligible to touch.
2. During any forward pass that crossed the neutral zone and has been touched by any player.

(*g*) A defensive player may not continuously contact an opponent's helmet (including the face mask) with hand(s) or arm(s). (*Exception*: the runner.)

Penalty: First down and 15 yards from the basic spot.

Player Restrictions

ARTICLE 5. (*a*) No player may position himself with his feet on the back or shoulders of a team-mate before the snap.

Penalty: Dead-ball foul 15 yards from the succeeding spot.

(*b*) No defensive player, in an attempt to block, bat or catch a kick, may:

1. Step, jump or stand on a team-mate.
2. Place a hand(s) on a team-mate to get leverage for additional height.
3. Be picked up by a team-mate.

Penalty: 15 yards from the previous spot.

When Ball is Loose

ARTICLE 6. When the ball is loose, no player shall hold an opponent or commit a personal foul.

Penalty: 5, 10 or 15 yards from the basic spot (Rules 10-2-2-*c*, 10-2-2-*d*, 10-2-2-*e* and 10-2-2-*f*).

SECTION 4. BATTING AND KICKING

Batting a Loose Ball
ARTICLE 1. (*a*) While a pass is in flight, any player eligible to touch the ball may bat it in any direction. (*Exception*: Rule 9-4-2.)

(*b*) Any player may block a scrimmage kick in the field of play or the end zone.

(*c*) No player shall bat other loose balls forward in the field of play or in any direction if the ball is in the end zone. (*Exception*: Rule 6-3-11.) *Penalty*: 15 yards from the basic spot and loss of down if not in conflict with other rules. (*Exception*: no loss of a down if the foul occurs when a legal scrimmage kick is beyond the neutral zone (Rules 10-2-2-*c*, 10-2-2-*d*, 10-2-2-*e* and 10-2-2-*f*).)

Batting a Backward Pass
ARTICLE 2. A backward pass in flight shall not be batted forward by the passing team in an attempt to gain yardage.
Penalty: 15 yards from the basic spot (Rule 10-2-2-*c*).

Batting Ball in Possession
ARTICLE 3. A ball in player possession may not be batted forward by a player of that team.
Penalty: 15 yards from the basic spot (10-2-2-*c*).

Illegally Kicking a Ball
ARTICLE 4. A player shall not kick a loose ball, a forward pass or a ball being held for a place kick by an opponent. These illegal acts do not change the status of the loose ball or forward pass; but if the player holding the ball for a place kick loses possession during a scrimmage down, it is a fumble and a loose ball; if during a free kick, the ball remains dead.
Penalty: 15 yards from the basic spot and loss of down if not in conflict with other rules (Rules 10-2-2-*c*, 10-2-2-*d*, 10-2-2-*e* and 10-2-2-*f*). (*Exception*: no loss of down if the foul occurs when a legal scrimmage kick is beyond the neutral zone.)

SECTION 5. FIGHTING

Fighting Prohibited
ARTICLE 1. (*a*) No person subject to the rules shall participate in a fight or incite a fight (Rule 2-32-1).

(*b*) No person subject to the rules shall leave their team area while a fight is going on in the field of play or end zones.

Penalty: 15 yards from the basic spot or the succeeding spot and disqualification.

RULE 10

Penalty Enforcement

SECTION 1. PENALTIES COMPLETED

How and When Completed
ARTICLE 1. (*a*) A penalty is completed when it is accepted, declined or cancelled according to rule or when the choice is obvious to the referee.

(*b*) Any penalty may be declined, but a disqualified player must leave the game.

(*c*) When a foul is committed, the penalty shall be completed before the ball is declared ready for play for any ensuing down.

(*d*) Penalties as stated are not enforced if in conflict with other rules.

Simultaneous with Snap
ARTICLE 2. A foul that occurs simultaneously with a snap or free kick is considered as occurring during that down.

Live-Ball Fouls by the Same Team
ARTICLE 3. When 2 or more live-ball fouls by the same team are reported to the referee, the referee shall explain the alternative penalties to the field captain of the offended team who may then elect only one of these penalties. (*Exception*: when a foul(s) for unsportsman-like conduct (non-contact fouls) occurs, the penalty(ies) is administered from the succeeding spot as established by the acceptance or declination of the penalty for any other foul.)

Off-setting Fouls
ARTICLE 4. If live-ball fouls by both teams are reported to the referee, each such foul is an off-setting foul and the penalties cancel each other and the down is replayed.
Exceptions:

1. When there is a change of team possession during a down or at the end of a down by rule, the team last gaining possession may decline off-setting fouls and thereby retain possession after completion of the penalty for its infraction if it had not fouled before its last gaining possession.

2. When Team B's foul is post-scrimmage kick enforcement, Team B may decline off-setting fouls and accept post-scrimmage-kick enforcement.

3. When a live-ball foul is administered as a dead-ball foul, it does not offset and is enforced in order of occurrence.

4. Rule 8-3-4-*c* (during a try after Team B possession).

Dead-Ball Fouls
ARTICLE 5. Penalties for dead-ball fouls are administered separately and in order of occurrence.

Exception: When dead-ball fouls by both teams are reported and the order of occurrence cannot be determined, the fouls cancel, the number or type of down established before the fouls occurred is unaffected, and the penalties are disregarded, except that any disqualified player must leave the game (Rules 5-2-6 and 10-2-2-*a*).

Live-Ball – Dead-Ball Fouls
ARTICLE 6. When a live-ball foul by one team is followed by one or more dead-ball fouls (including live-ball fouls penalised as dead-ball fouls) by an opponent or by the same team, the penalties are administered separately and in the order of occurrence.

Interval Fouls
ARTICLE 7. Fouls that occur between the end of the fourth period and the start of the extra period for overtime are enforced from the spot of the succeeding kick-off. (*Exception*: Rule 10-2-2-*g*.)

SECTION 2. ENFORCEMENT PROCEDURES

Spots
ARTICLE 1. The enforcement spots are: the previous spot, the spot of the foul, the succeeding spot and the spot where the run or kick ends.

Procedures
ARTICLE 2. The following procedures apply:

   (*a*) Dead-ball: the enforcement spot for a foul committed when the ball is dead is the succeeding spot. (*Exception*: Rule 8-3-5.)

   (*b*) Snap or free kick: the enforcement spot for a foul occurring simultaneously with a snap or free kick is the previous spot.

   (*c*) Running plays: the basic enforcement spots for fouls that occur during running plays in the field of play or end zone are as follows:

1. When the run ends beyond the neutral zone, the basic enforcement spot is the end of the related run (Rules 2-25-10-*a* and 2-30-4).

2. When the run ends behind the neutral zone before a change of team possession, the basic enforcement spot is the previous spot (Rules 2-25-10-*b* and 2-30-4).

3. When there is no neutral zone, the basic enforcement spot is the end of the related run. (*Exception*: Rule 8-5-1 *Exception*.) (Rules 2-25-10-*c*, 2-30-2, 2-30-3 and 2-30-4.)

(*d*) Pass plays: the basic enforcement spot for fouls during a legal forward pass play is the previous spot (Rules 2-25-10-*d* and 2-30-1).
Exceptions:

1. Team B pass interference spot fouls.

2. Roughing the passer enforcement on a completed forward pass from the end of the last run when that run ends beyond the neutral zone and there is no change of team possession.

3. Illegal touching.

(*e*) Kick plays: the basic enforcement spot for fouls that occur during a legal free or scrimmage kick play before possession is gained or regained or the ball is declared dead by rule is the previous spot (Rules 2-25-10-*e*, 2-30-2 and 2-30-3).
Exceptions:

1. Interference with the opportunity to make a catch spot foul (Rule 6-4-1).

2. Team A, during a scrimmage kick untouched by Team B beyond the neutral zone, bats a loose ball behind Team B's goal-line a violation and a touchback.

3. A block or foul after a valid, invalid or illegal signal for a fair catch by a Team B player who signalled for a fair catch during a free kick and had not touched the ball is a spot foul (Rule 6-5-4).

4. Illegal fair catch signal during a free kick is a spot foul (Rule 6-5-3).

5. Post-scrimmage kick enforcement: the basic enforcement spot is the spot where the kick ends when Team B fouls occur (Rule 2-25-11):

   (*a*) During scrimmage kick plays other than a try.

   (*b*) During a scrimmage kick play in which the ball crosses the neutral zone.

   (*c*) Three yards or more beyond the neutral zone.

   (*d*) Before the end of the kick.

   (*e*) When Team A does not have possession of the ball when the down ends.

6. Team B fouls behind the post-scrimmage kick spot are spot fouls.

(*f*) Behind the goal-line:

1. The enforcement spot is the goal-line for fouls by the opponents of the team in possession after a change of team possession (not on a try)

in the field of play when the run ends behind the goal-line. (*Exception*: Rule 8-5-1 *Exception*.)

2. The basic enforcement spot is the 20-yard line for fouls that occur after a change of team possession (not on a try) in the end zone and the ball remains in the end zone where it is declared dead.

3. The enforcement spot is the goal-line for fouls by the opponents of the team in possession after change of team possession in the end zone (not on a try) when the run ends behind the goal-line and any subsequent loose ball is recovered in the field of play.

(*g*) Fouls during or after a touchdown, field goal or try:

1. 15-yard penalties (including pass interference) for fouls by opponents of the scoring team during a down that ends in a touchdown may be penalised on the try or at the succeeding kick-off. The scoring-team captain will select the enforcement spot.

2. Defensive pass interference fouls on a touchdown play are penalised one-half the distance to the goal on the try or 15 yards on the succeeding kick-off. Defensive pass interference fouls on a try from the 3-yard line are penalised one-half the distance to the goal or, if the try is successful, 15 yards on the succeeding kick-off. The scoring team captain will select the enforcement spot.

3. When a foul(s) occurs after a touchdown and before the ball is ready for play on the try, enforcement is on the try or at the succeeding kick-off. The offended captain will select the enforcement spot.

4. 15-yard penalties for fouls by the opponent of the scoring team on a successful field goal are penalised on the succeeding kick-off. The field goal may be cancelled and the penalty enforced by rule. (*Exception*: Rule 10-2-2-*e*-5.)

5. Fouls during and after a try down are penalised under Rules 8-3-3, 8-3-4 and 8-3-5.

(*h*) Distance penalties for fouls by the receiving team may not extend the receiving team's restraining line behind its 5-yard line. Fouls that place the restraining line of the receiving team behind its 5-yard line are enforced from the next succeeding spot.

Half-Distance Enforcement Procedures

ARTICLE 3. No distance penalty shall exceed half the distance from the enforcement spot to the offending team's goal-line. (*Exception*: defensive pass interference penalties other than those from the 2-yard line or closer to the goal-line or on a try from the 3-yard line.)

Reprinted by permission of the British American Football Association, and with special thanks to the British American Football Referees'

Association. For reasons of space, Rules 11, 12 and 13 (The Officials: Jurisdiction and Duties; Football Variants; and Standards for Game Management) have been omitted. Copies of the Complete Rules and Interpretations of British American Football may be obtained from the British American Football Association.

THE LAWS OF

Cricket

Cricket

1. THE PLAYERS

1. Number of Players and Captain
A match is played between two sides each of eleven players, one of whom shall be captain. In the event of the captain not being available at any time a deputy shall act for him.

2. Nomination of Players
Before the toss for innings, the captain shall nominate his players who may not thereafter be changed without the consent of the opposing captain.

NOTE
    (*a*) *More or Less than Eleven Players a Side*.
A match may be played by agreement between sides of more or less than eleven players but not more than eleven players may field.

2. SUBSTITUTES AND RUNNERS: BATSMAN OR FIELDSMAN LEAVING THE FIELD: BATSMAN RETIRING: BATSMAN COMMENCING INNINGS

1. Substitutes
In normal circumstances, a substitute shall be allowed to field only for a player who satisfies the umpires that he has become injured or become ill during the match. However, in very exceptional circumstances, the umpires may use their discretion to allow a substitute for a player who has to leave the field or does not take the field for other wholly acceptable reasons, subject to consent being given by the opposing captain. If a player wishes to change his shirt, boots, etc., he may leave

the field to do so (no changing on the field) but no substitute will be allowed.

2. Objection to Substitutes
The opposing captain shall have no right of objection to any player acting as substitute on the field, nor as to where he shall field; however, no substitute shall field as wicket-keeper.

3. Substitute Not to Bat or Bowl
A substitute shall not be allowed to bat or bowl.

4. A Player for whom a Substitute has acted
A player may bat, bowl or field even though a substitute has acted for him.

5. Runner
A runner shall be allowed for a batsman who during the match is incapacitated by illness or injury. The player acting as runner shall be a member of the batting side and shall, if possible, have already batted in that innings.

6. Runner's Equipment
The player acting as runner for an injured batsman shall wear the same external protective equipment as the injured batsman.

7. Transgression of the Laws by an Injured Batsman or Runner
An injured batsman may be out should his runner break any one of Laws 33 (Handled the Ball), 37 (Obstructing the Field) or 38 (Run Out). As striker he remains himself subject to the Laws. Furthermore, should he be out of his ground for any purpose and the wicket at the wicket-keeper's end be put down he shall be out under Law 38 (Run Out) or Law 39 (Stumped) irrespective of the position of the other batsman or the runner and no runs shall be scored.

When not the striker, the injured batsman is out of the game and shall stand where he does not interfere with the play. Should he bring himself into the game in any way then he shall suffer the penalties that any transgression of the Laws demands.

8. Fieldsman Leaving the Field
No fieldsman shall leave the field or return during a session of play without the consent of the umpire at the bowler's end. The umpire's consent is also necessary if a substitute is required for a fieldsman, when his side returns to the field after an interval. If a member of the fielding

side leaves the field or fails to return after an interval and is absent from the field for longer than 15 minutes, he shall not be permitted to bowl after his return until he has been on the field for at least that length of playing time for which he was absent. This restriction shall not apply at the start of a new day's play.

9. Batsman Leaving the Field or Retiring

A batsman may leave the field or retire at any time owing to illness, injury or other unavoidable cause, having previously notified the umpire at the bowler's end. He may resume his innings at the fall of a wicket, which for the purposes of this Law shall include the retirement of another batsman.

If he leaves the field or retires for any other reason he may only resume his innings with the consent of the opposing captain.

When a batsman has left the field or retired and is unable to return owing to illness, injury or other unavoidable cause, his innings is to be recorded as 'retired, not out'. Otherwise it is to be recorded as 'retired, out'.

10. Commencement of a Batsman's Innings

A batsman shall be considered to have commenced his innings once he has stepped onto the field of play.

NOTE

(a) *Substitutes and Runners.*

For the purpose of these Laws allowable illnesses or injuries are those which occur at any time after the nomination by the captains of their teams.

3. THE UMPIRES

1. Appointment

Before the toss for innings two umpires shall be appointed, one for each end, to control the game with absolute impartiality as required by the Laws.

2. Change of Umpire

No umpire shall be changed during a match without the consent of both captains.

3. Special Conditions

Before the toss for innings, the umpires shall agree with both captains on any special conditions affecting the conduct of the match.

4. The Wickets

The umpires shall satisfy themselves before the start of the match that the wickets are properly pitched.

5. Clock or Watch

The umpires shall agree between themselves and inform both captains before the start of the match on the watch or clock to be followed during the match.

6. Conduct and Implements

Before and during a match the umpires shall ensure that the conduct of the game and the implements used are strictly in accordance with the Laws.

7. Fair and Unfair Play

The umpires shall be the sole judges of fair and unfair play.

8 Fitness of Ground, Weather and Light

(*a*) The umpires shall be the sole judges of the fitness of the ground, weather and light for play.

  (i) However, before deciding to suspend play or not to start play or not to resume play after an interval or stoppage, the umpires shall establish whether both captains (the batsmen at the wicket may deputise for their captain) wish to commence or to continue in the prevailing conditions; if so, their wishes shall be met.

(ii) In addition, if during play the umpires decide that the light is unfit, only the batting side shall have the option of continuing play. After agreeing to continue to play in unfit light conditions, the captain of the batting side (or a batsman at the wicket) may appeal against the light to the umpires, who shall uphold the appeal only if, in their opinion, the light has deteriorated since the agreement to continue was made.

(*b*) After any suspension of play, the umpires, unaccompanied by any of the players or officials shall, on their own initiative, carry out an inspection immediately the conditions improve and shall continue to inspect at intervals. Immediately the umpires decide that play is possible they shall call upon the players to resume the game.

9. Exceptional Circumstances

In exceptional circumstances, other than those of weather, ground or light, the umpires may decide to suspend or abandon play. Before making such a decision the umpires shall establish, if the circumstances allow, whether both captains (the batsmen at the wicket may deputise for their captain) wish to continue in the prevailing conditions; if so their wishes shall be met.

10. Position of Umpires
The umpires shall stand where they can best see any act upon which their decision may be required.

Subject to this over-riding consideration the umpire at the bowler's end shall stand where he does not interfere with either the bowler's run up or the striker's view.

The umpire at the striker's end may elect to stand on the off instead of the leg side of the pitch, provided he informs the captain of the fielding side and the striker of his intention to do so.

11. Umpires Changing Ends
The umpires shall change ends after each side has had one innings.

12. Disputes
All disputes shall be determined by the umpires and if they disagree the actual state of things shall continue.

13. Signals
The following code of signals shall be used by umpires who will wait until a signal has been answered by a scorer before allowing the game to proceed.

Boundary   – by waving the arm from side to side.

Boundary 6 – by raising both arms above the head.

Bye   – by raising an open hand above the head.

Dead Ball   – by crossing and re-crossing the wrists below the waist.

Leg Bye   – by touching a raised knee with the hand.

No Ball   – by extending one arm horizontally.

Out   – by raising the index finger above the head. If not out the umpire shall call 'not out'.

Short Run   – by bending the arm upwards and by touching the nearer shoulder with the tips of the fingers.

Wide   – by extending both arms horizontally.

14. Correctness of Scores
The umpires shall be responsible for satisfying themselves on the correctness of the scores throughout and at the conclusion of the match. See Law 21.6 (Correctness of Result).

NOTES

(a) *Attendance of Umpires*.

The umpire should be present on the ground and report to the ground executive or the equivalent at least 30 minutes before the start of a day's play.

(b) *Consultation Between Umpires and Scorers*

Consultation between umpires and scorers over doubtful points is essential.

(c) *Fitness of Ground*

The umpires shall consider the ground as unfit for play when it is so wet or slippery as to deprive the bowlers of a reasonable foothold, the fieldsmen, other than the deep-fielders, of the power of free movement, or the batsmen the ability to play their strokes or to run between the wickets. Play should not be suspended merely because the grass and the ball are wet and slippery.

(d) *Fitness of Weather and Light*

The umpires should only suspend play when they consider that the conditions are so bad that it is unreasonable or dangerous to continue.

4. THE SCORERS

1. Recording Runs

All runs scored shall be recorded by scorers appointed for the purpose. Where there are two scorers they shall frequently check to ensure that the score sheets agree.

2. Acknowledging Signals

The scorers shall accept and immediately acknowledge all instructions and signals given to them by the umpires.

5. THE BALL

1. Weight and Size

The ball, when new, shall weigh not less than $5\frac{1}{2}$oz (155.9g), nor more than $5\frac{3}{4}$oz (163g): and shall measure not less than $8\frac{13}{16}$in (22.4cm), nor more than 9in (22.9cm) in circumference.

2. Approval of Balls

All balls used in matches shall be approved by the umpires and captains before the start of the match.

3. New Ball

Subject to agreement to the contrary, having been made before the toss, either captain may demand a new ball at the start of each innings.

4. New Ball in Match of 3 or more Days' Duration

In a match of 3 or more days' duration, the captain of the fielding side may demand a new ball after the prescribed number of overs has been bowled with the old one. The governing body for cricket in the country concerned shall decide the number of overs applicable in that country which shall be not less than 75 six-ball overs (55 eight-ball overs).

5. Ball Lost or Becoming Unfit for Play

In the event of a ball during play being lost or, in the opinion of the umpires, becoming unfit for play, the umpires shall allow it to be replaced by one that in their opinion has had a similar amount of wear. If a ball is to be replaced, the umpires shall inform the batsmen.

NOTES

(a) *Specifications*

The specifications, as described in 1. above, shall apply to top-grade balls only. The following degrees of tolerance will be acceptable for other grades of ball.

(i) Men's Grades 2–4

Weight: $5\frac{5}{16}$ oz/150g to $5\frac{13}{16}$ oz/165g.

Size: $8\frac{11}{16}$in/22.0cm to $9\frac{1}{16}$in/23.0cm.

(ii) Women's

Weight: $4\frac{15}{16}$ oz/140g to $5\frac{5}{16}$ oz/150g.

Size: $8\frac{1}{4}$in/21.0cm to $8\frac{7}{8}$in/22.5cm.

(iii) Junior

Weight: $4\frac{5}{16}$ oz/133g to $5\frac{1}{16}$ oz/143g.

Size: $8\frac{1}{16}$in/20.5cm to $8\frac{11}{16}$in/22.0cm.

6. THE BAT

1. Width and Length

The bat overall shall not be more than 38in (96.5cm) in length; the blade of the bat shall be made of wood and shall not exceed $4\frac{1}{4}$in (10.8cm) at the widest part.

NOTE

(a) The blade of the bat may be covered with material for protection, strengthening or repair. Such material shall not exceed $\frac{1}{16}$in/1.56 mm in thickness.

7. THE PITCH

1. Area of Pitch

The pitch is the area between the bowling creases – see Law 9 (The

Bowling, Popping and Return Creases). It shall measure 5ft (1.52m) in width on either side of a line joining the centre of the middle stumps of the wickets – see Law 8 (The Wickets).

2. Selection and Preparation
Before the toss for innings, the executive of the ground shall be responsible for the selection and preparation of the pitch; thereafter the umpires shall control its use and maintenance.

3. Changing Pitch
The pitch shall not be changed during a match unless it becomes unfit for play, and then only with the consent of both captains.

4. Non-Turf Pitches
In the event of a non-turf pitch being used, the following shall apply:
   (*a*) *Length*: That of the playing surface to a minimum of 58ft (17.68m).
   (*b*) *Width*: That of the playing surface to a minimum of 6ft (1.83m).
See Law 10.7 (Rolling, Sweeping, Mowing, Watering the Pitch and Re-marking of Creases) Note (*a*).

8. THE WICKETS

1. Width and Pitching
Two sets of wickets, each 9in (22.86cm) wide, and consisting of three wooden stumps with two wooden bails upon the top, shall be pitched opposite and parallel to each other at a distance of 22yd (20.12m) between the centres of the two middle stumps.

2. Size of Stumps
The stumps shall be of equal and sufficient size to prevent the ball from passing between them. Their tops shall be 28in (71.1cm) above the ground, and shall be dome-shaped except for the bail grooves.

3. Size of Bails
The bails shall be each 4⅜in (11.1cm) in length and when in position on the top of the stumps shall not project more than ½in (1.3cm) above them.

NOTES
   (*a*) *Dispensing with Bails*
In a high wind the umpires may decide to dispense with the use of bails.

(b) *Junior cricket*
For junior cricket, as defined by the local governing body, the following measurements for the wicket shall apply:

Width – 8in/20.32cm
Pitched – 21yd/19.20m
Height – 27in/68.58cm
Bails – each 3⅞in/9.84cm in length and should not project more than ½in/1.3cm above them.

9. THE BOWLING, POPPING AND RETURN CREASES

1. The Bowling Crease
The bowling crease shall be marked in line with the stumps at each end and shall be 8ft 8in (2.64m) in length, with the stumps in the centre.

2. The Popping Crease
The popping crease, which is the back edge of the crease marking, shall be in front of and parallel with the bowling crease. It shall have the back edge of the crease marking 4ft (1.22m) from the centre of the stumps and shall extend to a minimum of 6ft (1.83m) on either side of the line of the wicket.

The popping crease shall be considered to be unlimited in length.

3. The Return Crease
The return crease marking, of which the inside edge is the crease, shall be at each end of the bowling crease and at right angles to it. The return crease shall be marked to a minimum of 4ft (1.22m) behind the wicket and shall be considered to be unlimited in length. A forward extension shall be marked to the popping crease.

10. ROLLING, SWEEPING, MOWING, WATERING THE PITCH AND RE-MARKING OF CREASES

1. Rolling
During the match the pitch may be rolled at the request of the captain of the batting side, for a period of not more than 7 minutes before the start of each innings, other than the first innings of the match, and before the start of each day's play. In addition, if, after the toss and before the first innings of the match, the start is delayed, the captain of the batting side shall have the right to have the pitch rolled for not more than 7 minutes.

The pitch shall not otherwise be rolled during the match. However, if in the opinion of the umpires, the delay has had no significant effect upon the state of the pitch, they shall refuse any request for the rolling of the pitch.

The 7 minutes' rolling permitted before the start of a day's play shall take place not earlier than half an hour before the start of play and the captain of the batting side may delay such rolling until 10 minutes before the start of play should he so desire.

If a captain declares an innings closed less than 15 minutes before the resumption of play, and the other captain is thereby prevented from exercising his option of 7 minutes rolling or if he is so prevented for any other reason the time for rolling shall be taken out of the normal playing time.

2. Sweeping
Such sweeping of the pitch as is necessary during the match shall be done so that the 7 minutes allowed for rolling the pitch provided for in 1 above is not affected.

3. Mowing
(*a*) *Responsibilities of Ground Authority and of Umpires*. All mowings which are carried out before the toss for innings shall be the responsibility of the Ground Authority. Thereafter they shall be carried out under the supervision of the umpires – see Law 7.2 (Selection and Preparation).

(*b*) *Initial Mowing*. The pitch shall be mown before play begins on the day the match is scheduled to start or in the case of a delayed start on the day the match is expected to start. See 3 (*a*) above (Responsibilities of Ground Authority and of Umpires).

(*c*) *Subsequent Mowings in a Match of 2 or More Days' Duration*. In a match of two or more days' duration, the pitch shall be mown daily before play begins. Should this mowing not take place because of weather conditions, rest days or other reasons the pitch shall be mown on the first day on which the match is resumed.

(*d*) *Mowing of the Outfield in a Match of 2 or More Days' Duration*. In order to ensure that conditions are as similar as possible for both sides, the outfield shall normally be mown before the commencement of play on each day of the match, if ground and weather conditions allow. See Note (*b*) to this law.

4. Watering
The pitch shall not be watered during a match.

5. Re-Marking Creases
Whenever possible the creases shall be re-marked.

6. Maintenance of Foot Holes

In wet weather, the umpires shall ensure that the holes made by the bowlers and batsmen are cleaned out and dried whenever necessary to facilitate play. In matches of 2 or more days' duration, the umpires shall allow, if necessary, the re-turfing of foot holes made by the bowler in his delivery stride, or the use of quick-setting fillings for the same purpose, before the start of each day's play.

7. Securing of Foot Holes and Maintenance of Pitch

During play, the umpires shall allow either batsman to beat the pitch with his bat and players to secure their footholds by the use of sawdust, provided that no damage to the pitch is so caused, and Law 42 (Unfair Play) is not contravened.

NOTES

(a) *Non-turf Pitches*

The above Law 10 applies to turf pitches.

The game is played on non-turf pitches in many countries at various levels. Whilst the conduct of the game on these surfaces should always be in accordance with the Laws of Cricket, it is recognised that it may sometimes be necessary for governing bodies to lay down special playing conditions to suit the type of non-turf pitch used in their country.

In matches played against touring teams, any special playing conditions should be agreed in advance by both parties.

(b) *Mowing of the Outfield in a Match of two or more days' duration*

If, for reasons other than ground and weather conditions, daily and complete mowing is not possible, the ground authority shall notify the captains and umpires, before the toss for innings, of the procedure to be adopted for such mowing during the match.

(c) *Choice of Roller*

If there is more than one roller available the captain of the batting side shall have a choice.

11. COVERING THE PITCH

1. Before the Start of a Match

Before the start of a match complete covering of the pitch shall be allowed.

2. During a Match

The pitch shall not be completely covered during a match unless prior arrangement or regulations so provide.

3. Covering Bowlers' Run-Up

Whenever possible, the Bowlers' run-up shall be covered, but the covers so used shall not extend further than 4ft/1.22m in front of the popping crease.

NOTE

(a) *Removal of Covers*

The covers should be removed as promptly as possible whenever the weather permits.

12. INNINGS

1. Number of Innings

A match shall be of one or two innings of each side according to agreement reached before the start of play.

2. Alternate Innings

In a two-innings match each side shall take their innings alternately except in the case provided for in Law 13 (The Follow-on).

3. The Toss

The captains shall toss for the choice of innings on the field of play not later than 15 minutes before the time scheduled for the match to start, or before the time agreed upon for play to start.

4. Choice of Innings

The winner of the toss shall notify his decision to bat or to field to the opposing captain not later than 10 minutes before the time scheduled for the match to start, or before the time agreed upon for play to start. The decision shall not thereafter be altered.

5. Continuation After One Innings of Each Side

Despite the terms of 1 above, in a one-innings match, when a result has been reached on the first innings the captains may agree to the continuation of play if, in their opinion, there is a prospect of carrying the game to a further issue in the time left. See Law 21 (Result).

NOTES

(a) *Limited Innings – One-Innings Match*

In a one-innings match, each innings may, by agreement, be limited by a number of overs or by a period of time.

(b) *Limited Innings – Two-Innings Match*

In a two-innings match, the first innings of each side may, by agreement, be limited to a number of overs or by a period of time.

13. THE FOLLOW-ON

1. Lead on First Innings
In a two-innings match the side which bats first and leads by 200 runs in a match of five days or more, by 150 runs in a three-day or four-day match, by 100 runs in a two-day match, or by 75 runs in a one-day match, shall have the option of requiring the other side to follow their innings.

2. Day's Play Lost
If no play takes place on the first day of a match of 2 or more days' duration, 1 above shall apply in accordance with the number of days' play remaining from the actual start of the match.

14. DECLARATIONS

1. Time of Declaration
The captain of the batting side may declare an innings closed at any time during a match irrespective of its duration.

2. Forfeiture of Second Innings
A captain may forfeit his second innings, provided his decision to do so is notified to the opposing captain and umpires in sufficient time to allow 7 minutes rolling of the pitch. See Law 10 (Rolling, Sweeping, Mowing, Watering the Pitch and Re-marking of Creases). The normal 10-minute interval between innings shall be applied.

15. START OF PLAY

1. Call of Play
At the start of each innings and of each day's play and on the resumption of play after any interval or interruption the umpire at the bowlers' end shall call 'play'.

2. Practice on the Field
At no time on any day of the match shall there be any bowling or batting practice on the pitch.

No practice may take place on the field if, in the opinion of the umpires, it could result in a waste of time.

3. Trial Run-Up
No bowler shall have a trial run-up after 'play' has been called in any

session of play, except at the fall of a wicket when an umpire may allow such a trial run-up if he is satisfied that it will not cause any waste of time.

16. INTERVALS

1. Length
The umpire shall allow such intervals as have been agreed upon for meals, and 10 minutes between each innings.

2. Luncheon Interval – Innings Ending or Stoppage within 10 Minutes of Interval
If an innings ends or there is a stoppage caused by weather or bad light within 10 minutes of the agreed time for the luncheon interval, the interval shall be taken immediately.

The time remaining in the session of play shall be added to the agreed length of the interval but no extra allowance shall be made for the 10 minutes interval between innings.

3. Tea Interval – Innings Ending or Stoppage within 30 Minutes of Interval
If an innings ends or there is a stoppage caused by weather or bad light within 30 minutes of the agreed time for the tea interval, the interval shall be taken immediately.

The interval shall be of the agreed length and, if applicable, shall include the 10-minute interval between innings.

4. Tea Interval – Continuation of Play
If at the agreed time for the tea interval, nine wickets are down, play shall continue for a period not exceeding 30 minutes or until the innings is concluded.

5. Tea Interval – Agreement to Forgo
At any time during the match, the captains may agree to forgo a tea interval.

6. Intervals for Drinks
If both captains agree before the start of a match that intervals for drinks may be taken, the option to take such intervals shall be available to either side. These intervals shall be restricted to one per session, shall be kept as short as possible, shall not be taken in the last hour of the match and in any case shall not exceed 5 minutes.

The agreed times for these intervals shall be strictly adhered to except that if a wicket falls within 5 minutes of the agreed time then drinks shall be taken out immediately.

If an innings ends or there is a stoppage caused by weather or bad light within 30 minutes of the agreed time for a drinks interval, there will be no interval for drinks in that session.

At any time during the match the captains may agree to forgo any such drinks interval.

17. CESSATION OF PLAY
NOTES
(a) *Tea Interval – One-day Match*
In a one-day match, a specific time for the tea interval need not necessarily be arranged, and it may be agreed to take this interval between the innings of a one-innings match.
(b) *Changing the Agreed Time of Intervals*
In the event of the ground, weather or light conditions causing a suspension of play, the umpires, after consultation with the captains, may decide, in the interests of time-saving, to bring forward the time of the luncheon or tea interval.

1. Call of Time
The umpire at the bowler's end shall call 'time' on the cessation of play before any interval or interruption of play, at the end of each day's play, and at the conclusion of the match. See Law 27 (Appeals).

2. Removal of Bails
After the call of 'time', the umpires shall remove the bails from both wickets.

3. Starting a Last Over
The last over before an interval or the close of play shall be started provided the umpire, after walking at his normal pace, has arrived at his position behind the stumps at the bowler's end before time has been reached.

4. Completion of the Last Over of a Session
The last over before an interval or the close of play shall be completed unless a batsman is out or retires during that over within 2 minutes of the interval or the close of play or unless the players have occasion to leave the field.

5. Completion of the Last Over of a Match
An over in progress at the close of play on the final day of a match shall

be completed at the request of either captain even if a wicket falls after time has been reached.

If during the last over the players have occasion to leave the field the umpires shall call 'time' and there shall be no resumption of play and the match shall be at an end.

6. Last Hour of Match – Number of Overs

The umpires shall indicate when one hour of playing time of the match remains according to the agreed hours of play. The next over after that moment shall be the first of a minimum of 20 six-ball overs (15 eight-ball overs), provided a result is not reached earlier or there is no interval or interruption of play.

7. Last Hour of Match – Intervals Between Innings and Interruptions of Play

If, at the commencement of the last hour of the match, an interval or interruption of play is in progress or if, during the last hour there is an interval between innings or an interruption of play, the minimum number of overs to be bowled on the resumption of play shall be reduced in proportion to the duration, within the last hour of the match, of any such interval or interruption.

The minimum number of overs to be bowled after a resumption of play shall be calculated as follows:

(a) In the case of an interval or interruption of play being in progress at the commencement of the last hour of the match, or in the case of a first interval or interruption a deduction shall be made from the minimum of 20 six-ball overs (or 15 eight-ball overs).

(b) If there is a later interval or interruption a further deduction shall be made from the minimum number of overs which should have been bowled following the last resumption of play.

(c) These deductions shall be based on the following factors:

(i) The number of overs already bowled in the last hour of the match or, in the case of a later interval or interruption in the last session of play.

(ii) The number of overs lost as a result of the interval or interruption allowing one six-ball over for every full three minutes (or one eight-ball over for every full four minutes) of interval or interruption.

(iii) Any over left uncompleted at the end of an innings to be excluded from these calculations.

(iv) Any over of the minimum number to be played which is left uncompleted at the start of an interruption of play to be completed when play is resumed and to count as one over bowled.

(v) An interval to start with the end of an innings and to end 10 minutes later; an interruption to start on the call of 'time' and to end on the call of 'play'.

(*d*) In the event of an innings being completed and a new innings commencing during the last hour of the match, the number of overs to be bowled in the new innings shall be calculated on the basis of one six-ball over for every three minutes or part thereof remaining for play (or one eight-ball over for every four minutes or part thereof remaining for play); or alternatively on the basis that sufficient overs be bowled to enable the full minimum quota of overs to be completed under circumstances governed by (*a*), (*b*), and (*c*) above. In all such cases the alternative which allows the greater number of overs shall be employed.

8. Bowler Unable to Complete an Over During Last Hour of the Match

If, for any reason, a bowler is unable to complete an over during the period of play referred to in 6 above, Law 22.7 (Bowler Incapacitated or Suspended during an Over) shall apply.

18. SCORING

1. A Run

The score shall be reckoned by runs. A run is scored:

(*a*) So often as the batsmen, after a hit or at any time while the ball is in play, shall have crossed and made good their ground from end to end.

(*b*) When a boundary is scored. See Law 19 (Boundaries).

(*c*) When penalty runs are awarded. See 18.6 below.

2. Short Runs

(*a*) If either batsman runs a short run, the umpire shall call and signal 'one short' as soon as the ball becomes dead and that run shall not be scored. A run is short if a batsman fails to make good his ground on turning for a further run.

(*b*) Although a short run shortens the succeeding one, the latter, if completed shall count.

(*c*) If either or both batsmen deliberately run short the umpire shall, as soon as he sees that the fielding side have no chance of dismissing either batsman, call and signal 'dead ball' and disallow any runs attempted or previously scored. The batsmen shall return to their original ends.

(*d*) If both batsmen run short in one and the same run, only one run shall be deducted.

(*e*) Only if three or more runs are attempted can more than one be short and then, subject to (*c*) and (*d*) above, all runs so called shall be disallowed. If there has been more than one short run the umpires shall instruct the scorers as to the number of runs disallowed.

3. Striker Caught
If the striker is caught, no run shall be scored.

4. Batsman Run Out
If a batsman is run out, only that run which was being attempted shall not be scored. If, however, an injured striker himself is run out no runs shall be scored. See Law 2.7 (Transgression of the Laws by an Injured Batsman or Runner).

5. Batsman Obstructing the Field
If a batsman is out obstructing the field, any runs completed before the obstruction occurs shall be scored unless such obstruction prevents a catch being made in which case no runs shall be scored.

6. Runs Scored for Penalties
Runs shall be scored for penalties under Laws 20 (Lost Ball), 24 (No-ball), 25 (Wide-ball), 41.1 (Fielding the Ball) and for boundary allowances under Law 19 (Boundaries).

7. Batsman Returning to Wicket he has Left
If, while the ball is in play, the batsmen have crossed in running, neither shall return to the wicket he has left even though a short run has been called or no run has been scored as in the case of a catch. Batsmen, however, shall return to the wickets they originally left in the cases of a boundary and of any disallowance of runs and of an injured batsman being, himself, run out. See Law 2.7 (Transgression of the Laws by an Injured Batsman or Runner).

NOTE
   (a) *Short run*
A striker taking stance in front of his popping crease may run from that point without penalty.

19. BOUNDARIES

1. The Boundary of the Playing Area
Before the toss for innings, the umpires shall agree with both captains on the boundary of the playing area. The boundary shall, if possible, be marked by a white line, a rope laid on the ground, or a fence. If flags or posts only are used to mark a boundary, the imaginary line joining such

points shall be regarded as the boundary. An obstacle, or person, within the playing area shall not be regarded as a boundary unless so decided by the umpires before the toss for innings. Sightscreens within, or partially within, the playing area shall be regarded as the boundary and when the ball strikes or passes within or under or directly over any part of the screen, a boundary shall be scored.

2. Runs Scored for Boundaries

Before the toss for innings, the umpires shall agree with both captains the runs to be allowed for boundaries, and in deciding the allowance for them, the umpires and captains shall be guided by the prevailing custom of the ground. The allowance for a boundary shall normally be 4 runs, and 6 runs for all hits pitching over and clear of the boundary line or fence, even though the ball has been previously touched by a fieldsman. 6 runs shall also be scored if a fieldsman, after catching a ball, carries it over the boundary: see Law 32 (Caught) Note (*a*). 6 runs shall not be scored when a ball struck by the striker hits a sightscreen full pitch if the screen is within, or partially within, the playing area, but if the ball is struck directly over a sightscreen so situated, 6 runs shall be scored.

3. A Boundary

A boundary shall be scored and signalled by the umpire at the bowler's end whenever, in his opinion:

(*a*) A ball in play touches or crosses the boundary, however marked.

(*b*) A fieldsman with ball in hand touches or grounds any part of his person on or over a boundary line.

(*c*) A fieldsman with ball in hand grounds any part of his person over a boundary fence or board. This allows the fieldsman to touch or lean on or over a boundary fence or board in preventing a boundary.

4. Runs Exceeding Boundary Allowance

The runs completed at the instant the ball reaches the boundary shall count if they exceed the boundary allowance.

5. Overthrows or Wilful Act of a Fieldsman

If the boundary results from an overthrow or from the wilful act of a fieldsman, any runs already completed and the allowance shall be added to the score. The run in progress shall count provided that the batsmen have crossed at the instant of the throw or act.

NOTE

(*a*) *Position of Sightscreens*

Sightscreens should, if possible, be positioned wholly outside the playing area, as near as possible to the boundary line.

20. LOST BALL

1. Runs Scored
If a ball in play cannot be found or recovered any fieldsman may call 'lost ball' when 6 runs shall be added to the score; but if more than 6 have been run before 'lost ball' is called, as many runs as have been completed shall be scored. The run in progress shall count provided that the batsmen have crossed at the instant of the call of 'lost ball'.

2. How Scored
The runs shall be added to the score of the striker if the ball has been struck, but otherwise to the score of byes, leg-byes, no-balls or wides as the case may be.

21. THE RESULT

1. A Win – Two-Innings Matches
The side which has scored a total of runs in excess of that scored by the opposing side in its two completed innings shall be the winners.

2. A Win – One-Innings Matches
(*a*) One-innings matches, unless played out as in 1 above, shall be decided on the first innings, but see Law 12.5 (Continuation After One Innings of Each Side).

(*b*) If the captains agree to continue play after the completion of one innings of each side in accordance with Law 12.5 (Continuation After One Innings of Each Side) and a result is not achieved on the second innings, the first innings result shall stand.

3. Umpires Awarding a Match
(*a*) A match shall be lost by a side which, during the match, (i) refuses to play, or (ii) concedes defeat, and the umpires shall award the match to the other side.

(*b*) Should both batsmen at the wickets or the fielding side leave the field at any time without the agreement of the umpires, this shall constitute a refusal to play and, on appeal, the umpires shall award the match to the other side in accordance with (*a*) above.

4. A Tie
The result of a match shall be a tie when the scores are equal at the conclusion of play, but only if the side batting last has completed its innings.

If the scores of the completed first innings of a one-day match are equal, it shall be a tie but only if the match has not been played out to a further conclusion.

5. A Draw
A match not determined in any of the ways as in 1, 2, 3 and 4 above shall count as a draw.

6. Correctness of Result
Any decision as to the correctness of the scores shall be the responsibility of the umpires. See Law 3.14 (Correctness of Scores).

If, after the umpires and players have left the field, in the belief that the match has been concluded, the umpires decide that a mistake in scoring has occurred, which affects the result, and provided time has not been reached, they shall order play to resume and to continue until the agreed finishing time unless a result is reached earlier.

If the umpires decide that a mistake has occurred and time has been reached, the umpires shall immediately inform both captains of the necessary corrections to the scores and, if applicable, to the result.

7. Acceptance of Result
In accepting the scores as notified by the scorers and agreed by the umpires, the captains of both sides thereby accept the result.

NOTES

(a) *Statement of Results*
The result of a finished match is stated as a win by runs, except in the case of a win by the side batting last when it is by the number of wickets still then to fall.

(b) *Winning Hit or Extras*
As soon as the side has won, see 1 and 2 above, the umpire shall call 'time', the match is finished, and nothing that happens thereafter other than as a result of a mistake in scoring, see 6. above, shall be regarded as part of the match.

However, if a boundary constitutes the winning hit – or extras – and the boundary allowance exceeds the number of runs required to win the match, such runs scored shall be credited to the side's total and, in the case of a hit, to the striker's score.

22. THE OVER

1. Number of Balls
The ball shall be bowled from each wicket alternately in overs of either six or eight balls according to agreement before the match.

2. Call of 'Over'
When the agreed number of balls has been bowled, and as the ball becomes dead or when it becomes clear to the umpire at the bowler's end that both the fielding side and the batsmen at the wicket have ceased to regard the ball as in play, the umpire shall call 'over' before leaving the wicket.

3. No-ball or Wide-ball
Neither a no-ball nor a wide-ball shall be reckoned as one of the over.

4. Umpire Miscounting
If an umpire miscounts the number of balls, the over as counted by the umpire shall stand.

5. Bowler Changing Ends
A bowler shall be allowed to change ends as often as desired provided only that he does not bowl two overs consecutively in an innings.

6. The Bowler Finishing an Over
A bowler shall finish an over in progress unless he be incapacitated or be suspended under Law 42.8 (The Bowling of Fast Short-pitched Balls), 42.9 (The Bowling of Fast High Full Pitches), 42.10 (Time Wasting) and 42.11 (Players Damaging the Pitch). If an over is left incomplete for any reason at the start of an interval or interruption of play, it shall be finished on the resumption of play.

7. Bowler Incapacitated or Suspended During an Over
If, for any reason, a bowler is incapacitated while running up to bowl the first ball of an over, or is incapacitated or suspended during an over, the umpire shall call and signal 'dead ball' and another bowler shall be allowed to bowl or complete the over from the same end, provided only that he shall not bowl two overs, or part thereof, consecutively in one innings.

8. Position of Non-Striker
The batsman at the bowler's end shall normally stand on the opposite side of the wicket to that from which the ball is being delivered, unless a request to do otherwise is granted by the umpire.

23. DEAD BALL

1. The Ball Becomes Dead, when:
(*a*) It is finally settled in the hands of the wicket-keeper or the bowler.

(*b*) It reaches or pitches over the boundary.

(*c*) A batsman is out.

(*d*) Whether played or not, it lodges in the clothing or equipment of a batsman or the clothing of an umpire.

(*e*) A ball lodges in a protective helmet worn by a member of the fielding side.

(*f*) A penalty is awarded under Law 20 (Lost Ball) or Law 41.1 (Fielding the Ball).

(*g*) The umpire calls 'over' or 'time'.

2. Either Umpire Shall Call and Signal 'Dead Ball', when:

(*a*) He intervenes in a case of unfair play.

(*b*) A serious injury to a player or umpire occurs.

(*c*) He is satisfied that, for an adequate reason, the striker is not ready to receive the ball and makes no attempt to play it.

(*d*) The bowler drops the ball accidentally before delivery, or the ball does not leave his hand for any reason other than in an attempt to run out the non-striker: see Law 24.5 (Bowler Attempting to Run Out Non-striker Before Delivery).

(*e*) One or both bails fall from the striker's wicket before he receives delivery.

(*f*) He leaves his normal position for consultation.

(*g*) He is required to do so under Laws 26.3 (Disallowance of Leg-byes), etc.

3. The Ball Ceases to be Dead, when:

The bowler starts his run-up or bowling action.

4. The Ball is Not Dead, when:

(*a*) It strikes an umpire (unless it lodges in his dress).

(*b*) The wicket is broken or struck down (unless a batsman is out thereby).

(*c*) An unsuccessful appeal is made.

(*d*) The wicket is broken accidentally either by the bowler during his delivery or by a batsman in running.

(*e*) The umpire has called 'no ball' or 'wide'.

NOTES

(*a*) *Ball Finally Settled*

Whether the ball is finally settled or not – see 23.1(*a*) above – must be a question for the umpires alone to decide.

(*b*) *Action on Call of Dead Ball*

(i) If 'dead ball' is called prior to the striker receiving a delivery the bowler shall not be allowed an additional ball, unless a 'no-ball' or 'wide' has been called.

24. NO-BALL

1. Mode of Delivery
The umpire shall indicate to the striker whether the bowler intends to bowl over or round the wicket, overarm or underarm, or right- or left-handed. Failure on the part of the bowler to indicate in advance a change in his mode of delivery is unfair and the umpire shall call and signal 'no-ball'.

2. Fair Delivery – The Arm
For a delivery to be fair the ball must be bowled not thrown. See Note (*a*) below. If either umpire is not entirely satisfied with the absolute fairness of a delivery in this respect he shall call and signal 'no-ball' instantly upon delivery.

3. Fair Delivery – The Feet
The umpire at the bowler's wicket shall call and signal 'no-ball' if he is not satisfied that in the delivery stride:
   (*a*) The bowler's back foot has landed within and not touching the return crease or its forward extension; or
   (*b*) Some part of the front foot whether grounded or raised was behind the popping crease.

4. Bowler Throwing at Striker's Wicket Before Delivery
If the bowler, before delivering the ball, throws it at the striker's wicket in an attempt to run him out, the umpire shall call and signal 'no-ball'. See Law 42.12 (Batsman Unfairly Stealing a Run) and Law 38 (Run Out).

5. Bowler Attempting to Run Out Non-Striker Before Delivery
If the bowler, before delivering the ball, attempts to run out the non-striker, any runs which result shall be allowed and shall be scored as no-balls. Such an attempt shall not count as a ball in the over. The umpire shall not call 'no-ball'. See Law 42.12 (Batsman Unfairly Stealing a Run).

6. Infringement of Laws by a Wicket-Keeper or Fieldsman
The umpire shall call and signal 'no-ball' in the event of the wicket-keeper infringing Law 40.1 (Position of Wicket-Keeper) or a fieldsman

infringing Law 41.2 (Limitation of On-Side Fieldsman) or Law 41.3 (Position of Fieldsman).

7. Revoking a Call

An umpire shall revoke the call 'no-ball' if the ball does not leave the bowler's hand for any reason. See Law 23.2 (Either Umpire Shall Call and Signal 'Dead Ball').

8. Penalty

A penalty of one run for a no-ball shall be scored if no runs are made otherwise.

9. Runs From a No-ball

The striker may hit a no-ball and whatever runs result shall be added to his score. Runs made otherwise from a no-ball shall be scored as no balls.

10. Out From a No-ball

The striker shall be out from a no-ball if he breaks Law 34 (Hit the Ball Twice) and either batsman may be run out or shall be given out if either breaks Law 33 (Handled the Ball) or Law 37 (Obstructing the Field).

11. Batsman Given Out Off a No-ball

Should a batsman be given out off a no-ball the penalty for bowling it shall stand unless runs are otherwise scored.

NOTES

(a) *Definition of a Throw*

A ball shall be deemed to have been thrown if, in the opinion of either umpire, the process of straightening the bowling arm, whether it be partial or complete, takes place during that part of the delivery swing.

(b) *No Ball not Counting in Over*

A no-ball shall not be reckoned as one of the over. See Law 22.3 (No-Ball or Wide Ball).

25. WIDE-BALL

1. Judging a Wide

If the bowler bowls the ball so high over or so wide of the wicket that, in the opinion of the umpire, it passes out of reach of the striker, standing in a normal guard position, the umpire shall call and signal 'wide-ball' as soon as it has passed the line of the Striker's wicket.

The umpire shall not adjudge a ball as being a wide if:

(*a*) The striker, by moving from his guard position, causes the ball to pass out of his reach.

(*b*) The striker moves and thus brings the ball within his reach.

2. Penalty
A penalty of one run for a wide shall be scored if no runs are made otherwise.

3. Ball Coming to Rest in Front of the Striker
If a ball which the umpire considers to have been delivered comes to rest in front of the line of the striker's wicket, 'wide' shall not be called. The striker has a right, without interference from the fielding side, to make one attempt to hit the ball. If the fielding side interfere, the umpire shall replace the ball where it came to rest and shall order the fieldsmen to resume the places they occupied in the field before the ball was delivered.

The umpire shall call and signal 'dead ball' as soon as it is clear that the striker does not intend to hit the ball, or after the striker has made one unsuccessful attempt to hit the ball.

4. Revoking a Call
The umpire shall revoke the call if the striker hits a ball which has been called 'wide'.

5. Ball Not Dead
The ball does not become dead on the call of 'wide-ball' – see Law 23.4 (The Ball is Not Dead).

6. Runs Resulting from a Wide
All runs which are run or result from a wide ball which is not a no ball shall be scored wide balls, or if no runs are made one shall be scored.

7. Out from a Wide
The striker shall be out from a wide ball if he breaks Law 35 (Hit Wicket) or Law 39 (Stumped). Either batsman may be run out and shall be out if he breaks Law 33 (Handled the Ball) or Law 37 (Obstructing the Field).

8. Batsman Given Out Off a Wide
Should a batsman be given out off a wide, the penalty for bowling it shall stand unless runs are otherwise made.

NOTE
 (*a*) *Wide Ball not Counting in Over*
A wide ball shall not be reckoned as one of the over – see Law 22.3 (No Ball or Wide Ball).

26. BYE AND LEG-BYE

1. Byes
If the ball, not having been called 'wide' or 'no ball', passes the striker without touching his bat or person, and any runs are obtained, the umpire shall signal 'bye' and the run or runs shall be credited as such to the batting side.

2. Leg-byes
If the ball, not having been called 'wide' or 'no ball', is unintentionally deflected by the striker's dress or person, except a hand holding the bat, and any runs are obtained the umpire shall signal 'leg-bye' and the run or runs so scored shall be credited as such to the batting side.

Such leg-byes shall only be scored if, in the opinion of the umpire, the striker has:
 (*a*) Attempted to play the ball with his bat; or
 (*b*) Tried to avoid being hit by the ball.

3. Disallowance of Leg-byes
In the case of a deflection by the striker's person, other than in 2(*a*) and (*b*) above, the umpire shall call and signal 'dead ball' as soon as one run has been completed or when it is clear that a run is not being attempted or the ball has reached the boundary.

On the call and signal of 'dead ball' the batsmen shall return to their original ends and no runs shall be allowed.

27. APPEALS

1. Time of Appeals
The umpires shall not give a batsman out unless appealed to by the other side which shall be done prior to the bowler beginning his run-up or bowling action to deliver the next ball. Under Law 23.1 (*g*) (The Ball Becomes Dead) the ball is dead on 'over' being called; this does not, however, invalidate an appeal made prior to the first ball of the following over provided 'time' has not been called. See Law 17.1 (Call of Time).

2. An Appeal 'How's That?'

An appeal 'How's That?' shall cover all ways of being out.

3. Answering Appeals

The umpire at the bowler's wicket shall answer appeals before the other umpire in all cases except those arising out of Law 35 (Hit Wicket) or Law 39 (Stumped) or Law 38 (Run Out) when this occurs at the striker's wicket.

When either umpire has given a batsman not out, the other umpire shall, within his jurisdiction, answer the appeal or a further appeal, provided it is made in time in accordance with 27.1 (Time of Appeals) above.

4. Consultation by Umpires

An umpire may consult with the other umpire on a point of fact which the latter may have been in a better position to see and shall then give his decision. If, after consultation, there is still doubt remaining the decision shall be in favour of the batsman.

5. Batsman Leaving his Wicket under a Misapprehension

The umpires shall intervene if satisfied that a batsman, not having been given out, has left his wicket under a misapprehension that he has been dismissed.

6. Umpire's Decision

The umpire's decision is final. He may alter his decision, provided that such alteration is made promptly.

7. Withdrawal of an Appeal

In exceptional circumstances the captain of the fielding side may seek permission of the umpire to withdraw an appeal providing the outgoing batsman has not left the playing area. If this is allowed, the umpire shall cancel his decision.

28. THE WICKET IS DOWN

1. Wicket Down

The wicket is down if:

(a) Either the ball or the striker's bat or person completely removes either bail from the top of the stumps. A disturbance of a bail, whether temporary or not, shall not constitute a complete removal, but the wicket is down if a bail in falling lodges between two of the stumps.

(b) Any player completely removes with his hand or arm a bail from the top of the stumps, providing that the ball is held in that hand or in the hand of the arm so used.

(c) When both bails are off, a stump is struck out of the ground by the ball, or a player strikes or pulls a stump out of the ground, providing that the ball is held in the hand(s) or in the hand of the arm so used.

2. One Bail Off
If one bail is off, it shall be sufficient for the purpose of putting the wicket down to remove the remaining bail, or to strike or pull any of the three stumps out of the ground in any of the ways stated in 1 above.

3. All the Stumps Out of the Ground
If all the stumps are out of the ground, the fielding side shall be allowed to put back one or more stumps in order to have an opportunity of putting the wicket down.

4. Dispensing with Bails
If, owing to the strength of the wind, it has been agreed to dispense with the bails, in accordance with Law 8 Note (a) (Dispensing with Bails), the decision as to when the wicket is down is one for the umpires to decide on the facts before them. In such circumstances and if the umpires so decide the wicket shall be held to be down even though a stump has not been struck out of the ground.

NOTE
(a) Remaking the Wicket
If the wicket is broken while the ball is in play, it is not the umpire's duty to remake the wicket until the ball has become dead – see Law 23 (Dead Ball). A member of the fielding side, however, may remake the wicket in such circumstances.

29. BATSMAN OUT OF HIS GROUND

1. When out of his Ground
A batsman shall be considered to be out of his ground unless some part of his bat in his hand or of his person is grounded behind the line of the popping crease.

30. BOWLED

1. Out Bowled
The striker shall be out bowled if:

(*a*) His wicket is bowled down, even if the ball first touches his bat or person.

(*b*) He breaks his wicket by hitting or kicking the ball on to it before the completion of a stroke, or as a result of attempting to guard his wicket. See Law 34.1 (Out–Hit the Ball Twice).

NOTE

(*a*) *Out Bowled – Not L.B.W.*

The striker is out bowled if the ball is deflected on to his wicket the ball has become dead – see Law 23 (Dead Ball). A member of the fielding side, however, may remake the wicket in such circumstances.

31. TIMED OUT

1. Out Timed Out

An incoming batsman shall be out timed out if he wilfully takes more than two minutes to come in – the two minutes being timed from the moment a wicket falls until the new batsman steps on to the field of play.

If this is not complied with and if the umpire is satisfied that the delay was wilful and if an appeal is made, the new batsman shall be given out by the umpire at the bowler's end.

2. Time to be Added

The time taken by the umpires to investigate the cause of the delay shall be added at the normal close of play.

NOTES

(*a*) *Entry in Score Book*

The correct entry in the score book when a batsman is given out under this Law is 'timed out', and the bowler does not get credit for the wicket.

(*b*) *Batsman Crossing on the Field of Play*

It is an essential duty of the captains to ensure that the in-going batsman passes the out-going one before the latter leaves the field of play.

32. CAUGHT

1. Out Caught

The striker shall be out caught if the ball touches his bat or if it touches below the wrist his hand or glove, holding the bat, and is subsequently held by a fieldsman before it touches the ground.

2. A Fair Catch

A catch shall be considered to have been fairly made if:

(*a*) The fieldsman is within the field of play throughout the act of making the catch.

(i) The act of making the catch shall start from the time when the fieldsman first handles the ball and shall end when he both retains complete control over the further disposal of the ball and remains within the field of play.

(ii) In order to be within the field of play, the fieldsman may not touch or ground any part of his person on or over a boundary line. When the boundary is marked by a fence or board the fieldsman may not ground any part of his person over the boundary fence or board, but may touch or lean over the boundary fence or board in completing the catch.

(*b*) The ball is hugged to the body of the catcher or accidentally lodges in his dress or, in the case of the wicket-keeper, in his pads. However, a striker may not be caught if a ball lodges in a protective helmet worn by a fieldsman, in which case the umpire shall call and signal 'dead ball'. See Law 23 (Dead Ball).

(*c*) The ball does not touch the ground even though a hand holding it does so in effecting the catch.

(*d*) A fieldsman catches the ball, after it has been lawfully played a second time by the striker, but only if the ball has not touched the ground since being first struck.

(*e*) A fieldsman catches the ball after it has touched an umpire, another fieldsman or the other batsman. However, a striker may not be caught if a ball has touched a protective helmet worn by a fieldsman.

(*f*) The ball is caught off an obstruction within the boundary provided it has not previously been agreed to regard the obstruction as a boundary.

3. Scoring of Runs
If a striker is caught, no runs shall be scored.

NOTES
(*a*) *Scoring from an Attempted Catch*
When a fieldsman carrying the ball touches or grounds any part of his person on or over a boundary marked by a line, 6 runs shall be scored.

(*b*) *Ball Still in Play*
If a fieldsman releases the ball before he crosses the boundary, the ball will be considered to be still in play and it may be caught by another fieldsman. However, if the original fieldsman returns to the field of play and handles the ball, a catch may not be made.

33. HANDLED THE BALL

1. Out Handled the Ball
Either batsman on appeal shall be out 'handled the ball' if he wilfully

touches the ball while in play with the hand not holding the bat unless he does so with the consent of the opposite side.

NOTES
 (*a*) *Entry in Score Book*
The correct entry in the score book when a batsman is given out under this Law is 'handled the ball', and the bowler does not get credit for the wicket.

34. HIT THE BALL TWICE

1. Out Hit the Ball Twice
The striker, on appeal, shall be out hit the ball twice if, after the ball is struck or is stopped by any part of his person, he wilfully strikes it again with his bat or person except for the sole purpose of guarding his wicket: this he may do with his bat or any part of his person other than his hands, but see Law 37.2 (Obstructing a Ball From Being Caught).
 For the purpose of this Law, a hand holding the bat shall be regarded as part of the bat.

2. Returning the Ball to a Fieldsman
The striker, on appeal, shall be out under this Law, if, without the consent of the opposite side, he uses his bat or person to return the ball to any of the fielding side.

3. Runs from Ball Lawfully Struck Twice
No runs except those which result from an overthrow or penalty, see Law 41 (The Fieldsman), shall be scored from a ball lawfully struck twice.

NOTES
 (*a*) *Entry in Score Book*
The correct entry in the score book when the striker is given out under this Law is 'hit the ball twice', and the bowler does not get credit for the wicket.
 (*b*) *Runs Credited to the Batsmen*
Any runs awarded under 34.3 above as a result of an overthrow or penalty shall be credited to the striker, provided the ball in the first instance has touched the bat, or, if otherwise, as extras.

35. HIT WICKET

1. Out Hit Wicket
The striker shall be out hit wicket if, while the ball is in play:

(*a*) His wicket is broken with any part of his person, dress, or equipment as a result of any action taken by him in preparing to receive or in receiving a delivery, or in setting off for his first run, immediately after playing, or playing at, the ball.

(*b*) He hits down his wicket whilst lawfully making a second stroke for the purpose of guarding his wicket within the provisions of Law 34.1 (Out Hit the Ball Twice).

NOTES

(*a*) *Not Out Hit Wicket*

A batsman is not out under this Law should his wicket be broken in any of the ways referred to in 35.1(*a*) above if:

(i) It occurs while he is in the act of running, other than in setting off for his first run immediately after playing at the ball, or while he is avoiding being run out or stumped.

(ii) The bowler after starting his run-up or bowling action does not deliver the ball; in which case the umpire shall immediately call and signal 'dead ball'.

(iii) It occurs whilst he is avoiding a throw-in at any time.

36. LEG BEFORE WICKET

1. Out LBW

The striker shall be out LBW in the circumstances set out below:

(*a*) *Striker Attempting to Play the Ball.* The striker shall be out LBW if he first intercepts with any part of his person, dress or equipment a fair ball which would have hit the wicket and which has not previously touched his bat or a hand holding the bat, provided that:

(i) The ball pitched in a straight line between wicket and wicket or on the off side of the striker's wicket, or in the case of a ball intercepted full pitch would have pitched in a straight line between wicket and wicket; and

(ii) the point of impact is in a straight line between wicket and wicket, even if above the level of the bails.

(*b*) *Striker Making No Attempt to Play the Ball.* The striker shall be out LBW even if the ball is intercepted outside the line of the off-stump, if, in the opinion of the umpire, he has made no genuine attempt to play the ball with his bat, but has intercepted the ball with some part of his person and if the other circumstances set out in (*a*) above apply.

37. OBSTRUCTING THE FIELD

1. Wilful Obstruction

Either batsman, on appeal, shall be out obstructing the field if he wilfully obstructs the opposite side by word or action.

2. Obstructing a Ball from Being Caught

The striker, on appeal, shall be out should wilful obstruction by either batsman prevent a catch being made.

This shall apply even though the striker causes the obstruction in lawfully guarding his wicket under the provisions of Law 34. See Law 34.1 (Out Hit the Ball Twice).

NOTE

(a) *Accidental Obstruction*

The umpires must decide whether the obstruction was wilful or not. The accidental interception of a throw-in by a batsman while running does not break this Law.

38. RUN OUT

1. Out Run Out

Either batsman shall be out run out if in running or at any time while the ball is in play – except in the circumstances described in Law 39 (Stumped) he is out of his ground and his wicket is put down by the opposite side. If, however, a batsman in running makes good his ground he shall not be out run out, if he subsequently leaves his ground, in order to avoid injury, and the wicket is put down.

2. 'No-ball' Called

If a no-ball has been called, the striker shall not be given run out unless he attempts to run.

3. Which Batsman is Out

If the batsmen have crossed in running, he who runs for the wicket which is put down shall be out; if they have not crossed, he who has left the wicket which is put down shall be out. If a batsman remains in his ground or returns to his ground and the other batsman joins him there, the latter shall be out if his wicket is put down.

4. Scoring of Runs

If a batsman is run out, only that run which is being attempted shall not be scored. If however an injured striker himself is run out, no runs shall be scored. See Law 2.7 (Transgression of the Laws by an Injured Batsman or Runner).

NOTES

(a) *Ball Played on to Opposite Wicket*

If the ball is played on to the opposite wicket neither batsman is liable to be run out unless the ball has been touched by a fieldsman before the wicket is broken.

(b) *Entry in Score Book*

The correct entry in the score book when the striker is given out under this law is 'run out', and the bowler does not get credit for the wicket.

(c) *Run Out off a Fieldsman's Helmet*

If, having been played by a batsman or having come off his person, the ball rebounds directly from a fieldsman's helmet on to the stumps, with either batsman out of his ground, the batsman shall be 'not out'.

39. STUMPED

1. Out Stumped

The striker shall be out stumped if, in receiving the ball, not being a no ball, he is out of his ground otherwise than in attempting a run and the wicket is put down by the wicket-keeper without the intervention of another fieldsman.

2. Action by the Wicket-Keeper

The wicket-keeper may take the ball in front of the wicket in an attempt to stump the striker only if the ball has touched the bat or person of the striker.

NOTE

(a) *Ball Rebounding from Wicket-keeper's Person*

The striker may be out stumped if in the circumstances stated in 39.1 above, the wicket is broken by a ball rebounding from the wicket-keeper's person or equipment other than a protective helmet or is kicked or thrown by the wicket-keeper on to the wicket.

40. THE WICKET-KEEPER

1. Position of Wicket-Keeper

The wicket-keeper shall remain wholly behind the wicket until a ball delivered by the bowler touches the bat or person of the striker, or passes the wicket, or until the striker attempts a run.

In the event of the wicket-keeper contravening this Law, the umpire at the striker's end shall call and signal 'no-ball' at the instant of delivery or as soon as possible thereafter.

2. Restriction on Actions of the Wicket-Keeper

If the wicket-keeper interferes with the striker's right to play the ball and to guard his wicket, the striker shall not be out, except under Laws 33

(Handled the Ball), 34 (Hit the Ball Twice), 37 (Obstructing the Field) and 38 (Run Out).

3. Interference with the Wicket-Keeper by the Striker
If in the legitimate defence of his wicket, the striker interferes with the wicket-keeper, he shall not be out, except as provided for in Law 37.2 (Obstructing a Ball From Being Caught).

41. THE FIELDSMAN

1. Fielding the Ball
The fieldsman may stop the ball with any part of his person, but if he wilfully stops it otherwise, 5 runs shall be added to the run or runs already scored; if no run has been scored 5 penalty runs shall be awarded. The run in progress shall count provided that the batsmen have crossed at the instant of the act. If the ball has been struck, the penalty shall be added to the score of the striker, but otherwise to the score of byes, leg-byes, no-balls or wides as the case may be.

2. Limitation of On-Side Fieldsmen
The number of on-side fieldsmen behind the popping crease at the instant of the bowler's delivery shall not exceed two. In the event of infringement by the fielding side the umpire at the striker's end shall call and signal 'no-ball' at the instant of delivery or as soon as possible thereafter.

3. Position of Fieldsmen
Whilst the ball is in play and until the ball has made contact with the bat or the striker's person or has passed his bat, no fieldsman, other than the bowler, may stand on or have any part of his person extended over the pitch [measuring 22yd (20.12m) × 10ft (3.05m)]. In the event of a fieldsman contravening this Law, the umpire at the bowler's end shall call and signal 'no-ball' at the instant of delivery or as soon as possible thereafter. See Law 40.1 (Position of Wicket-Keeper).

4. Fieldsmen's Protective Helmets
Protective helmets, when not in use by members of the fielding side, shall only be placed, if above the surface, on the ground behind the wicket-keeper. In the event of the ball, when in play, striking a helmet whilst in this position, 5 penalty runs shall be awarded, as laid down in Law 41.1 and Note (*a*) below.

NOTE

(a) Batsmen Changing Ends

The 5 runs referred to in 1 and 4 above are a penalty and the batsmen do not change ends solely by reason of this penalty.

42. UNFAIR PLAY

1. Responsibility of Captains

The captains are responsible at all times for ensuring that play is conducted within the spirit of the game as well as within the Laws.

2. Responsibility of Umpires

The umpires are the sole judges of fair and unfair play.

3. Intervention by the Umpire

The umpires shall intervene without appeal by calling and signalling 'dead ball' in the case of unfair play, but should not otherwise interfere with the progress of the game except as required to do so by the Laws.

4. Lifting the Seam

A player shall not lift the seam of the ball for any reason. Should this be done, the umpires shall change the ball for one of similar condition to that in use prior to the contravention, see Note 42.8 (a).

5. Changing the Condition of the Ball

Any member of the fielding side may polish the ball provided that such polishing wastes no time and that no artificial substance is used. No one shall rub the ball on the ground or use any artificial substance or take any other action to alter the condition of the ball.

In the event of a contravention of this Law, the umpires, after consultation, shall change the ball for one of similar condition to that in use prior to the contravention.

This Law does not prevent a member of the fielding side from drying a wet ball, or removing mud from the ball, see Note 42.8 (b).

6. Incommoding the Striker

An umpire is justified in intervening under this Law and shall call and signal 'dead ball' if, in his opinion, any player of the fielding side incommodes the striker by any noise or action while he is receiving a ball.

7. Obstruction of a Batsman in Running

It shall be considered unfair if any fieldsman wilfully obstructs a batsman in running. In these circumstances the umpire shall call and signal 'dead ball' and allow any completed runs and the run in progress or alternatively any boundary scored.

8. The Bowling of Fast Short-Pitched Balls

The bowling of fast short-pitched balls is unfair if, in the opinion of the umpire at the bowler's end, it constitutes an attempt to intimidate the striker, see Note (*d*) below.

Umpires shall consider intimidation to be the deliberate bowling of fast short-pitched balls which by their length, height and direction are intended or likely to inflict physical injury on the striker. The relative skill of the striker shall also be taken into consideration.

In the event of such unfair bowling, the umpire at the bowler's end shall adopt the following procedure:

(*a*) In the first instance the umpire shall call and signal 'no-ball', caution the bowler and inform the other umpire, the captain of the fielding side and the batsmen of what has occurred.

(*b*) If this caution is ineffective, he shall repeat the above procedure and indicate to the bowler that this is a final warning.

(*c*) Both the above caution and final warning shall continue to apply even though the bowler may later change ends.

(*d*) Should the above warnings prove ineffective the umpire at the bowler's end shall:

(i) At the first repetition call and signal 'no-ball' and when the ball is dead direct the captain to take the bowler off forthwith and to complete the over with another bowler, provided that the bowler does not bowl two overs or part thereof consecutively. See Law 22.7 (Bowler Incapacitated or Suspended during an Over).

(ii) Not allow the bowler, thus taken off, to bowl again in the same innings.

(iii) Report the occurrence to the captain of the batting side as soon as the players leave the field for an interval.

(iv) Report the occurrence to the executive of the fielding side and to any governing body responsible for the match who shall take any further action which is considered to be appropriate against the bowler concerned.

9. The Bowling of Fast High Full Pitches

The bowling of fast high full pitches is unfair.

A fast high full pitched ball shall be defined as a high ball that passes, or would have passed, on the full above waist height of a batsman standing upright at the crease. Should a bowler bowl a fast high full pitched ball, either umpire shall call and signal 'no-ball' and adopt the procedure of caution, final warning, action against the bowler and reporting as set out in Law 42.8.

10. Time Wasting
Any form of time wasting is unfair.

(*a*) In the event of the captain of the fielding side wasting time or allowing any member of his side to waste time, the umpire at the bowler's end shall adopt the following procedure:

(i) In the first instance he shall caution the captain of the fielding side and inform the other umpire of what has occurred.

(ii) If this caution is ineffective he shall repeat the above procedure and indicate to the captain that this is a final warning.

(iii) The umpire shall report the occurrence to the captain of the batting side as soon as the players leave the field for an interval.

(iv) Should the above procedure prove ineffective the umpire shall report the occurrence to the executive of the fielding side and to any governing body responsible for that match who shall take appropriate action against the captain and the players concerned.

(*b*) In the event of a bowler taking unnecessarily long to bowl an over the umpire at the bowler's end shall adopt the procedures, other than the calling of 'no-ball', of caution, final warning, action against the bowler and reporting as set out in 42.8 above.

(*c*) In the event of a batsman wasting time other than in the manner described in Law 31 (Timed Out), the umpire at the bowler's end shall adopt the following procedure:

(i) In the first instance he shall caution the batsman and inform the other umpire at once, and the captain of the batting side, as soon as the players leave the field for an interval, of what has occurred.

(ii) If this proves ineffective, he shall repeat the caution, indicate to the batsman that this is a final warning and inform the other umpire.

(iii) The umpire shall report the occurrence to both captains as soon as the players leave the field for an interval.

(iv) Should the above procedure prove ineffective, the umpire shall report the occurrence to the executive of the batting side and to any governing body responsible for that match who shall take appropriate action against the player concerned.

11. Players Damaging the Pitch
The umpires shall intervene and prevent players from causing damage to the pitch which may assist the bowlers of either side, see Note (*c*) below.

(*a*) In the event of any member of the fielding side damaging the pitch the umpire shall follow the procedure of caution, final warning and reporting as set out in 42.10 (*a*) above.

(*b*) In the event of a bowler contravening this Law by running down the pitch after delivering the ball, the umpire at the bowler's end shall first caution the bowler. If this caution is ineffective the umpire shall adopt the procedures, other than the calling of 'no-ball', of caution, final warning, action against the bowler and reporting as set out in 42.8 above.

(*c*) In the event of a batsman damaging the pitch the umpire at the bowler's end shall follow the procedures of caution, final warning and reporting as set out in 42.10 (*c*) above.

12. Batsman Unfairly Stealing a Run

Any attempt by the batsman to steal a run during the bowler's run-up is unfair. Unless the bowler attempts to run out either batsman – see Law 24.4 (Bowler Throwing at Striker's Wicket Before Delivery) and Law 24.5 (Bowler Attempting to Run Out Non-Striker Before Delivery) – the umpire shall call and signal 'dead ball' as soon as the batsmen cross in any such attempt to run. The batsmen shall then return to their original wickets.

13. Players' Conduct

In the event of a player failing to comply with the instructions of an umpire, criticising his decisions by word or action, or showing dissent, or generally behaving in a manner which might bring the game into disrepute, the umpire concerned shall, in the first place, report the matter to the other umpire and to the player's captain requesting the latter to take action. If this proves ineffective, the umpire shall report the incident as soon as possible to the executive of the player's team and to any governing body responsible for the match, who shall take any further action which is considered appropriate against the player or players concerned.

NOTES

(*a*) *The Condition of the Ball*

Umpires shall make frequent and irregular inspections of the condition of the ball.

(*b*) *Drying of a Wet Ball*

A wet ball may be dried on a towel or with sawdust.

(*c*) *Danger Area*

The danger area on the pitch, which must be protected from damage by a bowler, shall be regarded by the umpires as the area contained by an imaginary line 4ft/1.22m from the popping crease, and parallel to it, and within two imaginary and parallel lines drawn down the pitch from points on that line 1ft/30.48cm on either side of the middle stump.

(*d*) *Fast Short Pitched Balls*

As a guide, a fast short pitched ball is one which pitches short and passes, or would have passed, above the shoulder height of the striker standing in a normal batting stance at the crease.

(e) *The Bowling of Fast Full Pitches*
The bowling of one fast, high full pitch shall be considered to be unfair if, in the opinion of the umpire, it is deliberate, bowled at the striker, and if it passes or would have passed above the shoulder height of the striker when standing in a normal batting stance at the crease.

(f) *Time Wasting by Batsmen*
Other than in exceptional circumstances, the batsman should always be ready to take strike when the bowler is ready to start his run-up.

Reprinted by permission of MCC. Copies of the current edition of the official Laws of Cricket with full notes and interpretations can be obtained from MCC at Lord's Cricket Ground, London NW8 8QN.

Crown Green Bowls

Crown Green Bowls

1. The Game

1.1 The game shall be played on grass, or on an artificial surface as approved by the B.C.G.B.A.

1.2 The game shall be played by two players, each having two bowls, the players playing alternately until each shall have delivered both bowls, except in the event of the leader having forfeited his/her first bowl, in which case his/her opponent will then be allowed to deliver his/her two bowls consecutively.

1.3 A bowl must be played at least three metres from the footer to count, except when an opponent's bowls are out of play.

1.4 Before commencing play the number of points to be scored to make the game shall be fixed.

1.5 Where more than two players take part in a game, these Laws shall operate when applicable.

1.6 The 'entrance' (which must be near the centre of any one side of the playing area) shall be plainly marked.

2. Scoring

2.1 The winner of each end shall score one point for each bowl he/she has nearer to the jack than his/her opponent's nearest bowl and he/she shall lead out the jack at the succeeding end.

2.2 Only the winner of the end shall signal the result to the scorers, who must sit together and initial each other's score cards every third end to signify agreement.

2.3 Where the score cannot be agreed, it shall revert to the end where both markers show the score to be agreed as correct.

3. Commencement of the Game

3.1 At the commencement of the game, the footer must be placed, by the leader, within three metres either side of the entrance to the green, on either right or left side and one metre from the edge and from there play shall commence.

4. The Footer

4.1 The footer, which shall be round, shall have a diameter not less than 128mm (5 inches) and not more than 154mm (6 inches).

4.2 Every player must place his/her toe on the footer when bowling either the jack or a bowl and may retain possession of the footer until his/her bowl has ceased running.

4.3 A player bowling the jack with his/her right hand must play his/her bowls with his/her right hand and have his/her right toe on the footer and a player bowling the jack with his/her left hand must play his/her bowls with the left hand and must have his/her left toe on the footer. Nothing in this Law shall apply to any player who suffers from a disability.

4.4 A player must bowl with the same hand throughout the game.

4.5 Should players not conform with Laws 4.2, 4.3, 4.4., then any bowl not so played may be stopped by the referee and shall be played again. Should a player transgress again during the course of the game, the bowl wrongly played shall be deemed dead.

4.6 At no time may the footer be used within one metre from the edge of the green.

4.7 If a player takes up the footer after playing a bowl, which for any reason has to be replayed, or if the footer is displaced for any other reason during an end, it shall be replaced as near as possible to its former position.

4.8 After each end is concluded, the footer shall be placed at the jack by the last player. The leader in the succeeding end may, however, before bowling the jack, remove the footer anywhere he/she pleases within the space of one metre from the spot where the jack lay at the termination of the preceding end, subject to the provisions of Law 4.6.

5. A Mark

5.1 The leader shall bowl the jack to set a mark, the object of the players being to play their bowls as near as possible to the jack. To set a mark, the jack must be bowled and if it rests on the green, it shall be deemed a mark.

5.2 The following shall be deemed 'not a mark':–

If, after objection, the jack is proved by measurement to be less than 19 metres from the footer, the measurement to be taken from the nearest point of the jack to the centre of the footer.

5.3 If, when bowled, the jack shall go off the green.

5.4 If the leader in one trial shall fail to set a mark, his/her opponent is then entitled to set the mark with the same jack but not to play first at it. If the opponent fails in one trial to set a mark, the original leader shall then have one trial and so on alternately, until a mark has been set by one of them, the original leader to play the first bowl at it.

5.5 Objection to a Mark: Objection to a mark must be made verbally after the first bowl has come to rest. Any player objecting to a mark must raise his hand as an indication to the referee that an objection has been made.

5.6 If, after an objection to a mark has been made, it is proved by measurement to be a mark, the jack and bowl shall remain.

5.7 If the original leader fails to set a mark and objects to the mark set by his/her opponent, he/she shall not be allowed to bowl his/her wood until the objection has been settled, and if the measurement shall prove that a legitimate mark has been set, it must be accepted.

5.8 A tape or other certified measure (at least 19 metres long) must be used for the purpose of carrying out these Laws.

6. The Jack

6.1 Standard jacks as defined in Appendix A shall be used in all Competitions.

6.2 A jack must only be used for the sole purpose of setting a mark.

6.3 Delivery of the Jack: A player shall not bowl the jack without allowing his/her opponent the opportunity of seeing with what bias he/she bowls it and of watching its course from a point near the footer.

6.4 Jack Struck Off the Green: If the jack is struck off the green that end shall be deemed to have been played. Play shall resume, one metre in from the point where the jack left the green, the same player setting the mark.

6.5 Jack Impeded: If the jack in its course is impeded in any way, or stops on the land of other players, it must under all circumstances be returned and if two jacks are bowled near the same place, the one that is last stationary must be pronounced not a mark and be returned, no penalty being incurred.

6.6 Jack Displaced: If the jack is displaced by a bowl or the jack of any other players, or by an exterior cause and the players agree to the spot of replacement, the end must be continued, otherwise the end is void.

6.7 Jack or Bowl in Danger of Striking Still Bowl or Jack: If a running jack or bowl appears to be in danger of striking a still bowl or jack belonging to another set, such running jack or bowl should be stopped and returned to be replayed.

6.8 When, after delivery of the jack and a mark is set, the leader is prevented from delivering his/her first bowl through the tape being on the green during the measure of another mark, the leader may have the jack returned and again set the mark.

6.9 If a player strikes the jack with his/her bowl, and the jack comes in contact with a bowl or jack not belonging to the playing party, or if it comes in contact with any person on the green, the end becomes void.

6.10 If a jack comes in contact with a bowl belonging to the playing party, it must remain at the place to which it is removed by the strike.

6.11 Changing Jack or Bowls: No player shall be allowed to change the jack or bowls during the progress of a game except with the consent of the referee and then only if, in his/her opinion, the jack or bowls are so damaged as to be unplayable.

6.12 No player shall be permitted to play with bowls or jack which have a device for adjusting the bias, nor shall any player be permitted to alter the bias of bowls or jack, by any means during the course of play.

6.13 No player shall deliver a bowl while the jack or preceding bowl is in motion, otherwise his/her bowl shall be deemed dead and must be taken out of play.

7. The Bowl

7.1 A bowl shall not weigh less than 21lb.

7.2 Approaching a Running Bowl: A player must not approach nearer than one metre to a running bowl nor follow it up in such a manner as to obstruct the view of his/her opponent. If he/she offends the bowl shall be taken out of play and in the case of a further offence his/her bowls shall be taken off the green and the game awarded to his/her opponents, the defaulter to receive no score.

7.3 A player must not endeavour to accelerate or to impede its progress. If he/she offends the bowl shall be taken out of play and in the case of a further offence, his/her bowls shall be taken off the green and the game awarded to his/her opponent, the defaulter to receive no score.

7.4 Running Bowl Impeded: If a running bowl is impeded in any way other than by either player, it must be played again. If a running bowl is impeded by either player, both the offending player's bowls shall be forfeited at the end concerned.

7.5 If the leader's first bowl is impeded, he/she may, if he/she so desires, have the jack returned to him/her to set another mark.

7.6 If a running bowl comes into contact with the jack or any of the bowls in the set, such jack and/or bowls remain where they stop.

7.7 Playing Out of Turn: If a bowl is played out of turn it must be returned and played again in its proper turn.

7.8 Playing a Bowl Other than the Player's Own: If a bowl other than the player's own is delivered, whether by mistake or otherwise, it shall be deemed a dead bowl to that player and be returned to the proper owner to be played, the defaulter losing one of his/her bowls as a penalty. If, however, the jack or a bowl already played is disturbed by the bowl wrongly played, it shall be replaced as nearly as possible in its original position.

7.9 Disturbing a Still Bowl: If a still bowl is disturbed by any person other than the players concerned, or by a bowl or jack of any other players it must be replaced as near as possible to its original position but should either player touch or displace a still bowl before the end is completed, both the offending player's bowls shall be forfeited at the end concerned.

7.10 Bowl Falling from a Player's Hand: If a player has taken up his/her position and a bowl falls from his/her hand (even by accident) and runs so far that he/she cannot recover it without quitting the footer, such bowl shall be considered dead and must be taken out of play.

7.11 Blocking Opponent's Course: A player may play his/her bowl so as to block his/her opponent's course whenever he/she thinks proper, but he/she must not play his/her bowl a distance less than three metres from the footer, otherwise it shall be deemed dead and must be taken out of play. A bowl must be played, not placed, or it becomes a dead bowl.

7.12 Dead Bowls: A bowl or jack played or struck off the green or prevented from going off by resting against anything at the edge or in the channel, shall be dead.

7.13 Moving Jack or Bowls Before Opponent Agrees: At the conclusion of an end, neither the jack, nor a bowl claimed to count, may be moved without the consent of the opponent, until the points are counted and both players are satisfied, otherwise the opponent shall score one point for each of his/her bowls in play.

7.14 A player, when at the end where the jack lies, must not stand directly behind the jack or obstruct the view of his/her opponent.

8. The Referees, Measurers and Other Contingencies

8.1 Instructions to Referees and Measurers: The referee or measurers are not permitted to place either his/her thumb or finger on either the jack or bowl when measuring an end.

8.2 No measuring is permitted until the end is finished.

8.3 In the event of the displacement of the jack or bowl during measure the points already given shall count.

8.4 When an end is being measured, all players should stand away and not interfere with the actions of either the referee or measurer(s).

8.5 When measuring, the adjustable end of the pegs or permitted metal measures as approved by the British Crown Green Bowling Association must be taken to the jack.

8.6 Displacing Jack or Bowl during a Measure: If, during a measure, the jack or bowl is displaced by a player, he/she shall lose the point claimed.

8.7 Bowl Resting on Another: When a bowl rests on another, or is touching the jack and the bowl rested on has to be removed to allow a measure, it must be removed by the referee and the measure made after such removal.

8.8 Referee Not to Wait for an Objection: Referees are instructed to insist on and see that the games are carried out strictly in accordance with the Laws of the Game.

8.9 No person, other than the players and the referee, are allowed on the green, except measurers when their services are required.

8.10 Refusal or Inability to Continue the Game: If, after commencing a game, any player shall refuse or is unable to continue, the referee shall decide upon the point at issue.

8.11 Should a player leave the green without informing his/her opponent and obtaining the permission of the referee, he/she shall forfeit the game, no score to be given.

8.12 Any incident which necessitates a player having to stop play or leave the green and being unable to resume before the finish of the match, his/her opponent shall receive the maximum points and the score of the player who left the green to remain as it stood, but in the case of refusal of a player to continue the game, his/her opponent shall be awarded the maximum score and he/she shall receive no score.

8.13 Ungentlemanly and Unladylike Conduct: In the case of a wilful breach of the Laws of the Game or any unfair play or unsporting conduct, the referee may caution the offending players or spectators or order them to retire from the game or green and, in the case of a player, no substitute shall be allowed to take his/her place. The game shall be awarded to his/her opponent, who will receive the maximum score and the offending player to receive no score. If a player receives a second caution, he/she shall forfeit the game, his/her opponent receiving the maximum score and the offending player to receive no score.

8.14 Bad Light and Postponement of Game: If, during the course of a game, it becomes so dark that the jack cannot be distinctly seen from the footer, any player may have a light exhibited at the jack if he/she so requests, or he/she may appeal to the Referee, whose decision shall be final, for the game to be postponed. In the event of a postponement, owing to the above cause or any other unforeseen circumstances, the points scored by each player shall count and the position of the jack shall be marked.

8.15 Warnings Before Striking: All players are required to give a verbal warning and to take every precaution before striking to eliminate the possibility of causing injury to other players, referees, measurers and spectators, by being struck with bowls or jack. A player shall receive a caution for a first transgression of this law and for a second offence, the game shall be forfeited and awarded to the opponent who shall receive the maximum score, the defaulter no score.

8.16 Alterations of Laws: The British Crown Green Bowling Association is the interpreter of these laws, and from its decision there shall be no appeal either at Law or otherwise. None of these Laws shall be altered except as provided by the Association's Bye-Laws numbered 16 and 17 for the alteration of Rules and Bye-Laws.

8.17 Dispute Not Provided For in the Laws: Any dispute arising which is not provided for in the foregoing Laws, shall be decided by the referee, whose decision shall be final.

APPENDIX A

A Standard Jack

1. Standard jacks of 2 Full bias as approved by the British Crown Green Bowling Association, shall weigh a minimum of 567gms (20oz) and a maximum of 680gms (24oz) and the diameter shall be a minimum of 95mm (3¾ins.) and a maximum of 98.5mm (3⅞ins.). In respect of all standard jacks manufactured after 1st January, 1994, the minimum and maximum weight shall be 653gms (23oz) and 680gms (24oz) respectively and the diameter shall be a minimum of 97mm (3¹³⁄₁₆ins.) and maximum 98.5mm (3⅞ins.) respectively and conform to the agreed standard profile. Standard jacks manufactured after this date shall bear the appropriate year as Law 5. They shall be black in colour with white mounts and spots, white or yellow in colour with black mounts and spots. In place of mounts, composition jacks may have engraved circles of approximately the diameter of the mounts or spots and filled in the appropriate colour.

2. The mounts shall be approximately 20mm (13/16in.) diameter and bias side mounts shall not be hollow. The spots shall be approximately 6mm (¼in.) diameter and there shall be three spots on the non-bias side at a radius of approximately 19mm (¾in.) from the centre of the mount.

3. They shall not be numbered or lettered. Evidence of ownership shall be made on the non-bias side.

4. They shall be branded B.C.G.B.A. and the Code letter of the Official Tester. All new standard jacks shall bear the manufacturer's name.

5. New and renovated jacks shall be stamped with the year of expiry and for this purpose the year shall be reckoned from 1st October to 30th September the next year (i.e. jacks manufactured or retested between

1st October and 31st December will bear the stamp of expiry from the following year). All jacks shall be retested at not more than seven-yearly intervals.

Reprinted by permission of the British Crown Green Bowling Association.

THE RULES OF

Curling

The Rink

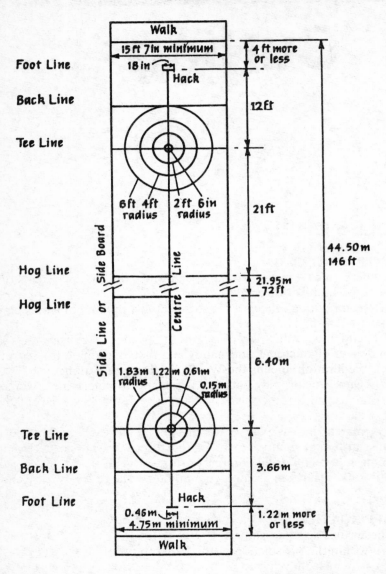

Curling

RULES OF PLAY

1. INTERPRETATION
In these rules, umpires' rulings, and other official documents of the Federation and its officers:

(*a*) 'competition' means a playdown by any number of teams playing games to determine a winner;

(*b*) 'end' means that part of a game in which the two opposing teams each deliver eight stones alternately and then determine the score;

(*c*) 'Federation' means the World Curling Federation;

(*d*) 'game' means play between two teams to determine a winner;

(*e*) 'house' means the area within the outside circle at each end of the rink;

(*f*) 'match' means play between two or more teams on one side against an equal number of teams on the other side to determine a winning side by the total number of shots or games;

(*g*) 'rink' means an area of ice marked in accordance with Rule 3.

2. APPLICATION
These rules apply to games:

(*a*) within the jurisdiction of the Federation; or

(*b*) to which they have been made applicable by the curling body having jurisdiction.

3. RINK
(1) Where possible, the rink shall be drawn on the ice in accordance with the diagram on facing page.

(2) Two rubber hacks of a style and size approved by the Federation shall be placed on the foot line with the inside edge of each hack 7.62cm (3 inches) from the centre line and on opposite sides of the centre line. The length of the hack shall not exceed 20.32cm (8 inches). The rubber of the hack shall be attached firmly to wood or other suitable material and the hack shall be recessed into the ice as much as is practical, but no more than 5.04cm (2 inches) in depth. There shall be no obstruction behind the hack structure.

(3) The back edge of the back line shall be at the outer edge of the outer circle where the centre line crosses the back line.

Interpretation: Because the outer markings of both the circle and back line are in fact one, it is important that prior to the beginning of the competition, the markings on all sheets are checked. The 6-foot measure should be exactly at the outermost marking. If this is not the case, all teams shall be informed of any discrepancies prior to the first game.

4. STONES

(1) Curling stones shall be of circular shape.

(2) No stone, including handle and bolt, shall be of greater weight than 19.96 kilograms (44lbs.) or of greater circumference than 91.44 centimetres (36 inches) or of less height than 11.43 centimetres (4.5 inches).

(3) If a stone is broken in play a replacement stone shall be placed where the largest fragment came to rest. The end in play and the game shall be completed using the replacement stone.

(4) A stone that rolls over in its course or comes to rest on its side or top shall be removed immediately from play.

(5) Where the handle of a stone quits the stone in delivery, the player is entitled to replay the stone, if the delivering team so desires.

Interpretation: The handle must be completely separated from the stone.

(6) A stone that does not clear the farther hog line shall be removed immediately from play except where it has struck another stone lying in play.

(7) A stone which comes to rest beyond and lying clear of the back line shall be removed from play immediately.

(8) A stone which hits a side board or touches a side line shall be removed from play immediately.

(9) No stone(s) shall be measured by instrument until the last stone of the end has come to rest except by the umpire, when requested by a skip, to decide whether or not a stone is in play.

Interpretation: If the position of the stones in the house makes it impossible to use the 6-foot measuring device to decide whether a stone is in play at the 6 o'clock position, the umpire shall do this visually and his decision shall be final.

(10) All sixteen stones assigned to a given sheet shall be delivered at each end unless the players in charge of the head have agreed a score for the end or the game has been conceded.

5. TEAMS

(1) At the start of a competition every team shall be composed of four players, each player playing two stones and playing each stone alternately with his opponent.

(2) No player shall use footwear or equipment that may damage the surface of the ice.

Interpretation: Any equipment which may possibly come into contact with the ice surface may be inspected by the Chief Umpire of the competition and rejected if that official feels that such equipment is either faulty or is being used in a manner to provide an unfair advantage (examples – faulty slider, extremely dry corn broom, shedding brush, etc.).

(3) The rotation of play stated on the lineup card shall be observed throughout the game.

Interpretation: The rotation of throwing by team members shall be submitted to the Chief Umpire on the lineup card at the team meeting prior to the beginning of the competition. The skip and the acting skip selected under 6(3) shall be designated on this card and the substitute player, if appropriate, shall be listed. Should there be any change, a new card shall be submitted to the Chief Umpire at least 30 minutes prior to the game in which the change is occurring.

(4) Prior to the game a disc, light coloured on one side and dark on the other, shall be tossed by an official in the presence of a member of each team. The team winning the toss shall decide which team shall lead at the first end after which the winner of the preceding end shall lead.

(5) Where a player is unable to continue to play in a game or to play at the start of a game, his skip may:

(*a*) finish the game then in progress and start any subsequent game with the remaining players, in which case the first two players shall throw three stones each; or

(*b*) bring in a qualified substitute for the game then in progress at the beginning of the next end, or at the start of any subsequent game.

(*c*) start the game with three players if one player is late for a reason adjudged valid by the umpire. The late player may enter the game in the next end, in his normal position.

(6) A player who has left a game because of illness, accident or other

extenuating circumstances may rejoin his team at any time during any game in the competition. If a substitute was selected the player may rejoin his team for the next game.

(7) No team shall play more than one substitute in a competition.

6. SKIPS

(1) The skip has the exclusive direction of the game for his team.

(2) Subject to Rule 5(3), the skip may play in any position in his team that he chooses.

7. POSITION OF PLAYERS

(1) Only skips and acting skips in charge of the house for the time being may stand within the house and the skip of the playing team has the choice of place and shall not be obstructed by the other skip, but behind the tee line the privileges of both in regard to sweeping are equal.

(2) The players, other than the skip and acting skip, shall not stand behind the house, but shall place themselves along the side of the rink between the hog lines, except when sweeping or about to deliver a stone.

Interpretation: Non-delivering team members shall not take a position or cause such motion that would obstruct, interfere with or distract the delivering team. The umpire shall not allow any action that could be interpreted as an attempt to intimidate an opponent.

8. DELIVERY

(1) Right handed players shall play from the hack on the left of the centre line and left handed players from the hack on the right of the centre line. Any stone delivered from the wrong hack shall be removed from play immediately.

(2) In the delivery of the stone, the stone shall be clearly released from the hand before the stone reaches the nearer hog line. If the player fails to so release the stone, it shall be removed from play immediately by the playing team. If the stone has struck another stone, the played stone shall be removed from play by the playing team and any displaced stone shall be replaced as nearly as possible where it originally lay to the satisfaction of the opposing skip.

Interpretation: Clearly released means that not only must the player release the stone, he must also ensure that his hand does not prevent the umpire from seeing that the stone is released.

(3) The following hog-line violation procedures shall be applied:

(*a*) The first warning shall be considered the instruction given by the Chief Umpire at the Pre-Event Meeting.

(*b*) Any infraction occurring subsequently during play shall result in the stone being removed by the team at the instruction of the umpire.

Interpretation: All hog-line violated stones shall be removed and any displaced stones shall be repositioned. Benefit to either team is not a factor.

(4) A stone that has not been released from the player's hand and that has not reached the nearer tee line may be returned to the hack and re-delivered.

(5) Each player shall be ready to deliver his stone when his turn comes, and shall not take an unreasonable time to play. Where the Chief Umpire considers that play is unnecessarily slow, he shall notify the skip of the team at fault that if their next stone is not delivered within 30 seconds from the time he gives a signal, he will order the stone to be removed from play immediately.

Interpretation: The lead and second shall be ready to deliver their stones whenever it is their turn to throw. If the third or skip has not moved towards the throwing end at two minutes, the skip shall then be informed that his player has 30 seconds to throw the stone.

(6) Where a player delivers a stone belonging to the opposing team, a stone belonging to his team shall be put in its place.

(7) Where a player delivers a stone out of proper rotation it shall be removed from play immediately by the playing team and returned to the player to be delivered in proper rotation, but when the mistake is not discovered until after the stone has come to rest or struck another stone, the end shall be continued as if the mistake had not occurred, and the missed stone shall be delivered by the player missing his turn as the last stone for his team in that end.

(8) Where the skips agree that a stone has been missed but are unable to agree as to which player missed his turn, the lead of the team that made the mistake shall play the last stone for his team in that end.

(9) Where two stones of a team are delivered in succession in the same end, the opposing skip shall remove the stone played by mistake, replace to his satisfaction any stone displaced by the stone played by mistake, and continue the end as if the mistake had not occurred, and the player who delivered the stone played by mistake shall re-deliver it as the last stone for his team in that end.

Interpretation: Should the infraction not be discovered until after further stones have been played, the end shall be replayed.

(10) Where a player delivers three stones in one end, the end shall be continued as if the mistake had not occurred and the fourth player of the team that made the mistake shall deliver one stone only in that end.

9. SWEEPING

(1) Between the tee lines, a running stone, or stone(s) set in motion by a running stone, may be swept by any one or more of the team to which it belongs.

Interpretation: Any stone in motion is a running stone. A stationary stone must be set in motion before it can be swept.

(2) Between the tee lines, no player shall sweep an opponent's stone.

(3) Behind the tee line, if the delivering team's choice is not to sweep, they shall not obstruct or prevent the opponent from sweeping the stone.

(4) Behind the tee line, only one player from each team may sweep at any one time. This may be the skip or acting skip from either team. Only the player in charge of the house shall be allowed to sweep behind the tee line, and shall not start to sweep an opponent's stone before the stone reaches the line.

Interpretation: (ai) The acting skip does not assume charge of the house until the skip leaves to throw his first stone, and then remains in charge.

(aii) If the skip throws other than fourth stones, he shall resume control of the house when his second stone has come to rest.

(bi) The sweeping motion shall leave no debris in front of the running stone.

(bii) The sweepers and their equipment must be seen to be clear of the stone at all times.

Penalty: If a team draws an infraction and the stone involved is their own it shall be removed from play at the discretion of the umpire. However if the stone involved belongs to the opposition the umpire shall direct the repositioning of the stone to where he considers it would have come to rest had it not been infracted. If in the opinion of the non-offending skip repositioning of the stone would benefit the offending team, it may be left where it came to rest.

(5) At the start of each game, each player shall decide which broom or brush he/she will use for sweeping purposes during the game and only that broom or brush may be used for sweeping by the player during that game. If the broom or brush becomes unfit for further use during the game it shall be replaced by the same type of broom or brush. The replacement shall be inspected and approved by an umpire prior to use. Brushes may be exchanged between players on the same team during a game – but a team broom may not be exchanged.

10. TOUCHED RUNNING STONES

(1) If a running stone is touched by any of the playing team or by his equipment, the touched stone shall be removed from play immediately by that team. However, if in the opinion of the opposing skip, removal of the stone would be beneficial to the offending team, then he may place the stone as nearly as possible to the position where he considers it would have come to rest had it not been touched. He may also reposition

any stone or stones that would have been displaced had the running stone not been touched and been allowed to continue.

Interpretation: For an opposing skip to reposition any potentially displaced stones, the infraction must have occurred inside the hog line at the playing end.

(2) If a running stone is touched by any of the opposing team or by his equipment, the stone shall be placed where the skip of the team to which it belongs considers it would have come to rest if it had not been touched.

(3) If the position of any stone is altered by a touched stone, the skip opposed to the team at fault may elect:

(*a*) to remove the touched stone and replace all other altered stones to the position where he considers they originally lay; or

(*b*) to leave the touched stone and all altered stones where they came to rest.

11. DISPLACED STATIONARY STONES

(1) If a stone which would have altered the course of a running stone is displaced by the playing team, the running stone shall be allowed to come to rest and may be left there or removed from play immediately at the discretion of the opposing skip.

(*a*) If the running stone is removed from play then all displaced stones shall be placed where the opposing skip considers they originally lay.

(*b*) If the running stone is left where it came to rest, then displaced stones shall remain where they came to rest.

(2) A stationary stone which is displaced and has no effect on the outcome of the running stone shall be replaced where it originally lay, by the opposing skip.

12. SCORING

(1) Games shall be decided by a majority of shots and a team scores one shot for each stone that is nearer the tee than any stone of the opposing team.

(2) Every stone that is within 1.83 metres (6 feet) of the tee is eligible to be counted.

Interpretation: The 6 foot measuring device shall be the sole instrument used to determine whether a stone is in the house, at the conclusion of the end.

(3) Measurements shall be taken from the tee to the nearest part of the stone.

Interpretation: Because a stone may vary in width, mesurements may not be taken from the outer edge of the stone.

(4) An end shall be considered as decided when the skips or acting skips in charge of the house at the time agree upon the score for that end.

Interpretation: Should any stone(s) be displaced before agreement has been reached, the non-offending team shall receive the benefit which may have accrued from a measurement. Should an umpire displace a stone when measuring one of the stones involved in the measurement, the stones shall be considered a tie.

(5) If two or more stones are so close to the tee that it is impossible to use a measuring device to determine the scoring stone, the determination shall be made visually by the Chief Umpire. If no decision can be made, the end shall be scored as a blank end.

13. UMPIRE

(1) The umpire has the general supervision of all games to which he is assigned.

Interpretation: The umpire shall function as directed by the Chief Umpire in accordance with the Rules of Play.

(2) The umpire shall determine any matter in dispute between opposing skips, whether or not the matter is covered in the rules.

14. CHIEF UMPIRE

(1) The Chief Umpire shall hear and determine appeals from decisions of umpires. His decision is final.

(2) Where the Chief Umpire had been so authorised, he may intervene at any time in any game and give such directions concerning the conduct of the game as he considers proper.

15. GENERAL

(1) Should any situation occur which is not covered by the rules, the decision will be made by the umpire in accordance with fairness.

Interpretation: Example – Any outside physical interference with the delivery or the course of a running stone shall result in the stone being replayed by the delivering team if so desired.

(2) In all situations involving penalties, a warning shall be issued by the umpire at the Pre-Event Meeting with the teams.

(3) The Pre-Event Meeting will involve all teams, the Chief Umpire and the Rules Committee Chairman or his designee.

Interpretation: All teams and coaches *must* attend the Pre-Event Meeting.

THE SPIRIT OF CURLING

Curling is a game of skill and of traditions. A shot well executed is a delight to see and so, too, it is a fine thing to observe the time-honoured traditions of curling being applied in the true spirit of the game. Curlers play to win but never to humble their opponents. A true Curler would prefer to lose rather than win unfairly.

A good Curler never attempts to distract an opponent or otherwise prevent him from playing his best.

No Curler ever deliberately breaks a rule of the game or any of its traditions. But, if he should do so inadvertently and be aware of it, he is the first to divulge the breach.

While the main object of the game of curling is to determine the relative skill of the players, the spirit of the game demands good sportsmanship, kindly feeling and honourable conduct. This spirit should influence both the interpretation and application of the rules of the game and also the conduct of all participants on and off the ice.

Reprinted by permission of the Royal Caledonian Curling Club, to whom copyright in these Rules belongs.

THE RULES OF
Golf

Golf

SECTION I ETIQUETTE: COURTESY ON THE COURSE

Safety
Prior to playing a stroke or making a practice swing, the player should ensure that no one is standing close by or in a position to be hit by the club, the ball or any stones, pebbles, twigs or the like which may be moved by the stroke or swing.

Consideration for Other Players
The player who has the honour should be allowed to play before his opponent or fellow-competitor tees his ball.

No one should move, talk or stand close to or directly behind the ball or the hole when a player is addressing the ball or making a stroke.

In the interest of all, players should play without delay.

No player should play until the players in front are out of range.

Players searching for a ball should signal the players behind them to pass as soon as it becomes apparent that the ball will not easily be found. They should not search for 5 minutes before doing so. They should not continue play until the players following them have passed and are out of range.

When the play of a hole has been completed, players should immediately leave the putting green.

Priority on the Course
In the absence of special rules, two-ball matches should have precedence over and be entitled to pass any three- or four-ball match, which should invite them through.

A single player has no standing and should give way to a match of any kind.

Any match playing a whole round is entitled to pass a match playing a shorter round.

If a match fails to keep its place on the course and loses more than one clear hole on the players in front, it should invite the match following to pass.

Care of the Course

Holes in Bunkers
Before leaving a bunker, a player should carefully fill up and smooth over all holes and footprints made by him.

Replace Divots; Repair Ball-Marks and Damage by Spikes
Through the green, a player should ensure that any turf cut or displaced by him is replaced at once and pressed down and that any damage to the putting green made by a ball is carefully repaired. Damage to the putting green caused by golf shoe spikes should be repaired on *completion of the hole*.

Damage to Green – Flagsticks, Bags, etc.
Players should ensure that, when putting down bags or the flagstick, no damage is done to the putting green and that neither they nor their caddies damage the hole by standing close to it, in handling the flagstick or in removing the ball from the hole. The flagstick should be properly replaced in the hole before the players leave the putting green. Players should not damage the putting green by leaning on their putters, particularly when removing the ball from the hole.

Golf Carts
Local notices regulating the movement of golf carts should be strictly observed.

Damage Through Practice Swings
In taking practice swings, players should avoid causing damage to the course, particularly the tees, by removing divots.

SECTION II DEFINITIONS

Addressing the Ball
A player has 'addressed the ball' when he has taken his stance and has also grounded his club, except that in a hazard a player has addressed the ball when he has taken his stance.

Advice

'Advice' is any counsel or suggestion which could influence a player in determining his play, the choice of a club or the method of making a stroke.

Information on the Rules or on matters of public information, such as the position of hazards or the flagstick on the putting green, is not advice.

Ball Deemed to Move

See 'Move or Moved'.

Ball Holes

See 'Holed'.

Ball Lost

See 'Lost Ball'.

Ball in Play

A ball is 'in play' as soon as the player has made a stroke on the teeing ground. It remains in play until holed out, except when it is lost, out of bounds or lifted, or another ball has been substituted under an applicable Rule, whether or not such Rule permits substitution; a ball so substituted becomes the ball in play.

Bunker

A 'bunker' is a hazard consisting of a prepared area of ground, often a hollow, from which turf or soil has been removed and replaced with sand or the like. Grass-covered ground bordering or within a bunker is not part of the bunker. The margin of a bunker extends vertically downwards, but not upwards.

Caddie

A 'caddie' is one who carries or handles a player's clubs during play and otherwise assists him in accordance with the Rules.

When one caddie is employed by more than one player, he is always deemed to be the caddie of the player whose ball is involved, and equipment carried by him is deemed to be that player's equipment, except when the caddie acts upon specific directions of another player, in which case he is considered to be that other player's caddie.

Casual Water

'Casual water' is any temporary accumulation of water on the course which is visible before or after the player takes his stance and is not in a water hazard. Snow and ice are either casual water or loose impedi-ments, at the option of the player, except that manufactured ice is an obstruction. Dew and frost are not casual water.

Committee
The 'Committee' is the committee in charge of the competition or, if the matter does not arise in a competition, the committee in charge of the course.

Competitor
A 'competitor' is a player in a stroke competition. A 'fellow-competitor' is any person with whom the competitor plays. Neither is partner of the other.

In stroke play foursome and four-ball competitions, where the context so admits, the word 'competitor' or 'fellow-competitor' includes his partner.

Course
The 'course' is the whole area within which play is permitted (see Rule 33-2).

Equipment
'Equipment' is anything used, worn or carried by or for the player except any ball he has played at the hole being played and any small object, such as a coin or a tee, when used to mark the position of a ball or the extent of an area in which a ball is to be dropped. Equipment includes a golf cart, whether or not motorised. If such a cart is shared by two or more players, the cart and everything in it are deemed to be the equipment of the player whose ball is involved except that, when the cart is being moved by one of the players sharing it, the cart and everything in it are deemed to be that player's equipment.
Note: A ball played at the hole being played is equipment when it has been lifted and not put back into play.

Fellow-Competitor
See 'Competitor'.

Flagstick
The 'flagstick' is a movable straight indicator, with or without bunting or other material attached, centred in the hole to show its position. It shall be circular in cross-section.

Forecaddie
A 'forecaddie' is one who is employed by the Committee to indicate to players the position of balls during play. He is an outside agency.

Ground Under Repair
'Ground under repair' is any portion of the course so marked by order of the Committee or so declared by its authorised representative. It includes material piled for removal and a hole made by a greenkeeper, even if not so marked. Stakes and lines defining ground under repair are in such ground. The margin of ground under repair extends vertically downwards, but not upwards.
Note 1: Grass cuttings and other material left on the course which have been abandoned and are not intended to be removed are not ground under repair unless so marked.
Note 2: The Committee may make a Local Rule prohibiting play from ground under repair.

Hazards
A 'hazard' is any bunker or water hazard.

Hole
The 'hole' shall be 4¼in (108mm) in diameter and at least 4in (100mm) deep. If a lining is used, it shall be sunk at least 1in (25mm) below the putting green surface unless the nature of the soil makes it impracticable to do so; its outer diameter shall not exceed 4¼in (108mm).

Holed
A ball is 'holed' when it is at rest within the circumference of the hole and all of it is below the level of the lip of the hole.

Honour
The side entitled to play first from the teeing ground is said to have the 'honour'.

Lateral Water Hazard
A 'lateral water hazard' is a water hazard or that part of a water hazard so situated that it is not possible or is deemed by the Committee to be impracticable to drop a ball behind the water hazard in accordance with Rule 26-1(*b*).
That part of a water hazard to be played as a lateral water hazard should be distinctively marked.
Note: Lateral water hazards should be defined by red stakes or lines.

Line of Play
The 'line of play' is the direction which the player wishes his ball to take after a stroke, plus a reasonable distance on either side of the intended direction. The line of play extends vertically upwards from the ground, but does not extend beyond the hole.

Line of Putt
The 'line of putt' is the line which the player wishes his ball to take after a stroke on the putting green. Except with respect to Rule 16-1e, the line of putt includes a reasonable distance on either side of the intended line. The line of putt does not extend beyond the hole.

Loose Impediments
'Loose impediments' are natural objects such as stones, leaves, twigs, branches and the like, dung, worms and insects and casts or heaps made by them, provided they are not fixed or growing, are not solidly embedded and do not adhere to the ball.

Sand and loose soil are loose impediments on the putting green but not elsewhere.

Snow and natural ice other than frost are either casual water or loose impediments, at the option of the player. Manufactured ice is an obstruction.

Dew and frost are not loose impediments.

Lost Ball
A ball is 'lost' if:

(*a*) It is not found or identified as his by the player within five minutes after the player's side or his or their caddies have begun to search for it; or

(*b*) The player has put another ball into play under the Rules, even though he may not have searched for the original ball; or

(*c*) The player has played any stroke with a provisional ball from the place where the original ball is likely to be or from a point nearer the hole than that place, whereupon the provisional ball becomes the ball in play.

Time spent in playing a wrong ball is not counted in the five-minute period allowed for search.

Marker
A 'marker' is one who is appointed by the Committee to record a competitor's score in stroke play. He may be a fellow-competitor. He is not a referee.

Matches
See 'Sides and Matches'.

Move or Moved
A ball is deemed to have 'moved' if it leaves its position and comes to rest in any other place.

Observer
An 'observer' is one who is appointed by the Committee to assist a referee to decide questions of fact and to report to him any breach of a Rule. An observer should not attend the flagstick, stand at or mark the position of the hole, or lift the ball or mark its position.

Obstructions
An 'obstruction' is anything artificial including the artificial surfaces and sides of roads and paths and manufactured ice, except:

(*a*) Objects defining out of bounds, such as walls, fences, stakes and railings;

(*b*) Any part of an immovable artificial object which is out of bounds; and

(*c*) Any construction declared by the Committee to be an integral part of the course.

Out of Bounds
'Out of bounds' is ground on which play is prohibited.

When out of bounds is defined by reference to stakes or a fence or as being beyond stakes or a fence, the out of bounds line is determined by the nearest inside points of the stakes or fence posts at ground level excluding angled supports.

When out of bounds is defined by a line on the ground, the line itself is out of bounds.

The out of bounds line extends vertically upwards and downwards.

A ball is out of bounds when all of it lies out of bounds.

A player may stand out of bounds to play a ball lying within bounds.

Outside Agency
An 'outside agency' is any agency not part of the match or, in stroke play, not part of a competitor's side, and includes a referee, a marker, an observer or a forecaddie. Neither wind nor water is an outside agency.

Partner
A 'partner' is a player associated with another player on the same side.

In a threesome, foursome, best-ball or a four-ball match, where the context so admits, the word 'player' includes his partner or partners.

Penalty Stroke
A 'penalty stroke' is one added to the score of a player or side under

certain Rules. In a threesome or foursome, penalty strokes do not affect the order of play.

Provisional Ball
A 'provisional ball' is a ball played under Rule 27-2 for a ball which may be <u>lost</u> outside a <u>water hazard</u> or may be <u>out of bounds</u>.

Putting Green
The 'putting green' is all ground of the hole being played which is specially prepared for putting or otherwise defined as such by the Committee. A ball is on the putting green when any part of it touches the putting green.

Referee
A 'referee' is one who is appointed by the Committee to accompany players to decide questions of fact and apply the Rules of Golf. He shall act on any breach of a Rule which he observes or is reported to him.

A referee should not attend the flagstick, stand at or mark the position of the hole, or lift the ball or mark its position.

Rub of the Green
A 'rub of the green' occurs when a ball in motion is accidentally deflected or stopped by any <u>outside agency</u> (See Rule 19-1).

Rule
The term 'Rule' includes Local Rules made by the Committee under Rule 33-8(*a*).

Side and Matches
Side: A player, or two or more players who are <u>partners</u>.
Single: A match in which one plays against another.
Threesome: A match in which one plays against two, and each side plays one ball.
Foursome: A match in which two play against two, and each side plays one ball.
Three-ball: A match play competition in which three play against one another, each playing his own ball. Each player is playing two distinct matches.
Best-ball: A match in which one plays against the better ball of two or the best ball of three players.
Four-ball: A match in which two play their better ball against the better ball of two other players.

Stance

Taking the 'stance' consists in a player placing his feet in position for the preparatory to making a stroke.

Stipulated Round

The 'stipulated round' consists of playing the holes of the course in their correct sequence unless otherwise authorised by the Committee. The number of holes in a stipulated round is 18 unless a small number is authorised by the Committee. As to extension of stipulated round in match play, see Rule 2-3.

Stroke

A 'stroke' is the forward movement of the club made with the intention of fairly striking at and moving the ball, but if a player checks his downswing voluntarily before the clubhead reaches the ball he is deemed not to have made a stroke.

Teeing Ground

The 'teeing ground' is the starting place for the hole to be played. It is a rectangular area two club-lengths in depth, the front and the sides of which are defined by the outside limits of two tee-markers. A ball is outside the teeing ground when all of it lies outside the teeing ground.

Through the Green

'Through the green' is the whole area of the course except:

(*a*) The teeing ground and putting green of the hole being played; and

(*b*) All hazards on the course.

Water Hazard

A 'water hazard' is any sea, lake, pond, river, ditch, surface drainage ditch or other open water course (whether or not containing water) and anything of a similar nature.

All ground or water within the margin of a water hazard is part of the water hazard. The margin of a water hazard extends vertically upwards and downwards. Stakes and lines defining the margins of water hazards are in the hazards.

Note: Water hazards (other than lateral water hazards) should be defined by yellow stakes or lines.

Wrong Ball

A 'wrong ball' is any ball other than:

(*a*) The ball in play,

(*b*) A <u>provisional ball</u> or

(*c*) In stroke play, a second ball played under Rule 3-3 or Rule 20-7(*b*).

Note: Ball in play includes a ball substituted for the ball in play when the player is proceeding under an applicable Rule which does not permit substitution.

SECTION III THE RULES OF PLAY

RULE 1

The Game

1-1 General

The Game of Golf consists in playing a ball from the <u>teeing ground</u> into the hole by a <u>stroke</u> or successive strokes in accordance with the Rules.

1-2 Exerting Influence on Ball

No player or caddie shall take any action to influence the position or the movement of a ball except in accordance with the Rules.

PENALTY FOR BREACH OF RULE 1–2:

Match play – Loss of hole; Stroke play – Two strokes.

Note: In the case of a serious breach of Rule 1–2, the Committee may impose a penalty of disqualification.

1-3 Agreement to Waive Rules

Players shall not agree to exclude the operation of any Rule or to waive any penalty incurred.

PENALTY FOR BREACH OF RULE 1–3:

Match play – Disqualification of both sides; Stroke play – Disqualification of competitors concerned.

(Agreeing to play out of turn in stroke play – See Rule 10-2*c*.)

1-4 Points Not Covered by Rules

If any point in dispute is not covered by the Rules, the decision shall be made in accordance with equity.

RULE 2

Match Play

2-1 Winner of Hole; Reckoning of Holes

In match play the game is played by holes.

Except as otherwise provided in the Rules, a hole is won by the side which holes its ball in the fewer strokes. In a handicap match the lower net score wins the hole.

The reckoning of holes is kept by the terms: so many 'holes up' or 'all square', and so many 'to play'.

A side is 'dormie' when it is as many holes up as there are holes remaining to be played.

2-2 Halved Hole
A hole is halved if each side holes out in the same number of strokes.

When a player has holed out and his opponent has been left with a stroke for the half, if the player thereafter incurs a penalty, the hole is halved.

2-3 Winner of Match
A match (which consists of a stipulated round, unless otherwise decreed by the Committee) is won by the side which is leading by a number of holes greater than the number of holes remaining to be played.

The Committee may, for the purpose of settling a tie, extend the stipulated round to as many holes as are required for a match to be won.

2-4 Concession of Next Stroke, Hole or Match
When the opponent's ball is at rest or is deemed to be at rest under Rule 16-2, the player may concede the opponent to have holed out with his next stroke and the ball may be removed by either side with a club or otherwise.

A player may concede a hole or a match at any time prior to the conclusion of the hole or the match.

Concession of a stroke, hole or match may not be declined or withdrawn.

2-5 Claims
In match play, if a doubt or dispute arises between the players and no duly authorised representative of the Committee is available within a reasonable time, the players shall continue the match without delay. Any claim, if it is to be considered by the Committee, must be made before any player in the match plays from the next teeing ground or, in the case of the last hole of the match, before all players in the match leave the putting green.

No later claim shall be considered unless it is based on facts previously unknown to the player making the claim and the player making the claim had been given wrong information (Rules 6-2(*a*) and 9) by an opponent. In any case, no later claim shall be considered after the result of the match has been officially announced, unless the Committee is satisfied that the opponent knew he was giving wrong information.

2-6 General Penalty
The penalty for a breach of a Rule in match play is loss of hole except when otherwise provided.

RULE 3

Stroke Play

3-1 Winner
The competitor who plays the stipulated round or rounds in the fewest strokes is the winner.

3-2 Failure to Hole Out
If a competitor fails to hole out at any hole and does not correct his mistake before he plays a stroke from the next teeing ground or, in the case of the last hole of the round, before he leaves the putting green, *he shall be disqualified*.

3-3 Doubt as to Procedure
(*a*) **Procedure**
In stroke play only, when during play of a hole a competitor is doubtful of his rights or procedure, he may, without penalty, play a second ball. After the situation which caused the doubt has arisen, the competitor should, before taking further action, announce to his marker or a fellow competitor his decision to invoke this Rule and which ball with which he will score if the Rules permit.

The competitor shall report the facts to the Committee before returning his score card unless he scores the same with both balls; if he fails to do so, *he shall be disqualified*.

(*b*) **Determination of Score for Hole**
If the Rules allow the procedure selected in advance by the competitor, the score with the ball selected shall be his score for the hole.

If the competitor fails to announce in advance his decision to invoke this Rule or his selection, the score with the original ball or, if the original ball is not one of the balls being played, the first ball put into play shall count if the Rules allow the procedure adopted for such ball.

Note: A second ball played under Rule 3-3 is not a provisional ball under Rule 27-2.

3-4 Refusal to Comply with a Rule

If a competitor refuses to comply with a Rule affecting the rights of another competitor, *he shall be disqualified*.

3-5 General Penalty

The penalty for a breach of a Rule in stroke play is two strokes except when otherwise provided.

CLUBS AND THE BALL

The Royal and Ancient Golf Club of St Andrews and the United States Golf Association reserve the right to change the Rules and make and change the interpretations relating to clubs, balls and other implements at any time.

RULE 4

Clubs

If there may be any reasonable basis for doubt as to whether a club which is to be manufactured conforms with Rule 4 and Appendix II, the manufacturer should submit a sample to the Royal and Ancient Golf Club of St Andrews for a ruling, such sample to become its property for reference purposes. If a manufacturer fails to do so, he assumes the risk of a ruling that the club does not conform with the Rules of Golf.

A player in doubt as to the conformity of a club should consult the Royal and Ancient Golf Club of St Andrews.

4-1 Form and Make of Clubs

A club is an implement designed to be used for striking the ball.

A putter is a club designed primarily for use on the putting green.

The player's clubs shall conform with the provisions of this Rule.

(*a*) **General**

The club shall be composed of a shaft and a head. All parts of the club shall be fixed so that the club is one unit. The club shall not be designed to be adjustable except for weight. The club shall not be substantially different from the traditional and customary form and make.

(*b*) **Shaft**

The shaft shall be generally straight, with the same bending and twisting properties in any direction, and shall be attached to the clubhead at the heel either directly or through a single plain neck or socket. A putter shaft may be attached to any point in the head.

(c) Grip
The grip consists of that part of the shaft designed to be held by the player and any material added to it for the purpose of obtaining a firm hold. The grip shall be substantially straight and plain in form and shall not be moulded for any part of the hands.

(d) Clubhead
The distance from the heel to the toe of the clubhead shall be greater than the distance from face to back. The clubhead shall be generally plain in shape.

The clubhead shall have only one face designed for striking the ball, except that a putter may have two such faces if their characteristics are the same; they are opposite each other and the loft of each is the same and does not exceed ten degrees.

(e) Club Face
The face shall not have any degree of concavity and, in relation to the ball, shall be hard and rigid. It shall be generally smooth.

(f) Wear
A club which conforms to Rule 4-1 when new is deemed to conform after wear through normal use. Any part of a club which has been purposely altered is regarded as new and must conform, in the altered state, to the Rules.

(g) Damage
If a player's club ceases to conform with Rule 4-1 because of damage sustained in the normal course of play, the player may:

    (i) Use the club in its damaged state, but only for the remainder of the stipulated round during which such damage was sustained; or

    (ii) Without unduly delaying play, repair it.

A club which ceases to conform because of damage sustained other than in the normal course of play shall not subsequently be used during the round.

(Damage changing playing characteristics of club – See Rule 4-2. Damage rendering club unfit for play – See Rule 4-4a.)

4-2 Playing Characteristics Changed
During a stipulated round, the playing characteristics of a club shall not be purposely changed by adjustment or any other means.

If the playing characteristics of a player's club are changed during a round because of damage sustained in the normal course of play, the player may:

    (i) Use the club in its altered state; or

    (ii) Without unduly delaying play, repair it.

If the playing characteristics of a player's club are changed because of damage sustained other than in the normal course of play, the club shall not subsequently be used during the round.

Damage to a club which occurred prior to a round may be repaired during the round, provided the playing characteristics are not changed and play is not unduly delayed.

4-3 Foreign Material
No foreign material shall be applied to the club face for the purpose of influencing the movement of the ball.
PENALTY FOR BREACH OF RULE 4-1, 4-2 or 4-3:
Disqualification.

4-4 Maximum of Fourteen Clubs
(a) Selection and Replacement of Clubs
The player shall start a <u>stipulated round</u> with no more than fourteen clubs. He is limited to the clubs thus selected for that round except that, without unduly delaying play, he may:

(i) If he started with fewer than fourteen, add as many as will bring his total to that number; and

(ii) Replace, with any club, a club which becomes unfit for play in the normal course of play.

The addition or replacement of a club or clubs may not be made by borrowing any club selected for play by any other person playing on the course.

(b) Partners May Share Clubs
Partners may share clubs, provided that the total number of clubs carried by the partners so sharing does not exceed fourteen.
PENALTY FOR BREACH OF RULE 4-4(a) or (b), REGARDLESS OF NUMBER OF EXCESS CLUBS CARRIED:
Match play – At the conclusion of the hole at which the breach is discovered, the state of the match shall be adjusted by deducting one hole for each hole at which a breach occurred. Maximum deduction per round: two holes.
Stroke play – Two strokes for each hole at which any breach occurred; maximum penalty per round: four strokes.
Bogey and par competitions – Penalties as in match play.
Stableford competitions – See Note to Rule 32-1(b).
(c) Excess Club Declared Out of Play
Any club carried or used in breach of this Rule shall be declared out of play by the player immediately upon discovery that a breach has occurred and thereafter shall not be used by the player during the round.
PENALTY FOR BREACH OF RULE 4-4(c):
Disqualification.

RULE 5

The Ball

5-1 General

The ball the player uses shall conform to agreed specifications of maximum weight, minimum size, spherical symmetry, initial velocity and overall distance when tested under specified conditions.

Note: In laying down the conditions under which a competition is to be played (Rule 33-1), the Committee may stipulate that the ball to be used shall be of certain specifications, and that it be of a size, brand and marking as detailed on the current List of Conforming Golf Balls issued by the Royal and Ancient Golf Club of St Andrews.

5-2 Foreign Material

No foreign material shall be applied to a ball for the purpose of changing its playing characteristics.

PENALTY FOR BREACH OF RULE 5-1 or 5-2:
Disqualification.

5-3 Ball Unfit for Play

A ball is unfit for play if it is visibly cut, cracked or out of shape. A ball is not unfit for play solely because mud or other materials adhere to it, its surface is scratched or scraped or its paint is damaged or discoloured.

If a player has reason to believe his ball has become unfit for play during play of the hole being played, he may during the play of such hole lift his ball without penalty to determine whether it is unfit, provided he announces his intention in advance to his opponent in match play or his marker or a fellow-competitor in stroke play and gives his opponent, marker or fellow-competitor an opportunity to examine the ball. If he lifts the ball without announcing his intention in advance or giving his opponent, marker or fellow-competitor an opportunity to examine the ball, *he shall incur a penalty of one stroke*.

If it is determined that the ball has become unfit for play during play of the hole being played, the player may substitute another ball, placing it on the spot where the original ball lay. Otherwise, the original ball shall be replaced.

If a ball breaks into pieces as a result of a stroke, the stroke shall be cancelled and the player shall play a ball without penalty as nearly as possible at the spot from which the original ball was played (see Rule 20-5).

*PENALTY FOR BREACH OF RULE 5-3:
Match play – Loss of hole; Stroke play – Two strokes.

If a player incurs the general penalty for breach of Rule 5-3, no additional penalty under the Rule shall be applied.

Note: If the opponent, marker or fellow-competitor wishes to dispute a claim of unfitness, he must do so before the player plays another ball.

(Cleaning ball lifted from putting green or under any other Rule – see Rule 21.)

RULE 6

The Player

Definition

A 'marker' is one who is appointed by the Committee to record a competitor's score in stroke play. He may be a fellow-competitor. He is not a referee.

6-1 Conditions of Competition

The player is responsible for knowing the conditions under which the competition is to be played (Rule 33-1).

6-2 Handicap

(a) **Match Play**

Before starting a match in a handicap competition, the players should determine from one another their respective handicaps. If a player begins the match having declared a higher handicap which would affect the number of strokes given or received, *he shall be disqualified*; otherwise, the player shall play off the declared handicap.

(b) **Stroke Play**

In any round of a handicap competition, the competitor shall ensure that his handicap is recorded on his scorecard before it is returned to the Committee. If no handicap is recorded on his scorecard before it is returned, or if the recorded handicap is higher than that to which he is entitled and this affects the number of strokes received, *he shall be disqualified* from that round of the handicap competition; otherwise, the score shall stand.

Note: It is the player's responsibility to know the holes at which handicap strokes are to be given or received.

6-3 Time of Starting and Groups

(a) **Time of Starting**

The player shall start at the time laid down by the Committee.

(*b*) **Groups**

In stroke play, the competitor shall remain throughout the round in the group arranged by the Committee unless the Committee authorises or ratifies a change.

PENALTY FOR BREACH OF RULE 6-3: *Disqualification*.

(Best-ball and four-ball play – See Rules 30-3(*a*) and 31-2.)

Note: The Committee may provide in the conditions of a competition (Rule 33-1) that, if the player arrives at his starting point, ready to play, within five minutes of his starting time, in the absence of circumstances which warrant waiving the penalty of disqualification as provided in Rule 33-7, the penalty for failure to start on time is *loss of the first hole in match play or two strokes at the first hole in stroke play* instead of disqualification.

6-4 Caddie

The player may have only one <u>caddie</u> at any one time, *under penalty of disqualification*.

For any breach of a Rule by his caddie, the player incurs the applicable penalty.

6-5 Ball

The responsibility for playing the proper ball rests with the player. Each player should put an identification mark on his ball.

6-6 Scoring in Stroke Play

(*a*) **Recording Scores**

After each hole the <u>marker</u> should check the score with the competitor and record it. On completion of the round the marker shall sign the card and hand it to the competitor. If more than one marker records the scores, each shall sign for the part for which he is responsible.

(*b*) **Signing and Returning Card**

After completion of the round, the competitor should check his score for each hole and settle any doubtful points with the Committee. He shall ensure that the marker has signed the card, countersign the card himself and return it to the Committee as soon as possible.

PENALTY FOR BREACH OF RULE 6-6(*b*): *Disqualification*.

(*c*) **Alteration of Card**

No alteration may be made on a card after the competitor has returned it to the Committee.

(*d*) **Wrong Score for Hole**

The competitor is responsible for the correctness of the score recorded for each hole. If he returns a score for any hole lower than actually taken, *he shall be disqualified*. If he returns a score for any hole higher than actually taken, the score as returned shall stand.

Note 1: The Committee is responsible for the addition of scores and application of the handicap recorded on the card – See Rule 33-5.
Note 2: In four-ball stroke play, see also Rule 31-4 and 31-7(*a*).

6-7 Undue Delay
The player shall play without undue delay. Between completion of a hole and playing from the next teeing ground, the player shall not unduly delay play.
PENALTY FOR BREACH OF RULE 6-7:
Match play – Loss of hole; Stroke play – Two strokes. For repeated offence – Disqualification. If a player unduly delays play between holes, he is delaying the play of the next hole and the penalty applies to that hole.

6-8 Discontinuance of Play
  (*a*) **When Permitted**
The player shall not discontinue play unless:
    (i) The Committee has suspended play;
    (ii) He believes there is danger from lightning;
    (iii) He is seeking a decision from the Committee on a doubtful or disputed point (see Rules 2-5 and 34-3); or
    (iv) There is some other good reason such as sudden illness.
    Bad weather is not of itself a good reason for discontinuing play.
    If the player discontinues play without specific permission from the Committee, he shall report to the Committee as soon as practicable. If he does so and the Committee considers his reason satisfactory, the player incurs no penalty. Otherwise, *the player shall be disqualified.*
    Exception in match play: Players discontinuing match play by agreement are not subject to disqualification unless by so doing the competition is delayed.
Note: Leaving the course does not of itself constitute discontinuance of play.
  (*b*) **Procedure When Play Suspended by Committee**
When play is suspended by the Committee, if the players in a match or group are between the play of two holes, they shall not resume play until the Committee has ordered a resumption of play. If they are in the process of playing a hole, they may continue provided they do so without delay. If they choose to continue, they shall discontinue either before or immediately after completing the hole, and shall not thereafter resume play until the Committee has ordered a resumption of play.
    When play has been suspended by the Committee, the player shall resume play when the Committee has ordered a resumption of play.
PENALTY FOR BREACH OF RULE 6-8(*b*): *Disqualification.*

(c) Lifting Ball When Play Discontinued

When during the play of a hole a player discontinues play under Rule 6-8(a), he may lift his ball. A ball may be cleaned when so lifted. If a ball has been so lifted, the player shall, when play is resumed, place a ball on the spot from which the original ball was lifted.

PENALTY FOR BREACH OF RULE 6-8(c):
Match play – Loss of hole; Stroke play – Two strokes.

RULE 7

Practice

7-1 Before or Between Rounds

(a) **Match Play**

On any day of a match play competition, a player may practise on the competition course before a round.

(b) **Stroke Play**

On any day of a stroke competition or play-off, a competitor shall not practise on the competition course or test the surface of any putting green on the course before a round or play-off. When two or more rounds of a stroke competition are to be played over consecutive days, practice between those rounds on any competition course remaining to be played is prohibited.

Exception: Practice putting or chipping on or near the first teeing ground before starting a round or play-off is permitted.

PENALTY FOR BREACH OF RULE 7-1(b): *Disqualification.*

Note: The Committee may in the conditions of a competition (Rule 33-1) prohibit practice on the competition course on any day of a match play competition or permit practice on the competition course or part of the course (Rule 33-2c) on any day of or between rounds of a stroke competition.

7-2 During Round

A player shall not play a practice stroke either during the play of a hole or between the play of two holes except that, between the play of two holes, the player may practise putting or chipping on or near the putting green of the hole last played, any practice putting green or the teeing ground of the next hole to be played in the round, provided such practice stroke is not played from a hazard and does not unduly delay play (Rule 6-7).

Exception: When play has been suspended by the Committee, a player may, prior to resumption of play, practise (a) as provided in this Rule, (b) anywhere other than on the competition course and (c) as otherwise permitted by the Committee.

PENALTY FOR BREACH OF RULE 7-2:

Match play – Loss of hole; Stroke play – Two strokes.

In the event of a breach between the play of two holes, the penalty applies to the next hole.

Note 1: A practice swing is not a practice stroke and may be taken at any place, provided the player does not breach the Rules.

Note 2: The Committee may prohibit practice on or near the putting green of the hole last played.

RULE 8

Advice; Indicating Line of Play

Definition

'Advice' is any counsel or suggestion which could influence a player in determining his play, the choice of a club or the method of making a stroke.

Information on the Rules or on matters of public information, such as the position of hazards or the flagstick on the putting green, is not advice.

The 'line of play' is the direction which the player wishes his ball to take after a stroke, plus a reasonable distance on either side of the intended direction. The line of play extends vertically upwards from the ground, but does not extend beyond the hole.

8-1 Advice

A player shall not give advice to anyone in the competition except his partner. A player may ask for advice from only his partner or either of their caddies.

8-2 Indicating Line of Play

(*a*) **Other Than on Putting Green**

Except on the putting green, a player may have the line of play indicated to him by anyone, but no one shall stand on or close to the line while the stroke is being played. Any mark placed during the play of a hole by the player or with his knowledge to indicate the line shall be removed before the stroke is played.

Exception: Flagstick attended or held up – See Rule 17-1.

(*b*) **On the Putting Green**

When the player's ball is on the putting green, the player, his partner or either of their caddies may, before but not during the stroke, point out a line for putting, but in so doing the putting green shall not be touched. No mark shall be placed anywhere to indicate a line for putting.

PENALTY FOR BREACH OF RULE:
Match play – Loss of hole; Stroke play – Two strokes.
Note: In a team competition with or without concurrent individual competition, the Committee may in the conditions of the competition (Rule 33-1) permit each team to appoint one person, e.g. team captain or coach, who may give <u>advice</u> (including pointing out a line for putting) to members of that team. Such person shall be identified to the Committee prior to the start of the competition.

RULE 9

Information as to Strokes Taken

9-1 General
The number of strokes a player has taken shall include any penalty strokes incurred.

9-2 Match Play
A player who has incurred a penalty shall inform his opponent as soon as practicable unless he is obviously proceeding under a rule involving a penalty and this has been observed by his opponent. If he fails to do so, he shall be deemed to have given wrong information, even if he was not aware that he had incurred a penalty.

An opponent is entitled to ascertain from the player, during the play of a hole, the number of strokes he has taken and, after play of a hole, the number of strokes taken on the hole just completed.

If during the play of a hole the player gives or is deemed to give wrong information as to the number of strokes taken, he shall incur no penalty if he corrects the mistake before his opponent has played his next stroke. If the player fails so to correct the wrong information, *he shall lose the hole*.

If after play of a hole the player gives or is deemed to give wrong information as to the number of strokes taken on the hole just completed and this affects the opponent's understanding of the result of the hole, he shall incur no penalty if he corrects his mistake before any player plays from the next <u>teeing ground</u> or, in the case of the last hole of the match, before all players leave the <u>putting green</u>. If the player fails so to correct the wrong information, *he shall lose the hole*.

9-3 Stroke Play
A competitor who has incurred a penalty should inform his marker as soon as practicable.

RULE 10

Order of Play

10.1 Match Play

(*a*) Teeing Ground

The side entitled to play first from the teeing ground is said to have the 'honour'.

The side which shall have the honour at the first teeing ground shall be determined by the order of the draw. In the absence of a draw, the honour should be decided by lot.

The side which wins a hole shall take the honour at the next teeing ground. If a hole has been halved, the side which had the honour at the previous teeing ground shall retain it.

(*b*) Other Than on Teeing Ground

When the balls are in play, the ball farther from the hole shall be played first. If the balls are equidistant from the hole, the ball to be played first should be decided by lot.

Exception: Rule 30-3(*c*) (best-ball and four-ball match play).

(*c*) Playing Out of Turn

If a player plays when his opponent should have played, the opponent may immediately require the player to cancel the stroke so played and play a ball in correct order, without penalty (See Rule 20-5).

10-2 Stroke Play

(*a*) Teeing Ground

The competitor entitled to play first from the teeing ground is said to have the 'honour'.

The competitor who shall have the honour at the first teeing ground shall be determined by the order of the draw. In the absence of a draw, the honour should be decided by lot.

The competitor with the lowest score at a hole shall take the honour at the next teeing ground. The competitor with the second lowest score shall play next and so on. If two or more competitors have the same score at a hole, they shall play from the next teeing ground in the same order as at the previous teeing ground.

(*b*) Other Than on Teeing Ground

When the balls are in play, the ball farthest from the hole shall be played first. If two or more balls are equidistant from the hole, the ball to be played first should be decided by lot.

Exceptions: Rules 22 (ball interfering with or assisting play) and 31-5 (four-ball stroke play).

(*c*) **Playing Out of Turn**

If a competitor plays out of turn, no penalty is incurred and the ball shall be played as it lies. If, however, the Committee determines that competitors have agreed to play in an order other than that set forth in Clauses 2(*a*) and 2(*b*) of this Rule to give one of them an advantage, *they shall be disqualified*.

(Incorrect order of play in threesomes and foursomes stroke play – See Rule 29-3.)

10-3 Provisional Ball or Second Ball from Teeing Ground

If a player plays a <u>provisional ball</u> or a second ball from a <u>teeing ground</u>, he should do so after his opponent or fellow-competitor has played his first <u>stroke</u>. If a player plays a provisional ball or a second ball out of turn, Clauses 1(*c*) and 2(*c*) of this Rule shall apply.

10-4 Ball Moved in Measuring

If a ball is moved in measuring to determine which ball is farther from the hole, no penalty is incurred and the ball shall be replaced.

RULE 11

Teeing Ground

Definition

The 'teeing ground' is the starting place for the hole to be played. It is a rectangular area two club-lengths in depth, the front and the sides of which are defined by the outside limits of two tee-markers. A ball is outside the teeing ground when all of it lies outside the teeing ground.

11-1 Teeing

In teeing, the ball may be placed on the ground, on an irregularity of surface created by the player on the ground or on a tee, sand or other substance in order to raise it off the ground.

A player may stand outside the <u>teeing ground</u> to play a ball within it.

11-2 Tee-Markers

Before a player plays his first stroke with any ball from the teeing ground of the hole being played, the tee-markers are deemed to be fixed. In such circumstances, if the player moves or allows to be moved a tee-marker for the purpose of avoiding interference with the stance, the area of his intended swing or his line of play, *he shall incur the penalty for a breach of Rule 13-2.*

11-3 Ball Falling off Tee

If a ball, when not in play, falls off a tee or is knocked off a tee by the player in addressing it, it may be re-teed without penalty, but if a stroke is made at the ball in these circumstances, whether the ball is moving or not, the stroke counts but no penalty shall be incurred.

11-4 Playing from Outside Teeing Ground

(*a*) **Match Play**

If a player, when starting a hole, plays a ball from outside the teeing ground, the opponent may immediately require the player to cancel the stroke so played and play a ball from within the teeing ground, without penalty.

(*b*) **Stroke Play**

If a competitor, when starting a hole, plays a ball from outside the teeing ground, *he shall incur a penalty of two strokes* and shall then play a ball from within the teeing ground.

If the competitor plays a stroke from the next teeing ground without first correcting his mistake or, in the case of the last hole of the round, leaves the putting green without first declaring his intention to correct his mistake, *he shall be disqualified*.

Strokes played by a competitor from outside the teeing ground do not count in his score.

11-5 Playing from Teeing Ground

The provisions of Rule 11-4 apply.

RULE 12

Searching for and Identifying Ball

Definitions

A 'hazard' is any bunker or water hazard.

A 'bunker' is a hazard consisting of a prepared area of ground, often a hollow, from which turf or soil has been removed and replaced with sand or the like. Grass-covered ground bordering or within a bunker is not part of the bunker. The margin of a bunker extends vertically downwards, but not upwards.

A 'water hazard' is any sea, lake, pond, river, ditch, surface drainage ditch or other open water course (whether or not containing water) and anything of a similar nature.

All ground or water within the margin of a water hazard is part of the water hazard. The margin of a water hazard extends vertically upwards and downwards. Stakes and lines defining the margins of water hazards are in the hazards.

12-1 Searching for Ball; Seeing Ball

In searching for his ball anywhere on the course, the player may touch or bend long grass, rushes, bushes, whins, heather or the like, but only to the extent necessary to find and identify it, provided that this does not improve the lie of the ball, the area of his intended swing or his line of play.

A player is not necessarily entitled to see his ball when playing a stroke.

In a hazard, if a ball is covered by loose impediments or sand, the player may remove by probing, raking or other means as much thereof as will enable him to see a part of the ball. If an excess is removed, no penalty is incurred and the ball shall be re-covered so that only a part of the ball is visible. If the ball is moved in such removal, no penalty is incurred; the ball shall be replaced and, if necessary, re-covered. As to removal of loose impediments outside a hazard, see Rule 23.

If a ball lying in casual water, ground under repair or a hole, cast or runway made by a burrowing animal, a reptile or a bird is accidentally moved during search, no penalty is incurred; the ball shall be replaced, unless the player elects to proceed under Rule 25-1(*b*).

If a ball is believed to be lying in water in a water hazard, the player may probe for it with a club or otherwise. If the ball is moved in so doing, no penalty is incurred; the ball shall be replaced, unless the player elects to proceed under Rule 26-1.

PENALTY FOR BREACH OF RULE 12-1:
Match play – Loss of hole; Stroke play – Two strokes.

12-2 Identifying Ball

The responsibility for playing the proper ball rests with the player. Each player should put an indentification mark on his ball.

Except in a hazard, the player may, without penalty, lift a ball he believes to be his own for the purpose of identification and clean it to the extent necessary for identification. If the ball is the player's ball, he shall replace it. Before the player lifts the ball, he shall announce his intention to his opponent in match play or his marker or a fellow-competitor in stroke play and mark the position of the ball. He must then give his opponent, marker or fellow-competitor an opportunity to observe the lifting and replacement. If he lifts the ball without announcing his intention in advance, marking the position of the ball or giving his opponent, marker or fellow-competitor an opportunity to observe, or if he lifts his ball for identification in a hazard or cleans it more than necessary for identification *he shall incur a penalty of one stroke* and the ball shall be replaced.

If a player who is required to replace a ball fails to do so, *he shall incur the penalty* for a breach of Rule 20-3(*a*), but no additional penalty under Rule 12-2 shall be applied.

RULE 13

Ball Played As it Lies; Lie, Area of Intended Swing and Line of Play; Stance

Definitions
A 'hazard' is any bunker or water hazard.

A 'bunker' is a hazard consisting of a prepared area of ground, often a hollow, from which turf or soil has been removed and replaced with sand or the like. Grass-covered ground bordering or within a bunker is not part of the bunker.

A 'water hazard' is any sea, lake, pond, river, ditch, surface drainage ditch or other open water course (whether or not containing water) and anything of a similar nature.

All ground or water within the margin of a water hazard is part of the water hazard. The margin of a water hazard is deemed to extend vertically upwards and downwards. Stakes and lines defining the margins of water hazards are in the hazards.

The 'line of play' is the direction which the player wishes his ball to take after a stroke, plus a reasonable distance on either side of the intended direction. The line of play extends vertically upwards from the ground, but does not extend beyond the hole.

13-1 Ball Played As It Lies
The ball shall be played as it lies, except as otherwise provided in the Rules. (Ball at rest moved – See Rule 18.)

13-2 Improving Lie, Area of Intended Swing or Line of Play
Except as provided in the Rules, a player shall not improve or allow to be improved:

   the position or lie of his ball,
   the area of his intended swing,
   his line of play, or a reasonable extension of that line beyond the hole or
   the area in which he is to drop or place a ball

by any of the following actions:

moving, bending or breaking anything growing or fixed (including immovable obstructions and objects defining out of bounds), or

removing or pressing down sand, loose soil, replaced divots, other cut turf placed in position or other irregularities of surface

except as follows:

as may occur in fairly taking his stance,

in making a stroke or the backward movement of his club for a stroke,

on the teeing ground in creating or eliminating irregularities of surface, or

on the putting green in removing sand and loose soil as provided in Rule 16-1(*a*) or in repairing damage as provided in Rule 16-1(*c*).

The club may be grounded only lightly and shall not be pressed on the ground.

Exception: Ball lying in or touching hazard – SeeRule 13-4.

13-3 Building Stance

A player is entitled to place his feet firmly in taking his stance, but he shall not build a stance.

13-4 Ball Lying in or Touching Hazard

Except as provided in the Rules, before making a stroke at a ball which lies in or touches a hazard (whether a bunker or a water hazard), the player shall not:

(*a*) Test the condition of the hazard or any similar hazard;

(*b*) Touch the ground in the hazard or water in the water hazard with a club or otherwise; or

(*c*) Touch or move a loose impediment lying in or touching the hazard.

Exceptions:

1. Provided nothing is done which constitutes testing the condition of the hazard or improves the lie of the ball, there is no penalty if the player (a) touches the ground in any hazard or water in a water hazard as a result of or to prevent falling, in removing an obstruction, in measuring or in retrieving or lifting a ball under any Rule or (b) places his club in a hazard.

2. The player after playing the stroke, or his caddie at any time without the authority of the player, may smooth sand or soil in the hazard, provided that, if the ball still lies in the hazard, nothing is done which improves the lie of the ball or assists the player in his subsequent play of the hole.

Note: At any time, including at address or in the backward movement for the stroke, the player may touch with a club or otherwise any obstruction, any construction declared by the Committee to be an integral part of the course or any grass, bush, tree or other growing thing.

PENALTY FOR BREACH OF RULE:
Match play – Loss of hole; Stroke play – two strokes.
(Searching for ball – See Rule 12-1.)

RULE 14

Striking the Ball

Definition
A 'stroke' is the forward movement of the club made with the intention of fairly striking at and moving the ball, but if a player checks his downswing voluntarily before the clubhead reaches the ball he is deemed not to have made a stroke.

14-1 Ball to be Fairly Struck At
The ball shall be fairly struck at with the head of the club and must not be pushed, scraped or spooned.

14-2 Assistance
In making a stroke, a player shall not accept physical assistance or protection from the elements.
PENALTY FOR BREACH OF RULE 14-1 or 14-2:
Match play – Loss of hole; Stroke play – Two strokes.

14-3 Artificial Devices and Unusual Equipment
If there may be any reasonable basis for doubt as to whether an item which is to be manufactured would, if used by a player during a round, cause the player to be in breach of Rule 14-3, the manufacturer should submit a sample to the Royal and Ancient Golf Club of St Andrews for a ruling, such sample to become its property for reference purposes. If a manufacturer fails to do so, he assumes the risk of an unfavourable ruling.

A player in doubt as to whether use of an item would constitute a breach of Rule 14-3 should consult the Royal and Ancient Golf Club of St Andrews.

Except as provided in the Rules, during a stipulated round the player shall not use any artificial device or unusual equipment:
  (*a*) Which might assist him in making a stroke or in his play; or

(*b*) For the purpose of gauging or measuring distance or conditions which might affect his play; or

(*c*) Which might assist him in gripping the club, except that plain gloves may be worn, resin, tape or gauze may be applied to the grip (provided such application does not render the grip non-conforming under Rule 4-1(*c*) and a towel or handkerchief may be wrapped around the grip.

PENALTY FOR BREACH OF RULE 14-3: *Disqualification*.

14-4 Striking the Ball More than Once
If a player's club strikes the ball more than once in the course of a stroke, the player shall count the stroke and *add a penalty stroke*, making two strokes in all.

14-5 Playing Moving Ball
A player shall not play while his ball is moving.
Exceptions:
Ball falling off tee – Rule 11-3.
Striking the ball more than once – Rule 14-4.
Ball moving in water – Rule 14-6.

When the ball begins to move only after the player has begun the stroke or the backward movement of his club for the stroke, he shall incur no penalty under this Rule for playing a moving ball, but he is not exempt from any penalty incurred under the following Rules:
Ball at rest moved by player – Rule 18-2(*a*).
Ball at rest moving after address – Rule 18-2(*b*)
Ball at rest moving after loose impediment touched – Rule 18-2(*c*).

14-6 Ball Moving in Water
When a ball is moving in water in a water hazard, the player may, without penalty, make a stroke, but he must not delay making his stroke in order to allow the wind or current to improve the position of the ball. A ball moving in water in a water hazard may be lifted if the player elects to invoke Rule 26.

PENALTY FOR BREACH OF RULE 14-5 or 14-6:
Match play – Loss of hole; Stroke play – Two strokes.

RULE 15

Playing a Wrong Ball

Definition
A 'wrong ball' is any ball other than:

(*a*) The ball in play;

(*b*) A provisional ball; or

(*c*) In stroke play, a second ball played under Rule 3-3 or Rule 20-7(*b*).

Note: Ball in play includes a ball substituted for the ball in play when the player is proceeding under an applicable Rule which does not permit substitution.

15-1 General

A player must hole out with the ball played from the teeing ground unless a Rule permits him to substitute another ball. If a player substitutes another ball when proceeding under an applicable Rule which does not permit substitution, that ball is not a wrong ball; it becomes the ball in play and, if the error is not corrected as provided in Rule 20-6, *the player shall incur a penalty of loss of hole in match play or two strokes in stroke play*.

15-2 Match Play

If a player plays a stroke with a wrong ball except in a hazard, *he shall lose the hole*.

If a player plays any strokes in a hazard with a wrong ball, there is no penalty. Strokes played in a hazard with a wrong ball do not count in the player's score. If the wrong ball belongs to another player, its owner shall replace a ball on the spot from which the wrong ball was first played.

If the player and opponent exchange balls during the play of a hole, the first to play the wrong ball other than from a hazard shall lose the hole; when this cannot be determined, the hole shall be played out with the balls exchanged.

15-3 Stroke Play

If a competitor plays a stroke or strokes with a wrong ball, *he shall incur a penalty of two strokes*, unless the only stroke or strokes played with such ball were played when it was lying in a hazard, in which case no penalty is incurred.

The competitor must correct his mistake by playing the correct ball. If he fails to correct his mistake before he plays a stroke from the next teeing ground or, in the case of the last hole of the round, fails to declare his intention to correct his mistake before leaving the putting green, *he shall be disqualified*.

Strokes played by a competitor with a wrong ball do not count in his score.

If the wrong ball belongs to another competitor, its owner shall place a ball on the spot from which the wrong ball was first played.

(Lie of ball to be placed or replaced altered – see Rule 20-3*b*.)

RULE 16

The Putting Green

Definitions

The 'putting green' is all ground of the hole being played which is specially prepared for putting or otherwise defined as such by the Committee. A ball is on the putting green when any part of it touches the putting green.

The 'line of putt' is the line which the player wishes his ball to take after a stroke on the putting green. Except with respect to Rule 16-1(*e*), the line of putt includes a reasonable distance on either side of the intended line. The line of putt does not extend beyond the hole.

A ball is 'holed' when it is at rest within the circumference of the hole and all of it is below the level of the lip of the hole.

16-1 General

(*a*) **Touching Line of Putt**

The line of putt must not be touched except:

(i) The player may move sand, loose soil and other loose impediments by picking them up or by brushing them aside with his hand or a club without pressing anything down;

(ii) In addressing the ball, the player may place the club in front of the ball without pressing anything down;

(iii) In measuring – Rule 10-4;

(iv) In lifting the ball – Rule 16-1(*b*);

(v) In pressing down a ball-marker;

(vi) In repairing old hole plugs or ball marks on the putting green – Rule 16-1(*c*), and

(vii) In removing movable obstructions – Rule 24-1.

(Indicating line for putting on putting green – See Rule 8-2*b*.)

(*b*) **Lifting Ball**

A ball on the putting green may be lifted and, if desired, cleaned. A ball so lifted shall be replaced on the spot from which it was lifted.

(*c*) **Repair of Hole Plugs, Ball Marks and Other Damage**

The player may repair an old hole plug or damage to the putting green caused by the impact of a ball, whether or not the player's ball lies on the putting green. If the ball is moved in the process of such repair, it shall be replaced, without penalty. Any other damage to the putting green shall not be repaired if it might assist the player in his subsequent play of the hole.

(*d*) **Testing Surface**

During the play of a hole, a player shall not test the surface of the putting green by rolling a ball or roughening or scraping the surface.

(*e*) **Standing Astride or on Line of Putt**

The player shall not make a stroke on the putting green from a stance astride, or with either foot touching, the line of the putt or an extension of that line behind the ball.

(*f*) **Position of Caddie or Partner**

While making a stroke on the putting green, the player shall not allow his caddie, his partner or his partner's caddie to position himself on or close to an extension of the line of putt behind the ball.

(*g*) **Playing Stroke While Another Ball in Motion**

A player shall not play a stroke while another ball is in motion after a stroke from the putting green except that, if a player does so, he incurs no penalty if it was his turn to play.

(Lifting ball interfering with or assisting play while another ball in motion – See Rule 22.)

PENALTY FOR BREACH OF RULE 16-1:

Match play – Loss of hole; Stroke play – Two strokes.

16.2 Ball Overhanging Hole

When any part of the ball overhangs the lip of the hole, the player is allowed enough time to reach the hole without unreasonable delay and an additional ten seconds to determine whether the ball is at rest. If by then the ball has not fallen into the hole, it is deemed to be at rest. If the ball subsequently falls into the hole, the player is deemed to have holed out with his last stroke, and *he shall add a penalty stroke to his score* for the hole; otherwise there is no penalty under this Rule.

(Undue delay – see Rule 6-7.)

RULE 17

The Flagstick

17-1 Flagstick Attending, Removed or Held Up

Before and during the stroke, the player may have the flagstick attended, removed or held up to indicate the position of the hole. This may be done only on the authority of the player before he plays his stroke.

If, prior to the stroke, the flagstick is attended, removed or held up by anyone with the player's knowledge and no objection is made, the player shall be deemed to have authorised it. If anyone attends or holds up the flagstick or stands near the hole while a stroke is being played, he shall be deemed to be attending the flagstick until the ball comes to rest.

17-2 Unauthorised Attendance
(*a*) Match Play
In match play, an opponent or his caddie shall not attend, remove or hold up the flagstick without the player's knowledge or authority while the player is making a stroke or his ball is in motion.
(*b*) Stroke Play
In stroke play, if a fellow-competitor or his caddie attends, removes or holds up the flagstick without the competitor's knowledge or authority while the competitor is making a stroke or his ball is in motion, *the fellow-competitor shall incur the penalty* for breach of this Rule. In such circumstances, if the competitor's ball strikes the flagstick, the person attending it or anything carried by him, the competitor incurs no penalty and the ball shall be played as it lies, except that, if the stroke was played from the putting green, the stroke shall be cancelled, the ball replaced and the stroke replayed.
PENALTY FOR BREACH OF RULE 17-1 or 17-2:
Match play – Loss of hole; Stroke play – Two strokes.

17-3 Ball Striking Flagstick or Attendant
The player's ball shall not strike:
    (*a*) The flagstick when attended, removed or held up by the player, his partner or either of their caddies, or by another person with the player's knowledge or authority; or
    (*b*) The player's caddie, his partner or his partner's caddie when attending the flagstick, or another person attending the flagstick with the player's knowledge or authority, or anything carried by any such person; or
    (*c*) The flagstick in the hole, unattended, when the ball has been played from the <u>putting green</u>.
PENALTY FOR BREACH OF RULE 17-3:
Match play – Loss of hole; Stroke play – Two strokes, and the ball shall be played as it lies.

17-4 Ball Resting Against Flagstick
If the ball rests against the flagstick when it is in the hole, the player or another person authorised by him may move or remove the flagstick and if the ball falls into the hole, the player shall be deemed to have holed

out with his last stroke; otherwise the ball, if <u>moved</u>, shall be placed on the lip of the hole, without penalty.

RULE 18

Ball at Rest Moved

Definitions
A ball is deemed to have 'moved' if it leaves its position and comes to rest in any other place.

An 'outside agency' is any agency not part of the match or, in stroke play, not part of a competitor's side, and includes a referee, a marker, an observer or a forecaddie. Neither wind nor water is an outside agency.

'Equipment' is anything used, worn or carried by or for the player except any ball he has played at the hole being played and any small object, such as a coin or a tee, when used to mark the position of a ball or the extent of an area in which a ball is to be dropped. Equipment includes a golf cart, whether or not motorised. If such a cart is shared by two or more players, the cart and everything in it are deemed to be the equipment of the player whose ball is involved except that, when the cart is being moved by one of the players sharing it, the cart and everything in it are deemed to be that player's equipment.
Note: A ball played at the hole being played is equipment when it has been lifted and not put back into play.

A player has 'addressed the ball' when he has taken his <u>stance</u> and has also grounded his club, except that in a <u>hazard</u> a player has addressed the ball when he has taken his stance.

Taking his 'stance' consists in a player placing his feet in position for and preparatory to making a stroke.

18-1 By Outside Agency
If a ball at rest is moved by an <u>outside agency</u>, the player shall incur no penalty and the ball shall be <u>replaced</u> before the player plays another <u>stroke</u>.

(Player's ball at rest moved by another ball – See Rule 18-5.)

18-2 By Player, Partner, Caddie or Equipment
  (*a*) **General**
When a player's ball is <u>in play</u>, if:
   (i) The player, his partner or either of their caddies lifts or moves it, touches it purposely (except with a club in the act of addressing it) or causes it to move except as permitted by a Rule; or

(ii) Equipment of the player or his partner causes the ball to move; *the player shall incur a penalty stroke*. The ball shall be replaced unless the movement of the ball occurs after the player has begun his swing and he does not discontinue his swing.

Under the Rules no penalty is incurred if a player accidentally causes his ball to move in the following circumstances:

In measuring to determine which ball farther from hole – Rule 10-4;
In searching for covered ball in hazard or for ball in casual water, ground under repair, etc. – Rule 12-1;
In the process of repairing hole plug or ball mark – Rule 16-1(*c*);
In the process of removing loose impediment on putting green – Rule 18-2(*c*)
In the process of lifting ball under a Rule – Rule 20-1
In the process of placing or replacing ball under a Rule – Rule 20-3(*a*)
In complying with Rule 22 relating to lifting ball interfering with or assisting play
In removal of movable obstruction – Rule 24-1.

(*b*) **Ball Moving After Address**

If a player's ball in play moves after the player has addressed it (other than as a result of a stroke), the player shall be deemed to have moved the ball and *shall incur a penalty stroke*. The player shall replace the ball unless the movement of the ball occurs after he has begun his swing and he does not discontinue his swing.

(*c*) **Ball Moving After Loose Impediment Touched**

Through the green, if the ball moves after any loose impediment lying within a club-length of it has been touched by the player, his partner or either of their caddies, and before the player has addressed it, the player shall be deemed to have moved the ball and *shall incur a penalty stroke*. The player shall replace the ball unless the movement of the ball occurs after he has begun his swing and he does not discontinue his swing.

On the putting green, if the ball or the ball-marker moves in the process of removing any loose impediment, the ball or the ball-marker shall be replaced. There is no penalty provided the movement of the ball or the ball-marker is directly attributable to the removal of the loose impediment. Otherwise, *the player shall incur a penalty stroke* under Rule 18.2(*a*) or 20-1.

18-3 By Opponent, Caddie or Equipment in Match Play

(*a*) **During Search**

If, during search for a player's ball, it is moved by an opponent, his caddie or his equipment, no penalty is incurred and the player shall replace the ball.

(*b*) **Other Than During Search**

If, other than during search for a ball, the ball is touched or moved by an opponent, his caddie or his <u>equipment</u>, except as otherwise provided in the Rules, *the opponent shall incur a penalty stroke*. The player shall replace the ball.

(Ball moved in measuring to determine which ball farther from the hole – See Rule 10-4.)

(Playing a wrong ball – See Rule 15-2.)

(Ball moved in complying with Rule 22 relating to lifting ball interfering with or assisting play.)

18-4 By Fellow-Competitor, Caddie or Equipment in Stroke Play
If a competitor's ball is moved by a fellow-competitor, his caddie or his <u>equipment</u>, no penalty is incurred. The competitor shall replace his ball.

(Playing a wrong ball – See Rule 15-3.)

18-5 By Another Ball
If a ball in play and at rest is moved by another ball in motion after a stroke, the moved ball shall be replaced.

*PENALTY FOR BREACH OF RULE:
Match play – Loss of hole; Stroke play – Two strokes.

  * If a player who is required to replace a ball fails to do so, he shall incur the general penalty for breach of Rule 18 but no additional penalty under Rule 18 shall be applied.*
Note 1: If a ball to be replaced under this Rule is not immediately recoverable, another ball may be substituted.
Note 2: If it is impossible to determine the spot on which a ball is to be placed, see Rule 20-3(*c*).

RULE 19

Ball in Motion Deflected or Stopped

Definitions
An 'outside agency' is any agency not part of the match or, in stroke play, not part of a competitor's side, and includes a referee, a marker, an observer or a forecaddie. Neither wind nor water is an outside agency.

'Equipment' is anything used, worn or carried by or for the player except any ball he has played at the hole being played and any small object, such as a coin or a tee, when used to mark the position of a ball or the extent of an area in which a ball is to be dropped. Equipment includes a golf cart, whether or not motorised. If such a cart is shared by two or more players, the cart and everything in it are deemed to be the equipment of the player whose ball is involved except that, when the cart is being moved by one of the players sharing it, the cart and everything in it are deemed to be that player's equipment.

Note: A ball played at the hole being played is equipment when it has been lifted and not put back into play.

19-1 By Outside Agency
If a ball in motion is accidentally deflected or stopped by any outside agency, it is a rub of the green, no penalty is incurred and the ball shall be played as it lies except:

(*a*) If a ball in motion after a stroke other than on the putting green comes to rest in or on any moving or animate outside agency, the player shall, through the green or in a hazard, drop the ball, or on the putting green place the ball, as near as possible to the spot where the outside agency was when the ball came to rest in or on it; and

(*b*) If a ball in motion after a stroke on the putting green is deflected or stopped by, or comes to rest in or on, any moving or animate outside agency except a worm or an insect, the stroke shall be cancelled, the ball replaced and the stroke replayed.

If the ball is not immediately recoverable, another ball may be substituted.

(Player's ball deflected or stopped by another ball – See Rule 19-5.)

Note: If the referee or the Committee determines that a competitor's ball has been deliberately deflected or stopped by an outside agency, Rule 1-4 applies to the competitor. If the outside agency is a fellow-competitor or his caddie, Rule 1-2 applies to the fellow-competitor.

19-2 By Player, Partner, Caddie or Equipment
(*a*) **Match Play**
If a player's ball is accidentally deflected or stopped by himself, his partner or either of their caddies or equipment, *he shall lose the hole*.

(*b*) **Stroke Play**
If a competitor's ball is accidentally deflected or stopped by himself, his partner or either of their caddies or equipment, *the competitor shall incur a penalty of two strokes*. The ball shall be played as it lies, except when it comes to rest in or on the competitor's, his partner's or either of their caddies' clothes or equipment, in which case the competitor shall through the green or in a hazard drop the ball, or on the putting green place the ball, as near as possible to where the article was when the ball came to rest in or on it.

Exception: Dropped Ball – See Rule 20-2(*a*).

(Ball purposely deflected or stopped by player, partner or caddie – See Rule 1-2.)

19-3 By Opponent, Caddie or Equipment in Match Play
If a player's ball is accidentally deflected or stopped by an opponent, his

caddie or his <u>equipment</u>, no penalty is incurred. The player may play the ball as it lies or, before another <u>stroke</u> is played by either side, cancel the stroke and play a ball without penalty as nearly as possible at the spot from which the original ball was last played (see Rule 20-5).

If the ball has come to rest in or on the opponent's or his caddie's clothes or equipment, the player may <u>through the green</u> or in a <u>hazard</u> drop the ball, or on the putting green place the ball, as near as possible to where the article was when the ball came to rest in or on it.

Exception: Ball striking person attending flagstick – See Rule 17-3(*b*).

(Ball purposely deflected or stopped by opponent or caddie – See Rule 1-2.)

19-4 By Fellow-Competitor, Caddie or Equipment in Stroke Play
See Rule 19-1 regarding ball deflected by outside agency.

19.5 By Another Ball
If a player's ball in motion after a stroke is deflected or stopped by a ball at rest, the player shall play his ball as it lies. In stroke play, if both balls lay on the <u>putting green</u> prior to the stroke, *the player incurs a penalty of two strokes*. Otherwise, no penalty is incurred.

If a player's ball in motion after a stroke is deflected or stopped by another ball in motion, the player shall play his ball as it lies. There is no penalty unless the player was in breach of Rule 16-1(*g*), in which case *he shall incur the penalty for breach of that Rule*.

Exception: Ball in motion after a stroke on the putting green deflected or stopped by moving or animate outside agency – See Rule 19-1(*b*).

PENALTY FOR BREACH OF RULE

Match play – Loss of hole; Stroke play – Two strokes.

RULE 20

Lifting, Dropping and Placing; Playing from Wrong Place

20-1 Lifting
A ball to be lifted under the Rules may be lifted by the player, his partner or another person authorised by the player. In any such case, the player shall be responsible for any breach of the Rules.

The position of the ball shall be marked before it is lifted under a Rule which requires it to be replaced. If it is not marked, *the player shall incur a penalty of one stroke* and the ball shall be replaced. If it is not replaced, *the player shall incur the general penalty* for breach of this Rule but no additional penalty under Rule 20-1 shall be applied.

If a ball or ball-marker is accidentally moved in the process of lifting the ball under a Rule or marking its position, the ball or the ball-marker shall be replaced. There is no penalty provided the movement of the ball or the ball-marker is directly attributable to the specific act of marking the position of or lifting the ball. Otherwise, *the player shall incur a penalty stroke* under this Rule or Rule 18-2(*a*).

Exception: If a player incurs a penalty for failing to act in accordance with Rule 5-3 or 12-2, no additional penalty under Rule 20-1 shall be applied.

Note: The position of a ball to be lifted should be marked by placing a ball-marker, a small coin or other similar object immediately behind the ball. If the ball-marker interferes with the play, stance or stroke of another player, it should be placed one or more clubhead-lengths to one side.

20-2 Dropping and Re-dropping

(*a*) **By Whom and How**

A ball to be dropped under the rules shall be dropped by the player himself. He shall stand erect, hold the ball at shoulder height and arm's length and drop it. If a ball is dropped by any other person or in any other manner and the error is not corrected as provided by Rule 20-6, *the player shall incur a penalty stroke*.

If the ball touches the player, his partner, either of their caddies or their equipment before or after it strikes a part of the course, the ball shall be re-dropped, without penalty. There is no limit to the number of times a ball shall be re-dropped in such circumstances.

(Taking action to influence position or movement of ball – See Rule 1-2.)

(*b*) **Where to Drop**

When a ball is to be dropped as near as possible to a specific spot, it shall be dropped not nearer the hole than the specific spot which, if it is not precisely known to the player, shall be estimated.

A ball when dropped must first strike a part of the course where the applicable Rule requires it to be dropped. If it is not so dropped, Rules 20-6 and 20-7 apply.

(*c*) **When to Re-Drop**

A dropped ball shall be re-dropped without penalty if it:

   (i) Rolls into a hazard;
  (ii) Rolls out of a hazard;
 (iii) Rolls on to a putting green;
 (iv) Rolls out of bounds;

(v) Rolls to a position where there is interference by the condition from which relief was taken under Rule 24-2 (immovable obstruction) or Rule 25-1 (abnormal ground condition);

(vi) Rolls and comes to rest more than two club-lengths from where it first struck a part of the course;

(vii) Rolls and comes to rest nearer the hole than its original position or estimated position (see Rule 20-2*b*) unless otherwise permitted by the Rules.

If the ball when re-dropped rolls into any position listed above, it shall be placed as near as possible to the spot where it first struck a part of the course when re-dropped.

If a ball to be re-dropped or placed under this Rule is not immediately recoverable, another ball may be substituted.

20-3 Placing and Replacing
(*a*) By Whom and Where
A ball to be placed under the Rules shall be placed by the player or his partner. If a ball is to be replaced, the player, his partner or the person who lifted or moved it shall place it on the spot from which it was lifted or moved. In any such case, the player shall be responsible for any breach of the Rules.

If a ball or the ball-marker is accidentally moved in the process of placing or replacing the ball, the ball or the ball-marker shall be replaced. There is no penalty provided the movement of the ball or the ball-marker is directly attributable to the specific act of placing or replacing the ball or removing the ball-marker. Otherwise, *the player shall incur a penalty stroke* under Rule 18-2(*a*) or 20-1.

(*b*) Lie of Ball to Be Placed or Replaced Altered
If the original lie of a ball to be placed or replaced has been altered:

(i) Except in a hazard, the ball shall be placed in the nearest lie most similar to the original lie which is not more than one club-length from the original lie, not nearer the hole and not in a hazard;

(ii) In a water hazard, the ball shall be placed in accordance with Clause (i) above, except that the ball must be placed in the water hazard;

(iii) In a bunker, the original lie shall be recreated as nearly as possible and the ball shall be placed in that lie.

(*c*) Spot Not Determinable
If it is impossible to determine the spot where the ball is to be placed or replaced:

(i) Through the green, the ball shall be dropped as near as possible to the place where it lay but not in a hazard;

(ii) In a hazard, the ball shall be dropped in the hazard as near as possible to the place where it lay;

(iii) On the <u>putting green</u>, the ball shall be placed as near as possible to the place where it lay but not in a hazard.

(*d*) **Ball Fails to Remain on Spot**

If a ball when placed fails to remain on the spot on which it was placed, it shall be replaced without penalty. If it still fails to remain on that spot:

(i) Except in a <u>hazard</u>, it shall be placed at the nearest spot not nearer the hole or in a hazard where it can be placed at rest;

(ii) In a hazard, it shall be placed in the hazard at the nearest spot not nearer the hole where it can be placed at rest.

PENALTY FOR BREACH OF RULE 20-1, 20-2 or 20-3:
Match play – Loss of hole; Stroke play – Two strokes.

20-4 When Ball Dropped or Placed Is in Play

If the player's <u>ball in play</u> has been lifted, it is again in play when dropped or placed.

A substituted ball becomes the ball in play if it is dropped or placed under an applicable Rule, whether or not such Rule permits substitution. A ball substituted under an inapplicable Rule is a <u>wrong ball</u>.

20-5 Playing Next Stroke from Where Previous Stroke Played

When, under the Rules, a player elects or is required to play his next <u>stroke</u> from where a previous stroke was played, he shall proceed as follows:

If the stroke is to be played from the <u>teeing ground</u>, the ball to be played shall be played from anywhere within the teeing ground and may be teed;

If the stroke is to be played from <u>through the green</u> or a <u>hazard</u>, it shall be dropped;

If the stroke is to be played on the <u>putting green</u>, it shall be placed.

PENALTY FOR BREACH OF RULE 20-5:
Match play – Loss of hole; Stroke play – Two strokes.

20-6 Lifting Ball Wrongly Dropped or Placed

A ball dropped or placed in a wrong place or otherwise not in accordance with the Rules but not played may be lifted, without penalty, and the player shall then proceed correctly.

20-7 Playing from Wrong Place

For a ball played from outside the teeing ground or from a wrong teeing ground, see Rules 11-4 and 11-5.

(*a*) **Match Play**

If a player plays a stroke with a ball which has been dropped or placed in a wrong place, *he shall lose the hole.*

(*b*) **Stroke Play**

If a competitor plays a stroke with:

(i) His original ball which has been dropped or placed in a wrong place;

(ii) A substituted ball which has been dropped or placed under an applicable Rule but in a wrong place; or

(iii) His ball in play when it has been moved and not replaced in a case where the Rules require replacement,

he shall, provided a serious breach has not occurred, *incur the penalty prescribed by the applicable Rule* and play out the hole with the ball.

If, after playing from a wrong place, a competitor becomes aware of that fact and believes that a serious breach may be involved, he may, provided he has not played a stroke from the next teeing ground or, in the case of the last hole of the round, left the putting green, declare that he will play out the hole with a second ball dropped or placed in accordance with the Rules. The competitor shall report the facts to the Committee before returning his score card; if he fails to do so, *he shall be disqualified*. The Committee shall determine whether a serious breach of the Rule occurred. If so, the score with the second ball shall count and *the competitor shall add two penalty strokes to his score with that ball*.

If a serious breach has occurred and the competitor has failed to correct it as prescribed above, *he shall be disqualified*.

Note: If a competitor plays a second ball, penalty strokes incurred by playing the ball ruled not to count and strokes subsequently taken with that ball shall be disregarded.

RULE 21

Cleaning Ball

A ball on the putting green may be cleaned when lifted under Rule 16-1(*b*). Elsewhere, a ball may be cleaned when lifted except when it has been lifted:

(*a*) To determine if it is unfit for play (Rule 5-3);

(*b*) For identification (Rule 12-2), in which case it may be cleaned only to the extent necessary for identification; or

(*c*) Because it is interfering with or assisting play (Rule 22).

If a player cleans his ball during play of a hole except as provided in this Rule, *he shall incur a penalty of one stroke* and the ball, if lifted, shall be replaced.

If a player who is required to replace a ball fails to do so, *he shall incur the penalty* for breach of Rule 20-3(*a*), but no additional penalty under Rule 21 shall be applied.

Exception: If a player incurs a penalty for failing to act in accordance with Rule 5-3, 12-2 or 22, no additional penalty under Rule 21 shall be applied.

RULE 22

Ball Interfering with or Assisting Play

Any player may:
   (*a*) Lift his ball if he considers that the ball might assist any other player; or
   (*b*) Have any other ball lifted if he considers that the ball might interfere with his play or assist the play of any other player, but this may not be done while another ball is in motion. In stroke play, a player required to lift his ball may play first rather than lift. A ball lifted under this Rule shall be replaced.
   If a ball is accidentally moved in complying with this Rule, no penalty is incurred and the ball shall be replaced.
PENALTY FOR BREACH OF RULE:
Match play – Loss of hole; Stroke play – Two strokes.
Note: Except on the putting green, the ball may not be cleaned when lifted under this Rule – see Rule 21.

RULE 23

Loose Impediments

Definition
'Loose impediments' are natural objects such as stones, leaves, twigs, branches and the like, dung, worms and insects and casts or heaps made by them, provided they are not fixed or growing, are not solidly embedded and do not adhere to the ball.
   Sand and loose soil are loose impediments on the putting green but not elsewhere.
   Snow and natural ice other than frost are either casual water or loose impediments, at the option of the player, except that manufactured ice is an obstruction.
   Dew and frost are not loose impediments.

23-1 Relief
Except when both the loose impediment and the ball lie in or touch a

hazard, any loose impediment may be removed without penalty. If the ball moves, see Rule 18-2(c).

When a player's ball is in motion, a loose impediment which might influence the movement of the ball shall not be removed.

PENALTY FOR BREACH OF RULE:

Match play – Loss of hole; Stroke play – Two strokes.

(Searching for ball in hazard – See Rule 12-1.)

(Touching line of putt – See Rule 16-1a.)

RULE 24

Obstructions

Definition

An 'obstruction' is anything artificial, including the artificial surfaces and sides of roads and paths and manufactured ice except:

(a) Objects defining out of bounds, such as walls, fences, stakes and railings;

(b) Any part of an immovable artificial object which is out of bounds; and

(c) Any construction declared by the Committee to be an integral part of the course.

24.1 Movable Obstruction

A player may obtain relief from a movable obstruction as follows:

(a) If the ball does not lie in or on the obstruction, the obstruction may be removed. If the ball moves, it shall be replaced, and there is no penalty provided that the movement of the ball is directly attributable to the removal of the obstruction. Otherwise, Rule 18-2(a) applies.

(b) If the ball lies in or on the obstruction, the ball may be lifted, without penalty, and the obstruction removed. The ball shall through the green or in a hazard be dropped, or on the putting green be placed, as near as possible to the spot directly under the place where the ball lay in or on the obstruction, but not nearer the hole.

The ball may be cleaned when lifted under Rule 24-1.

When a ball is in motion, an obstruction which might influence the movement of the ball other than an attended flagstick or equipment of the players shall not be removed.

24-2 Immovable Obstruction

(a) **Interference**

Interference by an immovable obstruction occurs when a ball lies in or on the obstruction, or so close to the obstruction that the obstruction interferes with the player's stance or the area of his intended swing. If the player's ball lies on the putting green, interference also occurs if an immovable obstruction on the putting green intervenes on his line of putt. Otherwise, intervention on the line of play is not, of itself, interference under this Rule.

(*b*) **Relief**

Except when the ball lies in or touches a water hazard or a lateral water hazard, a player may obtain relief from interference by an immovable obstruction, without penalty, as follows:

(i) **Through the Green:** If the ball lies through the green, the point on the course nearest to where the ball lies shall be determined (without crossing over, through or under the obstruction) which (*a*) is not nearer the hole, (*b*) avoids interference (as defined) and (*c*) is not in a hazard or on a putting green. The player shall lift the ball and drop it within one club-length of the point thus determined on ground which fulfils (*a*), (*b*) and (*c*) above.

Note: The prohibition against crossing over, through or under the obstruction does not apply to the artificial surfaces and sides of roads and paths or when the ball lies in or on the obstruction.

(ii) **In a Bunker:** If the ball lies in or touches a bunker, the player shall lift and drop the ball in accordance with Clause (i) above, except that the ball must be dropped in the bunker.

(iii) **On the Putting Green:** If the ball lies on the putting green, the player shall lift the ball and place it in the nearest position to where it lay which affords relief from interference, but not nearer the hole nor in a hazard.

The ball may be cleaned when lifted under Rule 24-2(*b*).

(Ball rolling to a position where there is interference by the condition from which relief was taken – See Rule 20-2(*c*)(v).)

Exception: A player may not obtain relief under Rule 24-2(*b*) if (*a*) it is clearly unreasonable for him to play a stroke because of interference by anything other than an immovable obstruction or (*b*) interference by an immovable obstruction would occur only through use of an unnecessarily abnormal stance, swing or direction of play.

Note: If a ball lies in or touches a water hazard (including a lateral water hazard), the player is not entitled to relief without penalty from interference by an immovable obstruction. The player shall play the ball as it lies or proceed under Rule 26-1.

(*c*) **Ball Lost**

Except in a water hazard or a lateral water hazard, if there is reasonable evidence that a ball is lost in an immovable obstruction, the player may, without penalty, substitute another ball and follow the procedure prescribed in Rule 24-2(*b*). For the purpose of applying this Rule, the ball shall be deemed to lie at the spot where it entered the obstruction. If the ball is lost in an underground drain pipe or culvert the entrance to which is in a hazard, a ball must be dropped in that hazard or the player may proceed under Rule 26-1, if applicable.

PENALTY FOR BREACH OF RULE:
Match play – Loss of hole; Stroke play – Two strokes.

RULE 25

Abnormal Ground Conditions and Wrong Putting Green

Definitions

'Casual water' is any temporary accumulation of water on the course which is visible before or after the player takes his stance and is not a water hazard. Snow and natural ice other than frost are either casual water or loose impediments, at the option of the player, except that manufactured ice is an obstruction. Dew and frost are not casual water.

'Ground under repair' is any portion of the course so marked by order of the Committee or so declared by its authorised representative. It includes material piled for removal and a hole made by a greenkeeper, even if not so marked. Stakes and lines defining ground under repair are in such ground. The margin of ground under repair extends vertically downwards, but not upwards.

Note 1: Grass cuttings and other material left on the course which have been abandoned and are not intended to be removed are not ground under repair unless so marked.

Note 2: The Committee may make a Local Rule prohibiting play from ground under repair.

25.1 Casual Water, Ground Under Repair and Certain Damage to Course

(*a*) **Interference**

Interference by casual water, ground under repair or a hole, cast or runway made by a burrowing animal, a reptile or a bird occurs when a ball lies in or touches any of these conditions or when such a condition on the course interferes with the player's stance or the area of his intended swing.

If the player's ball lies on the putting green, interference also occurs if such a condition on the putting green intervenes on his line of putt.

If interference exists, the player may either play the ball as it lies (unless prohibited by Local Rule) or take relief as provided in Clause (*b*).

(*b*) **Relief**

If the player elects to take relief, he shall proceed as follows:

(i) **Through the Green:** If the ball lies through the green, the point on the course nearest to where the ball lies shall be determined which (*a*) is not nearer the hole, (*b*) avoids interference by the condition, and (*c*) is not in a hazard or on a putting green. The player shall lift the ball and drop it without penalty within one club-length of the point thus determined on ground which fulfils (*a*), (*b*), and (*c*) above.

(ii) **In a Hazard:** If the ball lies in or touches a hazard, the player shall lift and drop the ball either:

(*a*) Without penalty, in the hazard, as near as possible to the spot where the ball lay, but not nearer the hole, on ground which affords maximum available relief from the condition; or

(*b*) *Under penalty of one stroke*, outside the hazard, keeping the point where the ball lay directly between the hole and the spot on which the ball is dropped.

Exception: If a ball lies in or touches a water hazard (including a lateral water hazard), the player is not entitled to relief without penalty from a hole, cast or runway made by a burrowing animal, a reptile or a bird. The player shall play the ball as it lies or proceed under Rule 26-1.

(iii) **On the Putting Green:** If the ball lies on the putting green, the player shall lift the ball and place it without penalty in the nearest position to where it lay which affords maximum available relief from the condition, but not nearer the hole nor in a hazard.

The ball may be cleaned when lifted under Rule 25-1(*b*).

(Ball rolling to a position where there is interference by the condition from which relief was taken – See Rule 20-2(*c*)(v).)

Exception: A player may not obtain relief under Rule 25-1(*b*) if (*a*) it is clearly unreasonable for him to play a stroke because of interference by anything other than a condition covered by Rule 25-1(*a*), or (*b*) interference by such a condition would occur only through use of an unnecessarily abnormal stance, swing or direction of play.

(*c*) **Ball Lost Under Condition Covered by Rule 25-1**

It is a question of fact whether a ball lost after having been struck toward a condition covered by Rule 25-1 is lost under such condition. In order to treat the ball as lost under such condition, there must be reasonable evidence to that effect. In the absence of such evidence, the ball must be treated as a lost ball and Rule 27 applies.

(i) **Outside a Hazard** – If a ball is lost outside a hazard under a condition covered by Rule 25-1, the player may take relief as follows: the point on the course nearest to where the ball last crossed the margin of the area shall be determined which (*a*) is not nearer the hole than where the ball last crossed the margin, (*b*) avoids interference by the condition, and (*c*) is not in a hazard or on a putting green. He shall drop a ball without penalty within one club-length of the point thus determined on ground which fulfils (*a*), (*b*) and (*c*) above.

(ii) **In a Hazard** – If a ball is lost in a <u>hazard</u> under a condition covered by Rule 25-1, the player may drop a <u>ball</u> either:

(*a*) Without penalty, in the hazard as near as possible to the point at which the original ball last crossed the margin of the area, but not nearer the hole, on ground which affords maximum available relief from the condition;

or

(*b*) *Under penalty of one stroke*, outside the hazard, keeping the point at which the original ball last crossed the margin of the hazard directly between the hole and the spot on which the ball is dropped.

Exception: If a ball lies in a <u>water hazard</u> (including a <u>lateral water hazard</u>), the player is not entitled to relief without penalty for a ball lost in a hole, cast or runway made by a burrowing animal, a reptile or a bird. The player shall proceed under Rule 26-1.

25-2 Embedded Ball
A ball embedded in its own pitch-mark in the ground in any closely mown area <u>through the green</u> may be lifted, cleaned and dropped, without penalty, as near as possible to the spot where it lay but not nearer the hole. 'Closely mown area' means any area of the <u>course</u>, including paths through the rough, cut to fairway height or less.

25-3 Wrong Putting Green
A player must not play a ball which lies on a <u>putting green</u> other than that of the hole being played. The ball must be lifted and the player must proceed as follows: the point on the course nearest to where the ball lies shall be determined which (*a*) is not nearer the hole and (*b*) is not in a <u>hazard</u> or on a putting green. The player shall lift the ball and drop it without penalty within one club-length of the point thus determined on ground which fulfils (*a*) and (*b*) above. The ball may be cleaned when so lifted.

Note: Unless otherwise prescribed by the Committee, the term 'a putting green other than that of the hole being played' includes a practice putting green or pitching green on the course.

RULE 26

Water Hazards (including Lateral Water Hazards)

Definitions
A 'water hazard' is any sea, lake, pond, river, ditch, surface drainage

ditch or other open water course (whether or not containing water) and anything of a similar nature.

All ground or water within the margin of a water hazard is part of the water hazard. The margin of a water hazard extends vertically upwards and downwards. Stakes and lines defining the margins of water hazards are in the hazards.

Note: Water hazards (other than lateral water hazards) should be defined by yellow stakes or lines.

A 'lateral water hazard' is a water hazard or that part of a water hazard so situated that it is not possible or is deemed by the Committee to be impracticable to drop a ball behind the water hazard in accordance with Rule 26-1(*b*).

That part of a water hazard to be played as a lateral water hazard should be distinctively marked.

Note: Lateral water hazards should be defined by red stakes or lines.

26-1 Ball in Water Hazard

It is a question of fact whether a ball lost after having been struck toward a water hazard is lost inside or outside the hazard. In order to treat the ball as lost in the hazard, there must be reasonable evidence that the ball lodged in it. In the absence of such evidence, the ball must be treated as a lost ball and Rule 27 applies.

If a ball lies in, touches or is lost in a water hazard (whether the ball lies in water or not), the player may *under penalty of one stroke*:

(*a*) Play a ball as nearly as possible at the spot from which the original ball was last played (see Rule 20-5); or

(*b*) Drop a ball behind the water hazard, keeping the point at which the original ball last crossed the margin of the water hazard directly between the hole and the spot on which the ball is dropped, with no limit as to how far behind the water hazard the ball may be dropped; or

(*c*) *As additional options available only if the ball lies in, touches or is lost in a lateral water hazard*, drop a ball outside the water hazard within two club-lengths of (i) the point where the original ball last crossed the margin of the water hazard, or (ii) a point on the opposite margin of the water hazard equidistant from the hole. The ball must be dropped and come to rest not nearer the hole than the point where the original ball last crossed the margin of the water hazard.

The ball may be cleaned when lifted under this Rule.

(Ball moving in water in a water hazard – see Rule 14-6.)

26-2 Ball Played Within Water Hazard
(*a*) Ball comes to Rest in Hazard

If a ball played from within a water hazard comes to rest in the hazard after the stroke, the player may:

(i) proceed under Rule 26-1; or

(ii) *under penalty of one stroke*, play a ball as nearly as possible at the spot from which the last stroke from outside the hazard was played (see Rule 20-5).

If the player proceeds under Rule 26-1(*a*), he may elect not to play the dropped ball. If he so elects, he may:

(*a*) proceed under Rule 26-1(*b*), adding the additional penalty of one stroke prescribed by that Rule; or

(*b*) proceed under Rule 26-1(*c*), if applicable, *adding the additional penalty of one stroke* prescribed by that Rule; or

(*c*) *add an additional penalty of one stroke* and play a ball as nearly as possible at the spot from which the last stroke from outside the hazard was played (see Rule 20-5).

(*b*) **Ball Lost or Unplayable Outside Hazard or Out of Bounds**

If a ball played from within the water hazard is lost or declared unplayable outside the hazard or is out of bounds, the player, after taking *a penalty of one stroke* under Rule 27-1 or 28(*a*), may:

(i) play a ball as nearly as possible at the spot in the hazard from which the original ball was last played by him (see Rule 20-5); or

(ii) *under an additional penalty of one stroke*, proceed under Rule 26-1(*b*) or, if applicable, Rule 26-1(*c*), using as the reference point the point where the original ball last crossed the margin of the hazard before it came to rest in the hazard; or

(iii) *under an additional penalty of one stroke*, play his next stroke as nearly as possible at the spot from which the last stroke from outside the hazard was played (see Rule 20-5).

Note 1: When proceeding under Rule 26-2(*b*), the player is not required to drop a ball under Rule 27-1 or 28(*a*). If he does drop a ball, he is not required to play it. He may alternatively proceed under Clause (ii) or (iii).

Note 2: If a ball played from within a water hazard is declared unplayable outside the hazard, nothing in Rule 26-2(*b*) precludes the player from proceeding under Rule 28(*b*) or (*c*).

PENALTY FOR BREACH OF RULE:

Match play – Loss of hole; Stroke play – Two strokes.

RULE 27

Ball Lost or Out of Bounds; Provisional Ball

If the original ball is lost in an immovable obstruction (Rule 24-2) or under a condition covered by Rule 25-1 (casual water, ground under repair and certain damage to the course), the player may proceed under the applicable Rule. If the original ball is lost in a water hazard, the player shall proceed under Rule 26.

Such Rules may not be used unless there is reasonable evidence that the ball is lost in an immovable obstruction, under a condition covered by Rule 25-1 or in a water hazard.

Definitions
A ball is 'lost' if:

(*a*) It is not found or identified as his by the player within five minutes after the player's side or his or their caddies have begun to search for it; or

(*b*) The player has put another ball into play under the Rules, even though he may not have searched for the original ball; or

(*c*) The player has played any stroke with provisional ball from the place where the original ball is likely to be or from a point nearer the hole than that place, whereupon the provisional ball becomes the ball in play.

Time spent in playing a wrong ball is not counted in the five-minute period allowed for search.

'Out of bounds' is ground on which play is prohibited.

When out of bounds is defined by reference to stakes or a fence, or as being beyond stakes or a fence, the out of bounds line is determined by the nearest inside points of the stakes or fence posts at ground level excluding angled supports.

When out of bounds is defined by a line on the ground, the line itself is out of bounds.

The out of bounds line extends vertically upwards and downwards.

A ball is out of bounds when all of it lies out of bounds.

A player may stand out of bounds to play a ball lying within bounds.

A 'provisional ball' is a ball played under Rule 27-2 for a ball which may be lost outside a water hazard or may be out of bounds.

27-1 Ball Lost or Out of Bounds
If a ball is lost outside a water hazard or is out of bounds, the player shall play a ball, *under penalty of one stroke*, as nearly as possible at the spot from which the original ball was last played (see Rule 20-5).
PENALTY FOR BREACH OF RULE 27-1:
Match play – Loss of hole; Stroke play – Two strokes.

27.2 Provisional Ball
(*a*) **Procedure**
If a ball may be lost outside a water hazard or may be out of bounds, to

save time the player may play another ball provisionally as nearly as possible at the spot from which the original ball was played (see Rule 20-5). The player shall inform his opponent in match play or his marker or a fellow competitor in stroke play that he intends to play a <u>provisional ball</u>, and he shall play it before he or his partner goes forward to search for the original ball. If he fails to do so and plays another ball, such ball is not a provisional ball and becomes the <u>ball in play</u> *under penalty of stroke and distance* (Rule 27-1); the original ball is deemed to be lost.

(*b*) **When Provisional Ball Becomes Ball in Play**

The player may play a provisional ball until he reaches the place where the original ball is likely to be. If he plays a stroke with the provisional ball from the place where the original ball is likely to be or from a point nearer the hole than that place, the original ball is deemed to be <u>lost</u> and the provisional ball becomes the ball in play under *penalty of stroke and distance* (Rule 27-1).

If the original ball is lost outside a water hazard or is out of bounds, the provisional ball becomes the ball in play, *under penalty of stroke and distance* (Rule 27-1).

(*c*) **When Provisional Ball to Be Abandoned**

If the original ball is neither lost outside a water hazard nor out of bounds, the player shall abandon the provisional ball and continue play with the original ball. If he fails to do so, any further strokes played with the provisional ball shall constitute playing a <u>wrong ball</u> and the provisions of Rule 15 shall apply.

Note: If the original ball lies in a water hazard, the player shall play the ball as it lies or proceed under Rule 26. If it is lost in a water hazard or unplayable, the player shall proceed under Rule 26 or 28, whichever is applicable.

RULE 28

Ball Unplayable

The player may declare his ball unplayable at any place on the course except when the ball lies in or touches a <u>water hazard</u>. The player is the sole judge as to whether his ball is unplayable.

If the player deems his ball to be unplayable, he shall, *under penalty of one stroke*:

(*a*) Play a ball as nearly as possible at the spot from which the original ball was last played (see Rule 20-5); or (*b*) Drop a ball within two club-lengths of the spot where the ball lay, but not nearer the hole; or

(*c*) Drop a ball behind the point where the ball lay, keeping that point directly between the hole and the spot on which the ball is dropped, with no limit to how far behind that point the ball may be dropped.

If the unplayable ball lies in a bunker, the player may proceed under Clause (*a*), (*b*) or (*c*). If he elects to proceed under Clause (*b*) or (*c*), a ball must be dropped in the bunker.

The ball may be cleaned when lifted under this Rule.

PENALTY FOR BREACH OF RULE:
Match play – Loss of hole; Stroke play – Two strokes.

RULE 29

Threesomes and Foursomes

Definitions

Threesome: A match in which one plays against two, and each side plays one ball.

Foursome: A match in which two play against two, and each side plays one ball.

29-1 General

In a threesome or a foursome, during any stipulated round the partners shall play alternately from the teeing grounds and alternately during the play of each hole. Penalty strokes do not affect the order of play.

29-2 Match Play

If a player plays when his partner should have played, *his side shall lose the hole.*

29-3 Stroke Play

If the partners play a stroke or strokes in incorrect order, such stroke or strokes shall be cancelled and *the side shall incur a penalty of two strokes.* The side shall correct the error by playing a ball in correct order as nearly as possible at the spot from which it was first played in incorrect order (see Rule 20-5). If the side plays a stroke from the next teeing ground without first correcting the error or, in the case of the last hole of the round, leaves the putting green without declaring its intention to correct the error, *the side shall be disqualified.*

RULE 30

Three-Ball, Best-Ball and Four-Ball Match Play

Definitions

Three-Ball: A match play competition in which three play against one another, each playing his own ball. Each player is playing two distinct matches.

Best-Ball: A match in which one plays against the better ball of two or the best ball of three players.

Four-Ball: A match in which two play their better ball against the better ball of two other players.

30-1 Rules of Golf Apply

The Rules of Golf, so far as they are not at variance with the following special Rules, shall apply to three-ball, best-ball and four-ball matches.

30-2 Three-Ball Match Play

(*a*) **Ball at Rest Moved by an Opponent**

Except as otherwise provided in the Rules, if the player's ball is touched or moved by an opponent, his caddie or equipment other than during search, Rule 18-3(*b*) applies. *That opponent shall incur a penalty stroke in his match with the player*, but not in his match with the other opponent.

(*b*) **Ball Deflected or Stopped by an Opponent Accidentally**

If a player's ball is accidentally deflected or stopped by an opponent, his caddie or equipment, no penalty shall be incurred. In his match with that opponent the player may play the ball as it lies or, before another stroke is played by either side, he may cancel the stroke and play a ball without penalty as nearly as possible at the spot from which the original ball was last played (see Rule 20-5). In his match with the other opponent, the ball shall be played as it lies.

Exception: Ball striking person attending flagstick – see Rule 17-3(*b*).

(Ball purposely deflected or stopped by opponent – see Rule 1-2.)

30-3 Best-Ball and Four-Ball Match Play

(*a*) **Representation of Side**

A side may be represented by one partner for all or any part of a match; all partners need not be present. An absent partner may join a match between holes, but not during play of a hole.

(*b*) **Maximum of Fourteen Clubs**

The side shall be penalised for a breach of Rule 4-4 by any partner.

(*c*) **Order of Play**

Balls belonging to the same side may be played in the order the side considers best.

(*d*) **Wrong Ball**

If a player plays a stroke with a wrong ball except in a hazard, *he shall be disqualified for that hole*, but his partner incurs no penalty even if the wrong ball belongs to him. If the wrong ball belongs to another player, its owner shall place a ball on the spot from which the wrong ball was first played.

(*e*) **Disqualification of Side**

 (i) *A side shall be disqualified* for a breach of any of the following by any partner:

Rule 1-3	Agreement to Waive Rules.
Rule 4-1, -2 or -3	Clubs.
Rule 5-1 or -2	The Ball.
Rule 6-2(*a*)	Handicap (playing off higher handicap).
Rule 6-4	Caddie.
Rule 6-7	Undue Delay (repeated offence).
Rule 14-3	Artificial Devices and Unusual Equipment.

(ii) *A side shall be disqualified* for a breach of any of the following by all partners:

Rule 6-3	Time of Starting and Groups.
Rule 6-8	Discontinuance of Play.

(*f*) **Effect of Other Penalties**

If a player's breach of a Rule assists his partner's play or adversely affects an opponent's play, *the partner incurs the applicable penalty in addition to any penalty incurred by the player*.

In all other cases where a player incurs a penalty for breach of a Rule, the penalty shall not apply to his partner. Where the penalty is stated to be loss of hole, the effect shall be to disqualify the player for that hole.

(*g*) **Another Form of Match Played Concurrently**

In a best-ball or four-ball match when another form of match is played concurrently, the above special Rules shall apply.

RULE 31

Four-Ball Stroke Play

In four-ball stroke play two competitors play as partners, each playing his own ball. The lower score of the partners is the score for the hole. If one partner fails to complete the play of a hole, there is no penalty.

31-1 Rules of Golf Apply
The Rules of Golf, so far as they are not at variance with the following special Rules, shall apply to four-ball stroke play.

31-2 Representation of Side
A side may be represented by either partner for all or any part of a stipulated round; both partners need not be present. An absent competitor may join his partner between holes, but not during play of a hole.

31-3 Maximum of Fourteen Clubs
The side shall be penalised for a breach of Rule 4-4 by either partner.

31-4 Scoring
The marker is required to record for each hole only the gross score of whichever partner's score is to count. The gross scores to count must be individually identifiable; otherwise *the side shall be disqualified.* Only one of the partners need be responsible for complying with Rule 6-6(*b*).
    (Wrong score – See Rule 31-7*a*.)

31-5 Order of Play
Balls belonging to the same side may be played in the order the side considers best.

31-6 Wrong Ball
If a competitor plays a stroke with a wrong ball except in a hazard, *he shall add two penalty strokes to his score for the hole* and shall then play the correct ball. His partner incurs no penalty even if the wrong ball belongs to him.
    If the wrong ball belongs to another competitor, its owner shall place a ball on the spot from which the wrong ball was first played.

31-7 Disqualification Penalties
(*a*) Breach by One Partner
A side shall be disqualified from the competition for a breach of any of the following by either partner:

Rule 1-3	Agreement to Waive Rules.
Rule 3-4	Refusal to Comply with Rule.
Rule 4-1, 4-2 or 4-3	Clubs.
Rule 5-1 or 5-2	The Ball.
Rule 6-2(*b*)	Handicap (playing off higher handicap; failure to record handicap).
Rule 6-4	Caddie.

Rule 6-6(*b*)	Signing and Returning Card.
Rule 6-6(*d*)	Wrong Score for Hole, i.e. when the recorded score of the partner whose score is to count is lower than actually taken. If the recorded score of the partner whose score is to count is higher than actually taken, it must stand as returned.
Rule 6-7	Undue Delay (repeated offence).
Rule 7-1	Practice Before or Between Rounds.
Rule 14-3	Artificial Devices and Unusual Equipment.
Rule 31-4	Gross Scores to count Not Individually Identifiable.

(*b*) **Breach by Both Partners**

A side shall be disqualified:

(i) For a breach by both partners of Rule 6-3 (Time of Starting and Groups) or Rule 6-8 (Discontinuance of Play); or

(ii) If, at the same hole, each partner is in breach of a Rule the penalty for which is disqualification from the competition or for a hole.

(*c*) **For the Hole Only**

In all other cases where a breach of a Rule would entail disqualification, *the competitor shall be disqualified only for the hole at which the breach occurred*.

31-8 Effect of Other Penalties

If a competitor's breach of a Rule assists his partner's play, *the partner incurs the applicable penalty in addition to any penalty incurred by the competitor*.

In all other cases where a competitor incurs a penalty for breach of a Rule, the penalty shall not apply to his partner.

RULE 32

Bogey, Par and Stableford Competitions

32-1 Conditions

Bogey, par and Stableford competitions are forms of stroke competition in which play is against a fixed score at each hole. The Rules for stroke play, so far as they are not at variance with the following special Rules, apply.

(*a*) **Bogey and Par Competitions**

The reckoning for bogey and par competitions is made as in match play. Any hole for which a competitor makes no return shall be regarded as a loss. The winner is the competitor who is most successful in the aggregate of holes.

The marker is responsible for marking only the gross number of strokes for each hole where the competitor makes a net score equal to or less than the fixed score.

Note: Maximum of fourteen Clubs – Penalties as in match play – see Rule 4-4.

(*b*) **Stableford Competitions**

The reckoning in Stableford competitions is made by points awarded in relation to a fixed score at each hole as follows:

Holes Played in	*Points*
More than one over fixed score or no score returned	0
One over fixed score	1
Fixed score	2
One under fixed score	3
Two under fixed score	4
Three under fixed score	5
Four under fixed score	6

The winner is the competitor who scores the highest number of points.

The marker shall be responsible for marking only the gross number of strokes at each hole where the competitor's net score earns one or more points.

Note: Maximum of fourteen Clubs (Rule 4-4) – Penalties applied as follows: From total points scored for the round, deduction of two points for each hole at which any breach occurred; maximum deduction per round: four points.

32-2 Disqualification Penalties

(*a*) **From the Competition**

A competitor shall be disqualified from the competition for a breach of any of the following:

Rule 1-3	Agreement to Waive Rules.
Rule 3-4	Refusal to Comply with Rule.
Rule 4-1, 4-2 or 4-3	Clubs.
Rule 5-1 or 5-2	The Ball.
Rule 6-2(*b*)	Handicap (playing off higher handicap; failure to record handicap).
Rule 6-3	Time of Starting and Groups.
Rule 6-4	Caddie.
Rule 6-6(*b*)	Signing and Returning Card.
Rule 6-6(*d*)	Wrong Score for Hole, except that no penalty shall be incurred when a breach of this Rule does not affect the result of the hole.

Rule 6-7	Undue Delay (repeated offence).
Rule 6-8	Discontinuance of Play.
Rule 7-1	Practice Before or Between Rounds.
Rule 14-3	Artificial Devices and Unusual Equipment.

(*b*) **For a Hole**

In all other cases where a breach of a Rule would entail disqualification, *the competitor shall be disqualified only for the hole at which the breach occurred.*

RULE 33

The Committee

33-1 Conditions; Waiving Rule

The Committee shall lay down the conditions under which a competition is to be played.

The Committee has no power to waive a Rule of Golf.

Certain special rules governing stroke play are so substantially different from those governing match play that combining the two forms of play is not practicable and is not permitted. The results of matches played and the scores returned in these circumstances shall not be accepted.

In stroke play the Committee may limit a referee's duties.

33.2 The Course

(*a*) **Defining Bounds and Margins**

The Committee shall define accurately:
  (i) the course and out of bounds,
  (ii) the margins of water hazards and lateral water hazards,
  (iii) ground under repair, and
  (iv) obstruction and integral parts of the course.

(*b*) **New Holes**

New holes should be made on the day on which a stroke competition begins and at such other times as the Committee considers necessary, provided all competitors in a single round play with each hole cut in the same position.

Exception: When it is impossible for a damaged hole to be repaired so that it conforms with the Definition, the Committee may make a new hole in a nearby similar position.

(*c*) **Practice Ground**

Where there is no practice ground available outside the area of a competition course, the Committee should lay down the area on which players may practise on any day of a competition, if it is practicable to do so. On any day of a stroke competition, the Committee should not normally permit practice on or to a <u>putting green</u> or from a <u>hazard</u> of the competition course.

(*d*) **Course Unplayable**

If the Committee or its authorised representative considers that for any reason the course is not in a playable condition or that there are circumstances which render the proper playing of the game impossible, it may, in match play or stroke play, order a temporary suspension of play or, in stroke play, declare play null and void and cancel all scores for the round in question. When play has been temporarily suspended, it shall be resumed from where it was discontinued, even though resumption occurs on a subsequent day. When a round is cancelled, all penalties incurred in that round are cancelled.

(Procedure in discontinuing play – Rule 6-8.)

33-3 Times of Starting and Groups

The Committee shall lay down the times of starting and, in stroke play, arrange the groups in which competitors shall play.

When a match play competition is played over an extended period, the Committee shall lay down the limit of time within which each round shall be completed. When players are allowed to arrange the date of their match within these limits, the Committee should announce that the match must be played at a stated time on the last day of the period unless the players agree to a prior date.

33-4 Handicap Stroke Table

The Committee shall publish a table indicating the order of holes at which handicap strokes are to be given or received.

33-5 Score Card

In stroke play, the Committee shall issue for each competitor a scorecard containing the date and the competitor's name or, in foursome or four-ball stroke play, the competitors' names.

In stroke play, the Committee is responsible for the addition of scores and application of the handicap recorded on the card.

In four-ball stroke play, the Committee is responsible for recording the better-ball score for each hole and in the process applying the handicaps recorded on the card, and adding the better-ball scores.

In bogey, par and Stableford competitions, the Committee is responsible for applying the handicap recorded on the card and determining the results of each hole and the overall result or points total.

33-6 Decision of Ties

The Committee shall announce the manner, day and time for the decision of a halved match or of a tie, whether played on level terms or under handicap.

A halved match shall not be decided by stroke play. A tie in stroke play shall not be decided by a match.

33-7 Disqualification Penalty; Committee Discretion
A penalty of disqualification may in exceptional individual cases be waived, modified or imposed if the Committee considers such action warranted.

Any penalty less than disqualification shall not be waived or modified.

33-8 Local Rules
(a) Policy
The Committee may make and publish Local Rules for abnormal conditions if they are consistent with the policy of the Governing Authority for the country concerned as set forth in Appendix I to these Rules.

(b) Waiving Penalty
A penalty imposed by a Rule of Golf shall not be waived by a Local Rule.

RULE 34

Disputes and Decisions

34-1 Claims and Penalties
(a) Match Play
In match play if a claim is lodged with the Committee under Rule 2-5, a decision should be given as soon as possible so that the state of the match may, if necessary, be adjusted.

If a claim is not made within the time limit provided by Rule 2-5, it shall not be considered unless it is based on facts previously unknown to the player making the claim and the player making the claim had been given wrong information (Rules 6-2a and 9) by an opponent. In any case, no later claim shall be considered after the result of the match has been officially announced, unless the Committee is satisfied that the opponent knew he was giving wrong information.

(b) Stroke Play
In stroke play no penalty shall be rescinded, modified or imposed after the competition has closed, except that a penalty of disqualification shall be imposed at any time after the competition has closed if a competitor:
(i) Returned a score for any hole lower than actually taken (Rule 6-

6*d*) for any reason other than failure to include a penalty which he did not know he had incurred; or

(ii) Returned a scorecard on which he had recorded a handicap which he knew was higher than that to which he was entitled, and this affected the number of strokes received (Rule 6-2*b*); or

(iii) was in breach of Rule 1-3.

A competition is deemed to have closed when the result has been officially announced or, in stroke play qualifying followed by match play, when the player has teed off in his first match.

34-2 Referee's Decision

If a referee has been appointed by the Committee, his decision shall be final.

34-3. Committee's Decision

In the absence of a referee, the players shall refer any dispute to the Committee, whose decision shall be final.

If the Committee cannot come to a decision, it shall refer the dispute or doubtful point to the Rules of Golf Committee of the Royal and Ancient Golf Club of St Andrews, whose decision shall be final.

If the point in doubt or dispute has not been referred to the Rules of Golf Committee, the player or players have the right to refer an agreed statement through the Secretary of the Club to the Rules of Golf Committee for an opinion as to the correctness of the decision given. The reply will be sent to the Secretary of the Club or Clubs concerned.

If play is conducted other than in accordance with the Rules of Golf, the Rules of Golf Committee will not give a decision on any question.

Reprinted by permission of the Royal and Ancient Golf Club of St Andrews and the United States Golf Association, by whom these Rules have been approved. The complete Rules of Golf (The Royal and Ancient Golf Club of St Andrews) includes Appendixes dealing in some detail with 'Local Rules', 'Design of Clubs' and 'The Ball', plus 'Rules of Amateur Status'. For reasons of space those Appendixes have been omitted. Copies of the complete Rules of Golf, including those Appendixes, can be obtained from the Royal and Ancient Golf Club of St Andrews.

Handball

The Playing Area

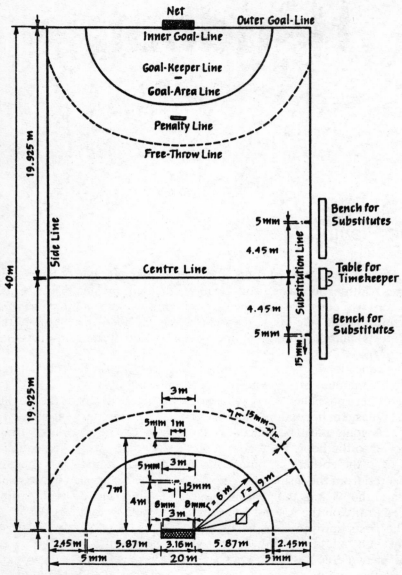

All lines 5mm wide

Handball

RULE 1

The Playing Area

1.1 The playing area (the court) shall be rectangular, 40m in length and 20m in width. The playing court shall be divided, by means of a centre line, into two equal halves. The longer boundary lines of the court shall be known as the side lines; and the shorter, the goal-line (between the goal-posts) and the outer goal-line, on either side of the goal-posts (see diagram).

The condition of the playing court must never, at any time, be altered in such a manner as to favour one of the playing teams.

Note: Where possible a safety zone should be included outside the playing area at least 1m beyond the side-lines and 2m behind the goal-lines.

1.2 The goals must be placed in the centre of the goal-line, firmly attached to the floor. Each goal consists of two upright posts, equidistant from the corners of the playing area, 3m apart and 2m in height, measured from the inside of the goal-posts. The outer edge of the goal-line and the back of the goal-post shall be in line. The posts should be placed firmly on the ground and joined by a horizontal cross-bar.

The posts and the cross-bar shall be square, 8cm × 8cm, made of wood, light metal or synthetic material. They shall be painted on all sides in two colours which contrast effectively with the background. Where the goal-posts and the cross-bar meet they shall be painted the same colour and the rectangles of colour shall be 28cm long. All other rectangles of colour shall be 20cm in length.

Each goal shall have a net attached in such a way that a ball, when thrown into it, cannot rebound immediately into the playing court.

1.3 The goal-area line is measured by marking a line 3m long at a distance of 3m from and parallel to the goal-line. The ends of this line are connected to the outer goal-line by two quarter-circles, each having a radius of 6m, measured from the back inside corner of the goal-posts. This line is known as the goal-area line.

1.4 A second line (the free-throw or 9m line) is drawn at a distance of 9m from the goal-area and marked in such a way that it is constantly at a distance of 3m from the goal-area line. This is achieved by connecting the line with two quarter-circles of 9m radius, measured from the rear inside corner of the goal-posts. The line is drawn on the court as a broken line. Both the lines and the spaces between shall measure 15cm in length.

1.5 Seven metres from the rear edge of the goal-line and parallel to it is drawn a line (the penalty or 7 metre line), 1 metre long, the ends of the line being equidistant from the sidelines of the playing court.

1.6 Inside the goal-area, and at a distance of 4m measured from the rear edge and from the centre of the goal-line, is drawn a line 15m in length. (This line which shall be parallel to the goal-line shall mark the limit of the goalkeeper's advance when a penalty throw is being executed.)

1.7 In the centre of the court is drawn a line exactly halfway between the two goal-lines. The line extends across the court and must connect with the inner edges of both side-lines.

1.8 The 15cm long substitution lines, which currently project into the court, on either side of the centre line, are to be marked, in addition, 15cm outside the court, making therefore a continuous line of 30cm.

1.9 All lines on the court shall be deemed to form part of the area they enclose. They shall measure 5cm in width and must be clearly visible. (see, however, 1.10.)

1.10 Between the goal-posts the goal-line shall measure the same width as the goal-posts – 8cm.

RULE 2

Duration of Play

2.1 For both male and female players and where the age is in excess of eighteen years, each game shall consist of two periods of 30 minutes, with a 10-minute interval.

2.2 The playing time shall begin with a throw-off from the centre of the court, following a whistle signal from the court referee. Playing time ends either by means of an automatic signal from the timing device or a final signal from the timekeeper.

Where an infringement of the Laws or an incident of unsporting conduct occurs, which cannot be penalised within the time, the resultant action, a free throw, a penalty or whatever it may be, shall be executed after the final signal and the game shall end only after the result of the throw has been established. However, any infringement during the execution cannot lead to the award of a free throw to the opposing team. *Note*: Where a public clock is used for the purpose of timing a game it should, where possible, be set to run from 0 to 30 minutes.

Where such a clock is not available, the timekeeper shall use a table clock or stop-watch and end the half or the game with an audible signal.

An automatic signal to denote the end of time is now permitted and recommended. The IHF are to consider this in greater detail, particularly in relation to free throws and penalty throws, which may be interrupted by the signal, and recommendations will be made available in due course.

2.3 The teams change ends for the second half of the game.

2.4 The referees shall decide if play is to be interrupted and when play shall be restarted, and indicate their decision clearly to the timekeeper.

Where the referees indicate an interruption of the time such shall be communicated to the timekeeper by means of three short blasts from the whistle and by the referee forming his hands into a 'T' shape.

A resumption of the playing time shall always be indicated by means of a whistle signal from the referee.

2.5 If during the execution of a free throw or a penalty throw (7-metre throw), the final signal is given, whilst the throw is being taken or the ball is in the air, the throw must be retaken. The game shall only be ended after the result of the second attempt has been ascertained.

Where an infringement of the laws or unsportsmanlike conduct occur during the execution of the retaken throw, the same must be punished.

2.6 Where the referees determine that the timekeeper has given the final signal prematurely, they shall keep the players on the court and play the time that is remaining. The game shall be restarted by a signal from the referee by the team that was in possession of the ball when the play was interrupted.

Where it is apparent that the timekeeper has signalled the end of the first period too late, the second half shall be shortened accordingly.

2.7 Extra time shall be played when the rules of a competition determine that a match must be won by one of the teams, if at the end of normal time the result is a tie. Extra time shall be played after an interval of five minutes has elapsed. The referee shall toss a coin to decide which team shall begin the period of extra time or which goal a team shall defend. The extra time shall consist of two periods of five minutes, without interval, for all categories of players. At the end of the extra time and where the result is still a tie, a second period of two halves of five minutes shall be played following an interval of five minutes. The referee shall once again toss a coin to decide which team shall start the first period and which goal is to be defended.

Where even after a second period of extra time the scores remain level, the regulations governing the competition shall be applied to determine the winner.

RULE 3

The Ball

3.1 The ball must be spherical and consist of an outer casing of leather or synthetic material. The outer case must not be too shiny or slippery and the ball should not be inflated too hard.

3.2 At the start of play, the ball for men and youths shall weigh between 425 and 475 gm and the circumference shall be between 54 and 56cm.

The ball for women and juniors shall weigh not more than 400gm and not less than 325gm and the circumference shall be not more than 56cm and not less than 54cm.

3.3 Two balls which conform to the Rules must be available at the beginning of every game. Both balls shall be checked by the referees and they shall decide which of the two shall be used in the game.

3.4 The ball chosen must be used for the whole of the game and shall only be changed for the most compelling of reasons.

3.5 Only balls marked with the Official IHF Logo shall be used for international games.

RULE 4

The Players

4.1 Each team shall consist of 12 players all of whom must be listed on the scoresheet.

A team must include a goalkeeper throughout the whole of the game.

A maximum of seven players (6 court players and 1 goalkeeper) may be present on the court at any one time. The remaining players are substitutes.

Only the substitutes, suspended players and up to four team officials are permitted to be in a team's substitution area.

The team officials must be listed on the scoresheet. They are not allowed to be replaced during the course of a game. One official shall be designated with responsibility for the team and only this named official shall have the right to address the timekeeper/scorer and, by consent, the referees.

4.2 At the commencement of a game each team must have at least 5 players present on the playing court. The number of players on the court may be increased to 7 and the total complement of the team to 12, at any time during the game (including extra time).

Once a game is in progress it is permitted for the game to continue, even when a team might be reduced to less than 5 players present on the court.

4.3 Prior to the commencement of a game each player shall have his/her name recorded on the official scoresheet. Each player so recorded shall be 'entitled to participate'.

Players entitled to participate may enter the court at any time, provided such entry is made from within the team's defined substitution area.

Players and officials who arrive late shall only be entitled to participate after explicit permission has been obtained from the timekeeper/scorer.

Where a player who is not entitled to participate enters the court, the opposing team shall be awarded a free throw and the offending player/s disqualified (see 17.5a).

4.4 Substitutes may enter the game repeatedly and at any time without notifying the timekeeper/scorer, provided the player being replaced has already left the court. (This rule shall also apply to the substitution of the goalkeeper.)

Players leaving or entering the court must do so within the boundaries of their team's substitution area.

During a 'time out' it is permitted to enter the court, from the substitution area i) for a normal substitution or ii) after permission from the referees has been obtained (see hand signal 18).

Note: Any player who leaves the court or who enters the court and in so doing commits an infringement of the substitution rule shall be penalised for such faulty substitution, except where the leaving of the court was unintentional.

4.5 A faulty substitution shall be penalised by a free throw awarded against the offending team (see 13.1a) taken from the place where the offending player crossed the sideline. The offending player shall be awarded a 2-minute period of suspension. Where the faulty substitution takes place during a stoppage in the game the offender shall be suspended and the game restarted by a throw appropriate to the original cause for the stoppage of the game.

In the event of serious unsporting conduct, or an assault in connection with, or immediately subsequent to, a faulty substitution, the offending player shall be disqualified or excluded respectively (see 17.5*d*, 17.7).

4.6 If an extra player enters the court, without substitution, or a player from within the substitution area interferes with the game, in contravention of the Rules, the player shall be suspended for 2 minutes. In addition another member of the offending team shall leave the court to ensure the team plays with reduced strength, for the period of the suspension.

Where a player serving a period of suspension enters the court before the period of suspension has expired, he/she shall be suspended for a further period of 2 minutes. In addition another member of the offending team present on the court shall be obliged to leave the court to serve the remainder of the original period of suspension.

Where a decision has to be made as to which player must leave the court, such decision shall be the responsibility of the team official. In the event of the official refusing so to choose, the decision as to which player must leave will be made by the referee.

Note: A player leaving the court to serve additional or remaining suspension time for another shall remain entitled to play and may enter the court as a substitute, during the suspension time.

Only the player awarded with a period of suspension shall have such recorded on the scoresheet. Players removed from the court to serve or continue a period of suspension, through the actions of another, shall not have their names entered onto the scoresheet.

4.7 All the court players in a team shall be uniformly dressed and the colours of the teams must be clearly distinguishable, one from the other. A player who is used as a goalkeeper shall wear colours which clearly distinguish him/her from either of the two teams and the goalkeeper of the opposing team (see 18.3).

Players shall be numbered 1 to 20. The numbers must be at least 20cm high on the back of the shirt and at least 10cm on the front of the shirt. The colour of the numbers must contrast clearly with that of the team uniform.

All players must wear sports shoes.

Bracelets, wrist-watches, rings, necklaces, chains, rimless or frameless spectacles and spectacles without solid frames or restraining bands, or any other objects, including head or face protection, which might be dangerous to other players are prohibited (see 18.3).

Any equipment which it is considered might constitute a hazard shall be removed before a player is deemed to be entitled to participate in a game.

The captain of each team must wear an armlet around the upper arm. This should be approximately 4cm wide and the colour must contrast with that of the uniform.

RULE 5

The Goalkeeper

5.1 A player playing as a goalkeeper may become a court player at any time, provided he/she changes into the appropriate team uniform. Likewise, a court player is entitled to undertake the role of goalkeeper. However, a goalkeeper's original number must be visible, front and back. Similarly a court player, playing in the goal, must also have the original numbers clearly visible.

All goalkeeping substitutions must be effected, via the substitution area.

The goalkeeper is allowed to:

5.2 Touch the ball with any part of the body, in the act of defence, when inside the goal-area.

5.3 Move around inside the area without restriction (see, however, 16.3b).

5.4 Leave the goal-area, provided he/she is not at the time in possession of the ball. After leaving the goal-area the goalkeeper is considered to be a court player and the Rules applying to court players shall also apply to the goalkeeper. The goalkeeper is considered to have left the goal-area as soon as any part of his/her body touches the ground outside the goal-area-line (see, however, 5.12).

5.5 Leave the goal-area with the ball, if, in the act of defence, he/she leaves the goal area, wholly or partially, whilst trying to get the ball under control. Where the goalkeeper, in this situation, wholly or partially leaves the goal-area, he/she shall be permitted to play the ball from outside the goal-area, and shall not be considered to have infringed the Laws.

The goalkeeper is not allowed to:

5.6 Commit an act which might endanger an opponent, whilst defending the goal.

5.7 Play the ball intentionally over the outer goal-line, once having the ball under control.

5.8 Leave the goal-area with the ball under control (see 13.1b).

5.9 Make contact with the ball, outside the goal-area, following a goal-throw, until the ball has been touched by another player (see 13.1b).

5.10 Touch the ball when it is lying or rolling on the floor, outside the goal-area while he/she is inside the goal-area (see 14.1b).

5.11 Take the ball into the goal-area whilst it is lying or rolling on the floor outside the goal-area-line (see 14.1b).

5.12 Re-enter the goal area from the playing court while in possession of the ball (see 14.1b).

5.13 Touch the ball with the feet or the legs below the knee whilst it is moving outwards in the direction of the playing area or it is stationary within the goal-area (see 13.1*b*).

5.14 Touch or cross the 4-metre line marked inside the goal-area before the ball has left the thrower's hand, when a penalty-throw is being executed (see 14.8).

Note: When a penalty-throw is executed and the goalkeeper places himself/herself immediately at the 4-metre line, he/she is allowed, provided one foot is placed firmly on the ground and behind the line, to move the other foot or any part of the body, in the air and in front of the 4-metre line.

RULE 6

The Goal-Area

6.1 The goal-area is that part of the court bounded by the goal-area-line. Only the goalkeeper is allowed to enter the goal-area (see, however, 6.3).

The goal-area-line is considered to be part of the area.

The goal-area is considered to have been entered when a court player touches it with any part of the body.

6.2 Court players who enter the goal-area shall be penalised as follows:

(*a*) Free throw when the player is in possession of the ball (see 13.1*c*).

(*b*) Free throw if the player is not in possession of the ball, but by entering the goal-area gains an advantage (see 13.1*c* and 6.2*c*).

(*c*) Penalty (7-metre)-throw when a player of the defending team enters the goal-area and thereby gains an advantage over the attacking opponent who is in possession of the ball (see 14.1*c*).

6.3 A court player entering the goal-area shall not be penalised when:

(*a*) He/she enters the goal-area after playing the ball, provided it causes no disadvantage to the opposing team.

(*b*) The player enters the goal-area without the ball and does not gain an advantage by so doing.

(*c*) A defending player enters the goal-area during or after making an attempt to defend, provided such action does not cause disadvantage to the opposing team.

6.4 When the ball is inside the goal-area it belongs to the goalkeeper. No court player shall be allowed to touch the ball whilst it is stationary or rolling on the floor or when the ball is in the possession of the goalkeeper. It is permitted, however, to play the ball when it is in the air above the goal-area (see 13.1*c*).

6.5 When at the end of its momentum the ball comes to rest in the goal-area it shall be returned to the field of play by the goalkeeper.

6.6 Play is not interrupted when a defending player legitimately and in the act of defence touches or deflects the ball into the goal-area where the ball comes to rest or is shaken by the goalkeeper.

6.7 Where a player intentionally plays the ball into his/her own goal-area the referee shall decide as follows:

(*a*) Goal – if the ball goes into the goal.

(*b*) Penalty-throw if the goalkeeper touches the ball and a goal is not scored (see 14.1*d*).

(*c*) Play to continue uninterrupted if the ball enters the goal-area and returns to the playing court, without having been touched by the goalkeeper and without having gone out of play.

6.8 A ball returning from the goal-area into the playing court remains in play.

RULE 7

Playing the Ball

It is permitted:

7.1 To throw, catch, stop, push or hit the ball using the hands (the hands may be open or closed), arms, head, torso, thighs and knees.

7.2 To hold the ball for a maximum of three seconds, even when it is lying on the floor.

7.3 To take a maximum of three steps, while in possession of the ball. One step is considered taken when:

(*a*) A player who is standing with both feet in contact with the floor lifts one foot and puts it down again, or moves one foot from one position to another.

(*b*) A player who is in contact with the floor with one foot only, catches the ball and then makes contact with the ground with the other foot.

(*c*) A player, after a jump, touches the floor with one foot only and then hops on the same foot or touches the ground with the other foot.

(*d*) A player after a jump touches the floor with both feet simultaneously and then lifts one and puts it down again, or moves one foot from one place to another.

Note: When one foot is moved from one place to another the player is allowed to move the other foot until it is level with the first without this being counted as a step.

7.4 While standing or running:

(*a*) To bounce the ball once and catch it with both hands.

(*b*) To bounce the ball or to roll the ball on the ground repeatedly with one hand and thereafter catch or pick up the ball in one or both hands.

Once the player takes possession of the ball in one or both hands it must be played within 3 seconds or after taking no more than three steps.

The act of bouncing, or dribbling, shall be deemed to have begun when the player touches the ball with any part of the body and in so doing directs the ball towards the floor.

Once the ball has touched another player or the goal the player is allowed to take possession of the ball again.

7.5 To place the ball from one hand to the other. (It is not allowed to throw the ball from one hand to the other.)

7.6 To play the ball while kneeling, sitting or lying on the ground.

It is not permitted:

7.7 To touch the ball more than once unless it has first touched the ground or another player or any part of the goal (see 13.1*d*).

Where in the act of catching or stopping the ball, the player does not control the ball cleanly at the first attempt, and thereby fumbles in his/her efforts, such action shall not be penalised. However, where control of the ball has been established the player must not touch it more than once after tapping or bouncing it.

7.8 To touch the ball with any part of the leg below the knee, except when the ball has been thrown against the legs of a player by an opponent, and where the striking of the leg by the ball does not cause advantage to be gained by the player or his team.

7.9 To dive for the ball while it is lying or rolling on the ground (see 13.1*d*).

Note: This Rule does not apply to the goalkeeper while he/she is inside the goal-area.

7.10 To play the ball intentionally over the side-line or the team's own outer goal-line (see 13.1*e*).

Note: This Rule does not apply to the goalkeeper who from within the goal-area and in the act of defending fails to control the ball and thereby directs the ball over his/her own outer goal-line. In such instances a goal-throw is awarded.

7.11 To keep the ball in the team's possession without making any recognisable attempt to attack or to score a goal.

Such action is considered to be 'passive play' and is penalised by a free throw against the offending team. The throw is executed from where the ball was when the play was interrupted (see 13.1*f*).

7.12 Where the ball makes contact with one of the referees, on the court, the play shall continue as the referee is, in this instance, considered to be part of the field of play.

RULE 8

Approach to an Opponent

A player is permitted:
8.1 To use hands and arms to gain possession of the ball.
8.2 To use an open hand, in any direction, to dispossess an opponent.
8.3 To obstruct an opponent with the torso, even if the opponent is not in possession of the ball.
A player is not permitted:
8.4 To obstruct or restrain an opponent by means of arms, hands or legs.
8.5 To force an opponent into the goal-area.
8.6 To pull or hit the ball with one or both arms out of the hand of an opponent.
8.7 To use the fist to dispossess an opponent.
8.8 To throw the ball intentionally or dangerously at an opponent or to feint with the ball in such manner as might be determined dangerous.
8.9 To endanger the goalkeeper.
8.10 To push an opponent or to hold an opponent with one or both arms.
8.11 To run or jump into, trip, hit, or, endanger an opponent in any other manner.
8.12 Infringements of the Rules governing Approach to an Opponent (see 5.6; 8.4-11) shall be penalised by the award of a free throw against the offending player/s (see 13.1g) or by a penalty-throw awarded to the opposing team (see 17.1a).
8.13 Infringement of the Rules governing Approach to an Opponent and where the action is mainly or exclusively directed at the opponent and not at the ball shall be penalised progressively (see 17.1b–17.3b). Where a player is considered guilty of an unsporting action, he/she shall also be penalised progressively (see 17.1d, 17.5c).
8.14 Serious infringements of the Rules governing Approach to an Opponent or any serious occurrence of unsporting conduct shall be punished by the disqualification of the offending player (see 17.5b, 17.5d).
8.15 A player who commits an assault upon another player or an official shall be excluded (see 17.7).

RULE 9

Scoring

9.1 A goal is scored when the whole of the ball has crossed the goal-line, between the goal-posts and underneath the cross-bar, provided no infringement of the Rules has been committed by the thrower or a team mate before or during the throw.

Where a defending player commits an infringement of the Rules, but the ball enters the goal, the goal shall be awarded. However, if a referee or the timekeeper has blown the whistle before the whole of the ball has crossed the goal-line then the goal cannot be allowed.

In the event of a defender, including the goalkeeper, throwing the ball into their own goal, a goal shall be awarded to the opposing team provided the ball had not previously crossed the outer goal-line.
Note: If the ball is prevented from entering the goal by someone or something not authorised to be on the court, for example, a spectator, the referees shall award a goal, if in their opinion such would have been the inevitable result had play not been interrupted.
9.2 When a goal is scored and is signalled by two blasts of the referee's whistle, the goal may be indicated immediately upon the scoreboard. There is no need to await the throw-off. The referee is entitled, however, to subsequently disallow the goal, until he/she has signalled a throw-off for the resumption of the game.

Where a goal is scored immediately before half-time or the end of the game and play cannot continue by means of a throw-off due to the appropriate signal having sounded to end the play, the referees must indicate clearly that a goal has been awarded, and ensure that the scorer and team officials are made aware of the validity of the goal.
Note: The awarding of a goal may be indicated on the scoreboard as soon as it has been signalled by the referees.
9.3 The team scoring the most goals in a match shall be declared the winner.
9.4 In the event of each team scoring the same number of goals the match shall be declared drawn.

RULE 10

Throw-Off

10.1 Prior to the commencement of the game, the referee shall toss a coin and the team winning the toss shall have the option of beginning the game by means of a throw-off, or alternatively choosing which end they wish to defend. In the event of the team choosing the latter option, then the team losing the toss shall begin the game with the throw-off.

The second half of a play is begun by a throw-off taken by that team which did not start the first half of the game.

In the event of extra time being deemed necessary, the teams shall toss a coin, again, to decide which team should begin the extra period.

10.2 After a goal is scored, play is resumed by a throw-off taken by the team conceding the goal.

10.3 The throw-off is taken from the centre of the court and may be executed in any direction. The throw shall only be made following a whistle signal from the referee and be executed within 3 seconds of the signal being made (see 13.1*h*).

10.4 At the throw-off, all the players must be in their own half of the court. Players of the team not in possession of the ball must be at least 3m from the player taking the throw.

RULE 11

Throw-In

11.1 A throw-in is awarded if the whole of the ball has crossed the side-line, either on the ground or in the air. Additionally a throw-in is also awarded if a defending player, other than the goalkeeper, deflects or causes the ball to cross the outer goal-line (see, however, 7.10).

11.2 The throw-in is taken without any whistle signal from the referee (see, however, 16.3*b*), by a member of the team whose players were not the last to touch the ball before it went out of play.

11.3 The throw-in is taken from the place where the ball crossed the side-line. Where, however, the throw is awarded for the ball crossing the outer goal-line, the throw is taken from the corner of the court where the side-line and outer goal-line connect, and from the side of the goal from which the ball left the field of play.

11.4 The player taking the throw-in must have one foot placed on the side-line until the ball has left the hand.

Whilst taking the throw the player is not allowed to place the ball on the ground and take it up again or to bounce the ball and catch it again (see 13.1i).

11.5 During the execution of the throw all members of the opposing team shall position themselves at least 3m from the thrower.

However, players of the opposing team are entitled, at all times, to position themselves immediately outside their own goal-area-line irrespective of whether this position is 3m from the thrower.

RULE 12

Goalkeeper's-Throw (Goal-Throw)

12.1 A goal-throw is awarded when the ball crosses the outer goal-line, having last been touched by a member of the team attacking the goal or by the goalkeeper in the act of defending the goal (see 5.7 and 7.10).

12.2 The goal-throw is executed by means of the goalkeeper throwing the ball into the playing area, from a position inside the goal-area. The throw is made without any whistle signal from the referee.

The throw is considered taken when the ball has crossed the goal-area line.

12.3 If the ball shall, on occasion, come to rest in the goal-area, the goalkeeper shall bring the ball back into play by throwing the ball into the playing court (see, however, 6.7c).

12.4 Following the execution of a goal-throw, the goalkeeper is not allowed to make contact with the ball again until it has first touched another player (see 5.9 and 13.1k).

RULE 13

Free Throw

13.1 A free throw is awarded for:

(a) Incorrect substitution or entering the court in a manner contrary to the Rules (see 4.4–6).

(b) Infringements by the goalkeeper (see 5.7-10 and 5.13).

(c) Infringements by court players in the goal area (see 6.2a–b and 6.4).

(d) Infringements when playing the ball (see 7.2-4 and 7.7-9).

(e) Intentionally playing the ball across the outer goal-line or the side-line (see 6.7c and 7.10).

(f) Passive play (see 7.11).

(g) Infringements in regard to the 'Approach to an Opponent' (see 8.12).

(h) Infringements in connection with the throw-off (see 10.3).

(i) Infringements in connection with a throw-in (see 11.4).

(k) Infringements in connection with a goalkeeper's throw (see 12.4).

(l) Infringements in connection with a free throw (see 13.3).

(*m*) Infringements in connection with a penalty (7-m) throw (see 14.2-4, 6).

(*n*) Infringements in connection with a referee's throw (see 15.3).

(*o*) Incorrect execution of formal throws (see 16.2-5).

(*p*) Unsporting conduct (see 8.13-14 and 17.1*d*).

(*q*) Assault (see 8.15 and 17.7-9).

13.2 A free throw is taken without any whistle signal from the referee (see, however, 16.3*a–h*), and from the place where the offence took place. However, when the offence was committed by the defending team between their goal-area-line and the free-throw-line, the throw shall be taken from the nearest point outside the free-throw-line.

13.3 Once the player who is to execute the throw has taken up his/her position, from which to take the throw, he/she is not permitted to bounce the ball and catch it again or to put it down and take it up again (see 13.1).

13.4 Players of the attacking team must not cross or touch their opponents' free-throw-line until the throw has been taken.

The referees shall correct the positions of any attacking players contravening this Rule and who in their opinion are gaining an advantage from the position they have adopted. Where such action is deemed necessary by the referee, the throw shall only be executed following a whistle signal from the referee (see 16.3*c*).

13.5 When a free throw is being taken, members of the team not in possession of the ball shall position themselves at least 3m from the thrower. However, where the throw is to be executed from the free-throw-line, members of the defending team are permitted to position themselves immediately outside their own goal-area-line.

13.6 The referee shall not award a free throw, if by so doing an advantage would be gained by the team causing the infringement and a disadvantage experienced by the team in possession of the ball.

Where an infringement causes an attacking team to be placed at a disadvantage a free throw, at least, must be awarded.

A free throw, at least, must be awarded if an infringement causes an attacking team to lose possession of the ball.

A free throw must not be awarded if a player remains in full control of the ball in spite of the infringement.

13.7 In the event of the game being interrupted without any infringement of the Rules having occurred, and one of the teams is in possession of the ball, the game shall be started by means of a free throw executed by the team having possession and from the place where the ball was at the time of the interruption. The free throw must be preceded by a whistle signal (see 16.3*a*).

13.8 The ball *must* be put down *immediately* by a player in possession of the ball, when a decision is made against him/her or his/her team.

RULE 14

Penalty-Throw (7m Throw)

14.1 A 7m throw shall be awarded:

(*a*) When a clear chance of scoring a goal is prevented, by an infringement, in any part of the court, and even where the offender is a team official.

(*b*) When the goalkeeper enters the goal-area in possession of the ball or, when standing inside the goal-area, takes it into the goal-area (see 5.11-12).

(*c*) When a court player enters his/her own goal-area to gain an advantage over an attacking opponent who is in possession of the ball (see 6.2*c*).

(*d*) When a court player deliberately plays the ball to his/her own goalkeeper inside the goal-area and the goalkeeper touches the ball.

(*e*) When there is an unwarranted whistle signal which destroys a clear goal scoring opportunity.

(*f*) When a clear goal-scoring opportunity is destroyed by interference of someone not authorised to be on the court.

14.2 The penalty-throw must be taken as a shot propelled towards the goal and within 3 seconds of the whistle signal given by the court referee (see 31.1*m*).

14.3 The player taking the penalty-throw must not touch or cross the 7-metre-line before the ball has left the hand.

14.4 Once the penalty-throw has been executed, the ball may not be played again until it has touched the goalkeeper or the goal.

14.5 While the penalty-throw is being taken all players with the exception of the thrower must be positioned outside the free-throw line (the 9-metre line).

14.6 Players of the defending team must be at least 3m from the 7-metre line, while a penalty-throw is being taken. Where a defending player touches or crosses the 9-metre line or encroaches nearer than 3m from the 7-metre line before the ball has left the thrower's hand, the referee shall decide as follows:

(*a*) Goal – if the ball goes into the goal.

(*b*) The retaking of the throw in all other cases.

14.7 The referees shall not award a 7-metre throw for an infringement of the Rules by a defending team if, by so doing, he/she causes a disadvantage to the attacking team.

A 7-metre throw, at least, must be awarded, if a clear goalscoring opportunity is destroyed and a goal does not result, due to an infringement of the Rules or an act of unsporting conduct, an unwarranted whistle signal, or by interference on the part of someone not authorised to be part of the game.

Where, in spite of an infringement, an attacking player retains full ball and body control, a penalty-throw shall not be awarded.

RULE 15

Referee's Throw

15.1 A game shall be restarted by means of a Referee's Throw when:

(a) The Rules have been infringed simultaneously, on the court, by players of both teams.

(b) The ball has touched the roof or fixed equipment above the playing court.

(c) An interruption of the game is caused through no infringement of the Rules and whilst neither side was in possession of the ball.

15.2 The referee's throw shall in future be executed always from the centre of the court accompanied by a whistle signal (see 16.3a). A time-out must be given for each referee's throw.

15.3 The execution of the referee's throw shall be from the centre of the court by the court referee throwing the ball vertically into the air, following a whistle signal.

15.4 With the exception of one player from each team all other players must be positioned at least 3m from the referee while the referee's throw is being executed.

The two competing players shall stand either side of the referee, each on that side which is nearer to their own goal. The referee shall throw the ball into the air and the two players shall jump to try to gain possession. However, the ball may only be played after it has reached its highest point.

RULE 16

Execution of Formal Throws

16.1 All players must adopt the positions prescribed for the throw in question.

Initially, an incorrect position shall be corrected by the referee (see, however, 13.4 and 16.7).

The ball must be in the hand of the thrower before it can be executed.

16.2 During the execution of the throw-off, throw-in, free-throw and penalty-throw, the thrower must keep at least a part of one foot in constant contact with the floor (see 13.10). It is permitted, however, for the player to repeatedly lift and put down the other foot.

16.3 The referee *must* give a whistle:

(*a*) When the game is to be restarted in certain situations (see 2.4, 10.3, 13.7, 14.2 and 15.2).

(*b*) When the execution of a throw-in, goal-throw, or free-throw has been delayed (see 11.2, 12.2, 13.2).

(*c*) After a correction or caution (see 13.4 and 16.7).

(*d*) Following a warning (see 17.1).

(*e*) Following the award of a period of suspension (see 17.3).

(*f*) Following a disqualification (see 17.5).

(*g*) Following an exclusion (see 17.7).

(*h*) Where the referees have indicated different opinions as to which team should be penalised (see 18.9).

In the execution of the throw and where a whistle signal has been given by the referee, the thrower must play the ball within 3 seconds (see 13.1*o*).

16.4 A throw is considered to have been executed once the ball has left the hand of the thrower.

When taking the throw the player concerned must actually release the ball. It is not permitted for the ball to be placed into the hands of or touched by a team colleague.

16.5 Once the player taking the throw has released the ball he/she is not allowed to play the ball again until it has first touched another player or the goal.

16.6 A goal may be scored directly from any throw (see, however, 9.1).

16.7 When a throw-in or free-throw is being taken, players of the team not in possession shall be at least 3m from the thrower. However, the referee does not correct the position of the players contravening the Rules if no advantage is gained and the attacking team are in a position to play the ball immediately.

The referee does, however, correct any wrong position if it is felt such is causing disadvantage to the attacking team (see 16.3*c*).

In those instances where the referee blows his whistle for a throw to be taken, despite the incorrect positioning of defenders, those players are fully entitled to participate immediately. They cannot be penalised retrospectively.

If a defending player deliberately causes delay or interferes with the taking of a throw, by standing too close to the opponents, thereby infringing the Rules, that player shall be cautioned and where the offence is repeated shall be suspended (see 17.1*c* and 17.3*c*. See, however, 12.2).

RULE 17

Punishments

17.1 A caution can be given for:

(*a*) Infringements concerning Approach to an Opponent (see 5.6, 8.4-11).

A caution shall be given for:

(*b*) Infringements concerning the approach to an opponent and which are to be punished progressively (see 8.13).

(*c*) Infringements of the Rules when an opponent is attempting to execute a throw (see 16.7).

(*d*) Unsporting conduct by a player or official (see 17.11, 17.12*a* and 17.12*c*).

17.2 The referee shall indicate the decision to issue a caution to an offending player by holding up a yellow card. The card shall be visible to the player and the timekeeper/scorer.

Note: The yellow card should measure approximately 12 × 9cm.

Individual players should not be given more than one caution and collectively not more than three cautions may be awarded against a team as a whole.

Where a player has served a period of 2 minutes suspension such player cannot subsequently be given a caution.

No more than one caution may be given to the officials of a team.

17.3 A suspension (2 minutes) shall be given:

(*a*) For an incorrect (faulty) substitution or for entering the court contrary to the Rules (see 4.4-6).

(*b*) For repeated infringements of the Rules governing the approach to an opponent, and which are to be punished progressively (see 8.13).

(*c*) For repeated unsporting conduct by a player on the court (see 8.13 and 17.11).

(*d*) When a player fails to place the ball down on to the floor, immediately, when a decision for an infringement has been made against an attacking team.

(*e*) For repeatedly infringing the Rules when the opposing team is executing a formal throw (see 16.7).

(*f*) In consequence of a disqualification of a player or team official (see 17.5).

In exceptional circumstances a suspension can be awarded without recourse to an initial caution.

17.4 The decision to suspend a player must be clearly indicated to the player concerned by the referee raising one arm in the air with two fingers extended. The action of the referee shall be clearly visible to the timekeeper/scorer.

In all cases a period of suspension shall be of 2 minutes duration. However, where a player is suspended on three occasions the third period of suspension shall automatically lead to the player being disqualified (see 17.5e).

A suspended player is not allowed to participate in the game until the period of suspension has expired and during the time of suspension the team shall play with reduced strength upon the court.

The period of suspension shall begin immediately the referee has whistled to signal a resumption of play.

If a period of suspension has not expired by the end of the first half, the unexpired time shall be carried forward to the second half. Similarly, where a game goes into extra time any unexpired period of suspension at the end of normal time shall be carried over into the extra period to be played.

17.5 A disqualification shall be awarded:

(*a*) If a player who is not entitled to participate enters the court (see 4.3 and 17.6).

(*b*) For serious infringements relating to the approach to an opponent (see 8.14).

(*c*) For repeated unsporting conduct by a team official or a player outside the court (see 17.6, 17.11 and 17.12*d*).

(*d*) For serious unsporting conduct (see 8.14) by a player or a team official (see 17.6, 17.11, 17.12*b* and *d*).

(*e*) For a third period of suspension (see 17.4).

(*f*) For an assault by a team official (see 17.6 and 17.7 Note).

The disqualification of a player or a team official during the playing time shall always result in a period of suspension and the team's strength on the court being reduced by one.

17.6 When awarding a disqualification the referee shall indicate the punishment by holding up a red card, which may be clearly seen by the player or official concerned and the timekeeper/scorer.

The disqualification of a player or official applies for the remainder of the playing time. The player or official must leave the court and the substitution area immediately.

A disqualification reduces the number of players and/or officials available to the team (except as in 17.12*b*). The team may, however, continue to play at full strength on the court following the expiry of the suspension time awarded against the disqualified player or official (see Note 4.6).

Where a referee decides to award a 2-minute suspension to an official on the bench or a player in the substitution area, a player already on the court must leave to serve the period of suspension. However, such suspension is not recorded against the name of the player subsequently removed from the court.

Note: The red card should measure approximately 9 × 12cm.

The requirement for disqualified players and officials to leave the substitution area shall also mean that the player and official must move away from any position from where they might be able to exert an influence on the team.

17.7 An exclusion shall be given:

In the event of an assault, during the playing time both on and outside of the court (see 2.1, 2.2, 2.7, 8.15 and 17.8-17.9).

Note: Assault is defined as a deliberate and particularly violent physical action made in contravention of the Rules and against the person of a player, referee, timekeeper/scorer, official or spectator.

For the purpose of this Rule spitting is to be interpreted as an assault.

17.8 In awarding an exclusion the referees shall call a 'time out' and must inform the guilty player and the timekeeper/scorer immediately.

The referee shall indicate the exclusion to the offending player by crossing his arms at head height.

An excluded player shall take no further part in the game and must leave the court and the substitution area immediately. Throughout the remainder of the game the team of the excluded player shall play at reduced strength on the court. It is not permitted for an excluded player to be replaced.

17.9 Any player having been given a period of suspension and who is guilty of another infringement, before the game is restarted shall be further punished by means of the most severe of the applicable punishments allowed for in the Rules.

17.10 In the event of a goalkeeper being suspended, disqualified or excluded another player must take up the position of goalkeeper (see 4.1).

17.11 The referrees must caution any player they deem guilty of unsporting conduct, irrespective of whether such takes place on or outside the court (see 17.1*d*).

If the offence is repeated and the player is on the court, that player shall be suspended. However, should the player be outside the court (for example, a substitute, or a suspended player) then that player shall be disqualified (see 17.5*c* and 17.6).

A team official committing an offence deemed to be unsporting conduct shall first be cautioned (see 17.1*d*), and where such action is repeated, he shall be disqualified (see 17.5*c*, 17.6).

If unsporting conduct or an assault takes place when the game is already interrupted, the game shall be resumed by the throw appropriate to the original interruption of play.

Note: Both physical and verbal expressions which are deemed to be incompatible with the spirit of good sportsmanship are to be regarded as unsporting conduct.

Team officials who enter the court without permission shall be considered guilty of unsporting or even serious unsporting conduct and punished accordingly (see 4.4).

If a player or team official is guilty of committing a series of offences (infringements, unsportsmanslike conduct, assault) simultaneously or in quick succession, each requiring serious punishment, then only the most severe of the punishments shall be awarded.

17.12 Unsporting conduct or assault taking place within the premises of where a game is played shall be penalised as follows:

Prior to the commencement of the game:

(*a*) For unsporting conduct a caution shall be given (see 17.1*d*).

(*b*) Serious unsporting conduct or assault shall be punished by disqualification of the offending player (see 17.5*d* and 17.5*f*). The team of the disqualified individual is allowed, however, to begin the game with 12 players.

During an interval:

(*c*) In the case of unsporting conduct a caution shall be issued to the offender (see 17.1*d*).

(*d*) Repeated or serious unsporting conduct or assault shall be punished by disqualification (see 17.5*c* 17.5*d-f*).

After the game has been completed:

(*e*) The preparation of a written report.

RULE 18

The Referee

18.1 Each game shall be conducted by two referees. Each shall have equal authority and they shall be assisted by a scorer and a timekeeper.

18.2 The referees shall monitor the conduct of the players from the moment they enter the premises where the game is to be played until the moment they leave.

18.3 Prior to the commencement of the game the referees shall examine the playing court, the goals and the balls (see 3.1). They decide which of the balls shall be used. Where there is failure to agree, the decision of the referee officially named first shall prevail.

The referees shall check the scoresheet ensuring that all details recorded are correct. They shall check that the uniforms of the teams are in accordance with the Rules, establish that the number of players and officials present in the substitution area is correct and determine the presence and identity of the 'responsible team official'.

Any discrepancies must be corrected (see 4.7).

18.4 The referee officially named first shall toss a coin before the beginning of the game, in the presence of his/her colleague and the two captains (see 10.1).

18.5 At the start of the game the referee officially named second shall take up the position of court referee, behind the team taking the throw-off and in their half of the court. The court referee shall give the whistle signal for the game to begin (see 10.3).

Note: The referees shall be known as the court referee and the goal-line referee. The court referee is so named because he/she is always in a position on the court and behind the attacking team. The other official adopts a position on the goal-line, outside the goal, while an attack is mounted and thus will be positioned behind the defence.

When the defending team ultimately gains possession, they become the attacking team and their opponents will fall back upon their own goal-area-line for the purpose of defence. The position of the referees is now reversed. The referee who was the court referee shall retreat before the now defending team and assume a position on their goal-line, outside the goal. The other referee moves forward behind the now attacking team to become the court referee. The action is repeated throughout the game, when the possession of the ball is once more exchanged between the teams.

From time to time the referees should change ends to ensure they are not always the goal-line and court referee for the same team throughout the game.

18.6 In principle a game shall be conducted by the same two referees. Jointly they must ensure that the game is played in accordance with the Rules and they must penalise infringements (see, however, 13.6 and 14.9).

In the circumstance of one referee being unable to continue throughout the game, the other referee shall continue alone.

18.7 The court referee shall, in principle, assume responsibility and signal for:

(*a*) The execution of all formal throws in accordance with the Rules 16.3 *a–h* and the restoration of play following a 'time out' (see 2.4).

(*b*) The expiration of the playing time if the automatic signal has not sounded or the timekeeper has failed to give the final signal.

In principle, the goal-line referee shall whistle:

(*c*) To signify a goal has been scored.

18.8 If on occasion both referees decide simultaneously that an infringement shall be penalised, but signify different opinions as to the severity of the punishment, the more severe of the two shall be applied.

18.9 Where both referees together interrupt the game, but differ as to which team should be penalised, the decision of the court referee shall prevail.

Upon such occasion the game shall be restarted following clear hand signals from the court referee and a whistle signal.

18.10 Both referees shall keep a record of the goals scored by both teams and they shall also record cautions, suspensions, disqualifications and exclusions.

18.11 Both referees shall be responsible for controlling the playing time. Where there is disagreement about the accuracy of timekeeping, the decision of the first named referee shall decide.

18.12 Upon completion of the game the referees shall assume responsibility for ensuring that all information recorded on the scoresheet is correct.

18.13 Decisions of the referees based upon their observations of the facts are considered final.

Appeals can be lodged against decisions considered not to conform to the Rules.

During the course of the game, team captains are entitled to address the referees.

18.14 Both referees shall have the right to order that a game be suspended temporarily or permanently. However, every effort must be made to continue with a game before a decision is made to suspend it permanently.

18.15 Only referees are permitted to wear black dress.

RULE 19

The Scorer and the Timekeeper

19.1 The scorer is responsible for the checking of team lists and only those players so recorded and eligible shall be considered 'entitled to participate'. The scorer, together with the timekeeper, regulates the entering of players arriving after the start of the game or who are re-entering the court following a period of suspension.

The scorer shall be responsible for the scoresheet and the entries to be recorded thereon (goals, cautions, suspensions, disqualifications and exclusions).

19.2 The timekeeper shall control:

(*a*) The playing time (see 2.1, 2.2, 2.4 and 2.7). The referees decide when the clock is to be stopped and restarted.

(*b*) The number of players and officials in the substitution area (see 4.1).

(*c*) Together with the scorekeeper the entering of players arriving after the game has commenced (see 4.3).

(*d*) The exit and entry of substituting players (see 4.4-4.5).

(*e*) The entering of players who are not entitled to participate (see 4.6).

(*f*) The signal of the referee to allow a substitute goalkeeper to enter the court, before the other goalkeeper has left, has been abolished.

(*g*) The suspension time of suspended players (see 17.4).

It is the responsibility of the timekeeper to give a loud signal to stop the game at the end of each half, if there is no public clock with automatic time signal available.

19.3 Where an interruption of play 'time out' occurs, it shall be the responsibility of the timekeeper, should there be no public clock available, to inform the responsible team official how much time has been played or how much time there is left to play.

19.4 The timekeeper shall assume responsibility for informing suspended players or the responsible team official when a period of suspension has expired (see 17.4).

Reprinted by permission of the British Handball Association. For reasons of space two Appendixes – Clarification of the Rules and Regulations Governing the Substitution Area – have been omitted. These are included in the Complete Rules of Handball, available from the Association.

THE RULES OF

Hockey

The Field of Play

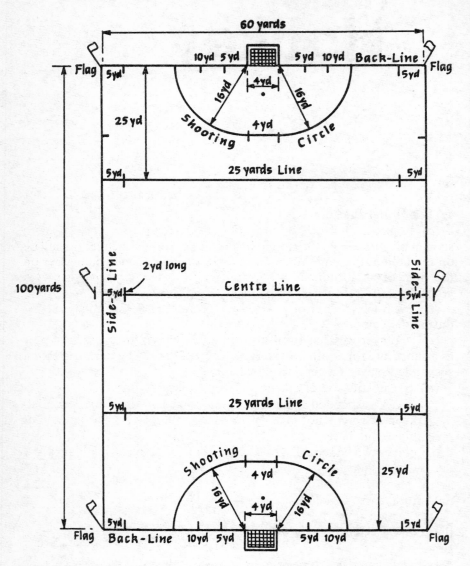

The front of the goal-posts must be touching the outer edge of the goal-line.
All lines must be 3in wide.
A spot 6in in diameter shall be marked 7yd in front of the centre of each goal.
All short indication marks must be inside the field only and shall be 12in in length.

Hockey

1. Teams and Duration of Play

(*a*) A game shall be played between two teams of not more than sixteen players each. Not more than eleven players of each team shall be on the field at the same time. Each team shall have one goalkeeper on the field or shall indicate a field player who has the privileges of a goalkeeper.

(*b*) Each team is permitted to substitute not more than five players during the game.

(*c*) A player who has been substituted may re-enter the field of play as a substitute for another player. No substitute shall be permitted for a suspended player (excepting a goalkeeper).

(*d*) (i) Substitution of players may take place at any time.

(ii) A suspended goalkeeper may be replaced by another goalkeeper, who is not taken from among the players on the field of play (this latter option is still available). If so replaced, a field player will be required to leave the field of play, so that team plays with 10 players.

(*e*) The duration of the game shall be two periods of 35 minutes each unless otherwise agreed before the game.

(*f*) At half-time the teams shall change ends, and the duration of the interval shall be between 5 and 15 minutes, as agreed before the game starts.

(*g*) The game starts when the umpire blows his whistle for the opening pass back. See also Rule 10(*a*).

2. Captains

Each team must have a captain on the field who must wear a distinctive arm-band and who shall:

(*a*) Toss for choice of start. The winner of the toss shall have:

(i) the right to choose which end his team will attack in the first half;
or

(ii) the right to have possession of the ball at the start of the game.

The winner of the toss having made his choice, the opposing side will automatically have the second option. The team not having started the game will have possession of the ball for re-starting after half-time.

(*b*) Before the start of play and on any change, indicate, if necessary, to each other and to the umpires, their respective goalkeepers subject to Rules 15(*c*)(ii) and 16(*b*)(i).

(*c*) In case he is substituted or suspended, pass his arm-band to another player who will replace him as captain.

3. Umpires and Timekeepers

(*a*) There shall be two umpires to control the game and to administer the rules. These umpires shall be the sole judges of fair and unfair play during the game.

(*b*) Unless otherwise provided, each team shall be responsible for providing one umpire.

(*c*) Each umpire shall be:

(i) Primarily responsible for decisions in his own half of the field, for the whole of the game without changing ends.

(ii) Solely responsible for decisions on the hit-in for the full length of his nearer side-line.

(iii) Solely responsible for decisions on corners, penalty corners, penalty strokes and goals in his own half and free hits in his own circle.

(*d*) The umpires shall be responsible for keeping time for the duration of the game. It shall be permissible to have a timekeeper or timekeepers. Such timekeepers shall take over those duties of the umpires which concern the keeping of time and the indication of the end of each half.

(*e*) Umpires shall allow the full or agreed time and shall keep a written record of the goals as they are scored.

(*f*) Time shall be allowed for all enforced stoppages and such time shall be added to that half in which the stoppage occurred.

(*g*) Umpires and timekeepers shall be debarred from coaching during a game and during the interval.

(*h*) Umpires shall only blow the whistle to:

(i) Start and end each half of the game.

(ii) Enforce a penalty.

(iii) Start and end a penalty stroke.

(iv) Indicate, when necessary, that the ball has passed wholly outside the field of play.

(v) Signal a goal.

(vi) Restart the game after a goal has been scored.

(vii) Suspend the game for any reason and restart after a suspension.

(*i*) Umpires shall satisfy themselves before the game that, as far as is practicable, Rules 4 to 9 inclusive are observed.

Umpires shall refrain from enforcing a penalty in cases where they are satisfied that by enforcing it an advantage would be given to the offending team.

4. Field of Play
(*See page 554*)

(*a*) All lines used in the measurements of the field are to be 3in wide. The side-lines and back-lines including the goal-lines are part of the field of play.

(*b*) The field shall be rectangular, 100yd long and 60yd wide. Its boundaries shall be clearly marked out with lines in accordance with the plan on page 554. The longer lines shall be called the side-lines and the shorter the back-lines, including that part of the back-line between the goal-posts called the goal-line.

(*c*) A centre-line and two 25-yards lines shall be marked throughout their length on the field; the middle of these lines to be 50yd and 25yd respectively from the outer edge of the back-lines.

(*d*) To assist in the control of the hit-in, across the centre-line and each 25-yards line, parallel to and 5yd from the outer edge of the side-lines a mark of 2yd in length shall be made.

(*e*) A mark 12in in length shall be placed inside the field of play on each side-line and parallel to the back-line and 16yd from its inner edge.

(*f*) For penalty corner hits, the field shall be marked inside the field of play on the back-lines on both sides of the goal at 5yd and 10yd from the outer edge of the nearer goal-post such distance being to the further edge of those lines. For corner hits the field shall be marked inside the field of play on the back-lines 5yd from the outer edge of the side-line. All these marks to be 12in in length.

(*g*) A spot 6in in diameter shall be marked in front of the centre of each goal; the centre of the spot shall be 7yd from the inner edge of the goal-line.

(*h*) No marks other than those shown on the plan are permissible on the playing surface.

(*i*) Flagposts of not more than 5ft nor less than 4ft in height shall be placed for the whole game at each corner of the field, and at the centre; those at the centre shall be 1yd outside the side-lines.

5. Goals and goalposts, etc.

(*a*) There shall be a goal at the centre of each back-line consisting of two perpendicular posts 4yd apart, joined together by a horizontal cross-bar 7ft from the ground (inside measurements). The front base of the goal-posts shall touch the outer edge of the back-line. The goal-posts shall not extend upwards beyond the cross-bar, nor the cross-bar extend sideways beyond the goal-posts.

(*b*) The goal-posts and cross-bar shall be rectangular and shall be 2in wide and not more than 3in nor less than 2in deep, and they shall be painted white.

(*c*) Nets shall be attached firmly to the goal-posts and the cross-bar at intervals of not more than 6in, and shall be attached firmly to the ground behind the goal or to the back-board/side-boards.

(*d*) A back-board, 18in in height and 4 yd in length, shall be placed at the foot of and inside the goal-nets. Side-boards 18in in height and a minimum 4ft in length shall be placed at right angles to the back-lines. The side-boards shall be fixed to the back of the goal-posts, so that the width of the goal-posts is not effectively increased.

(*e*) No chocks shall be placed inside the goal to support any of the boards.

6. Shooting Circles

In front of each goal shall be drawn a line, 4 yd long, parallel to and 16yd from the back-line. The 16yd shall be measured from the inside front corner of the goal-posts to the outer edge of that line. This line shall be continued each way to meet the back-lines by quarter circles having the inside front corner of the goal-posts as centres. The space enclosed by these lines, including the lines themselves, shall be called the shooting circle (hereinafter referred to as 'the circle').

7. The Ball

(*a*) The ball shall be spherical with the specifications mentioned in this Rule.

(*b*) The weight of the ball shall be not more than $5\frac{3}{4}$oz (163g), and not less than $5\frac{1}{2}$oz (156g).

(*c*) The circumference of the ball shall be not more than $9\frac{1}{4}$in (23.5cm) nor less than $8\frac{13}{16}$in (22.4cm).

(*d*) (i) The ball shall be hard; it may be solid or hollow, provided it meets the other specifications in this Rule.

(ii) The ball shall have an outer surface of any natural or artificial material. The surface shall be smooth, but a seam or indentations are permitted provided they do not alter the shape of the ball.

(iii) The inner portion of a solid ball may consist of any natural or artificial material in any composition or mixture, as long as it meets the other specifications in this Rule.

(*e*) The traditional colour of the ball is white, but the team captains may agree upon the use of a ball of any other colour, as long as it contrasts with the colour of the field of play.

(*f*) Umpires shall not permit the use of a ball that does, in their opinion, not comply with this Rule. Should a ball during a game deteriorate in such a way that it not longer meets the specifications of this Rule, it shall be replaced immediately. If the game has not been stopped for any reason and the ball is in play when it becomes unusable, the game shall be stopped and restarted using a new ball in accordance with Rule 10(*b*). See also Rule 11(*a*) and Rule 17 I and II.

8. The Stick

(*a*) The stick shall have a flat face on its left-hand side only. The face of the stick is the whole of the flat side and that part of the handle for the whole of the length which is above the flat side.

(*b*) The head (i.e. the part below the lower end of the splice) shall be curved and shall be of wood and shall not be edged with or have any insets or fittings of metal or any other substance, nor shall there be any sharp edges or dangerous splinters. The maximum length of the curved head of the stick, as measured from the lowest part of the flat face, shall not exceed 4in. It shall not be cut square or pointed, but shall have rounded edges.

(*c*) The total weight of the stick shall not exceed 28oz, nor be less than 12oz, and it shall be of such a size, inclusive of any covering, that it can be passed through a ring having an interior diameter of 5.10cm.

(*d*) Umpires shall forbid the use of any stick which in their opinion does not comply with this Rule. See Rule 3(i).

Penalty: For any breach of this Rule any player concerned shall not be allowed on the field of play until such time as he complied with this Rule.

9. Players' Dress and Equipment

(*a*) Each player shall wear the dress approved by his Association or Club, unless varied to avoid confusion in a particular game. Goal-keepers shall wear a colour different from that of their own team and that of their opponents. Players shall not have dangerous spikes, studs or protruding nails in footwear, or wear anything that may be dangerous to other players.

(*b*) The following equipment is permitted for use by goalkeepers only: Body Protectors, Pads, Kickers, Gauntlet Gloves, Protective Headgear (now mandatory), and Elbow Pads.

Penalty: For any breach of this Rule any player concerned shall not be allowed on the field of play until such time as he has complied with this Rule.

10. To Start or Restart the Game

(*a*) To start the game, restart it after half-time and after each goal scored, a 'pass-back' shall be played at the centre of the field. The pass-back for the start of the game shall be made by a player of the team which did not make a choice of ends (see Rule 2*a*), after half-time by a player of the opposing team, and after a goal has been scored by a player of the team against whom the goal has been awarded. The pass-back, which may be pushed or hit, must not be directed over the centre-line. At the moment when the pass-back is taken, no player of the opposing team shall be within 5yd of the ball and all players of both teams other than the player making the pass-back must be in their own half of the field. If the striker hits at but misses the ball, the pass-back still has to be taken. After taking the pass-back, the striker shall not play the ball nor remain or approach within playing distance until it has been touched or played by another player of either team. Time wasting shall not be permitted.

(*b*) (i) To restart the game in accordance with Rule 7(*f*), Rule 12 III, Rule 12 Penalties 4 or Rule 18(*b*)(i) a bully shall be played on a spot to be chosen by the umpire in whose half of the ground the incident occurred.

(ii) To bully, a player of each team shall stand squarely facing the side-lines, each with his own back-line on his right. The ball shall be placed on the ground between the two players. Each player shall tap with his stick, first the ground between the ball and his own back-line, and then, with the flat face of his stick, his opponent's stick, over the ball, three times alternately, after which one of these two players shall play the ball with his stick to put it into play.

(iii) Until the ball is in play, all other players shall not stand within 5yd of the ball.

(iv) A bully shall not be played within 16yd of the back-line or goal-line.

Penalties. 1. For a breach of Rule 10(*a*) a free hit shall be awarded to the opposing team.

2. For a breach of Rule 10(*b*)(ii) or (iii) the bully shall be played again.

3. For persistent breaches of Rule 10(*b*)(ii) and (iii), the umpire may award a free hit to the opposing team; or, for such breaches in the circle by a defender, a penalty corner.

11. Scoring a Goal

(*a*) A goal is scored when the whole ball, having been hit or deflected by the stick of an attacker whilst in the circle and not having gone outside the circle, passes completely over the goal-line between the goal-posts and under the cross-bar – except in circumstances detailed in Rule 15(*g*) and Rule 16. 15(*e*) and 15(*h*), when a goal may not be awarded, and in circumstances detailed in Rule 16 Penalty 1, when a goal may be awarded. It is immaterial if the ball subsequently touches, or is played by one or more defenders. If, during the game, the goal-posts and/or the cross-bar becomes displaced, and the ball passes completely over the goal-line at a point which, in the umpire's opinion, is between where the goal-posts and/or under where the cross-bar, respectively, should have been, a goal shall be awarded.

(*b*) The team scoring the greater number of goals shall be the winner.

12. Conduct of Play
I. A player shall not:

(*a*) Play the ball with the rounded side of his stick.

(*b*) Take part in or interfere with the game unless he has his own stick in his hand, or change his stick for the purpose of taking part in the game under Rules 14, 15, 16 and 17.

'Own stick' means the stick with which the player began to play, or any stick that he legitimately substitutes for it.

(*c*) Raise his stick in a manner that is dangerous, intimidating or hampering to another player when approaching, attempting to play, playing or stopping the ball. A ball above the height of a player's shoulder shall not be played or played at by any part of the stick. For goalkeepers see Rule 12 II(*c*).

(*d*) Stop the ball with his hand or catch it. For goalkeepers, see Rule 12 II(*c*). *There is nothing in this Rule which prevents a player using his hand to protect himself from a dangerously raised ball.*

(*e*) Hit wildly into an opponent or play or raise or kick the ball in such a way as to be dangerous in itself, or likely to lead to dangerous play or play the ball intentionally into an opponent's foot, leg or body.

(*f*) Stop or deflect the ball on the ground or in the air with any part of the body *to his or his team's advantage*, save as provided for in Rule 12 II(*c*).

(*g*) Deliberately raise the ball so that it will fall into the circle.

(*h*) Use the foot or leg to support the stick in order to resist an opponent.

(*i*) Kick, pick up, throw, carry or propel the ball in any manner or direction except with the stick. But see guidance 12 I(*f*), 12 I(*i*) and Rule 12 II(*c*).

(*j*) Hit, hook, hold, strike at or interfere with an opponent's stick.

(*k*) Charge, kick, shove, trip, strike at or personally handle an opponent or his clothing.

(*l*) Obstruct by running between an opponent and the ball nor interpose himself or his stick as an obstruction.

II. A player may:

(*a*) Play the ball only with the flat side of his stick, which includes that part of the handle above the flat side.

(*b*) Tackle from the left of an opponent provided that he plays the ball without previous interference with the stick or person of his opponent. See Rule 12 I, particularly (*k*), (*l*), (*m*).

(*c*) If he is a goalkeeper and the ball is inside his circle, be allowed – contrary to the provisions of Rule 12 I(*c*), (*d*), (*f*) and (*j*) – to kick the ball, stop it with any part of his body including his hand and stop it with his stick above his shoulder. No penalty shall be incurred if when stopping a shot at goal, the ball rebounds off any part of the goalkeeper's body or his stick.

III. (*a*) If the ball becomes lodged in one of the pads of a goalkeeper, or in the clothing of any player or umpire, the umpire shall stop the game and restart it by a bully on the spot where the incident occurred, subject to Rule 10(*b*)(iv).

(*b*) If the ball strikes an umpire or any loose object on the pitch, including any piece of playing equipment dropped accidentally, the game shall continue. Any deliberate action by a player in throwing his stick or other piece of playing equipment on to the pitch, at the ball, at an opponent or at an umpire, should be penalised under Rule 12 IV.

IV. *Misconduct. Rough or dangerous play, time-wasting, deliberate breaches of any rule, or any other behaviour which in the umpire's opinion amounts to misconduct shall not be permitted.*

Penalties.

1. *Outside the circle*: A free hit shall be awarded to the opposing team. An umpire shall award a penalty corner for an offence by any defender inside his own 25yd area, when, in the umpire's opinion, the offence was deliberate.

2. *Inside the circle – by an attacker*: A free hit shall be awarded to the defending team.

3. *Inside the circle – by a defender*: For a breach inside the circle by a defender a penalty corner shall be awarded or a penalty stroke if in the umpire's opinion, Rule 16(*a*) applies.

4. *Inside and Outside the circle*: For a simultaneous breach of this Rule by two opponents, the umpire shall order a bully to be played on the spot where the breach occurred, subject to Rule 10(*b*) (iv).

5. *Inside and Outside the circle*: For rough or dangerous play or misconduct, in addition to awarding the appropriate penalty, the umpire may:

(i) Warn the offending player(s), which may also be indicated by showing a green card;

(ii) Suspend him (them) temporarily, for not less than 5 minutes, which may also be indicated by showing a yellow card;

(iii) Suspend him (them) from further participation in the game which may also be indicated by showing a red card.

A temporarily suspended player shall remain on the team bench or in the sin-bin, until allowed by the umpire by whom he was suspended to resume play.

13. Off-side

(*a*) *At the moment when the ball is played*, a player of the same team as the pusher or striker is in an off-side position if he is in his opponents' 25-yd area unless:

(i) He is behind the ball; or

(ii) There are at least two opponents nearer to their own back-line or goal-line than he is.

(*b*) A player who is in an off-side position shall not play or attempt to play the ball or gain any advantage for his team or influence the play of an opponent.

Penalty: A free hit shall be awarded to the defending team.

14. Free Hit

(*a*) A free hit shall be taken on the spot where the breach occurred except that:

(i) *for a breach by an attacker within the circle* it shall be taken:
either from any spot within that circle,
or from any spot within 16yd of the inner edge of the defending team's back-line or goal-line on a line drawn through the place where the breach occurred and parallel to the side-line.

(ii) *for a breach by an attacker outside the circle but within 16yd of the defending team's back-line* it shall be taken from any spot within 16yd of the inner edge of the defending team's back-line on a line drawn through the place where the breach occurred and parallel to the side-line.

(*b*) The ball shall be stationary and the striker shall push or hit it. The ball must be moved and shall not be raised intentionally in such a way as to be dangerous in itself, or likely to lead to dangerous play.

(*c*) At the moment when the free hit is taken, no player of the opposing team shall remain within 5yd of the ball. However, for a free hit to the attacking team within 5yd of the circle, players of both teams, except the striker, shall be at least 5yd from the ball. Should the umpire consider that a player is standing within 5yd of the ball in order to gain time, the free hit shall not be delayed.

(*d*) If the striker hits at but misses the ball, provided that Rule 12 I(*c*) has not been contravened, the free hit still has to be taken.

(*e*) After taking the free hit, the striker shall not play the ball again nor remain or approach within playing distance until it has been touched or played by another player of either team.

Penalties.

1. *Inside the circle*: A penalty corner or a penalty stroke shall be awarded to the attacking team.

2. *Outside the circle*: A free hit shall be awarded to the opposing team. An umpire shall award a penalty corner for an offence by any defender in his own 25yd area, when, in the umpire's opinion, the offence was deliberate.

15. Penalty Corner

(*a*) A penalty corner shall be awarded to the opposing team if, in the umpire's opinion:

(i) There has been an *intentional* breach of Rules 12, 14 or 17 inside the 25yd area but outside the circle by a player of the defending team; or

(ii) An *unintentional* breach of Rule 12, 14 or 17 II(*b*) inside the circle by a player of the defending team; or

(iii) For persistent breaches of Rule 10(*b*)(ii) or (iii) in the circle by a defender.

(*b*) A player of the attacking team shall push or hit the ball from a spot on the back-line not less than 10yd from the goal-post, on whichever side of the goal the attacking team prefers. The player concerned is required to have at least one foot outside the field of play when taking the penalty corner. The ball shall not be raised, but the hit shall not be penalised if the ball lifts slightly off the ground without causing danger or appearing likely to lead to dangerous play.

(*c*) (i) At the moment when such push or hit is made, no other player shall be within 5yd of the ball. The rest of the attacking team shall be in the field of play with both sticks and feet outside the circle. Not more than 5 of the defending team shall stand with both sticks and feet behind their own goal-line or back-line. The rest of the defending team shall be beyond the centre-line.

(ii) In the event of the defending goalkeeper being incapacitated he shall be replaced immediately by another goalkeeper. If the defending goalkeeper be suspended, he may be replaced by another goalkeeper from his team bench (substitutes), but a field player must leave the field, thus leaving the team one player short. Replacement goalkeepers shall be permitted to put on protective equipment without undue delay (See Rule 9(*b*)).

(*d*) Until the ball is pushed or hit no attacker shall enter the circle, nor shall a defender cross the goal-line, back-line or centre-line.

(*e*) (i) No shot at goal shall be made from a penalty corner until the ball be stopped or come to rest on the ground outside the circle or has touched the stick or person of a defender. The defending goalkeeper shall remain on his feet until the first shot at goal has been made.

(ii) If the first shot at goal is a hit, the ball shall not cross the goal-line at a height higher than the back-board/side-boards (18in) unless it has touched the stick or person of a defender.

(iii) If the ball travels beyond 5yd from the outer edge of the circle-line, the penalty corner is ended and the special provisions mentioned in (i) and (ii) no longer apply.

Note: As a mandatory experiment, the ball must be stopped outside the circle. The ball may be deflected or passed one or more times by the attacking players, but it must be stopped or come to a stop at some time outside within 5yd of the circle before a shot at goal is made. If the ball travels beyond 5yd from the outer edge of the circle, there is no need for it to be stopped as the penalty corner has ended.

Although the first hit must not cross the goal-line above a height of 18in, there is no limit to the height of a push, flick or scoop or of any subsequent stroke, subject always to there being no danger. Nor is there any limit to the height of a hit before it crosses the line subject always to there being no danger.

At the moment when the penalty corner hit or push from the backline is taken, the goalkeeper may remain on the goal-line or move to another position but he is not allowed to lie down until the first shot at goal has been made. As soon as that first shot (be it a hit, push, flick, or scoop) has been made, the goalkeeper is permitted to dive, kneel, slide etc in the usual manner. It is the act of deliberately grounding himself before the first shot, that is denied to the goalkeeper by Rule 15(e) (i); consequently the goalkeeper shall not be penalised if he makes an involuntary fall or if his act be induced by the actions of his opponents, in which case the umpire may order that the penalty corner be taken again. The goalkeeper may also dive, slide, etc whenever he gets within playing distance of the ball before the first shot at goal has been made.

If the ball has not previously been touched by a defender, or has not been stopped on the ground, a flying hit following a pass or deflection from one attacker to another, should be penalised as a breach of this Rule.

(*f*) The player injecting the penalty corner hit or push from the back-line shall not, after striking the ball, play the ball again, nor approach or remain within playing distance of the ball, until it has been touched or played by another player of either team.

(*g*) If the injector of the penalty corner hits at or pushes at but misses the ball, the penalty corner still has to be taken.

(*h*) No goal shall be scored directly by the player injecting the penalty corner hit or push from the back-line, even if the ball is played into goal by a defender.

Penalties.

1. *For a breach of Rules* 15(*c*) (i) *or* 15(*d*), *viz*:

Attacker(s) entering the circle or defender(s) crossing the goal-line, back-line or centre-line too soon or coming from 5yd of the ball too soon – the penalty may, at the discretion of the umpire, be taken again.

2. *For persistent breaches of Rule* 15(*b*) (i) *or* 15(*d*) *by the attackers* – The umpire may award a free hit.

3. *For persistent breaches of Rules* 15(*c*) (i) *or* 15(*d*) *by the defenders* – The umpire may award a penalty stroke.

4. *For an unintentional breach of Rule* 15(*e*) (i) *by the goalkeeper* – The penalty corner may, at the discretion of the umpire, be taken again.

5. *For intentional or persistent breaches of Rule* 15(*e*) (i) *by the goalkeeper* – The umpire shall award a penalty stroke.

6. *For any other breach of Rule* 15 – A free hit shall be awarded to the defending team.

16. Penalty Stroke

(*a*) A penalty stroke shall be awarded to the opposing team if that team has possession or the opportunity to gain possession of the ball in the circle and, in the opinion of the umpire:

(i) There has been an *intentional* breach of Rules 12, 14 or 17 II (*g*) (v) inside the circle by a player of the defending team; or

(ii) A goal would probably have been scored had an *unintentional* breach of Rule 12 inside the circle by a player of the defending team not occurred.

(iii) Rules 15(*c*)(i) and/or 15(*d*) are persistently breached by the defenders.

(*b*) (i) The penalty stroke shall be either a push, flick or scoop stroke taken from a spot 7yd in front of the centre of the goal by a player of the attacking team and defended by the goalkeeper of the opposing team on the field at the time the breach occurred. In the event of the goalkeeper being incapacitated or suspended, the captain of the defending team shall immediately nominate another goalkeeper. This goalkeeper shall be permitted to put on or remove, without undue delay, protective equipment. Under the provisions of this Rule, before the taking of the stroke, a goalkeeper may also remove his face mask, headgear and/or his gauntlet gloves. See Rule 9(*b*).

(ii) Whichever stroke is used, the ball may be raised to any height.

(iii) During the taking of a penalty stroke all the other players of both teams shall stand beyond the nearer 25yd line and shall not influence or attempt to influence the conduct of the penalty stroke.

(*c*) (i) The attacking player shall not take the penalty stroke until the umpire, having satisfied himself that both defender and attacker are ready, has indicated that he may do so by blowing his whistle.

(ii) When taking the stroke the attacker shall stand close to and behind the ball and shall be permitted in making the stroke to take one stride forward. Dragging or lifting the rear foot is not a breach of this Rule, provided that it does not pass the front foot before the ball is moved.

(iii) The attacker shall touch the ball once only and thereafter shall not approach either the ball or the goalkeeper.

(*d*) (i) The goalkeeper shall stand on the goal-line. After the player taking the stroke and the goalkeeper are in position and the umpire has blown his whistle, the goalkeeper may not leave the goal-line or move either of his feet until the ball has been played.

(ii) The usual privileges of the goalkeeper shall be allowed to him, but he shall not be allowed to delay the taking of the stroke by making unnecessary changes or modifications of clothing. If the ball be caught and held by the goalkeeper, the penalty stroke is ended. See also clause (*e*) (iii). He shall not be penalised, if, in stopping a shot at goal, the ball, in the umpire's opinion, rebounds off his body, stick or his hand.

(iii) If any deliberate action by the attacker prior to striking the ball induces the goalkeeper to move either of his feet or, if the attacker feints at striking the ball, the attacker shall be penalised.

(*e*) If, as a result of the penalty stroke:

(i) The whole ball passes completely over the goal-line between the goal-posts and under the cross-bar, a goal is scored.

(ii) The ball should come to rest inside the circle, be lodged in the goalkeeper's pads, be caught by the goalkeeper, or pass outside the circle, in all cases the penalty stroke is ended. Unless a goal has been scored or awarded, the game shall be restarted by a push or hit to be taken by a defender from a spot in front of the centre of the goal and 16yd from the inner edge of that line.

(*f*) All time taken between the award of a penalty stroke and resumption of play shall be added to the time of play.

Penalties.

1. For a breach of any rule by the goalkeeper which prevents a goal from being scored, a goal shall be awarded to the opposing team (see penalty 3 below).

2. For a breach of any Rule by an attacker, the game shall be restarted with a free hit to be taken by a defender from a spot in front of the centre of the goal-line and 16yd from the inner edge of that line.

3. For a breach of clause (*b*) (iii) or (*d*) (i), the umpire may order the stroke to be taken again.

17. Ball Outside Field of Play

When the whole ball passes completely over the back-line, and no goal is scored, or over the side-line, it is out of play and the game shall be restarted as in Rules 17 I and 17 II.

I. *Over side-line*

(*a*) When the whole ball passes completely over the side-line, it or another ball shall be placed on the line at the spot at which it crossed the side-line. The ball shall be pushed or hit without undue delay by a player of the team opposed to the player who last touched it in play. This player is not required to be wholly inside or outside the side-line when making his push or hit.

(*b*) The ball shall be stationary and the striker shall push or hit it. The ball must be moved and shall not be raised intentionally or in such a way as to be dangerous in itself or likely to lead to dangerous play.

(*c*) At the moment when the push or hit is taken no player of the opposing team shall be within 5yd of the ball. If any player of the opposing team be within 5yd of the ball, the umpire may require the push or hit to be taken again. If, however, in the umpire's opinion, a player of the opposing remains within 5yd of the ball to gain time, the push or hit shall not be delayed.

(*d*) If the striker hits at but misses the ball, provided that Rule 12 I(*c*) has not been contravened, the push or hit still has to be taken.

(*e*) After taking a push or hit the player shall not play the ball again, nor remain or approach within playing distance of the ball until it has been touched or played by another player of either team.

Penalty. For any breach of this Rule, a free hit shall be awarded to the opposing team.

II. *Over back-line*

(*a*) By an attacker.

(i) When the ball passes completely over the opponents' back-line by or off one of the attacking team and no goal is scored, it or another ball shall be placed on a spot opposite the place where it crossed the back-line and not more than 16yd from the inner edge of that line. The ball shall be pushed or hit without undue delay by one of the defending team.

(ii) The ball shall be stationary and the striker shall push or hit it. The ball must be moved and shall not be raised intentionally or in such a way as to be dangerous in itself or likely to lead to dangerous play.

(iii) No player of the opposing team shall be within 5 yd of the ball when the push or hit is taken.

(iv) If the striker hits at but misses the ball, provided that Rule 12 I(*c*) has not been contravened, the push or hit still has to be taken.

(v) After taking the push or hit, the striker shall not play the ball again nor remain nor approach within playing distance of the ball until it has been touched or played by another player of either team.

(*b*) *By a defender*.

(i) When the ball has been unintentionally hit by, or glanced off, the stick or person of a defender and has gone over his own back-line or goal-line from within his own 25yd area, a push or hit shall be taken by the attacking team as follows, unless a goal has been scored.

(*a*) The player shall push or hit the ball from a spot on the back-line within 5yd of the corner flag nearer to the point where the ball crossed the back-line.

(*b*) The ball shall be stationary and the striker shall push or hit it. The ball must be moved and shall not be raised intentionally or in a way that is dangerous in itself or likely to lead to dangerous play.

(*c*) No player of the opposing team shall be within 5yd of the ball when the push or hit is taken.

(*d*) If the striker hits at but misses the ball, provided that Rule 12 I(*c*) has not been contravened, the push or hit still has to be taken.

(*e*) After taking the push or hit, the striker shall not play the ball again nor remain or approach within playing distance of the ball until it has been touched or played by another player of either team.

(ii) When the ball, in the umpire's opinion, is sent over his own back-line or goal-line by or off one of the defending team who is more than 25yd from the back-line, the game shall be restarted by a push or hit by one of the defending team from a spot opposite the place where it crossed the back-line or goal-line and not more than 16yd from the inner edge of that line.

(*a*) The ball shall be stationary and the striker shall push or hit it. The ball must be moved and shall not be raised intentionally or in a way that is dangerous in itself or likely to lead to dangerous play.

(*b*) No player of the opposing team shall be within 5yd of the ball when the push or hit is taken.

(*c*) If the striker hits at but misses the ball, provided that Rule 12 I(*c*) has not been contravened, the push or hit has to be taken.

(*d*) After taking the push or hit, the striker shall not play the ball again nor remain nor approach within playing distance of the ball until it has been touched or played by another player of either team.

Penalties:

1. For a breach of this Rule by an attacker, a free hit shall be awarded to the defending team.

2. For a ball raised dangerously from a free hit within the circle by a defender, a penalty corner shall be awarded.

3. For an unintentional breach of this Rule by a defender outside the circle a free hit shall be awarded to the attacking team.

4. For an unintentional breach of this Rule inside the circle or for an intentional breach of this Rule by a defender within the 25yd area but outside the circle, a penalty corner shall be awarded.

5. For an intentional breach of this Rule by a defender within the circle, a penalty stroke shall be awarded.

III. No player may deliberately play or deflect the ball over his own back-line or goal-line from an area enclosed by the 25yd line, including the circle.

Penalty: For a breach of this Rule, a penalty corner shall be awarded to the opposing team.

18. Accidents

(*a*) If a player or an umpire be incapacitated, the umpire or other umpire shall stop the game temporarily noting the time lost. See Rule 3(*f*).

In either case, if a goal be scored before the game be stopped it shall be allowed if, in the umpire's opinion, it would have been scored had the accident not occurred.

(*b*) The umpire shall restart the game as soon as possible, by:

(i) A bully – subject to Rule 10(*b*)(iv) – on a spot to be chosen by the umpire in whose half of the ground the accident occurred; or

(ii) The appropriate penalty when the accident was the result of a breach of the rules; or

(iii) The implementation of a decision given before the game was stopped.

(*c*) If the umpire concerned cannot continue, the other umpire or a replacement or reserve umpire shall restart the game.

Issued under the authority of the Hockey Rules Board on behalf of the International Hockey Federation and reprinted here with their permission. Guidance for Players and Umpires, Advice to Umpires and Equipment Specifications have been omitted for reasons of space but are given in the complete Rules of the Game of Hockey, available from the Board.

Ice Hockey

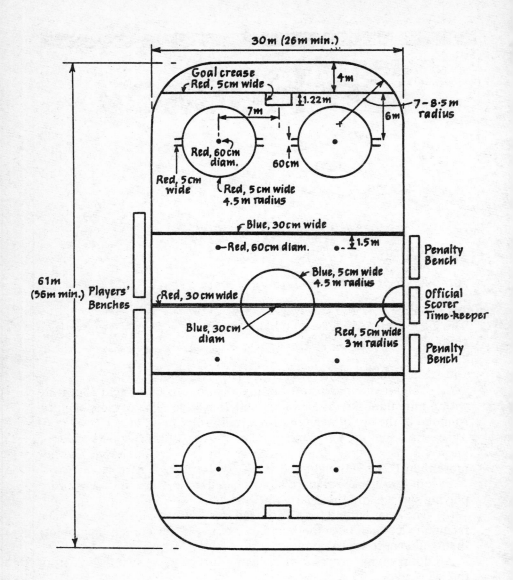

Ice Hockey

1. THE RINK

A glossary of terms may be found on pages 622–625

101. Rink
The game of Ice Hockey shall be played on an ice surface known as a **rink**.

102. Dimensions of Rink (see diagram on opposite page)
(*a*) The maximum size of the rink shall be 61m long and 30m wide with a minimum size of 56m long and 26m wide. The corners shall be rounded in the arc of a circle with a radius of 7 to 8.5m.

The rink shall be surrounded by a wooden or plastic wall or fence known as the **boards** which shall extend not less than 1.20m and not more than 1.22m in height above the level of the ice surface.

Except for the official markings provided for in these rules, the entire playing surface and the boards shall be white in colour.

(*b*) The boards shall be constructed in such manner that the surface facing the ice shall be smooth and free of any obstruction or any object that could cause injury to players.

All doors giving access to the playing surface must swing away from the ice surface.

All protective screens and gear used to hold them in position shall be mounted on the boards on the side away from the playing surface.

It is recommended that above the boards of the rink there be:

1. Protective glass 160–200cm in height on the ends between the goal-lines and 80–100cm along the sides.

2. Nets at the ends behind the goals above the glass to protect the spectators.

For the IIHF Championships the protective glass is obligatory.

103. Goals

(*a*) 4.00m from each end of the rink and in the centre of a red line 5cm wide drawn completely across the width of the ice and continued vertically up the side of the boards, regulation goal-posts and nets shall be set in such manner as to remain stationary during the progress of a game.

(*b*) The goal-posts shall be of approved design and material, extending vertically 1.22m above the surface of the ice and 1.83m apart, measured from the inside of the posts. A cross-bar of the same material as the goal-posts shall extend from the top of one post to the top of the other.

1. The inside measurement of the goal from the front of the goal-line to the rear of the net, at its deepest point, shall not be more than 1.12m or less than 60cm.

2. There shall be attached to the back of each goal-frame a net which is constructed in such a manner as to keep the puck within the confines of the goal.

(*c*) The goal-posts, cross-bar and the exterior surface of other supporting framework for the goal shall be painted entirely in red. The surface of the base plate inside the goal and supports other than the goal-posts shall be painted white and covered by a white cushion.

(*d*) The red line, 5cm wide, between the goal-posts on the ice and extended completely across the rink, shall be known as the **goal-line**.

104. Goal-Crease

(*a*) In front of each goal a **goal-crease** area shall be marked by a red line 5cm in width.

(*b*) The goal-crease shall be laid out as follows: 30cm from the outside of each goal-post, lines 1.22m in length and 5cm in width shall be drawn at right angles to the goal-line and the points of these lines farthest from the goal-line shall be joined by another line, 5cm in width.

(*c*) The goal-crease area shall include all the space outlined by the crease-lines and extended vertically 1.22m to the level of the top of the goal-frame.

105. Division of Ice Surface

(*a*) The ice area between the two goal-lines shall be divided into three equal parts by lines 30cm in width and blue in colour, extending completely across the rink, parallel with the goal-lines, and continuing vertically up the side of boards.

(*b*) That portion of the ice surface in which the goal is situated shall be called the **defending zone** of the team defending that goal; the central portions shall be known as the **neutral zone**, and the portion farthest from the defending goal as the **attacking zone**. The zone-line shall be considered part of the zone that the puck is in.

(*c*) There shall also be a line, known as the **centre line**, 30cm in width and red in colour, drawn completely across the rink in centre ice, parallel with the goal-lines, continuing vertically up the side of the boards.

106. Centre Ice Spot and Circle
A circular blue spot, 30cm in diameter, shall be marked exactly in the centre of the rink; and with this spot as a centre, a circle of 4.5m radius shall be marked with a blue line 5cm in width.

107. Face-off Spots in Neutral Zone
Two spots 60cm in diameter shall be marked with a red line 5 cm wide on the ice in the Neutral Zone 1.5m from each blue line, and the same distance from the boards as the end zone face-off spots. Within each face-off spot draw two parallel lines 7.5cm from the top and bottom of the spot. The area within the two lines shall be painted red, the remainder shall be painted white.

108. End Zones Face-off Spots and Circles
(*a*) Face-off spots and circles shall be marked on the ice in both end zones and on both sides of each goal. The face-off spots shall be 60cm in diameter and drawn with a red line 5cm wide. Within each face-off spot draw two parallel lines 7.5cm from the top and bottom of the spot. The area within the two lines shall be painted red, the remainder shall be painted white. The circles shall have a radius of 4.5m from the centre of the face-off spots and marked with a red line 5cm wide. Extending from the outer edge of both sides of each face-off circle shall be two lines 5.5m and 6.5m from and parallel to the goal-line, 60cm long and 5cm wide.

(*b*) The location of the face-off spots shall be fixed in the following manner.

Establish the imaginary point 6m directly in front of the centre of each goal; 7m on each side of this point, parallel to and 6m from the goal-line, shall be the centre of the end zone face-off spots.

109. Players' Benches
(*a*) Each rink shall be provided with seats or benches for the use of both teams, and the accommodations provided including benches and doors shall be uniform for both teams. Such seats or benches shall have accommodation for at least 16 persons of each team and shall be placed immediately alongside the ice, in the Neutral Zone, as near to the centre of the rink as possible, and convenient to the dressing-rooms.

The players' benches should be on the same side of the playing surface opposite the penalty bench and should be separated by a substantial distance.

Where physically possible, each players' bench shall have two doors opening in the Neutral Zone, and all doors opening to the playing surface shall be constructed so that they swing inward.

(*b*)   None but players in uniform, and not more than 6 team officials, shall be permitted to occupy the players' bench area so provided.

(*c*)   For the choice of players' benches, see Section B under Rule 632, Start of Game and Periods.

110. Penalty Bench

(*a*)   Each rink must be provided with benches or seats to be known as the **penalty bench**. It is preferable to have separate penalty benches for each team separated from each other and substantially separated from either players' bench. The penalty bench(es) must be situated opposite the Neutral Zone.

(*b*)   A semi-circle, 3m in radius, to be known as the **referees' crease**, shall be marked on the ice by a line 5cm wide immediately in front of the Penalty Timekeeper.

111. Signal and Timing Devices

(*a*)   Each rink shall be provided with a siren, or other suitable sound device, for the use of Timekeepers.

(*b*)   Each rink shall have some form of electrical clock for the purpose of keeping the spectators, players and game officials accurately informed as to all time elements at all stages of the game, including the time played in any period and the time remaining to be served by at least two penalised players on each team.

Note: In the IIHF Championships the time of the periods shall be counted up, from 0 to 20, and the time of the penalties down from the total minutes imposed to zero.

(*c*)   Behind each goal there shall be electrical lights for the use of the Goal Judges. A red light shall signify the scoring of a goal. Where automatic lights are available, a green light will signify the end of a period only.

Note: The purpose of the green light is to enable the Referee and Linesmen to observe the goal and light in the same sight line and know exactly when the period ends. The red light shall be connected to the timing device in such a manner so that when the period has ended it will not be possible for the goal judge to put it on. However, the fact that the goal judge may not be able to put on the red light does not necessarily mean that the goal is not valid. The determining factor is whether or not the puck is completely over the goal line and in the goal before the period ends.

112. Dressing-rooms and Rink Lighting

(*a*) Each rink shall provide a suitable room, equipped with sanitary toilet and shower suitable for 25 persons with equipment, for the use of the visiting team.

(*b*) A separate dressing-room equipped with sanitary toilet and shower shall be provided for the use of the Referees and Linesmen.

(*c*) No officer, manager, player or employee of any team may enter into an acrimonious discussion with any Referee or Linesman, during or after a game and no person, except as authorised by the Association concerned, shall be allowed to enter the Referees' dressing-room during the course of, or immediately following a game. For any infraction of this rule the matter shall be reported by the Referee to the proper authorities for further action.

(*d*) All rinks shall be sufficiently well lighted so that the players and spectators may conveniently follow play at all times.

Note: If, in the opinion of the Referee, there is not sufficient light to continue the game, the Referee shall have the authority to postpone the remainder of the game or take time out pending the necessary improvement to the lights. If one team is being handicapped to a greater extent by failure of lights and in the opinion of the Referee the game should not be cancelled, he shall have the authority to alternate the teams so as each team will play the same amount of time in each end of the rink.

2. TEAMS

201. Composition of Teams

(*a*) A team shall not have more than 6 players on the ice at any one time while the play is in progress. These 6 players shall be designated as follows: Goalkeeper, Right Defence, Left Defence, Centre, Right Wing and Left Wing.

(*b*) If at any time a team has more than 6 players on the ice, or the number to which they are entitled by reason of penalties, during the progress of play, they shall be assessed a bench minor penalty.

202. Captain of Team

(*a*) Each team shall appoint a Captain and not more than two Alternate Captains. On the ice, only the Captain or Alternate Captain shall have the privilege of discussing any questions with the Referee relating to interpretation of rules that may arise during the progress of a game. Only the Captain or an Alternate Captain may come off the bench if invited by the Referee when none are on the ice. If the Captain or Alternate Captain comes off the bench when not invited by the Referee, a bench minor penalty is to be assessed upon the team. When the Captain and an Alternate Captain are on the ice, only the Captain may talk to the Referee.

The Captain shall wear the letter 'C' and the Alternate Captain(s) the letter 'A' in a conspicuous position on the front of the sweater. The letters should be in a contrasting colour approximately 8cm in height.

If the letters are not worn, the privileges under this section will not be granted.

(*b*) The Referee and Official Scorer shall be advised, prior to the start of each game, the names and numbers of the Captain of the team and Alternate Captain(s).

(*c*) No goalkeepers shall be entitled to exercise the privileges of Captain or Alternate Captain.

(*d*) Only the Captain or Alternate Captain shall have the privilege of discussing with the Referee any point relating to the interpretation of rules. Any other player who comes off the bench and makes any protest or intervention with the officials for any purpose shall be assessed a misconduct penalty in addition to a minor penalty under Rule 601(*a*), Abuse of Officials.

A complaint about a penalty is *not* a matter 'relating to the interpretation of the rules' and a minor penalty under Rule 601(*a*) Abuse of Officials, shall be imposed against any Captain or Alternate Captain or other player making such a complaint.

(*e*) No playing Coach or playing Manager shall be permitted to act as Captain.

203. Players in Uniform

(*a*) At the beginning of each game the Manager or Coach of each team shall list the players and goalkeepers who shall be eligible to play in the game. A maximum of 20 players, plus 2 goalkeepers, shall be permitted.

(*b*) Each player shall wear an individual number at least 25cm in height on the back of his sweater.

All players of each team shall be dressed uniformly in colour of their helmet, sweaters, pants and stockings. Any player not complying with this provision shall not be permitted to participate in the game.

(*c*) A list of names and numbers of all eligible players and goalkeepers shall be handed to the Referee or Official Scorer before the game, and no change in the list or addition thereto shall be permitted after the commencement of the game.

(*d*) Each team shall be allowed one goalkeeper on the ice at one time. The goalkeeper may be removed and another 'player' substituted. Such a 'player' substitute shall not be permitted the privileges of the goalkeeper.

(*e*) Each team shall have on its bench, or on a chair immediately beside the bench, a substitute goalkeeper who shall at all times be fully dressed and equipped ready to play.

The substitute goalkeeper may enter the game at any time following a stoppage of play, but no warm-up shall be permitted (see Rule 205, Change of Players).

(*f*) Except when both goalkeepers are incapacitated, no player on the playing roster in that game shall be permitted to wear the equipment of the goalkeeper.

(*g*) In all games, where in the opinion of the Referee, the colours of the competing teams are so much alike that there is a possibility of a miscall by the Referee or Linesmen, it is the responsibility of the home team to change its sweaters if the Referee so orders.

204. Starting Line-up

(*a*) Prior to the start of the game, at the request of the Referee, the Manager or Coach of the visiting team is required to name the starting line-up to the Referee or the Official Scorer. At any time in the game, at the request of the Referee, made to the Captain, the visiting team must place a playing line-up on the ice and promptly commence play.

(*b*) Prior to the start of the game the Manager or Coach of the home team, having been advised by the Official Scorer or the Referee of the names of the starting line-up of the visiting team, shall name the starting line-up of the home team, which information shall be conveyed by the Official Scorer or the Referee to the Coach of the visiting team.

(*c*) No change in the starting line-up of either team, as given to the Referee or Official Scorer, or in the playing line-up on the ice, shall be made until the game is actually in progress. For an infraction of this rule, a bench minor penalty shall be imposed upon the offending team, provided such infraction is called to the attention of the Referee by the Captain of the opposing team before the second face-off in the first period takes place.

(*d*) Following a stoppage of play, the visiting team shall promptly place a line-up on the ice ready for play and no substitution shall be made for that time until play has been resumed. The home team may then make any desired substitution which does not result in the delay of the game.

If there is any undue delay by either team in changing lines, the Referee shall order the offending team or teams to take their positions immediately and not permit a line change.

Note: In the application of this rule, the change of one or more player(s) shall constitute a line change.

205. Change of Players

(*a*) Players may be changed at any time from the players' bench, provided that the changing players shall be within an imaginary area limited by the length of the respective players' bench and 3m from the boards and out of the play before any change is made.

A goalkeeper may be changed for another player at any time under the conditions set out in this section.

Note 1: When a goalkeeper leaves his goal area and proceeds to his players' bench for the purpose of substituting another player, the rear Linesman shall be responsible to see that the substitution made is not by reason of the premature departure of the substitute from the bench (before the goalkeeper is within 3m of the bench). If the substitution is made prematurely, the Linesman shall stop the play immediately by blowing his whistle, unless the non-offending team has possession of the puck, in which event the stoppage will be delayed until the puck changes hands. There shall be no time penalty to the team making the premature substitution, but the resulting face-off will take place on the centre 'face-off spot'.

The Referee shall request that the public address announcer make the following announcement: 'Play has been stopped due to premature entry of a player from the players' bench.'

Note 2: If, in the course of making a substitution, the player entering the game plays the puck with the stick, skates or hands or checks or makes any physical contact with an opposing player while the retiring player is actually on the ice, then the infraction of 'too many men on the ice' will be called.

If, in the course of a substitution, either the player entering the play or the player retiring is struck by the puck accidentally, the play will not be stopped and no penalty will be assessed.

Note 3: Goalkeepers shall not be permitted to go to the players' bench during a stoppage of play, except to be replaced or during the time-out. For a violation of this rule a minor penalty shall be assessed the goalkeeper.

(*b*) If, in the last 2 minutes of the game, a bench minor penalty is imposed for deliberate illegal substitution (too many men on the ice), a penalty shot shall be awarded against the offending team. The bench minor will not be served – see Rule 406(*d*), Penalty Shot.

(*c*) A player serving a penalty on the penalty bench, who is to be changed after the penalty has been served, must proceed at once, by way of the ice, and be at his own players' bench before any change can be made.

For any violation of this rule, a bench minor penalty shall be imposed.

(*d*) When a substitution for the goalkeeper has been made during a stoppage of play, the goalkeeper who left the game may not re-enter the game until the first stoppage of play thereafter.

There shall be no warm-up for any substitute goalkeeper. For violation of this rule a minor penalty shall be assessed to the goalkeeper returning to the game illegally.

(*e*) For player changes taking place during a stoppage of play, the Referee will assume the normal position for the ensuing face-off. The Referee will then allow a 5-second period during which the visiting team may make a player change. After this 5-second period has elapsed, the Referee will raise an arm to indicate that the visiting team may no longer change any player(s).

With the arm still up, the Referee will allow a 5-second period during which the home team may make a player change. After this 5-second period has elapsed, the Referee will drop the arm to indicate that the home team may no longer change any player(s).

Where a team attempts to make a player-change after their allotted period of time, the Referee shall send the player(s) back to their bench. Any subsequent infraction to this procedure at any time during the course of the game shall incur a bench minor penalty under this rule. A change of players may include from 1 to 6 players. A change of one player is considered a change under this rule.

206. Injured Players

(*a*) When a player, other than a goalkeeper, is injured or compelled to leave the ice during the game, he may retire from the game and be replaced by a substitute, but play must continue without the teams leaving the ice.

(*b*) If a goalkeeper sustains an injury or becomes ill, he must be ready to resume play immediately or be replaced by a substitute goalkeeper and no additional time shall be allowed by the Referee for the purpose of enabling the injured or ill goalkeeper to resume play – see also section (*d*).

If both goalkeepers of the team are incapacitated and unable to play, the team shall have 10 minutes to prepare, dress, and warm up another player in uniform to act as the goalkeeper. In this case, neither of the two regular goalkeepers may return to that game.

No warm-up shall be permitted for a substitute goalkeeper.

(*c*) The substitute goalkeeper shall be subject to the regular rules governing goalkeepers and shall be entitled to the same privileges.

(*d*) If a penalised player has been injured, he may proceed to the dressing-room without the necessity of taking a seat on the penalty bench. If the injured player receives a minor, major or match penalty, the penalised team shall immediately put a substitute player on the penalty bench who shall serve the penalty without change, except by the injured penalised player. For violation of this rule, a bench minor penalty shall be imposed.

The penalised player who has been injured and been replaced on the penalty bench shall not be eligible to play until his penalty has expired.

(*e*) When a player is injured so that he cannot continue play or go to his bench, the play shall not be stopped until the injured player's team has secured possession of the puck. If the player's team is in possession of the puck at the time of injury, play shall be stopped immediately, unless his team is in a scoring position.

Note 1: In the case where it is obvious that a player has sustained a serious injury, the Referee and/or Linesmen may stop the play immediately.

Note 2: When play has been stopped due to an injured player, excluding the goalkeeper, the injured player shall leave the ice and may not return to the ice until after play has resumed. If the player refuses to leave the ice a minor penalty for delay of game shall be assessed that player.

3. EQUIPMENT

301. Sticks

(*a*) The sticks shall be made of wood or other material approved by the IIHF such as aluminium or plastic and must not have any projections. The shaft of a player's stick must be straight. Adhesive tape of any colour may be wrapped around the stick at any place.

(*b*) No stick shall exceed 147cm in length, from the heel to the end of the shaft, nor more than 32cm from the heel to the end of the blade.

The blade of the stick shall not be more than 7.5cm and less than 5cm in width at any point.

All edges of the blade shall be bevelled.

The curvature of the blade of the stick shall be restricted in such a way that the distance of a perpendicular line measured from a straight line drawn from any point at the heel to the end of the blade to the point of maximum curvature shall not exceed 1.5cm.

(*c*) The blade of the goalkeeper's stick shall not exceed 9cm in width at any point, except at the heel where it must not exceed 11.5cm in width, nor shall the goalkeeper's stick exceed 39cm in length from the heel to the end of the blade.

The widened portion of the goalkeeper's stick extending up the shaft from the blade shall not extend more than 71cm from the heel and shall not exceed 9cm in width.

(*d*) A player who participates in the play while taking a replacement stick to his goalkeeper shall incur a minor penalty under this rule.

302. Skates

(*a*) All skates (except goalkeepers') shall be equipped with safety heel tips.

When the Referee becomes aware that any person is wearing a skate on which the protective heel tip is missing or broken, he shall direct its replacement at the next intermission between periods. If such replacement is not carried out and the player re-enters the game, the Referee shall assess a minor penalty to the offending player.

(*b*) The use of speed skates or fancy skates or any skate so designed that it may cause injury is prohibited.

303. Goalkeeper's Equipment

(*a*) With the exception of skates and stick, all the equipment worn by the goalkeeper must be constructed solely for the purpose of protection of head or body, and must not include any garment or contrivance which would give the goalkeeper undue assistance in keeping goal.
Note: Abdominal aprons extending down the front of the thighs on the outside of the pants are prohibited.

(*b*) The leg-guards worn by goalkeepers shall not exceed 30cm in extreme width when on the leg of the goalkeeper.

(*c*) Protective padding attached to the back or forming part of the goalkeeper's blocker glove shall not exceed 20.3cm in width nor 40.6cm in length at any point.

Cages on catching gloves are prohibited. A 'cage' shall mean any lacing or webbing or other material in the goalkeeper's catching glove joining the thumb and the index finger which is in excess of the minimum necessary to fill the gap when the goalkeeper's thumb and index finger in the glove are fully extended and spread and includes any pocket or pouch effect produced by excess lacing or webbing or other material between the thumb and index finger when fully extended.

304. Protective Equipment

(*a*) All protective equipment, except gloves, headgear or goalkeeper's leg guards, must be worn *entirely* under the uniform. For violation of this rule, after one warning by the Referee, a minor penalty shall be imposed on the offending player.

(*b*) All players must wear a hockey helmet, with chin-strap properly fastened.

(*c*) All goalkeepers must wear a full face-mask and a goalkeeper's full head protector or hockey helmet.

(*d*) Full face-masks shall be worn in all IIHF sanctioned games and tournaments in classifications of 20 years and younger. It is recommended that all senior players also wear full face-masks or at least eye protectors.

Full face-masks shall be worn in the IIHF Women's championships and in Women's international games.

(*e*) Full face-masks must be constructed in such a way that neither the puck nor the stick blade might get through it.

(*f*) Referees and Linesmen shall wear a black hockey helmet.

305. Dangerous Equipment

(*a*) The use of pads or protectors made of metal or any other material likely to cause injury to a player is prohibited.

Note: The Referee has the authority to prohibit a player from participating in the game while using or wearing any equipment that he considers dangerous to a player or game official.

(*b*) A glove from which all or part of the palm has been intentionally removed or cut to permit the use of the bare hand shall be considered illegal equipment and if any player wears such a glove in play, a minor penalty shall be imposed.

306. Puck

The puck shall be made of vulcanised rubber or other approved material, 2.54cm thick and 7.62cm in diameter, and be primarily black in colour. The puck shall weigh not less than 156g nor more than 170g.

4. PENALTIES

401. Penalties

Penalties shall be actual playing time and shall be divided into the following classes:

(1) Minor penalties
(2) Bench minor penalties
(3) Major penalties
(4) Misconduct penalties
(5) Match penalties
(6) Penalty shot

When penalties are imposed after the conclusion of any game and until the players have left the ice, such penalties shall be reported to the proper authorities by the Referees on the official game report.

In cases when any rule states that the Manager or Coach shall designate a player to serve any penalty and if the Manager or Coach refuses to name a player, the Referee shall have the authority to name any player of the offending team that he desires to serve the penalty.

402. Minor Penalties

(*a*) For a **minor penalty**, any player, other than a goalkeeper, shall be ruled off the ice for 2 minutes, during which time no substitute shall be permitted.

(*b*) A **bench minor** penalty involves the removal from the ice of one player of the team against which the penalty is imposed for a period of 2 minutes. Any player, except the goalkeeper of the team, may be designated to serve the penalty by the Manager or the Coach, through the Captain, and such player shall take his place on the penalty bench promptly and serve the penalty as if it was a minor penalty imposed on him.

(*c*) If, while a team is **short-handed** by one or more minor or bench minor penalties, the opposing team scores a goal, the first of such penalties served or assessed shall automatically terminate.

Note 1: 'Short-handed' means that the team must be below the numerical strength of its opponents on the ice at the time the goal is scored. Thus, an equal number of minor or major penalties to an equal number of players of both teams does not cause either team to be 'short-handed'.

This rule shall also apply when a goal is scored on a penalty shot.

When the minor penalties of two players of the same team terminate at the same time, the Captain of that team shall designate to the Referee which of such players will return to the ice first and the Referee will instruct the Official Scorer accordingly.

When a player receives a major penalty and a minor penalty at the same time, the major penalty shall be served first by the penalised player.

Note 2: This applies where BOTH penalties are imposed on the SAME player (see also Note to Rule 408, Delayed Penalties).

(*d*) When ONE minor penalty is assessed to ONE player on EACH team at the same stoppage of play, these penalties will be served without substitution provided both teams are at full strength on the ice.

Unless paragraph one of this rule section is applicable, when coincident minor penalties or coincident minor penalties of equal duration are imposed against players of both teams, the penalised players shall all take their places on the penalty benches and such penalised players shall not leave the penalty bench until the first stoppage of play following the expiry of their respective penalties. Immediate substitution shall be made for an equal number of minor penalties or coincident minor penalties of equal duration to each team so penalised and the penalties of the players for which substitutions have been made shall not be taken into account for the purpose of the Delayed Penalty Rule (408).

403. Major Penalties

(*a*) For the first **major penalty** in any one game, except to the goalkeeper, the offender shall be ruled off the ice for 5 minutes, during which time no substitute shall be permitted.

(*b*) For the second major penalty in the same game to the same player, or a major penalty for cross-checking, butt-ending, high-sticking, slashing, spearing and boarding the player, he shall be ruled off the ice for the balance of the playing time, but a substitute shall be permitted after 5 minutes' major penalty plus game misconduct penalty. (See Rules 604, 607, 615, 630, 631.)

(*c*) When coincident major and/or match penalties or coincident penalties of equal duration including a major or a match are imposed against players of both teams during the same stoppage of play, immediate substitutions shall be made for those penalties, and such penalties shall not be taken into account for the purpose of the delayed penalty. In the case where the penalised players remain in the game, they shall take their place on the penalty bench and shall not leave until the first stoppage of play following the expiry of their respective penalties.

When the Coincident Major/Match Penalty rule is applied and there is a differential in the total time penalties, those penalties causing the differential shall be served first in the normal manner and shall be taken in account for the purpose of applying Rule 402(*c*) Minor Penalties and Rule 408 Delayed Penalties. Any time difference or differential in the total time penalties may be served by any non-penalised player.

404. Misconduct Penalties

(*a*) A **misconduct penalty** to any player, except the goalkeeper, involves removal from the game for a period of 10 minutes. A substitute player is permitted to replace, immediately, a player serving a misconduct penalty. A player whose misconduct penalty has expired shall remain on the penalty bench until the next stoppage of play.

When a player receives a minor or major penalty and a misconduct penalty at the same time, the penalised team shall immediately put a substitute player on the penalty bench and he shall serve the minor or major penalty without change.

Any player receiving two misconduct penalties in one game shall automatically be assessed a game misconduct.

(b) A **game misconduct** penalty involves removal for the balance of the game and the offender shall be ordered to the dressing-room for the remainder of the game, but a substitute shall be permitted immediately.
Note 1: A 'game misconduct' penalty does not incur automatic suspension, except for that game. The proper authority shall have the power to increase the suspension period.
Note 2: In championship and tournament games any player shall be suspended for his second game misconduct penalty automatically for the next championship or tournament game of his team.

(c) A **gross misconduct** penalty involves the suspension of a player or team official for the balance of the game, but a substitution shall be permitted immediately.

Any player or team official incurring a gross misconduct penalty shall be suspended from participating in any further games until his case has been dealt with by the proper authorities.
Note: For game misconduct or gross misconduct penalties regardless of when imposed, a total of twenty minutes shall be charged in the records against the player, or against the team in the case of a team official incurring a gross misconduct penalty. Such penalties shall be reported by the Referee to the proper authorities immediately following the game. In championship games, league games, or in a tournament any player or team official assessed a gross misconduct penalty shall be suspended for the next game of his team as a minimum.

405. Match Penalties

(a) A **match** penalty involves the suspension of a player for the balance of the game, and the offender shall be ordered to the dressing-room immediately. A substitute player is permitted to replace the penalised player after 5 minutes' playing time has elapsed.
Note: For all match penalties, regardless of when imposed, a total of 20 minutes shall be charged in the records against the offending player.

(b) A player incurring a match penalty shall be suspended from playing in any further games until his case has been dealt with by the proper authorities.

406. Penalty Shot

(a) When there is an infraction of the rules that calls for a penalty shot not involving a major, misconduct, game misconduct, or match penalty, the non-offending team shall be given the option of accepting the penalty shot or having a minor penalty assessed to the offending player. If, however, a major, misconduct, game misconduct, or match penalty is incurred with the penalty shot, the shot shall be awarded and the penalty for the prescribed infraction shall be assessed.

(*b*) Any infraction of the rules which calls for a penalty shot shall be taken as follows:

The Referee shall cause to be announced over the public address system the name of the player designated by him or selected by the team entitled to take the shot (as appropriate). He shall then place the puck on the centre face-off spot and the player taking the shot will, on the instruction of the Referee, play the puck from there and shall attempt to score on the goalkeeper. Once the player taking the shot has possession of the puck he must proceed towards his opponent's goal-line, and once the puck is shot, the play shall be considered complete. No goal can be scored by a second shot of any kind, and any time the puck crosses the goal-line the shot shall be considered complete.

Only the goalkeeper or alternate goalkeeper or a player designated as a goalkeeper or alternate goalkeeper, may defend against the penalty shot.

(*c*) The goalkeeper must remain in his crease until the player taking the penalty shot has touched the puck, and in the event of violation of this rule or any foul committed by the goalkeeper, the Referee shall allow the shot to be completed, signalling such violation by raising his arm, and if the shot fails, he shall permit the penalty shot to be taken over again. If the goalkeeper leaves the goal crease too early:
  – The first time: warning and a new penalty shot
  – The second time: misconduct penalty and a new penalty shot
  – The third time: award a goal.

The goalkeeper may attempt to stop the shot in any manner except by throwing his stick or any other object in which case a goal shall be awarded.

Note: See Rule 633. Throwing Stick.

(*d*) In cases where a penalty shot has been awarded, the penalty shot shall be taken by any player selected by the Captain of the non-offending team except a player serving a penalty or a player to be assessed a delayed penalty. Such selection shall be reported to the Referee and cannot be changed.

If, at the time a penalty shot is awarded, the goalkeeper of the penalised team has been removed from the ice and substituted for by another player, including the substitute goalkeeper, the goalkeeper shall be permitted to return to the ice before the penalty shot is taken.

(*e*) While the penalty shot is being taken, players of both sides shall withdraw to the sides of the rink and behind the centre red line.

(*f*) If, while the penalty shot is being taken, any player of the opposing team shall have by some action interfered with or distracted the player taking the shot and, because of such action, the shot should have failed, a second attempt shall be permitted and the Referee shall impose a misconduct penalty on the player so interfering or distracting.

(*g*) If a goal is scored from a penalty shot, the puck shall be faced at centre ice in the usual way. If a goal is not scored, the puck shall be faced at either of the end face-off spots in the zone in which the penalty shot has been attempted.

(*h*) Should a goal be scored from a penalty shot, a further penalty to the offending player shall not be assessed unless the offence for which the penalty shot was awarded was such as to incur a major, misconduct, game misconduct, match or gross misconduct penalty, in which case the penalty prescribed for the particular offence shall be served.

If the offence for which the penalty shot was awarded was such as would normally incur a minor penalty, then regardless of whether the penalty shot results in a goal or not, the minor penalty shall not be served.

(*i*) If the foul upon which the penalty shot is based occurs during actual playing time, the penalty shot shall be awarded and taken immediately in the usual manner, notwithstanding any delay occasioned by a slow whistle by the Referee to permit the play to be completed which delay results in the expiry of the regular playing time in any period.

The time required for the taking of a penalty shot shall not be included in the regular playing time or any overtime.

407. Goalkeeper's Penalties

(*a*) A goalkeeper shall not be sent to the penalty bench for an offence which results in a minor, major or misconduct penalty, but instead the penalty shall be served by another member of his own team who was on the ice when the offence was committed, said player to be designated by the Manager or Coach of the offending team, through the Captain, and such substitute shall not be changed.

(*b*) Should a goalkeeper incur two major penalties in one game, he shall also receive a game misconduct penalty.

(*c*) Should a goalkeeper incur a game misconduct penalty, his place shall be taken by the substitute goalkeeper, if available, otherwise by a member of his team, who shall be permitted 10 minutes to dress in the goalkeeper's full equipment.

(*d*) Should a goalkeeper incur a match penalty, his place shall then be taken by the substitute goalkeeper, if available, otherwise by a member of his team, and such player will be allowed the goalkeeper's equipment. However, any additional penalties as specifically called for by the individual rules covering match penalties will apply, and the offending team shall be penalised accordingly. Such additional penalty shall be served by another member of the team on the ice at the time the offence was committed, said player to be designated by the Manager or Coach of the offending team through the Captain.

(*e*) A minor penalty shall be imposed on a goalkeeper who leaves the immediate vicinity of his crease during an altercation.

Note: All penalties imposed on a goalkeeper, regardless of who serves the penalty, shall be charged in the records against the goalkeeper.

(*f*) If a goalkeeper participates in the play in any manner when he is beyond the centre red line, he shall be assessed a minor penalty.

408. Delayed Penalties

(*a*) If a third player of any team is penalised while two players of the same team are serving penalties, the penalty time of the third player shall not commence until the penalty time of one of the two players already penalised shall have elapsed. Nevertheless, the third player penalised shall at once proceed to the penalty bench, but may be replaced on the ice by a substitute, until such time as the penalty time of the penalised player shall commence.

(*b*) When any team has three or more players serving penalties at the same time and because of the delayed penalty rule, a substitute for the third offender on the ice, none of the three penalised players on the penalty bench may return to the ice until play has been stopped unless, by reason of the expiration of penalties, the penalised team is entitled to have more than four players, including the goalkeeper, on the ice in which case the penalised player shall be permitted to return in the order of the expiry of their penalties. Otherwise, when play is stopped the player(s) whose penalty has expired may return to the game.

(*c*) If the penalties of two players of the same team will expire at the same time, the Captain of the team will designate to the Referee which of such players will return to the ice first and the Referee will instruct the penalty Official Scorer accordingly.

(*d*) When a major and a minor penalty are imposed at the same time on two or more players of the same team, the Official Scorer shall record the minor as being the first of such penalties.

409. Calling of Penalties

(*a*) Should an infraction of the rules which would call for a penalty be committed by a player of the side in possession of the puck, the Referee shall immediately blow his whistle and assess the penalty to the offending player. The resulting face-off shall be made at the place where the play was stopped, unless the stoppage occurs in the Attacking Zone of the player penalised, in which case the face-off shall be made at the nearest face-off spot in the Neutral Zone.

(*b*) Should an infraction of the rules, which would call for a penalty, be committed by a player of the team *not* in possession of the puck, the Referee shall signify the calling of a penalty by raising his arm and, upon completion of the play (as defined in Note 2 below) by the team in possession, will immediately blow his whistle and give the penalty to the offending player.

Note 1: The subsequent face-off shall be made at the place where the play was stopped, unless during the period of a delayed whistle due to a foul by a player of the side not in possession, the side in possession ices the puck, shoots the puck from its defensive zone so that it goes out of bounds or is unplayable, then the face-off following the stoppage shall take place in the Neutral Zone near the defending blue line of the team shooting the puck.

If the penalty or penalties to be imposed are minor penalties, and a goal is scored on the play by the non-offending team, the first minor penalty shall not be imposed, but all other minor, major or match penalties shall be imposed in the normal manner.

Note 2: 'Completion of the play by the team in possession' in this rule means that the puck must have come into the possession and control of or been intentionally directed by an opposing player or goalkeeper, or has been 'frozen'. This does not mean a rebound off the goalkeeper, the goal or the boards, or any accidental contact with the body or equipment of an opposing player.

Note 3: If after the Referee has signalled a penalty, but before the whistle has been blown, the puck shall enter the goal of the non-offending team as the direct result of the action of a player of that team, the goal shall be allowed and the penalty signalled shall be imposed in the normal manner.

If, when a team is short-handed by reason of one or more minor or bench minor penalties, the Referee signals a further minor penalty or penalties against the short-handed team a goal is scored by the non-offending team before the whistle is blown, then the goal shall be allowed, the penalty signalled shall be waived but penalties being served in the box will remain in effect.

(*c*) Should the same offending player commit other fouls on the same play, either before or after the Referee has blown his whistle, the offending player shall serve such penalties consecutively.

(*d*) If any fouls are committed after the play has been stopped, the offending players shall be penalised as though play were actually in progress.

410. Supplementary Discipline

In addition to the suspensions imposed under these rules, the proper disciplinary authority may, at any time after conclusion of the game, at their discretion investigate any incident that occurs in connection with any game, and may, if done before the next game of the offending team, assess additional suspensions for any offence committed during the pre-game warm-up, on the way between the dressing-room and the ice surface, during the course of a game or any aftermath thereof by a player or team official, whether or not such offence has been penalised by the Referee.

5. OFFICIALS

501. Appointment of Officials
For all International matches there shall be appointed one Referee and two Linesmen, one Game Timekeeper, one Penalty Timekeeper, one Official Scorer and two Goal Judges for each game.

National Associations have the authority to use the Two Referee system in games which are completely under their jurisdiction.

502. Referee
(*a*) The Referee shall have general supervision of the game, and shall have full control of game officials and players during the game, including stoppages; and in case of any dispute, his decision shall be final. The Referee shall remain on the ice at the conclusion of each period until all players have proceeded to their dressing-rooms.

(*b*) All Referees and Linesmen shall be garbed in black trousers and official sweaters.

They shall be equipped with approved whistles and metal tape-measures with minimum length of 2m.

(*c*) The Referee shall order the teams on the ice at the appointed time for the beginning of a game, and at the commencement of each period. If for any reason there be more than 15 minutes' delay in the commencement of the game or any undue delay in resuming play after the 15-minute interval between periods, the Referee shall state in his report to the proper authorities the cause of the delay and the team or teams which were at fault.

(*d*) The Referee may, at his own discretion, measure any equipment. The Referee shall check or measure the equipment worn by any player when requested to do so by the Captain of either team.

(*e*) The Referee shall, before starting the game, see that the appointed Game Timekeeper, Penalty Timekeeper, Official Scorer and Goal Judges are in their respective places, and satisfy himself that the timing and signalling equipment are in order.

(*f*) It shall be his duty to impose such penalties as are prescribed by the rules for infractions thereof, and to give the final decision in matters of disputed goals. The Referee, in matters of disputed goals, may consult with the Linesmen or Goal Judge before making his decision.

(*g*) The Referee shall announce to the Penalty Timekeeper all penalties, and for what such penalties are imposed. The infraction of the rules for which each penalty has been imposed will be announced correctly, as reported by the Referee, over the public address system. Where players of both teams are penalised on the same play, the penalty to the visiting player will be announced first.

(*h*) The Referee shall report to the Official Scorer the name or number of the goal scorer and any players entitled to assists. (In IIHF 'A' Pool Championships, assists will be determined by the Official Scorer.)

The Referee shall cause to be announced over the public address system the reason for not allowing a goal whenever the goal signal light is turned on in the course of play. This shall be done at the first stoppage of play regardless of any standard signal given by the Referee when the goal signal light was put on in error.

(*i*) The Referee shall see to it that players of opposing teams are separated on the penalty bench to prevent feuding.

(*j*) Should a Referee accidentally leave the ice or receive an injury which incapacitates him from discharging his duties while play is in progress, the game shall be stopped immediately by the Linesman, unless one of the teams has the puck in a scoring position, in which case the play shall be allowed to be completed. If it is obvious that the injury sustained is of a serious nature, play shall be stopped immediately.

(*k*) If, through misadventure or sickness, the Referees or Linesmen appointed are prevented from appearing, the team leaders of the two teams shall agree on a Referee or Linesman. If they are unable to agree, the proper authorities shall appoint the Officials.

If the regularly appointed officials appear during the progress of the game, they shall at once replace the temporary officials.

(*l*) Should a Linesman appointed be unable to act at the last minute or through sickness or accident be unable to finish the game, the Referee shall have the power to appoint a replacement, if he deems it necessary.

(*m*) If, owing to illness or accident, the Referee is unable to continue to officiate, one of the Linesmen shall perform such duties of the Referee during the balance of the game, the Linesman to be selected by the Referee, or, if necessary, by the team leaders of the competing teams.

(*n*) The Referee shall secure, from the Official Scorer, the Game Report immediately following each game. He shall sign and check this report and return same to the Official Scorer.

(*o*) The Referee is required to report on the official game report all game misconducts, gross misconducts, and match penalties immediately following the game involved giving full details to the Proper Authorities concerned.

503. Linesman

(*a*) The duty of the Linesman is to determine any infractions of the rules concerning:

Off-side – Rule 624, Off-side;

Off-side Pass – Rule 625, Passes;

Icing – Rule 618, Icing the Puck.

He shall stop the play when the puck:

(i) Goes out of playing area – Rule 626(*a*), Puck Out of Bounds or Unplayable;

(ii) When it is interfered with by an ineligible person – Rule 620, Interference by Spectators;

(iii) When the goal-post has been displaced from its normal position – Rule 608, Delaying the Game.

He shall stop the play:

(i) For off-sides occurring on face-off circles – Rule 610, Face-Offs;

(ii) When there has been a premature substitution for a goalkeeper – Rule 205, Change of Players;

(iii) For injured player(s) – Rule 206, Injured Players;

(iv) Interference by spectators – Rule 620, Interference by Spectators.

(*b*) He shall stop play if the puck has been batted with the hand from one player to a team-mate or again when the puck has been struck with a high stick and it has become obvious the Referee did not observe the infraction.

(*c*) He shall conduct the face-off at all times, except at the start of the game, at the beginning of each period and after a goal has been scored.

The Referee may call upon a linesman to conduct a face-off at any time.

(*d*) He shall, when requested to do so by the Referee, give his version of any incident that may have taken place during the playing of the game.

(*e*) He shall not stop play to impose any penalty except for violations of:

(i) Too many men on the ice – Rule 201(*b*), Composition of Teams;

(ii) Articles thrown on the ice from vicinity of the players' or penalty bench – Rule 601(*j*), Abuse of Officials and other Misconduct;

(iii) Stick thrown on to the ice from the players' or penalty bench – Rule 605, Broken Stick;

and he shall report such violations to the Referee, who shall impose a bench minor penalty against the offending team.

He shall report immediately to the Referee his version of the circumstances with respect to deliberately displacing the goal-post from its normal position – Rule 608, Delaying the Game.

He shall report immediately to the Referee his version of any infraction of the rules constituting a bench minor penalty, a major or match foul, misconduct, game misconduct or gross misconduct penalty.

504. Two Referees

(*a*) The Referees shall have general supervision of the game, and shall have full control of all game officials and players during the game, including stoppages; and in case of any dispute, their decision shall be final. The Referees shall remain on the ice at the conclusion of each period until all players have proceeded to their dressing-rooms.

(*b*) All Referees shall be garbed in black trousers and official sweaters.

They shall be equipped with approved whistles and metal tape-measures with minimum length of 2m.

(*c*) The Referees shall order the teams on the ice at the appointed time for the beginning of a game, and at the commencement of each period. If, for any reason, there be more than 15 minutes' delay in the commencement of the game or any undue delay in resuming play after the 15-minute interval between periods, the Referees shall state in their report to the proper authorities the cause of the delay, and the team or teams which were at fault.

(*d*) The Referees may, at their own discretion, measure any equipment, the Referee shall check the equipment worn by any player when requested to do by the Captain of either team.

(*e*) The Referees shall, before starting the game, see that the appointed Game Timekeeper, Penalty Box Attendants, Official Scorer and Goal Judges are in their respective places, and satisfy themselves that the timing and signalling equipment are in order.

(*f*) It shall be their duty to impose such penalties as are prescribed by the rules for infractions thereof, to stop play for any other infractions of the Rules, and to give the final decision in matters of disputed goals. The Referees may, in matters of disputed goals, consult with the Goal Judge before making a decision.

(*g*) The Referees shall report to the Official Scorer all penalties, and for what infractions such penalties are imposed.

The infraction of the Rules for which each penalty has been imposed will be announced correctly, as reported by the Referees, over the public address system. Where players of both teams are penalised at the same time, the penalty to the visiting player will be announced first.

(*h*) The Referees shall report to the Official Scorer the name or number of the goal scorer and any players entitled to assists.

The Referees shall cause to be announced over the public address system the reason for not allowing a goal whenever the goal signal light is turned on in the course of play. This shall be done at the first stoppage of play regardless of any standard signal given by the Referees when the goal signal light was put on in error.

(*i*) The Referees shall see to it that players of opposing teams are separated on the penalty bench to prevent feuding.

(*j*) Should a Referee accidentally leave the ice or receive an injury which incapacitates him from discharging his duties while play is in progress the game shall be stopped immediately by the other Referee, unless one of the teams has the puck in a scoring position, in which case the play shall be allowed to be completed. If it is obvious that the injury sustained is of a serious nature, play shall be stopped immediately.

(*k*) If, through misadventure or sickness, both Referees appointed are prevented from appearing, the team leaders of the two clubs shall agree on Referees.

If they are unable to agree, the proper authorities shall appoint the officials.

If the regularly appointed officials appear during the progress of the game, they shall at once replace the temporary officials.

(*l*) Should one of the appointed Referees be unable to act at the last minute or through sickness or accident be unable to finish the game, the other Referee shall have the power to appoint a replacement, if he deems it necessary.

(*m*) The Referees shall secure from the Official Scorer the Game Report immediately following each game. They shall sign and check this report and return it to the Official Scorer.

(*n*) The Referees are required to report on the official game report all game misconducts, gross misconducts and match penalties immediately following the game involved, giving full details to the proper authorities concerned.

505. Goal Judges

(*a*) There shall be one Goal Judge at each goal. They shall not be members of either team engaged in the game, nor shall they be replaced during its progress, unless after the commencement of the game it becomes apparent that either Goal Judge, on account of partisanship or any other cause, is guilty of giving unjust decisions, in which case the Referee may appoint a replacement Goal Judge.

(*b*) Goal Judges shall be stationed behind the goals, during the progress of play, in properly screened cages, so that there can be no interference with their activities. They shall not change goals during the game.

(*c*) The Goal Judge shall decide if the puck has passed between the goal-posts and completely over the goal-line and give the appropriate signal.

The Referee shall give the final decision in matters of a disputed goal.

He may consult with the Goal Judge or Linesman before making his decision or ask the Video Goal Judge for his decision.

506. Penalty Box Attendants

The Penalty Box Attendant (one per team penalty box) is responsible for permitting the penalised player(s) to return to the ice at the appropriate time upon the completion of their penalty(s). He shall also notify the Official Scorer if a player leaves the penalty box before the expiry of the penalty. He shall, upon request, give a penalised player correct information as to the unexpired time of his penalty.

507. Official Scorer

(*a*) Before the start of the game, the Official Scorer shall obtain from the Manager or Coach of both teams a list of all eligible players and the starting line-up of each team, which information shall be made known to the opposing team Manager and Coach before the start of play, either personally or through the Referee. (See Rule 203, Players in Uniform, and Rule 204, Starting Line-up.)

The Official Scorer shall secure the names of the Captain from the Manager or Coach at the time the line-ups are collected and will so indicate by placing the letter 'C' opposite their names on the score-sheet. The information shall be presented to the Referee for his signature at the completion of the game.

(*b*) The Official Scorer shall keep a record of the goals scored, the scorers, the players to whom assists have been credited, and shall indicate those players on the lists who have actually taken part in the game. He shall also record the time of entry into the game of any substitute goalkeeper. He shall record on the official score-sheet a notation where a goal is scored when the goalkeeper has been removed from the ice.

The Official Scorer shall keep, on the official game report, a correct record of all penalties imposed by the officials including the names of the players penalised, the infractions penalised, the duration of each penalty and the time at which each penalty was imposed. He shall report in the Penalty Record each penalty shot awarded, the name of the player taking the shot and the result of the shot. He shall check and ensure that the time served by all penalised players is correct. He shall be responsible for the correct posting of penalties on the scoreboard at all times and shall promptly call to the attention of the Referee any discrepancy between the time recorded on the clock and the official correct time, and he shall be responsible for making any adjustments ordered by the Referee.

The Official Scorer shall have announced the awards of points for goals and assists, the infraction of the rules for which each penalty has been imposed will be announced over the public address system. Where players of both teams are penalised on the same play, the penalty to the visiting player will be announced first. Changes in such awards shall also be announced in the same manner. He shall also have announced when only one minute of actual playing time remains in the first and second period, and two minutes remain in the third period and overtime. The decisions of the Video Goal Judge shall be announced as either 'A goal has been scored at . . .' or 'No goal has been scored'. Where a goal has been disallowed, he shall have announced the reason as reported by the Referee.

(*c*) No request for changes in any award of points shall be considered unless they are made before the conclusion of actual play in the game by the team Captain, or before the Referee has signed the Official Score Sheet.

(*d*) The Official Scorer shall advise the Referee when the same player has received his second major or misconduct penalty in the same game.

(*e*) The Official Scorer shall also prepare the Official Score Sheet for signature by the Referee and forward it to the proper authorities.

508. Game Timekeeper

(*a*) The Game Timekeeper shall record the time of the starting and finishing of each game and all actual playing time during the game.

(*b*) The Game Timekeeper shall signal the Referee(s) for the commencement of the game, for the start of second and third periods, and any overtime period or periods. He shall allow 15 minutes' intermission between each period after which Referee(s) shall start play. He shall also signal by ringing a gong, siren or by blowing a whistle, the ending of each period, any overtime period or periods and the ending of the game. This applies in rinks that are not provided with an automatic gong or siren, or if the automatic gong or siren should fail to operate.

(*c*) In the event of any dispute regarding time, the Referee's decision shall be final.

509. Proper Authorities

The term 'proper authorities' or 'proper disciplinary authority' as applied under these rules is defined as the immediate governing body of the games involved.

6. PLAYING RULES

601. Abuse of Officials and Other Misconducts

Note: In the enforcement of this rule, the Referee has, in many instances, the opinion of imposing a misconduct penalty or a bench minor penalty. In principle, the Referee is directed to impose a bench minor penalty in respect to the violations which occur on or in the immediate vicinity of the players' bench but off the playing surface, and in all cases affecting non-playing personnel or players. A misconduct penalty should be imposed for violations which occur on the playing surface or in the penalty bench area and where the penalised player is readily identifiable.

(*a*) Any player who challenges or disputes the rulings of any official during the game shall be assessed a minor penalty for unsportsmanlike conduct. If the player persists in such a challenge or dispute, he shall be assessed a misconduct penalty, and any further dispute will result in a game misconduct penalty being assessed.

(*b*) If any player is guilty of any one of the following, his team shall be assessed a bench minor penalty:

1. After being penalised he does not proceed directly and immediately to the penalty bench and take his place on the penalty bench, or to the dressing-room when so ordered by the Referee.

2. While off the playing surface, uses obscene, profane or abusive language to any person, or uses the name of any official coupled with any such remarks.

3. While off the playing surface, interferes in any manner with any game official, including the Referee, Linesmen, Timekeepers or Goal Judges in the performance of their duties.

(*c*) Any player who is guilty of any one of the following shall be assessed a misconduct penalty:

1. Using obscene, profane or abusive language to any person on the ice or anywhere in the rink before, during or after the game, except in the immediate vicinity of the players' bench – see 601(*b*)2.

2. Intentionally knocking or shooting the puck out of reach of an official who is retrieving it.

3. Deliberately throwing any equipment, except the stick (see Rule 633*c*, Throwing Stick) out of the playing area.

4. Banging the board with his stick or any other instrument at any time.

5. Failing to proceed directly and immediately to the penalty bench following a fight or other altercation in which he has been involved and which has been broken up, and for which he is penalised or causes any delay by retrieving his equipment. His gloves, stick, etc. shall be delivered to him at the penalty bench by a team-mate (this misconduct penalty shall be in addition to any other penalties incurred).

6. After a warning by the Referee, persisting in any course of conduct (including threatening or abusive language or gestures or similar actions) designated to incite an opponent into incurring a penalty.

7. Entering or remaining in the Referee's crease while the Referee is

reporting to, or consulting with, any game official, including Linesmen, Timekeeper, Penalty Timekeeper, Official Scorer or Announcer, except for the purpose of taking his place on the penalty bench.

(*d*) Any player who is guilty of any of the following shall, at the discretion of the Referee, be assessed a misconduct, game misconduct or gross misconduct:

1. Any physical attack by a player against any game official – touching him with hands or stick, such as holding, pushing with hands, stick or body, tripping, body checking, cross checking, slashing, checking from behind and the like.

2. Throwing a stick out of the rink – Rule 633(*c*). Throwing Stick.

3. Continuing or attempting to continue a fight or altercation after he has been ordered by the Referee to stop, or resisting a Linesman in the discharge of his duties.

(*e*) Any player who is guilty of any of the following shall be assessed a game misconduct:

1. Persisting in any course of conduct for which he has previously been assessed a misconduct penalty.

2. Using obscene gestures on the ice or anywhere in the rink before, during or after the game.

(*f*) Any player who is guilty of any manner of behaviour which makes a travesty of, interferes with or is detrimental to the conducting of the game shall be assessed a gross misconduct penalty.

(*g*) If any team official is guilty of any of the following, his team shall be assessed a bench minor penalty:

1. Banging the boards with a stick or other instrument at any time.

2. Using obscene, profane or abusive language to any person or using the name of any official coupled with such remarks anywhere in the rink.

3. Interfering in any manner with any game official, including the Referee, Linesmen, Timekeepers or Goal Judges in the performance of their duties.

(*h*) Any team official who is guilty of any type of misconduct shall be assessed a game misconduct penalty plus a bench minor penalty.

(*i*) Any team official who is guilty of holding or striking an official, or any manner of behaviour which makes a travesty of or interferes with or is detrimental to the conducting of the game, shall be assessed a gross misconduct penalty.

(*j*) Throwing anything on to the ice from anywhere in the rink is prohibited.

If this rule is violated by:

1. A player – he shall be assessed a minor plus game misconduct penalty.

2. A team official – he shall be assessed a game misconduct and his team a bench minor penalty.

3. An unidentified person of the team in the vicinity of the players' bench – the team shall be assessed a bench minor penalty.

If the player or team is penalised under Rule 633, Throwing Stick, this rule shall not apply.

(*k*) Any player or team official who deliberately spits on or at an opponent, team official or game official shall be assessed a gross misconduct penalty. When a team official is assessed a gross misconduct under this section the team shall also be assessed a bench minor penalty.

602. Adjustment of Equipment

(*a*) Play shall not be stopped nor the game delayed by reason of adjustments to clothing, equipment, shoes, skates or sticks.

(*b*) The onus of maintaining clothing and equipment in proper condition shall be upon the player. If adjustments are required, the player shall retire from the ice and play shall continue.

(*c*) No delay shall be permitted for the repair or adjustment of goalkeeper's equipment. If adjustments are required, the goalkeeper shall retire from the ice and his place shall be taken by the substitute goalkeeper immediately and no warm-up shall be permitted.

(*d*) For an infraction of this rule, a minor penalty shall be imposed.

603. Excessive Rough Play

(*a*) A match penalty shall be imposed on a player who commits an action not permitted by the rules that may cause an injury or that results in an injury to an opponent. The circumstances shall be reported to the proper authorities for further action. A substitute will be permitted at the end of the fifth minute.

(*b*) A gross misconduct penalty shall be imposed on any player who commits any of the above described actions against a team or game official.

604. Boarding

A minor or major penalty, at the discretion of the Referee based upon the degree of violence of the impact with the boards, shall be imposed on any player who body-checks, cross-checks, elbows, charges or trips an opponent in such manner that causes the opponent to be thrown violently into the boards. When a major penalty is assessed under this rule, the player shall automatically be assessed in addition a game misconduct penalty.

Note: Any unnecessary contact with a player playing the puck on an obvious icing or off-side play which results in that player being knocked into the boards is *boarding* and must be penalised as such. In other instances where there is no contact with the boards, it should be treated as *charging*.

Rolling an opponent (if he is the puck carrier) along the boards where he is endeavouring to go through too small an opening is not boarding. However, if the opponent is not the puck carrier, then such action shall be penalised as boarding, charging, interference or if the arms or stick are employed it shall be called holding or hooking.

605. Broken Stick

(*a*) A player without a stick may participate in the game. A player whose stick is broken may participate in the game provided he drops the broken portion. A minor penalty shall be imposed for an infraction of this rule.

Note: A broken stick is one which, in the opinion of the Referee, is unfit for normal play.

(*b*) A goalkeeper may continue to play with a broken stick until stoppage of play or until he has been legally provided with a stick.

(*c*) A player or goalkeeper whose stick is broken may not receive a stick thrown on to the ice from any part of the rink, but may receive a stick from a team-mate without proceeding to his players' bench.

For an infraction of this rule penalties will be assessed under Rule 601(*j*), Abuse of Officials and Other Misconducts.

(*d*) A goalkeeper whose stick is broken may not go to the players' bench during a stoppage of play for a replacement, but must receive his stick from a team-mate.

For an infraction of this rule a minor penalty shall be imposed on the goalkeeper.

606. Charging and Checking from Behind

(*a*) A minor or major penalty shall be imposed on a player who runs, jumps into or charges an opponent.

A minor plus a misconduct penalty or a major plus a game misconduct penalty shall be assessed any player who pushes, body checks or hits an opponent from behind in any manner anywhere on the ice.

A major plus a game misconduct penalty or a match penalty shall be assessed any player who injures an opponent as a result of checking that player from behind.

Where a player is high-sticked, cross-checked, body-checked, pushed, hit or propelled in any manner from behind into the boards in such a way that the player is unable to protect or defend himself, a major penalty plus a game misconduct Penalty shall be assessed.

Note: If more than two steps or strides are taken and with excessive force used to check a player, it shall be considered charging.

(*b*) A double minor or major penalty shall be imposed on a player who commits any foul against a goalkeeper while the goalkeeper is within the goal-crease.

A goalkeeper is *not* 'fair game' just because he is outside the goal-crease area. A penalty for interference or charging (minor or major) should be called in every case where an opposing player makes unnecessary contact with a goalkeeper.

Likewise, Referees should be alert to penalise goalkeepers for tripping, slashing or spearing in the vicinity of the goal.

(*c*) A minor or major penalty at the discretion of the Referee shall be imposed on a player who makes physical contact with an opponent after the whistle has been blown, if in the opinion of the Referee, the player has had sufficient time after the whistle to avoid such contact.

Note: In women's ice hockey a direct body-check shall be penalised by a minor penalty.

607. Cross-Checking

(*a*) A minor or major penalty, at the discretion of the Referee, shall be imposed on a player who cross-checks an opponent.

Note: 'Cross-check' shall mean a check delivered with both hands on the stick and no part of the stick on the ice.

(*b*) A major penalty shall be imposed on any player who injures an opponent by cross-checking.

(*c*) When a major penalty is assessed under this rule, the player shall automatically be assessed in addition a game misconduct penalty.

608. Delaying the Game

(*a*) A minor penalty shall be assessed on a goalkeeper who shoots the puck directly outside the playing area. A minor penalty shall be assessed on any player who deliberately shoots the puck outside the playing area. A minor penalty shall be assessed on any player or goalkeeper who throws or deliberately bats the puck with his hand or stick outside the playing area.

A bench minor penalty shall be imposed upon a team that, after scoring a goal, has more than one change of players on the ice.

(*b*) A minor penalty shall be imposed on any player (including the goalkeeper) who delays the game by deliberately displacing a goal-post from its normal position.

The Referee or Linesman shall stop play immediately when a goal-post has been displaced.

If the above mentioned delay is caused by any player or goalkeeper from the defending team in its defensive zone during the last 2 minutes of a game, or overtime, a penalty shot shall be awarded.

If the goal is deliberately displaced by a goalkeeper or player during the course of a break-away (see note), a penalty shot will be awarded to the non-offending team. Should this violation occur after the goalkeeper has been removed for another player, a goal shall be awarded to the non-offending team.

Note: A player with a 'break-away' is defined as a player in control of the puck with no opposition between him and the opposing goal and with a reasonable scoring opportunity.

(*c*) A bench minor penalty shall be imposed upon any team which, after warning by the Referee to its Captain to place the correct number of players on the ice and commence play, fails to comply with the Referee's direction and thereby causes any delay by making additional substitutions, by persisting in having players off-side, or in any other manner.

(*d*) The puck must be kept in motion at all times.

(*e*) Except to carry the puck behind its goal once, a team in possession of the puck in its own defence area shall advance the puck towards the opposing goal, except if it is prevented from so doing by players of the opposing team.

For the first infraction of this rule, play shall be stopped and a face-off shall be made at either end face-off spot adjacent to the goal of the team causing the stoppage, and the Referee shall warn the Captain of the offending team of the reason for the face-off. For a second violation by any player of the same team in the same period, a minor penalty shall be imposed on the player violating the rule.

(*f*) A minor penalty shall be imposed on any player including the goalkeeper who holds, freezes or plays the puck with his stick, skates or body along the boards in such a manner as to cause a stoppage of play unless he is actually being checked by an opponent.

(*g*) A player beyond his defensive zone shall not pass nor carry the puck backward into his defensive zone for the purpose of delaying the game, except when his team is below the numerical strength of the opponents on the ice.

(*h*) For an infringement of this rule, the face-off shall be at the nearest end face-off spot in the Defending Zone of the offending team.

(*i*) If a team is not on the ice and prepared to start play in 15 minutes after the start of the intermission (or previous period) a bench minor penalty shall be assessed under this rule.

609. Elbowing, Kneeing or Head-Butting

(*a*) A minor penalty shall be imposed on any player who uses his elbow or knee to foul an opponent.

(*b*) A major penalty plus a game misconduct penalty shall be imposed on any player who injures an opponent as the result of a foul committed by using his elbow or knee.

(*c*) A match penalty shall be imposed on any player who deliberately head-butts or attempts to head-butt an opponent.

610. Face-Offs

(*a*) The puck shall be faced-off by the Referee or the Linesman by dropping the puck on the ice between the sticks of the players facing-off. Players facing-off will stand squarely facing their opponents' end of the rink, approximately one stick length apart, with the blade of their sticks touching the ice.

When the face-off takes place at any of the end or Neutral Zone face-off spots, the players taking part shall take their positions so that they will stand squarely facing their opponent's end of the rink. The sticks of both players facing-off shall have the blade touching the ice in contact with the designated white area. The player of the attacking team in his attacking half of the rink shall place his stick within the designated white area first.

No other players shall be allowed to enter the face-off circle or come within 4.5m of the players facing-off and must stand on-side on all face-offs.

If a violation of this sub-section of this rule occurs, the Referee or Linesman shall re-face the puck, *unless* the non-offending team gained possession of the puck in which case the face-off will be considered valid and play shall be permitted to continue.

(*b*) If a player facing-off fails to take his proper position immediately when directed by the official, the official may order him replaced for that face-off by any team-mate on the ice.

No substitution of players shall be permitted until the face-off has been completed and play has been resumed, except when a penalty is imposed that will affect the on-ice strength of either team.

(*c*) In the conduct of any face-off anywhere on the playing surface, no player facing-off shall make any physical contact with his opponent's body by means of his own body or by his stick, except in the course of playing the puck after the face-off has been completed.

For violation of this rule the Referee shall impose a minor penalty or penalties on the player(s) whose action(s) caused the physical contact.

(*d*) Where a player has been removed from a face-off by an official, and another player of the same team delays taking up his proper position after a warning by the official, a bench minor penalty shall be assessed that team.

For end zone face-offs at the face-off circles, where a player not taking the face-off enters the circle or is in the circle before the puck is dropped, shall result in the player who is about to take the face-off being removed without a warning and replaced by any other player of that team on the ice.

A second violation by a team during the same face-off shall result in a minor penalty for 'face-off violation' to the player who commits the second violation by his team.

(*e*) When an infringement of a rule has been committed or a stoppage of play has been caused by any player of the attacking side in the Attacking Zone, the ensuing face-off shall be made in the Neutral Zone at the nearest face-off spot.

Note: This includes stoppage of play caused by a player of the attacking side shooting the puck on the back of the defending team's goal without any intervening action by the defending team.

(*f*) When an infringement of a rule has been committed by players of both teams the ensuing face-off will be made at the place where the puck was when the play was stopped.

(*g*) When stoppage occurs between the end face-off spots and the near end of the rink, the puck shall be faced-off at the end face-off spot, on the side where the stoppage occurs, unless otherwise expressly provided by these rules.

(*h*) When a goal is illegally scored as a result of a puck being deflected directly off or by an official, the resulting face-off shall be made at the end face-off spot in the defending zone.

(*i*) When the game is stopped for any reason not specifically covered in the official rules, the puck shall be faced-off where it was last played.

(*j*) The whistle shall not be blown by the official to start play. Playing time shall commence from the instant the puck is faced-off and shall stop when the whistle is blown.

(*k*) Following a stoppage of play, should one or both defencemen, who are playing near their attacking blue line, or any player coming from the bench of the attacking team enter into the attacking zone beyond the outer edge of the corner face-off circle, the ensuing face-off shall take place at the nearest face-off spot in the Neutral Zone near the blue line of the defending team.

611. Falling on the Puck

(*a*) A minor penalty shall be imposed on a player other than the goalkeeper who deliberately falls on or gathers a puck into his body.

Note: Any player who drops to his knees to block shots should not be penalised if the puck is shot under him or becomes lodged in his clothing or equipment, but any use of the hands to make the puck unplayable should be penalised promptly.

(*b*) A minor penalty shall be imposed on a goalkeeper who deliberately falls on or gathers the puck into his body or who holds or places the puck against any part of the goal or against the boards, when the puck is behind the goal-line and the goalkeeper's body is entirely outside the boundaries of his goal-crease, or who falls on or gathers the puck into his body when the puck is beyond the two lines on each side of the end face-off circles.

(c) No defending player, except the goalkeeper, will be permitted to fall on the puck or hold the puck or gather the puck into his body or hands when the puck is within the goal-creases.

For infringement of this rule, play shall immediately be stopped and a penalty shot shall be imposed against the offending team, but no other penalty shall be given.

If the goalkeeper has been removed from the ice, the Referee shall immediately award a goal to the non-offending team.

Note: This rule shall be interpreted so that a penalty shot will be awarded only when the puck is in the crease at the instant the offence occurs. However, in cases where the puck is outside the crease, Rule 611(*a*) may still apply and a minor penalty may be imposed, even though no penalty shot is awarded.

612. Fisticuffs or Roughing

(*a*) A match penalty shall be imposed on any player who starts fisticuffs.

(*b*) A minor penalty shall be imposed on a player who, having been struck, shall retaliate with a blow or attempted blow. However, at the discretion of the Referee, a double minor, major or match penalty may be imposed if such player continues the altercation.

Note 1: It is the intent and purpose of this rule that the Referee shall impose the match penalty in all cases when the instigator or retaliator of the fight is the aggressor.

Note 2: The Referee is provided very wide latitude in the penalties which he may impose under this rule. This is done intentionally to enable him to differentiate between the obvious degrees of responsibility of the participants, either for starting the fighting or persisting in continuing the fighting. The discretion provided should be exercised realistically.

(*c*) At the discretion of the Referee a minor or double minor penalty may be imposed on any player deemed guilty of unnecessary roughness.

When a major penalty is assessed under this rule, the player shall automatically be assessed in addition a game misconduct penalty.

(*d*) A misconduct or game misconduct penalty shall be imposed on any player involved in fisticuffs off the playing surface. If one player is on the ice and one is off the ice, both shall be considered on the ice for the application of this rule (*a*) and (*b*) above.

(*e*) A game misconduct penalty shall be imposed on any player or goalkeeper who is the first to intervene in an altercation already in progress. This penalty is in addition to any other penalty incurred in the same incident.

613. Goal and Assist

Note: It is the responsibility of the Referee to award goals and assists (except in IIHF 'A' Pool Championships) and his decision, in this respect, is final. Such awards shall be made or withheld strictly in accordance with the provisions of this rule. Therefore, it is essential that the Referee shall be thoroughly familiar with every aspect of this rule, be alert to observe all actions which could affect the making of an award and, above all, the awards must be made or withheld with absolute impartiality.

In case of obvious error in awarding a goal or an assist which has been announced, it should be corrected promptly but changes shall not be made in the official scoring summary after the Referee has signed the Game Report.

(*a*) A goal shall be scored when the puck shall have been put between the goal-posts below the cross-bar, and entirely across the goal-line by the stick of a player of the attacking side.

(*b*) A goal shall be scored if the puck is put into the goal in any way by a player of the defending side. The player of the attacking side who last played the puck shall be credited with the goal but no assist shall be awarded.

(*c*) If an attacking player kicks the puck and it is deflected into the goal by any player or goalkeeper the goal shall not be allowed.

(*d*) If the puck shall have been deflected into the goal from the shot of an attacking player by striking any part of the person of a player of the same side, the goal shall be allowed. The player who deflected the puck shall be credited with the goal. The goal shall not be allowed if the puck has been kicked, thrown or otherwise deliberately directed into the goal by any means other than a stick.

(*e*) A goal shall not be allowed if the puck has been deflected directly into the goal off an official.

(*f*) Should a player legally propel a puck into the goal-crease of the opposing team and the puck should become loose and available to another player of the attacking side, a goal scored on the play shall be valid.

(*g*) Unless the puck is on the goal-crease area, a player of the attacking side may not stand on the goal-crease line or in the goal-crease or hold his stick in the goal-crease area, and if the puck should enter the goal while such condition prevails except as in section (*h*) of this rule – a goal shall not be allowed, and the puck shall be faced in the neutral zone at the face-off spot nearest the Attacking Zone of the offending team.

(*h*) If a player of the attacking side has been physically interfered with by the action of any defending player so as to cause him to be in the goal-crease, and the puck should enter the goal while the player so interfered with is still within the goal-crease, the goal shall be allowed, unless, in the opinion of the Referee, he had sufficient time to get out of the crease, but stayed there of his own accord.

(*i*) No goal may be scored where an attacking player has kicked or batted the puck with the hand and the puck deflects off any player or his stick, goalkeeper or official. Any goal scored, other than as covered by the rules, shall not be allowed.

No goal may be scored if the net is off its moorings and/or the base of the net is not completely flat on the ice at the time the puck enters the net or crosses the goal line.

Note: No goal shall be disallowed after the face-off immediately following the scoring of that goal.

(*j*) A goal shall be credited in the scoring records to a player who shall have propelled the puck into the opponents' goal. Each goal shall count one point in the player's record.

(*k*) When a player scores a goal, an assist shall be credited to the player or players taking part in the play immediately preceding the goal, but not more than two assists can be given in any goal. Each assist so credited shall count one point in the player's record.

(*l*) Only one point can be credited to any one player on a goal.

(*m*) Where a player not listed on the Game Report scored a goal or is awarded an assist, the goal is to be disallowed, the player is to be removed from the game and no penalty is to be assessed.

(*n*) Where facilities are available, the video replay may be used to determine whether or not a goal shall count. The Referee at his discretion may call for a video replay judgement.

614. Handling the Puck with the Hands

(*a*) A player, except the goalkeeper, shall not close his hand on the puck.

(*b*) A goalkeeper shall not:

1. Hold the puck in his hand(s) for longer than 3 seconds or in any manner which in the opinion of the Referee causes a stoppage of play; or

2. Throw the puck forward towards his opponent's goal which is first played by a team-mate; or

3. Deliberately drop the puck into his pads or on to the goal-net.

Note: The object of this rule is to keep the puck in play continuously and any action by the goalkeeper which causes an unnecessary stoppage must be penalised.

(*c*) For a violation of this rule, the offending player shall be assessed a minor penalty.

(*d*) A defending player, other than the goalkeeper, shall not pick up the puck from the ice with his hands. For a violation of this rule, the player shall be assessed a minor penalty. However, if the puck was in the goal-crease at the time of the violation, a penalty shot shall be awarded the opposing team.

(*e*) A player shall be permitted to stop or 'bat' a puck in the air with his open hand, or push it along the ice with his hand. However, the play shall be stopped if, in the opinion of the Referee, he has deliberately and intentionally directed the puck to a team-mate, and the puck faced-off at the spot where the offence occurred. If this violation is committed by an attacking player in his Attacking Zone, the face-off shall take place at the nearest Neutral Zone face-off spot. Play shall not be stopped for any hand pass by a player in his own defending zone provided the hand pass is completed before the player and puck leave the zone.

Note: The object of this rule is to ensure continuous action and the Referee should not stop play unless he is satisfied that the directing of the puck to a team-mate was in fact deliberate and intentional.

The goal shall be disallowed if the puck was batted with the hand by an attacking player and deflected off any player or goalkeeper into the goal.

615. High-sticks

(*a*) The carrying of sticks above the normal height of the shoulder is prohibited, and a minor penalty may be imposed on any player violating this rule, at the discretion of the Referee.

(*b*) No goal may be scored when an attacking player contacts the puck with the stick above the height of the cross-bar. The face-off is to be conducted at one of the end zone face-off spots of the team committing the high-stick violation. Where a goal is scored from a stick so carried by a player of the defending team, the goal shall be allowed.

(*c*) When a player carries or holds any part of his stick above the height of the shoulders that causes an injury to the opposing player, the Referee shall have no alternative but to impose a major penalty plus a game misconduct penalty on the offending player.

If, however, such high-sticking action that causes the injury was judged to be accidental, a double minor penalty shall be imposed.

(*d*) Batting the puck above the normal height of the shoulders with the stick is prohibited and when it occurs play shall be stopped and a face-off conducted at one of the end face-off spots adjacent to the goal of the team committing the high-stick violation unless:

1. The puck is batted to an opponent, in which case the play shall continue; or

2. A player of the defending team bats the puck into his own goal, in which case the goal shall be allowed.

Note: When a player bats the puck to an opponent under subsection 1, the Referee shall give the 'washout' signal immediately. Otherwise he shall stop the play.

616. Holding an Opponent

(*a*) A minor penalty shall be imposed on a player who holds an opponent with his hands or stick or in any other way.

(*b*) A minor or major penalty plus a misconduct penalty shall be imposed on a player who grabs or holds the face mask, helmet, or pulls the hair of an opponent with his hand.

(*c*) A minor penalty shall be imposed on a player who holds an opponent's stick with his hands or in any other way. The penalty is announced as 'holding the opponent's stick'.

617. Hooking

(*a*) A minor penalty shall be imposed on a player who impedes or seeks to impede the progress of an opponent by hooking with his stick.

(*b*) A major penalty shall be imposed on any player who injures an opponent by hooking.

(*c*) When a player, in control of the puck on the opponent's side of the centre red line and having no opponent to pass other than the goalkeeper, is hooked or otherwise fouled from behind, thus preventing a reasonable scoring opportunity, a penalty shot shall be awarded to the non-offending team. The Referee, however, shall not stop the play until the attacking team has lost possession of the puck to the defending team.
Note: The intention of this rule is to restore a reasonable scoring opportunity which has been lost by reason of a foul from behind when the foul is committed on the opponent's side of the centre red line.

By 'control of the puck' is meant the act of propelling the puck with the stick. If, while it is being propelled, the puck is touched by another player or his equipment or hits the goal or goes free, the player shall no longer be considered to be 'in control of the puck'.

(*d*) If, when the opposing goalkeeper has been removed from the ice, a player in control of the puck is hooked or otherwise fouled with no opposition between him and the opposing goal, thus preventing a reasonable scoring opportunity, the Referee shall immediately stop the play and award a goal to the attacking team.

618. Icing the Puck

(*a*) For the purpose of this rule, the centre line will divide the ice into halves. Should any player of a team, equal or superior in numerical strength to the opposing team, shoot, bat, or deflect the puck from his own half of the ice, beyond the goal-line of the opposing team, play shall be stopped and the puck faced-off at the end face-off spot of the offending team nearest to where they last touched the puck, unless on the play the puck shall have entered the goal of the opposing team, in which case the goal shall be allowed.

For the purpose of this rule, the point of last contact with the puck by the team in possession shall be used to determine whether or not icing has occurred.

Note 1: If during the period of a delayed whistle due to a foul by a player of the side NOT in possession, the side in possession 'ices' the puck, then the face-off following the stoppage of play shall take place in the Neutral Zone near the Defending Blue Line of the team 'icing' the puck.

Note 2: When a team is 'shorthanded' as the result of a penalty and the penalty is about to expire, 'icing the puck' shall not be called if the team is below the numerical strength of the opposing team at the instant the puck is shot. The action of the penalised player remaining in the penalty box will not alter the ruling.

Note 3: When the puck is shot and rebounds from the body or stick or an opponent in his own half of the ice so as to cross the goal line of the player shooting, it shall not be considered as 'icing'.

Note 4: Notwithstanding the provisions of this section concerning 'batting' the puck in respect of the 'icing the puck' rule, the provisions of the final paragraph of Rule 614(*e*), Handling the Puck with the Hands, apply and no goal can be scored by batting the puck with the hand into the opponent's goal whether attended or not.

Note 5: If while the Linesman has signalled a slow whistle for a clean interception under Rule 624(*d*), Offsides, the player intercepting shoots or bats the puck beyond the opponent's goal-line in such a manner as to constitute 'icing the puck', the Linesman's 'slow whistle' shall be waived the instant the puck crosses the blue line and 'icing' shall be called in the usual manner.

(*b*) If the puck was so shot by a player of a side below the numerical strength of the opposing team, play shall continue and icing shall not be called.

(*c*) If, however, the puck shall go beyond the goal-line in the opposite half of the ice directly from either of the players participating in a face-off, it shall not be considered a violation of this rule.

(*d*) If, in the opinion of the Linesman, a player of the opposing team, except the goalkeeper, is able to play the puck before it passes his goal-line, but has not done so, icing shall not be called and play shall continue. If, in the opinion of the Referee, the defending side intentionally abstains from playing the puck promptly when they are in a position to do so, he shall stop the play and order a face-off on the end-zone face-off spot nearest the goal of the offending team.

(*e*) If the puck shall touch any part of a player of the opposing side, or his skates or his stick, or if it passes through any part of the goal-crease before it shall have reached the goal-line, or shall have touched the goalkeeper, or his skates or his stick, before crossing the goal-line, it shall not be considered as icing the puck and play shall continue.

(*f*) If the Linesman shall have erred in calling an icing the puck infraction (regardless of whether either team is short-handed) the puck shall be faced-off on the centre ice face-off spot.

619. Interference

(*a*) A minor penalty shall be imposed on a player who interferes with or impedes the progress of an opponent who is not in possession of the puck, or who deliberately knocks a stick out of an opponent's hand or who prevents a player who has dropped his stick or any other piece of equipment from regaining possession of it, or who knocks or shoots any abandoned or broken stick or illegal puck or other debris towards an opposing puck carrier in a manner that could cause him to be distracted – see also Rule 633(*a*), Throwing Stick.

Note: The last player to touch the puck – other than a goalkeeper – shall be considered the player in possession. In interpreting this rule the Referee should make sure which of the players is the one creating the interference – often it is the action and movement of the attacking player which causes the interference since the defending players are entitled to 'stand their ground' or 'shadow' the attacking players. Players of the side in possession shall not be allowed to 'run' deliberate interference for the puck carrier.

(*b*) A minor penalty shall be imposed on any player on the players' bench or on the penalty bench who by means of his stick or his body interferes with the movements of the puck or of any opponent on the ice during the progress of play.

(*c*) If an attacking player deliberately stands in the goal-crease, the Referee shall stop play, and the ensuing face-off shall take place in the Neutral Zone.

A minor penalty shall be imposed on a player who, by means of his stick or body, interferes with or impedes the movements of the goalkeeper while he is in his goal-crease area, unless the puck is already in that area.

(*d*) If, when the goalkeeper has been removed from the ice, any member of his team (including the goalkeeper) not legally on the ice, including any team official, interferes by means of his body or stick or any other object with the movements of the puck or an opposing player, the Referee shall immediately award a goal to the non-offending team.

(*e*) When a player in control of the puck on the opponents' side of the centre red line, and having no opponent to pass other than the goalkeeper, is interfered with by a stick or part thereof or any other object thrown or shot by any member of the defending team including a team official, a penalty shot shall be awarded to the non-offending side.

620. Interference by Spectators

(*a*) In the event of a player being held or interfered with by a spectator, play shall be stopped by the Referee or Linesman. If the team of the player interfered with is in possession of the puck at this time, the play shall be allowed to be completed before play is stopped. The puck shall be faced at the spot where last played at the time of the stoppage.

(*b*) Any player who physically interferes with a spectator shall, at the discretion of the Referee, be assessed a gross misconduct penalty and the Referee shall report all such infractions to the proper authorities.

(*c*) In the event that objects are thrown on to the ice which interfere with the progress of the game, the Referee shall stop the play and the puck shall be faced-off at the spot where play is stopped.

621. Kicking a Player

A match penalty shall be imposed on any player who kicks or attempts to kick another player.

622. Kicking the Puck

Kicking the puck shall be permitted in all zones, but a goal may not be scored by the kick of an attacking player. If an attacking player kicks the puck and it is deflected into the goal by any player (other than off a player's stick), or goalkeeper, the goal shall not be allowed.

623. Leaving the Players' or Penalty Bench

(*a*) No player may leave the players' bench or penalty bench at any time during the altercation. Substitutions made prior to the altercation shall be permitted provided the players so substituting do not enter the altercation.

(*b*) The first player to leave the players' or penalty bench during an altercation shall be assessed a double minor penalty and a game misconduct. If players of both teams leave their respective benches at the same time, the first identifiable player of each team to do so shall be penalised under this rule.

(*c*) Any other player or players (those not penalised under *b* above) who leave the players' bench during an altercation shall be assessed a misconduct penalty up to a maximum of five misconducts per team as designated by the Referee.

(*d*) Any player or players (other than in *b* above) that leaves the players' bench and incurs a minor, major or misconduct for his actions shall be automatically assessed a game misconduct.

Note 1: Any game misconducts assessed under (*b*) or (*d*) above shall be considered as part of 'five maximum' under (*c*).

Note 2: For the purpose of determining which player was the first to leave his players' bench during an altercation the Referee may consult with the linesmen or off ice officials.

(*e*) Except at the end of each period, or on expiration of a penalty, no player may at any time leave the penalty bench.

(*f*) A penalised player who leaves the penalty bench, whether play is in progress or not, before his penalty time has expired shall be assessed:

1. A minor penalty (except for *g* below) to be served at the expiration of his previous penalty.

2. If the violation occurred during a stoppage of play and an altercation was taking place, he shall also be assessed a game misconduct in addition to the minor penalty.

3. If the player is penalised under Rule 623(*b*) above, as the first player off the players' or penalty bench, he shall not be assessed any penalties under paragraphs 1 and 2 above.

(*g*) If a player leaves the penalty bench before his penalty is fully served, the Penalty Timekeeper shall note the time and advise the Referee at the first stoppage of play.

If the player returned to the ice prematurely because of an error of the Penalty Timekeeper, he shall not be assessed an additional penalty but must serve the amount of time remaining in his penalty when he re-entered the game.

(*h*) If a player shall illegally enter the game from his own players' bench or from the penalty bench by his own error or the error of the Penalty Timekeeper, any goal scored by his own team while he is illegally on the ice shall be disallowed, but all penalties imposed against either team shall be served as regular penalties.

(*i*) If a player is in possession of the puck and in such a position as to have no opposing player between himself and the opposing goalkeeper and he is interfered with by a player of the opposing team who has illegally entered the game, he shall be awarded a penalty shot.

(*j*) If, when the opposing goalkeeper has been removed from the ice, a player of the side attacking the unattended goal is interfered with by a player who shall have entered the play illegally, the Referee shall immediately award a goal to the non-offending team.

(*k*) Any team official who goes on the ice during any period, without permission of the Referees, shall be assessed a game misconduct.

624. Off-Sides

(*a*) Players of an attacking team may not precede the puck into the Attacking Zone.

(*b*) For a violation of this Rule, play shall be stopped and a face-off conducted.

If the puck was carried over the blue line at the time of the violation, the face-off shall take place at the nearest neutral zone face-off spot to where the puck crossed the line. If the puck was passed or shot over the blue line, the face-off shall take place where the pass or shot originated. *Note*: A player actually propelling and in control of the puck who shall cross the line ahead of the puck shall not be considered off-side.

(*c*) The position of the player's skates and not that of his stick shall be the determining factor in deciding an off-side violation. A player is off-side when both skates are completely over the blue line into his Attacking Zone.

Note 1: A player is 'on-side' when 'either' of his skates are in contact with or on his own side of the line at the instant the puck completely crosses that line, regardless of the position of his stick.

Note 2: It should be noted that while the position of the player's skates is what determines whether a player is 'off-side', nevertheless the question of 'off-side' never arises until the puck has completely crossed the line into the Attacking Zone, at which time the decision is to be made.

(*d*) If (an) attacking player(s) precedes the puck that is shot, passed or deflected into the Attacking Zone by a team-mate, or again deflected into the Attacking Zone off a defending player, but a defending player is able to play the puck, the Linesman shall signal a delayed off-side. The Linesman shall drop his arm to nullify the off-side violation and allow play to continue if:

1. The defending team passes or carries the puck into the Neutral Zone; or

2. All attacking players in the Attacking Zone (at the time the puck crosses the blue line) clear the Attacking Zone by making skate contact with the blue line.

If the puck is shot on goal, causing the goalkeeper to play the puck, play shall be stopped immediately for an off-side violation under this rule. If any attacking player touches the puck or attempts to gain possession of a loose puck while the puck is still in the Attacking Zone or forces the defending puck carrier further back in the Attacking Zone, the Linesman shall stop play.

Note: The Attacking Zone must be completely clear of attacking players before a delayed off-side can be nullified with the puck still in the Attacking Zone.

(*e*) If a player legally carries or passes the puck back into his own Defending Zone while a player of the opposing team is in such Defending Zone, the off-side shall be waived and play permitted to continue. (No delayed whistle.)

(*f*) If, in the opinion of the Linesman, a player has intentionally caused an off-side play, the puck shall be faced-off at the end face-off spot in the Defending Zone of the offending team.

Note: An intentional off-side is one which is made for the purpose of securing a stoppage of play, regardless of the reason, or where an off-side play is made under conditions where there is no possibility of completing a legal play.

625. Passes

(*a*) The puck may be passed by any player to a team-mate within any one of the three zones into which the ice is divided.

The puck, however, may not be passed by a player from his Defensive Zone to a team-mate who is on the opposite side of the centre red line unless the puck preceded the receiving player across the centre line.

(*b*) For a violation of this rule, play shall be stopped and a face-off shall take place at the place where the pass originated or the nearest face-off location.

Note 1: The position of the puck (not the player's skates) shall be the determining factor in deciding from which zone the pass was made.

Note 2: If a receiving player is beyond the centre red line at the time the puck crosses it he may make himself eligible to play the puck by coming back and touching the centre red line with either skate. Thus, the puck being considered to have preceded him across the centre red line.

Note 3: If any part of either skate of a receiving player is touching the centre red line, he shall be considered on his defensive side of the centre line.

Note 4: If the player receiving the pass has his skates over the centre red line, but plays the puck with his stick on his defensive side of the centre line, no violation of this rule shall occur until the puck is carried or shot over the centre line by such player. The official, however, shall use a 'delayed call' of this violation, and if the puck is intercepted by a player of the opposing team and carried or passed back over the centre line, the 'off-side' pass shall not be called.

If, in the same situation as above, the puck having crossed the centre line, shall go directly over the goal line, the 'off-side pass' shall not be called but instead the icing violation shall be imposed.

(*c*) Should the puck, having been passed, touch any player's body, stick or skates, between the passing player's Defensive Zone and the centre red line, it shall nullify any violation of this rule.

(*d*) If the Linesman errs in calling an off-side pass infraction, the puck shall be faced-off at the centre face-off spot.

626. Puck Out of Bounds or Unplayable

(*a*) When the puck goes outside the playing area at either end, or either side of the rink or strikes any obstacles above the playing surface other than the boards, glass or wire, it shall be faced-off at the place from where it was shot or deflected, unless otherwise expressly provided in these rules.

(*b*) When the puck becomes lodged in the netting on the outside of either goal so as to make it unplayable, or if it is frozen against the goal between opposing players intentionally or otherwise, the Referee shall stop the play and face-off the puck at the nearest end-zone face-off spots unless, in the opinion of the Referee, the stoppage was caused by a player of the attacking team, in which case the resulting face-off shall be conducted in the Neutral Zone.

Note: This includes the stoppage of play caused by a player of the attacking team shooting the puck on to the back of the defending team's goal without any intervening action by a defending player.

(*c*) A minor penalty shall be imposed on a goalkeeper who deliberately drops the puck on the goal netting to cause a stoppage of play.

(*d*) If the puck comes to rest on top of the boards surrounding the playing area, it shall be considered to be in play and may be played legally by hand or stick.

627. Puck Out of Sight and Illegal Puck

(*a*) Should a scramble take place, or a player accidentally fall on the puck, and the puck is out of sight of the Referee, he shall immediately stop the play. The puck shall then be faced-off at the point where the play was stopped unless otherwise provided for in the Rules.

(*b*) If, at any time while play is in progress, a puck other than the one legally in play shall appear on the playing surface, the play shall not be stopped, but shall continue with the legal puck until the play then in progress is completed by change of possession.

628. Puck Striking Official

Play shall not be stopped because the puck touches a Referee or Linesman anywhere on the rink, regardless of whether or not a team is short-handed, except when the puck has entered the goal in which case a face-off shall take place at the nearest end-zone face-off spot.

629. Refusing to Start Play

(*a*) If, when both teams are on the ice, one team for any reason shall refuse to play when ordered to do so by the Referee, he shall warn the Captain and allow the team so refusing 30 seconds within which to begin the game or resume play. If at the end of that time the team shall still refuse to play, the Referee shall impose bench minor penalty on the offending team, and the case shall be reported to the proper authorities for further action.

Should there be a recurrence of the same incident, the Referee shall have no alternative but to declare that the game is forfeited to the non-offending team, and the case shall be reported to the proper authorities for further action.

(*b*) If a team, when ordered to do so by the Referee, through its Captain, Manager or Coach, fails to go on the ice and start play within 2 minutes, the game shall be forfeited, and the case shall be reported to the proper authorities for further action.

630. Slashing

(*a*) A minor or major penalty, at the discretion of the Referee, shall be imposed on any player who impedes or seeks to impede the progress of an opponent by slashing with his stick.

(*b*) A major penalty shall be imposed on any player who injures an opponent by slashing.

Note: Referees should penalise as slashing any player who swings his stick at any opposing player (whether in or out of range) without actually striking him or where a player on the pretext of playing the puck makes a wild swing at the puck with the object of intimidating an opponent.

(*c*) Any player who swings his stick at another player in the course of any altercation shall be subject to a major or match penalty.

Note: The Referee shall impose the normal appropriate penalty provided in the other sections of this rule and shall, in addition, report the incident promptly to the proper authorities.

(*d*) When a major penalty is assessed under this rule, the player shall be automatically assessed a game misconduct penalty.

631. Spearing or Butt-ending

(*a*) A double minor plus a misconduct penalty shall be assessed a player who attempts to spear or butt-end an opponent. A major plus a game misconduct penalty shall be assessed a player who spears or butt-ends an opponent.

Note 1: 'Spearing' shall mean stabbing an opponent with the point of the stick blade whether or not the stick is being carried with one or both hands.

Note 2: 'Attempt to Spear' shall include all cases where a spearing gesture is made but no contact is made.

Note 3: 'Attempting to butt-end' shall include all cases where a butt-end gesture is made but no actual contact is made.

(*b*) If any injury results from spearing or butt-ending, a match penalty shall be imposed.

632. Start of Game and Periods

(*a*) The game shall be commenced at the time scheduled by a face-off at the centre face-off spot and shall be renewed promptly at the conclusion of each intermission in the same manner.

(*b*) Home teams shall have the choice of players' bench and shall start the game defending the goal nearest to its own players' bench. The teams shall change ends for each succeeding regular or overtime period.

(*c*) During the pre-game warm-up (which shall not exceed 20 minutes in duration) and before the commencement of play in any period, each team shall confine its activity to its own end of the rink so as to leave clear an area 9m wide across the centre of the Neutral Zone.
Note: Players shall not be permitted to come on the ice during a stoppage of play or at the end of the first and second periods for the purpose of warming-up.

(*d*) Twenty minutes before the time scheduled for the start of the game, both teams shall vacate the ice and proceed to their dressing rooms while the ice is being flooded. Both teams shall be signalled by the Game Timekeeper to return to the ice together in time for the scheduled start of the game.

633. Throwing a Stick

(*a*) When any player or goalkeeper or team official of the defending team deliberately throws or shoots a stick or any part thereof, or any other objects, in the direction of the puck in his Defending Zone, the Referee shall allow the play to be completed, and if a goal is not scored, a penalty shot shall be awarded to the non-offending team, which shot shall be taken by any player designated by the team Captain.

If, however, the goal being unattended and the attacking player having no defending player to pass and having a chance to score on an open goal, a stick or part thereof or any other object, be thrown or shot by any member of the defending team, including a team official, thereby preventing a shot on the open goal, a goal shall be awarded to the attacking team.

(*b*) A major penalty shall be imposed on any player or goalkeeper on the ice who throws his stick or any part thereof, or any other object in the direction of the puck in any zone, except when such act has been penalised by the assessment of a penalty shot, the awarding of a goal or a goal is scored on the play by the non-offending team.
Note: When a player or goalkeeper discards the broken portion of a stick by tossing it to the side of the ice (and not over the boards) in such a way

as will not interfere with play or opposing player, no penalty will be imposed for so doing.

(*c*) A misconduct or game misconduct penalty, at the discretion of the Referee, shall be imposed on a player or goalkeeper who throws his stick, or any part thereof, within or outside the playing area, unless a penalty was imposed under 633(*a*) or (*b*) above. If the offence is committed in protest at an official's decision, a minor penalty under Rule 601(*a*), Abuse of Officials, plus a game misconduct shall be assessed to the offending player.

(*d*) If the goalkeeper intentionally leaves his stick or part thereof in front of his goal and if the puck hits the stick, while the goalkeeper is on or off the ice, the Referee shall stop play immediately and award a goal to the opposing team.

634. Time of Match

(*a*) The game shall consist of three 20-minute periods of actual play with a rest intermission between periods. Play shall be resumed promptly following each intermission upon the expiry of 15 minutes from the completion of play in the preceding period. A preliminary warning shall be given by the Game Timekeeper to the officials and to both teams 3 minutes prior to the resumption of play in each period and the final warning shall be given in sufficient time to enable the teams to resume play promptly.

In games played in outside or uncovered rinks, teams shall change ends at the mid-way period of the third period and overtime period. Goalkeepers shall not be permitted to go to the players' bench, except to be replaced. For a violation of this rule, a minor penalty shall be assessed.

(*b*) The team scoring the greatest number of goals during the three 20-minute periods shall be the winner, and shall be credited with 2 points in the standings.

(*c*) In the intervals between periods, the ice surface shall be flooded unless mutually agreed to by the teams to the contrary.

(*d*) If any unusual delay occurs within 5 minutes of the end of the first or second periods, the Referee may order the next regular intermission to be taken immediately and the balance of play with the teams defending the same goals, after which the teams will change ends and resume play of the ensuing period without delay.

(*e*) Each team shall be permitted to take one time-out of 30 seconds' duration during the course of regular time or over-time and which must be taken during a normal stoppage of play. Any player designated by the Coach will indicate to the Referee who will report the time-out to the Game Timekeeper who shall be responsible for signalling the termination of the time-out.

Note: All players including goalkeepers on the ice at the time of the time-out will be allowed to go to their respective benches. Each team may take their time-out during the same stoppage of play. The team taking the second time-out during the same stoppage must notify the Referee before the completion of the first time-out.

635. Tripping

(*a*) A minor or major penalty shall be imposed on any player who shall place his stick, knee, foot, arm, hand or elbow in such a manner that it shall cause his opponent to trip or fall.

Note 1: If, in the opinion of the Referee, a player is unquestionably hook-checking the puck and obtains possession of it, thereby tripping the puck carrier, no penalty shall be imposed.

Note 2: Accidental trips occurring simultaneously with, or after, stoppage of play will not be penalised.

(*b*) When a player, in control of the puck in the opponent's side of the centre red line, and having no other opponent to pass than the goalkeeper, is tripped or otherwise fouled from behind, thus preventing a reasonable scoring opportunity, a penalty shot shall be awarded to the non-offending team. Nevertheless, the Referee shall not stop the play until the attacking team has lost possession of the puck to the defending team.

Note: The intention of this rule is to restore a reasonable scoring opportunity which has been lost by reason of a foul from behind when the foul is committed in the opponent's side of the centre red line.

By 'control of the puck' is meant the act of propelling the puck with the stick. If, while it is being propelled, the puck is touched by another player or his equipment or hits the goal or goes free, the player shall no longer be considered to be in control of the puck.

(*c*) If, when the opposing goalkeeper has been removed from the ice, a player in control of the puck is tripped or otherwise fouled with no opposition between him and opposing goal, thus preventing a reasonable scoring opportunity, the Referee shall immediately stop the play and award a goal to the attacking team.

Sections 7 and 8 – Medical Rules and Doping Rules – are given in full in the IIHF Official Rule Book.

GLOSSARY

Altercation is defined as any incident involving players leading to a penalty or penalties.

Attempt to or deliberate injury identifies an action by a player or team official who by use of a stick, skate or other object, or by use of his body, hits or attempts to hit an opposing player or team official or game official with the intention of causing injury.

Break-away can be defined as a player in full control of the puck and having no opposing player between himself and the opposing goal-keeper (or goal, if the goalkeeper has been removed).

Broken stick is one which, in the opinion of the Referee, is unfit for normal play.

Butt-ending identifies the condition whereby a player uses the shaft of the stick, above the upper hand, to check an opposing player in any manner or jabs or attempts to jab an opposing player with this part of the stick. A butt-ending penalty shall be called when any of these conditions arises.

Captain is a player, exclusive of a goalkeeper, who is selected or named by the team to represent the team with the officials in accordance with the rules. Wherever the word 'Captain' appears in the rule book, it defines those players who have been designated as Captain or Alternate Captain on the official game report.

Charging identifies the act of taking more than two steps or strides to contact an opposing player.

Coach is a person primarily responsible for directing and guiding the actions and efforts of his team. Along with the Manager he is respon-sible for the conduct of the players before, during and after the game in the arena.

Creases are the enclosed areas designed for the protection of the goalkeeper and the use of the Referee in the discharge of their respective duties. The lines which designate these areas are to be considered as part of the creases.

Cross-checking: Where a stick is being held with both hands, the action of using the shaft of the stick between the two hands and no part of the stick on the ice to check an opponent at any height shall constitute cross-checking.

Delayed off-side is a situation where an attacking player has preceded the puck across the attacking blue line, but the defending team is in a position to bring the puck back out of its defending zone without any delay or contact with an attacking player. The puck shall not have proceeded beyond the top of the circles.

Face-off is identified as a result of the action of the Referee or Linesman in dropping the puck between the sticks of two opposing players to start or resume play. The conduct of a face-off begins when the Referee indicates the location of the face-off and the official and the players take their appropriate positions, and ends when the puck has been legally dropped.

Game is a meeting of two teams playing for a specific length of time for the purpose of declaring a winner through the scoring of goals. The game consists of regular playing time and overtime, if such is required.

Game ejection means that a player or team official has been removed from the game by the Referee and must leave the area of the players' bench and must in no way direct, coach or assist the team in any manner for the remainder of the game.

Goalkeeper is a person designated as such on the game report, who is identified by the use of special and legal equipment and privileges to prevent the puck from entering the goal.

Goalkeepers' skates are specifically designed for the use of goalkeepers only. The blade of the skate is closed at both ends and is specially constructed so as to prevent the puck from passing through the blade.

Kicking is the motion of a player's foot towards an opponent with no intent to play the puck.

High-sticking is the action of the player carrying the stick or any part of the stick above the normal height of the shoulders.

Holding is any action by a player that impedes the progress of an opposing player who is in possession of the puck.

Hooking is the action of using the blade of the stick in a pulling or tugging motion to impede the progress of an opponent. The hooking action may apply to any part of an opponent's body or stick.

Heel of the stick is the portion between the straight part of the shaft and the flat part on the bottom of the blade.

Interference is any action which impedes the progress of an opponent who is not in possession of the puck.

Players are the members of the team physically participating in a game in accordance with the rules. Except where special rules apply to him, the goalkeeper is to be considered as one of the players.

Protective equipment is defined as the equipment worn by a player for the sole purpose of protecting himself from an injury.

Slashing is the action of hitting an opponent with a stick while holding the stick with one or both hands. Tapping the stick of the puck carrier is not considered slashing inasmuch as it is limited to hitting the stick of the opponent for the sole purpose of taking the puck. A player who swings his stick at an opponent and makes no contact shall still be guilty of slashing.

Spearing is the act of poking or attempting to poke an opponent with the point of the blade of the stick while holding the stick with one or both hands.

The term **Team Official** applies to all persons involved in the management of a team and includes coach, manager, trainers, stick boy, team doctor or any other non-playing member of teams' organisation.

Time-out: see Rule 634.

Reprinted by permission of the International Ice Hockey Federation. Copies of the complete Rules with Notes and Referees' Signals can be obtained from the Federation.

Korfball

The Indoor Field of Play

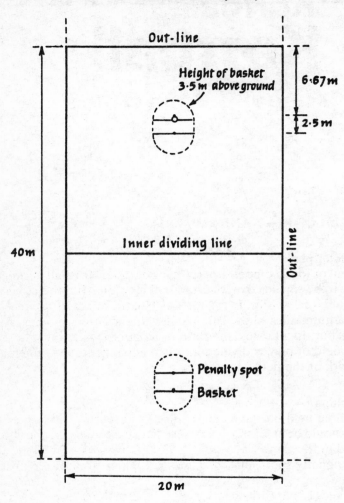

Out-line

Height of basket
3·5 m above ground

6·67 m

2·5 m

40 m

Inner dividing line

Out-line

Penalty spot
Basket

20 m

Korfball

1. FIELD OF PLAY AND MATERIAL

1. Field of play

National or local competition rules for outdoor Korfball permit the field of play to be smaller than the standard 60 × 30m but the recommended minimum is 50 × 25m. In indoor Korfball the dimensions are 40 × 20m. Competition rules allow still smaller dimensions in games for young players but, in all cases, the ratio of length to width must be 2:1.

The field of play is divided into two equal zones by a line parallel to the width of the field.

2. Marking

The whole field of play is marked out by clearly visible lines or tapes which should be at least 3–5cm wide. The line separating the two zones is marked in the same way.

The penalty spots must be marked 2.5m in front of the post as seen from the centre of the field.

On fields of play other than grass it is permissible to use lines, tapes or ropes. They must be clearly visible and their colour must contrast with the field's surface.

The width of the lines or tapes should be 3–5 cm; the diameter of the ropes, if used, must be at least 5mm.

In indoor Korfball, the field of play should be surrounded, if possible, by a border area kept free from obstacles which must be at least 1m wide.

3. Posts

Posts are erected in both zones on the longitudinal axes of the field, at a distance from the ends equal to 1/6th of the length of the field. The posts are round and may consist of solid wood or metal tubing with an external diameter of 4.5–8cm. They are fixed perpendicularly in or on the ground.

4. Baskets

In both outdoor and indoor Korfball a basket is fixed to each post. The basket must face towards the centre and the whole of its top edge must be 3.5m above the ground. The baskets are cylindrical without a bottom; they are 25cm high and have an inner diameter of 39–41cm. The rim (top edge) of the basket has a width of 2–3cm. The baskets must be made of cane and be of one colour, bright yellow.

The method of fixing the basket to the post must satisfy the following conditions:

(i) No movement is permitted between basket and post.

(ii) The post must not protrude above the basket.

(iii) No fixture of more than 1cm may protrude inside or outside the basket.

(iv) A metal support underneath the basket is only permitted over not more than one quarter of the circumference nearest to the post; metal strips against the outside of the basket are only permitted over one third of the circumference.

National or local competition rules may allow a basket of synthetic materials to be used. The behaviour of such a basket must resemble one made of cane in every respect. From time to time, the IKF decides what constitutes approved material and they shall then be certified as such.

5. Ball

Korfball is played with a round ball, the outer casing of which is made of leather or another approved material. When synthetic material is used, the outer casing must resemble a leather ball in all respects. From time to time, the IKF decides what shall constitute approved materials which must then be certified. The ball shall be one- or two-coloured (in indoor Korfball it must be two-coloured). No material shall be used in its construction which might prove dangerous to the players.

The circumference of the ball must be 68–71cm. It must be inflated hard. At the start of a match the weight of the ball must be not less than 425g and not more than 475g.

2. PERSONS

6. Players

(*a*) *Numbers and position.* The game is played by two teams, each consisting of 4 male and 4 female players, of whom 2 men and 2 ladies are placed in each zone.

(*b*) *Incomplete team.* When one or both teams are incomplete, the game can only start, or be continued, if a line-up is possible which ensures that no zone has less than 3 players from each side and that in no division one female and two male players are opposed by one male and two female players.

(*c*) *Substitution of players.* Up to 2 players of a team can be substituted without the approval of the referee. After the aforementioned two substitutions, players can only be substituted when they are injured and can no longer take part in the match. In these cases the referee must decide whether the substitution shall be allowed.

Once a player has been substituted he cannot return to the match.

A player sent off by the referee cannot be replaced.

(*d*) *Equipment of players.* The players of each side must be dressed in a uniform sports costume which is sufficiently different from that of the other side. The players must wear shoes. Players are prohibited to wear objects which can cause injuries during the game.

7. Captain and Coach

(*a*) *Captain.* One player of each team is captain. He* wears a clearly visible band on the upper part of his left arm. He represents the team and is responsible for the proper conduct of his players. In the absence of the team coach, he informs the referee of any change in the team. He has the right to draw the referee's attention to anything he thinks desirable in the interest of the good progress of the match.

(*b*) A coach is permitted to accompany his team to a match. When the coach is present at a match, it is his task to inform the referee of all changes in his team.

* *Whenever the word 'he' is used, it should be understood that this could be 'she'.*

8. Referee

The referee controls the game. His task is:

(*a*) To decide the suitability of the ball, field of play and material.

The referee ascertains before the match that hall and field of play are not unsuitable, that the materials satisfy the stipulations and that everything is ready for the commencement of the game. He pays attention to any changes which might occur during the game.

(*b*) To enforce the rules.

The referee punishes infringements of the rules, except when the punishment would be to the disadvantage of the non-offending side (Advantage Rule).

He takes action when one side obtains an unfair advantage from circumstances outside the game.

He decides in cases of doubt.

(*c*) To indicate the starting, stopping and restarting of the game by means of blowing a whistle.

To start or restart the game, the referee blows his whistle as soon as the player taking the throw is ready and all the requirements (Rules 19 and 20) are satisfied.

(*d*) To take action against misbehaviour by the players or interference by the public.

The referee can consider any unsporting action as misbehaviour, for example, inadmissible forms of appeal or demonstrative gestures against the referee. During the match the referee shall indicate a formal warning by showing a yellow card to the player or coach concerned. Should the player or coach concerned misbehave for a second time, then he must be sent off. In this case the referee shall first show a yellow card and then immediately follow this by showing a red card. If misconduct takes place during the half time and after the players have left the pitch, then the yellow or red card shall be shown to the person concerned at that time and the captain and coach of both teams informed before the start of the second half.

If the misconduct takes place after the game and the referee wishes to take action, then a card shall not be shown. However, the person concerned and the captain and coach of both teams shall be informed.

If during the match there is a case of serious misbehaviour, such as violent physical aggression, then the person concerned is sent off at once. The referee sends someone off by showing him a red card.

9. Timekeeper
If at all possible the referee will appoint a timekeeper whose duty it is to warn the referee just before the end of each half of the game.

3. THE GAME

10. Linesmen
In each match there are two linesmen whose duty is to make sure whether the ball is out, whether Rule 16(*m*) has been infringed and to draw attention to any foul made in their vicinity.

The linesmen indicate the spot where the free pass should be taken after the ball has gone out of play or after an infringement of Rule 16(*m*) on, or outside, the field of play.

The referee will tell the linesmen their positions. In the case of unpermitted interference, partiality, improper conduct, showing approval, disapproval or encouragement of one of the teams by a linesman, the referee has the right to deprive him of his function and to appoint a substitute.

11. Duration

A game of outdoor Korfball lasts 2 × 35 minutes with a half-time interval of 10 minutes.

A game of indoor Korfball lasts 2 × 30 minutes with an interval of 10 minutes though national or local competition rules may permit shorter times.

Interruptions not forming part of the normal play should be excluded from the timing of the game. If deemed sufficiently important by the referee, any delays in the first or second half caused by infringements of the rules, delaying changing of zones or any outside influence (including the treatment of injuries) may be deemed to be delays outside the course of the game and the referee may lengthen the duration of that half accordingly.

The referee may also lengthen the duration of that half accordingly whenever a free pass under rule 16g, or in some cases a penalty under rule 20a, for an infringement of rule 16g, is not given because it is not advantageous to the non-offending side.

12. Goals

(a) A team scores a goal when:

(i) The ball has fallen completely through the basket which is positioned in the attack zone of that team, except for the cases mentioned under (c).

(ii) It is sure that the ball would have fallen completely through the basket, but it is tapped back from underneath by a defender, except for the cases mentioned under (c).

(b) A goal stands even when the referee has previously blown for an infringement committed by a defender, provided the ball had left the hands of the shooting attacker at the moment of whistling and was outside the reach of any defender, except for the cases mentioned under (c).

(c) The referee does not allow the goal when:

(i) He has blown his whistle before the ball has fallen through the basket and the infringement was committed by an attacker, or because he has blown for the end of the first or the second half of the match.

(ii) He has observed an infringement committed by the attacking side but has not blown for the infringement until after the ball has gone through the basket.

(iii) He has previously observed an unfair advantage to the attacking side.

(iv) The ball is first thrown from underneath through the basket and then falls back again through the basket.

(*d*) The team scoring the most goals wins the match.

13. Line-up

(*a*) *Choice of line-up*. The home team decides into which basket they will shoot in the first half. They arrange their players in the two zones and the visiting team arranges their side accordingly.

(*b*) *Change in line-up*. Normally the same line-up is maintained throughout the match. If, however, during the game circumstances alter owing to the dropping out of a player, the referee can, at the request of a coach and after consulting the other coach, permit a change. He will order a change when this is necessary to comply with the conditions mentioned in Rule 6(*b*), or when the number of players with a direct opponent is less than absolutely necessary.

14. Zone changes and changes of end

Each time that two goals have been scored the players change zone. At half-time there is a change of ends. The players move to the other zone.

15. Throw-off

The throw-off is taken by an attacker from a point inside his zone near the centre of the field. A throw-off takes place at the start of the game, at the start of the second half and after every goal; in the first case the throw-off is taken by the home team, in the second case by the visiting team and in the last case by the team against which the goal has been scored.

The same stipulations apply as for a free pass (see Rule 19).

16. Infringements of the rules

During the game it is prohibited:

(*a*) To touch the ball with leg or foot. If the touching is unintentional and exerts no important influence upon the game, it will not be punished.

(*b*) To hit the ball with the fist.

(*c*) To take hold of the ball in a fallen position.

(*d*) To run with the ball. Running with the ball is contrary to the requirement of co-operation. Change of position with the ball is therefore only permitted when otherwise it would be impossible to throw the ball correctly or to stop with the ball.

In applying these principles, three cases are to be distinguished:

1. When seizing the ball the player stands at rest. In this case he may move one leg at will, provided the other one remains in its place.

Turning on the latter is permitted. It is also permitted to jump, provided that the leg which did not move is used for the take-off. If after a jump the player comes down with the ball still in his hands, this will only be an infringement of the rules if, in doing so, he has moved from his former position. In general, there can be no question of running with the ball if it did not result in a clear change of position.

2. When seizing the ball the player is running or jumping; first he stops and afterwards passes the ball. The requirement is that, after seizing the ball, he has immediately and fully tried to come to a stop. After coming to a stop, the same rules apply as mentioned under 1, above.

3. After seizing the ball while running or jumping, the player throws the ball before he has come to a stop. This is permitted provided the catching and throwing have only taken a very short time, or have been combined into one flowing movement, or if the player has tried hard to lessen his speed immediately after catching the ball.

(*e*) To avoid co-operation (solo-play).

Note: Solo-play is the deliberate avoidance of co-operation, i.e. a player tries to change his position with the ball in his possession without the help of another player.

Solo-play is not punishable:

1. When the player does not change his position appreciably.
2. When the avoidance of co-operation was not intentional.

(*f*) To hand the ball to another player of one's own team.

(*g*) To delay the game unnecessarily.

(*h*) To knock, take or run the ball out of an opponent's hand.

(*i*) To push, to cling to, or to hold off an opponent.

This unlawful hindering of an opponent has to be punished no matter whether this opponent does or does not possess the ball even if the ball is in another zone.

Every impediment of the free movement of an opponent is forbidden whether this is done deliberately or not.

This rule does not force a player to give way for another player, i.e. each player is allowed to position himself just as he pleases. He will only be punished when he jumps so suddenly in the path of a moving opponent that a collision becomes inevitable.

(*j*) To hinder an opponent excessively. This rule applies when the opponent has the ball in his possession.

The hindering player is allowed to hinder the throwing of the ball in the desired direction by actions which result in the ball being thrown against his hand or arm.

He is allowed to block the ball by bringing his arm in the path of the ball, but he must not:

1. Hinder his opponent in the free use of his body by blocking the arm instead of the ball.

2. Beat the ball or hit the throwing arm, i.e. the hindering arm or hand must not move towards the ball at the instance of contact.

Unexpected movements by an opponent will often cause a restriction in a player's freedom of movement. Such cases will not be punished, provided immediate action is taken by the opponent to restore the player's freedom of movement.

(k) To hinder an opponent of the opposite sex in throwing the ball.

(l) To hinder an opponent who is already being hindered by another player.

(m) To play outside one's zone.

(n) To shoot from a defended position.

The shot must be considered defended when the hindering defender satisfies each of the following three conditions:

1. He must be within arm's length of the attacker and must have his face turned towards him.

2. He must actually try to block the ball.

3. He must be nearer the post than the attacker, except when he and the attacker are near and on opposite sides of the post. In the latter case conditions 1 and 2 alone are sufficient.

(o) To shoot after cutting past another attacker.

'Cutting' occurs when a defender cannot follow an attacker, because the attacker runs so close past another attacker, that the defender collides with or is likely to collide with this attacker and therefore is forced to give up his hindering position. If at that instant the defender is at a considerable distance from the attacker, then there can be no question of 'cutting' and the shot must be allowed.

(p) To shoot from the defence zone, from a free-pass or from a referee-throw (throw-up).

(q) To shoot when one plays without a personal opponent.

This occurs when the defence has only three players against an attack of four players. In that case the captain of the attacking side must inform the referee and the other captain which of his attackers will not shoot.

The captain is entitled to change his decision during the match, but only after informing the referee and the other captain at a time when the ball is dead, i.e. the referee has blown for an infringement, a goal and so on. This change of attacker is only allowed twice between a change of zones. A goal can be made from a penalty by an attacker without a personal opponent.

(r) To influence a shot by moving the post.

(s) To take hold of the post when jumping, running or in order to move away quickly.

(t) To violate the conditions laid down for a free pass or a penalty.

17. Out-ball

The ball is out as soon as it touches a boundary line of the field of play, the ground, a person or an object outside the field of play.

The ball is also out when it touches the ceiling or an object above the field of play.

In the case of an out-ball a free pass is awarded against the side who touched the ball last.

18. Referee-throw (throw-up)

When two opponents seize the ball simultaneously, the referee will stop play and will throw the ball up.

The same applies when play must be restarted without one side being entitled to the ball. For this purpose the referee chooses two players from the zone concerned, who must be of the same sex and if possible of about the same height. These two players may touch the ball after the ball has reached its highest point during the throw-up. The other players must observe a distance of 2.5m and may only touch the ball after one of the two selected players has touched the ball or after the ball has been in contact with the ground.

The attacker, selected by the referee for the throw-up, is not allowed to shoot directly from the throw-up.

19. Free pass

(*a*) *When to award a free pass*. A free pass is awarded to the opposing side after the referee has indicated that one of Rules 16 or 17 has been violated. After the game has been stopped by the referee's whistle, an infringement of the rules is no longer possible though it is possible for a player to be guilty of misbehaviour.

After a goal has been awarded, the game is always resumed with a throw-off according to Rule 15 and any infringement shall not be penalised by a free pass to the opponents. A free pass must be retaken if the throw is taken before the referee has blown his whistle for the throw to be taken.

(*b*) *Place of the free pass*. The free pass is taken from the spot where the infringement was committed. If the infringement was committed against a certain person (Rule 16, *h*, *i*, *j*, *k*, *l* and sometimes *m*), then the free pass is taken from the spot where the person was standing.

In the case of an out-ball or when Rule 16(*m*) has been violated on or outside the boundaries of the field of play then the free pass is taken from outside the field near the boundary line where the ball or the offending player touched or crossed the line.

When the ball is out because it touches the ceiling or an object above the field of play, the free pass is taken near one of the long boundaries and nearest to the spot where the ball touches the ceiling or the object.

(c) *How to take a free pass*. The player taking the free pass must bring the ball into play within no more than 4 seconds after the whistle has gone for the commencement of play – see Rule 8(c).

The players of the opposing team must keep a distance of at least 2.5m until the taker of the free pass moves the ball. The players of the same team as the taker of the free pass must keep a distance of at least 2.5m until the ball is brought into play. If the free pass is to be taken in the attack zone, each player of the same team as the taker of the free pass must also remain at least 2.5m from each other until the ball is brought into play. The ball is brought into play when a player of the opposing team touches the ball, or when a player of the same team as the player taking the free pass touches the ball whilst standing at least 2.5m from the spot at which the pass is taken, or when the ball has travelled at least 2.5m from the place of the free pass. When after 4 seconds the taker of the free pass is still in possession of the ball, then the referee blows his whistle and awards a free pass to the other side.

Shooting after the taking of a free pass is only allowed after the ball has moved freely through the air and afterwards has been touched by another player.

When the person taking the free pass touches a boundary line, or the playing area on the other side of the boundary line before the ball has left his hands and after the referee has blown his whistle to indicate that the free pass can be taken, then the referee awards a free pass to the opposing side on the other side of the boundary line.

20. Penalty

(a) *When to award a penalty*. Infringements which result in the loss of a scoring chance are punished by the award of a penalty to the other side. A penalty can also be awarded for other infringements which repeatedly hinder the attack unfairly.

(b) *Place of penalty*. The penalty must be taken from the penalty spot (see Rule 2) which is 2.5m from the post as seen from the centre of the field.

(c) *How to take a penalty*. It is permitted to score directly from a penalty. The person taking the penalty must not touch the ground between the post and the penalty spot with any part of his body before the ball has left his hands. The penalty must be retaken if it is taken before the referee has blown his whistle to indicate that the penalty can be taken. The stipulation of Rule 19c that the opponents may move within the prescribed distance as soon as the person taking the free pass moves the ball, and the stipulation that players of the same team as the person taking the free pass in the attack zone must remain 2.5m from each other until the ball is brought into play, do not apply in the case of a penalty.

All other players must observe a distance of 2.5m (in all directions) from any point on the imaginary line between spot and post. They must refrain from any action or comments disturbing the person taking the penalty.

If necessary the first as well as the second half of the match will be prolonged for the taking of a penalty.

Reprinted by permission of the International Korfball Federation. Copies of the complete Rules of Korfball, including those for the above variations, and explanations of the Rules, can be obtained from the British Korfball Association.

Men's Lacrosse

The Field of Play

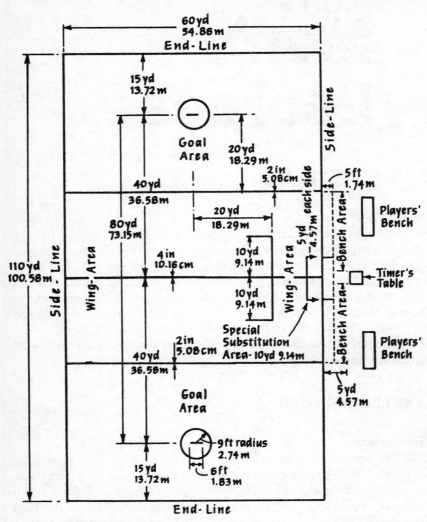

Note: Offside (centre) line – 4 in, 10.16cm
All other lines – 2 in, 5.08cm

Men's Lacrosse

THE GAME

Lacrosse is played by two teams of 10 players each. The purpose of each team is to score by causing the ball to enter the goal of its opponents, and to prevent the other team from securing the ball and scoring. The ball is kept in play by being carried, thrown or batted with the crosse, rolled or kicked in any direction, subject to the restrictions laid down in the following Rules and the Additional Rulings (ARs) which accompany them. The ARs have the same authority as the rules.

The ball may not be touched by the hand, except by a goalkeeper who is within his goal-crease.

1. THE PLAYING FIELD

1. Dimensions

1.1 The lacrosse playing field shall be, *where possible*, a rectangular field 110yd (100.58m) long and 60yd (54.86m) wide.

1.2 The boundaries of the field shall be marked with white lines. An extra heavy white line shall be marked through the centre of the field perpendicular to the side-lines; this line shall be designated the centre-line. The boundary lines on the long sides of the field shall be designated side-lines; those at each end shall be designated end-lines.

1.3 Flag markers or pylons shall be placed at the four corners of the field, at each end of the gate within the special substitution area, and at that end of the half-way line which is opposite the bench area. If flag markers are used, they must be made of flexible material so that they will bend a minimum of 90 degrees without breaking. If pylons are used, they must be made of plastic or rubber.

2. The Goals

2.1 Each goal shall consist of two vertical posts joined by a rigid cross-bar. These posts shall be 6ft (1.83m) apart and the top cross-bar shall be 6ft (1.83m) from the ground (all inside measurements). The goal-posts and cross-bar shall be collectively designated the pipes.

2.2 The goal-posts shall be centred and shall be placed 80yd (73.15m) apart and 15yd (13.72m) from each end-line.

2.3 The pipes shall be made of *wood or an approved metal or alloy and each shall be of not more than 3in (7.6cm) square or equivalent circular cross section. The material used and the shape shall be such as to prevent injury resulting from collision with them.* The pipes shall be painted orange *or white* and secured to the ground.

A line shall be drawn between the goal-posts to indicate the plane of the goal, and it shall be designated the goal-line.

2.4 *Where possible*, the goal-posts shall be:
either sunk into the ground so that no ground-pipes are used;
or supported by flat ground-pipes

2.5 *Where ground-pipes are used, there must be a board measuring 1in by 3in by 18in (2.54cm by 7.62cm by 0.46m) securely fastened to each ground-pipe directly behind the vertical post at an angle of 45 degrees.*

3. The Goal-Crease

3.1 Around each goal there shall be plainly marked a circle known as the goal-crease. This circle shall be marked by using the mid-point of the goal-line as the centre and drawing a circle around that point with a radius of 9ft (2.74m).

3.2 The goal-crease area is the circular ground territory about each goal within and including the goal-crease.

4. The Goal-Nets

4.1 Each goal must be fitted with a pyramidal-shaped cord netting which shall be fastened to the goal-posts, the cross-bar and the ground so as to prevent the passage of the ball. The mesh of the net shall not exceed 1.5in (3.81cm). The centre of the goal-net shall be fastened to the ground at a point 7ft (2.13m) behind the centre of the goal-line. The pipes and the goal-net shall be collectively designated the cage.

4.2 The goal-nets must be adjusted so that the ball may pass completely through the imaginary plane of the goal at any point.

4.3 Goal-nets may be any solid colour.

5. The Goal-Areas

5.1 At each end of the field a line shall be marked from side-line to side-line 20yd (18.29m) from the centre-line. These lines shall be designated goal-area lines.

5.2 The areas between the goal-area lines and the end-lines (but excluding the lines themselves) at each end of the field shall be designated the goal-areas.

6. The Wing-Areas

6.1 Lines parallel to the side-lines shall be marked on each side of the field 20yd (18.29m) from an imaginary line joining the centres of the goal-lines; the lines shall extend 10yd (9.14m) on each side of the centre-line. These lines shall be designated the wing-area lines.

6.2 The areas between the wing-area lines and the side-lines, and confined within the extremities of the wing-area lines, but excluding those lines, shall be designated the wing-areas.

7. The Centre of the Field

A point on the centre-line equidistant from each side-line shall be marked with an 'X' and shall be designated the centre.

8. The Special Substitution Area

8.1 The special substitution area shall be indicated by two lines marked on the side of the field *on the same side of the field as the benches*. These lines shall, *where possible*, be 20ft (6.1m) in length and shall extend away from the field of play at right angles to the side-line from points on the side-line 5yd (4.57m) from the centre-line.

8.2 That part of the side-line between the special substitution-area lines shall thus be 10yd (9.14m) in length, and shall be designated the gate.

9. The Timer's Table and the Benches

9.1 *Where possible, a timer's table shall be used.* The timer's table shall be placed, *where possible*, at least 5yd (4.57m) from the side-line at the centre-line.

9.2 Benches for the competing teams shall be placed *in each bench area at least 10yd (9.14m) from the imaginary extension of the half-way line and, where possible*, at least 6 yd (5.47m) from the side-line, parallel to the side-line.

10. The Bench Areas

The bench areas are located off the playing field and are between the special substitution area lines and the imaginary extensions of the goal-area lines.

11. The Coaches' Area

Where possible, a dotted restraining line shall be placed 9ft (2.74m) from the side-line. It shall be parallel to the side-line and extend the length of the bench area. The area bounded by the side-line, the dotted restraining line, the special substitution area line and the imaginary extension of the goal-area line shall be designated the coaches' area.

12. Lines

12.1 All lines referred to in this section (except the centre-line and the goal-lines) shall be 2in (5.08cm) in width. The centre-line shall be 4in (10.16cm) in width. The goal-lines shall be the same width as the pipes.

12.2 Where other lines appear on the field of play, the lines referred to in this section shall be all of one colour, and that colour shall contrast with the colour of the other lines.

13. The Penalty Box

The penalty box shall consist of two seats for each team at the centre of the field on the bench side of the field. *Where possible*, the seats shall be at least 5yd (4.57m) from the side-line.

2. EQUIPMENT

14. The Ball

14.1 The ball shall be of white, *yellow*, or orange rubber and between 7.75in (19.69cm) and 8in (20.32cm) in circumference. It shall be between 5 and 5.25 ounces in weight, and, when dropped on to a hard wooden floor from a height of 72in (1.83m), shall bounce to a height of between 45in (114.3cm) and 49in (124.46cm).

14.2 Balls shall be supplied by the home team and the ball in use at the end of the game shall become the property of the winning team.

14.3 *Where possible*, the home team shall supply ball boys with extra balls at each side and each end of the field. The ball boys shall wear helmets, gloves and boxes.

15. The Crosse

15.1 The crosse shall be of an overall length of between 40in (101.6cm) and 72in (182.88cm).

15.2 The head of the crosse shall measure between 4in (10.16cm) and 10in (25.4cm) inside measurement at its widest point.

15.3 The stick of the designated goalkeeper shall be an exception to Rules 15.1 and 15.2, above. There may be one stick up to 15in (38.1cm) inside measurement in use by each team at any one time, and it must be used by the designated goalkeeper. The goalkeeper's stick may be any desired length.

15.4 The head of the crosse shall be made of wood, laminated wood, plastic, or any other material approved by the *ELU*, and the shaft shall be made of wood, aluminium or any other material approved by the *ELU*. Where a handle is made of metal, it must have a plastic or wood plug on the end, or it must be adequately taped to prevent injury. The head of the crosse shall be approximately perpendicular to the handle.

15.5 The head of the crosse shall be constructed as follows:

Either both walls shall be of wood, laminated wood, plastic or other material approved by the *ELU*;

Or one wall shall be made of wood, laminated wood, plastic or other material approved by the *ELU*, and the other wall shall be made by weaving gut lacing from the tip of the head to the handle in such a manner that it prevents the tip from catching on an opponent's crosse.

15.6 The wooden or plastic walls of the crosse shall not be above 2in (5.08cm) in height; where a wall is made of gut, it may be any height.

15.7 The centre line of the handle shall cross the head approximately 2.5in (6.35cm) from the wall.

15.8 There shall be a guard stop at the throat of the crosse. The stop must be perpendicular to the handle of the crosse and wide enough to let the ball rest loosely on the stop. The guard stop shall be a minimum of 10in (25.4cm) from the outside edge of the head of the crosse. The stop shall be constructed so that no part of the ball can be under the stop.

15.9 The head and side(s) of the crosse shall have holes bored in them to facilitate the weaving of the stringing.

15.10 The net of the crosse shall be constructed of gut, rawhide, clock cord, linen or synthetic material and shall be roughly triangular in shape.

16. Prohibitions Relating to the Crosse

16.1 No player shall use a crosse in which the pocket has been permitted to sag to such a depth that the top surface of a lacrosse ball placed therein is below the bottom edge of the sidewalls when the crosse is held horizontal to the ground with the net to the bottom of the crosse. This prohibition shall not apply to the crosse of the designated goalkeeper.

16.2 No player shall use a crosse which is constructed or strung so as to be designed to withhold the ball from play.

16.3 No player shall use a crosse of trick construction or stringing which tends to retard the normal and free dislodgement of the ball by an opponent.

16.4 No stick may be tampered with in any way so as to give a player an advantage over his opponent.

16.5 Any strings which are not part of the stick as manufactured shall be limited to a hanging length of 2in (5.08cm).

16.6 The mesh of the net must be substantially all of one colour.

16.7 Adjustable length handles are illegal.

17. Personal Equipment

17.1 All players are required to wear protective gloves, suitable boots or shoes, and a protective helmet equipped with a face mask and a chinstrap which must be properly fastened on both sides.

All equipment, including helmets, gloves, shoulder pads, arm pads and kidney pads, shall be of the approved lacrosse pattern and style. It shall be manufactured by a recognised lacrosse manufacturer, and, in the opinion of the officials, it shall not endanger the wearer or any other player. Any equipment manufactured in the UK must be approved by the ELU before it is used.

The fingers may not be cut out of a player's gloves, and the entire finger must be encased within, and must be part of the glove. A player may not play with his fingers outside the glove. A player may cut the palms out of his gloves.

Boots or shoes shall be of non-metallic construction except for the studs and the eyelets. They shall have no sharp edges or points which may injure other players.

Play must be suspended immediately if a player loses any of the required equipment in a scrimmage area. Otherwise, the official shall delay the sounding of his whistle in the same manner as set forth in Rule 82, which deals with the slow whistle technique, except that the signal flag is not thrown under these circumstances.

17.2 *The normal dress shall be the team's registered jersey or shirt, shorts and socks.* Each player is required to wear a jersey with a contrasting block or Gothic number centred on the front and the back. The number on the front of the jersey shall be at least *6in (15.1cm)* high, and the number on the back shall be at least *8in (20.3cm)* high. The numbers on the front and back of a player's jersey shall be the same, and no duplicate numbers shall be permitted on the same team.

17.3 The visiting team shall notify the home team of the colour of the jerseys which they are going to wear in the game, and the home team must wear jerseys of a contrasting colour.

18. Prohibitions Relating to Personal Equipment

18.1 No player shall wear or carry equipment which, in the opinion of the officials, endangers himself or other players.

18.2 No player shall wear anything on the outside of his jersey which might obstruct the view of his numbers.

18.3 The special equipment worn by the goalkeeper shall not exceed standard equipment so far as shin guards, throat guards and chest protectors are concerned.

18.4 No player shall wear hockey goalkeeper gloves.

18.5 Track suit trousers may be worn by any player, but for a particular team they must be of the same colour, and it is recommended that they be of a different colour from those worn by the opponents.

18.6 Where members of a team wear leg-warmers or thigh-warmers, their colour(s) shall be uniform throughout the team.

3. THE TEAMS

19. Number of Players

19.1 Ten players shall constitute a full team. There shall be 1 goalkeeper, 3 defenders, 3 midfielders and 3 attackers.

19.2 If, because of injuries or men out of the game due to expulsion fouls, a team cannot keep 10 players in the game, then it may continue the game with fewer than 10 players, but no exceptions will be made to the regular rules for this situation.

20. Substitutes

20.1 A team may have up to 3 substitutes.

20.2 Only thirteen players in a squad may dress in team uniform for a game. Any others in the squad who are in the bench area must wear alternative strip or track-suits.

21. Captains

21.1 Each team shall designate a captain or co-captains, and they shall act as the representatives of their team on the field of play during the game. Where a team designates co-captains, one of them shall be designated the official representative of that team on the field.

21.2 The privilege of the captains to act as the representatives of the team on the field does not grant them the right to enter into argument with an official or to criticise any decision of an official.

21.3 Should the captain leave the field of play, either he or his coach should designate to the nearest Referee the name and number of the replacing captain. If a team is without a designated captain at any time during the play of the game, then one of the Referees may designate an acting-captain.

22. Coaches

22.1 A team may have any number of coaches but, *if more than one coach is to be used*, then a team shall designate one coach as its head coach. The head coach shall be responsible for making all decisions for his team which are not specifically delegated to his captain. Before the commencement of the game, the head coach shall nominate his captain(s), a defence-man to serve the goalkeeper's penalty time, and an In-home to the officials.

The In-home may be any member of the squad.

22.2 The head coach shall at all times conduct himself like a gentleman, and he shall endeavour in every way to have his players and substitutes also conduct themselves like gentlemen. He shall also be in control of and responsible for the actions and conduct of all non-playing members of his squad and any and all persons officially connected with his team. He shall assist the officials to keep the game under control at all times. It shall be his duty, upon the request of an official, effectively to control any actions of spectators which are not in conformity with good sportsmanship.

22.3 It shall be the responsibility of the home head coach to see:

(i) That the playing field is in proper condition for play.

(ii) That the players and substitutes are properly equipped to play.

(iii) That the *chief bench official and any other bench officials* are on hand with all the equipment necessary for them to carry out their respective functions.

(iv) That balls and, *where possible*, ball boys are provided.

22.4 One or more of a team's coaches may be a player/coach.

The officials must be informed of the shirt number of any such player/coach before the start of the game.

22.5 *Where a team does not have a coach, then the coach's duties specified in this rule shall be carried out by the captain(s).*

4. CONTROL OF THE GAME

23. The Officials

23.1 The game of lacrosse shall be controlled by *up to* 3 Referees, one of whom shall be designated the Head Referee. Their duties shall be equal in all respects, except that, in the settlement of any dispute, the decision of the Head Referee shall be final. The Referees shall have authority over the play of the game, with control and jurisdiction over the *bench officials*, players, substitutes, coaches, anyone officially connected with the teams, and spectators.

23.2 The authority of the Referees shall begin with their *arrival at the ground*, and terminate *at a reasonable time after the end of the match*.

23.3 By the sounding of his whistle, any of the Referees may suspend the play of the game for any reason which he deems necessary for the proper enforcement of the Rules of the Game.

23.4 The Referees shall keep a record of the goals scored by each team, and the number of the player scoring the goal. *Where a scorer is available, the Referees* shall check the score with the official scorer at the end of each period, but the Referees' score shall be the official score of the game. *Where no timekeeper is available, one of the Referees shall keep a record of the time played in each period. He shall endeavour to warn the teams 2 minutes before the end of each period, and 30 seconds before the end of each period.*

23.5 The Referees and the chief bench official shall wear similar uniforms. This shall be vertical black and white striped shirt, white shorts, black and white socks and a black cap.

24. The Chief Bench Official

24.1 A chief bench official (CBO) shall be *provided by the home club*, and he shall be equipped with a signal flag and a whistle. He shall supervise and hold complete jurisdiction over the timekeeper, penalty timekeepers, scorers, coaches, substitutes and any other officials within the bench areas, the special substitution area and the penalty box. *Where possible*, he shall wear the same uniform as the Referees, except that he shall also wear a suitably inscribed armband.

24.2 The CBO shall:

(i) Check the substitution of players going on to and off the field of play.

(ii) Check that each team has the correct number of players on the field of play.

(iii) *Where there is only one Referee on the field of play, check that each team obeys the Off-side Rule; where there is more than one Referee on the field of play*, assist the Referees in checking that each team obeys the Off-side Rule.

(iv) Check that no illegal stick exchange occurs.

(v) Check that no illegal actions are carried out by a coach or official member of either squad.

(vi) Check that no foul is committed by a player or substitute who is in the act of leaving the field of play or in the act of entering the field of play, or who is in the bench area, the special substitution area or the penalty box.

24.3 Where the CBO becomes aware of any of the above six infringements, he shall, depending on the circumstances, either throw a signal flag or blow his whistle, and subsequently advise the nearest Referee of the nature of the foul, as follows:

(i) If the ball is loose at the time that a foul is committed, then he shall blow his whistle immediately.

(ii) If one team has possession of the ball, and that team or both teams commits a foul or a number of fouls, then the CBO shall blow his whistle immediately.

(iii) If one team has possession of the ball, and its opponents commit a foul or a number of fouls, then the CBO shall throw a signal flag. The Referees shall then decide whether to throw a signal flag or blow the whistle.

24.4 The CBO shall acknowledge receipt and understanding of the Referees' signals relating to penalties, penalty periods or any other matters relating to the play of the game, by repeating the signal. He shall then relay the decisions of the Referees to the *other bench officials*, as appropriate.

24.5 The CBO shall advise the coaches, if so requested, as to the decisions of the Referees.

24.6 *Where there is no timekeeper, the CBO shall keep a record of the time taken during team time-outs and of the time intermissions between playing periods.* The CBO shall notify each team 30 seconds before the restart of play during a team time-out, and 1 minute before the start of each period.

24.7 *Where there is no scorer, the CBO shall keep a record of the number of each player upon whom a personal penalty is inflicted.* The CBO shall notify the nearest Referee if any player has incurred 5 personal fouls.

24.8 The CBO shall blow his whistle if a team legally asks him for a time-out.

24.9 *Where there is no penalty timekeeper, the CBO shall be equipped with a time-piece which can record time in seconds. He shall time the period of any penalty imposed by the Referees, and shall audibly count down the penalty time to the player concerned and to any substitute who may be about to go on to the field in place of the penalised player, as follows: 30 seconds, 15 seconds, 10, 9, 8 . . . 3, 2, 1, Release.*

24.10 *Where there is no scorer, the CBO shall keep an accurate record of the number of time-outs taken by each team, and he shall notify the nearest Referee immediately if a team exceeds the number allowed in a half or an overtime period.*

24.11 *The home team shall supply a competent CBO who is fully conversant with the rules of lacrosse. Should the home team fail to do so, then the head Referee shall instruct the coach or, where there is no coach, the captain(s) of the home team to select a player or substitute who is capable of undertaking the duties, to act as the CBO. The selected player shall take no further part in the playing of the game.*

25. The Timekeeper

25.1 A timekeeper *may* be appointed, and he must be equipped with a time-piece which is able to record time in seconds.

25.2 The timekeeper shall keep an accurate record of the time played in each period, and he shall go out on to the field of play for the last 30 seconds of play in each period to count down the remaining time to the closest Referee as follows; 30 seconds, 25 seconds, 20 seconds, 15 seconds, 14, 13 . . . 3, 2, 1, Time.

25.3 The timekeeper shall keep an accurate record of the time intermissions between playing periods, and he shall notify the chief bench official 1 minute prior to the start of each period of play.

25.4 The timekeeper shall keep an accurate record of the time taken during team time-outs, and he shall notify the chief bench official 30 seconds before the restart of play.

26. The Penalty Timekeepers

26.1 *One or* two penalty timekeepers *may* be appointed for each squad, and they shall be equipped with time-pieces which can record time in seconds. The penalty timekeepers shall be positioned at either side of the timer's table, behind the penalty box.

26.2 The penalty timekeepers shall time the period of any penalty imposed by the Referees, and shall audibly count down the penalty time to the player concerned and to any substitute who may be about to go on to the field in place of the penalised player, as follows: 30 seconds, 15 seconds, 10, 9, 8 . . . 3, 2, 1, Release.

27. The Scorers

27.1 Each team *may* provide a scorer and, unless otherwise designated by the Head Referee, the visiting scorer shall be the official scorer.

27.2 The scorers shall keep a record of the goals scored by each team, the name and number of the player scoring the goal, and the name and number of the player making an assist.

27.3 The scorers shall check with the Referees at the end of each period to ensure that they have the same score.

27.4 The scorers shall keep an accurate record of the number of time-outs taken by each team, and they shall notify the chief bench official immediately if a team exceeds the number allowed in a half or in an overtime period.

27.5 The scorers shall keep a record of the name and number of each player upon whom a penalty is inflicted, the type of foul, the duration of the penalty, and the game time of the penalty.

27.6 The scorers shall notify the chief bench official if any player should incur 5 personal fouls.

28. Mistakes by the Bench Officials

Where a chief bench official, timekeeper, penalty timekeeper, or scorer becomes aware that a mistake is being made which would result in a player or a team being penalised, then he shall promptly correct the mistake. If a goal is scored during the mistake and it is brought to the attention of the Referees before the next live ball, after the player in question has participated in the game, then the Referees shall allow or disallow the goal depending on the circumstances.

5. THE LENGTH OF THE GAME

29. Time of the Match

29.1 The match shall be divided into 4 periods of *20* minutes' duration each. 'Time-off' incurred in each quarter shall be added to the playing time of that quarter.

29.2 During the last 3 minutes of the fourth quarter, and during any overtime period, the game-clock and, if applicable, the penalty clock(s) shall stop whenever the ball becomes dead, and they shall restart whenever play is restarted.

This shall apply for all stoppages, including the scoring of a goal.

29.3 At the end of each quarter, the teams shall change ends.

The interval between the first and second quarters shall be of 2 minutes' duration.

At half-time, the interval shall be 10 minutes long.

At three-quarter time, the interval shall be 3 minutes.

29.4 Between the first and second periods, and between the third and fourth periods, the players shall, on leaving the playing field, assemble in the bench area only; to go beyond this area, they must have the permission of the Referees.

At half-time, the teams may leave the playing field.

30. Uncompleted Match

If less time than the regulation time has to be played either through failure of daylight or from any other cause, then the curtailment of playing time shall be at the discretion of the Referee who shall, if possible, arrange that all four quarters shall be of equal duration. If in any match it is not possible to play at least 60 minutes in all, then such a match shall not count in any competition and shall be replayed.

31. Tied Game

31.1 In the event of the scores being tied at the end of regulation playing time, then, *subject to Rule 31.3 below*, 2 periods of overtime shall be played. The following procedure shall apply:

(i) There shall be an interval of 5 minutes, during which the teams shall change ends.

(ii) Both periods of overtime shall start with a face-off as at the start of each quarter, subject to the provisions of Rule 34.1 being followed.

(iii) The overtime periods shall be of 4 minutes' duration, and there shall be a 2-minute interval between them.

(iv) The teams shall change ends between the 2 overtime periods.

31.2 If the scores are still tied at the end of the 2 overtime periods, then the following 'sudden death' procedure will take place:

(i) The captains will toss a coin during a 1-minute intermission, with the winner selecting the goal which he wishes to defend.

(ii) Play will then resume with a face-off at the centre of the field, subject to the provisions of Rule 34.1 being followed, for 4-minute periods until a goal is scored.

(iii) At the end of each 4-minute period, the teams shall change ends, but the team in possession of the ball at the end of a period shall retain possession of the ball in the same relative position of the field as when the period ended, except that the ball shall not be put into play closer than 20yd (18.29m) from the cage, or with an opponent nearer to the player who has possession of the ball than 5yd (5.47m); play will then continue immediately.

If a sudden-death overtime period ends when the ball is loose, then the next period will start with a face-off in the same relative position as when play ended.

31.3 *Where the governing body responsible for the organisation of a particular competition does not wish overtime to be played in matches in that competition, then it shall inform the clubs involved in that competition and the relevant Referees Association(s) of its decision. Where the scores in a game in such a competition are tied at the end of regulation playing time, then that match shall be declared a draw.*

32. Defaulted Game

32.1 *If any team fails to fulfil an engagement without, in the opinion of the relevant League Committee, giving adequate cause or reason, then that Committee shall either disqualify the defaulting team for that match and award its opponents a win, or it shall disqualify the team for the remainder of the competition, or it shall take any other action which it deems appropriate. In the first case, where relevant, the Committee may also deduct 1 point from the defaulting team's total points and, in the second case, where relevant, no points scored for or against the disqualified team shall count in the aggregates.*

6. THE PLAY OF THE GAME

33. Actions Prior to the Game

33.1 The Referee(s) and the CBO shall call together the captains of each team at the centre of the field approximately 5 minutes before the start of the game. The head Referee shall toss a coin to determine choice of goals; the visiting captain shall call the toss. At this time, any special ground rules shall be explained.

33.2 The Referees and the CBO shall then draw up the *squads* in lines facing each other at the centre of the field, with their left sides towards the goal they are defending. There shall be pre-game stick-checks or equipment-checks. Any special ground rule shall be explained.

34. Facing at the Centre

34.1 Play shall normally be started at the beginning of each period, and after each goal has been scored, by facing the ball at the centre of the field, subject to the following exceptions:

(i) In the event of an extra man situation at the conclusion of *any* period, then the next period shall be commenced by awarding the ball to the team which had possession at the conclusion of the prior period in the same relative position on the field. However, if the period ends with no team in possession, the ball shall be faced at the centre with all the usual restrictions.

(ii) Once a Referee has placed the ball between the sticks at a face-off, then the players are 'set', and any movement of a player's stick or gloves prior to the whistle will result in possession being awarded to the offended team. The player is allowed to move his feet or his body, provided that this movement is not transmitted to the gloves or stick.

(iii) If a face-off is about to take place, and a team is guilty of delaying the game, then possession shall be awarded to the offended team. At the discretion of the Referees, repeated commission of this foul may be construed as unsportsmanlike conduct.

34.2 The players facing shall stand on the same side of the centre-line as the goal each is defending, with their crosses resting on the ground along the centre-line and parallel to it. Each player must have both hands on the handle of his own crosse, not touching any strings, and both gloved hands must be on the ground. The feet shall not touch the crosse. No part of either crosse may touch, and the walls must be approximately 1in (2.54cm) apart, with the backs of the crosses facing each other. Both hands and feet must be to the left of the throat of the crosse. The left foot and the handle of the crosse may not cross the centre-line. Neither player may be in contact with his opponent's body by encroaching on his opponent's territory.

34.3 The Referee shall make certain that the heads of the crosses match evenly, and he then shall place the ball between and in the centre of the two crosses, resting on the lower wall of both crosses. The ball must not be touching the ground.

34.4 When the Referee sounds his whistle to start play, each player may attempt to direct the course of the ball by movement of his crosse in any manner he desires. Kicking or stepping on an opponent's crosse is illegal. A player may not 'kick through' his own crosse in order to move the crosse of his opponent.

34.5 Whilst the two players who are participating in the face-off are still down in the face-off position, and the ball is still between and in contact with their sticks, it shall be illegal for any other player to make contact with the body or crosse of either of those two players.

34.6 No player who is using a left-handed crosse shall take part in a face-off. A stick in which the net is woven to the head in such a manner that a lip or hook is formed which might ensnare the ball shall be illegal for use in face-offs.

34.7 At the time of a centre face-off, a team which has 10 players on the field of play (excluding the penalty box) shall confine the goalkeeper and 3 other players in its defence goal-area, 3 players in its attack goal-area, and 1 player in each of its wing-areas. When the whistle sounds to start play, the players in the wing-areas shall be released. All other players are confined to the specified goal-areas until possession of the ball is gained by any player, the ball touches or crosses a goal-area line, or the ball goes out-of-bounds.

34.8 In the above circumstances, when possession is gained by a player, the Referee shall rotate his right arm in full circular cranking motion and shout 'possession'. When the ball touches or crosses a goal-area line before possession has been called, the Referee shall rotate his right arm in full circular cranking motion and shout 'free ball'.

34.9 Where a team has 1 or more players out of the game on penalty, then that team shall be exempt from confining its players to the goal- and wing-areas to the extent of its players in the penalty box. Such a team shall have the right to choose the confining area(s) in which it shall exercise its exemption, but it must obey the off-side rule.

34.10 At a centre face-off, before 'possession' or 'free ball' have been called, if a Referee mistakenly blows his whistle, then the ball shall be re-faced at the centre of the field with the same restrictions as the original face-off.

34.11 If a foul is committed at a centre face-off before 'possession' or 'free ball' have been called, then confined players will not be released from the goal-area until the whistle blows to resume play.

34.12 If the ball goes directly out-of-bounds from a face-off, then it shall be re-faced at the same place as the previous face, and subject to the same restrictions as the previous face.

35. Facing Other Than at the Centre

35.1 When a face-off occurs other than at the centre of the field, then the following rules shall apply:

    (i) The crosses of the 2 players shall be placed at right angles to an imaginary line running from the ball to the centre of the nearest goal-line.

 (ii) The defending player shall stand between his crosse and his own goal, so as to have his back to his own goal.

(iii) The attacking player shall face towards the goal he is attacking.

(iv) The conditions laid down in Rule 34 apply as to the method of facing.

 (v) The ball shall not be faced closer to the cage than 20yd (18.29m) in any direction, and it shall be moved laterally to a point 20yd (18.29m) from the cage, if required.

(vi) The ball shall not be faced closer to a boundary line than 20ft (6.1m).

(vii) At the time the whistle sounds to start the face-off, no player shall be within 10yd (9.14m) of the players facing the ball.

36. The Status of the Ball

36.1 A ball is either a live ball or a dead ball.

36.2 Once the whistle has blown to (re)start play, for example at a face-off, or when the ball is being put back into play after going out-of-bounds, or when the ball is being put back into play after a foul has been committed, then the ball is a live ball.

36.3 When the whistle blows to stop play, for example because a goal has been scored, or because the ball has gone out-of-bounds, or because a whistle has blown denoting a foul, then the ball is a dead ball.

36.4 If a flag is thrown, and play continues, then the ball is still a live ball.

37. Free Play

37.1 When a player has been awarded the ball for any reason, no opposing player may take a position closer to him than 5yd (4.57m).

37.2 A free play shall not take place closer to the cage than 20yd (18.29m) in any direction, and the ball shall be moved laterally to a point 20yd (18.29m) from the cage, if required.

37.3 A free play shall not take place within 5yd (4.57m) of the gate, and the ball shall be moved laterally into the field of play until it is 5yd (4.57m) from the nearest part of the gate, if required.

38. Scoring

38.1 A goal counts 1 point, and is scored when a loose ball passes from the front completely through the imaginary plane formed by the rear edges of the goal-line as a base, the cross-bar as the top, and the goal-posts as the two sides. Should the ball be caused to pass through the plane of the goal by one of the defending players, it counts as a goal for the attacking team.

38.2 When the ball passes through the plane of the goal in the following circumstances, however, a goal does not count:

(i) After a Referee's whistle has sounded to indicate the end of a period.

(ii) After the period has ended, regardless of whether or not a Referee's whistle has sounded.

(iii) After a Referee's whistle has sounded for any reason, even though the sounding of the whistle was inadvertent.

(iv) When any part of the body of an attacking player is touching the goal-crease area.

(v) When the attacking team has more than 10 men on the field of play (including the penalty box) at the time.

(vi) When the attacking team has more men than it should have on the actual field of play (excluding the penalty box) at the time.

(vii) When the attacking team or both teams are off-side at the time.

39. Possession of the Ball

39.1 A player shall be considered in possession of the ball when he has control of it and could perform any of the normal functions of play such as carrying, cradling, passing or shooting.

39.2 A team shall be considered in possession of the ball when a player on that team has possession of the ball or when the ball is in flight from a player to a team-mate.

39.3 A ball not in a player's possession or a team's possession is a loose ball.

40. Ball Out-of-Bounds

40.1 Play shall be suspended at any time when the ball is out-of-bounds.

40.2 When a player with the ball in his possession steps on or beyond a boundary line, or any part of his crosse or body touches the ground on or beyond the boundary line, then the ball is out-of-bounds, and the player shall lose possession of it. The ball shall be awarded to any player of the opposing team who is ready immediately to make the free play, at the point where the ball was declared out-of-bounds.

40.3 When a loose ball touches the boundary line or the ground outside of a boundary line, or when it touches anything on or outside of a boundary line, then it is out-of-bounds, and the following rules shall apply:

(i) Except on a shot or a deflected shot at the goal, the ball shall be awarded at the point where it was declared out-of-bounds to any player on the opposing team to that player who last touched it who is ready immediately to make the free play.

(ii) When a loose ball goes out-of-bounds as a result of a shot or a deflected shot at goal, it shall be awarded to the team one of whose in-bound players was nearest to the ball when it became out-of-bounds. If two in-bound players of opposite teams are equidistant from the ball when it goes out-of-bounds, then it shall be faced.

(iii) A shot or deflected shot remains a shot until: The ball comes to rest on the field of play; or

A player gains possession of the ball; or

The ball goes out-of-bounds; or

A player deliberately causes the ball to go out-of-bounds.

40.4 If the ball goes directly out-of-bounds from a face-off, then it shall be faced again at the same place as the previous face-off, and subject to the same restrictions as the previous face-off.

40.5 If the ball is out-of-bounds within the confines of the gate, or within 5yd (4.57m) of any part of the gate, then it shall be moved laterally into the field of play until it is 5yd (4.57m) from the nearest part of the gate before play is resumed.

40.6 If the ball is out-of-bounds on the end-line, then it shall be put into play at the point at which it went out-of-bounds, notwith-standing the fact that this point may be less than 20yd (18.28m) from the cage.

40.7 *An exception to this shall be an undersized pitch where the distance from the goal-line to the end-line is less than 15yd (13.72m).*

In such a case, two lines shall be drawn on each end line. These lines shall be 2ft (60cm) in length and shall extend away from the field of play at right angles to the end-line from points on the end-line 15yd (13.72m) from the centre of the goal-line.

An out-of-bounds ball shall not be put into play between these two points and, where necessary, the ball shall be moved to the nearer of the two points before being put into play.

41. Body checking: *The Take-out and Shoulder-charging*

41.1 Body-checking *and taking-out* an opponent *are* permitted in the game of lacrosse, provided:

(i) the opponent is in possession of the ball or is within 9ft (2.74m) of a loose ball *or is within 9ft (2.74m) of a ball in flight*;

(ii) the contact is made from the front or side, not below the hip, and below the neck.

A body-check is the placing of the body in the way of and facing an opponent so that the latter is impeded.

A take-out is the hitting of an opponent with the shoulder.

See also Rule 70 concerning illegal body-checking and illegal take-outs.

41.2 *A player may use a shoulder-to-shoulder charge against an opponent with whom he is engaged or is about to be engaged in a ground scuffle, providing that the opponent is within 9ft (2.74m) of a loose ball.*

42. Checking with the Crosse

A player may check an opponent's crosse with his own crosse, provided that the opponent has possession of the ball, the opponent is within 9ft (2.74m) of a loose ball, or the ball is in flight within 9ft (2.74m) of the opponent. For the purpose of the Rules except the Off-side Rules, the Centre Face-off Possession Rules, and the Crease Rules, the gloved hand holding the crosse is considered as part of the crosse. See Rules 71 and 72 concerning illegal checking.

43. The Pick

The use of the pick by an offensive player is permitted, provided that the offensive player is stationary and motionless at the time the contact is made. See Rule 54 concerning an illegal pick.

44. Time-outs

44.1 There are two types of time-outs, those called by the officials, and those called by the teams.

44.2 A Referee or the chief bench official may call an official time-out for any reason which he deems necessary for the proper enforcement of the Rules of the game.

44.3 When a player is injured and, in the opinion of an official, the injury is serious, then play shall be suspended immediately. Otherwise, the Referee shall delay the sounding of his whistle as follows:

(i) If the attacking team is in possession of the ball and, in the opinion of the Referee, a scoring play is imminent, then the Referee shall delay the sounding of his whistle in the same manner as laid down under the 'slow whistle procedure', Rule 82, except that a signal flag is not dropped under these circumstances.

(ii) If the ball is loose, then the Referee shall delay the sounding of his whistle until possession is secured and, if a scoring play is imminent, the play is completed, in the same manner as laid down under the 'slow whistle procedure', Rule 82, except that the signal flag is not thrown under these circumstances.

44.4 (*International Rule omitted*)

44.5 A team may request a time-out provided:

The ball is dead; or

The team requesting the time-out has possession of the ball in its attacking half of the field.

44.6 A time-out may be called by a coach, a captain, or the player who has possession of the ball. The request may be made to a Referee or to the chief bench official.

44.7 A team time-out shall be 90 seconds long.

A team time-out may be foreshortened only if both teams are ready to restart before the full 90 seconds have elapsed.

44.8 A team shall be limited to *one time-out* per half, and one time-out per 4-minute overtime period.

No time-outs shall be allowed in a sudden death overtime period.

44.9 A time-out taken between periods is charged to the preceding period.

44.10 A team may not take consecutive time-outs without resumption of play.

45. Head Coach's Request for a Stick-check

45.1 A team's head coach may request the inspection of any crosse of the opposing team.

All aspects of the construction and dimensions of the crosse shall be considered.

Such a request may only be made when the ball is dead.

45.2 The game-time clock shall be stopped when a stick-check is requested, and it shall be re-started when the stick-check is complete.

45.3 Where applicable, the penalty clock(s) shall be stopped when a stick-check is requested, and they shall be re-started when the stick-check is complete.

45.4 If a stick is found to be legal after a stick-check has been requested by a given head coach then:

(i) On the first occasion that a stick is found to be legal after a stick-check has been requested by that coach, there shall be no penalty inflicted on the coach who asked for the stick-check.

(ii) For every subsequent occasion on which a stick is found to be legal after that coach has requested a stick-check, a technical penalty shall be inflicted on the coach.

45.5 If a goal has been scored with a stick and, before the next live ball, that stick is declared illegal for any reason, then the goal will not count.

45.6 *Where a team does not have a coach, then the coach's rights specified in this rule shall be granted to the captain(s).*

7. SUBSTITUTION

46. Substitution

46.1 Maximum substitution may take place at any time, subject to the following paragraphs.

46.2 The substituting player must wait in the substitution area for the player whom he is replacing to leave the field of play, and only then may he enter the field of play. Both players must go through the gate. Players may substitute on the fly, and they may do so on either side of the centre-line, provided that the Off-side Rule is observed.

46.3 If the player leaving the field of play is bound to the half of the field which he is in by the Off-side Rule, then the provisions of the Off-side Rule will be deemed to have been observed if the substitute steps out of the substitution area on to the field of play at the same time as the player leaving the field steps into the substitution area.

46.4 The following exceptions shall apply:

(i) On the scoring of a goal, at the end of a period, and during a time-out of any kind, substitution may be effected from any point on the side-line, and not necessarily through the gate. In such cases, it will not be necessary for the substituting player to remain on the side-line until his counterpart leaves the field of play, but his team must have the correct number of players on the field when play is restarted.

(ii) If an official time-out has been called because an injured player is unable to continue, then that player shall be removed from the field as soon as possible to the nearest boundary, and the substitute must report immediately.

8. THE GOAL-CREASE AND THE GOALKEEPER

47. The Designated Goalkeeper

47.1 Where a player on a team begins the game using a goalkeeper's stick, then that player shall be deemed to be the designated goalkeeper.

47.2 Where the designated goalkeeper is replaced by another player using a goalkeeper's stick, then that substitute shall be deemed to be the designated goalkeeper.

47.3 If the designated goalkeeper leaves the field of play and is not replaced by another player using a goalkeeper's stick, then the following rules shall apply:

(i) If the designated goalkeeper exchanges crosses with a team-mate prior to leaving the field, then that player shall be deemed to be the designated goalkeeper until such time as the crosses are re-exchanged.

(ii) If there is no goalkeeper's crosse in use by a team at any time, then the captain or coach of that team must nominate a player to act as the designated goalkeeper.

48. Privileges of the Designated Goalkeeper

48.1 While in his own goal-crease, the designated goalkeeper shall have the following privileges and protections:

(i) He may stop or block the ball in any manner with his crosse or body, and he may block the ball or bat it away with his hand, but he may not catch the ball with his hand: nor may he pick the ball up with his hand. He or any member of the defending team may receive a pass while in the crease area.

(ii) No opposing player may initiate contact with the goalkeeper or his crosse while the goalkeeper is within the goal-crease area whether the goalkeeper has the ball in his possession or not. An attacking player may reach into the goal-crease area to play a loose ball, so long as he does not initiate contact with the goalkeeper.

(iii) An exception to Rule 48.1(ii) above, is that the crosse of the goalkeeper, when extended outside the cylinder above the goal-crease area, except when the ball is in the crosse, is subject to being checked under the same circumstances as the crosse of any other player.

49. Prohibitions Relating to the Goal-Crease

49.1 An attacking player shall not be in his opponents' goal-crease area nor shall he touch any part of the cage with his body, at any time while the ball is live in his opponents' half of the field.

49.2 A goalkeeper or defending player who is outside the goal-crease area and who has the ball in his possession may not enter the goal-crease area.

49.3 A player who is in his goal-crease area may not remain in the goal-crease area with the ball in his possession for longer than 4 seconds. This shall be audibly counted by the nearest Referee as 1001, 1002, 1003, 1004. If a player tries to circumvent the 4-second rule by deliberately dropping the ball and then picking it up, then he will be assessed a technical foul.

49.4 For the purpose of this section, a player is considered to be within the goal-crease area when any part of his body is touching the goal-crease area, and he is considered to be outside the goal-crease area when no part of his body is touching the goal-crease area, and part of his body is touching the ground outside the goal-crease area.

9. TECHNICAL FOULS

50. The Penalty for Technical Fouls

50.1 The penalty for a technical foul shall be as follows:

(i) If the offending team has possession of the ball, or if the ball is loose at the time a technical foul is committed, then possession shall be awarded to the opposing team at the point where the ball was when the foul occurred.

(ii) If the opponents of the offending team have possession of the ball at the time a technical foul is committed, then the penalty shall be suspension from the field of play for 30 seconds for the player committing the foul.

50.2 If a technical foul occurs prior to the start of the game, or after the scoring of a goal or the end of a period, then the offending player is suspended from the game for 30 seconds and the ball is faced, subject to the exception specified in Rule 34.1(ii). If the technical foul occurs at some other time during the course of the game, but while the play is suspended, then the general Rule rather than this exception shall apply.

51. The Nature of a Technical Foul

Technical fouls are those of a less serious kind. Any breach of the Rules of play as set forth in this section shall be a technical foul unless that breach is specifically listed as a personal or expulsion foul in Sections 10 or 11. Some of the technical fouls which require definition are listed below, but this section is not intended to be comprehensive and all-inclusive.

52. Interference

52.1 A player may not interfere in any manner with an opponent in an attempt to keep him from a loose ball except when both are within 9ft (2.74m) of such loose ball.

52.2 A player may not, by the use of his body or his crosse, interfere with a player who is in pursuit of an opponent who has possession of the ball.

52.3 A player may not guard an opponent so closely as to prevent the opponent's free movement when the opponent is not in possession of the ball.

52.4 Nothing in this rule is intended to prohibit a legal offensive pick.

53. Pushing

53.1 A player may not push an opponent with his crosse.

53.2 A player may not push an opponent unless the opponent has possession of the ball or the opponent is within three yards of a loose ball.

53.3 A player may not push an opponent from the rear.

Pushing from the rear is defined as exerting enough pressure to force an opponent to move in a direction other than that in which he intends to go or, if in the direction he intends to go, then at a greater speed than he intends.

54. Illegal Pick

54.1 No offensive player shall move into and make contact with a defensive player with the purpose of blocking that defensive player from the man he is marking. Before any contact is made by the defensive player, the offensive player must be stationary and motionless, and he must be standing in his normal stance.

54.2 No offensive player shall hold his crosse rigid or extend his crosse rigid to impede the normal movement of a defender.

55. Holding

55.1 A player shall not hold an opponent or an opponent's crosse except as hereinafter permitted:

(i) A player may hold off an opponent who is in possession of the ball or who is within 3yd (2.74m) of a loose ball with either closed gloved hand on the handle of his crosse, or with either forearm. Both hands of the player who is doing the holding must be on his crosse. The holding off must merely be the exerting of equal pressure.

(ii) A player in possession of the ball may protect his crosse with his hand, arm, or other part of his body when an opponent makes a play to check his crosse. The hand, arm, or other part of his body may only be used to stop the stick-check, and it must not be used to hold, push, or control the direction of the movement of the checker's crosse or body.

55.2 A player may not hold an opponent with his crosse.

If a player holds an opponent with that portion of the handle of his crosse which is between his hands, then a cross-check hold has been committed.

56. Kicking an Opponent's Crosse

A player may not deliberately step on or kick the crosse of an opponent.

57. Handling the Ball

A player shall not touch the ball with his hand(s) while it is in play, except the goalkeeper in his crease as defined in Rule 48.1(i).

58. Withholding the Ball from Play

58.1 A player shall not withhold the ball from play in any manner.

A player shall not lie on a loose ball on the ground.

A player shall not trap a loose ball on the ground with his stick longer than is necessary for him to control the ball and pick it up in one continuous motion.

58.2 A player with the ball in his possession shall not hold his crosse in close proximity to his body with the purpose of preventing an opponent from dislodging the ball.

58.3 A player with the ball in his possession may not grasp any portion of the head of the stick with his hand.

59. Illegal Actions with the Crosse

59.1 A player shall not throw his crosse under any circumstances.

59.2 A player shall not take part in the play of the game in any manner unless he is grasping his crosse with at least one hand. A broken crosse is considered no crosse.

59.3 During the play of the game, a player may not exchange his crosse for another except to replace a broken crosse, but players who are legally on the playing field may exchange crosses.

59.4 Should a player lose his crosse in any legal way so that repossession of his crosse would cause him to violate a rule, then the 'slow whistle technique' (Rule 82) shall be employed by the Referees, except that the signal flag is not thrown under these circumstances. Should the crosse be in the crease so as possibly to interfere with the goalkeeper's play of an attempted shot at goal, then play shall be suspended immediately.

60. Illegal Actions by Team Officials

60.1 A coach, trainer or other person officially connected with a team shall not:

(i) Enter the field of play without the permission of an official, except during a team time-out or between periods.

(ii) Use artificial aids to communicate with players on the field of play.

(iii) Leave the area on his bench's side of the field between the special substitution area line and the imaginary extension of the goal-area line.

60.2 This rule does not prohibit a coach from communicating, from his bench area, with a player who is on the field of play or in the penalty box.

61. Illegal Procedure

61.1 Any action by a player or a substitute of a technical nature which is not in conformity with the rules and regulations governing the play of the game shall be termed illegal procedure. The following paragraphs give examples of illegal procedure.

61.2 Leaving the penalty box before being authorised to do so by the penalty time-keeper is a foul. The offending player shall be returned to the penalty box to serve out his unexpired time plus 30 seconds. If the ball is loose or in the possession of his own team, then it shall be awarded to the opposing team. If a goal is scored by the player's opponents, then any unexpired time on a technical foul shall be nullified, but he must still serve the 30 seconds for illegal entry into the game. During an authorised time-out or between periods, a player may leave the penalty box, but he must return at the commencement of play to complete his suspension.

61.3 Delaying the game is a foul. An individual player is guilty of delaying the game if, during a stoppage in play, he bats, kicks or throws the ball away. In such a case, if a time penalty is to be served, then the individual concerned must serve it himself. At the discretion of the Referees, such conduct may be construed as unsportsmanlike conduct.

A team is guilty of delaying the game when:

 (i) It is not ready to start the game at the beginning of a period, or after a time-out.

 (ii) It is not ready to start the game 30 seconds after a goal has been scored.

(iii) It is not ready to start the game when the Referees are ready to restart the game after a stoppage has occurred because of a foul or an out-of-bounds ball.

(iv) It is not ready to restart the game when the Referees are ready to restart the game after equipment has been adjusted.

 (v) It is not ready to restart the game after an injured player has been attended to.

When a team is guilty of delaying the game, and a time penalty is to be served, then it shall be served by the in-home.

61.4 Participation in the play of the game by an out-of-bounds player is a technical foul.

61.5 A team which does not have the required number of men in each designated area at the time the whistle is blown to start a centre face-off has committed a technical foul. See Rules 34.7 and 34.9.

61.6 Failure to be at least 10yd (9.14m) from a face-off at the time the whistle is blown is a technical foul.

61.7 Failure to be at least 5yd (4.57m) from an opponent having a free play is a technical foul.

61.8 Any breach of the rules relating to substitution as laid down in Rule 46 is a technical foul.

61.9 Any breach of the rules relating to the goal-crease as laid down in Rule 49 is a technical foul.

61.10 Any breach of the rules relating to time-outs as laid down in Rule 44 is a technical foul.

61.11 It is a technical foul for a team to have more than 10 men (including men in the penalty box) in the game at any time, except after the scoring of a goal, at the end of a period, and during a time-out of any kind.

61.12 It is a technical foul for a team to have more men than it should have on the actual field of play (excluding the penalty box) at any time, except after the scoring of a goal, at the end of a period, and during a time-out of any kind.

61.13 *Where a coaches' area is marked out*, only coaches, up to a maximum number of four, are allowed in the coaches' area, and it is thus a technical offence for more than four coaches to be in the coaches' area, except on the scoring of a goal, at the end of a period, and during a time-out of any kind. It is a technical offence for a player or substitute (other than a player/coach as specified in Rule 22.4) to enter the coaches' area, except on the scoring of a goal, at the end of a period, and during a time-out of any kind.

62. Stalling

62.1 Any deliberate action on the part of a team in possession of the ball to maintain possession of the ball outside the attack goal-area by holding or passing the ball without reasonable effort to attack its opponents' goal is a technical foul known as 'stalling'.

62.2 A team playing with fewer players than its opponents due to penalties cannot be guilty of stalling.

62.3 A team which has possession of the ball in their attack goal area cannot be guilty of stalling.

62.4 Where a Referee feels that a team in possession of the ball outside the attack goal-area is not making a reasonable attempt to attack its opponents' goal, then he shall ask that team to 'get it in'; the team must then carry or pass the ball into the attack goal-area within a reasonable time. Once the ball is in the attack goal-area, then the team in possession shall keep it in the attack goal-area. If the ball subsequently leaves the stalling area (the attack goal-area) before the defending team has had possession of the ball, except as a result of a foul by the defending team or a deflection by the defending team or a shot, then the team which has been asked to 'get it in' shall lose possession to their opponents.

62.5 Where a Referee feels that a team in possession of the ball inside the attack goal-area is not making a reasonable attempt to attack its opponents' goal, then he shall ask that team to 'Keep it in'; the team must then keep it in the attack goal-area.

If the ball subsequently leaves the stalling area (the attack goal-area) before the defending team has had possession of the ball, except as a result of a foul by the defending team or a deflection by the defending team or a shot, then the team which has been asked to 'Keep it in' shall lose possession to their opponents.

62.6 This rule shall not prevent a team from employing a careful passing game for the purpose of manoeuvring the opposing team out of position.

63. Illegal Crosse

63.1 Should it come to the attention of a Referee that a player is using a crosse (other than trick construction or stringing) which is illegal under the provisions of Rules 15 or 16, then the Referee shall demand that the player adjust the crosse to conform to specification, or exchange it for another.

63.2 For a second violation against the same player, the Referee shall inflict a technical penalty and place the illegal crosse in the custody of the official scorer for the remainder of the game.

64. Illegal Equipment

64.1 Should it come to the attention of a Referee that a player is wearing equipment which is illegal under the provisions of Rules 17 or 18, then the Referee shall demand that the player conform to specification. Should the player fail to do so, then he shall be compelled to withdraw from the game until such time as he has complied with the regulations governing equipment, a substitute being allowed for him immediately.

64.2 For a second violation by the same player, the Referee shall inflict a technical penalty, and he shall be compelled to withdraw from the game until such time as he has complied with the regulations.

65. Off-side

65.1 Except as provided for in Rule 65.4, a team is off-side, provided that the ball is in play, when:

(i) It has fewer than 3 men in its attack half of the field between the centre-line and the end-line; or

(ii) It has fewer than 4 men in its defensive half of the field between the centre-line and the end-line.

65.2 Except in cases where a goal is scored when one or both teams are off-side, the following rules shall apply:

(i) When only one team is off-side, a technical penalty shall be inflicted in accordance with Rule 50.

(ii) Where both teams are off-side, and one of the teams has possession of the ball, the teams shall be placed on-side, and play resumed with the team which had possession of the ball retaining possession.

(iii) Where both teams are off-side, and neither team has possession of the ball, the teams shall be placed on-side, and the ball shall be faced at the place where it was when the whistle went.

65.3 The following rules shall apply when one or both teams are off-side at the time a goal is scored:

(i) When only the defending team is off-side, then the goal shall stand, and no penalty shall be inflicted.

(ii) When only the attacking team is off-side, the goal shall not stand, and the ball shall be awarded to any member of the defensive team 20yd (18.29m) laterally from the cage.

(iii) When both teams are off-side, the goal shall not stand, and the ball shall be faced 20yd (18.29m) laterally from the cage.

65.4 The following exceptions shall apply to the foregoing rules concerning off-side.

(i) When 4 or more men from one team are in the penalty box at the same time, then that team is required to have 3 men in its attack half of the field and the remainder of its players in its defensive half of the field at all times. Under these conditions, no penalty shall result from the failure of such a team to have 4 players in its defensive half.

(ii) If a player, seeing that he is going to go off-side before he can stop, runs out-of-bounds instead of off-side, then no penalty shall result from the failure of his team to have the required number of players in that half of the field.

65.5 Where the governing body responsible for the organisation of a particular competition wishes to vary the off-side rule in cases where a team is playing with fewer than ten men, for example in the lowest division(s) of a league, then it shall inform the clubs involved in that competition and the relevant Referees Association(s) of its decision, and the following rules shall apply:

(i) Where a team starts a game with only 9 men, then that team shall be required to keep at least 2 men in its attack half of the field at all times, and it shall be required to keep at least 3 men in its defensive half of the field at all times.

(ii) Where a team starts a game with only 8 men, then that team shall be required to keep at least 1 man in its attack half of the field at all times, and it shall be required to keep at least 2 men in its defensive half of the field at all times.

(iii) Where a team starts a game with 7 or fewer men, then there shall be no requirement for it to keep a minimum number of men in its attack half, but it shall be required to keep at least 1 man in its defensive half of the field at all times.

(iv) A team starting with 10 men will play to the 'normal' rules regardless of the number of players which its opponents are fielding.

(v) If a team starts a game with, for example, 8 players and a further player then takes the field, then that team shall play under the rules for 9 men, as above, after the player's entry to the game.

If yet another man takes the field, then that team shall revert to the 'normal' rules.

(vi) An injury after the start of a game does not affect the above.

66. Thrusting Crosse at Face of Opponent

A player shall not push, thrust or flick his crosse at the face of an opponent.

67. Avoidable Lateness

When a team fails to appear on the field ready to play at the appointed time for the start of a match, then that team has committed a technical foul. The penalty shall be served by the in-home.

10. PERSONAL FOULS

68. The Penalty for a Personal Foul

The penalty for a personal foul shall be suspension from the game for a period of 1 to 3 minutes, depending upon the Referees' diagnosis of the severity and intention of the foul. If the foul occurs prior to the start of the game, or after the scoring of a goal or the end of a period, then the ball shall be faced. Otherwise, the ball shall normally be given to the team which has been fouled.

69. The Nature of a Personal Foul

Personal fouls are those of a more serious kind. Any breach of the rules of play as set forth in this section shall be a personal foul.

70. Illegal Body-check *and Illegal Take-out*

70.1 *A body-check is the placing of the body in the way of and facing an opponent, so that the latter is simply impeded. A take-out is the hitting of an opponent with the shoulder.* A body-check *or a take-out* of an opponent who is not in possession of the ball or within 9ft (2.74m) of a loose ball *or within 9ft (2.74m) of a ball in flight* is illegal.

70.2 An avoidable body-check *or take-out* of an opponent after he has thrown the ball is illegal.

70.3 A *take-out* of an opponent in which initial contact is from the rear, below the hip, or at or above the neck is illegal, unless the player *taken-out* turns his back or jumps or moves in such a manner as to make what started as a legal *take-out* appear illegal.

70.4 When a player uses his spread arm or arms in a body-check *or a take-out*, then they must be kept below the shoulders of the opponent throughout the entire body-check *or take-out*, and both hands must remain in contact with the crosse.

70.5 Blocking an opponent with the head, known as spearing, is illegal.

70.6 *Taking-out* an opponent who is lying on the ground, or who is down on one or both knees, is illegal.

70.7 *Unnecessary roughness must not be used during a body-check or a take-out.*

71. Slashing

71.1 Under no circumstances shall a player swing his crosse at an opponent's crosse with deliberate viciousness or reckless abandon, and a foul is committed in such circumstances whether or not the opponent's crosse or body is struck.

71.2 A strike by the crosse on the helmet or neck of an opponent is illegal, except when done by a player in the act of passing or shooting.

71.3 A player shall not strike any part of the body of an opponent, other than the gloved hand holding the stick, in an attempt to dislodge the ball from his opponent's crosse, but a check shall not be declared illegal if, in an attempt to protect his crosse, the player in possession uses some part of his body, other than his head or neck, to ward off the thrust of the defensive player's crosse and, as a result, the defensive player's crosse strikes some part of the attacking player's body other than his head or neck.

71.4 For the purpose of this Rule, mere contact is not a strike. The contact must be a definite blow, and not merely a brush.

72. Cross-check

A player may not check an opponent with that part of the handle of his crosse which is between his hands, either by thrusting his crosse away from him or by holding it extended from his body.

73. Tripping

A player shall not intentionally trip an opponent with any part of his crosse or body.

74. Unnecessary Roughness

74.1 An excessively violent infraction of the rules against holding or pushing is a personal foul, designated unnecessary roughness.

74.2 A deliberate and excessively violent contact made by a defensive player against an offensive player who has legally established a screening position shall be designated unnecessary roughness.

74.3 Any avoidable act by a player which is deliberate and excessively violent shall be designated unnecessary roughness, whether it be with the body or the stick.

75. Unsportsmanlike *or Ungentlemanly Conduct*

75.1 No player, substitute, non-playing member of a squad, coach or anyone officially connected with a competing team shall:

(i) Enter into argument with an official as to any decision which he has made.

(ii) In any way attempt to influence the decision of an official.

(iii) Use threatening, profane or obscene language or gestures to an official or to any member of the opposing squad.

(iv) Commit any act considered unsportsmanlike *or ungentlemanly* by the Referees.

(v) Repeatedly commit the same technical foul.

75.2 Where an unsportsmanlike *or ungentlemanly* conduct penalty has been inflicted, and the penalised person continues to act in an unsportsmanlike *or ungentlemanly* manner, the Referees have the right to banish him from the bench area.

75.3 No player or substitute shall use a crosse with trick construction or stringing which is designed to hold the ball and to retard the normal and free dislodgement of the ball by an opponent. A player using such a stick shall be given a 3-minute penalty, and the stick shall be placed in the custody of the official scorer for the remainder of the game.

75.4 A team which repeatedly abuses Rule 34 by breaking from a restricted zone at a centre face-off shall be guilty of unsportsmanlike *or ungentlemanly* conduct.

75.5 A team which repeatedly abuses Rule 34.1 (iii) by delaying the game at a face-off may be guilty of unsportsmanlike or *ungentlemanly* conduct.

76. Player Committing 5 Personal Fouls

76.1 Any player committing 5 personal fouls shall be 'fouled out' of the game, and shall not be allowed to take any further part in it.

76.2 A substitute for such a player shall be allowed to enter the game at such a time as the fouled out player would have been permitted to re-enter the game had he not committed 5 personal fouls.

11. EXPULSION FOULS

77. The Penalty for an Expulsion Foul

77.1 The penalty for an expulsion foul shall be suspension for the remainder of the game.

77.2 In the case of an expulsion foul against a player or a substitute, a substitution may be made after a lapse of 3 minutes.

77.3 In the case of an expulsion foul against a coach, non-playing member of a squad, or someone officially connected with a team, the in-home of the offending team shall be suspended from the game for 3 minutes, and he must remain in the penalty box for the entire 3 minutes.

77.4 *Should a player, substitute, coach, non-playing member of a squad or someone officially connected with a team commit an expulsion foul, then he shall be referred to the relevant Disciplinary Committee immediately. After the game, the Referee concerned shall, immediately and in writing, fully report the facts to the Secretary of the Referees' Committee of the Regional Association in whose area the game was played, and the Secretary shall immediately refer the case to the Disciplinary Committee of that Regional Association for attention.*

78. The Nature of an Expulsion Foul

78.1 The act of deliberately striking or attempting to strike an opponent, a non-playing member of the opponents' squad, a coach or anyone controlling the play of the game with the hand, crosse, ball or otherwise by a player, a substitute, non-playing member of a squad, a coach or anyone officially connected with a team may be an expulsion foul.

78.2 Refusal to accept the authority of the officials, or the use of foul or abusive language, *or unsportsmanlike or ungentlemanly conduct* may be an expulsion foul.

12. EXECUTION OF PENALTIES

79. Player Committing Foul

79.1 A player who has been sent out of the game by a Referee shall raise his stick at full arm's length above his head from the time he is sent off until the time he reaches the penalty box, and he shall report immediately to the timer's table. He must remain in the penalty box, subject to the rules below, until released by the *CBO* or the penalty timekeeper.

79.2 In the case of a time penalty, the time refers to the time for which the player will be off the field and out of the game. The timing of a penalty will begin when the penalised player sits down on one of the seats in the penalty box, or when the whistle blows to restart play, whichever is the later. If there are no empty seats left in the relevant penalty box, then the penalised player should kneel on one knee beside the seats.

79.3 If a penalised player is going to re-enter the game himself when his penalty time has expired, then he may spend the last 5 seconds of his penalty time on one knee beside the gate on his own team's side of the centre-line. He must then re-enter the game through the gate.

79.4 If a substitute is to replace the penalised player when the penalty time has expired, then the penalised player should spend the whole of the penalty time on the seat. The substitute may then spend the last 5 seconds of the penalty time on one knee beside the gate on his own team's side of the centre-line, prior to entering the field through the gate. The penalised player should then return to the players' bench.

79.5 Penalty time will only be served during normal playing time. Stoppages in play for all time-outs will also temporarily interrupt penalty time. During an authorised time-out, or between periods, a penalised player may leave the penalty box, but he must return at the commencement of play to complete his suspension.

79.6 Penalty time will end when the time of the penalty has expired, except that the scoring of a goal against a team having one or more players serving penalty time for technical fouls shall release the player or players from serving the balance of their penalty time. This shall not apply in the case of personal fouls, where the designated penalty time shall be served regardless of whether or not a goal is scored.

79.7 *Should a goalkeeper commit a technical or personal foul of a non-violent and non-abusive nature, then the nominated defender will serve the penalty time incurred, in order to prevent a possible injury to an inadequately protected deputy. In such circumstances, a personal foul will be recorded against the goalkeeper (and not against the defender) for the purpose of 'fouling out' after five personal fouls.*

Should the goalkeeper commit a foul of a violent or abusive nature, then he must serve the penalty time himself.

Should the goalkeeper commit an expulsion foul, or should he commit a fifth personal foul, then he must leave the game immediately.

79.8 *If the goalkeeper has to leave the field because of injury, or because he has committed a violent or abusive foul, or because he has been 'fouled out' after 5 personal fouls, or because he has committed an expulsion foul, then the Referees shall call an official time-out so that a deputy can don the goalkeeper's protective equipment. If the goalkeeper subsequently returns to the game then, at the next dead ball, the Referees shall call an official time-out so that the original goalkeeper can replace the deputy, and don his protective equipment.*

80. Restarting Play After a Penalty

80.1 When a penalty occurs in the offended team's defensive half of the field and penalty time is to be served, the ball shall be awarded to any player of the offended team on the offensive side of the centre-line.

80.2 In all other cases, the ball shall be awarded to any player of the offended team at the point where the ball was when play was suspended, the exceptions being as follows:

(i) Where the ball is within 20yd (18.29m) of the cage. In this case the ball shall be moved to a position laterally across the field 20yd (18.29m) from the cage and awarded to any player of the offended team.

(ii) In the event of the goalkeeper or a defending player offending against the crease rules, the ball shall be awarded to any player of the attacking team 20yd (18.29m) laterally from the cage.

(iii) In the event of a crease offence by an attacking player which does not involve a time penalty, the ball shall be awarded to a member of the defending team 20yd (18.29m) laterally from the cage.

80.3 If a goal is scored during a slow whistle play for a technical foul, then no penalty is given. If a goal is not scored during a slow whistle play, then a time penalty is given, and the ball is awarded to the attacking team at the place where it was when play was suspended, subject to Rule 80.2(i) being followed.

81. Simultaneous Fouls

81.1 When a member of a team commits a foul, and then a member of the opposing team commits a foul, then the fouls shall be considered simultaneous fouls, provided that the fouls are not separated by a whistle which has restarted play, or by the scoring of a goal.

81.2 When simultaneous fouls have been committed, the following rules shall apply:

(i) All fouls being technical, the fouls cancel, and the team in possession retains possession where the ball was when the whistle sounded. If no team is in possession, the ball is faced where it was when the whistle sounded.

(ii) If at least one of the fouls is a personal foul, then penalty time shall be served for all the fouls, and the following rules shall apply:

If one team incurs more total penalty time than the other, then the team with the lesser total penalty time shall be awarded the ball.

If the total penalty times are equal, then the team in possession of the ball shall retain possession of it.

If the total penalty times are equal, and neither team has possession of the ball, then the ball shall be faced where it was when the whistle blew.

(iii) For the purpose of totalling penalty time in the case of simultaneous fouls, an expulsion foul shall count as a 3-minute penalty.

(iv) There shall be no free clear after simultaneous fouls.

82. Slow Whistle Technique

82.1 If a defending player commits a foul, and the attacking team has possession of the ball at the time that the foul occurs, and, in the opinion of the Referees, a scoring play is imminent, and the act of fouling does not cause the attacking player who is in possession to lose the ball, then the Referee must drop a signal flag and withhold his whistle until such time as the scoring play has been completed.

82.2 The scoring play shall be considered to have been completed when:

(i) The attacking team has lost control of the ball.

(ii) The attacking team has clearly lost the opportunity of scoring a goal on the original play.

(iii) The attacking team has taken a shot.

(iv) In the case of the flag being dropped when the ball is in front of the defending team's goal, the attacking team, having caused the ball to go behind the goal, and having then brought it to the front of the goal, cause it to go behind their opponents' goal again.

(v) In the case of the flag being dropped when the ball is behind the defending team's goal, the attacking team, having brought the ball to the front of the goal, cause it to go behind the goal again.

82.3 The slow whistle technique shall be employed whether or not the foul is committed against the man in possession of the ball.

82.4 A pass is a movement of the ball caused by a player in control throwing or bouncing the ball to a team-mate.

82.5 During a slow whistle situation, a shot remains a shot until:

(i) It is clearly obvious that a goal will not be scored.

(ii) Added impetus is given to the ball by any member of the attacking team.

(iii) Possession is gained by a member of the defending team.

(iv) After hitting the goalkeeper and/or the pipe(s), the ball touches any player of either team other than the defending goalkeeper; at such time the ball shall be declared dead immediately.

82.6 Where a flag is thrown mistakenly then, when the whistle subsequently blows to stop the play, the ball shall be awarded to the team which has possession. If neither team has possession, then the ball shall be faced.

82.7 Where the CBO throws a signal flag to indicate that a foul has been committed in circumstances where a slow whistle could be employed, then the Referees must either throw a flag or blow the whistle depending on the circumstances.

83. Technical Foul

83.1 Where a player commits a loose-ball technical foul, and the offended team may be disadvantaged by the immediate suspension of play, then the Referee shall visually and verbally signal 'Play-on', and he shall withold his whistle until such time as the situation involving the potential advantage has been completed, as follows:

(i) If the offended team gains possession of the ball, then the play-on situation has lapsed, and the official will cease to signal.

(ii) If the offending team gains possession of the ball, then the whistle sounds, and the offended team is awarded the ball.

(iii) If the offended team commits a foul, then the whistle blows, and the usual simultaneous fouls rules apply.

13. SPECIAL SITUATIONS

84. Special Situations

84.1 Where an official is called upon to inflict a penalty against a team where no definite player is involved, or where the penalty is against someone other than a player in the game, then he shall inflict the suspension upon the in-home. If multiple fouls of this type occur, then the penalties shall be inflicted against additional attack players.

84.2 Where the person committing the foul is a substitute, then the foul shall be assessed against him so far as the record is concerned, and he may only re-enter the game subject to the same restrictions as though he were a player at the time the foul was committed.

84.3 If the ball becomes caught in a player's crosse, then a Referee shall audibly count 1001, 1002, 1003, 1004. If, at the end of those 4 seconds, the ball has not been dislodged, then play shall be stopped and the ball shall be faced.

84.4 If the ball becomes caught in a player's uniform or equipment, other than his crosse, then play shall be suspended immediately, and the ball shall be faced.

84.5 Rules 84.3 and 84.4 shall not apply to the designated goalkeeper when he is within his goal-crease. If, in such circumstances, the ball becomes caught in the stick, clothing or equipment of the designated goalkeeper, then the defensive team shall be awarded the ball 20yd (18.29m) laterally from the cage.

84.6 Should the ball become mired in the mud within the crease-area or *outside the crease*, time shall be suspended by the Referees and the ball shall be faced.

84.7 Should the ball become ensnared in the goal netting, time shall be suspended by the Referees and the ball shall be awarded to the defensive team 20yd (18.29m) laterally from the cage.

Reprinted by permission of the English Lacrosse Union. For reasons of space, the Additional Rulings (which have the same authority as the Rules) have been omitted. Copies of the complete Rules and additional Rules of Men's Lacrosse can be obtained from the Union.

Women's Lacrosse

Women's Lacrosse

1. FIELD MARKINGS (see diagram on page 684)

A. The playing area has no measured boundaries. The agreed boundaries shall be approximately 4m inside any natural or artificial objects, i.e. trees, bushes, athletic track, stands and so on. An area of 100m × 60m is desirable. An optional broken side-line and/or endline may be used to act as a visual guideline to indicate the playing boundaries.

B. A line called the goal-line shall be marked at each end of the field. These lines shall be no more than 92m and no less than 82m apart. They shall be 1.83m in length and shall be marked parallel to the width of the field.

There must be at least 9m playing space behind each goal-line running the width of the field.

C. Around each goal-line a circle, called the goal-circle, shall be marked. It shall have a radius of 2.6m, measured from the centre of the goal-line to the outer edge of the goal-circle.

D. Directions for 11m Area/Marking Area. (see diagram on page 684)

(1) Using D as centre, draw a circle of 2.6m radius. Mark A B B D.

(2) Using D as centre, draw (lightly) a semicircle of 11m radius. Mark G (as shown).

(3) Connect A to B and extend to semicircle. Mark C on each side (as shown).

(4) Make a hash mark (31cm) at G. Make 3 hash marks on semicircle every 4m on each side of G (as shown – total of 7 hash marks).

(5) Make another mark where semicircle intersects each side of the goal-line extended.

(6) Mark curve of the arc with a solid line from C to C. Mark each side of the arc with a solid line from B to C.

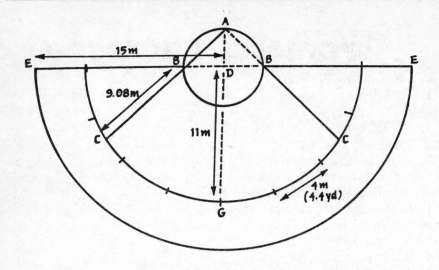

11m Area

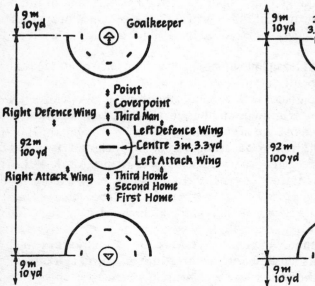

The Teams

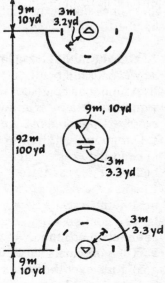

The Playing Area

(7) Measurements:

A – G = 13.6m
A – C = 12.7m
A – B = 3.7m
B – C = 9.9m
D – G = 11.0m
D – C = 11.0m

E. 15m Fan

Using D as centre, inscribe a semi-circle of 15m radius with a solid line from E to E (as shown). This semi-circle, called the 15m fan, designates the maximum distance for free space to goal.

F. In the centre of the field, a centre circle shall be marked with a 9m radius. In the centre of this circle, a 3m line, called the centre line, shall be marked parallel to the goal-lines.

G. All lines used in the marking of the field are 5cm wide.

H. The playing area must be flat and free of stones, glass and protruding objects. The boundaries must be determined by the captains and the umpires before the match.

I. No unauthorised marks may be added to the field and any unauthorised markings must be removed.

J. The coach and team personnel must remain outside the agreed boundary of the field. Neither a coach nor team personnel may stand by or pass in front of the opponents' bench.

2. GOALS AND GOAL-POSTS

A. A goal shall be placed in each goal-circle.

B. A goal shall consist of two perpendicular posts or pipes constructed of wood or metal, 1.83m high and 1.83m apart, joined at the top by a crossbar 1.83m from the ground (inside measurements). If a free standing goal is used, ground supports and/or side supports must be padded the entire length with material that limits the rebound of the ball.

C. The goal-posts/pipes must not extend upward beyond the crossbar, nor should the crossbar extend beyond the goal-posts.

D. The goal-posts and crossbar shall be 5cm square or 5cm in diameter and must be painted white.

E. The goal-line shall lie between the goal-posts, with the front of the goal-posts even with the front of the goal-line.

F. The mesh of the goal net must not be larger than 4cm. The goal net must be securely attached to the posts and crossbar and to a point on the ground 1.83cm behind the centre of the goal-line.

3. THE CROSSE

A. The crosse shall be constructed of wood, plastic, fibre glass, nylon, leather, rubber and/or gut. Only the handle may be constructed of aluminium or graphite. Recessed metal screws may be used to attach the head to the handle.

B. The head of the crosse shall be triangular. The head and handle, when joined, shall lie along the same plane.

C. The crosse shall not have sharp or protruding parts or be dangerous in any way.

D. Field player's crosse:

(1) The length of the crosse shall be 0.9m (minimum) to 1.1m (maximum). Small players may use a crosse shorter than 0.9m to allow the crosse to fit comfortably along the full length of the player's arm.

(2) The pocket of the crosse shall be strung with 4 or 5 vertical thongs and 8 to 12 stitches of cross lacing. Mesh pockets are not allowed.

(3) The width of the crosse head shall be 18cm (minimum) to 23cm (maximum). When measured 2.5 cm above the bridge or stop, the head shall have an inside measurement of 6.7 to 7.6 cm and an outside measurement of 7.6 to 10.1 cm. (The width is measured on a line perpendicular to the extension of the handle.)

(4) The length of the head, as measured from the centre of the stop or bridge to the top of the head, shall be 25.4cm (minimum) to 30.5cm (maximum).

(5) The walls of the head, measured at the highest point, shall be 3.2cm (minimum) to 4.5cm (maximum). The guard shall be 3.2cm (minimum) to 7.0cm (maximum).

(6) The depth of the wall and the pocket, with the ball, shall not exceed 6.3cm (the diameter of the ball). The top of the ball, when dropped into the pocket of the crosse held horizontally, must remain even with or above the top of the walls.

(7) The ball must move freely within all parts of the pocket. The ball must not become wedged between the walls, guard or bridge of a wooden crosse or in the stop of a moulded crosse.

E. Goalkeeper's Crosse

(1) The length of the crosse shall be 0.9m (minimum) to 1.22m (maximum).

(2) The pocket of the crosse may be mesh or may be strung with 4 or 5 vertical thongs and 8 to 12 stitches of cross lacing.

(3) The crosse head shall have a maximum inside measurement of 30cm and a maximum outside measurement of 32.5cm (The width is measured on a line perpedicular to the extension of the handle.)

(4) The head shall have a maximum length of 40cm.

(5) The walls of the head, measured at the highest point, shall be 7cm (maximum).

(6) The depth of the pocket with the ball shall be unlimited. The ball must be able to move freely within all parts of the pocket.

(7) The crosse shall not weigh more than 773g.

4. THE BALL

A. The ball shall be rubber, of any solid colour, with a circumference of 20cm (minimum) to 20.3cm (maximum).

B. The ball shall weigh not less than 142g or more than 149g. It must bounce between 1.1m and 1.3m when dropped from 1.8m onto concrete at a temperature between 18°C and 23°C.

5. TEAMS

A game is played between two teams. No more than 12 players per team are permitted on the field at the same time. Each team is allowed one goalkeeper on the field (see diagram 684).

6. PLAYERS' DRESS AND EQUIPMENT

A. All team members shall be dressed uniformly, with the exception of the goalkeeper whose shirt must be the same colour as her team's shirts; the bottom of her uniform must match the predominant colour of her team's uniform bottoms. All visible garments worn on the field of play are considered to be team uniform. The goalkeeper may wear her team shirt inside or outside her protective equipment. Her number must be visible.

B. Each player's uniform shirt shall be numbered, identically, on the front and back. Each team member shall have a different number. Numbers on the front of the shirt must be at least 10cm tall; numbers on the centre back of the shirt must be 20cm tall. If a team wears striped shirts, the numbers must be superimposed on a solid block background.

C. All visible garments worn under the kilt/shorts must be of the same predominant colour as the kilt/shorts. All visible garments worn under the top must be the same predominant colour as the top. All players wearing visible undergarments must be dressed in the same colour. This does not apply to medical sleeves.

D. Players must wear composition or rubber-soled boots/shoes. Plastic, leather or rubber cleats/studs may be worn. Spikes are not permitted.

E. All field players must wear mouthguards, Close-fitting gloves, nose guards, and eye guards may be worn. Field players are not permitted to wear headgear or face masks. Additional protective devices necessitated on genuine medical grounds may be worn, providing both the captains and the umpires agree that such equipment is not dangerous to other players.

All protective devices must be close-fitting and padded where necessary. They must not be of excessive weight.

F. The goalkeeper must wear a helmet with face mask, a chest or body pad, and a throat protector. She may also wear padded gloves, arm pads and leg pads. All padding must fit firmly and must not increase the width of the body beyond the thickness of the padding. The maximum thickness is 3cm. Padded gloves must be tied firmly at the cuff and have no webbing.

G. Players must not wear earrings, necklaces, bracelets and watches on the field of play. Medical jewellery with visible information, soft jewellery and rings must be taped securely to the players or be removed. Barrettes/hair slides are legal if they are not dangerous to other players.

H. No equipment, including protective devices, may be used unless it complies with the rules and is deemed safe by the umpire.

7. CAPTAINS

Each team must have a captain on the field who shall wear a distinctive arm band and:

A. toss for choice of ends to defend with the 'charge umpire'.

B. agree with the umpires on playing time and playing boundaries.

C. agree with the umpires on protective equipment, warranted by medical necessity, to be used during the game.

D. indicate a substitute for an injured player.

E. designate an acting captain if she leaves the field. Co-captains are not allowed.

F. confer with the umpires if weather conditions or any other extenuating circumstances make the continuation of the game questionable. The umpire's decision is final.

G. be permitted to request a crosse check. The captain on the field is the only player who may ask an umpire to check an opponent's crosse.

H. approach the umpire at halftime and immediately following the game for a rule(s) clarification. A coach may also request a rule(s) clarification from the umpires at halftime or after the game.

8. THE UMPIRE

The umpire shall control the game and administer the rules. The umpire should set a tone for the game by having a pleasant, professional demeanour. The umpire is solely responsible for judging fair and unfair play and shall:

A. The umpire should arrive at the field at least 30 minutes prior to the start of the game to allow enough time to inspect the grounds, goals, balls, crosses, clothing, boots/shoes, jewellery and protective equipment to be used to ensure they comply with the rules.

To check team crosses, the umpire should have players form a line. All crosses, whether to be used in the game or not, are checked at this time.

The umpire drops the ball into the horizontally held crosse. The top of the ball must remain even with or above the top of the wooden or plastic wall after pressure has been applied. The ball must move freely within the pocket. The umpire should look for splinters or rough edges on any part of the crosse.

If the crosse is illegal, the player is removed from the line. All players with illegal crosses and/or equipment should remain together, and adjust their equipment for re-inspection by the umpire.

If a crosse cannot be made legal, it must remain with the scorer throughout the game.

B. agree with the captains on protective equipment, warranted by medical necessity, to be used during the game.

C. ensure that the timer and scorer understand their responsibilities.

D. determine which umpire will be in charge of the game. The charge umpires will conduct the toss for choice of ends with the captains.

E. agree with the captains on the playing time and field boundaries.

F. umpire the game in accordance with IFWLA rules. The umpire has the responsibility to understand thoroughly the rules and to penalise any play that leads to or causes bodily injury, specifically dangerous shots, passes and checks to any part of the body. The IFWLA wants to keep excessive protective equipment off field players and this, to a great extent, will be ensured by the umpire diligently penalizing unsafe play.

G. umpire in the same field position both halves of the game if two umpires are working.

Three umpires may rotate their field positions clockwise after each goal.

H. report goals, warnings and suspensions to the scorer.

I. confer with the captains if weather conditions or any other extenuating circumstances make the continuation of the game questionable. The umpire's decision is final.

J. be available for rules clarifications from captains or coaches during halftime and immediately following the game.

K. make the game official by signing the score sheet.

L. wear a black and white vertical stripe (2.5cm) shirt/jacket. All other garments and accessories must be black

The umpire's decision is always final and without appeal.

9. SCORERS AND TIMERS

A. The scorer shall:

(1) record the lineups of both teams prior to the game.

(2) keep an accurate record of the goals scored. A goal scored by the defending team shall be recorded as an 'own goal' (o.g.).

(3) record all warnings and suspensions.

(4) record the numbers of all substitutes entering the game at a

stoppage of play. The scorer shall not allow a team to substitute beyond what is permitted in the rules.

B. The timer shall:

(1) confirm with the umpires, prior to the game, the length of the halves.

(2) start the clock at each draw on the umpire's whistle and arm signal.

(3) stop the clock on the umpire's whistle and arm signal after each goal. The clock is stopped on the umpire's signal:

– for substitution.

– after a goal is scored.

– for the removal of illegal substitutes.

– for warnings and suspensions.

– for injury or any other circumstances deemed necessary by the umpire.

The clock is stopped on every whistle during the last 2 minutes of each half and during overtime (if played).

(4) during the last two minutes of each half, stop the clock on every whistle. The clock is then restarted on the umpire's whistle and arm signal.

(5) notify the nearest umpire when there are 2 minutes remaining in each half.

(6) Notify the nearest umpire when there are 30 seconds remaining in each half.

(7) Verbally count to the nearest umpire the last 10 seconds of each half, sounding the horn when time is up.

(8) Notify the umpires when 5 and 10 minutes have elapsed between the halves.

(9) During an injury time-out, time the 2 minutes (5 minutes for goalkeepers) recovery time allowed to incapacitated players.

(10) Time the 3 minutes of lapsed playing time a substitute must wait before entering the game for a suspended player.

When play is stopped following the end of a suspension, the substitute may take one step on to the field of play, level with the centre-line. If a team has had 4 dead-ball substitutions, a replacement must wait for a goal to be scored before entering the game. In the event of a goalkeeper being suspended, a 2 minute time-out will be allowed to enable a player on the field to put on protective equipment. When she returns to the field of play, she must stand 4m behind the attack taking the 'free position'.

10. DURATION OF PLAY

A. The duration of the game shall be a maximum of two periods of 25 minutes each. (The length of the halves may be reduced in non-IFWLA sanctioned competition. The umpires and captains shall agree on the length of the halves.)

B. After halftime, which may not exceed 10 minutes, the teams shall change ends.

C. The game starts when the umpire simultaneously blows her whistle and drops her arm during the opening draw.

The whistle starts and stops play. To restart play, the umpire shall raise her arm above her head, then drop it to her side while blowing her whistle. The umpire should make certain the arm signal and whistle occur at the same time. In some instances the game will resume with a throw, whereby play restarts when the umpire tosses the ball forward while blowing her whistle.

The game restarts after goals and halftime with a draw.

D. All players must stand when the umpire blows her whistle to stop play. Players must not move until the game is restarted, unless directed by the umpire. The only exception shall be the goalkeeper (or a field player) within the goal-circle. When the game is restarted, the player with the ball may run, pass or shoot.

E. The clock is stopped on the umpire's whistle and arm signal after each goal and on every whistle to stop play during the last 2 minutes of each half. Additionally, the clock is stopped for warnings, suspensions, substitutions and the removal of illegal substitutes. This rule may be amended for non-IFWLA events by mutual agreement by the captains.

F. Play shall be continuous, but at the discretion of the umpire, time-out may be taken for unusual circumstances. Unusual circumstances may include injuries and/or accidents, inspecting a crosse, an animal on the field, a lost ball, a ball that has gone too far out-of-bounds and spectator interference.

G. If weather conditions or any other extenuating circumstances make play dangerous, the umpires may suspend the game after consultation with the captains. Umpires should be cautious when deciding to continue a game when weather conditions become a factor. Safety must be the primary concern. Secondary considerations include each team's travel time and expense. The umpire's decision is final.

H. A game is considered legal and complete if 80 per cent of the playing time has elapsed. If an interrupted game (one in which less than 80 per cent of the playing time has elapsed) is replayed, it must be replayed from the beginning.

11. SUBSTITUTION
Substitution of players is permitted only when play is stopped.

Time-out is taken for substitution.

A. Each team may substitute an unlimited number of players after every goal and at halftime. Only 4 players (per team) per half may be substituted during any other stoppage of play, with no more than 2 players per team entering the game at one time.

Before entering the game at a stoppage of play, the substitute must report to the scorer and indicate her number and the number of the player she is replacing.

The scorer must accurately record all substitutions to ensure that a team substitutes only 2 players per stoppage of play other than after goals or at halftime, with a maximum of 4 such substitutes allowed in each half. The scorer shall not allow additional substitutions beyond those stipulated in the rules.

B. Substitution may be made for a suspended player, but a suspended player can never re-enter the game unless she has been removed for a team offence. The substitute for a suspended player cannot enter the game until the first stoppage of play after 3 minutes of playing time has elapsed following the suspension. This player will be placed one step onto the field of play, level with the centre-line.

The timer shall time the 3 minutes of elapsed playing time.

If an injury or suspension occurs after a team has used its 4 allowed substitutions each half during stoppages other than goals and halftime, the team must, for the remainder of the half, play short unless a goal is scored.

C. If a field player is incapacitated for longer than 2 minutes, the game is restarted without her. Incapacitated goalkeepers are allowed 5 minutes recovery time. If no substitute has taken the incapacitated player's place, she may return with the umpire's permission while the game is in progress.

The timer shall time the 2 minute (5 minutes for goalkeepers) recovery time.

Players may drop their crosses and go to the side-line for water; however, there may be no coaching during an injury time-out.

No player is allowed on the field with an open wound or blood saturated clothing.

Substitution procedures:

After the substitute(s) has reported to the scorer, the timer will sound a horn at the next stoppage of play. Upon hearing this horn, the umpire will signal 'time-out' and beckon the substitute(s) onto the field. (No horn is needed for substitutions occurring at halftime.) Following a goal, a substitute(s) does not need to report, but must go onto the field when the horn is sounded. During substitution, a team may have more than 12 players momentarily on the field at the same time. (A substitute may enter the field before the player she is replacing has left the field.) This is only a violation if the player(s) leaving the game delays leaving the field.

All players who reported to the scorer prior to the sounding of the horn must enter the game at this time. The substitutes must enter the field without delay from the designated substitution area by the scoring/timing table.

Substitutes who report to the scorer after the sounding of the horn must wait until the next stoppage of play before entering the field.

The substitute must assume the same location as the person she is replacing, unless the substitution occurs after a goal or at halftime. The umpire must ensure that proper field positions are taken by the substituting players.

Any substitute(s) entering the game after a goal has been scored does not count as one of the 4 substitutes permitted in that half.

12. TO START OR RESTART THE GAME

To start the game and restart the game after halftime and after each goal scored, a draw is taken at the centre-line.

The centre-umpire administers the first and all subsequent draws and is responsible for fouls committed by the players taking the draw. The umpire should notify the other umpires when she cautions a player for an illegal draw.

The other umpires are responsible for fouls committed during the draw by all other players. The umpires should watch for players on the centre-circle using their bodies and/or crosses to hold/detain the opponent(s).

A. To draw, two opponents stand with one foot toeing the centre-line. Their crosses are held in the air above hip level, wood/plastic to wood/plastic, parallel to and above the centre-line. The crosses must be back to back, right wall facing downward, with each player's crosse between the ball and the goal she is defending. To determine the right wall, a player holds the crosse vertically, with the open pocket facing her.

B. The ball is placed between the crosses by the umpire. Once the crosses are set, the umpire will say 'Ready'. The players taking the draw may not move until the umpire blows the whistle. At that time, the players must immediately draw their crosses up and away.

When placing the ball between the backs of the crosses, the umpire should hold both crosses upright, with the wood or plastic together at the bottom. The ball is then placed between the crosses.

Once set, the two players taking the draw must not move until the umpire blows the whistle.

The umpire should vary the time interval between the command 'Ready' and blowing the whistle while backing out of the centre-circle to prevent the players anticipating the signal to play. The umpire should also plan the most expedient exit from the centre-circle by noting the positioning of the players on the circle.

C. The ball must go higher than the heads of the players taking the draw.
D. After one caution per game for an illegal draw by a specific player, the opponent is awarded a 'free position'. If both players draw illegally, having each previously received a caution, a throw is awarded. The umpire must remember the number of the player who is cautioned for an illegal draw. A substitute centre should not be penalised for her team-mate's violation.

During the free position, the offending centre is placed 4m in front of her opponent at a 45 degree angle from the centre-line.
E. All other players' feet must be outside the centre-circle until after the whistle.

This rule does not prohibit a player from hanging her crosse into the centre-circle. Entering the circle too soon during the draw should be called only when the player or her team gains an advantage because of her violation.

After two unsuccessful centre draws, a throw will be taken.
F. Following an accident, interference or any unusual circumstances see Rule 15.

13. SCORING
A. The team scoring the greater number of goals wins.
B. A goal is scored when the whole ball passes completely over the goal-line, between the goal-posts and under the crossbar from the front, having been propelled by the crosse of an attacking field player or the crosse or body of a defender.
C. A goal is not scored when:
    (1) the ball is put through the goal by a non-player.
    (2) the ball comes off the person of an attacking player.
    (3) the ball enters the goal after the whistle is blown or the horn is sounded.
    (4) the offensive shooter follows through over the goal-circle with any part of her person or her crosse, or any other attacking player enters the goal-circle. The umpire should watch the shooter's follow-through and body movement and whether the ball goes into the goal. If the ball enters the goal legally, the umpire should wait a little longer to watch for any goal-circle violations. The umpire should watch for the defence illegally causing the attack to enter the goal-circle.
    (5) the goalkeeper, while within the goal-circle, is interfered with in any way by an attacking player.
    (6) the umpire rules the shot or follow-through dangerous.
    (7) the ball enters the goal while the attacking team has an illegal player(s) on the field.
    (8) the ball enters the goal from an attacker's illegal crosse.

(9) the player who shot the goal adjusts her crosse after an umpire's request for a cross inspection.

14. BALL OUTSIDE FIELD OF PLAY
When the ball crosses the boundary, it is deemed outside the field of play, and the umpire must blow the whistle.

The umpire should blow the whistle as soon as the ball reaches the agreed boundary. However, to avoid potential injury to the players, the umpire should consider stopping play before the ball reaches the boundary.

A. If the ball is deliberately directed, carried or propelled out-of-bounds it is a minor foul.

The umpire must decide whether the player with the ball had other options which would keep the ball inbounds. A goalkeeper clearing to the side of the field should not be penalised for intentionally putting the ball out-of-bounds if she has a team-mate in the area potentially able to receive the ball.

B. If the ball is accidentally carried or propelled out-of-bounds, the player nearest the ball places the ball in her crosse and stands 4m inside the boundary from the spot where the ball went out of play. Play resumes on the umpire's whistle and arm signal.

Before blowing the whistle, the umpire should make every effort to determine which player is nearer the ball. 'Nearer' indicates any part of the player's body being closer to the ball. The umpire should know to whom the ball will be awarded prior to blowing the whistle.

(1) All players shall maintain their relative field position at the time the whistle was blown. No player may be closer to the boundary than the player awarded the ball. The umpire must ensure that no player gains an unfair advantage in the repositioning of players.

(2) The player with the ball must be given 1m clear space by her opponent(s).

(3) A throw is taken when the two opposing players closest to the ball are equidistant.

C. Play is not resumed within 11m of the centre of the goal-line.

15. THE THROW
Two opposing players stand with their feet and crosses at least 1m apart. Each is nearer the goal she is defending and is facing in toward the game. The throw must be taken at least 11m from the centre of the goal-line.

The umpire stands between 4m and 8m from the players, and as the whistle is blown, throws the ball with a short high arc toward the players so they catch it as they move in toward the game.

No other player may be within 4m of the players taking the throw. If the throw is inaccurate or is not touched by either player, it must be taken again.

The throw is taken when:

A. the ball goes into the goal off a non-player. The throw should be taken to the side of the goal by two opponents nearest the goal.

B. the ball goes out-of-bounds and two opposing players are equally near the ball.

C. there is an incident unrelated to the ball, and players are equidistant from the ball.

D. a ball lodges in the clothing of a field player or umpire.

E. two opponents foul simultaneously.

F. the game is restarted after an incident related to the ball when neither team had possession and two opposing players are equally near the ball, unless the accident has been caused by a foul.

G. the game is stopped for any reason not specified in the rules.

16. CONDUCT OF PLAY

A. A violation of any rule is a foul. The penalty for a foul is a 'free position'.

B. All players must stand when the whistle is blown. The umpire will indicate where the player taking the free position is to stand and where the offending player is to stand. The umpire must not allow a player on a minor field foul to move 4m in front of an opponent if that player was approaching from the side or rear when she fouled.

(1) No player or her crosse is allowed within 4m of the player taking the free position; if any player is within this distance she must move to a position indicated by the umpire. The umpire must resume play quickly so as not to delay the game while the clock is running. Time-out may be called to prevent undue delay in setting up a free position.

(2) A free position must not be taken within 11m of the centre of the goal-line.

(3) The player awarded the free position places the ball in her crosse, and on the umpire's whistle and visual arm signal she may run, pass or shoot.

(4) If two opposing players foul simultaneously and the fouls are equivalent (minor/minor or major/major), a throw is taken. If the fouls are not equivalent (major/minor), the team committing the major foul is penalised.

C. Held Whistle

An umpire may refrain from enforcing any rule when it would penalise the non-offending team. If a player retains possession of the ball, even though she has been fouled, the umpire will indicate that she has seen the foul by extending her arm in the direction of the player who is attacking.

17. GOAL-CIRCLE RULES

A. Only one player, either the goalkeeper or the person deputising for her, is allowed in the goal-circle at any one time. No other player is allowed to enter or have any part of her body or crosse on or over the goal-circle line at any time. A ball resting on the goal-circle line is the goalkeeper's.

B. The goalkeeper, while within the goal-circle:

(1) must clear the ball within ten seconds after it has entered the goal-circle.

(2) may stop the ball with either hand and/or body as well as her crosse. If she catches the ball with her hand she must put it in her crosse and proceed with the game.

(3) must remove a ball lodged in the goal netting or her clothing or pads, place it in her crosse and proceed with the game. The umpire may call time-out to assist the goalkeeper in dislodging the ball from her clothing, equipment or the goal-net.

(4) may reach out her crosse and bring the ball back into the goal-circle provided no part of her body is grounded outside the goal-circle. The goalkeeper or her deputy may step on, but not outside, the goal-circle line and still be considered in the goal-circle.

C. When the goalkeeper or anyone deputising for her is outside the goal-circle:

(1) she loses all her goalkeeping privileges.

(2) she may only re-enter the goal-circle without the ball.

(3) she may propel the ball into the goal-circle and then follow it in.

(4) she must return to the goal-circle to play the ball if it is inside the circle.

18. GOAL-CIRCLE FOULS AND PENALTIES

A. Goal-circle fouls.

(1) A player must not follow through over the goal-circle with any part of her body or crosse at any time unless she is deputising for the goalkeeper.

(2) Any unprotected field player:

(*a*) may only enter or remain in the goal-circle when her team has possession of the ball. A loose ball is deemed to be not in possession.

(*b*) must immediately leave the goal-circle when her team loses possession of the ball.

(*c*) may go into the goal-circle to play a rolling ball.

(*d*) while within the goal-circle, must clear the ball within 10 seconds after it has entered the goal-circle.

(*e*) while within the goal-circle, must remove a ball lodged in her clothing or crosse, place it in her crosse and proceed with the game.

(3) The goalkeeper or another player must not:

(*a*) allow the ball to remain within the goal-circle for longer than 10 seconds. The umpire should use a visible hand chopping motion to count each second that the ball remains in the goal-circle.

(*b*) when inside the goal-circle, reach beyond the goal-circle to play the ball with any part of her body.

(*c*) draw the ball into her goal-circle when any part of her is grounded outside the goal-circle. The goalkeeper or her deputy may step on but not outside the goal-circle line and still be considered in the goal-circle.

(*d*) when outside the goal-circle, step into the goal-circle with the ball.

(*e*) when outside the goal-circle, throw any of her equipment to another player.

B. Penalties for Goal-Circle Fouls.

(1) For all goal-circle fouls, except an unprotected field player illegally in the goal-circle, the 'free position' is taken 15m out from either side and level with the goal-line.

(2) For an unprotected field player illegally in the goal-circle, play must be stopped immediately and a major 'free position' awarded to the attack player nearest the centre hash mark on the 11m line. The offending player should be placed 4m behind and the penalty-lane cleared. The goalkeeper must not return to the goal-circle until play has restarted.

19. MINOR FOUL RULES AND PENALTIES

A. Minor Foul Rules

(1) A player must not cover a ground ball with her crosse or body.

(2) A player must not guard her crosse with her arm.

Elbows may not be used to protect the crosse. If one hand is removed from the crosse, the free arm must not be used to ward off an opponent, deliberately or otherwise, with or without contact.

Guarding the crosse should not be confused with the natural movement of the free arm when a player is running and holding the crosse with one hand.

(3) A player must not touch the ball with her hand or allow any part of her body to change the speed or direction of the ball to her team's distinct advantage, except as in Rule 17B2.

Ball contact from an unexpected deflection should not be penalised. The umpire must decide whether the body contact gave an offending team a distinct advantage and/or prevented an opponent from gaining possession of the ball.

A team does not gain an automatic advantage simply by retaining a ball off the body. The umpire must consider the proximity of the play to the goal, whether an opponent was close enough to play the ball, and whether the outcome of the play was any different than if there were no ball-to-body contact.

It is a major foul if the goalkeeper, while outside her goal-circle, blatantly plays the ball with any part of her body.

(4) A player must not check/tackle an opponent's crosse while the opponent is trying to gain possession of the ball.

A player does not need control of the ball before her crosse may be checked. If a player's crosse is contacting the ball, the crosse may be checked by an opponent. It is a legal play if the crosse check occurs simultaneously with the ball contacting the crosse.

(5) A player must not throw her crosse under any circumstance.

(6) A player must not take part in the game if she is not holding her own crosse.

A player's 'own crosse' is the crosse she possessed when entering the game or a substitute crosse obtained during a legal crosse obtained during a legal crosse exchange.

(7) A player must not draw illegally after one caution.

The right wall of the crosse must be toward the ground during the draw.

An illegal draw occurs when:

(*a*) a player taking the draw moves after the umpire says 'Ready' and but before the umpire blows the whistle.

(*b*) a player(s) does not draw her crosse up and away.

(*c*) the ball does not go higher than the heads of both centres.
The umpire administering the draw should watch for either centre laying back her crosse prior to drawing up and away.

(8) A player must not enter the centre-circle during the draw before the umpire blows her whistle.

Entering the centre-circle too soon during the draw should be called only when the player or her team gains an advantage because of her violation.

(9) A player must not intentionally delay the game.

(10) A player must not play with illegal equipment or in an illegal uniform.

When the ball lodges in the crosse of a field player, it must be dislodged immediately by striking the crosse on the ground; otherwise the crosse is illegal.

The umpire may inspect any equipment at any time during the game.

(*a*) If the equipment is legal, the game shall be restarted by giving the ball to the player who was in possession of the ball or nearest to the ball when the whistle was blown.

(*b*) If the equipment is illegal, it shall be placed with the scorer for the remainder of the half. The player may continue to play with legal equipment.

(c) If a goal was scored with an illegal crosse, and the illegal crosse is discovered prior to the next draw, the goal shall not count. All players must stand. Play is resumed with a 'free position' to the opposing goalkeeper.

(d) Illegal equipment may be adjusted at halftime and rechecked by the umpire. If it is legal, it may be used in the second half.

(e) The umpire should be alert to sagging pockets and crosses that hold the ball after successive hard checks.

(11) A player must not adjust the thongs of her crosse after an umpire requests to inspect her crosse during the game.

A player may adjust her crosse thongs at any time during the game except immediately after an umpire's request to check her crosse. There is no violation if a player adjusts her thongs after the opposing captain requests a crosse check but before the umpire asks to inspect the crosse.

If a player adjusts her thongs after the umpire asks to check her crosse, the crosse is ruled illegal automatically and is placed with the scorer for the remainder of the half.

(12) A player may not request, for a second time, the inspection of any crosse which meets rule specification.

(13) A player may not substitute illegally.

The penalty for an illegal substitution is a 'free position' awarded to the opponent closest to the ball. In addition, the umpire will call time-out and remove the illegal player.

If an illegal player is discovered on the attacking team after a goal is scored but before the next draw, the goal does not count, the illegal player is removed, and the opposing goalkeeper is awarded a 'free position'.

Illegal substitutes include any extra players on the field during the game and any suspended player who re-enters the game.

(14) A goalkeeper may not be beyond 15m of her goal-circle during a draw.

(15) A goalkeeper may not score a goal for her team or proceed beyond the centre-line at any time.

(16) A player must not hold the crosse of an opponent for a short time during a check/tackle.

(17) A player must not deliberately direct, propel or carry the ball out-of-bounds.

The umpire must decide whether the player with the ball had other options which would have kept the ball inbounds. A goalkeeper clearing out to the side of the field should not be penalised for intentionally putting the ball out-of-bounds, if she has a team-mate in the area potentially able to receive the ball.

B. Minor Foul Penalties

(1) For a minor foul, the offender is placed 4m from the player taking the 'free position', in the same direction from which she fouled. If committed by the defence, the 'free position' cannot be taken within 15m of goal, on a line which passes from the centre of the goal-line through the point where the foul occurred.

(2) Repeated minor fouls shall be penalised as major fouls. (Repeated is to do it a second time.)

20. MAJOR FOUL RULES AND PENALTIES
A. Major Foul Rules

(1) A player must not roughly or recklessly check/tackle an opponent's crosse.

A player must use extreme caution when checking from within a field/crosse width of an opponent's head or neck. If such a check is dangerous, it must be considered misconduct. The umpire should administer the appropriate warning card as well as the penalty for a major foul.

When determining whether a check is legal, the umpire should consider the amount of force used and the extent and direction of the backswing and follow through. An unbalanced body position and/or hands slipped together on the crosse handle often lead to rough/reckless checking.

A loud check is not necessarily rough and/or reckless.

(2) A player must not strike an opponent with her crosse or force an opponent's crosse into the opponent's body.

A yellow card must be given for a check to the head.

An attack player must not force her crosse or body into an opponent's crosse, thereby checking herself and potentially creating a dangerous situation. This often occurs when an attack player runs through a legal double-team. The umpire should watch the defender to see if she has established a legal position and is holding her crosse still.

The defender must never be penalised when the attack forces her crosse into the defender's crosse, even if contact occurs to the attacker's head or neck.

(3) A player must not hold her crosse within a field-crosse width of an opponent's head or neck.

(4) A player must not reach around or across her opponent's body to check her opponent's crosse when she is behind the opponent.

The act is a foul, whether or not there is contact with the opponent's crosse or body.

The defender's feet must be level with or ahead of her opponent's feet before she may reach across/around the opponent's body to check her opponent's crosse.

The umpire should look closely for contact with the attacker's arms, hands and torso. There must be space between the defender and the attacker.

(5) A player possessing the ball must not hold her crosse near her own face or body, or a team-mate's face or body, with or without cradling, making a legal check impossible.

This technique can lead to dangerous play. The defence must be allowed to legally check an opponent's crosse.

This is a foul only if the defender has a legal body position and the attacker prevents a legal check.

(6) A player may not charge, block, barge, shoulder, push with the hand or back into an opponent. A player must not move into the path of an opponent without giving the opponent sufficient time to stop or change directions.

When a player is running to receive the ball, a defensive player outside the opponent's visual field must give her enough time or space to change direction.

A player's legal body position is as wide as her shoulders. It includes the space in front of a player, extending only as far as the length of her arms when outstretched directly in front of her body. A player may not extend her crosse or body beyond this specified distance and impede (with contact) an opponent.

A player holding a position with outstretched arms must be in this position before the attacker reaches her. The defender must give the attacker time or space to change direction.

The umpire should watch for defenders extending hips or knees into an attacker who is changing her path to goal.

It is charging if an attacker uses her body or crosse to interfere with a defender maintaining a legal body position. This includes interference with a defender's legally held crosse.

(7) A player must not propel the ball or follow through with her crosse in a dangerous or uncontrolled manner at any time.

It is critical for the umpire to watch for contact to the defender on the follow through of the crosse after a shot. This is primarily the responsibility of the trail umpires.

A yellow card must be given for dangerously propelling the ball into an opponent.

(8) A player must not shoot dangerously or without control. A dangerous shot is judged on any combination of the shooter's distance from goal, the force of the shot, and/or the placement of the shot. A shot that does not give the goalkeeper time to react, may not be directed at her body, especially the head or neck. This does not apply to a goalkeeper who moves into the path of the shot. A shot may be judged dangerous and/or uncontrolled even if it misses the goal.

The attacker must know where her opponent(s) is before shooting. To judge a dangerous shot, the umpire should consider:

(*a*) whether an attacker's hand has slipped down the crosse.

(*b*) whether the shooter is off balance.

(*c*) whether the ball is batted or hurled at the goal and judged uncontrolled.

(*d*) whether a shot is taken blindly without regard for the opponent's position.

Shots which become dangerous after a defensive check or block should not be penalised.

The 'free position' for all dangerous shots is to be taken by the goalkeeper within her goal-circle.

(9) A player defending must not block the goal outside the goal-circle with any part of her body so as to obstruct the free space to goal which denies the attacking player the chance to shoot safely. This rule is enforced only when the attacking team possesses the ball within their 15m offensive area.

A defender must be outside the free space to goal when approaching the ball carrier until she is 2m away. A defender running through (she may not stop or hesitate) the free space to reach her opponent should not be penalised. Blocking this free space to goal requires an immediate whistle in order to prevent injury. This call should be made only if the player with the ball is looking to shoot. If she is being double or triple teamed and she has no opportunity to shoot for goal, the call should not be made.

(10) A player may not detain an opponent at any time by holding, tagging, pressing or pushing against her body, clothing or crosse with her arm, leg, body or crosse. A player must not hold an opponent's crosse after a check to the extent that the opponent's balance or movement is impeded. This applies to play on and off the ball.

(11) A player must not trip an opponent deliberately or otherwise.

(12) A player must not set a moving or stationary pick (screen) which cannot be seen by the opponent being screened. Picks must be set within the visual field of the opponent to be legal. Watch for offensive picks especially at the attacking end. This foul is a form of blocking and will be called when body contact occurs.

(13) A player may not swipe at her opponent. Swiping is the swinging of a crosse at an opponent's crosse or body with deliberate viciousness or recklessness whether or not the opponent's crosse or body is struck.

In addition to awarding the appropriate penalty, a yellow card must be given.

(14) A player when defending must not remain longer than 3 seconds in the 11m area at the front of the goal-circle unless she is marking an

opponent within a stick and arm's length (2m). To be exempt from the 3-second-rule, only one defender may mark the same non-ball player in the 11m area.

A defender who is marking an unmarked opponent standing directly behind the goal-circle is exempt from the 3-second-rule. She is not exempt from the free space to goal rule.

The 3-second-rule begins when the team in possession crosses the ball over the centre-line into the attacking half of the field.

When the attacking team crosses the centre-line the umpire has the option to show an 'advantage' arm signal if a defender is illegally in the marking area. Once the attacker is on a scoring play, the umpire should then use the 'advantage flag'.

B. Major Foul Penalties

(1) For a major foul, the offender is placed 4m behind the player taking the 'free position'. If the goalkeeper is fouled outside the goal-circle, she will take the 'free position' no closer than 11m from the centre of the goal-line.

(2) All players must clear the penalty-lane of crosses and any part of their body when a 'free position' is awarded for a major foul occurring within 11m of the front of the goal.

All players, except the goalkeeper, when instructed by the umpire, will clear sideways from the penalty-lane relative to their position at the time of the whistle. The goalkeeper, if she is outside the goal-circle and within the penalty-lane, may move back into the goal-circle if she has not fouled.

If a shot is taken that is dangerous to a defensive player and not the goalkeeper, the goalkeeper will still take the 'free position' within the goal-circle.

(3) If the foul prevented an almost certain goal, the umpire may move any players positioned between the 'free position' and the goal.

(4) If any defender is in the free space to goal when a 'free position' is set, she should not be penalised for blocking the free space to goal unless she does not immediately move out of this space after the umpire restarts play.

Play must be stopped immediately for a free space to goal violation. This violation is penalised at the spot where the ball is when the whistle is blown.

21. ADVANTAGE FLAG

A. Advantage flag is a 'held whistle' for a major foul by defence within 15m of goal. This includes the 15m fan and the playing area behind goal, which runs 9m deep and 15m to each side of the centre of the goal-line.

B. A yellow flag is raised by the umpire when an attack player, with or without the ball, is fouled on a scoring play. The umpire should keep the yellow flag in his/her waistband. If a scoring play is in progress and the defence commits a major foul, the umpire shall hold the advantage flag vertically above her head so it is visible, and call 'flag'. The umpire should note the numbers of both the attack and defence players concerned.

C. A scoring play is a continuous effort by the attacking team to move the ball toward the goal and complete a shot on goal.

D. The scoring play is over when:

(1) a shot is taken.

(2) the attacking team passes or carries the ball behind the level of the goal-line and fails to continue the initial momentum to score a goal.

(3) the attacking team stops its continuous effort to complete a shot on goal.

(4) the attacking team fouls. A throw will be taken beyond 15m, level with the goal-line extension. It is recommended that the C umpire (or closest umpire) takes the throw.

(5) the defence commits a subsequent foul which requires the game to be stopped.

During the advantage flag, play does not have to stop on the second defensive foul. Once a flag is raised, the umpire must be alert for a dangerous foul committed toward the ball carrier or her team-mate, even if the ball is not lost. The whistle may be blown immediately to prevent injury or dangerous play. Such a foul may be judged flagrant and therefore be carded.

(6) the attacking team loses possession of the ball. A bounce pass or bounce shot is not considered loss of possession.

The umpire must stop the scoring play immediately for a free space to goal violation, or for an unprotected player illegally in the goal-circle.

While the flag is raised, the umpire may stop the scoring play at any time to prevent injury.

E. Following the Advantage Flag:

(1) If a shot on goal is successful, the goal counts.

(2) If the attacking team chooses to shoot, the advantage indicated by the flag is complete and play continues.

Following a shot on goal (successful or not), the umpire shall return the flag to his/her waistband.

If the shot is affected by a foul, no advantage is gained and the attack will be awarded a 'free position'.

(3) If the scoring play ends without a further foul or shot on goal, a 'free position' will be awarded to the attack player who was fouled and the penalised defender will be placed 4m behind.

For a foul:

(*a*) between 11m–15m in front of goal, the 'free position' is awarded where the foul occurred.

(*b*) within 11m in front of goal, the 'free position' is awarded on the closest hash mark and the penalty-lane cleared.

(*c*) Behind goal, the 'free position' is awarded on the 11m mark on the goal-line extension.

(4) If any additional fouls by the defence end the scoring play, the 'free position' is awarded to the attack player who was fouled at the 11m hash mark nearest the most recent foul. The defender who fouled will be placed 4m behind and the penalty-lane cleared.

(5) If the attacking team fouls (major or minor), a throw will be taken beyond 15m, level with the goal-line extension.

(6) Whenever the penalty-lane is cleared and the goalkeeper is outside her goal-circle and has not fouled, she may return to her goal-circle.

22. MISCONDUCT AND SUSPENSIONS

A. Misconduct and Suspensions

A player must not:

(1) conduct herself in a rough, dangerous or unsportsmanlike manner.

(2) persistently cause infringement of the rules.

(3) deliberately endanger the safety of an opposing player.

(4) exhibit any type of behaviour which in the umpire's opinion amounts to misconduct.

B. Penalties

(1) Misconduct and/or suspension are treated as major fouls.

(2) In addition to awarding the appropriate penalty, the umpire may:

(*a*) give a verbal caution.

(*b*) warn the offending player with a yellow card. A yellow card must be given to the offender for:

– a check to the head.

– the dangerous propelling of a ball into an opponent.

– swiping.

– repeated fouls following a green card caution.

(*c*) suspend the offending player by showing a red card. In the event of a goalkeeper being suspended, a 2 minute time-out will be taken to enable a player already on the field, to put on protective equipment. When she returns to the field, she must stand 4m behind the attack who has been awarded the 'free position'.

A red card must be given to the offender if she has previously been given a yellow card. At this time, the umpire will present both a yellow card and a red card to the offender to indicate her second misconduct foul. She is suspended and may never re-enter the game.

(*d*) suspend from further participation in the game and/or send from the field without any previous warning, a player, coach or bench personnel guilty of dissent, misconduct, abusive language or flagrant/repeated violations of the rules.

(*e*) If a player, coach or bench personnel is warned or suspended, the game is restarted within 30 seconds with a 'free position' to the opponent nearest the ball when play was stopped. If the offender does not leave the field when requested by the umpire, her/his team must forfeit the game. If that team is behind in score, the score shall stand. If the forfeiting team is ahead, the score shall be 1–0 in favour of the opponents.

Warning cards should be constructed of thin sturdy plastic. Recommended size and shape are:

Green 6.5cm/triangle
Yellow 6.5cm/square
Red 6.5cm diameter/circle

23. TEAM FOULS AND PENALTIES

A. Team fouls

(1) Delay the game by failing to stand on a stoppage of play or respond to the umpire's directions.

(*a*) Failure to stand when the whistle is blown also includes creeping, false starts, and so on.

(*b*) Failure to move 4m away on a 'free position'.

(2) Persistent fouling.

B. Team Foul Penalties

(1) Delay of game.

(*a*) On the first deliberate delay of game, the umpire shall show the team's captain a green card and award the appropriate penalty.

(*b*) On the next delay of game, the umpire will show a green and yellow card to the offending player and award the appropriate penalty. All subsequent offenders on that team shall receive a green and red card suspension along with the appropriate penalty. The suspended player may return to the field on the next stoppage of play after a 3 minute lapse of playing time. The player re-entering the game will be placed one step on to the field of play, level with the centre-line.

(*c*) The fouls need not be identical, but simply some type of delay of game.

(2) Persistent Fouls

(*a*) The umpire shall show a green card to the team's captain for persistent team fouls. On the next similar offence by that team, the umpire will show the offender a green and yellow card. Regardless of the act, the offence will be penalised as a major foul.

The umpire may notice fouls occurring persistently due either to lack of skill, recklessness or an attempt to gain an unfair advantage.

The appropriate penalty is awarded and a time-out is taken. A green card is shown to the captain indicating that the repetition of such behaviour by any member of her team will be more severely penalised.

(*b*) The next player from the carded team who commits a subsequent team foul will receive a green and red card suspension in addition to the penalty for a major foul. The suspended player may return to the field on the next stoppage of play after a 3 minute lapse of playing time.

Arm Signals for Umpires

Blocking: Place open hands on the hips and move them to touch hips with an in-and-out motion.

Charging: Place right hand behind head.

Dangerous follow-through: Mimic follow-through motion with arm.

Dangerous propelling: Two-handed side arm swing or batting motion.

Dangerous shot: Open palm and move towards face.

Empty crosse check: Use the right hand with clapping motion on the left hand. Clap and hold for a held crosse.

Free position or possession of ball on out-of-bounds: Indicate the direction with one arm raised horizontally towards the goal of the team in possession.

Goal: Arms are raised above the head and the umpire then turns and points both arms horizontally towards the centre of the field.

Goal-circle foul: Point to goal-circle and then indicate direction of free position.

Held whistle: Arm raised horizontally shoulder level in the direction of the offended player's goal.

Illegal ball off the body: Indicate by pointing to the body part that touched the ball.

Illegal check on the body: Make a chopping motion with one hand on body part where contact was made.

No goal: With the arms extended toward the ground, swing them back and forth so they cross each other.

Obstruction of free space to goal: Arms held in front of the body with palms toward face, with one hand closer to the face, in a line about 16cm toward the face.

Pushing or body contact: Make a pushing motion with two arms out in front of the body.

Re-draw: Place arms fully extended horizontally in front of the body. Begin with hands together and extend them up and out with a quick motion.

Rough check: Use the arm to make a large chop motion against the wrist of the opposite arm.

Substitution: Make a beckoning motion with one arm to entering player.
Swipe: One arm in circular motion close to the head.
Ten-second count for ball in goal-circle: Make a small chop motion with one arm for each second counted.
Three-second-rule: Three fingers raised, palm away.
Time-in: Hand open above the head with arm fully extended; then drop the arm in a chopping motion to start the clock.
Time-out: Turn towards the timer and cross fully extended arms at the wrist above the head.

DEFINITIONS

(1) Advantage Flag is a held whistle for a major foul against an attack player, with or without the ball, while on a scoring play within 15cm of the goal. A yellow flag is raised by the umpire and a verbal call of 'flag'.

(2) Blocking is moving into the path of an opponent with the ball without giving that player sufficient time to stop or change direction, causing contact. When a player is running to receive the ball, a 'blindside' (unsighted) defence player must give her enough time and/or space to change her direction.

(3) Body Checking is a technique whereby a defender moves with an opponent without body contact occurring, following each movement of the opponent's body and crosse with her body thereby causing her opponent to slow down, change direction or pass the ball.

(4) Charging occurs when a player with the ball pushes into, shoulders or backs into, and makes bodily contact with her opponent who has already established her position (though not necessarily stationary).

(5) Clear is any action taken by the player within the goal-circle to pass the ball to her own team.

(6) Clear Space indicates the space between players which is free of crosses and any part of the body.

(7) Creeping is movement by a field player when she is to stand after a whistle is blown to indicate a stoppage of play for any reason.

(8) Crosse Checking is an extension of body checking whereby the defender attempts to dislodge the ball from her opponent's crosse by using a controlled or series of controlled tapping movements with her own crosse on her opponent's crosse.

(9) Directly Behind Goal Circle is the area between two imaginary lines extending perpendicularly and back from the goal-line extended, forming a tangent to the goal-circle.

(10) Free Space to Goal is an imaginary path to goal as defined by two lines extending from the ball to the outside of the goal-circle and within

15m of the goal. No defence player will be penalised if positioned below the extension of the goal-line, as shown.

(11) Grounded refers to any part of the goalkeeper's or her deputy's body touching the ground for support outside the goal-circle while she attempts to play the ball from inside the goal-circle.

(12) Penalty-Lane is the path to goal defined by imaginary lines that extend the width of the goal-circle to the ball carrier. All other players must clear this area when a 'free position' for a major foul is awarded within 11m in front of goal.

(13) Pick is an offensive technique in which a player without the ball uses her positioning to force an opponent to take another route. To be legal it must be set within the visual field of the opponent. The opponent must be given time and space to stop or change direction.

(14) Scoring Play is a continuous effort by the attacking team to move the ball toward the goal and to complete a shot on goal.

(15) A Shot is to propel the ball in the direction of the goal with the intent to score a goal.

(16) Swiping in the swinging of the crosse at an opponent's crosse or body with a deliberate viciousness or recklessness, whether or not the opponent's crosse or body is struck.

(17) Team/Bench Personnel includes the coach, assistant coaches, manager, medical staff and players.

(18) Toeing the Line refers to the placement of the foot up to, but not on, the centre-line.

(19) Within A Stick's Length is inside a crosse's length and arm's length extended. It is the distance a player must be to her opponent to be actively marking this opponent.

Reprinted by permission of the All-England Women's Lacrosse Association. Manufacturers' specifications for the crosse, ball, goals and nets, as well as Special Recommendations, are given in full in the IFWLA International Lacrosse Rules, which can be obtained from the All-England Women's Lacrosse Association.

Netball

The Court

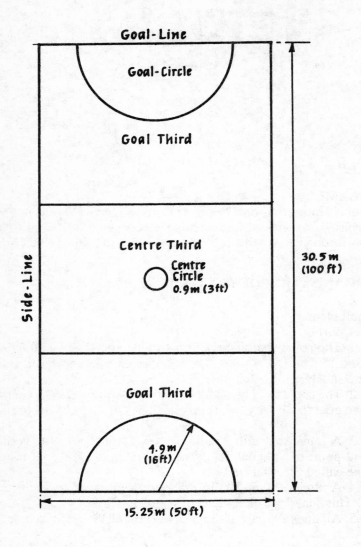

Netball

THE GAME
Netball is an International Sport. It is played by two teams of 7 players and is based on throwing and catching. Goals are scored within a defined area by throwing the ball into a ring attached to a 3.05m (10ft) high post.

I. ORGANISATION OF THE GAME

1. Equipment
1.1 *Court*
1.1.1 The court shall have a firm surface and shall be 30.5m (100ft) long and 15.25m (50ft) wide. The longer sides shall be called side-lines and the shorter sides goal-lines.

1.1.2 The court shall be divided into three equal parts – a centre third and two goal thirds – by two transverse lines drawn parallel to the goal-lines.

1.1.3 A semicircle with a radius of 4.9m (16ft) and with its centre at the mid-point of the goal-line, shall be drawn in each goal third. This shall be called the goal circle.

1.1.4 A circle, 0.9m (3ft) in diameter shall mark the centre of the court. This shall be called the centre circle.

1.1.5 All lines are part of the court, and shall be not more than 50mm (2in) wide.

1.2 *Goalposts*
1.2.1 A goalpost which shall be vertical and 3.05m (10ft) high shall be placed at the mid-point of each goal-line. A metal ring with an internal diameter of 380mm (15in) shall project horizontally 150mm (6in) from the top of the post, the attachment to allow 150mm (6in) between the

post and the near side of the ring. The ring shall be of steel rod 15mm (⅝in) in diameter, fitted with a net clearly visible and open at both ends. Both ring and net are considered to be part of the goalpost. If padding is used on the goalpost it shall not be more than 25mm (1in) thick and shall start at the base of the goalpost and extend between 2m (6.5ft) and 2.4m (8ft) up the goalpost.

1.2.2 The post, which shall be 65mm (2.5in)–100mm (4in) in diameter or 65mm (2.5in)–100mm (4in) square, may be inserted in a socket in the ground or may be supported by a metal base which shall not project on the court. The goalpost shall be placed so that the back of the goalpost is at the outside of the goal-line. For international matches the goalposts preferably should be inserted into the ground.

1.3 *Ball*

The ball shall be a netball or an association football size 5, and shall measure between 690mm (27in) and 710mm (28in) in circumference and weigh between 400g (14oz) and 450g) (16oz). The ball may be of leather, rubber or similar material.

1.4 *Players*

1.4.1 Shoes or boots may be worn. They shall be of lightweight material. Spiked soles are not allowed.

1.4.2 Registered playing uniforms, which shall include initials of playing positions, shall be worn at all times. Playing initials shall be worn both front and back above the waist and shall be 150mm (6in) high.

1.4.3 No sharp adornment or item of jewellery, except a wedding ring, shall be worn. If a wedding ring is worn, it shall be taped.

1.4.4 Fingernails shall be cut short.

2. Duration of Game

2.1 The game shall consist of four quarters of 15 minutes each, with an interval of 3 minutes between the first-second and third-fourth quarters and an interval of 5 minutes at half-time. An interval may be extended by the Umpires to deal with any emergency. Teams shall change ends each quarter.

2.2 Where any one team plays two or more matches in one day, or where time is limited, the duration of the games shall be as agreed by the teams' officials. In the event that agreement is not reached then the games shall consist of two halves of 20 minutes each with a 5 minutes' interval at half-time. Teams shall change ends at half-time.

2.3 Playing time lost for an accident or any other cause must be noted and added to that quarter or half of the game. In no case shall extra time be allowed except to take a penalty shot.

2.4 In certain climatic conditions the duration of the game shall be predetermined by the countries concerned.

3. Officials

The Officials are: umpires, scorers, timekeepers. The Team Officials are: coach, manager, captain, physiotherapist or doctor.

3.1 *Umpires*

3.1.1 There shall be two Umpires who shall have control of the game and give decisions. They shall umpire according to the rules and decide on any matter not covered by the rules. The decisions of the Umpire shall be final and shall be given without appeal.

3.1.2 The Umpire's whistle shall start and stop the game. Starting, or restarting the game after an interval, shall be controlled by the Umpire into whose half the play is to be directed.

3.1.3 After the players have taken their positions on the court, the Umpires shall toss for goal-end. The Umpire winning the toss shall control that half of the court designated the northern half.

3.1.4 Umpires shall wear clothes distinct from those of the players and preferably white or cream in colour. Suitable shoes shall be worn.

3.1.5 Each Umpire shall:

(i) Control and give decisions only in one half of the court unless appealed to by the other Umpire for a decision in the other half and be ready for such an appeal at all times. For this purpose the length of the court is divided in half across the centre from side-line to side-line.

(ii) Umpire in the same half of the court throughout the game.

(iii) Re-start the game after all goals scored in the half being controlled.

(iv) Give decisions for the throw-in for one goal-line and for the whole of one side-line and shall call 'play' when all other players are on the court. The Umpire responsible for the side-line is responsible for making decisions related to infringements by the player throwing in and the defending opponents.

(v) Keep outside the court except when it is necessary to enter it to secure a clear view of play, or to indicate the point from which a penalty must be taken, or to take a toss-up.

If the ball strikes the Umpire during play, or if an Umpire interferes with the movements of the players, play does not cease unless one team has been unduly penalised, in which case a free pass shall be awarded to that team.

(vi) When a toss-up has been awarded, appeal where necessary to the other Umpire to take the toss-up and that Umpire shall control points listed in section IV – Rule 18.4 (Toss-up 18.4.2–18.4.6).

(vii) Move along the side-line and behind the goal-line to see play and make decisions.

(viii) Refrain from blowing the whistle to penalise an infringement when by so doing the non-offending team would be placed at a disadvantage. An Umpire *may* call 'advantage' to indicate an infringement has been observed and not penalised. Having blown the whistle for an infringement the penalty must be taken unless a goal is scored which is to the advantage of the non-offending team.

(ix) Not criticise or coach any team while a match is in progress.

(x) Check that during a stoppage for injury or illness, other players remain on court. During this stoppage coaching is not permitted.

(xi) State the infringement and penalty and should use hand signals to clarify decisions.

3.2 *Scorers*

3.2.1 There shall be two scorers who shall:

(i) Keep a written record of the score together with a record of the centre pass.

(ii) Record each goal as it is scored unless notified to the contrary by the Umpire. This constitutes the official score of the game.

(iii) Keep a record of all unsuccessful shots.

(iv) Call the centre pass if appealed to by the Umpire, and inform the Umpire immediately if the incorrect centre pass is indicated.

(v) Record suspensions of players.

3.2.2 If the Umpires disagree with each other or with the scorers as to the centre pass they call for time to be taken while both Umpires and scorers consult the scoresheet.

3.3 *Timekeepers*

3.3.1 There shall be a timekeeper who shall:

(i) Take time when the game is started by the Umpire's whistle and shall signal the end of each quarter or half to the Umpire.

(ii) Take time when instructed by the Umpire who shall blow the whistle to stop play. To restart play the Umpire shall signal to the timekeeper and blow the whistle for play to be resumed.

(iii) Ensure that when instructed by the Umpire time lost for a stoppage is played in the quarter or half in which this occurs.

3.4 *Captains*
3.4.1   The captains shall:
(i) Toss for choice of goal or first centre pass and notify the Umpires of the results.
(ii) During an interval or after stoppage for injury or illness notify the Umpires and the opposing captain when substitutions and/or team changes are made.
3.4.2 The captains have the right to approach an Umpire during an interval or after the game for clarification of any rule.
3.4.3 During an interval either captain may appeal to the Umpires for extra time to deal with an emergency affecting a member of the team. If the appeal is granted the Umpires shall advise both the captains and the timekeeper of the expected length of the stoppage.
Penalty for 3.4.1(ii): A Free Pass shall be awarded after play restarts immediately an Umpire notices:–
(i) a substitute on court;
(ii) a player in a changed position.
The Free Pass shall be taken:–
(i) from the spot where the ball was when play stopped;
(ii) by a player allowed in that area;
(iii) after time has been allowed for the captain of the other team to substitute and/or make team changes if desired. The player concerned shall be permitted to remain in the position now being played.

4. The Team
4.1 The game is designed for single-sex competition.

4.2 A team shall consist of seven players whose playing positions shall be–

Goal Shooter (GS)
Goal Attack (GA)
Wing Attack (WA)
Centre (C)
Wing Defence (WD)
Goal Defence (GD)
Goalkeeper (GK)

4.3 Up to three substitutions are permitted by each team in any one game. Refer to Rule 6: Substitutions and Team Changes.

4.4 No team may take the court with fewer than five players.

5. Late Arrivals

5.1 No player arriving after play has started is allowed to replace a player who has filled the position of the late arrival except that the late arrival may be used as a substitute in the event of injury, illness or during an interval as provided for in Rule 6: Substitution and Team Changes.

5.2 If a player has not filled the position of the late arrival, the late arrival may not enter the game while play is in progress, but after notifying the Umpires may take the court:–

(i) after a goal has been scored. In this case the player must play in a position left vacant in the team;

(ii) immediately following an interval;

(iii) at a stoppage for injury or illness.

Penalty for 5.2: A Free Pass to the opposing team where the ball was when play stopped. The player concerned shall leave the court until the next goal is scored or until after the next interval.

6. Substitutions and Team Changes

6.1 Substitution occurs when a player leaves the court and is replaced by another player.

Team changes occur when players on court re-arrange playing positions.

6.1.1 Substitution and team changes are allowed on court:

(i) during an interval;

(ii) in the event of injury or illness;

(iii) in the event of a stoppage for failure to give notification of team changes.

In any one game each team may make up to three substitutions. A player who has previously been substituted may return to the game at a later stage but shall then be deemed to be one of the three permitted substitutions.

6.1.2 It is the responsibility of the team captain to notify the Umpires and the opposing captain if substitutions and/or team changes are made.

6.1.3 It is the responsibility of a team official to notify the official scorers of any substitutions or team changes.

6.1.4 When substitutions and/or team changes are made by a team sufficient time shall be allowed for the opposing team to make substitutions and/or team changes if desired.

6.1.5 If a team plays short while an injured or ill player is off the court, this player or a substitute may not enter the game while play is in progress but after notifying the Umpires may take the court:–

(i) after a goal has been scored. In this case the player or substitute must play in a position left vacant in the team;

(ii) immediately following an interval;

(iii) after stoppage for injury or illness;

(iv) in the event of a stoppage for failure to give notification of team changes.

6.1.6 Once three substitutions have been made, if a further substitution is made the Umpires shall require the player concerned to leave the court and that player shall not be replaced. Neither team shall be permitted to make team changes unless the player concerned is the Centre. That team then shall move only one player to allow play to continue.

Penalty for 6.1.2: A Free Pass shall be awarded immediately an Umpire notices:–

(i) a substitute on court;

(ii) a player in a changed position.

The Free Pass shall be taken:–

(i) from the spot where the ball was when play stopped;

(ii) by a player allowed in that area;

(iii) after time has been allowed for the captain of the other team to substitute and/or make team changes if desired.

The player concerned shall be permitted to remain in the position now being played.

7. Stoppages

7.1 Play may be stopped for injury or illness or any other cause. The decision to stop play shall be at the discretion of the Umpire.

7.2 When a player is injured or ill a stoppage of up to two minutes is allowed from when time is called to decide whether the injured or ill player is fit to continue to play. This decision shall be left to the team's officials.

7.3 During a stoppage for injury or illness time shall be allowed for both teams to make substitutions and/or team changes if desired. Also refer to Rule 3.1.5(x).

7.4 Play may be stopped by an Umpire for any emergency relating to:–

(i) the equipment, court, weather or interference by outside agencies;

(ii) a player's person or clothing;

(iii) officials officiating at the match.

7.5 To stop play the Umpire shall blow the whistle and instruct the timekeeper to take time. The Umpire shall decide the length of time for the stoppage and shall ensure that play is re-started as soon as possible.

7.6 To re-start play the Umpire shall signal to the timekeeper and blow the whistle for play to be resumed.

7.7 The game is continued from the spot where the ball was when play stopped other than when:–
(i) the ball is out of court, in which case a throw-in is taken;
(ii) the Umpire is unable to say who was in possession of the ball, or the ball was on the ground when play stopped, in which case a toss-up is taken between any two opposing players allowed in that area, as near as possible to the spot where the ball was when play stopped;
(iii) the stoppage is due to obstruction or contact, in which case a penalty pass or penalty pass or shot is awarded where the infringer was standing except where this places the non-offending team at a disadvantage, when the penalty shall be taken where the obstructed or contacted player was standing.

7.8 After injury or illness, when no substitution is made for a player unable to resume play, the injured or ill player may not enter the game while play is in progress, but after notifying the Umpires may take the court:–
(i) after a goal has been scored. In this case the player must play in a position left vacant by the team;
(ii) immediately following an interval;
(iii) at a stoppage for injury or illness.
Penalty for 7.8: A Free Pass is awarded to the opposing team where the ball was when play stopped. The player concerned shall leave the court until the next goal is scored, until the next interval, or until the next stoppage for injury or illness.

II. AREAS OF PLAY

8. Players' Areas
8.1 The playing area for each player is as follows and as shown in the diagram on the facing page:

Goal Shooter – 1, 2
Goal Attack – 1, 2, 3
Wing Attack –   2, 3
Centre   –   2, 3, 4

Playing Areas

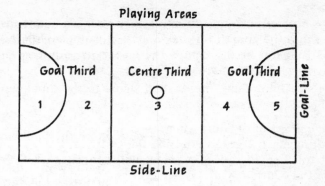

Penalty: See Penalty for 3.4.1(ii).

Wing Defence –   3, 4
Goal Defence –   3, 4, 5
Goalkeeper   –   4, 5
Lines bounding each area are included as part of that area.

8.2 Substitutions and team changes may be made as under Rule 6.

9. Off-side
9.1 *One player Off-side*
9.1.1 A player with or without the ball shall be off-side if any area other than the playing area for that designated position is entered.
9.1.2 A player may reach over and take the ball from an off-side area or may lean on the ball in an off-side area provided no body contact is made with the ground in the off-side area.
Penalty: A Free-Pass to the opposing team where the infringement occurred.

9.2 *Simultaneous Off-side*
When any two opposing players go off-side at the same moment:
(i) If neither makes any contact with the ball, they are not penalised and play continues.
(ii) If one of them is in possession of the ball or touches it, a toss-up is taken between those two players in their own area of play except as provided for under 9.2(iv).
(iii) If both of them are in possession of the ball or touch it, a toss-up is taken between those two players in their own area of play except as provided for under 9.2(iv).
(iv) If one player who is allowed only in the goal third goes off-side

into the centre third, and an opposing player simultaneously goes off-side into the goal third, one or both in contact with the ball, a toss-up is taken in the centre third between any two opposing players allowed in that area.

10. Out of Court

10.1 *The ball* is out of court when:
(i) It touches the ground outside the court.
(ii) It touches an object or person in contact with the ground outside the court.
(iii) It is held by a player in contact with the ground, an object or a person outside the court.
Penalty for 10.1: A throw-in to the team opposing the one who last had contact with the ball, to be taken where the ball crossed the line.

10.2 A *ball* which hits any part of the goalpost and rebounds into play is not out of court.

10.3 *A player in contact with the ball* is out of court when:
(i) The ground outside the court is touched.
(ii) Any object or person outside the court is touched.

10.4 *A player having no contact with the ball* may stand or move out of court, but before playing the ball the player must re-enter the court and no longer have contact with the ground out of court.
Penalty for 10.3 and 10.4: A throw-in to the opposing team at the point where the player was out of court.

10.5 Defending actions may only be attempted by players standing on court or jumping from the court.
Penalty for 10.5: Penalty pass or penalty pass or shot opposite the spot where the infringer attempted to defend.

10.6 If the ball is caught simultaneously by two opposing players one of whom lands out of court, a toss-up is taken on court between those two players opposite to the point where the player was out of court.

10.7 A player who has left the court to retrieve a ball or to take a throw-in must be permitted to re-enter the court directly.

Penalty for 10.7: Penalty pass or penalty pass or shot to the opposing team where the infringer was standing.

III. CONDUCT OF THE GAME

11. Positioning of Players for Start of Play
11.1 The Centre in possession of the ball shall stand in the centre circle. The Centre may stand on one or both feet, provided no part of this player's body is in contact with the ground outside the circle. The line is considered part of the centre circle.

11.2 The opposing centre shall be in the centre third and free to move.

11.3 All other players shall be in the goal third which is part of their playing area and free to move.

11.4 No other player is allowed in the centre third until the whistle has been blown to start the game.

Penalty for 11.4

1. If one player enters the centre third before the whistle is blown, a free pass to the opposing team where the infringement occurred.
2. When any two opposing players simultaneously enter the centre third before the whistle has been blown:
 (i) If neither makes contact with the ball, they are not penalised and play continues.
 (ii) If one of them touches or catches the ball, a toss-up is taken between those two players near to where the infringement occurred.

11.5 The Umpire shall ensure before starting play that all players are in their designated areas.

12. Start of Play
12.1 *Organisation of the Start of Play*
12.1.1 The Umpire shall blow the whistle to start and restart play.
12.1.2 The pass made by a Centre in response to the Umpire's whistle at the start and restart of play shall be designated a centre pass.
12.1.3 Play shall be started and restarted, after every goal scored and after each interval, by a centre pass taken alternately by the two Centres throughout the game.
12.1.4 If, at a centre pass, the ball is still in the Centre's hands when

the Umpire's whistle is blown to signal the end of a quarter or half, that team will take the pass after the interval.

12.2 *Controlling the Centre Pass*
12.2.1 When the whistle is blown the Centre in possession of the ball shall throw it within 3 seconds and shall obey the Footwork Rule.

12.2.2 The centre pass shall be caught or touched by any player who is standing or who lands within the centre third. A player who lands with the first foot, or on both feet simultaneously, wholly within the centre third, is judged to have received the ball in that third. That player's subsequent throw shall be considered to have been made from the centre third. A player who lands with any part of either foot in the goal third is judged to have received the ball in the goal third.

12.2.3 If a member of the team taking the centre pass catches the ball in the goal third, without it having been touched in the centre third by any player, a free pass shall be awarded to the opposing team, to be taken in the goal third close to the point where the ball crossed the line.

12.2.4 If a member of the opposing team touches or catches the centre pass in the goal third, or with feet astride the transverse line, play continues.

12.2.5 If the ball from the centre pass goes untouched over the side-line bounding the centre third, a throw-in is awarded to the opposing team where the ball crossed the line.

13. Playing the Ball
13.1 A player may:

(i) Catch the ball with one or both hands.

(ii) Gain or regain control of the ball if it rebounds from the goalpost.

(iii) Bat or bounce the ball to another player without first having possession of it.

(iv) Tip the ball in an uncontrolled manner once or more than once and then:

(*a*) Catch the ball; or

(*b*) Direct the ball to another player.

(v) Having batted the ball once, either catch the ball or direct the ball to another player.

(vi) Having bounced the ball once, either catch the ball or direct the ball to another player.

(vii) Roll the ball to oneself to gain possession.

(viii) Fall while holding the ball but must regain footing and throw within 3 seconds of receiving the ball.

(ix) Lean on the ball to prevent going off-side.

(x) Lean on the ball on court to gain balance.

(xi) Jump from a position in contact with the court and play the ball outside the court, provided that neither the player nor the ball makes contact with the ground, or any object or person outside the court while the ball is being played.

13.2 A player may not:

(i) Strike the ball with a fist.

(ii) Deliberately fall on the ball to get it.

(iii) Attempt to gain possession of the ball while lying, sitting or kneeling on the ground.

(iv) Throw the ball while lying, sitting or kneeling on the ground.

(v) Use the goalpost as a support in recovering the ball going out of court.

(vi) Use the goalpost as a means of regaining balance, or in any other way for any other purpose.

(vii) Deliberately kick the ball (if a ball is thrown and accidentally hits the leg of a player it is not a kick).

Penalty: Free pass to the opposing team where the infringement occurred.

13.3 A player who has caught or held the ball shall play it or shoot for goal within 3 seconds. To play the ball a player may:

(i) Throw it in any manner and in any direction to another player;

(ii) Bounce it with one or both hands in any direction to another player.

13.4 A player who has caught or held the ball may not:

(i) Roll the ball to another player.

(ii) Throw the ball and play it before it has been touched by another player.

(iii) Toss the ball into the air and replay it.

(iv) Drop the ball and replay it.

(v) Bounce the ball and replay it.

(vi) Replay the ball after an unsuccessful shot at goal unless it has touched some part of the goalpost.

Penalty: Free pass to the opposing team where the infringement occurred.

13.5 *Passing Distances*

13.5.1 *Short Pass*

(i) On the court: At the moment the ball is passed there must be room for a third player to move between *the hands* of the thrower and those of the receiver.

(ii) At the throw-in: At the moment the ball is passed there must be room on the Court between *the hands* of the thrower and those of the receiver for a third player to attempt an interception.

Penalty: Free pass to the opposing team where the ball is caught.

13.5.2 *Over a Third*

(i) The ball may not be thrown over a complete third without being touched or caught by a player who, at the time of touching or catching the ball, is wholly within that third or who lands in that third.

(ii) The player who lands with the first foot wholly within the correct third is judged to have received the ball in that third. The subsequent throw shall be considered to have been made from the third in which the player first landed.

(iii) The player who lands on both feet simultaneously with one foot wholly within the correct third and the other in the incorrect third shall be penalised.

Penalty: Free pass to the opposing team taken just beyond the second line that the ball has crossed, except where the ball thrown from the centre third passes out of court over the goal-line, when a throw-in shall be taken.

14. Footwork

14.1 A player may receive the ball with one foot grounded or jump to catch and land on one foot and then:

(i) Step with the other foot in any direction, lift the landing foot and throw or shoot before this foot is regrounded.

(ii) Step with the other foot in any direction any number of times, pivoting on the landing foot. The pivoting foot may be lifted but the player must throw or shoot before regrounding it.

(iii) Jump from the landing foot on to the other foot and jump again, but must throw the ball or shoot before regrounding either foot.

(iv) Step with the other foot and jump, but must throw the ball or shoot before regrounding either foot.

14.2 A player may receive the ball while both feet are grounded, or jump to catch and land on both feet simultaneously and then:

(i) Step with either foot in any direction, lift the other foot and throw or shoot before this foot is regrounded;

(ii) Step with either foot in any direction any number of times pivoting on the other. The pivoting foot may be lifted but the player must throw or shoot before regrounding it.

(iii) Jump from both feet on to either foot, but must throw or shoot before regrounding the other foot.

(iv) Step with either foot and jump but must throw the ball or shoot before regrounding either foot.

14.3 A player in possession of the ball may not:
(i) Drag or slide the landing foot.
(ii) Hop on either foot.
(iii) Jump from both feet and land on both feet unless the ball has been released before landing.
Penalty: A free pass to the opposing team where the infringement occurred.

15. Scoring a Goal

15.1 A goal is scored when the ball is thrown or batted over and completely through the ring by Goal Shooter or Goal Attack from any point within the goal circle including the lines bounding the goal circle:
(i) If another player throws the ball through the ring no goal is scored and play continues.
(ii) If a defending player deflects a shot for goal and the ball then passes over and completely through the ring a goal is scored.
(iii) Goal Shooter or Goal Attack may shoot for goal or pass if the ball is won at a toss-up in the goal circle.
(iv) If the whistle for an interval or 'time' is blown before the ball has passed completely through the ring, no goal is scored.
(v) If the whistle for an interval or 'time' is blown *after* a penalty pass or shot has been awarded in the goal circle, the penalty pass or shot shall be taken.

15.2 In taking a shot for goal a player shall:
(i) Have no contact with the ground outside the goal circle either during the catching of the ball or whilst holding it. It is not contact with the ground to lean on the ball, but if this happens behind the goal-line the ball is considered to be out of court.
(ii) Shoot within 3 seconds of catching or holding the ball;
(iii) Obey the Footwork Rule.
Penalty: A free-pass to the opposing team in the goal circle where the infringement occurred.

15.3 A defending player may not cause the goalpost to move so as to interfere with the shot at goal.
Penalty: Penalty pass or shot to the opposing team to be taken:
(i) From where the infringer was standing unless this places the non-offending team at a disadvantage.

(ii) If the infringer was out of court, on court near where the infringer was standing.

16. Obstruction

16.1 An attempt to intercept or defend the ball *may* be made by a defending player if the distance on the ground is not less than 0.9m (3ft) from a player in possession of the ball. When the ball is received, this distance is measured as follows:

(i) If the player's landing, grounded or pivoting foot remains on the ground, the distance is measured from that foot to the nearer foot of the defending player.

(ii) If the player's landing, grounded or pivoting foot is lifted, the distance is measured from the spot on the ground from which the foot was lifted, to the nearer foot of the defending player.

(iii) If the player is standing or lands on both feet simultaneously and remains grounded on both feet, the distance is measured from whichever is the nearer foot of that player to the nearer foot of the defending player;

(iv) If the player is standing or lands on both feet simultaneously and either foot is lifted, the other foot is considered to be the grounded foot from which the 0.9m (3ft) distance is measured.

16.2 From the correct distance, a defending player *may* attempt to intercept or defend the ball:

(i) By jumping towards the player with the ball, but if the landing is within 0.9m (3ft) of that player and interferes with the throwing or shooting motion, obstruction occurs.

(ii) If the player with the ball steps forward to lessen the distance of 0.9m (3ft) between them.

16.3 A player *may* be within 0.9m (3ft) of an opponent in possession of the ball providing no effort is made to defend and there is no interference with that opponent's throwing or shooting action.

16.4 From the correct distance, a defending player *may not* attempt to intercept or defend the ball by stepping towards an opponent with the ball.

16.5 *Obstruction of a player not in possession of the ball*

16.5.1 A player is obstructing if within a distance of 0.9m (3ft) (measured on the ground) from an opponent without the ball, any movements are employed by that player (whether attacking or defending) which take the arms away from the body, other than those involved in natural body balance. Within this distance a player is not obstructing if the arms are outstretched:

(i) To catch, deflect or intercept a pass or feint pass.

(ii) To obtain a rebound from an unsuccessful shot at goal.

(iii) Momentarily to signal for a pass, or to indicate the intended direction of movement.

16.6. *Obstruction by intimidation*

When a player with or without the ball intimidates an opponent it is obstruction.

Penalty for 16.1 to 16.6: Penalty pass or penalty pass or shot where the infringer is standing except where this places the non-offending team at a disadvantage, when the penalty shall be taken where the obstructed player was standing.

16.7 *Defending a player who is out of court*

16.7.1 A player may defend an opponent who has chosen to go out of court provided that the defending player does not leave the court or own playing area in order to defend.

Penalty: A penalty pass or penalty pass or shot from the point where the infringer leaves the court.

16.7.2 A player who goes out of court to collect a ball, to take a throw-in, or for any other valid reason, must be allowed back into the area of play near to the point at which the player left the court or took the throw-in. Any opponent attempting to prevent the player from re-entering the court is penalised.

Penalty: A penalty pass or penalty pass or shot on court immediately opposite the point where the infringer was standing.

16.8 *Obstruction by a player from out of court*

16.8.1 A player who is standing out of court may not attempt to defend a player who is on the court.

Penalty: A penalty pass or penalty pass or shot on the court opposite the point where the infringer was standing.

17. Contact

17.1 *Personal Contact*

17.1.1 No player shall come into personal contact with an opponent in such a manner as to interfere with the opponent's play either accidentally or deliberately.

17.1.2 In an effort to attack or defend or to play the ball a player shall not:–

(i) push an opponent in any way;

(ii) bump or rush into an opponent;

(iii) trip or knock an opponent in any way;

(iv) use any part of the body to interfere with an opponent's play;

(v) hold an opponent; this includes feeling to keep near an opponent;

(vi) charge an opponent, i.e. when jumping, bump against an opponent.

17.1.3 Whether attempting to attack or to defend, a player is responsible for any personal contact:–

(i) If taking up a position so near an opponent that contact cannot be avoided.

(ii) If moving so quickly into the path of a moving player that contact cannot be avoided.

17.1.4 A player shall not contact another on any other occasion or in any other way in such a manner as to interfere with the opponent's play.

17.2 *Contact with the ball*

17.2.1 A player, while holding the ball, shall not touch or push an opposing player with it in such a manner as to interfere with that opponent's play.

17.2.2 A player shall not, either accidentally or deliberately, place a hand or hands on, or remove from an opponent's possession, a ball held by an opposing player.

17.2.3 Where 17.2.1 and 17.2.2 occur simultaneously a toss-up is taken between those two players.

Penalty for 17.1 to 17.2.2: Penalty pass or penalty pass or shot where the infringer is standing except where this places the non-offending team at a disadvantage, when the penalty shall be taken where the contacted player was standing.

IV. CONDUCTING PENALTIES

The penalties awarded for the breaking of the Rules are:

Free Pass

Penalty Pass or Shot

Throw-in

Toss-up

18. General Rules

for the taking of penalties are:

(i) A penalty for an infringement on court is taken where the infringement occurred except:

(*a*) Where Advantage applies, i.e. the Umpire shall refrain from blowing the whistle to penalise an infringement when by so doing the non-offending team would be placed at a disadvantage.

(*b*) As provided for under Penalty for Rules 16 and 17, Obstruction and Contact.

(ii) The penalties, with the exception of the toss-up, are awarded to a team. Any member of the opposing team may take the penalty if allowed in the area where the penalty is awarded.

(iii) The player taking the penalty must throw the ball within 3 seconds after being in possession of the ball and taking up the position indicated by the Umpire.

(iv) In the taking of a Free Pass, penalty pass or shot or throw-in, the Footwork Rule applies as though the foot placed at the point indicated were equivalent to the landing foot in a one-foot landing or to receiving the ball with one foot grounded.

(v) If the player taking a Free Pass, or penalty pass or shot, infringes (iii) and (iv) above, a free pass is awarded to the opposing team.

18.1 *Free Pass*

18.1.1 A Free Pass is awarded for infringements of the Rules on the court with the exception of the Rules of Obstruction, Contact, simultaneous offences by two opposing players and interference with the goalpost.

18.1.2 When a Free Pass is awarded, the ball may be thrown by any player in the opposing team allowed in that area, but the ball may not be thrown over a complete third of the court without being touched or caught by a player who is standing or who lands within the third.

18.1.3 When a Free Pass is awarded in the goal circle to the attacking team, the player taking the penalty may not shoot for goal.

Penalty for 18.1.3: A Free Pass to the opposing team in the goal circle where the infringement occurred.

18.2 *Penalty Pass or Shot*

18.2.1 A penalty pass or a penalty pass or shot is awarded for infringement of the Rules of Obstruction and Contact.

18.2.2 A player penalised for Obstruction and Contact must stand beside and away from the thrower taking the penalty and must make no attempt to take part in the play until the ball has left the thrower's hands. If the infringer moves before the ball has left the thrower's hands the penalty shall be retaken unless the pass or shot is successful.

18.2.3 The penalty shall be taken from where the infringer was standing except where this places the non-offending team at a disadvantage, when the penalty shall be taken where the obstructed or contacted player was standing.

18.2.4 Any player allowed in the area may take the penalty.

18.2.5 (i) An attempt to intercept the penalty pass or shot may be made by any opposing player other than the offender.

(ii) If an opponent obstructs or contacts the thrower during the taking of the penalty pass or shot, a penalty pass or shot shall be awarded at the spot where the second infringer was standing unless this places the non-offending team at a disadvantage.

(iii) Both the original and second offenders must stand beside and away from the thrower taking the penalty and make no attempt to take part in the play until the ball has left the thrower's hands.

18.2.6 When two members of a team simultaneously obstruct or contact a member of the opposing team, each offender shall stand beside and away from the thrower taking the penalty. They must make no attempt to take part in the play until the ball has left the thrower's hands.

18.2.7 A Goal Shooter or Goal Attack taking a penalty pass or shot in the goal circle, may either pass or shoot for goal.

18.3 *Throw-in*

18.3.1 When the ball goes out of court, it shall be put into play by a member of the team opposing either:

(i) The player on court who last had contact with the ball.

(ii) The player who received the ball while any part of that player was touching the ground outside the court.

18.3.2 The player throwing the ball in shall:

(i) Stand outside the court and place one or both feet close to or at the point where the ball crossed the line.

(ii) Wait for the Umpire to say 'play' when all other players are on the Court.

(iii) Throw within 3 seconds of the Umpire calling 'play'.

(iv) Not enter the court until the ball has been thrown.

(v) Throw into the nearest third of the court from behind a goal-line, or the nearest or adjacent third from behind a side-line.

(vi) Throw only from behind a line bounding this player's playing area. If using the Footwork Rule the player must remain behind this area until the ball has been released.

(vii) Apply the Footwork Rule as in Section IV: Conducting Penalties – Rule 18: General Rules (iv).

Penalties for infringements occurring at the throw-in:

1. By the thrower – a throw-in is awarded to the opposing team at the spot where the infringement occurred except under (v) above when the penalty for breaking the 'over a third' Rule applies.

2. When a player obstructs or contacts during a throw-in, a penalty pass or penalty pass or shot is awarded on court.

3. If the ball fails to enter the court the penalty throw-in shall be taken by the opposing team from the original throw-in point.

4. When the ball from a throw-in goes out of court without being touched, a throw-in shall be taken by the opposing team from behind the point where the ball last went out.

5. If the ball is sent out of court simultaneously by two players in opposing teams or the Umpire cannot decide who touched the ball last, there shall be a toss-up opposite the point where the ball went out – see Rule 18.4.7(iii).

18.4 *Toss-up*

18.4.1 A toss-up puts the ball into play when:

(i) Opposing players gain simultaneous possession of the ball with either or both hands.

(ii) Opposing players simultaneously knock the ball out of court.

(iii) Opposing players are involved and the Umpire is unable to determine the last player to touch the ball before it goes out of court.

(iv) Opposing players are simultaneously off-side one in possession of or touching the ball.

(v) Opposing players make simultaneous contact which interferes with play.

(vi) After an accident the Umpire is unable to say who had the ball, or the ball was on the ground when play stopped.

18.4.2 The toss-up is taken on court between the two opposing players concerned as near as possible to the place where the incident occurred.

18.4.3 The two players shall stand facing each other and their own goal-ends with arms straight and hands to sides, but feet in any position. There shall be a distance of 0.9m (3ft) between the nearer foot of each player concerned. It is the responsibility of the Umpire to ensure that the players are standing correctly before taking the toss-up. They shall not move from that position until the whistle is blown. If one player moves too soon, a free pass is awarded to the opposing team where the infringement occurred.

18.4.4 The Umpire shall release the ball midway between the two players from just below the shoulder level of the shorter player's normal standing position. Momentarily, the Umpire shall be stationary and shall hold the ball in the palm of one hand and shall flick it vertically not more than 600mm (2ft) in the air as the whistle is blown.

18.4.5 The ball may be caught, or it may be batted in any direction except directly at the opposing player. All other players may stand or move anywhere within their playing area as long as they do not interfere with the toss-up.

18.4.6 Goal Shooter or Goal Attack may shoot for goal or pass if the ball is won at a toss-up in the goal circle.

18.4.7 When the toss-up cannot be taken where the incident occurred because of the boundaries involved, the following applies:

    (i) Where the incident involves two opposing players across a line dividing areas one of which is common to both players, the toss-up is taken between those two players in the common area.

    (ii) Where the incident involves two opposing players from adjoining playing areas across a transverse line and no area is common to both, the toss-up is taken in the centre third between any two opposing players allowed in that area.

    (iii) When two opposing players simultaneously knock the ball out of court over a line bounding an area which is not common to both, the toss-up is taken between any two opposing players allowed in that area, on court opposite the point where the ball crossed the line.

V. DISCIPLINE

19. Discipline of Players

19.1 The breaking of the Rules and/or the employment of any action not covered by the wording of the Rules, in a manner contrary to the spirit of the game, is not permitted. This includes:

(i) The breaking of rules:

    (*a*) Between the scoring of a goal and the restart of play.

    (*b*) Between a ball going out of court and the throw-in.

    (*c*) Between the awarding and taking of any penalty on court.

(ii) The deliberate delaying of play.

(iii) Dispute with the Umpire.

Penalty for 19.1(i): Immediately play restarts the Umpire shall penalise the infringement, by awarding a Free Pass, a Penalty Pass or a Penalty Pass or Shot, or Throw In as appropriate to the situation unless the non-offending team is placed at a disadvantage. In (*b*) and (*c*) above the Umpire may choose to penalise the infringement immediately it occurs.

Penalty for 19.1(ii): Free Pass unless the non-offending team is placed at a disadvantage.

Penalty for 19.1(iii): The Umpire may choose to penalise the disputing player with whatever action is considered appropriate under the Rules of the game.

19.2 Failure by a team to take the court at the end of any interval.

19.2.1 Play shall restart if the team has at least 5 players on court. In the event that the Centre is missing one player shall be moved to play in this position. The other player(s) may take the court in the position(s) left vacant after a goal has been scored or at the next interval.

19.2.2 If a team fails to take the court the Umpire shall give a 30-second warning and require that team to take the court within the specified period of time.

Penalty for 19.2.2: Free Pass to the team on court taken in the centre circle by any player allowed in the centre third. This Free Pass shall not count as a Centre Pass.

19.2.3 If the offending team fails to take the Court within a further 30 seconds of the above time the game shall be awarded to the non-offending team.

19.3 For rough or dangerous play or misconduct, in addition to awarding the appropriate penalty, an Umpire may:

(i) warn the offending player(s);

(ii) stand the offending player(s) off the court for a specified part of the game

(a) until the next goal is scored or

(b) until the next interval or

(c) for a specified period of time;

(iii) order the offending player(s) to leave the court and take no further part in the game. This action shall be taken only when the ordinary penalty is insufficient and except in extreme cases, only after a warning.

19.4 When a player is suspended that player may not be replaced. After completion of the suspension period the player may return to the game after a goal is scored or at the next interval.

19.4.1 When a Centre is suspended, that team shall move only one player to allow the play to continue and that player shall continue to play as Centre until the end of the suspension period. At the end of the suspension period both players must return to their original positions.

19.4.2 The suspended player(s) shall remain beside the score bench or in such other place as is designated before the game, until allowed to resume play by the Umpire.

20. Discipline of Others

20.1 During playing time an Umpire has the right to warn against any directing of play from off the court which is considered to assist one team unfairly. If such direction persists after a warning, the Umpire may penalise the team which it is felt may benefit.

20.2 In extreme circumstances, the Umpire may stop the game and require the exclusion of the person concerned from the area.

Reprinted by permission of the All-England Netball Association. For reasons of space, two Appendixes (dealing with Hand Signals and AENA Recommendations) have been omitted. A copy of the complete Rules of Netball, with those Appendixes, may be obtained from the Association.

THE LAWS OF

Rackets

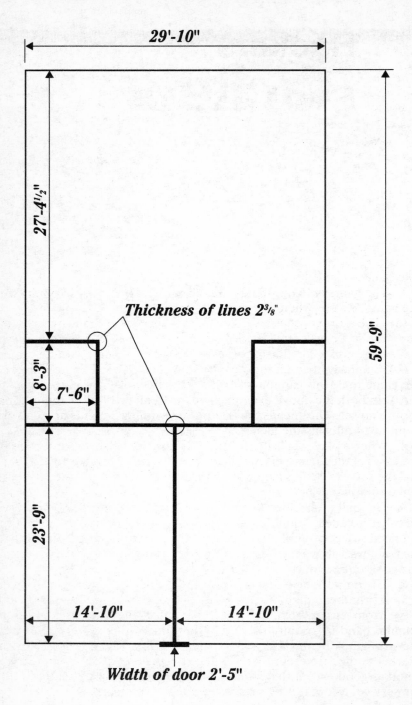

29'-10"

59'-9"

27'-4¹/₂"

Thickness of lines 2³/₈"

8'-3"

7'-6"

23'-9"

14'-10"

14'-10"

Width of door 2'-5"

Rackets

The Singles Game

1. The game is 15 up, that is, the player who first wins 15 points wins the game, except when:

(*a*) The score reaches 13-all for the first time in any game when hand-out – the receiver – may, before the next point has been started, set the game to 5, or to 3, i.e. the first player winning 5 or 3 points wins the game.

(*b*) Similarly at 14-all for the first time in any game hand-out may set the game to 3 (this cannot occur if set has been declared at 13-all).

(*c*) In both the above examples, i.e. at 13-all or 14-all, hand-out may choose no set. This means the first player winning 2 points at 13-all or 1 point at 14-all wins the game.

2. When a player fails to serve or to return the ball in accordance with the Laws of the Game, his opponent wins the rally. A rally won by hand-in – the server – scores a point. A rally won by hand-out – the receiver – makes him hand-in.

3. The ball after being served, whether the service is good or not – unless it is called a double fault by the Marker – is in play until it has bounced twice, or until after being properly returned it has failed to hit the front wall above the board, or until it has touched a player, or until it has gone out of court.

4. The right to serve first in a match is decided by the spin of a racket.

5. At the beginning of each game and of each hand the server may serve from either box, but must thereafter alternate as long as he remains hand-in, or until the end of the game. If the server serves from the wrong box by mistake and if this is not immediately noticed by the Marker and/or Referee, there shall be no penalty and the service shall count as good except that hand-out may, if he does not attempt to take the service, ask that it be served from the correct box.

6. Hand-in serves his hand-out and loses the right to serve:

(*a*) If the ball is served on to, or below, the board, or out of court, or against any part of the court before it strikes the front wall.

(*b*) If he fails to strike the ball, or strikes the ball more than once.

(*c*) If he serves two consecutive faults, i.e. a double-fault.

NB The ball is out of court when it touches the front, sides or back of the court above the area prepared for play, or when it touches, or passes over, any cross bars or other parts of the roof or electric light fittings of the court.

7. A service is a fault (except as provided by Law 6):

(*a*) If at the moment of striking the ball the server fails to have one foot at least on the floor within, and not touching, the line surrounding the service box. This is a foot fault.

(*b*) If the ball is served on to, or below, the service or cut line on the front wall.

(*c*) If the ball served first bounces on or before the short line (called short by the Marker).

(*d*) If the ball served first bounces in the wrong receiving half of the court, i.e. left of the court from the left-hand box and right from the right-hand box.

8. Hand-out may take a fault unless it has already been called a double fault by the Marker. If he attempts to do so the service becomes a valid start to the rally, fault or not.

9. A player wins a rally:

(*a*) Under Law 6.

(*b*) If his opponent fails to make a legitimate return of the ball in play.

(*c*) If the ball in play touches his opponent, or anything he wears or carries (other than his racket when in the act of striking), except:

(i) As is otherwise provided by Laws 11, 12 and 14.

(ii) In the case of a fault which hand-out does not attempt to take.

10. A return is good if the striker returns the ball above the board without it previously touching the floor, or the back wall, or any part of the striker's body or clothing, before it has bounced twice and if he does not hit the ball twice or hit it out of court. *No player may attempt to return the ball by boasting it off the back wall.*

11. If the ball, after being struck and before reaching the front wall, hits the striker's opponent, or his opponent's racket or anything he wears or carries, a let shall be allowed providing the return would have been good. If the return would not have been good the striker shall lose the rally.

NB Play shall cease even if the ball goes up.

12. Notwithstanding anything contained in these Laws, a let may be allowed, on appeal by either player, in the following circumstances:

(*a*) If the player is prevented from obtaining a fair view of the ball, or from reaching the ball, or from striking at the ball.

(*b*) If, owing to the position of the striker, his opponent is unable to avoid being touched by the ball.

(*c*) If the ball in play touches any other ball in the court.

(*d*) If the player refrains from hitting the ball owing to a reasonable fear of injuring his opponent.

(*e*) If the player in the act of striking the ball touches his opponent or his racket.

NB No let shall be allowed:

(i) In respect of any stroke which a player attempts to make, unless in making the stroke, he or his racket touches an opponent.

(ii) Unless the striker could have made a good return.

13. An appeal to the Referee may be made against any decision of the Marker provided that with regard to service the following Laws apply:

(*a*) A let shall be allowed if the receiver is not ready and does not in any way attempt to take the service.

(*b*) If the receiver attempts to take a first service no appeal may be made, but when he does not attempt to take it:

(i) If he appeals against the Marker's call of play and the Referee allows the appeal, the service becomes a fault.

(ii) If the server appeals to the Referee against a call or fault the Marker's decision is reversed, a let shall be allowed.

(*c*) When the Marker calls fault to a second service, the receiver shall not attempt to take it. If the Marker's decision is reversed on appeal by the server to the Referee, a let shall be allowed.

(*d*) When the Marker calls play and therefore deems good a second service, the receiver may appeal to the Referee even if he has taken the service. If the appeal is upheld the receiver is awarded the rally and immediately becomes the server or hand-in.

NB No appeal shall be made by the server (or receiver if he has taken that service) against foot faults called by the Marker or Referee.

14. If the player strikes at and misses a ball, he may make further attempts to return it but the following provisions shall apply:

(*a*) If the ball accidentally touches his opponent or his racket, the player shall lose the rally unless he could have made a good return in which case a let may be allowed by the Referee.

(*b*) In all other respects the Laws shall apply as if the player had not struck at the ball.

15. If in the course of play the Marker calls 'not up' or 'out of court' or 'time' or if any player appeals for a let, the rally shall cease immediately. If the Marker's call of 'not up' or 'out of court' is reversed on appeal to the Referee, a let shall be allowed.

16. If a let is allowed, the service or rally is void and the server must serve again from the same side. A let does not annul a previous fault.

17. After the first service is delivered, play shall be continuous, so far as is practical. During a game players must consult with the Referee before they leave the court except between games when one minute shall be allowed. The Referee may suspend play for bad light or unsuitable court conditions or for other reasons at his discretion. In the event of play being suspended for the day the match shall restart from the point at which it was suspended.

18. After the delivery of a service (i.e. after the start of a rally), no appeal shall be made for anything that occurred before the service was delivered except by appeal to the Referee to adjust the score if this is incorrectly called by the Marker.

19. A new ball may only be requested by the receiver, i.e. when he is hand-out but not between the first and second service or after a let has been given. The server may appeal to the Referee who may change the ball if he considers it unfit for play.

20. There must be a new ball to begin each game.

21. If the Referee is unable to decide an appeal he must allow a let to be played, except on service line or short line appeals.

22. The Referee is responsible for calling foot faults; he may also nominate one or two umpires specifically to watch for these, to help him keep the score and from which side the service is to be delivered.

23. Each player must get out of the way, after making a stroke, as much and as quickly as possible. He must do all he can to:

(a) Give his opponent a good view of the ball.

(b) Avoid interfering with him in getting to, and striking at, the ball.

(c) Leave him, as far as the striker's position allows, free to play the ball to any part of the court, i.e. directly to the front wall or side walls.

When a player fails to do any of these things, the Referee may on appeal, or without waiting for an appeal, award a let, or award the rally to his opponent, if in his opinion this is fair under the circumstances and taking into account what would have taken place had there been no such interference.

24. In the case of consistent interference by one player with another and/or in the case of negligent or dangerous play the Referee may halt play irrespective of any appeal being made and award the rally against the offending player.

25. The Referee has the power to order:

(a) A player, who has left the court, or who is wasting time during a game whilst on court, to play on immediately.

(b) A player to leave the court for any reason whatsoever and may award the match to his opponent if he feels this is appropriate.

26. There shall be a Marker and, whenever possible, a Referee for all

matches. In the absence of a Referee the Marker shall also act as Referee. The Referee shall give no decision unless an appeal is made, except for correcting an incorrect score (see Law 18) or to call a foot fault or as specifically noted in Law 24.

27. The Referee or, in his absence, the Marker has the power at his absolute discretion to award a rally to the opponent if a player, after due warning of the penalty to come, continues to:

(*a*) Dispute the Referee's decision.

(*b*) Make provocative or derogatory remarks to the Referee or Marker.

(*c*) Cause unnecessary delay between rallies (Law 25*a*) or to the resumption of play after a decision has been made by the Referee.

In the event of persistent offence by a player following a warning and the award of a rally, the Referee may award the match to the opponent. (See also Law 25*b*.)

The Four-handed or Doubles Game

1. The Laws of singles shall apply to doubles and wherever the words server, hand-out, striker, opponent or player are used in the Laws of singles, such words (wherever applicable) shall be taken to include his partner in doubles.

2. Only one of a pair shall serve in the first hand of a game.

3. The order of serving may be changed at the beginning of any game. The player who is serving when a game is won must continue to serve in the following game, but need not serve first thereafter in that game.

4. If the player, who should serve second, serves first by mistake, hand-out – either player in that pair – may object provided that he does so before a point has been scored or an attempt has been made to take the first service. If no such objection is made, the server may complete his hand and his partner shall then serve, but in subsequent hands if the error has been noted by any player on court, or by the Marker and/or the Referee, the pair must revert to their original order.

5. If in any hand a player serves again, after he has ceased to be hand-in, in other words if he serves a second time accidentally having been put out, that point shall not count provided the mistake is discovered before either of his opponents has served subsequently.

6. If a player does not serve when he should do so and one of his opponents serves instead, the player loses his right of service, unless it is claimed before he, or his partner, has attempted to take a service, or before a point has been scored.

7. In each pair one player shall receive service from the left and one player shall receive service from the right. This order of receiving service may only be changed at the start of each game but before the first rally has begun.

8. Appeals against service faults may be made by the striker receiving service as in Law 13 (Singles) and this right of appeal shall also apply to his partner when he himself is not receiving.

9. Hand-in scores a point if the player in the right-hand court returns or attempts to return a service which has been served to the left-hand court, and vice versa.

10. While the service is being delivered, the player who is receiving that service may stand where he pleases. His partner must stand behind the server, in such a position that the server has an unimpeded swing. The server's partner, at the moment of service, must stand near the back wall and in the court into which the service is not being delivered.

Note: In these Laws of singles and doubles the meanings of the following expressions are:

Court. The whole building in which the game of rackets is played; the back of the court is divided by a *half court line* into two halves, called the right (or forehand) court, and the left (or backhand) court.

Cut Line or Service Line. The line drawn on the front wall.

Half Court Line. The line on the floor, drawn from the short line to the back wall.

Hand-in. The player who serves.

Hand-out. The player who receives the service.

A Rally. The ensuing play after a serve.

To Serve. To start the ball in play by striking at it with a racket.

Service Board. The board across the lower part of the front wall.

Service Box. The small squares on each side of the court from which the service is delivered alternately.

Short Line. The line drawn across the floor parallel to the front wall.

Striker. The player whose turn it is to play and strike the ball after it has hit the front wall.

Reprinted by permission of the Tennis and Rackets Association. Copies of the complete Laws of Rackets, including Duties of the Referee, Guidance for Referees and Guidance for Markers, may be obtained from the Association.

THE LAWS OF

Real Tennis

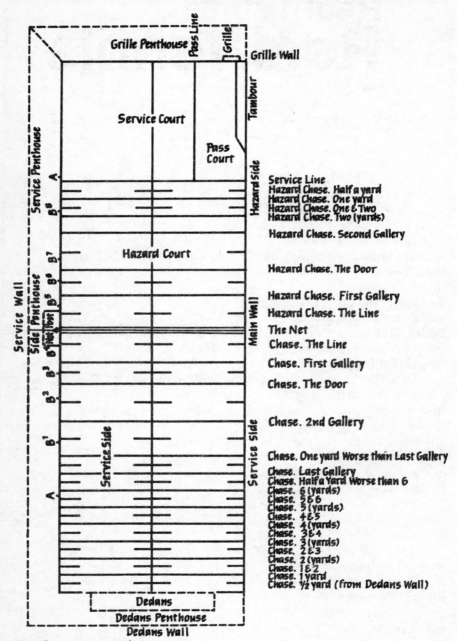

A, A Points where Galleries begin
B¹ to B⁹ Gallery Posts

Real Tennis

1. Definitions (see diagram of the court on the opposite page).
In these laws the following words have the following meanings:
Back Walls. The walls between the floor and the penthouses adjoining the main wall.
Bandeau. The strip of wall immediately below a penthouse, usually made of the same material as the penthouse.
Better. One chase is better than another if it is made on the same side of the court and further from the net (Law 8). In marking chases, better means that the ball makes a chase:
   (*a*) Further from the net than the line mentioned; and
   (*b*) Nearer to that line than to any other yard or gallery line (Law 8*b*).
Bisque. One stroke in a set conceded to an opponent (Law 22).
Chase. A chase is made whenever the ball falls in the hazard court, or anywhere on the service side, or enters a gallery, except the winning gallery (Law 8).
. . . *attacking a chase* – When a chase is being played for, the opponent of the player who made the chase is said to be attacking the chase (Laws 10 and 11).
. . . *calling a chase* – The marker calls a chase when he states the chase that is to be played for.
. . . *defending a chase* – When a chase is being played for, the player who made the chase is said to be defending the chase (Laws 10 and 11).
. . . *chase lines* – The lines marked on the floor to enable the marker to mark chases are called chase lines or chases (Law 7).
. . . *marking a chase* – The marker marks a chase when that chase is made.
. . . *chase off* – See Law 11(*b*).
. . . *chase the line* – See Line, Chase the.

Court. The enclosure in which the game is played. The court is divided into two sides, the service side and the hazard side (q.v.).

Dead. A ball is said to be dead when it ceases to be in play.

Dedans. The opening at the back of the service side.

Double. If the ball falls before it is struck it is a double.

Double Hit. A double hit shall not be called if the player has made one continuous stroke at the ball unless:

(*a*) During the course of such a stroke the ball has struck another surface of the court between one contact with the racket and another; or

(*b*) The ball remains in contact with the racket for so long a time as to constitute a throw.

Drop. A ball is said to drop when, after passing the net, it first touches the floor, or enters an opening, without having previously touched the floor.

Fall. A ball is said to fall when, after having dropped, it touches the floor again, or enters an opening.

Fault Line. The line on the floor nearest the grille and extending from the service line to the grille wall.

Gallery. An opening below the penthouse opposite to the main wall.

The starting galleries are named as follows, starting from the net:

(*a*) On the service side, the line, the first gallery, the door, the second gallery, the last gallery;

(*b*) On the hazard side, the line, the first gallery, the door, the second gallery, the winning gallery.

Gallery Post. The post between two galleries is considered to be part of the gallery nearer the net.

The part of the gallery net that surrounds a gallery post is part of that post.

Good Return. See Return.

Grille. The opening in the grille wall.

Grille Wall. The back wall on the hazard side.

Half-Court Line. The line that bisects the floor, between the main wall and the side wall.

Hazard Chase or Hazard Side Chase. A chase made on the hazard side of the court.

Hazard Court. The part of the floor of the court on the hazard side that lies between the net, the side wall, the main wall and the service line (but excluding that line).

Hazard Side. The side of the court on the left of the net when facing the main wall.

In Play. A ball served is in play until:

(*a*) The service becomes a fault; or

(*b*) Either player fails to make a good return.

Ledge. The horizontal surface of a wall that forms an opening.

Line, Chase the, is the chase at the line of the net. On the floor it is the area between the net and the first line. The line gallery is that between the net post and the post next to it.

Main Wall. The wall that has no penthouse.

Net Post. The post supporting the net under the penthouse.

Nick. The junction of the wall and the floor, or a return when the ball, as it drops or falls, touches the wall and the floor simultaneously.

Opening. Any gallery or winning opening.

Opening, Entering an. A ball enters an opening when a good return or service:

(*a*) Touches the post (see Gallery Post), net, or tray of that opening; or

(*b*) Touches anything lying in that opening (if an article is lying in an opening any part of it, even outside, is considered to be in that opening); or

(*c*) Comes to rest in or on the ledge of that opening; or

(*d*) In the case of the grille, touches the woodwork at the back of the framing of the grille.

Out of Court. A ball is out of court if it touches any part of:

(*a*) The walls above the area prepared for play; or

(*b*) The roof or roof beams or girders (in some courts a ball is out of court if it passes over a beam or girder); or

(*c*) The lighting equipment.

Passing the Net. The ball passes the net when it crosses it between the net post and the main wall, or when it crosses the line bisecting the side penthouse.

Rest. A stroke or series of strokes, commencing when the ball is served and terminating when the ball is dead.

Return, or Return of the Ball in Play. The return of the ball is good if:

(*a*) It is struck before it falls; and

(*b*) It is struck so that it passes the net without having previously touched the floor or anything lying on the floor, or the net post, or without having entered an opening; and

(*c*) It has not touched the player or anything he wears or carries except his racket in the act of striking the ball; and

(*d*) It does not go out of court; and

(*e*) It is struck definitely and is not a double hit; and

(*f*) It is not on the side of the net opposed to the player when he strikes it; and

(*g*) In courts where there is a wing net between the net post and the net, it does not touch the wing net before crossing the net.

Except that such a return is not good if:

(*h*) The player touches the net before striking the ball; or (*i*) The player touches the net after the ball and before the ball is dead; or

(*j*) The ball, after passing the net, comes back and drops on the side from which it was played. (Even if it touches the net before so dropping, the return is not good.)

Service. The method of starting a rest.

Service Court. The part of the floor on the hazard side that lies between the side wall, the grille wall, the fault line and the service line (including those two lines).

Service Line or Winning Gallery Line. The line which is nearest and parallel to the grille wall.

Service Penthouse. That part of the side penthouse which is on the hazard side of the court including the line that bisects the side penthouse.

Service Side. The side of the court on the right of the net when facing the main wall.

Service Wall. The wall above the side penthouse.

Side Penthouse. The penthouse above the galleries, up to its junction with the other penthouses.

Side Wall. The wall below the side penthouse.

Striker. The player who last struck the ball.

Striker-out. The player who is to take the service.

Tray. The inner part of the bottom of an opening behind the ledge, usually made of wood.

Uneven Odds. When points given and/or received are not the same in each game, and/or when one or more bisques or half-bisques are given.

Winning Gallery. The last gallery on the hazard side.

Winning Openings. The dedans, the grille, and the winning gallery.

Worse. One chase is worse than another if it is made on the same side of the court and nearer to the net (Law 8).

In marking chases, worse means that the ball makes a chase:

(*a*) Nearer to the net than the line mentioned; and

(*b*) Nearer to that line than to any other yard or gallery line (Law 8*b*).

2. Net

The height of the net above the level of the floor shall be:

(*a*) At the centre, 3ft; and

(*b*) At the main wall and below and edge of the penthouse, 5ft.

3. Balls

The balls shall be not less than $2\frac{7}{16}$in and not more than $2\frac{9}{16}$in in diameter. They shall not be less than $2\frac{1}{2}$oz and not more than $2\frac{3}{4}$oz in weight.

4. Rackets

Racket frames must be made of wood and designed for tennis unless, exceptionally, the Association approves another specification.

5. Sides

(*a*) The choice of sides at the beginning of a match is decided by spin of a racket.

(*b*) Subsequently the players change sides only when two chases have been scored or when one player is at 40 or advantage and one chase has been scored.

(*c*) If the players change sides before they should have done so, or do not change sides when they should, any strokes so played on the wrong side shall be scored and play shall continue as if no mistake had been made; except that any chase scored (Law 9) in excess of the proper number shall be annulled if the mistake is discovered before that chase has been played for (Law 10).

6. Service

The service is always given by the player who is on the service side.

A service is good if it is not a fault.

A service is a fault:

(*a*) If the server, while serving, does not stand on the floor further from the net than the second gallery line; or

(*b*) If the server misses the ball or does not definitely strike it or strikes it more than once; or

(*c*) If the ball served, before touching the side penthouse, touches any part of the court except the service wall (if the ball touches the edge of the penthouse before touching anything else it is a fault); or

(*d*) If the ball served leaves the penthouse or service wall without touching the service penthouse (if the ball, after striking the service wall or side penthouse, in dropping touches the edge of the service penthouse it is a good service); or

(*e*) If the ball served goes out of court; or

(*f*) If the ball served strikes the main wall before dropping; or

(*g*) If the ball served drops anywhere except in the service court or in the winning gallery.

A service that has become a fault may not be returned, but one that would otherwise become a fault may be volleyed provided that if the striker-out volleys a service before the ball has touched some part of the court he loses that point.

If the striker-out is not ready for a service and does not attempt to take it, a let (Law 16) shall be allowed.

7. Chase Lines, How Marked

Chase lines are marked on the floor as follows: See diagram on page 746:

Service Side:
  Half-a-yard,
  One yard,
  One and two,
and so on up to six, then:
  Half-a-yard worse than six,
  The last gallery,
  Half-a-yard worse than the last gallery,
  A yard worse than the last gallery,
  The second gallery,
  The door, and
  The first gallery.

Hazard Side: The same as on the service side, except that all chases between two and the second gallery are omitted and the last or winning gallery line is called the service line.

8. Chases, How Made

(*a*) When the ball enters a gallery (except the winning gallery) or falls on the floor (unless it falls on or further from the net than the service line) it makes a chase at the gallery it enters or at the line on which it falls.

(*b*) When it falls between two lines it makes a chase better or worse than the yard line or the gallery line nearest to the spot where it fell, except that:

(1) It makes chase better than half a yard when it so falls; and

(2) When it falls better or worse than the line 'a yard worse than the last gallery' the chase is called 'nearly a yard worse than the last gallery' or 'more than a yard worse than the last gallery'; and

(3) When it falls nearer to the net than the first gallery line it makes chase the line; and

(4) When it drops or falls in the net on the side opposed to the striker or drops on the side opposed to the striker and then falls on the side from which it was struck, it makes chase the line on the side opposed to the striker; and

(5) When it drops or falls on any item which is not an integral part of the court or a part of the player's clothing or equipment (though in the latter event a stroke is scored), it makes a chase as if it had fallen where that other item was lying.

9. Chase, How and When Scored

(*a*) When no chase is being played for, a chase is scored when made in accordance with Law 8.

(*b*) When a chase is scored, the score in strokes is unaltered.

10. Chases, When Played For

When two chases have been scored, or when one player is at 40 or advantage and one chase has been scored, the players change sides and the chase or chases in the order in which they were made are immediately played for.

A chase is played for once only, unless there is a let (Law 16).

11. Chases, How Won or Lost

When a chase is being played for:

(*a*) The player attacking the chase loses it if:

(1) He serves two consecutive faults; or

(2) He does not make a good return; or

(3) He makes a chase worse than the one being played for;

(*b*) It is a chase off when the player attacking the chase makes a chase equal to the one being played for (when it is chase off the chase is annulled and the score is unaltered);

(*c*) The player attacking the chase wins it if:

(1) His opponent serves two consecutive faults; or

(2) His opponent does not make a good return (unless the player attacking the chase makes a chase worse than or equal to the one being played for), in which case paragraph (*a*) or (*b*) of this rule applies; or

(3) He makes a chase better than the one being played for.

12. Errors Regarding Chases

(*a*) If the chase to be played for is wrongly called by the marker, the server may appeal before delivering the service, and the striker-out before attempting to take it. If there is no such appeal, the chase played for shall be that called by the marker immediately before the service is delivered, notwithstanding that this may be different from that marked when the chase was scored.

(*b*) If there has been any misunderstanding as to what chase the marker called, the rest as played shall stand or a let (Law 16) may be allowed, whichever the marker considers equitable in view of all the circumstances.

(*c*) If, through any mistake, at the end of the game there is a chase that has been scored and not played for, that chase is annulled.

(*d*) If the players change sides when too few or too many chases have been made, see Law 5(*c*).

13. Strokes, How Won

A player wins a stroke:

(*a*) If he wins a chase (Law 11*c*); or

(*b*) If his opponent loses a chase (Law 11*a*); or

(c) If a return or a good service played by him enters a winning opening, or falls on the service line or between the service line and grille wall; or

(d) If when no chase is being played for and provided that no chase is made his opponent does not make a good return; or

(e) If his opponent serves two consecutive faults (Law 6).

14. Strokes and Games, How Scored

In each game, when either player wins his first stroke his score is called 15; when he wins his second stroke, 30; when he wins his third stroke, 40; and when he wins his fourth stroke, he wins the game, except as below.

(a) When both players have won three strokes, the score is called deuce, and it is called advantage to the player who then wins the next stroke.

(b) If the player who is at advantage wins the next stroke, he wins the game; if he loses it, the score is again called deuce, and so on until the player who is at advantage wins a stroke and the game.

15. Sets, How Won

The player who first wins 6 games in a set wins it unless, extraordinarily, a different number of games is stipulated.

16. Let

In the case of a let:

(a) The rest to which it refers counts for nothing; and

(b) If a chase was being played for, it is then played for again; and

(c) If there was a previous fault, it is not annulled.

17. Continuous Play

(a) After the first service has been delivered, play shall be continuous and, having regard to all the circumstances, reasonably expeditious unless the referee (or, if none, the marker) decides otherwise.

(b) No player may leave the court without the express permission of the referee (or, if none, the marker) and then only for a good reason and for the shortest possible time.

(c) The referee (or, if none, the marker) has the power:

(i) To order any player who has left the court, with or without permission under (b) above, to return and play on; and

(ii) To order any player to leave the court or (as the case may be) to remain off the court; and

(iii) To order any player to resume or to expedite play; and

(iv) To give warnings and to award the match, as he, in his absolute discretion taking account of all the circumstances, thinks fit, to any player, and in the case of such an award, whether or not he has previously given a warning to the player in question.

18. Referee
A referee shall be appointed, if possible, before the start of a match if requested by the event organisers, the marker or a player. If the match has commenced without a referee, one may still be appointed at the request of the event organisers or the marker.

If so requested the referee shall:

(*a*) Call faults on the penthouse;

(*b*) Keep a written record of the score;

(*c*) Watch for cases in case the marker is unsighted and asks for the referee's opinion; and

(*d*) Correct errors in the calling of the score and of previously scored chases.

The referee shall also:

(*a*) Ensure that spectators in the dedans do not disturb the players;

(*b*) Be well versed in the *Laws of Tennis*;

(*c*) Ensure that Law 17 is complied with; and

(*d*) Be responsible for the conduct of the match. If, in his opinion, the behaviour of a player is thwarting his opponent(s) unfairly, or is bringing the game of tennis into disrepute, he shall warn the offending player that further offensive behaviour would result in forfeiture of the match. Should that player continue to offend, the referee shall award the match to his opponent(s) forthwith.

19. Marker
Save for the provisions of Laws 17 and 18 the marker has overall control of the match and his decisions are final. Although players are not allowed to appeal, either to the marker or the referee, on marking decisions, they may check the accuracy of the score and the calling of a previously scored chase. In the absence of a referee the marker shall assume all the duties and responsibilities of the referee.

20. Three- or Four-handed Games (also called Doubles)
(*a*) Before commencing each set the players on the service side select the partner who is to serve. He is then the server and striker-out for his side throughout the game, and for alternate games throughout the set, his partner serving and striking-out in the other games. Similarly the players on the hazard side then decide who is to be striker-out and server.

(*b*) A return of service is not good if made by striker-out's partner, unless the ball served has dropped in the service court between the half-court line and the fault line or on either of those two lines.

(*c*) Apart from the above, the Laws of Singles apply to Doubles and a player and his partner are in all cases subject to the same laws as a player in Singles.

(*d*) If the wrong player serves, whether or not the correct player returns the service, the marker shall call a let, but if the error goes unnoticed, all completed sets shall stand as if correctly scored.

HANDICAPS

21. Half Odds
When half odds handicaps are played, the position taken in the first game of each set is always that most favourable to the player conceding the handicap. If a handicap involves half odds received and owed, full odds when received will alternate with, rather than coincide with, full odds owed and vice versa (e.g. receive ½15 owe ½30 is played love owe 30 in the first game, receive 15 owe 15 in the second and so on).

22. Bisque
The player receiving the bisque may take it to win one stroke in each set at any time subject to the following:
(*a*) He may not take it during a rest; and
(*b*) If server, he may not take it after serving one fault; and
(*c*) If he takes it to win or to defend a chase, he may not do so before the time comes to change sides. Then, if there is only one chase, he may take it and need not change sides, or he may take it after changing sides but, after he has passed the net, he may not go back again.

If there are two chases the player must change sides before he takes it to win or to defend either of them.

23. Half-bisque
The player receiving a half-bisque may take it:
(*a*) To call chase off and so annul a chase about to be played for; or
(*b*) To annul a fault served by him; or
(*c*) To add a second fault to one served by his opponent; or
(*d*) The handicapper may give a half-bisque as being one bisque in alternate sets, in which case the bisque must be taken in the odds set.

Apart from (*b*) the conditions regarding taking a bisque (Law 22) apply equally to a half-bisque.

24. Cramped Odds
Unless specifically stated, the limiting conditions of cramped odds do not apply to service. Cramped odds may be such as are fixed by the handicapper but the more usual forms are as follows:

(*a*) *Bar the Openings*. The giver of the odds loses a stroke whenever a ball returned by him enters an opening.

(*b*) *Bar the Winning Openings*. The giver of the odds loses a stroke whenever a ball returned by him enters the dedans, the grille, or the winning gallery.

(*c*) *Chase*. When a player gives a specified chase this applies only to a chase on the service side. Any chase made by the giver of the odds worse than the one specified loses him a stroke. Any chase made by the receiver of the odds worse than the one specified is considered equal to the one specified.

(*d*) *Half-court*. The players shall agree or the handicapper decide to which half-court, on each side of the net, the giver of the odds shall play. He loses a stroke if a ball returned by him drops in the other half-court or in an opening or in half the dedans in the other half-court.

A ball that drops on the half-court line does not lose him a stroke.

After the ball has dropped the ordinary rules apply.

(*e*) *Round Services*. The striker-out may refuse to take any service that does not touch the grille penthouse. If he attempts to take such a service that service becomes good, if not otherwise a fault.

(*f*) *Touch No Side Walls*. The giver of the odds loses a stroke if the ball in play returned by him touches the side wall, the service wall, or the main wall, or enters a gallery.

(*g*) *Touch No Walls*. The giver of the odds loses a stroke whenever a ball in play returned by him touches any wall, or enters an opening.

A ball that falls a nick is not considered to have touched the wall.

A penthouse is not a wall.

A bandeau is part of a wall.

The above odds are also given in the form that the ball must drop before touching a wall, etc., but after dropping it may touch them without penalty. In this form it is usually called 'Touch no walls full pitch'.

25. Warm Up
In matches sanctioned by the Association, the players shall be permitted a warm-up period ending 5 minutes following:
(i) The scheduled start of play; or, if later,
(ii) The arrival of the last player on court.

DIRECTIONS TO THE MARKER
It is the duty of the marker:
To see that the net is at the correct height and that it remains correct.

To call faults.

To call the strokes when won or when asked to do so.

To mark the chases when scored.

To direct the players to change sides.

To call the chase or chases as the players change sides and to call each chase before it is played for, but not otherwise to repeat the chases.

To remove balls lying on the floor.

To keep the ball troughs replenished.

GLOSSARY OF TENNIS TERMS

(*See also the definitions contained in Law 1*)

Advantage. See Law 14.

All the Walls, also called Touch no Walls, see Law 24(*g*).

Attack. See Law 1: Chase, attacking a—.

Back Wall. See Law 1.

Bandeau. See Law 1.

Bar the Opening. See Law 24(*a*).

Bar the Winning Openings. See Law 24(*b*).

Batteries. The portions of wall between the openings and the floor.

Better. See Laws 1 and 8.

Bisque. See Laws 1 and 22.

Boast. A return that is struck against a wall on the same side of the net as the striker (presumably derived from *Bosse*).

Boasted Force. A boast that drops in a winning opening. The term is usually employed only for a force to the dedans.

Bobble Service. A slow service that bounces frequently on the service penthouse and that should drop near the grille wall.

Boomerang Service. A service that touches the service penthouse, the grille penthouse, the high back wall and then returns to the service penthouse before dropping close to and moving parallel with the grille wall.

Chase. See Law 1.

Coup de Brèche. A straight force that drops in the dedans near to one of its outer edges.

Coup de Cabasse. A return that drops in the dedans after first striking the wall between the last gallery and the dedans wall (called after a French professional of that name who played this difficult stroke).

Coups de Chandelle. A lofted return that drops or (more usually) falls in the dedans.

Coup d'Orléans. A return that is struck against the service wall and drops in the dedans direct (called after Philippe Egalité, Duc d'Orléans, who invented or practised this stroke).

Coup de Temps. The stroke usually attempted off the back wall when the ball is too near to the wall and floor for an ordinary return to be made. The stroke is commenced before the ball reaches the wall so that immediately it leaves it the stroke can be completed with the minimum amount of further movement and acceleration of the racket.

Court. See Law 1.

Cramped Odds. Handicaps that prohibit certain strokes or services. See Law 24.

Dead. See Law 1.

Dedans. See Law 1.

Defend. See Law 1: Chase, defending a—.

Deuce. See Law 14.

Door. See Laws 1 (Gallery) and 7.

Double. See Law 1.

Doubles. See Law 20.

Drop. See Law 1.

Drop Service. A high service, delivered from near the main wall, that should drop near to the grille wall.

Du Tout. The score of a player who requires one stroke to win the set. See Law 14 (Game-ball).

Enter a Gallery or an Opening. See Law 1.

Fall. See Law 1.

Fault. See Law 6.

Fifteen. See Law 14.

First Gallery. See Laws 1 (Gallery) and 7.

First Stroke. The return of the service.

Fly Net. Rarely used in modern courts. In some old courts there was a fly net high up in each of the four corners. A ball striking the fly net was not out of court.

Force. A stroke that drops into an opening, usually a winning opening. The term is not used for a slow lofted return.

Forty. See Law 15. Originally this score was 45, but was subsequently called 40 for the sake of brevity.

Four-handed Game. See Law 20.

Gallery. See Law 1.

Gallery Lines. Chase lines that correspond to galleries (see Laws 7 and 8*a*).

Gallery Net. The net attached to a gallery post to separate a gallery from the one next to it.

Gallery Post. See Law 1.

Game. See Law 14.

Giraffe Service. A high underhand service delivered from near the side penthouse. (After dropping on the service penthouse the ball should drop on the floor near to the fault line and to the grille wall.)

Good Return. See Law 1 (Return).
Good Service. See Law 6.
Grille. See Law 1.
Grille Penthouse. The penthouse above the grille wall.
Grille Wall. See Law 1.
Half a yard. See Law 7.
Half-bisque. See Law 23.
Half-Court. See Law 1.
Half Odds. See Law 21.
Hazard Chase. See Law 1.
Hazard Court. See Law 1.
Hazard Side. See Law 1.
Joues. The inner vertical walls of the dedans, grille, winning gallery and last gallery. A ball in touching a joue is not thereby deemed to have entered an opening (see Law 1).
Last Gallery. See Laws 1 (Gallery) and 7.
Ledge. See Law 1.
Let. See Law 16.
Line. The cord that supports the net.
Line, Chase the. See Law 1.
Love. The score of a player who has not yet won a stroke in the game or a game in the set in question.
Love Game. A game won by a player in which his opponent does not score a stroke.
Love Set. A set won by a player in which his opponent does not score a game.
Lune. A winning opening that was found in some old courts. There was no standard size, shape or position for lunes, but they were usually placed above the dedans and grille penthouses.
Net Post. See Law 1.
Nick. See Law 1.
Odds. Any form of handicap is called odds. See Laws 21 and 24.
Opening. Entering an. See Law 1.
Out of Court. See Law 1.
Passing the Net. See Law 1.
Penthouse. The sloping roof of the dedans, galleries and grille, extending along three sides of the court.
Piqué Service. The server stands near to the main wall and to the second gallery line. He serves overhead on to the service penthouse and as near as possible to the service line. After striking the service wall the ball should drop near to the grille wall and the fault line.
Play Line. The line painted on the walls to mark the upper limits of the area prepared for play (see Law 1, Out of Court).
Post. See Net Post and Gallery Post, Law 1.

Railroad Service. An overhead service usually delivered by the server standing near the side wall between the last gallery and the dedans wall. (The ball may touch the penthouse once or more times. On leaving the penthouse the ball, unless volleyed, should strike the grille wall with a twist on it that brings it back towards the side wall. A less common form of railroad service has the opposite twist on the ball so that it tends to go in the direction of the tambour after dropping.)

Referee. See Law 18.

Rest. See Law 1.

Rough. The side of the racket on which the knots are.

Second Gallery. See Laws 1 (Gallery) and 7.

Service. See Law 1.

Service Court. See Law 1.

Service Line. See Law 1.

Service Penthouse. See Law 1.

Service Side. See Law 1.

Service Wall. See Law 1.

Set. See Law 15. A match is won by the player who first wins an agreed number of sets. Each set is a separate unit and no game won in one set has any effect on another set. The method of scoring by sets appears to have been adopted in the 16th century. Prior to that, games only were scored. At first, 2 games won a set. At later periods, 3, 4, 6 and 8 game sets were usual.

Side Penthouse. See Law 1.

Side Wall. See Law 1.

Side Wall Service. Delivered from near the side penthouse. The ball usually touches the service wall before the service penthouse but need not do so. The twist on it should be such that it remains near to the grille wall after dropping.

Smooth. The side of the racket on which there are no knots.

Striker. See Law 1.

Striker-Out. See Law 1.

Stroke. See Laws 13 and 14.

Tambour. The projection on the main wall near the grille. The whole of the projection should be called the tambour though the term is commonly applied only to that part of it that is at an angle to the main wall.

Thirty. See Law 14.

Three-handed Game. See Law 20.

Touch No Walls. See Law 24(*g*).

Touch No Side Walls. See Law 24(*f*).

Twist Service. An underhand service delivered from near the side penthouse. The ball does not usually touch the service wall. The twist on it should be that, after striking the grille wall, it comes back towards the side wall.

Tray. See Law 1.
Uneven Odds. See Law 1.
Wing Net. A net put up in some courts for the protection of the marker in front of the net or post and attached to the underside of the service penthouse.
Winning Gallery. See Law 1.
Winning Openings. See Law 1.
Worse. See Law 1.
Yard. See Law 7.

Reprinted by permission of the Tennis and Rackets Association. Copies of the complete Laws of Tennis may be obtained from the Association.

THE RULES OF

Rounders

Ph/C

Rounders

1. THE PITCH

(A) Batting Square
The batting area shall be 2m square. The front line shall be parallel with and 7.5m away from the front line of the bowling square. All lines shall be considered as part of the square. There shall be a solid line extending from the front right hand corner of the batting square to the position of 1st post.

(B) Forward and Backward Areas
 (i) The front line of the batting square shall be extended in both directions by solid lines measuring at least 12m in length.
 (ii) This line and the area in front of it, and the imaginary continuation of it, shall be called the forward area.
(iii) The area behind this line and the imaginary continuation of it shall be called the backward area.
(iv) At least 10m behind the backward/forward area line, and 15m either side of the front right hand corner of the batting square, lines shall be drawn to mark the positions for waiting batters and batters out.
 (v) There shall be a 2m line from 4th post, extending into the backward area, at right angles to the forward/backward line.

(C) Bowling Square
The bowling area shall be 2.5m square. All lines shall be considered a part of the square.

(D) The Running Track
The running track shall be the area used by the batter when running, as

shown in the diagram on page 767 and will extend 2m beyond 4th post. The 2m line at 4th post shall be deemed part of the running track.

2. EQUIPMENT
All equipment should be manufactured for the purpose, and approved by the National Rounders Association.

(A) Bats
The bat shall be round and shall not measure more than 17cm round the thickest part, nor more than 46cm in length.

Wooden   – When spliced, the joint and any binding should be tight, firm and secure. The surface of the bat should be kept smooth and free from splinters and dirt.

Aluminium – Rubber caps and handles should be well fitted and not allowed to become loose.
Rubber grips or binding made for the purpose are recommended for all bats.

(B) Balls
The ball shall be leather, as approved by the N.R.A. It shall weigh a minimum of 70gm and a maximum of 85gm, it shall measure a minimum of 17cm and a maximum of 19cm in circumference. Only N.R.A. 'white' licensed balls shall be used in matches.

All stitching should be flush to the outer covering. There shall be no raised seams. Stitching should be uniform, tight and unfrayed. The outer covering should be free from tears and projections. The ball shall be kept clean and free from dirt. Whenever possible the ball shall be kept white.

(C) Posts
Each of the four posts shall be vertical and 1.2m above the ground. The four posts shall be supported in a base, and not fixed in the ground.

Posts should not shatter, splinter or break in a manner that could cause injury. All posts shall be cylindrical in shape. Wooden posts of less than 90mm in circumference should be sheathed in plastic. Flexible plastic posts should be avoided due to whiplash effect. Lightweight alloy posts are the only metal types allowed (no steel or iron). Posts that are tapered to fit the base shall not be tapered to less than 20mm diameter.

(D) Bases
Any corners of the base shall be to a minimum radius of 30mm. There shall be no sharp projections, points or surfaces. The collar of the base (where applicable) in which the post is fitted should be no higher than

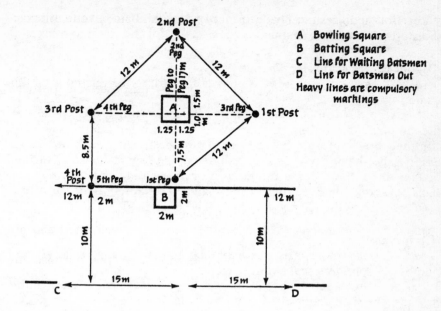

Heavy lines are compulsory markings

50mm. The base should be sufficiently weighted to be capable of supporting its post during inclement weather conditions.

The circumference and weight of the base should be sufficient to ensure that the post will remain static, or will return to its upstand position in inclement weather or if knocked. A minimum swing of ½m before returning to its correct position is recommended.

(E) Clothing

(*a*) Spiked footwear is prohibited.

N.B. Studs are allowed providing they measure more than 30mm in circumference at the base and are no longer than 12mm in length.

(*b*) All players, substitutes included, shall be clearly numbered. The numbers shall be clearly visible to the umpires at all times.

3. THE GAME

(A) Teams

(*a*) The games shall be played between two teams. A team shall consist of any number of players to a maximum of 15 and a minimum of 6, of whom no more than 9 may be on the field at any one time. In mixed sex matches a maximum of 5 male players must be observed at all times.

(*b*) Both umpires must be informed of a team's batting order prior to the start of its batting innings.

(B) Substitutes & Bowler Change

(*a*) Players, once substituted, may not return to the team during the game.

(*b*) A bowler can be changed only after delivering a good ball or at the umpire's discretion. In the event of a bowler being unable to continue bowling after being injured, or after being sent off by an umpire after having bowled a no-ball, the umpire shall allow a substitute bowler to continue, upon the request of the fielding captain. Any no-balls bowled by the previous bowler shall be accredited to the substitute bowler. During the change the ball shall be deemed dead.

(C) Innings

(*a*) A match shall consist of two innings and the team with the greater number of rounders shall win the game.

(*b*) A team leading by five or more rounders at the completion of the first innings shall require the team with the lower score to bat again. Should the team with the lower first innings score be unable to equal or better its opponents' score then the game shall be deemed to have finished at the conclusion of the third batting innings.

(*c*) The captain shall toss a coin for the choice of innings.

(*d*) The batter's umpire shall call by name or number the next player to bat. If a player receives a delivery before being called, a void ball will be declared.

Penalty: As for Batter Out (see Rule 4*c*(vi)).

(*e*) An innings shall start at the time the first ball is bowled, after the bowler's umpire has called 'play', and terminate when all the batters shall be declared out.

(*f*) A player put out in an innings shall not take the place of a missing batter.

4. BATTING

(A) A Batter

(*a*) whilst waiting for his/her turn to bat shall be in the backward area, well away from 4th post and batting square. His/her required position is shown on the diagram on page 767.

(*b*) shall stand with both feet within the batting square and shall not cross the front or back line of the square during hitting, or in the course of attempting to hit a good ball or until the ball has passed him/her.

N.B. This does not prevent a batter from leaving the batting square whilst the fielding side adjusts its fielding position, or during a break in play.

(c) shall have only one good ball bowled to him/her and shall also be deemed to have hit the ball if he/she strikes the ball with the bat or the hand holding the bat.

(d) must run to first post after having hit, attempted to hit, or let pass the first good ball delivered by the bowler.

(e) who hits a ball so that it pitches in the backward area shall have made a backward hit (this does not refer to balls that drop in the forward area and afterwards go behind).

(f) may, at his own discretion, take a no-ball and score in the usual way; he/she shall have been considered to have taken the ball if he/she has come within reach of, made contact with or passed first post.

(g) shall be entitled, if he/she is the only batter left in on entering the square:–

(i) to have the option of 3 good balls but shall forfeit the right to any remaining balls if he/she is caught or takes the ball. (He/she shall be considered to have taken the ball if he/she has come within reach of, made contact with or passed 1st post). He/she can then be put out in any of the usual ways or when the ball has been thrown full pitch or placed in the batting square.

(ii) to a rest of one minute after each rounder he/she may score.

(B) Obstruction – Batting Side

(a) While waiting to bat or after being given out, shall stand behind the marked line in the backward area out of the way of the backstop and 4th post fielders. (The required position is shown on the diagram on page 767.)

Penalty: The umpire shall award half a rounder to the fielding side in the event of obstruction.

(b) A batter shall be considered to have obstructed if he/she:

(i) impedes the player who is fielding the ball by deviating from the running track;

(ii) intentionally deflects the course of the ball;

(iii) verbally misleads the other team.

Penalty: The umpire shall declare the batter out and any rounder scored due to that obstruction shall be declared void.

(c) Whilst running round the track within the rules, a batter shall have right of way.

(d) A non-striking batter causing an obstruction and a rounder being scored by the striking batter on this ball, the rounder would be declared void, but the striking batsman would remain in.

(The obstructing batter would be declared out.)

(C) Batter Out

(*a*) A batter shall be declared out:

(i) if the ball be caught from bat or hand holding the bat except on a no-ball

(ii) if his/her foot projects over the front or back line of the batting square before he/she has hit the ball or it has passed him/her, except on a no-ball.

(iii) if he/she runs to the inside of a post, unless prevented from reaching it by an obstructing fielder.

(iv) if a fielder touches the post immediately ahead with the ball or the hand holding the ball while the batter is running to that post and before the batter has touched the post, except first post in the case of a no-ball.

N.B. IF ANY POST AND/OR BASE(S) SHOULD BE MOVED EITHER ACCIDENTALLY OR DELIBERATELY FROM THE CORRECT POSITION(S):

(*a*) IF THE BASE IS STILL IN THE CORRECT POSITION THEN CONTACT SHOULD BE MADE WITH THE BASE.

(*b*) IF BOTH THE POST AND THE BASE ARE MOVED OUT OF POSITION THEN CONTACT SHOULD BE MADE WITH THE GROUND MARKING INDICATING THE CORRECT POSITION OF THE POST(S).

(v) if he/she obstructs a fielder or intentionally deflects the course of the ball.

See Obstruction – Batting Side.

(vi) if he/she overtakes another batter.

(vii) if he/she loses contact or runs at any time when the bowler has the ball and is in his/her square (except an overrun or unless ordered to do so by an umpire.

(viii) during the bowler's action but before he/she releases the ball.

(ix) if after having been ordered to make contact with a post a batter has not done so.

(x) if he/she drops or throws his/her bat deliberately.

(D) Side Out

Where there is no batter awaiting his/her turn to bat, all the batters on the running track can be put out simultaneously, by the ball being thrown full pitch or placed by any fielder into the batting square before any batter has reached and touched 4th post.

(E) Procedure of Game

Whilst waiting at a post a member of the batting team shall have the advantage of running on if a no-ball is bowled and not taken by the batter. He/she can, at his/her discretion, continue to run round the track in the normal way. Similarly a batter need not run on for every ball bowled unless the next batter immediately behind him/her is obliged to run. More than one batter may be put out between the delivery of consecutive balls.

(F) Running Round the Track
A batter:

(*a*) shall run round the track carrying his/her bat in an attempt to reach 4th post having passed outside each post or the correct position of the post(s), if any has been displaced.

Posts must be passed in the order 1st, 2nd, 3rd, 4th and a batter is permitted to halt at one or more posts if he/she chooses.

On reaching 4th post he/she shall rejoin the waiting batters.
Penalty: The umpire shall declare the player out if he/she runs deliberately inside a post or deliberately drops or throws his/her bat. (When trying to make contact with a post, a batter who goes inside the post owing to obstruction by the fielder is not out.)

(*b*) shall not run beyond 1st post after a backward hit until the ball returns or has been returned to the forward area.
Penalty: The umpire shall order him/her back to 1st post.

(*c*) shall not wait between posts.
Penalty: The umpire shall order him/her to continue to and make contact with the next post.

(*d*) stopping (even temporarily) within reach of a post shall make and maintain contact with it using his/her hand or bat except that he/she may run on whenever the bowler is not in possession of the ball and in his/her square.
Penalty:

(1) If he/she does not make contact, the umpire shall order him/her to do so, and if he/she does not the umpire shall declare him/her out.

(2) If he/she loses contact or runs at any time when the bowler has the ball and is in his/her square (except an overrun) or unless ordered to do so by an umpire or during the bowler's action but before he/she releases the ball the umpire shall declare him/her out.

(*e*) shall continue his/her run to the next post if he/she is between posts when the bowler becomes in possession of the ball and is in his/her square but may not run past the post.
Penalty: The umpire shall order the player back to the post he/she passes.

(*f*) may not remain at the same post as another batter.
Penalty: The umpire shall order the player who batted first to run on and he/she may be put on in the usual ways.

(*g*) shall not return to a post unless he/she is ordered to do so by the umpire, or unless in the umpire's opinion he/she has over-run a post.
Penalty: The umpire shall order him/her on to the next post and he/she may be put out in the usual ways. A batter may return to 4th post to make contact before the next ball is bowled.

(*h*) when completing the track, shall not overtake any batter who is running ahead.
Penalty: The umpire shall declare the batter who overtakes to be out.

(*i*) must touch 4th post with his/her hand or bat.
Penalty: The umpire shall declare him/her out if 4th post is touched with the ball or with the hand holding the ball by the fielding side provided that another ball has not been bowled.

5. BOWLING

(A) The Bowler

(*a*) The bowler shall deliver one good ball to each incoming batter, except the last remaining incoming batter who is entitled to have the option of 3 good balls.

(*b*) A bowler may leave the bowling square to field the ball.

(*c*) A bowler may not deliver 2 consecutive no-balls to the same batter.
Penalty: a half rounder to the batting team.

(*d*) A dummy throw or bowl is not allowed. The ball must be delivered in the direction of the batting square. A player losing contact through this dummy ball will be allowed to return to his/her original position.

(B) No-Ball

(*a*) Decisions on height are based on the actual height of the batter.
Decisions on direction are based on position of batter when the bowler releases the ball.

(*b*) A no-ball is one that:

(i) is higher than the top of the head or lower than the knee when it reaches the batter.

(ii) hits the ground on the way to the batter.

(iii) would hit the batter.

(iv) is wide on the non-hitting side of the batter.

(v) is not delivered with a continuous and smooth underarm pendulum action (this does not prevent spin).

(vi) is bowled when the bowler fails to keep both feet within the square until the ball is released (the lines of the square are considered to be part of the square and the bowler should be penalised only when any part of his/her foot projects over the line).

(C) Bowling Substitutes
(See 3. **The Game.**)

6. FIELDING

(A) The Fielder
(*a*) If a fielder touches the post immediately ahead with the ball or the hand holding the ball, whilst the batter is running to that post and before the batter has touched the post the batter shall be declared out, excepting 1st post in the case of a no-ball.

(*b*) A fielder may put a batter out if he/she catches the ball directly from the bat or the hand holding the bat, excepting in the case of a no-ball.

(*c*) A fielder may prevent a live batter who is at or within reach of a post from scoring by touching the next post with the ball or the hand holding the ball. This does not prevent the batter from continuing his/her run.

(The live batter is defined as the batter to whom the most recent ball was bowled irrespective of whether this ball was no-ball or not).

(B) Side Out
Where there is no batter awaiting his/her turn to bat, all the batters on the running track may be put out simultaneously, by the ball being thrown full pitch or placed by any fielder into the batting square before any batter has reached and touched 4th post.

(C) Fielding Side Obstruction
(*a*) A fielder shall be considered to have obstructed if he/she impedes, in any way, a batter during his/her hitting action or when the batter is on the running track whether or not the fielder is holding the ball.

(*b*) He/she shall also be considered to have obstructed if he/she verbally misleads the other team.
Penalty: The umpire shall award half a rounder to the batting team and the batter shall be allowed to make contact with the post to which he/she is running.

7. SCORING

(A) One Rounder
(*a*) One rounder only may be scored from any one hit. In the case of a no-ball which is hit and caught, the batter may still score in the usual way.

(*b*) One rounder shall be scored if, after having hit the ball, the batter succeeds in running round the track and touches 4th post, or from 1st post when the ball returns or has been returned by a fielder to the forward area after a backward hit, provided that:

(i) he/she has not overtaken any other batter.

(ii) the bowler has not delivered another ball.

(iii) if he/she has stopped at a post, the post immediately ahead has not been touched by the fielder with the ball or the hand holding the ball.

(B) Half a Rounder

Half a rounder shall be scored by the batter if he/she completes the track fulfilling the same conditions as for one rounder but without hitting the ball.

(C) Penalty Half Rounder

A penalty half rounder shall be awarded to the batting team when:

(*a*) the bowler delivers two consecutive no-balls to the same batter. After a penalty half rounder for two consecutive no-balls is awarded, the previous no-balls are cancelled and the count starts again.

(*b*) a fielder obstructs a batter (see Rule 6*c* Fielding Side Obstruction).

A penalty half rounder shall be awarded to the fielding team when the waiting batters or batter out obstruct fielders (see Rule 4*b* Batting Side Obstruction).

(D) One Rounder and Penalty Half Rounders

It should be noted that the rounder may be scored with the addition of the award:

(*a*) one penalty half rounder if the ball that is hit is the second consecutive no-ball to that batter.

(*b*) one penalty half rounder if the batter is obstructed.

(*c*) two penalty half rounders if the ball that is bowled is the second consecutive no-ball to that batter and the batter is obstructed.

8. UMPIRES

For all matches played in accordance with these rules there shall be two umpires:

The batter's umpire shall stand in a position to judge the receipt of the ball by the batter in the batting square and then re-position to make decisions concerning 1st post and 4th post.

The bowler's umpire shall stand in a position so that he/she can see all the infringements of the rules for which he/she is responsible.

This will necessitate a change of position to facilitate a clear view of a left-handed batsman or a left-handed bowler.

The umpire's decisions on any aspect of the game shall be final, but they should appeal to each other on any point that is doubtful.

In the event of an unclear decision, the team *captains* may appeal to the umpires for clarification of the decision.

The umpire has the right to order a player off the pitch for unsportsmanlike conduct, with no substitution being possible.

(A) DUTIES OF THE BATTER'S UMPIRE

   (i) Call 'rounder' or 'half rounder' and give the score of both teams, after a rounder or half rounder is scored or awarded.

  (ii) Call 'no-ball' for balls that are not delivered with a continuous and smooth under-arm pendulum action.

 (iii) Call 'no-ball' for any ball bowled that passes the batter above head height.

 (iv) Call 'no-ball' for any ball bowled that passes the batter below the knee.

  (v) Call 'no-ball' for any ball bowled that hits the ground on the way to the batter.

 (vi) Call 'no-ball' if the bowler projects his/her foot over the front line of the bowling square.

 (vii) Give decisions concerning the front line of the batting square.

(viii) Give decisions concerning the back line of the batting square.

 (ix) Give decisions concerning backward hits and call 'backward hit'.

  (x) Give decisions concerning 1st and 4th posts.

 (xi) Give decisions concerning all catches.

 (xii) Call by name or number the next player to bat.

(B) DUTIES OF BOWLER'S UMPIRE

   (i) Call 'play' at the beginning of each inning.

  (ii) Call 'play' to restart the game after a dead ball situation.

 (iii) Call 'no-ball' for wides (any ball bowled which passes outside the normal reach of the batter).

 (iv) Call 'no-ball' for any ball that hits or which would have hit the batter and he/she remained in his/her original position.

  (v) Call 'no-ball' for any ball bowled to the non-hitting side of the batter.

 (vi) Give decisions concerning 2nd and 3rd posts.

 (vii) Call 'no-ball' if the bowler's foot projects over the back line of the bowling square.

(viii) Call 'no-ball' if the bowler's foot projects over the side lines of the bowling square.

(ix) Ensure that waiting batters and the batters out are behind their relevant lines.

(C) DUTIES OF BOTH UMPIRES

(*a*) Check the pitch markings and make sure that the playing area is free of all obstructions (with regard to safety policy).

(*b*) Check all equipment (with regard to safety policy).

(*c*) Check all clothing (with regard to safety policy).

(*d*) Keep record of scores and control the game.

(*e*) Keep check on batters out.

(*f*) Work as a team and consult over any decisions which are doubtful.

(*g*) Change position at the completion of two batting innings.

(*h*) Dismiss from the game, without the option of replacement, any player deemed to have committed any act of unsporting conduct.

(*i*) Shall call all decisions loudly and clearly so that all players and the other umpire can hear.

Reprinted by permission of the National Rounders Association. For reasons of space the paragraphs on Hints to Umpires have been omitted. Copies of the full Rules of the Game of Rounders and Hints to Umpires can be obtained from the National Rounders Association.

Rugby League Football

The Field of Play

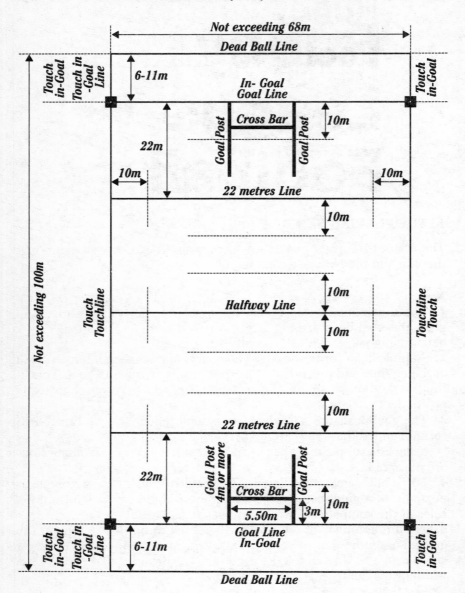

Rugby League Football

1. THE PLAYING FIELD

The plan of the playing field on the opposite page with the markings thereon and the Notes relating thereto are part of these Laws.

NOTES:
1. The touch-lines are in touch, the touch-in-goal lines are touch-in-goal, the goal-lines are in the in-goal area and the dead-ball line is beyond in-goal.
2. ⊡ Indicates a corner-post (see Glossary) placed at the intersection of each goal-line and touch-line. A corner-post is in touch-in-goal. Touch-judges should at all times ensure that corner-posts are correctly positioned.
3. The goal-posts are considered to extend indefinitely upwards. It is recommended that the bottom 2m of each upright be padded.
ⴸ shaped goal-posts are permissible provided the relevant dimensions are observed.
4. For adult games the dimensions should be as near maximum as possible. Minimum permissible dimensions should be laid down in the rules of the competition in which a match is played.
5. The broken lines in the plan shall consist of marks or dots on the ground not more than 2m apart. Transverse broken lines 10m from the goal-lines, 20m lines and half-way lines must be marked across the full width of the field.

2. GLOSSARY

The terms set out below shall have the following meanings assigned to them:

Advantage. Allowing the advantage means allowing play to proceed if it is to the advantage of the side which has not committed an offence or infringement.

Attacking team is the team which at the time has a territorial advantage. If a scrum is to be formed on the half-way line the team which last touched the ball before it went out of play is the attacking team.

Back as applied to a player means one who is not taking part in the scrum.

Ball back means to form a scrum where the ball was kicked from after it has entered touch on the full.

Behind when applied to a player means, unless otherwise stated, that both feet are behind the position in question. Similarly in front implies with both feet. When applied to a position on the field-of-play, behind means nearer to one's own goal-line than the point in question. Similarly in front of means nearer to one's opponents' goal-line.

Blind-side means the side of the scrum or of the play-the-ball nearer to touch (cf. open side).

Charging-down is blocking the path of the ball with hands, arm or body as it rises from an opponent's kick.

Converting a try is the act of kicking a goal following the scoring of a try.

Corner post is a post surmounted by a flag placed at the intersection of each touch-line and goal-line. The post shall be of non-rigid material and shall be not less than 1.25m high. The corner-posts are in touch-in-goal.

Dead ball means that the ball is out of play.

Defending team is the team opposing the attacking team (see above).

Differential penalty differs in one respect from a penalty kick in that a goal cannot be scored from it.

Drop goal, sometimes referred to as a field goal, is a goal scored by propelling the ball on the full, over the cross-bar by drop-kicking it.

Drop kick is a kick whereby the ball is dropped from the hands (or hand) and is kicked immediately it rebounds from the ground.

Drop-out means a drop-kick from between the posts or from the centre of the 20m line when bringing the ball back into play.

Dummy is the pretence of passing or otherwise releasing the ball while still retaining possession of it.

Field-of-play is the area bounded by, but not including, the touch-lines and goal-lines.

Forward means in a direction towards the opponents' dead-ball line. As applied to a player it means one who is at the time packing down in the scrum.

Forward pass is a throw towards the opponents' dead-ball line (see Section 10).

Foul play refers to the types of misconduct specified in Section 15, Law 1(*a*) (*b*) (*c*) and (*d*).

Free kick is the kick awarded to a team which kicks into touch from a penalty kick. The kick is taken 10m in from touch opposite the point of entry into touch and the ball may be kicked in any manner in any direction but a goal cannot be scored from it, nor can ground be gained by kicking into touch on the full.

Full time means the end of the game. Also referred to as no-side.

General play refers to all aspects of play after a match has been started or restarted by a place kick, drop-out, penalty kick, free kick or scrum.

Goal. See Section 6.

Grounding the Ball means:

(*a*) Placing the ball on the ground with hand or hands; or

(*b*) Exerting a downward pressure on the ball with hand or arm, the ball itself being on the ground; or

(*c*) Dropping on the ball and covering it with the part of the body above the waist and below the neck, the ball itself being on the ground.

Half-time means the end of the first half of the game.

Handover is the surrendering of the ball to the opposition after a team has been tackled the statutory number of successive times (Section 11, paragraph 7).

Heel is when a player propels the ball behind him with the sole or heel of his foot.

Hook is the act of the hooker when he strikes with a foot for the ball in the scrum.

In-goal. See the diagram on page 778.

In possession means to be holding or carrying the ball.

Kick means imparting motion to the ball with any part of the leg (except the heel) from knee to toe inclusive.

Kick-off. See Section 8.

Knock-on means to knock the ball towards the opponents' dead-ball line with hand or arm.

Loose arm is an offence by the hooker if he packs with one arm loose in the scrum.

Loose ball is when during play the ball is not held by a player and is not being scrummaged.

Loose head refers to the front-row forward in the scrum who is nearest to the referee.

Mark is the point at which a penalty kick or free kick is awarded or a scrum is formed.

Obstruction is the illegal act of impeding an opponent who does not have the ball.

Off-side, as applied to a player, means that he is temporarily out of play and may be penalised if he joins in the game (see Section 14).

On-side means that a player is not off-side.

Open-side means the side of the scrum or the play-the-ball further from touch (cf. blind side).

On the full means the ball is kicked over a given line without first bouncing.

Pack refers collectively to the forwards of any one team. To pack down means to form a scrum.

Pass is a throw of the ball from one player to another.

Penalise is to award a penalty kick against an offending player.

Penalty Kick. See Section 13.

Place Kick is to kick the ball after it has been placed on the ground for that purpose.

Playing area is the area enclosed by the fence, or other such line of demarcation, which prevents the encroachment of spectators.

Playing field is the area bounded by, but not including, the touch-lines and dead-ball lines.

Play-the-ball is the act of bringing the ball into play after a tackle (see Section 11).

Prop is the front-row forward in each team nearest to the scrum-half who is putting the ball into the scrum.

Punt is a kick whereby the ball is dropped from the hand or hands and is kicked before it touches the ground.

Put-in, also known as feeding the scrum, is the rolling of the ball into the scrum.

Scrum or scrummage or scrimmage (see Section 12). Where a team loses the advantages of the loose head and put-in the scrum is said to be awarded against that team.

Strike, as applied to the foot, means to attempt to secure possession of the ball, usually by heeling it, in a scrum or at a play-the-ball.

Tackle. See Section 11.

Touch-down is the grounding of the ball by a defending player in his own in-goal.

Touch-in-goal. See Section 9.

Try. See Section 6.

Upright tackle is where the player in possession is effectively tackled without being brought to the ground (see Section 11).

Voluntary tackle is where the player in possession voluntarily stops play when not effectively tackled (see Section 11).

3. THE BALL

1. The game shall be played with an oval air-inflated ball, the outer casing of which shall be of leather or other material approved by the

International Board, and nothing shall be used in its construction which might prove dangerous to the players.

2. The dimensions of the ball shall be:

	Desired Dimensions	Permissible Min.	Permissible Max.
Length	28cm	27cm	29cm
Longest circumference	74cm	73cm	75cm
Widest circumference	59cm	58cm	61cm
Weight (clean and dry)	410g	380g	440g

3. The referee shall blow his whistle immediately he notices that the size and shape of the ball no longer comply with the Laws of the Game.

4. THE PLAYER AND PLAYERS' EQUIPMENT

The game shall be played by two teams each consisting of not more than 13 players.

2. (*a*) Each team may effect up to four substitutions during the course of a match provided that the names of the substitute players are made known to the referee before the commencement of the match. A player once replaced shall take no further part in the match other than to replace a player who has been directed to leave the field to receive attention for bleeding.

Substitutions shall be sanctioned by the referee and will only be effected when the ball is out of play or play has been stopped owing to an injury, provided that when an injured player has left the field, his replacement may take the field immediately in an on-side position with the permission of a touch-judge.

(*b*) When a player is bleeding profusely, the referee shall direct him to leave the field for attention, in which event, he may be replaced and his replacement shall not count as one of the four substitutions referred to in the preceding paragraph. Should the player who left the field return, he must replace the player who replaced him.

3. For ease of identification it is permissible for players' clothing to bear numbers (1 to 13 with additional numbers for the substitutes), the numbers normally relating to the positions of the players in their respective teams, these positions being referred to by name as set out hereunder.

Backs:
1. Full-back
2. Right wing threequarter
3. Right centre threequarter
4. Left centre threequarter
5. Left wing threequarter
6. Stand-off half or five-eighth
7. Scrum half

Forwards:
8. Prop
9. Hooker
10. Front-row forward
11. Second-row forward
12. Second-row forward
13. Loose forward

4. (*a*) A player shall not wear anything that might prove dangerous to other players.

(*b*) A player's normal gear shall consist of a jersey of distinctive colour and/or pattern (preferably numbered), a pair of shorts, stockings of distinctive colour and/or pattern and studded boots or shoes.

(*c*) Protective clothing may be worn provided it contains nothing of a rigid nature.

(*d*) The referee shall order a player to remove any part of his equipment which might be considered dangerous and shall not allow the player to take any further part in the game until the order is obeyed. The player shall retire from the playing field to remove the offending item if the start or restart of the game would otherwise be delayed.

(*e*) The colours of the jerseys worn by competing teams shall be easily distinguishable and, if, in the opinion of the referee similarity between the jerseys might affect the proper conduct of the game he may, at his discretion, order either team to change jerseys in accordance with the Rules governing the competition in which the game is played.

(*f*) Studs on boots or shoes shall be no less than 8mm diameter at the apex and, if made of metal, shall have rounded edges.

5 MODE OF PLAY

1. The object of the game shall be to ground the ball in the opponents' in-goal to score tries (see Section 6) and to kick the ball over the opponents' cross-bar to score goals (see Section 6).

2. The captains of the two teams shall toss for choice of ends in the presence of the referee. The team of the captain losing the toss shall kick-off to start the game.

3. Once play has started any player who is on-side or not out of play can run with the ball, kick it in any direction and throw or knock it in any direction other than towards his opponents' dead-ball line (see Section 10 for Knock-on and Forward Pass).

4. A player who during play is holding the ball may be tackled by an opposing player or players in order to prevent him from running with the ball or from kicking or passing it to one of his own team (see Section 11 for Tackle).

5. A player who is not holding the ball shall not be tackled or obstructed (see Section 15).

6. SCORING – TRIES AND GOALS

1. A try shall count 4 points. A conversion goal or a penalty goal shall count 2 points. A drop goal during play shall count 1 point.

2. The game shall be won by the team scoring the greater number of points. If both teams score an equal number of points, or if both teams fail to score, then the game shall be drawn.

3. A try is scored when:

(*a*) A player first grounds the ball in his opponents' in-goal, provided that he is not in touch or touch-in-goal or on or over the dead-ball line.

(*b*) Opposing players simultaneously ground the ball in the in-goal area provided that the attacking player is not in touch or touch-in-goal or on or over the dead-ball line.

(*c*) A tackled player's momentum carries him into the opponents' in-goal where he grounds the ball even if the ball has first touched the ground in the field-of-play but provided that when the ball crosses the goal-line the player is not in touch or touch-in-goal or on or over the dead-ball line.

(*d*) The referee awards a penalty try which he may do if, in his opinion, a try would have been scored but for the unfair play of the defending team. A penalty try is awarded between the goal-posts irrespective of where the offence occurred.

(*e*) An attacking player carrying the ball comes into contact with the referee or a touch-judge or an encroaching spectator in the opponents' in-goal and play is thereby irregularly affected.

4. The try is awarded:

(*a*) Where grounded if scored as in 3(*a*) and 3(*b*) above.

(*b*) Where it first crosses the goal-line if scored as in 3(*c*) above.

(*c*) Between the posts if a penalty try.

(*d*) Where contact took place if scored as in 3(*e*) above.

5. Only the referee may award a try but he may take into consideration advice given by the touch-judges before arriving at his decision. He shall signal that a try has been scored by pointing to where the try has been awarded but should only do so after looking at the two touch-judges to ensure they are not reporting a prior incident.

6. A goal is scored if the whole of the ball at any time during its flight passes over the opponents' cross-bar towards the dead-ball line after being kicked on the full by a player (and not touching or being touched in flight by any other player) in any of these circumstances:

(a) By a place-kick after a try has been scored and counts 2 points.

(b) By a place-kick or a drop-kick when a penalty kick has been awarded and counts 2 points.

(c) By a drop-kick during play from any position in the field-of-play and counts one point.

7. A kick at goal after a try may be taken from any point on an imaginary line drawn parallel to the touch-line in the field-of-play and through the point where the try was awarded. A kick at goal from a penalty kick may be taken from the mark or from any point on an imaginary line drawn from the mark towards the kicker's own goal-line and parallel to the touch-line.

8. When a kick at goal is being taken following a try, the opposing players shall stand outside the field-of-play. Players of the kicker's team must be behind the ball.

When a kick at goal is being taken from a penalty kick, the opponents shall retire to their goal-line or not less than 10m from the mark (see Section 13).

It is illegal to attempt to distract the attention of a player who is kicking at goal.

9. For the purpose of judging a kick at goal, the goal-posts are assumed to extend indefinitely upwards.

10. When a kick at goal is being taken, the referee shall assign one touch-judge to each post. If a touch-judge is of the opinion that a goal has been scored he shall raise his flag above his head. If the kick is unsuccessful he shall wave his flag in front of him and below the waist. If there is no disagreement between the touch-judges their decision shall be accepted. In the event of disagreement, the referee shall decide.

7. TIME-KEEPING

1. The game shall normally be of 80 minutes' duration. At half-time there shall be an interval of 5 minutes, but this may be extended or reduced by the referee.

2. A team shall defend one in-goal for the first half of the game and then change ends for the second half.

3. If time expires in either half when the ball is out of play or a player in possession has been tackled and the ball has not been played, the referee shall immediately blow his whistle to terminate play. If the ball is in play when time expires, the referee shall terminate play when next the ball goes out of play or a player in possession is tackled but time shall be extended to allow a penalty kick or a kick at goal to be taken, in which case the half is terminated when next the ball goes out of play or a tackle is effected, unless a further penalty is awarded, in which case time is again extended for the kick to be taken.

4. Extra time shall be added to each half to compensate for time wasted or lost from any cause. The referee shall be the sole judge of extra time. He shall inform the respective captains how much extra time is to be played and shall keep a written record of same except where these duties have been delegated to a timekeeper.

5. (*a*) If the continuance of play endangers an injured player the referee may stop the game. If, when the game is stopped, a player is in possession of the ball the game shall be recommenced by that player playing-the-ball. Otherwise play shall be restarted with a scrum at the point where the ball was when play was stopped, with the team then in possession, or last in possession, having the loose head and the put-in.

(*b*) If a player in possession is injured in a tackle and unable to play the ball and play has been stopped, play shall be resumed by a colleague playing the ball at the point where the injured player was tackled.

(*c*) If a player in possession is injured in a tackle and unable to play the ball the referee may without stopping the game, provided he is satisfied that continuance of play would not endanger the injured player, direct a colleague of the injured player to play the ball at a point 5m in field from the point where the player was injured. In the event that a requirement to release the ball may endanger the injured player the referee may, at his discretion, order a scrum 5m in-field with the opponents of the team of the injured player having the loose head and the put-in.

8. THE KICK-OFF AND DROP-OUT

1. The kick-off is a place-kick from the centre of the half-way line. The team which loses the toss for choice of ends kicks-off to start the first half of the game and their opponents kick-off to start the second half.

When points have been scored, the team against which the points have been scored shall kick-off to restart the game.

2. The game is restarted with a place kick from the centre of the 20m line if:

(*a*) An attacking player last touches or is touched by the ball before it goes out of play over the dead-ball line, or into touch-in-goal except from a penalty kick (see 3 below) or from a kick-off from the centre of the half-way line (see 4*g* and 6*b* below).

(*b*) An attacking player infringes in the in-goal area. In the event of a deliberate breach by an attacking player a penalty kick is awarded 10m in the field-of-play in line with where the breach was committed (see Section 13).

(*c*) A defending player, in his in-goal, takes a kick in general play from an opponent on the full.

The ball may be kicked in any direction and is immediately in play. Opposing players shall retire 10m from the 20m line and shall not advance until the ball has been kicked. Defending players shall not advance in front of the ball before it is kicked. Any deliberate offence by either team shall incur a penalty to be awarded at the centre of the 20m line.

3. If the ball goes dead in the opponents' in-goal from a penalty kick (not necessarily a kick at goal) the game is restarted with a drop-out by a defending player from the centre of the 20m line.

4. The game is restarted with drop-out by a defending player from the centre of his goal-line if:

(*a*) A defending player last touches or is touched by the ball before it goes over the dead-ball line or into touch-in-goal.

(*b*) A defending player accidentally infringes in the in-goal area.

(*c*) A defending player touches down in the in-goal area.

(*d*) A defending player in possession is tackled in the in-goal area.

(*e*) A defending player kicks the ball into touch on the full from his own in-goal.

(*f*) The ball or a defending player carrying the ball touches the referee, a touch-judge, or an encroaching spectator in the in-goal area and play is thereby irregularly affected.

(*g*) The ball goes over the dead-ball line or into touch-in-goal other than on the full from a kick-off from the centre of the half-way line without being touched by or touching a defending player.

5. See Law 2 of this Section re ball caught on the full before being made dead in-goal.

6. A player who kicks-off or drops-out shall be penalised if he:

(*a*) Advances in front of the appropriate line before kicking the ball.

(*b*) Kicks the ball on the full over the touch-line, touch-in-goal line, or over the dead-ball line.

(*c*) Kicks the ball so that it fails to travel at least 10m forward in the field-of-play.

(*d*) Kicks the ball other than in the prescribed manner.

7. Any other player shall be penalised if he:

(*a*) Wilfully touches the ball from a kick-off or drop-out before it has travelled 10m forward in the field-of-play.

(*b*) Runs in front of one of his own team who is kicking-off or dropping-out.

(*c*) Approaches nearer than 10m to the line from which the kick is being taken when an opponent is kicking-off or dropping-out.

8. A penalty kick resulting from any offence at the kick-off shall be taken from the centre of the half-way line.

Any penalty kick resulting from the restarting of play from the 20m line shall be taken from the centre of that line.

A penalty kick resulting from any offence at the drop-out from between the posts shall be taken from the centre of the line drawn parallel to and 10m from the goal-line.

9. TOUCH AND TOUCH-IN-GOAL

1. The ball is in touch when it or a player in contact with it touches the touch-line or the ground beyond the touch-line or any object on or outside the touch-line except when a player, tackled in the field-of-play, steps into touch as he regains his feet, in which case he shall play-the-ball in the field-of-play.

The ball is in touch if a player jumps from touch and while off the ground touches the ball. The ball is not in touch if during flight it crosses the touch-line but is knocked back by a player who is off the ground after jumping from the field-of-play.

2. The ball is in touch-in-goal when it or a player in contact with it touches the touch-in-goal line, or any object on or outside the touch-in-goal lines.

3. When a ball has entered touch or touch-in-goal, the point of entry shall be taken as the point at which the ball first crossed the touch or touch-in-goal line.

4. If the ball is kicked by or bounces off a player in a forward direction – except from in-goal, Section 8, paragraph 4(*e*) – and it goes into touch on the full, a scrum is formed where contact with the ball was made except after the fifth play-the-ball (but not nearer than 10m to the touch-line or 10m to the goal-line) – see Section 12.

5. If the ball is kicked into touch from a penalty kick the game is restarted by a free-kick 10m infield opposite the point of entry into touch – see Section 13.

6. Other than as outlined in paragraphs 4 and 5 above, the game is restarted after the ball has gone into touch by forming a scrum 10m in-field opposite the point of entry into touch but not nearer than 10m to the goal-line – see Section 12.

10. KNOCK-ON AND FORWARD PASS

1. A player shall be penalised if he deliberately knocks-on or passes forward.

2. If, after knocking-on accidentally, the player knocking-on regains or kicks the ball before it touches the ground, a goal-post, a cross-bar or an opponent, then play shall be allowed to proceed. Otherwise play shall stop and a scrum shall be formed except after the fifth play-the-ball.

3. To charge-down a kick is permissible and is not a knock-on.

4. It is illegal to head the ball in a forward direction.

11. THE TACKLE AND PLAY-THE-BALL

1. A player in possession may be tackled by an opposing player or players. It is illegal to tackle or obstruct a player who is not in possession.

2. A player in possession is tackled:

(*a*) When he is held by one or more opposing players and the ball or the hand or arm holding the ball comes into contact with the ground.

(*b*) When he is held by one or more opposing players in such a manner that he can make no further progress and cannot part with the ball.

(*c*) When, being held by an opponent, the tackled player makes it evident that he has succumbed to the tackle and wishes to be released in order to play-the-ball.

(*d*) When he is lying on the ground and an opponent places a hand on him.

3. Once a player in possession has been tackled it is illegal for any player to move or try to move him from the point where the tackle is effected.

4. A player in possession shall not deliberately and unnecessarily allow himself to be tackled by voluntarily falling to the ground when not held by an opponent. If a player drops on a loose ball, he shall not remain on the ground waiting to be tackled if he has time to regain his feet and continue play.

5. If a tackled player, because of his momentum, slides along the ground, the tackle is deemed to have been effected where his slide ends – See Section 6, paragraph 3(*c*).

6. If any doubt arises as to a tackle, the referee should give a verbal instruction to 'play on' or shout 'held' as the case may be.

7. (*a*) A team in possession shall be allowed 5 successive 'play-the-balls'; but if tackled a 6th time, or there is an infringement by that team after the 5th play-the-ball, which in other circumstances would result in a scrum (other than a scrum following a ball being kicked into touch after landing in the field-of-play), the ball not having been touched by an opponent during the sequence of tackles, the ball shall be brought into play by an opposing player playing-the-ball at the point of tackle or infringement. The play-the-ball for this purpose shall not be counted for the purposes of the tackle count and shall operate as provided for in paragraph 10 of this Section.

(*b*) Where a player knocks-on and an opponent gathers the ball and is tackled before gaining any territorial advantage, the play-the-ball following that tackle shall not count for the purposes of the tackle count referred to in the preceding paragraph.

8. A tackled player shall not intentionally part with the ball other than by bringing it into play in the prescribed manner. If, after being tackled, he accidentally loses possession, a scrum shall be formed except after the fifth play-the-ball.

9. Once a tackle has been completed, no player shall take or attempt to take the ball from the tackled player.

10. The play-the-ball shall operate as follows:

(*a*) The tackled player shall be immediately released and shall not be touched until the ball is in play.

(*b*) The tackled player shall without delay regain his feet where he was tackled, lift the ball clear of the ground, face his opponents' goal-line and drop or place the ball on the ground in front of his foremost foot.

(*c*) One opponent may take up position immediately opposite the tackled player.

(*d*) Neither the tackled player nor the player marking him shall raise a foot from the ground before the ball has been released.

(*e*) When the ball touches the ground it may be kicked or heeled in any direction by the foot of either the tackled player or the player marking him. The ball is in play when it has come clear of the two players in the play-the-ball movement, i.e. the tackled player and the player marking him.

(*f*) A player of each team, to be known as the acting half-back, may stand immediately and directly behind his own player taking part in the play-the-ball and must remain in this position until the ball has come clear of the two players in the play-the-ball movement.

(*g*) Players of the side not in possession other than the acting half-back, are out of play if they fail to retire 10m from the point at which the ball is played or to their own goal-line. Players of the side in possession other than the player taking part in the play-the-ball and the acting half-back are out of play if they fail to retire 5m from the point at which the ball is played or to their own goal line.

(*h*) Having retired the distance prescribed in the preceding paragraph a player may not advance until the ball has come clear of the two players in the play-the-ball movement. A player who is out of play may again take part in the game when the advantage gained by not retiring has been lost.

11. The play-the-ball must be performed as quickly as possible. Any player who intentionally delays the bringing of the ball into play shall be penalised.

12. If part of the tackled player is on or over the goal-line but the ball is in the field-of-play the tackled player shall play the ball where it lies. If a player is tackled in an upright position bestriding the goal-line, he is deemed to be tackled in the in-goal area.

12. THE SCRUM

1. A scrum is formed to restart play whenever play is not being restarted with a kick-off, a drop-out (Section 8), a penalty kick (Section 13) or a play-the-ball (Section 11).

2. To form a scrum not more than 3 forwards of either team shall interlock arms and heads and create a clear tunnel at right angles to the touch-line. The forward in the centre of a front-row (i.e. the hooker) shall bind with his arms over the shoulders of the 2 supporting forwards. Not more than 2 second-row forwards on each team shall pack behind their respective front rows by interlocking arms and placing their heads in the two spaces between the hooker and his front-row forwards. The loose forward of each team shall pack behind his second-row forwards by placing his head in the space between them. All forwards must pack with their bodies and legs at right angles to the tunnel and the upper parts of their bodies horizontal. Once the ball has been put in the scrum no other player can lend his weight to it.

3. No more than 6 players on each team shall assist in the formation of a scrum and when the ball is in the scrum no more than 7 players of each team shall act as backs.

4. It is permissible for the forwards to push once the scrum has been correctly formed, but if it moves an appreciable distance to the disadvantage of any one team before the ball is put in, then the referee shall order the scrum to re-form in its original position.

5. (a) At the scrum the non-offending team shall have the loose head and the put-in.

(b) In the case of a mutual infringement, the attacking team shall have the loose head and the put-in.

6. (a) The ball shall be put into the scrum from the referee's side by holding it in a horizontal position with a point in each hand and rolling it along the ground. It must be put into the centre of the tunnel formed by the opposing front-row forwards.

(b) The ball shall not be put in before the scrum has been correctly formed.

(c) There shall be no undue delay in putting the ball into the scrum.

(d) The player putting it in shall not hesitate or dummy and after putting it in he shall immediately retire behind his own pack of forwards.

7. The scrum half of the team not having the put-in shall retire behind his last row of forwards. All other players outside the scrum (other than the scrum half putting the ball in) shall retire 5m or more behind the last row of forwards in their respective teams in the scrum and shall remain so until the ball has emerged correctly from the scrum.

8. When the ball is in the scrum it can only be played with the foot.

The front-row forwards shall not advance their feet into the tunnel or have one foot raised before the ball is put in or strike for the ball before the hookers.

A hooker may strike for the ball with either foot once it has contacted the ground in the centre of the tunnel.

After the hookers have struck for the ball the other forwards in the scrum may kick or heel the ball.

No player shall wilfully collapse a scrum or wilfully have any part of him other than his feet in contact with the ground.

A player shall not wilfully delay the correct formation of a scrum.

9. To be in play, the ball must emerge from between and behind the inner feet of the second-row forwards.

If the ball does not emerge correctly and the fault cannot be attributed to any one team then it should be put into the scrum once again.

10. If a scrum is ordered it shall normally be formed where the breach of Laws occurs. If such breach is within 10m of a touch-line or 10m of a goal-line the scrum shall be brought in 10m from the touch-line and 10m from the goal-line.

11. If a penalty kick is awarded relating to a scrum offence and the scrum has wandered from its original position, the mark is where the scrum was first formed.

12. If the ball emerges correctly from the scrum it is in play even though the scrum has wheeled. Any forward can detach himself from the scrum to gather or kick the ball. Any back can similarly play it provided he remained behind the scrum until the ball emerged.

13. PENALTY KICK

1. (*a*) A penalty kick shall be awarded against any player who is guilty of misconduct (Section 15) provided that this is not to the disadvantage of the non-offending team. Unless otherwise stated, the mark is where the offence occurs. If misconduct occurs in touch, the mark shall be 10m from the touch-line in the field-of-play and opposite where the offence occurred or, *in the case of obstruction, where the ball next bounces or is caught in the field-of-play, or 10m opposite the point of entry if the ball enters touch on the full, or 10m from the goal-line if the ball crosses the goal-line on the full, whichever is to the greater advantage of the non-offending side.* If the offence is committed by a defender in his own in-goal or an attacker in his opponents' in-goal, the mark is taken 10m into the field-of-play opposite where the offence occurred. In the event of further misconduct by the offending side, the referee shall advance the mark once only 10m towards the offending team's goal-line.

(*b*) In the event of a breach by the kicker's team a scrum shall be formed at the point where the penalty kick was awarded. In the event of a breach by the opposing team a further penalty kick shall be awarded at a point opposite where the breach occurred on a line parallel to the goal-line 10m from where the penalty kick was awarded.

2. A player may take a penalty kick by punting, drop-kicking, or place-kicking the ball from any point on or behind the mark and equidistant from the touch-line. Other than when kicking for goal the ball may be kicked in any direction, after which it is in play.

3. Players of the kicker's side must be behind the ball when it is kicked.

Players of the team opposing the kicker shall retire to their own goal-line or 10m or more from the mark towards their own goal-line and shall not make any attempt to interfere with or distract the attention of the kicker. They may advance after the ball has been kicked.

4. (*a*) If the ball is kicked into touch without touching any other player the kicking team shall restart play with a free kick. Opposing players shall retire 10m from the point of entry into touch or to their own goal-line.

In the event of a breach by the kicker's team, a scrum shall be formed at the point where the free kick was awarded. In the event of a breach by the opposing team a penalty kick shall be awarded at a point opposite where the breach occurred on a line parallel to the goal-line 10m from where the free kick was awarded.

(*b*) If the ball touches an opponent in flight and then enters touch a scrum shall be formed 10m in-field from where the ball crossed the touch-line with the kicker's team having the loose head and the put-in.

5. No player shall deliberately take any action which is likely to delay the taking of a penalty kick.

6. If the kick is not taken as stated or if a player of the kicker's team infringes, a scrum shall be formed at the mark.

7. When the referee penalises a player he must explain the nature of the offence.

8. If a penalty is awarded for an offence by the attacking team in the opponents' in-goal area the mark shall be 10m in the field-of-play opposite where the offence occurred. For an offence in-goal by the defending team which incurs a penalty, the mark is in the field-of-play 10m from the goal-line and opposite where the offence occurred, except for foul play against a try scorer (see paragraph 9 below).

9. If a player fouls an opponent who is touching down for a try, a penalty kick at goal shall be taken from in front of the goal-posts after the attempt to convert the try. After this kick has been taken the ball shall be deemed dead and play shall be restarted from the half-way line.

This Law applies to the period during which the ball is touched down for a try and not to any subsequent period.

10. (*a*) If a player fouls an opponent who is attempting a drop goal, a penalty kick shall be awarded in front of the goal-posts.

(*b*) If the attempt at drop goal is successful, a kick at goal must be taken from the penalty kick and play restarted from the centre of the half-way line irrespective of the outcome of that kick.

(*c*) If the attempt at drop goal is unsuccessful, the penalty kick can be taken in any manner provided for in the Laws and play restarted according to the outcome of that kick.

14. OFF-SIDE

1. A player is off-side except when he is in his own in-goal if the ball touches, is touched, held or kicked by one of his own team behind him.

2. An off-side player shall not take any part in the game or attempt in any way to influence the course of the game. He shall not encroach within 10m of an opponent who is waiting for the ball and shall immediately retire 10m from any opponent who first secures possession of the ball.

3. An off-side player is placed on-side if:

(*a*) An opponent moves 10m or more with the ball.

(*b*) An opponent touches the ball without retaining it.

(*c*) One of his own team in possession of the ball runs in front of him.

(*d*) One of his own team kicks or knocks the ball forward and takes up a position in front of him in the field-of-play.

(*e*) He retires behind the point where the ball was last touched by one of his own team.

15. PLAYER'S MISCONDUCT

1. A player is guilty of misconduct if he:

(*a*) Deliberately trips, kicks or strikes another player.

(*b*) When effecting or attempting to effect a tackle, makes contact with the head or neck of an opponent intentionally, recklessly or carelessly.

(*c*) Drops knees first on to an opponent who is on the ground.

(*d*) Uses any dangerous throw when effecting a tackle.

(*e*) Deliberately breaks the Laws of the Game.

(*f*) Uses offensive or obscene language.

(*g*) Disputes a decision of the referee or touch-judge.

(*h*) Re-enters the field-of-play without the permission of the referee or a touch-judge having previously temporarily retired from the game.

(*i*) Behaves in any way contrary to the true spirit of the game.

(*j*) Deliberately obstructs an opponent who is not in possession.

16. DUTIES OF REFEREE AND TOUCH-JUDGES

1. In all matches a referee and two touch-judges shall be appointed or mutually agreed upon by the contesting teams.

2. The referee shall enforce the Laws of the Game and may impose penalties for any deliberate breach of the Laws. He shall be the sole judge on matters of fact except those relating to touch and touch-in-goal (See paragraph 11 below).

3. He shall record the tries and goals scored during the match.

4. He shall be the sole timekeeper except where this duty has been delegated to another person (see Section 7).

5. He may, at his discretion, temporarily suspend or prematurely terminate a match because of adverse weather, undue interference by spectators, misbehaviour by players, or any other cause which, in his opinion, interferes with his control of the game.

6. He shall not allow anyone apart from the players on to the playing area without permission.

7. In the event of misconduct by a player, the referee shall, at his discretion, caution, temporarily suspend for 10 minutes, or dismiss the offender.

8. The players are under the control of the referee from the time they enter the playing area until they leave it.

9. The referee must carry a whistle which he shall blow to commence and terminate each half of the game. Except for these occasions the blowing of the whistle shall temporarily stop the play. The referee shall blow the whistle:

(*a*) When a try or a goal has been scored.

(*b*) When the ball has gone out of play.

(*c*) When he detects a breach of the Laws of the Game, except when to stop the play would be to the disadvantage of the non-offending team.

(*d*) When play is irregularly affected by the ball or the player carrying the ball coming into contact with the referee, a touch-judge, or with any person not taking part in the match or with any object which should not normally be on the playing field.

(*e*) When any irregularity, not provided for in these Laws, occurs and one team unjustifiably gains an advantage.

(*f*) When a stoppage is necessary in order to enforce the Laws or for any other reason.

10. If the referee judges on a matter of fact, he shall not subsequently alter that judgement but he may cancel any decision made if prior foul play of which he had no knowledge is reported to him by a touch-judge.

11. The referee shall accept the decision of a neutral touch-judge relating to touch and touch-in-goal play and to kicks at goal.

12. Each touch-judge shall remain in touch, one on each side of, and near to, the playing field except:

(*a*) When judging kicks at goal (see Section 6); and

(*b*) When reporting a player's misconduct which has escaped the notice of the referee.

13. Each touch-judge must carry a flag, triangular in shape, the longest sides being equal and not less than 30cm and the short side being not less than 23cm. The flag must be attached by the short side to a stick, the length of which shall be not less than 45cm.

14. A touch-judge shall indicate when and where the ball goes into touch by raising his flag and standing opposite the point of entry into touch except in the case of ball back (see section 9, Paragraph 4) when the touch-judge must indicate that no ground has been gained by waving his flag above his head accentuating the movements in the direction of the kicker's goal-line.

15. If the ball enters touch-in-goal the touch-judge shall wave his flag above his head and then point it towards the goal-posts if the ball last touched a defending player, or towards the 20m line if it was last touched by an attacking player.

16. Touch-judges shall assist the referee in judging kicks at goal (see Section 6, paragraph 10).

17. When a penalty kick is being taken, the nearer touch-judge shall take up a position near the touch-line 10m beyond the mark to act as a marker for the team which is required to retire. He shall wave his flag horizontally in front of him if any player fails to retire 10m.

18. In cases where circumstances in connection with the match are likely to be made the subject of official investigation, the referee and touch-judges shall report to the investigating authority only and shall refrain from expressing criticism or comment through other channels.

Reprinted by permission of the Rugby Football League. Full notes and interpretations of these Laws, and the Referee's signals, can be found in the official Rugby Football League's International Laws of the Game and Notes on the Laws, obtainable from the Rugby Football League.

THE LAWS OF

Rugby Union Football

The Field of Play

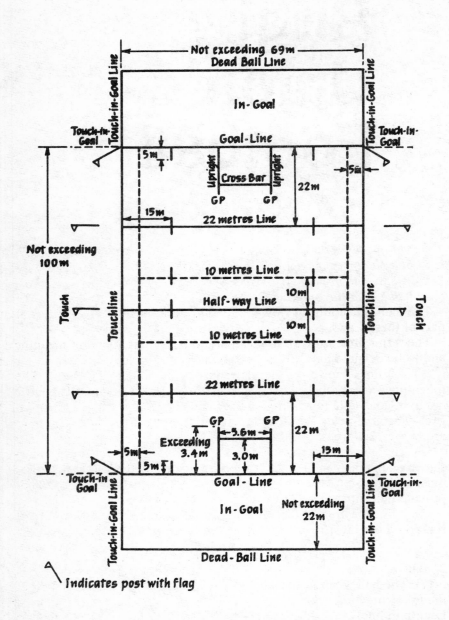

Not exceeding 69m
Dead Ball Line

In - Goal

Goal - Line

5m

Upright Cross Bar Upright

GP   GP

22m

5m

15m   22 metres Line

Not exceeding 100m

Touch   Touchline

10 metres Line

Half - way Line   10m

10 metres Line   10m

22 metres Line

GP   GP

5.6m

Exceeding 3.4m   3.0m   22m

5m

5m   Goal - Line   15m

Touch-in-Goal   In - Goal   Not exceeding 22m

Dead - Ball Line

Indicates post with flag

Rugby Union Football

LAWS

1. Ground

The field-of-play is the area shown on the plan on page 800, bounded by, but not including, the goal-lines and touch-lines. The playing area is the field-of-play and in-goal. The playing enclosure is the playing area and a reasonable area surrounding it.

The plan, including all words and figures thereon, is to take effect as part of these Laws.

The terms appearing on the plan are to bear their apparent meaning and to be deemed part of the definitions as if separately included.

(1) All lines shown on the plan must be suitably marked out. The touch-lines are in touch. The goal-lines are in-goal. The dead-ball line is *not* in in-goal. The touch-in-goal lines and corner posts are in touch-in-goal. The goal-posts are to be erected in the goal-lines. The 22m lines are in the 22m areas.

(2) The game must be played on a ground of the area (maximum) shown on the plan and marked in accordance with the plan. The surface must be grass-covered or, where this is not available, clay or sand, provided the surface is not of dangerous hardness.

(3) Any objection by the visiting team about the ground or the way it is marked out must be made to the referee before the first kick-off.

2. Ball

(1) The ball when new shall be oval in shape, of four panels, and of the following dimensions:

Length in line	280 to 300mm
Circumference (end on)	760 to 790mm

Circumference (in width)	580 to 620mm
Weight	400 to 440g

Note:

The ball, at commencement of play, should have a pressure equivalent to 9½–10lb per square inch (0.6697–0.7031 kilograms per square centimetre) at sea level.

(2) The dimensions of the ball may be reduced only for younger schoolboys.

(3) Balls may be specially treated to make them resistant to mud and easier to grip. The casings need not be of leather.

Note:

It is permissible to have spare balls available during a match, but a team may not gain or attempt to gain an unfair advantage through their use or by changing them.

3. Number of Players

(1) A match shall be played by not more than 15 players in each team.

Note:

As soon as a referee becomes aware that a team has more than the correct number of players on the field, he must require the captain of that team to reduce the number of players appropriately.

(2) When a Union authorises matches to be played with fewer than 15 players, the Laws of the Game shall apply except that there shall be no fewer than 3 players in a scrummage at all times.

(3) Replacement of players shall be allowed in recognised trial matches as determined by the Unions having jurisdiction over the match.

(4) In all other matches, a player may be replaced only on account of injury and subject to the following conditions.

(*a*) No more than 4 players in each team may be replaced.

Exceptions:

(i) up to 6 players may be replaced in domestic matches as determined by the Union having jurisdiction over the match.

(ii) up to 7 players may be replaced in matches between teams of schoolboys or teams where all players are under age 21, the age limitation being applied from the commencement of the official season of the visited Union.

(*b*) A player who has been permanently replaced must *not* resume playing in the match.

Note:

When a team names 7 replacements at least 2 of the reserves must cover front-row positions: loose-head prop, tight-head prop, hooker and one the second-row forward positions.

(5) (*a*) In matches in which a national representative team is playing, a player may be replaced *only* when, in the opinion of a medical practitioner, the player is so injured that he should not continue playing in the match.

(*b*) For such competitions and other domestic matches as a Union gives express permission, an injured player may be replaced on the advice of a medically trained person, or if a medically trained person is not present, with the approval of the referee.

(6) If the referee is advised by a doctor or other medically trained person or for any other reason considers that a player is so injured that it would be harmful for him to continue playing, the referee shall require the player to leave the playing area.

For this purpose the referee may also require a player to leave the field to be examined medically.

(7) Any objection by either team as regards the number of players in a team may be made to the referee at any time but the objection shall not affect any score previously obtained.

Attention is drawn to I.B. Resolution 5.5 which states that 'A player who has suffered definite concussion should not participate in any match or training session for a period of at least three weeks from the time of the injury, and then only subject to being cleared by a proper neurological examination'.

Replacements and Substitutes		
Domestic matches	3 players in attendance	3 replacements*
Matches between domestic teams and teams from other Unions	4 players in attendance	4 replacements
*See below	6 players in attendance	3 replacements*
U21	7 players in attendance	7 replacements
U19	6 players in attendance	Up to 7 replacements of which 3 may be substitutions
U15	7 players in attendance	Any number of replacements or substitutions by mutual agreement*

*RFU only

4. Players' Dress

(1) A player must not wear dangerous projections such as buckles or rings.

(2) Shoulder pads of the 'harness' type must not be worn. If the referee is satisfied that a player requires protection following an injury to a shoulder, the wearing of a pad of cottonwool, sponge rubber or similar soft material may be permitted provided the pad is attached to the body or sewn on to the jersey.

(3) Studs of a player's boots must conform to the British Standard BS 6366: 1983. They must be circular, securely fastened to the boots and of the following dimensions:

Maximum length (measured from sole)	18mm
Minimum diameter at base	13mm
Minimum diameter at top	10mm
Minimum diameter of integral washer	20mm

The wearing of a single stud at the toe of a boot is prohibited.

(4) The referee has power to decide before or during the match that any part of a player's dress is dangerous. He must then order the player to remove the dangerous part and permit him to resume playing only after it has been removed.

Note:

The moulded rubber multi-studded sole is acceptable under this Law.

5. Toss, Time

No-side is the end of a match.

(1) Before a match begins the captains shall toss for the right to kick-off, or the choice of ends.

(2) The duration of play in a match shall be such time not exceeding 80 minutes as shall be directed by the Union or, in the absence of such direction, as agreed upon by the teams or, if not agreed, as fixed by the referee. In International matches two periods of 40 minutes each shall be played.

(3) Play shall be divided into two halves. At half-time the teams shall change ends and there shall be an interval of not more than 5 minutes.

(4) A period not exceeding 1 minute shall be allowed for treatment of an injury to a player or for any other permitted delay. A longer period may be allowed only if the additional time is required for the removal of an injured player from the playing area.

Playing time lost as a result of any such permitted delay or of delay in taking a kick at goal shall be made up in that half of the match in which the delay occurred, subject to the power vested in the referee to declare no-side before time has expired.

6. Referee and Touch-Judges

A. Referee

(1) There shall be a referee for every match. He shall be appointed by or under the authority of the Union or, in case no such authorised referee has been appointed, a referee may be mutually agreed upon between the teams or, failing such agreement, he shall be appointed by the home team.

(2) If the referee is unable to officiate for the whole period of a match a replacement shall be appointed either in such manner as may be directed by the Union or, in the absence of such direction, by the referee or, if he is unable to do so, by the home team.

(3) The referee shall keep the time and the score, and he must in every match apply fairly the Laws of the Game without any variation or omission, except only when the Union has authorised the application of an experimental Law approved by the International Board.

(4) He must not give any instruction or advice to either team prior to the match. During the match he must not consult with anyone except only:

(*a*) Either or both touch-judges on a point of fact relevant to their functions, or on matters relating to Law 26(3); or

(*b*) In regard to time.

(5) During a match the referee is the sole judge of fact and of Law. All his decisions are binding on the players. He cannot alter a decision except when given before he observes that a touch-judge's flag is raised or before he has received a report related to Law 26(3) from a touch-judge.

(6) The referee must carry a whistle and must blow it:

(*a*) To indicate the beginning of the match, half-time, resumption of play after half-time, no-side, a score or a touch-down; and

(*b*) To stop play because of infringement or otherwise as required by the Laws.

(7) During a match no person other than the players, the referee and the touch-judges may be within the playing enclosure or the playing area unless with the permission of the referee which shall be given only for a special and temporary purpose.

Play may continue during minor injuries with a medically trained person being permitted to come on to the playing area to attend the player or the player going to the touch-line. Continuation of play during minor injuries is subject to the referee's permission and to his authority to stop play at any time. At half-time the referee shall allow the coach of each team onto the playing area to attend their teams.

(8) (*a*) All players must respect the authority of the referee and they

must not dispute his decisions. They must (except in the case of a kick-off) stop playing at once when the referee has blown his whistle.

(*b*) A player must when so requested, whether before or during the match, allow the referee to inspect his dress.

(*c*) A player must not leave the playing enclosure without the referee's permission. If a player retires during a match because of injury or otherwise, he must not resume playing in that match until the referee has given him permission.

(*d*) A player who has an open or bleeding wound must leave the playing area, until such time as the bleeding is controlled and the wound covered or dressed. Such a player may be replaced, once only, on a temporary basis until the wound is covered or dressed but after ten minutes the replacement becomes permanent. The ten-minute period begins when the player leaves the playing area.

Penalty. Infringement by a player is subject to penalty as misconduct.

B. Touch-judges

(1) There shall be two touch-judges for every match. Unless touch-judges have been appointed by or under the authority of the Union, it shall be the responsibility of each team to provide a touch-judge.

(2) A touch-judge is under the control of the referee who may instruct him as to his duties and may overrule any of his decisions. The referee may request that an unsatisfactory touch-judge be replaced and he has power to order off and report to the Union a touch-judge who in his opinion is guilty of misconduct.

(3) Each touch-judge shall carry a flag (or other suitable object) to signal his decisions. There shall be one touch-judge on each side of the ground and he shall remain in touch except when judging a kick at goal.

(4) He must hold up his flag when the ball or a player carrying it has gone into touch and must indicate the place of throw-in and which team is entitled to do so. He must also signal to the referee when the ball or a player carrying it has gone into touch-in-goal.

(5) The touch-judge shall lower his flag when the ball has been thrown in except on the following occasions when he must keep it raised;

(*a*) When the player throwing in the ball puts any part of either foot in the field-of-play;

(*b*) When the ball has not been thrown in by the team entitled to do so;

(*c*) When, at a quick throw-in, the ball that went into touch is replaced by another or is touched by anyone other than the players.

It is for the referee to decide whether or not the ball has been thrown-in from the correct place.

(6) In matches in which a national representative team is playing and

in such domestic matches for which a Union gives express permission, and where referees recognised by the Union are appointed as touch-judges, the touch-judges shall report incidents of foul play and misconduct under Law 26(3) to the referee for the match.

A touch-judge shall signal such an incident to the referee by raising his flag to a horizontal position pointing directly across the field at a right angle to the touch-line. The touch-judge must remain in touch and continue to carry out his other functions until the next stoppage in play when the referee shall consult him regarding the incident. The referee may then take whatever action he deems appropriate and any consequent penalties shall be in accordance with Law 26(3).

(7) When a kick at goal from a try or penalty kick is being taken both touch-judges must assist the referee by signalling the result of the kick. One touch-judge shall stand at or behind each of the goal-posts and shall raise his flag if the ball goes over the cross-bar.

7. Mode of Play

A match is started by a kick-off, after which any player who is on-side, and provided he does so in accordance with these Laws, may at any time:
Catch or pick up the ball and run with it;
Pass, throw or knock the ball to another player;
Kick or otherwise propel the ball;
Tackle, push or shoulder an opponent holding the ball;
Fall on the ball;
Take part in scrummage, ruck, maul or line-out;
Ground the ball in in-goal.

8. Advantage

The referee shall not whistle for an infringement during play which is followed by an advantage gained by the non-offending team. An advantage must be either territorial or such possession of the ball as constitutes an obvious tactical advantage. A mere opportunity to gain advantage is not sufficient.

9. Ball or Player Touching Referee

(1) If the ball or a player carrying it touches the referee in the field-of-play, play shall continue unless the referee considers either team has gained an advantage in which case he shall order a scrummage. The team which last played the ball shall put it in.

(2) (a) If the ball in a player's possession or a player carrying it touches the referee in that player's in-goal, a touch-down shall be awarded.

(b) If a player carrying the ball in his opponents' in-goal touches the referee before grounding the ball, a try shall be awarded at that place.

10. Kick-off

Kick-off is (a) a place kick taken from the centre of the half-way line by the team which has the right to start the match or by the opposing team on the resumption of play after the half-time interval, or (b) a drop kick taken at or from behind the centre of the half-way line by the defending team after the opposing team has scored.

(1) The ball must be kicked from the correct place and by the correct form of kick; otherwise it shall be kicked off again.

(2) The ball must reach the opponents' 10m line, unless first played by an opponent; otherwise it shall be kicked off again, or a scrummage formed at the centre, at the opponents' option. If it reaches the 10m line and is then blown back, play shall continue.

(3) If the ball is kicked directly into touch, the opposing team may accept the kick, have the ball kicked off again, or have a scrummage formed at the centre.

(4) If the ball crosses the opposing team's goal-line from a kick-off, without touching or being touched by a player, the opposing team has the option of grounding the ball, making it dead, or playing on. If the opposing team grounds the ball or makes it dead or the ball becomes dead by touching or crossing the dead-ball line, they will have the option of either having a scrummage formed at the centre of the half-way line, with the put-in, or having the other team kick-off again.

(5) The *kicker's team* must be behind the ball when kicked; otherwise a scrummage shall be formed at the centre.

(6) The *opposing team* must stand on or behind the 10m line. If they are in front of that line or if they charge before the ball has been kicked, it shall be kicked off again.

11. Method of Scoring

Try. A try is scored by first grounding the ball in the opponent's in-goal.

A try shall be awarded if one would probably have been scored but for foul play by the opposing team.

Goal. A goal is scored by kicking the ball over the opponents' cross-bar and between the goal-posts from the field-of-play by any place kick or drop kick, except a kick-off, drop-out or free kick, without touching the ground or any player of the kicker's team.

A goal is scored if the ball has crossed the bar, even though it may have been blown backwards afterwards and whether it has touched the cross-bar or either goal-post or not.

A goal is scored if the ball has crossed the bar notwithstanding a prior offence of the opposing team.

A goal may be awarded if the ball is illegally touched by any player of the opposing team and if the referee considers that a goal would otherwise probably have been scored.

The scoring values are as follows:

A try	5 points
A goal scored after a try	2 points
A goal from a penalty kick	3 points
A dropped goal (but not permitted from a free kick) or after a scrum taken in lieu of a free kick	3 points

12. Try and Touch-down

Grounding the ball is the act of a player who:

(*a*) *While holding the ball in his hand (or hands) or arm (or arms) brings the ball in contact with ground; or*

(*b*) *While the ball is on the ground either places his hand (or hands) or arm (or arms) on it with downward pressure, or falls upon it and the ball is anywhere under the front part of his body from waist to neck inclusive.*

Picking up the ball from the ground is not grounding it.

A. Try

(1) A player who is on-side scores a try when he carries the ball into his opponents' in-goal, or the ball is in his opponents' in-goal (and he first grounds it there).

(2) The scoring of a try includes the following cases:

(*a*) If a player carries, passes, knocks or kicks the ball into his in-goal and an opponent first grounds it.

(*b*) If, at a scrummage or ruck, a team is pushed over its goal-line and before the ball has emerged it is first grounded in in-goal by an attacking player.

(*c*) If the momentum of a player, when tackled, carries him into his opponents' in-goal and he first there grounds the ball.

(*d*) If a player first grounds the ball on his opponents' goal-line or if the ball is in contact with the ground and a goal-post.

(*e*) If a tackle occurs in such a position that the tackled player whilst complying with the Law is able to place the ball on or over the goal-line.

(3) If a player grounds the ball in his opponents' in-goal and picks it up again, a try is scored where it was first grounded.

(4) A try may be scored by a player who is in touch or in touch-in-goal provided he is not carrying the ball.

B. Penalty try

A penalty try shall be awarded between the posts if but for foul play by the defending team a try would probably have been scored, or it would probably have been scored in a more favourable position than that where the ball was grounded.

C. Touch-down

(1) A touch-down occurs when a player first grounds the ball in his in-goal.

(2) After a touch-down, play shall be restarted either by a drop-out or a scrummage.

D. Scrummage after grounding in case of doubt

Where there is doubt as to which team first grounded the ball in in-goal, a scrummage shall be formed 5m from the goal-line opposite the place where the ball was grounded. The attacking team shall put in the ball.

13. Kick at Goal after a Try

(1) After a try has been scored, the scoring team has the right to take a place kick or drop kick at goal, on a line through the place where the try was scored.

(2) If a kick is taken:

(*a*) It must be taken without undue delay.

(*b*) Any player including the kicker may place the ball.

(*c*) The *kicker's team*, except a placer, must be behind the ball when kicked.

(*d*) If the kicker kicks the ball from a placer's hands without the ball being on the ground, the kick is void.

(*e*) The *opposing team* must be behind the goal-line until the kicker begins his run or offers to kick when they may charge or jump with a view to preventing a goal.

(3) Neither the kicker nor a placer shall wilfully do anything which may lead the opposing team to charge prematurely. If either does so, the charge shall not be disallowed.

Penalty. For an infringement by the *kicker's team* – the kick shall be disallowed.

For an infringement by the *opposing team* – the charge shall be disallowed. If, however, the kick has been taken successfully, the goal shall stand. If it was unsuccessful, the kicker may take another kick under the original conditions without the charge and may change the type of kick.

14. In-goal

In-goal is the area bounded by a goal-line, touch-in-goal lines and dead-ball line. It includes the goal-lines and goal-posts but excludes touch-in-goal lines and dead-ball line.

Touch-in-goal occurs when the ball, or a player carrying it, touches a corner post, a touch-in-goal line or the ground or a person or object on or beyond it. The flag is not part of the corner post.

5m scrummage

(*1*) A 5m scrummage is a scrummage formed 5m from the goal-line opposite the place where the ball became dead in in-goal, but no closer than 5m from the touch line. The attacking team shall put in the ball.

(*2*) If a player carrying the ball in in-goal is so held that he cannot ground the ball, the ball becomes dead.

(*3*) A 5m scrummage shall be formed:

(*a*) If a defending player heels, kicks, carries, passes or knocks the ball into his in-goal, and it there becomes dead without an infringement having occurred, except where:

a try is scored; or

he wilfully knocks or throws the ball from the field-of-play into touch-in-goal or over his dead-ball line; or

(*b*) if a defending player carrying the ball in the field-of-play is forced into his in-goal and he then touches down; or

(*c*) if, at a scrummage or ruck a defending team, with the ball in its possession, is pushed over its goal-line and before the ball has emerged first grounds it in in-goal.

Drop-out

Except where the ball is knocked on or thrown forward in the field of play or in in-goal, if an attacking player kicks, carries, passes or charges down the ball from an opponent's ruck and it travels into the opponents' in-goal either directly or having touched a defender who does not wilfully attempt to stop, catch or kick it, and it is there:

grounded by a defending player; or

goes into touch-in-goal or over the dead-ball line;

a drop-out shall be awarded.

Penalties.

(*a*) A penalty try shall be awarded when by foul play in in-goal the defending team has prevented a try which otherwise would *probably* have been scored.

(*b*) A try shall be disallowed and a penalty kick awarded, if a try would *probably not* have been gained but for foul play by the attacking team.

(*c*) For foul play in in-goal while the ball is out of play the penalty kick shall be awarded at the place where play would otherwise have restarted and, in addition, the player shall either be ordered off or cautioned that he will be sent off if he repeats the offence.

(*d*) For wilfully charging or obstructing in in-goal a player who has just kicked the ball the penalty shall be either a penalty kick in the field-of-play 5m from the goal-line opposite the place of infringement, or at the option of the non-offending team, a penalty kick where the ball alights as provided under Law 26(3) Penalty (ii)(*b*).

(*e*) For other infringements in in-goal, the penalty shall be the same as for a similar infringement in the field-of-play except that the mark for a penalty kick or free kick shall be in the field-of-play 5m from the goal-line opposite the place of infringement and the place of any scrummage shall be 5m from the goal-line opposite the place of infringement but not within 5m of the touch-line.

Note

If from a free kick or penalty kick taken in in-goal the ball is made dead by the defending team before it has crossed the goal-line, a scrummage shall be awarded to the attacking team 5m from the goal-line opposite to where it was made dead.

15. Drop-out
A drop-out is a drop kick awarded to the defending team.

(1) The drop kick must be taken from anywhere on or behind the 22m line; otherwise the ball shall be dropped out again.

(2) The ball must cross the 22m line; otherwise the opposing team may have it dropped out again, or have a scrummage formed at the centre of the 22m line. If it crosses the 22m line and is then blown back, play shall continue.

(3) If the ball is kicked directly into touch, the opposing team may accept the kick, have the ball dropped out again, or have a scrummage formed at the centre of the 22m line.

(4) The *kicker's team* must be behind the ball when kicked; otherwise a scrummage shall be formed at the centre of the 22m line.

(5) The *opposing team* must not charge over the 22m line; otherwise the ball shall be dropped out again.

16. Fair-catch (Mark)
(*a*) *A player makes a fair-catch when in his 22m area or in his in-goal, he having at least one foot on the ground, cleanly catches the ball direct from a kick by one of his opponents and, at the same time, he exclaims 'Mark!'.*

A fair catch may be obtained even though the ball on its way touches a goal post or crossbar and can be made in in-goal.

(*b*) *A free kick is awarded for a fair-catch.*

(1) The kick shall be taken by the player making the fair-catch, unless he is injured in doing so. If he is unable to take the kick within 1 minute a scrummage shall be formed at the mark. His team shall put in the ball.

(2) If the mark is in in-goal, any resultant scrummage shall be 5m from the goal-line on a line through the mark.

17. Knock-on or Throw-forward

A knock-on occurs when the ball travels forward towards the direction of the opponents' dead-ball line after a player loses possession of it, or a player propels or strikes it with his hand or arm, or it strikes a player's hand or arm and touches the ground or another player before it is recovered by the player.

A throw-forward occurs when a player carrying the ball throws or passes it in the direction of his opponents' dead-ball line. A throw-in from touch is not a throw-forward. If the ball is not thrown or passed forward but it bounces forward after hitting a player or the ground, it is not a throw-forward.

(1) The knock-on or throw-forward must not be *intentional*.

Penalty. Free kick at the place of infringement or in accord with Law 14, Penalty (*e*). A penalty try may be awarded.

(2) If the knock-on or throw-forward is *unintentional*, a scrummage shall be formed either at the place of infringement or, if it occurs at a line-out, 15m from the touch-line along the line-of-touch unless:

The ball is knocked on by a player who is in the act of charging down the kick of an opponent but is not attempting to catch the ball; or

The ball is knocked on one or more times by a player who is in the act of catching or picking it up or losing possession of it and is recovered by that player before it has touched the ground or another player.

18. Tackle

A tackle occurs when a player carrying the ball in the field-of-play is held by one or more opponents so that while he is so held he is brought to the ground or the ball comes into contact with the ground. If the ball carrier is on one knee, or both knees, or is sitting on the ground or is on top of another player who is on the ground, the ball carrier is deemed to have been brought to the ground.

(1) (*a*) A tackled player must immediately pass the ball, or release the ball and get up or move away from the ball.

(*b*) After a tackle any other player must be on his feet when he plays the ball.

(*c*) A player who goes to the ground and gathers the ball or with the ball in his possession but who is not tackled must immediately get up on his feet with the ball, or pass the ball, or release the ball and get up or move away from the ball.

(2) It is illegal for any player:

(*a*) To prevent a tackled player from passing or releasing the ball, or getting up or moving away after he has passed or released it.

(*b*) To pull the ball from a tackled player's possession or attempt to pick up the ball before the tackled player has released it.

(*c*) While lying on the ground after a tackle to play or interfere with the ball in any way or to tackle or attempt to tackle an opponent carrying the ball.

(*d*) To wilfully fall on or over a player lying on the ground with the ball in his possession.

(*e*) To wilfully fall on or over players lying on the ground with the ball between them, or in close proximity.

(*f*) While lying on the ground in close proximity to the ball to prevent an opponent from gaining possession of it.

(3) A player must not fall on or over the ball emerging from a scrummage or ruck.

Penalty: Penalty kick at the place of infringement.

(4) A try may be scored if the momentum of a player carries him into his opponents' in-goal even though he is tackled.

19. Lying with, on or Near the Ball
The requirements of this Law are now incorporated into Law 18.

20. Scrummage
A scrummage, which can take place only in the field-of-play, is formed by players from each team closing up in readiness to allow the ball to be put on the ground between them but is not formed within 5m of the touch-line. If the ball in a scrummage is on or over the goal-line the scrummage is ended.

The middle player in each front row is the hooker, and the players on either side of him are the props.

The middle line means an imaginary line on the ground directly beneath the line formed by the junction of the shoulders of the two front rows.

Forming a scrummage

(1) A team must not wilfully delay the forming of a scrummage.

(2) Every scrummage shall be formed at the place of infringement or as near thereto as is practicable within the field-of-play. It must be stationary with the middle line parallel to the goal-lines until the ball has been put in.

Before commencing engagement each front row must be in a crouched position with heads and shoulders no lower than their hips and so that they are no more than one arm's length from their opponents' shoulders.

In the interest of safety each prop should touch on their opponent's upper arms and then pause prior to engagement in the sequence: crouch – touch – pause – engage.

(3) It is dangerous play for a front row to form down some distance from its opponents and rush against them.

(4) A minimum of 5 players from each team shall be required to form a scrummage. While the scrummage is in progress a minimum of 5 players shall remain bound on the scrummage until it ends. Each front row shall have 3 players in it *at all times*. The head of a player in the front row shall not be next to the head of a player of the same team.

(5) (*a*) While a scrummage is forming, the shoulders of each player in the front row must not be lower than his hips; all players in each front row must adopt a normal stance; both feet must be on the ground and not be crossed; the hookers must be in a hooking position; a hooker's foot must not be in front of the forward feet of his props.

(*b*) While the scrummage is taking place, players in each front row must have their weight firmly on at least one foot and be in a position for an effective forward shove and the shoulders of each player must not be lower than his hips.

(*c*) When 5 players of a team form the scrummage the 2 players in the second row must remain bound to each other until the scrummage ends.

Binding of players

(6) (*a*) The players of each front row shall bind firmly and continuously while the scrummage is forming, while the ball is being put in and while it is in the scrummage.

(*b*) The hooker may bind either over or under the arms of his props but, in either case, he must bind firmly around their bodies at or below the level of the armpits. The props must bind the hooker similarly. The hooker must not be supported so that he is not carrying any weight on either foot.

(*c*) The outside (loose head) prop *must* either bind his opposing (tight head) prop with his left arm inside the right arm of his opponent, or place his left hand or forearm on his left thigh. The tight head prop *must* bind with his right arm outside the left upper arm of his opposing loose head prop. He may grip the jersey of his opposing loose head prop with his right hand but only to keep himself and the scrummage steady and he must not exert a downward pull.

(*d*) All players in a scrummage, other than those in a front row, must bind with at least one arm and hand around the body of another player of the same team.

(*e*) No outside player other than a prop may hold an opponent with his outer arm.

Putting the ball into the scrummage

(7) When an infringement occurs the team not responsible shall put in the ball. In all other circumstances, unless otherwise provided, the ball

shall be put in by the team which was moving forward prior to the stoppage or, if neither team was moving forward, by the attacking team.

(8) The ball shall be put in without delay as soon as the two front rows have closed together. A team must put in the ball when ordered to do so and on the side first chosen.

(9) The player putting in the ball shall:

(*a*) Stand *1m* from the scrummage and midway between the two front rows.

(*b*) Hold the ball with both hands midway between the two front rows at a level midway between his knee and ankle.

(*c*) From that position put in the ball without any delay or without feint or backward movement, i.e. with a single forward movement, and at a quick speed straight along the middle line so that it first touches the ground immediately beyond the width of the nearer prop's shoulders.

(10) Play in the scrummage begins when the ball leaves the hands of the player putting it in.

(11) If the ball is put in and it comes out at either end of the tunnel, it shall be put in again, unless a free kick or penalty kick has been awarded. If the ball comes out otherwise than at either end of the tunnel and if a penalty kick has not been awarded play shall proceed.

Restrictions on front row players

(12) All front row players must place their feet so as to allow a clear tunnel. A player must not prevent the ball from being put into the scrummage, or from touching the ground at the required place.

(13) No front row player may raise or advance a foot until the ball has left the hands of the player putting it into the scrummage.

(14) When the ball has touched the ground, any foot of any player in either front row may be used in an attempt to gain possession of the ball, subject to the following:

Players in the front rows must not *at any time* during the scrummage wilfully:

(*a*) Raise both feet off the ground at the same time; or

(*b*) Adopt any position or take any action, by twisting or lowering the body or by pulling on an opponent's dress, which is likely to cause the scrummage to collapse; or

(*c*) Lift an opponent off his feet or force him upwards out of the scrummage; or

(*d*) Kick the ball out of the tunnel in the direction from which it is put in.

Restrictions on players

(15) Any player who is not in either front row must not play the ball while it is in the tunnel.

(16) A player must not:

(*a*) Return the ball into the scrummage; or

(*b*) Handle the ball in the scrummage except in the act of obtaining a 'push over' try or touch-down; or

(*c*) Pick up the ball in the scrummage by hand or legs; or

(*d*) Wilfully collapse the scrummage; or

(*e*) Wilfully fall or kneel in the scrummage; or

(*f*) Attempt to gain possession of the ball in the scrummage with any part of the body except the foot or lower leg.

(17) (*a*) The player putting in the ball and his immediate opponent must not kick the ball while it is in the scrummage.

(18) A scrummage must not be wilfully wheeled.

Penalty. (*a*) For an infringement of paragraphs 1, 2, 4, 5, 6*d*, 6*e*, 8, 9, 12, 13, 14*d*, 15, 16*a*, 16*b*, 16*c*, 16*f*, 17*a* and 17*b*, a free kick at the place of infringement.

(*b*) For an infringement of paragraphs 3, 6*a*, 6*b*, 6*c*, 14*a*, 14*b*, 14*c*, 16*d* and 16*e*, a penalty kick at the place of infringement.

Notes

(*1*) If in a scrummage a player whose feet are the 'hindmost' feet in that scrummage ceases to be bound while the ball is at his feet, the scrummage is over since the ball is deemed to be out of the scrummage.

(*2*) If a player repeatedly infringes he must be dealt with under Law 26(2).

(*3*) The referee should stop play if an unintentional wheel reaches 45 degrees.

For Off-side at Scrummage see Law 24b.

21. Ruck

A ruck, which can take place only in the field-of-play, is formed when the ball is on the ground and one or more players from each team are on their feet and in physical contact, closing around the ball between them. If the ball in a ruck is on or over the goal-line the ruck is ended.

(1) A player joining a ruck must have his head and shoulders no lower than his hips. He must bind with at least one arm around the body of a player of his team in the ruck.

Penalty. Free kick at the place of infringement.

(2) A player must not:

(*a*) Return the ball into the ruck.

Penalty. Free kick at the place of infringement.

(*b*) Handle the ball in the ruck except in the act of securing a try or touch-down.

(*c*) Pick up the ball in the ruck by hand or legs.

(*d*) Wilfully collapse the ruck.

(*e*) Jump on top of other players in the ruck.

(*f*) Wilfully fall or kneel in the ruck.

(*g*) While lying on the ground interfere in any way with the ball in or emerging from the ruck. He must do his best to roll away from it.

Penalty. Penalty kick at the place of infringement.

(3) When the ball in a ruck becomes unplayable a scrummage shall be ordered and the ball put in by the team moving forward immediately prior to the formation of the ruck. When neither team was moving forward or where the referee is unable to determine which team was moving forward, the ball shall be put in by the attacking team.

Note

Before whistling for a scrummage the referee should allow a reasonable time for the ball to emerge from the ruck particularly if either team is moving forward. If the ruck becomes stationary or in the opinion of the referee the ball will probably not emerge from the ruck without delay, he should order a scrummage.

22. Maul

A maul, which can take place only in the field-of-play, is formed by one or more players from each team on their feet and in physical contact closing round a player who is carrying the ball.

A maul ends when the ball is on the ground or the ball or a player carrying it emerges from the maul or when a scrummage is ordered or if the ball is on or over the goal-line.

(1) A player joining a maul must have his head and shoulders no lower than his hips.

Penalty. Free kick at the place of infringement.

(2) A player must not:

(*a*) Jump on top of other players in a maul.

(*b*) Wilfully collapse a maul.

(*c*) Attempt to drag another player out of the maul.

(3) A player is not in physical contact unless he is caught in or bound to the maul and not merely alongside it.

Penalty. Penalty kick at the place of infringement.

(4) (*a*) When the ball in a maul becomes unplayable or a maul becomes stationary a scrummage shall be ordered and the ball shall be put in by the team not in possession at the commencement of the maul, except where the referee is unable to determine which team was in possession then the ball shall be put in by the team which was moving forward prior to the stoppage or, if neither team was moving forward, by the attacking team.

(*b*) If a player catches the ball direct from a kick by an opponent, other than from a kick-off or from a drop-out, and is immediately held so that a maul ensues and the ball becomes unplayable or the maul becomes stationary, his team shall put in the ball at the ensuing scrummage.

Notes

(*1*) Before whistling for a scrummage, the referee should allow a reasonable time for the ball to emerge from the maul, particularly if either team is moving forward. If in his opinion the ball will probably not emerge from the maul without delay, he should not allow prolonged wrestling for the ball but should order a scrummage. If the maul has become stationary, but the ball is being moved and can be seen by the referee he should similarly allow a reasonable time for the ball to emerge.

(*2*) If any player in a maul goes to ground, including being on one knee or both knees or is sitting on the ground, a scrummage is to be ordered unless the ball is immediately available for the continuation of play.

23. Touch and Line-out

A. Touch

(1) The ball is in touch when it is not being carried by a player and it touches a touch-line or the ground or a person or object on or beyond it, or when it is carried by a player and it or the player carrying it touches a touch-line or the ground beyond it.

(2) If the ball is not in touch and has not crossed the plane of the touch-line, a player who is in touch may kick the ball or propel it with his hand but not hold it.

(3) The ball is deemed to have been kicked directly into touch if, from a kick, it is in touch without having pitched on the playing area or without having touched or been touched in flight by a player or the referee.

B. Line-out

The line-of-touch is an imaginary line in the field-of-play at right angles to the touchline through the place where the ball is to be thrown in.

Formation of line-out

(1) A line-out is formed by at least 2 players from each team lining up in single lines parallel to the line-of-touch in readiness for the ball to be thrown in between them. The team throwing in the ball shall determine the maximum number of players from either team who so line up. Such players are those 'in the line-out', unless excluded below.

(2) Each team must line up at least half a metre on its side of the line-

of-touch, so as to leave a clear space of one metre between the two lines of players.

(3) The line-out stretches from 5m from the touch-line from which the ball is being thrown in to a position 15m from that touch-line.

(4) Any player of either team who is further than 15m from the touch-line when the line-out begins is not in the line-out.

Throwing in the ball

(5) When the ball is in touch the place at which it must be thrown in is as follows:

(*a*) When the ball goes into touch from a penalty kick or from a kick including a free kick within 22m of the kicker's goal-line, at the place where it touched or crossed the touch-line, except as otherwise provided.

(*b*) When the kicker has received the ball outside his 22m line and retreated behind that line before kicking, and on all other occasions when the ball is kicked directly into touch, after having been kicked otherwise than as stated in (*a*), opposite the place from which the ball was kicked or at the place where it touched or crossed the touch-line if that place be nearer to the kicker's goal-line.

(*c*) When a quick throw-in is taken, from any point along the touch-line between where the ball went into touch and the goal-line of the team throwing in the ball.

(*d*) Otherwise when the ball is in touch, at the place where the ball touched or crossed the touch-line.

(6) (*a*) When kicked into touch from a penalty kick, the ball will be thrown in at the line-out by the team which kicked the ball into touch.

(*b*) Otherwise the ball is to be thrown in by an opponent of the player whom it last touched, or by whom it was carried before being in touch.

(*c*) In the event of doubt as to which team should throw in the ball, the attacking team shall do so.

(*d*) The player throwing in the ball must not put any part of either foot in the field-of-play.

(7) The ball may be brought into play at a formed line-out or by a quick throw-in without waiting for players to form a line-out.

(8) At a formed line-out the ball must be thrown in at the place indicated in (5) so that it first touches the ground or touches or is touched by a player at least 5m from the touch-line along the line-of-touch.

(9) At a quick throw-in, the ball that went into touch must be used and, after going into touch, it must have been handled only by the player throwing it in. The throw must be straight along the line-of-touch for a distance of not less than 5m.

(10) If any of the foregoing requirements for throwing in the ball are

infringed, the opposing team shall have the right, at its option, to throw in the ball or to take a scrummage. If the requirements are infringed at a quick throw-in, then the opposing team's options, to throw in the ball or to take a scrummage, shall be at the place where the quick throw-in occurred.

If, on the second occasion, the ball is not thrown in correctly, a scrummage shall be formed and the ball shall be put in by the team which threw it in on the first occasion.

Beginning and end of line-out

(11) The line-out begins when the ball leaves the hands of the player throwing it in.

(12) The line-out ends when:

(*a*) A ruck or maul is taking place and all feet of players in the ruck or maul have moved beyond the line-of-touch; or

(*b*) A player carrying the ball leaves the line-out; or

(*c*) The ball has been passed, knocked back or kicked from the line-out; or

(*d*) The ball is thrown beyond a position 15m from the touch-line; or

(*e*) The ball becomes unplayable.

Peeling off

Peeling off occurs when a player (or players) moves from his position in the line-out for the purpose of catching the ball when it has been passed or knocked back by another of his team in the line-out.

(13) When the ball is in touch players who approach the line-of-touch must *always* be presumed to do so for the purpose of forming a line-out. Except in the peeling off movement such players must not leave the line-of-touch, or the line-out when formed, until the line-out has ended. A player must not begin to peel off until the ball has left the hands of the player throwing it in.

Exception. At a quick throw-in, when a player may come to the line-of-touch and retire from that position without penalty.

(14) In a peeling off movement a player must move parallel and close to the line-out.

Restrictions on players in line-out

(15) *Before* the ball has been thrown in and has touched the ground or has touched or been touched by a player, any player in the line-out must not:

(*a*) Be off-side; or

(*b*) Use an opponent as a support to enable him to jump for the ball; or push, charge, shoulder or obstruct an opponent; or (*c*) Use any player of his team as a support to enable him to jump for the ball or lift any player of his team or bind with any player of his team; or

(*d*) Stand within 5m of the touch-line or prevent the ball from being thrown 5m.

(16) When jumping for the ball a player must use both hands or his inside arm to catch or deflect the ball.

(17) *After* the ball has touched the ground or touched or been touched by a player, any player in the line-out must not:

(*a*) Be off-side; or

(*b*) Hold, push, shoulder or obstruct an opponent not holding the ball; or

(*c*) Charge an opponent except in an attempt to tackle him or to play the ball.

(18) Except when jumping for the ball or peeling off, each player in the line-out must remain at least 1m from the next player of his team until the ball has touched or has been touched by a player or has touched the ground.

(19) A player in the line-out may move into the space between the touch-line and the 5m mark only when the ball has been thrown beyond him and, if he does so he must not move towards his goal-line before the line-out ends, except in a peeling off movement.

(20) Until the line-out ends, no player may move beyond a position 15m from the touch-line except as allowed when the ball is thrown beyond that position in accordance with the *Exception* following Law 24D(1)(*d*).

(21) A player participating in the line-out as defined in Law 24D may run into a gap in the line-out and take the ball provided he does not charge or obstruct an opponent in the line-out.

Restrictions on players not in line-out

(22) Players of either team who are not in the line-out may not advance from behind the line-out and take the ball from the throw-in except a player advancing at a long throw-in.

Penalty. (*a*) for an infringement of paragraps 1, 2, 3, 4, 13, 14, 15*c*, 15*d*, 18 or 19, a free kick 15m from the touch-line along the line-of-touch.

(*b*) For an infringement of paragraphs 15*a*, 15*b*, 17, 20, 21, a penalty kick 15m from the touch-line along the line-of-touch.

(*c*) For an infringement of paragraph 22 a penalty kick on the offending team's off-side line (as defined in Law 24D) opposite the place of infringement, but not less than 15m from the touch-line.

Place of Scrummage. Any scrummage taken or ordered under this Law or as the result of any infringement in a line-out shall be formed

15m from the touch-line along the line-of-touch. *For Off-side at Line-out see Law 24D.*

24. Off-Side

Off-side means that a player is in a position in which he is out of the game and is liable to penalty. In general play *the player is in an off-side position because he is in front of the ball when it has been last played by another player of his team. In play at* scrummage, ruck, maul *or* line-out *the player is off-side because he remains or advances or otherwise infringes, in front of the line or place stated in, the relevant sections of this Law.*

A. Off-side in general play

(1) A player is in an off-side position if the ball has been kicked, or touched, or is being carried by one of his team behind him.

(2) There is no penalty for being in an off-side position unless:

(*a*) The player plays the ball or obstructs an opponent; or

(*b*) he being within 10m of an opponent waiting to play the ball or of the place where the ball pitches does not retire without delay and without interfering with the opponent; or

(*c*) he, on all other occasions, moves towards the opponents waiting to play the ball or to the place where the ball pitches, before he is put on-side.

Exceptions:

(i) When an off-side player cannot avoid being touched by the ball or by a player carrying it, he is 'accidentally off-side'. Play should be allowed to continue unless the infringing team obtains an advantage, in which case a scrummage should be formed at that place.

(ii) A player who receives an unintentional throw-forward is not off-side.

Penalty. Penalty kick at the place of infringement, or, at the option of the non-offending team, a scrummage at the place where the ball was last played by the offending team. If the latter place is in-goal the penalty kick shall be taken or the scrummage shall be formed 5m from the goal-line on a line through the place.

For an infringement of (*2c*) by more than one player, the place of infringement will be that of the off-side player closest to the player waiting for the ball or to where the ball pitches.

B. Off-side at scrummage

The term off-side line means a line parallel to the goal-lines through the hindmost foot of the player's team in the scrummage.

While a scrummage is forming or is taking place:

(1) A player is off-side if:

(*a*) He joins it from his opponents' side; or

(*b*) He, not being in the scrummage nor the player of either team who puts the ball in the scrummage, fails to retire behind the off-side line or to his goal-line, whichever is the nearer, or places either foot in front of the off-side line while the ball is in the scrummage.

A player may leave a scrummage provided he retires immediately behind the off-side line. If he wishes to rejoin the scrummage, he must do so behind the ball. He may not play the ball as it emerges between the feet of his front row if he is in front of the off-side line.

Exception: The restrictions on leaving the scrummage in front of the off-side line do not apply to a player taking part in wheeling a scrummage providing he immediately plays the ball.

(2) A player is off-side if he, being the player on either team who puts the ball in the scrummage, remains, or places either foot, in front of the ball while it is in the scrummage.

(3) A player is off-side if he, being the immediate opponent of the player putting in the ball, takes up a position on or moves to the opposite side of the scrummage in front of the off-side line.

Penalty. Penalty kick at the place of infringement.

C. Off-side at ruck or maul
The term off-side line means a line parallel to the goal-lines through the hindmost foot of the player's team in the ruck or maul.

(1) *Ruck or maul otherwise than at line-out*
While a ruck or maul is taking place (including a ruck or maul which continues after a line-out has ended), a player is off-side if he:

(*a*) Joins it from his opponents' side; or

(*b*) Joins it in front of the off-side line; or

(*c*) Does not join the ruck or maul but fails to retire behind the off-side line *without delay*; or

(*d*) unbinds from the ruck or leaves the maul and does not *immediately* retire behind the off-side line or once he is on-side, if he rejoins the ruck or maul in front of the hindmost player of his team.

(*e*) Advances beyond the off-side line with either foot and does not rejoin the ruck or maul.

Penalty. Penalty kick at the place of infringement.

(2) *Ruck or maul at line-out*
The term 'participating in the line-out' has the same meaning as in Section D of this Law. A player participating in the line-out is not obliged to join or remain in the ruck or maul and if he is not in the ruck or maul he continues to participate in the line-out until it has ended. While a line-out is in progress and a ruck or maul takes place, a player is off-side if he:

(*a*) Joins the ruck or maul from his opponents' side; or

(*b*) Joins in front of the hindmost player of his team; or

(*c*) Being a player who is participating in the line-out and is not in the ruck or maul, does not retire to and remain at the off-side line defined in this section (*Penalty*. Penalty kick 15m from the touch-line along the line-of-touch); or

(*d*) Being a player who is not participating in the line-out, remains or advances with either foot in front of the off-side line defined in Section D of this Law.

Penalty. Penalty kick on the offending team's off-side line (as defined in Section D of this Law) opposite the place of infringement, but not less than 15m from the touch-line.

D. Off-side at line-out

The term participating in the line-out refers exclusively to the following players: those players who are in the line-out, the player who throws in the ball, his immediate opponent who may have the option of throwing in the ball, and one other player of either team who takes up position to receive the ball if it passed or knocked back from the line-out.

All other players are not *participating in the line-out.*

The term 'off-side line' means a line 10m behind the line-of-touch and parallel to the goal-lines or, if the goal-line be nearer than 10m to the line-of-touch, the 'off-side line' is the goal-line.

Off-side while participating in line-out

(1) A participating player is off-side if:

(*a*) *Before* the ball has touched a player or the ground he wilfully remains or advances with either foot in front of the line-of-touch, unless he advances while jumping for the ball provided that the jump is made from his side of the line-of-touch; or

(*b*) *After* the ball has touched a player or the ground, if he is not carrying the ball, he advances with either foot in front of the ball, unless he is lawfully tackling or attempting to tackle an opponent who is participating in the line-out. Such tackle or attempt to tackle must, however, start from the side of the ball; or

(*c*) *Before* the line-out ends he moves beyond a position 15m from the touch-line.

Exception: Players of the team throwing in the ball may move beyond a position of 15m from the touch-line for a long throw-in to them. They may do so only when the ball leaves the hand of the player throwing it in and if they do so their opponents participating in the line-out may follow them. If players so move and the ball is not thrown to or beyond them they must be penalised for off-side.

Penalty. Penalty kick 15m from the touch-line and along the line-of-touch.

(2) The player throwing in the ball and his immediate opponent must:

(*a*) Remain within 5m of the touch-line; or

(*b*) Retire to the off-side line; or

(*c*) Join the line-out after the ball has been thrown in 5m; or

(*d*) Move into position to receive the ball if it is passed or knocked back from the line-out provided no other player is occupying that position at that line-out.

Penalty. Penalty kick 15m from the touch-line and along the line-of-touch.

Off-side while not participating in line-out

(3) A player who is not participating is off-side if before the line-out has ended he advances or remains with either foot in front of the off-side line.

Exception: Players of the team throwing in the ball who are not participating in the line-out may advance for a long throw-in to them beyond the line-out. They may do so only when the ball leaves the hand of the player throwing in the ball and, if they do, their opponents may advance to meet them. If players so advance for a long throw-in to them and the ball is not thrown to them they must be penalised for off-side.

Players returning to on-side position

(4) A player is not obliged, before throwing in the ball, to wait until players of his team have returned to or behind the line-out but such players are off-side unless they return to an on-side position *without delay*.

Penalty. Penalty kick on the offending team's off-side line opposite the place of infringement, but not less than 15m from the touch-line.

25. On-side

On-side means that a player is in the game and not liable to penalty for off-side.

Player made on-side by action of his team

(1) Any player who is off-side in general play becomes on-side as a result of any of the following actions of his team:

(*a*) When the off-side player has retired behind the player of his team who last kicked, touched or carried the ball; or

(*b*) When one of his team carrying the ball has run in front of him; or

(*c*) When one of his team has run in front of him after coming from the place or from behind the place where the ball was kicked. In order to put the off-side player on-side, this other player must be in the playing area. But he is not debarred from following up in touch or touch-in-goal.

Player made on-side by action of opposing team
(2) Any player who is off-side in general play, *except* an off-side player within 10m of an opponent waiting to play the ball or where the ball pitches, becomes on-side as a result of any of the following actions: when an opponent carrying the ball has run 5m or when an opponent kicks or passes the ball, or when an opponent *intentionally* touches the ball and does not catch or gather it.

An off-side player within 10m of an opponent waiting to play the ball or where the ball pitches *cannot* be put on-side by *any* action of his opponents. Any *other* off-side player in general play is *always* put on-side when an opponent plays the ball.

Player retiring at scrummage, ruck, maul or line-out
(3) A player who is in an off-side position when a scrummage, ruck, maul or line-out is forming or taking place and is retiring as required by Law 24 (Off-side) becomes on-side when an opponent carrying the ball has run 5m, or when an opponent has kicked the ball.

An off-side player in this situation is *not* put on-side when an opponent passes the ball.

26. Foul Play
Foul play is any action by a player which is contrary to the letter and spirit of the Game and includes obstruction, unfair play, misconduct, dangerous play, unsporting behaviour, retaliation and repeated infringements.

Obstruction
(1) It is illegal for any player:
(*a*) Who is running for the ball to charge or push an opponent also running for the ball, except shoulder to shoulder.
(*b*) Who is in an off-side position wilfully to run or stand in front of another player of his team who is carrying the ball thereby preventing an opponent from reaching the latter player.
(*c*) Who is carrying the ball after it has come out of a scrummage, ruck, maul or line-out, to attempt to force his way through the players of his team in front of him.
(*d*) Who is an outside player in a scrummage or ruck to prevent an opponent from advancing round the scrummage or ruck.
Penalty. Penalty kick at the place of infringement. A penalty try may be awarded.

Unfair play, repeated infringements
(2) It is illegal for any player:

(*a*) Deliberately to play unfairly or wilfully infringe any Law of the Game.

(*b*) Wilfully to waste time.

(*c*) Wilfully to knock or throw the ball from the playing area into touch, touch-in-goal or over the dead-ball line.

(*d*) To infringe repeatedly any Law of the Game.

Penalty. For (*b*) and (*c*) a free kick, and for (*a*) and (*d*) a penalty kick at the place of infringement. A penalty try may be awarded. For offences under (*2c*) occurring in in-goal, Law 14 penalty (*e*) applies. For offences under (*2d*) a player may be cautioned and, if he repeats the offence, must be ordered off.

Misconduct, dangerous play

(3) It is illegal for any player:

(*a*) To strike an opponent.

(*b*) Wilfully to hack or kick an opponent or trip him with the foot, or to trample on an opponent lying on the ground.

(*c*) To tackle early, or late or dangerously, including the action known as a stiff arm tackle.

(*d*) Who is not running for the ball wilfully to charge or obstruct an opponent who has just kicked the ball.

(*e*) To hold, push, charge, obstruct or grasp an opponent not holding the ball, except in a scrummage, ruck or maul. (Except in a scrummage or ruck, the dragging out of a player lying close to the ball is permitted. Otherwise pulling any part of the clothing of an opponent is holding.)

(*f*) In the front row of a scrummage to form down some distance from the opponents and rush against them.

(*g*) In the front row of a scrummage wilfully to lift an opponent off his feet or force him upwards out of the scrummage.

(*h*) Wilfully to cause a scrummage or ruck or maul to collapse.

(*i*) While the ball is out of play to molest, obstruct or in any way interfere with an opponent or be guilty of any form of misconduct.

(*j*) To commit any misconduct on the playing area which is prejudicial to the spirit of good sportsmanship.

Penalty. A player guilty of misconduct and dangerous play shall either be ordered off or else cautioned that he will be ordered off if he repeats the offence. For a similar offence after caution the player must be ordered off.

In addition to a caution or ordering off a penalty try or a penalty kick shall be awarded as follows:

(i) If the offence prevents a try which would otherwise *probably* have been scored, a penalty try shall be awarded.

(ii) The place for a penalty kick shall be:

(*a*) For offences other than (*d*) and (*i*), at the place of infringement.

(*b*) For an infringement of (*d*) the non-offending team shall have the option of taking the kick at the place of infringement or where the ball alights, and if the ball alights:

in touch, the mark is 15m from the touch-line on a line parallel to the goal-lines through the place where it went into touch; or

within 15m from the touch-line, it is 15m from the touch-line on a line parallel to the goal-lines through the place where it alighted; or

in-goal, touch-in-goal, or over or on the dead-ball line, it is 5m from the goal-line on a line parallel to the touch-line through the place where it crossed the goal-line or 15m from the touch-line, whichever is the greater.

When the offence takes place in touch the 'place of infringement' in the optional penalty award is 15m from the touch-line opposite to where the offence took place.

If the offence takes place in touch-in goal, the 'place of infringement', in the optional penalty award, is in the field-of-play 5m from the goal-line and 15m from the touch-line.

(*c*) In the case of an offence against (*i*) at any place where the ball would next have been brought into play if the offence had not occurred, or, if that place is on or beyond the touch-line, 15m from the place, on a line parallel to the goal-lines.

(iii) For an infringement in in-goal, a penalty kick is to be awarded as provided for under Law 14 Penalties.

(iv) For an offence under Law 26(3)(*i*), the penalty kick is to be taken at whichever is the place where play would restart, i.e. at the 22m line (at any point the non-offending team may select), or at the centre of the halfway line, or if a scrummage 5m from the goal-line would otherwise have been awarded, at the place 15m from the touch-line on a line 5m from and parallel to the goal-line, whichever is the greater.

(v) For an offence which occurs outside the playing area while the ball is *still in play* and which is not otherwise covered in the foregoing, the penalty kick shall be awarded in the playing area 15m from the touch-line and opposite to where the offence took place.

(vi) For an offence reported by a touch-judge under Law 6B(6) a penalty kick may be awarded where the offence occurred or advantage may be played.

Player ordered off

A player who is ordered off shall take no further part in the match. When a player is ordered off, the referee shall, as soon as possible after the match, send to the Union, or other disciplinary body having jurisdiction over the match, a report naming the player and describing the circumstances which necessitated the ordering off. The Union or other disciplinary body having jurisdiction over the match shall consider such report and any other evidence they deem appropriate. They shall then take such action and impose such punishment as they see fit.

Citing of Players

Where a player commits an act of foul play which has not been detected by match officials, either of the Unions or affiliated organisations participating in the match have the discretion to cite that player to show cause why he should not be held accountable in the same way as a player who has been ordered off.

Under Law 26 when a player is ordered off the playing enclosure, or the match is abandoned under Law 26, in a match played under the jurisdiction of the RFU the procedure shall be as follows: the referee shall send his report within forty-eight hours to:

(a) The Disciplinary Secretary of the Constituent Body to which the player's club is allocated.

(b) The RFU when two or more players are ordered off together for offences arising from their involvement in the same incident and the Clubs for which they were playing are allocated to separate Constituent Bodies.

(c) The RFU if the Club for whom the player was playing is not allocated to a Constituent Body.

(d) The Union for which the player was playing in International matches.

Note

In all the above cases the referee shall send a copy of his report to his own Referee Society.

(e) The Constituent Body in whose area the match was played if he is not a member of a recognised Referee Society.

The report will then be dealt with by the RFU under their powers contained in Bye-Law 13 (*g*) or by the Constituent Body concerned under the powers delegated to it under the powers contained in Bye-Law 13 (*d*) (see 'Delegation of Powers' in RFU Handbook).

Club secretaries shall report to their Constituent Bodies, within four days, the name and address of any player of their Club who has been ordered off the playing enclosure. This applies irrespective of whether the referee is a member of a Society or not.

In the event of an abandoned match the referee should:

(1) identify the individual culprits who alone will be disciplined under Law 26;

(2) abandon the game under Law 6;

(3) explain to both captains the reasons why he is abandoning it.

27. Penalty kick

A penalty kick is a kick awarded to the non-offending team as stated in the

Laws. It may be taken by any player of the non-offending team and by any form of kick provided that the kicker, if holding the ball, must propel it out of his hands or, if the ball is on the ground, he must propel it a visible distance from the mark. He may keep his hands on the ball while kicking it.

(1) The non-offending team has the option of taking a scrummage at the mark and shall put in the ball.

(2) When a penalty kick is taken the following shall apply:

(*a*) The kick must be taken without undue delay.

(*b*) The kick must be taken at or behind the mark on a line through the mark, and the kicker may place the ball for a place kick. If the place prescribed by the Laws for the award of a penalty kick is within 5m of the opponents' goal-line, the mark for the penalty kick or a scrummage taken instead of it shall be 5m from the goal-line on a line through that place.

(*c*) The kicker may kick the ball in any direction and he may play the ball again, without any restriction except that if he has indicated to the referee that he intends to attempt a kick at goal, or has taken any action indicating such intention, he must not kick the ball in any other way. A player kicking for touch may only punt or drop kick the ball. Any indication of intention is irrevocable.

(*d*) The kicker's team, except the placer for a place kick, must be behind the ball until it has been kicked. Retiring players of the kicker's team who are in front of the ball will not be penalised if their failure to retire is due to the rapidity with which the kick has been taken but they must not stop retiring and enter the game until:

the offside player has retired behind the player who kicked the ball; or one of his team carrying the ball has run in front of him; or one of his team has run in front of him after coming from behind the place where the ball was kicked.

(*e*) The *opposing team* must run without delay (and continue to do so while the kick is being taken and while the ball is being played by the kicker's team) to or behind a line parallel to the goal-lines and 10m from the mark, or to their own goal-line if nearer to the mark, if a kick at goal is taken they must there remain motionless with their hands by their sides until the kick has been taken. Retiring players will not be penalised if their failure to retire 10m is due to the rapidity with which the kick has been taken, but they must not stop retiring and enter the game until an opponent carrying the ball has run 5m.

(*f*) The *opposing team* must not prevent the kick or interfere with the kicker in any way. This applies to actions such as wilfully carrying, throwing or kicking the ball away out of reach of the kicker.

Penalty. For an infringement by the *kicker's team* – a scrummage at the mark. For an infringement by the *opposing team* – a penalty kick

10m in front of the mark or 5m from the goal-line, whichever is the nearer, on a line through the mark. Any player of the non-offending team may take the kick.

28. Free Kick
A free kick is a kick awarded for a fair-catch, or to the non-offending team as stated in the Laws.

The team awarded a free kick may not score a dropped goal until after the ball next becomes dead or the ball has been played or touched by an opposing player. This restriction applies similarly following a scrummage taken in lieu of a free kick.

A free kick awarded for an infringement may be taken by any player of the non-offending team.

A free-kick may be taken by any form of kick, unless kicking for touch, provided that the kicker, if holding the ball, must propel it out of his hands or, if the ball is on the ground, he must propel it a visible distance from the mark. He may keep his hand on the ball while kicking it.

(1) The team awarded a free kick has the option of taking a scrummage at the mark and shall put in the ball.

(2) When a kick is taken, it must be taken without undue delay.

(3) The kick must be taken at or behind the mark on a line through the mark and the kicker may place the ball for a place kick.

(4) If the place prescribed by the Laws for the award of a free kick is within 5m of the opponents' goal-line, the mark for the free kick, or the scrummage taken instead of it, shall be 5m from the goal-line on a line through that place.

(5) The kicker may kick the ball in any direction and he may play the ball again without restriction. A player kicking for touch may only punt or drop kick the ball.

(6) The kicker's team, except a placer for a place kick, must be behind the ball until it has been kicked. Retiring players of the kicker's team who are in front of the ball will not be penalised if their failure to retire is due to the rapidity with which the kick has been taken but they must not stop retiring and enter the game until:

the offside player has retired behind the player who kicked the ball;

or one of his team carrying the ball has run in front of him; or

one of his team has run in front of him after coming from behind the place where the ball was kicked.

(7) The *opposing team* must not wilfully resort to any action which may delay the taking of a free-kick. This includes actions such as wilfully carrying, throwing or kicking the ball away out of reach of the kicker.

(8) The *opposing team* must retire without delay to or behind a line parallel to the goal-lines and 10m from the mark or to their own goal-line if nearer to the mark, or 5m from their opponents' goal-line if the mark

is in in-goal. Having so retired, players of the opposing team may charge with a view to preventing the kick, as soon as the kicker begins his run or offers to kick. Retiring players will not be penalised if their failure to retire 10m is due to the rapidity with which the kick has been taken, but they may not stop retiring and enter the game until an opponent carrying the ball has run 5m.

(9) If having charged fairly, players of the opposing team prevent the kick from being taken, the kick is void.

(10) Neither the kicker nor the placer shall wilfully do anything which may lead the opposing team to charge prematurely. If either does so, the charge shall not be disallowed.

Penalty. For an infringement by the *kicker's team* or for a void kick – a scrummage at the mark and the *opposing team* shall put in the ball. If the mark is in in-goal, the scrummage shall be awarded 5m from the goal-line on a line through the mark. For an infringement by the *opposing team* – a free kick 10m in front of the mark or 5m from the goal-line whichever is nearer, on a line through the mark. Any player of the non-offending team may take the kick.

Reprinted by permission of the International Rugby Football Board. Full notes and interpretation of these Laws, with IRFB Directives, RFU Rulings, Referee's Signals and a Mini-Rugby Directive can be found in The Laws of the Game of Rugby Football, obtainable from the Rugby Football Union.

Softball

Softball

Softball may be played as a Fast Pitch (FP) game or as a Slow Pitch (SP). The Pitching Regulations for the two alternatives are set out in Rule 6 between pages 864–876. Other variations between the two games are marked (FP) or (SP) in the Rules.

Wherever 'he' or 'him' or their related pronouns appear in the rules, either as words or as parts of words, they have been used for literary purposes and are meant in their generic sense (i.e., to include all human kind, or both male and female sexes). The words 'Junior Olympic' or the initials 'JO' refer to youth softball.

1. DEFINITIONS

1. Altered Bat. A bat is considered altered when the physical structure of a legal softball bat has been changed. Replacing the handle of a metal bat with a wooden or other type handle, inserting material inside the bat, applying excessive tape (more than two layers) to the bat grip or painting a bat at the top or bottom for other than identification purposes are examples of altering a bat. Replacing the grip with another legal grip is not considered altering the bat. A 'flare' or 'cone' grip attached to the bat is considered an altered bat.

2. Appeal Play. An appeal play is a play on which an umpire may not make a decision until requested by a manager, coach or player. The appeal must be made before the next legal or illegal pitch or before the pitcher and all infielders have clearly vacated their normal fielding positions and have left fair territory on their way to the bench or dugout area. At the conclusion of the game, an appeal can be made until the umpires leave the field of play.

3. Base on Balls. A base on balls permits a batter to gain first base without liability to be put out and is awarded to a batter by the umpire when four pitches are judged to be balls.

(SP only) If the pitcher desires to walk a batter intentionally, he may do so by notifying the plate umpire who shall award the batter first base.

4. Base Path. A base path is an imaginary line 1.0m (3ft) to either side of a direct line between the bases.

5. Batted Ball. A batted ball is any ball that hits the bat or is hit by the bat and which lands either in fair or foul territory. No intention to hit the ball is necessary.

6. Batter's Box. The batter's box is the area to which the batter is restricted, he may touch the lines, but no part of his foot may be outside the lines.

7. Batter-baserunner. A batter-baserunner is a player who has finished his turn at bat but has not yet been put out or touched first base.

8. Batting Order. The batting order is the official listing of offensive players by name and uniform number in the order in which members of that team must come to bat. When the line-up card is submitted, it shall also include each player's defensive position.

9. Blocked Ball. A blocked ball is a batted or thrown ball that is touched, stopped, or handled by a person not engaged in the game, or which touches any object which is not part of the official equipment or official playing area.

10. Bunt. A bunt is a legally tapped ball not swung at, but intentionally met with the bat and tapped slowly within the infield.

11. Catch. A catch is a legally caught ball which occurs when the fielder catches a batted or thrown ball with hands or glove. In establishing a valid catch, the fielder shall hold the ball long enough to prove he has complete control of the ball and that his release of the ball is voluntary and intentional. If a player drops the ball while in the act of throwing it, it is a valid catch. If the ball is merely held in the fielder's arm(s) or prevented from dropping to the ground by some part of the fielder's body or clothing, the catch is not completed until the ball is in the grasp of the fielder's hands or glove. It is not a catch if a fielder, immediately after he contacts the ball collides with another player or wall or falls to the ground, and drops the ball as a result of the collision or falling to the ground.

12. Catcher's Box. The catcher's box is an area defined by lines which are considered within the catcher's box. The catcher's body and equipment are considered within the box unless touching the ground outside the box. The catcher must remain in the box until:

(*a*) (FP only) The pitch is released.

(*b*) (SP only) The pitched ball is batted, touches the ground or plate or reaches the catcher's box.

13. Charged Conference. A charged conference takes place when:

(*a*) (*Defensive Conference*) The defensive team requests a suspension of play for any reason and a representative (not in field) of the defensive team enters the playing field and gives the umpire cause to believe that he has delivered a message (by any means) to the pitcher. When the manager crosses the foul line on the return to the dugout, the conference is over.

(*b*) (*Offensive Conference*) The offensive team requests a suspension of play to allow the manager or other team representatives to confer with the batter and/or runner(s).

14. Chopped Ball. (SP only) A chopped hit ball occurs when the batter strikes downward with a chopping motion of the bat so that the ball bounces high into the air.

15. Coach. A coach is a member of the team at bat who takes his place within one of the coach's boxes on the field to direct the players of his team in running the bases. Two coaches are allowed. One coach can have in his possession in the coach's box, a score book, pen or pencil, and an indicator, which shall be used for scorekeeping or record keeping purposes only.

16. Crow Hop. (FP only) A crow hop is defined as the act of a pitcher who steps or hops off the front of the pitcher's plate, replants the pivot foot, establishing a second impetus (or starting point), pushes off from the newly established starting point and completes the delivery.

17. Dead Ball. The ball is not in play and is not considered in play again until the pitcher has the ball in his possession and 'Play Ball' has been declared by umpire. A dead ball line is considered in play.

18. Defensive Team. The defensive team is the team in the field.

19. Dislodged Base. A dislodged base is a base displaced from its proper position.

20. Disqualified Player. Refers to a player who violates the slow pitch home run rule and is disqualified for that game.

21. Double Play. A double play is a play by the defence resulting in two offensive players being legally put out.

22. Fake Tag. A form of obstruction by a fielder who neither has the ball nor is about to receive the ball, and which impedes the progress of a runner either advancing or returning to a base. The runner does not have to stop or slide. Merely slowing down when a fake tag is attempted would constitute obstruction.

23. Fair Ball. A fair ball is a batted ball that:

(*a*) Settles or is touched on or over fair territory between home and first base or between home and third base.

(*b*) Bounds over or past first or third base which is in fair territory, regardless of where the ball hits after going over the base.

(*c*) While on or over fair territory, touches the person, attached equipment or clothing of a player or an umpire.

(*d*) Touches first, second or third base.

(*e*) First falls or is first touched on or over fair territory beyond first, second or third base.

(*f*) While over fair territory, passes out of the playing field beyond the outfield fence.

(*g*) Hits the foul pole.

Note: A batted ball shall be judged according to the relative position of the ball and the foul line, including the foul pole, and not as to whether the fielder is on fair or foul territory at the time he touches the ball. It does not matter whether the ball first touches fair or foul territory, as long as it does not touch anything foreign to the natural ground in foul territory and complies with all other aspects of a fair ball.

24. Fair Territory. Fair territory is that part of the playing field within, and including, the first and third base foul lines from the home plate to the bottom of the playing field fence and perpendicularly upwards.

25. Fake Tag. A form of obstruction by a fielder who neither has the ball nor is about to receive the ball, and which impedes the progress of a runner either advancing or returning to a base. The runner does not have to stop or slide. Merely slowing down when a fake tag is attempted would constitute obstruction.

26. Fielder. A fielder is any player of the team in the field.

27. Fly Ball. A fly ball is any fair or foul ball batted into the air.

28. Force-Out. A force-out is an out which may be made only when a runner loses the right to the base he is occupying because the batter becomes a batter-runner, and before the batter-runner or a succeeding runner has been put out. *Note*: If the forced runner, after touching the next base, retreats for any reason towards the base he had last occupied, the force play is reinstated and he may again be put out if the defence tags the runner or the base to which the runner is forced.

29. Foul Ball. A foul ball is a batted ball that:

(*a*) Settles or is touched on or over foul territory between home and first base or between home and third base.

(*b*) Bounds or rolls past first or third base on or over foul territory.

(*c*) While over foul territory, touches the person, attached equipment or clothing of a player or an umpire, or any object foreign to the natural ground.

(*d*) First hits the ground or is first touched over foul territory beyond first or third base.

(*e*) Touches the batter or the bat in the batter's hand(s) a second time while the batter is within the batter's box.

30. Foul Tip. A foul tip is a batted ball which goes directly from the bat, not higher than the batter's head, to the catcher's hand(s) or glove and is legally caught by the catcher. It is not a catch if it is a rebound unless the ball first touched the catcher's hand(s) or glove and does not touch the ground, batter or umpire.

31. Helmet.

(*a*) **Offensive**: All helmets must have double ear flaps and be approved by the National Operating Committee on Standards of Athletic Equipment (NOCSAE).

(*b*) **Defensive**: Any player may wear an approved helmet with or without earflaps. It must have a bill.

(*c*) **Catcher**: Skull helmets currently do not have NOCSAE standards.

32. Home Team. The home team shall be designated by mutual agreement or by a flip of a coin, unless otherwise stated in the rules of the organisation which the schedule of games is being played.

33. Illegal Bat. An illegal bat is one that does not meet the requirements of Rule 3, Section 1. (For Illegal Warm-Up Bat, see Rule 3, Section 2.)

34. Illegally Batted Ball. An illegally batted ball occurs when the batter hits the ball fair or foul and:

(*a*) The entire foot is completely outside the lines of the batter's box and on the ground.

(*b*) Any part of the foot is touching home plate.

(*c*) An illegal or altered bat is used.

35. Illegal Pitcher. A player legally in the game, but one who may not pitch as a result of being removed from the pitching position by the umpire because of:

(*a*) Two charged defensive conferences in one inning.

(*b*) (SP only) Pitching or warming up with excessive speed after a warning.

Effect: If an illegal pitcher returns to the pitching position and has thrown one pitch he is ejected from the game.

36. Illegal Substitute. A player who has entered the game without reporting.

37. Ineligible Player. A player who does not meet the requirements of ASA Code. The determination of eligibility is not the responsibility of the umpire. The use of an ineligible player will constitute a forfeit if properly protested.

38. In Flight. In flight is the term used for any batted, thrown or pitched ball which has not yet touched the ground or some object or person other than a fielder.

39. In Jeopardy. In jeopardy is a term indicating that the ball is in play and an offensive player may be put out.

40. Infield. The infield is that portion of the field in fair territory which includes areas normally covered by infielders.

41. Infield Fly. An infield fly is a fair fly ball (not including a line drive or an attempted bunt) which can be caught by an infielder with ordinary effort when first and second bases or first, second and third bases are occupied before two are out. Any defensive player who positions himself in the infield at the start of the pitch shall be considered an infielder for the purpose of this rule. The infield fly is ruled when the ball reaches the highest point based on the position of the closest infielder regardless who makes the play. When it seems apparent that a batted ball will be an infield fly, the umpire shall immediately declare, 'Infield Fly. The batter is out' for the benefit of the runners. If the ball is near a foul line, the umpire shall declare, 'Infield Fly. The batter is out if fair.'

The ball is alive and runners may advance at the risk of the ball being caught. The runner can tag up and advance once the batted ball is touched (prior to catching), the same as on any fly ball. If a declared infield fly becomes a foul ball, it is treated the same as any foul.

42. Inning. An inning is that portion of a game within which the teams alternate on offence and defence and in which there are three outs for each team. A new inning begins immediately after the final out of the previous inning.

43. Interference. Interference is the act of an offensive player or team member which impedes or confuses a defensive player attempting to execute a play.

44. Junior Olympic Player. Any player 18 years and under who has not reached their 19th birthday prior to September 1. *Note*: If Junior Olympic players play on an adult team, it is considered playing in an adult league and adult rules will be in effect.

45. Leaping. (FP only) An act by the pitcher which causes him to be airborne on his initial move and push from the pitcher's plate. The momentum built by the forward movement of the pitcher causes the entire body including both the pivot foot and the non-pivot foot to be in the air and moving toward home plate as the delivery is completed. With this style of pitching, the pitcher will release the ball simultaneously with his return to the ground. The pivot foot will then slide to the side and drag as the pitcher follows through or completes the delivery. This follow through should not be confused with replanting and gaining a second starting point (defined as the 'crow hop'), but simply a finish or follow through of the leap style of pitching. At the completion of the leap, the non-pivot foot is planted but will not allow the pitcher to gain further distance towards the plate, therefore the slide and drag of the pivot foot is a legal act.

46. Legal Touch. A legal touch occurs when a runner or batter-runner who is not touching a base is touched by the ball while it is securely held in a fielder's hand(s). The ball is not considered as having been securely held if it is juggled or dropped by the fielder after having touched the runner, unless the runner deliberately knocks the ball from the hand(s) of the fielder. It is sufficient for the runner to be touched with the glove or hand(s) holding the ball.

47. Line Drive. A line drive is a fly ball that is batted sharply and directly into the playing field.

48. Obstruction. Obstruction is the act of:

(*a*) A defensive player or team member which hinders or prevents a batter from striking at or hitting a pitched ball.

(*b*) A fielder, who is not in possession of the ball, in the act of fielding a batted ball, nor about to receive a thrown ball, which impedes the progress of a runner or batter-runner who is legally running bases.

49. Offensive Team. The offensive team is the team at bat.

50. On-deck Batter. The on-deck batter is the offensive player whose name follows the name of the batter in the batting order.

51. Outfield. The outfield is that portion of the field in fair territory which is not normally covered by an infielder.

52. Overslide. An overslide is the act of an offensive player when, as a runner, he overslides a base he is attempting to reach. It is usually caused when his momentum causes him to lose contact with the base which then causes him to be in jeopardy. The batter-runner may overslide first base without being in jeopardy.

53. Overthrow. An overthrow occurs when a thrown ball from a fielder goes beyond the boundary lines of the playing field (dead ball territory) or becomes a blocked ball.

54. Passed Ball. (FP only) A passed ball is a legally delivered ball that should have been held or controlled by the catcher with ordinary effort.

55. Pivot Foot. (FP only) The pivot foot is that foot which must remain in contact with the pitcher's plate. Pushing off with the pivot foot from a place other than the pitcher's plate is illegal.

(SP only) The pivot foot is the foot which the pitcher must keep in constant contact with the pitcher's plate until the ball is released.

56. Play Ball. Play ball is the term used by the plate umpire to indicate that play shall start and shall not be declared until all defensive players are in fair territory except the catcher, who must be in the catcher's box.

57. Protests. There are three types of protests:

(*a*) Misinterpretation of a playing rule – must be made before the next pitch or, if on the last play of the game, before the umpires leave the playing field.

(*b*) Illegal substitute of re-entry – must be made while they are in the game and before the umpires leave the playing field.

(*c*) Ineligible player – can be made any time during the game or before the offending team's next game. Eligibility is the decision of the protest committee.

58. Quick Return Pitch. A quick return pitch is one made by the pitcher with the obvious attempt to catch the batter off balance. This would be before the batter takes his desired position in the batter's box or while he is still off balance as a result of the previous pitch.

59. Runner. A runner is an offensive player who has reached first base and has not yet been put out.

60. Sacrifice Fly. A sacrifice fly is scored when, with fewer than two outs, the batter scores a runner with a fly ball or line drive that is:

(*a*) caught.

(*b*) dropped by an outfielder (or an infielder running into the outfield), and, in the scorer's judgment, the runner could have scored after the catch had the fly ball or line drive been caught.

61. Starting Pitcher. The player listed as a pitcher on the line up card or official score book.

62. Starting Player. A starting player shall be official when the lineup is inspected and approved by the plate umpire and team manager at the pre-game meeting. The names may be entered on the official score sheet in advance of this meeting; however, changes can be made at the pre-game meeting with no charged substitutions.

63. Stealing. (FP only) Stealing is the act of a runner attempting to advance during a pitch to the batter.

64. Strike Zone. When a batter assumes a natural batting stance, the strike zone is that space over any part of home plate between the batter's:

(*a*) (FP only) Arm pits and the top of his knees.

(*b*) (SP only) Back shoulder and his front knee.

65. Time. Time is the term used by the umpire to order the suspension of play.

66. Triple Play. A triple play is a continuous action play by the defence in which three offensive players are put out.

67. Turn at Bat. A turn at bat begins when a player first enters the batter's box and continues until he is put out or becomes a batter-runner.

68. Wild Pitch. (FP only) A wild pitch is a legally delivered ball that the catcher cannot catch or stop and control with ordinary effort.

2. THE PLAYING FIELD

Section 1. The playing field is the area within which the ball may be legally played and fielded. There shall be a clear and unobstructed area between the foul lines and within the radius of the prescribed fence distances from home plate.

Official Distance Table

Adult	Division	Bases	Pitching	Min. Fence	Max. Fence
Fast Pitch	Women	60' (18.29m)	40' (12.19m)	200' (60.96m)	250' (76.20m)*
	Men	60' (18.29m)	46' (14.02m)	225' (68.58m)	250' (76.20m)
	Jr. Men	60' (18.29m)	46' (14.02m)	225' (68.58m)	250' (76.20m)
Modified Pitch	Women	60' (18.29m)	40' (12.19m)	200' (60.96m)	
	Men	60' (18.29m)	46' (14.02m)	265' (80.80m)	
Slow Pitch	Women	65' (19.81m)	50' (15.24m)	265' (80.80m)	275' (83.82m)
	Men	65' (19.81m)	50' (15.24m)	275' (83.82m)	315' (96.01m)*
	Coed	65' (19.81m)	50' (15.24m)	275' (83.82m)	300' (91.44m)
	Super	65' (19.81m)	50' (15.24m)	300' (91.44m)	325' (99.08m)
16-inch Pitch	Women	55' (16.76m)	38' (11.58m)	200' (60.96m)	
	Men	55' (16.76m)	38' (11.58m)	250' (76.20m)	

Youth	Division	Bases	Pitching	Min. Fence	Max. Fence
Fast Pitch	G10-U	55' (16.76m)	35' (10.67m)	150' (45.72m)	175' (53.34m)
	G12-U	60' (18.29m)	35' (10.67m)	175' (53.34m)	200' (60.96m)
	G14-U	60' (18.29m)	40' (12.19m)	175' (53.34m)	200' (60.96m)
	G16-U	60' (18.29m)	40' (12.19m)	200' (60.96m)	225' (68.58m)
	G18-U	60' (18.29m)	40' (12.19m)	200' (60.96m)	225' (68.58m)
	B10-U	55' (16.76m)	35' (10.67m)	150' (45.72m)	175' (53.34m)
	B12-U	60' (18.29m)	40' (12.19m)	175' (53.34m)	200' (60.96m)
	B14-U	60' (18.29m)	46' (14.02m)	175' (53.34m)	200' (60.96m)
	B16-U	60' (18.29m)	46' (14.02m)	200' (60.96m)	225' (68.58m)
	B18-U	60' (18.29m)	46' (14.02m)	200' (60.96m)	225' (68.58m)
Slow Pitch	G10-U	55' (16.76m)	35' (10.67m)	150' (45.72m)	175' (53.34m)
	G12-U	60' (18.29m)	40' (12.19m)	175' (53.34m)	200' (60.96m)
	G14-U	65' (19.81m)	46' (14.02m)	225' (68.58m)	250' (76.20m)
	G16-U	65' (19.81m)	50' (15.24m)	225' (68.58m)	250' (76.20m)
	G18-U	65' (19.81m)	50' (15.24m)	225' (68.58m)	250' (76.20m)
	B10-U	55' (16.76m)	35' (10.67m)	150' (45.72m)	175' (53.34m)
	B12-U	60' (18.29m)	40' (12.19m)	175' (53.34m)	200' (60.96m)
	B14-U	65' (19.81m)	46' (14.02m)	250' (76.20m)	275' (83.82m)
	B16-U	65' (19.81m)	50' (15.24m)	275' (83.82m)	300' (91.44m)
	B18-U	65' (19.81m)	50' (15.24m)	275' (83.82m)	300' (91.44m)

* Effective 1996.

Note: If the base distances or the pitching distance is found to be at the wrong dimensions during the course of the game, correct the error, with no penalty, and continue playing the game. Every effort should be made by the umpire to obtain the correct dimensions.

Section 2. Ground or special rules establishing the limits of the playing field may be agreed upon by leagues or opposing teams whenever backstops, fences, stands, vehicles, spectators or other obstructions are within the prescribed area. Any obstruction on fair ground less than the prescribed fence distances from home plate should be clearly marked for the umpire's information.

Section 3. For the layout of the diamond, refer to drawing showing official dimensions for a softball diamond. This section serves as an example for laying out a diamond with 60-foot bases and a 46-foot pitching distance.

To determine the position of home plate, draw a line in the direction desired to lay the diamond. Drive a stake at the corner of home plate nearest the catcher. Fasten a cord to this stake and tie knots, or otherwise mark the cord, at 46 feet (14.02m), 60 feet (18.29m), 84 feet 10¼ inches (25.86m), and at 120 feet (36.58m). Place the cord (without stretching) along the direction line and place a stake at the 46-foot (14.02m) marker. This will be the front line at the middle of the pitcher's

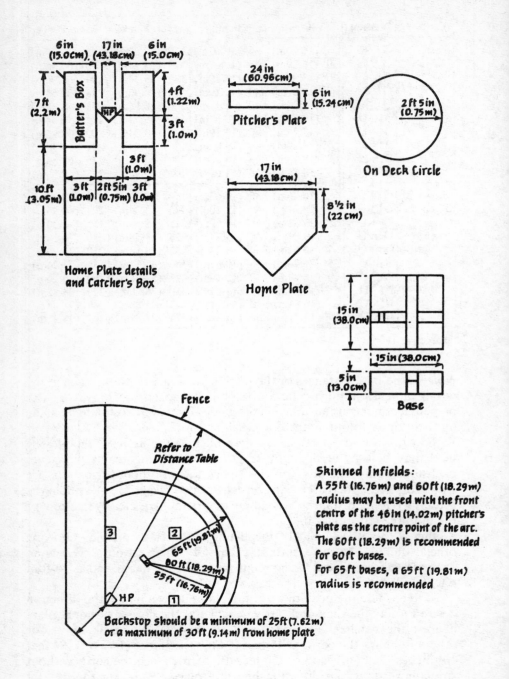

6 in
(15.0 cm)   17 in
(43.18 cm)   6 in
(15.0 cm)

7 ft
(2.2 m)   Batter's Box   4 ft
(1.22 m)

HP   3 ft
(1.0 m)

3 ft
(1.0 m)

10 ft
(3.05 m)   3 ft
(1.0 m)   2 ft 5 in
(0.75 m)   3 ft
(1.0 m)

Home Plate details
and Catcher's Box

24 in
(60.96 cm)

6 in
(15.24 cm)

Pitcher's Plate

2 ft 5 in
(0.75 m)

On Deck Circle

17 in
(43.18 cm)

8½ in
(22 cm)

Home Plate

15 in
(38.0 cm)

15 in (38.0 cm)

5 in
(13.0 cm)

Base

Fence

Refer to
Distance Table

3   2

65 ft (19.81 m)

60 ft (18.29 m)

55 ft (16.76 m)

HP   1

Backstop should be a minimum of 25 ft (7.62 m)
or a maximum of 30 ft (9.14 m) from home plate

Skinned Infields:
A 55 ft (16.76 m) and 60 ft (18.29 m)
radius may be used with the front
centre of the 46 in (14.02 m) pitcher's
plate as the centre point of the arc.
The 60 ft (18.29 m) is recommended
for 60 ft bases.
For 65 ft bases, a 65 ft (19.81 m)
radius is recommended

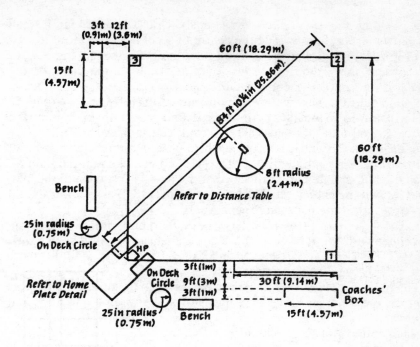

3ft 12ft
(0.91m) (3.6m)

60 ft (18.29m)

3

2

15 ft
(4.57m)

184 ft 10¼in (25.86m)

60 ft
(18.29m)

8 ft radius
(2.44m)

Refer to Distance Table

Bench

25 in radius
(0.75m)
On Deck Circle

Refer to Home
Plate Detail

HP

On Deck
Circle

1

3 ft (1m)

9 ft (3m)

3 ft (1m)

30 ft (9.14m)

Coaches'
Box

25 in radius
(0.75m)

Bench

15 ft (4.57m)

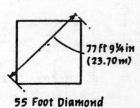

77 ft 9¼ in
(23.70 m)

55 Foot Diamond

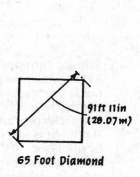

91 ft 11in
(28.07m)

65 Foot Diamond

plate. Along the same line, drive a stake at the 84-foot 10¼-inch (25.68m) marker. This will be the centre of second base. Place the 120-foot (36.58m) marker at the centre of second base and, taking hold of the cord at the 60-foot (18.29m) marker, walk to the right of the direction line until the cord is taut and drive a stake at the 60-foot (18.29m) marker. This will be the outside corner of first base and the cord will now form the lines to first and second bases. Again, holding the cord at the 60-foot (18.29m) marker, walk across the field and, in like manner, mark the outside corner of third base. Home plate, first base, and third base are wholly inside the diamond. To check the diamond, place the home plate end of the cord at the first base stake and the 120-foot (36.58m) marker at third base. The 60-foot (18.29m) marker should now check at home plate and second base.

In the layout of a 65-foot base path diamond, follow the same procedure with the following substitute dimensions: 65 feet (19.81m), 130 feet (39.62m), and 91 feet 11 inches (28.07m). Check all distances with a steel tape whenever possible.

A. The three-foot (0.91m) line is drawn parallel to the three feet (0.91m) from the baseline, starting at a point halfway between home plate and first base.

B. The batter's on-deck circle is a five-foot (1.52m) circle (2½-foot [0.76m] radius) placed adjacent to the end of the players' bench or dugout area closest to home plate.

C. The batter's box, one on each side of home plate shall measure three feet (0.91m) by seven feet (2.13m). The inside lines of the batter's box shall be six inches (15.24cm) from home plate. The front line of the box shall be four feet (1.22m) in front of a line drawn through the centre of home plate. The lines are considered as being within the batter's box.

D. The catcher's box shall be 10 feet (3.05m) in length from the rear outside corners of the batters' boxes and shall be eight feet, five inches (2.57m) wide.

E. Each coach's box is behind a line 15 feet (4.57m) long drawn outside the diamond. The line is parallel to the eight feet (2.44m) from the first and third base line, extended from the bases toward home plate.

F. The pitcher's plate shall be of rubber or wood, 24 inches (60.96cm) long and six inches (15.24cm) wide. The top of the plate shall be level with the ground. The front of the plate shall be the prescribed pitching distances from the back point of the plate. It shall be permanently attached to the ground at distances indicated in Rule 2, Section 1.

(FP only) There shall be a 16-foot (4.88m) circle, eight feet (2.44m) in radius, drawn from the pitcher's plate. The lines drawn around the pitcher's plate are considered inside the circle.

G. Home plate shall be made of rubber or other suitable material. It shall be a five-sided figure, 17 inches (43.18cm) wide across the edge facing the pitcher. The sides shall be parallel to the inside lines of the batter's box and shall be 8½ inches (21.59cm) long. The sides of the point facing the catcher shall be 12 inches (30.48cm) long.

1. (Seniors Men's SP) The second home plate shall be placed eight feet from the back tip of home plate on an extended line from first base. A line shall be drawn from third base to the second home plate.

H. The bases, other than home plate, shall be 15 inches (38.10cm) square, shall be made of canvas or other suitable material and not more than five inches (12.70cm) in thickness. The bases should be properly fastened in position.

1. The double base is approved for use at first base. This base is 15 by 30 inches and made of canvas or other suitable material. Half the base is white (over fair territory) and half is orange (over foul territory). It should not be more than five inches (12.70cm) in thickness.

Note: When using the double base at first, the following rules should be enforced:

(*a*) A batted ball hitting the white portion is declared fair and a batted ball hitting the orange portion is declared foul.

(*b*) Whenever a play is being made on the batter-runner, the defence must use the white portion and the batter-runner the orange portion. On extra base hits or balls hit to the outfield when there is no play being made at the double base, the runner may touch the white portion.

(*c*) The batter-runner must use the orange portion on the first attempt at first base; however, should he reach and go beyond first base, he must return to the white portion.

(*d*) Should the batter-runner round the base on a hit to the infield or the outfield, he must return to the white portion.

(*e*) When tagging up on a fly ball, the white portion must be used.

(*f*) On an attempted pick-off play (FP & 16-inch SP only), the runner must return to the white portion.

2. (Senior Men's SP) The double first base shall be used in this division of play.

3. EQUIPMENT
Section 1. The Official Bat:

(*a*) Shall be made of one piece of hardwood, or formed from a block of wood consisting of two or more pieces of wood bonded together with an adhesive in such a way that the grain direction of all pieces is essentially parallel to the length of the bat.

(*b*) Shall be metal, plastic, graphite, carbon, magnesium, fibreglass, ceramic or any other composite material approved by the ASA. Any new composite construction bat must be reviewed and approved by the ASA.

(*c*) May be laminated but must contain only wood or adhesive and have a clear finish (if finished).

(*d*) Shall be round or three-sided and shall be smooth. If the barrel end has a knurled finish the maximum surface roughness is not more than 250 if measured by a profilometer or 4/1000 if measured by a spectrograph.

(*e*) Shall not be more than 34 inches (87.0cm) long, nor exceed 38 ounces (1100.0g) in weight.

(*f*) If round, shall not be more than $2\frac{1}{4}$ inches (6.0cm) in diameter at its largest part; and if three-sided, shall not exceed $2\frac{1}{4}$ inches (6.0cm) on the hitting surface. A tolerance of $\frac{1}{32}$ inch (0.9mm) is permitted to allow for expansion on the round bat. *Note*: If the bat ring goes over the bat it should be considered a legal bat.

(*g*) If metal, may be angular.

(*h*) Shall not have exposed rivets, pins, rough or sharp edges or any form of exterior fastener that would present a hazard. A metal bat shall be free of burrs.

(*i*) If metal, shall not have a wooden handle.

(*j*) Shall have a safety grip of cork, tape (no smooth, plastic tape) or composition material. The safety grip shall not be less than 10 inches (25.0cm) long and shall not extend more than 15 inches (40.0cm) from the small end of the bat. Any moulded finger-formed grip made by the bat manufacturer, if used, must be permanently attached to the bat or attached to the bat with safety tape and must be approved by the Equipment Standards Committee. Resin, pine tar or spray substances placed on the safety grip to enhance the grip are permissible on the grip only. Tape applied to any bat must be continuously spiral. It does not have to be a solid layer of tape. It may not exceed two layers. Taping of a bat less than the required length is considered illegal.

(*k*) If metal, and not made of one-piece construction with the barrel end closed, shall have a rubber or vinyl plastic insert firmly secured at the large end of the bat.

(*l*) Shall have a safety knob of a minimum of $\frac{1}{4}$ inch protruding at a 90-degree angle from the handle. It may be moulded, lathed, welded or permanently fastened. A 'flare' or 'cone' grip attached to the bat will be considered altered. The knob may be taped as long as there is no violation of this section. The 'Power Pad' grip is approved.

(*m*) Shall be marked 'Official Softball' by the manufacturer. If the words 'Official Softball' cannot be read due to wear and tear on the bat, the bat should be declared legal if it is legal in all other aspects. *Note*: Softball bats used in ASA championship tournament play must be approved by the Equipment Standards Committee. Manufacturers must submit all new designed bats to the ASA Equipment Standards Committee for approval prior to sales.

Section 2. Warm-up Bats

No more than two official softball bats, one ASA approved warm-up bat or a combination of the two, not to exceed two, may be used by the on-deck batter in the on-deck circle. The warm-up bat should meet the following requirements to be approved:

(*a*) Stamped with $\frac{1}{4}$ inch letters WB on either end of the bat or marked in one-inch letters the words, 'warm-up bat' only on the barrel end of the bat.

(*b*) A minimum weight of 48 ounces (1360.0g).

(*c*) A minimum barrel diameter of $2\frac{1}{2}$ inches (6.0m).

(*d*) Shall have a safety grip of at least 10 inches (25.0cm) and no more than 15 inches (40.0cm) extended from the knob.

(*e*) Be of one-piece construction or a one-piece permanently assembled bat approved by the Equipment Standards Committee. *Note*: The Power Wrap warm-up attachment is legal.

Section 3. The Official Softball

(*a*) Shall be a regular, smooth-seamed, flat-surfaced, pebble or dimple-textured ball with concealed stitches.

(*b*) Shall have a centre core made of either No. 1 quality long fibre kapok, a mixture of cork and rubber, a polyurethane mixture or other materials approved by the ASA.

(*c*) May be hand or machine-wound with a fine quality twisted yarn and covered with latex or rubber cement.

(*d*) Shall have a cover cemented to the ball by application of cement to the underside of the cover and sewn with waxed thread of cotton or linen. If the cover is moulded, it may be bonded to the core or be of the same composition as the core. Either moulded type must have an authentic facsimile of stitching as approved by the ASA.

(*e*) Shall have a cover of chrome-tanned top-grain horsehide or cowhide, synthetic material or other materials approved by the ASA.

(*f*) The 12-inch (30.0cm) ball shall be between $11\frac{7}{8}$ inches (30.0cm) and $12\frac{1}{8}$ inches (3 1.0cm) in circumference and shall weigh between $6\frac{1}{4}$ ounces (180.0g) and seven ounces (200.0g). The smooth-seamed style shall not have fewer than 88 stitches in each cover, sewn by the two-needle method, or with an authentic facsimile of stitching as approved by the ASA.

(*g*) The 11-inch (27.0cm) ball shall be between $10\frac{7}{8}$ inches (27.0cm) and $11\frac{1}{8}$ inches (28.0cm) in circumference. It shall weigh between $5\frac{7}{8}$ ounces (165.0g) and $6\frac{1}{8}$ ounces (175.0g). The smooth-seamed style shall not have fewer than 80 stitches in each cover, sewn by the two-needle method, or with an authentic facsimile of stitching as approved by the ASA.

(*h*) The white-stitch 12-inch ball with a COR of .50 or under shall be

Softball	Thread colour	Min. size	Max. size	Min. weight	Max. weight	Marking
12" FP (30.0cm)	white	11⅞in 30.0cm	12⅛in 31.0cm	6¼oz 180.0g	7oz 200.0g	ASA Logo
12" SP (30.0cm)	red	11⅞in 30.0cm	12⅛in 31.0cm	6¼oz 180.0g	7oz 200.0g	MSP–47 ASA Logo
16" SP (41.0cm)	white	15⅞in 40.9cm	16⅛in 41.0cm	9oz 225.0g	10oz 283.0g	ASA Logo
11" SP (27.0cm)	red	10⅞in 27.0cm	11⅛in 28.0cm	5⅞oz 165.0g	6⅛oz 175.0g	GWSP–47 ASA Logo
11" FP (27.0cm)	white	10⅞in 27.0cm	11⅛in 28.0cm	5⅞oz 165.0g	6⅛oz 175.0g	ASA Logo

used in the following ASA play: men's and women's fast pitch, boys and girls 12-, 14-, 16-, and 18-under fast pitch, and boys 14-, 16-, and 18-under slow pitch.

(*i*)   The white-stitch 11-inch ball with a COR of .50 or under shall be used in the following ASA play: boys and girls 10-under fast pitch.

(*j*)   The red-stitch (and/or red indelible stamping as approved by the ASA) 12-inch ball with a COR of .47 and under shall be used in the following ASA play: men's slow pitch and coed (male batters only) slow pitch. It must be marked MSP-47.

(*k*)   The red-stitch (and/or red indelible stamping as approved by the ASA) 11-inch ball with a COR of .47 and under shall be used in the following ASA play: women's slow pitch, coed slow pitch (women batters only), boys 10- and 12-under slow pitch and girls 12-, 14-, 16-, and 18-under slow pitch. It must be marked GWSP-47.

Effect – (*j–k*): If the wrong ball is used, the manager of the offensive team has the option of taking the result of the play or having the last batter rebat and assume the ball and strike count prior to the wrong ball being discovered.

(*l*)   Softballs used in ASA play must meet standards set by the ASA as shown on the chart and **must be stamped with the ASA logo**.

Section 4. Gloves

May be worn by any player, but mitts may be used only by the catcher and first baseman. No top lacing, webbing or other device between the thumb and body of the glove or mitt worn by a first baseman or catcher, or a glove worn by any fielder, shall be more than five inches (12.70cm) in length.

(FP only) The pitcher's glove shall be of one solid colour other than white or grey.

Section 5. Masks, body protectors, shin guards and helmets

(*a*) (FP only) Adult catchers must wear masks with throat protectors. An extended wire protector may be worn in lieu of an attached throat protector.

(*b*) (SP only) Junior Olympic catchers must wear an approved batter's helmet with ear flaps, or the catcher's helmet and mask.

(*c*) (FP only) Junior Olympic catchers must wear a mask with throat protector, approved helmet with ear flaps, shin guards which offer protection to the knee caps and body protector. An extended wire protector may be worn in lieu of an attached throat protector.

Note: Any player warming up a Junior Olympic pitcher must wear a mask with throat protector and approved helmet with ear flaps.

(*d*) Helmets

1. Offence. All adult fast pitch and Junior Olympic fast and slow pitch offensive players, including the on-deck batter and Junior Olympic players acting as coaches in the coach's box, must properly wear batting helmets. *Exception*: Modified pitch players are not required to wear helmets.

Effect: Failure to wear the batting helmet when ordered to do so by the umpire shall cause the player to be ejected from the game. Wearing the helmet improperly or removing the helmet during a live ball play and judged by the umpire to be a deliberate act shall cause the violator to be declared out immediately. The ball remains alive.

Note: Calling a runner out for removing a helmet does not remove force play situations. Umpires should use discretion as to the intent of the rule concerning player safety.

2. Defence. Any defensive player may wear an approved helmet of similar colour as the team caps.

3. EQUIPMENT
Section 1. The Official Bat:

(*a*) Shall be made of one piece of hardwood, or formed from a block of wood consisting of two or more pieces of wood bonded together with an adhesive in such a way that the grain direction of all pieces is essentially parallel to the length of the bat.

(*b*) Shall be metal, plastic, graphite, carbon, magnesium, fibreglass, ceramic or any other composite material approved by the ASA. Any new composite construction bat must be reviewed and approved by the ASA.

(*c*) May be laminated but must contain only wood or adhesive and have a clear finish (if finished).

(*d*) Shall be round or three-sided and shall be smooth. If the barrel end has a knurled finish the maximum surface roughness is no more than

250 if measured by a profilometer or 4/1000 if measured by a spectrograph.

(*e*) Shall not be more than 34 inches (87.0cm) long, nor exceed 38 ounces (1100.0g) in weight.

(*f*) If round, shall not be more than $2\frac{1}{4}$ inches (6.0cm) in diameter at its largest part; and if three-sided, shall not exceed $2\frac{1}{4}$ inches (6.0cm) on the hitting surface. A tolerance of $\frac{1}{32}$ inch (0.90mm) is permitted to allow for expansion on the round bat. *Note*: If the bat ring goes over the bat it should be considered a legal bat.

(*g*) If metal, may be angular.

(*h*) Shall not have exposed rivets, pins, rough or sharp edges or any form of exterior fastener that would present a hazard. A metal bat shall be free of burrs.

(*i*) If metal, shall not have a wooden handle.

(*j*) Shall have a safety grip of cork, tape (no smooth, plastic tape) or composition material. The safety grip shall not be less than 10 inches (25.0cm) long and shall not extend more than 15 inches (40.0cm) from the small end of the bat. Any moulded finger-formed grip made by the bat manufacturer, if used, must be permanently attached to the bat or attached to the bat with safety tape and must be approved by the Equipment Standards Committee. Resin, pine tar or spray substances placed on the safety grip to enhance the grip are permissible on the grip only. Tape applied to any bat must be continuously spiral. It does not have to be a solid layer of tape. It may not exceed two layers. Taping of a bat less than the required length is considered illegal.

(*k*) If metal, and not made of one-piece construction with the barrel end closed, shall have a rubber or vinyl plastic insert firmly secured at the large end of the bat.

(*l*) Shall have a safety knob of a minimum of $\frac{1}{4}$ inch protruding at a 90-degree angle from the handle. It may be moulded, lathed, welded or permanently fastened. A 'flare' or 'cone' grip attached to the bat will be considered altered. The knob may be taped as long as there is no violation of this section. The 'power pad' grip is approved.

Section 6. Uniform
All players on a team shall properly wear uniforms that are alike in colour, trim and style. Coaches must be neatly attired and dressed alike or in team uniform and in accordance with the colour code of the team. All protective equipment should be worn properly.

(a) Headwear.

1. (FP Male) Ball caps are mandatory and must be alike.

2. (Female SP & FP) Ball caps, visors and headbands are optional for players. Players are not required to wear headwear, but if worn, all headwear must be of the same type (i.e., all caps, visors or headbands). Handkerchiefs do not qualify as headbands and cannot be worn around the head or neck. *Note*: Plastic visors are not allowed.

(b) **Pants/sliding pants.** All players' pants shall be either all long or all short in style. Players may wear a solid-coloured pair of sliding pants. It is not mandatory that all players wear sliding pants, but if more than one player wears them, they must be alike in colour and style. No player may wear ragged, frayed or slit legs on exposed sliding pants.

(c) **Undershirts**. Players may wear a solid-coloured undershirt (it may be white). It is not mandatory that all players wear an undershirt, but if more than one player wears one, those that are worn must be alike. No player may wear ragged, frayed or slit sleeves on exposed undershirts.

(d) **Numbers.** An Arabic number of contrasting colour at least six inches (15.24cm) high must be worn on the back of all uniform shirts. No players on the same team may wear identical numbers. (Numbers 3 and 03 are examples of identical numbers.) Players without numbers will not be permitted to play. If duplicate numbers exist, only one of the players may play at a time.

(e) **Casts.** Plaster or other hard substances in their final form may not be worn during the game. Any exposed metal may be considered legal if covered by soft material and taped.

(f) **Jewellery.** Exposed jewellery, which is judged by the umpire to be dangerous, must be removed and may not be worn during the game. Players who fail to do so will be ejected from the game.

(g) **Shoes** must be worn by all players. A shoe shall be considered official if it is made with either canvas or leather uppers or similar material(s). The soles may be either smooth or have soft or hard rubber cleats. Ordinary metal sole or heel plates may be used if the spikes on the plates do not extend more than $\frac{3}{4}$ of an inch (1.91cm) from the sole or heel of the shoe. Shoes with round metal spikes are illegal. No shoes with detachable cleats that screw on are allowed; however, shoes with detachable cleats that screw into the shoe are allowed. Junior Olympic/Coed/Men's Senior Play: No metal spikes nor hard plastic or polyurethane spikes similar to metal sole and heel plates are allowed.

4. PLAYERS AND SUBSTITUTES
Section 1. Players
(*a*) A team must have the required number of players present in the team area to start or continue a game. Players listed in the starting lineup and not available at game time may be substituted for and re-entered later.

1. Official lineup cards are to be completed and submitted to the official scorer or umpire at the start of each game. The lineup shall contain the first and last name, position and uniform number of each player. *Note*: If a wrong number is on the lineup sheet, correct it and continue playing with no penalty.

2. All available substitutes should be listed in the designated place by their last name, first name and uniform number.

3. Eligible roster members may be added to the available substitute list at any time during the game.

(*b*) Male rosters shall include only male players and female rosters shall include only female players.

(*c*) A team shall consist of players in the following positions:

1. Fast Pitch. Nine players – pitcher (F1), catcher (F2), first baseman (F3), second baseman (F4), third baseman (F5), shortstop (F6), left fielder (F7), centre fielder (F8) and right fielder (F9).

2. Fast Pitch with a Designated Player (DP). Ten players – same as fast pitch plus a DP. *Note*: Refer to Section 3 'designated player' for options resulting in nine players continuing the game.

3. Slow Pitch. Ten players – same as fast pitch plus an extra fielder (F10).

4. Slow Pitch With An Extra Player (EP). Eleven players – same as slow pitch plus an EP who bats in the lineup. Seniors may have 11 or 12 players using one or two EPs.

5. Coed. Ten players, five male and five female – same as slow pitch with the following positioning requirements: two males and two females in both the infield and the outfield, and one male and one female as pitcher and catcher.

6. Coed With Extra Players (EP). Twelve players, six male and six female – same as coed plus two EPs who bat in the lineup.

7. A physically challenged player can play as a defensive player only (DEFO). (See Section 2.)

(*d*) **Short-handed Rule** (SP only except Coed)
The short-handed rule may be used with the following requirements:

1. If a team begins play with 10 or 11 players, or a senior team with 10, 11 or 12, that team may continue a game with one less player than it started with whenever a player leaves the game for any reason other than ejection.

2. If the player leaving the game is a runner, he shall be declared out.

3. When the player who has left the game is scheduled to bat, an out shall be declared for each turn at bat.

4. The player who has left the game cannot return to the lineup.
Exception: A player who has left the game under the blood rule (Rule 4, Section 8 C) may return.

Effect – Section 1 (*a-d*): The game is forfeited for any violation of requirements.

Section 2. American Disability Act Rule (SP only)

Section 3. Designated Player (FP only)

(*a*) A designated player (DP) may be used for any player provided it is made known prior to the start of the game and his name is indicated on the lineup or score sheet as one of the nine hitters in the batting order.

(*b*) The name of the player for whom the DP is batting (DEFO) will be placed in the 10th position in the scorebook.

(*c*) The starting player listed as the DP must remain in the same position in the batting order for the entire game. The DP and his substitute, or the substitute's replacement, may never play offence at the same time.

(*d*) The DP may be substituted for at any time, either by a pinch-hitter, pinch-runner or the defensive player for whom he is hitting (DEFO). If the starting DP is replaced on offence by the DEFO or by a substitute, the DP is considered to have left the game and he may re-enter one time, as long as he returns to his original position in the batting order.

1. If replaced by the person playing defence only (DEFO), this reduces the number of players from 10 to nine. If the DP does not re-enter, the game may legally end with nine players.

2. If the DP re-enters and the DEFO was batting in his spot, the DEFO can return to the number 10 position and play defence only or leave the game.

Effect: Re-entering the DP into a batting position other than his original position is considered an illegal re-entry. The manager and the DP are ejected.

(*e*) The DP may play defence at any position. Should the DP play defence for a player other than the one for whom he is batting (DEFO), that player will continue to bat but not play defence, and is not considered to have left the game. The DP may play defence for the DEFO and the DEFO is considered to have left the game reducing the number of players from 10 to nine.

(*f*) The person being batted for (DEFO) may be substituted for at any time, either by a legal substitute or the DP for whom he is playing defence. The DEFO may re-enter the game one time, either in the number 10 position or in the DP's position in the batting order.

1. If returning to the number 10 position, he will again play defence only but may play any defensive position.

2. If the DEFO returns to the DP's position, he will play offence and defence; there will be only nine players in the batting order.

(*g*) Placing the defensive player only (DEFO) into one of the first nine positions for someone other than the original DP is considered an illegal re-entry. The manager and the DEFO are ejected.

Section 4. Extra Player (SP only)

(*a*) An extra player (EP) is optional, but if one is used, it must be made known prior to the start of the game and be listed on the scoring sheet in the regular batting order. If the EP is used, he must be used the entire game. Failure to complete the game with 11 batters as a result of an ejected player, results in a forfeiture of the game.

(*b*) The EP must remain in the same position in the batting order for the entire game.

(*c*) If an EP is used, all 11 must bat and any 10 may play defence. Defensive positions may be changed, but the batting order must remain the same.

(*d*) The EP may be substituted for at any time. The substitute must be a player who has not yet been in the game. The starting EP may re-enter.

(*e*) If the EP is used in coed, all 12 must bat and any 10 (five male and five female) may play defence. Defensive positions may be changed as long as the coed positioning is followed. The batting order must remain the same throughout the game.

(*f*) (Men's Senior only). One or two extra players may be designated at any place in the batting order. The EP(s) may enter a game on defence at any time, but the batting order must remain the same throughout the game.

Section 5. Re-entry

(*a*) Any of the starting players, including a DP (FP only) or an EP (SP only), may be substituted and re-entered once, provided players occupy the same batting positions whenever in the lineup. The starting player and the substitute(s) may not be in the lineup at the same time. If a manager removes a substitute from the game and re-enters the same substitute later in the game, this is considered an illegal re-entry.

(*b*) Violation of re-entry rule is handled as a protest when brought to the attention of the umpire by the offended team and may be made anytime during the game. The protest need not be made prior to the next pitch.

Effect – Section 5(*a–b*): Both the manager and illegal player are ejected. All play that occurred while the illegal re-entry was in the game will stand.

Note: If the re-entry violation also violates the unreported substitute ruling, those penalties would also be in effect.

(*c*) A starting player removed from the pitching position by the umpire and substituted for can re-enter the game at another position, but cannot return to the pitching position. *Effect*: If an illegal pitcher returns to the pitching position and has thrown one pitch he is ejected from the game. *Note*: This is not considered a re-entry violation so the manager is not ejected.

Section 6. Substitutes
A substitute may take the place of a player whose name is in his team's batting order. The following regulations govern player substitutions:

(*a*) The manager or team representative of the team making the substitution shall immediately notify the plate umpire at the time a substitute enters. The plate umpire shall then report the change to the scorer prior to the next pitch. If the violation is discovered prior to a pitch being made (legal or illegal), there is no penalty and the illegal substitute shall be declared legal.

(*b*) Substitute players will be considered in the game when reported to the plate umpire. A player will not violate the substitution rule until one legal or illegal pitch has been thrown. The use of an illegal substitute is handled as a protest by the offended team. If the team manager or player in violation informs the umpire prior to the offended team's protest, there is no violation regardless of how long the player or players were illegally in the game.

1. **Offence**. If the illegal player is discovered by the defence before the offensive manager, coach or player in violation informs the umpire and:

(i) after one legal or illegal pitch has been thrown while he is at bat, he is ejected and a legal substitute assumes the ball and strike count. Any advance of runners while the illegal batter is at bat is legal.

(ii) he has completed his turn at bat and prior to the next legal or illegal pitch, or before the defensive team has left the field, the illegal player is called out, ejected and any advance of runners as a result of obstruction, an error, a hit batter or a dropped third strike (FP), a walk, or a base hit is nullified.

(iii) he has completed his turn at bat and after the next legal or illegal pitch, or after the defensive team has left the field, the illegal player is ejected and any advance by runners while the illegal batter was at bat is legal.

2. **Defence**. If the illegal player is discovered by the offence before the defensive manager, coach or player in violation informs the umpire and:

(i) after he makes the play and prior to the next legal or illegal pitch, or before the defensive team has left the field, the offensive team has the option of taking the result of the play or having the last batter return and assume the ball and strike count he had prior to the discovery of the illegal player with each runner returning to the base at which he was prior to the play. The illegal player is ejected.

(ii) after a legal or illegal pitch to the next batter, all play stands but the illegal player is ejected.

Any player may be removed from the game during any dead ball.

Note: The pitcher no longer has to pitch until the first batter facing him has completed his turn at bat or the side has been retired.

Section 7. Ejected Player

A player or coach who has been ejected from the game is restricted to the bench unless the act is determined to be flagrant, when the player or coach must leave the grounds. Any ejected player discovered participating will constitute a forfeit.

Section 8. Blood Rule

A player, coach or umpire who is bleeding or who has blood on his uniform shall be prohibited from participating further in the game until appropriate treatment can be administered. If medical care or treatment is administered in a reasonable length of time, the individual will not have to leave the game. The length of time that is considered reasonable is left to the umpire's judgement. Uniform rule violations will not be enforced if a uniform change is required. The umpire shall:

(*a*) Stop the game and allow treatment if the injured player would affect the continuation of the game.

(*b*) Immediately call a coach, trainer or other authorized person to the injured player.

(*c*) Apply the rules of the game regarding substitution, short-handed player and re-entry if necessary.

5. THE GAME

Section 1. Home Team

The team designated as home team shall bat last in the inning.

Section 2. Fitness of the Ground

The fitness of the ground for a game shall be decided solely by the plate umpire.

Section 3. Regulation Game

(*a*) A regulation game shall consist of seven innings. A full seven innings need not be played if the team second at bat scores more runs in six and one-half innings and/or before the third out in the last of the seventh inning, or the run ahead rule is applied.

(*b*) A game that is tied at the end of seven innings shall be continued by playing additional innings until one side has scored more runs than the other at the end of a complete inning, or until the team second at bat has scored more runs in their half of the inning before the third out is made.

(c) A game called by the umpire shall be regulation if five or more complete innings have been played, or if the team second at bat has scored more runs in four or more innings than the other team has scored in five or more innings. The umpire is empowered to call a game at any time because of darkness, rain, fire, panic or other causes which place the patrons or players in peril. (For ASA national tournament play, see ASA Code 209 B.)

(d) Games that are considered regulation shall be resumed at the exact point where they were stopped.

(e) A regulation tie game shall be declared if the score is equal when the game is called at the end of five or more complete innings, or if the team second at bat has equalled the score of the first team at bat in the incomplete inning.

(f) Games that are regulation tie games shall be resumed at the exact point where they were stopped.

Section 4. Forfeited Games

A forfeited game shall be declared by the umpire in favour of the team not at fault in the following cases:

(a) If an umpire is physically attacked by any team member and/or spectator.

(b) If a team fails to appear on the field, or, being on the field, refuses to begin a game for which it is scheduled or assigned within a time set for forfeitures by the organisation which the team represents.

(c) If one side refuses to continue to play after the game has begun, unless the game has been suspended or terminated by the umpire.

(d) If, after play has been suspended by the umpire, one side fails to resume playing within two minutes after 'play ball' has been declared by the umpire.

(e) If a team employs tactics noticeably designed to delay or to hasten the game.

(f) If, after warning by the umpire, any one of the rules of the game is wilfully violated.

(g) If the order for the ejection of a player is not obeyed within one minute.

(h) If the ejection of a player or players from the game results in fewer than the required number of players to continue the game.

Section 5. Scoring of Runs

(a) One run shall be scored each time a runner legally touches first, second or third bases and home plate before the third out of an inning.

(*b*) No run shall be scored if the third out of the inning is the result of:

1. a batter-runner being called out prior to reaching first base or any other runner forced out due to the batter becoming a batter-runner.

2. a runner being put out by a tag or live ball appeal play prior to the lead runner touching home plate.

3. a preceding runner is declared out on an appeal play.

Note: An appeal can be made after the third out in order to nullify a run.

Section 6. Game Winner

The winner of the game shall be the team that scores more runs in a regulation game.

(*a*) The score of a called regulation game shall be the score at the end of the last complete inning, unless the team second at bat has scored an equal number or more runs than the first team at bat in the incomplete inning. In this case, the score shall be that of the incomplete inning.

(*b*) The score of a regulation tie game shall be the tie score when the game was terminated.

(*c*) The score of a forfeited game shall be seven to zero in favour of the team not at fault.

Section 7. Charged Conference

(*a*) **Offensive Conference.** There shall be only one charged conference between the manager and/or other team representative(s) and the batter or runner(s) in an inning. The umpire shall not permit any such conferences in excess of one in an inning. *Effect*: Ejection of the manager or coach who insists on another charged conference.

(*b*) **Defensive Conference.** There shall be only one charged conference between the manager or other team representative from the dugout with each pitcher in an inning. *Effect*: The second charge conference shall result in the removal of the pitcher from the pitching position for the remainder of the game.

Section 8. Home run Classification (Code Article 209 I)

A limit of over-the-fence home runs will be used in all men's and coed slow pitch divisions. All balls hit over the fence by a team in excess of the following limitations per game will be ruled on as shown:

(*a*) **Super Classification**. Unlimited.

(*b*) **Major Classification**. Twelve. The batter is ruled out for any in excess.

(*c*) **Class A Classification**. Six. The batter is ruled out for any in excess. (Includes Major Industrial.)

(*d*) **Major Coed Classification**. Five. The batter is ruled out for any in excess.

(*e*) **Class B Classification**. Three. The batter is ruled out for any in excess. (Includes Major Church, Class A Industrial, and all Masters and Seniors.)

(*f*) **Class A Coed Classification**. Two. The first batter hitting a home run in excess of two is ruled out and all other players hitting a home run are ruled out and disqualified from the game.

(*g*) **Class C Classification**. One. The first batter hitting a home run in excess of one is ruled out and all other players hitting a home run are ruled out and disqualified from the game. (Includes Class A Church.)

(*h*) **Class D Classification**. None. The batter is ruled out for the first in excess and all other players hitting a home run are ruled out and disqualified from the game.

Note:

1. Any fair fly ball touched by a defensive player which then goes over the fence in fair territory, should be declared a four-base award and shall not be included in the total of over-the-fence home runs.

2. Any time the batter is ruled out because of the excessive home run rule, the ball is dead and no runners can advance.

3. A home run will be charged for any ball hit over the fence whether runs score or not.

Section 9. Run Ahead Rule (Code Article 209 F)

(*a*) A run ahead rule must be used after five innings at all National Tournaments. *Exception*: Men's Super SP.

1. Fast Pitch – Eight.

2. Modified Pitch – Ten.

3. Slow Pitch – Twelve.

(*b*) Complete innings must be played unless the home team scores the run ahead limit while at bat. Whenever a run ahead limit is used and the visiting team reaches the limit in the fifth or sixth inning, the home team must have their opportunity to bat in the bottom half of the inning.

Section 10. Tie-breaker (Code Article 209 H)

(Women and Junior Olympic Girls FP only) If, after the completion of nine innings of play, the score is tied, the following tie-breaker will be played to determine a winning team.

(*a*) Starting with the top of the tenth inning, and each half inning thereafter, the offensive team shall begin its turn at bat with the player who is scheduled to bat ninth in that respective half inning being placed on second base. (e.g., if the number five batter is the lead off batter, the number four batter in the batting order will be placed on second base. A substitute may be inserted for the runner.) For scoring, see Rule 11, Section 10.

6. PITCHING REGULATIONS

FAST PITCH
Section 1. Preliminaries
Before starting the delivery (pitch), the pitcher shall comply with the following:

(a) Both feet must be on the ground within the 24-inch length of the pitcher's plate. The shoulders shall be in line with first and third bases.

1. (**Male only**) He shall take a position with his pivot foot in contact with the pitcher's plate and his non-pivot foot on or behind the pitcher's plate.

2. (**Female only**) She shall take a position with both feet in contact with the pitcher's plate.

(b) The pitcher shall take the signal from the catcher with the hands separated. The ball may be in the glove or pitching hand.

(c) The pitcher shall hold the ball in both hands for not less than one second and not more than 10 seconds before releasing it.

1. (**Male only**) If the pitcher decides to pitch with the non-pivot foot to the rear and off the pitching plate, the backward step may be taken before, simultaneous with or after the hands are brought together. The pivot foot must remain in contact with the pitching plate at all times prior to the forward step.

2. (**Female only**) Both feet must remain in contact with the pitching plate at all times prior to the forward step.

(d) The pitcher shall not be considered in pitching position unless the catcher is in position to receive the pitch.

(e) The pitcher may not take the pitching position on or near the pitcher's plate without having the ball in his possession.

Section 2. Starting Pitch
The pitch starts when one hand is taken off the ball or the pitcher makes any motion that is part of his windup.

Section 3. Legal Delivery
(a) The pitcher must not make any motion to pitch without immediately delivering the ball to the batter.

(b) The pitcher must not use a pitching motion in which, after having the ball in both hands in the pitching position, he removes one hand from the ball, takes a backward and forward swing, and returns the ball to both hands in front of the body.

(c) The pitcher must not use a windup in which there is a stop or reversal of the forward motion.

(d) The pitcher must not make two revolutions of the arm on the windmill pitch. A pitcher may drop his arm to the side and to the rear before starting the windmill motion.

(*e*) The delivery must be an underhanded motion with the hand below the hip and the wrist not farther from the body than the elbow.

(*f*) The release of the ball and follow through of the hand and wrist must be forward and past the straight line of the body.

(*g*) In the act of delivering the ball, the pitcher must take one step simultaneous with the release of the ball. The step must be forward and toward the batter within the 24-inch length of the pitcher's plate.
Note: It is not a step if the pitcher slides his foot across the pitcher's plate, provided contact is maintained with the plate. Raising the foot off the pitching plate and returning it to the plate creates a rocking motion and is an illegal act.

(*h*) Pushing off with the pivot foot from a place other than the pitcher's plate is illegal.

(*i*) (**Female Only**) The pivot foot must remain in contact with or push off and drag away from the pitching plate prior to the front foot touching the ground, as long as the pivot foot remains in contact with the ground.

(*j*) (**Male Only**) Both feet can be in the air at the same time. The leap is legal as long as the pivot foot does not replant and push off from a spot other than the pitching plate.

(*k*) The pitcher must not continue to wind up after releasing the ball.

(*l*) The pitcher shall not deliberately drop, roll or bounce the ball in order to prevent the batter from hitting it.

(*m*) The pitcher has 20 seconds to release the next pitch after receiving the ball or after the umpire indicates 'play ball'.

Section 4. Intentional Walk
If the pitcher desires to walk a batter intentionally all pitches must be legally delivered to the batter. A pitchout for the purpose of intentionally walking a batter is not considered an illegal pitch.

Section 5. Defensive Positioning
(*a*) The pitcher shall not deliver a pitch unless all defensive players are positioned in fair territory, except the catcher who must be in the catcher's box.

(*b*) A fielder shall not take a position in the batter's line of vision or, with deliberate unsportsmanlike intent, acts in a manner to distract the batter. A pitch does not have to be released. *Note*: The offending player shall also be ejected from the game.

(*c*) The catcher or any other fielder shall not step on or in front of home plate without the ball, or touch the batter or his bat with a runner on third base trying to score by means of a squeeze play or a steal.

Note: The batter shall also be awarded first base on the obstruction and the ball is dead.

Section 6. Foreign Substance
The pitcher nor any other player shall, at any time during the game, be allowed to use any foreign substance upon the ball. Under the supervision and control of the umpire, powdered resin may be used to dry the hands. The pitcher shall not wear tape on his fingers, a sweatband, bracelet, or similar type item on the wrist or forearm of the pitching-arm.

Section 7. Catcher
   (*a*) The catcher must remain within the lines of the catcher's box until the pitch is released.
   (*b*) The catcher shall return the ball directly to the pitcher after each pitch, except after a strikeout, put out or an attempted put out made by the catcher.
Exception: Does not apply with a runner(s) on base or the batter becoming a batter-runner.

Section 8. Throwing to a Base
The pitcher shall not throw to a base during a live ball while his foot is in contact with the pitcher's plate after he has taken the pitching position. If the throw from the pitcher's plate occurs during a live ball appeal play, the appeal is cancelled. *Note*: The pitcher may remove himself from the pitching position by stepping backwards off the pitcher's plate. Stepping forward or sideways constitutes an illegal pitch.
Effect – (*Sections 1–8*): Any infraction of Sections 1–8 is an illegal pitch. The ball is dead, a ball is called on the batter, and runners are entitled to advance one base without liability to be put out.
Exception: If the pitcher completes the delivery of the ball to the batter and the batter hits the ball, reaches first base safely and all runners advance at least one base, the play stands and the illegal pitch is nullified.
Note: If an illegal pitch hits the batter, the batter is awarded first base and all runners are awarded one base.

Section 9. Warm-up Pitches
At the beginning of each half inning, or when a pitcher relieves another, not more than one minute may be used to deliver not more than five pitches. Play shall be suspended during this time. For excessive warm-up pitches, a pitcher shall be penalized by awarding a ball to the batter for each pitch in excess of five. This does not apply if the umpire delays the start of play due to substitution, conference, injuries, etc. *Note*: A

pitcher returning to pitch in the same half inning will not receive warm-up pitches.

Section 10. No Pitch
No pitch shall be declared when:

(a) The pitcher pitches during the suspension of play.

(b) The pitcher attempts a quick return of the ball before the batter has taken his position or when the batter is off balance as a result of a previous pitch.

(c) A runner is called out for leaving a base prior to the pitcher releasing the pitch.

(d) The pitcher pitches before a runner has retouched his base after a foul ball has been declared and the ball is dead.

(e) No player, manager or coach shall call time, employ any other word or phrase, or commit any act while the ball is alive and in play for the obvious purpose of trying to make the pitcher commit an illegal pitch. *Note*: A warning shall be issued to the offending team, and a repeat of this type act by any member of the team warned shall result in the offender being ejected from the game.

Effect – Section 10 (*a–e*): The ball is dead, and all subsequent action on that pitch is cancelled.

Section 11. Dropped Ball
If the ball slips from the pitcher's hand during his delivery, a ball is declared on the batter, the ball will remain in play and the runners may advance at their own risk.

MODIFIED PITCH
Section 1. Preliminaries
Before starting the delivery (pitch), the pitcher shall comply with the following:

(a) He shall take a position with both feet in contact with the pitcher's plate. Both feet must be on the ground within the 24-inch length of the pitcher's plate. The shoulders shall be in line with first and third bases.

(b) The pitcher shall take the signal from the catcher with the hands separated. The ball may be in the glove or pitching hand.

(c) The pitcher shall hold the ball in both hands for not less than one second and not more than 10 seconds before releasing it.

(d) The pitcher shall not be considered in pitching position unless the catcher is in position to receive the pitch.

(e) The pitcher may not take the pitching position on or near the pitcher's plate without having the ball in his possession.

Section 2. Starting Pitch

The pitch starts when one hand is taken off the ball or the pitcher makes any motion that is part of his windup.

Section 3. Legal Delivery

(*a*) The pitcher must not make any motion to pitch without immediately delivering the ball to the batter.

(*b*) The pitcher must not use a rocker action in which, after having the ball in both hands in the pitching position, he removes one hand from the ball, takes a backward and forward swing, and returns the ball to both hands in front of the body.

(*c*) The pitcher must not use a windup in which there is a stop or reversal of the forward motion.

(*d*) The pitcher may take the ball behind his back on the back swing.

(*e*) The pitcher must not use a windmill or slingshot-type pitch or make a complete revolution in the delivery.

(*f*) The ball must not be outside the pitcher's wrist on the downward motion and during the complete delivery.

(*g*) The delivery must be underhanded motion with the hand below the hip and the pitcher's palm may be pointing downward.

(*h*) On the forward swing of the pitching arm, the elbow must be locked at the point of release and the shoulders and driving hip must be squared to home plate when the ball is released.

(*i*) The release of the ball must be on the first forward swing of the pitching arm past the hip. The release must have a complete, smooth follow-through with no abrupt stop of the arm near the hip.

(*j*) In the act of delivering the ball, the pitcher must take one step simultaneous with the release of the ball. The step must be forward and toward the batter within the 24-inch length of the pitcher's plate.
Note: It is not a step if the pitcher slides his foot across the pitcher's plate, provided contact is maintained with the plate. Raising the foot off the pitching plate and returning it to the plate creates a rocking motion and is an illegal act.

(*k*) Pushing off with the pivot foot from a place other than the pitcher's plate is illegal.

(*l*) The pitcher must not continue to wind up after releasing the ball.

(*m*) The pitcher shall not deliberately drop, roll or bounce the ball in order to prevent the batter from hitting it.

(*n*) The pitcher has 20 seconds to release the next pitch after receiving the ball or after the umpire indicates 'play ball'.

Section 4. Intentional Walk

If the pitcher desires to walk a batter intentionally all pitches must be legally delivered to the batter. A pitchout for the purpose of intentionally walking a batter is not considered an illegal pitch.

Section 5. Defensive Positioning

(*a*) The pitcher shall not deliver a pitch unless all defensive players are positioned in fair territory, except the catcher who must be in the catcher's box.

(*b*) A fielder shall not take a position in the batter's line of vision or, with deliberate unsportsmanlike intent, act in a manner to distract the batter. A pitch does not have to be released. *Note*: The offending player shall also be ejected from the game.

(*c*) The catcher or any other fielder shall not step on or in front of home plate without the ball, or touch the batter or his bat with a runner on third base trying to score by means of a squeeze play or a steal. *Note*: The batter shall also be awarded first base on the obstruction and the ball is dead.

Section 6. Foreign Substance

The pitcher nor any other player shall, at any time during the game, be allowed to use any foreign substance upon the ball. Under the supervision and control of the umpire, powdered resin may be used to dry the hands. The pitcher shall not wear tape on his fingers, a sweatband, bracelet, or similar type item on the wrist or forearm of the pitching arm.

Section 7. Catcher

(*a*) The catcher must remain within the lines of the catcher's box until the pitch is released.

(*b*) The catcher shall return the ball directly to the pitcher after each pitch, except after a strikeout, put out or an attempted put out made by the catcher. *Exception*: Does not apply with a runner(s) on base or the batter becoming a batter-runner.

Section 8. Throwing to a Base

The pitcher shall not throw to a base during a live ball while his foot is in contact with the pitcher's plate after he has taken the pitching position. If the throw from the pitcher's plate occurs during a live ball appeal play, the appeal is cancelled. *Note*: The pitcher may remove himself from the pitching position by stepping backwards off the pitcher's plate. Stepping forward or sideways constitutes an illegal pitch. **Effect** – (*Sections 1–8*): Any infraction of Sections 1–8 is an illegal pitch. The ball is dead, a ball is called on the batter, and runners are entitled to advance one base without liability to be put out.

Exception: If the pitcher completes the delivery of the ball to the batter and the batter hits the ball, reaches first base safely and all runners advance at least one base, the play stands and the illegal pitch is nullified.

Note: If an illegal pitch hits the batter, the batter is awarded first base and all runners are awarded one base.

Section 9. Warm-up Pitches
At the beginning of each half inning, or when a pitcher relieves another, not more than one minute may be used to deliver not more than three pitches. Play shall be suspended during this time. For excessive warm-up pitches, a pitcher shall be penalised by awarding a ball to the batter for each pitch in excess of three. This does not apply if the umpire delays the start of play due to substitution, conference, injuries, etc. *Note*: A pitcher returning to pitch in the same half inning will not receive warm-up pitches.

Section 10. No Pitch
No pitch shall be declared when:
 (*a*) The pitcher pitches during the suspension of play.
 (*b*) The pitcher attempts a quick return of the ball before the batter has taken his position or when the batter is off balance as a result of a previous pitch.
 (*c*) A runner is called out for leaving a base prior to the pitcher releasing the pitch.
 (*d*) The pitcher pitches before a runner has retouched his base after a foul ball has been declared and the ball is dead.
 (*e*) No player, manager or coach shall call time, employ any other word or phrase, or commit any act while the ball is alive and in play for the obvious purpose of trying to make the pitcher commit an illegal pitch. *Note*: A warning shall be issued to the offending team, and a repeat of this type act by any member of the team warned shall result in the offender being ejected from the game.
Effect – Section 10 (*a–e*): The ball is dead, and all subsequent action on that pitch is cancelled.

Section 11. Dropped Ball
If the ball slips from the pitcher's hand during his delivery, a ball is declared on the batter, the ball will remain in play and the runners may advance at their own risk.

SLOW PITCH
Section 1. Preliminaries
 (*a*) The pitcher must take a position with both feet firmly on the

ground and with one or both feet in contact with the pitcher's plate. The pitcher's pivot foot must be in contact with the pitcher's plate throughout the delivery.

(*b*) The pitcher must come to a full and complete stop with the ball in front of the body. The front of the body must face the batter. This position must be maintained at least one second before starting the delivery.

(*c*) The pitcher shall not be considered in pitching position unless the catcher is in position to receive the pitch.

Section 2. Starting Pitch

The pitch starts when the pitcher makes any motion that is part of his windup after the required stop. Prior to the required stop, any windup may be used.

Section 3. Legal Delivery

(*a*) The pitcher must not make any motion to pitch without immediately delivering the ball to the batter.

(*b*) The windup is a continuous motion.

(*c*) The pitcher must not use a windup in which there is a stop or reversal of the pitching motion.

(*d*) The pitcher must deliver the ball toward home plate on the first forward swing of the pitching arm past the hip with an underhanded motion.

(*e*) The pivot foot must remain in contact with the pitcher's plate until the pitched ball leaves the hand. If a step is taken, it can be forward, backward, or to the side, provided the pivot foot is in contact with the pitcher's plate and the step is simultaneous with the release of the ball.

(*f*) The pitcher must not pitch the ball behind his back or through his legs.

(*g*) The pitch shall be released at a moderate speed. The speed is left entirely up to the judgment of the umpire. The umpire shall warn the pitcher who delivers a pitch with excessive speed. If the pitcher repeats such an act after being warned, he shall be removed from the pitcher's position for the remainder of the game.

(*h*) The ball must be delivered with perceptible arc and reach a height of at least six feet (1.83m) from the ground, while not exceeding a maximum height of 12 feet (3.66m) from the ground.

(*i*) He does not continue to wind up after he releases the ball.

(*j*) The pitcher has 10 seconds to release the next pitch after receiving the ball, or after the umpire indicates 'play ball'.

Section 4. Defensive Positioning

(*a*) The pitcher shall not deliver a pitch unless all defensive players are positioned in fair territory, except the catcher who must be in the catcher's box.

(*b*) A fielder shall not take a position in the batter's line of vision or, with deliberate unsportsmanlike intent, act in a manner to distract the batter. A pitch does not have to be released. *Note*: The offending player shall also be ejected from the game.

Section 5. Foreign Substance

The pitcher nor any other player shall, at any time during the game, be allowed to use any foreign substance upon the ball, the pitching hand or the fingers. Under the supervision and control of the umpire, powdered resin may be used to dry the hands. The pitcher may wear a sweatband on the pitching arm. Tape on the fingers is legal.

Section 6. Catcher

(*a*) The catcher must remain within the lines of the catcher's box until the pitched ball is batted, touches the ground or plate, or reaches the catcher's box.

(*b*) The catcher shall return the ball directly to the pitcher after each pitch, except after a strikeout.

Effect: an additional ball is awarded to the batter.

Section 7. Quick Pitch

The pitcher shall not attempt a quick return of the ball before the batter has taken his position or when the batter is off balance as a result of a pitch.

Effect – (*Sections 1–7*): Any infraction of Sections 1–7 is an illegal pitch. A ball shall be called on the batter. Runners are not advanced.

Exception: If a batter swings at any illegal pitch, it is nullified and all play stands.

Section 8. Warm-up Pitches

At the beginning of each half inning, or when a pitcher relieves another, not more than one minute may be used to deliver not more than three warm-up pitches. Each warm-up pitch, if thrown underhand, must be at a moderate speed. Play shall be suspended during this time. For excessive warm-up pitches and warm-up pitches delivered with excessive speed including fast pitch-type deliveries, a pitcher shall be penalised by awarding a ball to the batter for each pitch. *Note*: After a warning for excessive speed pitches, the pitcher may be removed from the pitching position for the remainder of the game. A pitcher returning to pitch in the same half inning will not receive warm-up pitches.

Section 9. No Pitch
No pitch shall be declared when:

(*a*) The pitcher pitches during the suspension of play.

(*b*) A runner is called out for leaving his base before the pitched ball reaches home plate or is batted.

(*c*) The pitcher pitches before a runner has retouched his base after a foul ball has been declared and the ball is dead.

(*d*) The ball slips from the pitcher's hand during his windup or during the back swing.

(*e*) No player, manager or coach shall call time, employ any other word or phrase, or commit any act while the ball is alive and in play for the obvious purpose of trying to make the pitcher commit an illegal pitch. *Note*: A warning shall be issued to the offending team, and a repeat of this type act by any member of the team warned shall result in the offender being removed from the game.

Effect: Section 9(*a–e*): The ball is dead, and all subsequent action on that pitch is cancelled.

16-INCH SLOW PITCH
Section 1. Preliminaries

(*a*) The pitcher must take a position with both feet firmly on the ground and with one or both feet in contact with the pitcher's plate. The pitcher's pivot foot must be in contact with the pitcher's plate throughout the delivery.

(*b*) The pitcher must come to a full and complete stop with the ball in front of the body. The front of the body must face the batter. This position must be maintained at least one second before starting the delivery.

(*c*) The pitcher shall not be considered in pitching position unless the catcher is in position to receive the pitch.

(*d*) While the pitcher is in the pitching position, in the motion for his delivery, or in the act of faking a delivery prior to a hesitation, the pivot foot must be in contact with the pitcher's plate. After a hesitation, the foot may leave the pitcher's plate during an attempted pickoff or a fake throw. When the pitching motion is restarted, the restriction takes effect again.

(*e*) The pitcher may not take the pitching position on or near the pitcher's plate without having the ball in his possession.

Section 2. Starting Pitch
The pitch starts when the pitcher makes any motion that is part of his

windup after the required stop. Prior to the required stop, any windup may be used.

Section 3. Legal Delivery

(*a*) The pivot foot must remain in contact with the pitcher's plate until the pitched ball leaves the hand. If a step is taken, it can be forward, backward, or to the side, provided the pivot foot is in contact with the pitcher's plate and the step is simultaneous with the release of the ball.

(*b*) The pitcher must not pitch the ball behind his back or through his legs.

(*c*) The pitch shall be released at a moderate speed. The speed is left entirely up to the judgment of the umpire. The umpire shall warn the pitcher who delivers a pitch with excessive speed. If the pitcher repeats such an act after being warned, he shall be removed from the pitcher's position for the remainder of the game.

(*d*) The ball must be delivered with perceptible arc and reach a height of at least six feet (1.83m) from the ground, while not exceeding a maximum height of 12 feet (3.66m) from the ground.

(*e*) The pitcher must not continue to wind up after he releases the ball.

(*f*) The pitcher must not commit a third hesitation before the mandatory delivery of a pitch, legal or illegal. Hesitations are defined as:

1. Making any motion to pitch without immediately delivering the ball to the batter.

2. Using a windup which is not a continuous motion.

3. Using a windup in which there is a stop or reversal of the pitching motion.

4. Not delivering the ball toward home plate on the first forward swing of the pitching arm past the hip.

Note:

(*1*) After a hesitation of the pitching motion, and before a restart of that motion, the pitcher may attempt or fake a throw for a pickoff with his pivot foot still in contact with the pitcher's plate.

(*2*) Runners may be off the bases without penalty during the delivery or fake delivery.

(*3*) During the pickoff attempt of the pitcher, or the catcher following a pitch, each runner must return to the base at which he was when the pitch was started, and before he is touched with the ball.

(*4*) If the ball is overthrown, no runners may advance.

(*5*) If the thrown ball remains in playable territory, the runners are in jeopardy until they return to their original bases.

(*g*) The pitcher has 10 seconds to release the next pitch after receiving the ball, or after the umpire indicates 'play ball'.

Section 4. Defensive Positioning

(*a*) The pitcher shall not deliver a pitch unless all defensive players are positioned in fair territory, except the catcher who must be in the catcher's box.

(*b*) A fielder shall not take a position in the batter's line of vision or, with deliberate unsportsmanlike intent, act in a manner to distract the batter. A pitch does not have to be released. *Note*: The offending player shall also be ejected from the game.

Section 5. Foreign Substance

The pitcher nor any other player shall, at any time during the game, be allowed to use any foreign substance upon the ball, the pitching hand or the fingers. Under the supervision and control of the umpire, powdered resin may be used to dry the hands. The pitcher may wear a sweatband on the pitching arm. Tape on the fingers is legal.

Section 6. Catcher

(*a*) The catcher must remain within the lines of the catcher's box until the pitched ball is batted, touches the ground or plate, or reaches the catcher's box.

(*b*) The catcher shall return the ball directly to the pitcher after each pitch, except after a strikeout. *Effect*: An additional ball is awarded to the batter. *Exception*: Does not apply when the batter becomes a batter-runner or there are runners on base.

Section 7. Quick Pitch

The pitcher shall not attempt a quick return of the ball before the batter has taken his position or when the batter is off balance as a result of a pitch.

Effect – (*Sections 1–7*): Any infraction of Sections 1–7 is an illegal pitch. A ball shall be called on the batter. Runners are not advanced.

Exception: If a batter swings at any illegal pitch, it is nullified and all play stands.

Section 8. Warm-up Pitches

At the beginning of each half inning, or when a pitcher relieves another, not more than one minute may be used to deliver not more than three warm-up pitches. Each warm-up pitch, if thrown underhand, must be at a moderate speed. Play shall be suspended during this time. For excessive warm-up pitches and warm-up pitches delivered with excessive speed including fast pitch-type deliveries, a pitcher shall be penalised by awarding a ball to the batter for each pitch. *Note*: After a warning for excessive speed pitches, the pitcher may be removed from the pitching position for the remainder of the game. A pitcher returning to pitch in the same half inning will not receive warm-up pitches.

Section 9. No Pitch
No pitch shall be declared when:

(*a*) The pitcher pitches during the suspension of play.

(*b*) A runner is called out for leaving his base before the pitched ball reaches home plate or is batted.

(*c*) The pitcher pitches before a runner has retouched his base after a foul ball has been declared and the ball is dead.

(*d*) The ball slips from the pitcher's hand during his windup or during the backswing.

(*e*) No player, manager or coach shall call time, employ any other word or phrase, or commit any act while the ball is alive and in play for the obvious purpose of trying to make the pitcher commit an illegal pitch. *Note*: A warning shall be issued to the offending team, and a repeat of this type act by any member of the team warned shall result in the offender being removed from the game.

Effect – Section 9 (*a–e*): The ball is dead, and all subsequent action on that pitch is cancelled.

7. BATTING
Section 1. On-deck Batter

(*a*) The on-deck batter is the offensive player whose name follows the name of the batter in the batting order.

(*b*) The on-deck batter shall take a position within the lines of the on-deck circle nearest his bench.

(*c*) The on-deck batter may loosen up with no more than two official softball bats, an approved warm-up bat, or a combination not to exceed two. Any detachable piece placed on the bat must be approved by the Equipment Standards Committee following a one-year period observed by members of this Committee.

(*d*) The on-deck batter may leave the on-deck circle:

1. When he becomes the batter.

2. To direct runners advancing from third to home plate.

(*e*) The on-deck batter may not interfere with the defensive player's opportunity to make an out.

1. If it involves a runner, the runner closest to home plate at the time of the interference shall be declared out.

2. If it is with the defensive fielder fielding a fly ball, the batter is out.

Section 2. Batting Order

(*a*) The batting order of each team showing the players' names and uniform numbers must be on the lineup card and must be delivered before the game by the manager or captain to the plate umpire. The plate umpire shall submit it to the inspection of the manager or captain of the opposing team.

(*b*) The batting order delivered to the umpire must be followed throughout the game, unless a player is replaced by a substitute. When this occurs, the substitute must take the place of the removed player in the batting order.

(*c*) The first batter in each inning shall be the batter whose name follows that of the last player who completed his turn at bat in the preceding inning.

Effect – Section 2 (*b–c*): Except for a wrong batter at bat, batting out of order is an appeal play which may be made only by the defensive team. The defensive team forfeits its right to appeal batting out of order when one legal or illegal pitch has been made to the following batter, or when the pitcher and all infielders have clearly vacated their normal fielding positions and have left fair territory on their way to the bench or dugout.

1. If the error is discovered while the incorrect batter is at bat, the correct batter may take his place and legally assume any balls and strikes. Any runs scored or bases run while the incorrect batter was at bat shall be legal. *Note*: The offensive team may correct a wrong batter at the plate with no penalty.

2. If the error is discovered after the incorrect batter has completed his turn at bat and before a legal or illegal pitch has been made to the following batter or before the pitcher and all infielders have clearly vacated their normal fielding positions and have left fair territory on their way to the bench or dugout area, the player who should have batted is out. Any advance or score made because of a ball batted by the improper batter or because of the improper batter's advance to first base as a result of obstruction, an error, a hit batter, walk, dropped third strike or a base hit shall be nullified. The next batter is the player whose name follows that of the player called out for failing to bat. If the batter declared out under these circumstances is the third out, the correct batter in the next inning shall be the player who would have come to bat had the player been put out by ordinary play.

3. If the error is discovered after the first legal or illegal pitch to the next batter, or after the pitcher and all infielders have clearly vacated their normal fielding positions and have left fair territory on their way to the bench or dugout area, the turn at bat of the incorrect batter is legal, all runs scored and bases run are legal and the next batter in order shall be the one whose name follows that of the incorrect batter. No one is called out for failure to bat. Players who have not batted and who have not been called out have lost their turn at bat until reached again in the regular order.

4. No runner shall be removed from the base he is occupying except the batter-runner who has been taken off the base by the umpire as in (2) above to bat in his proper place. He merely misses his turn at bat with no penalty. The batter following him in the batting order becomes the legal batter.

(*d*) The batting order for coed shall alternate the sexes. Coed play will use an 11-inch red-stitch ball when the female bats and a 12-inch red-stitch ball when the male bats.

(*e*) When the third out in an inning is made before the batter has completed his turn at bat, he shall be the first batter in the next inning and the ball and strike count on him shall be cancelled.

Section 3. Batting Position

(*a*) The batter must have both feet completely within the lines of the batter's box prior to the start of the pitch. He may touch the lines, but no part of a foot may be outside the lines prior to the pitch.

(*b*) The batter must take his position within 10 seconds after 'play ball' has been declared by the umpire. *Effect*: The umpire will call a strike. No pitch has to be thrown and the ball remains dead.

The batter shall not step directly in front of the catcher to the other batter's box while the pitcher is in position to pitch. *Effect*: The ball is dead, the batter is out and the runners may not advance.

The batter shall not hinder the catcher from catching or throwing the ball by stepping out of the batter's box, or intentionally hinder the catcher while standing within the batter's box. *Effect*: The ball is dead, the batter is out and each runner must return to the last base that, in the judgment of the umpire, was touched at the time of the interference.

Section 4. A Strike is called by the Umpire:

(*a*) (FP only) For each legally pitched ball entering the strike zone. *Effect*: The ball is in play and the runners may advance with liability to be put out.

(SP only) For each legally pitched ball entering the strike zone before touching the ground and the batter does not swing. It is not a strike if the pitched ball touches home plate and then is swung at by the batter. Any pitched ball that hits the ground or plate cannot be legally swung at by the batter. *Note*: If the batter swings and misses the pitch prior to the ball hitting the ground or plate, it is a strike. *Effect*: The ball is dead.

(*b*) For each legally pitched ball struck at and missed by the batter. *FP Effect*: The ball is in play and the runners may advance with liability to be put out.

SP Effect: The ball is dead. If the batter swings at an illegal pitch, the illegal pitch is nullified.

(*c*) For each foul tip. *Effect*: (FP only) The ball is in play and runners may advance with liability to be put out. The batter is out if it is the third strike. (SP only) The ball is dead and the batter is out if it is the third strike.

(16-inch SP only) The ball remains live; however, runners cannot advance.

(*d*) (FP only) For each foul ball when the batter has fewer than two strikes.

(*e*) (SP only) For each foul ball, including the third strike.

(*f*) For each pitched ball struck at and missed which touches any part of the batter.

(*g*) When any part of the batter's person or clothing is hit with his own batted ball when he is in the batter's box and has fewer than two strikes.

(*h*) When a delivered ball by the pitcher hits the batter while the ball is in the strike zone.

(*i*) If the batter does not take his position within 10 seconds after 'play ball' has been declared.

Effect – Section 4 (*d–i*): The ball is dead and each runner must return to his base without liability to be put out.

Section 5. A Ball is called by the Umpire:

(*a*) (FP only) For each legally pitched ball which does not enter the strike zone, or touches the ground before reaching home plate, or touches home plate and the batter does not swing. *Effect*: The ball is in play and runners are entitled to advance with liability to be put out.

(SP only) For each legally pitched ball which does not enter the strike zone, touches the ground before reaching home plate, or touches home plate, and the batter does not swing. Any pitched ball that hits the ground or plate cannot be legally swung at by the batter. *Note*: If the batter swings at a pitch after the ball hits the ground or plate, it is a ball. *Effect*: The ball is dead and runners may not advance. (16-inch Slow Pitch only): The ball remains live; however, runners cannot advance.

(*b*) (FP only) For each illegally pitched ball not swung at. *Effect*: The ball is dead and runners are entitled to advance one base without liability to be put out. (SP only) For each illegally pitched ball not swung at. *Effect*: The ball is dead and runners may not advance.

(*c*) (SP only) When a pitched ball hits the batter outside the strike zone.

(*d*) When the catcher fails to return the ball directly to the pitcher as required.

(*e*) For each excessive warm-up pitch.

Effect – Section 5 (*c–e*): The ball is dead and runners may not advance.

Section 6. The Batter is out:

(*a*) When the third strike is struck at, missed and the pitched ball touches any part of the batter's person.

(*b*) When a batter enters the batter's box with or is discovered using an altered bat. The batter is also ejected from the game.

(*c*) When the batter enters the batter's box with or is discovered using an illegal bat.

(*d*) When an entire foot is touching the ground completely outside the lines of the batter's box when he hits a ball fair or foul.

(*e*) When any part of a foot is touching home plate when he hits a ball fair or foul.

(*f*) (FP only) When the batter bunts foul after the second strike. If the ball is caught in the air, it remains live and in play.

(*g*) (SP only) After a third strike, including a foul ball that is hit after two strikes.

(*h*) (SP only) When the batter bunts or chops the ball.

(*i*) When members of the team interfere with a player attempting to field a fly ball.

(*j*) When the batter hits a fair ball with the bat a second time in fair territory. *Exception*: If the batter is standing in the batter's box and contact is made while the bat is in the batter's hands, a foul ball is ruled even if the ball is hit a second time over fair territory. *Note*: If the batter drops the bat and the ball rolls against the bat in fair territory, and, in the umpire's judgment, there was no intention to interfere with the course of the ball, the batter is not out and the ball is live and in play.

Effect – Section 6 (*a–j*): The ball is dead and each runner must return to the base legally held at the time of the pitch.

(*k*) (FP only) When a called or swinging third strike is caught by the catcher.

(*l*) (FP only) When the batter has three strikes if there are fewer than two outs and first base is occupied. *Exception*: (Junior Olympic 10-Under) Any time the third strike is dropped.

(*m*) (All Slow Pitch Except Coed) Whenever the exception under Rule 4, Section 1*d* (Short-handed Rule) applies.

8. BATTER-RUNNER AND RUNNER
Section 1. The Batter becomes a Batter-runner

(*a*) As soon as he hits a fair ball.

(*b*) (FP only) When the catcher fails to catch the third strike before the ball touches the ground when there are fewer than two outs and first base is unoccupied, or anytime there are two outs. This is called the third strike rule. *Exception*: (Junior Olympic 10-Under) The ball is dead and the batter is out.

Effect – Section 1 (*a–b*): The ball is in play, and the batter becomes a batter-runner with liability to be put out.

(*c*) When four balls have been called by the umpire. The batter-runner is awarded one base without liability to be put out.

Effect:

1. (FP only) The ball is in play unless it has been blocked.

2. (SP only) The ball is dead and runners may not advance unless forced. If the pitcher desires to walk a batter intentionally, he may do so by notifying the plate umpire who shall award the batter first base. If two batters are to be walked intentionally, the second intentional walk may not be administered until the first batter reaches first base. *Note*: If the umpire mistakenly allows two walks at one time and the first batter fails to touch first base, no appeal will be honoured on the first batter.

3. (Coed) The ball is dead. On any walk to a male batter (intentional or not), the next batter – a female – has her choice of walking or hitting up until the first pitch. *Note*: Should the female batter-runner pass a male batter-runner when choosing to walk, no out shall be called during this dead ball period. A male batter-runner advancing to second without touching-first base shall be called out if properly appealed.

(*d*) When the catcher obstructs, hinders or prevents the batter from striking or hitting a pitched ball.

Effect:

1. The umpire shall give a delayed dead ball signal.

2. If the batter hits the ball and reaches first base safely, and if all other runners have advanced at least one base on the batted ball, catcher obstruction is cancelled. All action as a result of the batted ball stands. No option is given.

3. If the manager does not take the result of the play, obstruction is enforced by awarding the batter first base and advancing all other runners only if forced.

(*e*) When a fair batted ball strikes the person, attached equipment, or clothing of an umpire or a runner. If the runner is hit with a fair batted ball while touching a base, he is not out.

Effect:

1. If, after touching a fielder (including the pitcher), the ball is in play.

2. If, after passing a fielder other than the pitcher, and no other infielder had a chance to make an out, the ball is in play.

3. If, before passing a fielder without being touched, the ball is dead. If the runner is hit by the ball while off base, he is out and the batter-runner is entitled to first base without liability to be put out. Any runner not forced by the batter-runner must return to the base he had reached prior to the interference. When a fair ball touches a runner who is in contact with a base, the ball remains dead or live depending on the position of the fielder closest to the base.

(*f*) (FP only) When a pitched ball not swung at nor called a strike touches any part of the batter's person or clothing while he is in the batter's box. It does not matter if the ball strikes the ground before hitting him. The batter's hands are not to be considered a part of the bat. *Effect*: The ball is dead. The batter is entitled to one base without liability to be put out. *Exception*: If no attempt is made to avoid being hit, the umpire calls either a ball or a strike.

Section 2. Batter-runner is out:

(*a*) (FP only) When the catcher drops the third strike and he is legally put out prior to reaching first base.

(*b*) When after hitting a fair ball he is legally put out prior to reaching first base.

(*c*) When, after a fly ball is hit, the ball is caught by a fielder before it touches the ground, any object or person other than a defensive player. *Effect* – Section 2 (*a–c*): The ball is in play.

(*d*) When he fails to advance to first base and enters his team area after a batted fair ball, a base on balls, a hits batsman (FP only), a dropped third strike (FP only), or catcher obstruction. *Exception*: In slow pitch, the ball is dead on a base on balls, the batter-runner is out and runners cannot advance.

(*e*) When he runs outside the three-foot (0.91m) lane and, in the judgment of the umpire, interferes with the fielder taking the throw at first base; however, he may run outside the three-foot (0.91m) lane to avoid a fielder attempting to field a batted ball.

(*f*) When he interferes with a fielder attempting to field a batted ball, interferes with a thrown-ball, or (FP only) interferes with a dropped third strike. If this interference, in the judgment of the umpire, is an obvious attempt to prevent a double play, the runner closest to home plate shall also be called out. *Note*: A batter-runner being hit with a thrown ball does not necessarily constitute interference.

(*g*) When he interferes with a play at home plate in an attempt to prevent an obvious out at home plate. The runner is also out.

(*h*) When he moves back toward home plate to avoid or delay a tag by a fielder. *Effect* – Section 2 (*e–h*): The ball is dead and runner(s) must return to the last base legally touched at the time of interference.

(*i*) When he hits an infield fly.

(*j*) When an infielder intentionally drops a fair fly ball, including a line drive or a bunt, which can be caught with ordinary effort with first;

first and second; first and third; or first, second and third bases occupied with fewer than two outs. A trapped ball shall not be considered as having been intentionally dropped. *Effect*: The ball is dead, and each runner must return to the last base touched at the time of the pitch. *Note*: This rule would apply on an infield fly situation.

(*k*) When the immediate preceding runner who is not yet out intentionally interferes, in the umpire's judgment, with a fielder who is attempting to catch a thrown ball or throw a ball in an attempt to complete the play.
Effect: Batter-runner is out and the runner shall also be called out.

(*l*) (SP only) For excess over-the-fence home runs.

Section 3. Touching Bases in Legal Order

(*a*) When a runner must return to a base while the ball is in play or dead, he must touch the base(s) in reverse order. *Exception*: Should time out be called while a runner is touching a base, he must remain on the base occupied.

(*b*) When a runner or batter-runner acquires the right to a base by touching it before being put out, he is entitled to hold the base until he has legally touched the next base in order or is forced to vacate it for a succeeding runner.

(*c*) When a runner dislodges a base from its proper position, neither he nor the succeeding runner(s) in the same series of plays are compelled to follow a base out of position.
Effect – Section 3 (*a–c*): The ball is in play and runners may advance or return with liability to be put out.

(*d*) A runner shall not run bases in reverse order either to confuse the fielders or to make a travesty of the game. *Effect*: The ball is dead and the runner is out.

(*e*) Two runners may not occupy the same base simultaneously. *Effect*: The runner who first legally occupied the base shall be entitled to it, unless forced to advance. The other runner may be put out by being touched with the ball.

(*f*) Failure of a preceding runner to touch a base or to legally tag up on a caught fly ball, and who is declared out, does not affect the status of a succeeding runner who touches bases in proper order. If the failure to touch a base in regular order or to legally tag up on a caught fly ball is the third out of the inning, no succeeding runner may score a run.

(*g*) No runner may return to touch a missed base or one he had left too soon after a following runner has scored or once he leaves the field of play.

(*h*) Bases left too soon on a caught fly ball must be retouched prior to advancing to awarded bases.

(*i*) Awarded bases must be touched in legal order.

Section 4. Runners are entitled to advance with liability to be put out:

(*a*) (FP only) When the ball leaves the pitcher's hand on his delivery.

(*b*) On a thrown ball or a fair batted ball that is not blocked.

(*c*) When a legally caught fly ball is first touched.

(*d*) If a fair ball strikes an umpire or a runner after having passed an infielder other than the pitcher, and provided no other infielder had a chance to make an out, or when a fair batted ball has been touched by an infielder, including the pitcher.

Effect – Section 4 (*a–d*): The ball is in play.

Section 5. A runner forfeits his exemption from liability to be put out:

(*a*) If, while the ball is in play or on awarded bases, he fails to touch a base before attempting to make the next base. If the runner put out is the batter-runner at first base, or any other runner forced to advance because the batter became a batter-runner, this is a force out.

(*b*) If, after overrunning first base, the runner attempts to continue to second base.

(*c*) If, after dislodging a base, a runner attempts to continue to the next base.

(*d*) (16-inch SP only) A runner may lead off any base with the risk of being picked off by a throw from the pitcher or catcher. If a throw results in an overthrown or blocked ball, no runners may advance. Any runner advancing on a pitch not hit is liable to be put out if tagged before returning to his original base.

Section 6. Runners are entitled to advance without liability to be put out:

(*a*) When forced to vacate a base because the batter was awarded a base on balls. *Effect*: (FP only) The ball remains in play unless it is blocked. Any runner affected is entitled to one base and may advance farther at his own risk if the ball is in play. (SP only) The ball is dead.

(*b*) When a fielder not in possession of the ball, not in the act of fielding a batted ball, or not about to receive a thrown ball, impedes the progress of a runner or batter-runner who is legally running bases.

Note: Obstructed runners are still required to touch all bases in proper order, or they could be called out on a proper appeal by the defensive team.

Effect: When any obstruction occurs (including a rundown), the umpire will signal a delayed dead ball. The ball will remain alive.

1. If the obstructed runner is put out prior to reaching the base he would have reached had there not been obstruction, a dead ball is called and the obstructed runner and each other runner affected by the obstruction will always be awarded the base or bases he would have reached, in the umpire's judgment, had there not been obstruction. An obstructed runner may never be called out between the two bases where he was obstructed. This runner would either be advanced or returned to the last base touched. Should an act of interference occur following any obstruction, enforcement of the interference penalty would have precedence.

2. If the obstructed runner is put out after passing the base he would have reached had there not been obstruction, the obstructed runner will be called out. The ball remains live.

3. When a runner, while advancing or returning to a base, is obstructed by a fielder who neither has the ball nor is attempting to field a batted or thrown ball, or a fielder who fakes a tag without the ball, the obstructed runner and each other runner affected by the obstruction, will always be awarded the base or bases he would have reached, in the umpire's judgment, had there been no obstruction. If the umpire feels there is justification, a defensive player making a fake tag could be ejected from the game.

4. Catcher obstruction on the batter is covered under Rule 8, Section 1*d*.

(*c*) (FP only) When a wild pitch or passed ball lodges in or goes under, over or through the backstop. *Effect*: The ball is dead and all runners are awarded one base only. The batter is awarded first base only on the fourth ball.

(*d*) When forced to vacate a base because the batter was awarded first base.

(*e*) (FP only) When a pitcher makes an illegal pitch.

(*f*) When a fielder contacts or catches a fair batted or thrown ball with his cap, helmet, mask, protector, pocket, detached glove or any part of his uniform which is detached from its proper place on his person. *Effect*: The runners would be entitled to three bases from the time of the pitch if a batted ball, or two bases from the time of the throw if a thrown ball, and in either case, they may advance farther at their own risk. If the illegal catch or touch is made on a fair hit ball which, in the judgment of the umpire, would have cleared the outfield fence in flight, the batter-runner shall be awarded a four base award.

(*g*) When the ball is in play and is overthrown (beyond the boundary lines) or is blocked. *Effect*: All runners will be awarded two bases, and the award will be governed by the positions of the runners when the ball left the fielder's hand. If two runners are between the same bases, the award is based on the position of the lead runner.

Exception:

1. When a fielder loses possession of the ball, such as on an attempted tag, and the ball enters the dead ball area or becomes blocked, each runner is awarded one base from the last base touched at the time the ball entered the dead ball area or became blocked.

2. If a runner touches the next base and returns to his original base, the original base he left is considered the last base touched for the purpose of an overthrow award.

3. If the ball becomes blocked due to offensive equipment not involved in the game, the ball is ruled dead and runners are returned to the last base touched at the time of the blocked ball. If the blocked ball prevented the defence from making a play, the runner closest to home is called out.

(*h*) When a fair batted fly ball strikes the foul pole above the fence level or leaves the playing field in fair territory without touching the ground or going through the fence. It shall entitle the batter-runner to a home run, unless it passes out of the grounds at a distance less than the prescribed fence distances from home plate, in which case the batter-runner would be entitled to only two bases.

(*i*) When a fair ball bounces over or rolls under or through a fence or any designated boundary of the playing field. Also, when it deflects off a defensive player and goes out of play in foul territory, deflects off a runner or umpire after having passed an infielder excluding the pitcher and provided no other infielder had a chance to make an out. *Effect*: The ball is dead, and all runners are awarded two bases from the time of the pitch.

(*j*) When a live ball is unintentionally carried by a fielder from playable territory into dead ball territory. *Effect*: The ball is dead and each runner is awarded one base from the last base touched at the time the fielder entered dead ball territory. *Note*: A fielder carrying a live ball into the dugout or team area to tag a player is considered to have unintentionally carried it there.

(*k*) If, in the judgment of the umpire, a fielder intentionally carries, kicks, pushes or throws a live ball from playable territory into dead ball territory. *Effect*: The ball is dead. Each runner is awarded two bases from the last base touched at the time the fielder entered or the ball was kicked, pushed or thrown into dead ball territory.

Section 7. A runner must return to his base

(*a*) When a batted ball is foul.

(*b*) When an illegally batted ball is declared by the umpire.

(*c*) When a batter, batter-runner or runner is called out for interference. Each other runner shall return to the last base which, in the umpire's judgment, was legally touched by him at the time of the interference.

(*d*) (FP only) When the plate umpire or his clothing interferes with the catcher's attempt to throw out a runner stealing. *Exception*: If the runner being played on is ruled out, he will remain out.

(*e*) (FP only) When any part of the batter's person or clothing is touched by a pitched ball that is swung at and missed.

(*f*) (FP only) When a batter is hit by a pitched ball, unless forced.

Effect – Section 7 (*a*–*f*):

1. The ball is dead.

2. Each runner must return to his base without liability to be put out, except when forced to go to the next base because the batter became a batter-runner.

3. Runners need not touch the intervening bases in returning to base.

(*g*) (SP only) Base stealing is not allowed. *Effect*: Each runner may leave his base when a pitched ball is batted, touches the ground or reaches home, but must return to that base immediately after each pitch not hit by the batter. *Exception*: (16-inch SP only) Runners may lead off prior to a pitched ball.

(*h*) When an intentionally dropped ball is ruled.

(*i*) (FP Junior Olympic 10-Under only) Under no condition is a runner permitted to steal a base when a pitched ball is not batted. Each runner may leave his base when the ball leaves the pitcher's hand, but the ball is dead if not hit, and he must return to his base without liability to be put out.

Section 8. The runner is out:

(*a*) When running to any base in regular or reverse order and he runs more than three feet (0.91m) from a direct line between that base and the next one to avoid being touched by the ball in the hand(s) of a fielder.

(*b*) When the ball is in play and while he is not in contact with a base, he is legally touched with the ball in the hand(s) of a fielder.

(*c*) When, on a force play, a fielder contacts the base while holding the ball, touches the ball to the base or tags the runner before he reaches the base.

(*d*) When he fails to return to touch the base he previously occupied or missed and is properly appealed.

(*e*) When he physically passes a preceding runner before that runner has been put out.

Effect – Section 8 (*a*–*e*): The ball is in play and the runner is out.

(*f*) When he leaves his base to advance to another base before a caught fly ball has touched a fielder, provided the ball is returned to an infielder and properly appealed.

(*g*) When he fails to touch the intervening base or bases in regular or reverse order and the ball is returned to an infielder and properly appealed.

(*h*) When the batter-runner legally overruns first base, attempts to run to second base and is legally touched while off base.

(*i*) When running or sliding for home plate and he fails to touch it, makes no attempt to return to it, and a fielder holds the ball in his hand while touching the plate and appeals to the umpire for the decision.

Effect: Section 8 (*f*–*i*):

1. These are appeal plays, and the defensive team loses the privilege of putting the runner out if the appeal is not made before the next legal or illegal pitch, or before the pitcher and all infielders have clearly vacated their normal fielding positions and have left fair territory on their way to the bench or dugout area, or before the umpires have left the field at the conclusion of the game.

2. (Live Ball Appeal) If properly appealed during a live ball, the runner is out. (POE # 1 B)

3. (Dead Ball Appeal) Once the ball has been returned to the infield and time has been called, any infielder (including the pitcher or catcher), with or without possession of the ball, may make a verbal appeal on a runner missing a base or leaving a base too soon on a caught fly ball. The administering umpire should acknowledge the appeal and then make a decision on the play. No runner may leave his base during this period as the ball remains dead until the next pitch. *Note*:

A. If the pitcher has possession of the ball and is in contact with the pitching plate when making a verbal appeal, no illegal pitch is called.

B. If 'play ball' has been declared by the umpire and the pitcher then requests an appeal, the umpire would again call time and allow the appeal process.

(*j*) When he interferes with a fielder attempting to field a batted ball or interferes with a thrown ball. If this interference, in the judgment of the umpire, is an obvious attempt to prevent a double play and occurs before the runner is put out, the immediate succeeding runner shall also be called out. *Note*: If a ball ricochets off one defensive player and another player has the opportunity to make an out, the runner will be ruled out if he interferes with the second fielder.

(*k*) When he is struck with a fair untouched batted ball while not in contact with a base and before it passes an infielder, excluding the pitcher.

Note – Section 8 (*j*–*k*): When runners are called out for interference, the batter-runner is awarded first base and credited with a base hit.

(*l*) When he intentionally kicks a ball which an infielder has missed.

(*m*) When anyone, other than another runner, physically assists him while the ball is in play. If this assistance occurs prior to a caught batted fly ball, regardless of whether the ball is fair or foul, a delayed dead ball call will be made, after which he will be declared out. If the ball is caught, the batter-runner will also be declared out. *Effect*: The ball is dead if not caught. If a fair ball, award the batter-runner one base and if a foul ball, the batter will bat again. This includes a home run.

(*n*) When the coach near third base runs in the direction of home plate on or near the baseline while a fielder is attempting to make a play on a batted or thrown ball and thereby draws a throw to home plate. The runner closest to home shall be declared out.

(*o*) When one or more members of the offensive team stand or collect around a base to which a runner is advancing, thereby confusing the fielders and adding to the difficulty of making the play. *Note*: Members of a team include bat boy or any other person authorised to sit on team's bench.

(*p*) When a coach intentionally inteferes with a thrown ball while in the coach's box, or interferes with the defensive team's opportunity to make a play on another runner. The runner closest to home plate at the time of the interference shall be declared out.

Effect – Section 8 (*j–p*): The ball is dead and the runner is out. Each other runner must return to the last base legally touched at the time of the interference.

(*q*) When, after being declared out or after scoring, a runner interferes with a defensive player's opportunity to make a play on another runner. *Effect*: The runner closest to home plate at the time of the interference shall be declared out.

(*r*) When a defensive player has the ball and the runner remains on his feet and deliberately, with great force, crashes into the defensive player. *Effect*: The runner is out, the ball is dead, and each other runner must return to the last base touched at the time of the interference. *Note*: If the act is determined to be flagrant, the offender shall be ejected.

(*s*) (SP only) When he fails to keep contact with the base to which he is entitled until a pitched ball touches the ground, reaches home plate or is batted. *Exception*: (16-inch SP only) Any runner may leave his base as soon as the ball is declared in play.

(*t*) (FP only) When he fails to keep contact with the base to which he is entitled until the ball leaves the pitcher's hand.

Effect: Section (*s–t*): The ball is dead, 'no pitch' is declared and the runner is out.

(*u*) When a runner is legitimately off his base after a pitch or as a result of a batter completing his turn at bat, and while the pitcher has the ball within an eight-foot (2.44m) radius of the pitcher's plate, he must immediately return to his base or attempt to advance to the next base.

1. Failure to immediately return to his base or proceed to the next base once the pitcher has the ball within the eight-foot (2.44m) radius of the pitcher's plate will result in the runner being declared out.

2. Once the runner returns to a base for any reason, he will be declared out if he leaves the base, unless a play is made on him or another runner (a fake throw is considered a play), the pitcher no longer has possession of the ball within the eight-foot (2.44m) radius, or the pitcher releases the ball on a pitch to the batter. *Note*: A base on balls or dropped third strike on which any runner is entitled to run past any base is treated the same as a batted ball. The batter-runner may continue past any base and is entitled to run as long as he does not stop. If he stops after he rounds any base, he then must comply with (1) above.

(*v*) When he abandons a base and enters his team area or leaves the field of play.

(*w*) When he positions himself behind and not in contact with a base to get a running start on any fly ball. The ball remains alive.

(*x*) (SP only except Coed) Whenever the exception under Rule 4, Section 1*d* applies.

Section 9. Runner is not out:

(*a*) When he runs behind or in front of the fielder and outside the baseline in order to avoid interfering with a fielder attempting to field the ball in the base path.

(*b*) When he does not run in a direct line to a base, provided the fielder in the direct line does not have the ball in his possession.

(*c*) When more than one fielder attempts to field a batted ball and the runner comes into contact with the one who, in the judgment of the umpire, could not have made an out.

(*d*) When he is hit with a fair, untouched batted ball that has passed an infielder, excluding the pitcher, and, in the judgment of the umpire, no other infielder had a chance to make an out.

(*e*) When he is hit with a fair untouched batted ball that, in the judgment of the umpire, no infielder had a chance to make an out.

(*f*) When he is hit by a fair batted ball after it touches, or is touched by, any fielder, including the pitcher, and he could not avoid contact with the ball.

(*g*) When he is touched with a ball not securely held by a fielder.

(*h*) When the defensive team does not request the umpire's decision on an appeal play until after the next legal or illegal pitch, or until after the pitcher and all infielders have clearly vacated their normal fielding positions and have left fair territory on their way to the bench or dugout area.

(*i*) When a batter-runner overruns first base after touching it and returns directly to the base.

(*j*) When he is not given sufficient time to return to a base. He will not be called out for being off base before the pitcher releases the ball. 'No pitch' will be called by the umpire.

(*k*) When he has legally started to advance. He may not be stopped by the pitcher receiving the ball while on the pitching plate, nor by the pitcher stepping on the plate with the ball in his possession.

(*l*)   When he holds his base until a fly ball touches a fielder and then attempts to advance.

(*m*) When hit by a batted ball when touching his base, unless he intentionally interferes with the ball or a fielder making a play. (See Rule 8, Section 1 *e* (*1–3*).)

(*n*) When he slides into a base and dislodges it from its proper position. The base is considered to have followed the runner. *Effect*: A runner reaching a base safely will not be out for being off that base if it becomes dislodged. He may return without liability to be put out when the base has been replaced. A runner forfeits this exemption if he attempts to advance beyond the dislodged base before it is again in proper position.

(*o*) When a fielder makes a play on a batter, batter-runner or runner while using an illegal glove. The manager of the offended team is given two options:

1. He may have the entire play nullified with each runner returning to his original base and the batter batting over again, assuming the ball and strike count he had prior to the pitch he hit.

2. He may take the result of the play and disregard the illegal act.

Section 10. Running (Senior Men's)

(*a*) A courtesy runner shall be allowed once per inning for any reason. The courtesy runner must be the last recorded out (or the player scheduled to bat last, if in the first inning with no outs) and must be entered prior to the first pitch to the next batter. The courtesy runner is officially in the game when 'play ball' has been declared by the umpire. An ineligible courtesy runner is an appeal situation that must be made before a legal or illegal pitch to the next batter. *Effect*: The use of an ineligible courtesy runner shall result in the removal of the runner from the base and an out being recorded on the player whom he replaced.

(*b*) Runners must touch the second home plate located adjacent to the right handed batter's box in order to be safe at home. A runner may be retired at home plate on a non-force situation without a tag. The defensive player just has to hold the ball while touching the original home plate. If the runner touches the original home plate, he will be out if appealed by the defensive team. (See diagram under Rule 2, Section 3 *g*.)

(*c*) Once a runner crosses a line 20 feet from home plate, he cannot return to third base. *Effect*: The runner will be called out if he returns and the ball remains live.

9. PROTESTS

This is covered at length in the International Softball Federation Official Guide and Rule book.

10. UMPIRES

The umpires are the representative of the league or organisation by which they have been assigned to a particular game and, as such, are authorised and required to enforce each section of these rules. They have the power to order a player, coach, captain or manager to carry out or to omit any act which, in their judgment is necessary to give force and effect to one or all of these rules, and to inflict penalties as herein prescribed. The plate umpire shall have the authority to make decisions on any situations not specifically covered in the rules.

The responsibilities of the plate umpire and the base umpire, and other aspects of the umpire's role are covered in full in the International Softball Federation Official Guide and Rule book.

11. SCORING

Section 1 The Official Scorer

The official scorer shall keep records of each game as outlined in the following rules. He shall have the sole authority to make all decisions involving judgment. For example, it is the scorer's responsibility to determine whether a batter's advance to first base is the result of a hit in error. However, a scorer shall not make a decision which conflicts with the official playing rules or with an umpire's decision.

Section 2. The Box Score

A. Each player's name and the position or positions he has played shall be listed in the order in which he batted or would have batted had he not been removed or had the game not ended before his turn at bat.

1. (FP only) The designated player (DP) is optional, but if one is used, it must be made known prior to the start of the game, and be listed on the scoresheet in the regular batting order. Ten names will be listed, with the tenth name being the player playing defence only. The tenth player may bat only if he moves to the DP position in the batting order.

2. (SP only) The extra player (EP) is optional, but if one is used, it must be made known prior to the start of the game, and be listed on the scoresheet in the regular batting order. Eleven names will be on the official batting order (twelve for Coed SP), and all will bat.

B. Each player's batting and fielding record must be tabulated.

1. The first column shall show the number of times at bat by each player, but a time at bat shall not be charged against the player when:

(*a*) He hits a sacrifice fly that scores a runner.

(*b*) He is awarded a base on balls.

(*c*) (FP only) He hits a sacrifice bunt.

(*d*) (SP only) He is hit by a pitched ball.

(*e*) (FP only) He hits a sacrifice slap hit.

2. The second column will show the number of opponents put out by each player.

3. The third column shall show the number of base hits made by each player. A base hit is a batted ball that permits the batter to reach the base safely:

(*a*) On a fair ball which settles on the ground, clears the fence or strikes the fence before being touched by a fielder.

(*b*) On a fair ball which is hit with such force or such slowness or which takes an unnatural bounce, making it impossible to field with ordinary effort in time to retire the runner.

(*c*) When a fair ball which has not been touched by a fielder becomes dead because of touching the person or clothing of a runner or umpire.

(*d*) When the fielder unsuccessfully attempts to retire a preceding runner and in the scorer's judgement, the batter-baserunner would not have been retired at first base by perfect fielding.

4. The fourth column shall show the number of opponents put out by each player.

(*a*) A putout is credited to a fielder each time he:

(i) Catches a fly ball or line drive.

(ii) Catches a thrown ball which retires a batter-runner or runner.

(iii) Touches a runner with the ball when the runner is off the base to which he is entitled.

(iv) Is nearest the ball when a runner is declared out for being struck by a fair batted ball or interference with the fielder or when a runner is called out for being in violation of Rule 8, Section 8*e*.

(*b*) A putout is credited to the catcher:

(i) When a third strike is called.

(ii) When the batter bunts or chops the ball (SP only).

(iii) When the batter fails to bat in correct order.

(iv) When the batter interferes with the catcher.

5. The fifth column shall show the number of assists made by each player. An assist shall be credited:

(*a*) To each player who handles the ball in any series of plays which results in the putout of a runner or batter-runner. Only one assist shall be given to any player who handles the ball in any putout of a runner or batter-runner. Only one assist shall be given to any player who handles the ball on any putout. The player who makes the putout in a rundown or similar type of play shall be credited with both an assist and a putout.

(*b*) To each player who handles or throws the ball in such a manner that a putout would have resulted except for an error of a team-mate.

(*c*) To each player who, by deflecting a batted ball, aids in a putout.

(*d*) To each player who handles the ball in a play which results in a runner or batter-runner being called out for interference or for running out of base line.

6. The sixth column shall show the number of errors made by each player. Errors are recorded in the following situations:

(*a*) For each player who commits a misplay which prolongs the turn at bat of the batter or life of the present runner.

(*b*) For the fielder who fails to touch a base after receiving the ball to retire the runner on a force-out or when a runner is compelled to return to base, and provided the thrown ball could be caught by the fielder's ordinary effort.

(*c*) For the catcher if a batter is awarded first base because of catcher obstruction.

(*d*) For the fielder who fails to complete a double play because of dropping the ball.

(*e*) For a fielder, if runner advances a base, because of his failure to catch, stop or try to stop a ball accurately thrown to a base providing there was occasion for the throw. When more than one player could receive the throw, the scorer must determine which player gets the error.

Section 3 A base hit shall not be scored in the following cases:

(*a*) When a runner is forced out by a batted ball or would have been forced out, except for a fielding error.

(*b*) When a player fielding a batted ball retires a preceding runner with ordinary effort.

(*c*) When a fielder fails in an attempt to retire a preceding runner and, in the scorer's judgement the batter could have been retired at first base.

Section 4 A run batted in is a run scored because of one of the following reasons:

(*a*) A safe hit.

(*b*) A sacrifice bunt (FP), a sacrifice slap hit (FP), or a sacrifice fly (FP and SP).

(*c*) An infield putout or fielder's choice.

(*d*) A runner forced home because of obstruction, a hit batter or a base on balls.

(*e*) A home run and all runs scored as a result.

(*f*) Subject to the provisions of Rule 11, Section 4g, when the batter ends a game with a safe hit which drives in as many runs as are necessary to put his team in the lead. He shall be credited with only as many bases on his hit as are advanced by the runner who scores the winning run and then only if the batter runs out his hit for as many bases as are advanced by the runner who scores the winning run.

(*g*) When the batter ends a game with a home run hit out of the playing field, any runners on base are entitled to score.

Section 5 A pitcher shall be credited with a win in the following situations:

(*a*) When a starting pitcher has pitched at least four innings and his team is not only in the lead when he is replaced but remains in the lead for the remainder of the game.

(*b*) When a starting pitcher has pitched at least three innings and his team scores more runs than the opposing team in a game that is terminated after five innings of play; or in a game that is terminated after his team has scored more runs in four or more innings than the opposing team has scored in five or more innings, and provided that his team is not only in the lead if he is replaced after three innings of pitching but remains in the lead for the remainder of the game.

Section 6 A Pitcher's Loss.
A pitcher shall be charged with a loss regardless of the number of innings he has pitched if he is replaced when his team is behind in the score and his team thereafter fails to tie the score or gain the lead.

Section 7 The Summary
The summary shall list the following items in this order.

(*a*) The score by innings and the final score.

(*b*) The runs batted-in and by whom hit.

(*c*) Two-base hits and by whom hit.

(*d*) Three-base hits and by whom hit.

(*e*) Home runs and by whom hit.

(*f*) Sacrifice flies and by whom hit.

(*g*) Double plays and players participating in them.

(*h*) Triple plays and players participating in them.

(*i*) Number of bases on balls charged to each pitcher.

(*j*) Number of batters struck out by each pitcher.

(*k*) Number of hits and runs allowed by each player.

(*l*) The name of the winning pitcher.

(*m*) The name of the losing pitcher.

(*n*) The time of the game.

(*o*) The names of the umpires and scorers.

(*p*) (FP only) Stolen bases and by whom.

(*q*) (FP only) Sacrifice bunts and by whom.

(*r*) (FP only) The names of batters hit by a pitched ball and the names of the pitchers who hit them.

(*s*) (FP only) The number of wild pitches charged to each pitcher.

(*t*) (FP only) The number of passed balls charged to each catcher.

Section 8 Stolen Bases
(FP only) Stolen bases are credited to a runner whenever he advances

one base unaided by a hit, a putout, a force-out, a fielder's choice, a passed ball, a wild pitch, an error, an illegal pitch or obstruction.

Section 9 Records of a forfeited game
All records of a forfeited game shall be included in the official records except that of a pitcher's won-lost record.

Section 10 Tie Breaker Rule
In scoring, the run scored by the player starting as a runner at second base shall be charged to the defensive team and not the pitcher. Depending on the judgement of the official scorekeeper, a run scored by any other player will be charged to the pitcher's ERA.

Reprinted by permission of the International Softball Association. Some of the rules, those concerning umpires, for example, and a long appendix on Points of Emphasis, have been abbreviated or omitted for reasons of space. Copies of the Complete Official Rules of Softball may be obtained from the British Softball Federation.

Squash Rackets

Squash Court Dimensions
(All dimensions are in millimetres)

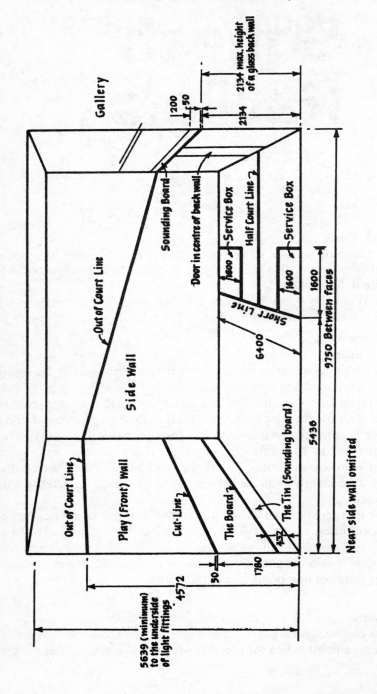

Squash Rackets

1. The Game

The game of squash is played between two players, each using a specified racket, with a specified ball, and in a court constructed to WSF specified dimensions.

Note: When the words 'he', 'him' and 'his' are used in the rules they shall also be taken to mean 'she' and 'her' as appropriate.

2. The Score

A match shall consist of the best of three or five games at the option of the organisers of the competition. Each game is to 9 points, in that the player who scores 9 points wins the game, except that, on the score being called 8-all for the first time, the receiver shall choose before the next service is delivered to continue that game either to 9 points (known as 'set one') or to 10 points (known as 'set two') in which latter case the player who scores 2 more points wins the game. The receiver shall in either case clearly indicate his choice to the marker, referee and his opponent.

The marker shall call either 'set one' or 'set two' as applicable before play continues.

The marker shall call 'game ball' to indicate that the server requires one point to win the game in progress or 'match ball' to indicate that the server requires one point to win the match.

3. Points

Points can be scored only by the server. When the server wins a stroke he scores a point; when the receiver wins a stroke he becomes the server.

4. The Service

4.1 The right to serve first is decided by the spin of a racket. Thereafter, the server continues to serve until he loses a stroke, whereupon his opponent becomes the server, and this procedure continues throughout the match. At the commencement of the second and each subsequent game the winner of the previous game serves first.

4.2 At the beginning of each game and each hand the server has the choice of serving from either box and thereafter shall serve from alternate boxes while remaining the server. However, if a rally ends in a let he shall serve again from the same box.

4.3 For a service to be good there shall be no foot fault and the ball, before being struck, shall be dropped or thrown and shall not hit the walls, floor, ceiling or any object(s) suspended from the walls or ceiling; it shall be served directly onto the front wall between the cut line and the out line so that on its return, unless volleyed, it reaches the floor within the quarter of the court opposite to the server's box. Should a player, having dropped or thrown the ball, make no attempt to strike it, the ball shall be dropped or thrown again for a service. A player with the use of only one arm may utilise his racket to propel the ball into the air before striking it.

4.4 A service is good when it does not result in the server serving his hand out. The server serves his hand out and loses the stroke if:

4.4.1 The ball, after being dropped or thrown for service, touches the wall(s), floor, ceiling or any object(s) suspended from the walls or ceiling before being served – called 'fault'.

4.4.2 At the time of striking the ball the server fails to have part of one foot in contact with the floor within the service box without any part of that foot touching the service box line (part of that foot may project over this line provided that it does not touch the line) – called 'foot fault'.

4.4.3 The server makes an attempt but fails to strike the ball – called 'not up'.

4.4.4 The ball is not struck correctly – called 'not up'.

4.4.5 The ball is served out – called 'out'.

4.4.6 The ball is served against any part of the court before the front wall – called 'fault'.

4.4.7 The ball is served onto or below the cut line – called 'fault' if above the board and 'down' if on or below the board.

4.4.8 The first bounce of the ball, unless volleyed by the receiver, is on the floor on or outside the short or half court lines of the quarter court opposite to the server's box – called 'fault'.

4.4.9 The ball, after being served and before it has bounced more than once on the floor and before it has been struck at by the receiver, touches the server or anything he wears or carries – called 'down'.

4.5 The server must not serve until the marker has completed calling the score.

5. The Play

After a good service has been delivered the players return the ball alternately until one fails to make a good return, the ball otherwise ceases to be in play in accordance with the rules or on a call by the marker or referee.

6. Good Return

6.1 A return is good if the ball, before it has bounced more than once upon the floor, is returned correctly by the striker onto the front wall above the board, without first touching the floor or any part of the striker's body or clothing, or the opponent's racket, body or clothing, provided the ball is not hit out.

6.2 It shall not be considered a good return if the ball touches the board before or after it hits the front wall and before it bounces on the floor, or if the racket is not in the player's hand at the time the ball is struck.

7. Let

A let is an undecided rally. The rally in respect of which a let is allowed shall not count and the server shall serve again from the same box.

8. Strokes

A player wins a stroke:

8.1 Under Rule 4.4 when the player is the receiver.

8.2 If the opponent fails to make a good return of the ball when the opponent is the striker, unless a let is allowed or a stroke is awarded to the opponent.

8.3 If the ball touches his opponent or anything he wears or carries when his opponent is the non-striker, except as is otherwise provided for in Rules 9, 10 and 13.1.1. In all cases the referee shall rule accordingly.

8.4 If a stroke is awarded to him by the referee as provided for in the rules.

9. Hitting an Opponent with the Ball

If the ball, before reaching the front wall, hits the striker's opponent or his racket, or anything he wears or carries, the ball shall cease to be in play and:

9.1 Unless Rule 9.2 applies, the striker shall win the stroke if the return would have been good and the ball would have struck the front wall without first touching any other wall.

9.2 If the return would have been good but the striker has either followed the ball round and turned or allowed it to pass around him – in either case by striking the ball to the right of his body after the ball had passed to his left (or vice versa) then a let shall be allowed in all cases. *Note to referees*: If the striker, having turned or allowed the ball to pass around him, chooses not to continue the rally due to reasonable fear of striking his opponent and, in the opinion of the referee, a reasonable possibility of this occurring did exist and the striker would have been able to make a good return, then a let shall be allowed.

9.3 If the ball either had struck or would have struck any other wall and the return would have been good, a let shall be allowed unless, in the opinion of the referee, a winning return has been intercepted, in which case the striker shall win the stroke. *Note to referees*: The stroke award provisions of Rule 9 do not apply to turning, ball passing around the striker, or further attempts to strike it.

9.4 If the return would not have been good, the striker shall lose the stroke.

10. Further Attempts to Hit the Ball

If the striker strikes at and misses the ball he may make further attempts to strike it. If, after being missed, the ball touches his opponent or his racket, or anything he wears or carries, then, if, in the opinion of the referee:

10.1 The striker could otherwise have made a good return a let shall be allowed, or

10.2 The striker could not have made a good return he shall lose the stroke.

If any such further attempt is successful resulting in a good return being prevented from reaching the front wall by hitting the striker's opponent or anything he wears or carries, a let shall be allowed in all circumstances. If any such further attempt would not have resulted in a good return, the striker shall lose the stroke.

11. Appeals

The loser of a rally may appeal against any decision of the marker affecting that rally.

An appeal to the referee under Rule 11 should be prefaced with the words 'Appeal please'. Play shall then cease until the referee has given his decision.

If an appeal under Rule 11 is disallowed the marker's decision shall stand. If the referee is uncertain he shall allow a let except where provided for in the *Note to referees* after Rule 11.2.1 and *Notes to referees C and D* after Rule 11.2.2.

Appeals upheld or referee intervention under Rule 20.4 are dealt with in each specific situation below.

11.1 Appeals on service

11.1.1 If the marker calls 'fault', 'foot fault', 'not up', 'down' or 'out' to the service the server may appeal. If the appeal is upheld a let shall be allowed.

11.1.2 If the marker fails to call 'fault', 'foot fault', 'not up', 'down' or 'out' to the service the receiver may appeal, either immediately or at the end of the rally if he has played or attempted to play the ball. If, in the opinion of the referee, the service was not good he shall stop play immediately and award the stroke to the receiver.

11.2 Appeals on play other than service

11.2.1 If the marker calls 'not up', 'down' or 'out' following a player's return, the player may appeal. If the appeal is upheld the referee shall allow a let except that if, in the opinion of the referee:

– The marker's call has interrupted that player's winning return, he shall award the stroke to the player.

– The marker's call has interrupted or prevented a winning return by the opponent, he shall award the stroke to the opponent.

Note to referees: In the latter case the referee shall also award the stroke to the opponent if he is unsure whether the marker's call was correct.

11.2.2 If the marker fails to call 'not up', 'down' or 'out' following a player's return the opponent may appeal either immediately or at the end of the rally if he has played or attempted to play the ball. If, in the opinion of the referee, the return was not good he shall stop play immediately and award the stroke to the opponent.

Notes to referees: A. No appeal under Rule 11 may be made after the delivery of a service for anything that occurred before that service.

B. Where there is more than one appeal in a rally (including an appeal under Rule 12) the referee shall consider each appeal.

C. If a return is called 'not up', 'down' or 'out' by the marker and that same return subsequently goes down or out the referee, on appeal, if he reverses the marker's call or is unsure, shall then rule on the subsequent occurrence.

D. If a service is called 'fault', 'foot fault', 'not up', 'down' or 'out' by the marker and that service subsequently goes down, not up or out, or is again a fault, the referee, on appeal, if he reverses the marker's call or is unsure, shall then rule on the subsequent occurrence.

12. Interference

12.1 When it is his turn to play the ball a player is entitled to freedom from interference by his opponent.

12.2 To avoid interference the opponent must make every effort to provide the player with:

12.2.1 Unobstructed direct access to the ball.

12.2.2 A fair view of the ball.

12.2.3 Freedom to hit the ball.

12.2.4 Freedom to play the ball directly to the front wall.

12.3 Interference occurs if the opponent fails to fulfil any of the requirements of Rule 12.2, irrespective of whether he makes every effort to do so.

Notes to referees: A. In 12.2.1 the opponent must move to allow the player direct access to the ball as soon as the opponent has completed his own return, i.e. at the completion of a reasonable follow-through of his racket swing. The player must also make every effort to get to and where possible play the ball.

B. In 12.2.2 fair view of the ball applies only to its rebound from the front wall.

C. In 12.2.3 freedom to hit the ball requires that the opponent permit the player an arc of racket swing comprising reasonable backswing, strike at the ball and reasonable follow-through.

Interference caused by a player's excessive backswing can not result in the award of a stroke to that player.

A player's excessive follow-through may cause interference for the opponent when it becomes the latter's turn to play the ball.

12.4 A player encountering what he considers to be interference has the choice of continuing with play or of stopping and appealing to the referee.

12.4.1 The correct method of appeal, whether a let or a stroke is sought by the player, is with the words 'Let please'.

12.4.2 An appeal may be made only by the player. The appeal must be made either immediately the interference occurs or, where the player clearly does not continue with play beyond the point of interference, without undue delay.

12.5 The referee shall decide on the appeal and shall announce his decision with the words 'no let', 'yes let' or 'stroke to . . . (name of appropriate player)'. In assessing the interference situation the only relevant opinion is that of the referee and his decision shall be final.

12.6 The referee shall not allow a let and the player shall lose the rally if:

12.6.1 There has been no interference.

12.6.2 Interference has occurred but either the player would not have made a good return or he has not made adequate effort to get to and where possible play the ball.

12.6.3 The player has clearly accepted the interference and played on.

12.6.4 The player has created his own interference in moving to the ball.

12.7 The referee shall allow a let if there has been interference which the opponent has made every effort to avoid and the player would have made a good return.

12.8 The referee shall award a stroke to the player if:

12.8.1 There has been interference which the opponent has not made every effort to avoid and the player would have made a good return.

12.8.2 There has been interference which the opponent has made every effort to avoid and the player would have made a winning return.

12.8.3 The player has refrained from hitting the ball which, if hit, would clearly have struck his opponent going directly to the front wall; or to a side wall but in the latter case would have been a winning return (unless in either case turning, ball passing around player or further attempt applies).

12.9 The referee is also empowered to allow a let under Rule 12.7 or to award a stroke under Rule 12.8 without an appeal having been made, if necessary stopping play to do so.

12.10 The provisions of Rule 17, Conduct On Court, may be applied in interference situations. The referee shall, stopping play if it has not already stopped, apply an appropriate penalty if:

12.10.1 The player has made unnecessary physical contact with his opponent or vice versa.

12.10.2 The player has endangered his opponent with an excessive racket swing.

13. Lets

In addition to lets allowed under other rules, lets may or shall be allowed in certain other cases.

13.1 A let may be allowed.

13.1.1 If owing to the position of the striker, the opponent is unable to avoid being touched by the ball before the return is made.

Note to referees: This rule shall include the cases where the striker's position is in front of his opponent, making it difficult for the latter to see the ball, or where the striker allows the ball to pass close to him, and the ball hits his opponent who is behind the striker. This is not, however, to be taken as conflicting in any way with the duties of the referee under Rule 12.

13.1.2 If the ball in play touches any article lying on the floor.

Note to referees: The referee shall ensure that no articles are placed on the floor by the players.

13.1.3 If the striker refrains from hitting the ball owing to a reasonable fear of injuring his opponent.

Note to referees: This shall include the case of the striker wishing to play the ball onto the back wall.

13.1.4 If, in the opinion of the referee, either player is distracted by an occurrence on or off the court.

13.1.5 If, in the opinion of the referee, a change in court conditions has affected the result of the rally.

13.2 A let shall be allowed:

13.2.1 If the receiver is not ready and does not attempt to return the service.

13.2.2 If the ball breaks during play.

13.2.3 If the referee is asked to decide an appeal and is unable to do so.

13.2.4 If an otherwise good return has been made but either the ball lodges in any part of the playing surface of the court preventing it from bouncing more than once upon the floor, or the ball goes out on its first bounce.

13.3 If the striker appeals for a let under Rules 13.1 (2 to 5), in order for a let to be allowed he must have been able to make a good return. For a non-striker appeal under Rules 13.1.2, 13.1.4 and 13.1.5 this is not a requirement.

13.4 No let shall be allowed under Rules 13.1.3 and 13.2.1 if the striker attempts to play the ball but may be allowed under Rules 13.1.2, 13.1.4, 13.1.5, 13.2.2, 13.2.3 and 13.2.4.

13.5 The appeals requirements of Rule 13 are:

13.5.1 An appeal by the player is necessary for a let to be allowed under Rules 13.1.3 (striker only), 13.1.4, 13.2.1 (striker only) and 13.2.3.

13.5.2 An appeal by the player or referee intervention without appeal is applicable to Rules 13.1.2, 13.1.5, 13.2.2 and 13.2.4.

13.5.3 Where a player is struck by the ball as described in Rule 13.1.1 the referee shall decide without appeal whether a let is to be allowed or the stroke awarded to the striker.

14. The Ball

14.1 At any time, when the ball is not in actual play, another ball may be substituted by mutual consent of the players, or on appeal by either player at the discretion of the referee.

Note to referees: Either player or the referee may examine the ball at any time it is not in actual play to check its condition.

14.2 If a ball breaks during play, it shall be replaced promptly by another ball.

Note to referees: The referee shall decide whether a ball is broken.

14.3 If a ball has broken during play but this has not been established, a let for the rally in which the ball broke shall be allowed if the server appeals prior to the next service or if the receiver appeals prior to attempting to return that service.

Note to referees: If the receiver appeals prior to attempting to return service and, in the opinion of the referee, the ball break occurred during that service, the referee shall allow a let for that rally only, but if unsure he should allow a let for the previous rally.

14.4 The provisions of Rule 14.3 do not apply to the final rally of a game. An appeal in this case must be immediately after the rally.

14.5 If a player stops during a rally to appeal that the ball is broken only to find subsequently that the ball is not broken, then that player shall lose the stroke.

15. Warm Up

15.1 Immediately preceding the start of play the two players together shall be allowed on the court of play a period of five minutes for the purpose of warming up the ball to be used for the match.

After two and a half minutes of the warm up, the referee shall call 'half-time' and ensure that the players change sides unless they mutually agree otherwise. The referee shall also advise when the warm up period is complete with the call of 'Time'.

An interval of up to ninety seconds shall be permitted between the end of the warm up and start of play.

15.2 Where a ball has been substituted under Rule 14 or when the match is being resumed after considerable delay, the referee shall allow the ball to be warmed up to playing condition. Play shall then resume on the direction of the referee, or upon mutual consent of the players, whichever is the earlier.

Note to referees: The referee must ensure that both players warm up the ball fairly (Rules 15.1 and 15.2). An unfair warm up shall be dealt with under the provisions of Rule 17.

15.3 The ball may be warmed up by either player between the end of the five-minute warm up and start of play, between games and when his opponent is changing equipment.

16. Continuity of Play

After the first service is delivered play shall be continuous so far as is practical provided that:

16.1 At any time play may be suspended, owing to bad light or other circumstances beyond the control of the players, for such period as the referee shall decide. The score shall stand.

If another court is available when the court originally in use remains unsuitable, the match may be transferred to it if both players agree or as directed by the referee.

In the event of play being suspended for the day the score shall stand unless both players agree to start the match again.

16.2 An interval of ninety seconds shall be permitted between all games. Players may leave the court during such intervals but must be ready to resume play by the end of the stated time. By mutual consent of the players play may recommence prior to the expiry of the ninety-second time interval.

16.3 If a player satisfies the referee that a change of equipment, clothing or footwear is necessary, the player may leave the court. He is required to effect the change as quickly as possible and shall be allowed a period not exceeding ninety seconds for this purpose.

16.4 When fifteen seconds of a permitted ninety-second time interval remain the referee shall call 'Fifteen seconds' to advise the players to be ready to resume play. At the end of this interval the referee shall call 'Time'.

It is the responsibility of the players to be within earshot of the court to hear the calls of 'Fifteen seconds' and 'Time'.

Notes to referees: A. Should one player fail to be ready to resume play when 'Time' is called, the referee shall apply the provisions of Rule 17.

B. Should neither player be ready to resume play when 'Time' is called the referee shall apply the provisions of Rule 17 for both players.

16.5 In the event of an injury to a player the referee shall decide if it was:

16.5.1 Self-inflicted

16.5.2 Accidentally contributed to or accidentally caused by his opponent

16.5.3 Caused by his opponent's deliberate or dangerous play or action.

Notes to referees: A. In all injury situations, the referee must determine that the injury is genuine.

B. In Rule 16.5.1, the referee may allow the injured player up to three minutes to recover from the injury. This time interval may be extended at the discretion of the referee. If additional recovery time is needed beyond that permitted by the referee, the referee shall require the player to continue play; or concede the game, accept the time interval and then continue play; or concede the match.

C. In Rule 16.5.2, the referee must not interpret the words 'accidentally contributed to' or 'accidentally caused by' to include the situation where the injury to the player is as a result of that player occupying an unnecessarily close position to his opponent.

D. In Rule 16.5.2 the referee shall allow reasonable time for the injured player to recover, having regard to the time schedule of the competition.

The injured player must by the end of this period of time resume play or concede the match. If play is resumed the score at the time of injury shall stand, except that if play is resumed on another day the match may start again if both players agree.

E. In Rule 16.5.3 the referee may, at his discretion, apply an appropriate Rule 17 penalty, except that if the injured player requires time to recover the referee shall award the match to the injured player.

F. In all cases a player shall not resume play while a wound which is bleeding remains uncovered and the flow of blood continues.

16.6 The referee shall apply the provisions of Rule 17 to a player who, in his opinion, delays play unreasonably. Such delay may be caused by:

16.6.1 Unduly slow preparation to serve or to receive service.

16.6.2 Prolonged discussion with the referee.

16.6.3 Delay in returning to the court, having left under the terms of Rules 15.1, 16.2 or 16.3.

17. Conduct on Court

If the referee considers that the behaviour of a player on court could be intimidating or offensive to an opponent, official or spectator, or could in any way bring the game into disrepute, the player may be penalised.

Offences which should be dealt with under this rule include audible and visible obscenities, verbal and physical abuse, dissent to marker or referee, abuse of racket or ball and coaching, other than during the interval between games. Other offences include unnecessary physical contact and excessive racket swing (Rule 12.10), unfair warm up (Rule 15.2 Note To Referees), late back on court (Rule 16.4 Notes to Referees A and B), deliberate or dangerous play or action (Rule 16.5.3) and time wasting (Rule 16.6).

For these and any other offences which, in the opinion of the referee, justify the application of this rule, one of the following penalty provisions may be applied.

Warning by the referee (called a conduct warning)

Stroke awarded to opponent (called a conduct stroke)

Game awarded to opponent (called a conduct game)

Match awarded to opponent (called a conduct match)

Notes to referees: A. If the referee stops play to give a warning a let shall be allowed.

B. If the referee stops a rally to award a conduct stroke then that stroke award becomes the result of the rally. If the referee awards a conduct stroke at the conclusion of a rally, the result of the rally stands and the conduct stroke award is additional but without change of service box.

A conduct stroke awarded at the end of a game shall be carried over to the next game.

C. If the referee awards a game that game shall be the one in progress or the next game if one is not in progress, in which latter case the interval between games shall not apply. The offending player shall retain any points already scored in the game awarded.

18. Control of a Match

A match is normally controlled by a referee, assisted by a marker. One person may be appointed to carry out the functions of both referee and marker. When a decision has been made by the referee he shall announce it to the players and the marker shall repeat it with the subsequent score.

19. Duties of a Marker

19.1 The marker shall call the play, followed by the score, with the server's score called first. He shall call 'fault', 'foot fault', 'not up', 'down', 'out' and 'hand-out' as appropriate, and shall repeat the referee's decisions.

19.2 If the marker makes a call the rally shall cease.

19.3 If play ceases and the marker is unsighted or uncertain he shall advise the players and shall call on the referee to make the relevant decision; if the referee is unable to do so a let shall be allowed.

20. Duties of a Referee

20.1 The referee shall allow or disallow appeals for lets, and award strokes; make decisions where called for by the rules, including all cases when a player is struck by the ball, and for injuries; and shall decide all appeals including those against the marker's calls or lack of calls. The decision of the referee shall be final.

20.2 The referee shall exercise control:

20.2.1 Upon appeal by one of the players, including an appeal against any specification.

20.2.2 As provided for in Rules 4, 8, 9, 10, 11, 12, 13, 14, 15, 16, 17, 18 and 19.

20.3 The referee shall not intervene in the marker's calling of the score unless, in the opinion of the referee, the score has been called incorrectly in which case he shall have the marker call the correct score.

20.4 The referee shall not intervene in the marker's calling of the play unless, in the opinion of the referee, the marker has made an error in stopping play or allowing play to continue, in which case the referee shall immediately rule accordingly.

20.5 The referee is responsible for ensuring that all rules relating to time are strictly enforced.

20.6 The referee is responsible for ensuring that court conditions are appropriate for play.

20.7 The referee may award a match to a player whose opponent fails to be present on court, ready to play, within ten minutes of the advertised time of play.

APPENDIX

DEFINITIONS (SINGLES)

Appeal A player's request to the referee to consider an on or off court situation. 'Appeal' is used throughout the rules in two contexts:

    1) Where the player requests the referee to consider varying a marker's decision

    2) Where the player requests the referee to allow a let. The correct form of appeal by a player is 'Appeal please' or 'Let please'.

Attempt The referee shall decide what is an attempt to play the ball. An attempt is made when, in the opinion of the referee, the striker has moved his racket towards the ball from the backswing position.

Board The lowest horizontal marking on the front wall, with the tin beneath it covering the full width of the court.

Box (Service) A square area in each quarter court bounded by part of the short line, part of the side wall and by two other lines, and from within which the server serves.

Competition A championship tournament, league or other competitive match.

Correctly The ball being hit by the racket (held in the hand) not more than once nor with prolonged contact on the racket.

Cut Line A line upon the front wall, 50mm in width, the top edge of which is 1.83m above the floor and extending the full width of the court.

Down The expression used to indicate that an otherwise good service or return has struck the board or tin or has failed to reach the front wall; or that a player has been struck by the ball before it has bounced more than once upon the floor. ('Down' is also used as a marker's call.)

Game Part of a match, commencing with a service and concluding when one player has scored or been awarded nine or ten points (in accordance with the rules).

Game Ball The state of the score when the server requires one point to win the game in progress ('Game ball' is also used as a marker's call).

Half-Court Line A line set upon the floor parallel to the side walls, dividing the back of the court into two equal parts, meeting the short line at its midpoint to form the 'T'.

Half Time The midpoint of the warm up ('Half time' is also used as a referee's call).

Hand The period from the time a player becomes server until he becomes receiver.

Hand-Out Condition when a change of server occurs. ('Hand-out' is also used as a marker's call to indicate that a change of hand has occurred).

Match The complete contest between two players, commencing with the warm up and concluding when both players have left the court at the end of the final rally (covers broken ball rule).

Match Ball The state of the score when the server requires one point to win the match. ('Match ball' is also used as a marker's call.)

Not Up The expression used to indicate that the ball has not been struck in accordance with the rules. 'Not up' applies when 1) the ball is not struck correctly by the server or striker, 2) the ball bounces more than once upon the floor before being struck by the striker, 3) the ball touches the striker or anything he wears or carries other than his racket, 4) the server makes an attempt but fails to strike the ball. ('Not up' is also used as a marker's call.)

Officials The marker and the referee.

Out The expression used to indicate that 1) the ball has struck the out line, or a wall above the out line, or the ceiling, or any fitting attached to the ceiling and/or wall above the out line or 2) the ball has passed through any fitting attached to the ceiling and/or wall above the out line or 3) in addition to 1) and 2) on courts which are not fully enclosed the ball has passed over the out line and out of the court without touching any wall or, if no out line is provided, passed over any wall and out of the court. ('Out' is also used as a marker's call.)

Out Line A continuous line comprising the front wall line, both side wall lines and the back wall line and marking the top boundaries of the court. *Note*: When a court is constructed without provision of such a line, i.e. the walls comprise only the area used for play, or without part of such a line (e.g. a glass back wall) and the ball in play strikes part of the horizontal top surface of such a wall and deflects back into court, the ball is out. The decision should be made in the normal manner by the marker, subject to appeal to the referee.

Point A unit of the scoring system. One point is added to a player's score when he is the server and wins a stroke.

Quarter (Court) One half of the back part of the court which has been divided into two equal parts by the half-court line.

Rally A service only or service and any number of returns of the ball, ending when the ball ceases to be in play.

Reasonable Backswing The initial action used by a player in moving his racket away from his body as preparation prior to racket movement towards the ball for contact. A backswing is reasonable if it is not excessive. An excessive backswing is one in which the player's racket arm is extended towards a straight arm position and/or the racket is extended with the shaft approximately horizontal. The referee's decision on what constitutes a reasonable as distinct from excessive backswing is final.

Reasonable Follow-Through The action used by a player in continuing the movement of his racket after it has contacted the ball. A follow-through is reasonable if it is not excessive. An excessive follow-through is one in which the player's racket arm is extended towards a straight arm position with the racket also extended with the shaft horizontal – particularly when the extended position is maintained for other than a momentary period of time. An excessive follow-through is also one in which the arm extended towards a straight position takes a wider arc than the continued line of flight of the ball, even though the racket is on the correct vertical position. The referee's decision on what constitutes a reasonable as distinct from excessive follow-through is final.

Service The method by which the ball is put into play by the server to commence a rally.

Short Line A line, 50mm in width, set out upon the floor parallel to and 5.44m from the front wall and extending the full width of the court.

Specified The description given to balls, rackets and courts that meet existing WSF specifications.

Striker The player whose turn it is to hit the ball after it has rebounded from the front wall, or who is in the process of hitting the ball, or who – up to the point of his return reaching the front wall – has just hit the ball.

Stroke The gain achieved by the player who wins a rally, either in the course of play or on award by the referee, and which results in either the scoring of a point or change of hand.

Tin Situated between the board and the floor covering the full width of the court and constructed in such a manner as to make a distinctive noise when struck by the ball.

Tournament Director The person responsible for the conduct of players and officials throughout the tournament.

Tournament Referee The person given overall responsibility for all marking and refereeing matters throughout the tournament, including the appointment and replacement of officials to matches.

General Note The use of the word 'shall' in the rules indicates compulsion and the lack of any alternative. The word 'must' indicates a required course of action with considerations to be taken into account if the action is not carried out. The word 'may' indicates the option of carrying out or not carrying out the action.

DEFINITIONS (DOUBLES)

All the definitions are the same as for Singles, except for:

Game Part of a match, commencing with a service and concluding when one side has scored or been awarded 15 or 17 points (in accordance with the rules).

Game Ball The state of the score when either side requires one point to win the game in progress. ('Game ball' is also used as a marker's call.)

Hand The period from the time a player becomes server until he loses the right to serve.

Hand-out Condition when the first server of side-in has served and side-in loses the stroke ('Hand-out' is also used as a marker's call).

Match The complete contest between two sides, commencing with the warm up and concluding when all players have left the court at the end of the final rally (covers broken ball rule).

Match Ball The state of the score when either side requires one point to win the match. ('Match ball' is also used as a marker's call.)

Match Ball, Game Ball Condition when one side requires one point to win the match and the opponents require one point to win the game in progress.

Point A unit of the scoring system. One point is added to a side's score when it wins a stroke.

Side-in The side which serves is called side-in.

Side-out Condition when the serving side becomes the receiving side, also the name of the receiving side ('Side-out' is also used as a marker's call).

Striker A partner of the striking side who attempts to hit the ball or who does hit the ball.

Striking Side The side whose turn it is to hit the ball after it has rebounded from the front wall, or which has one partner in the process of hitting the ball, or which, up to the point of the return reaching the front wall, has just had one partner hit the ball.

Stroke The gain achieved by a side which wins a rally, either in the course of play or on award by the referee, and which results in the scoring of a point.

DIMENSIONS OF A SINGLES COURT

Length:	9750mm between plaster faces
Breadth:	6400mm between plaster faces
Height to lower edge of cut line on front wall:	1780mm
Height to lower edge of front wall line:	4570mm
Height to lower edge of back wall line:	2130mm
Distance to nearest edge of short line from back wall:	4260mm
Height to upper edge of board from floor:	480mm
Thickness of board (flat or rounded at top):	15mm top to 45mm bottom (splayed)

Side wall line: the diagonal line joining the front wall line and the back wall line.

The service boxes shall be entirely enclosed on three sides within the court by lines, the short line forming the side nearest to the front wall, the side wall bounding the fourth side.

The internal dimensions of the service boxes shall be 1600mm.

All dimensions in the court shall be measured, from junction of the floor and front wall – 1 metre above the finished floor level.

All lines shall be 50mm in width. All lines shall be coloured red.

In respect of the outer boundary lines on the walls, it is suggested that the plaster should be so shaped as to produce a concave channel along such lines.

DIMENSIONS OF A DOUBLES COURT
Length: 9750mm between plaster faces
Width: 7620mm between plaster faces

All other dimensions shall be as for the Singles court.

Reprinted by permission of the Squash Rackets Association. For reasons of space, the following items have been omitted: Notes to Officials, Appendixes Concerning Markers' and Referees' Calls, the Dimensions of a Racket, the Specification for Squash Rackets Balls, the Colour of Players' Clothing, a Code of Conduct and Guidelines for National Federations, their Affiliated Associations and Tournament Organisers. Copies of the complete Rules of Squash can be obtained from the Association.

Table Tennis

Table Tennis

The masculine gender is used throughout but refers equally to men or women.

2.1 The Table

2.1.1 The upper surface of the table, known as the playing surface, shall be rectangular, 2.74m long and 1.525m wide, and shall lie in a horizontal plane 76cm above the floor.

2.1.2 The playing surface shall include the top edges of the table but not the sides of the table top below the edges.

2.1.3 The playing surface may be of any material and shall yield a uniform bounce of about 23cm when a standard ball is dropped on to it from a height of 30cm.

2.1.4 The playing surface shall be uniformly dark coloured and matt, but with a white side-line, 2cm wide, along each 2.74m edge and a white end-line, 2cm wide, along each 1.525m edge.

2.1.5 The playing surface shall be divided into two equal courts by a vertical net running parallel with the end-lines, and shall be continuous over the whole area of each court.

2.1.6 For doubles, each court shall be divided into two equal half-courts by a white centre-line, 3mm wide, running parallel with the side-lines; the centre-line shall be regarded as part of each right half-court.

2.2 The Net Assembly

2.2.1 The net assembly shall consist of the net, its suspension and the supporting posts, including the clamps attaching them to the table.

2.2.2 The net shall be suspended by a cord attached at each end to an upright post 15.25cm high, the outside limits of the post being 15.25cm outside the side-line.

2.2.3 The top of the net, along its whole length, shall be 15.25cm above the playing surface.

2.2.4 The bottom of the net, along its whole length, shall be as close as possible to the playing surface and the ends of the net shall be as close as possible to the supporting posts.

2.3 The Ball
2.3.1 The ball shall be spherical, with a diameter of 38mm.
2.3.2 The ball shall weigh 2.5gm.
2.3.3 The ball shall be made of celluloid or similar plastics material and shall be white, yellow or orange, and matt.

2.4 The Racket
2.4.1 The rackets may be of any size, shape or weight but the blade shall be flat and rigid.
2.4.2 At least 85% of the blade by thickness shall be of natural wood; an adhesive layer within the blade may be reinforced with fibrous material such as carbon fibre, glass fibre or compressed paper, but shall not be thicker than 7.5% of the total thickness or 0.35mm, whichever is the smaller.
2.4.3 A side of the blade used for striking the ball shall be covered with either ordinary pimpled rubber with pimples outwards having a total thickness including adhesive of not more than 2mm, or sandwich rubber with pimples inwards or outwards having a total thickness including adhesive of not more than 4mm.
   2.4.3.1 'Ordinary pimpled rubber' is a single layer of non-cellular rubber, natural or synthetic, with pimples evenly distributed over its surface at a density of not less than 10 per sq cm and not more than 50 per sq cm.
   2.4.3.2 'Sandwich rubber' is a single layer of cellular rubber covered with a single outer layer of ordinary pimpled rubber, the thickness of the pimpled rubber not being more than 2mm.
2.4.4 The covering material shall extend up to but not beyond the limits of the blade, except that the part nearest the handle and gripped by the fingers may be left uncovered or covered with any material.
2.4.5 The blade, any layer within the blade and any layer of covering material or adhesive shall be continuous and of even thickness.
2.4.6 The surface of the covering material on a side of the blade, or of a side of the blade if it is left uncovered, shall be matt, bright red on one side and black on the other; any trimming round the edge of the blade shall be matt and no part of it shall be white.
2.4.7 Slight deviations from continuity of surface or uniformity of colour due to accidental damage, wear or fading may be allowed provided that they do not significantly change the characteristics of the surface.

2.4.8 At the start of a match and whenever he changes his racket during a match a player shall show his opponent and the Umpire the racket he is about to use and shall allow them to examine it.

2.5 Definitions

2.5.1 A **rally** is the period during which the ball is in play.

2.5.2 A **let** is a rally of which the result is not scored.

2.5.3 A **point** is a rally of which the result is scored.

2.5.4 The **racket-hand** is the hand carrying the racket.

2.5.5 The **free hand** is the hand not carrying the racket.

2.5.6 A player **strikes** the ball if he touches it with his racket, held in the hand, or with his racket-hand below the wrist.

2.5.7 A player **obstructs** the ball if he, or anything he wears or carries, touches it in play when it has not passed over the playing surface or his end-line, not having touched his court since last being struck by his opponent.

2.5.8 The **server** is the player due to strike the ball first in a rally.

2.5.9 The **receiver** is the player due to strike the ball second in a rally.

2.5.10 The **Umpire** is the person appointed to control the match.

2.5.11 Anything that a player **wears or carries** includes anything that he was wearing or carrying at the start of the rally.

2.5.12 The ball shall be regarded as passing **over** or **around** the net assembly if it passes under or outside the projection of the net assembly outside the table or if, in a return, it is struck after it has bounced back over or around the net.

2.5.13 The **end-line** shall be regarded as extending indefinitely in both directions.

2.6 Service

2.6.1 At the start of service the ball shall be stationary, resting freely on the flat, open palm of the server's free hand, behind the end line and above the level of the playing surface.

2.6.2 The server shall then project the ball near vertically upwards, without imparting spin, so that it rises at least 16cm after leaving the palm of the free hand.

2.6.3 As the ball is falling from the highest point of its trajectory the server shall strike it so that, in singles, it touches first his court and then, passing directly over or around the net assembly, touches the receiver's court; in doubles, it touches successively the right half-court of server and receiver.

2.6.4 The ball and the racket shall be above the level of the playing surface from the last moment at which the ball is stationary before being projected until it is struck.

2.6.5 When the ball is struck, it shall be behind the server's end-line but not farther back than the part of the server's body, other than his arm, head or leg, which is farthest from the net.

2.6.6 It is the responsibility of the player to serve so that the Umpire or Assistant Umpire can see that he complies with the requirements for a good service.

2.6.6.1 If the Umpire is doubtful of the legality of a service but neither he nor the Assistant Umpire is sure that it is illegal he may, on the first occasion in a match, warn the server without awarding a point.

2.6.6.2 If subsequently in the match the same player's service is of dubious legality, for the same or for any other reason, he shall not be given the benefit of the doubt and shall lose a point.

2.6.6.3 Whenever there is a clear failure by the server to comply with the requirements for a good service no warning shall be given and he shall lose a point, on the first as on any other occasion.

2.6.7 Exceptionally, strict observance of any of the requirements for a good service may be waived where the Umpire is notified, before play begins, that compliance with that requirement is prevented by physical disability.

2.7 A Good Return

2.7.1 The ball, having been served or returned, shall be struck so that it passes over or around the net assembly and touches the opponent's court, either directly or after touching the net assembly.

2.8 The Order of Play

2.8.1 In singles, the server shall first make a good service, the receiver shall then make a good return and thereafter server and receiver alternately shall each make a good return.

2.8.2 In doubles, the server shall first make a good service, the receiver shall then make a good return, the partner of the server shall then make a good return, the partner of the receiver shall then make a good return and thereafter each player in turn in that sequence shall make a good return.

2.9 In Play

2.9.1 The ball shall be in play from the last moment at which it is stationary before being projected in service until:

2.9.1.1 It touches anything other than the playing surface, the net assembly, the racket held in the hand or the racket hand below the wrist; or

2.9.1.2 The rally is otherwise decided as a let or a point.

2.10 A Let

2.10.1 The rally shall be a let:

2.10.1.1 If in service the ball, in passing over or around the net assembly, touches it, provided the service is otherwise good or the ball is obstructed by the receiver or his partner.

2.10.1.2 If the service is delivered when the receiving player or pair is not ready, provided that neither the receiver not his partner attempts to strike the ball.

2.10.1.3 If failure to make a good service or a good return or otherwise to comply with the Laws is due to a disturbance outside the control of the player.

2.10.1.4 If play is interrupted by the Umpire or Assistant Umpire.

2.10.2 Play may be interrupted:

2.10.2.1 To correct an error in the order of serving, receiving or ends.

2.10.2.2 To introduce the expedite system.

2.10.2.3 To warn or penalise a player.

2.10.2.4 Because the conditions of play are disturbed in a way which could affect the outcome of the rally.

2.11 A Point

2.11.1 Unless the rally is a let, a player shall lose a point:

2.11.1.1 If he fails to make a good service.

2.11.1.2 If he fails to make a good return.

2.11.1.3 If he obstructs the ball, except as provided in Law 3.10.1.1.

2.11.1.4 If he strikes the ball twice successively.

2.11.1.5 If, except in service, the ball touches his court and then again the playing surface.

2.11.1.6 If he strikes the ball with a side of the racket blade whose surface does not comply with the requirements of 2.4.3.

2.11.1.7 If he, or anything he wears or carries, moves the playing surface.

2.11.1.8 If his free hand touches the playing surface.

2.11.1.9 If he, or anything he wears or carries, touches the net assembly.

2.11.1.10 If, in doubles, except in serving or receiving, he strikes the ball out of proper sequence.

2.11.1.11 If, under the expedite system, he serves and the receiving player or pair makes 13 successive good returns.

2.11.1.12 If the Umpire awards a penalty point against him.

2.12 A Game

2.12.1 A game shall be won by the player or pair first scoring 21 points unless both players or pairs score 20 points, when the game shall be won by the player or pair first scoring subsequently 2 points more than the opposing player or pair.

2.13 A Match

2.13.1 A match shall consist of the best of 3 games or the best of 5 games.

2.13.2 Play shall be continuous throughout a match except that any player shall be entitled to claim an interval of not more than 2 minutes between successive games.

2.14 The Choice of Serving, Receiving and Ends

2.14.1 The right to choose the initial order of serving, receiving and ends shall be decided by lot and the winner of this right may choose to serve or to receive first, to start at a particular end or to require the loser to make the first choice.

2.14.2 When one player or pair has chosen to serve or to receive first or to start at a particular end, the other player or pair shall have the other choice.

2.14.3 After each 5 points have been scored the receiving player or pair shall become the serving player or pair and so on until the end of the game, unless both players or pairs have scored 20 points or the expedite system is in operation, when the sequences of serving and receiving shall be the same but each player shall serve for only 1 point in turn.

2.14.4 In each game of a doubles match, the pair having the right to serve first shall choose which of them will do so and in the first game of a match the receiving pair shall decide which of them will receive first; in subsequent games of the match, the first server having been chosen, the first receiver shall be the player who served to him in the preceding game.

2.14.5 In doubles, at each change of service the previous receiver shall become the server and the partner of the previous server shall become the receiver.

2.14.6 The player or pair serving first in a game shall receive first in the next game of the match and in the last possible game of a doubles match the pair due to receive next shall change their order of receiving when first either pair scores 10 points.

2.14.7 The player or pair starting at one end in a game shall start at the other end in the next game of the match and in the last possible game of a match the players or pairs shall change ends when first either player or pair scores 10 points.

2.15 Out of Order of Serving, Receiving or Ends

2.15.1 If a player serves or receives out of turn, play shall be interrupted by the Umpire as soon as the error is discovered and shall resume with those players serving and receiving who should be server and receiver respectively at the score that has been reached, according to the sequence established at the beginning of the match, and, in doubles, to the order of serving chosen by the pair having the right to serve first in the game during which the error is discovered.

2.15.2 If the players have not changed ends when they should have done so, play shall be interrupted by the Umpire as soon as the error is discovered and shall resume with the players at the ends at which they should be at the score that has been reached, according to the sequence established at the beginning of the match.

2.15.3 In any circumstances, all points scored before the discovery of an error shall be reckoned.

2.16 The Expedite System

2.16.1 The expedite system shall come into operation if a game is unfinished after 15 minutes' play, unless both players or pairs have scored at least 19 points, or at any earlier time at the request of both players or pairs.

2.16.1.1 If the ball is in play when the time limit is reached, play shall be interrupted by the Umpire and shall resume with service by the player who served in the rally that was interrupted.

2.16.1.2 If the ball is not in play when the time limit is reached, play shall resume with the service by the player who received in the immediately preceding rally of the game.

2.16.2 Therefter, each player shall serve for 1 point in turn until the end of the game, and if the receiving player or pair makes 13 good returns the server shall lose a point.

2.16.3 Once introduced, the expedite system shall remain in operation for the remainder of the match.

These Rules have been adopted by the International Table Tennis Federation, are approved by the English Table Tennis Association and have been reprinted with their permission. For reasons of space some of the Rules have been abbreviated. Copies of the Rules of Table Tennis, including Disciplinary Regulations and Regulations for International Competitions, may be obtained from the Federation.

THE RULES OF

Tennis

The Tennis Court

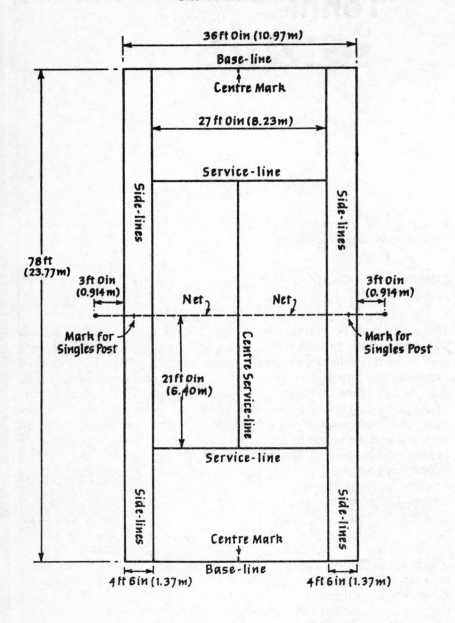

Tennis

Except where otherwise stated, every reference in these Rules to the masculine includes the feminine gender.

THE SINGLES GAME

1. The Court

The court shall be rectangular, 78ft (23.77m) long and 27ft (8.23m) wide. It shall be divided across the middle by a net suspended from a cord or metal cable of a maximum diameter of ⅓in (0.8cm), the ends of which shall be attached to, or pass over, the tops of the two posts, which shall be not more than 6in (15cm) square or 6in (15cm) in diameter. These posts shall not be higher than 1in (2.5cm) above the top of the net cord. The centres of the posts shall be 3ft (0.914m) outside the court on each side and the height of the posts shall be such that the top of the cord or metal cable shall be 3ft 6in (1.07m) above the ground.

When a combined doubles (see Rule 34) and singles court with a doubles net is used for singles, the net must be supported to a height of 3ft 6in (1.07m) by means of two posts, called singles sticks, which shall be not more than 3in (7.5cm) square or 3in (7.5cm) in diameter. The centres of the singles sticks shall be 3ft (0.914m) outside the singles court on each side.

The net shall be extended fully so that it fills completely the space between the two posts and shall be of sufficiently small mesh to prevent the ball passing through. The height of the net shall be 3ft (0.914m) at the centre, where it shall be held down taut by a strap not more than 2in (5cm) wide and completely white in colour. There shall be a band covering the cord or metal cable and the top of the net of not less than 2in (5cm) nor more than 2½in (6.3cm) in depth on each side and completely white in colour. There shall be no advertisement on the net, strap band or singles sticks.

The lines bounding the ends and sides of the court shall respectively be called the base-lines and the side-lines. On each side of the net, at a distance of 21ft (6.40m) from it and parallel with it, shall be drawn the service-lines. The space on each side of the net between the service-line and the side-lines shall be divided into two equal parts called the service-courts by the centre service-line, which must be 2in (5cm) in width, drawn half-way between, and parallel with, the side-line. Each base-line shall be bisected by an imaginary continuation of the centre service-line to a line 4in (10cm) in length and 2in (5cm) in width called the centre mark, drawn inside the court, at right angles to and in contact with such base-lines. All other lines shall not be less than 1in (2.5cm) nor more than 2in (5cm) in width, except the base-line, which may be 4in (10cm) in width, and all measurements shall be made to the outside of the lines. All lines shall be of uniform colour. If advertising or any other material is placed at the back of the court, it may not contain white or yellow. A light colour may only be used if this does not interfere with the vision of the players.

If advertisements are placed on the chairs of the linesmen sitting at the back of the court, they may not contain white or yellow. A light colour may only be used if this does not interfere with the vision of the players.

Note 1: In the case of the Davis Cup or other Official Championships of the International Tennis Federation, there shall be a space behind each base-line of not less than 21ft (6.40m), and at the sides of not less than 12ft (3.66m). The chairs of linesmen may be placed at the back of a court within the 21ft (6.4m) or at the side of the court within the 12ft (3.66m), provided they do not protrude into that area more than 3ft (0.914m).

Note 2: In the case of the stadium courts in the Davis Cup World Group and the Federation Cup Main Draw there should be space behind each base-line of not less than 27ft (8.23m) and at the sides of not less than 15ft (4.57m).

Note 3: At club or recreational level, the space behind each base-line should be not less than 18ft (5.5m) and at the sides not less than 10ft (3.05m).

2. Permanent Fixtures

The permanent fixtures of the court shall include not only the net, posts, singles sticks, cord or metal cable, strap and band, but also, where there are any such, the back and side stops, the stands, fixed or movable seats and chairs round the court, and their occupants, all other fixtures around and above the court, and the Umpire, Net-cord Judge, Foot-fault Judge, Linesmen and Ball Boys when in their respective places.

Note: For the purpose of this rule, the word Umpire comprehends the Umpire, the persons entitled to a seat on the court, and all those persons designated to assist the Umpire in the conduct of a match.

3. The Ball
The ball shall have a uniform outer surface and shall be white or yellow in colour. If there are any seams they shall be stitchless. The ball shall be more than $2\frac{1}{2}$in (6.35cm) and less than $2\frac{5}{8}$in (6.67cm) in diameter, and more than 2oz (56.7g) and less than $2\frac{1}{16}$oz (58.5g) in weight.

The ball shall have a bound of more than 53in (135cm) and less than 58in (147cm) when dropped 100in (254cm) upon a concrete base. The ball shall have a forward deformation of more than 0.220in (0.56cm) and less than 0.290in (0.74cm) and a return deformation of more than 0.315in (0.80cm) and less than 0.425in (1.08cm) at 18lb (8.165kg) load. The two deformation figures shall be the averages of three individual readings along three axes of the ball and no two individual readings shall differ by more than 0.030in (0.08cm) in each case.

For play above 4,000ft (1219m) in altitude above sea level, two additional types of ball may be used. The first type is identical to those described above except that the bound shall be more than 48in (121.93cm) and less than 53in (135cm) and shall have an internal pressure that is greater than the external pressure. This type of tennis ball is commonly known as a pressurised ball. The second type is identical to those described above except that they shall have a bound of more than 53in (135cm) and less than 58in (147cm) and shall have an internal pressure that is approximately equal to the external pressure and have been acclimatised for 60 days or more at the altitude of the specific tournament. This type of tennis ball is commonly known as a zero-pressure or non-pressurised ball.

4. Racket
Rackets failing to comply with the following specifications are not approved for play under the Rules of Tennis:

(*a*) The hitting surface of the racket shall be flat and consist of a pattern of crossed strings connected to a frame and alternately interlaced or bonded where they cross; and the stringing pattern shall be generally uniform, and in particular not less dense in the centre than in any other area. The strings shall be free of attached objects and protrusions other than those utilised solely and specifically to limit or prevent wear and tear or vibration, and which are reasonable in size and placement for such purposes.

(*b*) The frame of the racket shall not exceed 32in (81.28cm) in overall length, including the handle and $12\frac{1}{2}$in (31.75cm) in overall width. The strung surface shall not exceed 15½in (39.37cm) in overall length, and 11½in (29.21cm) in overall width.

(c) The frame, including the handle, shall be free of attached objects and devices other than those utilised solely and specifically to limit or prevent wear and tear or vibration, or to distribute weight. Any objects and devices must be reasonable in size and placement for such purposes.

(d) The frame, including the handle, and the strings, shall be free of any device which makes it possible to change materially the shape of the racket, or to change the weight distribution in the direction of the longitudinal axis of the racket which would alter the swing moment of inertia, during the playing of a point.

The International Tennis Federation shall rule on the question of whether any racket or prototype complies with the above specifications or is otherwise approved, or not approved, for play. Such ruling may be undertaken on its own initiative, or upon application by any party with a bona fide interest therein, including any player, equipment manufacturer or National Association or members thereof. Such rulings and applications shall be made in accordance with the applicable Review and Hearing Procedures of the ITF, copies of which may be obtained from the office of the Federation.

Case 1. Can there be more than one set of strings on the hitting surface of a racket?

Decision. No. The rule clearly mentions a pattern, and not patterns, of crossed strings.

Case 2. Is the stringing pattern of a racket considered to be generally uniform and flat if the strings are on more than one plane?

Decision. No.

Case 3. Can vibration dampening devices be placed on the strings of a racket and if so, where can they be placed?

Decision. Yes; but such devices may be placed only outside the pattern of the crossed strings.

Case 4. In the course of play, a player accidentally breaks the strings of his racket. Can he continue to play with the racket in this condition?

Decision: Yes.

5. Server and Receiver

The players shall stand on opposite sides of the net; the player who first delivers the ball shall be called the server, and the other the receiver.

Case 1. Does a player, attempting a stroke, lose the point if he crosses an imaginary line in the extension of the net,

(a) before striking the ball,

(b) after striking the ball?

Decision. He does not lose the point in either case by crossing the imaginary line and provided he does not enter the lines bounding his opponent's court (Rule 20(*e*)). In regard to hindrance, his opponent may ask for the decision of the Umpire under Rules 21 and 25.

Case 2. The server claims that the receiver must stand within the lines bounding his court. Is this necessary?

Decision. No. The receiver may stand wherever he pleases on his own side of the net.

6. Choice of Ends and Service

The choice of ends and the right to be server or receiver in the first game shall be decided by toss. The player winning the toss may choose or require his opponent to choose:

(*a*) The right to be server or receiver, in which case the other player shall choose the end; or

(*b*) The end, in which case the other player shall choose the right to be server or receiver.

Case 1. Do players have the right to new choices if the match is postponed or suspended before it has started?

Decision. Yes. The toss stands, but new choices may be made with respect to service and end.

7. The Service

The service shall be delivered in the following manner. Immediately before commencing to serve, the server shall stand with both feet at rest behind (i.e. further from the net than) the base-line, and within the imaginary continuations of the centre-mark and side-line. The server shall then project the ball by hand into the air in any direction and before it hits the ground strike it with his racket, and the delivery shall be deemed to have been completed at the moment of the impact of the racket and the ball. A player with the use of only one arm may utilise his racket for the projection.

Case 1. May the server in a singles game take his stand behind the portion of the base-line between the side-lines of the singles court and the doubles court?

Decision. No.

Case 2. If a player, when serving, throws up two or more balls instead of one, does he lose that service?

Decision. No. A let should be called, but if the Umpire regards the action as deliberate he may take action under Rule 21.

8. Foot-fault

The server shall throughout the delivery of the service:

(*a*) Not change his position by walking or running. The server shall not, by slight movement of the feet which do not materially affect the location originally taken up by him, be deemed 'to change his position by walking or running'.

(b) Not touch, with either foot, any area other than that behind the base-line within the imaginary extension of the centre-mark and side-lines.

9. Delivery of Service

(a) In delivering the service, the server shall stand alternately behind the right and left courts beginning from the right in every game. If service from a wrong half of the court occurs and is undetected, all play resulting from such wrong service or services shall stand, but the inaccuracy of station shall be corrected immediately it is discovered.

(b) The ball served shall pass over the net and hit the ground within the service court which is diagonally opposite, or upon any line bounding such court, before the receiver returns it.

10. Service Fault

The service is a fault:

(a) If the server commits any breach of Rules 7, 8 or 9(b).

(b) If he misses the ball in attempting to strike it.

(c) If the ball served touches a permanent fixture (other than the net, strap or band) before it hits the ground.

Case 1. After throwing a ball up preparatory to serving, the server decides not to strike at it and catches it instead. Is it a fault?

Decision. No.

Case 2. In serving a singles game played on a doubles court with doubles posts and singles sticks, the ball hits a singles stick and then hits the ground within the lines of the correct service court. Is this a fault or a let?

Decision. In serving it is a fault, because the singles stick, the doubles post, and that portion of the net or band between them are permanent fixtures. (Rules 2 and 10, and note to Rule 24.)

11. Second Service

After a fault (if it is the first fault) the server shall serve again from behind the same half of the court from which he served that fault, unless the service was from the wrong half, when, in accordance with Rule 9, the server shall be entitled to one service only from behind the other half.

Case 1. A player serves from a wrong court. He loses the point and then claims it was a fault because of his wrong station.

Decision. The point stands as played and the next service should be from the correct station according to the score.

Case 2. The point score being 15 all, the server, by mistake, serves from the left-hand court. He wins the point. He then serves again from the right-hand court, delivering a fault. This mistake in station is then discovered. Is he entitled to the previous point? From which court should he next serve?

Decision. The previous point stands. The next service should be from the left-hand court, the score being 30/15, and the server having served one fault.

12. When to Serve
The server shall not serve until the receiver is ready. If the latter attempts to return the service, he shall be deemed ready. If, however, the receiver signifies that he is not ready, he may not claim a fault because the ball does not hit the ground within the limits fixed for the service.

13. The Let
In all cases where a let has to be called under the rules, or to provide for an interruption to play, it shall have the following interpretations:

(*a*) When called solely in respect of a service that one service only shall be replayed.

(*b*) When called under any other circumstance, the point shall be replayed.

Case 1. A service is interrupted by some cause outside those defined in Rule 14. Should the service only be replayed?

Decision. No. The whole point must be replayed.

Case 2. If a ball in play becomes broken, should a let be called?

Decision. Yes.

14. The Let in Service
The service is a let:

(*a*) If the ball served touches the net, strap or band, and is otherwise good, or, after touching the net, strap or band, touches the receiver or anything which he wears or carries before hitting the ground.

(*b*) If a service or a fault is delivered when the receiver is not ready (See Rule 12).

In case of a let, that particular service shall not count, and the server shall serve again, but a service let does not annul a previous fault.

15. Order of Service
At the end of the first game the receiver shall become server, and the server receiver; and so on alternately in all the subsequent games of a match. If a player serves out of turn, the player who ought to have

served shall serve as soon as the mistake is discovered, but all points scored before such discovery shall be reckoned. A fault served before such discovery shall not be reckoned. If a game shall have been completed before such discovery, the order of service remains as altered.

16. When Players Change Ends
The players shall change ends at the end of the first, third and every subsequent alternate game of each set, and at the end of each set unless the total number of games in such set is even, in which case the change is not made until the end of the first game of the next set. If a mistake is made and the correct sequence is not followed, the players must take up their correct station as soon as the discovery is made and follow their original sequence.

17. The Ball in Play
A ball is in play from the moment at which it is delivered in service. Unless a fault or a let is called it remains in play until the point is decided.

Case 1. A player fails to make a good return. No call is made and the ball remains in play. May his opponent later claim the point after the rally has ended?

Decision. No. The point may not be claimed if the players continue to play after the error has been made, provided the opponent was not hindered.

18. Server Wins Point
The server wins the point:

(*a*) If the ball served, not being a let under Rule 14, touches the receiver or anything which he wears or carries, before it hits the ground.

(*b*) If the receiver otherwise loses the point as provided by Rule 20.

19. Receiver Wins Point
The receiver wins the point:

(*a*) If the server serves two consecutive faults.

(*b*) If the server otherwise loses the point as provided by Rule 20.

20. Player Loses Point
A player loses the point if:

(*a*) He fails, before the ball in play has hit the ground twice consecutively, to return it directly over the net, except as provided in Rule 24(*a*) or (*c*).

(*b*) He returns the ball in play so that it hits the ground, a permanent fixture, or other object, outside any of the lines which bound his opponent's court, except as provided in Rule 24(*a*) or (*c*).

(*c*) He volleys the ball and fails to make a good return even when standing outside the court.

(*d*) In playing the ball he deliberately carries or catches it on his racket or deliberately touches it with his racket more than once.

(*e*) He or his racket (in his hand or otherwise) or anything which he wears or carries touches the net, posts, singles sticks, cord or metal cable, strap or band, or the ground within his opponent's court at any time while the ball is in play.

(*f*) He volleys the ball before it has passed the net.

(*g*) The ball in play touches him or anything that he wears or carries, except his racket in his hand or hands.

(*h*) He throws his racket at and hits the ball.

(*i*) He deliberately and materially changes the shape of his racket during the playing of the point.

Case 1. In serving, the racket flies from the server's hand and touches the net before the ball has touched the ground. Is this a fault, or does the player lose the point?

Decision. The server loses the point because his racket touches the net whilst the ball is in play (Rule 20(*e*)).

Case 2. In serving, the racket flies from the server's hand and touches the net after the ball has touched the ground outside the proper court. Is this a fault, or does the player lose the point?

Decision. This is a fault because the ball was out of play when the racket touched the net.

Case 3. A and B are playing against C and D. A is serving to D, and C touches the net before the ball touches the ground. A fault is then called because the service falls outside the service court. Do C and D lose the point?

Decision. The call 'fault' is an erroneous one. C and D had already lost the point before 'fault' could be called, because C touched the net whilst the ball was in play (Rule 20(*e*)).

Case 4. May a player jump over the net into his opponent's court while the ball is in play and not suffer a penalty?

Decision. No. He loses the point (Rule 20(*e*)).

Case 5. A cuts the ball just over the net, and it returns to A's side. B, unable to reach the ball, throws his racket and hits the ball. Both racket and ball fall over the net on A's court. A returns the ball outside of B's court. Does B win or lose the point?

Decision. B loses the point (Rule 20(*e*) and (*h*)).

Case 6. A player standing outside the service court is struck by a service ball before it has touched the ground. Does he win or lose the point?

Decision. The player struck loses the point (Rule 20(*g*)), except as provided under Rule 14(*a*).

Case 7. A player standing outside the court volleys the ball or catches it in his hand and claims the point because the ball was certainly going out of court.

Decision. In no circumstances can he claim the point:

   (i) If he catches the ball he loses the point under Rule 20(*g*).

  (ii) If he volleys it and makes a bad return he loses the point under Rule 20(*c*).

 (iii) If he volleys it and makes a good return, the rally continues.

21. Player Hinders Opponent

If a player commits any act which hinders his opponent in making a stroke, then, if this is deliberate, he shall lose the point or if involuntary, the point shall be replayed.

Case 1. Is a player liable to a penalty if in making a stroke he touches his opponent?

Decision. No, unless the Umpire deems it necessary to take action under Rule 21.

Case 2. When a ball bounds back over the net, the player concerned may reach over the net in order to play the ball. What is the ruling if the player is hindered from doing this by his opponent?

Decision. In accordance with Rule 21, the Umpire may either award the point to the player hindered, or order the point to be replayed (see also Rule 25).

Case 3. Does an involuntary double hit constitute an act which hinders an opponent within Rule 21?

Decision. No.

22. Ball Falls on Line

A ball falling on a line is regarded as falling in the court bounded by that line.

23. Ball Touches Permanent Fixture

If the ball in play touches a permanent fixture (other than the net, posts, singles sticks, cord or metal cable, strap or band) after it has hit the ground, the player who struck it wins the point; if before it hits the ground, his opponent wins the point.

Case 1. A return hits the Umpire or his chair or stand. The player claims that the ball was going into court.

Decision. He loses the point.

24. A Good Return

It is a good return:

(*a*) If the ball touches the net, posts, singles sticks, cord or metal cable, strap or band, provided that it passes over any of them and hits the ground within the court.

(*b*) If the ball, served or returned, hits the ground within the proper court and rebounds or is blown back over the net, and the player whose turn it is to strike reaches over the net and plays the ball, provided that neither he nor any part of his clothes or racket touches the net, posts, singles sticks, cord or metal cable, strap or band or the ground within his opponent's court, and that the stroke be otherwise good.

(*c*) If the ball is returned outside the posts, or singles sticks, either above or below the level of the top of the net, even though it touches the posts or singles sticks, provided that it hits the ground within the proper court.

(*d*) If a player's racket passes over the net after he has returned the ball, provided the ball passes the net before being played and is properly returned.

(*e*) If a player succeeds in returning the ball, served or in play, which strikes a ball lying in the court.

Note: In a singles match, if, for the sake of convenience, a doubles court is equipped with singles sticks for the purpose of a singles game, then the doubles posts and those portions of the net, cord or metal cable and the band outside such singles sticks shall at all times be permanent fixtures, and are not regarded as posts or parts of the net of a singles game.

A return that passes under the net cord between the singles stick and adjacent doubles posts without touching either net cord, net or doubles post, and falls within the court, is a good return.

Case 1. A ball going out of court hits a net post or singles stick and falls within the lines of the opponent's court. Is the stroke good?

Decision. If a service: no, under Rule 10(*c*). If other than a service: yes, under Rule 24(*a*).

Case 2. Is it a good return if a player returns the ball holding his racket in both hands?

Decision. Yes.

Case 3. The service, or ball in play, strikes a ball lying in the court. Is the point won or lost thereby?

Decision. No. Play must continue. If it is not clear to the Umpire that the right ball is returned a let should be called.

Case 4. May a player use more than one racket at any time during play?

Decision. No. The whole implication of the rules is singular.

Case 5. May a player request that a ball or balls lying in his opponent's court be removed?

Decision. Yes, but not while a ball is in play.

25. Hindrance of a Player

In case a player is hindered in making a stroke by anything not within his control, except a permanent fixture of the court, or except as provided for in Rule 21, a let shall be called.

Case 1. A spectator gets into the way of a player, who fails to return the ball. May the player then claim a let?

Decision. Yes. If in the Umpire's opinion he was obstructed by circumstances beyond his control, but not if due to permanent fixtures of the court or the arrangements of the ground.

Case 2. A player is interfered with as in Case 1, and the Umpire calls a let. The server had previously served a fault. Has he the right to two services?

Decision. Yes. As the ball is in play, the point, not merely the stroke, must be replayed as the rule provides.

Case 3. May a player claim a let under Rule 25 because he thought his opponent was being hindered, and consequently did not expect the ball to be returned?

Decision. No.

Case 4. Is a stroke good when a ball in play hits another ball in the air?

Decision. A let should be called unless the other ball is in the air by the act of one of the players, in which case the Umpire will decide under Rule 21.

Case 5. If an Umpire or other judge erroneously calls 'fault' or 'out', and then corrects himself, which of the calls shall prevail?

Decision. A let must be called unless, in the opinion of the Umpire, neither player is hindered in his game, in which case the corrected call shall prevail.

Case 6. If the first ball served – a fault – rebounds, interfering with the receiver at the time of the second service, may the receiver claim a let?

Decision. Yes. But if he had an opportunity to remove the ball from the court and negligently failed to do so, he may not claim a let.

Case 7. Is it a good stroke if the ball touches a stationary or moving object on the court?

Decision. It is a good stroke unless the stationary object came into court after the ball was put in to play in which case a let must be called. If the ball in play strikes an object moving along or above the surface of the court a let must be called.

Case 8. What is the ruling if the first service is a fault, the second service correct, and it becomes necessary to call a let either under the provision of Rule 25 or if the Umpire is unable to decide the point?

Decision. The fault shall be annulled and the whole point replayed.

26. Score in a Game

If a player wins his first point, the score is called 15 for that player; on winning his second point, the score is called 30 for that player; on winning his third point, the score is called 40 for that player, and the fourth point won by a player is scored game for that player except as below:

If both players have won 3 points, the score is called deuce: and the next point won by a player is scored advantage for that player. If the same player wins the next point, he wins the game: if the other player wins the next point the score is again called deuce; and so on, until a player wins the 2 points immediately following the score at deuce, when the game is scored for that player.

27. Score in a Set

(*a*) A player (or players) who first wins 6 games wins a set; except that he must win by a margin of 2 games over his opponent and where necessary a set shall be extended until this margin is achieved.

(*b*) The tie-break system of scoring may be adopted as an alternative to the advantage set system in paragraph (*a*) of this rule, provided the decision is announced in advance of the match.

In this case, the following rules shall be effective:

The tie-break shall operate when the score reaches 6 games all in any set, except in the third or fifth set of a three-set or five-set match respectively when an ordinary advantage set shall be played, unless otherwise decided and announced in advance of the match.

The following system shall be used in a tie-break game.
Singles

(i) A player who first wins 7 points shall win the game and the set, provided he leads by a margin of 2 points. If the score reaches 6 points all the game shall be extended until this margin has been achieved. Numerical scoring shall be used throughout the tie-break game.

(ii) The player whose turn it is to serve shall be the server for the first point. His opponent shall be the server for the second and third points and thereafter each player shall serve alternately for 2 consecutive points until the winner of the game and set has been decided.

(iii) From the first point, each service shall be delivered alternately from the right and left courts, beginning from the right court. If service from a wrong half of the court occurs and is undetected, all play resulting from such wrong service or services shall stand, but the inaccuracy of station shall be corrected immediately it is discovered.

(iv) Players shall change ends after every 6 points and at the conclusion of the tie-break game.

(v) The tie-break game shall count as one game for the ball change, except that, if the balls are due to be changed at the beginning of the tie-break, the change shall be delayed until the second game of the following set.

Doubles

In doubles the procedure for singles shall apply. The player whose turn it is to serve shall be the server for the first point. Thereafter each player shall serve in rotation for 2 points, in the same order as previously in that set, until the winners of the game and set have been decided.

Rotation of Service

The player (or pair in the case of doubles) who served first in the tie-break game shall receive service in the first game of the following set.

Case 1. At 6 all, the tie-break is played, although it has been decided and announced in advance of the match that an advantage set will be played. Are the points already played counted?

Decision. If the error is discovered before the ball is put in play for the second point, the first point shall count but the error shall be corrected immediately. If the error is discovered after the ball is put in play for the second point the game shall continue as a tie-break game.

Case 2. At 6 all, an advantage game is played, although it has been decided and announced in advance of the match that a tie-break will be played. Are the points already played counted?

Decision. If the error is discovered before the ball is put in play for the second point, the first point shall be counted but the error shall be corrected immediately. If the error is discovered after the ball is put in play for the second point an advantage set shall be continued. If the score thereafter reaches 8 games all or a higher even number, a tie-break shall be played.

Case 3. If during a tie-break in a singles or doubles game, a player serves out of turn, shall the order of service remain as altered until the end of the game?

Decision. If a player has completed his turn of service the order of service shall remain as altered. If the error is discovered before a player has completed his turn of service the order of service shall be corrected immediately and any points already played shall count.

28. Maximum Number of Sets

The maximum number of sets in a match shall be five, or, where women take part, three.

29. Role of Court Officials

In matches where an Umpire is appointed, his decision shall be final; but where a Referee is appointed, an appeal shall lie to him from the decision of an Umpire on a question of Law, and in all such cases the decision of the Referee shall be final.

In matches where assistants to the Umpire are appointed (Linesmen, Net-cord Judges, Footfault Judges) their decisions shall be final on questions of fact, except that if in the opinion of an Umpire a clear mistake has been made he shall have the right to change the decision of an assistant or order a let to be played. When such an assistant is unable to give a decision, he shall indicate this immediately to the Umpire who shall give a decision. When an Umpire is unable to give a decision on a question of fact he shall order a let to be played.

In Davis Cup matches or other team competitions where a Referee is on court, any decision can be changed by the Referee, who may also instruct an Umpire to order a let to be played. The Referee, in his discretion, may at any time postpone a match on account of darkness or the condition of the ground or the weather. In any case of postponement the previous score and previous occupancy of courts shall hold good, unless the Referee and the players unanimously agree otherwise.

Case 1. The Umpire orders a let, but a player claims the point should not be replayed. May the Referee be requested to give a decision?

Decision. Yes. A question of tennis law, that is an issue relating to the application of specific facts, shall first be determined by the Umpire. However, if the Umpire is uncertain or if a player appeals from his determination, then the Referee shall be requested to give a decision, and his decision is final.

Case 2. A ball is called out, but a player claims that the ball was good. May the Referee give a ruling?

Decision. No. This is a question of fact, that is an issue relating to what actually occurred during a specific incident, and the decision of the on-court officials is therefore final.

Case 3. May an Umpire overrule a Linesman at the end of a rally if, in his opinion, a clear mistake has been made during the course of a rally?

Decision. No. An Umpire may overrule a Linesman only if he does so immediately after the mistake has been made.

Case 4. A Linesman calls a ball out. The Umpire was unable to see clearly, although he thought the ball was in. May he overrule the Linesman?

Decision. No. An Umpire may overrule if he considers that a call was incorrect beyond all reasonable doubt. He may overrule a ball determined good by a Linesman only if he has been able to see a space between the ball and the line; and he may overrule a ball determined out, or a fault, by a Linesman only if he has seen the ball hit the line, or fall inside the line.

Case 5. May a Linesman change his call after the Umpire has given the score?

Decision. Yes. If a Linesman realises he has made an error, he may make a correction provided he does so immediately.

Case 6. A player claims his return shot was good after a Linesman called 'out'. May the Umpire overrule the Linesman?

Decision. No. An Umpire may never overrule as a result of a protest or an appeal by a player.

30. Continuous Play and Rest Periods
Play shall be continuous from the first service until the match is concluded, in accordance with the following provisions.

(*a*) If the first service is a fault, the second service must be struck by the server without delay. The receiver must play to the reasonable pace of the server and must be ready to receive when the server is ready to serve.

When changing ends a maximum of 1 minute 30 seconds shall elapse from the moment the ball goes out of play at the end of the game to the time the ball is struck for the first point of the next game.

The Umpire shall use his discretion when there is interference which makes it impractical for play to be continuous. The organisers of international circuits and team events recognised by the ITF may determine the time allowed between points, which shall not at any time exceed 20 seconds from the moment the ball goes out of play at the end of one point to the time the ball is struck for the next point.

(*b*) Play shall never be suspended, delayed or interfered with for the purpose of enabling a player to recover his strength, breath, or physical condition. However, in the case of accidental injury, the Umpire may allow a one-time 3-minutes suspension for that injury. The organisers of international circuits and team events recognised by the ITF may extend the one-time suspension period from 3 minutes to 5 minutes.

(*c*) If, through circumstances outside the control of the player, his clothing, footwear or equipment (excluding racket) becomes out of adjustment in such a way that it is impossible or undesirable for him to play on, the Umpire may suspend play while the maladjustment is rectified.

(*d*) The Umpire may suspend or delay play at any time as may be necessary and appropriate.

(*e*) After the third set, or when women take part the second set, either player is entitled to a rest, which shall not exceed 10 minutes, or in countries situated between latitude 15 degrees north and latitude 15 degrees south, 45 minutes, and furthermore, when necessitated by circumstances not within the control of the players, the Umpire may suspend play for such a period as he may consider necessary. If play is suspended and is not resumed until a later day, the rest may be taken only after the third set (or when women take part the second set) of play on such a later day, completion of an unfinished set being counted as one set.

If play is suspended and is not resumed until 10 minutes have elapsed in the same day, the rest may be taken only after three consecutive sets have been played without interruption (or when women take part two sets), completion of an unfinished set being counted as one set.

Any nation and/or committee organising a tournament, match or competition, other than the international Tennis Championships (Davis Cup and Federation Cup), is at liberty to modify this provision or omit it from its regulations, provided this is announced before the event commences.

(*f*) A tournament committee has the discretion to decide the time allowed for a warm-up period prior to a match but this may not exceed 5 minutes and must be announced before the event commences.

(*g*) When approved point penalty and non-accumulative point penalty systems are in operation, the Umpire shall make his decisions within the terms of those systems.

(*h*) Upon violation of the principle that play shall be continuous, the Umpire may, after giving due warning, disqualify the offender.

31. Coaching

During the playing of a match in a team competition, a player may receive coaching from a captain who is sitting on the court only when he changes ends at the end of a game, but not when he changes ends during a tie-break game. A player may not receive coaching during the playing of any other match. The provisions of this rule must be strictly construed.

After due warning an offending player may be disqualified. When an approved point penalty system is in operation, the Umpire shall impose penalties according to that system.

Case 1. Should a warning be given, or the player be disqualified, if the coaching is given by signals in an unobtrusive manner?

Decision. The Umpire must take action as soon as he becomes aware that coaching is being given verbally or by signals. If the Umpire is unaware that coaching is being given, a player may draw his attention to the fact that advice is being given.

Case 2. Can a player receive coaching during an authorised rest period under Rule 30(*e*), or when play is interrupted and he leaves the court?

Decision. Yes. In these circumstances, when the player is not on the court, there is no restriction on coaching.

Note: The word 'coaching' includes any advice or instruction.

32. Ball Change

In cases where balls are to be changed after a specified number of games, if the balls are not changed in the correct sequence, the mistake shall be corrected when the player, or pair in the case of doubles, who should have served with new balls is next due to serve. Thereafter the balls shall be changed so that the number of games between changes shall be that originally agreed.

THE DOUBLES GAME

33. The Doubles Game
The above rules shall apply to the doubles game except as below.

34. The Doubles Court
For the doubles game, the court shall be 36ft (10.97m) in width, i.e. 4½ft (1.37m) wider on each side than the court for the singles game, and those portions of the singles side-lines which lie between the two service-lines shall be called the service side-lines. In other respects, the court shall be similar to that described in Rule 1, but the portions of the singles side-lines between the base-line and service-line on each side of the net may be omitted if desired.

35. Order of Service in Doubles
The order of serving shall be decided at the beginning of each set as follows:
> The pair who have to serve in the first game of each set shall decide which partner shall do so and the opposing pair shall decide similarly for the second game. The partner of the player who served in the first game shall serve in the third; the partner of the player who served in the second game shall serve in the fourth, and so on in the same order in all the subsequent games of a set.
> *Case 1.* In doubles, one player does not appear in time to play, and his partner claims to be allowed to play single-handed against the opposing players. May he do so?
> *Decision.* No.

36. Order of Receiving in Doubles
The order of receiving the service shall be decided at the beginning of each set as follows:
> The pair who have to receive the service in the first game shall decide which partner shall receive the first service, and that partner shall continue to receive the first service in every odd game throughout that set. The opposing pair shall likewise decide which partner shall receive the first service in the second game and that partner shall continue to receive the first service in every even game throughout that set. Partners shall receive the service alternately throughout each game.
> *Case 1.* Is it allowable in doubles for the server's partner or the

receiver's partner to stand in a position that obstructs the view of the receiver?

Decision. Yes. The server's partner or the receiver's partner may take any position on his side of the net in or out of the court that he wishes.

37. Service Out of Turn in Doubles
If a partner serves out of his turn, the partner who ought to have served shall serve as soon as the mistake is discovered, but all points scored, and any faults served before such discovery, shall be reckoned. If a game shall have been completed before such discovery, the order of service remains as altered.

38. Error in Order of Receiving in Doubles
If during a game the order of receiving the service is changed by the receivers, it shall remain as altered until the end of the game in which the mistake is discovered, but the partners shall resume their original order of receiving in the next game of that set in which they are receivers of the service.

39. Service Fault in Doubles
The service is a fault as provided for by Rule 10, or if the ball touches the server's partner or anything which he wears or carries; but if the ball served touches the partner of the receiver, or anything which he wears or carries, not being a let under Rule 14(*a*) before it hits the ground, the server wins the point.

40. Playing the Ball in Doubles
The ball shall be struck alternately by one or other player of the opposing pairs, and if a player touches the ball in play with his racket in contravention of this rule, his opponents win the point.

Reprinted by permission of the International Tennis Federation. Copies of the complete Rules of Tennis, including additional Notes, Regulations for Making Tests and the Rules of Wheelchair Tennis, may be obtained from the Federation.

THE RULES OF

Volleyball

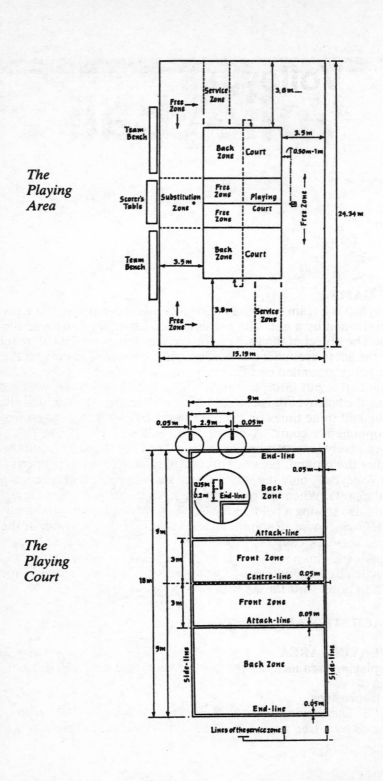

The Playing Area

The Playing Court

Volleyball

THE GAME

Volleyball is a team sport played by two teams of 6 players on a playing court divided by a net. The ball is played by hitting it with hands and arms. The object of the game is for each team to send the ball regularly over the net to ground it on the opponent's court, and to prevent the ball from being grounded on its own court.

The ball is put into play by the right back-row player, who serves, hitting the ball over the net to the opponent's court. A team is entitled to hit the ball three times (in addition to the block contact) to return it to the opponent's court. A player is not allowed to hit the ball twice consecutively (except when blocking). The rally continues until the ball touches the ground, goes out or a team fails to return it properly.

In volleyball, only the serving team may score a point (except in the deciding set). When the receiving team wins a rally, it gains the right to serve (also scoring a point in the deciding set) and its players rotate one position clockwise. Rotation ensures that players play both at the net and on the back court.

The team wins a set by scoring 15 points with a 2-point lead and wins the match by winning 3 sets. In the event of a 16-16 tie, the team scoring the 17th point wins the set with only a 1-point lead.

1. FACILITIES AND EQUIPMENT

1. PLAYING AREA

The playing area includes the playing court and the free zone.

1.1 Dimensions

1.1.1 The playing court is a rectangle measuring 18m × 9m, surrounded by a free zone a minimum of 3m wide and with a space free from any obstructions up to a height of a minimum of 7m from the playing surface.

1.1.2 For official international competitions, the free zone shall measure a minimum of 5m from the side-lines and of 8m from the end-lines. The free space shall measure a minimum of 12.5m in height from the playing surface.

1.2 Playing Surface

1.2.1 The surface must be flat, horizontal and uniform.

1.2.2 For official international competitions, only a wooden or synthetic surface is allowed. Any surface must be previously approved by the FIVB.

1.2.3 The playing surface must not present any danger of injury to the players. It is forbidden to play on rough or slippery surfaces.

1.2.4 On indoor courts the surface of the playing court must be of a light colour. For official international competitions, white colours for the lines, and other colours for the playing court and the free zone are required.

1.2.5 On outdoor courts, a slope of 5mm per metre is allowed for drainage.

Court lines made of solid materials are forbidden.

1.3 Lines on the Court

1.3.1 All lines are 5cm wide. They must be of a light and different colour from the floor and any other lines.

1.3.2 *Boundary lines.* Two side-lines and two end-lines mark the playing court. Both side-lines and end-lines are drawn inside the dimensions of the playing court.

1.3.3 *Centre Line.* The axis of the centre-line divides the playing court into two equal courts measuring 9m × 9m each. This line extends beneath the net from side-line to side-line.

1.4 Zones of the Playing Court

1.4.1 *Front Zone.* On each court the front zone is limited by the axis of the centre-line and the attack-line drawn 3m back from that axis (its width included). The front zone is considered to extend indefinitely beyond the side-lines.

1.4.2 *Service Zone.* The service zone is a 3m-wide area behind the end-line. It is laterally delimited by two short lines, each 15cm long drawn 20cm behind the end-line and perpendicularly to it, one as the extension of the right side-line and the other 3m to its left. Both are included in the width of the zone. In depth, the service zone extends to the edge of the free zone.

1.4.3 *Substitution zone.* The substitution zone is limited by the imaginary extension of both attack-lines up to the scorer's table.

1.5 Temperature

The minimum temperature shall not be below 10°C (50°F). For official international indoor competitions, the maximum temperature shall not be higher than 25°C (77°F) and the minimum not lower than 16°C (61°F).

1.6 Lighting

For official international indoor competitions, the lighting on the playing area should be 1000 to 1500 lux, measured at 1m above the playing surface.

2. NET AND POSTS

2.1 Net

The net is 1m in depth and 9.5m long, placed vertically over the axis of the centre-line. It is made of 10cm square black mesh. At its top there is a horizontal band, 5cm wide, made of two-fold white canvas and sewn along its full length. Each extreme end of the band has a hole through which passes a cord fastening the band to the posts to keep the top of the net taut. Within the band there is a flexible cable for fastening the net to the posts and keeping its top taut. At the bottom of the net (with no horizontal band) there is a rope, threaded through the meshes for fastening it to the posts and keeping the lower part of the net taut.

2.2 Side Bands

Two white bands, 5cm wide and 1m long, are fastened vertically to the net and placed above each side-line. They are considered as part of the net.

2.3 Antennae

An antenna is a flexible rod, 1.8m long and 10mm in diameter. It is made of fibre glass or similar material. Two antennae are fastened at the outer edge of each side band and placed on the opposite sides of the net. The top 80 cm of each antenna extend above the net and are marked with 10cm stripes of contrasting colours, preferably red and white. The antennae are considered as part of the net and laterally delimit the crossing space.

2.4 Height of the Net

2.4.1 The height of the net shall be 2.43m for men and 2.24m for women.

2.4.2 It is measured from the centre of the playing court with a measuring rod. The two ends of the net (over the side-lines) must both be at the same height from the playing surface and may not exceed the official height by more than 2cm.

2.5 Posts

2.5.1 The posts supporting the net must be rounded and smooth, with a height of 2.55m, preferably adjustable.

2.5.2 They must be fixed to the ground at a distance of 0.50m–1m from each side-line. Fixing the posts to the ground by means of wires is forbidden. All dangerous or obstructing devices must be eliminated.

2.6 Additional Equipment

All additional equipment is determined by FIVB regulations.

3. THE BALL

3.1 Characteristics

The ball shall be spherical, made of a flexible leather case with a bladder inside made of rubber or a similar material.
- Colour: uniform and light.
- Circumference: 65–67cm.
- Weight: 260–280g.
- Inside pressure: $0.40–0.45kg/cm^2$

3.2 Uniformity of Balls

All balls used in a match must have the same characteristics regarding circumference, weight, pressure, type etc. Official international competitions must be played with FIVB approved balls.

3.3 Three-ball System

For official international competitions 3 balls shall be used. In this case, 6 ball retrievers are stationed, one at each corner of the free zone and one behind each Referee.

2. PARTICIPANTS

4. TEAMS

4.1 Composition and registration

4.1.1 A team may consist of a maximum of 12 players, one coach, one assistant coach, one trainer and one medical doctor. For official international competitions, the medical doctor must be accredited beforehand by the FIVB.

4.1.2 Only the players recorded on the scoresheet may participate in the match.

4.1.3 Once the team captain and the coach have signed the scoresheet, the recorded players cannot be changed.

4.2 Captain

4.2.1 The team captain shall be indicated on the scoresheet.

4.2.2 The team captain is identified with a stripe of 8cm × 2cm, of a different colour to the shirt, underlining the number on the chest.

4.2.3 When the team captain is not on the court, the coach or the team captain will designate another player to act as the game captain.

5. PLAYERS' EQUIPMENT

5.1 Equipment

5.1.1 A player's equipment consists of a shirt, shorts and shoes.

5.1.2 Shirt, shorts and socks must be uniform, clean and of the same colour.

5.1.3 Shoes must be light and pliable with rubber or leather soles without heels.

5.1.4 (*a*) Players' shirts must be numbered from 1 to 18.

(*b*) The numbers must be placed in the centre of the front and back.

5.1.5 The numbers must be of a contrasting colour to the shirts and a minimum of 10cm in height on the chest and of 15cm on the back. The stripe forming the numbers shall be a minimum of 2cm wide.

5.2 Authorised Changes

5.2.1 If both teams arrive at a match dressed in shirts of the same colour, the home team must change. On a neutral site, the team listed first on the match programme shall change.

5.2.2 The first referee may authorise one or more players to:

– Play barefoot.

– Change wet shirts between sets or after substitution, provided that the colour, design and number of the new shirt(s) is (are) the same.

5.2.3 In cold weather, the first referee may authorise the teams to play in training suits, provided that they are of the same colour and design for the whole team and properly numbered (Rule 5.1.4).

5.3 Forbidden Objects and Uniforms

5.3.1 It is forbidden to wear any object that may cause an injury to a player or give an artificial advantage to the player.

5.3.2 Players may wear glasses at their own risk.

5.3.3 It is forbidden to wear uniforms without official numbers (Rules 5.1.4 and 5.1.5), or of a different colour from other players.

6. RIGHTS AND RESPONSIBILITIES OF THE PARTICIPANTS

6.1 Basic Responsibilities

6.1.1 Participants must know the Rules of the Game and abide by them.

6.1.2 Participants must accept referees' decisions with sportsmanlike conduct, without disputing them. In case of doubt, clarification may be requested through the game captain and only through the game captain.

6.1.3 Participants must behave respectfully and courteously in the spirit of *fair play*, not only towards the referees, but also towards other officials, the opponents, team-mates and spectators.

6.1.4 Participants must refrain from actions or attitudes aimed at influencing the decisions of the referees or covering up faults committed by their team.

6.1.5 Participants must refrain from actions aimed at delaying the game.

6.1.6 Both the team captain and the coach are responsible for the conduct and discipline of their team members.

6.1.7 Communication between team members during the match is permitted (Rule 6.3.4).

6.2 Captain

6.2.1 Prior to the match the team captain:

(*a*) Signs the scoresheet.

(*b*) Represents the team at the toss.

6.2.2 During the match the team captain functions as the game captain while on the court. The game captain is authorised to speak to the Referees while the ball is out of play (Rule 6.1.2):

(*a*) To ask for an explanation on the application or interpretation of the Rules. The game captain also submits to the referee involved the requests or questions of team-mates. If the explanation does not satisfy, the game captain must immediately indicate to the referee that he/she reserves the right to record a disagreement on the scoresheet as an official protest at the end of the match (Rule 26.2.4).

(*b*) To ask authorisation to:

– Change uniforms or equipment.

– Verify the positions of the teams.

– Check the floor, the net, the ball, etc.

(*c*) To request regular game interruptions (Rule 20.1).

6.2.3 At the end of the match, the team captain:

(*a*) Thanks the referees and signs the scoresheet to ratify the outcome.

(b) If he/she previously expressed a disagreement to the first referee, may confirm it as a protest, recording it on the scoresheet (Rule 6.2.2a).

6.3 Coach

6.3.1 Prior to the match, the coach records or checks the names and numbers of players on the scoresheet and then signs it.

6.3.2 Prior to each set, the coach gives the scorer or the second referee the line-up sheet duly filled in and signed.

6.3.3 During the match the coach must sit on the team bench nearest to the scorer (Rule 6.5.2).

6.3.4 During the match, the coach, as well as other members of the team, may give instructions to the players on the court but only while sitting on the bench or within the warm-up area, without disturbing or delaying the match.

6.4 Assistant Coach

6.4.1 The assistant coach sits on the team bench, but has no right to intervene in the match.

6.4.2 Should the coach have to leave the team, the assistant coach may assume the coach's function, at the request of the game captain and with the authorisation of the first referee.

6.5 Location of Participants

6.5.1 The team benches are located beside the scorer's table, outside the free zone.

6.5.2 The players not in play should sit on the team bench or stand in the warm-up area on their side of the court. The coach and other team members should sit on the bench.

6.5.3 Only team members are permitted to sit on the bench during the match and to participate in the warm-up session (Rule 4.1.1).

6.5.4 The players not in play may warm up without balls in the areas assigned to this purpose. The warm-up areas, sized approximately 3m × 3m, are located in the bench-side corners of the playing area, outside the free zone.

6.5.5 During the set intervals, balls may be used by the players in the free zone.

3. POINT, SET AND MATCH WINNER

7. SCORING SYSTEM

7.1 To Win a Match

7.1.1 A match is won by the team that wins 3 sets.

7.1.2 In the case of a 2-2 tie, the deciding (5th) set is played as a tie-break with the rally-point system (Rule 7.4).

7.2 To Win a Set
7.2.1 A set is won by the team that first scores 15 points with a minimum lead of 2 points. In the case of a 14-14 tie, the play is continued until a 2-point lead is reached (16-14, 17-15).

7.2.2 However, in the first four sets, a point limit is reached when, after a 16-16 tie, the team scoring the 17th point wins the set with only a one-point lead. In the deciding set, in the case of a 14-14 tie, play is continued until a two-point lead is reached. There is no point limit.

7.3 To Win a Rally
Whenever a team fails to serve or return the ball, or commits any other fault, the opposing team wins the rally, with one of the following consequences:

7.3.1 If the opposing team served, it scores a point and continues to serve.

7.3.2 If the opposing team received the service, it gains the right to serve without scoring a point (side-out) (except Rule 7.4).

7.4 To Win a Rally in the Deciding (5th) Set
In the deciding set, a point is scored when a team wins a rally, with one of the following consequences:

7.4.1 The serving team scores a point and continues to serve.

7.4.2 The receiving team gains the right to serve and scores a point.

7.5 Default and Incomplete Team
7.5.1 If a team refuses to play after being summoned to do so, it is declared in default and forfeits the match with the result 0–3 for the match and 0–15 for each set.

7.5.2 A team that, without justifiable reason, does not appear on the playing court on time is declared in default with the same result as in Rule 7.5.1.

7.5.3 A team declared *incomplete* for the set or for the match (Rules 9.2.2. and 11.4) loses the set or the match. The opposing team is given the points or the points and the sets needed to win the set or the match. The incomplete team keeps its points and sets.

4. PREPARATION OF THE MATCH: STRUCTURE OF PLAY

8. PREPARATION OF THE MATCH

8.1 Toss
8.1.1 Before the warm-up, the first referee carries out a toss in the presence of the two team captains.

The winner of the toss chooses:
– Either the right to serve or receive the service;
– Or the side of the court.
The loser takes the remaining alternative.

8.1.2 If a deciding (5th) set is to be played, the first referee will carry out another toss.

8.2 Warm-up Session

8.2.1 Prior to the match, if the teams have previously had another playing court at their disposal, each team will have a 3-minute warm-up period at the net; if not, they may have 5 minutes each.

8.2.2 If both captains agree to warm up at the net together, the teams may do so for 6 to 10 minutes, according to Rule 8.2.1.

8.2.3 In the case of consecutive warm-ups, the team that has the first service takes the first turn at the net.

9. TEAM LINE-UP

9.1 Starting Line-up

9.1.1 Before the start of each set, the coach has to present the starting line-up of the team on a line-up sheet. This sheet is submitted, duly signed, to the second referee or the scorer (Rule 10.1.2). The players who are not in the starting line-up of a set are the substitutes for that set.

9.1.2 Once the line-up sheet has been delivered, no change in line-up is authorised.

9.1.3 If there is a discrepancy between the line-up sheet and actual positions of players, the players must move to the positions indicated on the line-up sheet before the start of the set. There will be no penalty.

If one or more players on the court are not registered on the line-up sheet, the players on court must be changed according to the line-up sheet, without penalty.

However, if the coach wishes to keep such non-registered players on the court, a request for a regular substitution has to be made which will then be recorded on the scoresheet.

9.2 Rotation Order

9.2.1 Rotation order as determined by the starting line-up has to be maintained throughout the set.

9.2.2 There must always be six players per team in play.

10. PLAYERS' POSITIONS AND ROTATION

10.1 Positions

10.1.1 At the moment the ball is hit by the server, each team must be within its own court (except the server) in 2 rows of 3 players. These rows may be broken.

10.1.2 The 3 players along the net are front-row players and occupy positions 4 (left), 3 (centre) and 2 (right). The other 3 are back-row players occupying positions 5 (left), 6 (centre) and 1 (right). Each back-row player must be positioned further back from the centre-line than the corresponding front-row player.

10.1.3 The positions of players are determined and controlled according to the positions of their feet contacting the ground as follows:

(*a*) Each front-row player must have at least a part of one foot closer to the centre-line than the feet of the corresponding back-row player.

(*b*) Each right (left) side player must have at least a part of one foot closer to the right (left) side-line than the feet of the centre player in the same row.

10.1.4 Once the ball has been served, the players may move around and occupy any position on their own court and in the free zone.

10.2 Rotation

When the receiving team has gained the right to serve, its players must rotate one position clockwise (player in position 2 rotates to position 1 to serve, player in 1 rotates to 6, etc.).

10.3 Positional Faults

10.3.1 The players of a team commit a fault if they are not in their correct positions at the moment the ball is hit by the server (Rule 10.1.1).

10.3.2 If the server commits a serving fault (Rule 17.8) at the moment of hitting the ball, this fault prevails over a positional fault and is thus penalised. If, after the ball has been hit, the service becomes a fault (Rule 17.9), it is a positional fault that will be penalised.

10.3.3 A positional fault leads to the following consequences:

– The fault is penalised with the loss of a rally (Rule 13.2.1);

– The players are returned to their correct positions.

10.4 Rotation Faults

10.4.1 A rotation fault is committed when the service is not made according to the rotation order (Rule 9.2). This corresponds to a positional fault; the error must be corrected and the team at fault penalised according to Rule 10.3.3.

10.4.2 The scorer should determine the exact moment the fault was committed. All points scored subsequently by the team at fault must be cancelled. The opponent's points remain valid. If the points scored while the player was out of position or out of service order cannot be determined, a loss of rally is the only sanction.

11. SUBSTITUTION OF PLAYERS

11.1 Definitions
A substitution is the act by which the referees authorise a player to leave the court and another player to occupy his position.

11.2 Limitations of Substitutions
11.2.1 Six substitutions is the maximum permitted per team per set. One or more players may be substituted at the same time.

11.2.2 A player of the starting line-up may leave the game and re-enter, but only once in a set, and only to the player's previous position in the line-up.

11.2.3 A substitute player may enter the game only once per set, in place of a player of the starting line-up, and he can only be replaced by the same player.

11.3 Exceptional Substitution
An injured player who cannot continue playing should be legally substituted. If this is not possible, the team is entitled to make an *exceptional* substitution, beyond the limits of Rule 11.2.

11.4 Substitution for Expulsion
An *expelled* or *disqualified* player (Rule 24.2.3-4) must be replaced through a legal substitution. If that is not possible, the team is declared *incomplete* (Rule 7.5.3).

11.5 Illegal Substitution
11.5.1 A substitution is illegal if it exceeds the limitations indicated in Rule 11.2 (except Rule 11.3).

11.5.2 When a team makes an illegal substitution and the play is resumed (Rule 12.1), the following procedure shall apply:
– The fault is penalised with the loss of a rally;
– The substitution is rectified;
– The points scored by the team at fault after the fault was committed are cancelled. The opponent's points remain valid.

5. PLAYING ACTIONS

12. STATES OF PLAY

12.1 Ball in Play
The rally begins with the referee's whistle. However, the ball is 'in play' from the service hit.

12.2 Ball Out of Play
The rally ends with the referee's whistle. However, if the whistle is due to a fault made in play, the ball is 'out of play' the moment the fault was committed (Rule 13.2).

12.3 Ball 'In'
The ball is 'in' when it touches the floor of the playing court including the boundary lines (Rule 1.3.2).

12.4 Ball 'Out'
The ball is 'out' when it:
(*a*) Falls on the floor completely outside the boundary lines.
(*b*) Touches an object outside the court, the ceiling or a person out of play.
(*c*) Touches the antennae, ropes, posts or the net itself outside the antennae/sidebands.
(*d*) Crosses completely the vertical plane of the net, totally or even partly outside the crossing space (Rules 15.1.2 and 15.1.3).

13. PLAYING FAULTS

13.1 Definition
13.1.1 Any playing action contrary to the Rules is a playing fault.
13.1.2 The referees judge the faults and determine the penalties according to these Rules.

13.2 Consequences of a Fault
13.2.1 There is always a penalty for a fault; the opponent of the team committing the fault wins the rally according to Rule 7.3, or Rule 7.4 in the deciding set.
13.2.2 If two or more faults are committed successively, only the first one is counted.
13.2.3 If two or more faults are committed by opponents simultaneously, a *double fault* is counted and the rally is replayed.

14. PLAYING THE BALL

14.1 Team Hits
14.1.1 The team is entitled to a maximum of three hits (in addition to blocking, Rule 19.2.1) for returning the ball over the net.
14.1.2 The hits of the team include not only intentional hits by the player, but also unintentional contacts with the ball.

14.1.3 A player may not hit the ball two times consecutively (except Rule 19.2.2).

14.2 Simultaneous Contacts
14.2.1 Two or three players may touch the ball at the same moment.

14.2.2 When two (three) team-mates touch the ball simultaneously, it is counted as two (three) hits (except at blocking). If two (three) team-mates reach for the ball but only one player touches it, one hit is counted. If players collide, no fault is committed.

14.2.3 If there are simultaneous contacts by opponents over the net and the ball remains in play, the team receiving the ball is entitled to another three hits. If such a ball goes 'out', it is the fault of the team on the opposite side. If simultaneous contacts by opponents lead to a 'held ball' it is a *double fault* (Rule 13.2.3) and the rally is replayed.

14.3 Assisted Hit
A player is not permitted to take support from a team-mate or any structure/object in order to reach the ball. However, the player who is about to commit a fault (touch the net to cross the centre-line etc.) may be stopped or held back by a team-mate.

14.4 Characteristics of the Hit
14.4.1 The ball may be touched with any part of the body above and including the knee.

14.4.2 The ball must be hit cleanly and not held (including lifted, pushed, carried or thrown). It can rebound in any direction.

14.4.3 The ball may touch various parts of the body, provided that the contacts take place simultaneously.

Exceptions:

(*a*) At blocking, consecutive contacts may occur with one or more blocker(s) provided that the contacts occur during one action.

(*b*) At the first hit of the team (19.2), unless it is played over-head using fingers, the ball may contact various parts of the body consecutively, provided that the contacts occur during one action.

14.5 Faults in Playing the Ball
(*a*) *Four hits*: A team hits the ball four times before returning it (Rule 14.1.1).

(*b*) *Irregular hit*: The ball touches the player below the knee (Rule 14.4.1).

(*c*) *Assisted hit*: A player takes support from a team-mate or any structure/object in order to reach the ball (Rule 14.3).

(*d*) *Held ball*: A player does not hit the ball cleanly (Rule 14.4.2).

(*e*) *Double contact*: A player hits the ball twice in succession or the ball contacts various parts of the body successively (Rules 14.1.3 and 14.4.3).

15. BALL AT THE NET

15.1 Ball Crossing the Net
15.1.1 The ball sent to the opponent's court must go over the net within the crossing space. The crossing space is the part of the vertical plane of the net limited as follows:
– Below, by the top of the net;
– At the sides, by the antennae and their imaginary extension; and
– Above, by the ceiling.
15.1.2 A ball heading towards the opponent's side outside the crossing space may be played back, provided that it has not completely crossed the vertical plane of the net at the moment of contact.
15.1.3 The ball is 'out' when it crosses completely the lower space under the net.

15.2 Ball Touching the Net
While crossing the net (Rule 15.1.1), the ball may touch it except during the service.

15.3 Ball in the Net (other than the service ball)
15.3.1 A ball driven into the net may be recovered within the limits of the three team hits.
15.3.2 If the ball rips the mesh of the net or tears it down, the rally is cancelled and replayed.

16. PLAYER AT THE NET

16.1 Playing Area
16.1.1 Each team must play within its own playing area and space. The ball may, however, be retrieved from beyond the free zone.

16.2 Reaching Beyond the Net
16.2.1 In blocking, a blocker may touch the ball beyond the net, provided that there is no interference with the opponents' play before or during the latter's attack hit (Rule 19.3).
16.2.2 A player is permitted to pass a hand beyond the net after an attack-hit, provided that the contact has been made within the player's own playing space.

16.3 Penetration Under the Net

16.3.1 It is permitted to penetrate into the opponents' space under the net, provided that this does not interfere with the opponents' play.

16.3.2 Penetration into the opponents' court:

(*a*) to touch the opponent's court beyond the centre line with a foot or feet is permitted, provided that some part of the penetrating foot/feet remains either in contact with or directly above the centre line.

(*b*) to contact the opponent's court with any other part of the body is forbidden.

16.3.3 A player may enter the opponents' court after the ball is out of play (Rule 12.2).

A player may penetrate into the opponents' free zone provided that there is no interference with the opponent's play.

16.4 Contact With the Net

16.4.1 Contact with the net is a fault only when the action of playing the ball is in the front zone.

16.4.2 Once the player has hit the ball, the player may touch the posts, ropes or any other object outside the total length of the net provided that it does not interfere with play.

16.4.3 When the ball is driven into the net and causes it to touch an opponent, no fault is committed.

16.5 Player's Faults at the Net

It is a fault if:

(*a*) A player touches the ball in the opponent's space before or during the opponent's attack-hit (Rule 16.2.1).

(*b*) A player penetrates into the opponent's space under the net interfering with the latter's play (Rule 16.3.1).

(*c*) A player penetrates into the opponent's court (Rule 16.3.2).

(*d*) A player touches the net (Rule 16.4.1).

17. SERVICE

17.1 Definition

The service is the act of putting the ball into play by the right back-row player, placed in the service zone, who hits the ball with one hand or arm.

17.2 First Service in a Set

17.2.1 The first service of sets 1 and 5 is executed by the team that has obtained the right to serve at the toss (Rule 8.1).

17.2.2 The other sets will be started with the service of the team that did not serve first in the previous set.

17.3 Service Order
17.3.1 The players must follow the service order recorded on the line-up sheet (Rule 9.2.1).

17.3.2 After the first service in a set, the player to serve is determined as follows:

(*a*) When the serving team wins the rally, the player who served before, serves again.

(*b*) When the receiving team wins the rally, it gains the right to serve and rotates (Rule 10.2). The player who moves from the right front-row position to the right back-row position will serve.

17.4 Authorisation of the Service
The first referee authorises the service after having checked that the server is in possession of the ball in the service zone and that the teams are ready to play.

17.5 Execution of the Service
17.5.1 At the moment of the service hit or take-off for a jump service, the server must not touch the court (the end-line included) nor the ground outside the zone. After the service hit, the player may step or land outside the zone, or inside the court.

17.5.2 The server must hit the ball within 5 seconds after the first referee whistles for service.

17.5.3 A service executed before the referee's whistle is cancelled and repeated.

17.5.4 The ball shall be hit with one hand or any part of the arm after being tossed or released and before it touches the playing surface.

17.6 Service Attempt
17.6.1 If the ball, after having been tossed or released, lands without touching the server, it is considered a service attempt.

17.6.2 After a service attempt, the referee must authorise the service again and the server must execute it within the next 5 seconds.

17.6.3 One and only one service attempt is permitted for each service.

17.7 Screening
The players of the serving team must not prevent their opponents, through screening, from seeing the server and the path of the ball.

17.7.1 A player of the serving team makes an individual screen if he waves his arms, jumps or moves sideways etc. when the service is being executed, and the ball is served over him.

17.7.2 A team makes a collective screen when the server is hidden behind a group of two or more team-mates, and the ball is served over them.

17.8 Serving Faults

The following faults lead to a change of service, even if the opponents are out of position when the server:

(a) Violates the service order (Rule 17.3).

(b) Does not execute the service properly (Rule 17.5).

(c) Violates the rule of service attempt (Rule 17.6).

17.9 Serving Faults After Hitting the Ball

After the ball has been correctly hit, the service becomes a fault (unless a player is out of position) if the ball:

(a) Touches a player of the serving team or fails to cross the vertical plane of the net.

(b) Touches the net (Rule 15.2).

(c) Goes 'out' (Rule 12.4).

(d) Passes over an individual or collective screen (Rule 17.7).

18. ATTACK-HIT

18.1 Definition

18.1.1 All actions to direct the ball towards the opponent, except service and block, are considered attack-hits.

During an attack-hit tipping is permitted if the contact is clean, and the ball is not accompanied by the hand.

18.1.2 An attack-hit is completed the moment the ball completely crosses the vertical plane of the net, or is touched by an opponent.

18.2 Front-Row Player's Attack-hit

The front-row player may complete an attack-hit at any height provided that the contact with the ball has been made within the player's own playing space (except Rule 18.4d).

18.3 Restrictions to a Back-Row Player's Attack-hit

18.3.1 A back-row player may complete an attack-hit at any height from behind the front zone. At take-off the player's foot/feet must neither have touched nor crossed over the attack line. After the hit the player may land within the front zone (Rule 1.4.1).

18.3.2 A back-row player may also complete an attack-hit from the front zone, if at the moment of contact any part of the ball is below the top of the net.

18.4 Attack-hit Faults
An attack-hit fault is committed when:
(*a*) A player hits the ball within the playing space of the opposing team.
(*b*) A player hits the ball 'out' (Rule 12.4).
(*c*) A back-row player completes an attack-hit from the front zone, if at the moment of the hit the ball is entirely above the top of the net (Rules 18.1.2 and 18.3.2).
(*d*) A player completes an attack-hit on the opponent's service, when the ball is in the front zone and entirely above the top of the net.

19. BLOCK

19.1 Definition
Blocking is the action of players close to the net to intercept the ball coming from the opponents by reaching higher than the top of the net.
19.1.1 *Block attempt.* A block attempt is the action of blocking without touching the ball.
19.1.2 *Completed block.* A block is completed whenever the ball is touched by a blocker. Only front-row players are permitted to complete a block.
19.1.3 *Collective block.* A collective block is executed by 2 or 3 players close to each other and is completed when one of them touches the ball.

19.2 Block and Team Hits
A block contact is not counted as a team hit (Rule 14.1.1).
19.2.1 After a block contact, a team is entitled to 3 hits to return the ball.
19.2.2 The first hit after the block may be executed by any player, including the one who has touched the ball at the block.

19.3 Blocking within the Opponents' Space
In blocking the player may place hands and arms beyond the net, provided that the action does not interfere with the opponents' play. Thus, it is not permitted to touch the ball beyond the net until the opponent has executed an attack-hit.

19.4 Blocking Contact

19.4.1 Consecutive (quick and continuous) contacts may occur with one or more blockers provided that the contacts are made during one action.

19.4.2 These contacts may occur with any part of the body, above and including the knee.

19.5 Blocking Faults

(*a*) The blocker touches the ball in the opponent's space either before or simultaneously with the opponent's action (Rule 19.3).

(*b*) The ball touches the blocker below the knee (Rule 19.4.2).

(*c*) A back-row player completes a block or participates in a completed one (Rules 19.1.2 and 19.1.3).

(*d*) A player blocks the ball in the opponent's space from outside the antenna.

(*e*) A player blocks the opponent's service.

(*f*) The ball is sent 'out' off the block.

6. INTERRUPTIONS AND DELAYS

20. REGULAR GAME INTERRUPTIONS

20.1 Categories
Regular game interruptions are for *time-outs* and *player substitutions*.

20.2 Number of Regular Interruptions
Each team is entitled to a maximum of 2 time-outs and 6 player substitutions per set.

20.3 Request for Regular Interruptions
Interruptions may be requested only by the coach or the game captain, when the ball is out of play and before the whistle for service, by showing the corresponding hand-signal. A request for substitution before the start of a set is permitted and should be recorded as a regular game interruption in that set.

20.4 Sequence of Interruptions
One or two time-outs and one request for player substitution by either team may follow one another, with no need to resume the game. A team is not authorised to request consecutive interruptions for player substitutions unless the game has been resumed. However, 2 or more players may be substituted during the same interruption (Rule 20.6.2).

20.5 Time-out

20.5.1 A time-out lasts for 30 seconds.

20.5.2 During a time-out, the players in play must go to the free zone near their bench.

20.6 Player Substitution

20.6.1 A substitution shall last only the time needed for recording the substitution on the scoresheet, and allowing the entry and exit of players.

20.6.2 If the coach intends to make more than one substitution, the number must be signalled at the time of the request. In this case, substitutions must be made in succession, one pair of players after another.

20.6.3 At the moment of the request, the player(s) must be ready to enter, standing close to the coach (Rule 6.3.3). If that is not the case, the substitution is not granted and the team is sanctioned for a delay (Rule 21.2).

20.6.4 Substitutions must be carried out in the substitution zone (Rule 1.4.3).

20.7 Improper Requests

Among others, it is improper to request an interruption:

(*a*) During a rally or at the moment of, or after, the whistle to serve (Rule 20.3).

(*b*) By a non-authorised team-member (Rule 20.3).

(*c*) For player substitution before the game has been resumed from a previous substitution by the same team (Rule 20.4).

(*d*) After having exhausted the authorised number of time-outs and player substitutions (Rule 20.2).

Any improper request that does not delay the game shall be rejected without any sanction unless repeated in the same set (Rule 21.1*d*).

21. DELAYS TO THE GAME

21.1 Type of Delay

Any action of a team that defers resumption of the game is a delay and includes:

(*a*) Delaying a substitution.

(*b*) Prolonging other interruptions, after having been instructed to resume the game.

(*c*) Requesting an illegal substitution (Rule 11.2).

(*d*) Repeating an improper request in the same set (Rule 20.7).

(*e*) Delaying the game by a player in play.

21.2 Sanctions for Delays

21.2.1 The first delay by a team in a set is sanctioned with a *delay warning*. The sanction of a delay warning is a team sanction.

21.2.2 The second and subsequent delays of any type by any player or other member of the same team in the same set constitute a fault and are sanctioned with a *delay penalty*: loss of a rally.

22. EXCEPTIONAL GAME INTERRUPTIONS

22.1 Injury

22.1.1 Should a serious accident occur while the ball is in play, the Referee must stop the game immediately. The rally is then replayed.

22.1.2 If an injured player cannot be substituted, legally or exceptionally (Rule 11.3), the player is given a 3-minute recovery time, but not more than once for the same player in the match. If the player does not recover, his team is declared incomplete (Rules 9.2.2 and 7.5.3).

22.2 External Interference

If there is any external interference during the game, play has to be stopped and the rally is replayed.

22.3 Prolonged Interruptions

If unforeseen circumstances interrupt the match, the first referee, the organiser and the control committee, if there is one, shall decide the measures to be taken to re-establish normal conditions.

22.3.1 Should one or several interruptions occur, not exceeding 4 hours in total, then:

(*a*) If the match is resumed on the same playing court, the interrupted set shall continue normally with the same score, players and positions. The sets already played will keep their scores.

(*b*) If the match is resumed on another court, the interrupted set is cancelled and replayed with the same starting line-ups. The sets already played will keep their scores.

22.3.2 Should one or several interruptions occur, exceeding 4 hours in total, the whole match shall be replayed.

23. INTERVALS AND CHANGE OF COURTS

23.1 Intervals

The interval between all sets lasts 3 minutes. During this period of time, the change of courts and line-up registration of the teams on the scoresheet are made.

23.2 Change of Courts

23.2.1 After each set, the teams change courts, with the exception of the deciding set (Rule 8.1.2). Other team members change benches.

23.2.2 In the deciding set once a team reaches 8 points, the teams change courts without delay and the player positions remain the same. If the change is not made at the proper time, it will take place as soon as the error is noticed. The score at the time that the change is made remains the same.

7. MISCONDUCT

24. MISCONDUCT

Incorrect conduct by a team member towards officials, opponents, team-mates or spectators is classified in four categories according to the degree of the offence.

24.1 Categories

24.1.1 Unsportmanlike conduct: arguing, intimidation etc.

24.1.2 Rude conduct: acting contrary to good manners or moral principles, expressing contempt.

24.1.3 Offensive conduct: defamatory or insulting words or gestures.

24.1.4 Aggression: physical attack or intended aggression.

24.2 Sanctions

Depending on the degree of the incorrect conduct, according to the judgement of the first referee, the sanctions to be applied are:

24.2.1 *Misconduct warning*: For unsportsmanlike conduct, no penalty is given but the team member concerned is warned against repetition in the same set. The warning is recorded on the scoresheet.

24.2.2 *Misconduct penalty*: For rude conduct, the team is penalised with the loss of a rally which is recorded on the scoresheet.

24.2.3 *Expulsion*: Repeated rude conduct is sanctioned by expulsion. The team member who is sanctioned with expulsion must leave the playing area, the bench and the warm-up area for the rest of the set. The second expulsion of the same team member is regarded as a disqualification.

24.2.4 *Disqualification*: For offensive conduct and aggression, the player (or any other team member) must leave the playing area, the team bench and the warm-up area for the rest of the match.

24.3 Sanction Scale

The repetition of misconduct by the same person in the same set is sanctioned progressively as shown in the sanction scale below. Disqualification due to offensive conduct or aggression does not require a previous sanction.

Degree of Misconduct	Number of times	Sanction	Cards shown	Consequence
1. Unsportsmanlike Conduct	First	Warning	Yellow	Warning: no penalty
	Second	Penalty	Red	Loss of rally
	Third	Expulsion	Both jointly	Expulsion from the playing area, warm-up area and the team bench for the set
2. Rude Conduct	First	Penalty	Red	Loss of rally
	Second	Expulsion	Both jointly	Expulsion from the playing area, warm-up area and the team bench for the set
3. Offensive conduct	First	Disqualification	Both separately	Expulsion from the playing area, warm-up area and the team bench for the match
4. Aggression				

24.4 Misconduct Before and Between Sets

Any misconduct occurring before or between sets is sanctioned according to Rule 24.2 and sanctions apply in the following set.

Reprinted by permission of the British Volleyball Federation. For reasons of space, Section II, concerning Referees and Official Signals, has been omitted. Copies of the complete Volleyball International Rules may be obtained from the English Volleyball Association.

THE RULES OF

Water Polo

Water Polo

1. Field of Play and Equipment

1.1 The promoting organisation shall be responsible for the correct measurements and markings of the field of play and shall provide all stipulated fixtures and equipment.

1.2 The layout and markings of the field of play for a game officiated by two referees shall be in accordance with the following diagram.

Pools for Water Polo

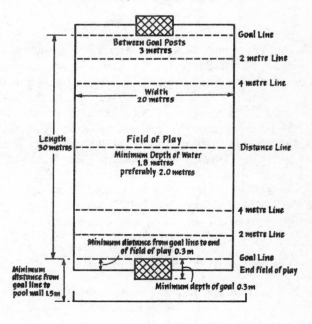

1.3 In a game officiated by one referee, the referee shall officiate on the same side as the official table, and the goal judges shall be situated on the opposite side.

1.4 The distance between the goal lines shall be not less than 20m and not more than 30m. The width of the field of play shall be not less than 10m and not more than 20m. For matches played by women, the maximum dimensions of the field of play shall be 25m in length and 17m in width. The boundary of the field of play at each end shall be 0.30m behind the goal line.

1.5 For FINA events the dimensions of the field of play, water depth and temperature, and light intensity shall be as set forth in FR 7.2, FR 7.3, FR 7.4 and FR 8.3.

1.6 Distinctive marks shall be provided on both sides of the field of play to denote the following:

white marks – goal line and half-distance line.

red marks – 2m from goal lines.

yellow marks – 4m from goal lines

1.7 A red mark shall be placed at each end of the field of play, 2m from the corner of the field of play on the side opposite to the official table, to denote the re-entry area.

1.8 Sufficient space shall be provided to enable the referees to have free movement from end to end of the field of play. Space shall also be provided at the goal lines for the goal judges.

2. Goals

2.1 Two goal posts and a crossbar, rigidly constructed, rectangular with a dimension of 0.075m facing the field of play and painted white shall be located on the goal lines at each end, equal distances from the sides and not less than 0.30m in front of the ends of the field of play.

2.2 The inner sides of the goal posts shall be 3m apart. When the water is 1.50m or more in depth, the underside of the crossbar shall be 0.90m from the water surface. When the water is less than 1.50m in depth, the underside of the crossbar shall be 2.40m from the floor of the pool.

2.3 Limp nets shall be securely fastened to the goal posts and crossbar to enclose the entire goal area and shall be attached to the goal fixtures in such a manner as to allow not less than 0.30m clear space behind the goal line everywhere within the goal area.

3. The Ball

3.1 The ball shall be round and shall have an air chamber with a self closing valve. It shall be waterproof, without external strappings or any covering of grease or similar substance.

3.2 The weight of the ball shall be not less than 400g and not more than 450g.

3.3 For matches played by men, the circumference of the ball shall be not less than 0.68m and not more than 0.71m, and its pressure shall be 90–97 kPa (kilo Pascals) (13–14 pounds per sq in atmospheric).

3.4 For matches played by women, the circumference of the ball shall be not less than 0.65m and not more than 0.67m, and its pressure shall be 83–90 kPa (kilo Pascals) (12–13 pounds per sq in atmospheric).

4. Flags

4.1 The referees shall each be provided with a stick 0.70m in length fitted with a white flag at one end and a flag of a contrasting colour at the other, each flag to be 0.35m × 0.20m.

4.2 The goal judges shall each be provided with separate red and white flags.

4.3 The secretaries shall be provided with separate red, white and blue flags.

4.4 The flags provided for the goal judges and the secretaries shall be 0.35m × 0.20m, on separate sticks 0.50m in length.

5. Caps

5.1 One team shall wear white caps and the other team shall wear caps of a contrasting colour, other than solid red, as approved by the referees, but also to contrast with the colour of the ball. The other team may be required by the referees to wear blue caps. The goalkeepers shall wear red caps. Caps shall be fastened under the chin. If a player loses his cap during play, he shall replace it at the next appropriate stoppage of the game. Caps shall be worn throughout the entire game.

5.2 For Olympic Games, World Championships and other FINA events, caps shall be fitted with malleable ear protectors. It is recommended that caps fitted with ear protectors be used for all other competitions. The ear protectors of a team shall be the same colour provided that the goalkeeper may have red ear protectors.

5.3 Caps shall be numbered on both sides with numbers 0.10m in height. The goalkeeper shall wear cap no. 1 and the other caps shall be numbered 2 to 13. A substitute goalkeeper shall wear the goalkeeper's cap. A player shall not be allowed to change his cap number during the game except with the permission of a referee and with notification to the secretary.

5.4 For international matches, the caps shall display on the front the international three letter country code and may display the international flag. The country code shall not be less than 0.06m in height.

6. Teams

6.1 Each team shall consist of seven players, one of whom shall be the goalkeeper and who shall wear the goalkeeper's cap, and not more than six reserves who may be used as substitutes. A team playing with less than seven players shall not be required to have a goalkeeper.

6.2 All players not in the game at the time, together with the coaches and officials, shall sit on the team bench and shall not move away from the bench from the commencement of play, except during the intervals between periods. Teams shall change ends and benches at half time and at the end of the first period of any extra time. The team benches shall both be situated on the side opposite to the official table.

6.3 The captains shall be playing members of their respective teams and each shall be responsible for the good conduct and discipline of his team.

6.4 Players shall wear non-transparent costumes or costumes with a separate undergarment and before taking part in a game shall remove any articles likely to cause injury.

6.5 Players shall not have grease, oil or any similar substance on the body. If a referee ascertains before the start of play that such a substance has been used, he shall order it to be removed immediately. The start of play shall not be delayed for the substance to be removed. If the offence is detected after the play has started, the offending player shall be excluded from the remainder of the game and a substitute permitted to enter the field of play immediately from the re-entry area nearest to his own goal line.

6.6 Before the start of the game and in the presence of the referees, the captains shall toss a coin, the winner to have the choice of ends.

7. Substitutes

7.1 Except as otherwise provided by the Rules, a player may only be substituted:

(*a*) during the intervals between periods of play, including any periods of extra time; or

(*b*) after a goal has been scored;

when he may enter the field of play from any place.

7.2 A substitute shall be ready to replace a player without delay; if he is not ready the referee may restart the game without him, in which event he may enter from the re-entry area nearest to his own goal lines at the next appropriate stoppage, by permission of a referee.

7.3 A goalkeeper who has been replaced by a substitute may, if he returns to the game, play in any position.

7.4 Should a goalkeeper retire from the game through any medical reason, the referees shall allow an immediate substitute, subject to one of the players taking the goalkeeper's cap.

8. Officials

8.1 For FINA events the officials shall consist of two referees, two goal judges, timekeepers and secretaries, each with the following powers and duties. Such officials shall also be provided wherever possible for other events, except that in a game refereed by two referees and no goal judges, the referees shall assume the powers and duties (but without making the specified flag signals) allocated to the goal judges in 10.2.

Note: Depending on the degree of importance, games can be controlled by teams of four to eight officials, as follows:

(*a*) Referees and goal judges:

Two referees and two goal judges; or two referees and no goal judges; or one referee and two goal judges.

(*b*) Timekeepers and secretaries:

With one timekeeper and one secretary: The timekeeper shall record the periods of continuous possession of the ball by each team, in accordance with 21.17. The secretary shall record the exact periods of actual play and the intervals between periods, and shall also record the respective periods, of exclusion of players ordered from the water in accordance with the Rules. The secretary shall also maintain the record of the game as set out in 12.1.

With two timekeepers and one secretary: Timekeeper No. 1 shall record the exact periods of actual play and the intervals between periods. Timekeeper No. 2 shall record the periods of continuous possession of the ball by each team, in accordance with 21.17. The secretary shall maintain the record of the game as set out in 12.1.

With two timekeepers and two secretaries: Timekeeper No. 1 shall record the exact periods of actual play and the intervals between periods. Timekeeper No. 2 shall record the periods of continuous possession of the ball by each team, in accordance with 21.17. Secretary No. 1 shall maintain the record of the game as set out in 12.1(*a*). Secretary No. 2 shall carry out the duties set out in 12.1(*b*)(*c*) & (*d*) relating to the exclusion of players and the third personal foul.

9. Referees

9.1 The referees shall be in absolute control of the game. Their authority over the players shall be effective during the whole time that they and the players are within the precincts of the pool. All decisions of the referees on questions of fact shall be final and their interpretation of the Rules shall be obeyed throughout the game. The referees shall not make any presumption as to the facts of any situation during the game but shall interpret what they observe to the best of their ability.

9.2 The referees shall whistle to start and restart the game and to declare goals, goal throws, corner throws (whether signalled by the goal judge or not), neutral throws and infringements of the Rules. A referee may alter his decision provided he does so before the ball is put back into play.

9.3 The referees shall refrain from declaring a foul if, in their opinion, such declaration would be an advantage to the offending player's team. The referees shall not declare an ordinary foul when there is still a possibility to play the ball.

Note: The referees shall apply this principle to the fullest extent. They should not, for example, declare an ordinary foul in favour of a player who is in possession of the ball and making progress towards his opponents' goal, because this is considered to give an advantage to the offender's team.

9.4 The referees shall have the power to order any player from the water in accordance with the appropriate Rule and to abandon the game should a player refuse to leave the water when so ordered.

9.5 The referees shall have the power to order the removal from the precincts of the pool any player, substitute, spectator or official whose behaviour prevents the referees from carrying out their duties in a proper and impartial manner.

9.6 The referees shall have power to abandon the game at any time if, in their opinion, the behaviour of the players or spectators, or other circumstances prevent it from being brought to a proper conclusion. If the game has to be abandoned the referees shall report their actions to the competent authority.

10. Goal Judges

10.1 The goal judges shall be situated on the same side as the official table, each on the goal line at the end of the field of play.

10.2 The duties of the goal judges shall be:

(*a*) to signal with the red flag when the players are correctly positioned on their respective goal lines at the start of a period;

(*b*) to signal with the white flag for an improper start or restart;

(*c*) to signal with the white flag for a goal throw;

(*d*) to signal with the red flag for a corner throw;

(*e*) to signal with both flags for a goal;

(*f*) to signal with the red flag for an improper re-entry of an excluded player or improper entry of a substitute.

10.3 Each goal judge shall be provided with a supply of balls and when the original ball has gone outside the field of play, he shall immediately throw a new ball to the goalkeeper (for a goal throw), to the nearest player of the attacking team (for a corner throw), or as otherwise directed by the referee.

11. Timekeepers

11.1 The duties of the timekeepers shall be:

(*a*) to record the exact periods of actual play and the intervals between the periods;

(*b*) to record the periods of continuous possession of the ball by each team;

(*c*) to record the exclusion times of players ordered from the water in accordance with the Rules, together with the re-entry times of such players or their substitutes;

(*d*) to announce the start of the last minute of the game and of the last minute of the second period of any extra time.

11.2 A timekeeper shall signal by whistle (or by any other means provided it is distinctive, acoustically efficient and readily understood), the end of each period independently of the referees and his signal shall take immediate effect except:

(*a*) in the case of the simultaneous award by a referee of a penalty throw, in which event the penalty throw shall be taken in accordance with the Rules;

(*b*) if the ball is in flight and crosses the goal line, in which event any resultant goal shall be allowed.

12. Secretaries

12.1 The duties of the secretaries shall be:

(*a*) to maintain the record of the game, including the players, the score, all exclusion fouls, penalty fouls, and the personal fouls awarded against each player;

(*b*) to control the periods of exclusion of players and to signal the expiration of the period of exclusion by raising the appropriate flag; except that a referee shall signal the re-entry of an excluded player or a substitute when that player's team has retaken possession of the ball;

(*c*) to signal with the red flag and by whistle for any improper re-entry of an excluded player or improper entry of a substitute (including after a flag signal by a goal judge to indicate an improper re-entry or entry), which signal shall stop play immediately;

(*d*) to signal, without delay, the award of a third personal foul against any player as follows:

(i) with the red flag if the third personal foul is an exclusion foul;

(ii) with the red flag and a whistle if the third personal foul is a penalty foul.

13. Duration of the Game

13.1 The duration of the game shall be four periods each of seven minutes actual play. Time shall commence at the start of each period when a player touches the ball. At all signals for stoppages, the recording watch shall be stopped until the ball is put back into play by the ball leaving the hand of the player taking the appropriate throw or when the ball is touched by a player following a neutral throw.

13.2 There shall be a two-minute interval between periods. The teams, including the players, coaches and officials, shall change ends before starting the third period and the second period of any extra time.

13.3 Should the scores be level at full time in any game for which a definite result is required, any continuation into extra time shall be after an interval of five minutes. There shall then be played two periods each of three minutes actual play with an interval of one minute for the teams to change ends. If at the end of the first two periods of extra time, the score is equal, there shall be an interval of one minute. A third period of extra time shall begin and the game shall end when a goal is scored.

13.4 Any visible clock shall show the time in a descending manner (that is, to show the time remaining in a period).

14. The Start of Play

14.1 At the start of each period, the players shall take up positions on their respective goal lines, about 1m apart and at least 1m from the goal posts. Not more than two players shall be allowed between the goal posts. No part of a player's body shall be beyond the goal line at water level.

14.2 When the referees are satisfied that the teams are ready, a referee shall blow the whistle to start and then release or throw the ball into play on the half-distance line.

14.3 If the ball is released or thrown giving one team a definite advantage, the referee shall call for the ball and award a neutral throw on the half-distance line.

15. Method of Scoring

15.1 A goal shall be scored when the entire ball has passed fully over the goal line, between the goal posts and underneath the crossbar.

15.2 A goal may be scored from anywhere within the field of play; except that the goalkeeper shall not be permitted to go or touch the ball beyond the half-distance line.

15.3 A goal may be scored by any part of the body except the clenched fist, provided that at the start or any restart of the game, other than at the taking of a penalty throw, at least two players (of either team but excluding the defending goalkeeper) have intentinally played or touched the ball. A goal may be scored by dribbling the ball into the goal.

A goalkeeper cannot score a goal by shooting after having taken a goal throw unless another player touches the ball intentionally after the goal throw has been taken.

15.4 A goal shall be scored if, at the expiration of 35 seconds possession or at the end of a period, the ball is in flight and enters the goal.

In the circumstances of this Rule, if the ball enters the goal after hitting the goal post, crossbar, goalkeeper or other defending player, and/or bouncing off the water, a goal shall be allowed. If the end of the period has been signalled and the ball is then played or touched intentionally by another attacking player on its way into the goal, the goal shall not be allowed.

If the ball is in flight towards the goal in the circumstances of this Rule and the goalkeeper or another defending player pulls down the goals, or a defending player other than the goalkeeper stops the ball with two hands or arms or punches the ball to prevent a goal being scored, the referee shall award a penalty throw if, in his opinion, the ball would have reached the goal line if the offence had not occurred.

If the ball which is in flight towards the goal in the circumstances of this Rule lands on the water and then floats completely over the goal line, the referee shall award a goal only if the ball floats over the goal line immediately due to the momentum of the shot.

16. Restarting After a Goal

16.1 After a goal has been scored, the players shall take up positions anywhere within their respective halves of the field of play. No part of a player's body shall be beyond the half-distance line at water level. A referee shall restart the game by blowing the whistle. At the time of the restart, actual play shall resume when the ball leaves the hand of a player of the team not having scored the goal. A restart not taken in accordance with this Rule shall be retaken.

17. Goal Throws

17.1 A goal throw shall be awarded:

(*a*) when the entire ball has passed fully over the goal line excluding between the goal posts and underneath the crossbar, having last been played or touched by a player of the attacking team;

(*b*) when the entire ball has passed fully over the goal line between the goal posts and underneath the crossbar or strikes the goal posts, crossbar or the defending goalkeeper direct from a free throw or corner throw, without having been intentionally played or touched by another player.

17.2 The goal throw shall be taken by the defending goalkeeper from anywhere within his 2-m area. If the goalkeeper is out of the water, the goal throw shall be taken by another defending player. A goal throw not taken in accordance with this Rule shall be retaken.

There should be no undue delay in taking a free throw, goal throw or corner throw, which must be taken in such a manner so as to enable the other players to observe the ball leaving the thrower's hand. Players often make the mistake of delaying the throw because they overlook the provisions of 20.4, which permit the thrower to dribble the ball before passing to another player. The throw can thus be taken immediately, even though the thrower cannot at that moment find a player to whom he might pass the ball. On such an occasion, he is allowed to take the throw either by dropping it from a raised hand on to the surface of the water or by throwing it into the air and he can then swim with or dribble the ball. In either case, the throw must be taken so that the other players are able to observe it.

18. Corner Throws

18.1 A corner throw shall be awarded when the entire ball has passed fully over the goal line excluding between the goal posts and underneath the crossbar, having last been played or touched by a player of the defending team.

18.2 The corner throw shall be taken by a player of the attacking team from the 2-m mark on the side nearest to which the ball crossed the goal-line. The throw need not be taken by the nearest player but shall be taken without undue delay.

(For the method of taking a throw, see 17.2.)

18.3 At the taking of a corner throw no players of the attacking team shall be within the 2-m area.

18.4 A corner throw taken from the wrong position or before the players of the attacking team have left the 2-m area shall be retaken.

19. Neutral Throws

19.1 A neutral throw shall be awarded:

(*a*) when, at the start of a period, a referee is of the opinion that the ball has fallen in a position to the definite advantage of one team;

(*b*) when one or more players of each team commit a foul at the same moment which makes it impossible for the referees to distinguish which player offended first;

(*c*) when both referees blow their whistles at the same moment to award ordinary fouls to the opposing teams;

(*d*) when a player of each team commits an exclusion foul simultaneously, whether during actual play or in dead time. The neutral throw is to be taken following the exclusion of the offending players;

(*e*) when the ball strikes or lodges in an overhead obstruction.

19.2 At a neutral throw, a referee shall throw the ball into the water at approximately the same lateral position as the event occurred in such a manner as to allow the players of both teams to have equal opportunity to reach the ball. A neutral throw awarded within the 2-m area shall be taken on the 2-m line.

19.3 If at a neutral throw the referee is of the opinion that the ball has fallen in a position to the definite advantage of one team, he shall call for the ball and retake the throw.

20. Free Throws

20.1 The referee shall blow his whistle to declare fouls and shall display the appropriate flag to indicate the team to which the free throw is awarded.

20.2 The time allowed for a player to take a free throw shall be at the discretion of the referees; it shall be reasonable and without undue delay but does not have to be immediate. It shall be an offence if a player who is clearly in a position most readily to take a free throw does not do so. (For the method of taking the throw, see 17.2.)

20.3 The responsibility for returning the ball to the player who is to take the free throw shall be that of the team to which the free throw is awarded.

20.4 The free throw shall be taken in a manner to enable the players to observe the ball leaving the hand of the player taking the throw, who shall also then be permitted to carry or dribble the ball before passing to another player. The ball shall be in play immediately when it leaves the hand of the player taking the free throw.

20.5 Should the game be stopped through accident, injury, illness, bleeding or other unforeseen reason, the team in possession of the ball at the time of the stoppage shall be awarded a free throw at the point of stoppage when the game is resumed.

20.6 A free throw taken from the wrong position shall be retaken.

21. Ordinary Fouls

21.1 It shall be an ordinary foul to commit any of the offences described in 21.2 to 21.18, which shall be punished by the award of a free throw to the opposing team, to be taken by one of its players from the point where the foul occurred. If the ball is further from the defending team's goal, the free throw shall be taken from the location of the ball. If a foul is committed by a defending player within his 2-m area, the free throw shall be taken on the 2-m line opposite to where the incident took place. (The referees must award ordinary fouls in accordance with the Rules to enable the attacking team to develop an advantage situation. However, the referees must have regard to the special circumstances of 9.3 (Advantage).)

21.2 To advance beyond the goal line at the start of a period, before the referee has given the signal to start.

21.3 To assist a player at the start of a period or at any other time during the game.

21.4 To hold on to or push off from the goal posts or their fixtures, to hold on to or push off from the sides or ends of the pool during actual play or to hold on to the rails except at the start of a period.

21.5 To take any active part in the game when standing on the floor of the pool, to walk when play is in progress or to jump from the floor of the pool to play the ball or tackle an opponent. This Rule shall not apply to the goalkeeper while within his 4-m area.

21.6 To take or hold the entire ball under the water when tackled.

It is an ordinary foul to take or hold the ball under the water when tackled, even if the player holding the ball has his hand forced under the water, with the ball, as a result of the opponent's challenge. It makes no difference that the ball goes under the water against his will. What is important is that the foul is awarded against the player who was in contact with the ball at the moment it was taken under the water. It is important to remember that the offence can only occur when a player takes the ball under when tackled. Thus, if the goalkeeper emerges high out of the water to save a shot and then while falling back takes the ball under the water, he has committed no offence; but if he then holds the ball under the water when challenged by an opponent, he will have committed an infringement of this Rule and if his actions prevented a probable goal, a penalty throw must be awarded under 23.2.

21.7 To strike at the ball with a clenched fist. This Rule shall not apply to the goalkeeper while within his 4-m area.

21.8 To play or touch the ball with two hands at the same time. This Rule shall not apply to the goalkeeper while within his 4-m area.

21.9 To impede or otherwise prevent the free movement of an opponent who is not holding the ball, including swimming on the opponent's shoulders, back or legs. 'Holding' is lifting, carrying or touching the ball but does not include dribbling the ball.

The first thing for the referee to consider is whether the opponent is holding the ball, because if he is doing so, the player making the challenge cannot be penalised for 'impeding'. It is clear that a player is holding the ball if he holds it raised above the water. The player is also holding the ball if he swims with it held in his hand or makes contact with the ball while it is lying on the surface of the water. Swimming with the ball (dribbling) is not considered to be holding.

A common form of impeding is where the player swims across his opponent's legs, thus reducing the pace at which he can move and interfering with his normal leg action. Another form is swimming on the opponent's shoulders. It must also be remembered that the foul of impeding can be committed by the player who is in possession of the ball, because any violent movement by the player in possession of the ball might constitute striking or even brutality. A player may also commit the offence of impeding even if he is not holding or touching the ball.

21.10 To push or push off from an opponent.

Pushing can take place in various forms, including with the hand or with the foot. In those cases, the punishment is a free throw for an ordinary foul. However, referees must take care to differentiate between pushing with the foot and kicking – which then becomes an exclusion foul or even brutality. If the foot is already in contact with the opponent when the movement begins, this will usually be pushing, but if the movement begins before such contact with the opponent is made, then this should generally be regarded as kicking.

21.11 For a player of the team in possession of the ball to commit an offence under 21.9 (to impede an opponent) or 21.10 (to push or push off from an opponent) before a free throw, goal throw or corner throw is taken.

21.12 To be within 2m of the opponent's goal except when behind the line of the ball. It shall not be an offence if a player takes the ball into the 2-m area and passes it to another player who is behind the line of the ball and who shoots at goal immediately, before the first player has been able to leave the 2-m area.

If the player receiving the pass does not shoot at goal, the player who passed the ball must immediately leave the 2-m area to avoid being penalised under this Rule.

21.13 To take a penalty throw other than in the prescribed manner. (See 24.4 for the method of taking a penalty throw.)

21.14 To delay unduly when taking a free throw, goal throw or corner throw. (See 17.2.)

21.15 For a goalkeeper to go or touch the ball beyond the half distance line.

21.16 To waste time.

It is always permissible for a referee to award an ordinary foul under this Rule before the 35 seconds possession period has elapsed.

If the goalkeeper is the only player of his team in his half of the field of play, it shall be deemed wasting time for him to receive the ball from another member of his team who is in the other half of the field of play.

In the last minute, the referees must be certain that there is intentional wasting time before applying this Rule.

21.17 For a team to retain possession of the ball for more than 35 seconds of actual play without shooting at their opponents' goal. The timekeeper recording the possession time shall reset the clock:

(*a*) when the ball has left the hand of the player shooting at goal. If the ball rebounds into play from the goal post, crossbar or the goalkeeper, the possession time shall not recommence until the ball comes into the possession of one of the teams;

(*b*) when the ball comes into the possession of the opposing team. 'Possession' shall not include the ball merely being touched in flight by an opposing player;

(*c*) when the ball is put into play following the award of an exclusion foul, penalty foul, goal throw, corner throw or neutral throw.

Visible clocks shall show the time in a descending manner (that is, to show the possession time remaining).

The timekeeper and referees must decide whether there was a shot at goal or not but the referees shall have the final decision.

21.8 To send the ball out of the field of play, including the ball rebounding from the side of the field of play above water level.

22. Exclusion Fouls

22.1 It shall be an exclusion foul to commit any of the offences outlined in 22.3 to 22.16, which shall be punished (except as otherwise provided by the Rules) by the award of a free throw to the opposing team and the exclusion of the player who committed the foul. The excluded player himself or a substitute shall be permitted to re-enter the field of play from the re-entry area nearest to his own goal line after the earliest occurrence of one of the following:

(*a*) when 20 seconds of actual play have elapsed, at which time the secretary shall raise the appropriate flag provided that the excluded player has reached his re-entry area in accordance with the Rules;

(*b*) when a goal has been scored;

(*c*) when the excluded player's team has retaken possession of the ball (which means receiving control of the ball) during actual play, at which time the defensive referee shall signal re-entry by a wave-in signal by hand (not using the flags);

(*d*) when play is restarted by a player of the excluded player's team after a stoppage, at which time the defensive referee shall signal re-entry by a wave-in signal by hand (not using the flags).

The excluded player shall move to the re-entry area nearest to his own goal line without leaving the water. An excluded player who removes himself from the water (other than following the entry of a substitute) shall be deemed guilty of an offence under 22.10 (Disrespect).

An excluded player (including any player excluded under the Rules for the remainder of the game) shall remain in the water and move (which may include swimming underwater) to the re-entry position on his own goal line without interfering with the play. He may swim from the field of play at any point on the goal line and may swim behind the goal to the re-entry area nearest to his own goal line provided he does not interfere with the alignment of the goal.

On reaching the re-entry area, the excluded player shall be required to rise to the surface of the water before he (or a substitute) shall be permitted to re-enter in accordance with the Rules. However, it shall not be necessary for the excluded player to then remain in the re-entry area to await the arrival of an intended substitute.

A change of possession does not occur merely because of the end of a period, but an excluded player or substitute shall be eligible to re-enter if his team wins the ball at the swim up at the start of the next period. The referees and the secretary should note which team was in possession of the ball at the end of a period if a player is excluded when the end of a period is signalled.

22.2 After the earliest occurrence referred to in 22.1, except when a goal has been scored, the excluded player himself or a substitute shall be permitted to re-enter the field of play from the re-entry area nearest to his own goal line, provided that:

(*a*) he has received a signal for the secretary or a referee;

(*b*) he shall not jump or push off from the side or wall of the pool or field of play;

(*c*) he shall not affect the alignment of the goal;

(*d*) a substitute shall not be permitted to enter in the place of an excluded player until that player has reached the re-entry area nearest to his own goal line.

These provisions shall also apply to the entry of a substitute when the excluded player has received three personal fouls or has otherwise been excluded from the remainder of the game in accordance with the Rules.

A substitute shall not be waved in by a referee and nor shall the secretary signal the expiration of the 20 seconds exclusion period until the excluded player has reached the re-entry area nearest to his own goal line. This shall also apply to the re-entry of a substitute who is to replace a player excluded from the remainder of the game. In the event of the excluded player failing to return to his re-entry area, a substitute shall not be permitted to enter until a goal has been scored or at the end of a period.

The primary responsibility for giving the wave-in signal for the re-entry of an excluded player or a substitute is with the defensive referee. However, the attacking referee may also assist in this regard and the signal of either referee shall be valid. If a referee suspects an improper re-entry or the goal judge signals such an improper re-entry, then he should first satisfy himself that the other referee had not signalled the re-entry.

Before giving the wave-in signal for the re-entry of an excluded player or a substitute, the defensive referee should wait momentarily in case the attacking referee whistles to restore possession to the opponent's team.

22.3 For a player to leave the water or sit or stand on the steps or side of the pool during play, except in the case of accident, injury, illness or with the permission of a referee.

22.4 To interfere with the taking of a free throw, goal throw or corner throw, including:

(*a*) intentionally to throw away or fail to release the ball to prevent the normal progress of the game;

(*b*) any attempt to play the ball before it has left the hand of the thrower.

A player is not to be penalised under the Rule if he does not hear the whistle as a result of being under the water. The referees must determine if the actions of the player are intentional.

Interference with a throw may take place indirectly when the ball is hampered, delayed or prevented from reaching the player who is to take the throw, or it may occur when the execution of the throw is interfered with by an opponent blocking the direction of the throw or by disturbing the actual movement of the thrower. For interference with a penalty throw, see also 22.15.

22.5 To splash in the face of an opponent intentionally.

Splashing is frequently used as an unfair tactic but is often only penalised in the obvious situation when players are facing one another. However, it can also occur less obviously when a player produces a curtain of water with his arm, seemingly without deliberate intent, in an attempt to block the view of the opponent who is about to shoot at goal or to make a pass.

The punishment for intentionally splashing an opponent is exclusion under 22.5 or a penalty throw under 23.2 if the opponent is inside the 4-m area and is attempting to shoot at goal. Whether to award a penalty throw or an exclusion is decided solely by the positioning and actions of the attacking player; whether the offending player is inside the 4-m area or outside is not a decisive factor.

22.6 To hold, sink or pull back an opponent who is not holding the ball. 'Holding' is lifting, carrying or touching the ball, but does not include dribbling the ball.

The correct application of this Rule is very important both as to the presentation of the game and in arriving at a proper and fair result. The wording of the Rule is clear and explicit and can only be interpreted in one way: to hold, sink or pull back an opponent who is not holding the ball is an exclusion foul. It is essential that referees apply this Rule correctly, without personal arbitrary interpretation, to ensure that proper limits to rough play are not exceeded. In addition, referees must note that an infringement of 22.6 within the 4-m area which prevents a probable goal must be punished by the award of a penalty throw.

22.7 To kick or strike an opponent intentionally or make disproportionate movements with that intent.

The offence of kicking or striking can take a number of different forms, including being committed by a player in possession of the ball or by an opposing player; possession of the ball is not a decisive factor. What is important is the action of the offending player, including if he makes disproportionate movements in an attempt to kick or strike, even if he fails to make contact.

One of the most serious acts of striking is elbowing backwards, which can result in serious injury to the opponent. Similarly, serious injury can occur when a player intentionally heads back into the face of an opponent who is marking him closely. In these instances, the referee would also be justified in punishing the offence under 22.9 (Brutality) rather than under 22.7.

22.8 To be guilty of misconduct, including the use of foul language, violent or persistent foul play, and so on. The offending player shall be excluded from the remainder of the game with substitution after the earliest occurrence referred to in 22.1.

Persistent foul play refers to play which is unacceptable within the spirit of the Rules and which is likely to bring the game into disrepute. Persistent foul play is entirely different and unrelated to 'persisting in an ordinary foul'.

22.9 To commit an act of brutality (including kicking or striking or attempting to kick or strike with malicious intent) against an opponent or official, whether during play or the interval between periods of play. The offending player shall be excluded from the remainder of the game and shall not be substituted.

In the last minute of the game, the referees may delay declaring a brutality offence until the next change of possession.

This Rule shall also apply if an act of brutality occurs during the interval between periods, except that the free throw shall not be awarded. The offending player shall be excluded from the remainder of the game, without substitution, and his team shall continue the game with six players only. These provisions shall not apply, however, before the game has actually commenced.

In the case of brutality at any time by a substitute who is not in the water during the play, the offending player shall be excluded from the remainder of the game. The captain shall be ordered to remove from the water a player of his choice and the team shall continue with six players only. The player who has been removed can subsequently be used during the remainder of the game as one of his team's six players in the water and no personal foul shall be awarded in relation to his removal from the water.

22.10 To refuse obedience to or show disrespect for a referee or official. The offending player shall be excluded from the remainder of the game, with substitution after the earliest occurrence referred to in 22.1.

If a member of a team commits an act of disrespect prior to the restart of play after the opposing team has scored a goal or during the interval between periods, he shall be excluded from the remainder of the game and his team shall be permitted to restart the game with seven players.

22.11 For a player of the team not in possession of the ball to commit any of the following offences before a free throw, goal throw, corner throw or penalty throw is taken or for a player of either team to commit any of the following offences before a neutral throw is taken:

21.9 – to impede an opponent

21.10 – to push or push off from an opponent

22.3 to 22.10 – to commit an exclusion foul

The original throw (including any neutral throw) shall be maintained. The player shall be excluded from the remainder of the game where the Rules so provide.

22.12 For a player of each team to commit any of the following offences simultaneously before a free throw, goal throw, corner throw, penalty throw or neutral throw is taken:

21.9 – to impede an opponent

21.10 – to push or push off from an opponent

22.3 to 22.10 – to commit an exclusion foul

Both players shall be excluded and a neutral throw awarded; except that if the offences are committed simultaneously at the taking of the penalty throw, the penalty throw shall be maintained. Players shall be excluded from the remainder of the game where the Rules so provide.

In the circumstances of this Rule, a change of possession is deemed not to have occurred merely because one team gains possession of the ball from the neutral throw. The players excluded under this Rule shall not be permitted to re-enter until the next earliest occurrence referred to in 22.1 following the neutral throw.

However, this only applies to the two players who were excluded simultaneously and any other players who were already excluded shall be permitted to re-enter if the neutral throw results in a change of possession.

If the two players who have been excluded under this Rule are eligible to re-enter before they have reached their respective re-entry areas, the defensive referee may wave in each player as soon as he is ready to re-enter. The referee does not have to wait until both players are ready to re-enter.

22.13 For a player of the team in possession of the ball to commit an offence under 22.3 to 22.10 (exclusion fouls) before a free throw, goal throw, corner throw or penalty throw is taken; except that:

(*a*) the player shall be excluded from the remainder of the game where the Rules so provide;

(*b*) if the offence is committed at the taking of a penalty throw, the penalty throw shall be maintained.

22.14 For an excluded player to re-enter or a substitute to enter the field of play improperly, including:

(*a*) without having received a signal from the secretary or a referee;

(*b*) from any place other than his own re-entry area, except where the Rules provide for immediate substitution;

(*c*) by jumping or pushing off from the side or wall of the pool or field of play;

(*d*) by affecting the alignment of the goal.

If this offence occurs in the last minute of the game, the last minute of the second period of any extra time, or at any time during a third period of extra time, the offending player shall be excluded from the remainder of the game, without substitution, and a penalty throw awarded to the opposing team.

It shall be an improper re-entry if an excluded player re-enters or a substitute enters without having received the referee's wave-in signal, even if the referee should have given the wave-in signal earlier.

22.15 To interfere with the taking of a penalty throw. The offending player shall be excluded from the remainder of the game with substitution after the earliest occurrence referred to in 22.1 and the penalty throw shall be maintained or retaken as appropriate.

The most common form of interference with a penalty throw is when an opponent aims a kick at the player taking the throw, just as the throw is about to be taken. It is essential for the referees to ensure that all players are at least 2m from the thrower, to prevent such interference from taking place. The referee should also allow the defending team the first right to take position in accordance with 24.2.

22.16 For the defending goalkeeper to fail to take up his correct position on the goal line at the taking of a penalty throw after having been ordered once to do so by the referee. Another defending player may take the position of the goalkeeper but without his privileges and limitations.

22.17 When a player of each team commits an exclusion foul or a penalty foul simultaneously during actual play, both players shall be excluded and a neutral throw awarded. (See also 22.12.)

22.18 When a player is excluded, the exclusion period shall commence immediately when the ball has left the hand of the player taking the free throw or when the ball has been touched following a neutral throw.

22.19 If an excluded player intentionally interferes with play, including affecting the alignment of the goal, a penalty throw shall be awarded to the opposing team and a further personal foul awarded against the excluded player. If an excluded player does not commence leaving the field of play almost immediately, the referee may deem this to be intentional interference under this Rule.

22.20 In the event of the game continuing into extra time, the exclusion period of any excluded player shall also continue into the extra time. Personal fouls awarded during the periods of normal time shall also carry forward into extra time and any player excluded under the Rules from the remainder of the game shall not be permitted to take part in any periods of extra time.

23. Penalty Fouls

23.1 It shall be a penalty foul to commit any of the following offences (23.2 to 23.8), which shall be punished by the award of a penalty throw to the opposing team.

23.2 For a defending player to commit any foul within the 4-metre area but for which a goal would probably have resulted.

In addition to the other offences preventing a probable goal, it is an offence within the meaning of this Rule:

(*a*) for a goalkeeper or other defending player to pull down or otherwise displace the goal;

(*b*) for a defending player to play the ball with two hands;

(*c*) for a defending player to play the ball with a clenched fist;

(*d*) for a goalkeeper or other defending player to take the ball under the water when tackled.

It is important to note that while the fouls described above, and other fouls such as holding, pulling back, impeding, and so on, would normally be punished by a free throw (and exclusion if appropriate), they become penalty fouls if committed within the 4-m area by a defending player if a probable goal would otherwise have been scored.

23.3 For a defending player within the 4-m area to kick or strike an opponent or to commit an act of brutality. In the case of brutality, the offending player shall also be excluded from the remainder of the game, without substitution, in addition to the award of the penalty throw.

23.4 For an excluded player intentionally to interfere with play, including affecting the alignment of the goal.

23.5 For a goalkeeper or any other defending player to pull over the goal completely with the object of preventing a probable goal. The offending player shall also be excluded from the remainder of the game, with substitution after the earliest occurrence referred to in 22.1.

23.6 For an excluded player to re-enter or a substitute to enter the field of play improperly prior to or at the expiration of an exclusion period with the object of preventing a goal. The offending player shall also leave the field of play to complete any of the original exclusion period remaining, if appropriate.

In the circumstances of this Rule, if the attacking team is in a position to shoot at goal, the referee shall wait to see if a goal is scored before stopping the play. If a goal is scored, the penalty throw is not awarded, but a personal foul is recorded against the offending player. If a goal is not scored, then the referee shall then immediately award a penalty throw in accordance with this Rule.

23.7 For an excluded player to re-enter or a substitute to enter the field of play improperly during the last minute of the game, the last minute of the second period of any extra time or at any time during a third period of extra time. The offending player shall also be excluded from the remainder of the game, without substitution.

23.8 For a player or a substitute who is not entitled under the Rules to participate in the play at the time to enter the field of play. The offending player shall also be excluded from the remainder of the game with substitution, where appropriate, after the earliest occurrence referred to in 22.1. This Rule shall not apply to an excluded player who re-enters or a substitute who enters the field of play before the earliest occurrence referred to in 22.1.

If an excluded player and a substitute both enter after the earliest occurrence referred to in 22.1, whichever player entered last shall be the player to be penalised under this Rule. If both players enter simultaneously, it shall be the substitute who is to be penalised.

24. Penalty Throws

24.1 A penalty throw shall be taken by any player of the team to which it is awarded, except the goalkeeper, from any point on the opponents' 4-m line.

24.2 All players shall leave the 4m area and shall be at least 2m from the player taking the throw. On each side of the player taking the throw, one player of the defending team shall have the first right to take position. The defending goalkeeper shall be positioned between the goal posts with no part of his body beyond the goal line at water level. Should the goalkeeper be out of the water, another player may take the position of the goalkeeper but without his privileges and limitations.

24.3 When the referee controlling the taking of the throw is satisfied that the players are in their correct postions he shall signal for the throw to be taken, by whistle and by simultaneously lowering the flags from a vertical to a horizontal position.

The lowering of the flag at the same time as the signal by whistle makes it possible under any conditions, even amidst noise by spectators, to execute the throw in accordance with the Rules. As the flag is lifted, the player taking the throw will concentrate, for he knows that the signal will follow immediately.

24.4 The player taking the penalty throw shall have possession of the ball and shall immediately throw it with an uninterrupted movement directly at the goal. The player may take the throw by lifting the ball from the water or with the ball held in the raised hand and the ball may be taken backwards from the direction of the goal in preparation for the forward throw, provided that the continuity of the movement shall not be interrupted before the ball leaves the thrower's hand.

There is nothing in the Rules to prevent a player taking the throw with his back to the goal while he adopts a half screw or full screw action.

24.5 If the ball rebounds from the goal post, crossbar or goalkeeper it remains in play and it shall not be necessary for another player to play or touch the ball before a goal can be scored.

24.6 If at precisely the same time as the referee awards a penalty throw the timekeeper whistles for the end of a period, all players except the player taking the throw and the defending goalkeeper shall leave the water before the penalty throw is taken. In this situation, the ball shall immediately be dead should it rebound into play from the goal post, crossbar or the goalkeeper.

25. Personal Fouls

25.1 A personal foul shall be recorded against any player who commits an exclusion foul or penalty foul. The referee shall indicate the offending player's cap number to the secretary.

25.2 Upon receiving a third personal foul, a player shall be excluded from the remainder of the game with substitution after the earliest occurrence referred to in 22.1. If the third personal foul is a penalty foul, the entry of the substitute shall be immediate.

26. Accident, Injury and Illness

26.1 A player shall only be allowed to leave the water, or sit or stand on the steps or side of the pool during play in the case of accident, injury, illness or with the permission of a referee. A player who has left the water legitimately may re-enter from the re-entry area nearest to his own goal line at an appropriate stoppage, with the permission of a referee.

26.2 If a player is bleeding, the referee shall immediately order the player out of the water with the immediate entry of a substitute and the game shall continue without interruption After the bleeding has stopped, the player is permitted to be a substitute in the ordinary course of the game.

26.3 If accident, injury or illness, other than bleeding, occurs, a referee may at his discretion suspend the game for not more than three minutes, in which case he shall instruct the timekeeper as to when the stoppage period is to commence.

26.4 If a player leaves the game through any medical reason including cramp, the referees shall allow the immediate entry of a substitute. Except in the circumstances of 26.2, the player shall not be allowed to take further part in the game if a substitute has entered. In the circumstances of this Rule, the substitute shall be permitted to enter from any point outside the field of play.

Appendix A – Instructions for the Use of Two Referees

1. The referees are in absolute control of the game and shall have equal powers to declare fouls and penalties. Differences of opinion of the referees shall not serve as a basis for protest or appeal.

2. The committee or organisation appointing the referees shall have power to designate the side of the pool from which each referee shall officiate.

3. At the start of the game and of each period, the starting signal shall be given by the referee on the same side as the official table.

4. After a goal, the signal to restart shall be given by the referee who was controlling the attacking situation when the goal was scored.

5. Each referee shall have the power to declare fouls in any part of the field of play but each referee shall give his primary attention to the offensive situation attacking the goal to his right. The referee not controlling the attacking situation (the defensive referee) shall maintain a position no closer to the goal being attacked than that player of the attacking team furthest back from the goal.

6. When awarding a free throw, goal throw or corner throw, the referee making the decision shall blow his whistle and both referees shall display the appropriate flag, to enable players in different parts of the pool to see quickly which team has been awarded the throw. If necessary to avoid doubt, the referee making the decision shall point to where the throw is to be taken.

7. The signal for a penalty throw to be taken shall be made by the attacking referee, except that a player who wishes to take the throw with his left hand may request the defensive referee to make the signal.

8. When simultaneous free throws are awarded by both referees to the same team, the award shall go to the player awarded the throw by the attacking referee.

9. When simultaneous awards are made for ordinary fouls but for opposing teams, the award shall be a neutral throw, to be taken by the attacking referee.

10. When one referee awards an exclusion foul and at the same moment the other referee awards a penalty foul but for opposing teams, both the offending players shall be excluded and a neutral throw awarded.

11. When simultaneous awards are made by both referees and one is for an ordinary foul and the other is for an exclusion foul or penalty foul, the exclusion foul or penalty foul award shall be applied.

12. In the event of simultaneous awards of penalty throws to both teams, the first throw shall be taken by the team last in possession of the ball. After the second penalty has been taken, the game shall be restarted with a neutral throw on the half-distance line.

Facilities
1. The water temperatures shall not be less than 26°± 1°C.
2. The light intensity shall not be less than 600 lux.

Age-Group Rules
1. All age-group competitors remain qualified from 1 January to the following 31 December at their age at the close of day (12 midnight) on 31 December of the year of competition.
2. Age-groupings are as follows:
    15 years of age and under
    16 and 17 years of age
    18, 19 and 20 years of age
The age for Junior World Championships is 20 years and under.

Reprinted by permission of the Amateur Swimming Association. Copies of the ASA Water Polo Referees' Handbook, incorporating the Rules of Water Polo with Appendixes and Notes, may be obtained from the ASA.

*To the
memory of
Berta Fantl*

Preface

While a major objective of this book is to survey current developments relevant to treatment approaches for the poor,[1] certain underlying themes guide the selection of articles:[2]

1. The effects of social class on mental health are uneven and complex. We are suspect of viewpoints that see a one-to-one relationship between class position and mental illness. Thus, we question the Hollingshead and Redlich conclusion that "a distinct inverse relationship does exist between social class and mental illness."[3]

2. Analysis of the poor is best directed through appraisal of various subgroupings rather than the disadvantaged as a whole, or any common denominator therof. Hence, we will be concerned with differences between the so-called lower class (largely unskilled laborers whose employment is more irregular) and the working class (semiskilled and skilled workers whose employment is more stable). Other typological breakdowns will also be considered. Unfortunately, however, many of the selections that of necessity have been included, do not explicitly make these distinctions. It is therefore suggested that the reader keep subgroupings of the poor constantly in mind.

3. Treatment approaches for the poor should be based not only on more service, but on more appropriate service. Basic revisions of traditional forms of psychotherapy are needed in order for psychotherapy to be maximally effective with the poor. We question the widely prevalent notion that psychotherapy is not the treatment of choice for blue collar people. This idea seems rooted in a very static, middle class centered view of therapy. The failure of psychotherapy with low income groups may be in large measure due to the insistence on a particular model of treatment, namely the psychodynamic, insight and reconstructive oriented approach.

vii

4. Low income groups may have considerably more potential for the basic aspects of psychotherapy than has hitherto been recognized. Characteristics of the poor that make them inappropriate for psychotherapy have been overemphasized to the exclusion of positive indications.

5. Much of social psychiatry, while indirectly associated with issues relevant to the disadvantaged, would profit from a more direct conscious orientation toward the poor and a concomitant class-focused technology.

6. The effectiveness of psychotherapy with the poor is contingent upon a far less detached therapeutic operation—one in which treatment agents are much more closely integrated with other institutions, such as the community, the world of work, and the church. This is particularly relevant in the rehabilitation of the delinquent (see Part IV) but is also applicable to the sociotherapeutic approaches discussed in Part III.

The new community directed plans, arising from the late President Kennedy's Mental Health-Retardation Centers Act, promise a tremendous break-through in the treatment of blue collar workers and low income people. The heart of the law calls for federal matching grants to the states for the construction of community mental health centers. The major decision now is what to put into these buildings; in other words, what adaptations and modifications of traditional treatment are needed in order to put content into the new forms. That is the goal toward which this book is directed.

Notes

1. Throughout we use the terms "poor," "disadvantaged," "deprived," "low income," "lower socioeconomic" interchangeably to refer in the main to the urban poor.

2. One additional factor has had an influence on the selection of materials: Articles published in other readers have for the most part been omitted so that as much fresh material as possible could be included.

3. A. B. Hollingshead and Frederich C. Redlich, *Social Class and Mental Illness* (New York, John Wiley & Sons, 1958), 217.

Acknowledgments

We should like to acknowledge the assistance and contributions of the following:

Roxane Cohen, Margaret Pearl, and Catherine Riessman for special assistance in the preparation of the manuscript;

Seymour Bellin, Maurice Connery, Irwin Deutscher, Kenneth Kindelsperger, S. M. Miller, Ned Polsky, Robert Reiff, Sylvia Scribner, Patricia Sexton, for their contributions to formulations found throughout the book;

The Victor Rabinowitz Foundation for its grant to the Blue Collar Project which provided valuable assistance to Frank Riessman in the preparation of the material for this book.

For typing the manuscript: Madelyn Anglin, Ray Antoine, Josephine Oravetz, Kay Tobey.

Contents

TREATMENT IN THE COMMUNITY

THE DRUG ADDICT

Part 1

Poverty,
Mental Illness,
and Treatment

Introduction

In the past decade the social and behavioral sciences have accumulated considerable research data displaying one of the serious paradoxes of our generation. While we are becoming increasingly aware of the mental health problems of the lower socioeconomic segments of our society, we have also recognized and documented the inadequacy of the mental health services available to them. The lack of knowledge and skill necessary to engage the poor in treatment further adds to their continually increasing dilemma. The low income person is bombarded with pleas and advice from the mass media, the schools, and the professional community to seek help with family and individual emotional problems. But he finds, after making a difficult decision to use such services, long waiting lists or costs for private care beyond his means. This, in addition to the requirements of agency bureaucratic organization, and aspects of the treatment process itself, leads to early withdrawal even after the patient's energies have been mobilized to do something about the problem. The purpose of this book is to bring together new psychotherapeutic, social, and casework approaches, techniques, and goals appropriate for low income and blue collar workers.

Anyone studying the problem of mental health in America must be impressed with the limitations in coverage and achievement of orthodox treatment. Traditional approaches do not seem to meet the problem of care for great numbers of people. The

3

investigations of Miller and Swanson have led them to the conclusion that:

> the increasing number of blue-collar workers who are seeking help for their personal problems has made it obvious that traditional goals and methods must be modified. In clinics which serve patients in both social classes, a disproportionate number of blue-collar workers drop out of therapy very early because of dissatisfaction with the therapeutic procedure. It is important that psychotherapists learn more about the characteristics of manual laborers and about conditions under which these people mature . . . our results indicate the desirability of exploring a variety of new psychotherapeutic techniques, particularly those in which words and concepts are subordinated to non-verbal and even motoric activity.[1]

Freud recognized that psychoanalytic therapy would have to be altered if it were to reach the multitude of people in need of help.

> . . . one may reasonably expect that at some time or other the conscience of the community will awake and admonish it that the poor man has just as much right to help for his mind as he now has for the surgeon's means for saving his life; . . . . The task will then arise for us to adapt our techniques to the new conditions. I have no doubt that the validity of our psychological assumptions will impress the uneducated too, but we shall need to find the simplest and most natural expressions for our theoretical doctrines. We shall probably discover that the poor are even less ready to part with their neuroses than the rich, because the hard life that awaits them when they recover has no attraction, and illness in them gives them more claim to help of others. Possibly, we may often be able to achieve something if we combine aid to the mind with material support.[2]

The articles chosen for the first section address themselves to a variety of issues concerning the study, diagnosis, and treatment of mental disorders among the lower two-thirds of our socio-economic strata. The extent and variety of the problems to be faced in the understanding of this heterogeneous group are not underestimated. There is no attempt to bring harmony to the scientific arena by choosing authors who are in complete agreement with one another. Evidence, criticism, and countercriticism are the ingredients that make up this initial statement of the problem.

The conditions of poverty in America and the implications of these conditions for the social services are pungently reviewed by S. M. Miller in a survey of recent literature documenting the existence of widespread poverty in the United States. He brings together the work of Harrington, Keyserling, Kolko, Lampman,

and Morgan, and further documents the nature and extent of the problem we face in meeting the mental health needs of the poor. He is concerned about the tendency to deal with the poor as if they were a homogeneous group, requiring uniform measures, and offers some suggestions regarding the variation that does exist and its implications for action.

Social Class and Mental Illness:
A Complex Relationship

Hollingshead and Redlich's basic conclusion that the "lower the socioeconomic class the higher the rate of mental illness" is seriously questioned by Miller and Mishler in their expository review of the New Haven study, *Social Class and Mental Illness*. The Miller and Mishler review provides a remarkably succinct summary of the problem and a significant re-evaluation of some of the main findings.

Miller and Mishler, in reinterpreting the data presented in the Hollingshead and Redlich report, demonstrate that a clear-cut continuum between social class and mental illness is lacking. They note great dissimilarity in classes IV and V, roughly equivalent to the lower and working classes with class IV actually showing the lowest incidence of mental disorder in comparison to all the class groupings—middle and upper included.

One of their more serious criticisms concerns the use of prevalence data in such a way that by implication it purports to answer questions beyond its scope.[3] Miller and Mishler aptly point out that one cannot conclude from prevalence data that the rate of morbidity varies by social class, or by any other characteristic. Prevalence rates (all the active cases discovered during a given interval of time) are affected by a number of factors that are particularly misleading in the understanding of the relationship between social class and mental disorders. For example, a higher rate of mental disorder among one segment of the population being studied might mean that this group had less access to the treatment resources available. In this case, a large number of untreated mental disorders would be accumulated over a period of time. It might also be that the particular kind of treatment offered is congenial and effective for only part of the population, again causing an uncommonly high morbidity rate in the remainder of the

population. What Miller and Mishler found adequately documented in the New Haven study is that differential treatment is accorded those suffering from mental disease by virtue of their social class position.

A summary table [4] from the second volume of the Midtown Study, by Langner, reports a definite inverse relationship between social class and mental illness. This conclusion is consistently supported by practically all of the data reported in the two volumes.[5]

The results of the Midtown Manhattan Study are of particular interest and value inasmuch as they are concerned with a large scale study of an *untreated* general population. While Ernest Gruenberg[6] raises some questions about the sample, particularly in terms of the exclusion of transient members of the population, he generally applauds the attempt to study a population not actively in treatment or institutionalized. He is, however, concerned about the fact that age standardization techniques were not used, inasmuch as age is known to be an extremely important variable connected with the rates of mental disease. He is critical of the use of the concept of "lifetime prevalence," which refers to the proportion of the population studied that had at any time displayed any of the symptoms being counted. He feels that retrospective data of this kind is highly unreliable. Gruenberg, like Miller and Mishler, views the research he reviewed as an important contribution but hopes that future studies will correct some of the errors.

It is important that such reviews be widely read by consumers of research. Final conclusions are often considered and remembered without taking into account the way in which the data was originally accumulated. Further, we may wonder about the growing tendency to be satisfied with correlation as a basis for cause and effect relationship. Perhaps we need more longitudinal studies related to the process of disease to enrich and clarify the findings of the cross-sectional investigations such as those of Midtown and New Haven. Moreover, highly structured interviews and large survey studies need to be complemented by the more laborious and difficult depth interviews necessary for understanding the context of responses. We are in danger of assuming that the poor are a completely homogeneous group requiring similar treatment for similar problems. Evidence to the contrary is growing. The poor, like others in our society, require help based upon an understanding of their specific needs. This is not to say that we cannot generalize but rather that we must be careful not to stereotype.

The research of Pasamanick, *et al.*, is of particular importance in highlighting the complexities of the relationship of mental disorder and social status. Unlike Hollingshead and Redlich, and Langner, who see a more direct lineal relationship between class and mental illness, Pasamanick views these variables as related in an uneven and highly complex manner. His research is of importance also in noting Negro-white differences, Negroes having decidedly lower rates of psychosis, psychoneuroses, and psychophysiological disorders.[7] This is of particular interest because his investigation was based on a noninstitutionalized population where a direct "clinical evaluation" of a subsample was made by psychiatrists (in contrast to the Midtown Study, where the evaluating psychiatrist never saw the subjects).

Kleiner and Parker [8] provide an excellent review of the recent literature on the relationship between status and mental disorder. They direct our attention to the conflicting data reported in many of the studies and attempt to relate these to the different methodologies that were used. They state: "the relationship between status and mental disorder is by no means a simple one and may be complicated by varying definitions of mental disorder, different case-finding methods, and the nature of the class system in the community being studied." However, their extensive investigation enabled them to locate at least one consistent relationship. They find a larger discrepancy between achievement and aspiration in populations with known psychopathology than is found in a "normal" control group. The social striving inherent in an upwardly mobile orientation would seem to be a crucial factor in poor mental health.

Kornhauser attempts to locate another class relevant dimension that may be related to mental health. His article points to the mental health hazards inherent in the occupational tasks of lower socioeconomic groups. He raises the question of whether mass production factory work is itself a mental health hazard. Are factory jobs peculiarly monotonous, frustrating, deadening, and hated? Or do persons with poor mental health find their way to factory jobs? Controlling for several background factors, such as education and early symptoms of emotional discomfort, he found a lower index of mental health among unskilled workers in an industrial plant than among skilled workers in the same plant. Kornhauser directs our attention to the potentially noxious influences inherent in the occupational tasks of the unskilled worker.

Miller and Swanson move from the gross recognition of differential mental health to a finer evaluation of the specific mechanisms most frequently used by the working and middle class strata of our society.

We were influenced primarily by the evidence of unequal proportions of certain personality disorders in the two social classes. Such disorders also reveal differences in the expression of aggression. In middle class disturbances, such as depression and obsession, anger is expressed by tortuous indirection. The depressive suffers from internal torment, but is predominantly passive in his reaction to other people. Obsessional neurosis is expressed by ritual, but almost never by physical attack. In contrast, pathologies like conversion hysteria and catatonic schizophrenia, which are common among working class patients, often impel direct expression of aggressive needs. The hysteric may have fits during which he unconsciously follows his first impulse; the aggressive catatonic may even become homicidal. Other characteristics of the disorders most common in the two socio-economic groups suggest differences in conceptual and motoric style. Patients with middle class disorders try to solve their problems conceptually. The oppressive ruminates; he may worry that he has not performed his ritual of checking the records in his office in just the right way, or he may fear that he has unintentionally offended a friend. In his brooding, he tries to recall all the events which led to the imagined offense so he can do something to straighten things out. The depressive is similarly preoccupied. He feels bowed down by the weight of his guilt; he constantly reviews his past sins; he wonders how he could have been so evil; he wishes he could undo some of his impulses or acts. Quite a different picture is conveyed by the disorders that are most prevalent among members of the working class. Disturbances in the functions of the voluntary muscles are fairly common. In hysteria the muscular disorder can often be traced to an early experience which created a fear of sexuality or aggression. Because of the fear, the hysteric represses his sexual needs. He may implement the repression by unconsciously distorting some sensory or muscular function that is usually under voluntary control. If his trunk is paralyzed, for example, he cannot make love. Sometimes the symptom expresses the need symbolically. If a limb is rigid, it may unconsciously symbolize tumescence. Catatonic schizophrenics, who also tend to come from the working class, resolve some of their conflicts about aggression by immobilizing in rigid position certain sets of muscles that might be used to express the forbidden need.[9]

Social Class and Treatment

Kingsley Davis, in a classic article first published in 1938,[10] analyzed the class bias in the basic conceptions of mental health

held by practitioners and theorists in the mental health field. The article abounds with evidence demonstrating the value bias of middle class ideology in the assumed "scientific" description of mental health characteristics. A recent article by Gursslin, *et al.,* using the Davis theme, provides a content analysis of recent mental health literature concerning the total population and purporting to describe the characteristics of mental health. The authors point to differences in the approach of middle class and "lower class" people to such things as problem solving, the cult of adjustment and conformity, the value of work, control of emotions, planning ahead, and community participation. This study not only brings the Davis position up to date by demonstrating the continuation of class bias in mental health formulations, it also points to the "social control" dangers inherent in its continuation through the expansion of mass media communication in the United States.

The research findings of Brill and Storrow, and of Overall and Aronson are examples of the growing evidence of the inadequacies of present psychotherapeutic methods in meeting the needs of the low income group. Consistently, one finds the greatest number of unplanned terminations in psychiatric clinics among the low income group. Brill and Storrow suggest that the crucial issue for psychiatrists and psychiatric clinics is the tendency to restrict treatment to one modality, psychotherapy. They point to the relative neglect of physical therapies and environmental modification in psychiatric clinics throughout the nation. Overall and Aronson document the specific differences in expectation between lower socioeconomic patients and their therapists. Highlighted in the results is the extent to which this group of patients relies on physical modalities of diagnosis and treatment.

Concluding Part I, Harry C. Bredemeier presents a clear view of the relationship between those who need services and those who attempt to provide them. Using the marketplace (exchange theory) as a paradigm for his analysis, he develops the position that social services are not organized and developed to meet the needs of the socially handicapped consumer. While many professionals may disagree with Bredemeier's point of view, he at least has a position that is stated with unusual clarity and substance. However, more important than consensus or its absence are the salient and piercing questions that are raised by his analysis. Among these are vital questions relating to service delivery and therapeutic efficiency.

The problem has been presented in its various forms. The

paucity of services for the poor, the inadequacies of present psychotherapeutic approaches for them, and the great difficulties in knowing and understanding how the conditions of life for different social
class positions affect the development of mental disease are the
factors that have generated this book of readings.

Notes

1. D. R. Miller and G. E. Swanson, *Inner Conflict and Defense* (New York: Holt, Rinehart & Winston, 1960) 397.

2. S. Freud, *Collected Papers,* Vol. II (London: Hogarth Press and the Institute of Psychoanalysis, 1950), 400–402.

3. The distinction between "prevalence" and "incidence" is extremely important. Prevalence refers to the total number of active cases in the population during some specified time; incidence refers to the occurrence of new cases during some specified time.

4. Thomas Langner, *Life Stress and Mental Health* (New York: The Free Press of Glencoe, 1963), 466–67.

5. An earlier report by Rennie and Srole on psychosomatic conditions in Midtown, indicates much more complex relationships between socioeconomic status and these disorders. Some disorders, such as colitis, hives, rashes, and hay fever, are more frequent in the high strata; others, like asthma and bladder trouble, are least prevalent in the middle range and most prevalent in the high and low status groups; heart ailments are most frequent in the middle range and least frequent at the two ex-

tremes; arthritis and hypertension are more prevalent in the lower strata. See Thomas Rennie and Leo Srole, "Social Class Prevalence and Distribution of Psychosomatic Conditions in an Urban Population," *Psychosomatic Medicine,* 18:6, 1956, 449–57.

6. Ernest Gruenberg, Review of *Mental Health in the Metropolis: The Midtown Manhattan Study,* Vol. I, in *Milbank Fund Quarterly,* XLI: 1 (Jan., 1963), 77–94.

7. Elsewhere Pasamanick offers some interesting hypotheses regarding these findings. See Benjamin Pasamanick, "Some Misconceptions Concerning Differences in the Racial Prevalence of Mental Disease," *American Journal of Orthopsychiatry* (Jan., 1963), 72–86.

8. R. J. Kleiner and S. Parker, "Goal Striving, Social Status, and Mental Disorder: A Research Review, *American Sociological Review,* 28:2 (April, 1963) 189–203.

9. Miller and Swanson, *Inner Conflict, op. cit.,* 309–11.

10. Kingsley Davis, "Mental Hygiene and the Class Structure," *Psychiatry,* I (1938), 55–56.

Social Class and Mental Illness:
A Complex Relationship

Poverty and Inequality in America: Implications for the Social Services

S. M. Miller

In the last months there has been a rediscovery of poverty in the United States which has upset some comforting myths. The expansion of gross national product and the misreading of Galbraith to believe that he was describing America as the affluent society rather than predicting possibilities have led to an easy complacency that the poor were few in number and declining through the "natural" operation of the economy. It was believed that we were living in an "income revolution" that not only was rapidly eliminating poverty but reducing inequalities of income and wealth as well. This panglossian picture has been battered by a number of recent books which have underlined the extent of poverty in the United States, the recent slowness of its elimination, the growing inequality in income and wealth and the corrosive character of poverty in a generally-high income society.[1]

Discussions of poverty are sometimes unclear because it is not recognized that poverty can be measured from two viewpoints: (1) Standard approach—an income level is specified as a poverty line and those below this level are considered poor; (2) Relative approach—a specified percentage of the population (say 20 per cent) are thought of as poor and one is concerned about changes in their conditions relative to that of other groups in society, for these changes reflect trends in equality. Most of the studies of poverty utilize the first principle. Obviously, one can argue about where the poverty line should be for different size and

Reprinted by permission of Child Welfare League of America from, *Child Welfare*, Vol. 42, No. 9, November 1963, 442–45.

types of consuming units. The surprising thing about the recent studies of poverty is that they have a fair degree of agreement in placing the poor at between 20 per cent and 25 per cent of the total United States population. If the poverty line is raised—and Harrington and Keyserling believe it to be too low by current American Standards—then more would be considered poor.

Harrington's book prevents us from looking at poverty as a "genteel" condition in which people are just somewhat worse off than we in the main society of relative high income and affluence. He feelingly etches what it means to be poor—the toll, the frustration. One cannot leave the book with the feeling that even a smaller poor can be ignored. His message is for a rich society to have a poor is a disgrace.

Morgan's conclusion is that this disgrace can be overcome with comparatively little funds in an economy that produces annually over 500 billions of goods and services: ten billion dollars a year would lift all families above the poverty line. Poverty has never before been so financially easy to eliminate.

Inequality is, however, another matter. Kolko and Lampman's works indicate that inequality is not now declining in the United States. Since 1949, Lampman's data show, the concentration of wealth in the hands of the upper one per cent has grown. The proportion of income going to the bottom 20 per cent of society is less today, Kolko charges, than it was in 1910. The upper 10 per cent, relative to other economic groupings, are not doing as well as in 1910, for it is the middle-income groups that have advanced the most from the expansion of the economy. As Herman Miller pointed out in a memorable article in the *New York Times* in 1962 ("Are We Closing the Income Gap? No.") the incomes of Negroes are no longer improving relative to that of whites. Although the general level of Negroes' incomes has been advancing, the income of whites has moved up at least as rapidly. The data assembled by Keyserling and Herman Miller suggest that there was a real improvement in the income position of low-income groups during World War II, but since then the economy has not drastically improved the conditions of the low-income population.

While Galbraith pointed out that our poor was a minority of the population unlike the majority poor of India and that we had the best-dressed poor in the history of the world, he under-played the possibility that the relative effects of poverty—relative deprivation—grows when a poor are a special part of the population. The Cloward-Ohlin theory of juvenile delinquency (see their *Delinquency and Opportunity: A Theory of Delinquent Gangs*) is based in part on this recognition of relative frustration. Material on revolutions indicates that a population is most likely to act not when its position is the worst in absolute terms but when conditions are improving but not as rapidly as they now are expected to. As the poor expect more—even though they may have more than the poor of other lands or they themselves had at an earlier point— then they feel most keenly their deprivation. Obviously, this analysis is pertinent to the current Negro Revolution.

The American poor are an extremely varied group. The Morgan and Keyserling data indicate that about 60 per cent live outside central cities and their suburbs; over a quarter, on the other hand, are in the central cities. Two-thirds of the heads of poor families are in the labor force, one-third are not. While 60 per cent of all Negroes are poor, most poor (80 per cent) are white. Only 10 per cent of the poor are people customarily employed who are now unemployed; about 25 per cent of the poor are in families headed by individuals over sixty-five. Poverty is concentrated, for almost 50 per cent of the poor live in the South.

A surprising finding of the Morgan study is that only one-fifth of the poor receive welfare aid. But one-tenth of all Americans have been "on welfare" at some time in their lives. The inadequacy of social security (27 per cent of the poor are in families headed by aged individuals) and welfare payments indicates the significance of public policy in permitting the existence of poverty.

Other causes of poverty lie in the great changes taking place in the American economy. Rural areas are producing the majority of the new poor, many of whom migrate to large cities. These cities not only already contain large numbers of poor (about one-third of their populations) but have no economic function to provide for the newly arriving poor. The changes in technology and in American industry are transforming American communities. Some industries are declining which means the end of many one-industry towns. Old plants are being closed down further aggravating the problems of many communities.

Skill and educational requirements of industries are increasing—whether industry really needs the level of skills it demands is not the issue; the important fact is that industry thinks it does or believes that it can get such labor. The effect is to make obsolete old skills, unemploying many workers as the demand for industrial labor declines. New labor is employable only if it is high skilled or educated; consequently, the low educated, especially the young, are more disadvantaged in relation to the economic system today than similarly low educated were a generation or two ago. The Second Industrial Revolution as presently conducted is destroying the economic potential of vast segments of the American population. Increasingly, formal schooling—not necessarily the ability to perform certain tasks—is the credential required for entry into the main economic system.

What are the implications of these findings for professionals dealing with the poor and their families:

1) Insufficient attention has been paid to the poor in America. Richard Cloward has written of social work's increasing disengagement from the poor. Other professions have never engaged or insufficiently engaged themselves with the plight of the poor. Each profession and social service has to confront itself with the issue of how much existing practice is aimed at dealing with the problems of the poor as they presently exist in the United States.

2) The "Welfare State" is a slogan rather than a reality. As Harrington has pointed out for the United States and Richard Titmuss for

Great Britain, the extension of welfare services in the "semi-affluent society" has not primarily benefited those at the bottom of the economic ladder. The upper working class and especially the middle classes have primarily gained from the extension of social services.

3) The varied character of the poor suggest that differential policies have to be carried out to deal effectively with particular segments of the poor. No one measure will be effective with all poor. For example, "heating up the economy" so that more jobs will be generated will not benefit those of the poor who are unable to work whether for physical or familial reasons (e.g., female head of households). On the other hand, the needed improvement in social services will not basically solve the problems of unemployment of distressed areas, even though it might alleviate them.

4) Consequently, it becomes especially important to clarify today the goals of professionals and the social services. If many of the poor are likely to be a permanent poor, what kind of programs will be most effective in ameliorating their conditions? On the other hand, those of the poor who can be helped to improve their conditions—who have some economic potential—need the kind of help which is aimed at their potential.

We do not have a coordinated and well-aimed set of policies to deal with the extent and character of poverty today. We are not dealing with the poverty of the 1930's nor the poverty of the turn of the century where all immigrant groups could be helped to "Americanize" with the facile goal in mind of rapidly working their way up the occupational ladder.

The goals of various social services have to be re-directed to meet the changed conditions of the Sixties. Many poor will be permanently poor as will be their children; other poor may escape into the main economy. Are the strategies and tactics of social services differentiated enough and suitable to deal with the varied kinds of poor with their different prospects and conditions?

5) Services aimed at individual treatment are not enough. Professionals and their organizations have to support and encourage action which will deal with the larger American scene where poverty is being produced and maintained. The professional role cannot end with the limited services that it can provide but must extend to pressure for the social changes which will make individualized professional services more meaningful and effective. Concentrating on the individualized services without concern for the forces outside the profession which are molding and limiting possibilities is adopting professional blinders. These blinders may promote confidence in one's expertise and effectiveness but ignore the barriers to deep and continuing change among the clientele.

6) Case-work services have to be flexible, adaptive, and ranging over a variety of activities. Are services predicated on the likelihood in the near future that the number of female-based families will not decrease and that most of them are permanently without a male figure?

Have we developed unmechanical "functional equivalents" which provide the kinds of experiences and feelings which a father might give to his children? And are we certain what these "experiences and feelings" are? In the effort to address such questions, case-work services must be remolded to deal more effectively with the pressing and continuing problems of today.

7) Is there adequate understanding of the styles of life of low-income groups? Are the programs of professional action based on and oriented to these styles of life or are the professional strategies and tactics extensions of what is believed to be important for middle-class individuals?

8) *Education is the escape-route from poverty.* Many services to families, consequently, should be more directly oriented to improving the educational chances and performances of the youth and, perhaps, the adults in low-income families. In this connection, it is important to recognize that many low-income families, especially Negro families, have a very high regard for education. Nonetheless, many children of these families are early school leavers. Among other reasons, this is due to parents' lack of ability to translate their general strong interest in education into effective support of the children in school and the inability (and frequent indifference) of schools to capitalize on the particular emphasis on education in many low-income families.

Public and private agencies dealing with the low income might seek to orient and concentrate their services on enhancing the educational prospects of low-income youth rather than having a less specific and less efficient emphasis on a "general improvement" in family and individual functioning.

9) This example of education underlines the importance of stressing the positive elements in low-income life. (For one of the few attempts to pursue this emphasis, see Frank Riessman, *The Culturally Deprived Child.*) In contrast to Harrington's portrait of a "culture of poverty" of apathy, indifference, and withdrawal, the professional must seek out the signs of strength and possibilities and accentuate them.

Notes

1. Leon Keyserling *et al.*, "The Keyserling Report," Conference on Economic Progress, "Poverty and Deprivation in the United States," Washington, 1961; Michael Harrington, *The Other America: Poverty in the United States* (New York: The Macmillan Company, 1962); Gabriel Kolko, *Wealth and Power in the United States* (New York: Frederick A. Praeger, 1962); Robert J. Lampman, *The Share of Top Wealth-Holders in National Wealth* (Princeton: Princeton University Press, 1962); James N. Morgan *et al.*, *Income and Welfare in the United States* (New York: McGraw-Hill and Company, 1962).

Social Class, Mental Illness, and American Psychiatry: [1] An Expository Review [2]

S. M. Miller and Elliot G. Mishler

This book may well have a marked effect upon the future practice of psychiatry. It reports the results of a major investigation by a sociologist-psychiatrist team of the relationships between social class and the appearance and treatment of mental illness. Fragmentary findings had been made available before (twenty-five articles have appeared over the last five years), but a great deal of important material is presented here for the first time and the authors have expanded their forthright interpretations of the study's implications for the treatment of the mentally ill.

The excitement of a pioneering study arises from the freshness of its point of view and the provocativeness of its findings. It poses new questions and places old ones in a new light. This quality of exciting discovery is present in the important and sometimes startling findings of this study. We can give some indication of the significance of the book by quoting the three major hypotheses which are the central concerns of the investigation: "(I) The prevalence of treated mental illness is related significantly to an individual's position in the class structure. (II) The types of diagnosed psychiatric disorders are connected significantly to the class structure. (III) The kind of psychiatric treatment administered by psychiatrists is associated with the patient's position in the class structure."

A major problem of such ground-breaking investigations is that the core discovery overwhelms both authors and readers alike by the

Reprinted from *Milbank Memorial Fund Quarterly*, Vol. 37, No. 2, April 1959, pp. 174–199.

brute fact of its existence. In the first wave of response there is often a neglect of fundamental questions concerning the approach, the methodology, and the interpretations placed upon the data. The chapter summaries tend to enter without qualifications into the folklore of the discipline.

The potential importance of this book for theory, research, and practice in the mental illness field is too great to permit such neglect.

I. Exposition of Findings

A. THE SOCIAL CLASS STRUCTURE

The basic data on social class composition are derived from interviews with respondents in a 5 per cent sample of all households in the metropolitan area of New Haven, Connecticut, which had a total population of about 236,940 persons. The New Haven population is divided into five social classes arranged in a hierarchal order. The family's class position is determined by the score of the head of the family on a weighted "Index of Social Position" that is derived from three separate scales measuring the social rank of his (a) area of residence; (b) occupation; and (c) education. The weights used in the formula for computing the summary index and the cutting points used to distinguish between classes were decided on specifically for this study and are not extrapolation from theory or other research. Roughly, occupation receives almost as much weight as the other two scores combined.

Class I, or the *upper class*, constitutes about 3 per cent of the population. It is composed of both "old" and "new" families who live in the most exclusive residential areas; the family head is a college graduate who is either an executive of a large firm or a professional. Class II, the *upper middle class*, is 8.4 per cent of the population and is made up occupationally of the managerial and professional groups. In Class III, the *lower middle class*, who make up 20.4 per cent of the population, about half are in salaried white collar work and the remainder either own small businesses, are semi-professionals, foremen, or skilled workers.

Class IV, the *working class*, is the largest group and accounts for half the households (49.8 per cent). Half of the group is semi-skilled workers, a third is skilled, and about a tenth is white collar employees. The overall educational level is much lower than in the class above it.

The *lower class*, Class V, which is 18.4 per cent of the population of New Haven, is made up of unskilled and semi-skilled workers of low education.

A rich and detailed description is provided of the historical background of the social class structure and of certain cultural characteristics of each of the classes such as their religious, family, ethnic, and leisure time patterns.

B. THE PREVALENCE OF PERSONS
IN PSYCHIATRIC TREATMENT

A "Psychiatric Census" was carried out in which an attempt was made to enumerate all persons from the New Haven metropolitan area who were "in treatment with a psychiatrist or under the care of a psychiatric clinic or mental hospital between May 31 and December 1, 1950."

The procedure here was remarkably thorough: systematic inquiries were made of relevant facilities and practitioners in New England and New York City and to special facilities further afield. The investigators' persistence brought response from every hospital and clinic contact and from 70 per cent of the private practitioners. In all, they believe that they may have missed only about 2 per cent of the community's residents who were receiving treatment. A total of 1,891 cases was enumerated on whom there was sufficient data for analysis. The data thus only permit discussion of *treated* mental illness, not of the total amount of mental illness in the community. To study the latter, a different type of research design with a psychiatric interview or some similar device of a cross-section of the community would be necessary. Thus, in the Hollingshead-Redlich study, there would have had to have been a psychiatric study of all of the individuals included in the 5 per cent sample of New Haven to enable statements to be made about "true" incidence and prevalence.

The major finding—one of the study's core discoveries—is of a systematic relationship between social class and the treated prevalence of mental illness. As can be seen in Table A, classes I through IV are somewhat underrepresented in the patient population, while Class V,

Table A—Class Status and the Distribution of Patients and Nonpatients in the Population

	POPULATION, PER CENT	
Class	Patients	Nonpatients
I	1.0	3.0
II	7.0	8.4
III	13.7	20.4
IV	40.1	49.8
V	38.2	18.4
	n = 1891	236,940

$$x^2 = 509.81, 4df, p < .001$$

Source: Hollingshead, A. B., and Redlich, F. C.: *Social Class and Mental Illiness*, Table 8, p. 199.

to which 38 per cent of the patient group are assigned by their scores on the Index of Social Position, is greatly overrepresented with twice as many patients as might be expected on the basis of their number in the community. Significant differences are also found in a comparison of

treated prevalence rates per 100,000 population (computed so as to adjust for age and sex differences among the classes) which are distributed as shown in Table B.

Table B—Class Status and Rate of (Treated) Psychosis per 100,000 Population (Age and Sex Adjusted)

Class	Adjusted Rate Per 100,000
I–II	523
III	528
IV	665
V	1,668
Total Population	808

Source: Text Table, p. 210.

In a more detailed analysis, Hollingshead and Redlich divide the patient group into specific diagnostic categories. A first glance reveals that the differences among the classes in treated prevalence rates are much greater for psychoses than for neuroses. The proportions of patients diagnosed as psychotic increase as one moves from Class I–II through Class V and conversely the proportions diagnosed as neurotic decrease (this reversal of the first relationship is automatic inasmuch as the two general categories make up the whole of the patient group). However, since this is a tempting finding to cite, it is important to point out that the authors discount its general importance and attribute it as possibly arising from the "differential use of psychiatric facilities by the population."

There are interesting differences among the social classes in regard to the specific neurotic disturbance which is modal among those who are in treatment: In Classes I and II the modal disturbance is character neuroses; in III and V, anti-social and immaturity reactions; while phobic-anxiety reactions are frequent in Class IV. Each of the above accounts for about one-third of the neurotic patients in each class as can be seen in Table C.

Table C—Percentage of Patients in Each Diagnostic Category of (Treated) Neurosis—by Class (Age and Sex Adjusted)

Diagnostic Category of Neurosis	Class			
	I–II	III	IV	V
Antisocial and Immaturity Reactions	21	32	23	37
Phobic-Anxiety Reactions	16	18	30	16
Character Neuroses	36	23	13	16
Depressive Reactions	12	12	10	8
Psychosomatic Reactions	7	9	13	11
Obsessive-Compulsive Reactions	7	5	5	0
Hysterical Reactions	1	1	6	12
	n = 98	119	182	65

$x^2 = 53.62$, df 18, $p < .001$

Source: Table 13, p. 226.

With regard to specific types of psychoses, much less variation in their percentage importance is found than is the case with the neuroses, as Table D reveals. In particular, for some of the major categories, differences are essentially non-existent—schizophrenia is the predominant

Table D—Percentage of Patients in Each Diagnostic Category of (Treated) Psychosis—by Class (Age and Sex Adjusted)

Diagnostic Category of Psychosis	Class			
	I–II	III	IV	V
Affective Psychoses	21	14	14	7
Psychoses Resulting from Alcoholism and Drug Addiction	8	10	4	8
Organic Psychoses	5	8	9	16
Schizophrenic Psychoses	55	57	61	58
Senile Psychoses	11	11	12	11
n =	53	142	584	672

$$x^2 = 48.23, \text{ df } 12, p < .001$$

Source: Table 14, p. 228.

psychotic disorder in all classes and the proportions of all psychotics who are schizophrenic run from a low of 55 per cent in Class I to 61 per cent in Class IV. This finding is striking since earlier studies have reported a much higher rate of schizophrenia in Class IV and V neighborhoods than in other neighborhoods. Little variation exists among the classes in diagnoses of senile psychoses (11 or 12 per cent in each). Class V is disproportionately low in the affective psychoses with 7 per cent, and the other classes give figures of 14 or 21 per cent. Organic psychoses are highest in Class V (16 per cent) and lowest in Class I (5 per cent), and Class IV with 4 per cent has half the rate of the other classes for psychoses resulting from alcoholism and drug addiction.

The treated prevalence rates for all of the separate neuroses (except hysterical reactions) show statistically significant differences among the classes. However, there is no ordering from a higher to a lower

Table E—Class Status and the Rate of Different Types of (Treated) Psychoses per 100,000 of Population (Age and Sex Adjusted)

Type of Disorder	Class			
	I–II	III	IV	V
Affective Psychoses *	40	41	68	105
Psychoses Due to Alcoholism and Drug Addiction †	15	29	32	116
Organic Psychoses ‡	9	24	46	254
Schizophrenic Psychoses §	111	168	300	895
Senile Psychoses ¶	21	32	60	175
n =	53	142	585	672

* $x^2 = 17.49$, 3df, p .001
† $x^2 = 77.14$, 3df, p .001
‡ $x^2 = 231.87$, 3df, p .001
§ $x^2 = 452.68$, 3df, p .001
¶ $x^2 = 88.36$, 3df, p .001

Source: Table 15, p. 232.

class that is consistent from one diagnostic category to another. The pattern of each neurosis with class must be examined and interpreted separately, as the authors do. Table E on the rates of persons in psychiatric treatment for different types of psychoses by class is the clearest demonstration in the book of an ordered inverse relationship of the type of disorder under treatment and social class. Although the curves for each disorder (affective, organic, schizophrenic, etc.) vary, in *every* case there is an increase in the rates as one moves from Class I–II to Class III, to Class IV, to Class V.

C. THE INCIDENCE OF MENTAL ILLNESS

One of the most important tools of epidemiological research and analysis is the distinction between *incidence,* i.e., the occurrence of new cases during some time, and *prevalence,* i.e., the total number of active cases in the population during some specified time. Although incidence is one of the components in a total prevalence picture, there is no systematic relation between the two since cases may be active currently that first appeared at any point in the past. In other words, as is generally known, prevalence rates do not directly reflect incidence rates since the former are dependent on rates of recovery and mortality from illness as well as on the occurring of illness.

All the figures reported above, and those in previous articles based on the study are for the prevalence of being in treatment. The most important new material in the volume is the presentation of incidence data for the psychiatric sample. It was derived by separating-out patients who entered or re-entered treatment during the interval of observation from those who had been in treatment at the beginning of the interval. It should be emphasized again that both incidence and prevalence rates refer to individuals *in treatment,* rather than to individuals with a mental disorder whether or not they are in treatment. Consequently, the appropriate definition of incidence data for this investigation might be the numbers or rate of those first coming into treatment and prevalence might be stated as the numbers or rate of those in treatment during the study period.

The rates of coming into treatment for all kinds of mental illness are reported in Table F.

Table F—Class Status and Rate of Incidence of (Treated) Neurosis and Psychosis per 100,000 Population (Age and Sex Adjusted)

Class	Rate
I–II	97
III	114
IV	89
V	139
Total	104

$$x^2 = 8.41, 3df, p < .05$$

Source: Text Table, p. 212.

The table shows that the overall differences remain statistically significant but the differentials are markedly reduced in comparison with the prevalence rates. Class IV now has the lowest rate. The authors summarize by stating: "Classes I and II contribute almost exactly the number of new cases (incidence) as could be expected on the basis of their proportion of the community's population. Class IV had a lower number than could be expected proportionately, whereas Class V had an excess of 36 per cent" (p. 215). In further analyses, Hollingshead and Redlich demonstrate that there is *no* significant statistical difference among the classes in the rate at which persons come under treatment for neuroses and show that the sharpest break in this rate for psychoses as a whole and for schizophrenia (both cases where the overall differences among classes are statistically significant) occurs between the rates for Classes I through IV (pp. 235–6). (We shall return at a later point to these important findings regarding incidence.)

The data on incidence and prevalence reveal that Classes IV and V comprise two-thirds of the community (68.2 per cent) and provide more than three-fourths (78.3 per cent) of the mental patients. Thus, due to the size of these two classes, the high psychotic incidence rates in Class V, and the long duration of illnesses in both classes, *psychiatry —whether or not it is aware of it—is largely concerned with Class IV and V patients.* Of course, private practitioners have few Class IV and V patients, but our calculations of the Hollingshead-Redlich data show that these two sources of treatment work with only 21 per cent of all New Haven mental patients.

D. PATHS TO TREATMENT

In an excellent discussion of the paths to psychiatric treatment, the authors make explicit their fundamental orientation that mental illness is a socio-cultural phenomenon as well as a psychological one. Thus, they state ". . . abnormal acts can be evaluated only in terms of their cultural and psychosocial contexts," and "Whether abnormal behavior is judged to be disturbed, delinquent, or merely idiosyncratic depends upon who sees it and how he appraises what he sees."

The sources of referral for treatment, i.e., the agencies or persons who decide that the behavior is that "type" of abnormality for which psychiatric treatment is appropriate, vary systematically by social class. Among neurotics, 55 to 60 per cent of those in Classes I through IV are likely to have been referred by physicians (almost entirely by private practitioners in the first three classes, and about half the time in Class IV by clinic physicians). The proportion of neurotic cases coming from medical referrals drops to 40 per cent in Class V; an equivalent proportion is referred by social agencies; with an additional 14 per cent directed to treatment by the police and courts (p. 186).

The differences are even more striking among psychotics where one-third of the patients in Class I were self-referrals and another 40

per cent came through family and friends. More than three-fifths of the Class III and IV patients were referred by physicians. For Class IV psychotics the police and courts are important, accounting for 19 per cent of the cases, and in Class V these two sources account for 52 per cent while social agencies contribute 20 per cent. The findings for schizophrenia are similar to those for psychosis in general (pp. 187–189).

The brief case reports that are presented to illustrate the different treatment consequences that follow on the same behavior when exhibited by persons of different classes should be required reading in all psychiatric residency programs. The authors note that "there is a definite tendency to induce disturbed persons in Classes I and II to see a psychiatrist in more gentle and 'insightful' ways than is the practice in Class IV and especially in Class V, where direct, authoritative, compulsory, and at times, coercively brutal methods are used."

And, their bitter, concluding epigram to this section is uncomfortably appropriate to their findings: "The goddess of justice may be blind, but she smells differences, and particularly class differences."

E. PATTERNS OF TREATMENT

At the end of their chapter on the Treatment Process, Hollingshead and Redlich state that "the data presented lead to the conclusion that treatment for mental illness depends not only on medical and psychological considerations, but also on powerful social variables to which psychiatrists have so far given little attention," and that "We have found real differences in *where, how, and how long* persons in the several classes have been cared for by psychiatrists."

These conclusions are based on a large number of detailed analyses of relations among diagnosis, treatment agency, treatment, and social class. We shall cite only a few of the most decisive findings.

First, the patient group as a whole divides into three relatively equal parts according to the principal type of therapy received: psychotherapies, organic therapies, or custodial care. Eighty-four per cent of the psychotic group is in treatment in a state mental hospital; 64 per cent of the neurotics are in the hands of private practitioners, and another 23 per cent are being treated in clinics.[3]

Despite the stress placed on diagnosis in psychiatric theory and practice, there is no overall relationship for neurotic patients between type of treatment and the specific diagnostic label attached to the patient. However, treatment is related directly to both social class and the agency in which the patient is treated. Even where treatment is received from the same facility, which is the most stringent test since it eliminates the selective bias that is present in the differential access to and choice of facilities by the different classes, there is a marked relationship between social class and type of treatment. For example, over 85 per cent of the Class IV and V neurotics in treatment with private practitioners receive "directive psychotherapy," while 45 per

cent of Class I and II private patients receive "psychoanalysis or analytic psychotherapy." Consistent with this is the inverse relationship between social class and the likelihood of receiving the traditional "50 minute hour." (Ninety-four per cent in Classes I and II, 45 per cent in Class V; Tables 28 and 29, pp. 268–70).

A similar relationship between the "depth" and duration of the therapy and social class is also found in clinics, and there is additional evidence in a separate study of one clinic that the "patient's class status determines the professional level of the therapist who treats him." Public hospitals appear to be more democratic in their assignment of treatment to neurotic patients, inasmuch as there is no overall relationship between social class and treatment in these institutions.

The findings with regard to class bias in the type of treatment given to psychotic patients and to schizophrenics are less clear and less consistent than for the neurotic group. On the other hand, the relations of class to the duration and history of treatment are very significant and very revealing. For example, as one moves down the class ladder, the likelihood for schizophrenics of having been in continuous treatment increases, while moving in the other direction there is an increased likelihood of periods of remission and re-entry into treatment. In other words, once he enters treatment the Class V schizophrenic is likely to be kept under psychiatric care (Table 38, p. 295). Further, for psychotics there is a direct increase from Class I to Class V in the time duration of their present course of treatment; while for a neurotic this relationship is reversed. In other words, while the lower class neurotic is dismissed from treatment much more quickly than patients from higher classes, the lower class psychotic is rarely perceived as "ready" to leave treatment.

In comparing patients of Classes III–V who have been admitted to the hospital for the first time with patients of the same classes who have been hospitalized previously, a striking finding emerges: The new patient is more likely to receive custodial care than the longer time patient! The implication is that patients of these classes are not given custodial care because of the failure of other methods but are somewhat routinely assigned to this very limited care. In Class V, for example, 64 per cent of the patients who are receiving custodial care had not had any previous treatment.

No discussion of treatment is complete that omits mention of expenditures and fees. The chapter dealing with this material contains more detailed comparative information than is available in any other source. One of the most salient findings is that the mean cost per day in private hospitals is higher for Class IV patients than for patients in the higher classes ($31.11 to $23.76 for a Class I person). This result which is contrary to expectation results from the discriminatory discounts granted higher status persons. Further, the higher status persons receive the most expensive therapies which leads the authors to state: "To use a metaphor, private hospitals are designed for the 'carriage trade' but they are supported by the 'shock box.' " A similar relationship

is found in clinics where treatment expenditures per patient are strongly related to class status, with the result that "Class II patients receive the most therapy and Class V patients the least." This finding is particularly disturbing since the clinics have presumably been developed to serve the psychiatric needs of lower status persons.

F. RECOMMENDATIONS

In a thoughtful and interpretive summary of the implications of their findings for the problem of the mentally ill in our society, Hollingshead and Redlich point to the gap between the extent of the need and the resources currently available to meet it. While they give proper emphasis to the financial problem (what America needs is a "good five-dollar psychotherapist"), they also point to the difficulties that result from the differences in cultural values and role expectations between psychiatrists and patients from the lower social classes. They note that psychiatrists tend to come from the upper and middle classes and have outlooks which lead many of them to dislike Class IV and V patients and to disapprove of the behavior patterns of Class V individuals.

More than money will be needed. Among the possible partial solutions to the problems that they suggest are proposals that psychiatrists themselves be trained to recognize and deal squarely with the differences between themselves and patients from other classes; that new forms and modes of therapy be developed to reach the "difficult" patient (whose difficulty seems to reflect the difference between his and his therapist's class positions more than his psychological disturbance); and, that new non-medical therapists, whose education would be less expensive than psychiatrists', be trained to treat the emotional disorders which do not have medical problems associated with them.

II. Discussion of Findings

This detailed and complex study touches on a large number of important issues concerning the social context of mental illness and its treatment. It represents a distinct step forward in a number of ways.

Three features of the study are especially notable: (a) The presentation of incidence figures as well as prevalence data is strongly to be commended. (b) The method of estimating the social class of patients and the community, despite the limitations indicated below, is an improvement over those employed in previous studies which tended to assume that all who lived in a particular area or paid a similar rent were in the same class. (c) Social class is linked to many more facets of mental illness than just the rate and kind of mental illnesses; in particular, the link of class to the treatment process is innovational.

In our discussion we have restricted ourselves to and organized our comments around three topics that are critical for the study: the concepts of social class and mental illness; the validation of the basic hypotheses; and, the implications of the study for psychiatric treatment.

A. CONCEPTS OF SOCIAL CLASS
AND MENTAL ILLNESS

Among sociologists, there is a variety of approaches to the problem of social stratification. Hollingshead and Redlich view the different classes as different primarily in their "styles of life" and use their combined scores on education, occupation, and residence as rough indices of these five different sub-cultures rather than as variables that are important in their own right.

In a study that directs explicit attention to the problems of getting "to" treatment and getting something "out of" treatment, the use of a combined index is unfortunate since it precludes analyses that might help to clarify what is involved in these processes. For example, it would have been of particular interest to be able to examine the relationships of education to the prevalence and treatment data in order to determine if an increase in education is associated with an increase in the propensity to view one's problems in psychological terms and therefore to benefit from psychological modes of treatment. Such a possibility is suggested by results in recent surveys of attitudes toward mental illness.[4] Enough evidence also exists to indicate that educational differences among individuals of the same occupational level are associated with differences in other characteristics, such as attitudes on public issues, so as to make the possibility of such crossbreaks especially desirable.[5]

In the Hollingshead system, some wage-earners are Class IV, others III or V, while white-collar workers are either III or IV. The class groupings thus become overlaps of various kinds, reducing their homogeneity, confusing comparisons and making generalizations difficult. An anomaly is that 18 per cent of New Haven was assigned to Class V in a time of prosperity. This figure seems high even with New Haven's migrant labor situation and may be due to a conceptualization of Class V which leads to a broad category characterized by widely varying behavior; for example, regular but unskilled workmen are lumped together with irregular but semi-skilled workmen.

Occupation scores correlate .88 with the original criterion on which the weighted index was based, and correlate less highly than this with residence and education (.50 and .72 respectively, p. 394). From this, it would appear that little would have been lost if occupation alone were used as the index of social class. On the other hand, much might have been gained by this procedure since, in addition to permitting potentially revealing analyses, it would have reduced the heterogeneity of the social class groups allowing for more precise interpretations of

the results. (If the data for occupation, education, and area of residence have been separately recorded by the researchers, it would be a comparatively simple procedure to see what variations by education exist within levels of occupations as classified, for example, by the Bureau of the Census. Such additional "runs" of the data would extend their usefulness, especially by permitting comparisons with other investigations.)

The importance of the study's findings, and our confidence in them, rests in large part on the fundamental assumption that the two basic variables of social class and mental illness have been measured independently of each other—if not, then the found relationships must be viewed skeptically as possibly spurious. This seems an easy enough accumption to accept. However, the findings in a recent study [6] raise serious doubts as to its validity. In this exceptionally well-controlled study, Haase is able to demonstrate that the same set of presenting symptoms is diagnosed as more severe when the patient is perceived by subtle cues to be a working class person than when he is seen as in the middle class. In the Hollingshead-Redlich study, despite the safeguards, this bias might be reflected in such findings as the relatively higher rates of psychoses as compared to neuroses when one moves down the populations coming into treatment as well as the prevalence rates of persons in treatment for the different classes. One such study, of course, is insufficient grounds for rejecting the findings presented here. The issue, however, is of such crucial importance that the final acceptance of the findings must rest on further investigations of the relationship of class to the diagnostic process itself.

B. THE VALIDATION OF HYPOTHESES

Compared to most investigations of complicated areas in social science, this book is a model of clarity with regard to the presentation of its guiding hypotheses and the procedures by which these hypotheses were tested empirically. The assumptions behind each decision in the development of the research design are stated explicitly and the basic instruments are described with sufficient detail so as to permit other researchers to replicate the study with exactitude.

This report is organized around three hypotheses that were formulated explicitly and tested directly. (Findings on two other hypotheses dealing with social mobility and the relation of class to developmental factors in psychiatric disorders will be reported in the companion volume by J. K. Myers and B. H. Roberts, *Family and Class Dynamics in Mental Illness*, New York, John Wiley & Sons, 1959.) Briefly, the hypotheses, which we have quoted earlier, state that the social class structure is related to the treated prevalence of mental illness, the specific types of diagnosed psychiatric disorders, and the types of treatment administered by psychiatrists to patients. The authors conclude that their findings confirm these hypotheses, and we have re-

ported the relevant findings in our expository section above. At this point, we shall re-examine their interpretations of some of the critical tables.

One of the major faults in the authors' approach to their findings is found in the first direct comparison that they present between the proportions of patients and the proportions of persons in the community in each of the five social classes (see Table A). Only *one* class, Class V, has disproportionately more patients than its frequency in the population, and *all* the other classes have less patients than would be expected. (If the data in this table are re-computed with the omission of Class V, the Chi Square test—the statistic used to evaluate all of the major findings—remains statistically significant but is markedly reduced in size, and the disproportionate contribution of Class IV is only 4 per cent more than expected, and of Class III, 3 per cent less than expected.)

While at various points they note that the major difference is between Classes IV and V, they include in their summary of this table the statement that "The lower the class, the greater proportion of patients in the population." The same interpretive tendency is found in their discussion of class differences on adjusted rates of mental illness (p. 210) where they ignore the fact that the Class III rate is actually *lower* than the rate in Class I–II. Again, in commenting on the class differences in incidence rates, they state (p. 212) "In a word, class status is linked to the incidence of treated mental illness." (The rates are shown in Table F.) A re-computation of these data, omitting Class V, reveals Class III and *not* Class IV as having a higher than expected number of patients.

Basing their remarks on the data we have just reviewed, Hollingshead and Redlich conclude their chapter by stating

> . . . enable us to conclude that Hypothesis I is true. Stated in different terms, a distinct inverse relationship does exist between social class and mental illness. The linkage . . . follows a characteristic pattern; Class V, almost invariably, contributes many more patients than its proportion of the population warrants. Among the higher classes there is a more proportionate relationship. . . . (p. 217).

What we are attempting to point out by this close review of their data is that the authors' tendency to report that there is a consistent and ordered inverse relationship between social class and mental illness is simply not an accurate interpretation of their findings. It would have been, as a matter of fact, more consistent with their "styles of life" view of social classes to have stressed what we believe is the major finding, namely the consistent differences between Class V and the other classes, with the differences that exist among the latter not clearly and consistently patterned in a hierarchal fashion.

Our attention was first called to this problem by the comments and remarks of other professionals and students who were summarizing the book's findings in seminars and staff meetings by statements

like "The lower the class the higher the rates of mental illness." The general tendency in discussions of class differences to group together Classes I–II versus Classes IV and V is another contributor to the misinterpretation of their findings. The book is so notable for its clarity in other respects that it is unfortunate that the interpretive summaries lend themselves so easily to confusion and distortion. (It might also be mentioned that synoptic statements of the order, "The lower the class the higher the rates of mental illness," ignore the nature of the Hollingshead-Redlich data which are of treated illnesses, not total illnesses. The relation between treated and total illnesses in different social classes is not known and the total rates cannot be assumed to be a standard coefficient of the treated rates.)

In interpreting the relationships between class and specific types of neurosis and psychosis (Hypothesis II) there is a tendency to use an overall significant statistic to report differences for specific disorders when the latter are less systematic and depend on rather small numbers of cases. For example, their two basic tables (Tables C and D) demonstrate that overall, there are statistically significant associations of the five classes with the seven specific neuroses and with the five specific psychoses. They then refer to an "extreme concentration" of hysterical patients in Class V. Examination reveals there are only eight Class V patients in this category and the reduction of the cell by two or three cases would erase its percentage difference from Class IV. Again, they state, "The higher the class, the larger the proportion of patients who are affective psychotics," yet a reduction of three cases among those in Classes I–II would completely eliminate the differences from Class I through Class IV, leaving only Class V as different from the others.

So far, except for one illustration, we have been concerned in our discussion with the reports and interpretations of prevalence data which permit specific tests of the authors' explicit hypotheses and form the major substantive findings around which the book is organized. We have already remarked on the important distinction between prevalence and incidence and will turn now to the findings on the incidence of specific disorders.

Hollingshead and Redlich separately compute rates for each of the "components" of prevalence: new cases arising during their six months interval of observation (incidence), cases that re-entered treatment during that period (re-entry), and those that had been in treatment at the beginning of the period (continuous). They then proceed to test for significant differences among the classes for each of these rates, separately for neuroses and psychoses. (See data presented in Table G. We consider them to be the most important findings in the book on social class and mental illness.)

They find significant differences among the classes for each of the component rates *except* for the incidence of neurosis. In other words, there is no systematic relationship between social class and the rates of coming into treatment for neurosis.

Table G—Incidence, Re-entry, Continuous, and Prevalence Rates per 100,000 for (Treated) Neuroses and Psychoses—by Class (Sex and Age Adjusted)

NEUROSES

Class	Incidence	Re-entry	Continuous	Prevalence
I–II	69	44	251	349
III	78	30	137	250
IV	52	17	82	114
V	66	35	65	97
$x^2 =$	4.40	8.64	69.01	56.05
df	3	3	3	3
p	$<.05$	$<.05$	$<.001$	$<.001$

PSYCHOSES

Class	Incidence	Re-entry	Continuous	Prevalence
I–II	28	44	117	188
III	36	38	217	291
IV	37	42	439	518
V	73	88	1344	1505
$x^2 =$	12.37	15.73	748.47	741.09
df	3	3	3	3
p	$<.01$	$<.01$	$<.001$	$<.001$

Source: Table 16, p. 235.

It appeared to us that the statistical significance of the other relationships of class and incidence rates (both new and old cases) might depend almost entirely on Class V. We re-computed incidence and re-entry rates for neuroses and psychoses, omitting Class V from the calculations. The test showed *no* significant differences among Classes I through IV. (Chi Square for the incidence and re-entry of neuroses are 1.96 and 3.36; for psychoses, the figures are .28 and .08. None of these is significant at the .05 criterion value.)

To summarize these findings: there are *no* significant differences among social classes I–V in the incidence of new cases of neuroses. There are *no* significant differences among classes I through IV in the incidence of new or old cases of neuroses *or* psychoses. Class V has significantly different and higher rates of new and old cases of psychosis (and the inclusion of Class V in the computations suggests that Class IV has a *lower* rate of re-entry of neurotics than the other classes).

The contrast between the significant differences in prevalence and the findings we have just reported of non-significant differences in incidence is extremely important. By concentrating on the prevalence data, an important finding for sociologists and psychiatrists—that Class IV has the lowest overall mental illness rate—is ignored, and some traditional views about the incidence of mental illness are left untouched. There is an implication at many points throughout the book that the prevalence findings may be interpreted as class differences in

the likelihood of developing various mental illnesses (the descriptions of class sub-cultures in Chapters 3 and 4, and the discussions of social class and the life cycle in Chapter 12 are presumably given an important place in the book because treated prevalence data are to some extent thought of in these terms). It is also likely that the findings will be discussed in both the lay and professional literature to some extent as if the prevalence findings did bear on questions of etiology.

Perhaps a recent statement on this by Dr. Redlich himself may serve to minimize such a tendency. "The New Haven study has not really brought out anything which is of etiological significance in explaining differences in prevalence, and prevalence in itself is not a very good measure from an epidemiological viewpoint. . . . We found, as far as the accumulation of schizophrenics in the lower classes is concerned, that although not entirely, it is mostly due to the fact that the lower socio-economic groups get different treatment and have different opportunities for rehabilitation." [7] It is unfortunate that this position was not stated as clearly in the book under review. In addition to these restrictions on the interpretation of the prevalence findings, and the fact that the data deal only with *treated* prevalence, our re-examination of the incidence data also supports the conclusion that the etiological significance of social classes for mental illness is yet to be demonstrated.

When the spurious issue of etiology is brushed aside, the book's major findings stand out quite clearly and they are of extreme importance. Essentially, these *refer* to the differential psychiatric treatment given to patients of different classes with the apparent result of an accumulation of cases in the lower classes. Besides the differences between the distributions of incidence and prevalence rates that we have discussed there are other findings that bear on this. The differences among classes on the paths to treatment, the types of treatment received, and the costs of treatment are important contributions to the understanding of the social aspects of medicine.

It should be noted that in many respects the study is an important followup of the Committee on Costs of Medical Care more than two decades ago.[8] By carefully studying how many and what kinds of persons are in psychiatric treatment, the nature and place of treatment, how much medical time is spent with them, and the costs of treatment, a baseline is provided for discussion of the most effective social utilization of psychiatric manpower and resources. Coupled with other data, the present study provides an opportunity to define the "psychiatrically indigent" category—undoubtedly a much more inclusive category than that of the "medically indigent."

The authors' conclusions regarding class bias in treatment do not depend on the other findings and do not suffer from the weaknesses of method and interpretation that we have discussed above. They are to be commended for their courage in facing this important issue squarely and for their no less courageous attempt to meet the problem by a forthright presentation of a number of proposals that are decidedly controversial in American psychiatric practice.

C. IMPLICATIONS OF THE STUDY

In view of the preceding discussion, we shall not take space to discuss the important theoretical issues about the relationship of social factors to the etiology of mental illness.[9] Rather, we shall restrict our remarks in this section to the study's implications for psychiatric practice.

It has been well known before this that the needs of the population for psychiatric treatment were not being met adequately. What this investigation demonstrates beyond this, is that the distribution of available resources is socially discriminatory. We believe that a serious moral question is also involved in this discovery, since the psychiatric profession legitimates its claim to high status and to social and economic rewards on the grounds that it functions in a "universalistic" nondiscriminatory way. Actually, it operates in such a way as to restrict its "best" treatments to persons in the upper social classes.

We agree that the need requires the development of new modes of treatment, better understanding by psychiatrists of social class patterns, and their reactions to them, and new types of non-medical therapists. We wish, however, to point to some of the assumptions involved in these recommendations and raise some questions that deserve further consideration. First, the authors appear to assume that psychoanalysis or some form of analytic psychotherapy is always ideally preferable to a directive or organic mode of treatment, and that therefore Class IV and V patients are being short-changed. At one level this is a value question since the different therapies are associated with different therapeutic goals, and the issues of what goals to select and who is to decide upon them lie in the realm of value. At another level, this is an empirical issue of whether other forms of treatment might not actually be more effective, rather than simply less costly and less demanding for certain groups of patients. Definitive empirical evidence does not yet exist to provide an answer to this question.

There also seems to be the assumption that it is the psychiatrist who relatively completely controls the type of treatment given. It may be that patients search out psychiatrists who will give them their preferred type of treatment and reject non-preferred treatments, both from private practitioners and within the clinics and hospitals. The selective process and pressures emanating from the patient cannot be ignored in a full account of the biased pattern of psychiatric treatment.

This leads to a related point. There is a tendency to discuss the problem of therapy with working class and lower class persons in a way that implies that the therapist wishes to give the patient "more" than the patient wishes. For example, some practitioners assert that the therapist wants to help the patient come to his own decisions, but the patient only wants to be told what to do; the therapist wants to establish a long term relationship with the patient, but the patient

wants a quick remedy; the therapist wants deep and lasting changes, but the patient is satisfied with superficial and transient results. The alternatives may be multiplied beyond this, but what is important is that they seem to imply a rejection of the therapist and the therapeutic process by the patient. We should like to suggest that quite the opposite may be happening. Rather than asking for "less" than he is offered, the working class and lower class patient may actually be asking for "more" in the sense that he wants a fuller, more extensive, and more permanent relationship than is possible either within the traditional definition of the therapeutic relationship or in terms of what the therapist wishes to enter into. In other words, it may be the therapist who drives the patient from treatment because he cannot handle the demands placed upon him, rather than the patient who drops treatment because its demands are too much for him.[10] (With the knowledge we have of working class and ethnic cultures it is difficult to subscribe without qualifications to assertions that patients from these groups do not like to talk or have special difficulties entering into relationships. The basic questions are: What kind of relationships, with whom, and under what conditions? In raising these questions we are suggesting that some prevailing interpretations of working class and lower class life may have to be re-evaluated.)

III. Research Perspectives in Social Psychiatry

Perhaps nothing emerges more clearly from the book viewed as a whole than the need for continued systematic research on the relationships of social factors to mental illness and psychiatric practice. Our critical comments on the Hollingshead-Redlich study have included suggestions as to how future studies of a similar nature might be improved. We should like at this point to note briefly some additional areas and questions for research that have been suggested by both the achievements and shortcomings of this work.

A. THE ETIOLOGY AND EPIDEMIOLOGY OF MENTAL DISORDERS

The etiological significance of social variables such as social class for various mental disorders remains an open question. Clearly, studies of "true" incidence will be needed before we are able to suggest answers to this question. In design these studies will have to be comparative and longitudinal and they will have to permit the isolation and control of different and changing forms of psychiatric practice. Field investigations of "true" prevalence such as the "Midtown" and "Stirling County" studies, reports from which are now in preparation, will provide a begin-

ning for understanding the relationships between such data and those for treated prevalence as reported by Hollingshead and Redlich. It is to be hoped that future investigations, in addition to including alternative indices of social class, will also be concerned with the effects of other social factors such as, for example, community and family structure, and ethnicity.[11]

More attention will have to be paid to the general problems of psychiatric diagnosis and classification. The nomenclature of the clinic is not particularly useful for field studies, but conceptual links must be forged among the different typologies and indices that are being developed. In all of this work it will be of particular importance not to neglect the fact that the process of psychodiagnosis is inherently a social process and full understanding requires the perspectives of sociological theory and analysis. In addition to data on types of disorders, the extension of a public health approach to the control of mental illness will require information on the severity and the extent of disability associated with mental illness so that large-scale social programs in the prevention, termination, or reduction of such disabilities may be undertaken.[12]

B. PATTERNS OF PSYCHIATRIC TREATMENT

The findings presented by Hollingshead and Redlich on the different paths to treatment followed by patients from different classes are very important, and this is an area in which we need to know much more. The history of the illness before the point of referral, the factors that enter into seeking help at a particular stage, the relation of time and type of referral to outcome, and the relationships of all of these to social class require exploration in further studies.

What variables and processes are involved in the initial phase of treatment that seems to be such an important determinant of later outcomes? How much choice is available to the patient and how does he exercise his choice? How does the process of class discrimination in assignment and treatment operate in clinics and other treatment facilities? How are the goals of treatment set and how are these goals related to the different values of patients and therapists and to their images of and attitudes toward each other?

The list of important research questions may be expanded easily. We wish to end with a special plea for evaluative studies of the effects of various forms of psychiatric treatment. There is a desperate shortage of systematic evidence in this area, and without such evidence our decisions regarding proper treatment tend to be determined by current fashions in psychiatry or by implicit social values and assumptions.

Although we have been critical of some of the methods and interpretations we should like to stress our respect and admiration for this fascinating and exciting study. It is a book of considerable significance that focuses our attention on a range of important problems which had

barely been discussed before. We regard it as a study of psychiatric practice rather than as one of epidemiology, and consider it a great contribution to the study of treatment. If it is not the definitive study that hopefully may be made in the next decade or two, that study will, in part, be possible because of the pioneering work of Hollingshead and Redlich.

Notes

1. Hollingshead, August B. and Redlich, Frederick C.: *Social Class and Mental Illness*, New York, John Wiley & Sons, 1958, 442 pp., $7.50.

2. A number of persons commented on earlier versions of this paper. In particular, the exposition has benefitted from the detailed comments of Ernest M. Gruenberg, M.D., Matthew Huxley, and Frank Riessman. Only the authors, of course, bear responsibility for the final formulations presented in this paper.

3. Calculating the data in terms of the psychiatric agency involved reveals some important practices: 30 per cent of the patients treated by private practitioners and by public clinics are suffering from various types of psychotic disorders.

4. See relevant findings in the forthcoming National Opinion Research Center study directed by Shirley Star; *People's Attitudes Concerning Mental Health*, New York: Elmo Roper, 1950; and Elaine and John Cumming, *Closed Ranks*, Cambridge: Harvard University Press, 1957.

5. Stouffer, Samuel: *Communism, Conformity and Civil Liberties*, New York: Doubleday, 1955. Riessman, Frank: "Workers' Attitudes Toward Participation and Leadership," unpublished doctoral dissertation, Columbia University, 1955.

6. Haase, William: "Rorschach Diagnosis, Socio-Economic Class, and Examiner Bias," unpublished Ph.D. dissertation, New York University, 1956. For a general discussion of diagnostic tests and social class, see Riessman, Frank, and Miller, S. M.: "Social Class and Projective Tests." *Journal of Projective Tests*, December, 1958, 22, pp. 432–439.

7. *Symposium on Preventive and Social Psychiatry*, April 15–17, 1957. Walter Reed Army Institute of Research, Washington, USGOP, 1958. (P. 199).

8. See the report by Lee, Roger I. and Jones, Lewis Webster: *The Fundamentals of Good Medical Care*. Chicago: University of Chicago Press, 1933. They quote Dr. Olin West that ". . . the outstanding problem before the medical profession today is that involved in the delivery of adequate, scientific medical service to all the people, rich and poor, at a cost which can be reasonably met by them in their respective stations in life." "Adequate medical care" is defined in both quantitative and qualitative terms: ". . . a sufficient quantity of good medical care to supply the needs of the people according to the standards of good current practice." (P. 3)

9. Nor shall we discuss a problem that we have alluded to several times—how representative the census of patients is of all of the mentally ill people in New Haven, especially in regard to the social class distribution of the total. Since individuals of different classes come to clinic and other treatment through different routes, it may not be assumed that the census sampled to the same degree the actual amount of all mental disorders in the different social classes.

10. Some evidence exists that many patients of other classes may have similar sets of expectations and present similar problems to psychiatrists. In a by-product of the study under review, it has been found that Class III and V patients exhibit strong resemblances in their expectations of therapy. Our hypothesis would be that it is the low-educated members of Class III who especially exhibit "non-psychiatric" attitudes. Redlich, F. C., Hollingshead, A. B., and Bellis, E.: "Social Class Differences in Attitudes Towards Psychiatry." *American Journal of Orthopsychiatry*, January, 1955, 25, pp. 60–70.

11. For an illustration of the relation of one aspect of community structure, namely, multiple- vs. single-family dwelling units, to cerebral arteriosclerosis and senile psychosis, see New York State Department of Mental Hygiene, *Fourth Annual Report of the New York State Health Commission*, 1954, pp. 31–33; on the impact of ethnic variations in family

structure, see Barabee, Paul and von Mering, Otto: "Ethnic Variations in Mental Stress in Families with Psychotic Children." *Social Problems,* October, 1953, 1, pp. 48–53; and Singer, J. L. and Opler, M. K.: "Contrasting Patterns of Fantasy and Motility in Irish and Italian Schizophrenics." *Journal of Abnormal and Social Psychology,* July 1956, 53, pp. 42–47.

12. Gruenberg, Ernest M.: "Application of Control Methods to Mental Illness." *American Journal of Public Health,* August, 1957, 47, pp. 944–952.

Comparison of Experience and Behavior of Lower and Higher Status Groups: Findings and Hypotheses

Thomas Langner

The differences between the socioeconomic strata can be summarized in tabular form (see Table 16-9). Those differences based upon data from the Midtown sample appear in roman type. Hypotheses based upon other research or impressions based upon the literature appear in italic type.

Table 16-9

	Lower Status	Higher Status
CHILDHOOD STRESSES	Slightly more broken homes before age seven. Greater proportion reporting economic deprivation in childhood.	Disagreed with parents more frequently.
ADULT STRESSES	Report worse adult physical health. More persons with poor interpersonal affiliation—especially lack of friends. Tend to feel children are more trouble than they are worth, to worry about them, and to have problems with them.	More likely to worry about work. More likely to worry about marriage.

Reprinted from *Life Stress and Mental Health,* New York: The Free Press of Glencoe, 1963, pp. 466–467.

Table 16-9 Continued

	Lower Status	Higher Status
STRESS AND IMPAIRMENT	More adult stress. Greater impairment per stress unit. *No financial or other reserves.* *Less resilience, less resistance.*	Less adult stress. Less impairment per stress unit. *Financial reserves, cushioning.* *Greater resilience and resistance.*
TYPE OF ADAPTATION TO STRESS	Exhibit increasingly greater proportion of psychotics with increasing stress. Show moderate increase in proportion of neurotics with increase of stress, ending in a plateau. Greater proportion of following gross types: 1. Probable psychotic type. 2. Probable organic type. 3. Probable personality trait type (character disorder). Greater proportion of following symptom groups and diagnostic types: Alcoholic, brain disease, dyssocial, psychosomatic, hypochondriacal, passive-dependent, depressed, rigid, schizoid suspicious, schizophrenic.	Exhibit a constant low proportion of psychotics, regardless of stress. Show sharp increase in proportion of neurotics with increase of stress. Greater proportion of following gross types: 1. Probable wells. 2. Probable neurotic type. Greater proportion of following symptom group: Aggressive (in interview situation, primarily).
MOBILITY	Passive-dependent, rigid, and suspicious individuals as well as alcoholics are moving downward from the high into the low stratum.	Anxious and obsessive-compulsive persons are moving upward from the low into the high stratum.

A Survey of Mental Disease in an Urban Population: Prevalence by Race and Income

Benjamin Pasamanick, Dean W. Roberts, Paul W. Lemkau, and Dean B. Krueger

The Commission on Chronic Illness, an independent agency founded jointly by the American Hospital Association, the American Medical Association, the American Public Health Association, and the American Public Welfare Association, financed by a series of grants from the National Institutes of Health and the Commonwealth Fund, has completed a study of the prevalence of chronic illness and needs for care in an urban area begun in 1952. The objectives of the investigation started in Baltimore were, broadly, to determine the prevalence of diagnosed and asymptomatic chronic disease and resulting disability, and its variations by socio-economic distribution, to estimate rehabilitation potentials, to evaluate multiple screening methods, and to develop new methods of studying the chronic disease problem.

The study was planned and carried out in four phases, of which only the first two are of relevance to this report and will be described briefly.

Step 1. A household canvass was carried out in the classical morbidity survey method by trained lay interviewers under the direction of the United States Bureau of the Census on approximately four thousand households, including about twelve thousand people representing a random sample of the population of Baltimore. Persons in medical institutions for long-term care, including mental hospitals, were not sampled. The sampling procedures, interview methods, preparation,

Reprinted from *Epidemiology of Mental Disorder*, Hans Nussbaum, ed., pp. 183–196. Copyright 1959 by the American Association for the Advancement of Science, Washington, D.C.

39

and findings will be described in detail in future reports of the Commission.[1] At this time it is sufficient to state that the sample surveyed was a probability sample of the city's population in terms of age, race and sex characteristics, and that interviews were completed in 97.7 per cent of the addresses selected for sampling.

Step 2. This consisted of the "clinical evaluation" of a subsample. About 10 per cent of the basic survey group of twelve thousand were chosen as the sample for this step. They were stratified in the following manner so that the bulk of the intensive evaluation would be devoted to persons with substantially disabling health conditions as determined by the household interview data: (1) 100 per cent of the persons reporting maximum disability; (2) 100 per cent of those reporting diabetes, CNS disease and neoplasm, 40 per cent of those reporting heart disease, 25 per cent reporting arthritis and rheumatism, 7 per cent of those reporting all other diseases; (3) approximately 6 per cent of the remainder reporting no disease or only short term or nondisabling conditions.

Of this stratified subsample, 731 individuals were examined at the Evaluation Clinic, 33 were examined at home, and an additional 45 whose current medical data were secured from physicians in hospitals in sufficient degrees of completeness were included to make a total of 809 and a response rate of 62.6 per cent. The report presented here will be limited to the data on mental illness gathered from step 2 of the Chronic Disease Commission survey. Details of subsampling, field work, evaluation, staff, and findings will be found in later reports of the Commission.

Briefly, the evaluation of the persons in this step was carried out at the Johns Hopkins Hospital by a panel of physicians specializing in internal medicine or pediatrics who were either full-time fellows in their respective departments or physicians in private practice with hospital staff appointments. These physicians performed the physical examinations and ordered any consultations, including psychiatric, or special diagnostic tests needed to clarify the medical status of the patient. A number of additional routine procedures were carried out, in all requiring some three to four hours for the complete clinic evaluation. For each evaluee, the examining physician completed a record in which significant chronic conditions were analyzed in terms of severity, history, disabling effects, treatment and care required, and prognosis. Each record was reviewed by the rehabilitation counselor to identify those who had any potential for rehabilitation, and a home visit was made by a counselor on these cases. Half of each of group 1 and group 2 described above were randomly selected, and in those who showed significant health disability thorough home investigation was made by either a public health nurse, social worker, or rehabilitation counselor, depending on the greatest apparent need. The records of all these cases so investigated were reviewed by the Commission staff and the home investigators to establish or confirm all the existing noted conditions.

After thorough perusal of the case material, the impressions, and

the diagnoses, every record which contained any material which might pertain to some factor associated with the possibility of mental illness was turned over to the psychiatrist for his "clinical evaluation." Approximately one quarter of the step 2 subsample cases were so reviewed. On the basis of the material contained in these records diagnosis of mental disorders was made using the definitions contained in the 1952 Diagnostic and Statistical Manual of the American Psychiatric Association.

Diagnoses were not allowed to stand unless the data recorded in the medical records supported the diagnosis. This resulted in one-third of the patients (32 per cent) for whom the examining physician recorded a psychiatric diagnosis having the diagnosis deleted on review by the psychiatrist. Change from one diagnosis to another was not accounted as a deletion. It is possible that some psychiatric diagnoses made by the examining internist were deleted merely because all the information available to the internist was not recorded and therefore was not available to the reviewing psychiatrist.

Examining internists recorded "impressions" but not diagnosis of psychiatric disease for 24 patients. For ten of these patients the reviewing psychiatrist considered the record and the data as supporting a diagnosis of psychiatric disease. Four additional diagnoses of psychiatric disease were made by the reviewing psychiatrist through changing a single diagnosis made by the examining internist into two psychiatric diagnoses, or by making a diagnosis in cases selected by the medical editing staff as probably involving psychiatric disease. In general, the effect of the review by the psychiatrist was to reduce substantially the figures on prevalence of psychiatric disease.

In addition, it must be noted that the findings to be presented represent prevalence as of the date of clinical evaluation, rather than the "lifetime" prevalence which some studies have reported. Some diagnoses were deleted because it was felt that there was no psychiatric illness present at the time of examination, although this had probably been present sometime in the past and might be again in the future. Along with diagnostic ratings, the psychiatrist made judgments of severity based on the degree of psychiatric impairment scaled in the Diagnostic and Statistical Manual of:

(a) No impairment where there were no medical reasons for changing employment or life situation.

(b) *Minimal* indicating incapacity of perceptible degree but not to exceed 10 per cent.

(c) *Mild impairment* in social and occupational adjustment of 20 per cent to 30 per cent disability.

(d) *Moderate,* indicating serious interference with a patient's ability to carry on premorbid social and vocational adjustment and having a 30 per cent to 50 per cent disability rating.

(e) *Severe,* indicating that for practical purposes the patient could not function at his premorbid social and vocational levels and had over 50 per cent disability.

Findings

The findings to be discussed in this preliminary report will be limited to the distribution of psychoses, psychoneuroses, and psychophysiologic autonomic and visceral disorders in our total sample of examined patients by race and economic status.

They do not include the category of "other mental, psychoneurotic, and personality disorders," which will be included in the general Commission report. This category which includes a number of childhood behavior disorders, mild mental defect, alcoholism, and other minor personality or behavior difficulties and has an adjusted rate of 15.2 per thousand is excluded from this report because the judgments of both the examining physicians and psychiatrists are probably not very reliable. This is particularly true in most of the judgments of mental deficiency and psychopathic personality. In a number of cases where it seemed apparent to the psychiatrist that the behavior or personality disorder, such as alcoholism, was symptomatic of a psychoneurosis or of another psychiatric disorder, the diagnosis was so changed. On the whole this was infrequent, and the category of "other mental psychoneurotic and personality disorders" usually containing vague or equivocal psychiatric illness, social maladjustment, and behavior patterns unacceptable to middle class diagnosticians was poorly recorded or judged in this survey as in most other similar studies. It was therefore thought best to confine this paper to those conditions generally considered as obvious mental illness.

The step 2 clinical evaluation sample was selected in such a fashion that adjustment of the data for differences in sampling proportions of the various groups and for differences in the proportions participating could be done through the application of weights. This permitted expression of the findings of the clinical evaluation in terms of the approximately twelve thousand persons surveyed in step 1, who in turn were found to be very similar to the total population of the city in terms of age and color. After proper weighting, our 809 evaluees were found to be distributed almost identically by age, color, and sex with the household survey sample. To the extent then that their distribution by these characteristics was significantly related to mental health, this sample is representative of the mental health of the noninstitutionalized population of the city of Baltimore.

Before we enter upon a discussion of our findings of mental disorder by race and economic status, we thought that it might be of some value to review briefly our findings of total prevalence and distribution by sex and age as well as severity which we have reported previously.

Table I presenting total prevalence and prevalence by sex of the clinical entities under consideration indicates that after conservative estimation approximately 10 per cent of a noninstitutional urban popu-

**Table I—Prevalence of Mental Disorder as a Rate per 1,000
Persons Evaluated by Diagnosis and Sex**

Diagnosis	Number of Cases Unweighted	RATE BASED ON WEIGHTED NUMBER OF CASES		
		Both Sexes	Males	Females
Psychoses	17	4.3	6.0	2.7
Psychoneuroses	51	52.6	35.6	68.0
Psychophysiologic, autonomic, and visceral disorders	18	36.5	18.9	52.4
Total	86	93.4	60.5	123.1

lation are at one moment in time mentally ill. There is approximately
twelve times as much psychoneurosis as psychosis while psychophysiologic autonomic and visceral disorders are two-thirds as common as
the neuroses. Male psychoses appear to be twice as frequent as those
in women, but, because of the small numbers involved, probably is not
statistically significant. On the other hand, females have more psychoneuroses and psychophysiologic autonomic and visceral disorders.

Table II containing the mental disorders classified by severity of

**Table II—Mental Disorders Classified by Severity of Impairment
as Defined by American Psychiatric Association**

Diagnosis	Number of Cases Unweighted	PERCENTAGE DISTRIBUTION BY SEVERITY OF IMPAIRMENT BASED ON WEIGHTED NUMBER OF CASES					
		Total	None	Minimal	Mild	Moderate	Severe
Psychoses	17	100.0	—	3.6	6.5	22.7	67.2
Psychoneuroses	50*	100.0	20.5	47.8	22.8	6.0	2.8
Psychophysiologic, autonomic, and visceral disorders	18	100.0	23.2	34.1	35.3	1.8	5.5

* Excludes one case with unknown severity.

impairment indicates, as might be expected, that the psychoses were
generally classified as being moderate to severe, while the psychoneuroses and psychophysiologic, autonomic, and visceral disorders had
either no significant impairment or ranged up to and including mild
impairment with below 30 per cent disability.

In Table III we present the prevalence of these types of mental dis-

**Table III—Prevalence of Mental Disorder as a Rate per 1,000
Persons Evaluated in Each Age Group**

Diagnosis	Number of Cases Unweighted	RATE BASED ON WEIGHTED NUMBER OF CASES				
		All Ages	Under 15	15–34	35–64	65 and Over
Psychoses	17	4.3	—	0.4	5.8	27.8
Psychoneuroses	51	52.6	8.3	68.8	69.2	70.8
Psychophysiologic, autonomic, and visceral disorders	18	36.5	—	78.7	38.6	—
Total	86	93.4	8.3	147.9	113.6	98.6

order by age group. Psychoses rise precipitously with increasing age. With no cases under 15, only 0.4 per thousand in the age group 15 to 34, increasing 14-fold in the group 35 to 64, which in turn is multiplied by 5 in the group 65 and over. In contrast, the psychoneuroses are almost uniformly distributed in the age groups over 15, but are less than 0.1 per cent under 15. The psychophysiologic disorders exhibit an entirely different pattern of distribution with no cases reported under 15 or over 65, but with more cases in the 15 to 34 group than in the 35 to 64.

Table IV offers our findings in respect to a distribution of mental

Table IV—Prevalence of Mental Disorder as a Rate per 1,000 Persons Evaluated by Diagnosis and Color

| | | RATE BASED ON WEIGHTED NUMBER OF CASES | | |
Diagnosis	Number of Cases Unweighted	Total White and Non-white	White	Non-white
Psychoses	17	4.3	5.8	0.3
Psychoneuroses	51	52.6	62.2	27.5
Psychophysiologic, autonomic, and visceral disorders	18	36.5	43.7	17.7
Total	86	93.4	111.7	45.5

illness by color. The designation non-white refers almost wholly to Negroes, and in our discussion these terms will be used interchangeably. It is apparent that in the three groups of clinical entities included in this report, whites have by far more mental illness recorded than non-whites. Approximately nineteen times as much psychosis, twice as much psychoneurosis, and almost three times as many autonomic and visceral disorders of psychophysiologic origin.

In Table V, we present the distribution of mental disorder by

Table V—Prevalence of Mental Disorder as a Rate per 1,000 Persons Evaluated by Diagnosis and Income

| | | RATE BASED ON WEIGHTED NUMBER OF CASES | | | | |
Diagnosis	Number of Cases Unweighted	All Incomes *	Under $2,000	$2,000– $3,999	$4,000– $5,999	$6,000 and Over
Psychoses	17	4.3	4.1	8.7	1.5	0.8
Psychoneuroses	51	52.6	80.1	55.4	13.4	62.5
Psychophysiologic, autonomic, and visceral disorders	18	36.5	—	18.2	47.2	72.5
Total	86	93.4	84.2	82.3	62.1	135.8

* Includes income not stated.

economic status as indicated by household income. In the group of psychoses, except for the lowest income category (under $2,000 a year) the prevalence of psychoses falls as income increases. In the neurotic

group prevalence is highest in the lowest income category and falls progressively only to rise again in the highest economic group of yearly income $6,000 and over. In the psychophysiologic, autonomic, and visceral disorders, prevalence increases directly with income.

Discussion

Before entering upon a discussion of the implications of these findings some comment on the limitations of the investigation other than the somewhat small numbers involved seems to be in order. Except for one characteristic, Baltimore differs very little from other urban centers, or indeed the rest of the country, in respect to age distribution and family income. However, it does differ markedly in having a higher proportion of non-whites, 26.7 per cent as contrasted to 13.2 per cent in all cities over 100,000 population in 1950. As was demonstrated, this characteristic tends to lower prevalence rates in our survey.

As was indicated before, the "response rates" for the clinical evaluation was 62.6 per cent. Unexpectedly, there was no significant difference in the response rate according to degree of disability and even absence of disability. There were, however, significant differences by age, color and sex, the rates being higher for children and lower for the aged, higher for the non-whites and slightly higher for males. With a non-response rate of 37.4 per cent, the question of bias must be considered carefully. With the data from the household survey for both respondents and non-respondents, it becomes possible to evaluate to some degree the bias due to non-response. Chronic conditions were reported during interviews at a slightly lower rate for the 809 individuals clinically evaluated (after weighting) than for the total survey sample. Our conclusion is that the amount of bias for all chronic disease due to non-response is probably quite small, and that the interview data available do not establish with certainty the direction of bias, though it seems likely to be in the direction of a little more disease among the persons clinically evaluated than among the total survey sample.

What can be said of the bias introduced by the method of having the original diagnostic impression made by a non-psychiatrist and supplemented by information from other sources? Very little, but impressions can be offered on this score. Since a fairly sizable group of physicians was employed in the clinical evaluations, it might be expected that considerable variation in psychiatric judgment and evaluation existed. These were largely well-trained and sophisticated young individuals alert to the psychiatric implications of illness. The impression is that the total direction of bias may be slightly toward overdiagnosis of mental disorder. There is some support for this in the finding that there was no significant impairment in over one-fifth of the cases of psychoneurosis and psychophysiologic disorders, while an additional two-fifths had only minimal impairment. On the other hand, the

psychiatrist reviewing these cases and eliminating approximately one-third where a diagnostic impression of mental disorder was made, because of lack of recorded supporting evidence or differing opinion, probably deleted a number of cases which on closer scrutiny and examination might have been included as mental disorders. The reliability of judgments of physicians and psychiatrist was not tested.

The total bias and direction is quite difficult to estimate. It may very well be that there is some tendency toward underreporting. However, this is not judged to be very great, and in any event nothing like the reports of approximately two-thirds of the population being mentally ill, as indicated in two recent surveys is approached. Our findings that approximately one-tenth of an urban population have one or more of the relatively well-defined mental disorders is sufficiently alarming and one obviously calling for serious and prompt consideration.

What explanations or hypotheses can be offered for some of the differences in the racial and economic distributions of mental disorder found in the Baltimore survey? How can we account for the much lower prevalence of mental illness among the Negro evaluees? First, as far as the psychoses are concerned, since we are apparently dealing largely with psychoses of old age in a non-institutionalized population, Negroes whose life expectancy is under 60 years would not be expected to contribute significantly to the population of psychotics. In addition, because of their social and economic circumstances they probably would not be as able to care for psychotic individuals at home as might those in easier circumstances. This is supported by the higher first admission rates to mental hospitals for Negroes. As for the difference in prevalence of psychoneuroses, how much of this may be attributable to the fact that the examiners were white, middle or upper class individuals with all that implies concerning cultural, class, and caste biases in interviewing and evaluation. Is this one of the reasons why the prevalence of "other mental psychoneurotic and personality disorders" was higher amongst the non-white? The latter would at least account for part of the difference. It is obviously not accountable for on the basis of economic status since in both the psychoses and the psychoneuroses the lower economic status groups had higher prevalence rates. Are these possible biases also operative in the group of psychophysiologic autonomic and visceral disorders where again the non-whites have a much lower rate? It is interesting to note that when we look at the rates of a number of disorders such as asthma, obesity, and hypertension without heart disease, which have been said to have psychogenic components, that the rates for non-whites are the same or even slightly higher than that for the white sample. Is the white examiner more likely to seek and therefore find psychologic components in members of his own race than in that of another?

The distribution of diagnostic categories by income offers a number of possible hypotheses by way of explanation. The prevalence of four psychoses per thousand in the category under $2,000 as contrasted to the next higher category with nine per thousand is probably attributable

to the fact that the lowest income group contains most of the Negroes, and since they had a much lower rate than that of whites in the non-institutionalized population, this finding could have been predicted. However, it appears that on the whole lowered economic status is associated with more psychoses. How much of this is cause and how much effect we cannot state from our data. It is quite likely that both mechanisms are operative here. A certain number have probably been forced into the lower economic status because of psychosis, and it is also probable that because of a number of factors associated with low income a sizable group of elderly individuals have been forced into this psychotic group. However, because of the small numbers involved too much emphasis cannot be placed upon the differences found.

Our findings relative to the prevalence of psychoneuroses in different income groups is rather interesting. Despite the fact that Negroes had a low rate of psychoneuroses reported, the highest rate of psychoneuroses recorded was in the lowest 70 per cent of the population with incomes under $4,000. The rate falls in the $4,000 to $6,000 group, which makes up 17 per cent of the population, and then rises again in the over $6,000 a year income group, which includes 11 per cent of the Baltimore population. This is in contrast to a number of other surveys which found psychoneuroses rising with income. Hypotheses of etiology might best be discussed in relation to specific psychoneurotic diagnoses. However, on the face it would appear that stress is greatest in the lowest and highest social economic strata, in the former due to deprivation and the frustrations consequent to deprivation and in the latter possibly due to various social and cultural inconsistencies and stress consequent to attempt to maintain status.

As in the case of the psychoses, it is unfortunate that we were unable to report more cases of autonomic and visceral disorders so that the reliability of our findings would be greater, but contrary to the findings in psychoses, there appears to be a definite trend toward increase in the prevalence of these disorders with increasing income. Is this a reflection of increased chronic tension and stress with income, or is it possibly another indication of bias in the examiners who might tend to find more psychogenicity in individuals of their own class? Were it not for the increase in psychoneuroses in the highest economic stratum, it might have been said that whereas psychoneuroses are unacceptable in our culture, autonomic and visceral disorders are permissible. One might even tortuously evolve the hypothesis that in these days of psychiatric sophistication in the well to do, it is fashionable for the rich to be neurotic, unacceptable to the middle class, but frequent in the lower class because of lack of sophistication and increased stress.

Undoubtedly many other explanations could be offered as acceptable as the above, or even more so, but these were advanced merely as examples of the large number of hypotheses which immediately offer themselves for testing. It is some indication of the dearth of our knowledge in this area and the long way still to be traveled toward the knowledge of etiology of mental disorders.

Summary

The Chronic Disease Commission's survey of mental disorder in Baltimore found that approximately one-tenth of a non-institutionalized population exhibited obvious mental illness. Whites were recorded as having much more disorder than non-whites. In the psychoses this may be due to the lower life expectancy of Negroes, but in psychoneuroses and autonomic and visceral disorders it may possibly be due to bias on the part of the examiners. Psychoses were more prevalent in the lower income groups; however, autonomic and visceral disorders of psychogenic origin increased with income. The psychoneuroses were most common in the lowest and highest income groups. Some hypotheses are offered for these differences.

Note

1. *Chronic Illness in a Large City*, Vol. 4 of *Chronic Illness in the United States*, Commonwealth Fund and the Harvard University Press, 1957.

Toward an Assessment of the Mental Health of Factory Workers: A Detroit Study

Arthur Kornhauser

Industrial psychology in America has been most concerned with productivity and organizational effectiveness. Working people are studied primarily as means to the ends of efficiency, whether of the single enterprise or of the larger society. Even when attention is directed to attitudes, feelings, and morale, interest usually centers on how these subjective states affect performance.

An alternative orientation focuses upon working people as themselves the significant ends. Interest attaches to the personal development and well-being of the men and women in industry, the improvement of their individual and social health—especially their "mental health." The present study belongs to this second category. It inquires about the impact of modern economic organization, particularly the demands of mass production manufacturing, on the people involved. What does the industrial way of life do to, and for, the men who man the machines? What does their work mean to them and what are the effects of their factory occupations on their spirit and their life adjustments?

Are factory workers—specifically Detroit auto-workers—happy and

Reprinted by permission of Society for Applied Anthropology, from *Human Organization*, Vol. 21, No. 1, Spring 1962, pp. 43–47.

This is a slightly revised form of a paper read at the American Psychological Association meetings in Chicago in September, 1960. It is a preliminary report of one part of a more extensive study. Principal support for the research was provided by the National Institute of Mental Health (Research grant M-460, 1951–57). Grateful acknowledgment is made to that agency and, for other assistance, to the Wayne State University College of Liberal Arts, the Computing Center, and the Wayne State Fund; also to the Institute of Labor and Industrial Relations of Wayne State University and the University of Michigan. Special thanks go to Dr. Otto M. Reid who shouldered a large share of responsibility for the conduct of the study.

well-adjusted in the main? Or are they predominantly bitter or depressed or anxious or apathetic? Are they enthusiastic, idealistic, self-reliant, zestful? Or cynical, alienated, dispirited? One can find assertions that they are all these contradictory things and many more. Evidence to support the assertions is scarce indeed. Even less is known about sub-groups, for example by job levels, age, income, and education. Are assembly line jobs peculiarly monotonous, frustrating, deadening—and hated? Does work on the line produce poor mental health? On this question, too, violent disagreement continues despite the debates which go on decade after decade.

In this article I shall sketch a few partial results from a study which attempted to secure evidence bearing on these issues. Along with the findings I shall briefly mention some possible implications and interpretations—and unanswered questions.

The research focuses on comparisons of the mental health of occupational groups in the Detroit automobile industry. The factory workers studied were selected by a systematic sampling procedure from the personnel files of 13 large and medium-sized automotive manufacturing plants. The sample includes only white, American-born men who had been with their present employer three years or more.

In reaching for methods to assess the mental health of these people we adopted two guiding principles: 1) We would begin with a variety of simple, commonly accepted ideas as to what constitutes good versus poor mental health and would proceed in subsequent steps to interrelate, test, and in some sense "validate" these ideas; and 2) we would rely primarily on data obtainable by means of interviews with the working people themselves, supplementing these findings by reports from interviewers, wives of respondents, and company records of absenteeism and medical department visits. Accordingly, several hundred detailed interviews were completed with workers and their wives, all at the homes of the interviewees.

The rationale of our mental health measures is this: We conceptualize mental health not as representing any psychodynamic unity but as a loose descriptive designation for an overall level of success, effectiveness, or excellence of the individual's functioning as a person. The emphasis is on mental health in a "normal" and positive sense; the inquiry does not deal with mental disease or illness. We proceed on the assumption that mental health is multi-dimensional—although this is not at all to imply that there are not certain dimensions of especially great importance relative to others. On the side of practical procedures, our search is not for any peculiarly crucial key measures of mental health but for useful indicators chosen from innumerable possible ones.

More specifically, the study relies upon reports by working men and their wives in regard to the workers' feelings of satisfaction and happiness; their attitudes and sentiments toward themselves, other persons, their world, and their future; their personal and social activities (at work, at home, and in the community); and their psychological and

bodily manifestations of disturbing stress or tensions. The interviews also included responses to lists of selected personality inventory items.

A number of indexes were derived from the interview responses. Those which enter into our general measure of mental health are indexes of:

Anxiety and emotional tension

Hostility versus trust in, and acceptance of, people

Sociability and friendship versus withdrawal

Self-esteem versus negative self-feelings

Personal morale versus anomie or social alienation

Overall satisfaction with life

"Validity" of the Mental Health Index

These component indexes were combined to form a total index of mental health. We then classified workers according to their scores on this general index. Although I shall freely refer to the "better" or "poorer" mental health of the men so classified, the statements are necessarily limited by the particular way in which the assessments are made. The meaning and justification of the appraisals must rest largely upon the "face validity" of the indexes—that is, upon the apparent reasonableness of the response material as indicative of what is ordinarily believed to characterize mental health in our culture (positive self-feelings, relative freedom from anxiety symptoms and hostile attitudes, and other qualities suggested by the above list of indexes).

An important additional type of evidence was obtained, however, as a check on whether our measure of mental health does in fact correspond with evaluations used and accepted by professional persons directly concerned with mental health in our society. Does the proposed index of mental health actually measure what the "experts" mean by mental health? Before proceeding to use the index we set up a small-scale "validation" study to answer this question. We arranged to have six experienced, highly qualified clinical psychologists and psychiatrists read the complete interview records of 40 cases and give their overall evaluation of each individual's mental health. Comparison of our quantitative indexes with these independent global ratings reveals that the indexes do, in fact, agree decidedly well with the clinicians' judgments. The tetrachoric correlation is .84; the Pearson coefficient is .76. It is thus apparent that the meaning of mental health represented by our index corresponds closely to what the clinicians also conceive to be better or poorer mental health.

A different type of validity check compared workers' responses with reports by their wives. These comparisons justify the further conclusion that the interview content represents behavior and attitudes possessing some reality in the eyes of another observer. When wives' estimates of whether their spouses are nervous, well satisfied with life, etc. are

compared with adjustment-indexes based on the man's own replies, the median correlations are above .50. When these several findings are taken together, they appear to offer considerable justification for employing our indexes for present purposes as presumptive measures, albeit crude ones, of mental health.

Mental Health Differences by Factory Occupational Categories

Our first question here is whether there are, in fact, differences of mental health associated with different types of factory jobs. If it is established that such differences exist, the next task is to search for explanations. As to the occurrence of significant differences our results are clear and unambiguous. When workers are classified by skill level and variety of work operations, mental health scores do show consistent correlation with the occupational hierarchy. The higher the occupational level the better the mental health.

One simple set of figures will suffice to make this more concrete. Let us compare occupations by the percentage of workers enjoying "good" mental health—i.e., having "high" mental health scores (the cutting point for "high" is, of course, arbitrary). We have two age groups—men in their 20's and those in their 40's. (See Table 1).

Table 1—Comparison of Occupations by the Percentage of Workers Enjoying "Good" Mental Health

	Percentages with Scores Indicating "Good" Mental Health	No. of Workers
298 men in their 40's		
Skilled workers	56	45
High semi-skilled	41	98
Ordinary semi-skilled	38	82
Repetitive semi-skilled	26	73
Repetitive, machine-paced only (subdivision of preceding category)	16	32
109 men in their 20's		
Skilled and high semi-skilled *	58	33
Ordinary semi-skilled	35	46
Repetitive semi-skilled	10	30
Repetitive, machine-paced only (subdivision of preceding category)	7	15

* The two categories are combined here because of small numbers.

A vital next question is whether these occupational differences are due to *effects of the jobs* and their associated conditions, or alternatively, do the differences result from *selection of certain kinds of persons* who go into and remain in the several types of work. Before I consider a

little of our evidence on this second question, I wish to emphasize the importance of the first results themselves. If more thorough studies confirm the findings I have reported, the social knowledge thus established may have large consequences. The poorer mental health of workers in lower level occupations cannot fail to affect not only their industrial behavior, as employees and labor unionists, but likewise their roles as citizens and as family and community members. As the knowledge of such differences becomes known (and again I repeat, if confirmed by additional studies), one may anticipate intensified efforts by the lower-placed groups, their leaders, and agencies concerned with their welfare to bring about social and industrial changes intended to eradicate the condition. Such social action programs will sorely need expanded research knowledge regarding crucial determining conditions and promising correctives. But demonstration of the existence of the problem is the first requirement.

These last comments are in no way intended to minimize the importance of the second question—the issue of whether and to what extent the observed occupational differences are attributable to the influence of the work and its correlates. We now turn to a brief analysis of this question. If the mental health differences are due to the type of persons in the occupations, differences among these people ought to be detectable in the pre-job period of their lives. A first suspicion that crosses one's mind, for example, is that the mental health results may all be "explained away" as due to educational differences. This could . occur by reason of the direct association of schooling with both occupational level and good mental health scores (the latter possibly meaning merely greater sophistication and self-protection in answering questions, thus giving the *appearance* of mental health).

Amount of schooling, then, affords one good test of the *selection* explanation of occupational mental health differences. Since substantial educational differences do occur between occupations and since education is also associated with better mental health, the possibility has to be examined whether this association is sufficient to produce the obtained results. Conversely, do occupational mental health differences persist apart from the influence of education—i.e., when only persons of like amounts of education are compared? Our findings strongly suggest that the latter is true. Proportions of workers having good mental health consistently decrease from higher to lower level occupations *for each of three educational categories separately*. Moreover, the magnitude of the differences is very nearly the same as when education is not controlled but is permitted to add its influence (see Table 2).

For the middle-age group (in which there are enough cases to permit more adequate analysis) occupation and education show a small additive effect on mental health as may be noted in Table 2A. Mental health is best among those high in education *and* occupation, poorest for those low in both education and occupation. This is contrary, of course, to the psychologically plausible hypothesis that mental health is adversely affected by lack of congruency between educational status and occu-

Table 2—Percentage of High Mental Health Scores by Groups Having Specified Occupation and Education

A. Middle-Age Factory Workers

| | EDUCATION | | | |
Occupation	Grade School	Some H.S.	H.S. Grad.	Total
Skilled	43% (7)	45% (20)	72% (18)	56% (45)
High semi-skilled	33 (46)	45 (33)	53 (19)	41 (98)
Ordinary semi-skilled	31 (35)	39 (36)	55 (11)	38 (82)
Repetitive semi-skilled	24 (46)	29 (21)	33 (6)	26 (73)
Total	30% (134)	40% (110)	57% (54)	39% (298)

Figures in parentheses show the number of cases in each cell on which the accompanying percentage is based.

B. Young Factory Workers

| | EDUCATION | | |
Occupation	Some H.S. or Less	H.S. Grad.	Total
Skilled and high semi-skilled	57% (14)	58% (19)	58% (33)
Ordinary semi-skilled	33 (36)	40 (10)	35 (46)
Repetitive semi-skilled	10 (21)	11 (9)	10 (30)
Total	31% (71)	42% (38)	35% (109)

Because of small numbers, we here combine the two lower educational groups and the two upper occupational groups.

pational status—the view that poorest mental health occurs among persons of better education in low-level jobs (and perhaps also among those of low education in high-level jobs). This hypothesis receives no support at all from our data, either for the middle-age group or the younger workers. In fact, the percentage of "good" mental health in lower-level jobs is *greater* for persons having more schooling.

Conclusions

The analysis of our data as a whole leads to the conclusion that educational differences, either by themselves or in interaction with job level, do not account for the observed mental health variations by occupation. To the extent that this conclusion is confirmed and to the extent that other pre-job personal characteristics (possible job *selection* factors) yield similar negative findings, it would indicate that the influences determining occupational mental health differences among factory workers are to be found in the jobs themselves and their associated life conditions.

We have analyzed a few other pre-job characteristics of workers in a manner parallel to that employed in respect to education. The material consists of responses to an extensive series of questions about the workers' boyhood conditions, behavior, attitudes, and aspirations. In a

word, the findings are similar to those for schooling though less clear-cut. That is to say, the occupational groups do differ by childhood characteristics (such as reported anxiety symptoms, success in school, self-confidence, economic deprivations, degree of happiness) but when occupations are compared for individuals having the same degree of these pre-job characteristics, occupational mental health differences persist even if somewhat reduced. In respect to childhood goals and values, the occupational groups show only minor differences and there is no evidence that these differences are responsible for any large part of the observed mental health variations.

In sum, then, the indications from our present data are: a) that mental health (as here assessed) is poorer among factory workers as we move from more skilled, responsible, varied types of work to jobs lower in these respects, and b) that the relationship is not due in any large degree to differences of pre-job background or personality of the men who enter and remain in the several types of work. The relationship of mental health to occupation, in other words, appears to be "genuine"; mental health is dependent on factors associated with the job.

This conclusion at once presents the further challenging question of what *aspects* of occupations are important. Which of the myriad characteristics of higher and lower-level jobs and associated conditions of life are the salient determinants of better or poorer mental health? More simply, *why* do we find poorer mental health in low-level occupations? I can do no more than touch upon these questions at this time.

One can readily offer a long list of plausible explanatory factors—from lower pay, economic insecurity, and disagreeable working conditions to the more intangible influences of status, promotion opportunities, type of supervision and work-group relations, simplicity and repetitiveness of job operations and lack of personal control over them, non-use of abilities with consequent feelings of futility, and many more such possible influences on and off the job. Some of these obviously may be more significant than others. We have analyzed data pertaining to many of these variables in an effort to estimate their saliency but I must leave these analyses for reporting at a later date.

Here, I wish merely to suggest that it would be a mistake to think in terms of this *or* that causal factor as important. Mental health is surely a product of complex combinations of influences—varied and shifting, dependent on the values currently emphasized and the expectations aroused as well as on the existing conditions of gratification and deprivation. Mental health is probably not so much a matter of freedom from specific frustrations as it is an overall orientation and balanced relationship to the world which permits a person to maintain realistic, positive belief in himself and his purposeful activities. Insofar as his entire job and life situation facilitate and support such feelings of adequacy, inner security, and meaningfulness, it can be presumed that mental health as we have assessed it will tend to be "good." The question becomes one of whether lower-level factory jobs do offer gen-

erally less favorable circumstances for the development and maintenance of this "healthy" personality than do "better" jobs—less favorable in many and varied ways a number of which I have mentioned. It appears to me there can be little doubt that this is true.

Furthermore, both on rational grounds and from our empirical evidence, I see no reason to think that it is useful to single out one or a few of the job-related characteristics as distinctively important—whether it be status, human relations at work, specialization of operations, lack of independence and control, or any other particular variable. What is important is *everything* that deprives the individual of purpose and zest, that leaves him with negative self-feelings, anxieties, tensions, a sense of lostness and futility, which distorts his thinking and obstructs effective behavior. If we are to understand why mental health is poorer in less skilled, more routine factory jobs, we must look at the entire pattern of work and life conditions of the people in these occupations—not at single variables.

Social Class and Treatment

Social Class and the Mental Health Movement

Orville R. Gursslin, Raymond G. Hunt, and Jack L. Roach

This paper is an analysis of the content of the mental health "message" found in mental health pamphlets, and the relationship of this content to the class characteristics of the audience reached. The nature of this relationship provides the foundation for a discussion of some broad consequences of mental health educational efforts designed to reach the general public.

During the last several decades, writing on the subject of mental health (which now comprises an imposing bibliography) has been criticized on several scores. Recent critiques (4; 7; 8; 14) have stressed the complexities involved in an accurate delineation of mental health, as well as the variety of conflicting opinions among authorities regarding its nature. In contrast, an earlier line of critical inquiry initiated by Kingsley Davis (5), although it has been widely cited and reproduced in the literature, has received little additional attention by authors in the field. Davis indicated there was an affinity between the protestant ethic and the concept of mental health as found in books and other works dealing with mental hygiene. He was concerned principally with documenting the middle class background of authorities writing on the subject of mental health, and in indicating that their middle class cultural orientation influenced their conception of mental health. In contrast, the present investigation is focused on mass media publications and treats the class orientation of the mental health message primarily as an independent rather than a dependent variable.

Reprinted from *Social Problems,* Vol. 7, No. 3, Winter 1959–60, pp. 210–218.

Procedure

The research consisted of a content analysis of mental health pamphlets in order to disclose dominant themes. The 27 pamphlets analyzed were obtained from a local mental health clinic, the New York State Department of Mental Hygiene and the National Association for Mental Health.

The basic criteria used in the selection of pamphlets were: they must have been concerned primarily with a description of the nature of mental health rather than mental illness; and they must have been addressed to the general public rather than to special groups (e.g., clergymen, nurses, teachers, etc.). Following the selection of pamphlets, the content was reviewed again and all text which did not fulfill the basic criteria was eliminated from consideration (even within pamphlets predominantly concerned with mental health, there was some discussion of the extent of mental illness, its causes and cures). This comprised about 30 per cent of the text.

In the material to follow, then, we shall be referring only to the remaining text, i.e., the content dealing specifically with the nature of mental health, in pamphlets primarily concerned with this subject. This text will be considered as a whole, and the presentation of findings is in terms of this totality.

Although the authors operated on the hypothesis that there would be a considerable amount of mental health text having a middle class orientation, there was no attempt made to select this material to the exclusion of possibly contradictory materials. An initial survey of the text indicated that our hypothesis seemed to be confirmed. To insure against bias, however, a check sheet was prepared and the frequency of specific content (i.e., words and phrases) was recorded using provisional categories. As far as the authors could determine, all repetitive content was included on the check sheet. The process of analyzing the pamphlets to ascertain repetitive material was repeated to insure the reliability of the authors' judgements. These judgements were found to be essentially the same in the second as they were in the first analysis.

Using this analysis as a basis, the themes in the literature were determined. A general criterion utilized was that words and phrases of the same basic content had to be repeated in at least one third of the pamphlets in order to be considered a "theme." These "themes," with examples, are presented in the "findings" section.

After the "themes" were ascertained, a determination was made as to whether they involved middle class values and orientations. This determination was based upon generalizations drawn from the sociological literature pertaining to differences between middle and lower class values and orientations. Most of these generalizations derive from an unpublished paper by Gross and Gursslin (9).

Findings

Approximately 60 per cent of the text referred to above (i.e., material expressly concerned with a description of mental health and its attainment) contained statements, either explicit or implied, which could be identified as falling within the middle class cultural mold. In addition, most of this content was accompanied by pictures portraying such scenes as middle class households and executives at work. Another 30 per cent of this material consisted of platitudes and an assortment of positively value-laden words. These directives concerning the finding and keeping of mental health were vague and/or ambiguous. Some illustrations of this kind of material are:

(1) "(Mentally healthy people) accept their responsibilities." (III p. 3)[1]

(2) "Being mentally healthy means feeling right about other people." (IV p. 11)

(3) "Such things as a happy childhood spent in a serene household with loving guidance from parents who are themselves well-balanced contribute to mental health." (X p. 28).

Several pamphlets, comprising roughly ten per cent of the content, were relatively free of the middle class "themes." One pamphlet in particular, entitled *How to Deal with Your Tensions*,[2] warrants special consideration, since many of the suggestions put forth in it concerning mental health and its attainment, attempt to modify some of the more tension-creating features of the middle class ethic. For instance, the reader of this pamphlet is advised to—" 'Escape for a while'—Sometimes, when things go wrong, it helps to escape from the painful problem for a while: —Making yourself 'stand there and suffer' is a form of self punishment, not a way to solve a problem."

Although some of this content could be seen as reflecting a lower class orientation in that it de-emphasizes "striving" and setting one's goals too high, it is set within a different context, namely, a middle class, rational, manipulative orientation toward the world. One "escapes for a while" in order that one may ultimately solve problems more effectively.

Dominant themes found in the literature examined, are presented below in the form of summary statements. These will be followed by quotations from the pamphlets which provide concrete examples of the material upon which they were based. The summaries and supporting material found in the left-hand column are opposite a statement of middle class versus lower-class values found in the right hand column.

The purpose of this presentation is to indicate certain basic parallels between the mental health content and the middle-class orientation

on the one hand, and a disjunction between this content and the lower-class orientation on the other.

MENTAL HEALTH PROTOTYPE | MIDDLE-CLASS VS. LOWER-CLASS PROTOTYPE

Adjustment and Conformity

The mentally healthy person is able to get along with others. He adjusts himself to the group and the prevailing norms.
Supporting examples:
(A) "If you're mentally healthy you can get along with other people" (I).
(B) "Success comes with the ability to work with . . . associates, not against them" (II, p. 1).
(C) "He [the mentally healthy child] learns the rules of group living. Rejection of the group is not only a symptom of poor adjustment but it may have serious consequences in its effect on the individual child. Many a bitter person could have been spared much unhappiness if he had learned early in life how to make himself acceptable to others" (XII, p. 4).

Adjustment and conformity have become the central watchwords of the "new middle class" man, who is typically a cog in the wheels of a large organization. He is not only an "organization man" but also an "other directed man." He seeks his source of direction in those about him and in mass media. His values shift as this guidance shifts. His only stable characteristics are striving and paying close attention to the signals about him.

Lower-class people have not learned these "skills." Although they are responsive to informal group pressures, they are more apt to express themselves spontaneously. In addition, since their chances for upward mobility are slight, they have less to lose from non-conformity (13; 16; 18; 20; 24).[3]

Problem-Solving

The mentally healthy person acts to solve problems as they arise. He faces up to his problems and then does something about them.
(A) "They [mentally healthy people] do something about their problems as they arise" (III, p. 3).
(B) "Ed [a poor example of mental health] ought to be honest with himself, try to face up to his own frustrations and do something about them" (IV p. 3).
(C) "Find out what you can do about your troubles and then do it!" (V p. 6).

Middle-class persons make a greater effort to control events in their lives and solve problems as they emerge. They make a conscious attempt to obtain knowledge which will be helpful in the control of their social and material environment.

Lower-class persons are more apt to blame "fate" or "bad luck" for their misfortuntes and to react with apathy and indifference to their problems. They seldom make an effort to obtain knowledge which would be helpful in such

control. Lower-class socioeconomic conditions result in lack of information and education and a general lack of environmental control. This, in turn, results in an adaptation to submission and failure as an adjustive life outlook (13; 16).

The Value of Work

The mentally healthy person enjoys work. He gets satisfaction out of doing a job and this contributes to his on-going state of mental health.

(A) "Those who have a zest for working . . . may be said to be mentally healthy" (IX p. 3).

(B) "He [the mentally healthy person] gets satisfaction out of doing a job" (VI p. 16).

(C) "Satisfactions gained from work help to keep people healthy" (X p. 4).

Middle-class persons place a great emphasis on the importance of a vocation. This along with other "virtues," such as thrift, respectability, and the accumulation of wealth, comprise the core values of the middle class.

Work is viewed by lower-class persons as something which is necessary in order to obtain money to buy the essentials of life (13; 16; 23).

Control of Emotions

The mentally healthy person controls his emotions and/or directs them into "harmless" outlets.

(A) "Don't let your emotions run you—you be the boss" (V p. 10).

(B) "We all have emotions but don't let them bowl you over" (VI p. 10).

(C) "Find a harmless outlet for your feelings—mow the lawn—scrub the floor—don't take it out on the boss or your wife" (V p. 8).

Middle-class people emphasize the importance of controlling one's emotions, whereas lower-class people give more direct expression to their emotions, particularly aggressive feelings. Middle-class children are taught to control their aggressive tendencies except when flagrantly provoked. Lower-class children are taught aggressive techniques and aggressive abilities are highly valued in lower-class society (11; 15; 21; 22).

Planning Ahead

The mentally healthy person plans ahead without fear of the future.

(A) "He [the mentally healthy person] plans for tomorrow with-

Middle-class people are future-oriented. They think in terms of long-range goals and make rational plans for the attainment of such goals. Since they have greater eco-

out being afraid of what's coming" (VII p. 6).

(B) "Plan for tomorrow but don't worry about it" (V p. 1).

(C) "They [mentally healthy people] plan ahead but do not fear the future" (III p. 3).

nomic security, they have less fear of the future. Lower-class people are present-oriented. They think in terms of immediate gratification. They see no value in planning for long-term goals, since the probability of their being attained is so slight (12; 13; 15).

Striving

The mentally healthy person establishes goals for himself that are within the limits of his capacity to reach and then he strives to his utmost to achieve these goals.

(A) "[Mentally healthy people] . . . make use of their natural capacities—they set realistic goals for themselves—they put their best effort into what they do and get satisfaction out of doing it" (III p. 3).

(B) "[The mentally healthy person] . . . does whatever he tackles to the best of his ability. If the result is not perfect, he doesn't fret about it, just tries to do better the next time" (VII p. 6).

(C) ". . . all tension is not bad. . . . The tension that comes from doing what you have to do with all your might, from striving for the best that is within you is the tension that makes you glad you are alive" (II p. 3).

Middle-class persons emphasize the importance of striving, particularly in the business and professional spheres. They aspire to higher status occupations and higher income levels than do lower-class persons. They set goals they think they can reach and are more optimistic about achieving the goals they set for themselves. They believe that ability will be rewarded with success.

Lower-class persons have very limited aspirations. They are more concerned with the satisfaction of immediate needs, and they feel that the likelihood of achieving long-range goals is remote. They tend, therefore, to devaluate the culturally defined success goals as well as the activities leading to the attainment of those goals (2; 3; 13; 26).

Community Participation

An example of less recurrent material:

(A) "Your community needs you. In such [community] activities people can make their own lives more meaningful. Most important—it provides emotional satisfaction" (VIII p. 3).

Middle-class people participate in many more community organizations and activities than do lower-class people, who participate, instead, in informal group associations. Lower-class people are less interested in "community betterment" activities and more interested in the immediate gratification of informal group participation (1; 12; 17; 24).

Discussion

The basic conclusion to be drawn from a sizable portion of the content under investigation is that the middle-class prototype and the mentally healthy prototype are in many respects equivalent. This conclusion involves a number of implications of which only a few will be touched upon in this paper.

Like Davis (5), we must also conclude that the mental health movement is unwittingly propagating a middle-class ethic under the guise of science. If anything, this conclusion has even greater import today than it had 20 years ago. There are two major reasons why this is true: (1) Educational efforts channeled through mass media have been greatly expanded over the past few years. For instance, in its first Annual Report (1950–1951) the National Association for Mental Health records that four million pamphlets were distributed during that year. By 1955, the number had increased to 12½ million. Although specific information regarding pamphlet distribution has not been published by the National Association for Mental Health since 1955, the organization does report that in 1957 nearly $425,000 was expended on education. This was the largest budget item for that year and was roughly double the 1956 figure (2). Since the 1930's it would appear that there has been increasing credence by the general public in psychiatric and mental health counsel. The foregoing is especially pertinent as far as influence on middle-class persons is concerned since this group is more apt to be the pamphlet receiving and reading group as well as the segment of the population most eager to grasp at the "latest" on how to raise one's children, live life to the utmost and yet have "peace of mind." The fact that the recipients as well as the disseminators of the mental health "message" are almost entirely middle class has been dealt with by the authors in another article (10).

A Functional Interpretation

From a functional point of view, we should like to consider the following proposition: the mental health movement contributes to the maintenance and persistence of the middle-class sociocultural structure by providing authoritative, "scientific" support to middle-class values and orientation. (We are speaking here, of course, of latent functions, since it is assumed that the consequences are neither intended nor recognized by proponents of the mental health movement.)

This proposition takes on particular significance when viewed from a historical perspective. The moral, religious, and economic underpinnings of "traditional" middle-class society have altered appreciably dur-

ing the past 50 years. It is of particular significance that with the decline of these old supportive institutions there has emerged a new movement giving "pseudo-scientific" authoritative support to the "new middle class" way of life. In many respects the mental health movement represents the functional equivalent of religion in the traditional middle-class structure.[4]

When the foregoing remarks are viewed from the standpoint of the formal goals of the mental health movement, a significant paradox is evident. If, as many sociologists and culturally oriented psychiatrists maintain, one of the primary roots of mental disorder lies in socially structured strains, then it may very well be that the mental health movement is helping to support a social system that is producing a high incidence of mental illness. In short, the mental health movement, whose purpose it is to contribute to personal organization and not necessarily social organization, may actually be contributing to the maintenance of middle-class social organization but not necessarily personal organization. These remarks are, of course, only suggestive. It is recognized that the relationship between personal and social organization is a complex one. It is also possible that a social movement which contributes to a modicum of social organization in an era of rapid social change may be in the long run doing more for "mental health" than a movement which sets up a disparate set of standards even though they be humanistically geared to a "fuller" attainment of man's "basic needs."

The foregoing remarks apply primarily to middle-class society. What, then, are some of the possible ramifications for lower-class society? Considering the differences in values and orientation, it is clear that the prototype of the lower-class individual is markedly different from the prototype of the "mentally healthy" individual. To the extent that the mental health movement is successful in advancing this mental health prototype as a desirable model to emulate, it may have a considerable personally disorganizing effect upon those lower-class persons who accept the mental health prototype. For example, the "message" sets forth a way of life which is most unrealistic for lower-class people, who must make some adjustment to the conditions and culture of the lower class. Lower-class people who take on forms of behavior implied in the mental health model are apt to find themselves alienated from lower-class society as well as subjected to other stresses of upwardly mobile types.

Again we are confronted with the paradox that the mental health educational effort may actually operate to produce that which it is manifestly intended to combat.

The corollary to the proposition that the mental health movement is functional for the middle-class sociocultural structure is that it is dysfunctional for the lower-class sociocultural structure since it promulgates an ethic which is contrary to some of the central values and orientation of lower-class society. The degree to which the mental health movement may have dysfunctional consequences for the lower-class structure at the present time is probably quite limited, since the movement's current mass media educational efforts probably have little appeal to lower-class

persons (10). To the extent, however, that more subtle and effective methods of social control are built around the mental health movement in the future, we may expect some pronounced dysfunctional consequences for the lower-class social structure.

The Extent of Coverage

Much of the foregoing may appear to be an overstatement of the effect of these "educational" efforts on the audience they reach. An examination of the popular literature of the day, however,—for example, middle-class, "ladies magazines"—should make it apparent that the influence of mental health education extends far beyond the distribution of pamphlets. For instance, an examination by the authors of five such magazines for only the latter half of 1958 disclosed nine feature articles dealing with mental health in terms generally similar to the pamphlet material. In short, the total effect, particularly on middle-class society, is much more pervasive than may superficially appear to be the case.

The extent to which the mental health "message" is affecting various segments of the population requires more systematic research. Likewise, there is a need for a more comprehensive study of the content of the "message." It is hoped that the present limited study will serve to stimulate further research.

Implications for the
Mental Health Movement

Mass media communication has been increasingly utilized by the mental health movement as a primary means for coming to grips with the problem of mental illness. Through its program of public education, the National Association for Mental Health, for example, has played a significant role in the public's growing awareness of the widespread incidence of mental illness. This organization has also been instrumental in breaking down some of the barriers and superstitions regarding the mentally ill. Here, the National Association for Mental Health seems on somewhat firmer ground, although, as some recent experiences have shown, the complexities involved demand a much more sophisticated base and plan of operation (4).

The situation concerning public enlightenment in the broader area of the nature of mental health and its attainment is far less encouraging. Much more research and theoretical development are required before the public can be approached with any degree of confidence that what is being offered as the substance of mental health has reasonable validity. In particular, the implication of the educational material offered for diverse subsystems and personality structures must be clearly thought

out. If they are not, the mental health educator is likely to discover belatedly that his purposive action has produced unanticipated consequences antithetical to his good intent. In brief, it would seem that a critical appraisal of these aspects of mental health education is required.

Notes

1. See pamphlet bibliography.
2. Stevenson, George S., *How to Deal with Your Tensions* (New York: National Association for Mental Health, 1958).
3. The supportive bibliography herein presented is by no means exhaustive of the breadth of material relating to class cultural differences. It is designed primarily to suggest some sources which touch upon the class characteristics referred to in the designated categories.
4. For a more general statement of this point of view from a longer historical perspective and a comparison of the mental health movement with the early Christian church see John R. Seely, "Social Values, The Mental Hygiene Movement and Mental Health," *The Annals of the American Academy of Political and Social Science*, 286 (March, 1953), 15–25.

References

1. Anderson, W. A., "Family Social Participation and Social Status Self Ratings," *American Sociological Review*, 11 (June, 1946), 253–258.
2. Centers, R., "Attitude and Belief in Relation to Occupational Stratification," *Journal of Social Psychology*, 27 (May, 1948), 159–185.
3. ———— and H. Cantril, "Income Satisfaction and Income Aspiration," *Journal of Abnormal and Social Psychology*, 41 (January, 1946), 64–69.
4. Cumming, E. and J. Cumming, *Closed Ranks* (Cambridge, Mass.: Harvard University Press, 1957).
5. Davis, K., "Mental Hygiene and the Class Structure," *Psychiatry*, 1 (February, 1938), 55–65.
6. Eaton, J., "The Assessment of Mental Health," *American Journal of Psychiatry*, 108 (August, 1951), 81–90.
7. *Evaluation in Mental Health: A Review of the Problem of Evaluating Mental Health Activities*, No. 413, U. S. Dept. of Health, Education and Welfare, Public Health Service, National Institutes of Health, National Institute of Mental Health (Bethesda, Maryland: Public Health Service Publication, 1955), 1–60.
8. Ginsburg, S. W., "The Mental Health Movement and Its Theoretical Assumptions," in *Community Programs for Mental Health*, edited by Kotinsky, R. and H. Witmer (Cambridge, Mass.: Harvard University Press, 1955).
9. Gross, L. and O. Gursslin, "A Simple Logical Scheme Using Social Class Models" (unpublished paper).
10. Gursslin, O., R. Hunt, and J. Roach, "Social Class, Mental Hygiene and Psychiatric Practice," *The Social Service Review*, 33 (September, 1959), 237–244.
11. Hollingshead, A., "Class Differences in Family Stability," *The Annals of the American Academy of Political and Social Science*, 272 (November, 1950), 39–46.
12. ————, *Elmtown's Youth* (New York: Wiley, 1949).
13. Hyman, H., "The Value Systems of Different Classes: A Social Psychological Contribution of the Analysis of Stratification," in *Class, Status and Power*, edited by Bendix, R. and S. Lipset (Glencoe, Ill.: The Free Press, 1953), 190–203.
14. Jahoda, M., *Current Concepts of Positive Mental Health* (New York: Basic Books, 1958).
15. Kluckhohn, C. and F. Kluckhohn, "American Culture: Generalized Orientations and Class Patterns," in *Conflicts of Power in Modern Culture* edited by

Bryson, L., L. Finkelstein, and R. Mac-Iver (New York: Harper, 1947), 106–128.

16. Knupfer, G., "Portrait of the Underdog," *The Public Opinion Quarterly*, 11 (Spring, 1947), 103–114.

17. Komarovsky, M., "The Voluntary Association of Urban Dwellers," *American Sociological Review*, 11 (December, 1946), 686–698.

18. Mills, C. W., *White Collar* (New York: Oxford University Press, 1953).

19. Redlich, F. "The Concept of Health in Psychiatry," in *Explorations in Social Psychiatry*, edited by Leighton, A., J. Clausen, and R. Wilson, (New York: Basic Books, 1957), 139–164.

20. Riesman, D., N. Glazer, and R. Denney, *The Lonely Crowd* (New Haven: Yale University Press, 1950).

21. Useeem, J., P. Tangent, and R. Useem, "Stratification in a Prairie Town," *American Sociological Review*, 7 (June, 1942), 331–342.

22. Warner, W. L., *American Life, Dream and Reality* (Chicago: University of Chicago Press, 1953).

23. Weber, M., *The Protestant Ethic and the Spirit of Capitalism*, (translated by T. Parsons) (New York: Charles Scribner's Sons, 1948).

24. Whyte, W. F., *Street Corner Society* (Chicago: University of Chicago Press, 1943).

25. Whyte, W. H., *The Organization Man* (New York: Simon and Schuster, 1956).

26. Williams, R., *American Society* (New York: Knopf, 1952).

MENTAL HEALTH PAMPHLETS *

I. *What is Mental Health?* (bookmark), New York State Dept. of Mental Hygiene, 1951.

II. *Your Balance of Power,* Wyeth Laboratories, Division of American Home Products Corporation, New York, 1957.

III. *Mental Health is—1-2-3-,* The National Association for Mental Health, 1951.

IV. *The Worry-Go-Round (How to Understand your Everyday Tensions),* The Connecticut Mutual Life Insurance Company, Hartford, Conn., 1955.

V. *Mental Health is For Everyday,* New York State Dept. of Mental Hygiene, 1952.

VI. *The Art of Happiness,* American Visuals Corporation, distributed by Mental Health Materials Corporation, New York, 1955.

VII. Christner, R., *Some Facts you should know about Mental Health,* (Montclair, New Jersey: The Economics Press Inc., 1955).

VIII. *The Middle Years* (Guideposts to Mental Health, No. 6), New York State Dept. of Mental Hygiene, 1951.

IX. *Mental Health Is A Family Affair,* Public Affairs Pamphlet, No. 155, Public Affairs Committee Inc., 1957.

X. *The Mind In Sickness and Health,* John Hancock Mutual Life Insurance Co., Boston, Mass., 1954.

XI. *Stress and What It Means to You,* Metropolitan Life Insurance Company, New York, 1958.

XII. *School Days* (Guideposts to Mental Health, No. 2), New York State Dept. of Mental Hygiene, 1957.

* Only pamphlets used as examples in the body of the article are included.

Social Class and Psychiatric Treatment

Norman Q. Brill, M.D., and Hugh A. Storrow, M.D.

Hollingshead and Redlich [1] have reported that patients in the upper social classes * who seek psychiatric treatment for any type of psychiatric disorder are more apt to receive intensive, insight-producing psychotherapy, while patients in the lower social classes are more apt to receive short-term supportive psychotherapy, pharmacologic, or other somatotherapy and if hospitalized, simple custodial care. It has been emphasized that this differential treatment or discrimination is in part the result of the inability of patients from lower social classes to afford the more costly and therefore presumably preferred intensive psychotherapy.

If the economic factors were of primary importance, it would be expected that this difference would not exist in a public clinic which excludes patients who are able to afford private psychiatric treatment. With the economic factor eliminated, intensive individual psychotherapy would be equally available to all patients regardless of their social class. Schaffer and Myers [2] tested this hypothesis in a study conducted in "a psychiatric outpatient clinic (for the medically indigent) in a major teaching hospital." They found that social class still seemed to play a role. Not only were patients from upper social classes accepted for treatment more often, but their treatment was more apt to be given by a more senior or more experienced member of the staff than was the case with patients from lower social classes. Other investigators, using patients' educational level as an index of social class have reported similar findings in both inpatient and outpatient settings (Kahn et al.,[3] Loor,[4] and Rosenthal and Frank [5]). This suggests the possibility of a

Reprinted by permission of American Medical Association, from *Archives of General Psychiatry*, Vol. 3, No. 10, October 1960, pp. 340–344.

relationship between education and sophistication and psychological mindedness and the possibility that, at least to some extent, it is these factors which determine the type of psychiatric treatment given to a patient, in addition to his social class or economic status.

Furthermore, where a clinic staff is primarily interested in doing intensive individual psychotherapy (as is often the case), patients who are believed to be not interested in, nor amenable to such treatment, are likely to be rejected at the outset. In an attempt to explore some of these possibilities, we reviewed the experience of our own clinic which is similar to the one studied by Schaffer and Myers.

Method

SETTING

This study was conducted in the Outpatient Department of the Neuropsychiatric Institute, University of California Medical Center, Los Angeles. This clinic functions primarily as a training center for medical students and psychiatric residents. Approximately 60 per cent of applicants are referred by physicians, while an additional 35 per cent are self-referred. The remainder are referred from nonmedical sources such as schools, social agencies, and courts. Both adults and children are accepted for treatment. Applicants who are financially capable of paying for private psychiatric care, however, are not accepted. The decision concerning financial eligibility is made by applying a sliding scale which considers family income, family size, and fixed family expenses. If a patient's family consists of three members, the maximum acceptable total family income is approximately $400.00 per month. This amount is scaled up or down for larger or smaller families. The clinic fees range from $0.50 to $10.00 per psychiatric interview, although the minimum fee may be further reduced if the patient's family is receiving public assistance. The average fee paid by patients is $1.47 per treatment hour.

Since the demand for clinic service exceeds the supply, selection of patients for therapy is necessary. This first contact is handled by a staff psychiatric social worker who conducts a preliminary financial and clinical screening. If a patient's financial resources exceed the clinic limits, he is, of course, referred for private care. Clinical reasons for referral elsewhere are (1) illnesses of very long duration that have not responded to a variety of therapies in the past; (2) severe depressions, particularly if associated with active suicidal tendencies and other psychiatric disorders requiring hospitalization. Most of the small number of psychotic patients who are accepted in the clinic have been previously treated in the psychiatric ward of the Medical Center and are carried in the clinic following discharge. Chronic alcoholics are excluded, since they are referred to a separate and special alcoholism unit in the clinic.

Patients accepted in the preliminary social service screening are further evaluated in an intake interview and by means of group psychologi-

cal testing. The intake interviewer is usually a psychiatric resident or medical student. The evaluative data are later considered in an intake conference which attempts to answer the question, "Is this patient likely to benefit from treatment?" In the vast majority of instances treatment means psychotherapy of a relatively short-term nonintensive nature. If the answer to this question is "yes" and if a therapist is available, the patient is accepted for treatment.

For the most part, and with relatively few exceptions, treatment is provided by medical students and psychiatric residents. The medical students (third year) are ordinarily assigned two patients whom they see once a week for supportive psychotherapy for an entire school year. The psychiatric residents (in all three years of training) provide most of the treatment. They have considerable freedom in the selection of their cases. Patients are not treated by the staff psychiatrists or faculty and what treatment social workers and psychologists do is of a collaborative type with members of patients' families.

Analysis of data on terminated cases reveals that the treatment done in the clinic is primarily short-term nonintensive psychotherapy. Seventy-five per cent of the patients are seen once or twice per week and the median total number of interviews per patient is 20. One-third of the patients seen are treated primarily with supportive psychotherapy and the remainder with psychotherapy characterized by some support but primarily focused on attempts to help the patient understand the psychological causes of his illness. Drugs are rarely prescribed.

DATA COLLECTION

Standardized data are collected on each patient at each stage of his progress through the clinic. These data are recorded on rating scales developed for this purpose and which permit direct tabulation of information on IBM cards. Identifying data such as age, sex, occupation, and education are obtained by the clinic psychiatric nurse at the time of the first clinic visit. The intake interviewer collects and records information which may have a bearing on a patient's suitability for therapy, and the therapist is asked to provide data on the therapy and its results. All interviewers are provided with coding instructions for the rating scales used and are trained in the coding process. This study is based on data obtained from these rating scales. This approach has advantages over those based on the extraction of information from clinic charts, since charts are frequently poor sources of data which are comparable from patient to patient.

SAMPLE STUDIED

Four hundred fifty patients over 18 years of age applied for and received an intake evaluation in the clinic between July 1, 1958, and June

30, 1959. Twenty-seven of these were seen in treatment by psychologists or social workers. Since these cases were all relatives of patients assigned for treatment to residents or medical students and were seen only as part of a collaborative effort, they were excluded from further analysis. The remaining 423 patients constitute the sample studied. The age range was from 18 to 55 with the median in the early 30's. Two-thirds were women and 95 per cent were white. Major diagnostic categories were as follows:

Disorder	Per Cent
Psychotic	8
Psychophysiologic	7
Psychoneurotic	44
Personality	36
Other diagnostic categories	5

Hollingshead's Two-Factor Index of Social Position was used to estimate each patient's social class level.[6] This Index employs the patient's education and occupation in the class level determination. Using the Two-Factor Index the resulting distribution of classes was as follows:

Class	Per Cent
I and II	13
III	33
IV	39
V	15

The presence of a small number of Class I individuals in the sample is attributable to the method of class level determination. A few highly educated professional individuals in relatively low income academic positions are financially eligible for clinic care, particularly if their families are large and other financial commitments heavy.

Of the 423 patients in the sample, 43 per cent were rejected as unsuitable for treatment in this clinic; 14 per cent were assigned for treatment to a medical student, and 43 per cent to a psychiatric resident. For 85 of the 423 patients in the sample, insufficient information was available to permit social class determination, and these patients were excluded from further study, leaving a sample of 338. Since the exclusion of this number of subjects might introduce a bias into the subsequent data analysis, the excluded subjects were compared with those remaining in terms of their progress through the clinic. No statistically significant differences were found between the two groups in terms either of probability of acceptance for therapy or in terms of the training and experience of the therapist assigned to those accepted. In this comparison and in all other analyses reported in this paper the χ^2 test of statistical significance was used.

Results

A number of analyses were done to test the relationship of the patient's progress through the clinic with social class. It was found that if

the social classes were combined into upper (I, II, and III) and lower (IV and V), there was a relationship at the 0.05 level of significance between social class and whether or not a patient was accepted for treatment. Patients in the upper class group were more likely to be accepted for treatment than were those in the lower class group. The percentages and numbers of patients in each category are given in Table 1. If the social classes were considered separately, statistically sig-

Table 1—Social Class of Patients and Acceptance for Psychiatric Treatment

	SOCIAL CLASS*					
	I, II, AND III		IV AND V		TOTALS	
Disposition	No.	Per Cent	No.	Per Cent	No.	Per Cent
No treatment	57	37	91	49	148	44
Treatment	97	63	93	51	190	56
Totals	154	100	184	100	338	100

* Determinations made using Hollingshead's Two-Factor Index of Social Position.[6]
Note: $\chi^2 = 4.78$ $p < 0.05$

nificant differences disappeared. It was also found that separating the therapy patients into two groups according to whether they were assigned a medical student or a resident therapist destroyed the significance of the relationship. The results in this clinic thus demonstrated a significant relationship between social class and whether or not a patient was accepted for treatment but no significant relationship between social class and the training and experience of the therapist assigned. The observed relationship between social class and acceptance for therapy could not be accounted for in terms of interrelationships between social class and age, sex, or diagnostic category since none of these latter variables were found to be significantly related to social class.

Comment and Conclusions

Our findings agree with those of Hollingshead and Redlich and those of Schaffer and Myers in that a relationship has been demonstrated between a patient's social class and whether or not he is accepted for therapy in our clinic. We have failed to confirm, however, the relationship observed by Schaffer and Myers between social class and the training and experience of the therapist assigned. Although the samples were comparable in terms of class distribution and percentage of patients accepted for treatment, this may be because our staff members do not function as therapists, and patients who are judged to be amenable to psychotherapy are assigned to medical students as well as to residents. A relationship between social class and acceptance for psychiatric treatment is thus demonstrated again in a clinic where the cost of such treat-

ment cannot be considered a contributing variable. This suggests that measures directed at reducing the cost of psychotherapy and making it more widely available do not offer *the* solution to the problem of providing needed psychiatric treatment to the lower class patient. It seems that if a series of applicants for psychiatric treatment is separated on the basis of social class into upper and lower groups, a larger proportion of patients who can be considered suitable for psychotherapy will be found in the upper group. There is a distinct tendency to view the lower class patient as less suitable for psychotherapy than the upper class individual.

Analyses of data obtained at intake relating to "psychological mindedness" of patients in relation to social class revealed the following: Low social class is found to be significantly related to lower estimated intelligence, less education, a tendency to see the presenting problem as physical rather than emotional, a desire for symptomatic relief only rather than over-all help, lack of understanding of the psychotherapeutic process, and lack of desire for psychotherapy. The intake interviewer tends to react less positively to the lower class patient and to see him as less treatable for psychotherapy than his upper class counterpart. Two variables not found to be related to social class are manifest anxiety and amount of obvious secondary gain associated with the illness. These findings are summarized in Table 2 in which the per cent of patients in each class group rating high and low on each variable are tabulated.

Table 2—Social Class Versus "Psychological Mindedness"

	CLASS I, II, AND III			CLASS IV AND V			
	High Rating (%)	Low Rating (%)	Total (%)	High Rating (%)	Low Rating (%)	Total (%)	Statistical Significance of Differences
Estimated intelligence	54	46	100	24	76	100	p <0.01
Amount of education	67	33	100	13	87	100	p <0.01
Degree of manifest anxiety	8	92	100	14	86	100	n.s.
Amount of obvious secondary gain yielded by illness	38	62	100	40	60	100	n.s.
Recognition of emotional factors in illness	57	43	100	44	56	100	p <0.05
Desire for over-all help rather than symptomatic relief only	64	36	100	47	53	100	p <0.01
Understanding of psychotherapeutic procedures	43	57	100	28	72	100	p <0.01
Desire for psychotherapy	89	11	100	80	20	100	p <0.05
Interviewer's positive feelings toward patient	71	29	100	56	44	100	p <0.01
Estimate of treatability by psychotherapy	88	12	100	77	23	100	p <0.01

Note: Each variable rated by intake interviewer with reference to each patient.

Imber, Nash, and Stone [7] studied a situation in which therapists were not allowed to select their patients and both therapists and patients were under administrative pressure to remain in psychotherapeutic contact. They found that lower class patients remained in treatment for significantly shorter periods than middle class individuals. In addition, lower

class patients were less likely to return for treatment after initial screening. When patients are not assigned randomly but are selected on the basis of suitability for psychotherapy, as in our clinic, this difference disappears. In 147 patients whose therapy had been terminated at the time of data analysis no significant social class differentials are found in total number of interviews, average frequency of interviews, or judged response to therapy.

We feel that clinical judgments which find a lower proportion of patients suitable for psychotherapy in the lower than in the upper classes are in general valid. In a review of the relationship of social factors to psychotherapy Reusch states: "The present methods of individual psychotherapy—psychoanalysis included—are methods which were designed for use between people who belong to approximately the same social class and who share in common a large number of assumptions." [8] This point of view has also been suggested by Schaffer and Myers,[2] Hollingshead and Redlich,[1] and other workers in the field. It is in part because of this that lower class patients may be more often assigned to inexperienced psychotherapists, or are offered treatments other than psychotherapy.

In no sense do we suggest that our clinic or others like it should abandon attempts to cope with this problem and continue to offer only the kind of treatment which psychiatrists with "dynamic" orientations seem to prefer to give. Rather we feel that such clinics should reexamine their emphasis on psychotherapy as their preferred method of treatment. Rather than being criticized on the grounds of discrimination against the lower class individual, we feel that many psychiatrists and psychiatric clinics are open to criticism for their tendency to restrict treatment to one modality. It may be that education will ultimately result in a more sophisticated and more psychologically minded public that will more uniformly seek psychotherapy for emotional disorders but until that time arrives, psychiatrists are obliged to employ treatment methods that are designed to help all patients and not just those which for a variety of personal reasons they prefer to use.

Note

* These authors use the system of class typing developed by Hollingshead. A person's social class is that of his family and is determined with reference to the education and occupation of the family head plus the location of the family place of residence. Five class levels are distinguished. These are briefly described as follows:

Class I: Families in this class usually have considerable wealth. The head of the family is highly educated and is a major professional person or an important executive in a large concern.

Class II: The heads of families in this group are college graduates. They are lesser professionals or second-line business executives.

Class III: The family head is a high school graduate with perhaps some further training in college or in a business or trade school. He is likely to be a shopkeeper, a salesman, a white-collar employee, or a skilled factory worker.

Class IV: In most cases the family head has not finished high school. He is likely to be employed as a semiskilled factory worker.

Class V: The family head, who is usually not educated beyond the elementary level, works as an unskilled factory hand or laborer.

Hollingshead has also developed a sim-

plified method of measuring class levels using education and occupation only.[6] This method was used in the present investigation.

References

1. Hollingshead, A. B., and Redlich, F. C.: Social Class and Mental Illness, New York, John Wiley & Sons, Inc., 1958.

2. Schaffer, L., and Myers, J.: Psychotherapy and Social Stratification, Psychiatry, 17:83–93 (Feb.) 1954.

3. Kahn, R. L.; Pollack, M., and Fink, M.: Social Factors in the Selection of Therapy in a Voluntary Mental Hospital, J. Hillside Hosp. 6: 216–228, 1957.

4. Lorr, M.: Survey Findings, VA Survey of Use of Tranquilizers for Psychiatric Patients, Transactions of The Third Research Conference on Chemotherapy in Psychiatry, edited by C. L. Lindley, Vol. 3, Washington, D.C., Veterans Administration, 1959, pp. 39–49.

5. Rosenthal, D., and Frank, J. D.: The Fate of Psychiatric Clinic Outpatients Assigned to Psychotherapy, J. Nerv. & Ment. Dis. 127:330–343 (Oct.) 1958.

6. Hollingshead, A. B.: Two Factor Index of Social Position (mimeographed), New Haven, Connecticut, A. B. Hollingshead, 1957.

7. Imber, S. D.; Nash, E. H., Jr., and Stone, A. R.: Social Class and Duration of Psychotherapy, J. Clin. Psychol. 11:281–284 (July) 1955.

8. Ruesch, J.: Social Factors in Therapy, in Association for Research in Nervous and Mental Diseases, Psychiatric Treatment, Vol. 31, edited by S. B. Wortis, M. Herman, and C. C. Hare, Baltimore, The Williams & Wilkins Company, 1953, pp. 59–93.

Expectations of Psychotherapy in Patients of Lower Socioeconomic Class

Betty Overall and H. Aronson

There are many obstacles to psychotherapy with the patient of lower socioeconomic class. One of the greatest is such a patient's minimal involvement in the initial phases of treatment.

This problem became apparent in one of our psychiatric clinics in which the patient population consists almost entirely of individuals of lower socioeconomic class. A six-month survey of new patients revealed a dropout rate of 57 per cent after the initial interview, that is, only 43 per cent of the patients seen returned for a second appointment. This rate, while not notably different from that reported from comparable settings,[2,10] indicated a waste of time and effort sufficient to warrant an examination of the clinic population and the psychotherapeutic procedures followed.

The present study represents an attempt to define one of the factors that might have produced so high a rate of attrition. Since so many patients terminated after only one interview, it was felt that an important cause of dropouts might be the patient's negative evaluation of his initial interview in terms of his original expectations of treatment.

Hollingshead and Redlich[4] in their discussion of class factors in psychotherapy point out what they believe the lower socioeconomic class expectations to be:

Reprinted from *American Journal of Orthopsychiatry*, Vol. 33, No. 3, April 1963, pp. 421–430. Copyright, the American Orthopsychiatric Association, Inc.

This study was supported in part by Grant OM-356-R1 of the National Institutes of Health. We thank Dr. G. D. Klee, Director of Adult Outpatient Service, for his support and encouragement. We also acknowledge Dr. Jean O'Connor, Director of Comprehensive Clinic, Dr. William Holden, Assistant Director of Adult Outpatient Service, and Mrs. Imogene Young, Director of Psychiatric Social Work.

Class V patients accept professional procedures which have no meaning to them and which often arouse their anxiety. . . . Practically all Class V neurotics drop out of treatment. The few who remain beyond the intake period are unable to understand that their troubles are not physical illnesses. They continue to hold these attitudes even when their therapist changes from insight therapy to directive-supportive therapy. These patients are disappointed in not getting sufficient practical advice about how to solve their problems and how to run their lives. They express in word and action their lack of confidence in a "talking treatment." They retain rigid attitudes toward mental illness and consider the psychiatrist a magical doctor who can miraculously cure their "physical ills." They expect "pills and needles" and, also as a gratuity, sympathy and warmth, and they are disappointed at not having such demands gratified. . . . The most frequent source of difficulty between the lower status patient in psychotherapy and the therapist is the patient's tacit or overt demand for an authoritarian attitude on the part of the psychiatrist and the psychiatrist's unwillingness to assume this role because it runs counter to certain therapeutic principles.

The present study focuses on a general description of the treatment expectations of patients of lower socioeconomic class, and relates the fulfillment of these expectations to their returning or not returning for treatment.

For this purpose, three specific hypotheses were formulated:

1. Patients of lower social class expect the therapist to assume an active, medical role in the initial interview.

2. The actual conduct of the therapist during the interview is less active and medically oriented than the patient expects.

3. Those patients whose anticipations are less accurate will be less likely to return for further treatment; that is, those patients who do not return for treatment will have a greater discrepancy between their expectations and their perception of the interview.

Since the patient may evaluate the events of the interview in terms of his own reactions or even perceive them in a distorted manner, it appears reasonable to study the differences between a patient's and a therapist's perceptions. With this added dimension, a fourth hypothesis can be added:

4. The discrepancy between a patient's expectations and his perception of the interview is a better predictor of return to treatment than is the discrepancy between a patient's expectations and his therapist's perception of the interview.

Procedure

SETTING

The locale of this study was a psychiatric clinic in the general outpatient department of a university hospital, but totally administered by the department of psychiatry. The therapists were fourth-year medical

students, who were rotated through the clinic on a monthly basis. Supervision was by advanced residents and staff members, and the philosophy of the staff was dynamic. Patients received one or two initial interviews of an hour's duration. They were then seen for 15 to 20 minutes once every two to four weeks for the remainder of their treatment.

SUBJECTS

The subjects were 40 patients who had come to the clinic for their first visit. Patients who were obviously psychotic or severely disoriented were screened out as untestable.

Although a student-therapist may have seen more than one intake patient during his rotation in the clinic, only his first was selected for examination. All further patients seen by the student-therapist were excluded from the study. The information was obtained, therefore, from 40 patients, each seen by a different student-therapist. Within these limits, the subjects were a random selection of those seen during a single school year.

The age range of the subjects was 16 to 66, with a mean age of 39.6. There were 26 females and 14 males; 27 Negro and 13 white patients. Thirty of the 40 patients declared themselves Protestant, and all but 2 were born in the South. Sixteen were married and 24 had no marital ties: that is, they were either single, separated, divorced, or widowed.

Educational level ranged from second grade to completion of high school: 55 per cent had completed ninth grade or less, 37.5 per cent had completed 10 to 12 grades and 7.5 per cent (three) were students in high school at the time of the study. In terms of income: (Only 39 of the subjects could supply complete information on income.) 33.3 per cent were recipients of public assistance, 41 per cent earned $50 or less weekly and 25.6 per cent earned more than $50 a week. The highest reported income was $85 a week.

This sample group meets the requirements of Hollingshead and Redlich for classification as social groups IV and V in terms of income, occupation, and education. It is interesting that the treatment setting is typical of that described by Hollingshead and Redlich, in that lower class patients are assigned to therapists of lower status.

Procedure. A questionnaire was constructed listing 35 statements of a therapist's possible behavior in an initial interview. (A number of the questions were suggested by the Libo Preference Form P-D-A.[7]) Each question was devised to tap one of five aspects of a therapist's behavior such than an affirmative response would indicate the presence of that aspect. Although the five points are not mutually exclusive, each question focuses on only one. The categories, chosen to represent the points suggested by Hollingshead and Redlich, were:

1. Active—The therapist actively instructs or directs the patient, for example, "Do you think the doctor will tell you what is causing your trouble?"

2. Medical—The therapist focuses on the organic or physical prob-

lems of the patient, for example, "Do you think the doctor will be interested in your digestion?"

3. Supportive—The therapist avoids charged material in an attempt to bolster or comfort the patient, for example, "Do you think the doctor will try to get your mind off your troubles?"

4. Passive—The therapist leaves the direction of the discussion to the patient, encouraging all patient communications, for example, "Do you think the doctor will expect you to do most of the talking?"

5. Psychiatric—The therapist focuses on emotional or dynamic material, for example, "Do you think the doctor will want to know how you get along with people?"

A pilot study was conducted to be sure the questions were comprehensible and could differentiate among the subjects, that is, that no question was given the same response by all patients. The questionnaire was then revised to its present form.

Each patient was given the questionnaire orally by a psychiatric social worker (B.C.O.) on his first visit to the clinic, immediately preceding his interview with the therapist. The patient was asked to state whether he felt each statement was descriptive of the interview he was about to have. At the conclusion of the initial interview, the patient was again given the questionnaire to obtain his perception of the therapeutic procedure. Three questions were added:

"Do you like the doctor?"

"Do you think the doctor seemed to understand you?"

"Do you feel the doctor can help you?"

The fact sheet data to determine social class (income, occupation, education, and so on) were obtained at this time.

The student-therapist completed a comparable questionnaire at the conclusion of the interview to determine his perception of the interview. There were four additional questions, asking:

"Would this type of patient benefit most by being seen for a few interviews only?"

"Do you think the interview went well?"

"Do you think the prognosis is good?"

"Do you think this patient can use psychiatric treatment?"

The therapist did not know the purpose of the questionnaire. He was told that the study was to investigate the kinds of therapeutic techniques necessary for the wide range of diagnostic problems seen in the clinic.

The patient's return for a second clinic appointment, scheduled for all patients, was the criterion for classification as Return or Non-Return.

Results

Hypothesis 1. Patients of lower social class expect the therapist to assume an active, medical role in the interview.

Table 1 indicates the wording of the questionnaire and shows the

Overall and Aronson

Table 1—Percentage of Affirmative Responses Made by Patients Before and After Their Initial Interviews and by Student-Therapists After the Initial Interviews †

PATIENTS' BEFORE	PATIENTS' AFTER	THERAPISTS' AFTER	
Do you think the doctor will . . .	Did the doctor . . .	Did you . . .	
58%	50%	58%	1. give you medicine?
23	08	16	2. not ask questions about your personal life?
60	15**	08**	3. tell you what is wrong with you
78	58*	54	4. try and cheer you up?
20	13	00	5. not want your opinions?
75	78	82	6. listen more than he talks?
68	18**	16**	7. give you definite rules to follow?
54	28*	29*	8. avoid subjects which might upset you?
80	43**	71	9. ask what medicines you have been taking?
78	43**	55	10. want to know what your childhood was like?
90	85	82	11. want to know what kinds of things make you unhappy?
63	15**	08**	12. tell you what is causing your trouble?
83	18**	45**	13. ask what physical illnesses have been in your family?
87	55**	47**	14. want you to look at the bright side of things?
85	88	100	15. want to know about your thoughts and feelings?
83	40**	82	16. want to know what other doctors you have seen lately?
70	55	50	17. ask you a lot of questions?
70	20**	24**	18. be interested in your digestion?
90	65*	84	19. want to know how you get along with people?
75	18**	13**	20. tell you ways to solve your problems?
65	08**	05**	21. have a list of things he will want to check over?
95	73*	82	22. want to know how happy you are?
68	85	95**	23. expect you to do most of the talking?
68	25**	24**	24. be particularly interested in your aches and pains?
80	63	39**	25. try to get your mind off your troubles?
70	20**	29**	26. ask questions about any operations you have had?
88	100	100	27. be interested in hearing any personal problems you have?
70	15**	05**	28. tell you what is wrong with what you do?
50	83*	97**	29. not give you a physical examination?
78	45**	68	30. ask you to describe the physical illnesses you have had?
80	58*	74	31. want to know what your friends are like?
55	00**	00**	32. take your pulse and blood pressure?
93	95	100	33. listen to your troubles?
45	08**	08**	34. tell you what kinds of food you should eat?
98	83	100	35. be interested in knowing if some things make you afraid or nervous?

† The first 35 questions have been stated in the preinterview form given to patients. Appropriate changes of person or tense were made on the postinterview questionnaires. While the N is usually 40, omission of responses occasionally reduced the N to 38 or 39. Only one question was omitted by as many as three subjects. The results quoted are, of course, based on the actual number of responses obtained for each question.

* P < .05 (two-tailed) by means of the McNemar test for the significance of changes when compared with patients' preinterview responses.

** P < .01 (two-tailed) by means of the McNemar test for the significance of changes when compared with patients' preinterview responses.

Table 1—Continued

Patients' postinterview only:

97	36. Did you like the doctor?
100	37. Do you think the doctor seemed to understand you?
97	38. Do you feel that the doctor can help you?

Therapists' postinterview only:

50	36. This type of patient would benefit most by being seen for a few interviews only. (Yes, No.)
78	37. Do you think the interview went well?
61	38. Do you think the prognosis is good?
76	39. Do you think that this patient can use psychiatric treatment?

percentage of affirmative responses to each question made by our subjects. Since there was no control group, it was arbitrarily considered a significant degree of affirmation when questions were answered affirmatively by 65 per cent or more of the subjects. Several categories are somewhat incompatible, yet only three questions are affirmed by less than 50 per cent of the subjects. This could indicate a general set by the patients to answer Yes, or it could reflect an actual expectation that the therapist be simultaneously active, medical, supportive, passive and psychiatric, as these traits are defined above. The particularly high percentage of affirmative responses to questions in the psychiatric category strongly indicates that, contrary to the Hollingshead and Redlich conceptualization and to a much greater degree than we ourselves foresaw, these patients do generally anticipate that psychiatric issues will be raised.

At present, the degree to which the expectations reported here differ from those held by other socioeconomic groups must be left to the judgment of the reader. We are planning a comparable study of a middle-class population treated in the same hospital, which will make possible a statistical comparison of patient's expectations.

Hypothesis 2. The actual conduct of the therapist during the interview is less active and medically oriented than the patient expects.

Table 1 shows the percentage of affirmative responses to the same statements made after the interview had been conducted. The patients' observations of the interview were significantly different from their expectations for 23 of the 35 questions when compared by the McNemar test for the significance of changes.[12] Table 2 presents a graph of these differences in terms of the category of expectation indicated by an affirmative response. It shows that most of the discrepancy between expectation and observation lies in the categories of Active, Medical and Supportive, in each of which the therapist's behavior was generally less than the patient anticipated. In the Passive and Psychiatric categories, the tendency to expect more than was observed is not as clear-cut and the proportion of incorrect anticipation is generally smaller.

Hypothesis 3. Those patients whose anticipations are less accurate will be less likely to return for further treatment; that is, those patients who do not return for treatment will have a greater discrepancy between their expectations and their perception of the interview.

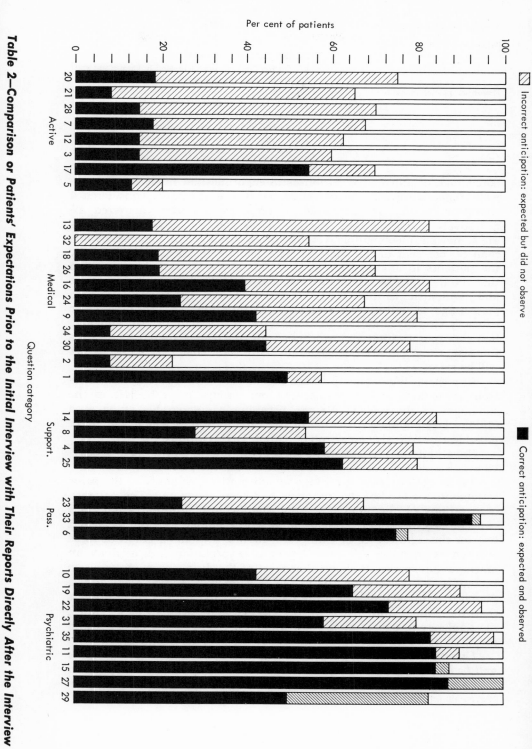

Table 2—Comparison or Patients' Expectations Prior to the Initial Interview with Their Reports Directly After the Interview

The 40 patients were subdivided into two groups: Return and Non-Return. There were 23 patients in the Return group and 17 in the Non-Return group. No significant differences were found between the two groups in terms of age, sex, race, income, education or marital ties; nor is this dropout rate of 42.5 per cent significantly different from that found through the six-month survey.

When the discrepancies between a patient's expectations and his view of the interview were totaled for the 35 questions, a single discrepancy score could be quantified for each patient. A Mann-Whitney U Test [12] showed the discrepancy scores of the Non-Return group to be significantly greater than those of the Return group. The difference was significant at the .01 level, corroborating the hypothesis that those patients whose expectations were most inaccurate were less likely to return for treatment.

Hypothesis 4. The discrepancy between a patient's expectations and his perception of the interview is a better predictor of return to treatment than is the discrepancy between a patient's expectation and his therapist's perception of the interview.

A single discrepancy score for each patient was also tabulated between the patient's expectations and the therapist's view of the actual conduct of the interview. The discrepancy scores of the Return and the Non-Return groups were then compared. In contrast to the significant difference noted above, no significant difference was found here (P < .25). Thus, our hypothesis that the patient's view is a better predictor of return is supported.

Since only three of the specific questions (namely, 9, 13 and 16, which are concerned with the adequacy of the medical history) show a significant difference between what the patient experienced and what the therapist felt had occurred, a Pearson product-moment correlation [9] was made between the two discrepancy scores described above, to determine the extent to which the patients disagreed with their therapists in terms of perception. The correlation was .72, which is significant at the level of 1 per cent. Thus, the patient and his therapist substantiately agree on the interview, indicating that little distortion of the events had taken place.

General questions: Of the 40 patients, only one answered No to the question, "Did you like the doctor?" and only one answered No to the question, "Do you feel that the doctor can help you?". Both patients were in the Non-Return group. All 40 patients answered Yes to, "Do you think the doctor seemed to understand you?". Apparently, questions such as these are of little value in understanding the dropout rate for the patients studied.

There was less unanimity in the student-therapists' responses. However, no differentiaton between the Return and Non-Return patients was made on questions 36, 37 and 38. There was a significantly greater number of affirmative responses for the Return group to, "Do you think that this patient can use psychiatric treatment?" (P < .05). There are two ways of interpreting this differentiation. The therapists could be

discerning some difference between the groups, whatever this difference might be. However, it is also possible that the patients are able to perceive acceptance or rejection on the part of the therapist, and that this perception influences their decision to return.

Discussion

The problem of high, initial dropouts has been investigated from a variety of viewpoints.[8] Seeman [11] points to the fact that the patients who are best integrated apparently have less need for treatment and thus leave treatment more readily.

Frank et al.,[1] in a series of carefully planned studies on dropout rates, found that patients who tend to remain in treatment could be differentiated from terminators in terms of "class, education and occupation, fluctuating illness with manifest anxiety, readiness to communicate distress and personal liabilities, influenceability, social integrity and perseverance" (p. 298).

The above studies investigate high dropout rates in order to define the patient variables pertinent to early termination of treatment by the patient. The philosophy behind such studies is an attempt to achieve a screening process whereby those patients who are less likely to continue will simply not be accepted for treatment. Relatively little has been written and few investigations have been reported which reflect the attitude that, since such patients need treatment, procedures that would lessen the likelihood of premature termination should be found. However, two very interesting studies with this focus have been carried out.

Imber, Nash, and Stone [6] raised the question of whether a high dropout rate among lower-class patients may be due to the fact that they are typically assigned to the more inexperienced therapists, that is, medical students and social workers. A study was therefore conducted in which the experience of the therapist was held at a constant, senior resident-staff level. This did not lower the dropout rate for the lower-class patients.

Freedman et al.,[2] in a study of ambulatory schizophrenic patients, obtained significant differences in dropout rate when the patient's denial or acknowledgment of his mental illness was examined in combination with a rating of the warmth or detachment of the therapist during the interview. They found that when such warmth or detachment in the first interview is compatible with the patient's attitude about treatment, the patient tends to remain in therapy. That is, when the patient acknowledges his mental illness and encounters a warm relationship, or when he denies his mental illness and encounters a detached relationship, he is more likely to remain in treatment than when the other combinations of attitude and reception are present.

Our own viewpoint is similar to Freedman's in that several variables may interact to produce premature termination. These include the indi-

vidual patient being treated. The personality of the patient may produce such factors of resistance as fear of dependency or fear of expressing hostility. These resistances would be present regardless of the social class of the individual.

Another factor, a cognitive one, is perceptual understanding based on experience and learning. Expectation, as used in this study, was delineated to investigate the cognitive phenomenon. Lower-class individuals, due to cultural factors, may have a different conception of therapy and the procedures involved. It is speculated that there is an inverse relationship between accuracy of expectations of psychotherapy and social class, since opportunity to learn about therapy is more available to the upper classes.

The above discussion emphasizes variables that may exist within the patient. Other factors producing dropouts may be present within the therapeutic procedures. Personality factors may exist within the lower-class patient that make the use of present psychotherapeutic techniques inadvisable. Hunt [5] points out that present psychotherapeutic techniques have been drawn from treatment and research on a biased sample, upper-middle-class and upper-class patients. He questions the validity of generalizing these principles to all social classes, since the principles of psychotherapy may well be class-linked. "To the extent that this is true," he writes, "it is likely that not only will psychotherapeutic treatment of lower class patients be difficult and inefficient, it may actually not be practical in any real sense. In short, the time appears to have arrived when we must consider the possibility that psychotherapy, at least as presently constituted, is a treatment process the efficacy of which is confined to middle and higher class patient populations."

Perhaps, in viewing therapy from a traditional perspective, the therapist unknowingly rejects the lower-class patient when he does not meet the therapist's expectations. Heine and Trosman [3] point out that a situation is created in which a patient with one set of expectations is rewarded by the therapist, while another patient with a different set of expectations—no less realistic in a medical setting—is rejected by the therapist. Their study indicates that as many continuers as discontinuers are hopeful about their anticipated experience with psychiatric treatment. However, the continuers apparently conceptualized the experience in a manner more congruent with the therapist's role image and were, therefore, more gratifying to the therapist. This might explain our finding that the student-therapists differentiated the people who returned on the question, "Do you think that this patient can use psychiatric treatment?".

The results of our study indicate that lower-class patients predominantly expect a medical-psychiatric interview with the therapist generally assuming an active but permissive role. They tend not to return when these expectation are not fulfilled. Such expectations may well be due to cognitive factors, and the problem, then, is to find some means by which these factors may be reduced. One way of reducing cognitive inaccuracies is to attempt, during the initial phases of treatment, to reeducate the patient as to both his own and the therapist's role in the treat-

ment. Since a great proportion of dropouts occur after the initial interview, it would seem particularly important to raise the question of expectations during the first hour. Moreover, it may be necessary to encourage a direct expression of expectations so that both patient and therapist can more easily view and modify their roles.

Summary

A study was conducted to test the effect of treatment expectations and their fulfillment on patients' early termination of therapy. Forty patients of lower socioeconomic class were seen prior to and after their initial interviews and a questionnaire was given them at both times. The therapists were also asked to complete a comparable questionnaire at the conclusion of the interview. The questionnaires were constructed to measure the areas of the therapist's activity or passivity, emphasis on medical or psychiatric problems, and use of supportive therapy. These areas were chosen to cover points raised by Hollingshead and Redlich as being pertinent to lower-class patient expectations.

The results indicate that lower-class patients tend to expect a medical-psychiatric interview with the therapist taking a generally active but permissive role. Those patients whose expectations were most inaccurate were significantly less likely to return for treatment. Moreover, patients and therapists substantially agreed as to the events that had taken place during the interview. However, the patient's observations of the interview were a better predictor of return to psychotherapy than the therapist's observations, when both were compared with patient expectations.

These results were discussed in terms of implications for therapy with patients of lower socioeconomic class.

References

1. Frank, J., L. H. Gliedman, S. D. Imber, E. Nash, Jr., and A. R. Stone. 1957. Why patients leave psychotherapy. A.M.A. Arch. Neurol. and Psychiat. 77:283.

2. Freedman, N., D. M. Engelhardt, L. D. Hankoff, B. S. Glick, H. Kaye, J. Buchwald and P. Stark. 1958. Drop-out from outpatient psychiatric treatment. A.M.A. Arch. Neurol. and Psychiat. 80:657.

3. Heine, R. W. and H. Trosman. 1960. Initial expectations of the doctor-patient interaction as a factor in continuance in psychotherapy. Psychiat. 23:275.

4. Hollingshead, A. B. and F. C. Redlich. 1958. Social Class and Mental Illness. John Wiley & Sons, Inc. New York, N.Y.: 340, 345.

5. Hunt, R. G. 1960. Social class and mental illness: some implications for clinical theory and practice. Am. J. Psychiat. 116:1065.

6. Imber, S., E. Nash, Jr., and A. R. Stone. 1955. Social class and duration of psychotherapy. J. Clin. Psychother. 11:281.

7. Libo, L. M. Preference Form P-D-A. Unpublished test.

8. Lief, H. I., V. F. Lief, C. O. Warren and R. G. Health. 1961. Low dropout rate in a psychiatric clinic. Arch. Gen. Psychiat. 5:200.

9. Peters, C. C. and W. R. Van Voorhes. 1940. Statistical Procedures and their Mathematical Bases. McGraw-Hill, New York, N.Y.

10. Rosenthal, D. and J. D. Frank. 1958. The fate of psychiatric clinic outpatients assigned to psychotherapy. J. Nerv. Ment. Dis. 127:330.

11. Seeman, J. 1955. Counselor judgments of therapeutic process and outcome. *In* Psychotherapy and Personality Change. C. R. Rogers and R. F. Dymond, Eds. University of Chicago Press, Chicago, Ill.

12. Siegel, S. 1956. Nonparametric Statistics for the Behavioral Sciences. McGraw-Hill, New York, N.Y.

The Socially Handicapped and the Agencies: A Market Analysis

Harry C. Bredemeier

A market is in equilibrium when suppliers find acceptance of all the items they want to supply at a "just profit"; *and* when consumers find available all the items they want to consume, also at a "just profit." The critical terms needing explication are: "find acceptance," "just," and "profit."

Finding acceptance of goods or services means three things: (a) *being in contact* with potential consumers, who are (b) *willing* and (c) *able* to accept the proffered items. Profit means rewards minus the costs incurred in either supplying or consuming the items. Costs, however, as George Homans has most recently reminded us,[1] are foregone rewards. Profits, then, are rewards received minus rewards foregone. (The real costs of supplying one's labor to a firm, for example, are all the alternative things one might have done with that time and energy; and the real costs of buying a bar of soap are all the alternative things one might have bought with that time, energy, and money.)

But profits might be too high or too low for equilibrium. If they are too high, tensions are likely to occur either in the form of "guilt" on the part of the profiteers (unlikely as that might seem to most American readers), or blame or censure on the part of persons on the other side of the market, or on the part of the public. In addition, the high profits reflect an unbalanced ratio of suppliers to consumers—either too few items are being supplied compared to the demand for them so that their price is bid up; or consumers are receiving windfalls in the sense that they would be willing to forego much more than they are required to forego for the items in question. In the first case (suppliers making

"too high" profits), the situation is likely to be changed by additional suppliers coming into the market to enjoy the profits (or tensions accumulating if something prevents their entry). In the second case (consumers enjoying "too high" profits), similarly, either additional consumers will be attracted to the windfalls or, if they are blocked, tensions will accumulate.

There is likely to be institutionalized some standard of a "just" profit. Homans has suggested an approach to understanding the standards through the concept of "investments." Investments are the costs *previously* incurred in entering the market—the money previously not spent and now invested, the time previously spent in medical school rather than in alternative ways, the children previously acquired for whom one is now responsible, and so on. They are stakes in the successful outcome of the market transaction; the greater the stakes, the greater must be the reward received in order to "break even." For a familiar example, the man who invests a thousand dollars must receive ten times as much as the man who invests a hundred dollars in order to receive the same *rate* of return. Similarly, the man who invested ten years in a medical education must receive much more than the high school graduate who went immediately into gainful employment, in order to be even with him.

In addition, if profits are to be felt as "just," the reward must often, or sometimes, include a component that does not represent the covering of past or current costs, but that rather *symbolizes* an honorific sentiment— that says, in effect, "This is a noble or honorable thing to be." The sentiment that men should receive more than women partly reflects such a sentiment (as the contrary sentiment of "equal pay for equal work" amply testifies); and the sentiments that Caucasians should receive more than Negroes and older people more than younger ones illustrate it also.[2]

Still further, market transactions vary with respect to the perceived riskiness of a successful, i.e., profitable, outcome. The greater the risk to which one exposes his foregoing of rewards, his investments, and his "honor," the greater must be the return, if he is to feel "properly" rewarded. This again is most familiarly seen in the higher rates paid on common stocks than on bonds, or in the low rates paid on government bonds. It is also partly reflected in the lower salaries paid to tenure professors than to persons with similar training, in private industry.

For a market to be in equilibrum, then, it is necessary that consumers and suppliers be in touch with one another, and that they be respectively willing to accept and to offer the items being traded at rewards to one another that fully compensate, but do not over-compensate, each side's costs, investments, sentimental expectations, and risks.

I shall elaborate on each of these conditions in the context of what I shall call at the outset "the market for social services." First, it is necessary to specify who is in this market—what the two sides are.

On the one hand, I suggest, stand Households; on the other, agencies, just as, in a more familiar market, stand households on one side and business firms on the other. Consider that more familar market for

a moment. Just as in any market, the persons or organizations on each side are *both* suppliers and consumers. Households supply labor to business firms and consume goods; business firms supply goods and consume labor.

In the social service market, what do Households supply and what do they consume? They supply, I want to suggest, human potentialities to be developed, in a sense quite analogous to households supplying labor services which then have to be productively organized by the managers of business firms. Put mechanistically, Households supply the raw materials that the socialization and social control Agencies manufacture into more productive and responsible role players. Put humanistically, Households supply the purpose of the entire system and all its markets: the potential human qualities of reason, joy, empathy.

In their role as consumers, Agencies consume those potentials, just as business firms consume labor. In their role as suppliers, the Agencies' job is to supply, as I have indicated, people who are at least more able than they would otherwise have been to lead productive lives character- ized by reason, empathy, and joy. Households, in turn, in their role as consumers, receive back the socialized capacities and abilities of the people aided by the Agencies, just as they receive back, in the form of goods, the products of the labor services they supply in the labor market. We are now ready to examine the factors making for equilibrium or disequilibrium in this market.

Households as Suppliers of Potentials

The human potential supplied to Agencies by Households is, of course, always handicapped potential. Universally, it is handicapped by age and lack of experience, in the case of the youthful potential sup- plied to those Agencies we call schools. In other cases, it is handicapped by language and cultural barriers, by old age, by emotional and mental disturbances, by technological obsolescence, by racial discrimination, by broken homes, by bad luck, by sickness, and so on.

The basic fact is that the productive process on this side of the market is, from a market point of view, disorganized to the point of chaos. There are no eugenics programs, and there are no effective powers by which cities or suburbs can choose the raw materials they want and keep the others out. In consequence, the products come with wide varia- tions in the *amount* of potentiality each has, in the degree to which any amount that may be present is buried under handicaps, in the location and veins of access by which the precious stuff can be reached, and so on. In short, the products come with varying kinds of handicaps, requir- ing highly various kinds of refining processes.

Now, the first requirement of market equilibrium, I have said, is that suppliers be in contact with consumers. So far as the under-age handicapped are concerned, this requirement seems to be met fairly

well through compulsory school attendance—although even here inform-
ants have asserted that in the slums of today's central cities there are
large numbers of rural in-migrants who are regularly missed by the
compulsory attendance machinery. With respect to other kinds of handicaps, however, even this elementary requirement of equilibrium seems
to be met rather poorly.

Several features of the structure of this market can be identified as
responsible for this. One is the fact that while the market has been
traditionally structured so as to put the burden of the contact problem
on the supplying Households rather than on the consuming Agencies—
Households have been expected to take the initiative in actively seeking
out Agencies to help them—many of the new handicapped are a different
breed. They are not so likely to take the initiative in seeking help; and
this, in turn, has several sources.

The first source is ignorance: Especially in the case of in-migrant
lower class Negroes and Puerto Ricans, there is probably considerable
ignorance of the very existence of such agencies as baby keep-well
stations, mental hygiene clinics, dental clinics, family service agencies,
visiting nurse associations, and perhaps even schools and welfare
departments. Behind ignorance of the existence of supplying Agencies,
there is very likely considerable ignorance of the very existence of any
"handicaps" that *might* be offered to Agencies. Put otherwise, many
handicaps are not translated into offers because they are not felt as
obstacles in need of elimination by their possessors. This is familiar
enough in the case of many children and their need for schooling to
overcome their age-handicap; and it is, doubtlessly, no less the case with
respect to many health conditions, guidance problems, and so on. The
cough or listlessness that spells tuberculosis, the bleeding gums and
toothaches that presage loss of teeth, the eye strain that prevents reading—all are probably taken as a normal part of the troubles that comprise human existence, among many people.

Behind both kinds of ignorance there is the structural fact that in
many cases there are no agencies to which a given problem could be
taken, even if it were recognized as a problem. In Newark, N.J., for
example, there are baby keep-well stations available (in what supply
and how well known is uncertain) for infants up to two years of age, and
there are school health services available for children over five. But no
agency has responsibility for children between two and five.

Beyond nonavailability and ignorance as barriers to supplying problems to Agencies, a second source of breakdown in contact is the vital
matter of costs. So far as contact is concerned, there is the cost in time
and effort. Service Agency "business firms" are neither vertically nor
horizontally integrated. Rather, potential users face a situation—or often
feel that they do—comparable to that of a patient with a toothache who
would have to go one place for the gold with which to have his cavity
filled, a second place on the other side of town for the anesthesia, a
third place to rent a drill, and then would have to carry them all to a
dentist at a fourth place—who might not deign to use that drill.

Is the Supplying of Potential
a Profitable Business?

Even if contact is established, or potentially establishable, a further requirement is that suppliers have some confidence that supplying their potentials will be profitable—that is, that the rewards will more than compensate for the pleasures and other rewards they forego, the amount they invest, and the stakes and honor they risk. In this respect the social service market seems to be in dreadful shape.

The situation of the handicapped persons who are supposed to make their potentials available for cultivation by Agencies might be glimpsed by paraphrasing Omar Khayyám and asking, "What buys the fully socialized half so sweet as what he sells?"

Workers, we may suppose, value the things they purchase with their wages more than they do the time and energy they expend in earning them; and what is more, they know that they do. The handicapped, however, especially the young and the culturally deprived, can scarcely be so sure. It may be that to trade impulsiveness for restraint, spontaneity for discipline, play for work yields a net profit in the long run; but this can scarcely seem certain to the not-fully-socialized. (Indeed, it may be that to be "fully socialized" primarily means having the conviction that it is profitable, and that such a conviction comes only as the product of socialization.)

In this respect, the handicapped are expected to take an extraordinary amount on faith; and, the way things are, it might be really quite irrational of them to do so. The benefits of the very behavior patterns that constitute "problems" from a middle class point of view—teen-age out-of-wedlock pregnancies, relief recipients who continue to have illegitimate children by an assortment of males, drunkenness, early-school leaving, truancy, narcotics addiction—the benefits of those patterns are clear and immediate. By contrast, in the first place, the costs attached to them are either delayed far into the future or even exist only in the minds of the middle classes; second, most of the benefits promised by Agency personnel for conformity to their way of life are benefits far in the future, by no means guaranteeable, and really only "benefits" to people who already look at the world through middle class lenses; and, third, the *costs* of the middle class way are immediate and clear.

In short, we have a situation in which, as many potential clients see it, Agencies seem to be saying, "Come to our firms. First, though, throw away all your present securities and pleasures. What we'll give you immediately in return will hurt pretty much. Much later on, though, we're pretty sure we'll give you something, or rather, we hope and have faith that other people not connected with us and over whom we have no control whatever will give you something you'll like. We can't describe it exactly, we can't guarantee you'll even get it, we can't compen-

sate you for your sacrifice. Therefore, rush right down to your nearest Agency and take advantage of this fabulous offer before we withdraw it."

It may be that it takes a certain amount of masochism to respond to such an advertisement, while healthy clients, no matter how handicapped, might be more likely to deal with such offers, if they deal with them at all, in the way you and I would deal with a powerful madman— at arms length and with a wary eye on the nearest exit.

There is another cost to the supplying of a handicapped potential. The fact is that to take one's tuberculosis to a physician is distinctly a better service to society than not to take it—to conceal it, or to claim that it is a cherished way of life. Yet there is resistance to doing this, even in the case of tuberculosis, venereal disease, or other illnesses. Part of the reason, at least, is that to be dependent—to say that one is handicapped—is, by American standards, not a worthy thing to do.

To take one's slowness at learning, or cultural retardation, or alcoholism, or sense of having to be a Don Juan, to a social agency is still less a good thing. If I know that my potentialities for productive rationality, empathy, and joy are not being expressed fully because the class is going too fast for me, I am not encouraged to feel pride for recognizing it and doing something about it. I am rather led to feel shame, to which I respond by hiding the fact or rejecting the school; not by taking my problem to an Agency.

When the psychiatrist in the cartoon says to his patient, "The reason you have an inferiority complex, Mr. Jones, is that you *are* inferior," what makes it "funny" is the collision of idea with the fundamental American premise that no one dares admit to inferiority. (There is nothing funny at all in a doctor saying, "The reason your stomach hurts, Mr. Jones, is that you have appendicitis.")

Children may be a partial exception to this—but only partial. Even children are not considered "worthy" for being handicapped; at best, they are considered lovable. Lower class, uneducated, non-work oriented, sexually promiscuous Negro women, on the other hand, are too often regarded as only contemptible. To the degree that this is so, the cost in self-respect of supplying potentiality to Agencies is enormous. As Kingsley Davis has pointed out, it is precisely the self-respect and public respect that the prostitute loses that makes it necessary to pay her for services that are otherwise costless to produce.

Clients of social agencies, strikingly enough, are often in a similar position, in the sense that what they produce is not considered respectable, the possession of a handicap being considered something degrading. Indeed, agency clients are sometimes even worse off than prostitutes, because even though the prostitute's services are considered unrespectable, there is still a demand for them, so people are willing to pay her for the cost she incurs by loss of respect. The traditional structure of the social service market, however, is such that, far from paying clients, agencies, if anything, expect to be paid by clients. It may very well be that this is the single most irrational aspect of the structure of this market: the tendency to carry over into a situation in which suppliers

need rewards a custom that can only work for clients who are already so "hooked" on socialization that they are willing to pay for more.

A still further deterrent to the willingness of culturally handicapped persons to supply their potentials to agencies is that a great deal is risked in so doing. When workers put themselves under the direction of management in the process of producing goods, they also risk many things: their time, energy, future careers, the welfare of their families, their ability to carry out their religious, political, recreational, and other roles, their dignity—even their lives. If they are to be willing to accept such risks, there must be some basis for them to trust the consumers of their labor services.

In the labor market, workers have learned to trust employers to pay them at the end of the week, to recognize that they have family responsibilities and social needs apart from their work roles, and to respect their privacy and the legitimacy of their non-work statuses. This is not to imply that the managers of business firms are any more trustworthy *in character* than the personnel of social agencies. If anything, the opposite may be closer to the truth. Rather, the point is that there are certain critical structural characteristics that make it more reasonable for workers to trust employers than for the handicapped to trust agencies.

One of these characteristics is the fact that workers are organized into unions, and consequently have enough bargaining power *vis a vis* employers to insure that their stakes will be protected. It is not so much that employers can be trusted, then, as that workers can, in effect, *make* them trustworthy.

The handicapped are in no such fortunate position. They have not become organized, although two qualifications to that statement must be made at once—an historical one and a pending one. The historical qualification is that in an earlier period a structure partly homologous to the union was the political machine. The machine, as Merton has observed, did for European immigrants many of the things that professionalized agencies now do for the new Negro and Puerto Rican immigrants to the city. The machine charged a price, too, of course; but it was not a price felt so immediately by the culturally handicapped. Even more important, the machine was often "their" machine, protecting them against the formal society and buying their loyalty with its loyalty and unsupercilious acceptance.

The pending qualification is that with the new militancy of today's urban Negroes—perhaps the largest single contemporary group of the deprived and handicapped—a new political bargaining power may be in the making. More than one observer has noted the "funny coincidence" that the Kennedy administration's activities in the form of the Committee on Juvenile Delinquency, the Youth Employment Bill, Civil Rights, and so on, came at a time when the Democrats badly needed the support of the nation's urban Negroes. It is likely that as central city after city becomes preponderantly Negro, these particular handicapped persons will move more toward the union's power to "make" Agencies reliable.

Certain additional differences in this respect between Agencies and business firms can be better taken up in the context of considering the market position of Agencies as consumers of potentiality.

Agencies as Consumers

One of the most significant characteristics of Agencies as consumers, analogous to business firms as consumers of labor services, is the fact that social Agencies have virtually no competition. Agencies not only tend to be professionalized, as compared to the political machine, they also tend to be more bureaucraticized. What competition there is among them tends to be competition for philanthropic dollars, often carried out in the budget meetings of United Funds or Community Councils. In fact, one may wonder theoretically whether the rise of United Funds has, to any extent, turned interagency relations into a cartel-like arrangement in which, in return for a reduction in open competition, Agencies have divided the market among themselves and have become careful not to tread in one another's preserves.

Competition is important, of course, in the present context, the context of factors underlying clients' ability to trust the Agencies, for two reasons. First, competition does, under certain conditions, tend to force heads-up playing; and second, competition on one side of the market means more alternatives for people on the other side, and more alternatives mean more freedom. Workers can afford to trust employers partly because employers have competition for labor service, and hence need to establish reputations as "good places to work."

Agencies, however, not only do not compete with one another; they also differ from business firms in not being so obviously dependent on their clients as employers are on their workers. In part, of course, the monopoly of services by Agencies contributes to their relative independence. In any case, Agency personnel are often shielded, by their lack of competition and by their independence of clients, from their failure to be considerate of clients' costs, investments, and risks. In this respect, the difference between teachers and social workers, on the one hand, and businessmen and entertainers, on the other, is clear. In the case of businessmen and entertainers, the sanctions for indifference to clients' needs are vivid and immediate. Agency personnel, however, are sheltered from the result of their insensitivity by the power of the state, which compels the audience to return every day, or by their monopoly of the housing, health, or welfare facilities urgently needed by clients.[3]

It is, then, the *structure of the situation* in which Agencies act as consumers, and not the character structure of Agency personnel, that makes it difficult for Agencies to engender in clients the requisite degree of trust and confidence that they will not be exploited. There is, to be sure, a possible substitute for bargaining power and competition as structures making for trustworthiness, viz., professional integrity.

Medical men and legal men have traditionally been the prime examples of personnel who take other people's lives in their hands, and whose integrity is guaranteed only by their own socialized commitment to a service ethic, plus the watchful eyes of their colleagues. Opinions may differ about how effective such professional ethics and ethical practices have been in the legal and medical professions, but I would not expect many serious claims for the effectiveness of those devices for teachers, social workers, housing authorities, probation officers, and so on. I don't mean, in saying that, to impugn the professional integrity of teachers or social workers. I mean, rather, to describe what seems to me to be a fact, viz., that the profession of social work has not succeeded in building the same degree of public confidence as has the medical profession. (I do not want, in this context, to imply anything about whether the reputations of medical men are deserved or not.)

On the consuming side of the market for potentials, as well as on the demand side, then, there are structural conditions depressing the profitability of households supplying their potentials.

Nor is this all. One of the conditions of market equilibrium, it will be recalled, is that consumers find all the consumption items they need. When there is more on the market than consumers want or can afford to accept, we speak of a glut and of a deflationary pressure. When there is not enough to satisfy consumer demand, we speak of scarcity and of inflationary pressures.

What I've suggested so far is that there is in fact virtually no demand for the supply of potentials pouring into the market from the assembly lines of fertility and fecundity.

A major reason there is not, of course, is that the demand for the productive and responsible role-players who are the *products* of the Agencies is itself severely limited. I shall return to this in the context of viewing Agencies as *suppliers*. The relevant point is that the equilibrium condition that "consumers find all the consumption items they need" is, in the social service market, over-met with such a vengeance that the market is seriously depressed, with no legitimate mechanism available for reducing the flood of consumption items pouring onto the market. The supply of potential is totally inelastic, so long as it is illegitimate to restrict it with contraceptives.

Like all consumers, Agencies want assurances that the products they consume are of good quality. Consumers run risks and incur costs also; and their profit is greater to the degree that what they consume is guaranteed top grade. The ideal of teachers, social workers, guidance counselors, and so on seems, understandably, to be to have only those clients whose gold is close to the surface or lying on the ground, and unencrusted with dross—whose potentialities, in other words, are not potentialities at all, but rather actualities.

This is not hard to understand, of course. It takes a greater investment of energy, time, and other resources to refine low-grade ore than it does to refine high-grade ore; and energy, time, and other resources are scarce. It must be remembered, however, that we are dealing here

with a market for services, not ores, and the fact is that relatively inaccessible potentialities are put out. There they are, on the market. Our task is to understand why the market is in such a depressed state; and I am pointing out that one reason is that social service agencies find it too costly to deal with, or at least to encourage, all but the easy cases.

The fact that schools, welfare departments, and similar agencies do physically "accept" the handicapped should not be allowed to obscure this. They often accept them merely in the sense of providing physical space for them, without, however, "consuming" them, that is, attempting to develop their potentials. The point here has been made in extreme form by Julius Horwitz, consultant on Public Welfare to the New York State Senate, majority leader.

> Who would pay $30 a week for two rooms chopped out of a railroad flat, with broken walls, vermin, furniture that belongs in an incinerator, a front door through which rats enter as freely as the swarming children? Who would pay $30 a week, $65 semimonthly, $130 a month? The City of New York would and does. Why? The landlords know the answer and the answer makes them inviolate. One of them said, "I run a pigsty for the City of New York. We're partners, see? The city pays me to keep these people off the street and out of everybody's sight, period. They aren't people. They're drunken, filthy, baby-producing pigs, and as soon as they die off, there are more to take their places. Nobody in City Hall would dare mention "birth control." They might lose votes. . . . Nobody down there (City Hall) knows how these people live, because if they did, they would scream in their sleep. Me? I sleep, because I'm doing everybody a favor. I give the pigs four walls, and the city appreciates it, or, instead of paying me so well, they'd close me down tomorrow, just like they close down bookie joints and hustlers. But they won't because there's no place else to put the 150 babies I've got urinating in my halls.[4]

The fact is that suppliers of handicapped potential can hardly "stand behind their product," in the same way as the suppliers of consumers' goods, largely because those products are so often merely by-products of other, more valued, activities, viz., sexual ones. What the supplying Households can offer in place of warranties is, at best, hope and care; but this, under present arrangements, is often not enough for the Agencies, who, as consumers, experience an unsatisfied demand for very high quality potential of the sort that requires little or no effort to develop.

From the point of view of Agencies-as-consumers, there is not a glut but a shortage of the kind of potential we want, as witness the inflationary competition among colleges and universities for high aptitude students. Public school teachers, welfare workers, settlement house personnel, case workers, and so on, similarly experience a scarcity of their ideal clients, who are bright, ambitious, eager to learn and to improve themselves, receptive to the "ego-strengthening" ideology of case work, and, perhaps above all, grateful. This disappointment with

the discrepancy between the potentials they want to develop and the deprivation-encrusted ones of the handicapped persons actually offered to them is an important source of the resentment of and hostility toward the clients they actually serve that I have sometimes noticed among teachers and social workers. That resentment and hostility, of course, becomes an additional cost to clients, whose willingness to submit their potentials to the Agencies is then even further depressed.

THE COST TO AGENCIES OF ACCEPTING

HANDICAPPED POTENTIALS

But let us return to the matter of the costs that Agencies must incur in consuming handicapped potential. As I have already indicated, the fact is that developing the potentials of handicapped persons is by definition much more expensive than developing those of privileged persons. It is more costly, in the first place, in time, attention, and energy. If often requires special equipment. It may require more elaborate control over the individual's environment, in those cases in which much of his environment is hostile to and destructive of his development. It may require, for example, special remedial reading teachers in schools, a special cadre of school-home liaison agents, special text books, lower teacher-student ratios, lower social worker and probation officer case loads, residential treatment centers, boarding schools, and so on.

Agencies do not have the resources with which to meet such costs, which is another reason for the depressed state of this market. This, of course, is an obstacle to consumption which is as simply and easily met as the inability of building contractors to employ bricklayers: expanded public expenditures on building removes the obstacle. I shall return to this issue later.

Another cost may be even more of a deterrent to consumption in this case, and may be somewhat more complicated to overcome. This is the cost of obsolescence of the methods used by Agency personnel, from "purchasing" methods, through "processing" methods, to "marketing" methods.

The professional skills and professional ideology of Agency personnel have been developed to deal with a different kind of material than is now being presented. Most importantly, they have relied heavily on the pre-existence of a home and community life that developed the motivation to make use of Agency services and that reinforced Agency techniques. Methods of teaching, of counselling, of referring to other agencies, that worked with middle-class oriented clients do not work with the terribly deprived of today's slums. The passive waiting-for-the-client-to-present himself that once worked does not work with clients who may not even recognize a problem, and who fear the Agency as an enemy even if they do. The practice of handing a client the name and address of the next counselor or Agency or clinic he should see, and

relying upon his incentive, knowledge, and wherewithal to go there may not work at all with clients who are skeptical of the use and ignorant of the procedures of Agencies, and too confused to move. The professional tendency to think that every difficulty represents an unresolved Oedipus Complex may not be the most appropriate starting point with a client who knows that his mother's income from the Welfare Department depends on her producing some more children.

But the fact seems to be that many Agency personnel are as wedded to their traditional methods as their most rigid clients are to theirs. The very suggestion that the expertise learned in professional schools might be inapplicable to different situations is enough to cause many teachers and social workers to become defensive. Why is this? One would not expect an experimental psychologist to be defensively hostile to the suggestion that his successful techniques for training rats ought to be changed when he approaches pigeons. But professional Agency personnel often seem to be different. Why is this?

Why does the writing-off as obsolete of methods that do not work represent such a high cost to many Agency personnel? What, actually, would they forego, or sacrifice, by scrapping a traditional mode of operation as readily as our experimental psychologist scraps a reinforcement trick that doesn't work?

I suggest that the answer is threefold. In the first place, Agency personnel, like all consumers, risk their self-respect and the respect of the public by the act of consuming certain items rather than others. Now, what seems to be the case is that the professional self-images of many Agency personnel appear to depend on the kind of clients they serve, rather than on their functional skills in serving them. Many of them feel compelled, then, not to identify themselves with their more handicapped clients, and to disengage themselves from their roles.[5] Such disengagement can be facilitated and made public by the apathy, cynicism, and client-derogation of many deprived-youth-serving personnel. It is as if our hypothetical psychologist, upon finding that his techniques for reinforcing rats did not work with pigeons, hastened to assure himself and all bystanders that pigeons are notoriously inferior creatures anyway, and he is not to be judged on the basis of his unfortunate association with them. This could, if believed, be a very convenient and hard-to-change stance, since the more the pigeons refused to act like rats, the greater the evidence the experimenter could produce that they were incapable of responding to his methods.

What it would in fact prove, of course, is that he was incompetent at training pigeons. If he were already threatened by some cultural norm that ranked rat-work above pigeon-work, the additional threat of incompetence could be expected to drive him even deeper into his infatuation with his methods. ("Even if they make me work with pigeons, I'm still like those rat-men, as witness my identical methods.")

A second kind of cost of obsolescence is generated by the fact that when people have invested considerable time and effort in the learning and perfection of certain skills, the scrapping of those skills means the

writing-off of those investments. This may be hard to do, and it is still harder to the degree that some portion of the individual's self was invested in the old approach—that is, to the degree that he had become ego-involved in it or personally identified with it. The obsolescence of the methods then means an obsolescence of part of the self, and is as likely to be resisted by Agency personnel as are efforts to change the ego-involved but self-defeating practices of their handicapped clients.[6]

A third cost of relinquishing old methods is the fact that, in situations in which *no* methods are *certain* to bring success, but in which success is still highly important, whatever methods are used are likely to be vested with the function of giving a sort of magical reassurance. They become more than instrumental methods, they become reassuring rituals, and they are not likely to be easily relinquished unless either reassurance is provided in other ways or the emotional investment in a successful but uncontrollable outcome is reduced.[7]

These three costs of changing methods to deal adequately with a different clientele—the need to identify with "superior" clients, the ego-involvement with previous investments, and the need for reassuring rituals—must be added to the other costs of dealing with the seriously deprived, which are the greater effort and more extensive facilities required and the threat of degradation by association. When they are added together, it becomes apparent that there are real reasons for the reluctance of Agencies to accept for cultivation the potentials of many handicapped persons. It is not surprising that the market is depressed.

A still further cost incurred by Agencies may be better understood in the context of considering Agencies as *suppliers* of developed potential.

Agencies as Suppliers

From the supply side of the market, it will be recalled, the conditions of equilibrium are that suppliers find acceptance of their outputs; and that their receipts be high enough to compensate for their costs, investments, and risks.

THE MARKETING OF PRODUCTIVE AND RESPONSIBLE ROLE-PLAYERS

One difficulty in connection with the first requirement is that Agencies, as a general rule, do nothing to market their products. Clients aren't "delivered" to consumers; they are "graduated," "expelled," "dismissed," "closed," "referred," "discharged"—all of which often means that they are simply steered out the door, with no systematic follow-up. To exaggerate, it is as if milk companies were simply to run hoses from their cows out the dairy windows and let the milk run, or as if the final

action on an automobile assembly line were for a worker to start the engine, put the car in gear, and let it roll down the highway. Even if the product were of excellent quality, this would, at least, complicate the problem of finding acceptance of it. The better mousetrap principle of marketing works only if there is a great demand for mousetraps and only if competitive suppliers don't hand-deliver them. It works only if one produces a *better* mousetrap.

The basic difficulty with disposing of the products of social service agencies is that no one believes they are very good products. In Essex County, New Jersey, there are well over 10,000 youths who have fled or been ousted from the schools and who are not at present employable. They are the Agency products.

Justified or not, there is widespread skepticism that probation officers do their charges any good, that reformatories do much besides harden delinquents into criminals, that schools do much besides baby-sit for youths under sixteen (and in the process sap their incentives and *lower* their abilities), that welfare workers do anything but write checks as rewards for irresponsibility, or that social workers do anything but exhort their clients to loftier ideals.

Some reasons for Agencies' failures to turn handicapped youth into productive and responsible citizens have already been touched upon, but it will help to mention them again. They include the use of ineffective methods, the failure to identify challenges early enough, the lack of genuine Agency acceptance of the role of socializer,[8] the lack of sufficient resources to invest in the task, and the lack of competitive or other outside pressure on Agencies to be efficient.

Very often, as suggested earlier, the fundamental defect in Agency "production methods" is the failure to include an essential ingredient: respect for the client.

In an earlier section, I observed that Agency personnel are protected from their failure to appreciate clients' needs, in a way that theatrical performers are not. The protection is, in the long run, self-defeating, however, for it results in no effective socialization taking place. Teachers and social workers must respect the structure of their clients' personalities and cultural worlds at least as much as the experimental psychologist respects the structure of his pigeons' present needs and past experiences, if their change efforts are to be anything but ritualistic gestures.

In addition, so far as human socialization is concerned, it seems clear that an essential condition of successful socialization is a strong "input" of diffuse, generalized support for the client. Human beings are not likely to give up a familiar pattern of behavior for a different one unless a distinction is made by the control agent between *them,* on the one hand, and the specific pattern of behavior, on the other. Not until the individual feels that not he but the behavior trait is what the control agent is rejecting is he likely to make the same distinction himself; and making that distinction is a necessary (although still not a sufficient) condition for his changing. To expect him to change because *he* is re-

jected is something like expecting a pigeon to peck a red dot instead of a blue one because he gets an electric shock no matter what he does.

All of the training attitudes and practices that prevent Agency personnel from accepting and supporting their clients as persons, then, prevent them from being successful in their change efforts and insure a product that is not likely to cause consumers to beat a path to Agency doors.

We have been talking only of the strategy and tactics of socialization—only of the conditions of an effective market. It happens that the point we are emphasizing also involves an important ideological issue.

The ideological issue might be put as the choice between regarding "integration," especially racial integration, as a one-way or a two-way street. Most often it is regarded as a one-way street: Lower class Negroes should come over to "us," which means becoming like us. This is the sentiment that motivates even the most well-meaning of northern white liberals when they insist that Negroes must learn to reform themselves before they can be accepted as equals.

From the two-way perspective, however, and from the premise of cultural pluralism, integration also means that liberal, or nonliberal, middle class whites (and Negroes) learn to recognize many aspects of lower class Negro or Puerto Rican life styles as equally legitimate variations on the complex themes of sex, love, life, death, marriage, family, religion, work, housing, play, and so on. I don't suppose that very many middle class Agency personnel these days would consciously claim that the American middle class has discovered or created the perfect symphony of life's themes and instruments, but when confronted with concretely different ones, many of them act as if that is exactly their preposterous claim.

I am not arguing here that middle class Agency personnel ought to be bloodlessly and nervelessly without preference and passions. I am only saying that in order to be truly pluralistic in their ideology they ought to be more respectful of the right of difference to exist (indeed, sufficiently curious about the difference to hope that everyone is not like themselves); and I am also saying, ideology aside, that unless they are thus respectful, their chances of inducing change in their clients approach zero.

The fact is, then, that although social service suppliers are more protected against their clients' needs than are business men and entertainers, the protection may well be more of a liability than a boon, so far as performing their manifest function is concerned.

THE REWARDS TO AGENCIES

A further special feature of Agencies' situation as suppliers is that they depend for their incomes and recognition on government allocations of tax dollars, on United Fund allocation of philanthropic dollars, or on their own ability to tax the community's philanthropic pocket-

book. They are not supported, for the most part, out of fees paid by those who consume their products, whether those consumers are the households whose members' handicaps were "treated" or other organizations or persons who make use of the clients' enhanced productivity and responsibility.

Since people who consume the products do not pay for them, it is difficult for them to pass any consumer judgment on the quality of the product, and hence it is difficult for Agencies to relate their success or failure as socialization and social control centers to their rewards. Also, since the people who do support the Agency are not the consumers of Agency products, it is difficult for them to balance their payments against their satisfaction with the product. The first effect of this is to reinforce the pressure on Agencies to become magically ritualistic, as discussed above.

A further effect is to put the Agencies in a paradoxical position, requiring a delicate balancing act and perhaps even some sleight of hand. On the one hand, they must impress the public with the need for tax and philanthropic support by pointing to the great quantity of unmet problems. On the other hand, they must persuade the public that they are able to deal with those problems. Too much emphasis on the first requirement might raise the question of what have the Agencies been doing all this time if things are so bad, while too much emphasis on the second might elicit the reaction, "If you're doing so well, why holler for more?"

This fact contributes to the pressure on Agencies, noted earlier, to prize above all the easily helped clients and to devote a large proportion of resources to them, in order to be able to demonstrate "success." At the same time (and this is the promised qualification to an earlier statement that Agencies do not need their clients), Agencies must attempt to deal with some "hard" cases, in order to avoid the criticism that they are irrelevant. Still, the chances of success with the hard cases being so much les, there is still further cause for resentment on the part of Agency personnel toward the seriously handicapped who threaten, in this way, the Agency's record.

In their effort to make the public aware of the need for further aid to the handicapped, Agencies are, furthermore, confronted by the fact that the handicapped have always been the focus of two contradictory elements in the American value system: a sentimental and romanticized conception of "the downtrodden Poor," who are to be "uplifted" and a ruggedly individualistic contempt for, or at best careless indifference to, anyone who cannot make his own way.

When social service agencies appeal to the public for support of their operations by appealing to the sentimentality side of that tradition (and especially insofar as they identify with, or are recruited on the basis of, such appeals), they risk destroying their effectiveness as socializers and social control agents. They risk it by tending to overemphasize the permissive and supportive aspects of socialization and underemphasizing the aspect of what Talcott Parsons calls "denial of

reciprocity" and "contingent reward" (that is, firm refusal of the socializing agent to accept the client's present behavior, and the consistent readiness to reward him for improved behavior). When Agency personnel err in this over-permissive and over-supportive direction, they almost necessarily fail in their change functions, and are likely to incur in addition contemptuous exploitation by their clients and cries of "coddling" from the rugged individualism side of their audience.

To protect themselves from this fate, as well as from the self-image of bleeding hearts and Lady Bountifuls, Agency personnel may swing to the other extreme of under-permissiveness, under-supportiveness, and rejection of the client (as contrasted with denial of reciprocity). They are, of course, as certain to fail in this case as in the other. The ambivalence between these two poles is probably what is reflected in the two contradictory stereotypes of social workers and teachers now current in American society, the sweet but incredibly naïve lady of charity, and the hatchet-faced sadist.[9]

Appeals to the other traditional view of the handicapped usually takes the form of appeals to a version of "enlightened self-interest." This, of course, is the warning that "Our cities are in danger," "A tidal wave of juvenile delinquency is upon us," "Tuberculosis is no respecter of suburban boundaries," and so on.

One of the consequences of this approach may be to reinforce the "tough-minded" approach to the socially handicapped, with its attendant self-defeating rejection of clients as "dangers" to be "curbed" instead of "potentials" to be "developed."

The paradox goes further. The kind of appeal that would probably maximize Agencies' chances of striking an appropriate balance between the extremes of over- and under-permissiveness may, in the United States today, be exactly the appeal that would minimize Agency chances of getting public support. This is an appeal to supporters on the ground of making sound and profitable *investments* in human productivity. Such a mode of address to the public might permit Agency personnel themselves to have a more productive orientation to their tasks, by constantly reminding themselves of the true nature of their undertaking.

If John Kenneth Galbraith is right, however, the public isn't as interested in the production of healthy people as it is in the production of consumers goods:

> In the general view it is privately produced production that is important, and that nearly alone. This adds to national well-being. Its increase measures the increase in national wealth. Public services, by comparison, are an incubus. They are necessary, and they may be necessary in considerable volume. But they are a burden which must, in effect, be carried by the private production. If that burden is too great, private production will stagger and fall.
>
> At best public services are a necessary evil; at worst they are a malign tendency against which an alert community must exercise eternal vigilance. Even when they serve the most important ends,

such services are sterile. "Government is powerless to create anything in the sense in which business produces wealth. . . ."

Alcohol, comic books, and mouth wash all bask under the superior reputation of the market. Schools, judges, and municipal swimming pools lie under the evil reputation of bad kings.[10]

The fact is, as I have pointed out before, that Agencies and their staffs make heavy investments in their socialization and social control "plants." They stake their careers, their reputations, their self-images, and their incomes on, at the very least, the "controlling" of the socially handicapped. If enough people of the right kind are to be motivated to make such investments, the rewards for doing so must be large enough to make the risks worthwhile. There must be some reason for them to believe that their investments will be reasonably safe—that they will be *able* to turn out a good "product," and that the public will reward them for doing so. (Agency personnel are no different from their clients in this respect: both will do what proves to be worthwhile, and neither will, for long, do what does not pay off.)

They are not, however, rewarded for socializing the handicapped. Rather, two other things happen: They are given inadequate facilities (including training) for carrying out their tasks; and they are made the objects of public castigation for every failure. If a rat in a maze is made to press five levers simultaneously for his food pellet, if all five are out of reach, if he gets the pellet at random even when he does by Herculean effort succeed, and if he gets an electric shock every time he tries and fails, no one would be surprised if he gave up, or if other rats, given a choice, avoided that particular maze.

Neither should it be surprising if teachers, social workers, probation officers, and other Agency personnel become less than enthusiastic about their assignments, leave for other jobs, "flee from the client" up the Administrative ladder, or vent their frustration in a cynical downgrading of their clients.

Households as Consumers

The socialized products of formal agencies are "returned" to Households, as the finished goods of business firms are returned. As consumers in both cases, Households have certain requirements that must be met if they are to play their roles in contributing to market equilibrium.

HOUSEHOLDS' NEEDS FOR
SOCIALIZED MEMBERS

Households need members who are healthy enough, skillful enough, and motivated enough both to carry out roles within the House-

hold and to contribute to the Household's adaptation to the economy, the political system, other Households, and so on. As we noted earlier, in relatively simple societies, Households perform for themselves the function of socializing and controlling their members in this way, just as they perform for themselves economic, political, recreational, and all other functions. In complex, changing socities, however, Households are dependent on external formal organizations for all these functions, including that of socialization and social control. This is doubly the case with respect to those members whose handicaps require that highly special skills be applied to the socialization process, and it is even more the case with respect to those Households whose members are already so handicapped as to make it impossible for them to perform those remaining, and highly strategic, socialization functions still reserved to the family.

Apparently a growing number of Households in central cities are not finding the productive and responsible role players they need from the formal agencies. In this context, the irrelevance and obsoleteness of schools' and other agencies' protest that they are being asked to do what "should really be done in the family" becomes clear. The fact is that the Households now in need of socialized personnel cannot provide them themselves, which is precisely what makes the formal agencies' responsibilities more critically important than they have ever been, and also more difficult. For the difficulty to elicit the protest, however, is rather like the difficulty of manufacturing automobiles causing General Motors to complain that Households aren't what they used to be. They are not, indeed, which is what creates the *raison d'être* of the specialized agencies.

"Multi-problem families," then, are very clearly not having their needs as consumers met, and in this sense the market is obviously in a deep depression. But the handicapped Households themselves are not the only consumers of the socialized products of health, education, and welfare agencies. All other Households equally, though less directly, need productive and responsible citizens, both in order to benefit from their contribution in the overall division of labor and to avoid the costs of their *un*socialized destructiveness and irresponsibility.

This, of course, is well-recognized by most "no-problem" families, as is evidenced by their vigorous complaints about the ineffectiveness of the Agencies. In this sense, it continues to be clear that the market is depressed. On the other hand, it is not at all clear that these latter Households in fact want better performance from Agencies badly enough to pay for it. From this point of view, it may be that, insofar as consumers are sovereign, the output of the Agencies is just what consumers in the aggregate want.

On the other hand, it may be that consumers of Agency products would really like and be willing to pay for better products but feel frustrated at their inability to find them. Certainly, when schools graduate students, reformatories release delinquents, child service agencies close cases, and so on, not much more is meant than that the space

occupied is needed by someone else. The returning of the client to the community does not carry with it anything like a warranty that he is now a "finished product," in any sense of the term. This reflects again the fact that many Agencies have been forced away from defining themselves as in the business of producing productive and responsible citizens. Many of them seem to have accepted the conception that they are warehouses for storing people until someone withdraws them, or they escape, or are otherwise conveniently gotten rid of.

Another difficulty of Households as consumers, as I noted earlier, is the discrepancy between the standards in terms of which "payments" (contributions) are made (empathy, charity, duty) and those in terms of which the products consumed are evaluated (efficiency, conformity).

When the "costs of welfare" or of education are considered, then, they tend to be considered only in outbursts of irritation over the supporting of ever-growing families through public assistance grants, or over the expensiveness of "frills and fads" in public schools. There has not developed a mechanism for making equally clear either the costs of not making investment in potential-development or the benefits of increased or differently allocated investments in techniques for improving such development. This is but another way of saying that the "business of formal socialization" is not well enough organized to permit rational choices to be made by consumers and suppliers alike.

Beyond this, of course, is the fact that the cost of accepting handicapped formal Agency products as compared to the cost of consuming the less-handicapped products of middle-class families is very high, because of the formers' inefficiency. "Hiring the handicapped" is very probably *not* "good business" in most cases.

Summary

By way of summary, I shall try to state several hypotheses that have been suggested in the text of the paper.

1. Many handicaps are not brought to the attention of formal agencies of socialization and social control because:
    a. The handicapped persons do not perceive their characteristics as handicaps.
    b. They do not know of the Agencies that might help them.
    c. There are no Agencies for coping with them.
    d. The lack of integration and coordination among Agencies make the bringing of handicaps to them too costly.
    e. There are no encouragements given to handicapped people to make their potentials available.
    f. Agencies do not give potential clients enough assurance that that the Agencies are effective.
    g. Agencies do not give clients enough assurance that their status-set and status-sequence interests will be respected.

    h. Professional bureaucratized Agencies do not experience experience enough competition from organizations more sympathetic to clients' needs, to force them to be more re- responsive.

    i. Professional ethics among Agency personnel have not been sufficient to generate client trust.

    j. The benefits to clients of behavior regarded as pathological are clear and immediate while the benefits of changing are vague and distant. The costs of changing are clear and im- mediate while the costs of not changing are vague and distant.

    k. It is considered degrading to have a handicap, and this leads potential clients to comprehensive assertions of independence.

2. Agencies do not accept the handicapped potentialities made available to them by households because:

    a. Agency personnel are under pressure not to develop any potentialities except the easiest ones.

    b. Agency personnel require the households who supply poten- tials to them to guarantee their products and to do much of the work that it is the manifest function of the Agencies to do.

    c. Developing the potentials of handicapped people is too costly in terms of time, effort, ingenuity, and obsolescence of tra- ditional methods.

    d. Agency personnel base their self-images on the kind of client they serve rather than their skills in serving them.

    e. Agency personnel disengage themselves from their roles as servers of the deprived in defense against their fear of degradation by association.

3. Agencies do not find public acceptance of their products because:

    a. The Agencies do not accept responsibility for getting them accepted.

    b. The Agencies do not do a good job of socializing the handi- capped. The principle reasons they do not are:

      (1) Agency personnel do not respect their clients.

      (2) Reliance for moral and financial support on appeals to sentimentality leads to over-permissive and over-sup- portive treatment of clients.

      (3) Reliance for support on appeals to fear-based self-interest leads to over-demanding and rejecting treatment of clients.

      (4) Agency personnel are not rewarded by the public for their efforts, are punished for their failures, and are not given adequate resources, including training, for carrying out their functions.

4. Households do not generate a sufficient demand for the developed potential of handicapped people because:

    a. Households that are handicapped by having such members cannot, by definition, be effective demanders.

  b. Unhandicapped households have alternative sources of supply of developed potential.

  c. Unhandicapped households are able to avoid the cost of underdevelopment of handicapped potential by moving to the suburbs.

  d. Households cannot trust the reliability of Agencies' outputs.

  e. The public has no appetite for enhanced abilities to experience joy, empathy, and reason.

Notes

1. *Social Behavior: Its Elementary Forms*, (New York: Harcourt, Brace & World, 1962).

2. Homans includes this component in the concept of "investment," but it is such a different phenomenon from that covered by the conventional meaning of investment that it may be better to reserve a different name for it.

3. It is not, of course, entirely accurate to say that agencies are not dependent on their clients. Without clients, agencies are out of business. I shall return to the nature of their dependency below, in the context of considering agencies as suppliers. In the present context, however, it seems important to note that the lesser degree and plainness of the dependency, coupled with the freedom from competition, makes it less certain, from the client's point of view, that his costs and risks will be appreciated enough to keep him from being, as he perceives it, exploited.

4. Julius Horwitz, "The Grim State of Welfare," *Look* (March 26, 1963), 77.

5. See Erving Goffman's discussion of "role distance," in *Encounters* (Indianapolis, Ind.: The Bobbs-Merrill Co., 1961).

6. I am indebted for clarification of this point, as well as others, to my colleague, Dr. Bernard Goldstein.

7. Cf. Robert K. Merton's discussion of ritualism in *Social Theory and Social Structure* (New York: The Free Press of Glencoe, 1957), 184–87. See also Harry C. Bredemeier and Richard M. Stephenson, *The Analysis of Social Systems* (New York: Holt, Rinehart & Winston, 1962), 255–61.

8. Erving Goffman, *Encounters, op. cit.*

9. The stereotype given expression in that penetrating analysis, "Officer Krupky," from *West Side Story* is the latter, with the former being attached to the Juvenile Court Judge.

10. John Kenneth Galbraith, *The Affluent Society* (Boston: Houghton Mifflin Co., 1958) 133, 135.

Low Income Behavior and Cognitive Style

Introduction

Low Income Behavior

An important element in the determination of appropriate treatment for low income individuals is knowledge regarding their behavior: how it is different from middle class behavior, what characteristics it has in common with middle class behavior (if any), and which significant subgroups come under the rubric "low income." [1]

Different writers portray somewhat different pictures of low income life, and some, like Hylan Lewis, are more impressed with its heterogeneity than with any supposed homogeneity of "culture." Our emphasis is on what appear to be important, therapeutically relevant behavior patterns in low income life. In addition, we are concerned with subgroups that we feel should be considered in developing an appropriate treatment strategy.

Different interpretation of low income behavior may arise from the fact that some investigators refer to a single subgroup within the low income complex. Thus, Walter Miller refers largely to Negro and Irish "lower class" *youths* and consequently accents peer-culture values more than family-determined values; Herbert Gans describes Italian "working class" and "lower class" groups with a heavy emphasis on working class *family* norms; Lee Rainwater is more concerned with "working class" wives and thus gives greater attention to consumer attitudes.

What, then, are some of the characteristic approaches to low income life? Walter Miller describes the "focal concerns" of this group as trouble, toughness, smartness, excitement, fate, autonomy.[2] Albert Cohen[3] lists the following characteristics: family and kinship stress, neighboring, restricted participation in voluntary associations, preference for the familiar, anti-intellectuality, authoritarianism, intolerance, pessimism, insecurity, cynicism, extra-punitiveness, patriarchy, toughness, consumption stress. The following is an attempt at an inclusive statement of major themes and characteristics.

Major Themes in Low Income Culture

1. Security vs. Status—the key
2. Pragmatism and anti-intellectualism
3. Powerlessness, the unpredictable world, and fate
4. Alienation, anger, and the underdog
5. Cooperation, gregariousness, equalitarianism, and humor
6. Authority and informality (not in contradiction)
7. Person centered outlook, particularism
8. Physicalism, masculinity, and health
9. Traditionalism and prejudice
10. Excitement, action, luck, and the consumer orientation
11. Non-joining
12. Special significance of the extended family. Stable, female based household.

There is a vast literature concerning the characteristics of lower socioeconomic groups, much of which is summarized in the first article in this section, "A Survey of Working- and Lower-Class Studies," by Herbert Gans. Gans's summary does not distinguish between what is sometimes referred to as "lower class" (largely unskilled laborers whose employment is more irregular) and "working class" (semiskilled and skilled workers whose employment is more stable). As we shall see in later sections, psychotherapeutic approaches have not typically directed attention toward distinctions between these two subgroups. This is unfortunate because it prevents a more attuned treatment strategy. It is for this reason that we summarize here some differences and similarities between the two groups.

The "Lower Class" and The "Working Class": Differences and
   Similarities

Differences—The "lower class":

1. lives under more difficult and depriving conditions
2. has less access to middle class goals and goods
3. has less access to working class means of organization (e.g.,
   unions)
4. has less stability in terms of jobs, neighborhood, and family
5. has fewer working class traditions and less urban experience
6. has a different ethnic composition, a larger proportion of
   Negro and Spanish speaking people;

Similarities—Both groups:

1. perform manual work for their livelihood
2. are essentially removed from the middle class prestige race
3. live a "realistic," concrete-centered, physical life, and the
   mental styles of both are quite similar
4. have a family and community life that constrains toward
   some degree of interdependence and cooperation (although
   there is a greater strain in the lower class group).

Jerome Cohen's "Social Work and the Culture of Poverty" includes a discussion of "lower class" and "working class" differences,
as well as some perspective regarding the increasingly popular
culture of poverty concept.

The next two articles are directed toward enriching our understanding of subgroups within the low income population: S. M.
Miller's "The American Lower Classes: A Typological Approach,"
contributes an important breakdown of possible subgroups, using
economic security and family stability as subdividing variables to
produce four subtypes or cells. Miller also notes some of the action
implications of this analysis. A second typological analysis is provided by another excerpt from Gans's *The Urban Villagers*. He
develops a fascinating typology that includes four groups: "The
maladapted, the *middle-class mobiles*, and—the two most important
ones—the *routine-seekers* and *action-seekers*. The former is based
on the search for a routine life, and the latter, on the pursuit of
adventurous episodes, or what West Enders call 'action.' " [4] "While
the action-seekers are more likely to be in the lower class," Gans
notes that not all action-seekers are "lower class." The routine

seekers are more often found in the "working class." It is extremely important for the "middle class observer" not to confuse the action-seekers with the maladapted group, the "people who are entirely unable to control their behavior because of alcoholism or other personal difficulties." The action-seekers "pursue episodes within a context of rules, and do not cut themselves off from family and peers . . . whereas the maladapted may be mentally ill, and lack the self-control and contact with reality to function in these groups." [5] The confusion of these two groups leads to an exaggeration of pathology among low income groups and to considerable misunderstanding of their behavior and concomitant errors in working with them.

Preparatory to a discussion of styles of disadvantaged groups, we present Melvin Kohn's intriguing interpretation of the connections between parent-child relationships (rather than techniques of child rearing), parental values, and conditions of life in the various social classes.

Cognitive Style and Language

The following is a brief list of broadly characteristic elements of the cognitive style of a variety of low income groups. [6]

1. physical and visual rather than aural
2. content-centered rather than form-centered
3. externally oriented rather than introspective
4. problem-centered rather than abstract-centered
5. inductive rather than deductive
6. spatial rather than temporal
7. slow, careful, patient, persevering (in areas of importance), rather than quick, clever, facile
8. games and action vs. tests oriented
9. expressive vs. instrumental oriented
10. one-track thinking and unorthodox learning rather than other-directed flexibility
11. words used in relation to action rather than word-bound orientation (inventive word power and "hip" language).

The lead article in this section, by Martin Deutsch, is based on the currently popular deprivation thesis. This viewpoint holds that the disadvantaged child has been essentially deprived of necessary stimulation early in life, by the conditions of poverty and resulting

types of family life. This deprivation is seen as fundamental in determining his cognitive style and ability, particularly as producing limited verbal ability.

An excerpt from Riessman's *The Culturally Deprived Child* attempts to challenge the "stimulus deprivation" thesis and to replace it with a "stimulus different" interpretation, including some questions regarding the presumed verbal deficit of the disadvantaged child. Since therapy obviously has to be communicative, the importance of understanding the language of the disadvantaged cannot be underestimated. Basil Bernstein's attempts at integration of social class, speech systems, and psycho-therapy provide another view of this language style or pattern.

Much has been written regarding the inadequate conceptual style of low income people. Miller and Swanson describe low income style as motoric ("some people can think through a problem only if they can work on it with their hands"), in contrast to middle class style which is more often symbolic ("they feel more comfortable if they can get a picture of the task and then solve it in their heads").[7]

Siller's research provides substantiation for a class difference in conceptual thinking.[8] But what is particularly significant about Siller's investigation is that it demonstrates that the statistically significant class differences in conceptual thinking are essentially produced by a subgroup within the low status population sample, who do very poorly. When this group is removed from comparison, class differences in conceptual ability disappear (there was no similar subgroup of extremely poor performers in the high status sample). This finding would seem to suggest that careful analysis of low income populations be made with an eye toward different treatment and educational procedures. The uneven effects of poverty (discussed in Part 1) are perhaps in evidence again, suggesting that we develop programs in terms of subgroups of the poor rather than in terms of common denominators.

Despite our emphasis on the subtypes of poverty, we conclude this section with a fascinating attempt by Warren Haggstrom to portray certain core psychological elements in the poor, particularly those related to chronic, enforced dependency. Haggstrom proposes a social action program, using the Saul Alinsky model, as an antidote to this condition. This proposal may provide a useful framework within which to view the treatment approaches presented in Part III, especially the sociotherapeutic suggestions.

Notes

1. The terms "low income," "disadvantaged," "poor," and "deprived" are used interchangeably.

2. See Walter B. Miller, "Lower Class Culture as a Generating Milieu of Gang Delinquency," *Journal of Social Issues,* XIV: 3, (1958), 5–19.

3. Albert Cohen and Harold Hodges, "Characteristics of the Lower Blue-Collar Class," *Social Problems,* 10; 4 (1963), 303–34.

4. Herbert Gans, *The Urban Villagers* (New York: The Macmillan Company, 1962), 18.

5. *Ibid.,* p. 31.

6. See Frank Riessman, *The Culturally Deprived Child* (New York: Harper and Roe, 1962), Ch. VII, VIII.

7. Daniel R. Miller, and Guy E. Swanson, *Inner Conflict and Defense* (New York: Holt, Rinehart & Winston, 1960), 24.

8. Jerome Siller, "Socioeconomic Status and Conceptual Thinking," *Journal of Abnormal and Social Psychology,* 55:3 (1957), 365–71.

Low Income Behavior

A Survey of Working- and Lower-Class Studies [1]

Herbert Gans

A wealth of evidence from other studies indicates that the peer group society is a class, rather than an ethnic, phenomenon. My survey of these studies will be cursory. It will consider various social structural and cultural characteristics in the order in which I have described them among the West Enders.

Although the existence of a peer group society has not been reported in other working-class populations, Walter Miller's study of an Irish and Negro neighborhood did conclude that: "Lower class society may be pictured as comprising a set of age-graded one-sex peer groups which constitute the psychic focus and reference group for those over twelve and thirteen." [2] The distinction between the peer group society and the outside world is much like Hoggart's dichotomy of "us" and "them" in the British working class.[3] He writes:

> . . . the world outside is strange and often unhelpful . . . it has most of the counters stacked on its side . . . to meet it on its own terms is difficult. One may call this, making use of a word commonly used by the working classes, the world of "Them.". . . The world of "Them" is the world of the bosses, whether those bosses are private individuals or . . . public officials. . . . "Them" includes the policemen and those civil servants . . . whom the working classes meet. . . . To the very poor, especially, they compose a shadowy but numerous and powerful group affecting their lives at almost every point. . . . "They" are "the people at the top" . . . who . . . "get yer in the end," "aren't really to be trusted," "are all in a clique together," "treat y'like muck." [4]

Reprinted from *The Urban Villagers*, New York: The Free Press of Glencoe, 1962, pp. 230–242.

Similarly, a study of American working-class women notes their separation from "the outer world," and their fear of its " 'chaotic and catastrophic' qualities." [5] In some ways Redfield's conception of the relationship between the peasant and the elite is like that between the West Ender and the outside world.[6] Moreover, Lewis's description of the Mexican "culture of poverty" bears a number of resemblances to the way of life of the poorest West Enders.[7]

My description of routine- and action-seekers is paralleled in many ways by S. M. Miller and Frank Riessman's distinction between the "unskilled, irregular worker . . . [who] . . . lacks the disciplined, structured and traditional approach of the stable worker and stresses the excitement theme." [8] Their analysis, based on a review of American working-class studies, reflects the general sociological distinction between working and lower class.[9] Walter Miller's study of lower-class culture describes in more systematic detail what I have called action-seeking. He notes its "focal concerns" with such qualities as toughness, daring, adroitness in repartee, excitement, and rejection of superordinate authority.[10] His discussion of excitement observes that:

> For many lower-class individuals the rhythm of life fluctuates between periods of relatively routine or repetitive activity and sought situations of great emotional stimulation. Many of the most characteristic features of lower-class life are related to the search for excitement or "thrill." [11]

The largest amount of data is available on family life. The segregation of family roles and the separate lives of husbands and wives have been reported in studies of the English working class,[12] among Puerto Ricans, both in Puerto Rico and in New York,[13] in a Mexican family,[14] and in a national American working-class sample.[15] A study of Polish-Americans describes this segregation as follows:

> . . . the pairs are not "one" . . . the marriage relation is not intensive. There is not a ceaseless seeking out of the other's motivations, no rigid set of expectations to which the other must conform.[16]

The same study also notes the men's need to display and defend their masculinity.[17] Similar findings have been reported in most working-class populations regardless of ethnic origin.[18] The subordinate role of children in what I have called the adult-centered family has been observed among New York Puerto Ricans [19] and in a general survey of working-class culture.[20] Two American studies point out the lack of interest in children as individuals.[21] The pattern of permitting freedom to boys, and of keeping girls at home has also been found among Puerto Ricans.[22]

The central role of the peer group has been suggested, as previously noted, by Walter Miller's study of Irish and Negro lower-class adolescents.[23] Another American study found that:

Husband and wife tend to have few, if any friends in common. Relationships with friends tend to be on a single-sex basis. . . . Often relatives are the only friends. If husband or wife do have friends who are not relatives, they have them as individuals and not as couples.[24]

Many studies have shown the existence of the family circle, notably in England,[25] and among New York Puerto Ricans.[26] The prevalence of spending one's social life with relatives more than with friends has been reported in England [27] and in a variety of American working-class groups.[28]

A number of findings on group life and personality have suggested that many of the elements I have summarized as person-orientation are found among working-class people generally, and one survey of American studies describes them as person-centered.[29] This article also notes the practice of personalizing bureaucracy and other outside world situations, as does an account of English working-class life.[30] A study of American working-class women describes their problems in regard to self-control, and shows how lack of self-control encourages their children in turn to express anger through violence.[31] It also suggests that working-class adolescents express themselves motorically, or physically, while middle-class adolescents use conceptual and symbolic modes.[32] Another study of American working-class women stresses the importance of group life, the fear of loneliness, and their concern with what others think of them.[33] An analysis of lower-class interview respondents has described in considerable detail their tendency to be concrete and particularistic, to think anecdotally, to personalize events, and to see phenomena only from their own perspective:[34] they do not "assume the role of another toward still others." [35] The limited repertoire of roles also has been described in a study of an English group,[36] and the inability or unwillingness of people to adopt other roles has been reported as lack of empathy in a previously mentioned study of Middle Eastern peasants.[37]

A number of American studies have shown the scarcity of working-class participation in what I have described as community life.[38] For example, the West Enders' pattern of being religious but not being identified with the church has been found among other American groups, both Protestant and Catholic,[39] and in England as well.[40]

Both American and English studies have reported the working-class detachment from work,[41] the concern with job security,[42] and the negative evaluation of white-collar workers and bosses.[43] The West Enders' ambivalence about education is also widely shared. The conception that school should teach children to keep out of trouble has been described by an English study; [44] that education must contribute to the occupational success of the individual, by many studies, including an American [45] and a Puerto Rican one.[46] Two studies have indicated that working-class mothers want more education for their children than do the fathers.[47]

I have already reported the prevalence of the general conception that

the outside world is not to be trusted. This extends also to a skepticism about caretakers,[48] a reluctance to visit settlement houses,[49] and a fear of doctors and hospitals that seems to be found in all countries.[50] Similarly, working-class people everywhere believe—or know—the police to be crooked, and politicians, corrupt. In America,[51] England,[52] and Mexico,[53] researchers have described the working- and lower-class antagonism toward law, government, and politics.

Conversely, the mass media are accepted, often more enthusiastically than by other classes. A recently published study of American television viewers has made this finding, and noted the working-class audience's interest in and identification with performers.[54] Several studies have also suggested the preference for action dramas over other forms of media content, not only in America,[55] but all over the world.[56] In Green's study of a Polish group, the rejection of romantic films by young working-class adults was described as follows: "At the local movie house, when the hero pauses in pursuit of the villain to proffer the heroine a tender sentiment, whistling and foot stamping greet his fall from grace." [57]

As I have not attempted to make a complete survey of the literature, I have mentioned here only some of the many similarities between the West Enders and other groups. Even so, it should be evident that, by and large, the peer group society is associated with working- and lower-class life. Moreover, the data shows that many of its features are found among other ethnic groups who have come to America from Europe—notably the Irish and Polish—as well as among racially differentiated groups, such as the Negroes and the Puerto Ricans. Incidentally, the peer group society also cuts across religious lines, for many of its characteristics appear not only among Protestants in England and America, but among European and Latin Catholics as well.

Some differences—including a few ethnic ones—do exist between the West Enders and other working-class people. Yet many of these differences can be traced to class factors operating in past and present generations. Italian-Americans, for example, differ from the Irish-Americans in a number of ways. The Irish are more respectful of paternal authority, of the older generation, of the church, and of authority in general. Irish men are also much closer to their mothers than are Italian men, a fact that has a number of implications for family structure, family dynamics, and even for the ways in which mental illness is expressed.[58]

Many of these differences can be related to the fact that the Irish immigrants came from landowning, peasant families. In Ireland, the father was the sole owner of the family farm, and thus was free to choose as to which of his sons would inherit it. As a result, sons were in a subordinate position.[59] One study of the Irish peasantry notes, in fact, that sons were called boys until the day the father surrendered the farm to one of them, even if they themselves were middle-aged adults.[60] The conditions which the Irish immigrants found in America evidently did not encourage any major change in family structure. Certainly, one could argue that those Irish-Americans who turned to politics

and the priesthood found that the relationship between the political boss
and his underlings and between the Bishop and his priests was much
the same as that between the farm owner and his sons. Needless to say,
not all Irish-Italian differences can be explained purely by class factors,
or by cultural differences which developed from economic conditions in
Europe. They do seem, however, to be of primary importance.

West Enders also differ from other working-class, and especially
lower-class, groups in the role that the mother plays in family life.
Studies of the English working class, for example, have stressed the
importance of the "Mum" and the dominance of the mother-daughter
relationship over all others, even when the daughter is married and has
children of her own.[61] Similarly, studies of the Negro, Puerto Rican, and
Carribean lower classes have shown the family to be what anthropologists call matrifocal.[62] The mother is the head of the household, and the
basic family unit includes her, her children, and one or more of her
female relatives, such as her mother or aunt. Often the man is a marginal
and only intermittent participant in this female-based household.[63]
American studies of the lower class have reported what Walter Miller
calls "serial monogamy"—a pattern in which a woman lives and has
children with a series of men who desert her or whom she asks to
leave.[64]

The reason for this pattern among Negroes can be found in the fact
that in past and present, they have lived under conditions in which the
male's position in the society has been marginal and insecure. Under
slavery, for example, the formation of a normal family was discouraged,
although the female slave was allowed to raise her own children. Since
the days of slavery, the Negro's economic position has been such as to
maintain much of this pattern. The man who has difficulty in finding a
steady job and is laid off frequently finds it difficult to perform the
functions of a male breadwinner and household head. Moreover, when
the woman is able to find steady employment or can subsist on welfare
payments, she tends to treat the man with disdain and often with open
hostility, especially if he complicates her life by making her pregnant.
Under these conditions, there is no incentive for the man to remain in
the family, and in times of stress he deserts. Moreover, when the male
children grow up in a predominantly female household—in which the
man is a powerless and scorned figure—their upbringing encourages
ambivalence as to male functions and masculinity. Thus, the pattern is
perpetuated into the next generation.[65]

The hypothesis that the female-based family can be traced to class
and, more specifically, to occupational factors is supported by studies
describing this family type among peoples who have not been slaves.[66]
It has been found, for example, among Puerto Ricans, both on the island
and in New York. It seems, however, to be more prevalent among Puerto
Ricans from sugar cane areas, which have a plantation economy much
like that under which the Negro endured slavery.[67] The hypothesis is
supported in another way by the fact that a somewhat similar family
constellation prevails when the man's occupation separates him from his

family for long periods. Thus, a study of sailors' families in Norway indicates that the woman takes over the dominant role in the family, and overprotects her children.[68] Although the girls show no negative consequences, the boys seem to develop what Tiller calls a defensive feminine identification, and compensatory masculine traits. When such boys become adults, they thus favor occupations that stress masculinity and minimize female contact and the family role.

The female-based family, however, is not found among West Enders, and the reasons perhaps can also be traced to occupational factors. Although the West Enders' ancestors suffered from unemployment, the totally agrarian economy of Southern Italian society and the extremely strenuous character of farm labor created no employment opportunities for women. Indeed, the family could best survive if the woman stayed home and bore a large number of children who could eventually add to the family's income. As a result, the woman did not take on an economic function, and the man maintained his position in the family even though he could not always support it adequately. This family constellation seems to have been strong enough to endure in America during those periods when the man was unemployed and the woman could find a job. Needless to say, some family instability and male marginality or desertion has occurred among the immigrants and the second generation, but such cases have been considerably fewer than among newcomers with female-based families.

Finally, the West Enders may be contrasted to the Jews, an ethnic group which came to America at about the same time as the Italians, but with a different occupational history.[69] The Jews who emigrated from Poland and Russia around the turn of the century were neither farm laborers nor peasants, but peddlers, shopkeepers, and artisans with a more middle-class occupational tradition. They also differed from their fellow immigrants in their belief in education, partly for reasons related to this tradition. Although they worked initially as unskilled and semi-skilled laborers in America, they reacted differently to their environment than did the ethnic groups from peasant and farm labor origins. Superficially, the Jewish family structure resembled the Italian one, with a nuclear household surrounded by a large family circle. Because of the high value placed on education, however, the immigrants did not restrain their children from contact with the outside world. As already noted, they encouraged the children to use the schools and settlement houses to prepare themselves for white-collar and professional occupations. Thus, the Jewish young people pursued careers that drew them apart from the parental generation at the same time that their Italian neighbors rejected such careers as "lonely ventures" that could only break up the cohesion of the family circle. Although the Jewish immigrants did bemoan the children's acculturation into styles of life congruent with their higher occupational level, they also took pride in the successful mobility of their offspring.[70]

I would not want to claim that the West Enders are like all other working-class and peasant ethnic groups, or that all differences between

them and other populations can be explained by class factors. Indeed, many differences between the ethnic groups must be attributed to other factors in their cultural traditions and in their American experience.[71] Until comparative studies of these groups are made that hold class constant, however, we will not know exactly where these differences are located, nor how they can be explained.

Notes

1. Most of the reported studies deal with the working class, some with the lower class, and others fail to distinguish between the two. Differences between the two classes will be discussed in the next section. In the survey, I shall use the term "working class" to describe both, unless the study cited refers specifically to lower-class people.

2. Walter B. Miller, "Lower Class Culture as a Generating Milieu of Gang Delinquency," *Journal of Social Issues*, vol. 14, No. 3 (1958), pp. 5–19, at p. 14.

3. Richard Hoggart, *The Uses of Literacy*, London: Chatto and Windus, 1957, Chap. 3.

4. *Ibid.*, p. 62.

5. L. Rainwater, R. Coleman, and G. Handel, *Workingman's Wife*, New York: Oceana Publications, 1959, pp. 44–45.

6. Robert Redfield, "Peasant Society and Culture," in *Little Community and Peasant Society and Culture*, Chicago: University of Chicago Press (Phoenix Books), 1960, pp. 36–39.

7. Oscar Lewis, *The Children of Sanchez*, New York: Random House, 1961, pp. xxiii–xxvii.

8. S. M. Miller and Frank Riessman, "The Working Class Subculture: A New View," *Social Problems*, vol. 9 (1961), pp. 86–97, at p. 95.

9. See, for example, W. Lloyd Warner and Paul S. Lunt, *The Social Life of a Modern Community*, New Haven: Yale University Press, 1941, which distinguishes between and describes upper-lower and lower-lower classes; and the work of his associates, for example, August B. Hollingshead, *Elmtown's Youth*, New York: Wiley and Sons, 1949.

10. Walter M. Miller, *op. cit.*, summarized from Chart I, p. 7.

11. *Ibid.*, pp. 10–11. See also his "Implications of Urban Lower-Class Culture for Social Work," *Social Service Review*, vol. 33 (1959), pp. 219–236; and Warren Miller's novel of the episodic life in a lower-class Negro gang, *The Cool World*, Boston: Little, Brown, 1959.

12. See, for example, J. M. Mogey,

Family and Neighborhood, London: Oxford University Press, 1956, p. 58; and Elizabeth Bott, *Family and Social Network,* London: Tavistock Publications, 1957, pp. 58 ff. Bott also cites a number of earlier studies with a similar finding, and notes that not all working-class families are segregated.

13. Helen Icken. "From Slum to Housing Project," unpublished study made for the Urban Renewal and Housing Administration, Commonwealth of Puerto Rico, 1960, mimeographed, p. 55; Elena Padilla, *Up from Puerto Rico*, New York: Columbia University Press, 1958, pp. 151–152.

14. Lewis, *op. cit.*, p. 335.

15. Lee Rainwater, *And the Poor Get Children*, Chicago: Quadrangle Books, 1960, p. 69; and Social Research, Inc., "Status of the Working Class in Changing American Society," Chicago: Social Research, Inc., February, 1961, mimeographed, p. 80.

16. Arnold W. Green, "The 'Cult of Personality' and Sexual Relations," in Norman W. Bell and Ezra F. Vogel, eds., *A Modern Introduction to the Family*, New York: The Free Press of Glencoe, 1960, pp. 608–615, at pp. 614–615.

17. *Ibid.*, p. 614.

18. Walter Miller, "Lower Class Culture as a Generating Milieu of Gang Delinquency," *op. cit.*, p. 9; Rainwater, *op. cit.*, pp. 84–85; Icken, *op. cit.* Lewis's study of a Mexican family gives innumerable examples of this phenomenon.

19. Padilla, *op. cit.*, pp. 179 ff.

20. Miller and Riessman, *op. cit.*, p. 92. They use the term "parent-centered."

21. L. Rainwater, R. Coleman, and G. Handel, *op. cit.*, p. 89; and Social Research, Inc., *op. cit.*, pp. 161, 163.

22. Icken, *op. cit.*, p. 57; Padilla, *op. cit.*, pp. 186 ff.

23. Miller, "Lower Class Culture as a Generating Milieu of Gang Delinquency," *op. cit.*, p. 14.

24. Social Research, Inc., *op. cit.*, p. 82.

25. Mogey, *op. cit.*, p. 97; Bott, *op. cit.*,

p. 112; Michael Young and Peter Willmott, *Family and Kinship In London*, London: Routledge and Kegan Paul, 1957, Chap. V.

26. Padilla, *op. cit.*, pp. 112 ff. She calls it "the great family group."

27. Madeline Kerr, *The People of Ship Street*, London: Routledge and Kegan Paul, 1958, pp. 106–108. Young and Willmott report the rejection of mobile relatives, *op. cit.*, pp. 143–144.

28. Floyd Dotson, "Patterns of Voluntary Association among Urban Working Class Families," *American Sociological Review*, vol. 16 (1951), pp. 687–693, at p. 691; Rainwater, Coleman, and Handel, *op. cit.*, p. 107; Bennett M. Berger, *Working-Class Suburb*, Berkeley: University of California Press, 1960, p. 68; and Social Research, Inc., pp. 63, 82. Rainwater, Coleman, and Handel also note the working-class woman's difficulty in making friends. *Op. cit.*, p. 108.

29. Miller and Riessman, *op. cit.*, pp. 93–94.

30. *Ibid.*, and Hoggart, *op. cit.*, p. 28.

31. Daniel R. Miller, Guy E. Swanson *et al.*, *Inner Conflict and Defense*, New York: Holt, Rinehart, and Winston, 1960, Chap. 14.

32. *Op. cit.*, Chap. 15. A national survey reports that "respondents with less education tend to be less introspective about themselves, whether about strong points or shortcomings." G. Gurin, J. Veroff, and S. Feld, *Americans View Their Mental Health*, New York: Basic Books, 1960, p. 69.

33. Rainwater, Coleman, and Handel, *op. cit.*, pp. 64–66. See also Hoggart, *op. cit.*, p. 72.

34. Leonard Schatzman and Anselm Strauss, "Social Class and Modes of Communication," *American Journal of Sociology*, vol. 60 (1955), pp. 329–338; and Anselm Strauss and Leonard Schatzman, "Cross Class Interviewing: An Analysis of Interaction and Communicative Styles," in Richard N. Adams and Jack J. Preiss, ed., *Human Organization Research*, Homewood, Ill.: Dorsey Press, 1960, pp. 205–213.

35. Schatzman and Strauss, *op. cit.*, p. 331.

36. Kerr, *op. cit.*, Chap. 17.

37. Daniel Lerner, *The Passing of Traditional Society*, New York: The Free Press of Glencoe, 1958.

38. Dotson, *op. cit.*, p. 688; Berger, *op. cit.*, p. 59; Rainwater, Coleman, and Handel, *op. cit.*, p. 114 ff. See also Morris Axelrod, "Urban Structure and Social Participation," *American Sociological Review*, vol. 21 (1956), pp. 13–18.

39. Berger, *op. cit.*, pp. 45 ff.; Rainwater, Coleman, and Handel, *op. cit.*, p. 123.

40. Hoggart, *op. cit.*, pp. 94–97; Kerr, *op. cit.*, pp. 135–136.

41. A concise review of studies of work patterns and attitudes of working-class and lower-class people is found in Joseph A. Kahl, *The American Class Structure*, New York: Holt, Rinehart and Winston, 1957, pp. 205–215.

42. Ephraim H. Mizruchi, "Social Structure, Success Values and Structured Strain in a Small City," paper read at the 1961 meetings of the American Sociological Association, mimeographed; Social Research, Inc., *op. cit.*, pp. 57–58.

43. Katherine Archibald, "Status Orientations among Shipyard Workers," in Reinhart Bendix and Seymour M. Lipset, eds., *Class, Status and Power*, New York: The Free Press of Glencoe, 1953, pp. 395–403; Young and Willmott, *op. cit.*, p. 14.

44. Hoggart, *op. cit.*, p. 98.

45. Social Research, Inc., pp. 51–53; see also Archibald, *op. cit.*, p. 399; and Mizruchi, *op. cit.*

46. Padilla, *op. cit.*, p. 198.

47. Herbert H. Hyman, "The Value System of Different Classes," in Bendix and Lipset, *op. cit.*, pp. 426–442, Tables III, IV; and Icken, *op. cit.*, p. 34.

48. Padilla, *op. cit.*, p. 264.

49. Albert Cohen, *Delinquent Boys: The Culture of the Gang*, New York: The Free Press of Glencoe, 1955, pp. 116–117.

50. Hoggart, *op. cit.*, p. 42; Kerr, *op. cit.*, p. 39; Lewis, *op. cit.*, p. xxviii.

51. Miller and Riessman, *op. cit.*, p. 91.

52. Hoggart, *op. cit.*, p. 87.

53. Lewis, *op. cit.*, pp. xxvii, 351, 389. On the personalization of government, see Miller and Riessman, *op. cit.*, p. 93; Padilla, *op. cit.*, p. 256; and Lewis, *op. cit.*, p. 332.

54. Ira O. Glick and Sidney J. Levy, *Living with Television*, Chicago: Aldine Publishing Company, 1962, Chap. III, VII.

55. See, for example, Berger, *op. cit.*, pp. 74–75.

56. Herbert J. Gans, "American Films and Television Programs on British Screens: A Study of the Functions of American Popular Culture Abroad," Philadelphia: Institute for Urban Studies, 1959, mimegraphed, Chap. 4.

57. Green, *op. cit.*, p. 613.

58. These differences between the Irish are reported in Ezra F. Vogel, *op. cit.*, and M. K. Opler and J. L. Singer, "Ethnic Differences in Behavior and Psychopathogy," *International Journal of Social Psy-*

chiatry, vol. 2 (1956), pp. 11–22. See also Mark Zborowski, "Cultural Components in Responses to Pain," *Journal of Social Issues*, vol. 8 (1952), pp. 16–30; and Paul Barrabee and Otto van Mering, "Ethnic Variations in Mental Stress in Families with Psychotic Children," *Social Problems*, vol. 1 (1953), pp. 48–53.

59. Conrad M. Arensberg and Solon T. Kimball, *Family and Community in Ireland*, Cambridge: Harvard University Press, 1940, pp. 47 ff.

60. *Ibid.*, pp. 51, 56.

61. The previously cited studies by Young and Willmott, and by Kerr describe this relationship in great detail.

62. See, for example, Raymond T. Smith, *The Negro Family in British Guiana*, London: Routledge and Kegan Paul, 1956; and for America, E. Franklin Frazier, *The Negro Family in the United States*, Chicago: University of Chicago Press, 1939.

63. Walter B. Miller, "Lower Class Culture as a Generating Milieu of Gang Delinquency," *op. cit.*, p. 14.

64. Walter B. Miller, "Implications of Urban Lower-Class Culture for Social Work," *op. cit.*, p. 225.

65. Walter B. Miller, "Lower-Class Culture as a Generating Milieu of Gang Delinquency," *op. cit.*, p. 9.

66. I have not been able to find any explanation of the dominant role of the "Mum" in the English working-class family. It should be noted, however, that this family is not female-based.

67. I owe this suggestion to Howard Stanton. In the sugar cane economy, there is work for only three to four months a year.

68. Per Olav Tiller, "Father Absence and Personality Development of Children in Sailor Families," Oslo: Institute for Social Research, 1957, mimeographed.

69. This account draws on Marshall Sklare, *Conservative Judaism*, New York: The Free Press of Glencoe, 1955; and Nathan Glazer, *American Judaism*, Chicago: University of Chicago Press, 1957.

70. For a detailed study of differences between American-born Italians and Jews, see Fred L. Strodtbeck, "Family Interaction, Values and Achievement," in D. C. McClelland, A. Baldwin, U. Bronfenbrenner, and F. Strodtbeck, *Talent and Society*, Princeton: D. Van Nostrand, 1958, pp. 135–194. He compares Jewish values, such as the belief in education, the desirability of individual achievement, and the striving for mobility and for rational mastery of the world to the Italians' familism and fatalism. Even so, he suggests that "differences between Italians and Jews are greatly attenuated when class level is held constant." *Op. cit.*, p. 154, based on an unpublished study by B. Tregoe.

71. See here especially Zborowski, *op. cit.*, and Opler and Singer, *op. cit.* Since the West End was a multi-ethnic neighborhood with relatively little variation in class, the studies now being conducted by the Center for Community Studies among the various ethnic groups may shed further light on these differences.

Social Work and the Culture of Poverty

Jerome Cohen

Concern about poverty is not exactly a "New Frontier" for social work. Even during the peak of intensive individual treatment, social work as an institution found expression for its concern with the larger issues of gross economic deprivation and its social consequences. It is undeniable that personnel and planning efforts have frequently been diverted to other matters, and that for long periods of time social work has distributed its resources unevenly among many demands other than those imposed by poverty that have been placed upon its energies. But while social work may have neglected its charge, it never abandoned it.

This paper is concerned with the "culture" of poverty and the members of the lower class who are an integral part of its complex. There is considerable confusion in sociological literature about what constitutes the lower and working classes. One might speculate about the basis of some of the confusion. In a democratic society the existence of social classes, invidiously perceived from lower to upper, is anathema. The social scientist, a participant in as well as an observer of his culture, may also suffer from the strain of defining the class system—especially the lower class. The social work profession, first borrowing from the confused literature of social stratification and then adding its own loose usage of the terminology, has compounded the confusion to the point that one rarely knows of what population an author is speaking when he refers to the lower-class or working-class population. Yet these two groups are quite different in many important ways. They are so different, in fact, that members of the working class, who since the 1930's have

Reprinted by permission of the National Association of Social Workers, from *Social Work*, Vol. 9, No. 1, January 1964, pp. 3–11.

achieved enough economic stability and political power that they can well care for themselves, have by many authors been lumped in with the middle classes of society. They do not belong there—they have retained a fairly distinctive style of life and value system.[1]

The working class accounts for at least half the population and makes up a large proportion of the clients served by the social work profession. This belief is in disagreement with those who claim that social work has been primarily concerned with a middle-class clientele. A review of the statistics of both public and private agencies staffed by trained social workers (those agencies served primarily by social workers without full professional training would certainly not be serving a middle-class clientele), including a recent FSAA study, will support this position. Approximately 70 per cent of the clients in the agencies participating in the study were members of the lower or working classes.[2] If *relative need* is viewed in terms of capacity and resources for self-help, then a case may be made for a different view of the equitable distribution of social services but the data do not *directly* support the charge that social work services are aimed primarily at a middle-class target.

The most important generative factor distinguishing the lower from the working classes seems to be the unstable employment characteristic of the lower class. In large part this accounts for their status as marginal people always on the edge of an affluent society. In this paper the term "lower class" will be used for the approximately 18 per cent of the population who suffer *severe* poverty as a result of unstable employment and the lowest paid service and unskilled work. This is the most seriously deprived group. The rest of the blue-collar work force, the minor white-collar workers, and the higher-paid service workers who are in stable employment will constitute the working class for the purposes of this paper.

On Cultures and Subcultures

Before discussing the culture of poverty and its inhabitants, attention will be given to the problems that arise out of using culture as an organizing concept. The past ten or fifteen years have seen a popularization of the concept of culture and its derivative, subculture. Social workers seem especially susceptible to taking over a new slogan, concept, or method from other disciplines and using it vigorously but not rigorously. Too often the concept's full meaning and implications are not understood. This is unfortunate, not because semantic purity is lost, but because the value of the concept for illuminating professional concerns is thereby diluted.

Unfortunately the mistake is often made of taking literally an Albert Cohen's or a Walter Miller's description of lower-class behavior and approaching the people in a particular neighborhood as if one really expected, upon knocking on a door, to find the modal type of which they

spoke. The confusion that occurs upon finding in the real-life situation a great deal more diversity than was anticipated frequently serves to disenchant the uninitiated. This misplaced concreteness has a number of such unfortunate consequences. Social science generalizations cannot be used in this way. Social workers must be careful that they do not promote the well-known, self-fulfilling prophecy by approaching people with expectations of behavior that call forth that very behavior. Such knowledge as can be absorbed from the social sciences as well as the behavioral sciences needs to be used discreetly at appropriate times and places.

While it is true that most human behavior is derived from a particular cultural experience in which the individual has learned to think and behave in certain defined ways, it is likewise true that he always has available a variety of alternatives. In a complex urban industrial society the alternatives are frequently numerous enough to make prediction quite hazardous. The notion of a subculture with a more narrowly defined population limits the alternatives to some extent, but still the variation is gross. Unfortunately, subcultures are not nice, clean, distinct entities within the larger culture. Rather, they frequently have fuzzy boundaries and there is much intermingling with the larger culture. From time to time ghetto-like pockets of isolation are found. These may have real enclosures like the old walled-in Jewish ghettos of eastern Europe or social enclosures like some modern public housing projects located on the fringes of middle-class neighborhoods. Or the isolating factor may be the remoteness of a rural community such as that of the Appalachian Mountains. But whatever the conditions, a great deal of behavioral variety among the inhabitants is still found.

In a way, the concept of subculture itself is an instance of "inconsistency" in the larger culture. Robin Williams put it well when he said:

> Every modern society that is at all complex carries a culture in which there are very many important strains and inconsistencies. With increasing size and complexity of the society, subcultures appear, carried by relatively autonomous groups or strata within the larger society . . . we may find only a tenuous linking together of a congeries of groups each with its own comparatively distinct value system, its special problems, its distinctive social perspectives.[3]

While Ralph Linton, an anthropologist, early recognized that members of a social class are shaped by their own subculture and that their personality norms are derived first of all from this subculture and only secondarily from the culture of the larger configuration of which their class is a part, he was also one of the earliest to recognize that considerable variation existed within subcultures. He was one of the first to introduce the distinction between ideal and real patterns of behavior. He was acutely aware that just because a people have developed an ideal pattern, a verbalization of what shall be done under certain circumstances, this does not mean that they will adhere any more closely to the norm than another group that has not bothered to verbalize the

pattern. Added to the problem of the "ideal types" and "patterns of behavior" frequently used by the social scientist to describe a culture is the fact that the culture often leaves an area of behavior socially undefined or that the social consequences of certain acts are not strictly sanctioned. This increases the opportunity for individual variation. Further, while a high frequency of certain traits may be found within a subculture, their combination will vary from individual to individual, producing a somewhat different total picture.[4]

Responses Reflect Values

Albert Cohen cites a study by L. K. Barker of seventy-five working-class and seventy-one middle-class boys in an Indiana junior high school. Barker asked a series of questions designed to pose dilemmas that could be resolved by a solution embodying either working-class or middle-class values. The specific questions reflected the characteristics cited most frequently as class-related, valued behavior. The results were heavily in the hypothesized direction and, as was strongly indicated by tests of significance, were not likely to be due to the vagaries of chance. Here are a few examples of the percentages of middle-class and working-class responses to the questions:

Do you ever like to play or do things by yourself? It is assumed that working-class boys are more dependent upon the society of their peers, that middle-class boys are more likely to find satisfaction in independent activity. Seventy-six per cent of the middle-class boys, forty-three per cent of the working-class boys answered "yes" to this question.

Do you have any hobbies? For instance, do you collect or make things, do you play an instrument, or do you raise animals? It was assumed that the cultivation of hobbies reflects the middle-class emphasis on the "constructive" use of leisure, on the conception of time as a commodity that ought not to be "wasted" entirely in random and idle play. Seventy-six per cent of the middle-class boys, thirty-seven per cent of the working-class boys answered "yes."

Suppose you and some of your friends go to a movie. One of the boys hasn't any money and you have some extra. O.K., you lend him the money. Now, in the bunch that you run with, what would you usually do? Would you expect him to (a) pay you back or (b) just do you a favor sometime? This question was designed to pit the middle-class conception of mutual aid as a quasi-contractual relationship, a sort of business transaction, against the working-class ethic of reciprocity ("You help me out when you're ahead of the game and I'll help you out when I'm ahead of the game"). Fifty-five per cent of the middle-class boys, seventy-six per cent of the working-class boys chose the second response.

A group of ten boys form a club. They all decide to go to Indianapolis to the auto races. It will cost about $6 a boy. They all get

jobs and save their money for a while. When the time of the races comes, they all have their money except one boy who is broke. One of his friends has earned and saved some extra money and says, "I'll pay your way." But the boy without money says, "No, you worked hard and saved the money. The money is yours and I have no right to it." The other boy says, "Yes, but you're my friend and friends are supposed to help one another. I'll pay your way. Even if you can't pay me back, that's O.K." Do you think the boy should let his friend pay his way, even if he's not sure he can pay it back? This question was designed to pose, in even sharper form, the same dilemma as the preceding question. Here the issue is raised of whether it is legitimate to accept aid from a primary group associate even if one is not sure he can repay it. The spirit of spontaneous giving and guiltless acceptance is pitted against the spirit of rational exchange and individual responsibility. Thirty-two per cent of the middle-class boys, sixty-three per cent of the working-class boys said "yes."

When these ten boys first thought of making this trip, nine of the boys were all excited about going and wanted to go very much. But one boy said, "It takes a long time to save $6.00. I'm studying to be an electrician and I'm saving to buy books and tools that will run me over $15.00. No, I can't afford to take this trip." All the other boys said: "The whole club ought to go together. Maybe it will take you a little longer to save your $15.00, but you won't feel right if you stay behind, and besides, the club ought to go as a whole." Do you think the boy should (a) go along with the rest of the club or (b) stay home? This question really involves two dilemmas: the long-run versus the short-run, and the corner boy emphasis on primary-group solidarity and loyalty versus the college-boy emphasis on personal advancement. Thirty-four per cent of the middle-class boys, fifty-one per cent of the working-class boys chose to "go along with the rest of the club."

Suppose you are out playing ball with the boys and having lots of fun. Do you (a) leave the boys and go home to eat because you are expected home for meals at a certain time, or (b) go home to eat whenever you get hungry or through playing or whenever you feel like it? The issue here is between middle-class time-consciousness, with its implications of punctuality, time-budgeting and self-discipline, and working-class preoccupation with the pleasures and pains of the here and now. Eighty-seven per cent of the middle-class boys, sixty-nine per cent of the working-class boys give the first answer.[5]

The trend is clear, and this is important and meaningful to know. Social science, like all science, is concerned with regularities in observed phenomena. Its findings are stated in propositions that are associated with a particular degree of probability. Such statements tell us that "x" and "y" are related to one another at a given rate and that the probability that this phenomenon did not occur by chance is such and such.

Nevertheless, in this case it is clearly evident that large numbers of middle-class boys responded like the working-class boys and an equally large number of working-class boys responded as if they held the same

value system as the middle-class boys. Social work has long accepted the maxim that "in some ways each man is different from every other man and in some ways he is like every other man." For many years considerable professional energy has been spent in the building of a science and art devoted to the discovery of the unique patterns in each individual's responses. More recently, increased attention is being given to the further discovery of the common socially determined elements in man's behavior. This is both necessary and proper, but let us hope that we can avoid putting the *old* "social" back into social work. We must aim toward the development of a "social" practice based upon all that we have painfully learned to date while incorporating relevant concepts from the social and behavioral sciences so we can ourselves master their meaning and derive principles of action based upon them. We need in social work a much more sophisticated knowledge than we have yet acquired of how to use social science propositions effectively. We must find a way to make use of these propositions both to understand the clients we serve and to stimulate the further development of practice principles founded upon such a growing scientific base.

Normative behavior, then, is not a simple concept to be understood quickly and in gross terms. To quote Robin Williams:

> It is especially necessary to stress the relation of individuals to their institutions. No one lives in a culture as a whole. We live in particular segments of a total culture—in a particular family, class, school, church, and so on. What we directly experience is always a variant of the patterns discernible by external scientific abstraction.[6]

Nevertheless, it is remarkable how much regularity, conformity, and predictability do exist. It is impressive how many practical insights derive from such a vantage point.

One of the important insights gained from the study of a particular culture is the manner in which adaptation, adjustments, and problem-solving are carried out. A culture inevitably offers ways to solve problems. For large-scale planning purposes it is frequently less important to know the individual variations on a subcultural theme than to know how the aggregate of individuals within this subculture solve their problems of living. It may then be possible to determine what is important and functional for them as a group and to plan interventions related to their patterned responses.

What are some of the implications, then, of using the culture concept as an analytic device for the understanding of lower-class behavior and the planning of action programs in their behalf? First, I think that if we use the concept of subculture, then we must concern ourselves with the subculture's process of development. Subcultures develop out of a set of conditions and in some particular manner. We may accept, on the one hand, the theory of *cultural evolution*, which states that there is a spontaneous development of each culture based upon a particular set of circumstances. This might support the position that "de-

linquent subcultures" arise out of specific conditions in the social structure and that the similar behavior seen in these subcultures are a function of that social structure. Or we may accept the theory of *cultural diffusion*, which states that cultural behavior is spread from one place to another. This might encompass theories of "differential association" as a basis of delinquent behavior. In either case, we must find some means of understanding the processes by which a particular culture was created and the circumstances that nurtured its development. For social action must in part be based on such an understanding.

Culture and Personality

In recent years it has been necessary to awaken not all, but many, in the social work community to the fact that personality is not the only variable at work in the production of lower-class behavior. It has been necessary to portray strongly and emphatically the ways in which the social structure shaped behavior as a natural consequence of the conditions it imposed. It would be unfortunate indeed, if we swung too far in the opposite direction and failed to recognize that a given social structure also profoundly affects the conditions under which personality is developed. It is obvious that personality and social structure both play important roles in the behavioral picture we see at any given moment. Only the narrowest proponents of effecting social change through large-scale modes of intervention in the social structure believe that such structural changes will automatically or quickly bring about the desired individual or group behavioral changes. Change takes time in human affairs. This is true whether we conceive of change within a psychotherapeutic model or in terms of the social structure. The absence of a realistic time perspective for *any* theory of change can only lead to disappointment and frustration.

It is important to note that "fiction" in this instance plays an important role. It is difficult, if not impossible, to bring about changes in an existing institution if ideas are not stated with conviction and certainty. People are not ready to give up their "tried and true" practices for a new plan that is presented subject to so many conditions that it begins to sound quite unusable. However, it is obvious that the same bit of behavioral data can be analyzed in many ways—chemically, biologically, sociologically, psychologically, historically, economically, and so forth. Learning theories, psychoanalytic theories, and theories of functionalism have all been used with some success in the efforts to account for specific human behavior. Are we still naïvely searching for the *true* theory? In the helping professions it has long been perfectly clear that human behavior can be legitimately analyzed on many levels and that the important questions are not so much which is right but rather which will most adequately serve the goal of professional intervention. The unified theory of human behavior, if one is ever achieved, will without question

combine in some form many theories now held and others not yet
conceived.

Similar Patterns of Behavior

Having examined some aspects of the concept of culture, let us turn
to the culture of poverty itself. To what extent can we really speak of
a "culture of poverty"? There is increasing evidence that regardless of
where poverty is found, it produces some readily identifiable patterns of
behavior. Oscar Lewis' studies of poverty in Mexico reveal patterns of
thought and behavior amazingly similar to those of equally poor people
in other parts of the world, even though the host cultures are quite
different.[7] For example, there is an interesting group of Oriental Jews
in Israel who comprise approximately thirty percent of the population.
Their circumstances of life are characterized by extreme poverty, and in
general, they represent the lowest class of the Israeli society. Because
they are largely Arabic and Yemenite, their skin is generally four or
five shades darker than that of most of the other Jews in Israel. (This
greater visibility may be one of the characteristics promoting their conditions of life.) The group has become the object of increasing social
research as a result of the government's great concern for this third of
its population. And what do they find? First, they find the rate of school
drop-out to be high. It appears that children leave school not only because they cannot afford to go on—their economic services being needed
by the family—but also because the school system is organized around
the learning styles of the more advantaged child. Therefore, the Oriental
Jew, who tends to particularize and has difficulty with conceptualization,
does not perform well in school. They also find a relative inability to
defer gratification in many areas of social functioning. Employment
with good possibilities for learning and advancement are often left for
other positions that bring a small but immediate increase in income.[8]
It begins to sound like a familiar pattern, does it not? *Our* "culturally
deprived" child, is *their* "culturally deprived" child, and the conditions
that produced the two may be quite similar.

To what extent can the conditions of poverty that yield this similar
behavior be identified? It was suggested earlier that the subculture
characteristic of the unstable employed segment of our population needs
to be separated analytically from that characteristic of the more stable
working-class population. Although both may need services of one kind
or another, there remains little doubt that they are quite different.
Working-class people are frequently members of unions, which protect
them, nourish them, and give them a sense of group pride in their
achievements—a sense of mastery and a measure of political power.
This latter ingredient, political power, is important psychologically as
well as practically. For it is through such power that the development
of alienation, which so often leads to an anomic world view, may be

tempered. The circumstances of working-class life are more favorable to the nurturing of family cohesion and a more stable family life.[9]

Members of the lower class have little opportunity for mastery and its anxiety-reducing function. A number of theoreticians have suggested that deviant behavior, though it creates problems in other ways, sometimes offers an opportunity for mastery in an area of life and as such serves the purpose of preventing a completely damaged sense of self-worth and a feeling of "nothingness." The shame that frequently accompanies limited opportunity for mastery often leads to heightened hostile aggressiveness and the destruction of trust in others. Living in poverty inevitably leads to questions about one's own adequacy as well as about the values of society. The "brave front" often seen is a protection against the core of depression that is a natural consequence of living under these conditions. The constant exposure to betrayal of confidence by others adds to the feelings of shame as the individual recognizes that he has built his confidence upon false assumptions. Anticipation of love and happiness which is not fulfilled furthers self-debasement.[10] The greater the expectation, the more acute the anxiety is likely to be. It is no wonder that withdrawal and suspicion are so common. Taking a chance simply hurts too much. These are some of the consequences of poverty in terms of human emotion. It follows that we must take great care that when opportunities for achievement are offered, they are offered with carefully planned assistance so as to maximize the likelihood of success.

It seems prudent in discussing the culture of poverty to take heed of the above warnings about the nature of subcultures. The culture of poverty, like any other culture, is not shared by inhabitants who are carbon copies of one another. There are the old; the physically, the mentally, and the socially handicapped; the downwardly mobile drifters and the upwardly mobile strivers. Some have shared in the culture for many generations and others are the new immigrants who have not yet been fully socialized by its norms, values, and behaviors. Furthermore, impoverished people differ greatly in the extent to which they can live beyond the moment. Some use religious convictions to absorb the pain of the moment. Others have different but equally deep attachments. They are all there, the differences and the similarities. The culture of poverty is shared by a multitongued people of great diversities and many "samenesses."

Questions for Investigation

Interestingly, a similar psychological description can be given of the lower class or economically deprived segment of our population and some types of the disturbed or emotionally deprived segment. The latter type is most frequently classified under the omnibus label "character disorder." In the severe cases of both we find anxiety defended against

by projection and denial. We find acting-out behavior that is pleasure oriented and so pervasive that it almost seems to be a way of life. We find immediate impulse gratification an almost necessary condition for psychological survival. That there are similarities in the behavior manifestations few seem to deny. The basis of the behavior, however, is an important issue of debate in which each side has found its champions. Is it social structure or basic personality structure that accounts for most of this behavior? The debate is occasionally illuminating but more often argumentative. More enlightening and productive would be the turning of energies to an investigation of *why* the behavior looks the same even though it arises from somewhat different circumstances of life. Is it a function of extreme deprivation regardless of whether this is economic or emotional? If so, what are the specific ingredients that form the similar essence of the deprivation? To what extent does the behavior disappear in each case if the conditions of life are changed? How much deprivation is necessary before an irreversible process occurs? What is the developmental process that accompanies each form of deprivation as it moves through time?

This last question constitutes a most important and fruitful area for investigation. E. Wight Bakke, in his socioeconomic study of the depression family, carefully describes the process of change in individuals and families as they were affected by the existing economic conditions.[11] What he did for the stable working-class family, who were well organized to begin with and were supported by the recognition that a majority of the society were in the same condition as they, might well be done for those who participate in the culture of poverty—for those who suffer, as Labor Secretary Wirtz suggested, from the "human tragedy of life without opportunity" and "the gnawing fear of permanent uselessness."

We need to know more about the origins of the culture of poverty and about the permeability of its boundaries and the degree of isolation it produces. We need to know more about how those who are subjected to it live; what kind of remedial help is needed to alleviate the problem; how far institutional services can be utilized as they exist and where they have to be changed to meet the needs of this group. We need to know more about how these "culturally different" people among us function intellectually and socially and what modes of political activity will arouse them and generate self-involvement so that the communities they live in may become more effective agents of self-change.

In spite of our increased attention to the problems of poverty and our investment of an increasing proportion of our resources in efforts to effect change, our intervention leaves much to be desired. We are still faced with the reality of mass poverty and its consequences. We are still faced with overwhelming needs for social services. We are still faced with the inadequacy of our present methods to induce change on a large enough scale. We cannot do it all within the context of social work, and we need not continue to indict ourselves, but perhaps we can do more. We can continue to seek out means by which to under-

stand the conditions in which the culture of poverty is generated and perpetuated. We can seek out measures that, even if they are not yet based upon solid evidence, appear to be effective in ameliorating the problems with which we are concerned, and we can continue, in the tradition of social work, to be the voice that is raised loud and strong in behalf of the poor, the hurt, the disenfranchised members of our society.

Notes

1. S. M. Miller and F. Riessman, "Are Workers Middle Class?" *Dissent,* Vol. 3, No. 4 (Autumn 1961), pp. 507–513.

2. D. F. Beck, *Patterns in Use of Family Agency Service* (New York: Family Service Association of America, 1961), p. 10.

3. R. M. Williams, Jr., *American Society* (New York: Alfred A. Knopf, 1951), p. 349.

4. *See* Ralph Linton, *The Study of Man* (New York: Appleton Century, 1936), and S. Stansfeld Sargent and Miriam W. Smith, eds., *Culture and Personality* (New York: Wenner-Gren Foundation for Anthropological Research, 1949). In the latter book, Lawrence K. Frank makes this point exceedingly well.

5. *Delinquent Boys* (Glencoe, Ill.: Free Press, 1955), pp. 105–108.

6. Williams, *op. cit.,* p. 366.

7. Oscar Lewis, *Five Families* (New York: Basic Books, 1959).

8. *See* S. W. Eisenstadt, *The Absorption of Immigrants* (Glencoe, Ill.: Free Press, 1955), pp. 90–104, and *The Falk Project for Economic Research in Israel,* Fifth Report 1959–1960 (Jerusalem, Israel: Jerusalem Post Press, 1961), pp. 117–125.

9. The growing technology reflected in automation and other economic conditions of production in mining and industry may be once more reversing these circumstances for many workers long a part of the stable working class. Once again, many are finding themselves displaced, unemployed and drifting down to the lower classes.

10. *See* Helen Merrell Lynd, *On Shame and the Search for Identity* (New York: Science Editions, 1961), and Gerhart Piers and Milton B. Singer, *Shame and Guilt* (Springfield, Ill.: Charles C Thomas, 1953), for an excellent analysis of the consequences of shame.

11. E. W. Bakke, *The Unemployed Worker* (New Haven: Yale University Press, 1940).

The American Lower Classes:
A Typological Approach

S. M. Miller

In recent years, increasing attention has been directed to "the lower class"—those existing at the economic and social margins of society. The current concern with the limited economic prospects of dropouts,[1] the discussions of "hard-core," and "multi-problem" families,[2] the casualties of the welfare state,[3] the analysis of the numbers living below the "poverty line" in America [4] and the conditions of the "submerged fifth" in Britain [5]—all reflect the growing awareness of the "underprivileged" in presumably affluent welfare societies of high industrialization.

Much confusion exists in these discussions. Those concerned with psychological and social dislocations ("disorganization" is the commonly used word) tend to understress the importance of economic pressures, and those interested in economic deprivation frequently discount the role of social and psychological problems in preventing people from coping with their difficulties. Who is or is not "lower class" is a moot point, as different axes of demarcation are utilized. As I have explained elsewhere, I prefer to use terms like the "new working class" rather than that of the "lower class." Since most of the literature is couched in terms of the "lower class," I have used this term despite my objections to it.

Reprinted from *Social Research,* 1964.

The author is indebted to the Louis M. Rabinowitz Foundation for financial assistance. He has benefitted from the suggestions and comments of Frank Riessman, Bernard Kramer, Bernard Goldstein, Helen Icken Safa, and Jerome Cohen. A version of this paper was presented at the annual meetings of the American Sociological Association, Los Angeles, August, 1963.

A way of classifying a population is a way of thinking about them.
A frequent practice is to classify that large number of people who are
members of households where the breadwinner is not involved in some
kind of white collar (i.e. middle class) occupation as "lower class." [6]
This category is then considered to have high homogeneity and treated
as though it constituted a group with great centrality of attitudinal and
behavioral patterns. This orientation has probably led to much of the
confusion and conflict in discussions of the characteristics of those at
the lower end of the social structure. For example, the inconsistent
child-rearing results may be due to the variations from study to study in
those who are sampled as members of "the lower class."

It is becoming more common, though not a consistent practice,
to mark off distinctions within the manual category. Frank Riessman
and I [7] have argued that a working class of skilled and semi-skilled
regular workers should be distinguished from unskilled, irregular workers
who might be called "lower class." Preferably, the latter group might be
called by less invidious terms like "the unskilled," "marginal workers" or
"underprivileged workers," restricting this latter term of Allison Davis'
to a narrow scope. [8] But even where a distinction is made between the
"working class" and the "lower class," the criteria of classification are
frequently obscure or conflicting.

Two approaches, not always clearly noted, are employed in defining
the "lower class." One approach emphasizes the definition of groups
in terms of "class" characteristics, especially economic role or income.
The other employs "cultural" or "status" criteria such as style of life.
The Hollingshead index—occupation, education, place of residence—
is in the tradition of the first approach. [9] Walter Miller's discussion [10] of
"the lower class subculture" is along the lines of the second. Social
workers' discussions of "the lower class client" and the "multi-problem
family" almost always employ style-of-life indicators.

The two approaches intertwine but seem to make independent contributions to elucidating the characteristics of the "lower class" or the
poor. Consequently, I have brought them together in an effort to move
away from a broadly and vaguely defined "lower class" into a specification of types of lower-class individuals. The effort is to utilize class and
status variables in categorizing a population. The combination of the
two produces problems, but these may be overweighed by the difficulties
and obscurities produced by the current shifting between the two sets
of dimensions in discussing groupings and issues: Walter Miller's
"lower class" [11] is not Lee Rainwater's. [12]

Obviously other dimensions like education or region should also be
employed. Class and status dimensions should be more carefully marked
off than in the following discussion. Unfortunately the material to do
an adequate job is lacking. The purpose here is to show one way of
approaching the problem of differentiation within the poor. The intent
is to direct more attention to the recognition of variations among the
poor.

The Class Criterion

The advantage of using an economic indicator in defining the lower class is that it specifies a political-economic category to which legislation and other remedial programs could be devoted. Emphasis on style-of-life indicators can be confusing because the meaning of an attitude or behavior or what it leads to can be quite different for the rich, for the middling well-off, for those "getting by" and for the poor. The same behavior may have different roots and consequences in varying milieus.

On the other hand, the class or occupational criterion is not as clear-cut as it appears. Some unskilled workers have stable, fairly well-paid jobs and are thus not a pressing social or economic problem. (This is particularly true where the unskilled worker is employed in a unionized, mass-production factory.) Many semi-skilled and fewer skilled workers suffer some degree of irregularity of employment, especially due to seasonal factors. Another problem is that a considerable number of poor families (35 per cent to 50 per cent) have no member in the labor force.[13]

Consequently, I would suggest that an income criterion is more useful today than an occupational criterion in the definition of the lower class. The recent analyses of poverty in the United States can be employed for this purpose.[14] They show remarkable agreement, despite their different procedures, in estimating that one-quarter to one-fifth of the United States population lives below the poverty line. The level of income defining poverty varies depending on family size, composition, age, region, type of community. For our purposes, we can ignore these complexities and put the poverty line at $4,000 family income, following Keyserling. It is this population which, if we want to use the term could be called "lower class" or "low income" or "the poor."

The advantage of utilizing the economic criterion, and particularly the income definition, is that it specifies a socio-economic category towards which policy can be directed. For example, Morgan reports,[15] following Lampman's earlier lead, that 10 billion dollars would bring all spending units now below the poverty line to an income level above poverty. Questions of the distribution of income and of social services can be pinpointed then in terms of how they affect this particular population.

Obviously, income levels and sources of income vary considerably among the "low-income" population. Keyserling distinguishes between the very poor, the poor, and a higher income group who suffer what he terms "deprivation" but not outright poverty. What income level is used affects deeply the characteristics of the poor. Lampman uses lower income limits than Keyserling or Morgan. Consequently, he describes a poor population with 50 per cent of the heads of households out of the labor market, while the others, using a higher income level to define

poverty, report only 35 per cent of the heads as out of the labor market. We do not have data but it is reasonable to deduce that a higher percentage of Lampman's poor are on welfare than is true of Morgan's or Keyserling's.

Clearly, different income cutoff points shape the characteristics of the "low income." The lower the income level used, the more economically and socially different are the poor.

Definitions of poverty and the poor are not technical problems but social and ideological issues. The low income are not basically a "welfare poor." Only one-fifth of Morgan's poor receive welfare assistance. The social scientists and social service specialists who write of the "welfare poor" are discussing only a slice of the poor; those concerned with "hard-core" and "multi-problem families" are, in turn, analyzing only a very thin wedge of this small slice.

The income criterion has several components: the level of income, the stability or regularity of income, the source of income (employment or welfare). A number of observers believe that it makes a difference, holding income constant, whether a family is supported by welfare or not. The knowledge to make a fine classification of these components is lacking. I have resorted therefore to combining them into one indicator of economic security (roughly combining income and stability), and then dichotomizing this indicator into the two simple dimensions of high (security) and low (insecurity). Lumping together these components and dichotomizing them is inadequate.[16] But we cannot at present describe each of the cells of what should be an 8-fold or 16-fold table. I think, however, that the cells of a 4-fold table can be usefully discussed. This capsulated table should rapidly be expanded as we acquire more knowledge and understanding.

The Style-of-Life Criterion

The style-of-life variable also offers difficulties. It refers at least to attitudes and behavior in the areas of family relationships and consumption patterns. A major difficulty is that the content of the "lower class style-of-life" is debatable. Further, evaluative judgments (as implied in the concepts of "family disorganization," "social disorganization" or "family instability") are invariably involved. As yet, it is not possible to formulate a clean-cut classification which avoids cultural biases and still is able to render a judgment about the impact of life style on individuals. For example, does the absence of a permanent male figure mean that the family is inevitably "unstable" and that children are necessarily psychologically deformed by living in such a family? Assessments such as these are difficult to make because much of our knowledge and theorizing about fatherless families is based on middle-class situations.

I employ the notion of "familial stability/instability," a dichotomization of style of life, to summarize a variety of elements. Familial stability patterns are characterized by families coping with their problems—the children are being fed, though not necessarily on a schedule; the family meets its obligations so that it is not forced to keep on the move; children are not getting into much more trouble than other children of the neighborhood. These are not satisfactory indicators; they are, at best, suggestive of the kind of behavior which is characteristic of stability among the "low income." The aim is to be able to describe the degrees of effectiveness of different styles of life in handling the same environment. Our vocabulary is inadequate for this task.

Class and Status

The two approaches can be welded together by cross-tabling the two dimensions of the two variables of economic security and familial stability in a 2 × 2 table:

Types of Economic Security and Familial Stability

			Familial Stability +	Familial Instability −
Economic	Security	+	++(1)	+−(2)
	Insecurity	−	−+(3)	−−(4)

Cell 1 is referred to as the stable poor; cell 2, the strained; cell 3, the copers, and cell 4, the unstable.

To some extent, life-cycle stages may be involved here, as some young people escape from cell 4 via cell 2 or cell 3 to cell 1, a more stable pattern, and beyond. Or families may drop with age from cell 1 to cell 3, where they have lowered economic security but maintain family stability.

Each of the cells contains many variants. While I believe the four types are an improvement over analysis in terms of "*the* lower class," it is important to recognize that each type has many variations. One difference, of course, is whether the family is stationary in its particular pattern or moving to greater or less security-stability. *My general orientation is to emphasize flux rather than assuming a permanent position in a pattern.*

The Stable Poor

Cell 1 (*the stable poor*) is characterized by stability, economically and familially. This cell points to the regularly employed, low-skill, stable poor families.

Farm, rural and rural non-farm persons undoubtedly make up the bulk of the stable poor since they are the majority of the American poor: a re-calculation of Morgan's data suggests that only 30 per cent of the poor live in metropolitan areas. The majority of all the poor and of the stable poor are white rural Southern populations. In addition, the non-urban poor are probably represented in this cell to a greater extent than they are among all the poor. Aged persons are also over-represented and constitute a large part of the downwardly mobile poor since most of them were better off at earlier points in their lives. Left-over third generation immigrant populations in large cities are probably under-represented.[17]

A number of Negro families are of the stable poor. They have higher social status in the Negro community than their economic counterparts have in the white community because of the general scaling down of incomes and occupational levels of Negroes in the United States. For reasons discussed below, Negroes and other discriminated groups are probably becoming more important politically as well as in relative size among the urban stable poor.

The children of cell 1 families are most likely of all the children of the poor to be educationally and occupationally mobile. Cell 1 might be the "takeoff" cell, the phase necessary before many can really make a big advance. But this is a dangerous metaphor for obviously many youth from families in more difficult circumstances are able to make considerable gains.

The stable poor, then, are a varied group; one component, the aged, has a poor economic future, except to the extent that social security and old-age payments improve, and a declining future as an intact family unit.

The Strained

Cell 2 (*the strained*) portrays a secure economic pattern, but an unstable family one. This might be a life-cycle problem, i.e., at certain points, the families of low-wage, unskilled workers are likely to exhibit unstable patterns. Examples might be "wild" younger workers or alchoholic older workers who disturb family functioning. Or, the pattern could manifest the beginning of a move into cell 4, as a low-income family finds increasing difficulty in maintaining its economic security because

of family and personal problems or the economic situation. Obviously, the two possibilities may be closely connected.

Movement may be viewed inter-generationally as well as in terms of life-cycle patterns. Many of the offspring of strained families "may fail to match the economic security of their parents" and experience inter-generational skidding.[18]

Strained familial relations may not, however, result in skidding. In earlier periods, immigrant groups faced considerable internal strain arising from the conflict between the younger and older generations in the course of acculturation. Nonetheless, the second generation generally improved its economic circumstances. The instability of today's strained families is regarded as more "pathological" than that of the immigrant populations, although some social work accounts of families at the turn of the century differ little from current reports of "poor family functioning." The current stress is on fighting and drinking among parents, illicit sexual relations of parents, and neglect or brutality towards the children. Whether the economically secure and familially unstable are characterized by these patterns is not clear. If they are not, then, the offspring of the strained family may not be as prey to skidding. Further, not all children of deeply conflicted or hostile families are inevitably unable to maintain or improve their economic position.

I have looked at cell 2 as a transitional condition. This view may be misleading: many families persist with a low but steady income and a great deal of internal strain

The Copers

The copers of cell 3 manifest economic insecurity and familial stability—families and individuals having a rough time economically but managing to keep themselves relatively intact. This group probably increases considerably during extensive layoffs. Probably a considerable number of Negroes are in this group and their children are more likely to be mobile than those living in cell 2-type situations.

This cell probably contains a disproportionate number of families which have been downwardly mobile. Both Morgan [19] and I [20] have shown the sizable number of sons of nonmanual workers who end up in manual (and sometimes low-income) positions. In Great Britain, 40 per cent of those born in nonmanual families move into manual occupations. Many of these downwardly mobile are probably more likely to retain a stable family style than others in the same economic predicament. As in many other situations, however, a minority of the downwardly mobile may manifest extreme familial instability, which would place them in cell 4. Limited data suggest that children of downwardly mobile families have a better chance of rising occupationally than children of families which have been at this low level for some generations.[21]

The Unstable

In cell 4, *the unstable* have neither economic nor personal stability. It is this group which is probably most generally called "the lower class," and Jerome Cohen has suggested to me that the term "lower class" might be usefully restricted to this group. Since this recommendation is unlikely to be consistently utilized by social workers, economists, sociologists, political scientists and others interested in low-income populations, I have not adopted it, preferring to focus attention on the varied segments of the low-income population. Within the unstable group, there are degrees of stability and strain—*not every family is a "hard-core case" or has a "multi-agency problem."* Nor do we have sufficient longitudinal data to assert that once in cell 4, always in cell 4. It may be that families and individuals occasionally manifest both economic and personal instability, then overcome these problems for a while. Later they may again suffer from illness, unemployment, emotional upset, or familial instability.

As important in some ways as distinguishing cell 4 from the other three cells which make up the "lower class," is to note that cell 4 is a very varied grouping. In it are partially urbanized Negroes new to the North and cities, remaining slum residents of ethnic groups which have largely moved out of the slums, long-term (intergenerational) poor white families, the *déclassé* of Marx. Also included are the physically handicapped and the aged who have dropped through the class structure. *The low-income class generally and the unstable in particular is a category of unskilled, irregular workers, broken and large families, and a residual bin of the aged, physically handicapped, and mentally disturbed.*

In some cases, social characteristics handicap the low-income groups: recent rurality (unfamiliarity and lack of skills with urban problems) and discrimination. These groups—Negroes, former mountaineer whites —would have the worst problems. They would also have perhaps the greatest potential because removing their social limitations would lead to big change. Their handicaps are less self-inflicted and self-sustaining. This may not be as true for mountaineer whites as for Negroes. Aside from people dropping into the poverty class along the life-and-physical-cycle, the whites in the lower class who have no good, i.e., social, reason for being there, are most likely to be intractable to change.

Hylan Lewis [22] has suggested the categories of clinical, pre-clinical and sub-clinical to delineate patterns among the poor. I would substitute the word "chronic" for "clinical." The chronics refer to the long-term dependents, part of whom would be the "hard-core"; the pre-chronics would be a high-risk group which is moving toward a chronic situation but have not yet become chronically dependent. The sub-chronics are

those who have many characteristics of dependence but have a greater ability to cope with their problems.[23]

A number of forces can lead individuals into chronic dependence. *"Lower-class" life is crisis-life, constantly trying to make-do with string where rope is needed.* Anything can break the string. Illness is one of the most important—"Got a job but I got sick and lost it"; "We managed until the baby got sick." The great incidence of physical afflictions among the poor—frequently unknown to the victim—are obvious to any casual observer. Particularly striking are the poor teeth of many. The tendency of lower class people to somaticize their emotional difficulties may be influenced by the omnipresence of illness.

Familial and personal instability may be the sources as well as the consequences of difficulties. While some frequent concomitants of low income life such as matrifocality do not inevitably produce grave difficulties in family life, they frequently do. Alchoholism, an inability to handle aggression, hostility or dependence—one's own or other's toward one—can deeply disturb family functioning. A variety of direct personal aid may be necessary.

Sophistication along these lines of analysis has frequently tended to denigrate the importance of structural factors in producing "personal inadequacies," "social disabilities," "familial instability." The work of Raymond Smith [24] and Edith Clarke [25] strongly suggests that illegitimacy is related to economic conditions—the better the economic conditions among the "lower class" Negroes of the Caribbean, the lower the rate of illegitimacy. Kunstadter [26] similarly argues that matrifocality as a "lower class" trait is related to a particular set of economic characteristics.

Prolonged unemployment, irregular employment, low income are important forces leading to a chronic pattern. Low-paid and irregularly employed individuals do not develop an image of the world as predictable and as something with which they are able to cope. Controlling or directing events appears (and frequently is) an unattainable achievement. When they suffer long-term unemployment, they are less likely than other unemployed who have had the experience of fairly regular employment, to maintain a personal stability. (Maslow [27] has argued that those who have had a stable past are more able to manage in disastrous circumstances than those who have had considerable prior deprivation.) A high-employment economy has relatively fewer "hard-core" cases than a low-employment economy. The American community studies suggest that the "lower class" is smaller in numbers in times of prosperity than in periods of depression. Peter Townsend in an informal lecture recently declared that during the 1930's in England it was believed that 500,000 to 1,000,000 of those not working were "unemployable." In 1940 with the pressures of the war, it was discovered that only 100,000 were really unemployables. Structural change would be of great importance in reducing chronic dependence.

Strategies

Three basic policies are possible: (1) direct economic change, such as providing better employment, or directly raising incomes through the provision of a national minimum level of income; (2) direct services, such as case-work activities to strengthen the ego-functioning of the individual or family assistance through home-maker help; (3) indirect change by affecting the climate—social, psychological, political—of the neighborhoods in which the poor live.

What would lead one type of a low-income population in a given direction would not work at all for another type. A panacea does not work because there is no one thing which will have a pervasive impact in all cases if changed. What is dynamic for one type may be insignificant for others.

I find the concept of elasticity useful here.[28] It points to the extent of change resulting from input of additional services or income. Some types of the poor have high income elasticity—a little change in income produces a big change in behavior; other types may have low income elasticity but have high education elasticity or high casework elasticity. Still other types will respond rapidly and deeply to new housing, to a steady job, to counseling, or a package of such ingredients rather than to, say, casework. The concept of elasticity introduces frontally the issues of variable remedies for different types. The issues of costs, substitution and choice of different services or resources are made vivid by the notion of elasticity and productivity (the return per unit of expenditure).

The stable, those in cell 1, would be immediately helped if their incomes were raised so that they came closer to the American standard of life. Unionization of their industries (especially in service trades and occupations), shifts from low productivity land and industries to high productive industries, and occupational retraining would be important. In some situations, individuals have to be prepared for retraining (where, for example, the level of literacy is low) or aided in moving to new localities where opportunities are greater. They may need help in adjusting to new urban conditions, but this adjustment would probably not be very difficult where jobs and housing are adequate. The stable poor, in short, would have a high income elasticity, rapidly improving and adjusting to increases in their income.

The inadequacy of social services and payments in the United States forces many into cell 1. Improving and extending social security, which keeps many in penury and does not help a substantial number in non-covered occupations and industries, would move many from cells 2, 3, and 4 into cell 1 and lead many of the stable poor into the main society. Harrington [29] and Titmuss [30] have pointed out that social services in the United States and Britain do not seem to be benefitting the poor as much

as the middle income. Obviously, changes in social policy are necessary here.

Some of the strained of cell 2 might require some casework help in improving family conditions and operations, but other approaches might be effective. If they live in a locality that manifests high rates of disturbances, they might be helped by moving to new areas. For some, an improvement in economic conditions may be necessary in order to get deeper family changes. Undoubtedly, a number are not sensitive to income changes or to neighborhood climate change and sustained casework help would be necessary.

Familial instability may be a carryover from an earlier period when the family suffered from economic insecurity; the family has not caught up with its economic improvements. But, as Seymour S. Bellin and Jerome Cohen have pointed out, in some families where economic conditions have improved after a long period of economic deprivation and family difficulties, withdrawing the stress of economic insecurity may be insufficient. The toll of the stress frequently must be overcome. Special help may be necessary to bring about familial changes of great importance. The adaptation of social agencies would be important so that they are able to meet the requirements of these families at the time of need and to provide aid in ways which fit the outlook of these families.

The copers of cell 3, who maintain family stability in the face of grave economic difficulties, obviously need economic aid. Many of them would be helped by improvement in welfare payments and practices; others, where there is a working head of household, would be advanced by regularization of work and/or shifting to more remunerative fields. The needs of the stable and the copers would seem to be similar. Improvement on the economic dimension would push more of the copers into the mobility possibilities of the stable poor of cell 1 and beyond.

Cell 4, the unstable, is the most discussed grouping of the poor today. Many, if not most, are on welfare allotments; women head many of the family units. A general improvement in economic conditions would not have much economic impact on the unstable because they are largely out of the labor force and out of the economy. It is widely believed that unstable families do not have a high income elasticity but the evidence is not strong. Specific programs aimed at this group would be important. Present-day welfare services are insufficient since they have largely been budgetary and policing activities. Concentration on improving the educational achievement of the youth of these families would be more important perhaps, than a diffuse effort to achieve better family functioning.[31] A number of interesting and aggressive casework services have been offered; their degree of long-term success is unclear. A variety of direct services may be effective with some of these families— including continuous homemaking and baby-sitting services, provisions of nurseries, all-day schools, and consumer buying protection.

It may be that a less direct approach would be effective. It would involve trying to mobilize politically the communities in which the unstable live with the more stable poor so as to provide greater feelings

of strength and control. The anticipated but side effect would be the improving of family conditions. A general change in a low income community precipitated perhaps by the mobile, the strained, and the copers, may spread to affect the unstable of the community. The social actionists, of whom Saul Alinsky is the best-known, have this implicit strategy.

In all of the strategies it is necessary to be clear about who exactly is the target population. This is frequently determined on the basis of the numbers involved, though there is always the delicate choice of helping a lot of people a little or a few people a lot. The second step is to discover what works with whom. There is probably nothing that will help all "lower class" people in one move although, as suggested above, a steady, meaningful, well-paid job as a general base of action should not be underestimated. A decent level of living as the minimal responsibility of an affluent society, no matter what people do around this level, may be an important point to maintain in a period when government welfare payments are under criticism. But there are some things that will help certain types. We have to find the right things for the right groups at the right time.

Political Action

The poor are not rapidly declining; income and wealth inequality appear to be increasing in recent years; the incomes of Negroes are no longer advancing relative to those of whites; pension and assistance schemes are maintaining many in poverty rather than providing a "Welfare State" standard. The decline in the number of poor between 1947 and 1957 has been due, Lampman contends, to general economic advance rather than to a redistribution of income and wealth in favor of the poor. Improvements in social services and a decrease in inequality would require a shift in the allocation of national product towards improving the relative position of the bottom 20 per cent.

These issues are political ones. They will be affected by the possibility that the present American poor may prove to be more politically active than is usually true of the poor. If this happens, it will be because a large slice of the urban poor is made up of Negroes who have ethnic as well as economic forces moving them. Samuel Lubell [32] has argued that Negroes in large cities will furnish a new base for Democratic ward machines. They are becoming more and more politically active and demanding. This self-organization is not only important in getting changes from the government, but it is also serving to change "lower-class" Negro communities from within. Local leaders are developing and the orientation of many community agencies to provide leadership and direction to "lower-class" communities will become increasingly ineffective. The conservative orientation of gaining change and social advance through an harmonious arrangement with local power forces is being superseded by disadvantaged groups themselves actively pres-

suring for the kinds of changes—in housing, in schools and the like—
that they believe to be important.

In the course of these pressures, it is likely that the *desegregation
issue will emerge as a social class issue* affecting all "lower-class" persons, and not only as a racial issue affecting Negroes alone. Mexican-
Americans and Puerto Ricans, who with Negroes increasingly make the
poor of the large metropolis a "colored poor," are increasingly moving
into the stable and coping patterns and beginning to develop political
effectiveness. Poverty may not be treated as a racial issue affecting only
Negroes. *Even where Negroes operate alone, the impact of their demands
will affect all the poor as they achieve better schools, better housing,
better jobs, better social services.*

Cause and Consequence

A good deal of the tone of discussions of the "lower class," even by
sociologists, has a negative quality. On the other hand, a few seem to
have a romantic feeling about the "lower class," particularly their juvenile delinquents, and see them as rebels against the horrors of middle-
class, conformist America. The former view suffers from the assumption
that they have little potential for change; the latter, that there is nothing
better in present-day America to which they can change.

Among other things, the glorification theme ignores, as Riessman has
pointed out, the impact on the "lower class" of its limited education.[33]
The negative view frequently confuses, as Keyserling has noted, cause
and consequence. The personal instability of many "lower-class" persons
may be a consequence of economic instability as well as a cause of it.
The chain of cause-and-effect over time frequently becomes blurred.
Where is there an effective way of cutting into the chain so that change
will occur?—that becomes the issue. My feeling is that structural forces
have been underplayed recently as a mode of change, as "the culture
of poverty" has been overstressed.[34]

The negative view has the danger of not seeing positive elements in
"lower-class" life. By ignoring these elements, social policies can frequently worsen them. For example, in an exciting study of a Puerto
Rican slum, Helen Icken Safa has reported the community and familial
solidarity of the residents of a slum barrio. When families were moved
into public housing, community ties were weakened. The project social
workers centered on the wife. The husband's role and responsibility in
the family and community diminished.[35]

It is perhaps a "heuristic" fallacy, as Frank Riessman has said, to
believe that "lower-class" people are willing and capable of positive
change. This is not always true, but if professionals and social reformers
lack confidence in the poor, little can be accomplished in the social
services or in political action. One might fail with this optimism—as we
frequently do—but without it, it is doubtful if anything can be moved.

Frequently, disenchantment and cynicism capture accurately a slice of life. They are also immobilizing, for they ignore the constructive and energizing role of hope.[36]

Conclusion

A clearly defined "lower class" does not exist—it is a varied, changing group as Peter Townsend has noted:

> A misconception is that in a relatively prosperous society most individuals have the capacity to meet any contingency in life. Only a poor and handicapped minority need special protection or help. This ignores the infinite diversities and changing conditions to be found in any population. Men gain or fall in status and living standards; at one stage of their life their dependencies are minimal, at others unduly numerous; sometimes they need exceptional help to achieve qualifications and skills held to be desirable by society; and at all times they are susceptible to the vicissitudes of prolonged ill health, disability, redundancy of unemployment, and bereavement which they are usually powerless to control or even reasonably anticipate. Unanticipated adversity is not the peculiar experience of one fixed section of the working class.[37]

In England, Dahrendorf contends,[38] the unskilled category is a temporary position—individuals at various stages of the life cycle may drop into it, but for only a comparatively few is it a permanent position. In the United States, this is not as true, and if caste pressures grow, it will be even less true.

The changing economy of America is producing new property relations; at the same time it is producing new working classes and lower classes.[39] The analysis of data and the development of our concepts have not kept up with the increasing differentiation within these populations. Many pressures and counter-pressures exist in any stratum. Despite a modal pattern, considerable variety in values and behavior occurs. Since cross-pressures affect the "lower class" to a considerable extent,[40] we should look for *types* of behavior patterns even among people apparently very similar in objective characteristics. Those at the social bottom see only a vague and ill-defined "them" up there—and those above believe that those below are all rather similar. But the tops know how much differentiation within the top actually takes place; the bottoms are aware of much more differentiation than are the outsiders looking in. In particular, what has been taken as typical of the most unstable bottom-group has been generalized to apply to all who are poor or manual workers.

The label—"the lower class"—increasingly distorts complicated reality. We must begin to demarcate types of poor people more sharply if we are to be able to understand and interpret behavior and circumstance and to develop appropriate social policies. Evaluations of com-

mentators are frequently masked as description. *Ways of coping with hard reality are interpreted as normatively prescribed when they frequently are weakly dissanctioned behavior.*

The resurgence of interest in the poor augurs well for a re-thinking of the new kind of poverty in the "Welfare State," which is unlike the mass unemployment of the 1930's or the grinding poverty of the employed workers of the 19th century. Our "received wisdom" should be superseded by new categories and concepts. New wine is being poured into old conceptual bottles and the specialness of the new is being lost.

Notes

1. Cf. Patricia Cayo Sexton, *Education and Income: Inequalities in our Public Schools,* New York: Viking Press, 1961, pp. 10 ff. S. M. Miller, Carolyn Comings and Betty Saleem, *The School Dropout Problem—Syracuse,* Albany: New York State Division for Youth and the Syracuse University Youth Development Center, 1963. Herman P. Miller points out that the disadvantage of not having a college diploma grew from 1939 to 1958. See his "Money Value of an Education," *Occupational Outlook Quarterly* (September, 1961), p. 4.

2. Janet E. Weinandy, *Families Under Stress,* Syracuse: Syracuse University Youth Development Center, 1962.

3. Audrey Harvey, *Casualties of the Welfare State,* Fabian Tract 321, London: Fabian Society, 1959.

4. Michael Harrington, *The Other America: Poverty in the United States.* New York: The Macmillan Company, 1962; Conference on Economic Progress, *Poverty and Deprivation in the United States,* Washington: Conference on Economic Progress, 1961; the main author of this analysis is Leon Keyserling and it is known as the "Keyserling Report"; Gabriel Kolko, *Wealth and Power in the United States,* New York: Frederick Praeger, 1962; Robert J. Lampman, "The Low Income Population and Economic Growth," Study Paper No. 12, Joint Economic Committee, Congress of the United States, December 16, 1959, Washington: Government Printing Office, 1959; James N. Morgan et al., *Income and Welfare in the United States,* New York: McGraw-Hill and Company, 1962. These books are reviewed in S. M. Miller, "Poverty and Inequality in America: Implications for the Social Services," *Child Welfare,* XLII (November, 1963), pp. 442–5 (republished in the Syracuse University Youth Development Center Reprint Series).

5. Brian Abel-Smith, "Whose Welfare State?" Norman MacKenzie, ed., *Conviction,* London: MacGibbon and Kee, 1958.

6. "The terms 'lower class' and 'middle class' are used here to refer to systems of behavior and concerns rather than groups defined in conventional economic terms." William C. Kvaraceus and Walter B. Miller, *Delinquent Behavior: Culture and the Individual,* Washington: National Education Association, 1959, p. 62.

7. S. M. Miller and Frank Riessman, "The Working-Class Subculture: A New View," *Social Problems,* IX (Summer, 1961), pp. 86–97. Reprinted in this volume.

8. Allison Davis, "The Motivation of the Underprivileged Worker," in William Foote Whyte, ed., *Industry and Society,* New York: McGraw-Hill and Company, 1946, pp. 84–106.

9. August B. Hollingshead and Frederick C. Redlich, *Social Class and Mental Illness: A Community Study,* New York: John Wiley & Sons, 1958, pp. 387–97.

10. Walter B. Miller, "Lower Class Culture as a Generating Milieu of Gang Delinquency," *Journal of Social Issues,* XIV, No. 3 (1958), p. 6, footnote 3. In his penetrating analysis, Miller notes the existence of "subtypes of lower class culture" but does not pursue this point. While his emphasis is on cultural characteristics such as "female-based" household and "serial monogamy" mating patterns, he elsewhere employs educational, occupational and income variables to define the lower class. See his "Implications of Urban Lower-Class Culture for Social Work," *Social Service Review,* XXXIII (September, 1959), pp. 229 ff. His major stress is on cultural or status characteristics as defining the lower class culture.

11. *Ibid.*

12. Lee Rainwater assisted by Karol

Kane Weinstein, *And the Poor Get Children,* Chicago: Quadrangle Books, 1960. See also the distinctions made within the lower-lower class by Martin Loeb, "Social Class and the American Social System," *Social Work,* 6 (April, 1961), p. 16.

13. Keyserling, *op. cit.,* Lampman, *op. cit.*

14. See footnote 4.

15. Morgan, *op. cit.,* p. 3.

16. Not all families receiving welfare assistance should automatically be classified in the economically insecure category. For the aged, perhaps, welfare assistance does not constitute a lack of security. In general, however, the fact of welfare assistance would put a family in the economically insecure category.

17. Richard Cloward and Lloyd Ohlin, *Delinquency and Opportunity,* New York: The Free Press of Glencoe, 1960.

18. Dennis Wrong, in a personal communication, has influenced this and the following paragraph. "Skidding" is discussed in Harold Wilensky and Hugh Edwards, "The Skidder: Ideological Adjustments of Downward Mobile Workers," *American Sociological Review,* 24 (April, 1959), pp. 215–231.

19. Morgan, *op. cit.*

20. S. M. Miller, "Comparative Social Mobility," *Current Sociology,* IX, no. 1, 1960, pp. 1–89.

21. *Ibid.,* pp. 32–33.

22. Hylan Lewis, "Child Rearing Among Low Income Families," Washington Center for Metropolitan Studies, June 8, 1961. This paper and others by Lewis are among the most stimulating on the problems of low-income patterns. Also see Hyman Rodman, "The Lower-Class Value Stretch," *Social Forces,* 42, December, 1963.

23. I have used the terms "dependent" and "dependence" here for want of a sharper term; I find the concept of dependence murky and frequently used to cover a variety of conditions which a writer does not like.

24. Raymond T. Smith, *The Negro Family in British Guiana,* London: Routledge & Kegan Paul, Ltd., 1956.

25. Edith Clarke, *My Mother Who Fathered Me,* New York: Humanities Press, 1957.

26. Peter Kunstadter, "A Survey of the Consanguine and Matrifocal Family," *American Anthropologist,* 65 (February, 1963), pp. 56–66.

27. A. H. Maslow, *Motivation and Personality,* New York: Harper & Bros., pp. 80–106.

28. Carlsson has reintroduced the concept of elasticity into sociological thinking. Gosta Carlsson, "Okonomische Ungleichheit und Lebenschanchen," *Kolner Zeitschrift fur Soziologie,* 5, 1961, pp. 189–199.

29. Harrington, *op. cit.*

30. Richard Titmuss, *Essays on "The Welfare State,"* London: George Allen & Unwin, 1958, chapter 2, "The Social Division of Welfare," and *Income Distribution and Social Change,* Toronto: University of Toronto Press, 1962. Although Titmuss is a seminal thinker in analyzing changes in the social structure of the modern society, he has been almost completely ignored by American sociologists.

31. Cf. S. M. Miller, "Poverty and Inequality in America," *op. cit.*

32. In his syndicated column which appeared in the *Syracuse Herald-Journal* November 14, 1961.

33. Frank Riessman, *The Culturally Deprived Child,* New York: Harper & Brothers, 1962.

34. Harrington seems frequently to write and speak as though all low-income persons are bound in an immutable chain of apathy and ineffectiveness, characteristics of "the culture of poverty." He has obviously extended this term beyond the intent of Oscar Lewis who introduced it in his *Five Families,* New York: Basic Books, 1959, and in *The Children of Sanchez,* New York: Random House, 1961. Warren Haggstrom has countered this view in his "The Power of the Poor," Syracuse University Youth Development Center, 1963.

35. Helen Icken Safa, *From Shanty Town to Public Housing,* Syracuse University Youth Development Center, 1962. The peculiar stresses of public housing life may be functional equivalents of the economic conditions of matrifocality discussed by Kunstadter.

36. Cf. S. M. Miller and Frank Riessman, "Working Class Authoritarianism: A Critique of Lipset," *British Journal of Sociology,* September, 1961.

37. Peter Townsend, "Freedom and Equality," *New Statesman,* LXI, No. 1570, April 14, 1961, p. 574.

38. Ralf Dahrendorf, "Unskilled Labour in British Industry," unpublished Ph.D. thesis in sociology, London School of Economics, 1956, pp. 429–30.

39. S. M. Miller, "Poverty, Race and Politics," in Irving Louis Horowitz, ed., *The New Sociology: Essays on Social Values and Social Theory in Honor of C. Wright Mills,* New York: Oxford University Press, 1964.

40. See Miller and Riessman, "The Working-Class Subculture," and Hylan Lewis, *op. cit.*

Routine-Seekers and Action-Seekers

Herbert Gans

From the list of controllable and uncontrollable criteria of class, it is possible to isolate four major behavior styles that predominate among West Enders and separate them into strata and subcultures. These are: the *maladapted*, the *middle-class mobiles*, and—the two most important ones—the *routine-seekers* and *action-seekers*. The former is based on the search for a routine life, and the latter, on the pursuit of adventurous episodes, or what West Enders call "action." They will be described first.[1] The two terms distinguish between conceptions of living and between ways of responding to opportunities and of making choices. These, in turn, result in differences in rhythm of life, in the patterns of family relationships, work, leisure, religious behavior, attitudes toward authority, and, indeed, in the very purpose of human existence.

The routine-seekers are people whose aim is the establishment of a stable [2] way of living, in which the economic and emotional security of the individual and of his family are most important. Their way of life is marked by a highly regular and recurring scheduling of behavior patterns, and nearly all their activities are organized into a routine. There may be a regular menu for every day of the week, which differs little from one week to the next. And the same people may be visited or entertained on the same evening every week. A similar regularity is observable in the celebration of holidays, giving of gifts, and in many of the other spheres of life in which the middle-class person strives for novelty and variety. As this regularity is especially striking among West Enders, I have therefore used the term "routine." [3]

Reprinted from *The Urban Villagers*, New York: The Free Press of Glencoe, 1962, pp. 28–32.

For the action-seeker, life is episodic. The rhythm of life is dominated by the adventurous episode, in which heights of activity and feeling are reached through exciting and sometimes riotous behavior.[4] The goal is action, an opportunity for thrills, and for the chance to face and overcome a challenge. It may be sought in a card game, a fight, a sexual interlude, a drinking bout, a gambling session, or in a fast and furious exchange of wisecracks and insults. Whatever the episode, the action-seeker pursues it with a vengeance, and lives the rest of his life in quiet—and often sullen—preparation for this climax, in which he is usually said to be "killing time."

In most instances, routine-seekers are more likely to have stable jobs, which require more skills and pay higher wages than do those of action-seekers. But this is not always so. Indeed, should society not make stable jobs and adequate income available in sufficient amounts, people may try to achieve a routine life style, but be unable to overcome the many obstacles to it. When work, income, and education equivalent to working-class status are available, those who seek routine can usually find it, unless their desire for it is frustrated by personal or familial disabilities.

Among the West Enders, action-seekers generally occupy jobs of minimal stability, skill, and pay. This is partly cause and partly effect. As their upbringing has not prepared them for work or interest in work, they often gravitate into the least satisfying jobs. This, in turn, encourages them even further to find gratifications in episodes of action.

The search for action is a male prerogative. As children reach school age, the boys are allowed to roam the streets and to look for childhood adventures, more so in lower-class than in working-class families. Girls, however, are expected to stay home, and thus are less likely to want action—at least overtly.

Action-seekers also are more apt to be found among adolescents than adults, for adolescence, especially in the working and lower class, is peculiarly suited to the episodic life. The routine portions of existence, such as school and work, are usually based on adult rules, and unsatisfying to the adolescent. Thus, the teenage boy can be himself only during adventurous episodes that are interspersed between periods of time-killing. Most adolescents graduate into the routine pattern when they marry, and develop stable family relationships. Others, however, may marry, and then pay little attention to their families, spending their non-work hours with male companions and "playing around" with other women on the side. These, West Enders describe as being "unable to get off the corner."

The differences between the two styles range over many areas of life. Routine-seekers are more likely to be regular churchgoers, to live by the ethical norms of the religion, and to favor moderation in all pursuits. They will accept the authority of the more powerful as long as it is wielded equitably, and they are willing to grant the possibility that the government may act with good intentions, although they believe that it does not do so often. The action-seeker goes to church mainly to seek

absolution from sins committed during episodes, is belligerent in the presence of authority, and is certain that government is always exploitative and corrupt.

Routine-seekers are thrifty; they spend extra funds on the family, or save if for emergencies. Action-seekers spend the same monies on nightclubs, new clothes, appliances, automobiles, or gambling sprees, even if their impulsive spending leaves them no funds for what they consider to be necessities. Routine-seekers also spend money for impulse goods, but they buy clothes only for the holidays and postpone more expensive items until the need or desire for them becomes pressing. When they gamble, they set a limit on their losses and stop playing when it is reached.

Although the action-seekers are less concerned with behavior control than the routine-seekers, they must be distinguished from a third group, the maladapted—people who are entirely unable to control their behavior because of alcoholism or other personal difficulties. To the middle-class observer there may be little difference between them and the more impulsive action-seekers. But whereas the latter pursue episodes within a context of rules, and do not cut themselves off from family and peers, the maladapted may be mentally ill, and lack the self-control and contact with reality to function in these groups. If these people behave in nonthreatening ways, West Enders often call them "characters." And, as noted earlier, they also may call them "bums," although routine-seekers use this term as well to describe action-seekers.

For the most part, the action- and routine-seekers are socially nonmobile. Another set of West Enders, however, is mobile. Bearing a superficial resemblance to the routine-seekers, these people strive to move themselves—or, more often, their children—into the middle class. But since West Enders reject the middle class, those who seek to rise into it must do so either as individuals or as individual family units. Moreover, since no middle-class culture exists among West Enders, the mobile have to model themselves on outsiders. As a result, they must detach themselves from relatives and old friends and are often rejected by these.

Placing the West Enders into classes depends on the definition of class that one uses. If working class is equated to the holding of a relatively stable skilled or semiskilled job, and lower class, to the holding of an unstable, unskilled one, most West Enders can be described as working class. This holds true both for the routine- and action-seekers. If a class is defined by life-style, however, action-seekers can be described as lower class; routine-seekers, as working class. But not all action-seekers are lower class. The analysis of the American class system in Chapter 11 will clarify this qualification by showing that action-seeking is a prevalent but not the distinguishing characteristic of lower-class culture.

For the purpose of summarizing this discussion, however, the West Enders can be divided into four major strata: The lower-lower-class maladapted, the lower-class action-seekers, the working-class routine-seekers, and the middle-class mobiles.

Sociologists rank the classes in terms of their economic, social, and

political influence in the larger society, and on that basis, the middle-class mobiles are most important, followed by the routine-seekers, the action-seekers, and the maladapted. But while West Enders would accept the notion of a class hierarchy, they would reject this ranking. Generally speaking, each group—except the last—considers itself to be most desirable, using criteria of evaluation that would support its judgment. Thus, while the routine-seekers deplore the impulsive behavior of the action-seekers, the latter are scornful of the routine-seekers' inability to have fun, as well as for the dullness of their lives. Both see the middle-class mobiles as snobs or renegades.

In terms of number of people in the West End, the routine-seekers are most important, followed by the action-seekers, the middle-class mobiles and the maladapted.

Notes

1. The distinction bears some resemblance to that drawn by English sociologists between "respectable" and "rough" members of the working class. Kuper, for example, distinguished respectables by their high standards of domestic and personal cleanliness, speech and manners, personal appearance, and upkeep of the home; roughs, by the absence of these criteria. Leo Kuper, "Blueprint for Living Together," in Leo Kuper, ed., *Living in Towns*, London: Cresset Press, 1953, pp. 1–202, at pp. 78–82. Kuper's criteria would also distinguish between routine- and action-seekers, but what he describes are the most visible elements in a pattern that can be traced to the more fundamental differences I have suggested.

2. This term I have taken from S. M. Miller and Frank Riessman, "The Working-Class Subculture: A New View," *Social Problems*, vol. 9 (1961), pp. 86–97, at p. 91.

3. I do not use the term deprecatingly, for there is more than enough spontaneity and surprise in everyday life to counteract the regularities. West Enders do not seem to be unwilling slaves to a routine, or to be bored by it. In fact, I did not really develop the concept until after I left the West End, and owe it to a middle-class informant in another community, married to an Italian, who complained bitterly that her in-laws had a set and never deviating menu for every day of the week.

4. The conception of action-seeking and the episodic rhythm of life struck me one night early in the field work, after I had spent an evening in a tavern, listening to a West Ender's riotous life history. The concept of episode comes from Nelson N. Foote, "Concept and Method in the Study of Human Development," in Muzafer Sherif and M. O. Wilson, eds., *Emergent Problems in Social Psychology*, Norman: University of Oklahoma Press, 1957, pp. 29–53. For a detailed description of action-seeking which has clarified my own conception, see Walter B. Miller, "Lower Class Culture as a Generating Milieu of Gang Delinquency," *Journal of Social Issues*, vol. 14, No. 3 (1958), pp. 5–19.

Social Class and Parent-Child Relationships:
An Interpretation

Melvin L. Kohn

This essay is an attempt to interpret, from a sociological perspective, the effects of social class upon parent-child relationships. Many past discussions of the problem seem somehow to lack this perspective, even though the problem is one of profound importance for sociology. Because most investigators have approached the problem from an interest in psychodynamics, rather than social structure, they have largely limited their attention to a few specific techniques used by mothers in the rearing of infants and very young children. They have discovered, *inter alia*, that social class has a decided bearing on which techniques parents use. But, since they have come at the problem from this perspective, their interest in social class has not gone beyond its effects for this very limited aspect of parent-child relationships.

The present analysis conceives the problem of social class and parent-child relationships as an instance of the more general problem of the effects of social structure upon behavior. It starts with the assumption that social class has proved to be so useful a concept because it refers to more than simply educational level, or occupation, or any of the large number of correlated variables. It is so useful because it captures the reality that the intricate interplay of all these variables creates different basic conditions of life at different levels of the social order. Members of different social classes, by virtue of enjoying (or suffering) different conditions of life, come to see the world differently—to develop different

Reprinted by permission of The University of Chicago Press, from *American Journal of Sociology*, Vol. 68, No. 4, January 1963, pp. 471–480.

conceptions of social reality, different aspirations and hopes and fears, different conceptions of the desirable.

The last is particularly important for present purposes, for from people's conceptions of the desirable—and particularly from their conceptions of what characteristics are desirable in children—one can discern their objectives in child-rearing. Thus, conceptions of the desirable—that is, values [1]—become the key concept for this analysis, the bridge between position in the larger social structure and the behavior of the individual. The intent of the analysis is to trace the effects of social class position on parental values and the effects of values on behavior.

Since this approach differs from analyses focused on social class differences in the use of particular child-rearing techniques, it will be necessary to re-examine earlier formulations from the present perspective. Then three questions will be discussed, bringing into consideration the limited available data that are relevant: What differences are there in the values held by parents of different social classes? What is there about the conditions of life distinctive of these classes that might explain the differences in their values? What consequences do these differences in values have for parents' relationships with their children?

Social Class

Social classes will be defined as aggregates of individuals who occupy broadly similar positions in the scale of prestige.[2] In dealing with the research literature, we shall treat occupational position (or occupational position as weighted somewhat by education) as a serviceable index of social class for urban American society. And we shall adopt the model of social stratification implicit in most research, that of four relatively discrete classes: a "lower class" of unskilled manual workers, a "working class" of manual workers in semiskilled and skilled occupations, a "middle class" of white-collar workers and professionals, and an "elite," differentiated from the middle class not so much in terms of occupation as of wealth and lineage.

Almost all the empirical evidence, including that from our own research, stems from broad comparisons of the middle and working class. Thus we shall have little to say about the extremes of the class distribution. Furthermore, we shall have to act as if the middle and working classes were each homogeneous. They are not, even in terms of status considerations alone. There is evidence, for example, that within each broad social class, variations in parents' values quite regularly parallel gradations of social status. Moreover, the classes are heterogeneous with respect to other factors that affect parents' values, such as religion and ethnicity. But even when all such considerations are taken into account, the empirical evidence clearly shows that being on one side or the other of the line that divides manual from non-manual workers has profound consequences for how one rears one's children.[3]

Stability and Change

Any analysis of the effects of social class upon parent-child relationships should start with Urie Bronfenbrenner's analytic review of the studies that had been conducted in this country during the twenty-five years up to 1958.[4] From the seemingly contradictory findings of a number of studies, Bronfenbrenner discerned not chaos but orderly change: there have been changes in the child-training techniques employed by middle-class parents in the past quarter-century; similar changes have been taking place in the working class, but working-class parents have consistently lagged behind by a few years; thus, while middle-class parents of twenty-five years ago were more "restrictive" than were working-class parents, today the middle-class parents are more "permissive"; and the gap between the classes seems to be narrowing.

It must be noted that these conclusions are limited by the questions Bronfenbrenner's predecessors asked in their research. The studies deal largely with a few particular techniques of child-rearing, especially those involved in caring for infants and very young children, and say very little about parents' over-all relationships with their children, particularly as the children grow older. There is clear evidence that the past quarter-century has seen change, even faddism, with respect to the use of breast-feeding or bottle-feeding, scheduling or not scheduling, spanking or isolating. But when we generalize from these specifics to talk of a change from "restrictive" to "permissive" practices—or, worse yet, of a change from "restrictive" to "permissive" parent-child relationships—we impute to them a far greater importance than they probably have, either to parents or to children.[5]

There is no evidence that recent faddism in child-training techniques is symptomatic of profound changes in the relations of parents to children in either social class. In fact, as Bronfenbrenner notes, what little evidence we do have points in the opposite direction: the over-all quality of parent-child relationships does not seem to have changed substantially in either class.[6] In all probability, parents have changed techniques in service of much the same values, and the changes have been quite specific. These changes must be explained, but the enduring characteristics are probably even more important.

Why the changes? Bronfenbrenner's interpretation is ingenuously simple. He notes that the changes in techniques employed by middle-class parents have closely paralleled those advocated by presumed experts, and he concludes that middle-class parents have changed their practices *because* they are responsive to changes in what the experts tell them is right and proper. Working-class parents, being less educated and thus less directly responsive to the media of communication, followed behind only later.[7]

Bronfenbrenner is almost undoubtedly right in asserting that middle-

class parents have followed the drift of presumably expert opinion. But why have they done so? It is not sufficient to assume that the explanation lies in their greater degree of education. This might explain why middle-class parents are substantially more likely than are working-class parents to *read* books and articles on child-rearing, as we know they do.[8] But they need not *follow* the experts' advice. We know from various studies of the mass media that people generally search for confirmation of their existing beliefs and practices and tend to ignore what contradicts them.

From all the evidence at our disposal, it looks as if middle-class parents not only read what the experts have to say but also search out a wide variety of other sources of information and advice: they are far more likely than are working-class parents to discuss child-rearing with friends and neighbors, to consult physicians on these matters, to attend Parent-Teacher Association meetings, to discuss the child's behavior with his teacher. Middle-class parents seem to regard child-rearing as more problematic than do working-class parents. This can hardly be a matter of education alone. It must be rooted more deeply in the conditions of life of the two social classes.

Everything about working-class parents' lives—their comparative lack of education, the nature of their jobs, their greater attachment to the extended family—conduces to their retaining familiar methods.[9] Furthermore, even should they be receptive to change, they are less likely than are middle-class parents to find the experts' writings appropriate to their wants, for the experts predicate their advice on middle-class values. Everything about middle-class parents' lives, on the other hand, conduces to their looking for new methods to achieve their goals. They look to the experts, to other sources of relevant information, and to each other not for new values but for more serviceable techniques.[10] And within the limits of our present scanty knowledge about means-ends relationships in child-rearing, the experts have provided practical and useful advice. It is not that educated parents slavishly follow the experts but that the experts have provided what the parents have sought.

To look at the question this way is to put it in a quite different perspective: the focus becomes not specific techniques nor changes in the use of specific techniques but parental values.

Values of Middle- and Working-Class Parents

Of the entire range of values one might examine, it seems particularly strategic to focus on parents' conceptions of what characteristics would be most desirable for boys or girls the age of their own children. From this one can hope to discern the parents' goals in rearing their children. It must be assumed, however, that a parent will choose one characteristic as more desirable than another only if he considers it to be both important, in the sense that failure to develop this characteristic would

affect the child adversely, and problematic, in the sense that it is neither to be taken for granted that the child will develop that characteristic nor impossible for him to do so. In interpreting parents' value choices, we must keep in mind that their choices reflect not simply their goals but the goals whose achievement they regard as problematic.

Few studies, even in recent years, have directly investigated the relationship of social class to parental values. Fortunately, however, the results of these few are in essential agreement. The earliest study was Evelyn Millis Duvall's pioneering inquiry of 1946.[11] Duvall characterized working-class (and lower middle-class) parental values as "traditional" —they want their children to be neat and clean, to obey and respect adults, to please adults. In contrast to this emphasis on how the child comports himself, middle-class parental values are more "developmental" —they want their children to be eager to learn, to love and confide in the parents, to be happy, to share and co-operate, to be healthy and well.

Duvall's traditional-developmental dichotomy does not describe the difference between middle- and working-class parental values quite exactly, but it does point to the essence of the difference: working-class parents want the child to conform to externally imposed standards, while middle-class parents are far more attentive to his internal dynamics.

The few relevant findings of subsequent studies are entirely consistent with this basic point, especially in the repeated indications that working-class parents put far greater stress on obedience to parental commands than do middle-class parents.[12] Our own research, conducted in 1956–57, provides the evidence most directly comparable to Duvall's.[13] We, too, found that working-class parents value obedience, neatness, and cleanliness more highly than do middle-class parents, and that middle-class parents in turn value curiosity, happiness, consideration, and—most importantly—self-control more highly than do working-class parents. We further found that there are characteristic clusters of value choice in the two social classes: working-class parental values center on conformity to external proscriptions, middle-class parental values on *self*-direction. To working-class parents, it is the overt act that matters: the child should not transgress externally imposed rules; to middle-class parents, it is the child's motives and feelings that matter: the child should govern himself.

In fairness, it should be noted that middle- and working-class parents share many core values. Both, for example, value honesty very highly— although, characteristically, "honesty" has rather different connotations in the two social classes, implying "trustworthiness" for the working-class and "truthfulness" for the middle-class. The common theme, of course, is that parents of both social classes value a decent respect for the rights of others; middle- and working-class values are but variations on this common theme. The reason for emphasizing the variations rather than the common theme is that they seem to have far-ranging consequences for parents' relationships with their children and thus ought to be taken seriously.

It would be good if there were more evidence about parental values —data from other studies, in other locales, and especially, data derived from more than one mode of inquiry. But, what evidence we do have is consistent, so that there is at least some basis for believing it is reliable. Furthermore, there is evidence that the value choices made by parents in these inquires are not simply a reflection of their assessments of their own children's deficiences or excellences. Thus, we may take the findings of these studies as providing a limited, but probably valid, picture of the parents' generalized conceptions of what behavior would be desirable in their preadolescent children.

Explaining Class Differences in Parental Values

That middle-class parents are more likely to espouse some values, and working-class parents other values, must be a function of differences in their conditions of life. In the present state of our knowledge, it is difficult to disentangle the interacting variables with a sufficient degree of exactness to ascertain which conditions of life are crucial to the differences in values. Nevertheless, it is necessary to examine the principle components of class differences in life conditions to see what each may contribute.

The logical place to begin is with occupational differences, for these are certainly pre-eminently important, not only in defining social classes in urban, industrialized society, but also in determining much else about people's life conditions.[14] There are at least three respects in which middle-class occupations typically differ from working-class occupations, above and beyond their obvious status-linked differences in security, stability of income, and general social prestige. One is that middle-class occupations deal more with the manipulation of interpersonal relations, ideas, and symbols, while working-class occupations deal more with the manipulation of things. The second is that middle-class occupations are more subject to self-direction, while working-class occupations are more subject to standardization and direct supervision. The third is that getting ahead in middle-class occupations is more dependent upon one's own actions, while in working-class occupations it is more dependent upon collective action, particularly in unionized industries. From these differences, one can sketch differences in the characteristics that make for getting along, and getting ahead, in middle- and working-class occupations. Middle-class occupations require a greater degree of self-direction; working-class occupations, in larger measure, require that one follow explicit rules set down by someone in authority.

Obviously, these differences parallel the differences we have found between the two social classes in the characteristics valued by parents for children. At minimum, one can conclude that there is a congruence between occupational requirements and parental values. It is, more-

over, a reasonable supposition, although not a necessary conclusion, that middle- and working-class parents value different characteristics in children *because* of these differences in their occupational circumstances. This supposition does not necessarily assume that parents consciously train their children to meet future occupational requirements; it may simply be that their own occupational experiences have significantly affected parents' conceptions of what is desirable behavior, on or off the job, for adults or for children.[15]

These differences in occupational circumstances are probably basic to the differences we have found between middle- and working-class parental values, but taken alone they do not sufficiently explain them. Parents need not accord pre-eminent importance to occupational requirements in their judgments of what is most desirable. For a sufficient explanation of class differences in values, it is necessary to recognize that other differences in middle- and working-class conditions of life reinforce the differences in occupational circumstances at every turn.

Educational differences, for example, above and beyond their importance as determinants of occupation, probably contribute independently to the differences in middle- and working-class parental values. At minimum, middle-class parents' greater attention to the child's internal dynamics is facilitated by their learned ability to deal with the subjective and the ideational. Furthermore, differences in levels and stability of income undoubtedly contribute to class differences in parental values. That middle-class parents still have somewhat higher levels of income, and much greater stability of income, makes them able to take for granted the respectability that is still problematic for working-class parents. They can afford to concentrate, instead, on motives and feelings —which, in the circumstances of their lives, are more important.

These considerations suggest that the differences between middle- and working-class parental values are probably a function of the entire complex of differences in life conditions characteristic of the two social classes. Consider, for example, the working-class situation. With the end of mass immigration, there has emerged a stable working class, largely derived from the manpower of rural areas, uninterested in mobility into the middle class, but very much interested in security, respectability, and the enjoyment of a decent standard of living.[16] This working class has come to enjoy a standard of living formerly reserved for the middle class, but has not chosen a middle-class style of life. In effect, the working class has striven for, and partially achieved, an American dream distinctly different from the dream of success and achievement. In an affluent society, it is possible for the worker to be the traditionalist—politically, economically, and, most relevant here, in his values for his children.[17] Working-class parents want their children to conform to external authority because the parents themselves are willing to accord respect to authority, in return for security and respectability. Their conservatism in child-rearing is part of a more general conservatism and traditionalism.

Middle-class parental values are a product of a quite different set of

conditions. Much of what the working class values, they can take for granted. Instead, they can—and must—instil in their children a degree of self-direction that would be less appropriate to the conditions of life of the working class.[18] Certainly, there is substantial truth in the characterization of the middle-class way of life as one of great conformity. What must be noted here, however, is that *relative to* the working class, middle-class conditions of life require a more substantial degree of independence of action. Furthermore, the higher levels of education enjoyed by the middle class make possible a degree of internal scrutiny difficult to achieve without the skills in dealing with the abstract that college training sometimes provides. Finally, the economic security of most middle-class occupations, the level of income they provide, the status they confer, allow one to focus his attention on the subjective and the ideational. Middle-class conditions of life both allow and demand a greater degree of self-direction than do those of the working class.

Consequences of Class Differences in Parents' Values

What consequences do the differences between middle- and working-class parents' values have for the ways they raise their children?

Much of the research on techniques of infant- and child-training is of little relevance here. For example, with regard to parents' preferred techniques for disciplining children, a question of major interest to many investigators, Bronfenbrenner summarizes past studies as follows: "In matters of discipline, working-class parents are consistently more likely to employ physical punishment, while middle-class families rely more on reasoning, isolation, appeals to guilt, and other methods involving the threat of loss of love." [19] This, if still true,[20] is consistent with middle-class parents' greater attentiveness to the child's internal dynamics, working-class parents' greater concern about the overt act. For present purposes, however, the crucial question is not *which* disciplinary method parents prefer, but when and why they use one or another method of discipline.

The most directly relevant available data are on the conditions under which middle- and working-class parents use physical punishment. Working-class parents are apt to resort to physical punishment when the direct and immediate consequences of their children's disobedient acts are most extreme, and to refrain from punishing when this might provoke an even greater disturbance.[21] Thus, they will punish a child for wild play when the furniture is damaged or the noise level becomes intolerable, but ignore the same actions when the direct and immediate consequences are not so extreme. Middle-class parents, on the other hand, seem to punish or refrain from punishing on the basis of their interpretation of the child's intent in acting as he does. Thus, they will punish a furious outburst when the context is such that they interpret it

to be a loss of self-control, but will ignore an equally extreme outburst when the context is such that they interpret it to be merely an emotional release.

It is understandable that working-class parents react to the consequences rather than to the intent of their children's actions: the important thing is that the child not transgress externally imposed rules. Correspondingly, if middle-class parents are instead concerned about the child's motives and feelings, they can and must look beyond the overt act to why the child acts as he does. It would seem that middle- and working-class values direct parents to see their children's misbehavior in quite different ways, so that misbehavior which prompts middle-class parents to action does not seem as important to working-class parents, and vice versa.[22] Obviously, parents' values are not the only things that enter into their use of physical punishment. But unless one assumes a complete lack of goal-directedness in parental behavior, he would have to grant that parents' values direct their attention to some facets of their own and their children's behavior, and divert it from other facets.

The consequences of class differences in parental values extend far beyond differences in disciplinary practices. From a knowledge of their values for their children, one would expect middle-class parents to feel a greater obligation to be *supportive* of the children, if only because of their sensitivity to the children's internal dynamics. Working-class values, with their emphasis upon conformity to external rules, should lead to greater emphasis upon the parents' obligation to impose constraints.[23] And this, according to Bronfenbrenner, is precisely what has been shown in those few studies that have concerned themselves with the over-all relationship of parents to child: "Over the entire twenty-five-year period studied, parent-child relationships in the middle-class are consistently reported as more acceptant and equalitarian, while those in the working-class are oriented toward maintaining order and obedience." [24]

This conclusion is based primarily on studies of *mother*-child relationships in middle- and working-class families. Class differences in parental values have further ramifications for the father's role.[25] Mothers in each class would have their husbands play a role facilitative of the child's development of the characteristics valued in that class: Middle-class mothers want their husbands to be supportive of the children (especially of sons), with their responsibility for imposing constraints being of decidedly secondary importance; working-class mothers look to their husbands to be considerably more directive—support is accorded far less importance and constraint far more. Most middle-class fathers agree with their wives and play a role close to what their wives would have them play. Many working-class fathers, on the other hand, do not. It is not that they see the constraining role as less important than do their wives, but that many of them see no reason why they should have to shoulder the responsibility. From their point of view, the important thing is that the child be taught what limits he

must not transgress. It does not much matter who does the teaching, and since mother has primary responsibility for child care, the job should be hers.

The net consequence is a quite different division of parental responsibilities in the two social classes. In middle-class families, mother's and father's roles usually are not sharply differentiated. What differentiation exists is largely a matter of each parent taking special responsibility for being supportive of children of the parent's own sex. In working-class families, mother's and father's roles are more sharply differentiated, with mother almost always being the more supportive parent. In some working-class families, mother specializes in support, father in constraint; in others, perhaps in most, mother raises the children, father provides the wherewithal.[26]

Thus, the differences in middle- and working-class parents' values have wide ramifications for their relationships with their children and with each other. Of course, many class differences in parent-child relationships are not directly attributable to differences in values; undoubtedly the very differences in their conditions of life that make for differences in parental values reinforce, at every juncture, parents' characteristic ways of relating to their children. But one could not account for these consistent differences in parent-child relationships in the two social classes without reference to the differences in parents' avowed values.

Conclusion

This paper serves to show how complex and demanding are the problems of interpreting the effects of social structure on behavior. Our inquiries habitually stop at the point of demonstrating that social position correlates with something, when we should want to pursue the question, "Why?" What are the processes by which position in social structure molds behavior? The present analysis has dealt with this question in one specific form: Why does social class matter for parents' relationships with their children? There is every reason to believe that the problems encountered in trying to deal with that question would recur in any analysis of the effects of social structure on behavior.

In this analysis, the concept of "values" has been used as the principal bridge from social position to behavior. The analysis has endeavored to show that middle-class parental values differ from those of working-class parents; that these differences are rooted in basic differences between middle- and working-class conditions of life; and that the differences between middle- and working-class parental values have important consequences for their relationships with their children. The interpretive model, in essence, is: social class—conditions of life—values—behavior.

The specifics of the present characterization of parental values may prove to be inexact; the discussion of the ways in which social class position affects values is undoubtedly partial; and the tracing of the consequences of differences in values for differences in parent-child relationships is certainly tentative and incomplete. I trust, however, that the perspective will prove to be valid and that this formulation will stimulate other investigators to deal more directly with the processes whereby social structure affects behavior.

Notes

1. "A value is a conception, explicit or implicit, distinctive of an individual or characteristic of a group, of the desirable which influences the selection from available modes, means, and ends of action" (Clyde Kluckhohn, "Values and Value Orientations," in Talcott Parsons and Edward A. Shils (eds.), *Toward A General Theory of Action* [Cambridge, Mass.: Harvard University Press, 1951], p. 395). See also the discussion of values in Robin M. Williams, Jr., *American Society: A Sociological Interpretation* (New York: Alfred A. Knopf, Inc., 1951), chap. xi, and his discussion of social class and culture on p. 101.

2. Williams, *op. cit.*, p. 89.

3. These, and other assertions of fact not referred to published sources, are based on research my colleagues and I have conducted. For the design of this research and the principal substantive findings see my "Social Class and Parental Values," *American Journal of Sociology*, LXIV (January, 1959), 337–51; my "Social Class and the Exercise of Parental Authority," *American Sociological Review*, XXIV (June, 1959), 352–66; and with Eleanor E. Carroll, "Social Class and the Allocation of Parental Responsibilities," *Sociometry*, XXIII (December, 1960), 372–92. I should like to express my appreciation to my principal collaborators in this research, John A. Clausen and Eleanor E. Carroll.

4. Urie Bronfenbrenner, "Socialization and Social Class through Time and Space," in Eleanor E. Maccoby, Theodore M. Newcomb, and Eugene L. Hartley (eds.), *Readings in Social Psychology* (New York: Henry Holt & Co., 1958).

5. Furthermore, these concepts employ a priori judgments about which the various investigators have disagreed radically. See, e.g., Robert R. Sears, Eleanor E. Maccoby, and Harry Levin, *Patterns of Child Rearing* (Evanston, Ill.: Row, Peterson & Co., 1957), pp. 444–47, and

Richard A. Littman, Robert C. A. Moore, and John Pierce-Jones, "Social Class Differences in Child Rearing: A Third Community for Comparison with Chicago and Newton," *American Sociological Review*, XXII (December, 1957), 694–704, esp. p. 703.

6. Bronfenbrenner, *op. cit.*, pp. 420–22 and 425.

7. Bronfenbrenner gives clearest expression to this interpretation, but it has been adopted by others, too. See e.g., Martha Sturm White, "Social Class, Child-Rearing Practices, and Child Behavior," *American Sociological Review*, XXII (December, 1957), 704–12.

8. This was noted by John E. Anderson in the first major study of social class and family relationships ever conducted, and has repeatedly been confirmed (*The Young Child in the Home: A Survey of Three Thousand American Families* [New York: Appleton-Century, 1936]).

9. The differences between middle- and working-class conditions of life will be discussed more fully later in this paper.

10. Certainly middle-class parents do not get their values from the experts. In our research, we compared the values of parents who say they read Spock, Gesell, or other books on child-rearing, to those who read only magazine and newspaper articles, and those who say they read nothing at all on the subject. In the middle class, these three groups have substantially the same values. In the working class, the story is different. Few working-class parents claim to read books or even articles on child-rearing. Those few who do have values much more akin to those of the middle class. But these are atypical working-class parents who are very anxious to attain middle-class status. One suspects that for them the experts provide a sort of handbook to the middle class; even for them,

it is unlikely that the values come out of Spock and Gesell.

11. "Conceptions of Parenthood," *American Journal of Sociology,* LII (November, 1946), 193–203.

12. Alex Inkeles has shown that this is true not only for the United States but for a number of other industrialized societies as well ("Industrial Man: The Relation of Status to Experience, Perception, and Value," *American Journal of Sociology,* LXVI [July, 1960], 20–21 and Table 9).

13. "Social Class and Parental Values," *op. cit.*

14. For a thoughtful discussion of the influence of occupational role on parental values see David F. Aberle and Kaspar D. Naegele, "Middle Class Fathers' Occupational Role and Attitudes Toward Children," *American Journal of Orthopsychiatry,* XXII (April, 1952), 366–78.

15. Two objections might be raised here. (1) Occupational experiences may not be important for a mother's values, however crucial they are for her husband's, if she has had little or no work experience. But even those mothers who have had little or no occupational experience know something of occupational life from their husbands and others, and live in a culture in which occupation and career permeate all of life. (2) Parental values may be built not so much out of their own experiences as out of their expectations of the child's future experiences. This might seem particularly plausible in explaining working-class values, for their high valuation of such stereotypically *middle-class* characteristics as obedience, neatness, and cleanliness might imply that they are training their children for a middle-class life they expect the children to achieve. Few working-class parents, however, do expect (or even want) their children to go on to college and the middle-class jobs for which a college education is required. (This is shown in Herbert H. Hyman, "The Value Systems of Different Classes: A Social Psychological Contribution to the Analysis of Stratification," in Reinhard Bendix and Seymour Martin Lipset [eds.], *Class, Status and Power: A Reader in Social Stratification* [Glencoe, Ill.: Free Press, 1953], and confirmed in unpublished data from our own research.)

16. See, e.g., S. M. Miller and Frank Riessman, "The Working Class Subculture: A New View," *Social Problems,* IX (Summer, 1961), 86–97.

17. Relevant here is Seymour Martin Lipset's somewhat disillusioned "Democracy and Working-Class Authoritarianism," *American Sociological Review,* XXIV (August, 1959), 482–501.

18. It has been argued that as larger and larger proportions of the middle class have become imbedded in a bureaucratic way of life—in distinction to the entrepreneurial way of life of a bygone day—it has become more appropriate to raise children to be accommodative than to be self-reliant. But this point of view is a misreading of the conditions of life faced by the middle-class inhabitants of the bureaucratic world. Their jobs require at least as great a degree of self-reliance as do entrepreneurial enterprises. We tend to forget, nowadays, just how little the small- or medium-sized entrepreneur controlled the conditions of his own existence and just how much he was subjected to the petty authority of those on whose pleasure depended the survival of his enterprise. And we fail to recognize the degree to which monolithic-seeming bureaucracies allow free play for—in fact, require—individual enterprise of new sorts: in the creation of ideas, the building of empires, the competition for advancement.

At any rate, our data show no substantial differences between the values of parents from bureaucratic and entrepreneurial occupational worlds, in either social class. But see Daniel R. Miller and Guy E. Swanson, *The Changing American Parent: A Study in the Detroit Area* (New York: John Wiley & Sons, 1958).

19. Bronfenbrenner, *op. cit.,* p. 424.

. 20. Later studies, including our own, do not show this difference.

21. "Social Class and the Exercise of Parental Authority," *op. cit.*

22. This is not to say that the methods used by parents of either social class are necessarily the most efficacious for achievement of their goals.

23. The justification for treating support and constraint as the two major dimensions of parent-child relationships lies in the theoretical argument of Talcott Parsons and Robert F. Bales, *Family, Socialization and Interaction Process* (Glencoe, Ill.: Free Press, 1955), esp. p. 45, and the empirical argument of Earl S. Schaefer, "A Circumplex Model for Maternal Behavior," *Journal of Abnormal and Social Psychology,* LIX (September, 1959), 226–34.

24. Bronfenbrenner, *op. cit.,* p. 425.

25. From the very limited evidence available at the time of his review, Bronfenbrenner tentatively concluded: "though the middle-class father typically has a warmer relationship with the child, he is also likely to have more authority and status in family affairs"

(*ibid.*, p. 422). The discussion here is based largely on subsequent research, esp. "Social Class and the Allocation of Parental Responsibilities," *op. cit.*

26. Fragmentary data suggest sharp class differences in the husband-wife relationship that complement the differences in the division of parental responsibilities discussed above. For example, virtually no working-class wife reports that she and her husband ever go out on an evening or weekend without the children. And few working-class fathers do much to relieve their wives of the burden of caring for the children all the time. By and large, working-class fathers seem to lead a largely separate social life from that of their wives; the wife has full-time responsibility for the children, while the husband is free to go his own way.

Cognitive Style and Language

The Disadvantaged Child and the Learning Process

Martin P. Deutsch

This paper will discuss the interaction of social and developmental factors and their impact on the intellectual growth and school performance of the child. It will make particular reference to the large number of urban children who come from marginal social circumstances. While much of the discussion will be speculative, where appropriate it will draw on data from the field, and will suggest particular relationships and avenues for future investigation or demonstration.

Among children who come from lower-class socially impoverished circumstances, there is a high proportion of school failure, school dropouts, reading and learning disabilities, as well as life adjustment problems. This means not only that these children grow up poorly equipped academically, but also that the effectiveness of the school as a major institution for socialization is diminished. The effect of this process is underlined by the fact that this same segment of the population contributes disproportionately to the delinquency and other social deviancy statistics.

The thesis here is that the lower-class child enters the school situation so poorly prepared to produce what the school demands that initial failures are almost inevitable, and the school experience becomes negatively rather than positively reinforced. Thus the child's experience in school does nothing to counteract the invidious influences to which he is exposed in his slum, and sometimes segregated, neighborhood.

We know that children from underprivileged environments tend to

Reprinted from *Education in Depressed Areas*, A. Harry Passow, ed., New York: Bureau of Publications, Teachers College, Columbia University, 1963, pp. 163–179.

come to school with a qualitatively different preparation for the demands of both the learning process and the behavioral requirements of the classroom. These are various differences in the kinds of socializing experiences these children have had, as contrasted with the middle-class child. The culture of their environment is a different one from the culture that has molded the school and its educational techniques and theory.

We know that it is difficult for all peoples to span cultural discontinuities, and yet we make little if any effort to prepare administrative personnel or teachers and guidance staff to assist the child in this transition from one cultural context to another. This transition must have serious psychological consequences for the child, and probably plays a major role in influencing his later perceptions of other social institutions as he is introduced to them.

It must be pointed out that the relationship between social background and school performance is not a simple one. Rather, evidence which is accumulating points more and more to the influence of background variables on the patterns of perceptual, language, and cognitive development of the child and the subsequent diffusion of the effects of such patterns into all areas of the child's academic and psychological performance. To understand these effects requires delineating the underlying skills in which these children are not sufficiently proficient. A related problem is that of defining what aspects of the background are most influential in producing what kinds of deficits in skills.

Environmental Factors

Let us begin with the most macroscopic background factors. While it is likely that slum life might have delimited areas that allow for positive growth and that the middle-class community has attributes which might retard healthy development, generally the combination of circumstances in middle-class life is considerably more likely to furnish opportunities for normal growth of the child. At the same time, slum conditions are more likely to have deleterious effects on physical and mental development. This is not to say that middle-class life furnishes a really adequate milieu for the maximum development of individual potential: it doesn't. The fact that we often speak as though it does is a function of viewing the middle-class environment in comparison to the slum. Middle-class people who work and teach across social-class lines often are unable to be aware of the negative aspects of the middle-class background because of its apparent superiority over the less advantageous background provided by lower-class life. We really have no external criterion for evaluating the characteristics of a milieu in terms of how well it is designed to foster development; as a result we might actually be measuring one area of social failure with the yardstick of social catastrophe.

It is true that many leading personalities in twentieth-century

American life have come from the slums, and this is a fact often pointed out by nativistic pragmatists in an effort to prove that if the individual "has it in him" he can overcome—and even be challenged by —his humble surroundings. This argument, though fundamentally fallacious, might have had more to recommend it in the past. At the turn of the century we were a massively vertical mobile society—that is, with the exception of certain large minority groups such as the Negroes, the Indians, and the Mexican-Americans who were rarely allowed on the social elevator. In the mid-twentieth century, it is now increasingly possible for all groups to get on, but social and economic conditions have changed, and the same elevator more frequently moves in two directions or stands still altogether. When it does move, it goes more slowly, and, most discouragingly, it also provides an observation window on what, at least superficially, appears to be a most affluent society. Television, movies, and other media continually expose the individual from the slum to the explicit assumption that the products of a consumer society are available at all—or, rather, as he sees it, to all but him. In effect, this means that the child from the disadvantaged environment is an outsider and an observer—through his own eyes and those of his parents or neighbors—of the mainstream of American life. At the same time, when the child enters school he is exposing himself directly to the values and anticipations of a participant in that mainstream— his teacher. It is not sufficiently recognized that there is quite a gap between the training of a teacher and the needs limitations, and unique strengths of the child from a marginal situation. This gap is, of course, maximized when the child belongs to a minority group that until quite recently was not only excluded from the mainstream, but was not even allowed to bathe in the tributaries.

What are some of the special characteristics of these children, and why do they appearently need exceptional social and educational planning? So often, administrators and teachers say, they are children who are "curious," "cute," "affectionate," "warm," and independently dependent in the kindergarten and the first grade, but who so often become "alienated," "withdrawn," "angry," passive," "apathetic," or just "troublemakers" by the fifth and sixth grade. In our research at the Institute for Developmental Studies, it is in the first grade that we usually see the smallest differences between socio-economic or racial groups in intellectual, language, and some conceptual measures, and in the later grades that we find the greatest differences in favor of the more socially privileged groups. From both teacher's observations and the finding of this increasing gap, it appears that there is a failure on some level of society and, more specifically, the educational system. Was the school scientifically prepared to receive these children in the first place? And, in addition, were the children perhaps introduced to the individual demands of the larger culture at too late an age—that is, in first grade?

Before discussing these psychological products of social deprivation, it is appropriate to look more closely at the special circumstances of

Negro slum residents. In the core city of most of our large metropolitan areas, 40 to 70 per cent of the elementary school population is
likely to be Negro. In my observations, through workshops in many
of these cities, I have often been surprised to find how little real comprehension of the particular problems of these youngsters exists as part
of the consciousness of the Negro or white middle-class teachers. While
in middle-class schools there is great sensitivity to emotional climates
and pressures and tensions that might be operating on the child in
either the home or the school, in lower-class schools the problems of
social adaptation are so massive that sensitivity tends to become
blunted.

In the lower-class Negro group there still exist the sequelae of the
conditions of slavery. While a hundred years have passed, this is a
short time in the life of a people. And the extension of tendrils of the
effects of slavery into modern life has been effectively discouraged only
in the last few decades, when there have been some real attempts to
integrate the Negro fully into American life. It is often difficult for teachers and the personnel of other community agencies to understand the
Negro lower-class child—particularly the child who has come, or whose
parents have come, from the rural South. There is a whole set of implicit
and explicit value systems which determine our educational philosophies,
and the institutional expectation is that all children participate in these
systems. And yet for these expectations to be met, the child must
experience some continuity of socio-cultural participation in and sharing
of these value systems before he comes to school. This is often just not
the case for the child who comes from an encapsulated community,
particularly when the walls have been built by the dominant social and
cultural forces that have also determined the value systems relating to
learning.

A recent article in *Fortune* magazine asked why the Negro failed
to take full advantage of opportunities open to him in American life.
At least part of the answer is that the Negro has not been fully integrated into American life, and that even knowledge about particular
occupations and their requirements is not available outside the cultural
mainstream. Implications of this for the aspirations and motivations of
children will be discussed later.

Another source of misunderstanding on the part of school and social
agency people is the difficulty of putting in historical perspective the
casual conditions responsible for the high percentage of broken homes
in the Negro community. Implications of this for the child's emotional
stability are very frequenly recognized, but the effects on the child's
motivation, self-concept, and achievement orientation are not often
understood.

The Negro family was first broken deliberately by the slave traders
and the plantation owners for their own purposes. As was pointed out
earlier, the hundred years since slavery is not a very long time for a total
social metamorphosis even under fostering conditions—and during that

period the Negro community has been for the most part economically marginal and isolated from the contacts which would have accelerated change. The thirteen depressions and recessions we have had since Emancipation have been devastating to this community. These marginal economic and encapsulated social circumstances have been particularly harsh on the Negro male. The chronic instability has greatly influenced the Negro man's concept of himself and his general motivation to succeed in competitive areas of society where the rewards are greatest. All these circumstances have contributed to the instability of the Negro family, and particularly to the fact that it is most often broken by the absence of the father. As a result, the lower-class Negro child entering school often has had no experience with a "successful" male model or thereby with a psychological framework in which effort can result in at least the possibility of achievement. Yet the value system of the school and of the learning process is predicated on the assumption that effort will result in achievement.

To a large extent, much of this is true not only for the Negro child but for all children who come from impoverished and marginal social and economic conditions. These living conditions are characterized by great overcrowding in substandard housing, often lacking adequate sanitary and other facilities. While we don't know the actual importance, for example, of moments of privacy, we do know that the opportunity frequently does not exist. In addition, there are likely to be large numbers of siblings and half-siblings, again with there being little opportunity for individuation. At the same time, the child tends to be restricted to his immediate environment, with conducted explorations of the "outside" world being infrequent and sometimes non-existent. In the slums, and to an unfortunately large extent in many other areas of our largest cities, there is little opportunity to observe natural beauty, clean landscapes or other pleasant and aesthetically pleasing surroundings.

In the child's home, there is a scarcity of objects of all types, but especially of books, toys, puzzles, pencils, and scribbling paper. It is not that the mere presence of such materials would necessarily result in their productive use, but it would increase the child's familiarity with the tools he'll be confronted with in school. Actually, for the most effective utilization of these tools, guidance and explanations are necessary from the earliest time of exposure. Such guidance requires not only the presence of aware and educated adults, but also time—a rare commodity in these marginal circumstances. Though many parents will share in the larger value system of having high aspirations for their children, they are unaware of the operational steps required for the preparation of the child to use optimally the learning opportunities in the school. Individual potential is one of the most unmarketable properties if the child acquires no means for its development, or if no means exist for measuring it objectively. It is here that we must understand the consequences of all these aspects of the slum matrix for the psychological and cognitive development of the child.

Psychological Factors

A child from any circumstance who has been deprived of a substantial portion of the variety of stimuli which he is maturationally capable of responding to is likely to be deficient in the equipment required for learning.

Support for this is found in Hunt who, in discussing Piaget's developmental theories, points out that, according to Piaget:

> . . . the rate of development is in substantial part, but certaintly not wholly, a function of environmental circumstances. Change in circumstances is required to force the accommodative modifications of schemata that constitute development. Thus, the greater the variety of situations to which the child must accommodate his behavioral structures, the more differentiated and mobile they become. Thus, the more new things a child has seen and the more he has heard, the more things he is interested in seeing and hearing. Moreover, the more variation in reality with which he has coped, the greater is his capacity for coping. (2, pp. 258–259).

This emphasis on the importance of variety in the environment implies the detrimental effects of lack of variety. This in turn leads to a concept of "stimulus deprivation." But it is important that it be correctly understood. By this is not necessarily meant any restriction of the quality of stimulation, but, rather, a restriction to a segment of the spectrum of stimulation potentially available. In addition to the restriction in variety, from what is known of the slum environment, it might be postulated that the segments made available to these children tend to have poorer and less systematic ordering of stimulation sequences, and would thereby be less useful to the growth and activation of cognitive potential.

This deprivation has effects on both the formal and the contentual aspects of cognition. By "formal" is meant the operations—the behavior —by which stimuli are perceived, encouraged, and responded to. By "contentual" is meant the actual content of the child's knowledge and comprehension. "Formal equipment" would include perceptual discrimination skills, the ability to sustain attention, and the ability to use adults as sources of information and for satisfying curiosity. Also included would be the establishment of expectations of reward from accumulation of knowledge, from task completion, and from adult reinforcement, and the ability to delay gratification. Examples of "contentual equipment" would be the language-symbolic system, environmental information, general and environmental orientation, and concepts of comparability and relativity appropriate to the child's age level. The growth of a differentiated attitudinal set toward learning is probably a resultant of the interaction between formal and contentual levels.

Hypothesizing that stimulus deprivation will result in deficiences in either of these equipments, let us examine the particular stimuli which are available and those which are absent from the environment of the child who comes from the conditions discussed above. This reasoning suggests also certain hypotheses regarding the role of environment in the evolving of the formal and contentual systems.

As was pointed out in the previous section, the disadvantaged environment as well as certain aspects of the middle-class circumstance offers the child, over-all, a restricted range of experience. While one does see great individual variability in these children, social conditions reduce the range of this variation; with less variety in input, it would be reasonable to assume a concomitant restriction in the variety of output. This is an important respect in which social poverty may have a leveling effect on the achievement of individual skills and abilities. Concomitantly, in the current problem of extensive under-achievement in suburban lower-middle-class areas, the over-routinization of activity with the consequent reduction in variety may well be the major factor.

In individual terms, a child is probably farther away from his maturational ceiling as a result of this experiential poverty. This might well be a crucial factor in the poorer performance of the lower socio-economic children on standardized tests of intelligence. On such tests, the child is compared with others of his own age. But if his point of development in relation to the maturational ceiling for his age group is influenced by his experience, then the child with restricted experience may actually be developed to a proportionately lower level of his own actual ceiling. If a certain quantum of fostering experience is necessary to activate the achievement of particular maturational levels, then perhaps the child who is deficient in this experience will take longer to achieve these levels, even though his potential may be the same as the more advantaged child. It might be that in order to achieve a realistic appraisal of the ability levels of children, an "experience" age rather than the chronological age should be used to arrive at norms.

This suggests a limitation on the frequent studies comparing Negro and white children. Even when it is possible to control for the formal attributes of social class membership, the uniqueness of the Negro child's experience would make comparability impossible when limited to these class factors. Perhaps too, if such an interaction exists between experiential and biological determinants of development, it would account for the failure of the culture-free tests, as they too are standardized on an age basis without allowing for the experimental interaction (as distinguished from specific experimental *influence*).

Let us now consider some of the specifics in the child's environment, and their effects on the development of the formal, contentual, and attitudinal systems.

Visually, the urban slum and its overcrowded apartments offer the child a minimal range of stimuli. There are usually few if any pictures on the wall, and the objects in the household, be they toys, furniture, or utensils, tend to be sparse, repetitious, and lacking in form and color

variations. The sparsity of objects and lack of diversity of home artifacts which are available and meaningful to the child, in addition to
the unavailability of individualized training, gives the child few opportunities to manipulate and organize the visual properties of his environment and thus perceptually to organize and discriminate the nuances
of that environment. These would include figure-ground relationships
and the spatial organization of the visual field. The sparsity of manipulable objects probably also hampers the development of these functions in the tactile area. For example, while these children have broom-
sticks and usually a ball, possibly a doll or a discarded kitchen pot to
play with, they don't have the different shapes and colors and sizes
to manipulate which the middle-class child has in the form of blocks
which are bought just for him, or even in the variety of sizes and shapes
of cooking utensils which might be available to him as playthings.

It is true, as has been pointed out frequently, that the pioneer child
didn't have many playthings either. But he had a more active responsibility toward the environment and a great variety of growing plants
and other natural resources as well as a stable family that assumed
a primary role for the education and training of the child. In addition,
the intellectually normal or superior frontier child could and usually
did grow up to be a farmer. Today's child will grow up into a world of
automation requiring highly differentiated skills if he and society are to
use his intellect.

The effect of sparsity of manipulable objects on visual perception
is, of course, quite speculative, as few data now exist. However, it is an
important area, as among skills necessary for reading are form discrimination and visual spatial organization. Children from depressed
areas, because of inadequate training and stimulation, may not have
developed the requisite skills by the time they enter first grade, and the
assumption that they do possess these skills may thus add to the frustration these children experience on entering school.

The lower-class home is not a verbally oriented environment. The
implications of this for language development will be considered
below in the discussion of the contentual systems. Here let us consider
its implication for the development of auditory discrimination skills.
While the environment is a noisy one, the noise is not, for the most
part, meaningful in relation to the child, and for him most of it is
background. In the crowded apartments with all the daily living stresses,
is a minimum of non-instructional conversation directed toward the
child. In actuality, the situation is ideal for the child to learn inattention. Furthermore, he does not get practice in auditory discrimination
or feedback from adults correcting his enunciation, pronunciation, and
grammar. In studies at the Institute for Developmental Studies at New
York Medical College, as yet unreported in the literature, we have found
significant differences in auditory discriminaion between lower-class
and middle-class children in the first grade. These differences seem to
diminish markedly as the children get older, though the effects of their
early existence on other functioning remain to be investigated. Here

again, we are dealing with a skill very important to reading. Our data indicate too that poor readers within social-class groups have significantly more difficulty in auditory discrimination than do good readers. Further, this difference between good and poor readers is greater for the lower-class group.

If the child learns to be inattentive in the pre-school environment, as has been postulated, this further diminishes incoming stimulation. Further, if this trained inattention comes about as a result of his being insufficiently called upon to respond to particular stimuli, then his general level of responsiveness will also be diminished. The nature of the total environment and the child-adult interaction is such that reinforcement is too infrequent, and, as a result, the quantity of response is diminished. The implications of this for the structured learning situation in the school are quite obvious.

Related to attentivity is memory. Here also we would postulate the dependence of the child, particularly in the pre-school period, on interaction with the parent. It is adults who link the past and the present by calling to mind prior shared experiences. The combination of the constriction in the use of language and in shared activity results, for the lower-class child, in much less stimulation of the early memory function. Although I don't know of any data supporting this thesis, from my observations it would seem that there is a tendency for these children to be proportionately more present-oriented and less aware of past-present sequences than the middle-class child. This is consistent with anthropological research and thinking. While this could be a function of the poorer time orientation of these children or of their difficulty in verbal expression, both of which will be discussed below, it could also relate to a greater difficulty in seeing themselves in the past or in a different context. Another area which points up the home-school discontinuity is that of time. Anthropologists have pointed out that from culture to culture time concepts differ and that time as life's governor is a relatively modern phenomenon and one which finds most of its slaves in the lower-middle, middle-middle, and upper-middle classes. It might not even be an important factor in learning, but it is an essential feature in the measurement of children's performance by testing and in the adjustment of children to the organizational demands of the school. The middle-class teacher organizes the day by allowing a certain amount of time for each activity. Psychologists have long noticed that American Indian children, mountain children, and children from other non-industrial groups have great difficulty organizing their response tempo to meet time limitations. In the Orientation Scale developed at the Institute, we have found that lower-class children in the first grade had significantly greater difficulty than did middle-class children in handling items related to time judgments.

Another area in which the lower-class child lacks pre-school orientation is the well-inculcated expectation of reward for performance, especially for successful task completion. The lack of such expectation, of course, reduces motivation for beginning a task and, therefore, also

makes less likely the self-reinforcement of activity through the gaining of feelings of competence. In these impoverished, broken homes there is very little of the type of interaction seen so commonly in middle-class homes, in which the parent sets a task for the child, observes its performance, and in some way rewards its completion. Neither, for most tasks, is there the disapproval which the middle-class child incurs when he does not perform properly or when he leaves something unfinished. Again, much of the organization of the classroom is based on the assumption that children anticipate rewards for performance and that they will respond in these terms to tasks which are set for them. This is not to imply that the young lower-class child is not given assignments in his home, nor that he is never given approval or punishment. Rather, the assignments tend to be motoric in character, have a short time-span, and are more likely to relate to very concrete objects or services for people. The tasks given to pre-school children in the middle-class are more likely to involve language and conceptual processes, and are thereby more attuned to the later school setting.

Related to the whole issue of the adult-child dynamic in establishing a basis for the later learning process is the ability of the child to use the adult as a source for information, correction and the reality testing involved in problem solving and the absorption of new knowledge. When free adult time is greatly limited, homes vastly overcrowded, economic stress chronic, and the general educational level very low— and, in addition, when adults in our media culture are aware of the inadequacy of their education—questions from children are not encouraged, as the adults might be embarrassed by their own limitations and anyway are too preoccupied with the business of just living and surviving. In the child's formulation of concepts of the world, the ability to formulate questions is an essential step in data gathering. If questions are not encouraged or if they are not responded to, this is a function which does not mature.

At the Institute, in our observations of children at the kindergarten level and in our discussions with parents, we find that many lower-class children have difficulty here. It follows that this problem, if it is not compensated for by special school efforts, becomes more serious later in the learning process, as more complex subject matter is introduced. It is here that questioning is not only desirable but essential, for if the child is not prepared to demand clarification he again falls farther behind, the process of alientation from school is facilitated, and his inattentiveness becomes further reinforced as he just does not understand what is being presented.

It is generally agreed that the language-symbolic process plays an important role at all levels of learning. It is included here under the "contentual" rubric because language development evolves through the correct labeling of the environment, and through the use of appropriate words for the relating and combining and recombining of the concrete and abstract components in describing, interpreting, and communicating perceptions, experiences, and ideational matter. One

can postulate on considerable evidence that language is one of the areas which is most sensitive to the impact of the multiplicity of problems associated with the stimulus deprivation found in the marginal circumstances of lower-class life. There are various dimensions of language, and for each of these it is possible to evaluate the influence of the verbal environment of the home and its immediate neighborhood.

In order for a child to handle multiple attributes of words and to associate words with their proper referents, a great deal of exposure to language is presupposed. Such exposure involves training, experimenting with identifying objects and having corrective feedback, listening to a variety of verbal material, and just observing adult language usage. Exposure of children to this type of experience is one of the great strengths of the middle-class home, and concomitantly represents a weakness in the lower-class home. In a middle-class home also, the availability of a great range of objects to be labeled and verbally related to each other strengthens the over-all language fluency of the child and gives him a basis for both understanding the teacher and for being able to communicate with her on various levels. An implicit hypothesis in a recent Institute survey of verbal skills is that verbal fluency is strongly related to reading skills and to other highly organized integrative and conceptual verbal activity.

The acquisition of language facility and fluency and experience with the multiple attributes of words is particularly important in view of the estimate that only 60 to 80 per cent of any sustained communication is usually heard. Knowledge of context and of the syntactical regularities of a language make correct completion and comprehension of the speech sequence possible. This completion occurs as a result of the correct anticipation of the sequence of language and thought. The child who has not achieved these anticipatory language skills is greatly handicapped in school. Thus for the child who already is deficient in auditory discrimination and in ability to sustain attention, it becomes increasingly important that he have the very skills he lacks most.

The problem in developing preventive and early remedial programs for these children is in determining the emphasis on the various areas that need remediation. For example, would it be more effective to place the greatest emphasis on the training of auditory discrimination, or on attentional mechanisms, or on anticipatory receptive language functions in order to achieve the primary goal of enabling the child to understand his teacher? In programming special remedial procedures, we do not know how much variation we will find from child to child, or if social-class experiences create a sufficiently homogeneous pattern of deficit so that the fact of any intervention and systematic training may be more important than its sequences. If this is so, the intervention would probably be most valid in the language area, because the large group of lower-class children with the kinds of deficits mentioned are probably maturationally ready for more complex language functioning than they have achieved. Language knowledge, once acquired, can be self-reinforcing in just communicating with peers or talking to oneself.

In observations of lower-class homes, it appears that speech sequences seem to be temporally very limited and poorly structured syntactically. It is thus not surprising to find that a major focus of deficit in the children's language development is syntactical organization and subject continuity. In preliminary analysis of expressive and receptive language data on samples of middle- and lower-class children at the first- and fifth-grade levels, there are indications that the lower-class child has more expressive language ability than is generally recognized or than emerges in the classroom. The main differences between the social classes seem to lie in the level of syntactical organization. If, as is indicated in this research, with proper stimulation a surprisingly high level of expressive language functioning is available to the same children who show syntactical deficits, then we might conclude that the language variables we are dealing with here are by-products of social experience rather than indices of basic ability or intellectual level. This again suggests another possibly vital area to be included in an enrichment or a remedial program: training in the use of word sequences to relate and unify cognitions.

Also on the basis of preliminary analysis of data, it appears that retarded readers have the most difficulty with the organization of expressive language.

In another type of social-class-related language analysis, Bernstein (1960), an English sociologist, has pointed out that the lower-class tends to use informal language and mainly to convey concrete needs and immediate consequences, while the middle-class usage tends to be more formal and to emphasize the relating of concepts. This difference between these two milieus, then, might explain the finding in some of our recent research that the middle-class fifth-grade child has an advantage over the lower-class fifth grader in tasks where precise and somewhat abstract language is required for solution. Further, Bernstein's reasoning would again emphasize the communication gap which exists between the middle-class teacher and the lower-class child.

Though it might belong more in the formal than in the contentual area, one can postulate that the absence of well-structured routine and activity in the home is reflected in the difficulty that the lower-class child has in structuring language. The implication of this for curriculum in the kindergarten and nursery school would be that these children should be offered a great deal of verbalized routine and regulation so that expectation can be built up in the child and then met.

According to Piaget's theories, later problem-solving and logical abilities are built on the earlier and orderly progression through a series of developmental stages involving the active interaction between the child and his environment. This is considered a maturational process, though highly related to experience and practice. Language development does not occupy a super-ordinate position. However, Whorf, Vygotsky, and some contemporary theorists have made language the essential ingredient in concept formation, problem-solving, and in the relating to an

interpretation of the environment. Current data at the Institute tend to indicate that class differences in perceptual abilities and in general environmental orientation decrease with chronological age, whereas language differences tend to increase. These might tentatively be interpreted to mean that perceptual development occurs first and that language growth and its importance in problem solving comes later. If later data and further analysis support this interpretation, then the implication would be that the lower-class child comes to school with major deficits in the perceptual rather than the language area. Perhaps the poverty of his experience has slowed his rate of maturation. Then by requiring, without the antecedent verbal preparation, a relatively high level of language skill, the school may contribute to an increase in the child's deficit in this area, relative to middle-class children. Meanwhile, his increased experience and normal maturational processes stimulate perceptual development, and that deficit is overcome. But the child is left with a language handicap. The remedy for such a situation would be emphasis on perceptual training for these children in the early school, or, better, pre-school, years, combined with a more gradual introduction of language training and requirements.

This theory and interpretation are somewhat, but by no means wholly, in conflict with the previous discussion of language. In an area where there is as yet much uncertainty, it is important to consider as many alternatives as possible, in order not to restrict experimentation.

In any event, whether or not we consider language skills as primary mediators in concept formation and problem solving, the lower-class child seems to be at a disadvantage at the point of entry into the formal learning process.

The other contentual factors that so often result in a poorly prepared child being brought to the school situation are closely interrelated with language. Briefly, they revolve around the child's understanding and knowledge of the physical, geographic, and geometric characteristics of the world around him, as well as information about his self-identity and some of the more macroscopic items of general information. It could be reasonably expected, for example, that a kindergarten or first-grade child who is not mentally defective would know both his first and last names, his address or the city he lives in, would have a rudimentary concept of number relationships, and would know something about the differences between near and far, high and low, and similar relational concepts. Much of what happens in school is predicated on the prior availability of this basic information. We know that educational procedures frequently proceed without establishing the actual existence of such a baseline. Again, in the lower-class child it cannot be taken for granted that the home experience has supplied this information or that it has tested the child for this knowledge. In facilitating the learning process in these children, the school must expect frequently to do a portion of the job traditionally assigned to the home, and curriculum must be reorganized to provide for estab-

lishing a good base. This type of basic information is essential so that the child can relate the input of new information to some stable core.

From all of the foregoing, it is obvious that the lower-class child when he enters school has as many problems in understanding what it is all about and why he is there as school personnel have in relating traditional curriculum and learning procedures to this child. Some reorientation is really necessary, as discussion of these problems almost always focuses on the problems the school has, rather than on the enormous confusion, hesitations, and frustrations the child experiences and does not have the language to articulate when he meets an essentially rigid set of academic expectations. Again, from all the foregoing, the child, from the time he enters school and is exposed to assumptions about him derived from experience with the middle-class child, has few success experiences and much failure and generalized frustration, and thus begins the alienating process in the direction of the apathetic and disgruntled fifth grader described earlier.

The frustration inherent in not understanding, not succeeding, and not being stimulated in the school—although being regulated by it, creates a basis for the further development of negative self-images and low evaluations of individual competencies. This would be especially true for the Negro child who, as we know from doll-play and other studies, starts reflecting the social bias in his own self-image at very early ages. No matter how the parents might aspire to a higher achievement level for their child, their lack of knowledge as to the operational implementation, combined with the child's early failure experiences in school, can so effectively attentuate confidence in his ability ever to handle competently challenge in the academic area, that the child loses all motivation.

It is important to state that not all the negative factors and deficits discussed here are present in every or even in any one child. Rather, there is a patterning of socially determined school-achievement-related disabilities which tends initially to set artificially low ceilings for these children: initially artificial, because as age increases it becomes more and more difficult for these children to develop compensatory mechanisms, to respond to special programs, or to make the psychological readjustments required to overcome the cumulative effects of their early deficits.

It is also important to state that there are strengths and positive features associated with lower-class life. Unfortunately, they generally tend not to be, at least immediately, congruent with the demands of the school. For example, lack of close supervision or protection fosters the growth of independence in lower-class children. However, this independence—and probably confidence—in regard to the handling of younger siblings, the crossing of streets, self-care, and creating of their own amusements, does not necessarily meaningfully transfer to the unfamiliar world of books, language, and abstract thought.

School Conditions

Educational factors have of course been interlaced throughout this discussion, but there are some special features that need separate delineation.

The lower-class child probably enters school with a nebulous and essentially neutral attitude. His home rarely, if ever, negatively predisposes him toward the school situation, though it might not offer positive motivation and correct interpretation of the school experience. It is in the school situation that the highly charged negative atitudes toward learning evolve, and the responsibility for such large groups of normal children showing great scholastic retardation, the high drop-out rate, and to some extent the delinquency problem, must rest with the failure of the school to promote the proper acculturation of these children. Though some of the responsibility may be shared by the larger society, the school, as the institution of that society, offers the only mechanism by which the job can be done.

It is unfair to imply that the school has all the appropriate methods at its disposal and has somehow chosen not to apply them. On the contrary, what is called for is flexible experimentation in the development of new methods, the clear delineation of the problem, and the training and retraining of administrative and teaching personnel in the educational philosophy and the learning procedures that this problem requires.

In addition, the school should assume responsibility for a systematic plan for the education of the child in the areas that have been delineated here by the time the child reaches kindergarten or first grade. This does not mean that the school will abrogate the family's role with regard to the child, but rather that the school will insure both the intellectual and the attitudinal receptivity of each child to its requirements. Part of a hypothesis now being tested in a new pre-school program is based on the assumption that early intervention by well-structured programs will significantly reduce the attenuating influence of the socially marginal environment.

What might be necessary to establish the required base to assure the eventual full participation of these children in the opportunity structure offered by the educational system is an ungraded sequence from age 3 or 4 through 8, with a low teacher-pupil ratio. Perhaps, also, the school system should make full use of anthropologists, sociologists, and social psychologists for description and interpretation of the cultural discontinuities which face the individual child when he enters school. In addition, the previously discussed patterning of deficits and strengths should be evaluated for each child and placed in a format which the teacher can use as a guide. In the early years this would enable diagnostic reviews of the intellectual functioning of each child, so that learning procedures, to whatever extent possible, could be appropriate to a par-

ticular child's needs. New evaluation techniques must be developed for this purpose, as the standardized procedures generally cannot produce accurate evaluation of the functioning level or achievement potential of these children.

Possibly most important would be the greater utilization by educators in both curriculum development and teacher training of the new and enormous knowledge, techniques, and researches in the social and behavioral sciences. Similarly, social and behavioral scientists have in the school a wonderful laboratory to study the interpenetration and interaction of fundamental social, cognitive, psychological, and developmental processes. Close and continuing collaboration, thus, should be mutually productive and satisfying, and is strongly indicated.

References

1. Bernstein, B., "Language and Social Class," *Brit. J. Psychol.*, 11:271–276, September 1960.

2. Hunt, J. McV., *Intelligence and experience*. New York: Ronald Press, 1961.

Are the Deprived Non-Verbal?

Frank Riessman

Early Environment and the Changeability of the I.Q.

Few people still maintain the old asumption that the I.Q. is necessarily stable or constant throughout life. There is too much evidence showing that it can be changed under varying conditions. But an allied view has been advanced that is related to the "constancy" assumption.

This argument holds that the underprivileged child has been immersed in an early "impoverished" environment in which there is insufficient stimulation, thus producing a *basic retardation,* so that, in effect, his I.Q. remains relatively low throughout life.[1]

One version of this argument maintains that the early environment of the deprived child produces behavior similar to that sometimes found in institutional children, and in children brought up in isolation from society. At its extreme, this view sees the behavior of deprived children as being similar to that found in the stimulus deprivation experiments, where volunteers are put in special respiratory tanks for twenty-four hours. (Following these experiments, the subjects are unable to concentrate, their I.Q. performance and problem-solving ability temporarily deteriorates, and they are in a general fog.) The stimulus deprivation thesis presumes that the underprivileged child has suffered some similar lack of stimulation over a long period of time, particularly in his early life, and that this accounts for his low I.Q. There are three levels at which this argument may be challenged:

Reprinted from *The Culturally Deprived Child,* New York: Harper and Row, 1962, pp. 57–58, 74–78. Copyright 1962 by Frank Riessman.

1. In the first place, the stimulus-depriving tank analogy seems extremely far-fetched because, whatever one may say about the environment of these children, it certainly is not lacking in stimulation per se. Witness the crowded homes and streets, the noise, parties, TV sets, the sports, games, fights, etc.

2. Moreover, the family life includes a good deal of sibling interaction, physical punishment, definite toilet training, masturbation inhibition, breast feeding, and various responsibility demands. Regardless of the particular evaluation one may wish to place on these practices, they do appear to provide stimulation. This environment seems quite distinct from that of children reared in isolation from society.

3. Haggard's findings further call into question the inference concerning "basic retardation," because if the I.Q. can be so markedly improved by only three hours of special training, surely the childhood experiences cannot have been so limiting or irreversible. It might also be added that much of the behavior of deprived children, in non-academic spheres, gives evidence of considerable spontaneity, a trait not ordinarily associated with a history of deficient stimulation.

The greatest block to the realization of the deprived individual's creative potential appears to be his verbal inadequacies. He seems to have enormous difficulty expressing himself verbally in many situations. For example, when interviewing underprivileged individuals one of the most characteristic comments encountered is "You know what I mean." It is liberally appended to all kinds of answers and occurs even when the respondent is at ease with the interviewer. This difficulty of expression also takes place in the school; consequently, there has arisen a rather firm belief that the deprived child is basically inarticulate.

While it would be easy enough to conclude that the underprivileged are essentially non-verbal, careful examination indicates that the problem is not nearly so simple. Because verbal ability is so important, it is necessary to try to specify the exact nature of the deprived individual's verbal functioning, rather than simply to assume that he is non-verbal or less verbal.

The Nature of the Verbal Deficit

Eells and Havighurst [3] point out that deprived children use a great many words with a fair amount of precision, but these are not the words used in the school. Success in school is based on facility with a middle-class vocabulary, not with the language of the underprivileged.

What then is the vocabulary pattern of the deprived? Basil Bernstein, the British sociologist, believes that deprived groups are at home with what he calls "public language," but are deficient in "formal language." Public, or informal, language is characterized by "short, gram-

matically simple, often unfinished sentences . . . simple and repetitive use of conjunctions (so, then, and, because); frequent use of short commands and questions, etc." [4]

Walter Murray reminds us that in everyday conversation deprived individuals demonstrate a language that is often rich in simile and analogy.[5] This is seen in their use of slang and in cursing. A large proportion of the new words that have become part of our language (*e.g., oomph*) are said to have had their origins among deprived groups. Some of the words come in via musicians, while others come in through the hipsters and the Beatniks who have been much influenced by the culture of the underprivileged. Newspapers like the *New York Daily News* also reflect some of this vivid abbreviated language. The communication of the deprived is famous for its use of imaginative nicknames and shortenings—the British "never-never" for installment buying, "telly" for TV, "pub" for bar or public place.

The inventive word power of the deprived is also shown in the language of the gang:

bop—to fight
bread—money
cool it—take it easy
dig—to understand
jazz—worthless talk
pad—room
rank—to insult
pecks—food
snake—spy
sound—talk

The Institute for Developmental Studies, under Martin Deutsch, is currently conducting a series of investigations of the language patterns of deprived children. Preliminary findings, while not conclusive, are suggestive:

In our own study, we have already encountered interesting surprises. We assumed that the lower-class child, when confronted with a word-association task, will respond in a somewhat stereotyped or rigid manner; instead we find that both first and fifth grade lower-class children give rich associations that sometimes lack logical continuity. Example: to the stimulus word "home," one of our subjects associated, "well, living with your mother and father, and taking care of it so the ceilings won't fall down, just like my house almost the whole ceiling is falling down. If you want a good home, you have to get all the furniture that belongs in the home." Thus, it is possible that the oft-stated conclusion on the verbal impoverishment of the child from the culturally deprived home is most striking when he is presented with highly structured tasks. and that verbal enrichment techniques, which take advantage of his freer flow of language in more unstructured situations, may help him to meet his language and scholastic potential.[6]

Deutsch's staff utilizes a novel technique to elicit the child's "spontaneous language," which in the case of the deprived child seems to be more developed than might be expected. The child is presented with a large toy clown; the clown's nose lights up when the child talks, and the child is free to choose his topic, or even to repeat himself; the clown's nose fails to light up when the child is silent, and the child is told this means "the clown is sad." Deprived children are much more verbally expressive in this situation.[7]

Other findings reported by the Institute are:

1. Deprived children appear to be poor in the use of verbs, but much better with descriptive adjectives.

2. Deprived children seem to understand more language than they speak (their "receptive" linguistic ability is much better than their "expressive" language).

3. Deprived children demonstrate a surprising ability for phantasy (as seen in the clown situation).

4. Deprived children express themselves best in spontaneous, unstructured situations.[8]

In role-playing sessions we have had occasion to observe that the verbal performance of deprived children is markedly improved in the discussion period following the session. When talking about some *action* they have *seen,* deprived children are apparently able to verbalize much more fully. Typically they *do not verbalize well in response to words alone.* They express themselves more readily when reacting to things they can see and do. Words as stimuli are not sufficient for them as a rule. Ask a juvenile delinquent who comes from a disadvantaged background what he doesn't like about school or the teacher and you will get an abbreviated, inarticulate reply. But have a group of these youngsters act out a school scene in which someone plays the teacher, and you will discover a stream of verbal consciousness that is almost impossible to shut off.

Words and Creativity

Irving Taylor, formerly Project Coordinator on the staff of the Institute for Developmental Studies, has some novel ideas about untapped creative potential in disadvantaged children. He believes that these children are not nearly so non-verbal as is generally thought. He says that they use words in a different way and are not as dependent on words for their sole form of communication, but that nevertheless they are imaginative at the verbal level.[9]

Taylor finds on word association tests that deprived children give responses that are often less conventional, more unusual, original, and independent. They seem to be more flexible and visual with language. For example, to the word "stone," deprived children are more willing to

give associations such as "solid" and "hard," responses that encompass the perceptual qualities of the object. They are also more likely to say "throw it in a lake," "chop things up with it." Non-deprived children restrict their associations more to standard synonyms like "rock," "pebbles." The deprived child includes these words also—he knows that they "belong" with "stone"—but his is freer in including other words.[10]

Taylor feels that deprived individuals are not as restricted by verbal forms of communication, but tend to permit language to interact more with non-verbal means of communication, such as gestures and pictures. This interaction with other kinds of communication gives them them the potential for "breaking through the language barrier"; they are not forced to think in terms of the structure of language as are so many people. *They are less word-bound.*

Taylor believes that their wide range of associations indicates a freer use of language, which may be an important attribute of one type of creativity. He contends that not only do studies of creative people indicate that they have greater "semantic flexibility," but also that they respond well to visual, tactile, and kinesthetic cues. In general, their non-aural senses seem to be especially acute. Taylor notes that this pattern resembles the mental approach of the underprivileged child in many respects.

Finally, Taylor points out that when the creative potential of deprived children remains educationally untapped, there is a much greater possibility of its finding outlets in delinquency and destructive behavior.[11]

Notes

1. Ralph W. Tyler, "Can Intelligence Tests Be used to Predict Educability," in Kenneth Eells, *et al.*, *Intelligence and Cultural Differences,* (Chicago: University of Chicago Press, 1951), p. 43.

2. Donald Hebb, a leading psychologist, makes the assumption that the early childhood period is of decisive importance in determining later intelligence. He believes that Negro and poor white children have had insufficient stimulation in their early development, and that this accounts for their lower *functioning* intelligence at a later age. He accepts the intelligence test performance as an accurate indicator of operating intelligence although he believes it to be a completely inaccurate index of *capacity*—inherent intelligence. See Donald O. Hebb, *Organization of Behavior,* (New York: John Wiley & Sons, 1949), Chapter II.

3. Kenneth Eells *et al.*, *Intelligence and Cultural Differences* (Chicago: University of Chicago Press, 1951), p. 43.

4. By contrast, some characteristics of formal language are: "Accurate order and syntax regulate what is said; and logical modifications and stress are mediated through a gramatically complex sentence construction, especially through the use of a range of conjunctions and relative clauses. Frequent use of prepositions which indicate logical relationships as well as prepositions which indicate temporal and spatial contiguity; frequent use of impersonal pronouns, 'it,' 'one,' etc." See Basil Bernstein, "A Public Language," *British Journal of Sociology,* December, 1959, pp. 311–323.

5. Personal communication from Walter Murray.

6. Mimeographed report from the Institute for Developmental Studies, Department of Psychiatry, New York Medical College.

7. *Ibid.*

8. *Ibid.*

9. Personal communication from Irving Taylor.

10. Taylor recognizes the possibility that the wide range of associations of

deprived children may simply reflect a laxity or looseness with language; in other words, they may have many different associations because they do not know the meaning of words. He tested this alternative interpretation with a carefully constructed, Thurstone-type, ordinal word-distance scale, in which the children are asked to select from a large list the words which "go with" the original stimulus word and the words which do not belong with it. Preliminary results appear to support the thesis that deprived children do know the meanings of the words, but have a wider range of associations. They do not include words at random that are inappropriate.

11. Personal communication from Irving Taylor.

Social Class, Speech Systems, and Psycho-therapy [1]

Basil Bernstein

Today various forms of psycho-therapy are being extended to include a greater number of individuals from different social backgrounds. Training programmes for probation officers, social workers, psychologists, and members of the prison and borstal services are gradually being extended at different rates to include an understanding of psycho-dynamic processes and a therapy oriented relationship. I shall start from an assertion that sensitivity to the psycho-therapeutic relationship and the form of communication considered to be appropriate is less available to members of the lower working-class, not by virtue of innate deficiencies in intelligence but because of a culturally induced speech system whose dimensions of relevance and significance do not orient the lower working-class patient in the therapy relationship. Conversely the speech system of the therapist creates for him sets of expectations which are not met by the lower working-class patient. By lower working-class I refer to individuals who are employed in lower manual occupations, approximately 30 per cent of the labour force.

Let us start by examining some general aspects of the psycho-therapy relation with which I shall be concerned.

1) It is a form of social relationship which exterts a tension on the patient to structure and re-structure his discrete experience in a verbally significant form. In terms of the patient's other relationships the therapy relationship attempts to elicit from the patient a unique order of communication.

Reprinted from *British Journal of Sociology*, March, 1964.
Paper delivered to the British Association for the Advancement of Science, Aberdeen, September 1963.

2) The referent for this communication is the patient—or rather his motivational processes and the implicit or explicit social relationships which they engender. The "I" of the patient is undergoing a continuous transformation by virtue of those unique communications.

3) The form of authority within the therapy relationship is unclear and ambiguous. The patient often is given no clear understanding of what is or is not expected of him. The shape of the social relationship is not defined in any detail. Differences in social status which serve as orientation for behaviour outside of the therapy relationship do not serve to indicate appropriate behaviour with it.

4) In as much as the patient's communications are filtered through the purposes, goals, beliefs, and emotional imperatives of the patient's natural group then the patient's appropriate perception of himself is often considered to be hindered. The conventions which confer upon the patient his social identity are viewed from the point of view of the therapist as material to be worked through. Put more simply the form of the therapy relationship involves the patient in a position of suspended isolation; he stands in relation to his group rather like a figure differentiated from his ground.

5) Finally, successful therapy is based upon "mutual belief on the part of both therapist and patient that the illness may be removed by participation in a social relationship where the major activity is the transformation of discrete experience through the medium of communication essentially through speech."

Summarising these points we get something like this.

The therapy relationship is based upon the belief that the conditions which brought the patient into the relationship may be ameliorated by communication in a context where the normal status relationships serve as no guide for behaviour in a context which involves a suspension of the patient's social identity and where the referent for the communication is the discrete experience of the patient.

This is a somewhat unusual social relationship involving some strange requirements. It will be argued that members of the lower working-class who are limited to a particular speech system are likely to find these requirements difficult to meet. Such individuals are likely to benefit less from therapy, to break off treatment early, whilst the therapist will tend to find the relationship unrewarding. He will require a sensitivity towards his patient of a different order than that necessary for a middle-class patient. From the therapist's point of view the lower working-class patient's communication will seem to be inadequate, there will be a low level of insight, the patient may seem to be negative and passive, so forcing the therapist into taking a more dominant role than he would wish, above all the therapist will meet an unwillingness on the part of the patient to transform his personal feelings into unique verbal mean-

ings. The lower working-class patient will have difficulty in verbalizing his personal experience and in receiving communications which refer to the sources of his motivations. I shall argue that these difficulties do not necessarily stem from low intelligence but originate in the speech system the child learns in his culture and that this speech system creates for the developing child dimensions of relevance and learning wholly appropriate for his natural environment but inappropriate for orientating the individual in special relationships like therapy.

Research indicates that the verbal I.Q. scores of members of the lower working-class are likely to be severely depressed in relation to scores at the higher ranges of non-verbal tests. Furthermore, research based upon small groups of middle- and working-class subjects matched for average verbal I. Q. and non-verbal I.Q. indicates that the working-class groups use a markedly different speech system than the matched middle-class groups. The working-class groups' speech is characterized by a reduction in qualifiers, adjectives, adverbs, particularly those which qualify feelings, the organisation of the speech is comparatively simple, there is a restriction on the use of the self-referent pronoun "I" and an increase in personal pronouns. The written work of matched groups of middle- and working-class boys indicates a similar pattern of differences and also that the working-class prefer much more concrete than abstract propositions. As these limited studies were of small groups matched for I.Q. the sources of the differences in the speech and the relations to which the speech creates access must lie in differences between the cultures.

These differences found in the speech I shall take as indices of a particular form of communication; they are not in any sense accidental but are contingent upon a form of social relationship, or more generally, a social structure. These differences I shall argue indicate the use of a linguistic code. It is a code which does not facilitate the verbal elaboration of meaning; it is a code which does not help the user put into words his intent, his unique purposes, beliefs, and motivations. It also does not help him to receive such communications from others. It is a code which sensitises the user to a particular form of social relationship which is unambiguous, where the authority is clear cut and serves as a guide to action. It is a code which helps to sustain solidarity with the group at the cost of the verbal signalling of the unique difference of its members. It is a code which facilitates the ready transformation of feeling into action. It is a code where changes in meaning are more likely to be signalled non-verbally than through changes in verbal selections.

From this perspective the psycho-therapy relationship involves, for a member of the lower working-class, a radical change in his normal coding process. What requires to be made relevant for this relationship is almost the antithesis of what *is* made relevant by the coding process the individual normally uses in his cultural environment. How does this way of translating experience come about? What in the culture is responsible for the speech system? To begin with there is nothing unusual

or unique about the speech system. It is not helpful to consider it a form of sub-standard English. It is not a speech system induced by innate intelligence.

Different social structures will generate different speech systems. These speech systems or codes entail for the individual specific principles of choice which regulate the selections he makes from language at both the syntactic and lexical level. What the individual actually says, from a developmental perspective transforms him in the act of saying.

As the child learns his speech or in our terms learns specific codes which regulate his verbal acts he learns the requirements of his social structure. From this point of view every time the child speaks, the social structure of which he is a part is reinforced in him, and his social identity develops and is constrained. The social structure becomes for the developing child his psychological reality by the shaping of his acts of speech. If this is the case, then the processes which orient the child to his world and the kind of relationships he imposes are triggered off initially and systematically reinforced by the implications of the speech system. Underlying the general pattern of the child's speech are critical sets of choices, in-built preferences for some alternatives rather than others, planning processes which develop and are stabilised through time—coding principles through which orientation is given to social, intellectual and emotional referents. Children who have access to different speech systems, and so to the coding principles which sustain them, by virtue, and only by virtue of their arbitrary position in the class structure, may take quite different lines of development, may adopt quite different intellectual and social procedures which are only tenuously related to their purely psychological abilities.

I shall start by asking the following questions: What kinds of social relationships generate what kinds of speech systems? What kinds of principles or planning procedures control the speech systems? What kinds of relationships in the environment do these planning procedures, or rather the linguistic options which are taken up, both give access to and stabilise?

I shall confine my attention to one speech system or code. I am going to define this speech system in terms of the ease with which it is possible to predict the syntactic alternatives which are taken up to organise meaning. If it is fairly easy to predict the syntactic alternatives used to organise meaning across a range of speech I shall call this system a restricted code. It is possible to predict these syntactic alternatives because the range of alternatives used in this code are relatively few. The speech is comparatively simple in structure. We can go a little further and say that in the case of a restricted code the vocabularly will be drawn from a narrow range. Although the code has been defined in terms of syntax we can go on to suggest certain psychological correlates of this code. If a speaker is moving towards a restricted code then the code, that is the linguistic options he is taking up, will not facilitate the speaker in his attempt to put into words his purposes, his intent, his

unique experience in a verbally explicit form. Further, the events in the environment which are given significance create a particular order of learning.

Let us start off by asking what is responsible for the simplification of the structure of the speech in this code, what is responsible for the narrow range of vocabularly choices, what is responsible on a psychological level for the constraints on the verbal signalling of the unique experience of the speaker? If we know this we shall begin to have an idea of the social learning which this code gives access to and stabilises. I shall suggest that both the simplification in the structure and the constraint upon the verbal signalling of intent have their origin in the form of the social relationship constraining the speakers.

In the case of a restricted code the speech is played out against a back-cloth of assumptions common to the speakers, against a set of shared interests and identifications, in short against a cultural identity which reduces the need for the speakers to elaborate verbally their intent and make it explicit. If you know somebody very, very well, an enormous amount may be taken for granted; you do not have to put into words all that you feel because the feelings are common. But knowing somebody very well is a particular kind of social relationship; knowing somebody very well indicates common interests, identifications, expectations, although this need not necessarily mean common agreements. Concretely a restricted code is not necessarily class linked but will arise in closed communities like a prison, combat units in the armed services, but also between close friends, in the peer group of children and adolescents. In fact, wherever the form of the social relationship is based upon some extensive set of closely shared identifications self-consciously held by the members.

In these social relations which generate a restricted code the speech will tend to be fast, fluent, with reduced articulatory clues, the meanings are likely to be condensed, dislocated and local to the relationships. There will be a low level of vocabulary and syntactic selection. The how rather than the what of the communication becomes relevant. Finally, and of critical importance, the unique meaning of the person will tend to be implicit and not verbally elaborated.

In fact the sequences will have the same *general* forms as this.

Examples

It's all according like well those youths and that if they get with gangs
    and that they most
they most
have a bit of a lark around and
say it goes wrong
and that and they probably knock some off I think they do it just to be a
    bit big you know
getting publicity here and there

                        V.I.Q. average (lower working-class).
                        Transcript of a tape-recorded discussion.

The point I want to make is that a restricted code is available to all members of society as the social conditions which generate it are universal. But it may be that a considerable section of our society, in particular members of the lower working-class who work in unskilled or semi-skilled occupations, 30 per cent of the labour force, are limited to this code and have no other. We have a special case, a case where children or adults can use only one speech system. What this code makes relevant to them, the learning generated by the apparently spontaneous acts of speech may not be appropriate for the demands of the psycho-therapeutic relationship.

I would like to look more closely at some of the psychological and sociological implications of this code with psycho-therapy in mind.

When a child learns a restricted code he learns to perceive language in a particular way. Language is not perceived as a set of theoretical possibilities which can be transformed into a facility for the communication of unique experience. Speech is not important media for communicating relatively explicitly the experience of separateness and difference. Speech is not a primary means for a voyage from one self to the other. In as much as this is so then areas of the self are not likely to be differentiated by speech and so become the object of special perceptual activity. It is also likely that the motivations of others will not serve as starting points for enquiry and verbal elaboration. Of some importance the identity of the individual will be refracted to him by the concrete symbols of his group rather than creating a problem to be solved by his own unique investigations. In a sense a person limited to a restricted code has a problem of identity because this problem is irrelevant.

I would like to consider next a family where only a restricted code is used. Here the "I" of the mother, her uniqueness, the way she communicates separateness and difference is likely to be conveyed non-verbally rather than through controlled verbal discriminations. If this is so then much of the wareness of the developing child of his mother is less available for verbalisation because it has rarely been verbalised. A powerful bond of a non-verbal form is forged. The motivations, the intents of mother and child are less available to each because these are not objects of verbal inquiry.

A critical aspect of the family is the means of expression of authority particularly the type of verbal inter-action, authority relationships create. I shall argue that associated with parents limited to a restricted code is a specific form of authority relations.

Authority can be expressed so as to limit the chances of verbal interaction within the relationship, or authority can be expressed so as to increase verbal inter-action. The area of discretion available to the child may be reduced to an uncompromising acceptance, withdrawal, or rebellion within the authority relationship, or the social context of control may permit a number of responses on the part of the child. Authority may be expressed through commands and threats or it may rest on

appeals. These appeals used by authority may be of two basic kinds: person-oriented or status-oriented. If the appeals are status-oriented then the behaviour of the child is referred to some general or local rule which constrains conduct "shouldn't you clean your teeth," "you don't behave yourself like that on a bus," "children in grammar schools are expected to behave rather differently." [1] Status appeals may also relate the child's behaviour to the rules which regulate his conduct with reference to age, sex or age relationships. e.g. "Little boys don't play with dolls," "you should be able to stop doing that by now," "you don't talk to your father, teacher, social worker, etc., like that." These are important implications of status appeals. If they are not obeyed the relationship can quickly change to reveal naked power and may become punitive. Status appeals are impersonal. They rely for their effectiveness upon the status of the regulator. The effect of these appeals is to transmit the culture or local culture in such a way as to increase the similarity of the regulated with others of his group. If the child rebels he is challenging very quickly the culture of which he is a part and it is this which tends to force the regulator into taking punitive action. Finally the social context of control is such that the relationship is unambiguous—the relative statuses are clear-cut.

The person-oriented appeals are very different. In these appeals the conduct of the child is related to the feelings of the regulator (parent) or the significance of the act, its meaning is related explicitly to the regulated, to the child, e.g. "Daddy will be pleased, hurt, disappointed, angry, ecstatic if you go on doing this." "If you go on doing this you will be miserable when the cat has a nasty pain."

In the case of person-oriented appeals the conduct of the child is referred to the *feelings* of the regulator, in the second case the significance of the act, its meaning, is related directly to the child. There are important consequences of the *person-oriented* appeals. Control is effected through either the verbal manipulation of feelings or through the establishing of reasons which link the child to his acts. In this way the child has access to the regulator as a person and he has access to the significance of his own acts as they relate to him as consequences. The person-oriented appeals tend to work through the verbalising of intent, whereas the status-oriented appeals, especially if they move quickly to power, are concerned with consequences of actions and not with intent. The status-oriented appeals rely for their effectiveness upon differences in status whereas the person-oriented appeals rely more upon the manipulation of thought and feeling. The person-oriented appeals elicit guilt in the child in terms of the effects of his actions upon persons and things. The child learns to adapt to the tensions involved in relating to persons and things mainly by being able to tolerate guilt and through having a more conscious awareness, through language, of the consequences of his actions. Where the child is subject to status-oriented appeals which change swiftly to a power relationship then a whole order of relationships are not learned. I suggest that where the sole speech

system of the parents is a restricted code, then power and status-oriented appeals will be used more. The child will become sensitive to a particular kind of control and the learning involved and may well be bewildered in a context of control where person-oriented means are used.

I should like to consider some areas of affective difficulty which may be elicited, maintained, and strengthened by a role relationship where both members are limited to a restricted code. It has been argued that extra-verbal channels will carry messages bearing the mutual intents of mother and child. Inter-personal aspects of this relationship in which each will uniquely qualify each other's experience will tend *not* to be raised to the level of verbal elaboration and be made explicit. The areas of discrete intent will not be areas of elaborated speech. This does not mean that these areas have no significance, only that whatever significance they may have is less available for linguistic regulation. Tensions arising in these areas are more likely to be denied as the means of dealing with them consciously are less available.

Further, if it is the case that authority relationships within the family tend to be status and power relations rather than person-oriented relations then the focus of the discipline of relation will be upon the consequences of the act rather than upon the intent of the child. Thus it could be argued that where the focus is upon *consequence* the relationship moves towards one of an inter-status type whereas if the focus is upon intent the relationship moves towards one of an inter-personal type. What is made available for learning, what is made relevant in person or status-oriented relations is radically different. The linguistic codes which transmit these relationships, behaviourally, are also different. The *speech* in a status or power-oriented relation is such that what is taken over by the child is the status aspect of the relation *not* the personal aspect of the relation. Again it should be noted that this reinforces the primacy of the extra-verbal channels for the perception or decoding of discrete intent. It is necessary to repeat that the perception of discrete intent occurs but the orientation of the perception is towards the extra-verbal channels.

Lack of clarity or ambiguity in the inter-status relation is likely to raise the level of tension for an individual limited to a restricted code and these tensions are less subject to verbal control. It is then much more likely that these tensions will be dissipated quickly through some immediate channel; changes in muscular tension, somato-motor set, or expressive behaviour. Further the individual may try to neutralise his affective involvement in a situation of inter-personal strain by denial or attributing the responsibility for the strain to an encumbent of another status. There is a probability that although the individual will hold notions of wrongness and justice, feelings of guilt and personal involvement may be dissociated from the notions of wrongness. On the other hand the level of unconscious guilt may well be high.

Psychopathology will tend to be shaped in terms of high guilt thresholds, low anxiety thresholds, and an inability to tolerate anxiety. In

situations which elicit perceptions of ambiguity or ambivalency the individual may be unable to tolerate the resultant tension involved in loss of structure. He will tend to move towards a well articulated social structure where hierarchy, age, age relations, and sex will provide clear unambiguous prescriptions for appropriate behaviour as a means of controlling stress.

Thus a special group of defence mechanisms of an unconscious order are likely to be associated with this code which help to maintain its stability. The defences are likely to include denial, disassociation, and displacement rather than more elaborate defences which rely upon verbal procedures like rationalisation. These defences may help to shape the type of psychopathology.

The is one further point of a more sociological nature which needs to be made. Different modes of speech issue from different role relations. Individuals may be unable to produce appropriate speech modes because they are unable to dead with the role relation necessary for the appropriate communication. If a person is using an elaborated code, that is, where the person's intent is raised to the level of verbal explicitness, where his "I" is mediated by extensive verbal discriminations, a range of discretion must inhere in his role if such speech is to be produced at all. Further, the person's social history must have included practice and training for the role which social relations require. Role here refers to the particular relations necessary for the production of a restricted or elaborated code. In the case of an elaborated code the role relations receive less support from implicit identifications shared by the participators. The orientation of the individual will be based upon the expectation of psychological difference, his own and others. Individuated speech pre-supposes a history of a particular role relation if it is to be prepared and delivered appropriately. Inasmuch as difference is part of the expectation there is less reliance or dependency on the listener; or rather this dependency on the listener is reduced by the verbal explication of meaning. The dependency underpinning the use of a restricted code is upon the closely shared, extensive range of identifications which serve as a back-cloth to the speech and define the role relation. The dependency underpinning the use of an elaborated code is upon the verbal explication of meaning. The sources of role strain which inhere in these codes and so in the social relations which generate them are different. Simply, to produce an elaborated code, the person must be able to cope with the measure of social isolation which inheres in the role relations which these communications generate. This kind of isolation does not inhere in role relations which generate a restricted code. In terms of what is *said verbally* a restricted code is a *status* oriented code, whilst an elaborated code is a *person* oriented code.

I shall now try and pull together these various implications of a restricted code. The code is generated in social relationship where the intent of others may be taken for granted. This sharing or expectation of common intent simplifies the structure of the speech and so makes it

predictable. It removes the need in the speakers to elaborate verbally their unique experience. Hence the reduction of qualifiers of various kinds. The speech is relatively impersonal and serves to transmit similarity rather than differences in personal experience. The code functions to permit the signalling of social rather than personal identity. The latter tends to be signalled through non-verbal and expressive means rather than through elaborate varying of verbal selections. The code tends to make relevant the concrete here and now action situation rather than point to reflective, abstract relationships.[2] It does not facilitate a sustained interest in processes, particularly motivational processes. The self is rarely the subject of verbal investigation. Speech is not used as a means for a voyage from oneself to the other person. Behaviour is controlled in a social context in which status is unambiguous and in which the intent of the regulated and regulator is rarely verbally explored and so feelings of guilt and personal involvement in misdemeanours may be reduced. The code strengthens solidarity with the group by restricting the verbal signalling of personal difference. This does not mean that no differences will be signalled but that they will rarely be systematically explored. A strong sense of social identity is induced probably at the cost of a sense of personal identity.

Finally the code is not generated by I.Q. but by the culture acting through the family relationships.

From this point of view the psycho-therapy relationship involves, for an individual limited to a restricted code, a relationship where the signals are antithetic to his own way of making relationships. For the status relationships are ambiguous, give no indication for here and now behaviour. It is a person-oriented relationship which increases the tension upon the individual to structure and re-structure his experience in a verbally unique way. For the patient it involves a loss of social identity which his very code promotes and exposes the patient to the reflections on his personal identity in a social relationship which from the patient's point of view is unsupporting. A lack of insight into the sources of motivation combined with the dependency of the patient will tend to force the therapist into taking, from his point of view, too active or dominant a role in the relationship. The restricted code patient's main defence against the tensions induced by the therapy relationship is a great passivity and dependency. The therapist has to deal with feeling in himself that this kind of relationship invokes. Thus, the therapy relationship involves for the restricted code patient a situation of change of code and with this, a major change in the means whereby the patient orients to his natural world.[3] It is thought that if the therapy is successful there will be a change in the patient's code.

I am not suggesting that therapy with patients limited to a restricted code cannot be rewarding and beneficial. The absence of so-called appropriate communication is pregnant with meaning and significance for the therapist if he has a more sensitive understanding of the predicament of the patient and a willingness to adapt his technique.

Notes

1. Intonation can, of course, give these statements the character of commands; however, they do permit further interaction of a kind that serves to clarify the norms which inhere in the specific status of the regulated. On the other hand, the regulator may shift the basis of the appeal to that of person-oriented or fall back on power.

2. It is important to qualify at this point. Often powerful *descriptions* of feelings are offered, e.g., "The smoke from the factories makes me lonesome," "It hurts like my head's coming off my neck," "It's like broken glass inside me." Difficulty often occurs when one moves away from metaphor and simile.

3. A point may well be reached where therapist and patient face each other in an unproductive silence. The therapist not knowing how to elicit responses from the patient and the patient not knowing how to give them.

Bibliography—

Bernstein, B. (1958) "Some Sociological Determinants of Perception," *British Journal of Sociology*, IX, p. 159.

———. (1960) "Language and Social Class," *British Journal of Sociology*, XI, p. 271.

———. (1961) "Social Class and Linguistic Development" in *Education, Economy, and Society*, eds. Halsey, A. H., Floud, J. and Anderson, C. A., Free Press, N.Y., p. 288.

———. (1962) "Linguistic Codes, Hesitation Phenomena, and Intelligence," *Language and Speech*, 5, p. 31.

———. (1962) "Social Class, Linguistic Codes, and Grammatical Elements," *Language and Speech*, 5, p. 221.

Fifteen to Eighteen. (1959) *Report of the Central Advisory Council for Education*, Vol. I, Ministry of Education, London, H.M.S.O., specifically p. 376 on the relationships between verbal and nonverbal intelligence tests.

Hollingshead, A. B., and Redlich, F. C. (1958) *Social Class and Mental Illness*, John Wiley & Sons, N.Y.

Koln, M. L. (1959) "Social Class and Parental Authority," *American Sociological Review*, 24, 352–366.

———. (1959) "Social Class and Parental Values," *American Journal of Sociology*, 64, 337–351.

Lawton, D. (1963) "Social Class Differences in Language Development," *Language and Speech*, Oct.–Dec. 1963.

Miller, D. R., and Swanson, G. E. (1959) *Inner Conflict and Defense*, Henry Holt & Co., N.Y.

Riessman, F. (1962) *The Culturally Deprived Child*, Harper & Row, N.Y.

———. (1963) "New Models for a Treatment Approach to Low Income Clients," Paper presented to American Orthopsychiatric Association Convention, March 1963.

The Power of the Poor

Warren C. Haggstrom

On the average, the poor in the United States have bad reputations. They are regarded as responsible for much physical aggression and destruction of property; their support is alleged to be a heavy burden on the rest of the community; and they are said not even to try very hard to meet community standards of behavior or to be self-supporting. Poverty, it is said, is little enough punishment for people so inferior and so lacking in virtue.

Roughly speaking, these common opinions about the poor have some accuracy. Socially notorious varieties of deviancy and dependency do flourish in areas of poverty to a greater extent than in the remainder of our society. The middle classes, of course, have their own faults, which are sometimes perceptively observed and described by the poor. The relatively prosperous tend to use their verbal facility to conceal aspects of social reality from themselves and tend to use word-magic to make themselves comfortable about being in their generally undeserved positions of affluence, positions in which they manage to obtain the most pay and security for doing easy and interesting kinds of work.

Since the United States is a middle class society, those who emphasize the bad reputations of the poor are regarded as hard-headed realists, while those who stress the phoniness of the middle classes are considered rather extreme and overly suspicious. When a social worker reports that the lower classes tend in the direction of schizophrenia and character disorders, he is viewed as having made a sober report of the existing state of affairs. Or when a social scientist discovers that the poor are unsocialized, childlike, occupy an early category in *his* category

Revised version of a paper prepared for presentation at the 71st Annual Convention of the American Psychological Association in Philadelphia, Pennsylvania, August 29–September 4, 1963.

system of degrees of socialization, his discovery is treated as an important basis for further scientific work. But suppose that a leader of the poor announces that social workers tend to be "phonies" and "half-queer" as well, or suggests in his own language that social scientists are usually fuzzy-minded and socially irrelevant. This invidious description is not seen as a suitable hypothesis for investigation and research; it is rather said (without benefit of evidence) to be a symptom of the ignorance or of the personal or political needs of the person making the statement.

We cannot, of course, simply shed the presuppositions which attach to our social positions, and those of us who see the poor from above are likely not to have viewed them from the most flattering perspective. But let us, in the following discussion, attempt to be critical and scientific by orienting ourselves to reasons and evidence rather than to common sense conceptual refinements of our current prejudices. We will first analyze a popular contemporary account of the psychology of poverty, and then advance a different orientation as a more precise explanation for available data.

Psychological Characteristics of the Poor

Social scientists have arrived at a rough consensus about the modal personality in neighborhoods of poverty:

(1) The poor tend to have a keen sense of the personal and the concrete; their interest typically is restricted to the self, the family, and the neighborhood. There is a particular stress on the intimate, the sensory, the detailed, the personal. Not struggling to escape their circumstances, the poor often regard their ordinary lives as being of much intrinsic interest. This is related to their primary concern with the problem of survival rather than with the problem of moving up in society, and to the value which they attach to skills needed in coping with deprivation and uncertainty as distinguished from skills required to make progress. It has frequently been reported that persons in areas of poverty appear to be apathetic, to have little motivation, to be unable to cooperate with each other in the solution of problems which they regard as important, and to lack occupational and verbal skills and leadership traits; and are characterized by parochialism, nostalgic romanticism, and prescientific conceptions of the natural and social orders. Instead of having love for one another as fellow human beings, they achieve positive mutual attitudes through seeing themselves as all in the same boat together.

(2) Caught in the present, the poor do not plan very much. They meet their troubles and take their pleasures on a moment-to-moment basis; their schemes are short-term. Their time perspective is foreshortened by their belief that it is futile to think of the future. Thus, when the poor use conventional words to refer to the future, those words tend

to be empty of real meaning. They have little sense of the past and they go forward, but not forward to any preconceived place. Their pleasures and rewards are sought in the present; they find it difficult to delay gratification, to postpone satisfaction.

(3) There is much egoism, envy, and hostility toward those who prosper. There is a feeling of being exploited. There are many negative attitudes and few positive ones. The unity of the poor comes about through suspicion of and resentment toward outsiders, through opposition to common enemies and hostility to powerful groups. Disillusion about the possibility of advancement stems from a victim complex in relation to the powerful. There is a sense of inability to affect what will happen, a lack of conviction that it is within their power to affect their circumstances. The outside world cannot be trusted; it must be defended against. Outsiders and the outside are seen as risky, likely to injure you when you least expect it. Pessimism and fatalism about being able to affect one's own situation stems from a feeling of being victimized by superordinate, capricious, and malevolent natural and social forces. Their lives appear to them to be fixed by the immutable forces of fate, luck, and chance. While well-to-do people tend to attribute causality to inner forces, the poor tend to make external attributes of causality, seeing themselves as subject to external and arbitrary forces and pressures.[1]

The Social Problem of Poverty and Its Natural Solution

The poor, in short, are commonly seen as apathetic, child-like, not very competent, and hostile-dependent. Other research, emphasized in the past few years, has pointed out the extent to which the poor tend to occupy specific social categories (minority racial and ethnic groups, the elderly, ADC families, and the like), as well as the continuing large proportion of the population who have low incomes even in such an affluent society as the United States. It has been natural to get concerned about a large proportion of the population, the members of which have behavior patterns and psychological characteristics that tend to place them in opposition to or dependence on the remainder of the community.

Poverty has therefore again become a publicly recognized social problem in the United States. The general perception of a social problem leads to a search for its solution. Since a lack of money is the most universal characteristic of poverty, and since a general increase of income for some social groups would automatically abolish poverty, it seems clear to many persons that certain known steps are suitable to end poverty in the United States. Their view is that public policies should be developed and implemented that emphasize provision of jobs, increased access to education that leads to jobs, and higher minimum wage levels and welfare payments. Scientists, according to this view,

can contribute by learning how to measure poverty with greater accuracy and by studying its adverse psychological and other consequences, and they should seek to understand how these consequences might be controlled.

In this natural line of reasoning it is assumed rather than demonstrated that the major problem of the poor is poverty, a lack of money. But this assumption is essential to the associated recommendations for scientific work and social policy. It may be well, therefore, to inquire in a more searching fashion whether the problems of the poor primarily result from a lack of money.

There are a number of phenomena which one could hardly anticipate on the basis of such an assumption:

(1) A given level of real income has various consequences depending upon the circumstances in which a person receives the income.

Among the poor, there are many subgroups, the members of which do not display the presumed psychological consequences of poverty. These include most of that portion of the leadership of the poor which is itself poor, those low income families with high educational aspirations for their children, low income members of religious groups such as the Hutterites, university student families with little income, and the like. In the past, of course, members of the lower middle class have survived on real incomes below those received today by comparable public welfare families—and without losing their capacity to struggle in the pursuit of distant ends. Many from the intelligentsia today in such countries as India and Japan have incomes that, in the United States, would place them with the poor. They may differ from educated Americans in personality characteristics, but they do not have the alleged psychology of poverty either.

(2) Increases in income often do not lead to a diminution of the expected psychological consequences of poverty.

For example, the rise in real per capita public welfare expenditures in the United States have not had a demonstrated effect on the psychological functioning of welfare recipients.

(3) Differences in income between otherwise comparable groups of poor do not appear to be accompanied by differences in psychological functioning.

For example, states vary greatly in the size of their payments to comparable welfare recipient families. Comparable families appear to resemble one another in psychological orientation regardless of relatively major differences in their incomes.

(4) When income remains constant, but persons in a neighborhood of poverty become involved in successful social action on important issues, in their own behalf, their psychological orientation does extend over a greater period of time, their feeling of helplessness does lessen, their skills and activities do gradually change.

For example, no one could have predicted on the basis of articles in the relevant scholarly journals that lowly Negroes from areas of poverty would, with some help, begin to organize with such effect that they

would carry timid and ultra-conventional members of the Negro middle classes along with them into a militant struggle for freedom. It has also been reported that many "lower class" Negroes who have become part of the Muslim movement have had their lives transformed in the direction of greater order and achievement.

During this past summer I gathered some data concerning The Woodlawn Organization (TWO), a primarily "lower class," predominantly Negro organization which was initiated about two years ago in Chicago with the assistance of Saul Alinsky and the Industrial Areas Foundation. The poor constitute the bulk of active members, and are an important segment of the leadership of this community organization, which has already demonstrated its effectiveness and power. For example, TWO has delivered a majority of the votes from a Negro area to elect a white alderman who takes a strong civil rights position; the unsuccessful opponent was a Negro from the regular political organization. It has been able to secure its own conditions for implementation of an urban renewal development proposed by the University of Chicago for part of the Woodlawn area. TWO has carried out rent strikes and has taken other successful actions against owners of dilapidated slum buildings; it has organized picketing of stores that sell merchandise to people who cannot afford the high interest on installments; it has organized successful city hall demonstrations of more than a thousand persons. Over this period of widespread involvement, the poor appear to have gradually acquired skills of organization, longer range planning, and other qualities contrary to those which reputedly characterize areas of poverty. I observed a similar process occurring in "lower class" white neighborhoods in Northwest Chicago, where the Northwest Community Organization, another Alinsky associated enterprise, has been in existence for less than two years.

(5) When members of some groups lose or give up their wealth, they do not thereby acquire the psychology of poverty.

One has only to consider the vows of poverty taken by members of some religious orders to illustrate this assertion.

Since the psychology of poverty obtains only under specific and describable circumstances, one cannot therefore use poverty as an explanation for these psychological characteristics which often are associated with poverty.

We might briefly mention other problems involved in the ready identification of poverty as the major problem of the poor. First, it is invalid reasoning to proceed without evidence from the fact that the poor have distinctive failings to the assumption that poverty is important in the etiology of these failings. It is incorrect simply to take the defining characteristics of a social category to which a group of people belong (the category "poverty" in this case) and use it without further evidence to account for the peculiar afflictions of that group of people. Second, even if *all* poor today were to exhibit the psychology of poverty, this may be merely an accidental connection, and the fact of having little money could remain only distantly related, for example, to feelings of

being dominated by irrational external forces. One should not confuse an observed regularity with an inevitable regularity, a conventional law with a natural law. Third, when a scientist observes that a group of persons, the poor, have adopted their own patterns of behavior and system of beliefs, this does not mean that the behavior and belief patterns are cultural or subcultural or that these patterns represent durable characteristics of the people involved over a wide variety of social situations. The patterns and beliefs may be situational, not internalized, and may shift readily as the situation changes. Just when social scientists appear to be getting the poor firmly in mind, the poor are transformed. Thus, the "psychology of the poor" may be quite different from the psychology of a neurosis the basis of which *is* internalized.

It is therefore likely that the natural solution to the problem of poverty is naïve: it merely assumes the determinants of the psychology of poverty.[2]

The Self-Help Doctrine and Its Consequences for Dependent Persons

In rapidly industrializing societies in which there are many opportunities for individual advancement there typically arises some form of the doctrine of self-help. The common core of self-help views can be stated as follows: A person is good to the extent to which he has assumed responsibility for and accomplished the realization of his potentialities for maximum use of his native capacities in a long, sustained, and arduous effort to reach a distant legitimate goal. With enough effort any normal person can attain such goals; no special ability is needed.

In the older Western industrial nations a growing appreciation of the limitations of opportunity has provided increasing support for modification of the traditional doctrine, with the qualification that ability as well as effort is necessary to success, and that some persons have been born with more ability than others. Also, since the nineteenth century, the common legitimate goal has changed from entrepreneurship of a prosperous independent business to a high position in a large work organization, and the struggle begins in the institutions of learning before the transfer to a work setting.

According to the doctrine of self-help, *anyone*, given enough time and enough effort, could achieve success. Thus, to be poor could have either of two meanings. On the one hand, poverty was regarded as the original accompaniment of the highest development of character, the struggling poor who were later to become successful were most worthy of respect. On the other hand, poverty indefinitely prolonged might mean a character defect, a lack of will power. Poverty, therefore, was ambiguous; from it alone one could reach no conclusion about virtue.

However, an economy with limited opportunities for success plus the belief in equal opportunity for success according to merit made inevitable an assault on the self-esteem of the permanently unsuccessful.

Officially defined dependency was not usually regarded as ambiguous. The person on Welfare has left the struggle altogether and has sat back to allow others to furnish his sustenance. It is true that some persons, the crippled, the very young, the seriously ill, and so forth, clearly could not have avoided dependency. But as for the rest, the presumption of their ability to work and succeed if they only tried hard enough led to the inevitable conclusion that those who have left off trying are bad. The intensity with which this conclusion was known was also related to the fact that dependent persons were seen to be living at the expense of the rest of the community. Not only did the scoundrels manage to exist without honest labor, but they actually made of the rest of the community a duped partner to their idleness. Inexcused dependency became a social symbol communicating defective character, toward which there was a feeling of superiority tinged with contempt. Even in the best of circumstances professional helpers were automatically considered morally as well as materially superior to those helped, and thus the helping relationship became a concrete carrier of the general meaning of dependency: the unworthiness of the dependent.

In affecting the psychology of dependency, the self-help doctrine has also, of course, affect the *behavior* of persons who are in need. One way to evade the unpleasantness of being dependent is to avoid getting help at all in a dependent situation. Families in trouble, as was discovered in various studies, often hide away when they need help the most. The stigma attached to receiving assistance prevents the use even of available resources.

Official dependency in modern society is a residual category of persons unable to enter into the normal types of income-producing relationships. Such persons are unable to relate to the normal avenues for gaining support, and the presence and location of such avenues is therefore the major immediate condition or cause of dependency in modern society. Inability to relate to normal avenues of support symbolizes failure, and perception by a dependent person of his own dependency is sufficient to produce shame and guilt and their complications. Official dependency is fundamentally the perception of the use of relative social power within a superordinate-subordinate relationship; the doctrine of self-help in a contractual economy made financial dependency the focal point for this definition in modern society. The official assumption is that all working adults are equal in that they have entered into work contracts on an equal basis, contracts which they could have chosen to enter or not to enter.

The financially self-responsible person is assumed to be responsible also in other areas of his life. For this reason dependency can concern any area of superordinate-subordinate relationship, and there is always some stigma associated with any dependency relationship, even though there is often pleasure in divesting oneself of the burden of self-

responsibility. Even the relationship of citizen to expert can be distasteful since it makes the citizen intellectually dependent on the expert.

The sharpest psychological impact of dependency has occurred where it is officially defined and therefore clearly perceived and sanctioned by the community. However, most dependency is not so explicitly defined; most of the poor are not "on welfare." Even so, the poor are generally perceived, however unclearly, as having failed, and this perception has hardened the community against them. In the latter case, the doctrine of self-help has intensified the feelings of hopelessness among the poor.

The extent of self-support is only one measure of the extent of dependency, a measure stressed only in connection with the doctrine of self-help. More generally, dependency is the placement of one's destiny in other hands. It is therefore especially characteristic of the areas of poverty, but also characterizes many other aspects of society, including the low echelons of large organizations, organization men at any echelon, and so forth. In a general sense dependency is also destructive, but more subtly so. If extent of self-realization is a measure of personality development, then dependency, which erodes self-realization with the loss of self-responsibility, is a measure of personality inadequacy. If the human personality develops as a decision process through self-responsible choices, then the taking away of self-responsible choices through assuming the subordinate position in a dependency relationship necessarily destroys personality.

The Social Situation of the Poor

Most of the poor are heavily dependent on outside forces. In many places, a poor person is much more likely to be subject to police interrogation and search, or to public identification as the object of police activity, than is a member of a middle class family. Urban renewal programs periodically disrupt the neighborhoods of poverty, scattering the families in several directions in accordance with standards which the poor do not understand or support. Schools function impervious to the concerns of the low income families whose children attend, or else schools may seek themselves to "lead" in the areas of poverty in which they are located, that is, they seek to impose school standards and definitions on the neighborhoods. Settlement houses run recreation programs that meet their own traditional criteria, but neighborhood youth often do not understand these criteria, often cannot engage in accustomed and legal modes of behavior and still participate in settlement house activities, often, involuntarily and without understanding, have to disperse friendship groups in order to participate in a recreation program.

Many families, having bought more than they can afford, especially through high-interest installment financing, have no way to know

whether or when their furniture will be repossessed or their check garnisheed. Medical and psychiatric care are inadequate, inadequately understood, and uncertainly available, especially to the poor who do not have connections through welfare. The securing of general relief or categorical assistance is a humiliating experience at best for people imbued with self-help ideas, but the deliberate rudeness intended to discourage as many applicants as possible, the complex agency rules which are not so much bases for action as after-the-fact rationales to provide support for decisions already made, and the subjective and unpredictable decisions of social workers representing agencies to the poor, all combine to place the economic foundation of many families at the mercy of completely incomprehensible forces.

The poor who seek employment must find it in a dwindling supply of jobs available to unskilled and semiskilled persons (including domestics), often seasonal or temporary work. In addition, the landlords of the poor are frequently discourteous, seldom inclined to make adequate repairs on their buildings, and likely to blame the tenants for the condition of the ancient and crumbling structures for which high rents are charged.

In other words the poor, by virtue of their situation, tend to be more dependent than other groups on a larger number of powerful persons and organizations, which are often very unclear about the bases for their actions and unpredictable in their decisions, and which further render the poor helpless by condescending or hostile attitudes, explicit verbal communications which state or imply the inferiority of the poor, and callousness or actual harassment. If we divide the powerful persons affecting the poor into two groups, the benevolent in intention on the one hand, and the callous or punitive on the other, we will find that the majority of both type of power figure treat the poor as inferior and reach down to relate to them.[3]

The situation of poverty, then, is the situation of enforced dependency, giving the poor very little scope for *action,* in the sense of behavior under their own control which is central to their needs and values. This scope for action is supposed to be furnished by society to any person in either of two ways. First, confidence, hope, motivation, and skills for action may be provided through childhood socialization and continue as a relatively permanent aspect of the personality. Second, social positions are provided which make it easy for their occupants to act, which make it possible for decisions of their occupants to be implemented in their futures. Middle class socialization and middle class social positions customarily both provide bases for effective action; lower class socialization and lower class social positions usually both fail to make it possible for the poor to act.

Thus, the dependency of the poor is not primarily a neurotic need to occupy dependency positions in social relationships, but rather it results from a deprivation of those minimal social resources, at every period of their lives, which the poor need and therefore must seek. The poor are not victims of the social system in the sense that "organization

men" are victims. They are rather, as Michael Harrington has emphasized, the *other* America, outsiders to the major society. In consequence,
members of the majority society are usually outsiders to the poor.

The initial dependency and its consequences are reinforced by the
hardening of a consensus in the majority community about the nature
of the poor, stabilization of the patterns of behavior in areas of poverty,
and partial internalization of ideas and patterns of behavior in the
children who grow up in both communities. Thus, the positions of poor
persons in relationship to superordinate forces are expressions of two
communities, a superior and powerful community and an inferior and
weaker community; two communities with institutionalized ways of
living which prop up the superordinate position of the one in relation
to the other.

People isolate and segregate those they fear and pity. The stronger
of the two communities has traditionally acted to alleviate the results
perceived to be undesirable without changing the relationship of the
two communities or ending the division into two communities. Since
persons designing and implementing such programs did not consider
the consequences of the division for their aims, they were able to maintain an intention to bring the poor into their society. The recommendations have been for improved law enforcement; public welfare; public
housing; social settlements; higher horizons educational programs;
social work with "hard core" families; urban renewal, clean-up, paint-up,
and fix-up programs; block and neighborhood organizations; and the
like. All these plans and programs have usually shared two characteristics: (1) they are initiated and supported from outside the neighborhoods of poverty and imposed on the poor; and (2) they fail to make
any lasting positive impact on neighborhoods of poverty. That is, although a few persons and families become affluent and leave the
neighborhoods, the majority remain poor and continue in an atmosphere
of apathy, disorganization, and hostility, toward the programs designed to
rescue them. These programs, presupposing the inferiority of the people
in the area, perpetuate and exacerbate the inequality. Definitions of
the poor are carried by the institutionalized helping hands. Insofar as
these agencies have any *social* impact, the definitions embedded in
them become self-fulfilling. But, although the powerful external social
agencies—powerful in relation to the poor—are not very effective in
carrying out their official tasks in areas of poverty, they do enable the
stronger community to believe that something is being done about the
social problem of poverty, reducing guilt and shame to such an extent
that there remains little motivation to develop some effective means to
bring the poor into the larger society.

On the basis of this sketch of the dynamics of the situation of the
poor, the following classification can be made of the sources of the
"psychology of poverty."

(a) In any modern industrial society the overall amount of power
of the society tends constantly to increase, although the rate of increase
may vary. Although everyone in the society may secure ownership of

additional *material* goods as a result of technological progress, the additional *power* tends to be secured only by those persons and social systems with preexistent power. The poor boy with strong internalized drives and skills for success and the large corporation with effective control over technological advances in its field both illustrate the tendency for socially created power to attract to itself additional power. But the poor most often have neither the power created through childhood socialization nor that to be secured through attachment to a strong social system in which they have influence. In some countries, the population is predominantly poor, and this populace may have some power through the political process. But, in the United States the poor are an unorganized or ineffectively organized minority, unable even to exert influence in the political sphere. Thus, increments in power tend to attach to those with power, and the balance of power in a country such as the United States tends naturally to tilt against the poor.

(b) The fact of being powerless, but with needs that must be met, leads the poor to be dependent on the organizations, persons, and institutions which can meet these needs. The situation of dependency and powerlessness through internal personality characteristics as well as through social position leads to apathy, hopelessness, conviction of the inability to act successfully, failure to develop skills, and so on.

(c) As a consequence of the self-help doctrine, this "psychology of poverty" arouses the anger of the affluent toward the poor. Thus, the affluent can avoid the necessity to alter the social situation of the poor by assuming that the poor are bad and deserve their situation. This additional meaning of poverty makes rigid the dependency aspects of the social situation of the poor, and, to some extent, the poor accept the prevalent view of themselves. However, since the poor are not together in an unambiguously clear social category, they, at the same time, may reject being placed in such a category subject to the assumption of their dependency and inferiority. For example, persons eligible to live in public housing are not affected only by the convenience, space, and other physical characteristics of their living quarters. A large proportion seem to prefer dilapidated private housing operated by an indifferent landlord to better maintained, less crowded, less expensive quarters in a public housing project in which the management is concerned with tenant needs. The meaning of living in such a project may offset the superiority of the physical living arrangements.

(d) Over time the dependency relationship of the poor becomes institutionalized and habits, traditions, and organizations arise in both the affluent community and in the neighborhoods of poverty, maintaining the relationship between them. The poor react in part to the institutionalization itself. For example, "lower class" delinquency does not only stem from the fact that the poor have few and drab job opportunities. There is also the perception that the conforming poor tend to remain indefinitely in low social positions as well as the angry rejection by the adolescent poor of attempts, through law enforcement and

social agencies, to control and manipulate them without altering their situation.

Consequences of this social process for the poor have been indicated at several points in the preceding discussion; we will only briefly recapitulate some of them here.

First, people tend either to retreat from or to attack forces controlling their lives which they cannot affect and which are not inescapable. For this reason the poor typically stand aloof from settlement houses, get minimally involved with social workers, drop out of school. Only forces too omnipresent to be escaped may ensure normative affiliation through identification with aggressors. It is easy to see the poor as paranoid since they are so often hostile to and suspicious of powerful objects which they may perceive in a distorted fashion. However, paranoia presumably requires origins in early childhood, while the hostility and suspicion of the poor naturally arise from their social position and their necessarily over-simplified and naturally personified perceptions of it.

Second, with less of their selves bound up in their self-conceptions than is the case with other groups, the poor do not entirely accept these definitions of themselves, but protect themselves by various psychological strategies from fully accepting the implications of their situation. The impact of the definitions then is primarily indirect; the definitions have consequences by creating the situation of the poor through the meaning of poverty to those who possess power. The situation gives rise to the typical absence of that hope which is associated with action and which gives salience to intentions and attitudes. Thus, the poor frequently verbalize middle-class values without practicing them. Their verbalizations are useful in protecting their self-conceptions and in dealing with the affluent rather than in any pronounced relationship to non-verbal behavior. This does not imply deliberate falsification; a poor person may have the necessary sincerity, intention, and skill to embark on a course of action but there is so much unconscious uncertainty about achieving psychological returns through success that the action may never be seriously attempted. As has been discovered in social surveys, the poor may not only pay lip service to middle class notions, but may, for similar reasons, say to any powerful person what they believe he wants to hear. That is, much of the behavior of the poor does not relate primarily to their own basic values, beliefs and perceptions held by others about the poor. The poor are normally involved in partly involuntary self-diminution; their behavior may therefore be remarkably transformed when, as has happened through social action, they begin to acquire a sense of power, of ability to realize *their* aspirations. Thus, the so-called differential values of the poor, which are ill-defined at best, are more nearly comprehensible as the psychological consequences of a long continued situation of perceived powerlessness in contemporary industrial society. They become a subculture to the extent that the traditions, orientations, and habits of dependency become internalized.

Third, the situation of the poor, the inability of the poor to act in

their own behalf, creates a less complex personality structure for them than is the case with affluent persons with more linguistic skills. This does not necessarily mean that the poor have less effective personalities, or are unsocialized in comparison, since the personalities of more highly educated persons are often partly constituted by social elaborated fantasies which conceal reality and rationalize avoidance of problem solving.

Fourth, awareness of their common fate typically leads the poor to engage in mutual aid activities, activities which, in spite of involving only very minor skills, are precursors to the joint social action which develops naturally as the poor acquire organizational skills and confidence in using them.

Fifth, because of the social situation of the poor and the fact that the majority society has relatively little normative basis for social control in areas of poverty, these areas are often characterized by high rates of publicly discernible types of deviance: juvenile delinquency, school dropouts, alcoholism, illegitimacy, mother-centered families, and the like.

Finally, there are differential consequences of institutionalized, uncompensated powerlessness for the poor who have various social positions within areas of poverty. For example, because of the greater expectation for men to be powerful and to be sources of power, the consequences of powerlessness for "lower class" men is usually greater than that for women.

All of this suggests that the problems of the poor are not so much of poverty as of a particularly difficult variety of situational dependency, a helplessness to affect many important social factors in their lives, the functioning or purpose of which they do not understand, and which are essentially unpredictable to them.

Not Enough Money Versus Situational Dependency

With increased money the poor could at least be better able to cope with such forces, could be less dependent on some. What, then, is the relationship between the poverty of the poor and their situational dependency?

Money is a generalized source of power over people through a right to control over goods and services. As such, money is one of many kinds of power. Poverty, therefore, is one of many kinds of powerlessness, of being subject to one's social situation instead of being able to affect it through action, that is, through behavior which flows from decisions and plans. Since there are several varieties of generalized power, an absence of money is often replaceable *insofar as the psychological reactions to powerlessness are concerned*. An American Indian who lives in poverty may have considerable influence through authority relation-

ships traditional in his culture. Members of religious orders who have taken vows of poverty remain able to exercise influence through their order and through relationships of interdependence with colleagues. The college student with a very low income has influence through the expectations of his future social position. When the poor engage in successful social action they gain power, even when their incomes remain unchanged.

In other words, when social scientists have reported on the psychological consequences of poverty it seems reasonable to believe that they have described the psychological consequences of powerlessness. And many persons without money have, or get, other varieties of power, or else identify with powerful persons or groups and therefore fail to exhibit these consequences. Even the poor do not react entirely on the basis of the social definition of them. There are counter institutions and traditions (churches, unions, and clubs) which deflect the impact of the majority definition. Primary groups (family and peer) also mediate and modify the community definitions they transmit. The behavior of the poor may not, therefore, reflect their self-conceptions; we should not suppose that the poor feel as would middle class persons in their situations, or as their behavior suggests they feel. This very resistance of the poor makes it possible to attempt the otherwise herculean task of trying to get the major society to alter its relationship to poverty by helping the poor themselves to build a backfire, to become strong and effective enough to challenge the invidious definitions that have been made of them.

Human personality is a process of decisions and actions on the basis of decisions. One becomes fully human only through acting in important areas of one's life. All social arrangements which take responsibility out of the hands of the poor, which make decisions and action more difficult or operative over a more restricted area, feed the psychology of powerlessness which is so widely (and correctly) regarded as undesirable. For example, it is often noted that the poor lack a time perspective. But only through action (important decisions and behavior on their basis) does one acquire a history and, with the history, a practical concern with the future.

What consequences does the social situation of the poor have for programs to help the poor? We will next consider some general answers to this question.

Redefining the Social Situation of the Poor

We can reject two possible alternatives.

First, the solution most frequently suggested is to help the poor secure more money without otherwise changing present power relationships. This appears to implement the idea of equality while avoiding any necessary threat to established centers of power. But, since

the consequences are related to *powerlessness,* not to the absolute supply of money available to the poor, and since *the amount of power purchasable with a given supply of money decreases as a society acquires a larger supply of goods and services,* the solution of raising the incomes of the poor is likely, unless accompanied by other measures, to be ineffective in an affluent society. Where the poor live in serious deprivation of goods and services, an increase in the supply of those goods and services would be an important source of power, that is, of access to resources which satisfy crucial needs. However, when the poor do not live in actual deprivation, increases in money make relatively little impact on the dependency relationships in which they are entangled. The opportunity to participate in *interdependent* relationships, as a *member* of the majority society, requires an increase in *power.*

Second, the *self-help* doctrine is normally related to conventional criteria of success, and persons who have not met these conventional criteria therefore are threatened with feelings of guilt and shame. One theoretically possible solution would seem to involve redefinition of success, allowing social support to lives which are now viewed as failures. This, however, presupposes an ability to meet some alternative criteria of success through action, a possible solution for philosophers, poets, or beatniks, but not now generally possible for the poor. It may, however, be that the meaning of the self-help doctrine could be adequately extended to reward the social action of the poor who can act successfully through their own organizations.

Along these lines the criteria for an effective solution are reasonably clear. In order to reduce poverty-related psychological and social problems in the United States, the major community will have to change its relationship to neighborhoods of poverty in such fashion that families in the neighborhoods have a greater stake in the broader society and can more successfully participate in the decision-making process of the surrounding community.

It is frequently said that we must provide opportunities for the poor. To render more than lip service to this objective demands more power and more skill and more knowledge than we now possess for the bureaucratic provision of such opportunities. For example, there are a finite number of jobs available, fewer than the number of people looking for work. There are severe limits to the extent to which the adult poor can be trained for existing openings. A large proportion of the poor have jobs which do not remove them from the ranks of the powerless. Any great shift in opportunities made available to the poor within the structure of the majority community will threaten more powerful groups with vested interests in those limited opportunities, and the proponents of creating opportunities for the poor cannot themselves affect the political or economic process enough to implement their good intentions.

It is important to develop opportunities in sensitive relation to the perception by the poor of their own needs. When this is not done, the poor are not likely to be able to use efficiently the opportunities created

for them. And, most central of all, rather than to provide opportunities for the "lower class," the poor must as a group be helped to secure opportunities for themselves. Only then will motivation be released that is now locked in the silent and usually successful battle of the neighborhoods of poverty to maintain themselves is an alien social world. This motivation which will enable them to enter the majority society and make it as nurturant of them as it is at present of the more prosperous population.

The involvement of the poor in successful and significant social action provides both immediate and compelling psychological returns and also the possibility of initiative to help the bureaucratic organizations related to the poor to fulfill their officially stated purposes. The institutions of the major community can be forced to establish relationships of interdependence, not of dependence, with the poor; professionals can help by accepting professional roles as employees of the organizations of the poor.

In our society inner worth as expressed in action, striving, the struggle is held eventually to result in attainment of aspirations. If one is not successful, one is viewed as worthwhile so long, and only so long, as one struggles. The poor tend to be regarded as failures and not struggling, and hence as worthless. This perception of worthlessness is incorporated in the conception which others have of the poor and also, to some extent, in the conceptions which the poor have of themselves. One way in which the poor can remedy the psychological consequences of their powerlessness and of the image of the poor as worthless is for them to undertake social action that redefines them as potentially worthwhile and individually more powerful. To be effective, such social action should have the following characteristics:

1. the poor see themselves as the source of the action;
2. the action affects in major ways the preconceptions, values, or interests of institutions and persons defining the poor;
3. the action demands much in effort and skill or in other ways becomes salient to major areas of the personalities of the poor;
4. the action ends in success; and
5. the successful self-originated important action increases the force and number of symbolic or nonsymbolic communications of the potential worth or individual power of individuals who are poor.

The result of social action of this kind is a concurrent change in the view which the poor have of themselves and in the view of the poor by the outside world. There is a softening of the destructive social reality and immediate psychological returns to the poor, although not without hostile reactions from advantaged persons and organizations with known or hidden vested interests in maintenance of the areas of poverty.[4]

The only initial additional resources which a community should provide to neighborhoods of poverty should be on a temporary basis: organizers who will enable the neighborhoods quickly to create powerful,

independent, democratic organizations of the poor. These organizations will themselves then seek from the rest of the community resources necessary to the neighborhoods for the solution of the problems they perceive. Agencies for the provision of training and education and opportunities can be developed under the control of the neighborhoods of poverty, thereby ensuring that the poor are in interdependent rather than dependent positions in relation to the agencies. This would meet the professed objectives of most communities since it would effectively motivate the poor to maximum use of opportunities, since the requirements of professional practice will ensure the quality of services rendered, and since the communities state their intention not to allow their help to become an instrument of domination.

The comment that "We know the needs of the poor" is accurate in a very general sense. But there is a great distance between this observation and a knowledge of how, in practice, those needs can be met. If a community is not merely giving lip service to meeting them, if a community wants to be effective as well as to have good intentions, then the way of meeting needs must be appropriate to the personal and social characteristics of those being helped. In this case, effectiveness requires that the only *unilateral* additional help be given at the outset and in the form of temporary assistance in the creation of democratic and powerful organizations of the poor. Through such organizations, the poor will then negotiate with outsiders for resources and opportunities without having to submit to concurrent control from outside. The outcome will be maximal motivation to take advantage of resources and opportunities which are sensitively tailored to their needs.

Summary

There are two alternative ways to understand the psychological characteristics of the poor. These characteristics can be naïvely understood as resulting from poverty. But there are a number of reasons why it is more precise to view them as the psychology of the *powerlessness* of the poor.

These alternative points of view have also different consequences for social policy. If the problem were only one of a lack of money, it could be solved through provision of more and better paying jobs for the poor, increased minimum wage levels, higher levels of welfare payments, and so on. There would be, in that case, no real need for the poor to undertake any social action on their own behalf. This view is consistent with the idea that the poor are unable to participate in and initiate the solution of their own problems.

However, since it is more likely that the problem is one of powerlessness, joint initiative by the poor on their own behalf should precede and accompany responses from the remainder of society. In practice this initiative is likely to be most effectively exercised by powerful conflict organizations based in neighborhoods of poverty.[5]

Notes

1. This summary social scientists' image of the psychological characteristics of the poor was prepared on the basis of a survey of articles and books relating to poverty published by social scientists during the past fifteen years. Any particular author would be likely to differ on one or more points and would probably want to add others not recorded here. For example, in *The Children of Sanchez* (New York: Random House, 1961), Oscar Lewis includes "a strong present time orientation with relatively little ability to defer gratification and plan for the future, a sense of resignation and fatalism based upon the realities of their difficult life situation, a belief in male superiority which reaches its crystallization in *machismo* or the cult of masculinity, a corresponding martyr complex among women, and finally, a high tolerance for psychological pathology of all sorts." (Pages xxvi-xxvii) Lewis, of course, restricted his account to urban Mexican poor.

2. The personality characteristics of the poor may themselves be different from those reported. Much of the scientific literature is based on reports of verbal or other behavioral responses of the poor in the presence of researchers, usually middle class persons of much higher status and greater power than those being studied. It is not easy for a powerful person accurately to understand one who is weak since the behavior of the latter in the research situation may depend very much on the behavior of the former. The massive failure of intelligent and educated Southern whites to withstand Negroes with whom they had maintained years of presumably close relationship should provide reason for researchers to use caution in their claims based on a few hours' contact with persons much different from their usual associates.

3. It should be remembered that not all sections of the poor are so much at the mercy of outside forces. The stably employed working class poor are less dependent on mysterious, unpredictable, arbitrary, and capricious forces. There are degrees and kinds of poverty, and the differences among them will be set forth elsewhere to supplement the general description contained in this paper.

4. The Syracuse University School of Social Work has developed a field placement in which graduate students are now receiving training in initiating social action projects by the poor to resolve problems of broad concern in neighborhoods of poverty. Experience indicates that social work students can learn to help the poor jointly to engage in efforts which meet these criteria. Social action efforts by the poor in areas of poverty have occurred in several places. For example, several years ago, Hope and Dan Morrow moved with their family into a block in East Harlem, New York City. With their help, the families in the block organized themselves formally and informally for a number of important purposes ranging from keeping streets clean to reducing juvenile delinquency. On a larger scale, some of the social action organizations originated by Saul Alinsky of the Industrial Areas Foundation have involved large numbers of people in neighborhood improvement through a conflict process around crucial neighborhood issues. IAF organizations have enabled areas to decrease or end exploitation by some absentee landlords and unethical businesses. They have also ended police brutality and secured police protection, street cleaning, and other services which low income neighborhoods had not previously received at a level equivalent to that of the remainder of the community. Several of the IAF organizations are engaging in "self-help" nonfederally assisted urban renewal. It remains true, however, that most social action programs in low income areas do not meet the above criteria. Such programs frequently attempt to mobilize neighborhoods of poverty without jeopardizing any existing power arrangement, even temporarily, and thus pursue two contradictory objectives simultaneously. They may, in any case, perform such useful functions as providing symbolic satisfaction for the conscience of the majority community and jobs for some estimable persons.

5. Because of the nature of this paper there has been no attempt in it to marshal the data relevant to the various assertions made in the discussion of the psychology of areas of poverty as the psychology of powerlessness. This paper has not been designed as a contribution to science in the sense in which science is understood to be a body of verified statements. In the area under consideration

there is no such body of statements now available. Contributions to science remain possible, but must be put forward as relatively tentative formulations in the early stages of a process which will move to the collection of additional data relevant to specific points. It is my hope that the above formulation can serve such a purpose.

Part 3

Psychotherapeutic Approaches for Low Income People

Introduction

█n light of the low income person's failure to seek psychiatric treatment, the greater likelihood of his being rejected for it, and his higher drop-out rate should he begin treatment, what are the alternatives for a treatment approach oriented toward the poor? [1]

One possibility, suggested by Hunt, is to confine psychotherapy entirely to middle and higher classes. He argues that the principles of psychotherapy may well be "class-linked." [2] Ruesch adds: "The present methods of individual psychotherapy—psychoanalysis included—are methods which were designed for use between people who belong to approximately the same social class and who share in common a large number of assumptions." [3]

Consistent with this view is the recommendation offered by Brill and Storrow:

> We feel that such clinics should re-examine their emphasis on psychotherapy as their preferred method of treatment. Rather than being criticized on the grounds of discrimination against the lower class individual, we feel that many psychiatrists and psychiatric clinics are open to criticism for their tendency to restrict treatment to one modality. It may be that education will ultimately result in a more sophisticated and more psychologically minded public that will more uniformly seek psychotherapy for emotional disorders, but until that time arrives, psychiatrists are obliged to employ treatment methods that are designed to help all patients and not just those which for a variety of personal reasons they prefer to use. [4]

Closely related to this alternative is the thesis that more authoritative, directive, suggestive, techniques be utilized with the poor because this is their preference. Conversely, it is suggested that less insight therapy (psychodynamic therapy) be employed.

Others, like Hollingshead and Redlich, center their recommendations on efforts to reduce the cost of psychiatric treatment and to make it more readily available.[5] Another proposal concerns pretraining for the low income person on the nature of psychotherapy. Overall and Aronson stress the need to "reeducate the patient as to both his own and the therapist's role in treatment." [6]

Other proposals focus more on the setting of the therapy, stressing a reaching out on the part of the treatment agent toward the locale of the low income patient—a kind of "psychiatrist in the poolroom" approach.

It is possible, also, to argue, as in the case of the compensatory education thesis for the disadvantaged pupil, that more and better psychotherapy be supplied for the low income client; that he receive the best therapists, the most time, and so on.

The recommendations thus include:

1. no psychotherapy
2. more psychotherapy
3. other types of therapy
4. more accessible psychotherapy
5. preparation for existing forms of psychotherapy
6. selective utilization of different types of psychotherapy
7. more appropriate psychotherapy

Most of this section is directed toward the various revisions of psychotherapy that have been proposed to meet the needs of low income groups.

The Positive Potential of the Low-Income Client

Psychotherapy was originally developed to treat certain kinds of disorders, mainly symptom neuroses, common in Freud's day.[7] In the present era, therapy appears to have been generalized to other problems (delinquency, drug addiction, learning difficulties) without appropriate modification and development. However, psychotherapy has many functions: reassurance, tension reduction,

catharsis, objectification, exposure and change of irrational problem solving mechanisms, among others. In light of these, the
failure of therapy with low income individuals is somewhat surprising.

It is frequently maintained that psychotherapy is effective only
with intraceptive, intellectual people. Thus, it is argued, psychotherapy is not the treatment of choice for blue collar people whose
problems are largely environmental and whose mode of approach
is not introspective.[8] We believe this notion is rooted in a static
concept of psychotherapy. Our thesis is that psychotherapy as
presently organized is highly congenial to a middle class population, especially to the professional strata. It fits in with the goals,
values, and ways of thinking of the professional. It is not congenial to the style, outlook, traditions, or expectations of the low
income person.

The widely held view which assumes that psychotherapy is not
the treatment of choice for low income clients can be challenged.
This view is based on the selective emphasis on certain categories,
e.g., the low-income person's nonintrospective orientation, his
desire for direction, suggestion, and the like. But ignored in the
diagnosis are other qualities that may indicate a positive potential
for psychotherapy. Perhaps most important here is the low-income
individual's tendency not to isolate and intellectualize. Indeed, this
is an extremely important asset for treatment. There are other
dimensions of the low income person's culture and style that might
especially prepare him for psychotherapy or for treatment such as
role playing, group therapy, family therapy, hypnosis, hypnodrama,
therapies that include physical aspects, play therapy, and so on.

Diagnosis should not be selectively geared to those features
of the low income person's make-up that are unsuited for psychotherapy, and more attention should be directed toward those aspects
that may be positively relevant. If emotionally corrective experience rather than cognitive insight is the heart of modern psychotherapy—the key to deep behavior modification—then the poor
may be far better therapy risks than is generally realized.

New Approaches to Intake and Diagnosis

Before discussing new treatment approaches for low income
people, it might be useful to examine problems involved in diag-

nosis across class lines. There is increasing evidence that most of the clinician's diagnostic tools, whether in the cognitive sphere (e.g., intelligence tests) or in the emotional sphere, are class linked and class biased. The first article in this section, by William Haase, is especially important in raising questions of middle class bias in the use of the Rorschach test.

Haase reports that essentially identical Rorschach records are interpreted quite differently depending upon the designated social class origin of the patient. The protocols of individuals reported as lower class are diagnosed as more maladjusted with poorer prognosis than are their middle class counterparts with essentially similar records who were used as controls. It is also interesting to note that the lower class records were more frequently categorized in terms of psychosis and character disorder while the essentially identical middle class records were diagnosed as neurotic and normal. Haase does not object to a class differential analysis *per se*, but to the fact that the analysis unwittingly, but consistently, concludes that the "lower class" is more maladjusted. Considering the lack of opportunity and difficult life conditions of the poor, a "lower class" record identical to one of a middle class person might be presumed to indicate greater health and better prognosis.

This is not an isolated finding. Increasing evidence indicates that the traditional personality tests including the projective tests, and perhaps the testing situation itself, are not attuned to the low income individual, his life style, experience, and motivation. Riessman and Miller's survey of a variety of personality tests supports this contention.

Some of the limits of traditional verbal and projective tests may be reduced by greater use of situational and performance tests, where role playing, for example, is used as a diagnostic tool.[9] The article by Beker, Eliasoph, and Resnik represents a preliminary effort in this direction.

That special cross-cultural barriers may affect the testing situation even when the subject is very young is suggested in the Pasamanick-Knobloch article. Here the issue is not class, but race, and the report indicates that race may affect the subject's responses as early as two years of age. The effect is a lowered estimate of the verbal ability of the Negro child.

"A Short Story on the Long Waiting List," by Rachel Levine, is included because it raises some important questions and provides some direction for a new approach to problems involved in intake of low income clients as a mental hygiene clinic.

New Treatment Approaches

Introducing this section, Edmund Gordon raises some important questions regarding current methods of counseling low income youngsters. He contrasts two approaches to guidance and counseling, namely, the projective and the interaction (or reflectional) viewpoints, and indicates some of their implications for counseling disadvantaged youth. McMahon provides a somewhat provocative reformulation and criticism of traditional views of the working class patient.

This leads directly into the imaginative discussion by Spiegel regarding transference and countertransference in an interclass context. The author provides a cogent summary of the Florence Kluckhohn system for classifying value orientations of different cultures and its implication for examining working class subcultures. Spiegel draws some highly instructive proposals for the revision of psychotherapy, resulting in the reinterpretation of the meaning of "benevolent neutrality" (on the part of the therapist) and the relaxation "to a considerable extent of the principle of non-reciprocity." In essence, Spiegel argues that certain modifications of traditional practice are necessary in the interest of achieving rapport and transference, and he feels that he has been able to reach patients "who would otherwise have been rejected or would have dropped out of treatment."

Riese's "Educational Therapy, A Methodical Approach to the Problem of the 'Untreatable' Child," represents another significant program in reaching the supposedly unreachable, severely deprived child. Most of the children at Riese's Educational Therapy Center have previously been rejected by all other treatment agencies. Her approach combines milieu therapy and a psychodynamic orientation with particular stress on education:

In child psychotherapy, *education* cannot be underestimated. It contributes to intellectual maturation and thus furnishes a safer ground for emotional growth. It is one means of promoting constancy of effort, and thus self-confidence, composure and poise. Analogous to play therapy in early childhood, certain educational endeavors may provide material for psychotherapy with the older child. We have had children assert that the teaching afforded in the Center has helped in solving their problems of maladjustment—their inability to learn having been their greatest worry and the cause of their fears, delinquency, isolation, and hostility.[10]

A most interesting parenthetic observation of Riese's concerns the strength of these deprived children:

> It remains one of our most unexpected, challenging and rewarding experiences that the most destitute and neglected children proved to have the greatest strength in adjusting to the living conditions in the Educational Therapy Center and in coping with the menaces of their home and community.[11]

Another novel approach for reaching severely deprived people is a type of family therapy originated by Rachel Levine at the Henry Street Mental Hygiene Clinic in New York City. She developed an unusual and apparently effective type of "treatment in the homes" which she calls the technique of demonstration. In essence, the approach consists of the treatment agent bringing simple games, cards, and clay to the "multi-problem" home, and engaging as many members of the family as possible in these activities. When family conflicts arise around the games, they are discussed and worked with by the social worker right on the spot. Aside from the fact that this approach is much more involving than most office discussions, "it also eliminates the distortions which are common when conflict situations are reported after the fact and discussed in the office."

Perry, in discussing home treatment, reports some interesting changes in the image of the therapist and his role:

> First of all, there is a reversal of the host-guest positions. The professional is invited into the home of the patient; he is not inviting the patient into his office. This shows up in a thousand little ways. One is the fact that all the minor gestures which one becomes acustomed to use in one's office to establish an atmosphere in which appropriate communication can take place are completely out of order in the patient's home. For example, one does not have an ashtray to shove more conveniently toward the patient's reach. It is not one's own ashtray that lies there on the living room table. The worker cannot even offer a cigarette until he has found out that it is all right to smoke in the parlor.[12]

Levine in her home treatment approach uses role playing in addition to games and activities. It would seem that much of the family therapy and group therapy approaches currently gaining wider acceptance might profit from judicious use of games and role playing approaches, both of which appear to be more attuned to the cognitive style of lower socioeconomic groups than is verbal discussion isolated from concrete references.

We have already pointed to the use of role playing (and situational testing) as an approach to diagnosis. The article by Riessman and Goldfarb goes further into the question of why a role play format may be especially appropriate in group therapy approaches with low income people. A significant side effect of role play is that it can enable the therapist to gain much greater identification with his low income patients. Through the technique of role reversal (where the therapist can take over various roles of the client and/or his family), the treatment agent gains a tremendous opportunity to achieve a deepening identification with the low income person. Short of direct participation in the life of the client, there is little chance of obtaining this type of "inside" understanding. But perhaps the most important use of role playing lies in its potential for eliciting and developing verbal expression in the low income client.

Scheidlinger's article presents a more psychodynamic approach to group therapy for low-income youngsters along with some pertinent modifications.

This section closes with two articles representing some new trends (or the reappearance of old trends) in social work. Fantl's "Preventive Intervention" reminds us of the social context, its significance in analyzing a case, and its intervention implications. Weinandy offers a casework approach for multiproblem families that stresses action (social worker must take the initiative), directness (don't be subtle), be practical (aid in home management), authority (provide controls), be giving, and coordinate.

Sociotherapy

We now turn to treatment approaches at a more indirect level. Frequently the psychological difficulties of an individual appear to diminish in importance when he becomes involved in some commitment, activity, or social movement. This involvement can vary from a religious activity to a hobby, to a labor union, to participation in a block committee. In the article by Wittenberg that introduces this section, the author notes that participation in a neighborhood block committee led to marked personality development and growth in a woman receiving welfare aid, who, despite some leadership potential, had considerable personal difficulty. Wittenberg's approach combined casework, group work, and community organi-

zation principles in a program directed toward "personality adjust-ment through social action," or what might be termed sociotherapy. Here "the organization is the tool, while personality growth is the goal. . . . Essentially this is using whatever available healthy ego structure there is and building from there by using the environ-mental pressures as a catalytic agent."

Many of today's low income clients who are members of the Negro and Spanish-speaking minority groups have considerable interest, sometimes manifest, sometimes latent, in movements and community organizations representing their aspirations. Treat-ment agents, accustomed to more clinical models, tend to under-emphasize the therapeutic possibilities of encouraging these types of involvement. Rosen and Frank present some valuable guides regarding "Negroes in Psychotherapy." [13]

Fishman and Solomon, in their study of adolescents in the student sit-in movement, depict the behavior of these youths as an alternative way of coping with problems, both internal and ex-ternal. They characterize this behavior as "prosocial acting out" (in contrast to the anti-social acting out presumed to be typical of delinquents). "Public action for social goals is their way of at least temporarily resolving issues of identity formation, conscience and aggression. They see themselves as prodders of the national con-science, and derive satisfaction and self-esteem from this role."

While certainly opposing pressuring of all Negro clients to become interested in the Negro movement, we would argue that treatment agents should be alert to such possibilities whenever the client shows even slight interest in this direction.

We are reminded of the success claimed by the Black Muslim movement in curtailing the use of drugs and alcohol by members who previously had been active addicts and alcoholics. If this con-tention is accurate, the effect of social ideology is quite impressive, regardless of one's convictions about the Muslim movement.

Marshall [14] points up the issue by noting that the social worker who just tries to change the drug addict "without offering him a faith in addition"—without embodying this change in a "central ideology" that might involve the addict—has a much harder task than does the Muslim movement. (In this connection, it is striking that there appears to have been "a sharp decline in the incidence of crime among the Negro population of Montgomery, Alabama, during the year of the boycott (1955).") [15]

In countering the sociotherapeutic approach, it is sometimes

contended that although a particular symptom may disappear, the problem is merely displaced and expressed in different form, in the new involvement. In support of this thesis, irrational, distorted, and inappropriate aspects of the client's behavior in the new activity are sought for and cited. There is little doubt that this pattern operates on some occasions and perhaps partially in all such cases, but as an overall answer it appears far too over-simplified. It overlooks at least two important possibilities. One is that the new behavior may have emerged from, or taken root in, nonpathologic aspects of the patient's personality—(the "conflict-free portion of the ego").[16] The other possibility, perhaps more appealing to the traditional clinician, is the likelihood that the new behavior pattern may be a well sublimated expression of the patient's character. In either case, there is much room for therapeutic guidance to insure against negative symptom displacement.

The Mobilization For Youth program represents a sociotherapeutic approach stressing indirect social strategies, keyed to low income populations. Brager provides an excellent overview of this project, and one of its most important contributions, the use of nonprofessional, indigenous personnel. Neighborhood people drawn from low income communities can perhaps play a decisive role in the reorganizing of treatment approaches for low income people. These nonprofessionals have already been employed with considerable success as homemakers, parent education aides, interviewers and research aides, visiting nurses, recreation leaders, and community organizers.[17] They appear to be highly successful in developing rapport with low income "clients," some of whom are among the most deprived, disadvantaged individuals in the community.[18] Their success seems to result from the fact that they are similar to their clients in terms of background, style, language, ethnicity, and interests. Perhaps the model of the future will see an increasing ratio of nonprofessionals to professionals in low income treatment programs, with the professionals charged mainly with program and policy development, along with training and supervision of the new nonprofessionals who will have main responsibility for direct contact and immediate service.

The nonprofessionals should be people who have themselves come out of lower-class culture, and have successfully moved into a more stable way of life—either working- or middle-class—but have not rejected their past. Many mobile people tend to turn their backs on the culture from which they have come, and become more

hostile toward it than anyone else. Yet there are some people who, in making the change, have developed a considerable amount of empathy toward both old and new culture. Since they know the conditions and the culture that are to be changed, and the way of life that is being sought by and for lower-class clients they should be more successful in achieving rapport with such clients than are middle-class professionals. But, while these empathic people exist in large numbers, they are hard to find. Some have been drawn into settlement houses and into group work with adolescent gangs. Most of them, however, probably earn their living in factories and offices, without ever using their talent.[19]

Pills and Needles

Hollingshead and Redlich led the way in noting the low income person's physical orientation toward treatment: most of the class V clients believe that their problems are physically caused and should be physically (chemically, organically) treated via "pills and needles." [20]

Overall and Aronson found with regard to low income clients' expectations concerning psychotherapy that 70 per cent thought the doctor would be interested in their digestion, 78 per cent thought the doctor would ask them to describe the physical illnesses they have had, 55 per cent thought the doctor would take their pulse and blood pressure, and 45 per cent thought the doctor would tell them what kinds of food they should eat.[21]

In light of these findings it may be in order to suggest greater consideration of all types of physical treatment on the grounds that these approaches are consistent with the low income individual's expectations and style. Where possible auxiliary treatment might include the use of drugs (tranquilizers, LSD, sedatives, stimulants, procaine, hormones, vitamins), diets, massages, baths, heat treatment, breathing exercises, muscle relaxation techniques,[22] the somniatron,[23] sleep treatment (the new Soviet machine, the electrosone, for inducing a full night's sleep in two hours is relevant). To the low income individual, pills, machines, and massages are direct and knowable. Talk is vague and suspect. Often physical symptoms are involved in the emotional ailments of workers, so forms of medical treatment are especially attractive. Another advantage of medical treatment is that it can be explained to others —those who invariably inquire about your ailments. How can verbal talk therapy be explained?

Efforts of the National Institute of Mental Health and other groups to encourage the training of general practitioners to handle psychiatric problems in their usual medical rounds seem a positive trend. Such training might enable low income people to receive earlier psychiatric treatment. The break from the neighborhood physician to the special setting of the psychiatric clinic is a deep one for workers. In addition, treatment by a general practitioner clearly defines the distress as a "medical illness" and makes acceptance of treatment easier.

Unfortunately, there are too few illustrations in psychiatry or community psychiatry of attempts to integrate the physician and the psychotheraptist in a program specifically for low income groups. An outstanding exception is the Chicago Area Plan for Workers' Mental Health, jointly sponsored by Roosevelt University and various labor and community health agencies. The article by Ted Ruhig furnishes an overview of this plan.

Following this is a short article on the potential psychotherapeutic value of a "20-minute hour" utilizing physicians. It is argued that "a general practitioner who has at least a nodding acquaintance with basic psychiatric principles can now help to relieve the emotional distress of many of his patients by means of a series of eight to ten psychotherapeutic sessions, each of 20 minutes' duration." While this article does not purport to have direct bearing on lower socioeconomic populations, it is included because it would appear to have special significance for these strata.

Brief Approaches

Like the "20-minute hour," most of the treatment approaches presented in this section have not been developed with explicit focus on low income populations, but they clearly have important implications for these groups. Purcell's article is something of an exception here in that he consciously directs his attention toward providing a rationale for the "brief contact" in serving lower socioeconomic groups; hence his article is particularly pertinent in beginning this section. The article from the United Automobile Workers newspaper highlights the special implications of the "Open (day) Hospital" for workers and also discusses the relevance of the "Night Hospital."

There are numerous articles that space limitations prevent us

from including on the use of work, sheltered workshops, and the like in the treatment of mental illness.[24] We suspect that this work approach might have special therapeutic value for low income groups, but once again this is generally not the intent of these projects.

Broader Training for Therapists

Increasing evidence regarding the conditions for the effectiveness of psychotherapy suggests that it is not the psychotherapeutic system (be it Freudian, Sullivanian, or whatever type) that is decisive, but rather the strong mutual expectation of improvement by patient and doctor.[25]

There is increasing evidence that a muliplicity of techniques can be effective provided that the client and the treatment agent believe in them. But the techniques that low income clients believe in are different from those that the middle class practitioner believes in. Is it possible that treatment agents (including social workers) can be exposed to and trained in a wider variety of techniques, including those that are possibly more congenial to low income people? Another possible solution is the combination of some of these techniques with the more cognitive, psychodynamic approaches so attractive to the therapists. Reich combined muscle relaxation techniques with psychoanalysis. Robertiello, *et al.,* approach the integration of psychodramatic techniques with psychoanalysis. Drugs have been used adjunctively with "depth" treatments. Hypnosis has been combined with psychoanalysis, in hypnoanalysis. Activity diagnosis and treatment have been utilized in a psychoanalytic context.

Trends and the Future

In the past decade, two trends have emerged in the field of psychiatry: a physiological trend highlighted by a variety of new drugs; and an environmental-social trend reflected in community psychiatry, social psychiatry, milieu therapy, and the like.[26] It is striking that these two developments appear to be most in harmony with the treatment expectations and desires of low income patients. It is possible that physiological and environmental psychiatry are

also most relevant not only to the treatment expectations of the poor, but to their actual problems as well.

It may be that intrapsychic, psychodynamic treatment is more suited to middle class expectations and problems, while social and physiological therapies are more appropriate for low income problems. This is undoubtedly an oversimplification, however. More likely, the *emphasis* in treatment should be class related, but each stratum can probably benefit from treatment at the various levels: intrapsychic (and interpersonal), environmental, and physiological. Thus, low income treatment programs might utilize social and physiological orientations as their starting points (and in general, use them more extensively), but nevertheless could be concerned with internal psychological forces, which would be given greater attention as the therapy progressed. On the other hand, therapy attuned to middle class clients might begin with the psychological level, and move outward toward the environment and inward toward the physiological.

Part III concludes with an over-all analysis by Reiff and Scribner of the implications of the new comprehensive community mental health program for the treatment of low income groups.

In a sense, the emphasis on environmental and physiological causes, in part powered by the needs of a low income clientele, may contribute to the further development of a universal psychiatry. Hence, what has been said in this section may have much wider application than our low income focus might imply.

Notes

1. Hugh A. Storrow, "Psychiatric Treatment and the Lower-Class Neurotic Patient," *Archives of General Psychiatry*, 6 (1962), 473.

2. R. G. Hunt, "Social Class and Mental Illness: Some Implications for Clinical Theory and Practice," *American Journal of Psychiatry*, 116 (1960), 1065.

3. J. Reusch, "Social Factors in Therapy," *Psychiatric Treatment*, 31, ed. S. B. Wortis, M. Herman, and C. C. Hare (Baltimore, The Williams & Wilkins Company, 1953), 59–93.

4. Norman Q. Brill and Hugh A. Storrow, "Social Class and Psychiatric Treatment," *Archives of General Psychiatry*, 3 (1960), 344.

5. A. B. Hollingshead and F. C. Red-lich, *Social Class and Mental Illness* (New York: John Wiley & Sons, 1958), 372.

6. Betty Overall and H. Aronson, "Expectations of Psychotherapy in Patients of Lower Socioeconomic Class," *American Journal of Orthopsychiatry*, 33:13 (1963), 430.

7. Wheelis notes a related problem confronting psychoanalysis today arising out of the shift from the traditional symptom neuroses (phobias, obsessions, compulsions) characteristic in Freud's period to the now prevalent character disorders. See Allen Wheelis, *The Quest For Identity* (New York: W. W. Norton, 1958), 41.

8. See Norman Q. Brill and Hugh

Storrow, "Social Class and Psychiatric Treatment," *Archives of General Psychiatry*, 3 (1963), 340–44.

9. Cartoon-like tests such as the Rosenzweig Frustration Test and simple picture selection instruments such as the Szondi may be valuable. Moreover, the use of hypnosis and dreams as diagnostic devices may be indicated.

10. Hertha Riese, "Educational Therapy," *Psychiatry*, 13:4 (1950), 470–71.

11. Hertha Riese, "Educational Therapy, A Methodical Approach to the Problem of the 'Untreatable' Child," *Group Psychotherapy*, 12:1 (1959), 61

12. Stewart E. Perry, "Home Treatment and the Social System of Psychiatry," *Psychiatry*, 26 (1963), 61–63.

13. For a fuller discussion of this issue see Martin Grossack, *Mental Health and Segregation* (New York: Springer Publishing Co., 1963).

14. Kenneth Marshall, Speech on Negro Culture, given at Mobilization for Youth Training Program, September 12, 1962, p. 33.

15. Reported by T. Kahn, "Unfinished Revolution." Igal Rodenko Printer, New York, quoted by J. R. Fishman and F. Solomon, "Youth and Social Action," *American Journal of Orthopsychiatry*, 33:5 (1963), 876.

16. See John Cumming and Elaine Cumming, *Ego and Milieu* (Englewood Cliffs: Prentice-Hall, 1962), 13–14, for an illuminating application of Heinz Hartman's concept of a "conflict-free portion" of the ego.

17. See F. Riessman, "The Revolution in Social Work: The New Nonprofes-

sional" (Mobilization For Youth Report, 1963).

18. *Ibid.*

19. Herbert Gans, *The Urban Villagers* (New York: The Free Press of Glencoe, 1962), 277.

20. A. B. Hollingshead and F. C. Redlich, *Social Class and Mental Illness* (New York: John Wiley & Sons), 340–45.

21. Betty Overall and H. Aronson, "Expectations of Psychotherapy in Patients of Lower Socioeconomic Class," *American Journal of Orthopsychiatry*, 33:3 (1963), 425.

22. See E. Jacobson, *Progressive Relaxation* (Chicago: University of Chicago Press, 1938).

23. The Somniatron purports to produce deep relaxation or sleep through electrodes affecting the cortex. (Reported by Lafayette Instrument Company, Indiana).

24. See L. Bellak, B. J. Black, A. Lurie and J. S. A. Miller, "Rehabilitation of the Mentally Ill Through Controlled Transitional Employment," *American Journal of Orthopsychiatry*, 26:2 (1946), 285–96.

25. For a suggestive discussion related to this question see J. D. Frank, *Persuasion and Healing* (Baltimore: The Johns Hopkins Press, 1961).

26. While the social and psysiological trends have developed in parallel fashion, we do believe that they are of equal importance. Our own view is that the social-environmental approaches will prove decisive for most problems, with the physiological measures serving largely in an auxiliary fashion.

New Approaches to
Intake and Diagnosis

The Role of Socioeconomic Class
in Examiner Bias

William Haase

Recent literature has begun to investigate the role of the examiner's influence upon the subject, and the projection of his own personal traits into the report. Most of the focus has been upon personality variables with much less attention given to the function of socioeconomic factors. It is one aspect of this function that the present experiment purports to measure.

Summarizing the effect of the clinician upon the results of the personality tests that he administers, a whole host of studies [1] indicates that he most assuredly influences both the results he will elicit from any given test and the significance assigned to them. With this in mind, it becomes feasible to formulate the following hypotheses:

Hypothesis I. Appended social service reports identifying the environmental origin and socioeconomic status of the patient will influence estimates of adjustment obtained from Rorschach protocols.

Hypothesis II. Rorschach protocols interpreted as originating from a "lower class" level of society will tend to be diagnosed as less adjusted than the same records designated as of a higher class.

It is appropriate to discuss a bit of the rationale for selecting the Rorschach as the experimental instrument. The Rorschach is without doubt the most widely used and important projective technique in diagnostic practice. Review articles [2] accumulate bibliographies of the studies devoted to it in clinical research. Each year the list grows longer. The basis for its popularity may lie in the fact that it combines objective scoring with the widest possible latitude for clinicians to utilize their clinical insight and intuitions.

Projective method in general, and the Rorschach in particular, are

241

in keeping with the most recent developments in the philosophy of science,[3] in that they permit the study of process with the minimum interference with that process. Their use runs parallel with the trend toward focusing more and more scientific research upon the problems of patterns and configurations. Although this is indeed true, the vital importance of the Rorschach interpreter in these investigations must not be ignored. Therefore, the interpretation of the protocol given by the patient is of extreme importance. After testing is completed, the psychologist has in his possession a protocol—a collection of words. As MacFarlane,[4] Rose,[5] Frank,[6] and Warner[7] have pointed out, these words may have different meanings between patient and examiner, and between the different examiners. A study by Greyson and Tolman [8] of the fifty most widely used words in the psychologist's clinical reports found wide discrepancies of definition between the participating psychologists and psychiatrists and even among the psychologists themselves.

In one sense, prior to the interpretation and writing of the psychological report these words may be looked upon as raw material. Wolfe [9] states that a fundamental principal of personality measurement is that, "an individual reveals his own personality to any change he makes upon any type of material." This being the case the protocol becomes a projectile device in reverse, in that now the transition from raw materials to report will allow the examination of the examiner. The psychological report or statement of findings can be classified as a "personal document." Allport [10] defines the term as "any self revealing record that intentionally or unintentionally yields information regarding the structure, dynamics and functioning of the author's mental life." Evidence has already been offered that this indeed true of the clinician's report.[11]

Procedure

A total of 75 psychologists participated in the experiment; 21 were employees of county or city government units, 28 were staff members of the Veterans Administration, and 26 were third or fourth year trainees in the Veterans Administration clinical psychology training program.

A word about the experimental design and its relation to the composition of the Rorschachs and social service reports is in order. Because we were desirous of conducting an intra-psychologist's statistical test as well as inter-psychologist's evaluation, it became necessary to seek out Rorschachs that could be compared and equated for number of responses, projections, reaction times, color shock, shading shock, significant determinants, important ratios, A H per cent, number of populars, and the like. In short, we wanted Rorschachs whose psychograms were practically identical and whose content was roughly similar.

In addition, one of each pair should be given by a lower class patient and the other by a patient of a higher class. Also, ideally, the psycho-social history of the two patients should have been identical except for socioeconomic status, in order not to introduce other uncontrolled variables whose presence would influence the appraising psychologist. Finally, in order to insure judgments that were reliable it was decided that the minimum number of Rorschachs that could be presented to the psychologists for evaluation would be eight (four pairs).

It became apparent to the experimenter in a relatively short period of time—and possibly to the reader in an even shorter period—that this assignment was well-nigh impossible. The only practical course was to construct four pairs of Rorschachs and the four pairs of accompanying social service histories artificially. This was done so that the paired psychograms were almost identical and their content as alike as they could be without making them duplicates. (We had to be sure not to arouse the suspicion of the participating psychologists.)

We turn now to the construction of what was called "a selected and abridged social and economic history." This task was somewhat easier. The histories were limited to one page and all contained the following information:

1. A brief identifying and introductory paragraph concerning the "client."
2. A description of the residence and how contact was established.
3. Client's occupational history.
4. A description of each significant member of the family and statements about the client attributed to them.

The social histories were also paired and for identification were labelled as 1L for lower and 1M for middle, 2L and 2M, and so on. L stands for lower class and M for middle class. A quick inspection of the pairs would reveal that the family constellations are identical, statements about the "client" were made by the same people and conveyed the same meaning, and so forth.

The only factors that distinguish a pair of histories are socioeconomic ones. Thus in 1L and 1M one client has a Cornell education, the other, three years of high school. The father of the first is a Certified Public Accountant averaging $10,000 a year, while the father of the second is a fruit and vegetable dealer earning $45 a week. One lives in a "beautiful home" close to the tennis stadium in Forest Hills, Long Island, the other lives in a "four-room apartment on the fourth floor of a walk-up tenement in Greenpoint, Brooklyn."

The present experiment was designed to ask: "What will happen when Rorschach A1 is seen with social service history 1L, and Rorschach A2 is seen with social service history 1M? What effect will the differing socioeconomic set have upon the same psychologists?" Another question is asked: "What will happen when the one psychologist sees Rorschach A1 with social history 1L and another psychologist sees Rorschach A1 with social history 1M?"

Discussion of Results

In all, sixteen different evaluations involving three basic statistical techniques were applied to the collected data. In every case except one they were biased in favor of the middle classs with a probability beyond the .01 level. Whether we examine the clinicians impressions prior to diagnosis, the diagnosis itself, or the prognosis, *the direction of the bias is always the same*—it favors the middle class.

Under rating scales there were items that were divided for purposes of this investigation into two categories. Those requiring less speculation on the part of the psychologist were called "direct" and those requiring more speculation were called "indirect." For the indirect scores the basic effect of status attribution remains the same—biased in favor of the higher class. But on those items where the diagnostician can, if he desires, refer directly to psychogram for possible leads, and where the criteria for the presence or absence of pathology is more clearly defined in terms of a few indicators, the bias completely disappears.

Because these items formed the spade work for the eventual diagnosis and prognosis, one sees that they can be extremely influential. Therefore, there are two valuable insights to be derived from our findings here. (1) Content analysis alone with the greater freedom for speculation that it implies, can lead to increased opportunity for socioeconomic bias to make its appearance. (2) Increasing efforts should be directed toward the establishment of quantitatively verifiable signs and patterns for variables such as psychosexual adjustment, kind of fantasy and defense mechanisms, presence of hostility, etc., in order to avoid the opportunity for the projection of bias.

Without such signs and indicators as are available for anxiety depression, oppositional tendencies, and the like, the clinician relies more upon intuitional integration and this increased distance between himself and the record eventuates in bias detrimental to evaluation of Rorschachs considered to be lower class in origin.

What exactly is the meaning of our findings that bias in favor of the more middle class Rorschach is a pervasive characteristic and not one that varies with the psychologist's group origin, employment, experience, or theoretical position?

The immediate interpretation is the one that emphasizes the formal, academic preparation and the correlative social processes that inculcate the class identification upon the noviate professional. We would agree with K. Davis [12] that the content of mental hygiene is predominantly middle class and that there is unverbalized agreement among the practitioners of psychology that the lower class cannot totally assimilate the ways of thinking and behaving that alone can insure prevention and cure of maladjustment.

Regardless of class origin, psychologists, by virtue of their training, eventually attain close similarity in their approaches to patients of different classes. Whatever the initial differences in personality and social perception, it would seem that, at least insofar as orientation where class is concerned, the psychologist's attitudes and values are modified in the direction of norms relatively common for his discipline. Our study seems to indicate that these norms produce clinical judgments that are prejudiced with regard to the lower class.

We begin to see that whether the lower classes produced the same or different sets of responses to personality measurements, the same or different symptomatology as a result of inner personal difficulties, the likelihood is that they would be adjudged "sicker."

Two Possible Interpretations

The results can be thought of as falling within one of two basic frames of reference. (1) The bias is not in keeping with the clinician's fundamental objective of an impartial evaluation of any given personality, and this shortcoming must be labeled an irrational and unfortunate consequence of our insufficiently explored social, economic, and professional experiences. (2) Our results indicate neither bias nor irrationality but stem from a realistic appraisal by the clinician of the patient's condition and potential in the light of the structure of present-day society and the opportunities afforded to members of its various segments.

The latter point of view argues that our findings are not prejudicial at all, that the "bias" is not an unconscious inability to understand and emphathize with the lower class, but rather the result of an inescapable conclusion that class membership—attainment and maintenance of middle class standing—in and of itself is a criterion determining better prognoses and less pathology. What can be said of such a position? First of all, if it is prevalent, it should be stated explicitly so that this rather fundamental tenet could be subjected to scrutiny. We feel that such a position would be difficult to defend within the limits of present-day research and theory. That groups with different values, perceptions, and experiences, may fall prey to different mental problems has been shown to be a feasible potential. But that these psychic conflicts are more insidious and more destructive of the personality in a person of the lower class remains to be demonstrated.

Implications for Other Studies in
Mental Hygiene

The implications of our findings are rather disturbing when one begins to examine all the other areas where such a bias might operate

to the detriment of the lower class patient. One of the major implications of our study is the absolute importance of rigidly controlling
socioeconomic status in studies concerned not only with diagnosis but
with other aspects of abnormal psychology as well. Such controls would
prevent the existence of "double identity" groups with hidden potential
stimulus variables, e.g., the possibility that two groups designated as
schizophrenic and nonschrizophrenic are not actually lower class versus
middle class in make up. Such controls might prevent studies of psychotherapy from finding that those who "profited from therapy" are
mostly middle class, while those receiving "no benefit" are mostly lower
class. One might wonder if all socioeconomic material were kept from
the person responsible for selecting eventual candidates for the various
organic therapies, whether we would find such a large preponderance
of these selected to be from the lower class.

A number of crucial questions should be constantly kept in mind.
We should ask whether the concept of an optimally healthy psychological environment is identical for the various social classes. We should
be interested in the problem of whether the various symptoms of psychological maladjustment mean the same thing to the members of the
different classes. In clinical psychology, research should be directed
toward aiming to discover how members of the various classes differ
from one another in their responses to personality tests, and if differences exist and are verified, what is the proper interpretation of them
in terms of psychopathological or personality diagnosis.

We do not, of course, want to go so far beyond our data that our
ruminations become pure conjecture, but we cannot help but wonder
about fields of study that, while only tangentially related to our research
problem, are none the less of great importance to the concept of mental
hygiene. What of studies in education, for example? Do investigators
control for socio-economic status when deciding who are the students
who benefit most from modern educational procedure? What effect does
this socioeconomic variable play in the selection of students for vocational high school?

Psychiatric social work is another discipline where our findings may
be of some importance. Which families are judged to respond best to
the efforts of the case worker? What approaches are taken by social
agencies toward families of middle class status as opposed to those of
lower class status? Do "closed" cases represent optimum benefit, "non-
cooperation," or an attitude of the social worker? All of these questions
bear investigation to ascertain whether bias exists and what role it plays.

Whatever explanation one wishes to ascribe to our results, they
necessitate a thorough reexamination of the thinking about socioeconomic phenomena and their relationship to mental disorder. What new
insights may be possibly brought to the conclusion of Hollingshead and
Redlich that: "The data we have assembled demonstrate conclusively
that mental illnesss, as measured by *diagnostic prevalence* is not distributed randomly in the population. . . ." [13]

To MacFarlane's [14] warning that a projective tool may easily de-

generate into one that discloses the dynamics of the interpreter rather than the subject, we may now add, "and discloses his socioeconomic attitudes as well."

Our investigation adds a good deal of cogency to Auld's [15] conclusion that the psychologist "is likely to assume a bias in favor of his own social class." Grey's [16] question, "could it not be that middle class clinicians are subject to an unconscious bias in favor of those patients who most closely approximate their own values . . . ?" can tentatively be answered in the affirmative.

Notes

1. R. N. Filer, "The Clinician's Personality and His Case Reports," Ph.D. dissertation, University of Michigan, 1951; L. K. Frank, "Understanding the Individual Through Projective Techniques," *Am. Council on Educative Studies*, Ser. 1, 14, 56–62; W. Joel, "The Interpersonal Equation in Projective Methods," *Rorschach Res. Exch.*, 13 (1949), 479–82; G. A. Kimble, "Social Influence on Rorschach Records," *Journal of Abnormal Soc. Psychology*, 40 (1945), 89–93; Edith Lord, "Experimentally Induced Variations in Rorschach Performances," *Psychol. Monogr.*, 64 (1950), 1–34; Joan W. MacFarlane, "Problems of Validation Inherent in Projective Methods," *American Journal of Orthopsych.*, 12 (1942), 405–510; Benjamin Meeblman, "The Reliability of Psychiatric Diagnoses," *Journal of Abnormal Social Psychology*, 47 (1952), 577–78; Daniel R. Miller, "Prediction of Behavior by Means of the Rorschach Test," *Journal of Abnormal Social Psychology*, 48 (1954), 367–75.

2. Marguerite R. Hertz, "Rorschach, Twenty Years After," *Psychol. Bull.*, 39 (1942), 529–72; also in D. Brower and L. E. Apt, *Progress in Clinical Psychology, Vol. I* (New York: Grune & Stratton, 1952).

3. L. K. Frank, *Projective Methods* (Springfield, Ill.: Charles C Thomas, 1948).

4. Joan W. MacFarlane, "Problems of Validation Inherent in Projective Methods," *American Journal of Orthopsych.*, 12 (1942), 405–510.

5. A. W. Rose, "Projective Techniques in Sociological Research," *Soc. Forces*, 28 (1949), 175–83.

6. L. K. Frank, "Understanding the Individual Through Projective Techniques," *American Council on Educative Studies*. Ser. 1, 14, 56–62.

7. W. L. Warner, M. Mesker and K. Eells, *Social Class in America* (Chicago: Service Research Associates, 1949).

8. H. M. Greyson and R. S. Tolman, "A Semantic Study of Concepts of Clinical Psychologists and Psychiatrists," *Journal of Abnormal Social Psychology*, 45 (1950), 216–31.

9. H. M. Wolfe, "A Fundamental Principle of Personality Measurement," *Psychol. Rev.*, 56 (1949), 273.

10. G. W. Allport, *The Use of Personal Documents in Psychological Science* (New York: Social Science Research Council, 1942).

11. R. N. Filer, *The Clinician's Personality and His Case Reports.*" Ph.D. dissertation, University of Michigan, 1951.

12. K. Davis, "Mental Hygiene and The Class Structure," *Psychiatry*, 1 (1938), 55–65.

13. A. B. Hollingshead and F. C. Redlich, "Social Stratification and Psychiatric Disorders," *American Sociol. Rev.*, 18 (1953), 163–69.

14. Joan W. MacFarlane, "Problems of Validation Inherent in Projective Methods," *American Journal of Orthopsych.*, 12 (1942), 405–510.

15. B. F. Auld, Jr., "Cultural Influences on Personality Test Responses," *Psycho. Bull.*, 49 (1952), 318–32.

16. Alan L. Grey, "Social Status and Psychological Characteristics of Forty Patients," Ph.D. dissertation, University of Chicago.

Social Class and Projective Tests [1]

Frank Riessman and S. M. Miller

Allison Davis (6), Ernest Haggard (13) and their associates have demonstrated that various test relevant variables, such as motivation, practice, etc., can markedly affect intelligence test performance. In particular, Haggard has indicated that such factors as test taking experience, rapport with the examiner, motivation, language used in the test items, reading ability, and speed required can decidedly limit the test performance of the lower class child,[2] and thus contaminate our picture of his intelligence.

It is possible that similar factors are operative with regard to many other kinds of measurement. In this article we shall begin to examine possible effects of some of these variables on two very different types of projective tests—the Rorschach and the F (Fascism)—scale. Residual attention will be given to the Thematic Apperception Test.

Auld (2) has observed that most personality tests indicate that the lower class is more maladjusted or neurotic. He raises the possibility, however, that the observed class differences may be artifacts of the tests rather than valid differences. An example of the difficulties of tests is found in a personality test for high school students which contains the question, "Are you often left out of things other kids do?" An affirmative reply is interpreted as indicating shyness while a negative response signifies sociability. But it is quite possible, Auld states, that the answer is simply an accurate reflection of the situation, observed by Hollingshead (15) as well as by a number of other writers, that the lower class adolescent is in fact frequently left out of school affairs. An affirmative reply may mean that the lower class adolescent is not shy but that he is accurately reporting the reality situation.

Reprinted from *Journal of Projective Techniques*, Vol. 22, No. 4, November 1958, pp. 432–439.

Another more striking example reported some years ago by Rosenberg (25) concerns the Bernreuter Neurotic Inventory, on which working class individuals score in the neurotic direction more often than do middle class subjects. The following items on the Bernreuter are defined as normal and well adjusted by the tests:

1. Do you see more fun or humor in things when you are in a group than when you are alone? (The supposedly "normal" answer is "no.")

2. Can you usually understand a problem better by studying it alone than by discussing it with others? (The well-adjusted answer is "yes.")

3. Do you usually face your troubles alone without seeking help? ("Yes" is the non-neurotic answer.)

4. Do you like to bear responsibilities alone? ("Yes" is the "normal" answer.)

The responses required for "normalcy" by this test are of a highly individualistic order. Responses of this type may not be congruent with co-operative group norms and traditions of the worker (7). The appreciable class differences found on the Bernreuter, particularly on the "self-sufficiency" sub scale (2), *may reflect class differences in norms of individualism rather than neurotic tendencies!*

It is interesting to observe in this connection that a more recent article on the Bernreuter found that this test was sharply biased toward middle-class values; the authors concluded that the "working-class scores on the inventory are spuriously high (neurotic)." (14).

Another source of difficulty in interpreting scores of working-class individuals on these tests arises from the probability that middle-class subjects are probably much more adept at giving the conventional "adjusted" responses. Gough (11) found on the Minnesota Multiphasic Personality Inventory that the middle class students were much more evasive in their replies, tending to deny having problems of adjustment.

The Rorschach

In a recent study, Haase (12) found that essentially identical Rorschach records were *interpreted* quite differently depending upon the designated social class origin of the patient.

The protocols of individuals reported as lower class were diagnosed as more maladjusted with poorer prognosis than were their middle-class counterparts with essentially similar records who were used as controls. It is also interesting to note that the working-class records were more frequently categorized in terms of psychosis and character disorder while the essentially identical middle-class records were diagnosed as neurotic and normal.

Haase does not object to a class differential analysis *per se*, but rather he notes that the analysis unwittingly, but consistently, concludes that the lower class is more maladjusted. Haase points out that considering the lack of opportunity and difficult life conditions of the

worker, a lower-class record which is identical with that of a middle-class person might be presumed to indicate greater health and better prognosis.

While data are somewhat sparse on actual class differences in response to the Rorschach, a trend is suggested by a number of the studies. Auld (2) in presenting class differences on the Rorschach, based on a comparison of two previous studies, notes a number of significant differences including a greater total number of responses for the middle class group, as well as proportionately more color and movement responses. (It should also be noted that the lower-class profile includes an equal number of animal and human movement responses, while the middle-class profile shows a greater proportion of human movement.)

Color responses on the Rorschach are interpreted as revealing the emotional life of the person, how responsive he is to other people and the environment. The lower class boys tested would seem to be less responsive to their environment and lacking in the emotional warmth, since they have fewer color responses of all kinds (2).

A recent study by Stone and Fiedler (28) also reports class differences in Rorschach responses of children although not all of the differences are in the same direction as in the two studies summarized by Auld. Consistent with the previous findings, Stone and Fiedler find that the lower-class group shows a higher proportion of FM (animal movement), a higher A% (animal responses), less CF (color form), less W% (whole responses) and a lower Dd% (small details). However, they found the lower-class group exhibiting a higher R (number of responses) and more FC (form-color), contrary to previous findings. Stone and Fiedler also report a special breakdown made for them by Carlson for the eight-year-old children used in Carlson's study (4). Here, the lower-class group had significantly less FC (form-color) and CF (color-form) responses and the middle-class group used far more color in general, consonant with the Auld report.

Auld (2) recommends that psychologists using the Rorschach should be provided with lower-class norms in order to avoid making misleading (and negative) interpretations of lower-class protocols because of the inadequacy of the usual standards of Rorschach analysis and interpretation which are predominantly based on middle-class subjects. This suggestion may not be an adequate solution. To see if it is, we must study the factors, following the Davis-Haggard model, which may affect the performance of working-class individuals on this test.

Eichler (8) in discussing the relationship of situational stress to Rorschach scores, points out that there is likely to be a decrease in color responses in stress situations. Klatskin (20) in reviewing the literature on the effect of the *test situation* on Rorschach responses notes that color responses, of all responses, are most affected by stress. Kimble (19) found that subjects tested under standard (usual formal) conditions give significantly fewer M (movement) and C (color) responses than others tested in the more informal atmosphere of a cafeteria.

It is quite possible that the worker experiences much more stress

in the Rorschach test situation than does the average middle class individual.

An important factor probably contributing to a more stressful reaction to the situation on the part of the worker is his lack of familiarity with the Rorschach test, as well as his lack of skill in test taking in general. Moreover, he is likely to have poorer rapport with the middle class examiner.

Haggard (13) found with regard to intelligence test administration, that rapport with the examiner and experience in test taking were important variables limiting the performance of lower class children.

It is possible then, that the test situation may produce situational stress for the worker. It is interesting to note that, as Eichler (8) reports, experimentally induced stress produces Rorschach response patterns which resemble those of the worker with regard to color responses.

An alternative hypothesis which should be explored further is that lower class responses to the Rorschach are more characterized by lack of interest and apathy than by stress or anxiety. This view is consistent with Davis' report (6) that on intelligence tests lower class children endeavor to finish as quickly as possible and typically are uninterested in the task.

Impressionistically, it appears that workers find the test material of the Rorschach particularly unstimulating. It is not the kind of task which is found to be immediately meaningful to them. The ambiguity of the Rorschach task may be in opposition to workers' *desire for structure* and definiteness (24). In .a sense the "easiest" responses to give on the Rorschach are those determined by form and animal: that is, these responses can be given when the person is least involved or interested in the test as well as when one is situationally anxious. These are the more predominant responses of the lower-class subjects.

Undoubtedly, many clinicians would contend that these responses to the test are indicative of personality characteristics of the lower class and therefore can be utilized in interpretations. There are a number of important objections to this view. As pointed out above, the lower class response may indicate a localized situational reaction, not an enduring, deep personality trend. Furthermore the precise determinants of the lower-class responses are uncertain, and cautious procedure would call into question the imputing of personality interpretations to these responses. The responses may be reactions to the nature of the test and test situation rather than to the content of the Rorschach. While the former may have importance for certain kinds of differential diagnosis, the Rorschach itself does not provide a mode of interpreting such extra-test reactions except by considering the Rorschach session as an interview or by assuming that these responses are symmetrical with all other responses.

A challenging point is that Rorschach responses and interpretations of the worker are difficult to reconcile with conclusions about his personality as inferred from other kinds of evidence. For example, community studies of the worker furnish a very different picture of him

than one would obtain from the Rorschach syndrome. While data are often coerced to fit an interpretation of the worker as impulsive and over-emotional, there is considerable evidence pointing to a personality pattern built around a cooperative, solidaristic, outgoing, emotionally responsive orientation, hardly reflected in the Rorschach pattern, especially the lack of color responses (7, 29).

For a variety of reasons then, the Rorschach may, at the present time, be an inadequate test for working class subjects. Providing lower-class norms for clinicians would not completely overcome these difficulties. Employing separate norms in analyzing a lower-class record may tell us how the individual compares with other lower class subjects in response to situational test anxiety, skill in test taking, etc., but still does not give us an adequate picture of his basic, enduring personality tendencies. It is possible that the Rorschach may be one of the various tests that are not equally applicable to different cultural groups, because of the nature of the test material in relation to the background of the group.

The Thematic Apperception Test

The Thematic Apperception Test is another projective technique applied across class lines without awareness of the difficulties which may arise. Mason and Ammons (22) report a number of class differences in response to the TAT, including language differences, differences related to the recording of the stories, differences in willingness to participate, and differences in stories elicited by the various cards. "For example, burglar stories were told to Card 14 by every class, but the burglar was clever and escaped in upper class stories, while he was caught in lower class stories" (22).

Korchin (21) found that middle class subjects gave longer stories on the TAT than did lower-class subjects. Again we may hypothesize that rapport difficulties and concomitant situational stress may partially explain the shorter stories of the lower class subjects.[3]

Nevertheless in, many respects this test may be more appealing than the Rorschach to working-class individuals. The task seems more stimulating to them and what is required is perhaps clearer. However, two difficulties limit the usefulness of this instrument. In the first place, most of the pictures include people who appear to be middle class; some are ambiguous, but very few suggest working class individuals, symbols or situations. In the second place, very few lower class individuals have had much experience making up stories from pictures. This second objection is not quite as serious as the first, because working-class individuals have been exposed to movies and television stories and might be able to participate in this task if the pictures were more suggestive of working class people, themes, and symbols. We do not mean to imply that such pictures should include labor struggles and strike scenes. More probably, everyday scenes which included workers'

homes, manner of dress, and recreational activities would be more effective.

One adaptation of the TAT which makes an effort in this direction was developed in Mexico for rural children (27). Thus far no similar test has emerged for urban working-class subjects.

Some of the difficulties involved in instituting such tests is revealed by the several grounds on which Riess *et al.* (23) criticize the Thompson TAT cards for Negro subjects. Perhaps the most troubling difficulty with the Thompson cards is that they explicitly and unambiguously portray Negro figures. This situation may constrain against full relaxation and involvement on the part of many Negro subjects who find this experience strikingly different from most test situations which customarily do not involve Negroes. Providing Negroes with "familiar" material is unfamiliar (and perhaps disturbing) to them in this particular context. It is for this very reason that we have suggested that a "working-class TAT" not employ strike scenes and labor issues, but rather introduce in a more indirect manner situations and symbols reflecting lower-class life. We might also suggest that Negro TAT cards be constructed in which the race of the characters is ambiguous, rather than explicitly white or Negro. These cards night evoke more response from many Negro subjects. Also, it might be possible to develop new cards reflecting themes and symbols emanating from Negro culture and not simply reproduce a standard TAT with the characters blackened to appear Negro as in the Thompson TAT.

It is interesting that there are special cards for different age and sex groups within the regular TAT set but not for different class groups.

The F Scale—Fascism Scale

Another very important projective test on which significant class differences appear, is the so-called Fascism Scale or F scale as it is usually called (1). This test unlike the Rorschach of the TAT is highly structured in the sense that only certain definite, forced choice responses may be given in answering the questions. (It is projective (3) in the sense that the implication or meaning of the question is *disguised*.) One of the most important attributes of this scale is its definite relationship with social attitudes such as leadership, prejudice, and political apathy.

A few of the items from an abbreviated form of the F scale (26), called the A–E scale (authoritarianism-equalitarianism), will clarify its meaning:

1. There are two kinds of people in the world: the weak and the strong. (A positive answer is scored in an authoritarian direction.)

2. A few strong leaders could make this country better than all the laws and talk. (A positive answer is recorded in the authoritarian direction.)

Results from a number of studies indicate that the working class is more authoritarian on both the F and the A–E scales (17).

Again the question arises—what does this mean? Adorno *et al.* (1) indicate that the original F scale was developed on an almost entirely middle-class sample. Hyman and Sheatsley (16) point out that differences in response may simply reflect differences in formal education, rather than be symptomatic of deep personality trends.

In support of this position, Riessman (24) found that education was a very decisive factor accounting for differences in response to the authoritarianism-equalitarianism scale. Of the grade school educated workers, 62 percent gave authoritarian responses while only 37 percent of the high school educated workers responded in an authoritarian direction. It is, therefore, possible that the scale items may have a very different meaning for the educated individual than they have for the less educated person.

If this is the case, we can expect the scale to be much more predictive of authoritarian relevant attitudes within the middle class, the group with more formal education.

Riessman (24) found no relationship for the working class group between authoritarianism, as measured by the A–E scale, and response to leaders as "people oriented" (likes people, kind, understanding, etc.). That is, the workers who were classified as authoritarian in terms of the A–E scale, showed just as many "people oriented" responses to leadership as the equalitarian workers. In the middle-class group, on the other hand, the authoritarian individuals as measured by the A–E items were much less likely to select "people oriented" humanitarian characteristics in indicating their response to leadership than were the middle class equalitarians.

This lack of predictive value of the F scale for working-class groups is further corroborated by Farris (9) in a study of the relationship of authoritarianism and political behavior (political activity, confidence, information, etc.). He concludes that "within groups of working-class respondents. . . . authoritarianism does not usually correlate with observed variations in political behavior or attitudes." (9).

There is then considerable reason to believe that the F scale and its derivatives are not applicable to the working-class subculture, while it may be appropriate for the middle class, on which the scales were originally developed.

One final point is relevant here: Christie (5) points out that the middle-class person who feels that people are prying into his affairs (a standard F-scale item) may suffer from paranoid tendencies, whereas an individual in the working class, where probing by various public functionaries is not uncommon, may *realistically* offer the same response. Also the statement "There are two kinds of people in the world: the weak and the strong" might have quite different implications for those whose class membership places them among the "strong," i.e., middle-class, and the "weak" i.e., lower-class. It is a reasonable hypoth-

esis that those in a favorable hierarchical position are not as aware of the discrepancy in freedom of action or of their own privileges as those who are constantly faced with the reality of status differences.

Florence Goodenough (10) in reappraising her own work on the Draw-a-Man Test, has eloquently stated the issue: "The search for a culture-free test, whether of intelligence, artistic ability, personal-social characteristics, or any other measurable trait is illusory." While this view may be prematurely skeptical, it seems that, at least in their present form, authoritarian tests are limited in application by their middle-class orientation.

Conclusion

1. The typical response tendencies of lower class individuals on the Rorschach may not be indicative of enduring personality tendencies. Rather, they may simply reflect a response to a localized stress situation—namely the stress involved in taking the test from a middle class examiner in the context of workers' general lack of experience in test taking. There is evidence that situational stress is associated with fewer color responses which appear to be one of the typical characteristics of workers' records. It also appears possible that situational stress will diminish those responses which require a more relaxed, interested involvement on the part of the testee—such as W, M, R, O.

We also suggest another hypothesis (not necessarily in contradiction to our major point): the workers' Rorschach response may be characterized by lack of interest and involvement. The worker shows a higher proportion of the responses which are "easiest" to give when least involved (A, F, etc.). It is possible that both lack of interest and test anxiety characterize workers' response at different times, but considerable research is needed before anything conclusive can be said.

The Rorschach may, at the present time, be a very limited test for determining personality patterns of lower class individuals. The difficulties in using the instrument with these individuals cannot be surmounted by simply providing lower class norms for the examiner.

2. There appears to be a need for a test, like the Thematic Apperception Test in form, but *including* working class people, symbols and situations. At the present time no such test is available for workers.[4]

In the absence of such a test, the need for caution on the part of psychiatrists and clinicians utilizing the standard personality tests is considerable. *Even if a new test equally appropriate in structure for both working-class and middle-class subjects were to become available, problems of rapport, experience in test taking, etc. would have to be overcome* before a full and accurate picture of the worker could be obtained from a battery of personality tests.

3. Although the lower-class individual scores in an authoritarian direction on the F-scale and its derivatives, the items probably have a very different meaning or referent in his sub-culture; consequently we should be very cautious in inferring anything about his personality, authoritarian tendencies, etc., from these scales. It is most striking that the scales are not predictive of authoritarian relevant attitudes (such as people oriented leadership and political apathy) in the lower class, while they are predictive in the middle class.

Many of the difficulties encountered in personality tests when they are applied across cultural and subcultural lines arise also on the *attitude* tests and polls employed by social psychologists and sociologists. While the authoritarianism scales were developed as projective personality tests, they are actually quite similar to numerous attitude scales. Kaltz's (18) finding that white-collar interviewers received fewer pro-labor responses from workers than did working-class interviewers is highly relevant in this connection.

4. Considerable research is needed in order to determine exactly how the test relevant variables, such as practice, motivation, etc., affect the performance of different groups on various projective tests. We need to know more about how the lower-class individual responds to different tests, which he likes better, and, more particularly, how he responds to test anxiety. Are there class differences in response to test (situational) anxiety, and if so, what are they? In regard to the Rorschach, specifically, we need to know whether workers' responses are characterized by lack of interest, anxiety or both. This knowledge, of course, would have to be flexibly, not mechanically, applied. For example, it is not always true that a Negro psychologist will have better rapport with every Negro child, although the presence of a Negro psychologist in the clinic would probably provide a more favorable climate for relationship between Negro children and white examiners.

If new TAT pictures apparently more suited to the lower class are developed, research will be needed to ascertain whether in fact these pictures lead to a more full response on the part of the worker, and whether they provide a more accurate portrayal of his personality.

5. Clinicians utilizing projective tests with members of different class groups should consider the possible effects of the test situation, language (and referents) used in the test, educational differences, motivation, timing of the test (speed factors), and cross-class rapport problems. In order to be able to do this effectively clinicians need considerable training in sociology as well as fairly extensive knowledge concerning the culture of the subgroups with which they are likely to be working.

Many of the test relevant variables we have been considering apply to any individual in any class, and clinicians have to attempt to appraise their role in making a diagnosis.

These variables probably function, however, in a more consistent and decisive fashion across class and cultural lines.

Notes

1. Data presented in this article are based, in part, on Frank Riessman, "Workers' Attitudes Toward Participation and Leadership," unpublished doctoral dissertation, Columbia University, 1955. Special thanks are due the Institute for Research in Human Relations for making portions of the data available.

2. "Lower class" and "working class" are used interchangeably in this article because of the widespread practice in this regard.

3. Length of story may not be the best index of lower class involvement as educational deficiencies would probably limit the length of the story regardless of how deeply the worker identified with the individuals in the pictures.

4. A number of projective picture tests similar to the TAT have been developed but these are oriented toward determining social attitudes rather than personality patterns. See, for example, H. Lennard and F. Riessman, "A Proposed Projective Attitude Test," *Psychiatry*, 1946, 9.

References

1. Adorno, T. W., *et al. The Authoritarian Personality*. New York: Harper and Row, 1950.

2. Auld, F. The influence of social class on tests of personality, *Drew University Studies*, No. 5, December 1952, 1–16.

3. Campbell, D. The indirect assessment of social attitudes. *Psychol. Bull.*, 1950, 47, 15–38.

4. Carlson, Rai. A normative study of Rorschach responses of eight-year-old children, *J. Proj. Tech.*, 1952, 16, 56–65.

5. Christie, R. Authoritarianism reexamined. In Christie and Jahoda (Ed.) *Studies in the scope and method of the authoritarian personality*. New York: The Free Press of Glencoe, 1954.

6. Davis, A. *Social Class Influences upon Learning*. Cambridge: Harvard University Press, 1948.

7. Douvan, Elizabeth. Social status and success striving, *J. Abnorm. Soc. Psychol.*, 1956, 52, 219–223.

8. Eichler, R. Experimental stress and alleged Rorschach indices of anxiety, *J. Abnorm. Soc. Psychol.*, 1951, 46, 344–355.

9. Farris, D. Authoritarianism as a Political Behavior Variable. *J. Polit.*, 1956, 18.

10. Goodenough, Florence and Harris, D. *Psychol. Bull.*, 1950, 5.

11. Gough, H. G. A New Dimension of Status II. *Amer. Sociol. Rev.*, 1948, 13, 401–409.

12. Haase, W. Rorschach Diagnosis, Socio-economic Class, and Examiner Bias. Unpublished doctoral dissertation, New York University, 1956.

13. Haggard, E. Social Status and Intelligence: An Experimental Study of Certain Cultural Determinants of Measured Intelligence, *Genet. Psychol. Monogr.*, 1954, 49, 145–185.

14. Hoffman, K. and Albizer-Miranda, C. Middle Class Bias in Personality Testing. *J. abnorm. soc. Psychol.*, 1955, 51, 150–152.

15. Hollingshead, A. B. *Elmtown's youth*. New York: John Wiley and Sons, 1949.

16. Hyman, H. and Sheatsley, P. The Authoritarian Personality—A Methodological Critique. In Christie and Jahoda (Eds.), *Studies in the scope and method of the authoritarian personality*. New York: The Free Press of Glencoe, 1954.

17. Janowitz, M. and Marvick, D. Authoritarianism and Political Behavior. *Pub. opin. Quart.*, 1953, 17, 185–201.

18. Katz, D. Do Interviewers Bias Poll Results? *Pub. opin. Quart.*, 1942, 6, 248–268.

19. Kimble, G. A. Social Influences on Rorschach Records. *J. abnorm. soc. Psychol.*, 1945, 40, 89–93.

20. Klatskin, Ethelyn. An Analysis of the Effect of the Test Situations upon the Rorschach Record. *J. proj. Tech.*, 1952, 16, 193–198.

21. Korchin, S. J., Mitchell, H. E. and Meltzoff, J. A Critical Evaluation of the Thompson TAT. *J. proj. Tech.*, 1950, 14, 445–452.

22. Mason, Beth and Ammons, R. B. Note on Social Class and the Thematic Apperception Test. *Percept. and mot. Skills*, 1956, 6, 88.

23. Riess, B. F., Schwartz, E. K. and

Cottingham, Alice. An Experimental Critique of Assumptions Underlying the Negro Version of the TAT. *J. abnorm. soc. Psychol.*, 1950, 45, 700–709.

24. Riessman, F. Workers' Attitudes towards Participation and Leadership. Unpublished doctoral dissertation, Columbia University, 1955.

25. Rosenberg, M. The Social Roots of Formalism, *J. soc. Issues*, 1949, 5, 14–23.

26. Sanford, F. H. *Authoritarianism and Leadership.* Philadelphia: The Institute of Research in Human Relations, 1950.

27. Shore, A. *Autoritarismo y agresion en una aldea Mexicana.* Mexico: D. F., 1954.

28. Stone, L. J. and Fiedler, Miriam F. The Rorschachs of Selected Groups of Children in Comparison with Published Norms: II The Effect of Socio-economic Status on Rorschach Performance, *J. proj. Tech.*, 1956, 20, 276–279.

29. Useem, J., Tangent, P. and Useem, Ruth. Stratification in a Prairie Town. *Amer. J. Sociol.*, 1942, 7, 331–342.

Situational Testing of Social Psychological Variables in Personality [1]

Jerome Beker, Eugene Eliasoph, and David Resnik

There is a growing awareness among behavioral scientists concerned with personality that verbal and projective tests provide incomplete and inadequate data, especially with relation to overt, coping behavior. The movement toward performance or situational testing in this area has been surveyed by Santostefano (1962), who notes that projective tests seem to tap fantasy behavior that may or many not be directly and positively actualized in overt behavior. Traditional "objective" tests, on the other hand, elicit largely verbal responses to largely verbal items and may not be subject to generalization in terms of other forms of behavior either because of conscious or unconscious distortion or because a different dimension or level of behavior is being tapped. Both kinds of test require a large measure of inference between test performance and other behavior or personality characteristics.

In the same paper, Santostefano presents criteria for an effective situational test, describing it as one which "(a) allows the free expression of personality dimensions in situations requiring S to cope with people and objects; (b) provides identical stimuli to all Ss in settings containing significant realism; (c) produces unequivocally identifiable responses; (d) yields measures, the meanings of which are not completely dependent on judgments; (e) elicits natural behavior which would be minimally affected by S's knowledge that he is dealing with a test; and (f) is feasible for use in ordinary clinic and research settings." These criteria are worthy of further examination in themselves, in the context of a research project reported by the same investigator (Santo-

259

stefano, 1960), and in the context of current research being conducted by the writers of the present paper.

Quite properly, the criteria listed above specifically include opportunities for subjects to interact with people as well as with objects. Interaction with another person beyond the first exchange, however, presupposes some sort of essentially unpredictable feedback since the subject's response to the other person's presumably standardized initial behavior cannot be anticipated. Therefore, the criterion of identical stimuli to all subjects cannot realistically be maintained in any but the simplest interpersonal situations. As will be demonstrated below, this criterion is not essential to effective situational testing. It is also hard to see how some degree of inference can be avoided, unless the test "result" is simply an objective report of the subject's behavior. Thus, the criterion that response "meanings" should not depend completely on judgments is methodologically, and perhaps semantically and logically, unrealistic.

In his own research, Santostefano (1960) presented subjects with forced choices between twenty sets of two tasks each and found five factors which he labeled as, for example, "expressing overt forceful aggression vs. inhibiting overt forceful aggression." It would seem that some degree of inference is required to obtain this label from, for example, the choice to break a large light bulb rather than a small one. The inference seems to be an obvious one, but it is nonetheless an inference. A further inference is required if these results are to be generalized to overall behavior, especially social behavior. Either it must be inferred that choices like this reflect life styles or personality traits, or one is left with basically the same kinds of problems that led to the search for alternatives to projective and verbal tests. It is the position of the writers of the present paper that the use of inferences and judgments such as this cannot be avoided if one hopes to study more significant variables than preferences for breaking light bulbs of a particular size. It is felt that the significant advantages of situational or performance tests derive from a different source; namely, the closer correspondence of the test situation and, presumably, the behavior it evokes, with non-test aspects of life. The inference involved may be smaller, but its presence must be recognized if one hopes to avoid the inappropriate exclusion of particular test techniques in which the inferential or judgmental aspect is, perhaps, more obvious. Rather, effort should be directed toward finding ways of improving the quality (or validity) of inference and judgment in situational testing.

One approach may involve presenting subjects with a standardized social situation as a stimulus to which they are asked to respond by enacting a particular role in the fictitious situation. One or more "testers" enact the other role or roles required, and observers are present to rate the subject's behavior on selected dimensions. This "role testing" technique has been applied elsewhere (Mouton, *et al.*, 1960), resulting in support for Borgatta's (1955) finding of "relatively high consistency in behavior for individuals from role playing to actual situations . . . ." (Mouton, *et al.*, 1960).

The study reported here was incidental to a larger project [2] being conducted at a training school for delinquent adolescent boys. It seems to suggest that role testing can, indeed, provide a reliable and—to the extent that it resembles non-test "real life" and evokes similar patterns of behavior—a valid instrument for the testing of social variables in personality. The technique would seem to be practical for use in most clinical and research settings, and although it inevitably requires more staff time and effort than do many of the more traditional verbal measures, it is no more demanding in this respect than are the projectives. Whether the verbal measures (e.g., the California Psychological Inventory or the MMPI) can provide essentially equivalent data with less time and effort, or at least in what areas they can do so, awaits further investigation.

The subjects in this study included 32 adolescent boys who had been adjudicated delinquent and subsequently institutionalized.[3] Although the diversity of backgrounds and personalities that may be included in a group such as this is well known, it seems a fair conclusion that the group was more homogenous than would have resulted from a random or a representative stratified selection from the general population. We know that this is the case with respect to age, sex, the low socioeconomic backgrounds from which all or nearly all of the boys came, and the fact that all were adjudicated delinquent and institutionalized. Therefore, one would expect as much or more difficulty in establishing adequate reliability of measures within this group than within a more diverse one, assuming the variables concerned not to be a direct function of the homogeneity of the group. For reasons concerned with the broader study of which the data presented here represent a part, all boys were "role-tested" between two and four weeks after their arrival at the institution. Thus, it seems likely that the results are largely uncontaminated either by transitory first reactions to institutionalization or by the impact of the institutional milieu (including treatment services) itself.

The entire testing procedure took about twenty minutes per boy and in each case involved a "tester" and three observer-raters. Ratings were made on ten scales, five for each of two situations or roles the subject was asked to enact. The tests were conducted in a room with a small stage or platform on which the subjects and the tester stood or sat, depending on the situation and the way it developed. When a subject entered the room, he was greeted by the tester and introduced to the raters. Then the subject was told that he was one of a number of boys who had been selected to help the institution learn more about the boys. He would be asked to act out two scenes, he was told, and he was assured that nothing he said or did would influence his personal record or such factors as his discharge date in any way. This introduction was conducted informally, after which the boy was asked to sit on a chair on the platform and the following instructions were read to him by the tester:

You are a judge in court. A boy who has stolen a car and run over a child who is in the hospital is in court and you are talking to him to

decide what to do about his case. You have to talk to him about what
he did and find out why he did it. You have to talk to him about the
law and what is going to happen to him if the child dies, if the child
is crippled for life, or if the child turns out all right after being
checked over in the hospital. You can talk to him about whatever
else you want. Now, I'm the boy and you're the judge, and I'm coming into the courtroom.

The tester then assumed the role of the boy. He slowly walked onto the
stage with his head down and sat in a chair in front of the "judge." If
the boy did not say anything or asked a question about the procedure,
the tester simply asked, "You wanted to see me, Your Honor?" After that,
the playlet proceeded spontaneously rather than in a standardized
fashion, depending on the subject's behavior, except that the tester attempted to direct some attention to each of the variables, unknown to
the boy, being rated. It continued until the raters indicated that they had
completed their five ratings, usually within about five minutes.

The tester then ended the scene, walked off the platform, and invited
the boy to get up and stretch or walk around. After this, the next set of
instructions were read, as follows:

Now we have one more scene. This time I want you to be yourself
and I'll be one of your best buddies. I've just stolen thirty bucks
from a cash box that was left in the open on a newspaper stand. I
stole the money because the man who owns the stand ranked on
(insulted) me, and I waited 'til his back was turned and took the
box. Now I'm meeting you and I tell you about it. You and I make
plans.

Both actors then walked onto the platform and the tester excitedly
started the conversation. "Hey, buddy, you know that old louse who runs
the newspaper stand on the corner? The guy that's always yellin' at us
kids? Well, this time I really took care of him. I stole his cash box and
got thirty bucks. What do you think we should do with it?" From this
point, except for the tester's attempts to focus on variables being rated,
the interaction was unplanned and spontaneous, continuing, as before,
until the raters indicated that they had completed their ratings. The
subject was then dismissed with thanks.

These two situations were chosen arbitrarily as seeming likely to
provide information about particular variables. Likewise, the five-point
rating scales used were developed simply for face validity, and it was
recognized that some were likely to prove inadequate in practice. For
the first role test (Role Test A), the variables for which rating scales
were devised were these:[4]

A-1. Ability to play the role of the judge effectively;
A-2. Rejection or acceptance of stealing (in the role of the judge);
A-3. Concern for the suffering of the injured child and his family;
A-4. Concept of authority as a dual function involving both guidance
      and control; and
A-5. Interest in probing for causes underlying the behavior.

Rating scales for the second role test (B) involved the subject's:

B-1. Ability to play the "self" role effectively;
B-2. Feelings about the stolen money;
B-3. Reactions to peer pressure;
B-4. Relationships with his parents; and
B-5. Feelings about his parents.

The tester attempted through his performance as has already been noted, to elicit some reactions from each subject relating to each of these general areas.

As is obvious from the brief description given above, this research represented a pilot study of the effectiveness of fairly simple situational tests in the measurement of complex personality variables directly involving social behavior. The reliability of the ratings is, of course, a critical factor. Reliability coefficients were computed for the mean of three raters using the method suggested by Ebel (1951) as outlined by Guilford (1954). Although only three raters rated any one subject, a total of eleven raters (many of whom were largely unacquainted with the scales used) participated in the project. This suggests that the reliability coefficients may be lower than would have been the case if the same three raters had participated throughout, but at the same time it provides a more stringent test of the scales and the procedure. All raters, however, were professionally trained in human behavior, and included nine social workers, one educator, and one psychologist. The reliability coefficients for each of the ten rating scales are presented in Table 1.

Table 1—Rating Scale Reliability Coefficients

Scale	A-1	A-2	A-3	A-4	A-5	B-1	B-2	B-3	B-4	B-5
Reliability	.90	.70	.68	.81	.86	.87	.94	.91	.50	.78

Reliability of the mean for three raters.

On the basis of this data, the three scales yielding reliability coefficients below .75 were eliminated from further analysis for this particular group. Further exploration is proposed to determine whether modification of the role tests designed to evoke relevant behavior by the subjects or modification of the scales themselves can result in improved reliability for all scales and for these three in particular. The seven remaining scales were then inter-correlated in an effort to establish the number of independent measures they represented. These correlation coefficients are presented in Table 2.

The clearest conclusion indicated by these data is that scales B-2 and B-3 were measuring essentially the same thing, not only because they were so highly correlated with each other but also because they correlated virtually identically with each of the other scales. This confirms the existence of an ambiguity in the test procedure that had been suspected in advance: in the nature of the test, conformity to peer pressure suggests acceptance of stealing and vice versa since the staged peer pressure was in this direction. Thus, these two parameters have not yet been

Table 2—Pearsonian Correlations Among Rating Scales

Scale	A-1	A-4	A-5	B-1	B-2	B-3	B-5
A-1	—	75	70	83	20	28	38
A-4	75	—	80	45	22	26	41
A-5	70	80	—	49	16	12	39
B-1	83	45	49	—	27	28	28
B-2	20	22	16	27	—	85	71
B-3	28	26	12	28	85	—	69
B-5	38	41	39	28	71	69	—

Correlations are presented only among those scales which produced reliabilities exceeding .75. N = 31; a coefficient of .29 is required for statistical significance at the .05 level. All correlations are positive, and signs and decimal points are omitted. The top and bottom portions of the table duplicate each other, but both are presented to facilitate the comparisons suggested in the text.

successfully differentiated—perhaps a third role test in which the roles in Test B are reversed (with the boy acting as the thief) is needed. It may also be, of course, that delinquent adolescent boys who conform most to peer pressure tend also to accept stealing most easily, but even this conclusion cannot be drawn without further evidence. For the purposes of the present paper, the significant finding is that this complex variable, involving conformity to peer pressures in favor of stealing, was rated with high reliability from informal situational test behavior before any empirical refinements of either the test or the scales had been introduced. Nor can the reliability be attributed to a lack of distribution in the ratings. Although there was a tendency for ratings to be high or low rather than in the middle (which itself suggests that the situational test evoked clearly identifiable behavior differentials among subjects), an approximately equal number of subjects were rated toward each extreme and the reliability coefficients attest to the fact that raters agreed on the behavior classifications.

The data also provide evidence for the existence of "role-playing ability" as a general variable, since subjects who were rated highly in their ability to take one of the roles (e.g., Scale A-1) tended also to be rated highly on the other (e.g., Scale B-1). Both of these scales had reliability coefficients in the area of .9, and it seems plausible to hypothesize for future research that: (a) role-playing ability tends to be a general ability rather than specific to the role; (b) ability to play the role of another correlates with the ability to project one's self-image effectively; and (c) situational or role tests, dependent on ratings by observers, provide an effective tool for investigation in this area. This finding is the more convincing because, while there seems to be a tendency for the scales used within each of the two role tests to cluster separately by test, this is not true of Scale B-1, which was closely correlated only with Scale A-1. It was only slightly related, if at all, to comfort about the stolen money, conformity to peer pressure, or the subject's feelings about his family. Scale B-1 tended, in fact, to relate more closely to Scales A-4 and A-5, concerned with the role of authority and interest in the causes of behavior. This seems to lend further credence to the idea of the existence of a general role-playing ability as suggested above.

Scales A-4 and A-5 also seem to represent a single variable in view

of their high correlation, virtually as high as the reliability of either, and their virtually identical correlations with each of the other scales. This is not surprising because a high rating on Scale A-4 implies that the subject is aware of the guidance function of authority as well as its control function. This would seem to imply, further, a concern with the causes of behavior, precisely the subject of Scale A-5. Here again, the need for further investigation is apparent, this time toward a clearer differentiation of concepts of authority as well as a refinement of the scales in an effort to increase reliabilities. For the purposes of the present paper, however, the data further demonstrate the feasibility of obtaining reliable and consistent ratings from situational tests.

Among the scales with reliability coefficients exceeding .75, only Scale B-5, with the lowest of the acceptable reliabilities, has yet to be discussed. The relatively low reliabilities of the two scales relating to parents (B-4 and B-5) were not unexpected, since it became increasingly evident as the study progressed that Test B did not provide an adequate source of relevant information even when the tester consciously tried to bring parental factors into purview. Possibly a separate situational test would be helpful in studying familial variables more intensively. The reliability of Scale B-5 was, however, high enough to permit some tentative inferences. In spite of their relatively low reliability, ratings of subjects' feelings about their parents correlated moderately—around .4— with their ability to take the role of the judge, their conception of the dual functions of authority noted above, and their interest (in the judge role) in probing for the causes of behavior. The correlations were much higher—on the order of .7—with Scales B-2 and B-3, discussed at length above, suggesting a close relationship between feelings toward parents as measured by the role tests and rejection of peer pressure to participate in the use of stolen money. All these correlations seem to "make sense" on both intuitive and theoretical grounds, supporting further the apparent validity of the role test findings.

All 21 correlation coefficients were positive, suggesting that some halo influence may have been present, but nine of the 21 were not significantly different from zero at the .05 level and fourteen of the 21 were below .5, so it seems apparent that a considerable degree of differentiation among the scales occurred. This is especially evident in Scales B-2 and B-3 (essentially equivalent scales, as has been pointed out above), which showed statistically significant correlations only with Scale B-5 and with each other.

Obviously, refinements are needed in the technique in the directions indicated and implied above. It seems equally clear, however, that the role tests provided convincing and useful "scores" for a variety of complex social and personality variables, including role-playing ability, concepts of the functions of authority, resistance to anti-social peer pressure, and to perhaps a somewhat lesser degree, feelings about parents. Additional variables that evolve from these suggest themselves as accessible to the same testing methods; for example, the mechanisms used for resisting peer pressure by those who do, and even the study of

such mechanisms that tend to succeed compared with those that tend to fail.

One of the most provocative and promising outcomes of the study was unanticipated. Most of the raters, practicing clinicians, reported that they frequently achieved more understanding of subjects' patterns of social behavior in the twenty minutes of role test observation than would usually be gained in a fairly lengthy initial phase of treatment. This suggests not only the obvious conclusion that the kind of situational test outlined above can enhance and speed clinical insight, but also that here may lie an untapped source of needed insight into some of the obscure variables on which the clinical process depends.

Thus, situational tests may offer a feasible method for identifying and studying complex social and personality variables and their inter-relationships as well as for testing individuals on such variables. It is doubtful whether either of these objectives can be as effectively realized in the absence of the kind of inductive approach and relatively spontaneous and unstructured test situations, implying the need for the use of ratings, that have been reported here. What is sought is not a standardized test but a sample of behavior directed so as to evoke actions illustrative of the non-fragmented personality variables with which the tester is concerned. At this stage, it is felt that the most productive effort in this area will be devoted to the development and refinement of evocative situational tests and reliable and valid rating scales for complex variables, rather than to the search for greater objectivization of situational testing and scoring alone.

Notes

1. This investigation was undertaken during the senior author's tenure in the United States Public Health Service Fellowship No. MPD-13,256-C1 fom the National Institute of Mental Health.

2. The overall project from which the present paper is a methodological extraction is an attempt to develop an empirical typology of juvenile delinquents with implications for differential approaches to prevention and rehabilitation.

3. One subject rejected the test situation almost completely, and most raters were unable to rate him on most of the scales used. Therefore, except for reliability figures on a few scales, data presented below are based on N-31. Exploration of the meaning of the rejection of the test is, of course, indicated, but it appeared likely that, for reasons unknown, the boy involved would have rejected any form of test at that particular time.

4. Copies of these preliminary rating scales are available from the senior author to interested readers.

References

Ebel, R. L. "Estimation of the Reliability of Ratings," *Psychometrika*, 16 (1951), 407–24.

Guilford, J. P. *Psychometric Methods*. (2nd ed. New York: McGraw-Hill, 1954).

Mouton, Jane S., Bell, R. L., and Blake, R. R. "Role Playing Skill and Sociometric Peer Status." In J. L. Moreno (Ed.), *The Sociometry Reader* (New York: The Free Press of Glencoe, 1960), 388–98.

Santostefano, S. "An Exploration of Performance Measures of Personality," *J. Clin. Psychol.*, 26 (1960), 373–77.

———. "Performance Testing of Personality," *Merrill-Palmer Quart.*, 8 (1962), 83–97.

Early Language Behavior in Negro Children and the Testing of Intelligence

Benjamin Pasamanick and Hilda Knobloch

Much has been written concerning Negro-white differences in growth, development, and intelligence. With continued investigation, environmental causes for these differences are being discovered so that it is no longer possible to state that they are unequivocally innate or racial (3).

The most controversial area, that of intelligence, has been studied intensively and the responsible sociocultural variables fairly well delineated. Among these has been described awareness of race, even in the preschool child, with consequent loss of rapport and lowering of score on psychometric examination. Poor performance on verbal items, attributable to cultural factors, has also been implicated (1).

In a longitudinal study of a low socioeconomic Negro group in New Haven, no significant Negro-white differences in either physical growth or behavioral development were found during the first eighteen months (7). It was hypothesized that growth and development were causally related and that poor nutrition rather than innate inferiority was therefore responsible for differences previously reported in both growth and development of Negro infants (6). A third examination of the group (40 children) at the mean age of 24.4 months supported this hypothesis (4). Growth and development for the group as a whole continued at white rates.

With continued use of the Gesell Developmental Examination on this third examination, interesting findings were noted in two behavior areas.

Reprinted by permission of American Psychological Assoc., Inc., from *Journal of Abnormal and Social Psychology*, Vol. 50, No. 3, May 1955, pp. 401–402.

Gross motor behavior was found to be markedly accelerated. Language behavior of the Negro infants while not retarded (mean DQ = 101) when compared to the white norms was significantly lower than the other fields of behavior. In addition, it was lower than the scores achieved in the first (DQ = 106) and second (DQ = 104) examinations, the difference between first and third being statistically significant ($p < .01$).

In a recent and still unpublished study done by one of the authors with Williams and Scott (8), a probable explanation for the discrepant scores in gross motor behavior was found. Gross motor development in a series of Negro clinic and private patients was found to be negatively correlated with socioeconomic status, the latter being negatively correlated with permissiveness. This probably accounts for the high quotients in the New Haven group which is largely of low socioeconomic status.

In an attempt to explain the comparatively low scores in the language area, the hypothesis was advanced that awareness of the examiner's different skin color caused sufficient inhibition to decrease verbal responsiveness by the children. This point had been raised by one of the parents who offered it as an explanation for her child's almost total lack of speech during examination.

This hypothesis was tested by somewhat crudely dividing the language behavior items on the Gesell Developmental Examination into three spheres, reported language behavior, comprehension of language, and verbal responsiveness. This was done to compare verbal responsive behavior, which might be impaired, with reported and comprehension behavior. Language maturity levels were assigned on the basis of recorded schedules in each of these spheres and quotients derived by the formula $DQ = \dfrac{CA}{MA}$ (Table 1). The mean quotients arrived at in this fashion were quite revealing.

Table 1—Mean Developmental Quotients of Various Aspects of Language Behavior

Language Behavior	Mean DQ	SD
Total	101	10.8
Reported	101	12.6
Verbal responsiveness	94	17.7
Comprehension of speech	104	15.7

Verbal and comprehension behavior spheres are significantly different ($p < .001$). Reported behavior is not significantly different from the other two. It is also apparent that verbal responsiveness varied more ($SD = 17.7$) than did comprehension or reported behavior; this might be due to variation in awareness of racial differences.

Although reported language behavior fell between the other two spheres and was essentially the same as total language behavior in mean

score, it was thought advisable to test accuracy of reporting by mothers. This was done by comparing the reported and observed gross motor behavior in the same manner. The mean reported behavior quotient was 131 and the observed 132; these are of course not significantly different indicating that, on the whole, the mothers of our subjects were fairly reliable reporters of gross motor behavior. There is no reason to believe their reporting of language differed from the actual performance of the child.

Discussion

The hypothesis that racial awareness plays a significant role during the examination process for the assessment of development seems to have some validity, even in the early preschool years. Comparative studies of ethnic group and racial psychologic differences by investigators from backgrounds and with physical characteristics differing from those of the group under investigation are inherently biased by this variable. One could speculate as to the source of these difficulties. How much of the observed reserve and inhibition is due to physical differences in the examiner and how much due to learning of attitudes from parents and siblings? In any event, it is a factor to be reckoned with in projected studies and in the evaluation of past studies.

Another implication from these findings is the difficulty of interpreting differences found when verbal response items are used in intelligence testing. Investigators have noted these sources of error (2), and it is of interest that our findings show that they may arise at a surprisingly early age.

Landreth and Johnson have shown that by three years of age Negro children have learned and accepted the majority stereotypes about Negroes (5). If our interpretation of the cause of lack of verbal responsiveness in the Negro children is correct, the awareness of racial differences apparently occurs much earlier than has been previously demonstrated.

Summary

Forty Negro children examined by a white examiner were found to have lowered language scores on third examination at two years of age. This was apparently due to lack of verbal responsiveness, rather than poor comprehension of language. This apparent early awareness of racial differences and loss of rapport has serious implications in the field of ethnic group psychology, particularly in the use of verbal items on intelligence testing.

References

1. Anastasi, Anne, and D'Angelo, Rita Y. A comparison of Negro and white preschool children in language development and Goodenough Draw-a-Man IQ. *J. genet. Psychol.*, 1952, *81*, 147–165.

2. Brown, F. An experimental and critical study of the intelligence of Negro and white kindergarten children. *J. genet. Psychol.*, 1944, *65*, 161–175.

3. Klineberg, O. Race differences: the present position of the problem. *Bull. World Fed. Ment. Hlth*, 1951, *3*, 3–11.

4. Knobloch, H., and Pasamanick, B. Further observations on the development of Negro children. *J. genet. Psychol.*, 1953, *83*, 137–157.

5. Landreth, C., and Johnson, B. C. Young children's responses to a picture and inset test designed to reveal reactions to persons of different skin color. *Child Develpm.*, 1953, *24*, 63–80.

6. McGraw, M. B. A comparative study of a group of Southern white and Negro infants. *Genet. Psychol. Monogr.*, 1931, *10*, 1–105.

7. Pasamanick, B. A comparative study of the behavioral development of Negro infants. *J. genet. Psychol.*, 1946, *69*, 3–44.

8. Williams, J., Scott, R., and Pasamanick, B. Unpublished data available at Howard Univer., Wash., D.C.

A Short Story on the Long Waiting List

Rachel A. Levine

The Henry Street Settlement Mental Hygiene Clinic (supported by Henry Street Settlement with matching funds from the New York City Community Mental Health Board), situated on the Lower East Side of New York City, was recently asked by some of its social agency and clinic neighbors, how were you able to abolish the waiting list? This question is still posed as though it were in the nature of a riddle.

Perhaps the question has reached the proportions of a riddle because waiting lists for mental health services round the town have been with us for a long time. Like many riddles which on first glance appear insoluble, the answer to this one too can easily be provided, if thinking is unencumbered by elements which deflect attention from the cause of waiting lists.

Proceeding to the core, this clinic looked first at two primary objectives. First, different from services offered in settings whose primary function is training, or research, this community clinic was established to bring the benefits of psychiatry to people who need it most but can afford it least. Second, in order to utilize the motivation which brings a person to seek help, that help must be available when it is requested.

If these are valid objectives, then it appears that when demand grows in excess of personnel available, it is incumbent upon a community clinic to seek new ways of meeting it by utilizing a variety of techniques rather than putting names on a waiting list, an act which is tantamount to turning people away. It is this proposition which evokes rationalizations in defense of the status quo because it touches off long-held beliefs based

Reprinted by permission of National Association of Social Workers, from *Social Work*, Vol. 8, No. 1, January 1963, pp. 20–23.

upon past training and personal investment. These in turn have the effect of deflecting attention from the core purpose of service to people in need to that of satisfying needs in therapists.

The reflection, however well-intentioned, is built up on personal views of such matters as goals and methodology. A counterpart of deflection from the core purpose then follows in the amount of time diverted from service to many to service to a few, as well as to meetings, conferences, supervision, case recording, etc. The way out of this dilemma has been to press for more staff.

More staff as the solution to increasing demand for services is becoming less and less viable with the slow but sure realization that the availability of qualified professional personnel will not in the foreseeable future keep pace with demand for mental health services, let alone the question of money. Receding too is the long-held premise that the waiting list is the incontrovertible proof of demand to convince Boards of Directors, Foundations, State, and Municipal governments of critical need for larger allocations for personnel. This no longer works because, weighed against the consequences of waiting lists, namely, drop-outs, progression into more serious manifestations of maladjustment and mental illness, delinquency and family disorganization, the waiting list principle is untenable and also yields its own ratio of attrition and diminishing return.. Community agencies which have steadfastly held to this condition are now confronted with the ironic situation of a diminishing case load and are casting about for referrals—or will inevitably reach this point. In a follow-up procedure in which immediate service was offered to some 150 applicants on the waiting list of two months to two years, conducted by the writer in another community mental health clinic in 1959, two-thirds of the applicants were no longer available. Some had moved, a few had found another resource, most had lost the initial stimulus and refused service. The one-third who accepted service had been waiting the shortest length of time.

Holding to the core purpose, this clinic abandoned the traditionally held solution of "more staff" to meet increased demand, and began to revise clinic policy and practices in February, 1961. The first major step with the assessment of all clinic functions and their relative expendability. It was concluded that direct service to people was the least expendable, and therefore a maximum of time was allotted for this purpose, with commensurate reduction of time for meetings and conferences. Classical supervision for experienced staff was eliminated, and case recording was cut to the barest essentials.

Simultaneously, intake which had been closed for approximately one year except for emergencies, was reopened and the waiting list abolished by action. Intake procedures were reorganized for more rapid processing as follows:

Applications and referrals for service are processed daily via telephone or brief interview in the case of a walk-in, so that the clinic knows at least what the need for service is, and the applicant knows whether or not the clinic can help. In cases where it appears the clinic can help,

the applicant is given an appointment for the initial interview the same day if an emergency, or within two weeks. Applicants who can be better served by another agency are immediately referred with follow-through. Although the first interview is generally with a social worker, it can also be with a psychiatrist or psychologist, depending upon the apparent need. Adequate diagnostic work-up included in referral is not repeated and psychological testing is done on a selective basis.

Where a complete diagnostic study is indicated, the intake process including team disposition conference is completed within a month or so of the application or referral date, priority being given to cases which appear urgent. Moreover, where indicated, patients can receive treatment pending the completion of the diagnostic study.

Having hurdled the barrier with respect to Intake, the equally critical one of eliminating a waiting list for treatment was tackled next, to allow for absorption of cases from Intake.

Reexamination of treatment practices proceeded with confrontation of reality considerations. If the community clinic is to serve people in its community to a maximum of its resources, it cannot concentrate services upon a few for indefinite lengths of time. There must be turn-over which is effected through termination of cases by plan. Turn-over in caseload is possible when the principle of limited goals is acceptable. Termination by plan is possible under the following conditions:

1. When the patient and the therapist together at the outset define the goal which in turn leads to consideration of length of treatment.
2. When the therapist sustains the treatment process selected to reach the goal.
3. When the patient is continuously involved in evaluating progress toward the specified goal and termination.

Parenthetically, it should be mentioned that experience has shown that for many patients, the above conditions when unequivocally applied have salutary affects. They remove initial fears of loss of control, lift the veil of mystery surrounding treatment in a mental health clinic, permit expression of their choice in problem solving. Above all, they tend to stimulate patients to mobilize themselves and their energies for the task, and are hence less apt to become a drop-out statistic.

The principle of limited goals is predicated upon the unqualified position that goals are patient-centered which means understandable to the patient, and hence attainable, clearly specified, rather than the therapists' preconceived goals, generalized in terms of speculations on potentials of attainability. Patient-centered goals derive from accurate assessment of patients' immediate problems, needs, capacities for change, as well as the best way they can make use of help. This concept is not new but is open to wide interpretation. The intent here is to narrow interpretation to literal meaning. If different goals and treatment methods are specified for different patients based upon accurate assessment of social, cultural, educational, economic, and clinical determinants,

the setting of time limits follows as a natural sequence. These can vary from one interview to a series of six, ten, or fifty or more in consecutive or intermittent fashion. Within a range of time-limit possibilities it is known that some patients need and can use only brief service, whether it is directed toward concrete supports like help with household management, housing, nursery school or recreation placement of children, or toward correcting misconceptions and destructive patterns of child rearing; other patients can benefit most from treatment focused on environmental change, others from psycho-therapeutic treatment of short duration to rebuild defenses which may have temporarily broken down in a crisis situation, others from modified insight therapy, still others from intermittent periods of supportive contact. In short, in the whole spectrum of treatment possibilities, goals, and time limits can be specified whether the modality selected be individual, or group, or family, or in combination.

The willingness in this clinic to examine Intake and Treatment practices long embedded as gospel in our profession, and to experiment with different approach in the light of a community clinic's primary function and in the light of the changing patient population and needs, has allowed for termination of cases by plan and serving more people at the time they need help. At no time during the past year has there been the necessity to reinstate a waiting list for either Intake or Treatment despite increase in demand.

Included in the foregoing is the recognition that demands for service vary from low to high but tend to level out to a manageable average over a period of a year. Should the average substantially rise beyond the manpower available to give service to patients, but remain within realistic objectives of a community clinic, then other solutions must be found. The magnitude of this task can be matched only by an equally wide undertaking on the part of all community agencies acting in concert to develop patterns of community organization and practice which are more effective than those we have today.

New Treatment Approaches

Counseling Socially Disadvantaged Children

Edmund W. Gordon

Among the factors which influence social status in our society are ethnic, economic, cultural, and religious group identification. The differences in status and group identification operate in many ways to influence the behavior of group members. Among them is the manner in which individuals in the various subgroupings relate to the norms assumed to be operative among white, middle class, U.S. Nationals. Numerous studies point to the higher incidence of variance from these norms among subgroups relegated to lower status. However, the data from these studies could also be analyzed to show the wide range of variations within subgroups, including those variations within the group upon which the accepted norms are based. When this is done, specific instances and patterns of norm variance are found in such wide distribution as to leave only the incidence of variance as a possibly significant factor, with type of variance being generic to all groupings. Thus, we may possibly account for the wide variety of characteristics, sometimes contradictory, which are reported to be found in a sub-subgroup like "school dropouts" or "juvenile delinquent" or "underachievers" or "socially disadvantaged" or "minority group youth" or "children of the poor" or "children in urban depressed areas."

It is the high incidence of norm variance with respect to school adjustment, school achievement, and persistence in school attendance in some members of these sub-subgroups that has led to much of our current concern with the counseling and educational problems of these children. Recognizing, as all of us do, that many disadvantaged children require no more or less counseling than do more privileged group children, I have interpreted my assignment to be that of wrestling with some of the special problems that may require attention in the guidance of

275

children who are *handicapped* by social, ethnic, cultural, or economic differences in status.

My topic suggests that there are special considerations, unique problems and specific approaches to guidance that must be taken into account when we apply these processes of guided behavioral development and guided behavioral change to youth so handicapped. I will deal with some of these in this paper. However, I seriously doubt that there are any such factors that are fundamental to guided behavioral development and change. Our focus on a handicapped group and some of the special problems and considerations involved, however, may lead us to the identification and support of concepts and theoretical positions that *are* fundamental to behavioral change. In medicine, when concerted attention has been given to the epidemicity and control of pathological syndromes we have often gained insight into and understanding of basic postulates. It also may be that as we look more closely at the guided development of children who are handicapped by differences in social status, we may gain a better understanding of some of the postulates basic to the process of guided behavioral development and change.

The manner in which investigators or practitioners approach the understanding of the organization of behavior or the modification of behavioral organization is influenced by their theoretical position on the genesis of patterned behavior. Problems raised for investigation, research design chosen, as well as phenomena observed, generally reflect the theoretical bias of the investigator. Goals and practices to be used in approaches to behavioral change are usually determined by the practitioner's view of the mechanism underlying behavioral organization.

Theories of behavior may be divided into those which posit an essentially projective view and those which posit an essentially reflectional or interactive view of the mechanisms underlying behavioral organization. In the projective view, predetermined, intrinsic patterns are thought to be released by stimulation and projected onto the environment where their specific form is facilitated or inhibited. Among persons adhering to this position, emphasis is given to hypotheses concerning the existence in the organism of intrinsic drive states which exist prior to and independently of life experiences and which are the basic forces in the determination of behavior. Certain behavioral patterns are seen as performed, stored, and waiting for the proper time and condition for emergence. Capacities and traits are seen as determined by these intrinsic factors which can only be modified somewhat by the environment. The fundamental character of patterned behavior is seen as genetically established and bound. Environmental forces are considered to influence the organization of behavior by determining: 1) the directions taken by the primary energies and drives; 2) the environmental objects to which they become attached; and 3) the specific time and form in which they will emerge.

On the other hand, the interactionist or reflectional position holds that all organized patterned behaviors are reflections of the interaction between the organism and its environment. Environmental interaction is

seen as the crucial determinant and molder of patterned organismic function. Temporal and situational phenomena are regarded not as *releaser* but as *causative* and *mediating* agents. Behavioral characteristics, traits, species, typical behaviors, all organized patterned behaviors are seen to exist only as results of sensory input flowing from interaction of the organism and environment. Behavioral potentials are said to be genetically seeded in the sense that the organism includes structural responsivity which is largely determined by the nature of the genes, but the behavioral patterns, behavioral characteristics, and quality of functions are determined by interactions between organism and environment with the nature of these interactions being critical for organized behavior.

When behavior theory is used to determine practice in guided behavioral development and change, the differences in the two positions are manifested in the goals, design, and management of guided behavioral development. (Guided behavioral development is used here as an inclusive term to cover pedagogy, counseling, and psychotherapy.) The dominance of the projective view in guided behavioral development has been reflected in:

1. A laissez-faire or neglectful attitude toward the training and development of intelligence;
2. A monitoring as opposed to a stimulating approach to academic and social readiness and personality development;
3. An exaggerated emphasis on the predictive value of the classification and quantification of psychological appraisal data and the neglect of qualitative appraisal data as a basis for planning and intervention;
4. Distortion of aspiration and expectation levels based upon unjustified ceilings on potentials for human development and adaptation;
5. Placement of the burden of proof (a) on the examiner rather than on the appraiser or appraisal methods; (b) on the learner rather than on the teacher or teaching methods, and (c) on the counselee rather than on the counselor or counseling method.
6. Emphasis on adjustment or acceptance of assumed realities rather than on modification of the environment and the individual's interaction with same;
7. Overemphasis on selection and placement (educational and vocational) with an underemphasis on the nurturing of interests and aptitudes and the development and training of capacities and skills;
8. An eclectic and empirical approach to research in directed learning with little application of the scientific method in exploration, experimentation and investigation.

Now, despite my negative view of these influences of projectionist theory on guided behavioral development, the theory has worked for many learners, or at least many learners have learned something despite

its influence. But what of those who do not learn or who have not learned at the same rate and in the same way as have our successful learners? What is the relationship of this controversy to guidance for children handicapped by social, ethnic, cultural, or economic status differences?

A problem of increasing proportion in eductaional and social planning is providing educational opportunities appropriate to the characteristics and needs of large numbers of children who live in communities where income level and social status are low; where general intellectual stimulation is inappropriate to a high level of academic achievement; and where patterns of social organization, cultural characteristics, and cultural values differ markedly from those dominant in middle class society.

Several studies of children attending school in many of our disadvantaged communities have pointed to atypicalities in development, in attitudes toward teachers, and in school achievement. Children living under varying conditions of deprivation and social-cultural atypicality are also reported to show disproportionately high rates of social maladjustment, behavioral disturbance, physical disability, and mental subnormality. Academic deficiency among a high percentage of this population is also well documented. The specific nature of these deficiencies is not so celarly documented, but in the few attempts at specifying the characteristics of these learners, several conditions seem commonplace. Among these are:

1. Contradictory attitudes toward self and toward others, with low self-concept and the resultant exaggerated positive and negative attitudes toward others prevalent;
2. Utilitarian and materialistic attitudes, not unlike those dominant in our society, but which, in the light of limited horizons and opportunities, function as depressants on motivation, aspiration, and achievement;
3. Low-level aspiration and motivation relative to teachers and academic products, as well as in relation to some social norms;
4. Low-level academic task orientation and variable levels of general task involvements;
5. Styles and modes of perceptual habituation that do not complement the emphasis important to traditional academic efficiency;
6. Weaknesses in the utilization of traditional abstract symbols and dominant group language forms to interpret and communicate;
7. Weaknesses in the utilization of abstractions, with a marked tendency to favor concrete, stimulus-bound cognitive processes;
8. Marked sociocultural patterns in conditions of life which tend to be noncomplementary to traditional standards of academic achievement and social stability. These include hypermobility, family instability, distorted model relationships, economic insufficiency, housing inadequacy, repeated subjection to discriminatory treatment, as well as forced separation from many of the main channels of our society.

Even fewer attempts have been made at identifying some of the positive characteristics of socially disadvantaged children. However, among these the following have been observed:

1. Selective motivation, creativity and proficiency
2. Complex symbolization reflected in in-group language forms and ritual behavior
3. Functional computational skills
4. Accuracy of preception and generalization around some social, psychological and physical phenomena
5. Selective recall, association, and generalization
6. Capacity for meaningful and loyal personal relationships.
7. Capacity for meaningful and sustained selective task involvement
8. Ingeniousness and resourcefulness in the pursuit of self-selected goals and in coping with the difficult conditions of life peculiar to states of economic insufficiency and poverty, low social class status, and low racial-caste status.

These positive and negative characteristics may be viewed as intrinsically determined, environmentally fixed patterns that lend themselves to but modest modification. Such a view would be consistent with a projectionist view of behavior and is certainly the position implied in many of our attitudes and traditional approaches to the rehabilitation of socially disadvantaged children. These characteristics may also be viewed as the products of social, economic, and cultural factors that have imposed patterns of organismic-environmental interaction inappropriate to the mastery of developmental tasks peculiar to traditional standards of academic, social and personal achievement. Since it is clear that the dominant influence of projectionist theory in pedagogy, counseling, and psychotherapy has not enabled these disciplines to deal effectively with the problems of children handicapped by social disadvantage and cultural atypicality, it is of crucial importance that we examine some of the implications of an alternative theoretical position.

I have provided some examples of the manner in which the projectionist theory is reflected in the design and management of learning experiences. I have also pointed to some of the special characteristics of socially and culturally disadvantaged children. Many of these characteristics identify this population as an underdeveloped and handicapped group when compared to the norms we have come to associate with middle class white children for whom much of our procedure in education and guidance has been developed. When social and cultural atypicalities result in disadvantages for the learner, differences in the design and management of learning experiences become crucial. What then are some of the implications of the interactionist position for directed learning in socially and culturally disadvantaged children?

Theorists and investigators working within the context of interactionist theory suggest that the concept of fixed intelligence is no longer tenable. Intelligence is seen as a *non-static, variable* phenomenon

based upon the nature and quality of central processes or cell assemblies which are the products of organismic-environmental interactions. The quality of intellect is á function of the nature of the interaction between organism and environment. Much of what we see as adequate or inadequate intellectual functioning is a product of processes that man can influence.

Motivational and attitudinal factors are experientially determined and experientially modified. This postulate is best reflected in Hebb's and Hunt's use of the Incongruity-Dissonance Principle, which Hunt sees as making both motivation and reinforcement "intrinsic to the organism's relations with its environment, intrinsic if you will, to the organism's information processing. It is as if the organism operated like an error-actuated feedback system where the error is derived from discrepancy between receptor-inputs of the present and the residues of past experience which serve as the basis for anticipating the future." What we reflect as motivation and attitude are the products of current sensory inputs interacting with residuals of earlier experience. These earlier experience residuals are thought to gain sequential organization. Grossly incongruous inputs disrupt this organization while slight degrees of incongruity lend interest and are stimulating. What we see as *no* motivation and negative attitude are instances of environmental encounters which are grossly incongruous with residues of prior experience.

The interactionist position leads us to conclude that the dialectics of development give temporal and sequential factors critical roles in determining the appropriatenesss of procedures in behavioral development and change. It appears that the so-called normal patterns of development gain their temporal and sequential regularity from a natural history that is common to a given species. Where variations and deprivations occur, expected patterns are disturbed. This is evident in some of the work in sensory deprivation, critical periods, and developmental tasks.

In the applied area disturbed learning patterns are coming to be recognized as the products of specific learning disabilities. The interactionist position suggests that learning disability may be a primary disorder reflecting the nature of the child's formal and informal learning experiences and should not be routinely regarded as a secondary disorder representing a projection of intrinsic disturbances or limitations. Atypicalities in any one or combination of the above points may result in disturbances in learning, and remedy that does not take these into account will be ineffective.

If we view the learner as a product of the interaction between organism and environment, psycho-educational design in directed learning for socially and culturally disadvantaged children must be dictated by the topography of the learner—analysis of the specific and detailed character of the learner—and the topology of the learner's experience—analysis of the specific and detailed history of the learner's experience. This kind of analysis can only result from qualitative ap-

praisal, descriptively reported and leading not simply to diagnosis and classification but to prescription and treatment appropriate to the topography and topology identified.

If environmental encounters—interactions—are the crucial determinants, it may well be that our preoccupation with the interpersonal relationship we call counseling and interviewing may be entirely inappropriate. Our theory and the needs of our children may force us to adopt new models and new techniques of guided behavioral development and behavioral change. It may be that we depend too heavily on vicarious experience when the situation requires real life experience in healthy situations, under growth-stimulating circumstances, with appropriate resources, supports, and direction. Nonradical modifications could be made through greatly improved teaching, group guidance, guided group interaction, interfamily consultation, or sheltered work, study, or social situations. More radical moves take us into the old-fashioned approach to social service, into community organization, into politics, into the manifold jobs of developmental facilitation—facilitating development through the management of environmental encounters at school (curricular and extra curricular), home (family relations and conditions of life) and community (economic growth, jobs, equality of opportunity, democratic living).

As an educational psychologist and specialist in guidance, I have the feeling that I should say something practical about counseling disadvantaged children. However, I must say that I am not at all certain that *we* know how best to *counsel* or that *counseling* is our most effective tool of guided behavioral development and change. I am not at all sure that what I do in the counseling relationship is meaningful in the life of a child whose conditions of life deny at crucial points the validity of democracy's promise and humanity's hopes. I can make him feel better. If we are lucky, he may see in me a spark of humanity with which he may identify and use as a model. Or I may be able to help him gain insight into the ways his own behavior helps to defeat his purposes. But we who have worked with these children know that once the process of social maladaptation has begun and is consistently reinforced by negative life experience, our successes are the exception rather than the rule.

If I am asked in which direction we should move to achieve maximal behavioral change and growth in minority group children, in socially disadvantaged children, and probably in all children, I can only suggest that the experiencing of self in interaction with objective and subjective reality is the only way in which consciousness and behavior develop and the only way in which they change. In my frame of reference, it is not so much in the isolated and insulated counseling relationship or the expanded group learning situation that the classroom provides, but in the main stream of life experience that these interactions are maximally operative. Consequently our focus in our efforts at behavioral growth and behavioral change (guidance and education) should be on the guided interaction of self with the environment, a focus on the

design and provision of environmental encounters calculated to best complement individual human potential, style, and need.

I do not feel that the school has the sole responsibility for meeting these needs. The kinds of problems we are talking about are in large measure products of factors intrinsic to the society in which we live. These factors include our system of economic relationships, the political realities of our time, the fact of widespread racial, religious and class prejudices, the real and artificial barriers to equal opportunity, and questions of war and peace. We can relieve, improve, and ameliorate, but will not fundamentally change these problems in the absence of fundamental changes in our society—in the organization, structure and relationships of our communities.

The Working Class Psychiatric Patient:
A Clinical View

James T. McMahon

Introduction

The purpose of this essay is four-fold: (1) A description will be sketched of what is known about the working class patient as he approaches a psychiatric facility; (2) A frame of reference will be outlined that may facilitate understanding of the working class person's initial and ongoing difficulty and reluctance in contracting for psychosocial intervention; (3) An exploration will be attempted of some of the major prejudicial stereotypes which often impede the poor from obtaining relief from daily distress; and (4) An illustration will be proffered of what can be learned and accomplished in assuming a novel stance toward one segment of the poor—working class fathers.[1]

The definition of working class is not by any means precise in contemporary sociological literature. There are generally two ways in which to delimit the concept of working class. The criteria of definition can be drawn from socioeconomic levels of income, education, occupation, and residence. This approach has its limitations, but it does convey a concrete, although incomplete, picture of the differentiation within the American social class stratification system. The more interesting and earthy criterion for social class is that of life style of different groups of people. For the purposes of this paper, however, we will choose the former approach when speaking of lines of demarcation between the social classes. The author feels that the life style criteria, although

283

necessarily complementary to the economic, may tend to lead the reader to the very same perception that must be avoided, that is, prejudicial stereotypes about low income families. Who is poor depends on how poverty is defined. It is difficult to define a baseline for poverty. Lampman, for example, states $2,500 for an urban family of four as his base, while Keyserling uses $4,000 total family income without specific reference to family size. Estimates of poverty, then, understandably vary, ranging between 16 per cent and 25 per cent of the total American population. We will take median figure of 20 per cent as comprising the poor; $4,000 will be our baseline in defining the poor. For the remainder of the paper, the constructs "working class," "lower socioeconomic," and "the poor" will be used interchangeably, although there are important differences that could be made, e.g., not all working class individuals are economically poor; and not all poor are working-class, e.g. students, intellectuals and so on.

Knowledge of the Working Class Psychiatric Patient

That different socioeconomic classes on the American scene respond variously to social and psychological intervention has by now become a truism. The plethora of studies of the working class response to psychotherapy [2] gives ample testimony to this fact. Since Hollingshead and Redlich (3) compiled their New Haven study, there has been no dearth of replication regarding the five classes of patients described in this fine piece of research. The cumulative results of these mental health field studies are quite clear even to the casual reader: namely, *the lower one finds himself on the social class status ladder, the more unavailable does effective psychiatric care become.* The underlying reasons adduced for this unhappy situation are many. Most articles on the subject of social class and mental illness have little difficulty in listing the "correlates" (not necessarily the causes) of the working class response to middle class intervening techniques. The variables that are most frequently found in the poor's response to psychotherapy can be divided into two broad categories: environmental and psychological. To gain a more specific appreciation of the working class response to psychosocial intervention, particular elements of these two broad categories will be briefly discussed.

Clinical administrative procedures have recently come under severe attack. The red tape of bureaucratic institutions is said to impede the working class patient from obtaining proper and immediate psychiatric attention. For example, most psychiatric facilities are plagued with waiting lists. It has been alleged that clinic waiting lists and application procedures feed into the middle class bias because of the latter's ability to defer impulse gratification. Although an attempt should be made to modify and simplify these procedures for the uninitiated, few would

argue for sweeping changes in clinical administrative procedures. It is noteworthy that in research studies where waiting periods were waived altogether, the results in psychotherapy were not significantly better. (8, 13). Other, more significant barriers to understanding and effective intervention must be looked for in dealing with the poor.

Seward (4), among others, has pointed out that the "time-concept" of the poor is manifested in terms of the here and now—the present. Due to the catastrophes that the poor face, their "relative" paucity of social and psychological resources, and their conditioning to failure, some feel that they do not enjoy the luxury of postponing gratification, particularly when seeking help for personal problems. Others (5) point out that even when the working class patient becomes engaged in some form of therapy, it usually is of short duration; that is, his middle class counterpart survives psychotherapeutic endeavors much longer. The factual data bears out the above findings regarding impulse renunciation and therapeutic longevity; but at times this statistic is used with certain undertones of disdain for low income patients. The data may also appear to warrant a subtle rationale for noninvolvement with the poor on the part of the treatment agent because of "unreachable qualities of the patientele." At times our middle class irritation over the low prestige with which the poor endow "talking therapy" is ludicrous, particularly in view of the dearth of evidence that any one method of therapy is more effective than another, or, for that matter, the lack of definitive evidence that the treatment method per se has a significant causal relationship to a patient's progress over time. (24). Success in treatment endeavors "appears" to be more significantly related to the personal attributes of the therapist rather than to his "middle-class methodology or sophisticated technique." (20, 21, 22, 23, 24).

Other practical issues faced daily by the poor often prove to be impediments to proper and effective psychiatric care. The very real problems of the cost of transportation and baby-sitters and the loss of hourly wages seem to bias the help offered to prospective patients in favor of the upper classes. In response to the above, graduated free systems are established for "therapeutic" instead of economic reasons. Evening hours become an "innovation." Social workers "deem" it necessary to make home visits. Often an air of condescension can cloak the consideration of the stark realities of the poor.

Working class fathers are labeled "inadequate" (6). Husbands are said to fear contact with clinics lest their already fragile egos be exposed to further hurt and shame. Wives are characterized as dominant and domineering, usurping the authority of the absent husband, who may be caricatured as a Caspar Milquetoast. Many of these inferences, mind you, are "confirmed and verified" with the male parent absent from the transaction—that is, evaluation by proxy, sight unseen.

Family organization is said to be quite different as we vary social class indicators. Family relationships among the low income groups are characterized as "involved." For example, the poor person from different ethnic backgrounds, is said to act less independently and less

individually in treatment situations than his white collar brother. More collateral service is needed; more involvement of relatives is desirable. Reports are heard that other family members tend to undermine and sabotage the therapeutic relationship of Johnny with his therapist.

With regard to personality characteristics, a number of studies attempt to identify the type of patient most likely to survive the initial diagnostic interview. The following traits are often mentioned as positive indicators for excellent prognosis in psychotherapeutic endeavors: The *good* prospect for therapy should evidence the following: psychological thinking rather than magical expectations; internalization of problems and the tendency to self-blame rather than acting out and projection; a wish to actively change one's environment instead of a passive fatalistic stance toward reality; self-control; a need to relate to people; and a desire to talk with others about personal problems. And on the litany continues, with "high motivation," "strong ego strength," and so on. In looking over these prized personal characteristics in prospective patients, one becomes acutely aware that they are personality correlates of the middle class. Furthermore, many are more indicative of mental health than emotional disturbance.

From another vantage point, many research studies, in an endeavor to crystallize the sentiments of lower socioeconomic patients toward psychiatric care, have enumerated the "expectations" of working class individuals. (7, 8, 9). The consensus is that the working class person expects his therapist to be more active, medically oriented, and immediately helpful in relieving his symptomatic distress. The patient is inclined to expect that the therapist will act "on" him, and "do" something for him. In essence, then, these studies have made it patently clear that the working class patient looks to the mental health specialist to display his expertise—now. This working class expectation of immediate help has at times been viewed as incongruous with the value, behavior, and treatment orientation of many middle class therapists. A therapist often becomes irritated at being put into the role of the medical or surgical man who works instantaneous magic. He bemoans the working class preoccupation with vague somatic complaints, omnipotent thinking, and projection upon the environment. The kinds of symptom formation that appear to be more syntonic with the middle class therapist's wishes and skills are: the introspective schizoid, the inwardly depressed, the symbolic neurotic, and the intelligent paranoid. As therapists we often find it terribly difficult and frustrating to understand the working class person's concept of time being bound by the present, his concept of past tragedies as negligible (why cry over spilt milk), and his prospects for the near future as realistically and shockingly nebulous. The psychoanalyst may explain away his disengagement from the poor with "superego lacunae"; the sociologist, with "non-deferred gratification patterns." The social worker ofen deftly labels every enigma that does not neatly fit into the psychoanalytic model as "cultural or subcultural"—that is, "What else can you expect with that kind of a background?"

Research study after research study continues to "beat the dead horse." Each new study on the characteristics of the working-class stance toward psychotherapy reinforces the middle class rationalization of noninvolvement with low income groups because "they are hard to reach, not amenable to casework, and so on." They are said to be the hard core—"We must find new ways to reach them"—but the replication of characteristics of the working class goes on like a litany. The social, economic, and psychological facts of these studies are probably quite accurate in their characterization of the low income groups. But in granting them validity, we must ask, "Does the continuance of corroborated data from many sources about the working class, give us the scientific rationalization by which we can be exonerated from a *de facto* practice of disengagement from the poor?" It is certainly not enough to validate findings; we must initiate action programs of intervention. Professional inaction cannot be rationalized on the finding that "they are hard to reach as shown by several recent research reports."

One might reasonably wonder, "How do low income persons become hard to reach, distant, or suspicious in the face of honest efforts to help them?" One assumption is that the poor have internalized many hard-core traits much as middle class persons become imbued with the values of upward mobility, deferred gratification, and an appreciation and ability to talk out problems in sophisticated language. One wonders, however, how much thought is given to the realities of being poor when treatment facilities and programs are set up. The poor suffer the most from severe illness. They have the highest incidence of communicable disease. They pay more for housing because of weekly rent systems. We are quick to tag the complaining poor with paranoid labels. That they are more prone to projection is probably true. The content of these projections, however, is often not recognized or recorded as realistic. Psychiatrists have been reminding us of this fact for many years with the remark "that there is a grain of truth to every paranoid's projection or delusion." Certainly the political, economic, and social class structures serve as a fertile ground for this proneness to projection. The fact that the poor do project onto their environment is not nearly as disturbing as the fact that they are often quite accurate regarding the content of their complaints. There may well be a plot out there— not a personal one of a psychiatric nature—but a very impersonal and impervious political and economic system that has a built-in bias in favor of the upper classes.

In essence then, what do these studies actually tell us of the working class response to social and psychological intervention? They convey one irreversible fact. The poor's response is different. Thus, the change agent (mental health personnel's skills, ideology, and optimism) must be more in tune with the working class needs, life style, and expectations. To be sure, if we could make every member of the working class a consumer of middle class values, behavior, and orientation, our only problem would become a dearth of therapists. But the real problem has

to be redefined, that is, how can we change our therapeutic stance, tactics, and strategy toward the poor?

Since there has been reported no widespread mental health success with low income families, one can hardly embark on an ex post facto evaluation of the proper and specific treatment modalities to be utilized. It appears to the author that the arena which offers the most immediate hope in dealing effectively with low income groups in a clinical setting lies in action research. This avenue of approach has been advocated by the Family Centered Project in St. Paul (11) and the work of Kaufman and Reiner (12) at the Judge Baker Guidance Center in Boston. These very empirical endeavors seem to be the best kind of clinical research in an effort to obtain heuristic clues about working class families, life style, expectations, and how they can be approached. (20) From this raw data more refined results could be obtained later in a much more sophisticated and scientific manner.

Frame of Reference: Expectation as Determining the Initial Modality of Intervention

As professionals, we stand committed to alleviate and ameliorate the personal plight of those suffering the pangs of social and psychological illness. If we are to extend effective help to low income families, it goes without saying that we must understand their needs as well as the mode in which they can most readily accept this assistance. To say that we can carefully delineate the characteristics of the low income families; that furthermore these traits set them apart from the middle class response to psychotherapy; and that finally, these findings explain why we find it so difficult to intervene, is certainly begging the question. The reasoning is circular. If these patients do not conform to white collar standards of psychiatric care, then obviously we are committed to engage them in some other fashion. Not only does the practice of psychoanalytically oriented psychotherapy seem to be upper class linked, but some feel that even the *basic principles* of psychotherapy are linked to these classes. (13) Where, then, do we obtain clues as to how the working class can be helped? Do we help them intuitively? Is it to be done in a trial and error fashion? Do we have any information that would aid us in addressing our intervention to the needs of the low income family?

There does seem to exist an entire body of untapped material that may gives clues as to the most effective approach to the working class patient. The *attitudes* and *expectations* of patients about the kind of help that is available to them can certainly clarify the initial difficulties that will have to be confronted before the blue collar patient can be significantly engaged at the clinical level of intervention. It is true that

the value of these items—that is, attitudes and expectations—do not carry much weight with the scientific researcher. But in the face of the practitioner's inability to understand and effectively deal with many low-income persons, they can give clues to the direction initial intervention must take. The key then to this espoused frame of reference seems to be satisfactorily expressed in the following proposition: There is more likely to be a favorable response among working class patients to initiate and continue needed psychiatric care, if, and only if, the therapist's participation in the transaction is congruent, at least temporarily, with the patients' request, attitude, and expectation. For example, if a patient comes to an out-patient facility, with an expectation of a direct, medically oriented reception, and he is met with a very passive psychoanalytic stance, he will immediately feel that he is misunderstood and cannot be helped, and more than likely he will be lost to contact. One might more easily engage a patient in worthwhile work on his problem if his initial expectation met immediate gratification. If the patient's legitimate but untutored request were met with a congruent response, he could more easily be helped, at a later time, to pursue more subtle kinds of help, if this were necessary and/or desirable. Freedman and others (9) found that they:

> obtained significant differences in drop-out rates when the patient's denial or acknowledgment of his mental illness was examined in combination with a rating of the warmth or detachment in the first interview is compatible with the patient's attitude about treatment, the patient tends to remain in therapy. That is, when the patient acknowledges his mental illness and encounters a warm relationship, or when he denies his mental illness and encounters a detached relationship, he is more likely to remain in treatment than when the other combination of attitude and reception are present.

Much can be accomplished with low income families by taking a more active and congruent initial role. The direction or stance that the therapist assumes (e.g. warmth-detachment, active-passive) will in large measure be determined by the expectation that is overt or elicited from the patient in the initial interview. Much of the misunderstanding, distortion, and ignorance about the working class patient can be attributed to the paucity of contacts that middle class personnel have with them regarding psychiatric treatment. The drop-out rate can easily become a rationalization for ignorance of working class dynamics as well as ultimate nonintervention. The first few interviews appear to be crucial. For example, in the past three years, the New York State Department of Mental Hygiene's statistics for out-patient facilities has recorded the "median number of persons interviews per patient termination" as hovering between 3.2 and 3.7 interviews. There appears then to be a large number of patients lost to contact. Many appear on the clinic rolls as having "no treatment given.'

In general, then, we are espousing a rather open-minded agnostic

approach to the working class patient. We do not have the answers. We should be willing to go along with his defenses until we can more readily understand the person in his situation. At times we become a bit slothful. We allow many people to refuse treatment without enabling them to know what they are rejecting. On the other hand, there should be no attempt to "sell" psychotherapy. For as Guze and Murphy state, "it is very rare that psychotherapy can be offered as a specific and exclusive treatment modality." (10) But certainly many people might be informed that although no specific cause or remedy is known for their distress, an exploration of their feelings might help them make up their mind regarding treatment and possibly diminish their anxiety depression.

Stereotypes That Often Impede Continuing Therapy with the Working Class

Fortunately, there are many working class patients who survive the initial ineptness of therapists. These people, however, fall heir very shortly to many stereotypes that impede understanding and effective intervention. It would seem, then, appropriate to comment on some of the more common cliches regarding continuing treatment with low income families.

(1) PSYCHOLOGICAL VERSUS MAGICAL THINKING

The verbal expectation and mental orientation that a patient manifests toward his problem often give clues to the advisability of ongoing psychotherapy. When the patient thinks and verbalizes psychologically, he is thought to be introspective, willing to accept personal responsibility—in short, a good prospect on whom the therapist can test out his psychotherapeutic wares. Many diagnostic work-ups are filled with psychological cliches of this nature. The above orientation appears to immediately register a certain amount of "credit" to the prospective patient for wanting to drink from the "waters of middle class therapeutic values." It is not long, however, before these same evaluators become disenchanted with the patient because of "intellectual insight." It should be thoroughly borne in mind that to those who have had the benefit of education, a certain amount of economic and familial security, and the like, psychological words and sentiments come easy. Prospective patients from the middle class find it relatively simple to verbalize glibly psychological jargon which has become rather institutionalized in our books, movies, newspapers, magazines, and plays.

How detrimental is magical thinking to the problem solving process? Psychological sophistication gives no assurance of effective therapy.

People who feel comfortable only when bantering about intellectual concepts are often lost when they have to become specific and relate on the *feeling level of therapy.* Conversely, omnipotent thinking in those who have severe environmental problems can be a veritable asset to the therapist in initial contact with the patient, since he is more amenable to the authority person's "prescription." Since childhood the model of the helping process that is deeply imprinted on all of us, regardless of class, is the doctor-patient relationship. This is often viewed as an authoritarian relationship. The patient is expected to be a consumer of the therapist's expertise. It is only because many of us are exposed to liberal and equalitarian orientations, through reading, education, and status, that we are able to look upon psychotherapeutic relationships with an eye toward the mutual participation of the parties involved.

The working class patient, for a variety of realistic reasons, often looks for help and advice in a direct and forthright manner. Since he spells out his problems in concrete fashion, it would seem that his expectations of immediate help make him more amenable to influence and suggestion. The latter, as we all know, plays a large role in therapy regardless of social class orientation. It is a matter of clinical experience that all patients take a certain amount of time "to learn their role in the therapeutic relationship." Psychotherapy does not have to be limited to the facile-tongued middle class patient. With a few modifications, particularly in the early handling of the interviews, many working-class patients find it rather easy and beneficial to enter into the work of therapy.

With today's bulging waiting lists and the over-selling of psychiatric help for personal problems, the practice of determining limited concrete goals seems to be timely and crucially relevant. Heretofore, the duration of treatment was often thought to be the criterion of its effectiveness. (22) This gradually diminishing orientation has often retarded the specific delimitation of feasible goal-directed therapy. Certainly in the area of clinical evaluation, one method of setting up criteria of accomplishment in psychotherapeutic endeavors would necessarily involve a system of limited observable goals. The goals could readily be determined largely by the specifics of the *presenting problem* and the *chief complaint* elicited from the patient at the time of initial application (finding out accurately what the patient wants from an agency may well take up to five or more sessions). This orientation may appear simplistic, trite, and prosaic. However, the value of eliciting from a patient a set of specific concerns is inestimable in enabling that person to clarify and cope with his network of problems. Once the major concerns of the patient are carefully delineated, one or more of these emerges as a limited goal. The entire therapeutic encounter becomes predicated on the achievement of this objective. The techniques, strategies, and tactics become means to its accomplishment. When the resolution comes about and termination of the patient seems to be in order, new goals can come under consideration, if they appear necessary and desirable to the patient and the therapist. These goals can range from

enabling the phobic child to enter kindergarten to helping the elderly psychiatric patient get back into activities with her former friends. This may be considered palliative treatment and symptomatic resolution —and oftentimes it is. It might furthermore be construed as providing a coping mechanism which happens to be socially acceptable. But in the face of unknown etiology of the common psychiatric disorders, these psychosocial strategies may be as beneficial to the psychiatric patient as the ingestion of aspirin is to the common cold sufferer or the injection of insulin is to the diabetic. No cure is wrought—just better, and, as Karl Menninger says, "weller" functioning. (25)

(2) PRACTICAL ACTION VERSUS INSIGHT DEVELOPMENT

The psychoanalytic concept of insight-development had become, until very recently, so prestige-laden that social workers often tended to evaluate their work with a patient in terms of its absence or presence. In the first place, it is extremely difficult to specifically define insight; to be really concrete about its essential components, and to determine definitively how one develops this elusive condition during the task of therapy. I have shown elsewhere how it appears that research psychologists have been the only ones to date to clearly convey the purpose, content, and process behind this often overworked and misunderstood concept. (15) When this concept is commented upon or utilized in social work practice, the technique has so many qualifying conditions and safeguards to be observed in its use (training, experience, analytical supervision and the rest) that one seriously doubts that it has an *essential* place among social work treatment modalities. This is probably doubly true when social workers become concerned with the concrete stresses of the low income patient.

One is impressed that the *actual experience* of *doing* and *struggling* toward a goal often brings more results and encouragement to the less sophisticated than all the attempts at time-consuming and penetrating self-analysis. Mendl and Rapport demonstrate how this *existential view* of therapy can work with chronic psychiatric patients (16). In dealing with the lower socioeconomic groups, it appears that immediate action and constant supportive encouragement augur well in overcoming the inertia that is due to the chronicity of their illness.

(3) INTERVENTION: IN TIME OF CRISIS OR STABILITY

Psychoanalysts, to whom social workers owe a great and lasting debt, have put a high premium on relative environmental stability for the emergence of effective personality change. Anna Freud (17), among others, has argued that psychoanalysis is contra-indicated for adolescents because of the constant flux in their psychological moods. It is argued

that it is more expedient to await the solidification of neurotic defenses in young adulthood, rather than make futile attempts to intervene in any significant manner during the turmoil of puberty.

In another realm, Eugene Litwak (18), a social psychologist from the University of Michigan, has argued that the most effective time to gain political converts is in the period of time between elections, when the enthusiasm of the campaign has waned and the commitment of adamant political affiliations loosens. Although these two approaches may merit more attention in their respective spheres, social workers have taken this "stability theme" and applied it out of context. This is particularly true when dealing with working class patients who labor under innumerable environmental problems as they approach the psychiatric facility.

The poor constantly live with crisis at their door. To await environmental stability is tantamount to inaction for them. Furthermore, people seldom ask for help unless there is some form of crisis emerging in their lives. To inform an alcoholic that he is to return for therapy when he has decided to abstain is to ask a starving man to pray. Social workers are constantly asked to help people in crises. They are rightfully put into a position of societal "fixers" standing between the community at large and the individual in society. It is interesting to note that in out-patient clinic work, no matter how long-standing or chronic a given condition might be, there is not only a precipitating factor that brings people to the clinic door, but, more importantly, there is often a very *critical precipitating factor* in determining why this person is motivated (out of fear, pain, or whatever) to call or come in person on this particular day, rather than two weeks ago or three days hence. Crisis seems to be an essential element in helping people to move toward a desired end—relief from suffering.

Even in the more stable therapeutic relationships, the most effective changes takes place during crisis—e.g. with the onslaughts of interpretation and the emergence of insight. It is a rather common occurrence in long-term therapy, with even the most sophisticated neurotic, that crisis upsets the deadening tones of treatment plateaus. Often the turning point in any given phase of therapy is precipitated by a realistic trauma or a confrontation of patient's resistance to change from the lips of the therapist. Furthermore, even those patients who suffer from chronic, intransigent character disorders, on coming to an out-patient facility, often have a superimposed neurotic, psychotic, or marital reaction for which they need immediate attention.

Crisis, in many instances, works in favor of the therapist. It often becomes a rationale for entering into a situation. It furthermore affords the therapist the opportunity to become a change-agent in the intolerable sufferings of people. To say, then, that people with many environmental stresses are not amenable to psychiatric care is to discriminate against the low income families who have a disproportionate amount of social and psychological stress. The above position can only be defended if psychiatric care is equated and synonymous with intensive psychotherapy of middle class vintage. But this is a *non sequitur*.

(4) ACTING OUT: A FUNCTION OF SUPEREGO
LACUNAE OR NUCLEAR DEPRESSION

Adelaide Johnson has written one of the most insightful articles regarding the acting out processes of adolescence. (19) In essence, her
work at the Institute of Juvenile Research in Chicago points out that
the parents of adolescents were often found to vicariously act out their
own antisocial desires and resentments through their adolescent children. The parents were said to have an under-developed or under-
socialized superego. Thus, both the parents and the child, through
identification, suffered from an occasional or "spotty" (lacunae-gaps)
conviction about socially acceptable behavior.

Irving Kaufman and Beatrice Simcox Reiner (12) take a different
view of parents and adolescents who have a proclivity to destructive
acting out. Concerned with the derogatory labels often pinned on adolescents and their parents, this group embarked on a qualitative research
design that spanned five years. Their work at the Judge Baker Child
Guidance Center in Boston convinced them that many of the low
income nonpsychotic group among whom they were laboring acted out
in an attempt to keep the lid on a deeply buried anxiety. Outwardly
calm, these parents and children acted out in an attempt to adjust
to a "nuclear depression." The impulse gratification could take on many
forms, such as sexual promiscuity, stealing, malicious mischief, or even
impulse buying. The central issue here is that this research demonstrates that these children and their parents, who were suffering from
character disorders, were also plagued by a deeply buried depression
not *qualitatively* different from their psychoneurotic cousins. Many
patients from the lower socioeconomic classes who suffer from character
disorders are often sloughed off as psychopaths unable to have feeling
and loyalty for any group. Kaufman and Reiner's work has raised some
real questions about the validity of stereotypes regarding people from
the lower socioeconomic classes who come into conflict with their
environment through behavioral routes rather than through the more
socially acceptable way of neurotic or psychotic symptom formation.
Admittedly, the kind of treatment that they administered took several
years. But it must also be borne in mind that this endeavor was also
clinical research done to test out whether there was a way of reaching
people suffering from pregenital character disorders.

(5) FINANCIAL AND EMOTIONAL DEPENDENCY:
A LACK OF DIFFERENTIATION BETWEEN
THE GOAL AND THE METHOD

The concept of emotional and financial dependency has a rather
negative value among social work personnel, though it is dealt with

daily. Social workers, particularly in welfare departments, have been harassed for years by politicians and public officials on this score. Both have deplored the dependency of welfare recipients on the tax dollar. In the socialization of the professional social worker, there are strong caveats regarding financial and emotional dependency of his clientele. This warning has a pan-phobic effect on social workers, particularly in psychiatric and welfare settings. In an earlier era, when social workers and psychoanalysts were more closely affiliated, the treatment modalities of each were differentiated by the stance each assumed toward the artificially induced transference neurosis. The psychoanalyst has always advocated that this phenomenon is essential for the successful resolution of the infantile neurosis, by bringing it forward in time and projecting it onto the therapist. To the social worker, the dependence of the transference neurosis appeared dangerous and was to be avoided at all costs. It was the bane of his professional existence, and rightly so. However, the net result of these and other caveats has been unwittingly transferred into other areas of intervention. It has helped, I think, the social work profession to cast its lot with middle class patients and thus imperceptibly move away from those who are most dependent in our society—the poor.

Unfortunately, however, even the many social workers who are still earnestly committed to the poor have made little or no differentiation between the goal of independence and the means to achieve it. As a result, the social worker has prematurely assumed in treatment relationships a firmness and possibly an aloofness toward the poor in both financial and emotional matters. That the goal should be independence, everyone would agree. But that the method be so inflexible as to disallow temporary financial and/or emotional dependence is both appalling and therapeutically unsound.

In child guidance settings, social workers have long feared the development of over-dependency in mother-child relations. We have come up with neat strategies, particularly with the over-protective mother. The mother is often prematurely encouraged "to allow her child to develop, to grow up and away from the silver cord." Dutifully, out of guilt, she obeys. She becomes firm and grits her teeth. Johnny is now reluctantly encouraged and firmly urged to relate more to his personal environment. He is told that he must mix with the boys, belong to the group. Often however, after so many years of indulgence, Johnny does not possess the developmental skills for his chronological age, that is, to throw a ball well, to compete, to accommodate, and to compromise. Because he is unskilled in these physical, social, and psychological endeavors, he may soon face the rejection of his peers. Result of this strategic therapeutic suggestion? Johnny is back again at mother's door more dependent than before. This is a classic example of confusing the ultimate goal of therapy and the methods appropriate to the attainment of this objective.

Kaufman and Reiner developed and identified four distinct phases of the treatment process that have particular relevance to this concept of

emotional dependency in psychotherapeutic endeavors. They are outlined as follows: (1) establishing a relationship; (2) ego-building
through identification; (3) helping the client establish a separate
identity; and (4) helping the client gain self-understanding. This approach can be summarized as leading the patient along ascending
maturational levels of development until stage four emerges. This last
phase of the treatment process discussed by the authors might well be
characterized as the *level of entry* at which many verbally sophisticated
middle class neurotics might initiate the process of psychiatric treatment.
Although this fourfold approach may be vulnerable to criticism on the
implicit "presumption" of fitting working class patients into a middle
class treatment slot or model, the first two phases are of particular
interest to us at the moment. In any event, most of the criticism that
might be leveled at this approach to the treatment of personality disorders can be discounted, since in any scientific or therapeutic endeavor,
one is limited by what is known and what works in a given situation.
There is certainly nothing unsound about making rather extended and
elaborate preparations with a patient (surgical or psychiatric) in order
to bring him to a level of psychosocial development where the better
known and time-honored techniques of treatment work best.

My main purpose in referring to this work is that the authors addressed themselves particularly to the initial stages of treatment with
working class patients. These patients were, furthermore, allowed to
become socially and emotionally dependent on the therapist for rather
extended periods of time. Dependence was even fostered temporarily,
largely through utilization of the mechanism of identification. In this
sense, then, identification was viewed as a temporary regressive phenomenon—a leaning on someone else's ego and and superego. To a
large extent this phase of identification with an ego-ideal was re-educa-
tional. The study gives the impression that these patients were helped to
gradually rise up the pathology ladder to a point where the better known
psychotherapeutic methods could more easily and successfully be
utilized in the resolution of problems. Whether one agrees with this
procedure clinically or ideologically, the important component is that
these people allowed themselves to be "used" in this way in an endeavor
to obtain a clearer idea of the attitudes, expectations, and potentialities
of the working class family.

The modern problem of widespread financial and emotional dependency among low income groups in American society poses many
questions for the profession of social work. The causes of this corrosive condition are many and multifaceted, e.g., education, work, and
mobility opportunities. The increasing inequality among the social
classes is even more frightening than the absolute numbers of the poor
and their income standards today. Increasing inequality among the
classes cuts off opportunity systems in many areas of personal and
social endeavors. Thus, because of increasing inequality, poverty becomes a greater problem in absolute numbers and relative percentages
with each succeeding generation. In the face of this situation, what

can a social worker do? He has been called the "guardian of the poor—the poor man's advocate." If this true, what are the needs of the modern social worker in confronting this immense poverty issue? Does he need more technology? This must be answered affirmatively. But we must go further. Does he need an ideology—a commitment—and to whom? Has social work, in its attempt to overcome the appellation of "do-gooder" and to consummate its pursuit of a "body of theory," gone native, that is, middle class? Will social work return to the house of its father—the poor? One would not quibble that more *accurate* translation of appropriate and *relevant* psychoanalytic findings are needed in dealing with even the concrete problems of the working class. More *precise* social science formulations need relevant application to the conditions that the modern social workers falls heir to in his daily tasks. But possibly even more attention needs to be focused, in the light of recent interracial events, on social work's future ideological stance toward the poor.

A Word About Working Class Fathers: An Illustration

The social work literature reports a universal value—that fathers should participate in the evaluation and treatment of their children. The statistics of clinic rolls, however, do not confirm this stated value. Fathers are infrequently seen. Fathers are said to be too busy; to be threatened by intense interpersonal involvement; to fear that contact with a psychiatric facility may be construed as masculine weakness; to have relegated child care responsibilities to the mother. (6)

This indictment of the father, particularly the working class father, leads to distorted inferences, because he is often evaluated through the eyes of the mother. More consideration should be given to contact with fathers. However, time and again, we hear the "rational" cliche: "If these men had to attend to some medical, legal, or dental necessity, they would take time off from work." Too often the above remark is uttered by a professional observing middle class banking hours. At a deeper level, there may well be a note of envy of the time-honored professions.

The author recalls quite vividly his own limited experience with working class fathers. After the clinic had received applications for the treatment of a number of boys between the ages of eight and twelve, it was decided that a group of five fathers would be seen individually after regular clinic hours. The general purpose of this decision was twofold: (1) the interviews would assist the clinic with collateral information and participation in the evaluation and treatment of the children; and, (2) the opportunity of contact with these fathers would serve as a test of the general stereotypes and cliches about the father's participation in the child guidance case situation. The results of

these sessions were quite enlightening to the author, and to some extent remarkable.

In the first place, these fathers, all in their mid-thirties, were hourly wage earners who would be docked from time away from the job. The author formulated an informal set of decisions before the fathers came in for the initial interview. The purpose of the visit was to be clearly stated to the fathers, that is, the need for collateral information relative to their sons' evaluation and treatment. The boys were to be evaluated and treated regardless of the fathers' response to this invitation. The fathers, on the other hand, would be allowed upon arrival to discuss a wide range of topics of their choosing. No attempt was to be made to steer the interview toward the behavior and poor school performance of the children. They were to be allowed a full complement of mechanisms (denial, evasion, projection, overcompensation, and so on) through which they might feel temporarily comfortable. No notes were to be taken; an air of informality was to be encouraged.

Several noteworthy tendencies were revealed. Perhaps fortuitously, each of the fathers conveyed in the first few interviews a great deal of physical fatigue. All of them held unskilled positions and worked arduously each day. Although the purpose of the meeting was the behavior and school performance of their children, the fathers spent on the average ten sessions in unstructured discussions of topics about which they felt quite comfortable. There was no recounting of personal tensions, anxieties, depressions, fears, and so on. Most of the complaints verbalized were of a physical and work nature. It became quite clear that these men could easily complain of physical woes indicative of their hard labors on the job. To feel tired or even "weak" because of a hard day's work did not in any way deflate or depreciate their masculine self-image. It was not until the men had seen the author for about ten sessions did they risk more ego-shattering psychological complaints. Two fathers, in particular, were a little more dramatic in the way they conveyed their tiredness and possible resentment in being asked to come to the clinic. They would routinely come to my office, set their rather large lunch pails squarely on the desk, plunk themselves down heavily in the awaiting chair, and thus eloquently communicate the toil of their laborious day.

Another interesting trait that was characteristic of the group was that each father manifested a good deal of enthusiasm for his work, and the day's accomplishment and failures had real meaning for him. It was not difficult to elicit the pride that these men felt in their manual work, provided they were given cues about the author's interest in the exact nature of their daily task. Each father readily responded in detail about what he "did," his achievement, this one slice of his "adequate" profile. The therapeutic task, then, for the first ten hours was really relating and administering to the father's need—to be understood, on the one hand, and to be approved of, on the other.

It was not long, however, before each of these fathers began to feel comfortable in recounting his own background and feelings in real

depth: the father he recalled, his boyhood memories, his aspirations for his children, the lack of time with his family because of not-so-lucrative moonlighting, the occasional impulsiveness on Friday evenings with the "boys," the thrill and oftentimes novelty of "doing something for" his children, e.g., fishing, hunting, and the like.

The surprising element of these interviews was that none of these fathers talked predominantly of his son's development unless there was some connecting link with the father's own background. There was a constant back and forth movement between the development of father and son. Due to the concreteness of their language, many of the analogies used by these fathers were astonishingly insightful of the similarities between father and son in aspiration, self-image and demeanor. Without exception each father identified with the son's plight and became a veritable ally with him, usually against the mother, the school, or the court. Time and again, it became increasingly obvious that the father, on a rather realistic basis, did not acutely feel personal responsibility for his son's misdeeds, since greater and more significant influence on the child's development was considered the wife's prerogative.

Possibly as a result of the above, the fathers set a low premium on the prospects of personal identification and/or occupational identification of the son with the father. A derivative of the following comment was often voiced: "Can I ask my son to be like me—a factory worker?" On the other hand, none of these fathers felt particularly disturbed or personally threatened when talking of his son's school performance. Often the comment, "I wasn't much of a whiz in school either," was verbalized with undertones of minimizing and/or condoning a given piece of behavior. On many occasions a father would at first mouth a middle class norm about education or behavior, only to inform me later that he felt constrained to appease the white collar gentleman. He would reveal: "I really don't understand why it is not *good for my child* to be whipped; it always helped to straighten me out quickly."

These fathers were forgotten men. Nobody had ever given them this much attention. They rarely had the opportunity to ramble on in such a formal and professional setting. What was thought to be the most difficult area in which to engage them—feelings about themselves—was actually quite easy. They often verbalized more like patients than collaterals. They spontaneously gave strong opinions on a wide range of topics from child rearing to labor unions to political affiliation, in an endeavor to alternately impress, test, and practice their verbal acumen on an authority person. Often the imparting of information had very good results in so-called attitude change, for example, "Mr. Jones, we often find in our work with children that it is sometimes wise to find out why Johnny took this money or that candy before we take action. We have often learned that some children take things and share them in an effort to enlarge their circle of friends." Many times the responses would be: "I never thought of that angle; I guess it does sort of makes sense; It is hard at times to control myself; I wonder about that kid of mine." In working with these fathers, the author found that

speaking in innocuous generalities and allowing the fathers to *particularize* often can aid the therapist in avoiding the dangerous position of "making accusations."

At first, some colleagues felt that this approach was merely allowing these fathers to dodge the main issues—their sons' unacceptable behavior. However, for this group of fathers, at any rate, it was ascertained that a period of relating to their physical needs was needed to better enable them to talk later, and sometimes much later, of their psychological fatigue and hurt. Discussion of employment tasks allowed these men to convey a certain expertise to the gentleman across the desk who possibly was unable to perform their work demands with any degree of dexterity and/or endurance. The focus on work accomplishment also better enabled them to balance any feeling of masculine weakness experienced in the process of "asking for help." This experience led to the tentative conviction that it may well take as long as ten to fifteen sessions to establish any kind of comfortable working relationship with working class men.

After a period of ten to fifteen hours, the therapeutic relationship was tested. Each father was asked to come to the clinic at 4:00 P.M. This arrangement of course was designed to see if the father had received enough benefit from the initial ten hours so that he would sacrifice hourly wages or make special arrangements with his superior about compensatory time commitments. Every father passed the test and was seen for an additional ten to fifteen hours. Over a period of seven months, then, each father was seen at the clinic for a minimum of twenty-four sessions. When the initial period of ten interviews was completed, none of the fathers asked for evening appointments. Each was surprisingly conscientious about telephoning to cancel, postpone, or announce delays in coming for an appointment. The wives, concurrently in treatment with the author, registered amazement at their husband's continuance. (This is not unique in mother-oriented child guidance cases.) The wives reported an increasing degree of companionship in the marriage and more comradeship in the father-son relationship. Startling personality changes were not affected. This expectation was never entertained. But the delicate balance of stress forces on the interfamilial relationships was certainly altered in a more favorable direction.

The experience with these five fathers cannot be generalized. This was a mere illustration of a way of orienting oneself to the working class father. That these men continued to keep appointments may have been fortuitous even with the strong encouragement supplied by the author. But the fact that they could manifest interest and ask "indirectly for help in clarifying their feelings" after a rather long initial period, should be investigated more thoroughly with more sophisticated research tools than mere clinical impressions.

In conclusion, I suggest that there are ways of reaching and understanding the working class psychiatric patient clinically. But accommodations have to be made. Since there is so little information relative

to successful intervention with low income groups, it appears that practical action-research can give heuristic clues and data that can be utilized at a later date by more extensive research investigations. To attune our methods to the attitudes, expectations and requests of the working-class patient is one way to enlist his cooperation and learn from him in the process. This course of action on the clinical front in no way discounts other modalities of intervention, such as social action groups and social changes on more macroscopic levels of social organization. But if public and private funds are to be spent effectively on the working class patient, then we should be committed to ascertain the acceptable modes (to him) of dispensing relevant treatment. In the last analysis, if this type of ideological committment does not emerge in mental health endeavors, and we insist on passing the responsibility elsewhere because of outmoded stereotypes, then we shall reap the harvest of poor clinics instead of clinics for the poor.

Notes

1. Data were collected on fathers at the Foery Clinic of St. Joseph's Hospital, Syracuse, New York. At the clinic, at any given period of time the number of children's cases approximates 50 per cent of the total patient population. The general treatment orientation of the staff is eclectic and family centered with strong emphasis on the treatment of the working class (lower socioeconomic) as well as the lower middle class patient.

2. Throughout this essay the term "psychotherapy" will be utilized because of the setting. Without further elaboration on this controversial term, the author will consider the meaning of the term to be generic regardless of the discipline of the mental health specialist.

References

1. S. M. Miller, "The American Lower Classes: A Typological Approach." Presented at the Los Angeles meetings of the American Sociological Association, August, 1963, pp. 1–22.

2. Leon Keyserling, Poverty and Deprivation in the United States (Washington: Conference on Economic Progress, 1961); Michael Harrington, The Other America (New York: The Macmillan Company, 1962); Gabriel Kolko, Wealth and Power in the United States (New York: Frederick A. Praeger, 1962); Robert J. Lampman, The Share of Top Wealth-Holders in National Wealth (Princeton: Princeton University Press, 1962); James N. Morgan et al., Income and Welfare in the United States (New York: McGraw-Hill Book Company, 1962).

3. A. B. Hollingshead and F. C. Redlich, Social Class and Mental Illness

(New York: John Wiley and Sons, 1958).

4. G. Seward and J. Marmor, Psychotherapy and Culture Conflict (New York: The Ronald Press Co., 1956).

5. Raymond G. Hunt, "Social Class and Mental Illness: Some Implications for Clinical Theory and Practice," The American Journal of Psychiatry, 116:12 (June, 1960), 1065–69.

6. Fiori Bronga, et al., "The Father Role in Social Agency Planning." Unpublished Master's thesis, Syracuse University School of Social Work, May, 1961.

7. James T. McMahon, "Attitudes and Expectations of Families of Neuropsychiatric Patients to First Trial Visit." Unpublished Master's thesis, Syracuse University School of Social Work, May, 1960.

8. Betty Overall and H. Aronson, "Expectations of Psychotherapy in Patients of Lower Socioeconomic Class," The

American Journal of Orthopsychiatry, 32:3 (April, 1963), 421–30.

9. H. Freedman *et al.,* "Drop-outs from Outpatient Psychiatric Treatment," *The A.M.A. Archives of Neurology and Psychiatry,* 80 (1958), 567 ff.

10. Samuel B. Guze and George E. Murphy, "An Empirical Approach to Psychotherapy: The Agnostic Position," *The American Journal of Psychiatry,* 120:1 (July, 1936), 53–57.

11. Alice Overton, Catherine H. Tinker, and associates, *Casework Notebook* (St. Paul, Minn.: Family Centered Project, 1959).

12. Beatrice Simcox Reiner and Irving Kaufman, *Character Disorders in Parents of Delinquents* (New York: Family Service Association of America, 1959).

13. Nila J. Cole *et al.,* "Some Relationships between Social Class and the Practice of Dynamic Psychiatry," *The American Journal of Psychiatry,* 118:11 (May, 1962), 1004–12.

14. Alvin Zander *et al., Role Relations in the Mental Health Professions* (Ann Arbor: University of Michigan Press, 1957).

15. James T. McMahon, "Insight Development: Its Nature and Place in Social Work Practice." Unpublished paper, May, 1960.

16. W. M. Mendel and S. Rapport, "Out-patient Treatment of Chronic Schizophrenic Patients: An Existential View," *Archives of General Psychiatry,* VIII: 2 (February, 1963), 190–96.

17. Anna Freud, address delivered at Clark University, 1957.

18. Eugene Litwak, "Communication Theory and Program Planning: Some Policy Implications." Presented at the Council on Social Work Education Conference, Philadelphia, January, 1960.

19. Adelaide Johnson, "Superego Lacunae in Parents of Delinquents," in *Searchlights on Delinquency,* Kurt R. Eissler, ed., 1949.

20. Charles W. Slack, "Experimenter-Subject Psychotherapy: A New Method of Introducing Intensive Office Treatment to Unreachable Cases," *Mental Hygiene,* 1962.

21. H. J. Eysenck, "Behavior Therapy, Spontaneous Remission and Transference in Neurotics," *The American Journal of Psychiatry,* 116:2 (August, 1963), 867–71.

22. Ian Stevenson, "The Challenge of Results in Psychotherapy," *The American Journal of Psychiatry,* 112:2 (August, 1959), 120–23.

23. H. J. Eysenck, "The Effects of Psychotherapy: An Evaluation," *Journal of Consulting Psychology,* 16 (1952), 319–24.

24. H. J. Eysenck, "The Effects of Psychotherapy," in *Handbook of Abnormal Psychology,* H. J. Eysenck, ed. (New York: Basic Books, 1961), 697–725, esp. 719–21.

25. Karl Menninger, *The Vital Balance* (New York: Basic Books, 1963), 406ff.

Some Cultural Aspects of Transference
and Countertransference

John P. Spiegel, M.D.

I am going to discuss some of the cultural aspects of transference and countertransference as these phenomena appear in the course of psychotherapy.[1] I would like to leave classical psychoanalysis out of this discussion. The reason for confining the subject matter to psychotherapy is that my information regarding cultural influences has been gathered in large part through the application of this technique. It has been derived from an investigation of the impact of cultural variations on the interpersonal relations within the family and on the psychologic adjustment of the family members. This study, (1) which I have been conducting with Florence R. Kluckhohn and a number of co-workers, assumes that families can be compared in terms of the factors which contribute to the psychologic "health" or "illness" of the family as a whole. Because we wished to give special attention to the culturable variable, our sample of families was chosen from three subcultural groups: Irish-American, Italian-American, and so-called Old American, all at the working class level. So that we could distinguish emotionally healthy from ill families, we divided this total sample into two parts. The first part, consisting of so-called "sick" families, was obtained through the Outpatient Psychiatric Clinic of the Children's Medical Center, Boston, to which these families had been referred because of an emotionally ill child. The second group, the so-called "well" or "normal" families, were selected from the wider metropolitan community. In most instances, contacts with them were arranged through public health and social agencies.

Reprinted by permission, from *Individual and Familial Dynamics*, Jules H. Masserman, ed., New York: Grune & Stratton, Inc., 1959, pp. 160–182.

Although in all cases we have maintained contact with the family as a whole, where the "sick" families were concerned contact was carried on through psychotherapy with the mother, father, and at least one child. Because of out interest in observing the social role conflicts in the family (8): individual interviews in the clinic setting were supplemented by visits to the home. This also permitted us to observe the functioning of the family as a unit. In addition, the therapists have at times attended family celebrations, have accompanied the father to his place of work, and have conducted therapeutic interviews in this setting, as well as in trucks, bars, and other unusual places. It is apparent from this brief description that we have regarded the usual setting of psychotherapy—the office with its desk, chair, couch and other props—as merely one aspect of the cultural definition of the therapist-patient roles. We have experimented with the possibilities of other settings. Thus, the observations which form the basis of this report are drawn from a greater variety of therapeutic contacts than are usually included in the definition of therapy. The reasons for this flexibility will, I hope, become more evident after I have discussed the various cultural issues involved in it.

In recent decades, the cultural anthropologists have brought to everyone's attention the extraordinary variety in patterns of living and in basic values throughout the world. As Florence Kluckhohn has stated, (6) continuous cross-cultural research has demonstrated that although people everywhere face much the same problems and choices between alternatives, they do not find the same solutions for them. Moreover, it has been shown that the cultural value orientations guiding these solutions are not superficial, nor are they present in conscious awareness. On the contrary, although they pervade every area of thought and activity, they can usually be formulated only in the most fragmentary fashion, if at all. They thus represent an example of a phenomenon which has recently been called "behavior without awareness." (1) This phenomenon refers to the making of an unconscious discrimination between two or more choices of behavior when the act of discrimination cannot be brought to the status of a conscious report because it has never at any time existed in consciousness. Since the value orientations of a culture are outside of awareness to begin with and are learned in childhood only through their indirect impact on conscious behavior, they can be expected to have a powerful effect on the therapeutic relationship.

In spite of the difficulties, there have been several attempts on the part of contemporary philosophers and anthropologists to formulate the "philosophy," "way of life," or "unconscious assumptions" of various cultures. The formulation which we have used in our study and which I will describe in a moment has been proposed by Florence Kluckhohn (3, 4, 5, 6) as a theory of variation in cultural value orientations. The theory is based on a classification of value orientations which can be used for the description of the similarities and differences between and within cultures. For the sake of the discussion of transference and countertransference which follows, I am going to give illustrations of the application of the theory to the similarities and differences between the

American middle class family and the Irish-American working class family. However, before undertaking this, I would like to present in summary outline the classification scheme itself and the presuppositions on which it is based (Table 1), quoting directly from Florence Kluckhohn

Table 1—Classification of Value Orientations

	Evil	Neutral: Mixture of Good and Evil	Good
Innate Human Nature			
	Mutable-Immutable	Mutable-Immutable	Mutable-Immutable
Man's Relation to Nature and Supernature	Subjugation to Nature	Harmony with Nature	Mastery over Nature
Time Focus	Past	Present	Future
Modality of Human Activity	Being	Being-in-Becoming	Doing
Modality of Man's Relationship to Other Men	Lineal	Collateral	Individualistic

Note: Since each of the orientations is considered to be independently variable, the arrangement in columns of sets of orientations is only the accidental result of this particular diagram. Any of the orientations may be switched to any one of the three columns.

for this purpose. (4) Three major assumptions underlie both the classification system of value orientations and the theory of variation in value orientations. First, it is assumed that *there is a limited number of common human problems for which all peoples at all times must find some solution*. This is the universal aspect of value orientations because the common human problems to be treated arise inevitably out of the human situation. But, however universal the problems, the solutions found for them are not the same. Hence the next consideration is the degree of relativity or, better, the range of variability. The second assumption, then, is that *while there is variability in solutions of all the problems, it is neither limitless nor random but is definitely within a range of possible solutions*. The third assumption, which provides the key to the later analysis of variation in value orientations, is that *all variants of all solutions are in varying degrees present in all societies at all times*. Thus, every society has, in addition to its dominant profile of value orientations, numerous *variant* or *substitute* profiles. And in both the dominant and the variant profiles, there is always a *rank ordering* or preferred sequence of value orientations rather than a single emphasis.

Five problems have been tentatively singled out as the crucial ones, universal to all human societies. These problems are stated here in the form of questions, and in each case there is a parenthetic designation of the name that will be used hereafter for the range of orientations relating to the question:

1. What is the character of innate human nature? (*Human-Nature Orientation*)
2. What is the relation of man to nature or supernature? (*Man-Nature Orientation*)

3. What is the temporal focus of human life? (*Time Orientation*)
4. What is the modality of human activity? (*Activity Orientation*)
5. What is the modality of man's relation to other men? (*Relational Orientation*)

I would now like to illustrate the ranges of variability and the rank ordering of solutions in these value orientation categories through a discussion of their configuration in the case of the urban Middle-class American family, and the Irish-American working class family (Table 2).

Table 2—Ranges of Variability in Value Orientation Categories

Orientation	Middle Class American	Italian-American	Irish-American
Relational	Ind. > Coll. > Lin.	Coll. > Lin. > Ind.	Lin. > Coll.> Ind.
Time	Fut. > Pres. > Past	Pres. > Past > Fut.	Pres. > Past. > Fut. (but some indication of an earlier Past Pres. Fut.)
Man-Nature	Over > Subj. > With	Sub. > With > Over	Subj. = With > Over (doubt about first order here and some doubt that there is a clear-cut first order preference)
Activity	Doing > Being > Being-in-Becoming	Being > Being-in-Becoming > Doing	Being > Being-in-Becoming > Doing
Human-Nature	Evil > Mixed > Good Mixed Evil and Good > Evil Good	Mixed Good and Evil predominantly	Most definitely an Evil basic nature with perfectibility desired but problematic

The following abbreviations are used in the above table:
Coll.—Collateral
Ind.—Individualistic
Lin.—Lineal
Over—Mastery-over-Nature
Subj.—Subjugation-to-Nature
With—Harmony-with-Nature

In the latter case, the value orientations are those brought to this country by the first generation of immigrants from rural Southern Ireland.

Human-Nature Orientation. All socities have found it necessary to orient in some way to the innately given possibilities for good or evil within human beings. Some have solved the contradictions between these two principles by assuming that man is born predominantly evil in nature but that he is prefectible by the application of effort. Others have regarded man as basically evil and unalterable. Still others have regarded man either as a hopeless mixture of good and evil, or as a mixture subject to change depending on internal and external circumstances. Akin to this position, but distinguishable from it, is the neutral point of view which is characteristic of psychotherapy and all the so-called "helping professions." Finally, there is the view of the romantic philosophers that man is born basically good but can be corrupted by external social cir-

cumstances, and the rare utopian view that man is immutably good and only seems bad to the jaundiced eye.

With regard to this value orientation, the American middle class family is in a complicated, transitional state. The view we have inherited from our Puritan ancestors is that man is basically evil, but perfectible. Effort, will power, and constant watchfulness were necessary in order to avert wickedness and temptation. Although there is now much variability here, depending on the religious affiliation of the family, there is considerable evidence of a change which puts the formerly second order mixed position into the dominant emphasis. This is in part due to the ever increasing influence of the psychologic and social sciences and to the concomitant weakening of religious convictions. It is probably fair to say that most middle class Americans are either in transition or in conflict or both with respect to this orientation.

The Irish family very definitely views man as basically evil and almost immutable. Perfectibility is desired but is regarded as highly problematic —something that will be achieved only by a select few. This results in a rather harsh morality, and a heavy load of guilt and shame. Associated with this are specialized procedures for the relief of guilt and shame whose implications for the transference-countertransference situation will be discussed shortly. The second order Mixed position is much less harsh but is possible for the Irish only in certain social activities such as the consumption of alcohol which is usually described as "a good man's weakness."

Man-Nature Orientation. The three-point breakdown of this orientation—Subjugation-to-Nature, Mastery-over-Nature, and Harmony-with-Nature—is rather self evident. The Subjugation-to-Nature position is characteristic of the Judeo-Christian tradition. The story of Job expresses with crystal clarity the essential helplessness and weakness of man. The position requires that man admit his weakness in order to gain any control at all over his fate. The Mastery-over-Nature position is characteristic of science, technology and an industrialized society. It assumes that, given enough time, effort, and money, nature can be tamed to man's will, and that control of his fate resides within his own skill and resources. The Harmony-with-Nature position assumes that there is no real separation or distinction between man, nature and supernature. Accordingly problems of fate and destiny are settled through recognition of and conformity with the patterned wholeness of the Universe. This was the position of classical Greece, and, in recent times, of Chinese and Japanese culture.

The American middle class family puts a first order emphasis on the Mastery-over-Nature position. Subjugation-to-Nature is in second position, the Harmony-with-Nature orientation is in the least favored, third order position, and accordingly has little influence on behavior in this country. This rank ordering is associated with the technologic organization and professionalization of activity in the American family. Since all problems are considered essentially solvable with the help of a suitable expert, there is no sympathy for a fatalistic or tragic attitude toward life.

However, some problems, such as chronic illness and death, fit badly into this scheme of things. Their significance must therefore either be denied, or handled by a shift to Subjugation-to-Nature.

In the Irish-American family Subjugation-to-Nature is given dominant emphasis; Harmony-with-Nature is in the second position, and Mastery-over-Nature in the least valued third position. Resignation and a tragic view of life are deeply ingrained attitudes. Problems are not expected to be resolved, but rather, in the absence of supernatural help, to recur over and over again. The strong, but second order emphasis on Harmony-with-Nature appears in the form of a naive, implicit animistic view of life. The "wee folk," animal and vegetable life all share in the joys and sorrows of man's existence, often assuming responsibility for the joy and blame for the sorrow. This orientation sanctions a good deal of active fantasy and, in fact, blurs the distinction between fantasy and reality. How this shapes certain aspects of the transference-countertransference situation will be discussed shortly.

Time Orientation. The possible cultural interpretations of the temporal focus break logically into the range of Past, Present, and Future. Much can be predicted about a particular society, particularly the expected direction of change, if one knows what the rank order emphasis is in this category. The American family places its dominant emphasis on the Future, with a second order stress on the Present and the Past a poor third. No American wants to be called "old fashioned." Anything new— a new car, a new song or a new idea—is clearly better than anything old. Children and youthfulness in general are considered important because of their connection with the future while old age is a painful condition and the elderly, without much prestige accorded to their years, do their best to appear young. Planning for a long range future, inevitably conceived as bigger and better, leads the American family to live its life by clock, calendar and schedule. The present can be given importance for certain social activities, but very definitely as "time-out" from the compulsive loyalty to the future.

The Present, on the other hand, is of the first importance to the Irish-American family, with the Past second and the Future a weak third. The future is not expected to be any different from the present, and, therefore, making elaborate plans is unnecesary. It is enough to cope with the exigencies of the present. Furthermore, the second order emphasis on the past is quite strong so that any controversy with respect to change whether in the area of morality or of everyday life is apt to be settled in favor of the traditions of the past.

Activity Orientation. The threefold range of variation suggested for this orientation is Being, Being-in-Becoming, and Doing. The Being orientation stresses the "is-ness" of behavior, the spontaneous inclination to act in accordance with one's moods, feelings, desires and impulses. In distinction to such wholehearted spontaneity, the Being-in-Becoming orientation emphasizes the rounded, integrated development of the personality, bringing into focus different interests at different times. The Doing variable, on the other hand, puts aside the "inner man" in favor of

externally judged successful performance. Thus, in this orientation, inner impulses have to be suppressed if they get in the way of the striving for competence and achievement on the road to success.

It is probably obvious to everyone that the American family puts primary emphasis on the Doing orientation. Parents value each other and their children in accordance with their competence and success in performance. This preference is well suited to the importance of hard work in an industrialized society. The first question an American asks of any stranger is, "What has he done?" or "What does he do?" Husbands and wives busily rate each other's performance as parents, and compare themselves and their children with the Smith's next door and the Jones's across the street. Thus competition becomes the pivot of interpersonal relations. On occasion, however, the extraordinary inhibition of inner impulse demanded by this orientation leads to revolt. Then the second order emphasis of Being is invoked, and impulsive activity is allowed free reign, particularly if aided by alcohol or drugs. The Being-in-Becoming orientation is so weak that activity of this nature is likely to be described as frivolous, dilettant-ish or a waste of valuable time.

In the Irish-American family, Being comes first in importance, with Being-in-Becoming in second position and Doing in third. Thus the Irish family values the free expression of inner states. Fighting, loving, fun-making, bickering and elaborate expression of sentiment are considered more interesting than work for the sake of work. The Being-in-Becoming second order variable is manifested in an appreciative attitude toward art, drama and poetry and toward the need to express the many facets of life. Thus relations between husbands and wives, parents and children are characterized by rapid transitions of mood. Extreme candor gives way suddenly to disguise and deceit. Humor replaces sadness and leads unexpectedly to anger. Finally, such kaleidoscopic shifts are experiences not only in their own right, but also for the sake of the wonderful tale that can be woven out of them in the presence of an appreciative audience.

Relational Orientation. The last of the common human problems to be discussed concerns the relation between the individual and the group. The three subdivisions of this orientation are the Lineal, the Collateral, and the Individualistic. As might be expected, the Individualistic emphasizes the importance of the individual ahead of any group considerations. The Lineal stresses the significance of the vertically structured group hierarchy while the Collateral values the horizontal, "one for all and all for one" aspect of group loyalty.

In American families the Individualistic orientation is in first position, the Collateral second, while the Lineal is the least favored. Thus, there is a certain amount of resentment felt toward any hierarchy and toward anyone who acts too "bossy." Husbands share authority, as well as other domestic roles, with their wives. Parents hope that their children will voluntarily manifest correct behavior so that the issue of discipline and authoritarian controls can be avoided. Every attempt is made to foster the autonomy of the individual family member and to allow

children to make their own decisions. Thus independence and self reliance form an important part of the egalitarian ethos. However, if group loyalty is to be invoked (as in organized games and sports) or when the family is to be represented in the community, then it is the collateral, groupwide emphasis that comes to the fore.

In the Irish-American family the lineal principle holds first rank; collaterality is second and individualism in the third order position. The group, whether the family, a bureaucratic political organization, or the church, always comes ahead of the individual. The ordered succession to hierarchical positions over time is constantly emphasized. For example, the father is very much the head of the family and never hesitates to express his authority over the wife and children. But if his own father is still alive, he owes him the same kind of respect and obedience which he showed as a child. In contrast to the American family, the Irish family trains its children for dependent behavior which is expected to remain a constant throughout life. This tends to backfire in a certain amount of hostility to authority, of which the political rebel in Irish history is a good example. Nevertheless, dependency training is on the whole thoroughly accepted, and is well reinforced through the mutual care and aid offered by the extended family, religious and community networks.

I would like to close this brief comparison of the value orientations in the two family systems with a note of warning concerning the stereotyping it would seem to imply. All ethnic labelling is an oversimplification, and falsifies the degree of variation and nonconformity in any social group. Some of the first generation Irish families in this country have been closer to American values from the beginning while many middle class American families have held values similar to the Irish. Still, for our purposes, such modifications would represent variations from the modal positions which I have described.

Let us now turn our attention to some of the considerations governing the appearance of transference and countertransference behavior within the psychotherapy situation.[2] It is ordinarily held that the word transference denotes behavior which is clearly an inappropriate response to the behavior of the therapist and which functions as a resistance to therapy. It is understod to derive from some aspect of the childhood relation with a parent or some other significant person. It is assumed that the memory of this earlier relationship has been repressed, but that the patient hopes to recapture with the therapist some of the actual or hoped for satisfactions of the original relationship. It is one of the aims of treatment to recover the repressed memory, wish, or fantasy and thus to dissipate the transference behavior.

There is little to be added to these considerations where the therapist's countertransference is concerned. It is held that countertransference describes an attitude in the therapist—whether or not it is actually manifested in action—which is inappropriate and unrealistically related to the current behavior of the patient. It is therefore presumed to have its origin in an incompletely resolved childhood relation or wish. The principle difference is that the therapist alone has responsibility for identifying

his countertransference responses and for exploring their significance.

An objection may be raised at this point that these considerations have been developed in the context of the standard psychoanalytic technique and that they cannot be applied without modification to the therapist-patient relation in psychotherapy. The objection derives from the fact that the heightened activity of the therapist and the relative paucity of his information make it much more difficult to keep track of what aspects of the mutual transaction either partner may be responding to. I would agree with this objection. However, the fact remains that transference and countertransference responses do occur in psychotherapy and must be dealt with in some way. I believe that the point of view which I am about to propose may represent an auxiliary tool for identifying and controlling such responses.

Let me first ask in what way are we to understand the meaning of the word "reality" as used in psychotherapy? Reality is a slippery concept, and the implicit assumptions buried in it are usually left unexamined. The best way of getting at whatever reality may mean in the context of psychotherapy is through an examination of the most general and standardized expectations established by professional practice for the behavior of the therapist and of the patient.

Looking first at the patient, I think it is fair to say that the person is expected to tell as much about himself as he is able. He is expected to work toward a recovery from his difficulties in a responsibile way without depending on outside help from his family or friends. It is hoped that he will not withhold important information or refuse to discuss certain topics because of loyalty to external persons, beliefs or institutions. It is expected that he will want, for the sake of his own emotional health and maturity, to become as autonomous and as independent in the making of choices and decisions as is possible, considering his life circumstances. In connection with this personal aim, it is expected that he will wish to have a future different from his past and present, and that he will wish to take individual responsibility for seeing that it is different. It is assumed that he will perceive the therapist as a professional person who has no ax to grind and nothing to contribute to him but his technical ability. It is assumed that he either begins with or soon develops confidence in the benefits to be expected from communication, from insight into himself, and from the use of words rather than physical action in expressing himself. Finally, it is hoped that he will be able to limit his expressive emotional behavior, both within and without the treatment situation, so that he neither escapes from his thoughts and memories through too much overt action, nor from his feelings through too much inhibition of action.

These are the goals set up professionally for the patient. Because of the operations of "resistance," it is not expected that the patient will actually be able to adhere consistently to these standards. On the contrary, it is believed that a large amount of treatment time will be spent in discovering why he is unable to behave in accordance with such goals. Nevertheless, it is hoped that by the time the treatment has ended, he

will have *achieved* many, if not all, of them. For these are the standards, in this country, of what is called "mental health." It should also be clear by now that they represent, in vivid detail, the value orientations of the American middle class family.

Now let us look at the expectations for the psychotherapist. It is expected that, like any expert or professional person, he will confine his activity with the patient to serious, responsible work on the patient's problems. In connection with the "work-oriented" relation he has with the patient, he is expected to exclude the ordinary social, recreational and personal aspects of human relations. Though he is permitted a modicum of so-called "educative" activity, he is expected to refrain from influencing the patient in accordance with his own personal, as opposed to professional, goals, standards or values. Indeed, he is expected to display a "benevolent neutrality" in this area, neither approving nor disapproving anything the patient says or does. In the place of a value attitude, he is to substitute "reality testing," helping the patient to discover the actual consequences in "external reality" and in the "reality" of the treatment situation, of anything the patient does, feels, or thinks. This neutral attitude with respect both to the good and the evil in the patient's behavior is maintained for the sake of helping the patient obtain maximum autonomy and independence in the formulation of his own goals and standards. He is expected to believe firmly in the patient's capacity to master his problems, neither overestimating, nor underestimating the degree to which actual change is possible. Concerning the probability of change, the therapist is expected to keep a weather eye on the future, but to concentrate mostly on the past and the present. There is some difference of opinion and even controversy as to whether the past or the present is to be given greater consideration, but most therapists would emphasize a balanced perspective between the two.

Such controversy, however, is indicative of a wider area of tension and indecision in the definition of the therapist's role. This has to do with the degree to which he should be free to change or modify the techniques he uses. On the one hand, he is expected to express his individuality in the moment to moment exercise of his technique. But on the other, he is expected to preserve the theories, concepts and techniques inherited from the past. Accordingly, he inevitably experiences some conflict between the conservative and the experimental aspects of his role. Furthermore, the tension between these two contradictory goals is heightened by the structure of the organizations with which he is affiliated. These organizations, such as hospitals, clinics and professional associations tend to be more heirarchically structured and more conservative of the past than is altogether congruous with the goals of scientific and technical activity.

If one scrutinizes this description of the standards for the "reality" structure of the therapist's behavior, it becomes evident that they, too, are guided by the American middle class value orientations. Slight variations appear in the *Nature-of-Man*, the *Relational*, and the *Time Orientations*. The first emphasizes the intensely neutral attitude toward good and evil more than is characteristic of the American middle class family

at the present time. The *relational* orientation gives a stronger stress to the Lineal structure than one finds in middle class values, and is probably representative of a value conflict in this orientation. Similarly, the therapist is expected to carry on this technique in an independent and individualistic way, but not to violate the canons of theory and practice imposed by the hierarchically structured organizations to which he belongs. In the same vein, the *time* orientation stresses the tradition and importance of the past somewhat more than is called for in American middle class values.

In spite of these mild incongruities between the values governing the definition of "reality" for the patient and for the therapist, the fit is on the whole a fairly good one. The roles are matched to each other on the basis of their conformity with the dominant American middle class values. On this basis, it can then be stated that transference and counter-transference phenomena will be identified, insofar as they have cultural determinants, on the basis of their departure from these value orientations. This means that resistance, from the cultural point of view, is resistance against dominant American values. One might say, without being altogether facetious, that to resist is to be un-American!

Although this statement of the cultural determinants of transference and countertransference resistance may sound overgeneralized, it is certainly not unexpected, nor does it require any apology or defense. Psychotherapy is a scientific and technical procedure and it is only natural that it should be based on the same set of values which govern the socio-economic class most representative of the scientific and technical outlook of the society as a whole. It may even turn out to be the case that the slight incongruity in the values governing the two roles is necessary to the maintenance of an optimum tension between the patient and therapist.

Good as the matching of the roles may be at this professional level, there is abundant evidence that the goodness of fit is subject to several weaknesses which I would now like to examine. Theoretically, it could be expected to remain stable if both the patient and the therapist come from American middle class families. In such cases there should be nearly perfect agreement about the "reality" toward which both parties are to strive. However, psychotherapists come from all classes and ethnic groups in this country, and, with the increasing development of mental health education and facilities, so do patients. So, one must ask, what happens when the value orientations of the family of origin of both the patient and therapist are discrepant with each other, and with dominant American values?

There is a presumption that the therapist is spared from difficulties in this matter in two ways: through a personal psychoanalysis, and through identification with the professional values and goals which I have just described. A personal analysis is designed to free the therapist from excessive bondage to his archaic super-ego and for this reason he is supposed to be able to remain relatively flexible in the presence of values different from those in which he was trained as a child. Corre-

lated with this lack of anxiety toward new or different values is the internalization of the "benevolent neutrality" and the other standards of the image of the perfect therapist.

Although there is no doubt, to my mind, about the validity of both these assumptions, there is much question about the extent to which the therapist can actually be freed of his original values. The experiences my colleagues and I have had, working with patients whose cultural backgrounds differed greatly from our own, is that the value discrepancy sets up a very complicated strain within the therapist. The conflict between the original values of the patient and the original values of the therapist stimulates a strain between the therapist's archaic super-ego and his new, professional identifications. A three-way conflict is precipitated in him which becomes fertile soil for the growth of countertransference difficulties. But before examining the details of such value conflicts and their consequences, let us turn to the patient and look at the difficulties he may experience on contact with the therapist.

For purposes of illustration, let us take a father in one of our Irish-American families, possessing the value orientations I have already described. How will he perceive the "reality" of the behavior which the therapist expects of him? He is expected to tell everything he knows about himself. But his training is that one does not tell intimate details about oneself even to family or friends, much less a total stranger. If the details are shameful or guilt-ridden, one doesn't even admit such things to oneself. They are too suffused with evil, and there are only two ways to handle such things. Either deny their existence, or confess them to a properly constituted authority, such as a priest. But isn't the therapist such a properly constituted authority, somewhat different from a priest perhaps, but a person entitled to hear such things? Certainly not. By virtue of what organization and what authorization would he possess such a right? I must confess that when we hear this question, which is usually implicit rather than directly stated, we are tempted to answer, "On the authority of Freud, the American Psychiatric Association and the Children's Hospital!" However, even this answer would not help since these authorities and organizations are already perceived as either unknown or possibly sinful. To the lineal values of the Irish-American, any hierarchy is better than no hierarchy at all, but one that is unknown or remote is likely to be regarded as hostile until it has proved itself otherwise.

But, one might well ask, how about the "benevolent neutrality?" Won't this neutral attitude help to counteract the fear of sinfulness, and its associated hostility to the sinner? Unfortunately, the answer is again no. In the perceptions of the Irish-American patient, such an attitude is hypocritical. It smacks of the benevolence of the upper classes toward the "deserving poor." It signifies merely that one's real feelings remain undeclared behind a concealing mask of condescension. Hiding one's real feelings is a familiar affair, and, according to his experience, is inevitably followed by brutal frankness when it is least expected. So this "neutrality" is merely a matter of waiting for the ax to fall.

Still, looking at the problem all this presents to the therapist, one might ask whether it is really so different from run-of-the-mill difficulties which always crop up at the beginning of therapy. Won't the suffering experienced by the patient encourage him to continue with therapy despite these hurdles? There are two answers to this question. In the first place, if the patient is the father of a disturbed child, he may very well not experience much suffering in his own personality. The only emotional disturbance he may be aware of is that caused him by his child's illness. But, secondly, even if he is aware of inner disturbance, this will probably not in itself be sufficient to make him want to work hard on the overcoming of obstacles. Hard work in an independent, self-responsible way for the sake of long distance goals has not been a part of his value training. In this area, the Present Time, Being, Lineal value structure are all firmly opposed to psychotherapy as understood by the therapist. Such a patient is not used to working on his own problems for the sake of vague future gains. He is accustomed to being told what to do, right now, in the present. Therefore he repeatedly asks the therapist what he is supposed to be doing, and, if he is not told, he is paralyzed. He feels that nothing is happening and he is wasting his time. And, even if the therapist, sensing this hopelessness, tries repeatedly to instruct him on how to conduct himself in the interview, this will prove to be of little help. For the Subjugated-to-Nature and Present Time Orientation lead the patient to see little possibility of change or improvement in the future. What will be, will be, and evil must be punished. In fact, the only hope of the future, as he sees it, is to cling grimly to the sense of evil, wistful for forgiveness, but never abandoning the sense of the power of evil, since this is his only guide to realistic conduct.

Exposed to these responses, which constitute the "reality" of the patient, how will the therapist conduct himself? For a while he may identify the patient's response as "resistance" and keep on trying to use his usual techniques. However, after a variable length of time, he will fell intensely frustrated. This frustration will stimulate the three-way conflict which I have already mentioned. On the one hand, his therapeutic values will order him to stick to his technique. The strong Mastery-Over-Nature position will make him feel guilty if he wants to stop the treatment before the patient appears ready to quit. For the American therapist, unlike the European,[3] feels that no patient or situation should be identified as "untreatable," at least until all possibilities have been exhausted, But if he continues under the guidance of these values, he will reach a stalemate, not being able to make progress or to terminate treatment. Meanwhile, the original values attached to his archaic super-ego tend more and more to assert themselves into the gap created by the stalemate. As this happens, a conflict develops between his original values and his newer therapeutic values. In addition, a conflict develops between his original values and the values on which the patient is acting. Since there already exists a conflict between his therapeutic values and the values which are guiding the patient, his ego is caught in a three cornered struggle which in most cases proves too much for

its integrative capacity. When this point has been reached, the archaic super-ego wins the struggle, though usually concealing its activity behind the facade of the therapeutic super-ego.

For example, suppose the therapist treating an Irish-American comes from an American-Jewish background. The values of this culture, insofar as they can be discerned at present, are characterized by the first order position of Evil, Subjugated-to-Nature, Future time, Doing, and Collaterality. Thus his Doing and Future Time orientations clash violently, with the Being, Present Time behavior of the patient. The Evil and Subjugated-to-Nature orientations of patient and therapist coincide. Therefore he comes to feel more and more hostile to the patient for not making a sufficient effort, and comes to characterize this default as evil, just as he would originally have characterized such a trend within himself. As the patient comes to stand increasingly for a rejected and bad part of the therapist, his ego tends to give in by finding a way to characterize the patient as deserving of rejection. However, the therapeutic part of his super-ego will still be strong enough to insist that such a rejection be justified on technical grounds, or at least clothed in professional jargon. The final resolution of his inner conflict is obtained through a termination of treatment on the grounds that the patient is too immature, too narcissistic, too dependent, too well defended, or any of a multitude of expressions which indicate that he has found the patient burdensome.

Is this description too cynical, or too cavalier in respect to the psychodynamic issues? The question is valid, because there is always a danger of explaining too much through the use of a cultural analysis. Certainly, much more is involved in the development of the transference-countertransference impasse than the value content of the super-egos of the patient and therapist. I do not wish to ignore the complex questions of ego psychology with which the conflict in cultural values is also associated. Unfortunately, it would take more time and space than is available to go into these questions. If I have somewhat overstressed the cultural analysis at the expense of other psychodynamic issues, it is because it is usually totally neglected. I would, however, like to take up one psychodynamic issue in order to lead into the concluding section of this paper.

While it is perfectly true that one aspect of the Irish-American patient's resistance is associated with the Subjugated-to-Nature value position, this is, as I have just stated, by no means the whole story. The value orientation accounts for the patient's resignation, his inability to conceive of the possibility of change, in the cognitive area. A real change within the personality has not been in his experience and he just doesn't see that it is possible. However, there is an emotional as well as a cognitive side to this kind of resistance. On the emotional side it is associated with the identification with the angry, critical parents. The attachment to the internalized parental images is intensely ambivalent, and masochistically satisfying. The treasuring of the sense of sin is, from one point of view, a conscious derivative of the highly libidinal, unconscious cathexis of the internalized, scolding parents. In addition, the scolding

parent within becomes a tender forgiving parent whenever a confession takes place. The alternation between sinning and confessing is necessary to the maintenance of the internal, libidinal dynamics. Furthermore, sinning or the alerting of the sense of sin in the external object, is the primary way of getting the object's attention.

These considerations are directly pertinent to the transference problem in the management of such a patient. It is not only that the patient remains cognitively unaware of the possibility of change. In addition he has no wish to change in the direction which the therapist expects him to. Giving up the crushing sense of sin means, essentially, renouncing the relation with the internalized parents. This might be possible if the therapist could capture the attention of the patient. It is an accepted fact that psychotherapy cannot take place without the establishment of at least a minimum positive transference. But the value neutrality of the therapist operates precisely at this point to prevent the establishment of a positive transference. The patient feels he cannot get the therapist's attention. Furthermore, he has no other reason to care about the therapist since the latter is not associated with any of his prestige systems or organizations. As a result he withdraws, and the therapist then realizes that *he* cannot get the *patient's* attention. This is the beginning of the therapeutic impasse.

I would like to conclude this paper with a consideration of some suggestions for the handling of this impasse. There are several possibilities. One could resign oneself to the acceptance of defeat. The conclusion then offers itself that not everyone can profit from psychotherapy, and that it is important not to let therapeutic ambition overrule good diagnostic judgment. This view involves a shift from the Mastery-over-Nature position which is difficult for most Americans to effect. Another possibility is to persist, doggedly, neither modifying the technique of psychotherapy, nor abandoning the attempt to help. Some Irish-American families have made a sufficient transition to dominant American values so that they may be able to respond to the standard techniques. However, the payoff in success is low and thus the price of sticking to the Mastery-over-Nature position in this fashion is very high. It can be done only by extremely patient therapists who have a high tolerance for frustration.

A third alternative preserves the Mastery-over-Nature position, but abandons the Past Time orientation insofar as this inhibits change and experimentation. This is the approach we adopted in our work with Irish-American patients. We have experimented with various methods for overcoming the resistance and for establishing a positive transference so that we could be in a position to exert some psychotherapeutic influence. The steps we took, however, were not set up on the basis of trial and error, but arose out of our theoretic point of view. We had already become convinced of the close connection between the pathology of the individual and the interpersonal and cultural value relations within the family. But the modifications which we adopted were made primarily for the sake of carrying on research. Only gradually and secondarily did

we perceive their relevance for the handling of transference and countertransference problems.

Our approach emphasizes the importance of the extended family and the community to the functioning of the individual. Although therapy concentrates mainly on the mother, father, and child, we attempt to see and make ourselves known to a wide assortment of relatives. This means that we become assimilated, to a certain extent, to the lineal chains of influence which bear upon the pathologic deviations in the family members. In additon, members of the therapeutic team become known, not simply as individuals, but also as members of a readily identifiable organization. This approximation of individuals and organizations reduces the fear of the strange, unknown group and, simultaneously, raises its prestige. At the same time, we have shown our willingness to depart from the routine of regular office appointments whenever this is necessary. Seeing family members when and where they are available is closer to the Present Time and Being orientations. Therefore it is more apt to be perceived as a valid act of attention than strict adherence to a Future oriented appointment book, and other bureaucratic routines.

In further validation of the Irish-American value orientations, we have relaxed to a considerable extent the principle of non-reciprocity. We answer personal questions about ourselves and do not hesitate to reveal our own value attitudes upon a variety of issues. Although our therapeutic standards have made us somewhat uneasy about such conduct, we have gradually become more comfortable with it. Especially has it become easier as we have come to understand how the Irish-American patient perceives nonreciprocity. Failing to answer a question, directing it back to the patient, or interpreting it are perceived as evasive maneuvers. Withholding a personal attitude is seen as having something to be ashamed of. Concealment, evasion, and denial are so ubiquitous in Irish-American culture that they are easily projected to the therapist. Such projections can be handled by interpretation only after the relationship has been established.

Finally, we have come to reinterpret the meaning of "benevolent neutrality." As ordinarily understood, this principle involves the adoption of a strictly neutral attitude with respect to the matters about which the patient feels guilty or ashamed. We have found that if the impulses of which the patient is ashamed would also make us feel ashamed if discovered within ourselves, it is best to be quite frank about it. And vice versa. That is to say that, if his impulses would leave us truly neutral and unmoved, we have to be frank about that, too. Since the sense of sin is a primary vector of interpersonal feeling, it cannot be hidden from those who are highly sensitive to its manifestations. Thus the reinterpretation of "benevolent neutrality" involves the recognition and admission that we all think of ourselves as sinners in some way. On this basis, denial is more easily renounced and the evil impulse more easily held in consciousness because the therapist is seen as someone who recognizes the patient's problem and has established his right to deal with it. This point

of view also makes it easier to deal with the characteristic denial through the use of humor. Since the therapist is not denying anything through the assumption of "neutrality," he can appreciate the humor and still insist on the expression of the feelings it is meant to conceal.

These are the major modifications which we have used in our research. The results of using them are not spectacular. They have not led to dramatic relief of symptoms. This is not the place to review the results of our work, nor are we ready to report final conclusions. But we have gained the conviction that we have been able to establish and maintain therapeutic contact with patients who would otherwise have been rejected or would have dropped out of treatment. We have been able to produce small increases in insight in individual family members. We have been impressed with the fact that a small gain in one or two family members is registered as a large gain in the total functioning of the family.

I hope it is clear that the modifications in approach which I have described are not to be considered general prescriptions for the field of psychotherapy as a whole. On the contrary, the value of a cultural analysis of the psychotherapeutic situation is that it clarifies the relation between variations in technique and the specific transference (and countertransference) responses which can be expected from members of different cultural groups. The general principle that emerges from this point of view is that modifications in technique should be rationally adapted to the varieties of cultural value orientations which exist among patients. A corollary of this proposition is the need, in the future, to give as much consideration to problems of cultural dynamics as has been given, in the past, to purely psychologic processes. It is my firm belief that such a program is necessary if we have to extend the range of effectiveness of psychotherapy to groups who have, up till now, proved refractory in the face of our best efforts.

Notes

1. The investigation has been supported by a grant from the National Institute of Mental Health, and from the Pauline and Louis G. Cowan Foundation. It is sponsored by the Laboratory of Social Relations, Harvard University, and the Children's Medical Center, Boston.

2. I am here ignoring the confusions and controversies over the exact meanings of the words transference and countertransference which have troubled the literature on these subjects. Excellent historical reviews of the semantic and conceptual problems involved have been published by Orr (7) and by Zetzel (10).

The topic is further complicated by the almost complete absence of any discussion of the countertransference in the literature of psychotherapy, as distinct from psychoanalysis.

3. See, for example, the contrast between the contribution of an American analyst, Leo Stone (9) and a British analyst, Anna Freud (2) to the topic "The Widening Scope of Indications for Psychoanalysis."

The difference between the two analysts in value orientations as related to therapeutic indications is striking.

References

1. Adams, J. K.: Laboratory studies of behavior without awareness. Psychological Bulletin 54:383–405, 1957.

2. Freud, Anna: The widening scope of indications for psychoanalysis: discussion. J. Am. Psychoanalyt. A. 2:607–620, 1954.

3. Kluckhohn, Florence R.: Dominant and substitute profiles of cultural orientations: Their significance for the analysis of social stratification. Social Forces 28:276–293, 1950.

4. ———: Dominant and Variant Value Orientations. In: Personality in Nature, Society, and Culture. Clyde Kluckhohn and Henry A. Murray, Eds., New York, Alfred A. Knopf, 1953.

5. ———: Variations in the basic values of family systems. Social Casework 39:63–72, 1958.

6. ———, Strodtbeck, Fred L., et al.: Variations in Value Orientations, Row Peterson & Co., Evanston, Ill, 1961.

7. Orr, Douglass W.: Transference and Countertransference: A Historical Survey. J. Am. Psychoanalyt. A. 2:567–594, 1954.

8. Spiegel, John P.: The resolution of role conflict within the family. Psychiatry 20:1–6, 1957.

9. Stone, Leo: The widening scope of indications for psychoanalysis. J. Am. Psychoanalyt. A. 2:567–594, 1954.

10. Zetzel, Elizabeth R.: Current concepts of transference. Internat. J. Psychoanalyt. 37:369–376, 1956.

Educational Therapy: A Methodical Approach to the Problem of the "Untreatable" Child

Hertha Riese, M.D.

Justification of a New Approach

Educational therapy is a psychotherapeutic endeavor aimed at assisting emotionally disturbed children who are considered nonamenable to treatment in the classic child guidance clinic. Contrary to the classic stipulations we are interested in the child who is not necessarily of average mentality, who does not relate or communicate verbally, and whose mental and emotional development does not give immediate promise that the child will be able to establish a transference or symbolic relation as needed for psychotherapy. As a rule, these negative attributes reflect a further handicap to treatment, for example, the inadequacy of the parents to meet the basic requirements of the usual approach. Their own needs are too concrete, their attitude toward life and the human society too negative in every conceivable way, their sense of isolation and incompetence too overpowering for finding a common ground for communication and a common goal in reference to the child's welfare. In particular, responsibilities can not easily be perceived or accepted by the parents.

To acknowledge helplessness in the face of one of the major human tragedies, child or infant rejection and neglect also means admitting that a populous sector of mankind is lost for human culture from one generation to the next. From the point of view of the child, to deny him the only assistance that could possibly reach the core of his problem amounts

Reprinted from *Group Psychotherapy*, Vol. 12, No. 1, March 1959, pp. 58–66, J. L. Moreno, M.D. ed., Beacon House Inc., publishers.

to punishment for having already been punished, and new rejection and neglect by the human family at large.

Amenability to Treatment Further Obviated by Disqualification for Treatment

For the victimized child the validity of the parents' censure of his whole existence is thus confirmed, as is the distorted self-image conceived through identification with parental rejection. But equally, the community has become a rejecting parent to which the child extends his hopeless longing, but to which his approach is by hostility and negation.

The children are aware of the inequality of fate that has placed them in an underprivileged position. Deprivation as well as "badness" are taken as an inexorable destiny against which they revolt covertly "by obeying the verdict." In effect they resort desperately to "badness" which is not only the main source of palliation of as well as compensation for deprivation, but also the only language spoken by the resource-less child. However, there could be no revolt unless motivated by the longing for better things, above all love, and in particular the mother's love as essential to the joy of being.

The Method

In the Educational Therapy Center in Richmond, Virginia, a Mental Hygiene Clinic operating under the Mental Hygiene Act, a professional and educational team with clerical assistants treat twenty to twenty-five children, one fifth of them girls, throughout the day. The average age is 8-14 years at intake. The purpose is to create a "psychological home," where the children can feel spontaneous, free, and accepted, and through which they will in turn accept the world.

PSYCHIATRIC SOCIAL WORK

Intensive work is being done with the families. The mothers generally can be reached with less difficulty than the fathers. Those fathers living in the home are often despondent, indifferent or withdrawn. Home visits are often highly appreciated and give a true picture of the child's human and material surroundings.

THE INTAKE

Due to the emergency of these children's plight, assistance has to be immediate from the point of view of the child, the family, and the community. Therefore, delay at intake and waiting lists are out of the ques-

tion. We meet the problem of the emergency at intake which exists in reference to all day-care children, by setting them on the "inside waiting list," when none of the therapists is able to take one more child in individual therapy or cannot be fitted into a therapy group. The number of children in the classrooms vary, the teachers' personalities and their approach are different, a highly qualified and experienced supervisor is available for individual sessions and extended contacts, consequently much can be done to gratify, protect and support the children until therapy proper can be started. The new child's behavior in the group can be observed and adequately dealt with. For some children to become familiar and comfortable in the day-care group and live as though anonymously in a "crowd" is a basic prerequisite before they can meet anyone on a relevant relation of "twosomeness."

Differential Criteria of Our Method

Other clinics treat children on scheduled individual sessions or group sessions, while simultaneously at least one of their parents or guardians is seen by the psychiatric social worker or a therapist equally in individual or group sessions.

In contrast our children live in a children's group with their teachers throughout the day every day of the week. They are given opportunity to gratify their vital needs as being accepted, sheltered, fed, taught, allowed to shape and own things, to move.

Other clinics use specific devices such as doll houses, the target, etc., in order to elicit significant responses primarily in terms of stages of libido.

In contrast we try to capture them through pure and unrestricted observation of the children's spontaneous behavior.

Other clinics establish therapeutic object relations in *symbolic* terms. In contrast we foster in the group a *living* experience of home, family, and companionship. Individual psychotherapy remains unaffected thereby.

Other clinics rely on a psychotherapy designed for children having attained social standing as reflected by communication and verbalization.

In contrast, we try to reach the asocial child unable or unwilling to communicate by words. More than once we had the experience that the simple- and at first silent-sharing of the same space initiates relevant relationship, thus has communicative power of its own.

Institutional confinement of such children whose early development has been severely interfered with to the extent that protection by a structured milieu is needed, can in certain cases be avoided. If the home placement meets the child's needs of discriminate attention and the child's transportation to the clinic occurs under parental protection, if similar protection in a child-adult, one to one therapeutic and later edu-

cational relationship is warranted, the daily routine of change represents a well tolerated, soon desired way of and to life. Under such protection and the precisely dovetailed routine between foster home and clinic, the child yields early to the lure of the community, to play with children in the neighborhood and interplay with the children in the clinic. The average clinic population can immediately be exposed to the advantage implied in our methods which lies in the fact that children, while being exposed to the test of reality, are prepared and trained in time to meet this test. In no other area is selection according to carefully established criteria more important. It remains one of our most unexpected, challenging and rewarding experiences that the most destitute and neglected children proved to have the greatest strength in adjusting to the living conditions in the Educational Therapy Center and in coping with the menaces of their home and community. However, placement in foster homes often cannot be avoided and often is requested by the children themselves as their only road to recovery and adjustment.

We offer:

(a) Individual psychotherapy, spatially remote from the area of activities and study, the opportunity for a review of the first object relation. This remoteness evidently is required not only for privacy and quiet, but also as a means to promote the symbolic aspects of the therapeutic relation. Group psychotherapy represents one special aspect of psychotherapy.

(b) Life in the day-care group in the permanent presence of an understanding and permissive educational staff. Here the majority of the children's concrete needs on various levels of developments are answered to the extent that it is possible.

(c) Opportunity is given for play and recreation or in other terms the manipulation of legitimately owned objects and the enjoyment of sensorimotor experience which conveys a sense of freedom, intensified by the recognized title to joy and leisure.

(d) Crafts, trades (carpentry and cabinet making) which are redeemed hostility and destruction, through mastery of matter and the offering of the exteriorated self through the achieved opus; the children are taught home economics and the preparation of meals which Bachelard [1] calls the festival at its morn. It is a lesson in suspended gratification, certainty gained through one's own contribution as well as the active enjoyment of the hours of necessary delay. Maintenance work on house and yard is spontaneously and well understood by the children as the fond tending of the "mother," who is kept well and alive that she may go on protecting them by her warming and enfolding arms. Maintenance is the symbol of reparation and rehabilitation. The wounds that the child could not help inflicting by impulsive destruction he can bind and he will increasingly enjoy the liberty to change, to give and to be an important helper and an accepted partner. The sense of his share in ownership and his partaking in the blessings of this world is thus intensely underscored.

(e) Academic Studies: A rewarding world in which we share, receive, own, and are thus enabled to give, is no longer feared and is therefore intriguing, challenging and worth exploring. The children's curiosity can now be gratified in their academic classes. (All day-care children at the time of referral are unteachable in public school because of their emotional condition.)

All children know each other well. They meet at meal time, at special activities and sports, at camping, and at outings in and out of town.

Rationale of the Method

Due to the intensity and quality of the disturbance which ties these children to the natural mother, individual therapy is rendered difficult. The children long for treatment, but fear and resist it, due to the false lure of motherliness to which they have been exposed throughout their existence. They also fear their own angry insistence on breaking through to the evasive mother, because new rejection will be incurred. The need therefore arises for displacing hostility on a suitable substitute, thus to hit the mother without annihilating her. This target is found in the day-care milieu which thus absorbs much of the negative transference against the symbolic mother.

This we have learned to be of extreme importance. The children impressed us by the way they were using their individual therapy sessions. Regression was manifested predominantly by expression of dependency needs which naturally are extreme. Hostility, once total negativism in the most withdrawn children is overcome, contrary to the behavior in the group, is subtle. The children may turn their glances away from the therapist to loafers, alcoholics, and prostitutes on the street corner to express "that is what I am and cannot help being, I defy you to prove it to be otherwise." Hostility, moreover, is displaced in the session and in the children's play and the bid for ego boost and the investment of the psychotherapist with an infinite variety of ideal characteristics is impressive at times and astonishing as to its graciousness. A young girl, given away by her mother at birth to an unknown woman who proved to be a prostitute of the most unsophisticated order, had been referred by the State for temper tantrums and a sex problem. One day during her session the telephone rang and was not answered. Desirous to be pleasant and generous, the girl exclaimed: "why don't you pick up your beautiful Queen Elizabeth telephone?" The initial interview usually also is revealing of these children's intense ambivalence between the longing for and the distrust and resentment against the mother image of the locked entrance to the world. The greater the impact of the first meeting with the psychiatrist, the greater is the fear of deception, of loss of stature and face, therefore, the greater the child's need for over-securing himself by aggression elsewhere, because he still clings to the mother as the origin of all hope.

The children's group first represents the street gang or so many hostile doubles. They need reinforcement for intensification of the pleasures derived from expressed hostility as a defense against the temptation to yield to dependency needs upon the mother figure. This phase is desirable. It carries the street gang into the house and acting out is localized on the therapeutic scene, where it can be observed and therapeutically dealt with. In particular the children will be necessarily confronted with the results of their behavior, reflect upon it, feel responsible or guilty and learn to deal with uneasiness or conflict.

The gang is taken for granted by the psychotherapist and not denied. This attitude alleviates the children's prejudice that he and all of his companions are inherently bad and they begin to discriminate between the person and undesirable individual acts. The gift of the gang and the alteration of its meaning intensify the positive elements of the transference to the gratifying mother figure, a fact which benefits individual therapy.

As long as the child recognizes the gang in the children's group, the teachers who are constantly in their presence are widely ignored, annoyed, or evaded. But what happens is that the children's group will answer his needs, but also change him. This is due to the permanent presence of the permissive and understanding adult group, and the insidious influence which necessarily results.

The children's group in day-care is sweeping. We accept children all through the year as the need arises and agencies or parents request our help. The degree of improvement varies, as for instance their sense of adequacy, familiarity, identification with the Center, dedication and pride as well as their curiosity and constructive activity. Mutual pathological needs will therefore be arouse by the newcomer or he will be used and it is inevitable that an epidemic of pathological interaction of some kind will occasionally flare up. But there are also the old-timers of the Center who recognize their former self in the newcomer and the recidivist; they help the newcomers to understand what they are doing and what it does to them when you thus behave. He becomes a more readily acceptable parental figure or an elder sibling and a bridge to identification with the adults. They have learned to trust. The teachers, as evident, also answer dependency needs when they represent impartial, disinterested and ever present support and comfort to the children when they act out mutual hostility violently. Thus, insidiously, the gang is infiltrated by adult love; it cannot be used any more as a hard tool against them. The child cannot disregard them; they are needed, leaned and relied upon. The children's group no longer represents the gang to the child, but his siblings. Love and hate, subtle rivalries, pathological and sound complementations are now settled in the familiar milieu, the symbolic scene of the home as the origin of his problems. At this stage an intense rivalry for the psychotherapist's love regularly is in evidence, no longer as in the past for who receives most and is first, but who deserves love most. The group thus becomes a testing ground for a child's character, because it is here that he is challenged in his faith. To support

his convictions he will for some time resort to the dialogue in individual sessions, but become more and more discursive and at times enthusiastically declamatory in the group as well.

Language, in particular the gentle and pondered discourse, stimulated by the adults' approach, their reflecting with them about what has gone on when difficulties arose, the insight thus gained as well as the gratification derived from one's understanding of people and their relations, stimulate the children's spontaneity for a similar approach. They first search the other fellow's motives suspiciously, then more and more objectively, then their own as well as their interaction with others. In his individual therapy session, the child will now be eager to discuss the emotional interaction in the group and see what happens there in the light of his previous experiences which are increasingly revealed.

Results

In a small random sampling of test results,[2] an increase of the Intelligence Quotient was noted in several cases, subsequent to therapy in one instance of 20 points, one non-reader achieved mental growth of three years in one year of therapy. In several cases both the intelligence test and projective tests indicated a broadening of interests with consequent drop in perseveration and stereotypy. There was also noted in these children increased productiveness, and more concreteness in perceiving environment where before their approach had been vague and global, or on the other hand, ability to combine and synthesize parts into a whole, where before their approach had been too concrete.

In certain cases shock reaction to the ink blots disappeared after therapy. In others, fantasy reactions appeared for the first time, indicating growing ability to try out various roles where before acting-out had been the child's only means of expression. In one child who was withdrawn and a day-dreamer retesting uncovered emerging responsiveness to his environment. The falling off of anxiety indicators was observed in several instances.

While the Rorschach is the most sensitive instrument for detecting personality changes, stories given to TAT, Blacky, and CAT in some few cases suggest a channeling of hostile and aggressive impulses into acceptable or at least limited objects. These stories also sometimes reveal that identification with substitute parents has taken place, subsequent to therapy.

Withdrawal, negativistic and ambivalent attitudes, paranoid ideation and sensitivity are relinquished. Dependency yields to reciprocal relationship and at times to profound and lasting dedication, as reflected in the visits of former patients returning from the Armed Forces and combat (Korean War) or now married men and fathers coming from distant homes to assure us that they will never be of any concern to us again.

Children who were blocking off remembrance begin to recover trau-

matic memories, to face their emotions, consent to reason and reflect on the changed and more realistic attitude toward their own behavior or the altered, no less realistic outlook on their disturbed family relationships.

Language development is impressive in all its spheres. Most obvious is the fundamental change from exclamatory or interjectional language, cursing, or clamoring to a formulated expression of thought, attuned to the person addressed. Progress is least in articulation, but sentence structures develop though certain constitutents such as tenses may lag behind. Vocabulary is enriched and abstract concepts emerge.

The children gain a sense of security, of being accepted; consequently they reach self-acceptance. They lose the feeling of being different and singled out by destiny. They rise to constructive leadership in the group, in others envy and competition yield to cooperation, responsible attitude toward property replaces wastefulness and destructiveness, interest is awakened in the outside world, in the future, in the will "to get an education," in an active and sustained effort to perform manual work in the group and an ardent will to find a job, to provide for their own needs and contribute to the family budget. Many of the children keep their jobs for long periods of time, some of them have enrolled in long term Army Services. While improving under treatment, the children begin spontaneously to associate with children in the community, attend recreation facilities, join outside boys' clubs, the Y.M.C.A.; they request to go to Public School.

Treatments last from 18 months to four or five years.

Failures are due above all to insistent interference by the mother who tends to commit the child to a definite need of her own or to a lack of community resources as adequate foster homes, or small group homes.

A number of hostile and withdrawn children may not be reached and finally be hospitalized; others belatedly referred, are lost to the State Industrial Schools when they act out in the community.

Notes

1. Gaston Bachelard: La Terre et les rêveries de la volonté, José Corti, Paris.

2. Compiled by Mrs. Percy Smith, Psychologist.

Treatment in the Home: An Experiment With Low Income, Multi-Problem Families

Rachel A. Levine

In August of 1961 the Mental Hygiene Clinic of the Henry Street Settlement began an experiment to bring mental health services to low income, multi-problem families, in ways they might be able to use. The experiment was named Treatment In The Home. It was devised to circumvent the well known resistance among such families to social agencies in general, and to mental health clinics in particular; to break the cycles of broken appointments in the clinic, new appointments and eventual closing of the case for "lack of motivation." This cycle reflects agency disregard of the reasons underlying the "lack of motivation," even while these are expounded learnedly in theory. For example, despite the knowledge of the alienation which exists between the social class represented by these families and the middle class structure of our social agencies, the agencies' expectations that these families will conform to the agencies' requirements, and practices is not altered.

The major features of the experiment lie in the methodology: shifting treatment from the clinic to the home, and use of the techniques of demonstration and intervention. It has as the main objective, to reduce the alienation by introducing a new learning experience— learning from going through a treatment process together, one which is tailored to what these families can understand and accept. To amplify further:

Paper presented at the United Neighborhood Houses Conference, November 18, 1963.

1) the treatment in the home insures continuity of regular appointments;
2) in place of discussion with the patient or parents only, all members of the family are present and the social worker relates to all the members and their problems;
3) the social worker brings into the home a variety of materials such as arts and crafts and simple games which all members can play. These serve as media through which conflicts between members are revealed as they take part in activity and as free responses occur;
4) as family members interact, the social worker takes the role of catalyst to dramatize the particular conflict, or intervenes to break into the destructive pattern of interaction, and proceeds to demonstrate on the spot ways and means of settling the dispute, with all members participating in testing out and talking about the new ways;
5) concrete services are provided to any member of the family who needs them.

A group of seven families was selected for this experiment; there is in all of them a concentration of socio-pathological problems in pervasive and extreme forms. These are families of boys whose emotional disturbance was so severe that they could not be contained in any public school class. They and their families were the subjects of a three-year pilot project which ended in June of this year, undertaken in collaboration with the Board of Education and subsidized in part by the New York City Community Mental Health Board. Schooling was conducted in the clinic with a teacher provided by the Board of Education, while the clinic provided treatment and recreational activities. Without exception, the impulsive acting-out behavior in school was but a reflection of home conditions. Parents, severely deprived themselves, wanted good lives for their children but did not know how to accomplish this and were excessively restrictive and punitive as their means of control. They lived under one roof, in isolation, their only mode of communication being verbal or physical abuse, born of deep anger. Absent were demonstrable affection, structure, reasonable limits consistently applied, and other elements so necessary in child rearing. Clinical treatment provided in traditional ways during the first year of the project yielded negligible results.

Hence, the experiment was based upon some broadly defined assumptions, which also represented the hope of finding some answers to the discouragement prevalent in the field concerning this segment of our community. The assumptions to be tested were:

1) For this "non-motivated" social class, clinic appointments are alien. Psycho-pathology has been part and parcel of their way of life from one generation to another. Is it any wonder that help for an intra-psychic problem alone has little or no meaning to people bedeviled by grim problems of survival? Also, suspicion and fear born

of ignorance, superstition, and misconceptions about mental health practically forces them to reject the service. Among our Puerto Rican population we often hear the word "loco" muttered. Who among us wants to be thought crazy? The assumption is that bringing the service to them in their own setting, divested of the authority of such agencies as the Department of Welfare, Police, or Housing Authority, should reduce the suspicion. Also, appointments planned for the time fathers are home include them in a natural way.

2) Psycho-pathology which is part and parcel of social and economic pathology cannot be treated in isolation from other problems and from other family members who are contaminated by the same set of influences. It is understandable that family members should distrust help which ignores the realities of their manifold problems. Therefore help for whatever problems emerge should also pave the way for trusting other community resources and should teach people how to use them.

3) The substitution of the technique of demonstration for verbal discussion of abstract ideas should bridge the gap in communication between the therapist and these families who are marginally educated, whose lives are a cultural wasteland. Doing or demonstrating what is needed should be more effective because the social worker's action, combined with talk about what is going on shows how the conflict develops and how it can be resolved without recourse to fighting or beating.

4) The use of play materials as the medium of treatment takes into account parents who are immature, inadequate, in rivalry with each other and with their children. It should lessen the gap in emotional distance, should let them derive pleasure with their children, should alter emotional tones in communication, and permit teaching of reasonable limits, of fair play, of tolerance and respect for individual need and difference. Moreover, in place of discussions of failure, success is demonstrated as disputes are settled in which all members can feel a sense of accomplishment.

5) Finally, treatment in the home should in the long run prove more economical for these families. Because problems are revealed in the living situation, distortions are eliminated, there is greater accuracy in diagnosis, the treatment process can be initiated quickly and progress more rapidly towards the resolution of conflict. Because all members of the family participate, all can benefit and need not be referred individually or in succession. Above all, time, money, effort and manpower are conserved, and the effort expended initially to reach the sources of problems for all family members should insure more lasting improvement. To what extent the method and the assumptions have been tested and evaluated can be illustrated here by the experience with one of these families.

At the start of the experiment, the "M" family, Puerto Rican, consisting of thirteen persons, lived in a five-room, low-cost housing project on marginal income, supplemented by the Department of Welfare.

Both parents, in their early forties, had minimal comprehension of English. Of the young children, one was in a residential treatment center, a second had been discharged from a state hospital, a third was mentally defective. Henry, then age ten, who was in our school therapy project, was diagnosed as "borderline schizophrenic." The home was always dirty and in a state of chaos. Both parents either allowed unbridled behavior or beat the children viciously and indiscriminately. The sixteen-year-old girl was ready to drop out of school; the six-year-old girl always unkempt, withdrawn, and doing poorly in school; the defective child just vegetated; and the youngest child, age two, was neglected and mistreated by everyone. The father lived like a privileged boarder, keeping all his personal possessions locked in a closet. He never participated in the life of the family except to administer beatings. The mother appeared like a disinterested bystander. Home was like a shell, devoid of adequate furnishings and toys because "they would only be broken." Henry was obliged to sleep in the same bed with the mentally ill brother and the mentally defective child, both of whom interfered with his proper rest.

The social worker arranged the visits after the family's evening meal, taking along simple play materials. From the first, the children eagerly gathered around the table, but the parents sat apart, watching, while the two-year-old was thrust aside. Gradually, both parents began to join in the games and the worker began to include the two-year-old by showing him how to hold and use materials, indirectly demonstrating to the older children and to the parents how he could be taught. In the activity, both parents manipulated, competed, and cheated just as the children did. Gently, the worker introduced rules. In the weeks that followed, as rivalries, cheating, and angry outbursts occurred, the worker would stop the activity, allow each one to have his say, encourage them to bring out their feelings of anger and hurt, and introduce, gradually, acts of fairnesss and respect for each other. Before many sessions had passed, the visits were awaited with eagerness by all the family. These weekly visits were supplemented with inclusion of family members in Settlement recreational programs, and additional time set aside for talks with the parents about problems they were now willing to bring up, either at home or in the office, to which they were now willing to come. They talked first about sex and birth control, during which it became evident that fears and ignorance accounted for their lethargy. The worker gathered information accompanied the parents to sources to help and in the process cleared away their misconceptions. A similar process of accompanying the parents and child through complicated processing in various agencies eventuated in the placement of the defective child in a state school, the readmission of the mentally sick child to the state hospital, the working out of a satisfactory plan for the sixteen-year-old to remain in school, the acceptance of a Big Sister for the six-year-old, and enrollment of the remaining younger children in after-school playschool.

The first period of ten month's work showed tangible evidence of

beginning change. Some relief from the pressures of many children allowed the mother to attend better to household tasks. The house was cleaner and beginning to take on the semblance of a home. There was more effort between parents and children to talk out their grievances, hence fewer tantrums, less fighting, and fewer beatings. Programs outside the home provided not only cultural enrichment but also learning to conform to reasonable discipline and limits, and learning that authority can be understanding. The six-year-old withdrawn girl began to change from an uncommunicative, unkempt, unhappy child, to a responsive, spirited youngster. All the children were doing better in school. Emotional distance had lessened and the general home atmosphere was less hostile. For the first time in their lives the parents made a birthday party for one of the children.

The use of adverbs like "less" fighting, and "more" effort in communication implies change which is a matter of degree, is relative, and is in contrast to attitudes and behavior prior to the experiment. It also implies change which is in flux and so, subject to relapse. The relapse into former patterns when treatment was interrupted for a few months was to be expected in view of the fragile nature of beginning improvement. However, with the beginning of the second year, it took only a few visits to reestablish the family on the track toward progress. During the balance of the second year of this experiment the "M" family made substantial advances. The father, for example, having experienced success with his own children, went so far as to offer his services to the clinic as a volunteer. The same rate of progress was made by all but one family.

The questions at this point would logically be, what really has been accomplished in the experiment, and do the assumptions hold up? First, the stimulus for change or improvement was imposed by external means, in a repetitive, consistent way, to bring about some environmental change. The intra-psychic or unconscious was not directly touched. The effectivenesss of such improvement could therefore be questioned by colleagues who believe real change can only come from within the personality. Whatever its shortcomings, can there be much dispute over the possibility that environmental change may be all that we can accomplish with certain people, given our present limited knowledge, tools, and resources? Also, is it not possible that environmental change can lead to inner change? If something is done often enough it eventually becomes habitual. Showing how something needs to be done is concrete and so, more understandable since people can see, and do, and feel the gratification of immediate success, rather than talking about it and being left to do it alone, when they do not know how. Then, the recognition for accomplishment and ensuing feelings of importance led the families to ask for help for other pressing problems, for which concrete services were given. Therefore shifting treatment to the home did enable them to use help and did bring about substantial improvement. Concrete services then provided satisfying experiences in the use of other community resources

which they so desperately needed. Was their indifference toward social and authoritative agencies so surprising when one stops to think about the bureaucratic procedures characteristic of so many agencies—procedures which are often mystifying and frustrating even to professional groups? Telephoning, filling out forms, innumerable trips, and waiting only to be told to return another time, harassed workers who are brusque, impersonal, quoting directives or regulations which defy anyone's intelligence. All of these are incomprehensible, especially to people who are not proficient in the language, are unfamiliar with our customs, cannot leave babies at home to travel long distances—and achieve no satisfaction. All of this represents to them a monstrous machine of which they are afraid. Teaching them how to use community resources by sharing the experience reduced these fears.

Second, to return to the external stimulus for change, the technique of Demonstration should not be construed as the "taking over" of parental role or responsibility. On the contrary, the treatment process demands from the worker the utmost in alertness and sensitivity to undercurrents of parental feelings of resentment to what they may feel to be usurpation of their control. Despite their inadequacies, and perhaps because of them, they are apt to withdraw if they feel their "rights" as parents preempted. Mindful of this, the worker did not plunge into directing. To begin with, he told them he was there to learn what their difficulties were and see if with his help they could work them out. There was often patient waiting, just being there. He verbalized feelings they might have had about what he was doing and to what end. He had to judge their readiness to move on, and measure how much and how far he would intervene and direct, but he was always reassuring by setting straight in their minds (parents and children alike) that the parents hold the authority and control. When such fears are truly allayed, and the participation of the parents gained, the change can become part of daily living. Hence, Demonstration as a technique in treatment was understandable and had meaning for these families. It also bridged some gaps in communication and improved family relationships.

Third, perhaps the best that can be put forth on the question of economy and prevention, is the consideration that in acting on all the problems of all family members simultaneously, there takes place the breaking up of maladjustment in the incipient stage when patterns of behavior can be reversed; thus the individual is enabled to cope better with problems with fewer crippling symptoms. There is also less interference from the impinging pathology of other family members. In the case illustration given, the pathology of other siblings had a direct bearing upon the difficulties of the project child, and this was also true of the other project children. The extent to which this is significant can be judged by our experience where for the caseload of seven children and their families, sixty-nine individuals, including close relatives, received services of one kind or another during the same period.

Finally, the method, Treatment in the Home, and the technique of Demonstration can be further evaluated by the research findings on the relationship between progress in the parents and improvement in the project children. Quoting from the research: "If, we reasoned, treatment in the home was instrumental in the childrens' behavior there should be a positive correlation between degree of improvement in the child and parents. If treatment in the home was ineffectual, one would expect no correlation between child and parental progress.

Each child was periodically rated by his teacher, social worker and recreation workers, on a five point behavioral rating scale. Taken together, these ratings provided a quantitative index of each child's progress or lack of it. The parents were independently ranked by the social worker who conducted the treatment in the home. At the end of each year's period the research findings showed conclusively a striking correspondence between parental progress (improvement in family milieu) and children's progress. Although all the children in the project have made some progress in educational achievement in varying degrees, the most marked changes are in behavioral adjustment and personality functioning, the very reasons for which they were suspended from the public school three years earlier. All were returned to the public school in September of this year and as of this date are making a satisfactory adjustment.

In closing, it should be said there is no intent to imply that the method in this experiment can succeed with all low income, multi-problem, or disadvantaged families, nor that all such families are the same. On the contrary, there is a wide range of individual differences, as with all families, so that no one method or technique can be applied to all, or be successful in all instances. The experiment shows merely that some families commonly classified as multi-problem, appear to be responding to the method described.

Role Playing and the Poor [1]

Frank Riessman and Jean Goldfarb

Role playing [2] techniques have long been popular with blue collar workers in labor unions and industry. Our own experience at Mobilization For Youth and various community organizations further indicates an exceptionally positive response to role-play technology by low income people. While more systematic research is needed regarding these observations, it may be useful to present some illustrations and a rationale for the special potential of this technique in work with lower socioeconomic groups.

Teaching Academic Material

1. TO NONPROFESSIONAL PERSONNEL

One of the most important "subjects" that had to be mastered by the Mobilization for Youth Parent Education Aids (indigenous non-professionals from lower socioeconomic groups) was the full program of the agency. Rather than give a lecture about the mobilization program, role playing was used in having the aids try to act out situations in which they would be telling families in the community about Mobilization For Youth. One aid would act as a member of the community, while another aid would act as herself. In the group discussion that followed each role-playing incident, the group leader (who had detailed knowledge about the program) could easily and meaningfully add to the information of the group.

This proved to be a very stimulating and yet informal experience and provided the interest for more intensive lecture-discussion presentations by representatives of the various subprograms of Mobiliza-

Reprinted by permission from *Group Psychotherapy*, Vol. 17, No. 1, March, 1964, pp. 36–48.

tion For Youth (work, education, community organization, individual services).

Goldberg's report on the Homemaker Program at Mobilization For Youth indicates the special value of role play in training nonprofessionals:

> One value of role play is that it offers the chance not only to understand the client but to test the practice in a simulated worker-client relationship. We usually let each homemaker take a crack at a siutation (e.g., how you could handle a very demanding client who sent her child to give you an order after she had exhausted her own quota). Then we criticize each other or try to say why one way was better than the others.
>
> One advantage of the role play is that it gives the supervisors a better picture of what homemaking is like or of what actually goes on. We have discovered, for example, that it is very difficult for them (the homemakers) to discuss budgeting with a family. In fact the homemakers, despite their antipathy for the "welfare way," were handling budgets very much like social investigators until we caught them in role play and began to explore ways of doing it less mechanically and dictatorially.[3]

2. TO PROFESSIONAL PERSONNEL

In a program concerned with conveying low income culture to teachers in the Mobilization For Youth community, one of the major approaches is to have the teachers visit the homes of their pupils. This is valuable, but is limited in that only two visits of about an hour each take place during the term. Role playing can be utilized effectively here by having groups of teachers meet together and act out some of the situations they have seen or in which they have participated at the homes.

The experience of each teacher can be added to that of all the others, but more important, through the technique of role-reversal the teachers can begin to know how the parents feel. Here the group leader plays a decisive part. During the discussion he can point out the meaning of much of the low income behavior and culture that has been enacted. He can bring in considerable academic content around the situations that have been witnessed by the audience. He can raise important questions that different members of the group, because of their varying experiences in the homes, can shed light upon. The reading of the group can also be integrated around the situations that have been enacted.

3. TEACHING CHILDREN

Role playing can have beneficial results in teaching academic material in the school.[4] Considerable excitement is added to a lecture when

a point is illustrated by the instructor with role playing. Most likely the incident will be long remembered by the audience. If an inquiring student should wonder what Abraham Lincoln, for example, would think of our present civil rights program, let Lincoln and Johnson stage a debate enacted by two students! The impossibilities of distance and time are eliminated, and the civics lesson will be well remembered.

Role playing can be utilized in countless ways (in school) such as acting out a history lesson (George Washington signing the Constitution), teaching arithmetic and economics by playing "store" and "bank." The role playing itself is a marvelous stimulus for discussion, and it appeals to the deprived child's love of action. It provides for a much more vivid presentation and fits in with his desire for excitement and movement; . . . role playing should be a trigger for advanced discussion and thinking. . . . [5]

Developing Teacher Styles

One of the special values of role playing sessions is that the new teacher, or the student teacher, can discover and develop her own repertoire of skills. For example, we often suggest that a teacher in a deprived setting express herself physically and visually as much as possible: walk around the room, use gestures, touch the children, etc. But for many people this is simply not possible; it is not within the framework of their personality, and there is nothing more dangerous than attempting to manufacture a style for which you have no feeling. It will go over like a lead balloon. The teacher will feel stiff and uneasy in imitating what "doesn't come naturally," and the children, who are surprisingly sensitive, will know it is contrived. The role playing sessions will soon ascertain whether the new teacher has any potential feeling for this "physical" pattern. If the teacher does, the ensuing sessions can bring out this potential, can encourage her, and can help her to shape her future style. If she does not have this particular skill, no matter, because fortunately there are innumerable ways of being an effective teacher, and role playing can assist in finding and integrating the best approaches for the particular teacher. Depending on what kind of personality style she has, she will probably select different approaches and techniques from the things we have suggested. If she is a careful, meticulous person herself, she can perhaps synchronize more readily with the slow style of the disadvantaged child. If she has great patience, she may be able to appreciate the tenacious persistence that evidences itself in these children once they have become absorbed, and she may be able to bring them to this point more rapidly. If she is vivid and exciting, and much interested in the subject, she should be encouraged to impart this enthusiasm to the children. If the teacher is a physically strong man, he should convey this to the children, not by display of his prowess, but by what one counselor at Wilt-

wick so aptly called the "suggestion of strength"—"you never hit the kid, but your size and strength are always *there*, by the way you touch the boy, lift things, handle yourself, and so on."

But strength, of course, is not only established through the physical. The thin, small-voiced female teacher can be just as effective as the big baritone. Role playing should help the new teacher to discover the manifold sources of strength and authority, and particularly her own resources in this capacity. Strength can be reflected to these children by definiteness, quiet, firm tones, consistency, standing by a statement, determination to teach, and so on. It is a tremendous mistake to think that authority and respect can only be commanded through physical power. The climax in role playing comes when the new teacher begins to feel and act in the sessions as though the classroom were her fortress. You cannot tell people to be confident—but you can provide the conditions, knowledge, and practice that build confidence. Role playing is one of the best confidence builders we know of for the new teacher.[6]

Some Illustrations of Role Playing
With Low Income Groups

Through its informality, easy pace, and use of humor, role playing can take some of the anxiety out of everyday situations that the low income individual finds threatening. For example, if he fears an approaching job interview, playing the part of the employer makes the latter a less threatening person. There is a secondary gain involved in this technique, for role playing is a little like witchery: by playing another person you "take his sting away" and gain some of his "magic power" for yourself.

If a low income group is forming a tenant's council in a housing project, role playing can give practical experience in "knocking on doors" and in learning how to present the plan to new tenants. In this way natural leaders in the community can be developed and trained. Many other types of problems can be profitably role played: family and marital disputes, gang conflicts and conflicts with authority, disputes between youth and parents. People can be taught how to address a PTA meeting, how to be a shop steward or a labor negotiator, and so on.

Role playing has been used in work with alcoholics, drug addicts, suicidal patients, psychotics, and the like. Freedom Riders have been screened through role playing to see how they would react to difficult situations that might arise.

There are at least four reasons why role playing may be valuable with the disadvantaged:

1. It appears to be congenial with the low income person's style, which is physical (action oriented, doing vs. talking); down to earth,

concrete, problem directed; externally oriented rather than introspective; group centered; game-like rather than test oriented; easy and informal in tempo.

2. It allows the practitioner (social worker, psychiatrist, educator) to reduce, in an honest fashion, the role distance between himself and the disadvantaged individual who is often alienated from him. It also permits the practitioner to learn more about the culture of the low income person from the inside (through playing the latter's role in role reversal).

3. It changes the setting and tone of what often appears to be, to the low income person, an office ridden, bureaucratic, impersonal, foreign world.

4. It appears to be an excellent technique for developing verbal power in the educationally deprived person, who is said to be largely inarticulate. Moreover, it seems to be especially useful for the development of leadership skills.

The Style of the Poor: Doing vs. Talking

Miller and Swanson, on the basis of a number of different investigations, arrive at the conclusion that an outstanding characteristic of the low income person's style is its emphasis on the physical, in particular the motoric (the large muscles involved in voluntary action).[7] It is not simply that the poor *are* physical; that their labor is characterized by working with things; that their child rearing typically utilizes physical punishment; that their religious expression very often includes physical manifestations of emotion such as hand-clapping; that when they become mentally ill they are more likely to develop motoric symptoms such as conversion hysteria and catatonia (disorders involving malfunctions of the voluntary muscles); that they are strongly interested in sports; that they are especially responsive to extra-verbal forms of communication, such as gesture.[8] The significant factor is that low income people *work through mental problems best when they can do things physically.* This is their habit, or style of work, and it appears when they work on academic problems or personal problems.

Miller and Swanson draw certain implications for therapy from their observations regarding the motoric style of the poor. "Our results indicate the desirability of exploring a variety of new psychotherapeutic techniques, particularly those in which words and concepts are subordinated to nonverbal and even motoric activities." [9]

A number of other investigators have also drawn attention to the physical bent of the poor as reflected in their expectations regarding psychotherapy, their presenting symptoms, their learning styles, and so forth. (See Overall and Aronson, Hollingshead and Redlich, Brill and Storrow).[10]

Role playing appears admirably suited to this physical, action-centered, motoric style. The process itself requires wholistic *doing* or acting out of situations, not merely talking about them. This is a mode of problem solving that low income males, and young males in particular, find attractive. They frequently have a strong dislike for talk; they want "action" and they *prefer talk that is related to action*. They also like vivid (e.g., hip, slang), down-to-earth, situation-rooted talk, and this, too, is likely to emerge in the role-play format. Role playing is much more lively, physical, and active than the typical interview.

Numerous other dimensions of role playing are congruent with characteristics of the low income person's style:

Low income patterns of working together, responding to one another, concern with human contact, are favored by role playing. Problems are shared and solutions are arrived at communally. Frequently, one low income individual has successfully dealt with (or is capable of dealing with) problems that are overpowering to another disadvantaged person. Sometimes the experience of people like himself is more influential for an individual (i.e., is a better model) than the therapist's aid. Role playing promotes group feeling and understanding through its informality, easy pace, and natural humor.

Low income groups typically do not like the traditional test format, and this limits diagnostic work with them. The requirements of their style seem to be better fulfilled by game-like atmospheres and situational measures both of which are readily found in role play technology.[11]

Low income people are generally less introspective, less introverted, less concerned with self. They respond more to the external, to the outside, to action. They are likely to see the causes of their problems in external forces; they project more and tend to externalize their guilt.[12] Kohn notes that their child rearing patterns center on conformity to external prescriptions "in contrast to the self-direction focus of the middle class."[13] He relates this partly to the fact that "working-class" occupations require that one follows explicit rules prescribed by an authority, while middle class occupations are subject to more self-direction.[14]

We postulate that low income psychology, rooted as it is in a more external (nonintrospective mold), might be appealed to more readily by a therapeutic system based on an outer-inner change nexus rather than on the inner-outer focus characteristic of traditional casework and psychiatry.[15]

Role playing as a technique is consistent with a model emphasizing external action, and with role taking as an impetus to change as well as a stimulus for introspection. (While low income people probably do not like to introspect in the abstract, they may be more introspective in response to external signals).

While the style of the poor includes a strong emphasis on informality, humor, and warmth, these individuals also like to have content that is structured, definite, and specific. It is often assumed that role-

playing is highly unstructured and free. In part this is true, particularly in the early phase of establishing the problem and mood. But in the middle and later phases (especially the role training stage), where the effort is made to teach very specific behaviors, role playing can be highly structured, reviewing in minute detail the various operations to be learned (such as how to run a meeting, organize a conference, talk to a housing manager). Educationally disadvantaged people appear to prefer a mood or tone of feeling that is informal and easy, but a content that is structured and task centered. Role playing may satisfy both these needs.

Breaking the Office Barrier

Role playing, apart from its likely congeniality with low income culture and style, has numerous other advantages. Perhaps most important is that the technique per se begins to break through the traditional office atmosphere with its implicit role segmentation and desk-supported distance, its interview method of "getting to know you," and its concomitant physical stasis. The entire office fabric, rooted as it is in fact-to-face verbalization about things not present, is inappropriate for the low income person who verbalizes best in response to things he can see and do and to which he can physically relate. Role playing breaks the office barrier, is more directly involving and spontaneous, and most important, provides a setting in which the therapist and the low income client are on an equal footing, at least in terms of style.

Role Play vs. Role Distance

Many practitioners, in an effort to be "one of the boys," attempt to imitate the language, clothes, manners, and style of low income youngsters with whom they work. Aside from the fact that this approach is essentially patronizing, it often fails because it is perceived as "phony." A much better way to cope with the problem of role distance is through one particular aspect of role playing. As leader of the session, the practitioner can, early in the role-playing process, participate directly by taking a role. In other words, he can remove himself from the distant leadership position by accepting a role as the client's brother, friend, boss, or the role of the client himself.

The practitioner will discover that he will be regarded in the light of the role he is playing. Informality becomes legitimate in this context, and the worker can take his tie off, behave differently, change his language. Participants understand what he is doing and enjoy it, and thus the constraint felt because of the role distance is reduced.

One of the virtues of role playing is that it allows for honest, open manipulation (and thus mitigates one of the primary difficulties of all therapy).

A Route to Verbalization

In role-playing sessions we have had occasion to observe that the verbal performance of deprived children is markedly improved in the discussion period following the session. When talking about some action they have seen, deprived children are apparently able to verbalize much more fully. Typically, they do not verbalize well in response to words alone. They express themselves more readily when reacting to things they can see and do. Words as stimuli are not sufficient for them as a rule. Ask a juvenile delinquent who comes from a disadvantaged background what he doesn't like about school or the teacher and you will get an abbreviated, inarticulate reply. But have a group of these youngsters act out a school scene in which someone plays the teacher, and you will discover a stream of verbal consciousness that is almost impossible to shut off.[16]

This point is nicely illustrated in the Syracuse Madison Area Project devoted to developing new methods for educating disadvantaged youngsters.[17]

Gerald Weinstein, curriculum coordinator of the project, introduced the youngsters to a poem by Langston Hughes called "Motto," in which one of the lines is: "I play it cool." The students liked the poem very much but had difficulty at first explaining the meaning of this line.[18] They decided to act out (role play) a situation to see if it would help.

Weinstein took the part of a teacher and a boy pretended he was walking down the hallway. "Hey you," said the teacher, "you're on the wrong side of the hall. Get over where you belong." Without looking up, the boy very calmly and slowly walked to the other side and continued without any indication of what was going on in his mind. That was playing it cool.

When Weinstein asked a boy to show what he would do when not playing it cool, a verbal battle ensued.

The class began offering definitions for "playing it cool": calm and collected, no strain.

Weinstein suggested another—nonchalant. A new word.[19]

Adaptations of Role Playing
With Low Income Groups

As Young and Rosenberg pointed out some years ago, role playing with low income groups should assiduously avoid the technical as-

pects connected with psychodrama.[20] Role playing seems to be more easily accepted by disadvantaged people when there is no stage and no special lighting effects, and when it is conducted very simply and directly.

In working with homemakers and school aids drawn from low income groups, we found that they were able and willing to participate in role playing immediately, with practically no warm-up or even preparatory discussion or explanation of the technique.

It is best to begin with a problem-centered approach aiming to arouse interest in a specific issue (e.g., how to convince a tenant to join a tenant's council). It is very easy then to suggest that we "do" the problem so that we can deal with it more effectively. The more preparation and discussion there is prior to role playing, the more resistant and fearful low income people become. Moreover, while low income people readily accept the basic technique of role reversal, they are far less accepting of the use of doubles, soliloquies, and the like. The more advanced techniques seem to arouse feelings of inadequacy, "I'm not an actor," and so on. It is possible to use these different techniques but considerably more preparation is needed than with middle class audiences. In a sense, the time saved in the warm up and initial explanatory period has to be utilized eventually in applying the advanced techniques, if they are to be used at all.

Low income groups with whom we have worked prefer an everyday, informal setting, a small group of no more than ten people, and no introductory didactic presentation describing the technique. It is also important, as Levit and Jennings [21] warn, to guard against the over use of the technique, and to employ it rather as an appropriate stimulus for discussion.

Role Playing and the Middle Class

It might well be asked, "Don't all the special functions of role playing that have been cited also appeal to professionals and to other middel class people? Don't they like learning in an informal, game-like manner?" While role playing could be an attractive technique for middle class people, it is, in fact, both approached and resisted by these individuals in very different ways for different reasons. Moreover, we would employ it with somewhat different ends in mind. For example, role playing is an excellent technique for reducing intellectualization and isolation, defense mechanisms that are favored by the professional stratum. Thus, its aim with these individuals might be to bring them down to earth, to unite their affect and cognition. The entire role play procedure might be focused on this deviation. With low income people, in whom over-intellectualization is not typically a problem, the aim is rather to utilize role playing in order to develop verbalization, self-consciousness, and intellectual ability; hence the role

playing would be organized very differently, perhaps moving toward reducing the emotional components.

Factors related to style produce certain class differences in response to the role-play technique. Many middle class individuals who find the technique lacking in appeal may be reacting negatively to the very physical action properties which are attractive to low income people. The middle class group may favor a more cerebral format.

Another issue relevant in middle class groups is exhibitionism. Ambivalence with regard to exhibitionism appears to be more prominent in the middle class audience. There are more individuals desiring to find an outlet for their exhibitionism, and thus very willing to volunteer to play roles, while others are especially inhibited by the exhibitionistic potential in the situation. We find the entire exhibitionistic focus far less important in disadvantaged groups.

We find, too, that psychiatrists, social workers, and educators are often resistant to role playing because they fear what they believe to be its sensationalistic charlatan-like overtones (similar reactions are evidenced with regard to hypnosis). They feel it is an in-group gimmick lacking in dignity (and status)!

In order to overcome some of these resistances, we would recommend that:

1. The theatrical elements be sharply reduced;
2. Simple (different) language be further developed to refer to the role play technology (role therapy might be a useful term for role playing in therapeutic context);
3. Role play techniques be combined with other familiar techniques in use in the "helping" professions. Rachel Levine uses role playing in family therapy in the home; [22] Robertiello et al. combine psychodramatic techniques with psychoanalysis; [23] Spotnitz's ego echo technique, whereby the therapist verbalizes the negative self image of the patient, strongly resembles the use of the mirror technique in role play technology; [24] role playing is an excellent technique for providing an *emotionally corrective experience*, one of the major goals of psychodynamic therapy.[25]
4. The various psychotherapeutic functions of role playing be made explicit: catharis, support, self awareness (mirror), problem objectification, insight (through controlled emotionally reeducative experiences), relearning (role training);
5. The specific uses of role playing be carefully elaborated and exemplified in great detail both didactically and by illustration;
6. It be made clear that role playing is not necessarily tied to any particular theory or treatment system; that although it owes a great debt to Moreno, it has been widely used without any reference to Moreno's system. (The further integration of role playing with role theory in sociology and learning theory in psychology would undoubtedly be beneficial).[26] It should be clear that role play technology can be combined with a great variety of treat-

ment systems, and that it is not a therapeutic system in itself. Over-reliance on any technique, divorced from a substantive theory of behavior change, is likely to be no more fruitful than the use of the interview technique by itself;

7. There is considerable research evidence regarding the effectiveness of role playing in modifying emotionally held attitudes such as attitudes toward integration.[27] In general, though, there is great need for more systematic research on various aspects of role playing both in terms of diagnosis (as a predictor of future performance) and of behavior modification;

8. Finally, role playing may represent an extremely valuable approach in working with low income populations who have been somewhat estranged from the "helping" professions: it may be useful as a diagnostic device in the development of rapport, in both individual and group therapy, in the office, "milieu," hospital, and home, as an adjunctive technique.

Notes

1. The following terms are used interchangeably in this article to refer to members of lower socioeconomic groups: "poor," "disadvantaged," "deprived," "educationally deprived," "low income."

2. Role playing is the flexible acting out of various types of problems in a permissive group atmosphere, e.g. a caseworker interviewing a withdrawn client, a person being interviewed by a housing project manager. As few as two people can role play, such as therapist and client in an office; but most role playing is done in groups where two people act out a situation and the group discusses it. Since it is free of the tensions of an actual problem situation, role playing stimulates the trying-out of new alternatives and solutions in lifelike situations without the consequences which in reality may be punishing. Role playing thus increases the participant's role flexibility in an atmosphere where he can safely take a chance with different kinds of behavior.

3. Gertrude Goldberg, "Report on Visiting Homemakers," Mobilization For Youth, 1963, unpublished.

4. Role playing has been employed as an aid in improving reading ability. See Sylvia Heimbach, "Role Playing As An Aid In Improving Reading Ability," *Group Psychotherapy*, 12 (1959), 42–51.

5. F. Riessman, *The Culturally Deprived Child* (New York: Harper & Row, 1962), 32–33.

6. Riessman, *op. cit.*, 96–97.

7. Daniel Miller and Guy Swanson, *Inner Conflict and Defense*, Holt, Rinehart and Winston, 1960, p. 24.

8. For a discussion of many of these items see Miller and Swanson, *op. cit.*

9. *Ibid.*, p. 397.

10. B. Overall and H. Aronson, "Expectations of Psychotherapy in Patients of Lower Socio-Economic Class," *American Journal of Orthopsychiatry*, 33 (November 3, 1963), 421–30; A. B. Hollingshead and F. C. Redlich, *Social Class and Mental Illness* (New York: John Wiley & Sons, 1958), 340–45; N. Q. Brill and H. Storrow, "Social Class and Psychiatric Treatment," *Archives of General Psychiatry*.

11. See Jerome Beker *et al.*, "Situational Testing of Social Psychological Variables In Personality," 259–66.

12. Miller and Swanson, *op. cit.*, 396.

13. Melvin L. Kohn, "Social Class and Parent-Child Relationships: An Interpretation," *American Journal of Sociology*, 68:4 (1963), 11.

14. *Ibid.*, p. 11.

15. We suspect that is an important reason for stressing a variety of environment oriented (community milieu) therapies for the low income stratum.

16. F. Riessman, *The Culturally Deprived Child* (New York: Harper and Row, 1963), 77.

17. See Robert Kanasola, "Students Dig Jive When It's Played Cool," *Syracuse Herald Journal* (Nov. 11, 1963), 17.

18. *Ibid.*

19. *Ibid.*
20. B. F. Young and M. Rosenberg, "Role Playing as a Participation Technique," *Journal of Social Issues,* 5:1 (1945), 42–45.
21. G. Levit and H. Jennings, "Learning through Role Playing," in *How to Use Role Playing* (Chicago: Adult Education Association, 1960), 10.
22. Rachel Levine, *Treatment in the Home,* 1962.
23. R. C. Robertiello, *et al., The Analyst's Role,* The Citadel Press, 1963.
24. Leo Nagelberg and Hyman Spotnitz, "Strengthening The Ego Through The Release of Frustrations-Aggression," *American Journal of Orthopsychiatry,* 28:4 (1958), 794–801.
25. Often in Milieu Therapies it is difficult to manipulate aspects of the environment to produce the emotionally reeducative stimulus. Role-play technology allows for a widening of the range of possible interventions.
26. See Milton Schwebel, "Role Playing In Counselor-Training," *Personnel and Guidance Journal* (Dec. 1953), 200–201.
27. See F. M. Culbertson, "Modification of an Emotionally Held Attitude Through Role Playing," *Journal of Abnormal and Social Psychology,* 54 (1957), 230–33; I. L. Janis and B. T. King, "The Influence of Role Playing on Opinion Change," *Journal of Abnormal and Social Psychology,* 49 (1954), 211–218.

Experiential Group Treatment of Severely Deprived Latency-Age Children

Saul Scheidlinger

There has been an increasing interest during the last two decades in the problem of children with severe ego pathology. They have variously been termed "severe non-neurotic ego disturbance," "borderline," "atypical," "pre-psychotic," "autistic" or "schizophrenic" (3). The treatment efforts described in the literature involve most frequently the provision of a therapeutic environment in an institution. There has also been some experimentation in extramural settings, modifying the usual techniques of individual psychotherapy to suit the special needs of these children. In line with the frequently held view of a guarded prognosis unless treatment be initiated prior to age six (2), much of this work has been carried on at the preschool age level.

This paper deals with an experimental use of activity group therapy for such *latency-age* [1] *children* (aged 8–13), who have experienced marked deprivation in their lives and consequently developed serious disturbances in ego functioning. Carried out within the framework of a nonsectarian family service agency, the observations and techniques to be discussed were gradually evolved in the course of our six years of work with these clients. (A few of our groups contain a majority of such cases—in most of them, they are in a minority. In all, they constitute about one third among the total number of 60 children currently in group treatment at the agency.)

Reprinted from *American Journal of Orthopsychiatry*, Vol. 30, No. 2, April 1960, pp. 356–368. Copyright, the American Orthopsychiatric Association, Inc. Reproduced by permission.

Presenting Problems

What about the backgrounds of these children? About 90 per cent Negro, with a sprinkling of whites and Puerto Ricans, these boys and girls came invariably from families with severe social and economic pathology. Marked emotional deprivation, especially in the earliest years, absence of parental figures (usually father), and transient relationships by the mother with several men were repetitive features. Such problems as lack of mothering, frequent parental neglect with inconsistent handling, and harsh physical punishment stood out. Not infrequently the child was exposed to direct sexual seductiveness and delinquent patterns.

How in greater detail do some of these children appear?

Carl, 9½, was extremely moody, sullen and withdrawn. His moods seemed unrelated to external factors. He had no close relationships with anyone and gave the surface impression of passivity. Suspiciousness and shyness with adults were noted. There was a twitching of the face, and both fear and fascination at the theme of death. At school Carl stood out as different and aloof. He worked far below his capacity, and was markedly retarded in reading. Of Negro background, Carl insisted that he was of Indian blood.

The psychotic mother had been in and out of mental hospitals for years. During these periods the children (including an older brother and a younger sister) were neglected, often without any adult in the picture for a number of days. Later on a great-aunt, a sickly woman over 70 years old, would assume care of the children until her niece's return from the hospital. The parents were divorced when Carl was a baby.

Bernice, 9, was brought to the agency because of disobedience, poor social relationships, fighting with siblings, playing with matches, bed-wetting and occasional thumb-sucking. She was described as an impulsive, slightly delinquent youngster who exhibited little capacity for control. At school she was defiant with adults. She stole money and small objects, mostly to "buy" favor with other children.

Bernice was born out of wedlock, as were her two younger siblings. Each of them had a different father, which served to enhance their own confusion regarding their identity. The family unit, consisting of the mother and the three children, lived in a one-room apartment. Bernice and her sister had to share a bed with their mother.

Bernice became enuretic at the age of seven after the mother had forced her to stop sucking her thumb. Once the restrictions were removed (bitter fluids on the thumb—described to the child as poison), Bernice began sucking her thumb again, and the bed-wetting ceased. Shortly before the group treatment commenced, Bernice broke herself of the thumb-sucking habit by putting a piece of tape on her thumb. While successful in stopping the habit,

Bernice became more withdrawn and depressed, sulking or crying
frequently for no apparent reason.

Vivian, 10, was described by her mother and her teacher as a
"nervous" child. She reacted to stress situations by becoming frightened and going to bed. Threats of whipping by the mother left
Vivian shaking and trembling. She was also very fearful of insects.
The mother further described her as a restless sleeper who cried out
in her sleep and sleepwalked on occasion. There was rivalry and
aggressiveness with an older brother. Vivian was depicted by our
agency's homemaker as quiet and withdrawn. She did not play like
the other children and would often go off to a corner, sit in a chair
and rub her lip.

The school spoke of Vivian as fidgeting and as talking out of
turn. At camp she displayed occasional temper outbursts and rapid
mood shifts. Vivian became more "nervous" after the death of a
brother several years before. Vivian and her sister had to help in
caring for the youngest child.

The mother was described as a dull woman, noncommunicative
and markedly depressed. She was hospitalized for cardiac disease,
and during this time a homemaker helped in caring for the children.
Upon the mother's return, she became pregnant again. She did not
want a fifth child—the four children were already too much for her.
The father, a passive and ineffectual person, was extremely dependent on his own domineering mother.

Vivian's severe pathology emerged with particular clarity during
the first few group sessions. She looked at times as though she were
in a trance. She made faces, smiled, talked to herself and even addressed inanimate objects. She was completely unable to relate to
the other girls, staying close to the adult.

These case illustrations readily suggest a similarity of our children
with the severe ego-disturbed cases described by Rank (8), Alpert (1),
Mahler (7), and especially those depicted by Weil (15). The latter had
discussed in considerable detail the failure in adequate ego development
characterized by poor social-emotional adaptations, problems of control,
and various anxiety manifestations, ranging from fears to obsessive-
compulsive mechanisms. Perhaps because of the greater amount of
actual deprivation and want (in addition to the emotional one), we were
particularly impressed in our children with the degree of oral fixations,
of a primitive, oral greediness coupled with an impatient, hostile expectation that these needs would not be met. Hand in hand with poor
reality testing, with difficulty in distinguishing between inner and outer
sources of tension, went serious distortions in the perceptions of other
people, especially adults. Related to this was an underlying tone of depression with an extremely low self-concept and the problem of confused
identity.

While none of these clients fitted into the concept of latency as summarized by Fries (4), it is also noteworthy that we never worked with
any in whom the ego pathology was all-embracing. Thus, hand in hand
with arrested or regressed ego functions went others which were reason-

ably well-developed and served as anchorage points for the therapeutic intervention.

Group Therapy Techniques

The group treatment techniques we evolved for these children constituted in effect a modification of the activity group therapy developed by S. R. Slavson in the late thirties (12, 13). Briefly, this method, devised for less severely disturbed children, stresses the *acting out* of conflicts and deviant behavior patterns within the framework of a permissive environment. The basic therapeutic elements accrue from the interaction of the children with each other and from their relationship to the therapist. An activity group consists of about eight members of the same sex and similar age, carefully selected with a view toward achieving a balance of adaptive behavior patterns—ranging from aggressiveness to withdrawal. The physical setting of such a group comprises a large room, equipped with simple furnishings, tools, crafts supplies and games, chosen from the standpoint of their therapeutic effectiveness (9, 10).

The potentialities inherent in activity group therapy for helping children with severe ego pathology suggested themselves to us through coincidence. This was in connection with the use of our groups for observation of children on whom there were inadequate diagnostic data. In the course of this observation the striking pathology of these children emerged readily enough to view. What emerged in addition was that the group experience seemed to assume a positive meaning for them from the very beginning. Considering that most of these clients were totally inaccessible to individual casework contact without motivation for help or change, this was an important observation. We began to experiment with more and more such children, modifying our techniques along the way in line with their special needs.

The changes we introduced experimentally differ in a number of ways from the techniques usually associated with activity group therapy. First of all, the therapist had to abandon from the very beginning the role of neutrality and extreme permissiveness which had worked so well with less damaged personalities. These children's ego faculties were simply not sufficiently developed to perceive the adult as a warm and helpful figure when he kept his verbal responses to a minimum, and particularly when he planfully failed to interfere in the face of what appeared to them as psychologically threatening group developments. As Slavson had stated regarding the general kinds of activity groups, they require children with at least "a minimal development of ego strength and superego organization so that impulses can be brought under control through reactions of other children and the demands of the group" (14, p. 25). Thus, for the children under discussion the therapist had to become more open and direct in his emotional reactions and verbalizations.

As to restraint, the therapist had to be readier to use it (preferably indirectly) in the face of verbal or physical impulsive acting out. It should be noted that direct physical attacks rarely occur in our groups. First of all, there is the careful selection and "balancing" of the membership. Then, there is the amazing tolerance of these groups for individuals who are "different" and particularly vulnerable. However, when restraint has to be instituted it is rarely perceived as a hostile act; quite to the contrary, we have had indications that as with nursery-age children, it is viewed with relief and relaxation as the adult's help to the ego against the threat of uncontrollable impulsivity. Prior to this shift in the therapist's role, these children, when asked about the groups, would describe the leader as "not caring," or as "being afraid of the kids."

Another related modification referred to the planful structuring of the broader group climate, even further than is usually the case, toward constancy, nurturing and feeding. Besides the availability of plentiful supplies, especially in the early stages of the group, the traditional snack became for us a full-fledged meal carefully prepared by the therapist. While planfully providing a few "extras" (plus the food of absentees) for the group to deal with as it pleases, the therapist did not permit the customary free group interaction with respect to basic portions. These were assured to each child no matter how persistent the attempts to grab on the part of the more aggressive group members.

We also decided that with these children's deficiencies in reality testing, the well-known nonverbal techniques of situational interference were inadequate. They required, in addition, frequent verbal interventions on the part of the therapist. These could be in the direction of confrontations of behavioral responses; i.e., "You are now quite upset," or "You are taking the wood which belongs to Fred"; more frequently these comments are in the nature of clarifying external reality. For instance, in a boys' group some of the members giggled and playfully threatened to beat Robert up after the meeting. The therapist clarified the reality for the child by saying, "They are only teasing." Or, the adult might say, "I will not let anyone in this club beat you." In a girls' group a child said to the therapist, "Get the girls out of the bathroom or they will fall in the toilet and get swallowed up." The therapist replied, "This cannot happen."

The Treatment Process

With the above kinds of modifications we found activity group therapy eminently suitable for helping such clients with severe disturbances in ego development. It is well known that in *all* children, acting is the natural form of communication. Also, with their more pliant personality structure, they respond more readily than adults to new perceptions inherent in a current experience. Expressing problems through

action rather than words is especially true of personalities with early fixation levels. For the earliest form of communication in life is non-verbal. Consequently, *the actual experiencing of gratifications* and the *reliving of earliest traumata* inherent in this approach are most valuable. Insofar as the group treatment constitutes in effect a *guided gratification, regression and upbringing,* current conflicts as well as earlier unresolved interpersonal experiences can be relived, but with different actors, and what is even more important—a different ending. As one girl put it when her mother questioned her on her not overeating as much at home as she used to: "They stuff you so much all the time in the club that I don't care to eat as much now." The therapist's feeding her once a week during the sessions had begun to carry her for the whole week!

In both of the illustrative cases at the end of this paper, the reactivation of oral conflicts in relation to the group therapist as a maternal figure is underscored. This is no coincidence, for as we have noted at another point regarding our groups, ". . . it is around the theme of food—the buying of it, the bringing of it to the meeting room, the cooking and serving—that the most dramatic and meaningful interactions occur. The conflicts re-enacted here involve not only the re-living of the earliest problems in mother-child relationships, but they are at the same time anchored in the current reality of the children's home experiences" (10). In this context, sibling rivalry actually became a struggle for mother's food—for her milk in a symbolic sense.

Bernice, the earlier-mentioned impulsive child, who sucked her thumb, fought with her sister, wet her bed, and played with fire, was enraged at other girls for bringing visitors to the group meetings. Her anger about this kind of sharing of the food was so intense that, in retaliation, she brought her hated younger sister to some sessions provisionally, just in case another girl had again invited her friend to attend. Quoting from a session:

"Like a racing locomotive suddenly brought to a halt, Bernice stopped short at the ping-pong table. Her sister Doris followed behind. Bernice did not bother to say hello or to take off her coat. After greeting Bernice I asked her if she wanted to have her sister visit for today. Bernice said it depended on whether or not Sally's friend was going to stay. When Sally announced that she had brought Dora at the designation of the girls, Bernice bellowed at Doris to take off her coat."

The fact that by bringing her sister she had further diluted the food available for sharing, did not count. One of the prime factors was that she had to get even. Perhaps also on a deeper level, her sister constituted an extension of herself, thus neutralizing the food given to the outsider, to Sally's friend. A similar self-defeating mechanism on the part of the same girl, which ended in her destroying the food, is seen in the following incident:

"Once again Bernice claimed the food of the absent club member. She and Sally raced for the empty seat, with Bernice pushing Sally out of the way. Sally asked Bernice if her mother did not teach

her manners. Bernice warned Sally not to talk about her mother that way, but Sally provocatively repeated her question. Bernice slapped Sally, and Sally hit Bernice back. Bernice landed a hard smack on Sally's arm and the latter began to cry. After Barbara's intervention 'to break it up,' Sally cried a little while longer. Bernice seemed somewhat apologetic and told Sally she had warned her not to say anything about her mother. She offered Sally the contested seat, but Sally refused it. After some further angry interchange, Bernice poured soda all over the sandwiches. She sat at the table pouting. Sally asked why she did that, spoiling the food for everybody, but Bernice did not reply."

As we have noted earlier, such reliving of conflicts in the sphere of orality alone encompasses much of the treatment process with these severely deprived children. This should not be construed, however, as meaning that in this kind of guided regression other psychosexual levels and their related fixations, particularly preoedipal ones, do not get stimulated as well. This could occur in relation to food or any other aspect of the group interaction, i.e., bathroom play, use of materials or tools. To quote from another session:

"As I continued to go around the table to serve the franks, Doreen said, 'It looks like we are stealing something from the boys.' Mary impatiently asked Doreen what she was talking about. After a second Sandra looked at Doreen and said, 'I get you.' Then all the girls laughed. As she bit into her frankfurter Doreen said, 'Mm. Mm.' Sandra said, 'Very funny.' Nonie added sarcastically, 'Ha-ha.'" Mary was the only girl who failed to perceive the phallic reference.

Therapeutic Success and Failure

The children in our groups frequently show open awareness of the changes which occur in them and in others. Take this illustration: "Jean took hold of Winnie's hand and began whirling her around. 'Last year,' she said to her, 'you used to be afraid of me. I told you that I would beat you up and you believed me. What about that now?' Winnie laughed at her in an easy way and said, 'I don't think you'd better try it now.'"

While the group treatment depicted so far has been markedly successful in modifying to a degree at least the functioning of a large majority of these severely disturbed clients, we have of course also had our failures. These seemed to fall into two major categories: (a) The overly provocative children, who despite the therapist's repeated interventions continued to so goad the other group members that counterattack and scapegoating could not be prevented. Eventually these children had to be removed from the group. (b) The children who improved in the group but failed to carry this over to the outside. This seemed related most often to a highly charged mutual provocativeness or sadomasochistic

pattern operating at home which defied modification through the case-work efforts with the family.[2]

Jane exemplifies a child with extremely provocative behavior in the group. She was referred by the school because of a violent temper and constant arguments with her peers. With adults, Jane was anxious for attention and affection. The mother openly preferred Jane's older sister and complained that Jane was willful, lied and stole money. She was generally dissatisfied with what anyone tried to do for her. From the very beginning Jane behaved aggressively toward all the girls in the group. Her major efforts seemed focused on hoarding supplies and food to take home with her, and on provocative teasing of the other children. The girls tried to put up with her, tolerating much of her provocativeness. Instead of calming her down, this only made things worse as she continued her sarcastic barrage directed at almost everyone. The girls soon verbalized the truth that whenever Jane came she caused trouble. The therapist's efforts to get close to Jane and to support her were of no avail, as she could not perceive the therapist as trying to help her. Her projection mechanisms and denial were so pervasive that in the face of all reality confrontations, she kept on insisting: "I never do anything to the girls. They pick on me, so I must hit back."

Bernice, whom we mentioned earlier in this paper, belongs to the other category, namely, the children who fail to transfer the changes achieved in the group to the outside world. This severely impulsive, hostile girl with complex symptomatology began to show signs of responding to the treatment after a year and a half. Aside from conscious efforts to control her intense oral-sadistic tendencies, she began to accept limitation, to cooperate with the adult and with group decisions. Her consistently warmer feelings toward the therapist were striking. On Valentine's Day she was the one who suggested that the girls make a heart for the adult. In addition, she herself made a change purse for her, delaying her eating for a considerable period of time. Quite an achievement for this voracious youngster! When the gifts were presented, Bernice called out twice: "Mrs. K, we love you," to which the therapist replied gently, "Yes, Bernice."

Despite these changes in the group, Bernice continued to get herself into difficulties in the community. It was felt that this was due to the continuing pathology in the mother-daughter relationship. The mother admitted that since the birth of her latest out-of-wedlock child, the "lickings" she administered to Bernice gave her satisfaction, "relieving everything I feel inside." Besides these whippings, there were frequent trips to the local police precinct, coupled with threats to send Bernice away. This mutual provocativeness at home is still being studied. The caseworker has been seeing both Bernice and her mother. It is quite likely that placement of Bernice away from home will be the only solution. In this event, the group experience, which demonstrated this girl's capacity to change and grow in a supportive environment, will have served as a significant steppingstone.

The Group Treatment of Carl and of Eileen

The problem of reliving earlier traumatic experiences especially in the sphere of orality could be exemplified through Carl's group treatment. This is the earlier-mentioned 9½-year-old boy with extreme mood swings, a marked distrust of adults, fear of death, no social relationships and severe retardation in reading. His lack of "mothering" was due to the psychotic mother's frequent hospitalizations with resultant neglect of the children.

During the first period Carl began by relating to the group with extreme caution. He was very suspicious toward the adult. In spite of the fact that he spent most of his time away from the others at the "isolates'" table, he was the first boy to announce during the eating that the group should meet more often than once a week and for longer periods. Of particular significance was his voracious manner of eating, his grabbing for food and stuffing it into his mouth, using the fingers of both hands. This behavior was so much more exaggerated than that of any of the other boys, also deprived, that they quickly dubbed him "Greedy." This would always cause Carl to glower at them, but in no way deterred his grabbing for all extras. The boys rather quickly accepted his tremendous needs and would usually, by tacit agreement, allow him the extra food without competition.

While there was a gradual improvement in the boy's relationship to the others by the second year, there was little change in his attitude toward food, or the therapist. By the third year, Carl became friendlier with the therapist, coupled with an increasing dependence on him for help with tools and materials. Concurrently, there was a dramatic change in Carl's consumption of food. At times he would pass up seconds, or would be slow enough in reaching for them so that other boys began competing more actively and directly. Carl didn't seem to be upset if they got ahead of him. His table manners had by now become quite acceptable. The mood swings were hardly in evidence. The summer camp noted for the first time a marked gain in impulse control. In contrast to the previous year, Carl would become realistically angry without "flying to pieces" or appearing to have to "sit on himself" to keep from blowing up.

During the fourth year the therapist noted a definite relationship between Carl's attitude toward him and his food consumption. When he was particularly hostile to the adult, he did not even take his basic portion. During this same year Carl brought some candy for the therapist after the latter had kept a chocolate rabbit for him from the Easter party which the boy could not attend.

The case of Eileen, who was not described previously, could serve to illustrate the group treatment with an even more seriously disturbed youngster.

Eileen was referred to the agency at the age of 8½. She was withdrawn, fearful, and had difficulties in relating to children and adults. Her hands trembled at times and she cried easily. She had expressed concern over "sin," which seemed related to sex and to growing up, generally. She had a great many fears of noises, insects and animals. At school she was on the fringe of the group, working far below capacity. A camp report from a prior year stressed her bizarre behavior. She would roll her eyes, ask seemingly unrelated questions, had poor reality orientation. There were also difficulties in physical coordination, some involuntary movements, and considerable overweight. Eileen, on occasion, would speak of herself as "crazy."

Eileen's mother, a primitive, self-centered woman with delinquent tendencies, had a very unhappy childhood. She had lost her mother at an early age. Following an out-of-wedlock pregnancy in her early teens, she was treated by her relatives as an outcast. Eileen was the later product of a short-lived marriage characterized by much conflict from the very beginning. Eileen was especially upset when her father deserted during her early childhood.

The group therapist described Eileen as pretty, somewhat overweight, with smooth brown skin and rounded regular features. She was quiet and unobtrusive with a façade of social ease. When ignored by the other girls, as she often was, she resorted to a mannerism in which she smiled, raised and lowered her eyes slowly, sighed, then smiled again, and turned away. Underneath, there was a mild depressive quality. When thus left out, Eileen spent much time working with materials. In this she needed considerable help from the adult. To the first girl using a tool, Eileen said, "Do you want to be a boy—I mean carpenter?" thus suggesting primitive thinking and confusion regarding her identity. In the seventh session she was greeted as "Fatso," and criticized for not talking. Her response was to smile again in the manner indicated above. Eileen announced that she was dieting because of her overweight. She never competed for extra food, quoting her mother as saying: "You eat like a bird, his beak, that is." In contrast, during one trip to a restaurant, Eileen ate with fascinated gluttony. Eileen related to the therapist with a dependent, superficial charm. The therapist also observed peculiar twitching or rotating motions of her hips when Eileen was engrossed in her work. She stopped this when another child brought it to her attention. Eileen continued to talk about her diet, but put so much mayonnaise or ketchup on her sandwiches that they literally dripped. Although usually alone or withdrawn, Eileen joined promptly in games when she was invited to do so. She was compliant and passive in relation to all requests made of her. She frequently did not seem to understand group decisions, being markedly preoccupied with herself. Her work with clay seemed unique and represented considerable fantasy with sexual symbolism. The same held true for her colorful, abstract paintings. Eileen preserved in the group's cabinet the head of a male, with the notion of sending it to a well-known comedian, an older man. She was unaware that the girls viewed her repeated preoccupation with this piece as bizarre.

For a few months there was a difficult period during which the girls derided Eileen as "crazy." Through the intensive activity of the therapist, involving both direct support of Eileen and indirect restraint of the others, there occurred a significant shift in the group attitudes. Most of the group, in identification with the adult, began to be supportive of the girl, including her in their games. They insisted, however, on her stopping her "crazy" acts, i.e., singing or talking to herself or hip movements; and she complied readily. Not only did the girls accept the special closeness Eileen required of the adult, but they often even drew her attention to Eileen's needs. At the end of 36 sessions, Eileen had shifted from a position of scapegoat to that of being a source of group concern and support.

Eileen responded with mild, tenuous expressions of affection to the therapist's activity in her behalf. Her awareness of support was evidenced by her revealing some of her concerns about the outside world such as school or camp. Each time the therapist brought these concerns to the attention of the family caseworker who helped out with them, there seemed to be another spurt of improvement in Eileen. She related better to the girls and her reality perceptions seemed improved. Eileen would on occasion bring bizarre-sounding fantasy material to the adult. While not discouraging her, this was handled always through enabling her to focus on the reality aspect.

The mother reported marked improvement in Eileen's functioning. The girl was cooperative and helpful around the house. She began going out to play with the children in the neighborhood. With support from her caseworker, the mother could permit Eileen to be on her own now. At camp Eileen enjoyed herself more than during the previous year. She was less fearful and could participate in group activities much of the time. Occasionally, she still seemed confused, unable to grasp the reality expectations, being content to remain by herself. Her relationship to the counselor was one of clinging, warm dependency.

During the second year of group therapy the girl's attendance continued to be excellent. She was noted to be taller and slimmer with marked gains in her physical coordination. The bizarre behavior patterns had disappeared. The therapist felt that there had been a definite gain in self-concept and mastery of environmental demands. While alone during part of each session, she was infinitely more involved with the others. She joined in when the girls initiated games. She withdrew, however, when they discussed boys and sex. While still in need of support, and functioning less adequately than all others, she hardly stood out as different to observers. (Our group sessions can be observed through one-way screens.) Eileen now rarely expressed fantasies to the adult or the group and was seldom noted to be idle or self-absorbed. Her efforts to be like the others and master conventional projects occurred apparently at the cost of the more creative fantasy-laden projects of the previous year. While still needing the support of the adult, Eileen paid little attention to her when really involved in activity with the group. Not only had she become a fully accepted member, but on rare occasions she even stood up to another girl.

After the family moved to larger and more attractive living quar-

ters, there was an interesting change in Eileen's use of the special club cabinet. Heretofore (until 53rd session), it had been for her a repository for her many "treasures," including the earlier-noted head of the comedian. She valued it so highly and constantly as to give the impression that an important part of her emotional life had centered there. It was as though with a room of her own in the new apartment she no longer needed this cherished, private place. Perhaps, in addition, it connoted her broader freedom to move out of the protective setting of the group.

Following the second period of group treatment, the caseworker reported further improvement in Eileen's symptomatology and functioning. This was particularly significant inasmuch as there had been some upsetting developments in the family. Not only did the mother marry again but she also became pregnant prior to this marriage. She sent her youngest child, Eileen's stepsister, out of the state to the child's father. This move, as well as her decision to offer the expected baby for adoption, upset Eileen considerably. On the constructive side, there was more consistency in Eileen's father's contacts and he began visiting her once a week.

While the relationship with the mother was much better— "Eileen's no trouble"—the latter's primitive punitive measures continued on occasion. She described, for instance, how about once a month she would make Eileen kneel on the floor and would beat her with a strap.

Eileen's schoolwork improved to the extent that, upon her move to the new apartment, she was promoted from an "opportunity class" to a regular one. Her reading advanced noticeably, and the mother was pleased that Eileen was now eager to read the newspaper.

Despite these gratifying changes for the better in Eileen, the psychiatric consultant recommended that the long-range plan be to place all the children away from home. This was because of the mother's severe personality pathology and her complete inability to tolerate assertiveness and independence in any of her children. In agreement with this recommendation, Eileen was assigned to a separate caseworker for supportive contact three months prior to the termination of the group treatment.

Discussion and Summary

It should be noted that an important next step in our experimental work should involve careful follow-up evaluations of our cases especially during and after adolescence. The few instances in which we were able to undertake this in an organized fashion seemed promising. They suggested that the clients had generally managed to at least maintain the gains in ego functioning achieved through the group treatment (6). On the other hand, we suspect that Weil's contention of a remaining underlying "deficient personality structure" (15, p. 277) in these kinds of individuals is probably true.

In trying to assess in general the therapeutic possibilities in this group approach, the following observations emerge:

1. The children are offered a benign familylike setting where, in contrast to their homes, there is a maximum of constancy and of gratification, and a minimum of frustrations. All this is enhanced by the special modifications we introduced in the therapist's role of greater directness, protective restraint, and verbal clarification.

2. The group as an entity represents a physical and a psychological reality with which even a deficient ego can cope. It permits new perceptions, possibly ranging from the deepest unconscious levels (i.e., primitive identification with the mother-group) to the initially unsettling conscious realization of this uniquely different kind of "club" (11).

3. Within the climate of a controlled gratification and regression, early conflicts are re-enacted with a consistent, strong and accepting parental figure. The stress is on the anticipation and on the unconditional meeting of needs.

4. Various degrees and types of relationships are possible—none are demanded. These range from isolation through the most tenuous primitive identifications involving the borrowing of another object's ego strengths—to real object ties.

5. The dosage of gratifications (love offerings) is determined by the child on the basis of his readiness to accept them, thus permitting gradual removal of defenses. At the same time, demands made upon him are minimal.

6. The support of the other group members, the reality-geared group environment, and the nondirective role of the therapist tend to minimize and counteract the fears of overwhelming impulsivity and of domination or destruction by the adult so frequently inherent in these kinds of problems (5).

7. While no attempt is made to enter the children's inner autistic worlds with their primitive fantasies, the boundaries between reality and fantasy are repeatedly emphasized.

8. With the free flow of emotional gratifications, arrested ego development can be resumed, step by step. The child learns to postpone immediate satisfactions; to recognize and respond to the requirements of reality; to find pleasure in playing games, or working with tools and materials.

9. Inevitable changes in individual self-concepts are closely intertwined with healthier perceptions of the adult, of other children and the group as an entity, thus counteracting identity confusions.

In summary, we have depicted the usefulnesss of a guided gratification, regression and upbringing through a modified form of activity group therapy for severely deprived latency-age children. Conflicts are expressed and reexperienced in this kind of setting through action, rather than words. The direct gratification of unmet oral and other pregenital needs through food, arts and crafts materials, and the like, offered by the adult, was found to be markedly effective in fostering improved ego functioning. The consistent, accepting parental figure,

coupled with the benign image of a group entity, promoted changes in the client's perceptions and expectations of the environment and of the people in it. The cumulative effects of these group experiences were an improved self-concept, better ego control over impulses, and enhanced reality testing.

We hope that further experimentation with such groups may well show the way toward reaching children during the latency period who, if not treated, tend to succumb to active psychoses or to develop highly destructive antisocial patterns in adolescence.

Notes

1. The term latency-age is employed loosely here, and is meant to include pre-adolescents.

2. In line with common practice in the family service field, a caseworker always assumes responsibility for the treatment planning for the family and for each of its members. While the children discussed in this paper are treated in the group, individual contact with the parents is maintained. However, because of the marked pathology in these cases such contacts are frequently sporadic and of limited effectiveness. For a discussion of the integration of casework and group therapy, see (10).

References

1. Alpert, A. *A Special Therapeutic Technique for Certain Developmental Disorders in Prelatency Children.* Am. J. Orthopsychiatry, 27:256–270, 1957.

2. Buxbaum, E. "Technique of Child Therapy: A Critical Evaluation," in *The Psychoanalytic Study of the Child,* Vol. IX. New York: Internat. Univ. Press, 1954.

3. Ekstein, R., K. Bryant, and S. W. Friedman. "Childhood Schizophrenia and Allied Conditions," in *Schizophrenia: A Review of the Syndrome* (L. Bellak, Ed.). New York: Logos Press, 1958.

4. Fries, M. E. *Review of the Literature on the Latency Period.* J. Hillside Hosp., 7:3–16, 1958.

5. Kaufman, I., E. Rosenblum, L. Heims, and L. Willer. *Childhood Schizophrenia: Treatment of Children and Parents.* Am. J. Orthopsychiatry, 27:683–690, 1957.

6. King, C. H. *Activity Group Therapy with a Schizophrenic Boy: Follow-up Two Years Later.* Int. J. Group Psychother., 9:184–194, 1959.

7. Mahler, M. S. "On Child Psychosis and Schizophrenia: Autistic and Symbiotic Infantile Psychoses," in *The Psychoanalytic Study of the Child,* Vol. VII. New York: Internat. Univ. Press, 1952.

8. Rank, B. "Treatment of Young Children with Atypical Development by Psychoanalytic Technique," in *Specialized Techniques in Psychotherapy* (G. Bychowski, et al., Eds.). New York: Basic Books, 1952.

9. Scheidlinger, S. *Group Psychotherapy.* Am. J. Orthopsychiatry, 24:140–145, 1954.

10. ———, M. Douville, C. Harrahill, C. H. King, and J. Minor. *Activity Group Therapy in a Family Service Agency.* Soc. Casewk, 40:193–201, 1959.

11. ———. *Group Process in Group Psychotherapy.* Am. J. Psychother., 14:104–120, 346–363, 1960.

12. Slavson, S. R. *An Introduction to Group Therapy.* New York: Internat. Univ. Press, 1954.

13. ———. *Some Elements in Activity Group Therapy.* Am. J. Orthopsychiatry, 14:578–588, 1944.

14. ———. *Criteria for Selection and Rejection of Patients for Various Types of Group Psychotherapy.* Int. J. Group Psychother., 5:3–30, 1955.

15. Weil, A. P. "Certain Severe Disturbances of Ego Development in Childhood," in *The Psychoanalytic Study of the Child,* Vol. VIII. New York: Internat. Univ. Press, 1953.

Preventive Intervention

Berta Fantl

The term "preventive intervention" may take on more specific meaning as those equipped with knowledge of individual psychodynamics move into an era in which sociocultural factors can be comprehended with pertinence and greater differentiation. Environment is no longer seen as restricted to what is accessible to immediate perception and open manipulation.[1] A new kind of awareness of the person-in-the-situation configuration is evolving which is significant for helping professions concerned with broad human issues.[2]

Conspicuous features of our time are the rapid changes in family and community life, the growth of bureaucratic structures, the professionalization of services, and the cultural and educational assimilation of different ethnic groups in urban centers. Along with these changes we are experiencing a new broadening of community responsibility for those in crisis or in a permanent dependent status—new at least in this country. It is not as if all the old patterns had vanished, but life has become complicated enough for the sophisticated and educated, let alone those whose earlier experiences have had little emotional enrichment and who have lacked opportunity to develop differential skills and competence for new kinds of social living.[3] The complexity of city life, the pattern of taking and sharing in new community structures, the establishment of new and meaningful interpersonal relationships in family affairs and organizational systems, cannot be left to chance alone. Simpler tasks than these we do not expect to accomplish without support and guidance, and without margin for experimentation and error.

Reprinted by permission of the National Association of Social Workers, from *Social Work*, Vol. 7, No. 3, July 1962, pp. 41–47.

Concept of a Neighborhood

In the fall of 1958 a small unit of social workers left the centralized downtown school child guidance services in which they had been working to take up residence in a lower-lower-class district. Psychological testing and psychiatric consultation were provided from the central agency by request. This move reflected a growing sense that clients who normally would not flock in significant numbers to the doors of social agencies need to be studied and more fully understood in their natural setting, and that social workers and their agencies need to become part of the neighborhood in order to make services available which are physically as well as psychologically accessible, when crises arise that readily motivate clients to use help—if help can be offered in a style congenial to their spontaneous ways of expressing problems as well as solving them.

Concern soon shifted from the traditional one-to-one relationships and work with "collaterals" to a broad awareness of the daily life of clients, their immediate dilemmas and crises, their family ties or lack of them.[4] Once enmeshed in the human problems of the neighborhood, the consideration arose of how much or how little casework services for a few families would accomplish in view of the type and number of problems encountered and the over-all needs of the neighborhood. This is not meant to imply that there is not a crying need for more and better diagnostic and treatment facilities for clients with emotional problems. But with social problems as they increasingly exist, every social agency needs to take an honest look at how well it serves the population it thinks and says it is serving, and whether in our present knowledge and skills there is perhaps room for innovations of service that might benefit larger numbers of people, in different dimensions of human behavior and relations.

Once the major areas of strength and weakness of the neighborhood were identified as compared to the rest of the city, as well as major social institutions, the composition of ethnic groups, the neighborhood pattern, and ways in which people communicated and related to each other, a new conception evolved of the work to be done, which, despite gaps and imperfections, seemed more realistically related to the welfare needs of the total neighborhood than were the traditional clinical services. Casework services continued to be provided for a limited number of clients, and increasing time was spent in collaboration and consultation with some of the "caretaking agents" who exercise a profound influence on the lives of clients.[5]

A keen awareness developed of the existing social distance between clients and the caretaking agents, their prejudices about each other, and the breakdown of meaningful communication, which seemed to defy every effort and good intention of either party for a more positive

interaction that might make full use of the meager number of services available in the neighborhood. One was aware not so much of lack of interaction as of opposing interaction and negative attitudes. Invariably prejudices and stereotyped perceptions were intensified by fear of "what people might think"—ignorance of another way of life and hopeless discouragement after repeated failure to establish rapport. People were often not sure what was expected of them, or how to act or what to say, or how to time their requests.

It is perhaps of interest to note that, as the social workers gradually became recognized and accepted by the client group as persons from whom one could "get help," the first few self-referrals were requests for help in conveying ideas and information to the schools, to public welfare officials, or to the police, or questions regarding them. It became apparent that not just the "doing of things" is important in initial relationships with multiproblem clients, but also ability to convey the feeling that we are not afraid to grapple with the complicated role relationships and interactions of their social environments.[6] These clients may not have had opportunity to develop the type of personality structure that fosters introspection and psychological awareness more commonly attributed to middle-class clients; be this as it may, most of them showed considerable awarenesss and discomfort about some of the more obvious social and cultural factors that interfere negatively with their social relationships and functioning.

Prejudices and stereotyped perceptions may have deep psychological roots; yet one gained the firm conviction that with patient, skillful, repeated intervention, and given a minimum of favorable attitudes, prejudices and stereotyped perceptions could be sufficiently modified to permit more satisfying behavior. One saw teachers become less discouraged with their jobs, policemen discover that they and certain groups of children did not need to be enemies—or at least not all the time—and the school social worker feeling at home in situations which not long before had been incomprehensible and would therefore have resulted in closing a case through the withdrawal of either the client or the agency.

Emerging Focus

Although an effort was made in the same way to understand other social institutions, it seemed logical as a school agency to try especially to understand the social structure and position of the schools in the neighborhood.

Such questions were asked as: How, on the whole, do school people in our neighborhood view their pupils and their families? How do the various ethnic groups view education as a goal for their children? Are there conflicting aims in the over-all educational system which put unbearable pressure on administrators and teachers, making a favor-

able response to their pupils more difficult? At what points does the value system of the educator conflict with those to be educated? Why is there such great turnover of teachers, nurses, and social workers in a neighborhood like this? Why is the neighborhood so little challenge to anyone? When and at what points are expectations about each other not met? What is the status problem in working in this district? [7]

We were concerned with what the low self-concept of our clients might mean to their interpersonal relationships and interactions. Were they taking out social and emotional frustration on each other? Was the societal strain (poverty, unemployment, discrimination) so high that impulsive behavior was one way of releasing tensions—taking also into account that waiting for any kind of gratification was not the usual neighborhood pattern? Many Negro clients maintained that living in the South had not been "too bad." Was it so bad that they needed to use denial as a defense, or were role expectations fewer, more personal in nature, better defined, and thereby less confusing? Could one realistically expect less stealing and violence (which might reflect a change of values) so long as social conditions did not leave room for equal and useful opportunities and outdated laws did not "fit the crime"? [8] Not only individuals but whole neighborhoods need to find their identity in society, and we need to understand the latent function performed by these "bad" neighborhoods in relation to the rest of the city.

By such questions one would not expect to find specific answers to problem situations in their own way as unique as individuals under close analysis. But the questioning broadened our psychological frame of reference to include the social systems, norms, values, and customs of the recipients of general welfare services and the helping professions; it provided a beginning for a more appropriate and flexible approach to mastering the environment while meeting inner personal needs.

Focus was on the problem situation, on the quality of interaction, on possible problems in communication. One tried to understand the inner and outer stresses to which people were responding and the expectations they had of themselves and of others. By disentangling, clarifying, and supporting complicated role relationships in the context of sociocultural factors and personal needs, it was hoped to re-establish an equilibrium for better communication and social functioning, and more mutually satisfying relationships. Recognizing the gaps and limitations of our present conceptual frame, the ultimate goal was to create a more benign neighborhood climate for clients by widening understanding of psychological, cultural, and social factors in the light of recent knowledge.

Sometimes it seemed that the mere presence of the social workers, their desire to understand, and their frank appraisal of what could be done or what did not seem possible brought a lessening of tension. More often they were more than mere listeners and observers. While paying attention to the minute details of what was going on between people and the types of stresses they were reacting to, they often intervened carefully with words or actions, taking pains not to overdo and

letting the client or consultee handle the situation the moment he seemed able to, yet leaving the door open for further intervention for the same or other problems.

Case Excerpt

The following case excerpt can illustrate only a few among several points which are the concern of this paper.

Tony. The counselor of a high school phoned the school social worker when she learned that the couple she had asked to come to school as Tony's parents were in fact foster parents, and that the public welfare department was planning to place Tony with his father, who had been released from prison a few months previously after serving a ten-year sentence for murdering Tony's mother, in Tony's presence, when the child was 3 years old. As distant relatives, and with their own children nearly grown, this couple had taken Tony into their home, showered him with affection, and much later, when their finances were no longer sufficient, asked the public welfare department for financial assistance, to which they were entitled as foster parents.

The counselor, who also carried teaching responsibilities, was not only new in her position as "personal problems counselor"; she was also new to the district and not without anxiety and inner tension in meeting her professional obligations. She had asked Tony's "parents" (they had registered him as their child) to come to school, since she considered him emotionally disturbed and in need of professional help. Tony was just sitting, not learning, and was completely inarticulate when questioned by teachers, although seen talking a few times to his classmates. The foster parents presented their story in poorly spoken English, with many gestures and references to the Lord. The counselor, bewildered and upset, wavered between deep sympathy and utter disbelief that so much human tragedy could be possible, of which only the barest details are reported here.

The social worker went over to the school immediately; the foster parents, without really knowing who she was, repeated eagerly and helplessly some of their story. A few telephone calls to public welfare and the probation department confirmed what they had to say. In one department the case load had not been covered because of a long-standing job vacancy, while in the other the worker was new and unfamiliar with his case load; there had been no planning for co-ordination of services. Tony's father showed a long history of emotional outbursts and instability; living by himself and without a steady job, he was left without the support of a worker who might have helped him to get re-established in the community. The foster parents had sought physical protection from him because he was threatening them, but the police had not believed them "because people come with stories like this every day."

After this crisis was settled through appropriate interventions by

the school social worker, when it had been clarified who was going to do what next, she noticed that the family had been repeatedly out of money and food and that the $70 they were receiving monthly from the public welfare department for Tony's care was their only steady source of income. (In order to save this amount the public welfare department had "considered" placing Tony with his father.) The foster mother was in need of an operation and unable to carry on with her job; the foster father had suffered two strokes several months earlier which disabled him. His social security payments had not come through. Dressed in his best suit, he had gone downtown several times to settle this matter. Again his limited ability to express himself in the situation and his lack of sophisticated know-how prevented him from dealing effectively with the bureaucratic structure of our social agencies. Because of complications in verifying his birth, it took the school social worker several weeks to locate his application and see that it was moved into the right channels.

Possible Lines of Intervention

One point about this case not unlike other cases is that there was a family in extreme despair, hanging on to each other and surrounded by agencies set up to protect and help people to function more adequately. Yet because of the complexity of structural processes inherent in any large-scale organization, agencies frequently create a climate that defeats much of their original intent. Frequently they are dealing with people who have never had opportunity to acquire the skills and competence to relate in the more impersonal and differential ways to the various officeholders of our growing bureaucratic structures. It is of no use to stay away from these situations and say, "If only the other agencies (police, court, public welfare, and so on) knew what they were doing!" and "We are the only ones who know what is right," since one must realize that all agencies, including our own, are interrelated in the client's social field. If structural or educational changes are necessary, we ourselves must become involved in this aspect of the client's life as one among several ways to bring about change.

1. The school social worker, in her dual role as a caseworker with clients and as a consultant to school personnel, saw several possible avenues for intervention. She could have "reached out" to this family, establishing a continued casework relationship and, with some awareness and attention to the social situation, focusing mainly on the psychological make-up of the clients. By "strengthening their ego" through primarily psychological means she might have hoped that eventually they would be able to deal more effectively with relationships in their environment.

In all probability this approach would have failed, since the worker very quickly recognized that "ego strength" was not lacking, but that these clients had never had the socializing experience to know how to

handle themselves in these types of situations. It cannot be said too often or emphatically that not being able to make the right connection in our social systems (including social agencies and clinics), or not following the right societal track from our point of view, is *not necessarily* a sign of poor ego organization.

In this case the point is perhaps plain, but the same often holds true in less extreme situations. Recent studies of character disorders which elaborate on the individual's psychodynamics without looking at the elements in the environment pertinent to his problem miss important clues for psychological treatment, social intervention, or a combination of both. "More casework services" or even "selected case loads" —as a highly desirable and well-intended aim—will not meet our expectations without development of problem formulations and treatment approaches as appropriate for specific client groups as they are realistic for casework. Moreover, as we shoulder the heavy responsibility of being consultants and collaborators in other agencies, we need to clarify what conceptual framework to adopt when the behavior and problems of clients are defined and discussed and social issues are at stake— even when nontechnical language is used, and though the clients are in need of psychological treatment.

Social policy and casework practice with clients of lower classes operate under the same roof. The increasing interdependence of man in relation to man and man in relation to his wider environment, as well as his internal functioning, need the most careful and flexible exploration. The point is not that any one conceptualization is "right" while others are wrong; but to find the conceptualization that will provide us with the most helpful leads in looking at the total needs of clients.[9] It is of little comfort to know that other professions are searching for similar reformulations, differentiations, and refinements. Albert Cohen in recent writing has the following so say: "A major task before us is to get rid of the notion . . . that the deviant, the abnormal, the pathological and in general, the deplorable always come wrapped in a single package." [10]

2. As a school consultant the social worker could have focused mainly on the conflict situation of the counselor as it related to her professional role. By recognizing her anxiety in being confronted with a perplexing situation and relieving some of her guilt for not being able to handle the situation more adequately—and, in general, through emotional support and some clarifying information—the counselor might have been enabled to deal more effectively with the clients. There were many other cases in which just this occurred.

In this instance the role of the counselor was extremely taxing, in a position new to her and a district quite different from her own background and previous professional experience. Her professional training had prepared her to meet parents who would recognize her as an educator and be concerned about the emotional aspects of their child's nonlearning. Instead she was presented with a family constellation and background she did not expect, while the foster parents in their personal way looked to her as a last resort for help, after telling their story

to a number of people. It was not that the counselor was basically inflexible about her role or that she lacked emotional warmth. But it often happens in lower-lower-class districts that the social distance and discouragement between clients and the caretaking agents—whether teachers, social workers, or others—are very great, and the perception of each other becomes blurred. In addition, the types of problems encountered are often dramatically aggressive; they are differently handled and seemingly unrelated to one's own social and emotional world, so that one's defense system may become quite threatened. The fluid give-and-take of feelings and words urgently needed with these clients *could not be produced without more adequate understanding and genuine empathy* for the various aspects of the total situation.

3. By remaining centered on the clients' needs, but focusing on the problem situation in all its emotional, social, and cultural facets, the school social worker decided to relieve the counselor of a pressing task which was more than she could be expected to handle at the moment. By intervening at this point the social worker established immediate rapport, not only with the foster parents but also with the counselor, with whom she had worked before. Through the disentangling of role relationships, the clarification of tasks and responsibilities, the re-establishment of channels of communication, and a sensitive awareness of the spoken and unspoken feelings of all persons involved, the family received the help they needed most. After the counselor got a "feel" of the neighborhood and the particulars of Tony's situation, she established good rapport with the foster parents, who often came to see her to discuss informally various events of their life.

Since Tony was a fearful child with emotional problems, and no treatment facilities were available for this type of "unmotivated" family, the social worker saw him for diagnostic purposes while the counselor explored resources within the school which would give him some opportunity to develop academically, emotionally, socially, and physically. Frequent and increasingly frank discussions with the school social worker made it possible for the counselor to air some of her own feelings of professional disappointment, her high self-expectations, and her physical fears of the neighborhood. Clarification of some of her misconceptions as they related to particular situations of children and their families lent support to the positive concern of the counselor for her students. After she had experienced the satisfaction and security of handling a few cases well, her warm and spontaneous behavior reappeared and she became keenly interested in her students and an active participant in neighborhood affairs.

Conclusions

This case is not set down as a success story, and deals with only one aspect of the work.[11] The experience of finding and mobilizing potential resources in a neighborhood said to have few potentials was

most rewarding. This mobilization occurred through social action, work on community committees, or—as has been suggested here—through work with caretaking agents and short-term contacts with clients during varied crisis situations.

With this broader conception of the work a different type of social worker evolved—one who saw himself as a part of the client's social field, who was ready to enter and deal with crisis situations in a new context and was perceived by others in that way. Being accused of "superficiality" and "lack of depth" in treatment became inadvertently a compliment, as the realization grew that casework sensibility, awareness, and skills can be used in more ways than one to enrich different dimensions of human behavior and help to unfold human relationships.

What emerged from this venture into social and cultural horizons was not the generality still attributed to social science theory, but the richness it added to a limited understanding and way of dealing with human problems. A more positive perspective was also gained on the inner strength of individuals and their drive for adaptation in an increasingly complex world.

Notes

1. Herman D. Stein, "The Concept of the Social Environment in Social Work Practice," *Smith College Studies in Social Work*, Vol. 30, No. 3 (June 1960), pp. 188–210.

2. Bertram Beck, "Prevention and Treatment," based on the work of the Subcommittee on Trends, Issues, and Priorities of the NASW Commission on Social Work Practice, 1959. (Mimeographed.)

3. Nelson N. Foote and Leonard S. Cottrell, *Identity and Interpersonal Competence* (Chicago: University of Chicago Press, 1955).

4. Berta Fantl, "Casework in Lower Class Districts," *Mental Hygiene*, Vol. 45, No. 3 (July 1961), pp. 425–438.

5. Gerald Caplan, *Concepts of Mental Health and Consultation* (Washington, D.C.: U.S. Dept. of Health, Education, and Welfare, 1959).

6. For a similar conceptualization of differential interventions *see* Ludwig Geismar, "Three Levels of Treatment for Multiproblem Families," *Social Casework*, Vol. 42, No. 3 (March 1961), pp. 124–128.

7. Elizabeth D. de Losada and Berta Fantl, "Working Papers." Unpublished manuscript, 1958–1960. We wish to express our gratitude to Edmund H. Volkart, Ph.D., professor of sociology at Stanford University, California, for his sustaining interest in our work and for the opportunity to discuss this type of question with him.

8. Richard A. Cloward and Lloyd E. Ohlin, *Delinquency and Opportunity* (New York: The Free Press of Glencoe, 1960); Erik H. Erikson, "On the Nature of Clinical Evidence," *Daedalus*, Proceedings of the American Academy of Arts and Sciences, Vol. 87. No. 4 (Fall 1958).

9. How can we think in the framework of "limited goals" for the neediest in our midst and for families burdened with a constellation of troublesome problems, when "expanding goals and sight" are needed? How is it that as social workers we need to be reminded that "constructive attitudes" are essential for working with certain client groups?

10. Albert K. Cohen, "The Study of Social Disorganization and Deviant Behavior," in *Sociology Today* (New York: Basic Books, 1959), p. 463. This is not unlike what Fritz Redl has to say in more psychological terminology, describing delinquent types, in *New Perspectives for Research on Juvenile Delinquency* (Washington, D.C.: U.S. Dept. of Health, Education, and Welfare, Children's Bureau, 1955).

11. For other aspects *see* Fantl, "Casework in Lower Class Districts," *op. cit.*

Techniques of Service

Janet E. Weinandy

Just as there are differences in the values and needs of problem families in the low socio-economic groups, it follows that the techniques employed in helping them have to be modified. I have said earlier in this report that experience has taught us that the clients will not seek help with their social and emotional problems, although they are receptive to this help when it is brought to them. This despite the fact that when under stress of physical needs they will go to the Welfare for financial assistance or to a clinic or hospital for medical care. In the following pages, I will try to describe what I have found to be the most useful techniques in working with the study group of families. Although these may sound somewhat primitive, it goes without saying that their successful employment must be based on an understanding of both individual and family dynamics, as well as cultural factors.

Action

This, as I see it, is one of the basic components in this type of social work. Starting with the first approach to the case, the worker has to take the initiative. She must seek out the client and explain why she has been sent to see him (in many instances after actively ferreting out from other agencies what their experience has been with this client and what they see as the problem). In extreme cases, where the

Reprinted from *Families Under Stress: A Report on the First Year of a Three Year Family Consultation Service in Public Housing,* Youth Development Center, Syracuse University publication, 1962, pp. 14–19.

371

worker is unwelcome the first time, she has to keep returning until some working basis is established. The *Casework Notebook* (St. Paul, Minn.: Family Centered Project, 1957) is specific on the point that where families and children are in jeopardy because of their handicapping attitudes and neglectful behavior, society gives the social worker the right to intervene.

Once having established a working basis, the worker must continue taking the initiative by going to the client. Seldom can he be expected to keep an office appointment except for a very specific reason. In my experience, even after long contact with the social worker, seldom will he call for help unless specifically taught to do so. Furthermore, because of weak ego and lack of initiative and courage, it is necessary to do many things actively with the client for his welfare, such as taking him to health and legal resources where other kinds of help can be initiated.

But that's not all. While in the home calling on the family, one does not just sit and observe while the mother tries to cope with six screaming children. Many useful lessons on child care can be taught by demonstration. This has to be done tactfully, realizing that the mother is in charge, and enlisting her support. So, in the course of a year I have done many things I never dreamed of doing in casework with middle-class clientele. I have done a family's mending on the spot with my portable sewing machine. I have baby-sat to allow the mother to keep a clinic appointment. I have taken a frightened parent to the hospital to register for surgery. I have been in court on almost all non-support hearings and juvenile delinquency hearings. When one impulsive woman deserted her children and was wanted by the police, I went after her, brought her to the Youth Bureau, and stuck with her until the matter was settled.

Then, of course, there are the financial problems. With many families I appear weekly with the notebook, see the paycheck stub (if I am lucky) and plan with the wife on how the money is to be spent. In a few instances, at their request, I have served as banker, holding money for rent or other necessities until it is due. In crisis periods and if there is a good reason, I run innumerable errands, get prescriptions filled, take the family to pick up surplus foods. I have gone with clients to see creditors and discuss refinancing of debts. There have been innumerable calls and visits to Welfare to interpret special problems, to clarify the family's budget so I can help them live within it, and to generally coordinate our efforts. This kind of activity also goes on with health agencies, and with corrective agencies as it becomes necessary.

Directness

To get anywhere with these clients, one has to spell out pretty frankly, in the very beginning if possible, what has gone wrong with

their situation, and why one is there. This is not easy for a caseworker accustomed by training and experience to practice subtleties. Though clients sometimes react with mild hostility or defensiveness to "accusations," in the long run they seem to appreciate being told where they stand, how society looks at them, and what is expected of them. This is not to say that a wholesale tearing down is the recommended technique. Far from it. One should, at the same time that one is presenting negatives, also let the client know what positives one sees in the situation, and indicate some faith in the client's ability to grow and change with help.

The offer of help of a practical, constructive nature should be given immediately. This is one of the best devices for establishing a relationship which enables one to build on. I had one experience with a young woman who was serenely producing out-of-wedlock babies each year, with no real effort being made by her or the other agencies involved to assume responsibility. Her only effort was to call the Welfare after each delivery and announce the new arrival. Her children were all over the neighborhood, uncontrolled, spreading ringworm as they went, and getting into minor difficulties. After my first attempt to talk with her about what she was doing and what she was expecting of society, she remarked, I felt with real feeling rather than habitual politeness, "I wish someone had talked to me like this before." Six weeks after the last baby was born she enrolled at Planned Parenthood, and announced to me that she had been given two methods of contraception! Sometime later we had another frank discussion on her neglect of the children, in which she owned up to her desperation on how to handle them since the strap seemed to do no good.

In another situation I had assumed, because the client was intelligent and came from a little higher level on the socio-economic scale, that she could be approached in a more sophisticated fashion. Here I again resorted to directness, and it paid off. This woman had a long history of mismanagement of money. I had rescued her from many dilemmas with Welfare and with the landlord, thinking each time after fairly frank discussions with her that she had learned something. We had, after 10 months of working together, a close relationship, and were on the brink of getting her rehabilitated on a job which was important to her and which had required hours of active effort to effect. At this point she impulsively misused some money which had been advanced for another purpose, and said nothing about it until I brought it up. Then I frankly stated that this was a pattern of hers which had gotten her into repeated difficulties, and she seemed always to expect to be rescued. She was then able to see that she had been confused about the concept of independence; that whereas she had thought she had been acting independently in spending money and had prided herself on her desire to be independent, actually her lack of planning had resulted in her being more dependent on others. She was a greatly sobered young woman as she thought back to all the times she had behaved in this way. The next time I saw her, we worked out a course of action for the future with some safeguards against her impulsiveness.

The Practical Approach

This is probably self-evident from the foregoing discussion, but deserves a little emphasizing. Casework on any level is impossible when the client has an empty stomach, requires immediate medical attention, or is in imminent danger of losing his home or possessions. Many clients, because of lack of foresight or because of being impulse-ridden, go from one crisis to another. One has to handle the crisis, or help the client do so at the outset, in the hope that in the brief interval between crises one has a chance to get at the underlying causes and perhaps do a preventive job. On the other hand, it is during a crisis that the anxiety is highest, and it is sometimes possible to capitalize on this. In any case, the social worker who is inexperienced in community resources, inexperienced in the practical aspects of life (such as home management, budgeting, care of children), and who is mainly clinically oriented, will have a miserable time in this kind of work.

I often think, and I am sure this is not an original idea, that what we are attempting to do in multi-problem family work is to revive the best of the reaching-out, neighborhood-centered approach of the early days of social work in this country, the days of Hull House and Mary Richmond. But we are attempting to include in this approach something of the modern theoretical knowledge and techniques which social work has developed within the past 25 years.

I also feel that the question of social legislation should not be ignored; casework alone cannot do the job that needs doing, although it helps. Great advances have been made in social legislation since the days of Jane Addams, but I can see some areas on the local scene where improvement is indicated. Of immediate concern to me are the laws for the protection of children, emotional neglect, enforcement of support orders for either legitimate or adjudicated fathers, and above all, the need for quicker action on violation of such orders. Another problem is that of easy credit and the whole area of collection practices.

Use of Authority

This is a concept relatively new in social work thinking, and though I have given it considerable attention during the past year, I am still trying it out and do not consider myself by any means an expert. However, I feel it may be one of the most valuable techniques in work with multi-problem families, if used correctly. Its theoretical base seems diametrically opposed to the concept which has recently been popular in clinically oriented social work, namely, the right of the individual to self-determination. How far can society allow its members to go in

self-destruction, particularly when it endangers the rights and safety of others? The concept of the employment of authority in social work is predicated on the theory that social workers represent sanctioned values of society and as such have an obligation to help their clients internalize these values. I believe that the clients often sense this authority more fully than the social worker does. We have too long bent over backwards being understanding and non-moralistic and non-judgmental, which has often served no useful purpose to the client. Other agencies in the community have set certain standards of behavior. The schools have expected children to be regular and prompt in attendance, and to conform to certain standards of cleanliness and behavior. The Welfare expects clients to be honest about their resources, and has set up machinery to punish fraudulent behavior. Public Housing has set minimum standards for housekeeping, behavior, and payment of rent. Then there are the laws governing public behavior, for protection of property and human safety, which are enforced differently depending on the age of the offender. If one really thinks about it, the behavior of one person always has implications for another person.

So it seems that the social worker's first task is to recognize that his clients are bound by the laws of society, just as any other citizen is, and to devise ways of helping the client learn this for his own welfare. This is sometimes done by pointing out to him that if he fails in certain areas, there will be consequences. If he allows his children to truant, he may be charged with neglect; if he fails to provide proper physical care for the children or is abusive to them, they may be taken away from him; if he does not pay his rent or take adequate care of his property, he can be evicted; if he fails to support his family, he will be sent to jail. Call it threatening, if you will. It's a very useful device providing that the threats are not idle ones, but are backed up by substantial enforcement if necessary. And provided, also, that if some anxiety can be aroused in this way, the social worker stands ready to implement whatever program of improvement is agreed upon and sticks with the client long enough to obtain results.

Another fact is that for reasons which are not hard to understand, many adult clients in this group are immature in their psycho-social development; in plain basic English, they are kids themselves. They need and want, sometimes even ask for, controls. The only way I can see to help them emerge from their immaturity is through intelligent use of appropriate controls, accompanied, of course, by large doses of encouragement as they show signs of growth. A little knowledge of child psychology can be of great value. So can a sense of humor, as one points out to them that they are being just as "hard-headed" as their children. Time limits are also useful—giving a mother a month to clean up her house, but not forgetting to go back and inspect at the appointed time.

We can learn many useful lessons from probation officers, who have been playing an authoritative role much longer than other social workers. One lesson is not to be too easily led on by promises, unless

they are backed up by concrete results. Another is that it is just as well to do a little checking during a program of improvement so that when the client falters, as he may, he can be spurred on, rather than letting the whole program fail. The social worker must constantly keep his sights on the goal. In doing this he again takes the initiative, recognizing that the client does not have the strength to do this for himself, as yet.

Giving

"Conscious use of self" may be the euphemism as it applies to behind-the-desk counselling, but I have in mind something more primitive. One gives all kinds of services. One gives by going to the house, by listening to the latest tribulations, by trying to find solutions. Sometimes one brings needed articles for the household, scrounged from somebody's attic or clothing exchange. Sometimes one gets the neighbors to come in and help. Giving is also imparting courage to the client to face whatever he has to face. Above all, giving is letting him know that you like him and have confidence in his ability to grow and change.

Coordinating

This is perhaps more a function than a technique, but the social worker serves as a coordinator with multi-problem families, and this may be one of his more important functions. We talk about how, in the past multi-problem families were treated in fragments by many agencies, with some services overlapping, and often without any sense of direction. Also, we went through an era of case conferences in which representatives of the agencies attempting to help the family met and discussed the situation. They tried to formulate some plan for the family and some decision regarding coordination of future services. This was fine, but consumed hours of expensive staff time, and all too often the group who had met continued to carry on their duties with fragments of the family as before. Nobody had assumed responsibility for the coordination of efforts based on a sound plan, the family was frequently confused by several workers contacting them about different matters, and nothing significant happened to the family as a result of all this.

Therefore, I have strong feelings that there is no alternative in multi-problem family work to having one person or agency carry the major responsibility for the working relationship with the family, and then helping the family initiate contacts with other services as needed. These services should be considered for this particular family as adjuncts to and secondary to the casework service. The caseworker then

assumes responsibility for keeping informed about what is going on in the other services. This is not to say that if the major problem is medical, and the medical social worker at the clinic or hospital is prepared to give the long-term coordinating service that is required, the family cannot "belong" to the medical social worker. It is merely a proposal to focus the responsibility for working with the family on one agency and worker, rather than dispersing and frittering away the efforts of many and ending in frustration for the social workers and failure for the family.

Sociotherapy

Personality Adjustment Through Social Action

Rudolph M. Wittenberg

Around the turn of the century state hospitals in Illinois were supposed to have used a startlingly naive test to determine the degree of sanity of their patients. They were locked in a room, equipped with a mop, where water was flowing from an open faucet. There were two types of patient: one group would grasp the mop and sweep madly, the other group would first turn off the faucet.

It is said that Jane Addams classified herself in the group of insane people who sweep madly, because intake at Hull House grew year by year while conditions creating the need for more and more social and psychiatric services were ignored, like the open faucet.

Perhaps this is all we can do, sweep madly and with more and more efficiency. Possibly the modification or even cure of social pathology is not the function of mental hygiene. Or is it possible to use knowledge gained in psychiatry, case work, and group work not only to help the individual reach his highest potential, but to direct his energies toward modifying some of the conditions which have caused some of his maladjustment? Can we use our tools to enable people to take initiative and develop leadership in their own behalf?

In order to find some of these answers, a research project (set up by Union Settlement Association, New York City, October 1945, and supplemented by a grant of the Greater New York Fund) was set up known as the Neighborhood Center For Block Organization. The area selected was most typical of people who showed the effects of social pathology in their personalities.

Reprinted from *American Journal of Orthopsychiatry*, Vol. 18, No. 2, April 1948, pp. 207–221. Copyright, The American Orthopsychiatric Association, Inc. Reproduced by permission.

The area chosen is characterized by the well known pattern of an urban slum: incomes on or slightly above the level of public welfare allowances, average rentals of $28 monthly, inadequate housing, lack of recreation and of social services, interracial and intercultural friction, and the concomitant symptoms of family breakdown, delinquency, gang warfare, prostitution, and gambling.

The 1940 census showed a population in this area of 24,141, divided as follows: Negro, 5336 (22.1%); native white (including Puerto Ricans) 13,142 (54.5%); foreign-born white 5553 (23.1%); other races 110 (.3%).

Since the census included the Puerto Ricans as native white citizens, it is not possible to secure a total figure on that group, but a fairly close estimate is 25 per cent of the population.

The area abounds with children; 29 per cent being under age 15, and 41 per cent under 21. During the last four years, in spite of razing the most hazardous buildings, the population has increased through the filling of empty apartments and the crowding of two or more Negro or Puerto Rican family units into one dwelling unit. The population in 1946 was approximately 26,000. Until the housing shortage arose, the population in this area was very mobile, but recently there has been little or no moving about with a resulting stability of population that is favorable to this project.

The experiment technically falls into the category of community organization, although it is different in goals and methods from the typical pattern associated with this term. It is clear that in this experiment the organization is the tool, while personality growth is the goal.

The unit of work chosen for this experiment was the two sides of a street, in this paper called the "block." This term also differs from the accepted meaning which applies to a square. There was common interest between the people who lived opposite and next to one another, while little natural group basis existed for the people living in back of the square. The common interest of such a unit, called the block project, differed from block to block. The four blocks organized at the time of this report are concerned with gang warfare, prostitution, housing violations, child care, and recreation.

In order to illustrate the methods used in the experiment, one block has been chosen, and one of its potential leaders and her own development. The population of this block consists of approximately 800 people, predominately American Negro, a small percentage of West Indians, Puerto Ricans, and a minority of Italians. It is a typical urban street, teeming with life, a public school without a playground, two vacant lots, a poolroom, and two grocery stores. A high percentage of people in this block are on relief and there is a minority of families where both parents live together.

The people were concerned with the large number of children playing on the street while cars and trucks passed through at rapid speed. While the police had done all they could within the limit of the law to effect a slowing down of traffic, nevertheless one or two accidents

occurred weekly. The public school was able to control this further during lunch hours and until school was out. However, during the summer months when the school was closed, the customary patrol car was no longer on duty near the school exit.

A few of the mothers brought this concern to the P.T.A. of the school, and it was from this beginning that the present block organization developed. Mrs. Smith, whose nine year old son was injured one day, suggested to the P.T.A. a petition directed to the police asking for a sign that would close the street to traffic. There was enough interest in the block to obtain nearly two hundred signatures. The Captain of the police precinct received the petitions and assured the people of his and the city's interest, but cars and trucks continued to drive full speed through the block. At this point the people asked for help for more effective organization. They had heard of the Neighborhood Center from brief visits, leaflets, and some referrals which had been made to social agencies. Since the office of the Neighborhood Center was located in a store nearby, they found it easy to come in and discuss their problem. In the first interview Mrs. Smith appeared sufficiently concerned to take the initiative in interesting other people. She became the Block President.

Mrs. Smith: 35 years old, a tall, attractive Negro woman whose common law husband had deserted, leaving her with the responsibility for her three children. Prior to this, she had worked as a domestic. She had to choose between accepting public welfare or again accepting a job as a domestic. The choice involved feelings about herself and her children. She felt that accepting a job would mean independence. At the same time her children would have to be taken care of by neighbors or left to their own devices. The alternative was to go into the difficult process of applying for relief and becoming dependent on the public agency, but with it the possibility of taking care of her children. She had chosen the latter course and been on relief for over two years when she came to the Neighborhood Center to ask for help with organization of the block.

Mrs. Smith said freely that she felt hopeless about the future because she did not get enough satisfaction for herself from the life she had to lead. She had been interested in going to college when she had left high school; she continued to read intensively, was concerned with racial, cultural, and political issues. The continuous disregard for human lives, illustrated by trucks and cars injuring small children, was to her a challenge that she felt had to be met by the people themselves.

She had been active with a private family agency and a child guidance clinic because of one of her children. Child guidance study had clearly established a rejection of the male child, who was identified with the husband, an irresponsible good-looking man, an only child deserted by his own father.

Mrs. Smith had apparently gotten some help from the clinic, because she was able to handle the rejection with more insight. Perhaps

she was caring for her children as well as she possibly could, with her background and family constellation. She had also used the family service well, gotten help with budgeting and nutrition, and was managing her relief allowance as adequately as could any trained home economist. Child guidance and case work had done their job well; Mrs. Smith had made the most of her situation, used the resources in the community and made a good adjustment.

Now she had come to get help of a different nature. She was concerned with the street in which her child had been injured, and she moved in the direction of a modification of her environment. The next step was the recognition that such changes can only be effected together with other people. She had to learn to cope with groups. As we know from work with groups, the process involving several people with common interests also has an effect on each individual member. Mrs. Smith, while hoping to change some of the conditions of the street, underwent some changes herself.

The Use of Group Techniques

The role of the professional worker becomes that of a group leader working with an indigenous group of people from the community. The group has both the elements of a natural and an interest group. These people have lived together in the same block for years, shopped in the same stores, gone to the same church, and suffered from the same speeding traffic. Their common interest was to modify the disturbing conditions and create instead something more satisfying to all of them. The worker has to operate through the natural leader just as he would in a social club at a settlement house. Based on a sound relationship, he must use his skill to: 1) offer constructive opportunities for sublimation; 2) permit release of hostilities and aggressions without damaging group process; 3) meet the dependency needs of members while enabling them to move toward more independent action; 4) encourage voluntary and self-developing interaction toward the group by using the common interest (project or program) as a catalytic agent; 5) enable individual members to function better inside the group and their block; 6) lead the group, through the natural leader, toward a successful achievement of their project.

Of particular significance is the relationship the worker must establish in this setup whch has a more completely voluntary character than is possible even in a voluntary agency. Basic is the acceptance of aggression against the professional worker, as well as recognition of limitations imposed by the tension and interaction which exists in spite of the common interest that brought the group together. Knowledge of when to be active or passive as the group's needs require, is fundamental. Simultaneously, the worker must be aware of the following dynamics: 1) his own relationship to each member of the group; 2) relationship of mem-

bers toward one another (interaction); 3) relationship to the group; 4) group's reaction toward him; 5) progress of the program which must not advance at the cost of group interaction; 6) relationship between group and the larger community of which it is a part (the block).

Because it would go beyond the frame of this paper to show the group process in this or any other block, we have concentrated on the development of Mrs. Smith who was elected to be the group's spokesman. Her reaction to this decision was decidedly ambivalent. It had great ego value to her and as she later expressed it, she felt that she "counted." At the same time, there was a great deal of fear, acute awareness of her status as a Negro, a relief recipient, a woman deserted by her husband, and a tenant living in a rat infested, dingy three room flat. She expressed her fear by saying, "I feel funny going to the police. I haven't done anything."

The role of the worker was to accept her ambivalent feelings and help her to work through them in a few informal brief interviews. The concrete issue around which this was handled was her talk with the police captain. Premature reassurance would have been as damaging as over-indulgence; it was the worker's job to find the exact point from which Mrs. Smith could go ahead. At the same time, the worker had to be aware of a primary community organization law: not to undertake projects which are not feasible or only possible in the distant future. Failure on this count would have been damaging both to Mrs. Smith and to the group. The worker had therefore first checked whether traffic laws permitted a play street in this block, and whether the particular precinct and captain were accessible to such a request by people from the blocks. The captain had been prepared for this step by a simple interpretation of the project, and the request was granted.

Once the play street stanchion was put up, Mrs. Smith and the others in the block became vigilant about speeding cars. Mrs. Smith asked how the law could be enforced and was advised to call the captain of the precinct about it. Although she had spoken to him, she needed help with this call. She asked the worker to dial the number after discussing the questions she would ask. The worker sat in the same room while Mrs. Smith explained to the captain clearly and simply the problem of through traffic. She was advised to take down license plate numbers of cars violating the law and to report them to the police. In one of the first meetings of the small group that took an interest in this problem, Mrs. Smith reported the suggestion made by the police captain. The people, particularly those who were home during the day, proved very willing to keep track of cars that raced through the block. After reporting a few violators, they found that word had apparently gotten around among truck drivers that it was cheaper to avoid this block.

Encouraged by this success, Mrs. Smith and the small group felt that the next problem would be to get a safe place for the children to play. This was a particularly realistic request because the public school had no playground. Just as they had found the police captain interested in their self-help attempt, they found the school principal eager to

cooperate. Talking this problem through with the worker helped them to realize that they would need mass support to exert sufficient pressure on the Board of Education to turn the empty lot next to the school into a playground.

One of the members of the small block committee thought that it would help to use some influential names in such a campaign and the committee wrote their first joint letter to a prominent and liberal Councilman. The worker's role in this letter, as in the past, was to stand by and make occasional suggestions when asked. But the actual writing and composition was done by Mrs. Smith and two other mothers who had become more active since the play street extension had appeared. The answer of the Councilman was extremely encouraging. He went through the files and discovered that there had been for the past five years a plan, tabled year after year, to purchase the land next to the school for a public playground. He thought that the chances for taking title to the land were good if the people kept after the powers that be.

It was at this point that Mrs. Smith thought of involving more citizens in the block than had hitherto been active. The block committee decided on their first leaflet. The worker asked if the committee would want to combine the appeal with a call for a public meeting in the very school under discussion.

There followed several weeks of increased activity on the part of the committee consisting of their first contact with the Board of Education for a permit to use the auditorium. It is significant to mention that this was perhaps the first time they had felt free to discuss the problem with some of the Italian as well as Puerto Rican neighbors.

Since the auditorium permit called for signatures of officers, the small committee elected Mrs. Smith temporary president and two women to the other offices. The Councilman who had been so encouraging in his letter was invited to speak at the meeting and Mrs. Smith, although hesitatingly, agreed to chair the meeting. Several new people who had not been interested earlier came forth and suggested some friends or relatives as entertainers. At the meeting, Mrs. Smith had her speech ready but found it difficult to read it to the end. She became increasingly agitated, faltered, and was near tears when she stopped abruptly and sat down. The Councilman took over and, by the time he had finished, Mrs. Smith had regained her composure sufficiently to close the meeting.

Case Work and Psychiatric Techniques

In discussing her confusion with the worker, Mrs. Smith began by saying that she would never again make a speech in her life. Since her feelings of discouragement were accepted and she was not reassured about the relative value of the meeting, she felt free to talk about some of the reasons for her difficulty. Quite naturally, she thought that the lack of experience in speaking was responsible for her excitement. She

believed that a course in public speaking might help her to have more composure before a group. She asked about courses the way a client in a case work agency might ask for a nursery school, or an unmarried mother for temporary shelter.

Just as the trained case worker would use such a request to get more understanding of the underlying causes, the worker at the Center helped Mrs. Smith to express the real feelings that had led to her anxiety on the platform. She told the worker that what upset her were several people in the front row who had grinned, giggled, and whispered to each other.

She related this with a great deal of feeling and laughed nervously when the worker asked whether she knew the people who had irritated her. Yes, they were neighbors; in fact, they lived on the same floor. And then, leaning forward and speaking with intensity, she said that the woman who had giggled was really the woman who had wrecked her marriage. This woman, Jane, had kept Mr. Smith in her apartment late in the evenings while Mrs. Smith was under the impression he was working overtime. It ended in his leaving both women, but Mrs. Smith said it was hard to be laughed at by the woman who, she felt, had taken Mr. Smith away. It was particularly hard, she said, when everybody was supposed to be interested in the playground and the children. "I think Jane did not come to the meeting to help with the playground but to watch me make a fool of myself. She probably sat there and thought: 'Look at her up there on the platform when she can't even hold on to her husband.' "

Accepting Mrs. Smith's feelings with warm reassurance, the worker said that this might well have been Jane's reason for coming to the meeting and wondered how Mrs. Smith felt about such a neighbor. She did not know what to think, she said, but wasn't it awful for people to act that way. Again it was helpful to her to talk to someone who was able to accept both her feelings and the behavior of the neighbor. She verbalized that perhaps this was the way Jane was and it didn't do any good to sulk about it.

The worker brought her back to talking about her own feelings about her husband and her resentment against Jane. Mrs. Smith had been aware of the relationship between the two for a long time and had compensated for it by trying to be friendly with Jane, who apparently had had too much guilt to accept Mrs. Smith and avoided her. Mrs. Smith found it hard to understand such behavior until the worker gave some simple interpretation. When he explained Jane's giggling as part of her guilt reaction, Mrs. Smith felt better and did not see it purely as an aggressive act against her but as part of Jane's own problems. She said that she wouldn't have had to act the way she had on the platform if she had understood why Jane laughed.

In a few informal interviews, separate from committee meetings, it was possible to help Mrs. Smith express deeper feelings about her husband and her father. Since there was clearly a need for deeper therapy, the possibility of referral was explored, but she did not see this need as urgent enough to go back to the family agency. She thought she did not

need to talk more about her husband. He had tried to come back to her several times in the last two years and she had always made it clear to him that she did not want a reconciliation. She thought it more important to her if she could accomplish something through the block committee on the street. "It would make me feel awfully good if we could really get something done for ourselves."

This process, which might be called social sublimation, was perhaps her way of working out some of her deeper problems. The brief contact freed her sufficiently to establish a less hostile and more natural relationship with Jane. She had become less vulnerable to Jane's hostility and succeeded in penetrating the defense Jane had built around herself. She then discovered another neighbor whose husband had deserted, a neighbor much more burdened than herself and in greater need of help.

While the episode on the platform had been of real significance to Mrs. Smith, the people on the block thought little of it. The Councilman's encouragement, the local talent, the attendance of nearly one hundred people had been sufficient stimulation to the block committee to meet regularly at the Neighborhood Center.

At a meeting following the school rally, the committee planned to announce that there would be a school playground. However, the worker pointed out realistically that this was not to materialize for a year in as much as it was too late in the year for visible results. The people accepted this limitation but asked what their children could do eight weeks hence when school would be over. They were firm in their belief that roaming the street was not the answer.

Mrs. Smith wondered whether it might be possible for the people of the block to run their own playground, right on the street. They had heard of recreational programs run by the PAL but none of them felt that this kind of mass recreation would do. They had all had experiences with their own or friends' children where individual behavior had been handled by untrained workers in a mass setup.

The Neighborhood Center interpreted the difference between professional and lay standards with the result that the people felt a play street run by their organization would require professional, trained group workers. Characteristic of their reaction was the statement of one mother, "We have to take handouts, but for our children, we want the best."

The problem of fund raising had to be faced; if this block was to run its own supervised program, it would need to finance it. In order to determine how many workers were necessary, the committee embarked on a simple survey of the children in this and the adjoining block. The committee was given the salary scale for group workers, graduates of professional schools of social work. They would need at least five workers if each were to be responsible for eight to ten children. They also got an approximate picture of the age range of children. We wish to emphasize again that the majority of people on the block committee were living on public welfare allowances and in no position to pay the salary of one worker for a period of eight or ten weeks. It is interesting that there was

little or no resentment against the idea of paying a man nearly twice as much as one of them got from the relief office. In a very realistic discussion they decided that the best they could do was to raise the salary for one professional leader. The Center worker made it clear that even if they succeeded in this difficult fund-raising campaign, it would be necessary to have at least four regular assistants. Fund raising and training of mothers and assistants occupied the committee until the day the program opened.

Fund raising began by getting from the drugstore quart-sized ice cream containers with covers, fastened with scotch tape and slit in the top. The newly elected treasurer was responsible for keeping track of the fifteen cans circulated in stores, beer parlors, poolrooms and in a number of homes in the block. When the collection boxes were turned in and the pennies, nickels, and dimes piled up on the large wooden table at the Center, less than one week's salary for the prospective worker was counted. They decided to use this money to run a block party to raise more funds. This plan drew approximately another hundred people into the Block Organization who were willing to help with the preparation of food and drink. One of these new members had known a now famous and very prominent band leader. She went with the committee to see him at one of the large downtown theaters and managed to get him to promise to appear at their block party without charge.

By now, Mrs. Smith and the original committee found it easy to write effective copy, and leaflets reporting progress had become a routine matter. Old and young alike participated in decorating their street with streamers from house to house, leaflets hanging from the fire escapes, and posters in poolrooms and grocery stores. They installed large borrowed spotlights on the fire escape opposite the lot, having gotten permission from the Puerto Rican tenant on the second floor. The Italian poolroom owner, inspired by this program, contributed funds for renting a loud speaker. Committee members brought tables and dishes. Other volunteers served food and drink. In the evening there was music and dancing. The treasurer announced over the microphone that the party was given to raise funds for a well run play street. Later when the famous band leader appeared, nearly six hundred young people crowded around to hear him and two colleagues sing and play on the primitive band stand.

A nearby gang took the opportunity to provoke a knife fight with some of the youngsters in the block, and the police asked the block committee at about one o'clock in the morning to start closing up. It was interesting to note that people in the block, to a man, swore that the gang had come from a different block. This reaction is emphasized because of the erroneous conception that there is no common interest within such units as the block.

The people were beginning to ask when the playground would open. The block committee was holding sessions because some of the profit from the block party had disappeared. Mrs. Smith discussed this with the Center worker, because she had lived in this block long enough to

know who might have taken the money. Mrs. Smith gave a surprising amount of background material for three suspects. With the worker's help she saw the need for help rather than humiliation for these people. One of the three, Mrs. Jones, was a member of the original block committee. Mrs. Smith felt it might be possible for the worker to help her not only with this problem, but some of her "purely personal" problems.

Interagency Coordination

Mrs. Smith herself offered to talk with Mrs. Jones to arrange an interview for her with the worker. The interview took place and yielded enough material to clear the case.

Mrs. Jones' case had been active with the Department of Public Welfare and she had had a number of brief service contacts with a private family agency. In a joint conference between the Neighborhood Center and the two other agencies, it was learned that both the public welfare worker and the private family agency worker considered Mrs. Jones not accessible for treatment. Outstanding in their reasoning was the belief that she had proven unable to accept any responsibility for herself or her family. It was startling to learn from the Center worker that Mrs. Jones had been one of the few people in the block who had not only come regularly to the meetings but had taken a great deal of initiative in carrying out assignments as distribution of leaflets, preparation of food for the party, bringing in several collection boxes, etc. She was also one of four women who regularly served four hours daily on the playstreet as assistants to the professional leader.

She had an immature demanding attitude toward the Department of Welfare, her sole support for the past seven years. Because of this, she had brought only emergency requests to the family agency. The case worker had referred her back to the relief office, so that at no time had there been possibility of more intensive and deeper treatment.

After the conference in which the strong and healthy aspects of Mrs. Jones' personality had been highlighted, the Neighborhood worker, because of his relationship to Mrs. Jones as a member of the block committee, undertook to open the way for intensive case work at the private family agency. Since overlapping between the two agencies had also been cut to a minimum, it was now possible for Mrs. Jones to use the community resources more constructively. One evidence of her growth might be the fact that she herself, some months later, volunteered the information that she had kept some of the money from the block party and meant to pay it back like any other debt.

In the meantime the block committee had continued to raise funds by appealing to unions whose members lived in the neighborhood, political parties, and a few individuals who could afford to contribute more than small change. The Neighborhood Center worker was delegated to interview possible candidates for the job of playground director. While

the worker accepted this assignment, he made it clear that the final choice would have to be made by the executive committee of the block.

Before the people saw the workers, two problems had to be cleared up. One was a request by the veterans in the block to be considered for the job. The second was a need for a better understanding of criteria for selection of a leader, with further interpretation of mental hygiene standards.

The question of hiring a veteran from the block proved extremely interesting, particularly since in the field of delinquency prevention there is a school of thought that advocates the use of "indigenous" leadership. The block committee discussed this problem freely, and all except Mrs. Smith felt that the veterans who had played baseball in the Army and handled soldiers should make good recreation leaders. Mrs. Smith told about her own growth since the beginning of the Block Organization. She described the insight she had developed, the better understanding of her neighbors and even her own children, her ability to express herself, to write, to handle money. She felt she had more self-confidence than before. She was certain she still had much to learn, and since she, who had learned so much did not consider herself qualified, the veterans would be much less ready for the job. She gave concrete examples of the veterans' behavior in the block.

Mrs. Smith said that the Negro veterans in her block, as well as the Italians in the next, had not shown any leadership. They all drew their twenty dollars for fifty-two weeks, an occupation known as belonging to the "52-20 Club." They did no work, few went to school, and this attitude was not a good example for youngsters. She said that gambling all hours of the night did not fit them for a whole day with children. Nevertheless she and other members of the committee agreed that if they wanted to apply for the job, their applications should be considered on the basis of their qualifications, not because they were friends and neighbors.

After a routine screening by the worker, the choice narrowed down to two candidates. One was very good looking, suave, with an excellent lingo of group work, but no specific plans and an apparent inability to work with people on their own level. The other candidate was a quiet, unpretentious, small man who came for the second interview with a very detailed plan, broken down into age groups, with suggestions for equipment within the budget and a real understanding of the unique setup in which he was to work. Both were Negroes with adequate references, both were graduates from a professional social work school. They were told by the director of the Center that each of them would have to be interviewed by the executive committee of the block, comparable to a Board of Directors of an agency.

The committee saw both applicants and was impressed with the talkative, good-looking one. They thought the second one might be too quiet. The qualifications were briefly compared by the block committee and the Center worker. When asked for his opinion, he gave it, but still left the decision to the block committee. After some debate, they concurred in the choice of Mr. Green, the less assuming but more able of the

two candidates. One of the first steps taken by the committee and their playground director was to plan for a brief training course so that the mothers could assist Mr. Green.

The training course for mothers had so many significant aspects that a full description would go beyond the frame of this paper. Suffice it to say that the session on behavior gave considerable material on their attitudes toward themselves and their children, as well as further insight into the difficult job they were about to undertake. Of the eight mothers present, four participated actively in the discussion, the same four who were to go out on the block every day for the next eight weeks. The other four had really come along for a day in the country. They showed more interest in the afternoon session, led by Mr. Green who taught them recreational skills and such techniques as getting a group together, setting up games and using equipment constructively. It was possible to make clear to the four mothers interested in problems of behavior that behavior is purposive. They applied this knowledge to the problems of their own children, several of whom had come along, and there were opportunities to help the mothers understand behavior symptoms on that very day by handling them on the spot. While such experiences would have to be repeated over a period of time in order to have validity, it would seem as though experimentation of this approach should be encouraged. It ties in with an experiment by Dr. David M. Levy several years ago in which a worker lived in the home of a mother who was unable to handle her twins, in order to help her with the day-by-day problems rather than in the one-hour interview in the clinic.

Mr. Green kept statistical and recreational records while the mothers, particularly Mr. Smith, made notes about the behavior of some of the children.

The program began as planned; the street divided in three age groups with several sessions planned each week for making new equipment. The police cooperated by roping off one side of the block, and a sign bearing the name of the Block Organization was installed on the rope. After about two days, the block committee was running an effective program serving an average of fifty children a day, a total of 1200 for the next eight weeks.

The most difficult thing for the four mothers was to accept the fact that so many women, whose children enjoyed the playground, refused to help, even for a short time. This discouragement about the apathy of neighbors remained one of the more prominent problems in this and other blocks.

Illustration of Interracial Practice

A most helpful by-product was the fact that for the first time in the history of this block, Italian and Negro mothers worked together in the interests of all the children. It seems significant that of the four

mothers assisting Mr. Green daily, two were Negro and two Italian. They had lived in the same block for years, but until this time had never even greeted one another. While the term intercultural education has never been used, it would seem that in practice, common activities had been possible. It would be wrong to generalize from this example because only one block further down, the prejudice between Puerto Ricans and Italians seemed to be the only common interest, after a worker attempted to test for the possibility of an organization. Perhaps it would be safe to say that intercultural experiences in one block do not necessarily carry over into the next one.

The narrative of the development of this particular block organization could be continued to include the next project which had to do with housing violations, but perhaps enough material has been presented to give a picture of the function and method of this particular experiment and to emphasize some of the underlying principles. While only four blocks are organized at this time with different projects and different populations, it seems possible to reach some tentative conclusions about the experiment which is continuing into the future.

Some Tentative Values

Essentially the value of this experiment seems to lie in release of hostilities and frustrations which, when channelled and organized, can be directed toward modifying the environment. Both individual and group growth seemed possible with this method. There is ample evidence to substantiate the impression that Mrs. Smith has made a better adjustment within herself and toward her children. She gained in self-respect and in status in her own block. She is no longer the bedraggled-looking, hopeless relief recipient.Through release she has become able to free a considerable amount of energy. Her contributions in her own block meetings, recently broadcast on the radio, and in several community-wide affairs, show her to be a grass roots leader who, however, has not moved away from her original soil. She is at the present time taking several courses, and spending some of her spare time reading good books on mental hygiene.

This one case was chosen for presentation, but there is similar evidence of growth in varying degrees in the lives of other members of the block committee. In every block there are a number of members who show definite growth of leadership patterns. While the effect on the total population of each block cannot be as readily measured, it would seem that there have been some modifications of behavior. For example, one block which succeeded in getting nearly every apartment painted and repairs made after having checked 750 violations by using the city housing official's help, learned that attitudes toward neighbors are expressed in such simple things as not throwing garbage into dumb-waiters or areaways, and by showing more respect for the other fellow's life.

Although such developments are of small significance, it is conceivable that if growth is stimulated with the best methods known in diagnosis and therapy, and affecting a wide enough area, such experiments might have deeper reaching effects.

Before discussing some of the methods used, it is necessary to speak about the structure of the agency. A most significant difference from the orthodox agency setup is the fact that here the worker goes to the people to test their ability to use help and put their share into the common helping experience. This immediately puts a different emphasis on the role of the professional worker and makes it necessary for him to gain the respect of the client purely by his personality and his skills. He does not have the protection of the agency's setting with its well known limitations. He does not give direct services of any kind, but attempts to enable the client to develop his own potential by offering him specific projects after having established the need through a survey.

Essentially, this is using whatever available healthy ego structure there is and building from there by using the environmental pressures as a catalytic agent. The therapeutic values would lie both in the social action process and in the relationship between worker and client. This facilitates referral to considerable extent because of the completely voluntary character and the fact that no direct services are given. It is more nearly the relationship that the client has with an interested neighbor.

In the initial interview, both at home and in the office of the agency, case work principles are needed to help work through resistance and carry the client from the opening problem of the community into his own intrapersonal ones. At the same time, it is necessary for the worker in this setting to have group work skills since most of his time is spent in working through small natural or interest groups. Such problems as development of leadership of individuals within the sub-group without moving too far ahead of the larger group, the block, require, in addition, techniques that the field of community organization has taught us in the last years.

Since the experiment was of interest to the New York School of Social Work, the project was used as a training center with three mature students taking their field work in this project. With these students an attempt was made to develop some criteria for methods which might be of value to the field at large.

Some Criteria for Methods

As a result of a separate research project, the following tentative principles were drawn from the analysis of work in four blocks.

1. The issue or project around which each block is organized must be determined by a cross-section of people in the block itself and not be super-imposed by outside professional workers or social agencies.

2. Intake in this process has the same generic character as it does

in case work or group work. The worker tries to ascertain in his first visits the client's willingness to utilize the services of the agency.

3. The particular issue chosen by each block needs to be one that unites rather than divides them. Thus, although in some instances a campaign against gambling on a block would be worthwhile, it was found that in some blocks such a drive would divide rather than unite.

4. The issues around which the blocks are organized should be simple and represent in a sense the common denominator of interest of the majority. The goal should be realizable within a definite span of time.

5. Continued home visits to the members of the small committee and with them to the people in the block is one of the basic steps in this method. The techniques of home visits and interviews require the same sensitivity and skill as is necessary in any intensive treatment relationship.

6. Just as in group work, the program itself must not be in advance of the experience of the organization and the growth of individuals within it. Thus a worker can conceivably effect some environmental changes herself by using a few influential people in the community, but if the people in the block themselves do not grow and develop both as individuals and organizationally, such block achievement is of dubious value. It would result in getting things done for people, increasing dependency, and in that sense be contrary to the function of the project.

Because the material gathered must be evaluated at a later time, there is strong emphasis on recording, both professional and lay, and consequently two sets of records are kept: the staff record and the block record. The staff record, as in good group work, is concerned with movement of individuals and the leader's role in the group. The block record, written by each secretary of each separate block organization, may be compared to the minutes of a social club or group and deals only with program.

Negroes in Psychotherapy [1]

Harold Rosen, M.D., and Jerome D. Frank, M.D.

Until less than a decade ago, almost the only psychiatric treatment available to the Negro was through public clinics and state mental hospitals. This is no longer the case. Two trends are now making private psychiatric care progressively more available to Negroes. One is the increasing number of psychiatrists including, we are glad to note, Negroes. The other is the rapidly rising socio-economic level of the Negro and the crumbling of interracial barriers (1, 5). Even in a border State such as Maryland most private psychiatrists now treat Negroes, and all but one of the major private hospitals accept them on a non-segregated basis,[2] although 10 years ago none admitted Negroes. There has in addition been a concomitant expansion and improvement of state hospital and clinic care and a widening range of available forms of therapy, both group and individual. It therefore seems appropriate to study the relationship between white therapist and Negro patient, since this affects the course of therapy.

This relationship is determined by the personal characteristics of therapist and patient, and by the cultural attitudes of Negro and white towards each other. The therapist must be aware that such factors exist and be able to focus on them when it seems therapeutically indicated, but without being so concerned with them as to overlook more strictly personal issues.

Negroes, when seen in psychiatric consultation, present the same general personality and treatment problems (8) and fall into the same general diagnostic categories (9) as do whites of approximately the same class status (6). Similarities between white and Negro are greater

Reprinted from *American Journal of Psychiatry*, Vol. 119, No. 5, November 1962, pp. 456–460.

than differences (4). The latter are nevertheless present (14) and must be given serious consideration. Negroes have the adjustment problems of all underprivileged minority groups—we have seen almost identical phenomena in Irish, Italians, Poles, Jews (and even among "Georgia crackers" and so-called poor whites)—but in Negroes the problems are apt to be more intense and pervasive, because they wear with the color of their skin an undisguisable sign of their minority group status (3).

The present, rapidly changing status of the Negro is an additional source of stress. The 1954 Supreme Court decision (1, 2), with the pressures for de-segregation to which it has given rise, is making itself felt with increasing sharpness in political, economic, religious, educational, and cultural areas. The Negro is fighting to win recognition, in both Southern and border States, as a mature human being (3a). As, with the passage of time, his social, economic, and class status improves (5), special problems will be posed in the fields of individual and social psychiatry (3a).

Neither can be considered apart from the other, since there is an inter-reaction between the two. When our society becomes healthier in this respect and, so we hope, no longer emotionally traumatizes the Negro in his formative years, the reactive guilt of the white—and what this means to him emotionally—will disappear. But at present the paranoid insecurity and guilt not only of the bigot but even of those without conscious race prejudice may at times be intensified as the problem, during the course of its ultimate solution and dis-solution, at first comes into sharper and sharper focus.

Few of us are entirely free from race prejudice; with some, this is overt; with others it may be below the level of conscious awareness. It may express itself in overt activity; it may—more happily—never be allowed such expression.

Certain aspects of the problem become highlighted in the psychotherapeutic relationship. The white therapist, vis à vis his Negro patient, need seldom contend with *conscious* prejudice in himself, because if this were present he would not have accepted the patient for treatment. He must, however, be alert to the possibility of *unconscious* prejudice. This may manifest itself either directly or through reaction formation. He may, for example, subtly reject Negro patients so that they stop coming to see him. Or conversely, especially if he is a member of a minority group himself, he may over-identify with them and lean over backwards by, for example, scheduling certain patients for extensive or intensive treatment when neither is indicated.

The more pronounced the unconscious insecurties and guilt of the white psychotherapist in this area are, the more ineffective his treatment contact with these patients must necessarily be. As his own guilt begins to disappear, he will find himself able to treat Negro patients more effectively instead of, unwittingly and for personality reasons of his own, traumatizing them still further.

The Negro, as a member of a minority group, inevitably brings certain attitudes into treatment; three—resentful anxiety, distrust, and "self-hatred"—require comment. Resentment and anxiety are produced by past experiences of discrimination.[3] Negroes never know how they will be received by whites in new situations. Almost all have suffered unexpected humiliating rebuffs. Moreover, at least in many Southern and border States, they are even now still denied equal protection of the law and as a result not infrequently undergo genuinely threatening experiences. One colored physician, for instance, while driving with a light-skinned companion in a Southern State, was arrested and threatened with jail because his companion's protestations that she was colored were disbelieved. There were veiled hints that, if this girl would permit sexual advances by the officer, the charge would be dropped. If freedom from fear is desirable for any citizen, as Tomkins has stated, it must be desirable for all citizens (6a).

Because of experiences like this, Negroes characteristically develop distrust of all whites (the second of the three attitudes so frequently seen during treatment), and unwillingness to reveal weakness to them. This, incidentally, is a greater obstacle in group than in individual therapy (12). The Negro's distrust of white patients in a therapy group is greater than his distrust of the white psychotherapist whose professional status tends to counteract this attitude.

The third commonly found culturally induced attitude, "self-hatred," has been noted in all underprivileged minority groups. Whiteness represents full personal dignity with complete participation in American society. The Negro, therefore, who is most nearly white in appearance, class, and educational status, and attitude has tended to be embarrassed by and to look down upon Negroes who more closely resemble the white stereotype of the Negro (15), while the Negro who is more closely identified with his group resents the attitudes of the more "assimilated" Negro, and at the same time may secretly envy him. Such attitudes connected with "self-hatred" are particularly difficult to reveal in the presence of whites, but eventually do appear if therapy is sufficiently prolonged.

These points may be illustrated by an example from a mixed white and Negro psychotherapy group. Such groups present particular problems for therapy arising out of these culturally induced attitudes; they also throw such attitudes into relief. This example highlights the protective reticence of Negroes in the presence of whites, contains a hint of the "self-hatred" phenomenon, and indicates this distrust of whites. This experience occurred in a border state (Maryland) where such attitudes are prominent.

Through an unusual concatenation of circumstances a mixed group, ordinarily conducted by a white therapist, had one meeting in which two members only were present, both Negroes; this time the therapist, likewise, was a Negro. One of the patients, Mrs. B., a school-

teacher, explained, "It will be much easier to talk since we are all the same," and then discussed what she felt to be her husband's irresponsibility, something which she could not bring up when whites were present because, in her opinion, this coincided with the whites' stereotype of the Negro male. Later she mentioned her annoyance, which she had never previously expressed in the group, because Mrs. G., a colored housewife of clearly inferior social and educational status, at an earlier meeting had said something critical about schoolteachers. These reciprocal attitudes, manifested by Mrs. G. and Mrs. B., could be interpreted as representing an example of "self-hatred" expressed in an oblique way. At the end of the meeting she told of her inability to trust a certain white social worker because, although this worker was friendly to Mrs. B., she had made remarks which Mrs. B. interpreted as uncomplimentary to Negroes in general. The therapist felt that Mrs. B. was referring also to the therapy group situation but this did not become explicit, nor did it seem at this particular time as though it should be raised for therapeutic discussion.

Racial discrimination may contribute to the psychopathology of the individual Negro patient in a variety of ways. Specific incidents occasionally serve as precipitating factors in the onset of severe neurotic or psychotic symptoms. Racist discrimination may help determine the content of grandiose or persecutory delusions (7). It may serve as a chronic precipitant for repetitious anixety-producing situations which, over a lifetime, predispose the individual concerned to see racial (or religious) discrimination where none exists. It may channelize the antisocial behavior of individuals with severe personality disorders and so-called character neuroses (11). Some may use it as an alibi for their own inadequacies. By making it possible for exploited individuals to vent aggresion against members of their own or other minority (or majority) groups, it may constitute a defense against the onset of neurotic or even psychotic symptomatology. In any case, patients concerned continue to be chronically psychogenically traumatized. So, frequently, are all with whom they come in contact.

Some specific implications of these points for the psychotherapeutic relationship may now be considered. First, the distrust which the Negro often brings to the white therapist may manifest itself in obscure ways which lead either therapist or patient to misinterpret what is going on. For example, patients without motivation for treatment are told they must learn how to live with their symptoms. If the patient be a Negro, he may attribute this to anti-Negro prejudice in the psychiatrist. This poses special problems for the therapist. Leaning over backwards and scheduling such patients for treatment is not only a waste of what otherwise could be productive psychiatric time, but is as much evidence of underlying race prejudice as refusal to accept Negro patients.

Similarly, the Negro for whom psychiatric hospitalization seems advisable, or members of his family, may feel that if he were white he would be accepted for treatment on an office basis. Four of our private

patients, for instance, were convinced that the recommendation for hospitalization was a thinly disguised means of rejecting them. If the white psychiatrist does not realize this and take the time to correct it, the recommendation for hospitalization may not be accepted.

If the patient accepts hospitalization, he may find that since no private psychiatric beds at the time are available he must be placed on a waiting list. This situation arises even in the total absence of discriminatory policies, but the Negro will almost certainly interpret it as race prejudice on the part of the referring psychiatrist or hospital administration. This, therefore, also must be discussed during the consultation sessions.

Membership in a minority group tends to lead to certain habitual ways of relating initially to a member of the majority group. The white therapist who sees Negro patients needs to be aware of these. Such patients are still apt to show either sullen reserve, or loquacious and obsequious over-affability. If the therapist permits himself to be antagonized by the former, or to be deceived into accepting the latter as expressing his patient's actual feelings, the development of a good psychotherapeutic relationship will be handicapped. Furthermore, many Negroes, especially of lower class status, tend to defend themselves against anticipated demands from the white by assuming an exaggerated air of indifference and stupidity.[4] The white psychiatrist may be misled by this into making an unwarranted diagnosis of mental deficiency or even of simple schizophrenia; yet the same patient may show normal responsiveness and intelligence when interviewed by a colored psychiatrist.[5]

The Negro's position as a member of a minority group subjects him to experiences which differ from those of the white of corresponding socio-economic status, and the therapist must evaluate the patient's history with this in mind. Intermittent school attendance or frequent change of job may indicate not emotional instability but the effort to survive. Nor need a jail sentence have the same implications for a Negro as for a white patient (14). Freedom from psychopathic traits and a high degree of morality do not necessarily protect the Negro from arrest on suspicion in many communities.

Traumatic experiences which the Negro patient has suffered, as a direct or indirect result of discrimination, may become intertwined with his personal neurotic difficulties. Various authorities comment on the frequency in the matriarchal home, so characteristic of the American Negro, of a harsh and unstable father (13); others stress the large number of broken homes among their patients, the death of one or both parents, the desertion of the father, and the strong emotional attachment to a frustrated and insecure mother (4).

The discrimination and segregation which the patient suffers from a rejecting, frustrating social order, frequently revivifies emotions experienced during infancy and early childhood. Both aspects of the problem must be worked through with some patients if even symptomatic relief is to be obtained.

While an understanding discussion of problems of prejudice may be of therapeutic value, this can readily be utilized, by therapist as well as by patient, for armchair philosophizing which prevents a good treatment relationship from developing. Unless he is aware of his own underlying problems in this area, the psychiatrist may use such a discussion, while apparently treating his patient, in actuality to reject him.

Although the psychiatrist can do little to change the real situation, he can discuss its emotional concomitants and how these bear on the patient's present emotional maladjustment. If treatment is to be successful, no such discussion, however, can remain on an intellectual basis.

This can be illustrated with the sharpness of caricature by a consideration of patients under psychiatric treatment on hypnotic levels. If the problem of race prejudice comes up during early sessions, especially during the first two or three, race-consciousness may be expressed in the patient's resentment against the white man as such, and especially against his therapist. This may take the form, if the therapist be Jewish, of anti-Semitic remarks (10). If it occurs later during treatment, the patient almost invariably ties it up with childhood experiences toward an authority figure.

A normal school student while being hypnotized, felt what she characterized as an irresistible urge to punch one of us (H.R.) in the jaw. She tried to keep from doing so. As her fist shot out, barely missing his face (which he had inclined somewhat to the side), she was regressed by direct hypnotic suggestion to that other time when, so she was told, she had felt exactly the same way. She immediately became a 5-year old, had just swallowed the food which her father was forcing down her throat, and wanted to kill him (10). This was handled in the same way as it would have been with a white patient.

In conclusion, two points may be stressed:

1. Most Negro patients whom we have seen in psychiatric consultation, evaluation or treatment are, as a result of the experiences to which they were subjected because of the color of their skin, both race-conscious and resentful of the imperfections of our democracy. If therapy be attempted, whether privately or in a clinic, these feelings must be brought out into the open and collaboratively discussed. The blind spots of the therapist are of prime importance in determining the outcome of such discussions.

2. The patient is applying for psychiatric treatment. He has symptoms that are incapacitating or invaliding him. It is treatment for these —and not an intellectual discussion of race prejudice—that he needs. The personal problems of each patient are unique regardless of the color of his skin, and each must be treated as an individual.

If the white therapist bears these points in mind, his Negro patients, both private and clinic, whether individually or in groups, can and do make gratifying, very steady progress.

Notes

1. Based on a preliminary report presented December 28, 1956, to the fourth annual congress, the Inter-American Society of Psychology, University of Puerto Rico (San Juan, Puerto Rico).
2. The State Hospital System does not. Negroes requiring psychiatric hospitalization are admitted to the Crownsville State Hospital; while white patients go to the other State Hospitals.
3. There, for instance, have been over 3700 arrests since February 1, 1960, when 4 first-year students at an all-Negro college in Greensboro, North Carolina, started the sit-in by refusing to leave a segregated lunch counter which had denied them service, but remained seated reading their Bibles and studying their texts. On the bright side, over 5000 eating facilities have now desegregated as a result of sit-ins, "Freedom Rides," *etc.*, since. In the past year-and-a-half such demonstrations in the Washington suburban area have attracted large numbers, including five U.S. Congressmen. The psychiatric implications of this are discussed in detail in a very thought-provoking article by Fishman and Solomon (3a).
4. This seems to be in a process of change. During the past year-and-a-half, these attitudes have been rejected, at least in our clinical experience, by patients seen *privately* in consultation or for brief, goal-limited psychotherapy, who were under 23 years of age.
5. We are indebted to the late Dr. Ethel Nixon for demonstrating this point to us with several psychiatric clinic patients.

Bibliography

1. Ashmore, H. S.: Epitaph for Dixie. New York: W. W. Norton, 1958.
2. Blaustein, A. P., and Ferguson, C. L., Jr.: Desegregation and the Law. Rutgers Univ. Press, 1957.
3. Dollard, J.: Caste and Class in a Southern Town. Yale Univ. Press, 1937.
3a. Fishman, J. R., and Solomon, F.: Psychological Observations on the Student Sit-In Movement. Read at the Third World Congress of Psychiatry, Montreal, Canada, June 8, 1961.
4. Frank, J. D.: (a) J. Nerv. Ment. Dis., 105:647, 1947; (b) Am. J. Psychiat., 103:97, 1946.
5. Frazier, E. F.: Black Bourgeoisie—The Rise of a New Middle Class in the United States. Glencoe, Ill.: Free Press, 1957.
6. Hollingshead, A. B., and Redlich, F. C.: Am. J. Psychiat., 110:695, 1954.
6a. Karon, B. P.: The Negro Personality. New York: Springer, 1958.

7. Myers, H. J., and Yochelson, L.: Psychiatry, 11:39, 1948.
8. Prudhomme, C.: Psychoanal. Rev., 25:187, 372, 1938.
9. Ripley, H. S., and Wolf, S.: Am. J. Psychiat., 103:499, 1947.
10. Rosen, H.: The Hypnotherapy of a Patient with a Sudden Incapacitating Stutter. *In* Hypnotherapy in Clinical Psychiatry. New York: Julian Press, 1953.
11. ———, and Kiene, H. F.: (a) Am. J. Psychiat., 103:614, 1947; (b) J. Nerv. Ment. Dis., 103:291, 1949.
12. Sommers, V. S.: Int. Group Psychother., 3:254, 1953.
13. St. Clair, H. R.: Am. J. Psychiat., 108:113, 1951.
14. Stevens, R. B.: Am. J. Psychiat., 103:493, 1947.
15. Warner, W. L., Junker, B. H., and Adam, W. A.: Am. Council on Ed., Wash., D.C., 7:301, 1941.

Youth and Social Action: Perspectives on the Student Sit-In Movement

Jacob R. Fishman, M.D., and Fredric Solomon, M.D.

This is the initial report of a study of the psychodynamics of adolescent and student participation in public, risk-taking activities for racial desegregation. The major participants in this movement have been Negro and white college students in the Southern United States. Their most dramatic and perhaps most effective weapon has been a form of public passive resistance known as the sit-in demonstration. Indeed, the whole movement has come to be known as the student sit-in movement, and the term has quickly become part of our contemporary culture.[1]

The original targets of these demonstrations were variety stores, which customarily welcome Negro patrons in most departments but exclude them from service at lunch counters. The first student sit-in took place on February 1, 1960, when four freshmen at an all-Negro college in Greensboro, North Carolina, deliberately decided to request service at such a segregated lunch counter. (18) When service was denied them because of their color, they refused to leave; instead they remained seated, reading schoolbooks and Bibles. Since that time demonstrations have spread through many parts of the country where such policies are in effect and have been aimed at all kinds of segregated public facilities.

There are several possible results from a sit-in. At one extreme, the segregation policy may be promptly ended and the students served. At the other, the demonstrators may be heckled and assaulted, or arrested, jailed, and charged with trespassing or disorderly conduct. Whatever

Reprinted from *American Journal of Orthopsychiatry*, Vol. 33, No. 5, October 1963, pp. 872–882. Copyright, The American Orthopsychiatric Association, Inc. Reproduced by permission.

the outcome, the pattern of social crisis is always the same: The students aggressively cross the color line, and then passively allow the consequences to rest on the co-operation of other like-minded people and on the decisions of civic authorities and businessmen in the dominant white majority. In the space of three years the South has witnessed thousands of demonstrations, which have also included boycotts, picketing, mass marches, hunger strikes of jailed students and the "freedom rides" on interstate buses. As of April, 1961 (before the freedom rides), demonstrators had numbered in the tens of thousands and had been active in some 75 Southern towns and cities. Three thousand five hundred demonstrators had been arrested; of these, an estimated 95 per cent were young people of both sexes in their teens or early twenties, both Negro and white.[2]

These demonstrations have resulted in the desegregation of more than 5,000 eating facilities, as well as hundreds of libraries, places of recreation and churches. The local, national and international news media have provided wide coverage, and the impact has been felt on campuses all over the country. For the Southern United States, this has represented a rate of social change far more rapid than any it has known since the Negro people were emancipated from slavery nearly 100 years ago. (6, 17, 21) In view of the social significance of this student movement, an understanding of the psychodynamic background and motivation of these young people should illuminate some of the relationships among personality, society and social change.

During the past two years we have studied the development of this movement, particularly in the Washington, D.C., area. The present paper represents our tentative psychosocial formulations of some motivational and personality factors in these students. Further data collection and analysis is under way. (5, 18–20) This report focuses mainly on young Negroes, whereas future papers will deal more extensively with the white student demonstrators, as well as with opponents and supporters in surrounding communities. Reports have already been presented on the very first of the organized sit-in demonstrations (18) and on the dynamics of nonviolent action. (20)

Picketing demonstrations in the Washington area have on occasion attracted as many as 200 participants, including, at one point in the summer of 1960, five United States Congressmen. However, the decision-making core of regular demonstrators consisted of about 40 students, calling themselves "NAG," "Nonviolent Action Group." They felt this name exemplified the group's determination to "nag the conscience of the community." (It also symbolizes the recurrent theme of a passive-aggressive, persevering style of action.) White and Negro students, both male and female, were about evenly represented in the group. The average age was 18 years and six months, most members having completed one year in college, with little or no comparable prior experience with interracial organizations. In its first year of activity, the group succeeded in desegregating about 25 facilities, including restaurants, lunch counters, a movie theatre and the area's only amusement

park. In addition, they were an important factor in stimulating the development of a council on human relations in suburban Montgomery County. During the course of these activities, about 100 arrests of demonstrators were made by local authorities. Several members of the original group later went on to become involved in freedom rides and other risk-taking actions for desegregation in the Deep South. (20)

Seventeen students (7 Negroes and 10 whites) in the Washington group were interviewed both individually and in groups. Three others (2 young Negro men who were major leaders, and one young white woman) were interviewed individually in some depth over a period of six months. Of primary interest in the interviews were those factors leading up to a student's decision to involve himself in a public, risk-taking activity for desegregation; a second focus was on family background and parental reactions to the student's participation. The demonstrators readily volunteered to discuss these and related matters, and two of the young Negro leaders have continued to maintain close contact with us. (20) In addition to interviews, direct observations were made of demonstrations and other group activities, and public reaction was followed through the extensive coverage of the local news media.

Emergence of a New Social Character

One of the 19-year-old Negro students recalled his reaction, which was typical, when he read the newspaper report of the very first organized sit-in in Greensboro, North Carolina. He and his friends at Howard University "all rejoiced, and we all felt the opportunity was here; and the fact that college students were doing it is one of the powerful reasons for participating ourselves . . . but more than anything . . . we all realized we had been *wanting to do something* and now was the time." Many of these students remembered that they first began "wanting to do something" in 1954 when they first heard about the Supreme Court decision for school desegregation; the student quoted above was 13 years old at that time, as were most of the young demonstrators in this study.

Thus it was at the threshold of their adolescence that the United States Supreme Court ruled unanimously that the segregated schools these youngsters had been attending were illegal. The Court had decided that systems of separate schools for Negroes and whites were inherently unequal because they generated in Negro students "a feeling of inferiority as to their status in the community that may affect their hearts and minds in a way unlikely ever to be undone." A unique and significant precedent was set in the use of statements of psychologists and social scientists to support this ruling.

This Supreme Court decision immediately received widespread publicity, discussion, denunciation and praise. It was apparent from talking to all of our Negro subjects that its message had been deeply imprinted on their minds and outlook. This public and legal recognition of the

desirability of desegregation and its possible achievement in the near future was an experience in the adolescent development of these young people quite different from that of their parents and older siblings. They felt that the older generation had come to accept segregation and social inferiority as the natural order of things. They were aware of the Southern tradition that, when dealing with white people, one should present the appearance of a contented subordinate. However, feeling that desegregation was now their right, these students experienced increasing frustration with its painfully slow implementation and with the seeming hypocrisy of adults who paid lip service to principles but took no risks for implementation. Such feelings were intensified by the contrast of their own situation with that of many African peoples who were aggressively achieving independence and total public recognition as adults in the family of nations.

Many observers have pointed out that the psychosocial history of the Southern Negro has been largely characterized by his need to suppress and displace elsewhere his feelings of hostility toward the dominant whites. (1, 15, 16) Similarly he has had to suppress and displace any motivation to compete in economic and social spheres. He has been forced to assume a manifest role of passivity and submission, a role which has its social roots in economic and legal dependency on the white majority as well as in fear of punitive retaliation for overstepping color boundaries. These characteristics are expressed and further reinforced through the incorporation by the Negro of certain aspects of Christianity—especially the child-like trust in God, acceptance of one's lot in life, turning the other cheek and a belief in a happy afterlife coming to those good Christians who suffer and endure. (15)

Outbreaks of this bottled-up aggression in the South through crimes directed against whites have been dealt with traditionally in an extraordinarily harsh manner, for example, lynchings. Crimes within the Negro community, however, have received greater toleration from the white authorities, who viewed them as the behavior of irresponsible children who could be taught no better. The inhibited anger against the whites commonly has been turned on the self and displaced into the greatly disguised, stereotyped patterns of laziness, apathy, passivity and unreliability. The hostile roots of such behavior have been so well masked and denied by the defensive operations of both racial groups that, until very recently, the prevalent Southern white's view of the Negro was that of a rather irresponsible but essentially contented child. The Negro's needs were thought to be amply taken care of by a paternal system of social relationships modeled on the traditions of slavery. It comes as a real shock to many Southerners to see a discontented Negro forcefully displaying his discontent in a public, vocal manner. This confrontation is very threatening to some white Southerners, as shown in some of their violent reactions to sit-ins.

The Negro student in the sit-in movement proves he is neither child-like nor contented. The protests are neither indirect nor patient, as tends to be the behavior of the older generation. At the same time they

express publicly the frustration and resentment that has been so long hidden. Through the force of the moral and democratic principles they invoke to justify their action, they channel aggression into a positive identification with the traditional ego-ideal of the white majority, as well as with that of the world community. Using the terms of Erich Fromm, we may describe this as the emergence of a new social character for the Southern Negro. (8) One prominent white Southern politician has remarked, "These kids seem to be completely new Negroes, the likes of which we've never seen before." This new social character has emerged from the psychological reaction of adolescent members of a social group to changed external realities. It is built upon certain long-standing personality and cultural traits shared by the group's members, as well as the changing events, ideas, and circumstances around them.

Identity Formation and "Prosocial Acting Out"

Along with these factors of changing social history and new social character, an additional perspective is necessary to understand the student sit-in movement. One must take into account certain features of the developmental and group psychology of late adolescence—with special emphasis on interrelationships between action and identity formation. As Erik Erikson has intimated, the unique needs and strengths of late adolescence frequently focus on the social and intellectual crises of the era, translating issues into the ideology and action of the youth movement. Thus ideology and social action may have a fundamental role in the development of identity in adolescents.

We have already remarked the childlike nature of the Negro stereotype in the eyes of the white Southerners (vividly symbolized in the custom of hailing any adult Negro male as "Boy," instead of "Mister" or "Sir"). Until recently the Negro could either accept that role, or move to the North. In the South he has been largely denied the opportunity to express normal aggressive and masculine strivings through dignified and respected occupations in the general society and in competition with the white male. Under these conditions the Negro male is degraded and depreciated and cannot serve as an adequate ego ideal or model for identification for his children. (12)

The young Negro demonstrators are acutely aware of the lack of adult identity that has characterized their fathers in the South. Both the conscious and unconscious strivings for potent male identification became very apparent in talking to them. In 1955, Rev. Martin Luther King led the entire Negro community of Montgomery, Alabama, in a boycott of the city's transit buses; after one year's struggle, the buses were desegregated. (13) This occurred when many of the students were only 15, two years after the Supreme Court had told them that their anger against segregation was justified and sanctioned. Young people

all over the South were vastly impressed with the Montgomery boycott. They felt it was a lesson in the practical and emotional "advantages of direct action" in expressing legitimate Negro discontent.[3] King became the image of an assertive Negro male assuming freedom of action with dignity, and achieving respectful recognition through successful struggle with the white community (that is, male community). In a sense he became the figure the Negro adolescent wished his father might have been, and as such he was incorporated as part of the ego-ideal. Three years later, soon after leaving home for college, Negroes were acting on the dictates of this identification model through the sit-in. Thus, for the late adolescent in the vanguard of the sit-in movement, the search for recognition as an adult that so characterizes his age group has been intimately interwoven with the struggle of Southern Negroes as a social group for recognition as mature human beings. For the 19-year-old student, then, the creation of a new social character for his people has become identical with the development of his own personality as a young adult.

As part of their struggles to achieve emancipation and identity, many of the Negro students seem to display significant ego-syntonic processes that suggest an acting out through the sit-ins of early childhood frustrations and parental conflicts and wishes. Although the concept of acting out has been used primarily in connection with certain forms of anti-social behavior (10) and problems of psychotherapy, (9) data in the current study suggest a more general role for acting out in character and identity formation. (5, 18) This is illustrated in the following description of B., a seemingly typical, poor, ambitious 19-year-old male Negro college freshman from the Deep South who became a leader of the Washington group of demonstrators. The data and formulations are based on a six-month series of research interviews and subsequent follow-up.

B. was brought up in a matriarchal family in which his step-father was absent most of the time, or jobless and degraded when home. His real father had left when he was still an infant. He is the oldest of eight brothers and sisters. His mother worked as a domestic for a white Southern family. He grew up feeling contemptuous and resentful of his father, but guilty about this resentment and perhaps responsible for the father's failures and absences. B. has ambivalent feelings toward his mother whom he fantasies really loved him most, but was forced to give prime attention to his younger siblings as well as the white family that employed her. He wore the white family's cast-off clothing. His mother was quite harsh with him if ever he expressed resentment about their status or about white people. She told him that they must know their place, and it would do no good to antagonize the whites. She feared losing the meager job which was their only source of income. He associates the lives of his parents with submission to the white community, and displaces onto this social submission much of the resentment, frustration and deprivation he experienced within his family. At the same time he recognizes his parents' passive-aggressive

ambivalence to the whites and the different levels of meaning in his mother's prohibitions against open hostility. This perception helps him develop an idealized image of his parents in which they are really eager for and capable of self-assertion (which would mean more love, attention and recognition for him); but their self-assertion is blocked by circumstance or fear.

B.'s decision to participate in a sit-in demonstration was at first quite impulsive, with a great deal of subsequent rationalization. His personal involvement and dedication have been intense, and actions result in much discharge of affect, as anger and depression are transformed into elation. This discharge of affect is related not only to the stimuli of immediate circumstances but also to symbolic mastery of childhood frustrations. Thus, on the one hand, he acts out his long-standing resentment of his parents derived from his repeated experiences of deprivation and displacement as a youngster, which he now sees as a consequence of his parents' social role. On the other hand, when he takes risks and tests the retaliatory dangers of which he has been warned by his family, he may threaten his mother, but he also wins her secret approval. He thereby enhances his self-esteem as an autonomous, masculine adult. He has acted out his family's suppressed resentment of the social system in a dignified and passive-aggressive manner and has responded to his mother's fantasied need for a socially potent male. (It is of interest that, in follow-up interviews two years later, he reports that his whole family has "come around" to open support of his activities.) It can be inferred that for some adolescents acting out has an important role in identity formation and progressive development of ego functions.

In an historical context, B. feels "caught between Uncle Tom and Jim Crow." Uncle Tom represents the internalized ambivalence of his parents in telling him he must be passive. Jim Crow represents the traditional pattern of segregation and sanctions applied by the whites, which also thwarts his aggressive strivings. He is able successfully to act out unconscious parental hostility to the whites that they themselves have been unable to express overtly. Consciously he has an idealized image of what his parents "really" feel or ought to feel about what is right. He also perceives that he is acting according to the dictates of the conscience of the total community and that he is doing what others fear, hesitate or are "too hypocritical" to do.[4] This perception of the super-ego or conscience of the community and of his parents allows him to rationalize his rebellion against his own family thereby decreasing guilt and anxiety. He feels he is doing what his parents (and the nation) really want him to do but they are afraid to say so openly. We have found similar dynamics in all but two of the young white demonstrators as well. One after another they reported that their parents were both definitely against racial segregation and definitely against doing anything about it. Some were consciously aware of the mixture of anxiety and pride their parents felt about their activities. As it were, they are acting out the conscience of the community.

The acting out of suppressed parental wishes and problems of deprivation, frustration, and moral ambiguity has been frequently reported in the psychodynamics underlying adolescent delinquency and antisocial behavior. (10) However, the acting out we have observed here is consciously based on moral imperatives, that is, on the perceived super-ego or conscience of the community, which becomes incorporated into the individual and group functional self-image. Since this perception began in childhood and, as we have shown, was dramatically reinforced during early adolescence, it becomes part of the ego-ideal; action based on its dictates becomes an important source of self-esteem. Therefore, we suggest the term "prosocial" acting out to describe this behavior. (5) This distinction is important. Delinquent acting out is described as antisocial precisely because of its opposition to the morality of the community. Acting out occurs through the delinquent's rebellion against severe super-ego dictates or in the framework of defective super-ego development (for example, "lacunae"). (10) In prosocial acting out, however, the ego-ideal and resultant functional self-image are much more in accord with the dictates of the community morality and conscience. Those involved in the latter require some level of social or moral approval, and their goals are rationalized in the direction of social welfare. This allows a gratifying and self-enhancing resolution of emotional conflict and social identity formation. They feel they are "doing society's work for it." The answers to the typical adolescent questions of autonomy, time perspective, work and ideals (2) are vastly different in these two forms of behavior. However, the dynamics seem to have many similarities. It may be that a more detailed understanding of the differing determinants of these two adolescent pathways would have significant implications for the social health of a community, as well as for a new approach to the prevention and treatment of delinquency.

One aspect of the group dynamics of acting out is worthy of note here. Through the conversion of their own anger into a seemingly passive and pious stance these students threaten the bigoted and volatile defenses of the white extremists. In so doing, the demonstrators accomplish a remarkable psychosocial feat, much to their advantage. The white extremists are provoked by the young Negroes to act out for them the very anger and resentment that they (the Negroes) have themselves felt. However, the anger and violence have now been externalized and projected onto the "aggressor," so that the students feel guiltless and even exhilarated in their justifiable indignation. It also helps win the sympathy of the observing public and reduces the fears of whites that Negroes intend to retaliate violently for past suppression. (13) This is probably a prominent feature of the dynamics of nonviolent action as a political weapon.

It is extremely important for these young students to be able to express publicly and directly their discontent and indignation against restriction, dependency, and inequity. It allows them to identify their aggressive strivings for independence and recognition, which are intrinsic to the adolescent phase of development, with their desperate

need for social emancipation and equality. These demonstrations are certainly aggressive. However, the dignified, well-disciplined, nonviolent style of the student action is calculated to be an effective propaganda weapon that will encourage the more moderate white southerners to accept some measure of desegregation, as well as win the sympathy and support of news media and public in other parts of the country. The students are also keenly aware of the attention they receive in news media in other parts of the world; they are surprisingly sophisticated in their political and social awareness. Although they are preoccupied with the task at hand, they readily identify with students and movements for recognition and emancipation in other parts of a total world community.

Ideology and Identity

The use of nonviolent resistance means that the students will picket, sit-in, ride buses and use facilities that are segregated, but they will not resist when heckled, attacked or arrested. It is consciously conceived of by many as a pragmatic political weapon applicable to the problem of segregation, and is consistent with Christian religious training. Although Biblical and Christian teachings and the traditions of Ghandi and civil disobedience are incorporated into their ideology as formulated by Martin Luther King, (13) these students are generally not pacifists. This is exemplified in the remarks of B., who was very much committed and dedicated to the principles of nonviolence in the sit-in. Soon after quoting from the Scriptures and Ghandi in support of nonviolence, he went on to talk with pride of his own personal ambitions to be a jet pilot in the U.S. Air Force.

At the same time, the philosophy of nonviolence is consistent with the long tradition of minimizing offense to the white community. It is a natural outgrowth of the traditional passive and submissive role in the face of white domination and potential retaliation. The internal prohibition against hostility to the whites is deep-seated; this hostility is more readily expressed by first being transformed into love for those who hate you. This process reduces guilt and anxiety and makes easier the students' departure from parental stereotypes; yet at the same time it allows them to identify with the parental religious ego-ideal. The ideology helps the adolescent maintain super-ego control over angry impulses while simultaneously internalizing an ego-ideal of love and respect for all human beings including the enemy, which in turn enhances the sense of identity and self-esteem. This illustrates the connection of ideology and identity formation for many adolescents. (3)

In one sense, then, the sit-in can be described as a passive-aggressive act. For a few it provides the arena for masochism and martyrdom. For all it is a demand to be seen, heard, and recognized. As is usual with adolescent movements, it is never anonymous. Names are freely given

and no one hides his face when pictures are taken. However, one should not underestimate the intensity of the aggression and hostility being channeled here, especially in the Negro students. We did not need to probe very deeply to find resentment and hostility built on layers of social and personal frustration in the demonstrators we interviewed. The aggression is manifest in the very circumstance that they are coercing people to accept or react to the accomplished fact of sitting-in at a segregated establishment, as well as in the evident satisfaction at stirring social turmoil by what seems to be such a small, quiet initial action; moreover, this is done frequently in areas where the violent and explosive potential of white segregationists is well known.

In our interviews with them, all these students, both Negro and white, saw its high moral purpose as a major feature of their activity. Desegregation and the philosophy of nonviolent resistance are seen primarily as moral rather than political principles. (20) As Erikson has pointed out in describing the process of ideology formation in adolescents, (3) these students take literally the moral commitment of the community and, denouncing what are perceived to be the hypocrisies of the current social and political situation, demand a substantial change. Here the goals of conscience of the students represent not only the traditional Christian morality of the nation but also the well-known and basic American social and political principles of equal rights and freedom of choice. Thus the Negro sit-in youth thinks of. himself as more Christian than the white community in the South. He also thinks of himself as more in accord with the highest principles of American democracy than the white hecklers on the sidelines. He derives considerable ego support from thus identifying with the ideals of the white majority and a great feeling of compensatory gratification from the experience of superior moral dedication. This helps him offset traditional feelings of racial inferiority that have been so long a part of the Southern milieu.

Although the ideology is highly moral, this is by no means an intellectual movement. There is a heavy orientation to action and work, even to the point of impatience with prolonged intellectual discussion. During the organization of the first sit-in in the Washington area, the original students, in recruiting others in their dormitory to join them, used as their rallying cry, "There's work to be done." Again and again there was an emphasis on getting down to the work at hand, the picketing or sitting-in, with a minimum of fuss or preliminary discussion. A great deal of gratification was derived from their sense of dedicated work, and it undoubtedly has an important function in the formation of individual and group identity. (2) However, it also illustrates the impulsive urge to immediate action so characteristic of adolescent time perspective and so different from that of the older generation. This sense of immediacy is exemplified in the students' frustration with "plenty of ideals but no action." Such an action orientation leads to considerable risk taking. Since deciding to take a risk is done by an individual student quite on his own (albeit with group support), such a decision helps to

develop a feeling of autonomy, as well as proving bravery and the willingness to endure suffering on behalf of one's principles. (4) The mutual experience of action, risk taking, and injury does a great deal to solidify the feelings of unity and identity of the group and to assure individual loyalties. Thus the sit-in groups derive great strength from their experiences in jail or in the midst of hostile crowds.

The assertion of freedom of choice in one's own behavior is interestingly parallel to the emphasis on freedom of choice in the principle of desegregation. For example, an 18-year-old white girl with a mixed group being arrested at a suburban bowling alley asked simply, "If these are my friends and I want to bowl with them, why should we be arrested?" For this girl, the need for freedom of choice and action so typical of the adolescent has become identical with the strivings of Negroes in the community at large.

It seems that an element of renunciation of former dependency gratifications is almost always present in the process of growing up. As they approach maturity, social groups as well as individuals must lose some of the security of their former social and economic relationships. A young person feels most free or independent only after having done something active and aggressive to win that independence. In this context, perhaps an "independent" identity can never be freely given—it must be at least partially *taken* by adolescents and, possibly, by young nations as well.

In summary, we would emphasize that one can find in the student sit-in movement patterns of adolescent identity strivings similar to those in many other adolescent groups. These young people, however, are caught on a wave of psychosocial transition and upheaval. For the Negroes, inferiority, submission, and deprivation are their childhood experience; passive-aggressive resolutions their heritage; Christianity their moral background; the Supreme Court decision and the coming of age of new African nations part of the tempo of change. Through these influences are filtered the typical internal pressures and new ego capacities of early and late adolescence. Public action for social goals is their way of at least temporarily resolving issues of identity formation, conscience, and aggression. They see themselves as prodders of the national conscience, and derive satisfaction and self-esteem from this role. As a result, they have been forced into synthesizing a new social character with its new problems and anxieties, with its risks and violence, but also with a vitality and optimism for a future that they feel they have had a hand in shaping.

Recent student activities in this and other countries suggest that the motivation and psychodynamics of student involvement in political and social action represents an important area of study. (14, 19, 22) Such studies may help in understanding the effects of social change and crises on personality and identity formation, as well as the converse effects of adolescent striving for recognition and identity on social and political change.

Notes

1. Merriam-Webster Dictionary (unabridged), 1962.
2. Statistics provided by the Congress of Racial Equality, New York, N.Y.
3. It is interesting to note reports that indicate a sharp decline in the incidence of crime among the Negro population of Montgomery, Alabama, during the year of the boycott. (11)
4. An interesting parallel may exist between the messianiclike feelings and identification of this young Negro leader and those formulated about Moses by S. Freud. (7)

References

1. Dollard, J. 1939. Caste and Class in a Southern Town. Harper & Bros., New York, N.Y.
2. Erikson E. 1956. The problem of ego identity. J. Amer. Psychoanal. Assn. 4(1):56–121.
3.———. 1958. Young Man Luther. W. W. Norton & Co., Inc. New York, N.Y.
4. ———. 1962. Youth; fidelity and diversity. Daedalus 91(1):5.
5. Fishman, J. R. and F. Solomon. Pro-social Acting out. In preparation.
6. Fleming, H. 1960. The new South and the sit-ins. J. Intergroup Relations 2(1):56–60.
7. Freud, S. 1934. Moses and Monotheism. Hogarth Press. London, Eng.
8. Fromm, E. 1941. Appendix: Social character and social process. In Escape from Freedom. Farrar & Rinehart. New York, N.Y.
9. Greenacre, P. 1950. General problems of acting-out. Psychoanal. Quart. 19:455–467.
10. Johnson, A. M. and S. A. Szurek. 1952. The genesis of antisocial acting-out in children and adults. Psychoanal. Quart. 21(3):323–343.
11. Kahn, T. 1960. Unfinished Revolution (Pamphlet). Igal Rodenko, Printer. New York, N.Y.:28.
12. Kardiner, A. and L. Ovesey. 1951. The Mark of Oppression: A Psychosocial Study of the American Negro. W. W. Norton & Co., Inc. New York, N.Y.
13. King, M. L. 1958. Stride Toward Freedom: The Montgomery Story. Harper & Bros. New York, N.Y.
14. Laquer, W. Z. 1962. History of the German Youth Movement. Basic Books, Inc. New York, N.Y.
15. Myrdal, G. 1944. An American Dilemma. Harper & Bros. New York, N.Y.
16. Powdermaker, H. 1943. The channeling of Negro aggression by the cultural process. Amer. J. Sociol. 48:750–758.
17. Rexroth, K. 1960. The students take over. The Nation. 191(1):4–9.
18. Solomon, F. and Fishman, J. R. Identity formation and crisis in student demonstrators against racial segregation. Presented at the Annual Meeting of the American Psychiatric Association, Toronto, Canada. May 7, 1962.
19. ———. Youth and social action: students participating in a large "peace" demonstration. Presented at the Annual Meeting of the American Orthopsychiatric Association, Washington, D.C. March, 1963.
20. ———. Non-violence in the South: a psychosocial study. Presented at the Annual Meeting of the American Psychiatric Association, St. Louis, Mo. May 6, 1963.
21. Wilson, J. Q. 1961. The strategy of Negro protest. J. Conflict Resolution. 5(3):291–303.
22. Youth: change and challenge (a symposium). 1962. Daedalus 91(1).

New Concepts and Patterns of Service: The Mobilization For Youth Program [1]

George Brager

The Mobilization program is based primarily upon the belief that no effort to prevent or control juvenile delinquency can succeed which does not provide young people with *genuine* opportunities to behave differently. We contend that obstacles to economic and social betterment are chiefly responsible for delinquency among low income groups. Unless the members of these groups, particularly those who are also members of minorities, are given a stake in the future—a tangible reason for conformity—they will become alienated from the values of the society, and delinquency will result.[2] This means that creative and exciting educational and work programs must be devised and made available, and that local residents must be involved directly in efforts to improve the social and economic opportunities which their community affords to young people. These are the broad goals of the Mobilization program.

The Mobilization Program

The Mobilization program plan is the product of two years of planning, the culmination of efforts by a professional staff engaged to develop a proposal, a research staff responsible to a school of social work, and the Mobilization board of directors. Near the end of the planning period, representatives of the school of social work were added to the board, and ultimately more than twenty New York City commissioners and officials joined the Mobilization councils; however,

the board group which was most active in the planning operation consisted of representatives of the local social agencies, local clergymen, and the assistant superintendent of the local school district.

Cooperative planning by groups with varying specialized interests may produce little more than a justification of "things as they are" or a solution that represents the least controversial, rather than the best possible way out of the problem. That the Mobilization proposal avoids this pitfall is indicated by the program itself. Three factors may be responsible. First is the experience of agencies on the Lower East Side in cooperative undertaking, and their awareness that, whatever the strains, funding support depended upon cooperation. Second, the theoretical point of view undergirding the Mobilization program gave unity to planning. By its interest in the theory, the National Institute of Mental Health, whose financing made the planning period possible, helped to turn the attention of community representatives to these theoretical perspectives. A third factor was the willingness of staff to bear the tensions required to maintain a particular point of view in the face of disagreement.

The program itself, as set forth in Mobilization's "A Proposal for the Prevention and Control of Delinquency by Expanding Opportunities," is as follows:

> One of the most important resources necessary on the Lower East Side is *employment,* since occupation is the chief determinant of social status in our culture. The objectives here are to increase employment opportunities for lower-class youth, to increase the visibility of existing job opportunities, and to increase the employability of lower-class adolescents. The action programs developed to do these jobs include a Youth Job Center, an employment and counseling agency, and an Urban Youth Service Corps, established to provide subsidized work experiences and training for unemployed, out-of-school youth sixteen to twenty-one, and focused on projects of value and utility to the neighborhood.
>
> A second important resource is expanded opportunity for *education.* This includes teacher training to reduce the social and psychological distance between teachers and parents; two laboratory schools to demonstrate methods of teaching lower income youngsters; in-service training courses aimed at improving verbal skills in culturally deprived children; improved curriculum materials and methods adapted to lower-class culture; experimental approaches to reading technology, including self-directing materials; parent education; language arts enrichment for nursery school, kindergarten, and early primary grades; a tutorial or "homework-helper" program; and a range of guidance, therapy, and visiting teacher service.
>
> A *community organization* program is aimed at organizing unaffiliated lower-income groups to take action on community issues.
>
> *Specialized services to individuals and families* include developing four neighborhood service centers, or "helping stations," offering families active assistance in dealing with service bureaucracies; providing a wide range of planning and referral services; establish-

ing an experimental narcotics program; using a visiting homemaker service; and providing a mental hygiene referral service.

Specialized services to groups include two coffee-shop projects, which are really social-cultural centers with a secondary referral center function; a detached-worker program to reduce conflict gang activity; an Adventure Corps aimed at providing recreational, educational, and vocational activities to potentially delinquent boys, 9–13 years of age; and a pre-adolescent project using community centers, camping trips, and a host of other resources and activities.

Some Program Assumptions

The program described above is based upon the following assumptions, among others:

1. *Lower-class persons are inadequately served by social welfare and educational organizations.* Voluntary social agencies serve such clients far less than is generally believed. Nonvoluntary agencies, such as public welfare and public education, do serve lower class persons, but in ways that are insufficiently congenial or meaningful to the life patterns of the clients.

A recent study conducted by the Family Service Association of America is illuminating. Its findings indicate that clients of family agencies across the country have proportionately more high school and college education than the population at large. In income distribution, the client group is an almost perfect cross-section of the national population. This parallel suggests a proper and democratic allocation of service. However, the need for service is not distributed in this fashion. The lower income group, whose need is obviously and historically greatest, is therefore grossly underserved.

Nor do neighborhood councils and other community organizations that represent themselves as spokesmen for "the people" in fact serve the lower class. Even in areas of significant minority-group population, most observers of meetings report not a single Puerto Rican among those present and only a smattering of Negroes (and these often are staff members of agencies).

The assertion that nonvoluntary programs are insufficiently meaningful to the lives of lower income people is supported by examination of the public school in many slum communities. Teachers are middle class in orientation, often alien to the slum neighborhood in which they work. Slum schools have high teacher turnover; consequently, instructors are less experienced and instructional time is reduced. In addition, the typical school curriculum is oriented to middle class values. As a result, lower class children are regarded as inferior, however great their demonstrated capabilities may be. A study of one lower class school in New York City charges that society's expectation of inferior performance from Negro children causes these children to strongly question

their own competencies. At the same time, "the middle-class orientation of the school . . . contributes little toward the development of value systems and activities directed toward breaking this circular dynamic process." [3]

Public agencies such as the Department of Welfare do, of course, serve the slum community, albeit inadequately. Because of restrictive legislation, inadequate budgets, and a scarcity of trained professionals in their staffs, they are unable to cope with the expanse of human misery that society has created. To add grievous insult to critical injury, they are made the target of conservative attack from the United States Senate to the John Birch Society, held to be the cause of the very problem they have been rendered helpless to solve.

2. *Understanding of the reciprocal, dysfunctional relationship between client "defects" and institutional "defects" is necessary for operational clarity.* Too often, service systems define defects only in terms of the client group. Families are described as multi-problem, although the same families might as accurately be called multi-deprived. In designing programs, it is necessary to pay attention to both parties to the interaction: the served and the service system. Public school programs, for example, must take into account features of lower class life that make it difficult for lower income youngsters to do well in school: the inexperience of the parents, their shyness and suspicion of the schools, lack of intellectual stimulation, noisy, crowded homes, and the like. At the same time, it is necessary to identify those features of the educational system itself that further reduce the possibility of academic success for lower income students: e.g., textbooks with vocabulary and content geared to the life of white, middle class children in the suburbs; overcrowded classes; and the middle class orientation of instructors.

Similarly, an effective program of community organization must take into account (1) the circumstances of lower income life (preoccupation with day-to-day problems and with survival, pessimism that discourages efforts to improve and so reduces changes still further, informal modes of behavior, lack of verbal facility); (2) the nature of the community (e.g., residential mobility, which destroys institutions and leadership; massive and impersonal bureaucracies, intergroup tensions, the opposition of entrenched organizations); and (3) the traditional form of community organization (leaders defined, in essentially middle class terms, as persons who can manage the forms rather than those who can influence others, the limitations of issues and activities imposed by established sponsors, the formal organizational nature of many efforts, and the tendency to focus on alleviating conflict and to avoid "gut" problems).

3. *Our technology, whether it be social work, education, or vocational counselling, tends to be culturally inflexible.* The professions, inevitably owned and operated by middle class persons, have developed methodology which has largely failed to take into account the different style

and needs of low income culture.[4] For example, although the verbal facility required by traditional psychotherapeutic processes is ordinarily not found in lower-income socialization, few attempts have been made to develop treatment methods more relevant to lower income persons.

The contrast between typical treatment emphases and low income culture and expectations highlights this point.

Typical Therapeutic Emphases	*Low-Income Culture and Expectations*
Do it yourself, change yourself, assume responsibility	Desire for authority, direction
Introspective, think-centered, word focus	Preference for work, action (talk deprecated)
Unstructured, permissive	Desire for structure and organization
Stress on the past	Focus on present
Self-focus	Emphasis on family and group
Stress on resistance and transference	Problem focus
Symbolic, often circuitous, interpretations and explanations	Desire for simple, concrete, objectively demonstrable explanations
Intensive transference and counter-transference	Desire for less intense relationships; preference for informal friendliness, respect, sympathetic, nonpatronizing understanding.*

* Frank Riessman, "Some Suggestions Concerning Psychotherapy with Blue-Collar Patients." Mimeographed, Mobilization For Youth, 1962.

Furthermore, what knowledge we have regarding the ways behavior may be influenced as a consequence of organizational patterns has yet to be incorporated systematically into the methodology of the practice professions. We may be aware, for example, that certain housing policies are likely to trigger aberrant behavior, but in practice the behavior is the exclusive object of intervention efforts, rather than the policies themselves. Similarly, we explore the motivation of a low income youngster who is unwilling to take a job, without giving appropriate attention to welfare policy that will reduce his family's allotment by the amount of the boy's earnings.

4. *Lower income people themselves must be involved in attempts to reshape their environment.* A program devised without this involvement of local citizens will represent little more than "middle class colonialism."

Many, if not all, of the service professions profess a belief in the individual's right to self-determination. At the same time, each profession considers itself, by virtue of its special knowledge, skill, and goals, uniquely qualified to define the limits of that right. Each supports and facilitates client participation in certain issues or activities but is somewhat disapproving if others are chosen. Too often, these limits to self-determination are the result of patronizing attitudes ("We know what's best for you"), professional shibboleths, organizational self-interest, or class bias.

Some Controversial Aspects of the Plan

Consideration of some of the issues provoked by the proposal may shed more light on the program's over-all point of view. These early points of disagreement also indicate the significant sources of tension with which the organization must come to terms in its day-to-day practice.

There was considerable disagreement concerning the auspices of the community organization program. Would it be preferable for Mobilization to operate the program directly or contract for its operation with an already existing community organization? Which alternative was more likely to accomplish the goal of involving hitherto unaffiliated lower income groups and persons in an attempt to increase their power to influence their environment? Could previous failures be attributed primarily to a lack of resource (staff and money) or to problems in the structure and methodology of existent community organizations?

Another focus of criticism was the social welfare emphasis of the casework program. Was this stress on concrete needs and assistance, rather than on personality disabilities and psychiatric services, a throwback to traditional casework practice, or is there in actuality (if not in principle) a separation between the concrete and environmental, on the one hand, and the psychological, on the other?

Certain aspects of the public school program also came under attack. In the hope of improving school-community relations, helping teachers to understand their pupils' home environment, and helping parents to help their children achieve in school, it was proposed that classroom teachers make regular visits to the homes of all their pupils. Some agreed that home visiting imposed noneducational functions on teachers. More important to school personnel, others questioned whether it would be safe for teachers to call on their pupils.

Some Program Strategies

To design programs, service, and community resources that would be attractive, meaningful, and responsive to the needs of lower income persons was the major task of planning. In this regard, three aspects of the over-all program were explored: (1) its content, (2) its structure and organization, and (3) its methodology or techniques.

CONTENT

The original Mobilization program (developed prior to the formal planning period) called for group work, mental hygiene (casework), and

community organization activities, in that order of priority. Public education and employment services (omitted from the original plan) now assume major priority.

Within the area of education, the most significant content focus has been on such matters as curriculum revision, teacher orientation and approach, and a reward system for success in high school, rather than on remediation and guidance. In other words, Mobilization's efforts has been as much to bring the system into harmony with lower income educational needs as to repair the damage that has already been done—some of it by the system itself.

Within other program areas as well, content emphasis shifted from the original plan. As has already been suggested, services to individuals stress concrete social assistance rather than clinical intervention. The major efforts of the community organization program are directed to the involvement of unaffiliated groups and individuals, rather than to maximizing the spokesman role of the already predisposed middle class "leadership." Such meaningful issues as employment, housing, discrimination, and youth problems are being emphasized with the full recognition that these issues may well engender controversy.

In the area of services to groups also, content has been chosen to increase the program's appeal to lower income persons. Traditionally, group workers have felt special affection for such program media as square dancing (as "basic, of the people, indigenous to America"). The Adventure Corps reflects the fact that many lower income youth prefer the rituals, symbols, and activities of a paramilitary organization to the soft, folksy styles of another day.

STRUCTURE AND ORGANIZATION

The nature of a program will be heavily influenced by the character of the sponsoring institution. Within a community center, for example, the presence of all age groups, the rules necessitated by it, the agency's physical facilities, its history and the like, and the resultant atmosphere of the institution will make it a desirable auspice for some programs but a problematic one if, for example, a sense of the youngsters' ownership is intrinsic to a program plan. The sponsoring institution will also affect a program's permanence—i.e., whether or not it will take root within the existing communal structure. If this is the goal, local institutions need to be active in program formulation and practice.

Wherever possible, the operation of Mobilization programs has been contracted to local institutions, with standards and a structure for compliance specified to ensure that service would be provided to deviation-prone lower income persons. In many instances, however, it seemed preferable not to draw on existent institutions. We posited that lower income people would not participate in organizations with a subtle middle class cast (e.g., parent associations, community councils). More

important, already existing organizations tend to resist the "invasion" of new members—particularly members of minority groups—because of the changes in power relationships that this brings about. While much lip service is given to the concept of integration, older community groups often regard Negroes and Puerto Ricans as "unready" for leadership. The help they offer therefore tends to be of a sort and in a manner that preserves unreadiness. For these reasons, then, the program to organize the unaffiliated could not be turned over entirely to established community powers.[5]

Similarly, to perform a "social brokerage" function, the worker can not be placed within the service system with which the client is engaged. Bureaucratic systems are, at best, difficult to manage, and low income persons, who need them most, are least able to manage them. This is due to their lack of knowledge, combined with the attitudes of bureaucratic personnel toward them, and the very complications of bureaucratic practices and policies. The broker insures at least minimal redress in the balance. Since the broker is a representative of the client's interests, not a neutral party, he must be free from institutional pressures.

Another major structural issue was developing a program style more reflective of lower income patterns and needs. Thus, the Neighborhood Service Center has aspects of the corner luncheonette: it is highly visible, informal, nonbureaucratic, and open in the evenings. Spanish is spoken, and staff may be seen without appointment.

The Youth Jobs Center also tries to avoid an institutionalized atmosphere. The fact that application blanks are filled out by clerical staff rather than the applicants thembselves allows the youngster who cannot read or write to apply without embarrassment. That vocational counseling is part of the work operation itself, rather than, as is traditionally the case, a process that precedes job placement. It involves less talk than action, and, as such, is more congenial to lower income style.

Another organizational concern relates to the staff. Professionals are, by definition, middle class. Within that inevitable limitation, however, an effort was made to recruit persons with the ideological orientation, basic understanding, and style to work effectively with lower income persons.

Furthermore, extensive use of personnel recruited from the community was an integral part of the program plan. Fifty positions have been provided for visiting homemakers, parent education aides, community organizers, coffee shop managers, case aides, and group leaders. Those who hold these positions represent the major ethnic groups in the community and are drawn from the six low-cost housing projects in the area. Some of them were removed from the relief rolls as a result of their employment by Mobilization. Indigenous staff are regarded as "bridges" —able (ideally) to interpret community life and values to the professionals, and to serve as interpreters of the professionals and as role models for their lower income neighbors.

METHODOLOGY OR TECHNIQUES

Mobilization's program draws on the vast body of practice knowledge accumulated by the service professions. It is also expected that new techniques will be developed as a consequence of the project's ideological orientation, content, and unique structural features.

Much of the long-accepted sociocultural and structural theoretical material, we believe, has not been sufficiently incorporated into daily practice methodology. The importance of this material is recognized, but it is ordinarily accepted as "given," a feature of diagnostic understanding rather than a basis for specific application. It is hoped that the use of staff with sociological and social-psychological expertise, plus the focus upon cultural content, will offer a practical test of methodological changes.

The Mobilization program requires a shifting of professional role emphases, such as a shift in the role of the detached worker. We view the worker as a channel, concerned with relating the street gang to the major institutional orders that impinge upon it (school authorities, potential employers, the courts, the police, and the like). Previously, the primary functions of the gang worker were to develop a personal relationship with individual youngsters or to redirect the group's energies into socially acceptable types of leisure-time activity. Similarly, the social case worker has become a social broker, intervening directly to bring the client and the community's institutions and services into a more congenial and beneficial juxtaposition.

In summary, Mobilization For Youth focuses upon social class as a major variable in the development of community services and resources. It is, we believe, the urgent responsibility of social engineers to design more effective ways of applying public and private resources to human need. What this paper describes, and what the experience of the next few years will test, are the underlying issues, assumptions, and strategies of one such attempt.

Notes

1. Mobilization For Youth is a comprehensive demonstration and research project in delinquency prevention and control, located in the Lower East Side of New York City. It is supported by the City of New York, the National Institute of Mental Health, the President's Committee on Juvenile Delinquency, and the Ford Foundation.

2. Richard A. Cloward and Lloyd C. Ohlin, *Delinquency and Opportunity* (New York: The Free Press of Glencoe, 1960).

3. Martin P. Deutsch, "Minority Group and Class Status as Related to Social and Personality Factors in Scholastic Achievement" (New York: Society for Applied Anthropology, Monograph No. 2, 1960), 11.

4. American professionals, along with other Americans, tend to resist notions of class difference. Many would deny Michael Harrington's contention that "There is . . . a language of the poor, a psychology of the poor, a world view of the poor," in short a culture of

poverty (*The Other America,* New York: The Macmillan Company, 1962), 17.

5. As noted in the Mobilization proposal, "There is . . . a contradiction inherent in the proposal to establish (independent) lower-class community organizations under Mobilization sponsorship. Mobilization is responsible to a wide variety of groups. Issues with which lower-class organizations deal may threaten some of these groups, in which case pressure may be exerted to control the fledglings. Unless they are formed spontaneously under the impetus of an inflammatory issue, lower-class groups cannot be organized without the financing and support of such established (i.e., middle-class) organizations as Mobilization. The fact that Mobilization constitutes a new structure partially mitigates the problem of control. So, too, does the Mobilization intent to protect the organizations' independence from both outside pressure and Mobilization's own opinions about their mistakes. This is no real solution, however; it will be necessary for Mobilization to divest itself of responsibility for the project as soon as feasible. Encouraging the organizations to raise their own funds will be a step in that direction." *A Proposal for the Prevention and Control of Delinquency by Expanding Opportunities* (Mobilization For Youth, 1961), 136–37.

Pills and Needles

||||||||||||||||||||||||||||||||||||||||||||||||||||||||||||||||||||||||||||||||||||||||||||||||||||||||||||||||||||||||||||||||||||||||||||||||||||||||||||||||||||||||||||||||

The Chicago Area Plan for Workers' Mental Health

Ted Ruhig

There is no certainty that the emotional illnesses of workers can be treated successfully in the present institutional and theoretical framework of psychiatry and psychology. If adequate treatment is to result, new facilities and approaches are required. It is probable that one will have to re-examine the roles of both the medical profession and psychotherapy in relation to workers, and redefine treatment, when speaking of their problems. This will involve, among other factors, the development of special approaches and techniques applicable to the circumstances of the clinical treatment of workers.

There can be no dispute that early and more adequate diagnosis and treatment for workers with mental health problems is needed. It is clear that workers as a group now get far less adequate treatment than many other social groups.

A recent national survey in this area, conducted under the auspices of the Joint Commission of Mental Illness and Health, stated:

> Where psychiatric treatment facilities were available in the community, as distinguished from public mental hospitals, they were used predominantly and most effectively by people with better education and higher income who thought in psychological terms, who were more aware of the presence and purposes of these facilities and who could best afford them.[1]

The lack of mental health resources uniquely designed for and uniquely appealing and available to workers virtually guaranteed the past failure of any large-scale attempt to deal with their mental health problems. In order to solve these problems, the Chicago Area Plan for

422

Workers' Mental Health is developing a new approach to reaching, motivating, educating, and treating workers and their mental health problems. This is being accomplished by using the resources and facilities
of the four Chicago area union health centers in an interrelated, four
year education and research project financed by the Chicago Unions concerned, the State of Illinois, and the National Institute of Mental Health.
The three aspects of the Chicago area plan are:

1. Creating a demonstration workers' mental health clinic to treat
   certain workers, to test new approaches, and to provide the necessary setting in which educational ventures can take place.
2. Educating, through seminar workshops, a group of physicians
   from the staffs of the union health centers (who generally have
   had no previous specialized training in psychiatry) to play a
   major role in identifying and minimally treating the emotional
   problems of their patients.
3. Educating the boards of directors and those other leaders of the
   unions who direct the union health centers to understand and
   thus to support newly developing approaches to workers' mental
   health.

The goals of the Chicago Area Plan are: (1) a method of overcoming workers' resistance to treatment by blurring the sharp distinction
between physical and mental illness; (2) better identification of workers'
mental health problems through more effective communication between
the worker and the physician; (3) more effective therapeutic approaches
to workers along the lines of a short-term crisis-oriented therapy;
(4) more effective union leadership that might increasingly encourage
their membership and themselves to make use of the advances in the
mental health field.

It is the hope of the plan that the physical connection of the mental
health clinic with the union health clinics, the involvement of the entire
staff of the union health clinics and the continuing support of the union
leaders will create a successful venture to overcome the traditional deep-
seated worker resistance to therapy.

Workers are accepting of treatment for physical illness. Using the
physical illness setting and the workers' acceptance of it as the device
to introduce treatment for mental illness, it should be relatively easier
for workers to accept treatment, particularly when each mental health
case will be given a prior complete physical workup. This intake procedure should lower the threshold of resistance to mental illness treatment to a treatment accepting point.

There are several unique circumstances surrounding this new approach. The most important one is the built-in patient load. There will be
less difficulty in motivating workers to initially use the proposed mental
health clinic because each union physical health clinic has a clientele of
union workers, many of whom have emotional problems and who are
seeking treatment. The treatment they all seek is on a physical basis, but
according to the estimates of the various heads of the union health

centers, approximately 30 per cent of the cases are thought to have an emotional basis. This factor of self-motivation and consequent self-referral may overcome the traditional problems in this field.

Another important innovation of the Chicago Plan is that the psychiatric clinic will not be identified as such. It will not have a name with a mental health connotation, but will include within its scope diagnostic treament and educational functions. Because it will appear to the worker as part of the physical health clinic, the psychiatric clinic will be able to explore the possibilities of psychiatric care for workers within the context of the worker's health.

As indicated, experience with workers shows that they take a negative view of mental health problems. In fact, when workers recognize maladaptive behavior in a fellow worker, a common reaction is to ask to have him fired. A likely problem is that the worker referred to the psychiatric clinic from a union health clinic would be "lost in transit" if he thinks he is being sent to a "head shrinker."

Workers strongly resist most treatment of psychiatric disorders. The lack of foresight, the shame and stigma that they feel about psychological probems is so great that they and their unions have not effectively pressed for treatment. Perhaps because the ordinary worker resists typical pyschiatric treatment, there has been a previous disinclination by union leadership to move in this direction. They have felt that efforts in this area somehow were not proper.

For example, in 1959, Group Health Insurance, Inc. of New York City launched a trial psychiatric insurance benefit program for a sample group of 30,000 subscribers.

> Interestingly, Group Health Insurance reports that those who least availed themselves of the psychiatric service during the test program were the blue collar workers. Without doubt, this weakness would be on its way toward correction if it were possible for an attending physician to refer patients directly to a participating psychiatrist.[2]

Our solution to this problem is to have this psychiatric clinic located in an existing union health clinic. The Medical Center of the Beef Boners, one of the four participating clinics, will house the Chicago Plan Psychiatric Clinic (but the psychiatric clinic will not be identified as such). In this way, the four union clinics hope to cut their losses "in transit" and also to avoid the stigma attached to mental health treatment per se.

The problem of workers as patients with mental health problems is indeed acute. They almost never "walk in" or self-refer, even when facilities are available. One reason so little is known in this field is that there has been so little recognition on the part of the patient himself, of the need for treatment, to say nothing of the physician actually treating the worker. The Chicago Plan clinic partially overcomes this problem in its initial barrier, because the worker presents himself as sick at the union health clinics.

Self-referral is very important to the project. It is the means to the short-term psychotherapy we propose: crisis-oriented or coping therapy. It is an important reason for thinking that the Chicago Area Plan has an excellent chance for more success than others.

Once the clinic is fully functioning, the procedure we envision is as follows: The worker will come to a union health clinic complaining of illness. He will go through the usual clinic procedure up to the point where one of the doctors treating him thinks the disorder may be psychosomatic, or mainly emotional. If the doctor is not familiar with problems of this kind, he will send the patient to one of his own clinic doctors who is seminar trained. The first doctor will know about the second because all the doctors in the seminar will be identified to the rest of the staff.

The psychiatrically-sensitized doctor will, during and after his training, act as a screener and therapist. He will minimally treat these patients with whom he feels competent and secure (because of his seminar-workshop training). He will consult with the psychiatric clinic team concerning those about whom he feels less certain. The type of case he will handle will be predetermined in the workshop sessions. He will refer other cases to the psychiatric clinic team. In every case, the worker will get a complete medical workup before he comes to the psychiatric clinic.

The kind of case the clinic will handle is not subject to rigid predetermination. From the beginning, it will screen all cases the doctors of the union health clinics suspect involve mental health problems. Cases will be selected for treatment after the screening process establishes their suitability for the clinic's specialized services. If the case load is light, more treatment will be done by the clinic with clinic personnel. If the case load is heavy, other resources and ways of handling the problem will be evolved.

The clinics may limit intake and exclude such mental health problems as alcoholism, deviant sexual behavior, psychoses, or addictions. Clinic staff will restrict themselves to problems the doctors refer—unless, of course, the staff doctors do not make enough referrals. In this unlikely possibility, the intake of cases may then be broadened.

The significance of the project lies in the fact that we are dealing with the problems of workers' mental health in a unique way, that is, across the broad spectrum of medical care, union management, and worker education. More specifically, the significance lies in the fact that we are trying out solutions to five intimately related major problems that face workers. These problems are:

1. Workers are poorly motivated for mental health treatment and do not easily accept treatment. This involves the nature of the workers' understanding of mental health, problems of education, the stigma associated with mental illness, the kinds of mental health problems workers have, and other factors.
2. Union leaders are often suspicious and uncomfortable about work in this field. Therefore, the assets of union intervention that

protect the worker in physical illness are not used in emotional illness.

3. There is a lack of sound identification of workers' mental health needs.

4. Most doctors who treat workers in medical clinics have little training in diagnosis (not to mention treatment) of emotional illnesses. These doctors and their clinic staff may also need their own feelings (sometimes negative) clarified regarding psychiatric care in their approaches to the worker patient.

5. The lack of an adequate treatment methodology, as well as diagnostic and treatment facilities, for workers with mental health problems.

The unusual combination of interest, facilities, and human resources assembled in the Chicago Area Plan makes possible significant advances in certain of the problem areas cited above. If successful, the project will have established a psychiatric clinic that will be integrated into union medical care programs. The existing union health centers will be better able to diagnose workers' emotional illnesses and will have a place to which these patients can be readily referred.

The doctors in union clinics will be better able to diagnose emotional illnesses, workers will be better able to accept help, union officials will have greater understanding of the problems of mental health, and psychiatrists will be better able to treat workers' emotional illnesses. A method will have been established by means of which a more promising approach can be made to workers' mental health problems. The desired rehabilitation approaches in mental illnesses of workers can be effected only through these preliminary steps.

Notes

1. *Action for Mental Health,* Final Project of the Joint Commission on Mental Illness and Health (New York: Basic Books, 1961), 103.

2. Abe Magriso and Donald Rubin, "Money and Mental Illness," *Industrial Union Department Digest,* AFL-CIO, 7: 1 (Spring, 1962).

"20-Minute Hour" Therapy Held
Sound GP Procedure

In Torrance, California, a general practitioner who has at least a nodding acquaintance with basic psychiatric principles can now help to relieve the emotional distress of many of his patients by means of a series of 8 to 10 psychotherapeutic sessions, each of 20 minutes' duration, *Factor* has been told by Dr. Pietro Castelnuovo-Tedesco, chief of the psychiatric service at Harbor General Hospital here and an assistant professor of psychiatry at UCLA.

The "20-minute hour" technique, he said, is devised primarily for the GP, internist and other nonpsychiatric physicians. Among its main features, he declared: It fits readily into a closely scheduled office practice; It makes minimal demands on the doctor's resources; It is reasonably free of untoward complications; It enlists the patient's strivings for health so that he becomes an active participant in the treatment process.

Most important, Dr. Castelnuovo-Tedesco said, the technique often brings about a significant symptomatic improvement.

Treatment is generally supportive and no special attempt is made to impart insight, he said. Despite the limited aims of treatment, after a few interviews patients generally appear more relaxed, more comfortable and a little happier, and "their involvement with their symptoms tends to fade as they become more involved with their physician."

"In 8 or 10 visits, relief of symptoms may be only partial," he said, "yet something usually is accomplished and patients are often distinctly grateful for it. If no improvement is noted by the tenth interview, if the patient's distress is in no way diminished, he should be referred to a psychiatrist who can treat him more intensively."

Reprinted from *Factor*, September 1962.

427

Patients suitable for the "20-minute hour" technique include the more common neurotic disorders seen daily in every office practice, and especially those where the chief symptoms are anxiety, depression, or preoccupation with multiple physical complaints.

Dr. Castelnuovo-Tedesco ruled out as suitable candidates the obviously psychotic, including depressed patients with even a hint of suicidal risk; the obviously psychopathic, including the drug addict and the confirmed alcoholic; the severely phobic patient, and those with the more serious psychosomatic disorders, such as ulcerative colitis.

In outlining his concept of short-term supportive treatment with limited goals, Dr. Castelnuovo-Tedesco emphasized that 50 minutes are not needed to treat a patient psychotherapeutically. It's only a matter of tradition, he said, and does not bear any necessary relationship to supportive therapy. He chose the 20-minute period, he said, because it represents an interval of time that a practitioner can reasonably be expected to spend with a patient.

Another bit of tradition that Dr. Castelnuovo-Tedesco questioned is the belief that psychotherapy is predominantly a matter of passive listening on the part of the physician. "It's certainly no sin to give advice or to speak to the patient in an ordinary give-and-take conversational way," he said.

There are four steps in the "20-minute hour" approach. The first, according to the psychiatrist, is to establish a relationship with the patient in the usual way by obtaining a good, basic medical history and by performing a complete physical. In taking the medical history, he said, it is helpful "if special emphasis is given to the chief complaint, to the present illness and in particular to the social context in which it has arisen."

Understanding the Patient

"In other words," he continued, "the doctor should want to know not only what the patient's complaints are and how they evolved, but also how they relate to his characteristic mode of living. This means that the doctor needs to know about the patient's work, his family relationships, his daily activities and something about his background.

"The doctor's first task is to use this initial basic history to understand what sources of friction and dissatisfaction are currently at work in the patient's life, especially in the areas of occupation and family relationships. Then, in his subsequent contacts with the patient, he must do what he can to alleviate them."

Step No. 2 entails the doctor's evolving a plan both for himself and the patient. Dr. Castelnuovo-Tedesco suggests: "If the doctor decides at the completion of his workup that the patient's problem is primarily emotional in origin, he should tell the patient so tactfully, but directly and

without equivocation. The patient will usually not resent this, since this is offered not as a casual opinion but as the conclusion to a painstaking workup. He should also tell the patient that to help him with his emotional problems he would like to see him each week for 20 minutes, and to do this he should set up at least five consecutive weekly appointments."

Step No. 3 is the treatment itself. This, of course, will vary from case to case, but generally "the plan should be to encourage the patient to talk freely about his complaints and his present life situation."

"One should keep in mind," he continued, "that there will always be an intimate relationship between these two items, the complaints and the life situation, and the doctor should listen intently for this connection as the story unfolds. It is distinctly helpful if the doctor interacts and converses with the patient about his problem in a friendly and spontaneous way.

"The role of advice needs clarification. In many instances where the patient is immobilized by self-doubt and anxiety so that he is unable to come to grips with a problem, it may be helpful if the physician, speaking as a friend who is interested and yet dispassionate, can review the practical realities and suggest a way out of the predicament. The only caution is that the advice should make sense to the patient and represent a course of action that he can reasonably be expected to follow. It should not be what the doctor would do if he were in the patient's shoes."

Parallel Cited

In developing understanding of the patient, the psychiatrist had this to say:

"Think, for example, what you would do if a close friend came to you upset and told you he was having trouble with his boss or that he was not getting along with his wife. Probably, you would begin by listening to him. You might ask some questions to clarify your picture of the problem. You would probably show concern and sympathy about his predicament. You might then point out some aspects of the problem that your friend had overlooked and that would tend to place the situation in a different, more hopeful light.

"You might even suggest to him certain steps that he could take to resolve the difficulty, and finally you would probably indicate that you would like to talk to him again. The second time you saw your friend you would listen to the further developments, perhaps praise him for his efforts to resolve the problem, or perhaps you might indicate to him why, on the basis of past performance, he stood a good chance of clearing up his difficulty.

"You can treat your patient in very much the same way. The essence is to allow him to express himself freely and for you to convey interest, friendliness, encouragement and also a measure of good sense."

Ending Therapy

Step No. 4 pertains to termination of treatment. After about eight to 10 weekly interviews, the patient usually has improved sufficiently so that he can be discharged. In some cases, however, he may need to return, perhaps some months later, for further psychotherapy. The criterion for discharge is the occurrence of moderate but evident symptomatic relief.

"I should like to add," Dr. Castelnuovo-Tedesco concluded, "that because of the brevity and limited scope of the '20-minute hour,' a marked dependence by the patient on the doctor does not develop. Therefore, one does not have to worry about the patient becoming excessively attached or dependent or about difficulties in terminating treatment."

Brief Approaches

The Helping Professions and the Problems of the Brief Contact in Low Income Areas

Francis P. Purcell

Recent federal legislation has permitted and encouraged certain urban areas to develop means of dealing with social problems and their individual manifestations by comprehensive social rehabilitation, prevention, and treatment programs.[1] These programs seek to influence the course of individual behavior and the social conditions underlying this behavior, and to plan broad community development programs.

Such projects are deeply concerned with what has been identified as the lower one-fifth of the population and with those who, in many instances, correspond to the lower half of this group. They serve the economically and socially disfranchised whose children participate in the only social structure readily available, the delinquency subculture. Attempts are being made to demonstrate that legitimate opportunity structures are as inviting and compelling as the illegitimate ones if skilled, sensitive and timely help is quickly made available, and new social structures are erected.[2]

The planners of these projects subscribe to the point of view that conformity is the outcome of a social system that is able to integrate socially defined, desirable goals with the prescribed and preferred means to their attainment. A disparity between the goals and the means to achieve them often leads to antisocial behavior. All too frequently these conditions are invidiously referred to as sociopathic reactions, when in essence they are a direct outcome of the external social conditions of life in this group and constitute an expected response. Responses, while expected, hence normal, nonetheless require sensitive and speedy attention

431

lest they become intractable, as in cases of addiction or serious patho-logical states. In short, direct services to individuals, families and groups are a necessary corollary to the creation of an opportunity structure, should these groups fail to manifest the needed capacity and motivation to successfully participate in such a structure.

What, then, should be the function of counseling, casework, and various helping organizations? The question of brief services versus long-term supportive or uncovering techniques often becomes more a question of meeting the professional's need than of responding effectively to the problems posed by certain client groups.

Even a casual study of community services will quickly disclose the problems confronted by planners and what certainly must be unhappy compromises and bitter retreats in the face of militant professionalism. The denouement is obvious enough. For example, the social work pro-grams in many communities are organized along the lines of method specializations. Thus, we have agencies employing caseworkers, agencies using group workers, agencies using community organization workers, and so on. Rather than the nature and scope of the problems defining the organizational structure, the structure of the profession appears to have, at least in part, defined the nature and scope of the services.

While other professional groups must accept equal culpability for the state of affairs that leads them to decreasing sensitivity to the needs of lower class clients, the profession of social work is most vulnerable be-cause of the mandate to service this group. Furthermore, if this is true of the social work profession, how much more true it must be of those after whom social work models itself. Emphasis in this paper is on the family service type of agency, although what is said could be as easily said of mental health clinics, school counseling bureaus, vocational counseling, and others.

Accepting that changes in individual modes of adaptation are indeed possible through the employment of self and social resources, or that individuals can be helped to fulfill role expectations and requirements, or that egos can be induced to higher levels of maturity, or that through planned intervention an individual may give meaning to his existence, it is still proper to design and offer services that *may* fall somewhat short of such lofty goals, if it is determined that in one instance only a speci-fied few can be reached while in another many can be served. If we were to divide the amount of professional time available for this kind of help by the number in the urban slum areas that require it, we prob-ably would be offering as little as a few minutes of treatment each month!

There is a growing body of evidence reported in the literature that indicates that the psychiatric pathology or long-term dependency prob-lems seen in day-to-day clinical practice, if described in terms of con-crete acts of behavior, are related significantly to at least two factors involving persons in the social structure.[3] They are powerlessness, or alienation, and social knowledge, or social learning.[4] Before elaborating on these, what is meant by concrete behavior should be clarified: it is

concrete in the sense that it is observable, while such conceptual formulations as ego strengths, inferiority feelings, self-images, identifications, ambivalences, and so on, are not social behaviors but are, for the most part, systems for organizing and explaining observable behavior by referring it to an inner determinant.[5] Such formulations may be incorrect, insufficient, or superfluous. Worst of all, they may point to constitutional variables over which little control can be exercised. At best, they are useless verbal frills that create a professional screen.

The significant feature of behavior for the practitioner is how behavior is learned and the way in which it is functional or dysfunctional for the individual, the group, and the community. Social workers are coming to understand that behavior which is functional for the individual may not be for the groups, family and others, of which he is a member.[6] It would, in these terms, not be too much to suppose that long-term treatment, or counseling, or casework may be functional for the individual practitioner or even the worker-client system, and at the same time dysfunctional for the family service or mental health centers as services organized to meet community needs.

There is substantial evidence from a number of surveys [7] and from other research that the phenomena of the lower classes externalizing and concretizing their problems, and their tendency to feel that forces such as fate control their destiny, arise out of a personal sense of powerlessness.[8] This sense of powerlessness is a variant of the individual's alienation from significant community ties and tends to isolate the person within the confines of a limited social world.[9] Such isolation is not an uncommon occurrence in a mass society, with its impersonal bureaucratic structures that often dominate man and are apparently impervious to his needs. Such a society frequently isolates and alienates individuals who, for whatever reason, such as in-migration or accident of birth, fail to master the requisite learning to negotiate their social environment. Such failure frequently results in personal adjustments that are dysfunctional for the individual and further reduce his capacity for social learning, since individuals who believe that fate, luck, or chance control events regard knowledge as irrelevant.[10] Various authorities have expressed their discouragement about such a sequence of events.[11]

The projects using opportunity theory [12] acknowledge deficits in social learning and the sense of powerlessness that occurs in urban living. They therefore strive to provide services in family centers organized to arrest self-defeating modes of adaptation by supplying the skills necessary to deal with the complexities of urban social life, encouraging the nondeviant adaptations of children and youth who have shown signs of incipient deviant behavior or have committed delinquent acts, and easing the dislocating aspects of migration into the community. They expressly set out to do such things as providing information about a wide range of community resources—from the school system to the subway system; teaching skills in such matters as budget management, purchasing, home management, and child care; acting as intermediaries in dealings with bureaucratized services and inequities; offering their services as

nurses, baby sitters, homemakers, and escorts, in order that the burdens of lower income living may be eased, and educational, vocational, medical, and other community services may be used more fully; offering enabling social resources with professional sensitivity and psychological insight; offering immediate help in time of trouble or emotional distress, i.e., "emergency psychological first aid"; making available intensive diagnosis and treatment services to selected low income persons.

To carry out these activities may be self-defeating, if the social instructions do not transfuse a sense of power to the clients. The knowledge that such services must be rendered at all could focus individuals on their own sense of futility and dependence on forces (fate) external to themselves. The major task here would be to communicate to these individuals a sense of control and mastery over the services being rendered.

The social knowledge of lower class people—the products of a culture of poverty—is not necessarily less complex. It, too, is a kind of coping knowledge, but a knowledge that provides for adaptation in a culture of poverty does not enable the individual to negotiate the socioeconomic aspects of the culture of affluence. It is not even less drab. It provides opportunities for a life style that affords numerous outlets for aggression, sexual expression, adventure, and interpersonal loyalties rarely available to middle class children.[13] Still, it provides standards of living below the minimums that safeguard health, and the level of observed anxiety is high. The clients in the slum are poorly housed, frequently in rat-infested tenements without adequate heat. Or they are diverted into cold, austere, modern brick housing projects that resemble human ant hills. Hunger is common, health needs are not met, little provision is made for recreation, and even less is done to assure youth education beyond high school—should they, indeed, manage to get through twelve grades. While we may become enamored with the positives of lower class culture with its rich opportunity for earthy, human contact and expression, we must remember that poverty, filth, disease and social anxiety are also typical.

According to the Mertonian model, social learning occurs indirectly as the community at large impresses on its members the goals to be valued. Simultaneously, *instruction* is provided in "acceptable modes of reaching out for these goals." Certain means, fraud or force, are excluded and other means greatly encouraged. Learning may stress goals far more than it makes explicit the means for reaching them. That is, the prescribed means may be cathected with far less concern or emotion than is attached to the ends. "With such differential emphasis upon goals and institutional procedures, the latter may be so vitiated by the stress on the goals as to have the behavior of many individuals limited only by considerations of technical expediency."[14] The members of the community "learn" (without having been directly taught) that achieving the goal is all-important while the means are of relative significance.

In the typical slum area, more than 40 per cent of the residents subsist on some form of public financial aid,[15] while others struggle on

minimal incomes. If only a small per cent of these received direct help, the services of thousands of professionals would allow each client only fifty minutes per week in terms of the standard clinical model transplanted via professionalism into community mental health centers and family agencies. If you subtract from the available "treatment" time that which of necessity must be spent in conferences and the like, the actual figure becomes so ridiculously small that observers tend to dismiss the whole business as playing with numbers. The issue is never satisfactorily or honestly confronted. Casework or counseling clinicians, being confronted with such data, often respond with resignation, classify the problem as hopeless, resign, and move to the suburbs!

The solutions to this problem set forth by professionals in the past have been varied. It has been suggested that we work with groups of clients, thereby spreading ourselves further (this is implicit even though we protest that group treatment is the treatment of choice). It has been suggested, of course, that the poor, because of the multiplicity of problems, chronicity of needs, resistance to treatment, and negative attitudes, are not treatable.[16] It has been suggested that we increase tenfold the number of social workers and clinicians, and that we use our skills to render a brief, time limited, direct, concrete, single problem-oriented help. The use of group methods and giving short-term help, "problem by problem," deserve careful attention. The findings of many surveys regarding the low level of group participation among the poor,[17] even on an informal basis, would indicate that group processes alone would be beneficial if we could succeed in forming client groups, not to mention the problem solving that might accrue.

The reputed inability of lower class people to look ahead or postpone immediate concerns for greater future reward, and their tendency to externalize, would indicate the efficacy of the brief contact. That is, clinicians would be of greater use to clients through ego-supportive, limited goal techniques which would focus on the administration of concrete services, while showing concern for the realities of the clients' social existence. This approach would require the clinician to forgo his "once and for all" orientation and recognize that problems in social living are as recurring as the common cold. The social worker, like the physician, would, under these circumstances, treat each condition as an entity. The client would return to service centers as the need was experienced, and when he terminated it would be with the expectancy that problems do arise from time to time, and it is natural enough to receive help with them. This would be particularly true since the help would not be invading the domain of his private life and world. Instead, the premises upon which services are offered under short-term conditions would hold that the problems result from the fact that individuals may not possess enough information about their environment to cope with their problems; therefore, *information* would be an important commodity to be distributed.

Frequently, information cannot be used because of the lack of *social skills*. Thus direct help in household management, budgeting, filing

claims and applications would be given. All that may be needed is the *allocation* of agency resources, such as homemakers. Or the sense of alienation felt as a direct outgrowth of the clients' frustrated inability to utilize the systems that control resources—e.g., employers, schools, housing, welfare—would be reduced by access to these organizations. These services are designed with the hope that large numbers could be immediately served. In addition, psychological disturbances can be defined as an intervening variable that cannot be approached when reality needs are intense. In psychiatric parlance, this is to say that the integrative capacity [18] of the ego varies with the nature of the integrative task and with the affective state (anxiety or depression) that attends to the task or autonomously presses down upon the ego, limiting its capacity. This, in turn, affects the size of the integrative task. The approach herein advocated seeks to reduce the task, hence increasing the integrative capacity of the ego, rather than the reverse. The kind of center envisioned here would function as a social emergency way station which would not only alleviate emergent problem-producing conditions, but would function as a humanizing agent with the bureaucratic structure in the area.

But even this model is only a variation of a theme, and simple arithmetic indicates that as an approach it is limited. The brief contact, too, is based on a clinical model which, I think, no longer merits the support it now receives in psychiatric clinics or family service agencies.

It is time to abandon this clinical model and develop a model based on a new definition of the situation. The new definition would focus on the culture of poverty, its nature and consequences for the person. The old definition of the situation suggested that psychological adaptive problems cause individuals to create social structures that fail to meet their needs individually and collectively, and that individuals incapacitated by psychological problems drift into the area or are unable to leave. The solution to the problem, therefore, is to effect, case by case in a face-to-face relationship, the needed psychological changes. This point of view, drawn to its logical conclusion, holds to the notion of characterological and psychological inferiority or inadequacy. The diagnostic categories emphasized to fulfill this definition are character disorders or, in standardized psychiatric nomenclature, personality trait disturbance with inadequate personality.[19] With this definition, ingenious modifications of the clinical model can be erected, but essentially the model and the assumptions remain the same.

While it may not be entirely accurate to think that current public assistance families have simply modeled their behavior after their parents who were on public assistance, a significant number of parents now receiving aid to dependent children, throughout the nation, were reared in families that received public assistance. (According to Burgess and Price,[20] this was true in 40 per cent of the five thousand aid to dependent children cases they studied.) What is more likely is that the socialization process in these families does not prepare the children with adaptive behaviors that would provide upward socioeconomic

mobility. The Burgess and Price study, for example, indicates that school dropout rate is high and the school retardation rate is twice that of the national average. Children of these families hold low status employment, if they are employed at all. (Fewer than 7 per cent attained the level of craftsman.)

Yet, many social welfare agencies seemingly ignore such facts; programs dealing with individual expressions of this group phenomenon continue to assume causation in terms of individual psychopathology. In an annotated bibliography of three hundred items considering the so-called multi-problem family, Schlesinger [21] concludes the following:

> To sum up this approach to definition, the term multi-problem family denotes those families which are of public concern because of their social and economic cost to the community and are characterized by:
>
> 1. A "pathological" family type as shown by (a) inadequate or destructive parent-child relationships by both parents, (b) inadequate social functioning on the part of the parents and/or children, and (c) extreme emotional immaturity of either or both parents.
> 2. Dependent and/or exploitative behavior towards the community and community agencies.
> 3. Persistent failure to respond to help or treatment offered.
> 4. A state of chronic dependency on the social services.

A redefinition of the situation, which would view the problem from the standpoint of *cultural change*, is called for. The definition would focus on specific behaviors that would indicate need for specific changes. It would recognize that coping behavior, collectively viewed, is learned and not just reactive or symptomatic, and it would, therefore, shift the focus from invisible entelechies to the social environment as a source and determinant of human conduct. If those in the low income areas are to be helped and given opportunity to pattern their life differently, it seems clear that basic modification must occur within this sub-culture of poverty. It is also clear that new combinations of knowledge must emanate from the human relations field, specifically, technologies and strategies aimed toward producing community change and development. In social work the technology to be further developed would be work with communities, in addition to social work with groups and individuals. Such efforts would emanate from family service centers, but workers would focus as much attention on the social environment as on the individual. The model of a social work with communities would see multi-problem families as multi-problem*ed* and would seek to identify with the family those elements in the community felt as being problems (e.g., housing, public assistance, employment, school, lack of opportunity, recreation, and so on). It would not seek to locate problems in the family or within individuals in the family.

One writer seems to express the social casework bind and trained incapacities when she says, "There is a particular client group which

traditionally has been the concern of all social agencies as well as social service departments in medical settings. These are the *individuals and families* who seem incapable of independent functioning for more than brief periods. *Their immaturity and emotional and financial dependence keeps them returning to social agencies for help."* She does, however, indicate that it's not all the clients' fault and points to the need for an improved technology. She criticizes short cuts and dealing only with immediate problems "as being self-defeating." "There is a tendency to believe such cases hopeless, and therefore not worthy of the full and careful diagnostic evaluation given to other cases. Perhaps we have found it easier to escape responsibility by placing the onus on the client 'who has no strengths to work with' than to search honestly for *techniques* that can be effective and practical in helping." [22] Clearly, this is a definite, if muted, appeal to break the mold.

The formation of a radically new social practice would not command wholesale abandonment of hard-earned knowledge and skills. This proposal calls for the array of clinical knowledge and skills to be distributed, organized, and administered in a different kind of structure. The model herein advocated does, however, command additional knowledge largely to be derived from the social sciences.

Schwartz [23] produced what may prove to be for social work the outline of the profession in the future. Essentially, he calls for a social work generalist who can apply social work knowledge and skills with equal facility as they are demanded by the *nature of the problem.* Furthermore, agencies or services of the future will not be organized along the line of specialists with varying numbers of clients. Schwartz challenges the specializations in social work and points out the disturbing fact that people with problems do not readily lend themselves to convenient arbitrary divisions of labor.

If we were to place this social work practice in the setting of a family service center, for example, the notion of the brief contact as such loses much of its significance. This would be particularly true if we were to define the situation in terms of the problems individuals and families were having with the community.

We would envision here social workers, each with a number of case aides who could adequately provide many of the brief services listed herein under professional supervision. Where the problem with the community is severe, the worker with this kind of *direct support* would move from the individual member of the family to the family as a functioning unit of the community. When a number of such families had been identified, the groups formed by the delegates of these families could meet with professional help to explore the mutual problems they were experiencing with the community, such as the way services (public and private) were falling short of their intended purposes, and ways of effecting needed changes.

With this kind of process, the major block to mutuality between the individual, his family, and the community could be expressed and identified. The symbiosis necessary between persons and their society

might be effected. The family service center would be designed to mediate this process and the various individual-social transactions worked out. It would be the objective here to clarify the need the community has for the family and the family for the community.

In this process the worker would consistently be providing access to new ideas, knowledge and social skills, and helping *individuals* understand the relevance this social learning has for them. The worker would clarify with family constellations the social reality that they are not simply pawns of fate or destiny.

Notes

1. "Juvenile Delinquency Control Act of 1961," *Public Law*, 87–274.

2. R. A. Cloward, and L. E. Ohlin, *Delinquency and Opportunity* (New York: The Free Press of Glencoe, 1960).

3. E. S. Jaco, "The Social Isolation Hypothesis and Schizophrenia," *American Sociological Review*, 19 (Oct., 1954).

4. Melvin Seeman, "On the Meaning of Alienation," *American Sociological Review*, 24 (Dec., 1959).

5. J. B. Rotter, *Social Learning and Clinical Psychology* (New York: Prentice Hall, 1954).

6. R. K. Merton, *Social Theory and Social Structure* (New York: The Free Press of Glencoe, 1957).

7. Mobilization For Youth, Inc., "A Proposal for the Prevention and Control of Delinquency by Expanding Opportunity." Mimeographed, 1962.

8. J. W. Evans, and M. Seeman, "Alienation and Learning in a Hospital Setting," *American Sociological Review*, 27 (Dec., 1962).

9. E. C. Banfield, *The Moral Basis to a Backward Society* (New York: The Free Press of Glencoe, 1958).

10. Seeman, *op. cit.*

11. Thomas Gladwin, "The Anthropologist's View of Poverty," *The Social Welfare Forum: Official Proceedings* (New York: Columbia University Press, 1961).

12. Mobilization For Youth, Inc., *op. cit.*

13. John R. Seely, "The Slum: Its Nature, Use, and Users," *Journal of the American Institute of Planners*, 25:1.

14. Merton, *op. cit.*, pp. 133–35.

15. Mobilization For Youth, Inc., *op. cit.*

16. State Charities Aid Association, "Multi-Problem Families—A New Name or a New Problem" (New York, State Charities Aid Assn. Social Research Service, 1960).

17. Mobilization For Youth, Inc., *op. cit.*

18. Thomas French, *The Integration of Behavior*, Vol. 1 (Chicago: University of Chicago Press, 1952).

19. American Psychiatric Assn., "Mental Disorders." Diagnostic and Statistical Manual, Washington, 1952.

20. M. E. Burgess, and D. D. Price, *An American Dependency Challenge* (Chicago, American Public Welfare Assoc., 1963).

21. Benjamin Schlesinger, *The Multi-Problem Family* (Toronto: University of Toronto Press, 1963).

22. Norma Fike, "Social Treatment of Long Term Dependency," *Social Work*, 2 (Oct., 1957).

23. William Schwartz, "The Social Worker in the Group," *Social Welfare Forum* (New York: Columbia University Press, 1961).

"Open Hospital" for Mental Ills
May Aid Worked-Up Workers

Modern medicine more and more is coming around to the view that mental illness is not necessarily helped by hiding the patient behind walls in an isolated institution away from the rest of the world.

If anything, psychiatrists are taking the opposite stand—that many mental disturbances can be more readily cured (or at least helped) by working with the patient in surroundings he's used to.

That's the report made by Mike Gorman, executive director of the National Committee Against Mental Illness, in an article published in the New York Times magazine.

In England particularly, he pointed out, mental hospital staff members for a long time now have been spending more and more of their working day out of the asylum and in the community and home. The results have attracted American psychiatrists.

These English psychiatrists work in out-patient clinics in general hospitals. They make home visits to the mentally sick. They spend a large amount of time in homes for the aged, ex-patients' clubs and child guidance clinics.

In effect, mental rehabilitation is becoming an out-in-the-open community project. Gorman calls it the "open hospital" method.

The most widely-publicized phase of this modern approach to assisting the mentally ill is the "day hospital." It takes patients from 9 A.M. to 5 P.M., sending them home at night.

During the day the patient takes part in group activity, treatment, and occupational therapy. At night he's at home with his family.

One result has been the withering of that dreaded feeling by the patient that he is a social outcast. This way, the patient does not lose

Reprinted from *Solidarity*, August 24, 1958, p. 6, a publication of the United Automobile Workers.

his ties with his family, an important emotional anchor to some mentally ill persons.

The reverse is also true, Gorman says. Very often, if a mentally ill member has been away for a long time, there is a tendency for the others in the family to regroup themselves.

So when a patient finally does return from a long stay in a hospital, he may find himself a stranger in his own home.

But under the day hospital method, the family itself becomes involved in the day-to-day job of bringing the mentally sick back to good health.

Good Night's Sleep

An equally interesting development in new methods of treating mental illness that Gorman reported on is the "night hospital."

Under the high pressures of modern industry, more and more workers are struggling with anxieties and depressions—an intense desire to please the boss, a nagging fear of failure, a reluctance to assume more responsibility even if they're perfectly capable of handling it.

Sometimes when a person is besieged with these fears, nighttime brings no relief. Darkness and loneliness only make the panic more vivid.

For such people the night hospital has proved a boon.

They can go directly from the job and check into the night center. If they need physical treatment, it is usually given before supper.

Bosses Okay Idea

After the evening meal, patients have their group—or individual— therapy and, often, recreational activity. They go to bed about 10 P.M., rise about 7 A.M., have breakfast and go to work.

In Canada, and particularly Montreal, success at one night hospital has been so remarkable that industrial firms are even sending their people there for treatment, Gorman says.

Still another heartening new phase of modern mental treatment is the growing effort to make the family general practitioner more familiar with the symptoms of mental disturbance.

"The general practitioner," Gorman says, "should be the first line of defense in the community against the initial onset of mental illness."

Because of that, the family physicians' union, the American Academy of General Practice, is sponsoring short seminars in psychiatric training for general practitioners.

On top of that, with the help of the American Psychiatric Associa-

tion, the AAGP is preparing manuals on these matters for the family doctor.

The aim is not only to help prevent mental illness. It is also to give the GP a hand in following up on those patients who have been discharged after mental treatment.

Issues in the New National Mental Health Program Relating to Labor and Low Income Groups

Robert Reiff and Sylvia Scribner

The plan for a nationwide system of comprehensive community mental health services has been widely acclaimed as both scientifically sound and socially desirable. To an extent unusual in the field of public health policy, there has been near-unanimous agreement on the validity of the underlying concepts of the program and the treatment principles it embraces. Moreover, many thoughtful recommendations dealing with these professional services have been presented in testimony before Congress, in studies and reports of expert groups, and in an increasing number of papers in professional journals.

It is not the purpose of this report either to repeat or evaluate these recommendations. We have reached certain conclusions, however, as a result of our own studies about the *implications* of these recommendations for meeting the mental health needs of blue collar workers and other large sections of the population who up to now have been inadequately served. We would like to review these implications here because we believe they have an important bearing on the ultimate success of the new program in meeting the objectives outlined for it.

One of the primary objectives, as stated by the late President Kennedy, is to reduce the state mental hospital population by providing services that will make possible treatment in the community of a large number of people who are at present confined in these institutions. While in principle the state hospital is available to the community at large, in practice its population is overwhelmingly drawn from lower

Part of a report by the National Institute of Labor Education Mental Health Project, June, 1963, New York City.

income groups. To bring about a reduction in state mental hospital population, therefore, requires that treatment and rehabilitation services be created in the community which can effectively reach lower socio-economic groups.

But this represents a new and challenging task. While we cannot review the evidence here, it has been convincingly established in the last decade that workers and individuals in lower socioeconomic groups are consigned to state hospitals in the first place because of the failure of existing community services to meet their needs.[1] The reasons for this failure have been explored from many theoretical points of view but there is common agreement that the deficiencies have not merely been quantitative, but qualitative as well. To a large extent, the orientation and treatment methods of existing community facilities have been based on service to middle and upper class individuals. They have neither attracted blue collar workers nor found them to be suitable clients when and if they presented themselves for help. Whether the new community centers will in fact function as an alternative to state mental hospitals, therefore, will be crucially determined by their ability to break away from old patterns and to offer types of services and treatment methods which are appropriate to the blue collar and low income patient.

Additional and broader objectives have been posed for the new program. Its purpose is not only to provide treatment facilities for the seriously disordered but to function as a total resource for all the community mental health needs. Prevention, as well as treatment, is a major responsibility. Consultation with other community agencies, mental health information, and education are among the principal activities recommended.

In order to fulfill these objectives, it again becomes crucial to take into account what is known about the relationship between socio-economic status and the treatment of mental illness. Prompt detection and early treatment are the basis for programs of secondary prevention, but it is well known that in the lower socioeconomic groups particularly, the need for psychiatric service is rarely recognized until the condition is of long duration or impairment is marked. Workers' attitudes toward mental illness and psychiatry militate against self-referral and early and effective treatment. Mental health personnel today generally have little contact with blue collar or low income individuals except when they are already suffering from fully developed illness.

For these and other reasons, whatever might be said about the prevalence of mental illness in lower socioeconomic groups as compared to other groups in the community, there is no question that their unmet needs for mental health services are greatest. The greatest needs demand high priority. This means that in many communities, the strengthening of mental health programs of prevention and treatment will call for emphasis on achieving more effective coverage of blue collar and low income families. In the light of past experience, more effective coverage will be measured by the extent to which a greater number of such fam-

ilies make voluntary use of mental health facilities and by the increasing proportion of less severe cases on the patient load.

Having discussed the vital importance of gearing the work of the new community centers to the problem of securing higher utilization by blue collar and low income groups, we should like now to turn our attention to some of the factors affecting such utilization. While these are interwoven and interdependent, they can be roughly grouped into the three areas of *programming, financing,* and *education.*

Programming

NATURE OF PROFESSIONAL SERVICES

Treatment Modalities.–It has generally been agreed that, in order to achieve comprehensiveness of service within the community, all modalities of treatment should be provided: outpatient, day care, night care, twenty-four hour inpatient care. Experiences of the several community-based programs already developed in this country show that the use of these "transitional modalities"—especially day treatment—can dramatically reduce the necessity for around-the-clock hospitalization.[2]

Such modalities commend themselves particularly for the care of blue collar workers. The threat of the breadwinner's "being sent away" for a long period of time adds to the catastrophic view which the working class family holds of mental illness. Treatment in the community on a day basis, while it may result in loss of income for a period of time, does not entail a total disruption of the family's way of life. Availability of these transitional modalities can thus act as an inducement to working people to seek help when it is needed without the dreaded prospect of long-term institutionalization.

Experience also indicates that it is more advantageous to have all modalities available under a *unified* clinical and administrative program so that continuity in care of the individual patient can be assured. This, too, is of special importance to the blue collar or low income patient. He is generally not sophisticated in maneuvering within the labyrinth of the community's medical and social services and tends to become "lost" in the process of referral and re-referral. Integrated programming which permits flexible use of treatment modalities without imposing endless red tape upon the patient is wholly desirable.

Treatment Methods.–While there is a growing body of knowledge about treatment methods which appear to be effective with lower socio-economic groups, it should be borne in mind that meaningful programs have not yet been fully developed for either the seriously disturbed or the more mildly disturbed individuals in these groups. Up to the present time, nine out of every ten psychotic individuals in lower income groups have been institutionalized and given protective or custodial care instead of active treatment. As for the less severely disturbed, most clinics, finding traditional therapies ineffective, have been content to let the

blue collar patient drop away, rather than break with custom and tradition to develop alternative treatment methods.

These facts emphasize that the first need in programs serving lower income groups is continued experimentation and flexibility in treatment methods. At the same time, certain observations seem to be emerging from even the limited experiences to date.

1. Effective treatment of blue collar and low income groups seems to require *multiple forms of intervention*. Historically, there have been three lines of approach to the treatment of mental illness: the physical (chemical-somatic), the psychological, and the social. While all three forms of intervention are utilized to one extent or another at the present time, it is characteristic for particular clinical settings to rely on one "best technique" to the exclusion of the others. Conditions of life of blue collar workers and low income families are such, however, that a simultaneous attack on all levels is frequently required—for example, combining active environmental manipulation such as job modification with physical therapies to effect the speediest amelioration of symptoms, with appropriate forms of psychological intervention.

Since so many present-day outpatient services are characterized by exclusive reliance on either psychological or physical therapies to the neglect of social forms of intervention, it is particularly important that attention be paid to means by which changes in the functioning of blue collar and low income patients might be effected by changes in their work or living milieus. Rehabilitation programs and broad community action programs developed for low income groups in the population have demonstrated the effectiveness of efforts to reduce stress on the job or at home, and have indicated the usefulness of such facilities as halfway or "boarding" houses. job training programs, and various types of self-help programs as adjunctive forms of therapy.

2. Treatment methods which place a heavy reliance on the use of some form of *social process* as a technique of treatment rather than on individual, face-to-face psychotherapy appear to be more effective with blue collar and low income groups. We have in mind such techniques as group therapy of various kinds, role-playing, family treatment, and work therapy programs.[3]

3. It has been found that with blue collar workers and lower socio-economic groups it is more practical to set *direct and immediate treatment goals* (helping the worker meet a crisis which contributed to his illness; overcoming specific impairments interfering with job or social performance, and so on) rather than gear treatment toward long-range personality reorganization. In general, blue collar workers appear more ready to participate in such goal-oriented treatment than in attempts at personality reorganization.

This requires a major shift in the attitude of the psychiatrist, psychologist, and social worker participating in community mental health programs. The dominant point of view has been that only those treatment methods which lead to personality reorganization can effectively deal with the problems of mental illness. This attitude has un-

doubtedly contributed to excluding from mental health services a large segment of the community which finds the product offered too luxurious and apparently unrelated to its needs.

Greater use of limited-goal techniques of treatment may lead to an interesting paradox: While existing psychotherapeutic techniques appear suitable for middle and upper class sections of the community and unsuitable for the lower socioeconomic groups, there are indications that the new techniques and approaches which are appropriate and effective with lower socioeconomic groups may meet the needs of middle and upper class segments of the community equally well.

Array of Services.–There seems to be some evidence that the provision of a broad range of mental health services, including family counseling, child guidance, and the like, encourages utilization of treatment facilities by blue collar workers.[4] In many communities, however, counseling and guidance services have developed separate from psychiatric treatment services, especially those based in hospitals; and it is not unusual to find adult and child treatment programs conducted in separate facilities under separate auspices. Special attention may have to be given, therefore, to the means by which the whole broad spectrum of mental health services can be offered under one roof.

Integration with Community Agencies.–There is a pressing need to achieve fuller integration of mental health services with other social, educational, health, and welfare services in the community. Discussions on the new program frequently refer to the need for close working relationships with such community agencies as the department of correction, welfare department, and the like. The emphasis appears to be on consultation and collaboration for the purposes of early detection and/or case management to lessen the need for referral to a treatment facility as such. Important as are these objectives, close working relationships among all community helping resources are also needed, as we have indicated, for effective *treatment* and rehabilitation of blue collar workers and lower socioeconomic groups. Any program that has as its objective the maintaining of the emotionally disturbed and mentally ill in the community must be prepared to concern itself with a whole host of problems confronting the patient—living arrangements, family attitudes, and the like—which are more easily ignored when the patient is withdrawn from the community and confined in a distant mental institution.

Families on the lower rungs of the economic ladder have a multiplicity of unmet health, economic, and social needs. It is difficult to see how effective mental health services can be rendered by a community mental health facility which pays no attention to this totality of needs and which endeavors to dispense a psychological prescription without regard to the whole life situation of the patient. It follows from this that a community mental health service will more effectively meet blue collar and low income needs if it is an integral part of the fabric and structure of the community and has strong ties with schools, health facilities, social agencies, and citizen groups. This implies that one of

the greatest needs is a unified framework of community services. The present situation of fragmentation of services poses an important problem for the future development of mental health programs: How can community mental health facilities achieve integration of services in behalf of the individual patient without duplicating existing programs? [5]

Not only does the fragmentation of community services pose a serious obstacle to the provision of effective treatment but it also seriously impedes the development of effective preventative programs which many social scientists and clinicians feel will require broad social action programs aimed at changes in the organization and morale of deprived and disadvantaged communities.

AVAILABILITY OF SERVICES

We have talked about the nature and type of psychiatric, psychological, and social work services which might contribute toward higher utilization and more effective work with blue collar and lower income groups. Another important aspect of programming to meet their needs is assurance that the services are readily available and offered in such a way as to maximize the patient's involvement.

1. *Services must be immediately available.*–There are several reasons why we stress the importance of immediacy of service in connection with blue-collar and lower income groups.

The first is their relatively high need for emergency service. Mental health attitude surveys have repeatedly demonstrated that working people equate mental illness with the most severe kinds of disorders only. They therefore tend not to seek professional help until their problem resembles this concept or, in other words, until it is acute. In the past, this has often meant almost automatic "emergency" hospitalization.

If the community mental health service is to function successfully as an alternative to institutionalization, provisions for first aid emergency treatment should be a high priority feature of its program. In urban areas this might take the form of a walk-in clinic open on a twenty-four hour basis. In areas with dispersed populations, mobile units for emergency home services might be desirable.

Immediacy of service has other aspects besides the problem of meeting emergencies. We have stressed the need to take special steps to increase the use of community mental health facilities by blue collar workers. One of the greatest obstacles to utilization is the waiting list. This may be an official list or merely a delay between the date of application for service and the first interview. Waiting lists and delays in service, we know, are a barrier to full utilization by all groups, but in the case of blue collar and low income groups they mean more than just postponement of treatment—they are likely to mean no treatment at all. Since, as we have already pointed out, there are many negative attitudes toward psychiatric treatment among blue collar workers, delay

in service is construed as one more instance of lack of interest and can quickly extinguish motivation for treatment. This means that it should be a matter of policy in serving blue collar workers and lower socio-economic groups to make the first contact a meaningful one—one in which a professional worker sees a patient and gives him professional attention no matter how brief.

2. *Facilities should be accessible.*—This applies not only to geographical location but to the hours when the centers are open. Working people can usually avail themselves of medical and other services only outside of regular working hours. It is important, therefore, that mental health centers routinely schedule a full range of services during evenings and weekends, and not rely on making after-hour services available only on an occasional basis or by individual arrangement.

3. *Staff should have multi-language abilities.*—This is an almost self-evident requirement but one that is frequently overlooked in the planning of a professional program. Minority groups in some communities make up a large proportion of individuals in the lower socioeconomic brackets. Among these may be many non-English-speaking families. Even among English-speaking families, older members born out of the country may still have greater ease and comfort when communicating in their native tongues. As soon as one becomes concerned with giving *active* treatment to these groups and not just custodial or protective care, the ability of professional staff to communicate with the patient becomes crucial unless steps are taken to overcome the language barrier, thousands of families will continue to be shut off from effective help.

4. *Services should be available on a nondiscriminatory basis.*—Discriminatory practices bear down most heavily on blue collar workers and those in the lower socioeconomic groups. The development of new community-based programs offers both an obligation and an opportunity to break away from any remaining discriminatory practices in state mental hospital programs. This is an essential step if we are to bestow the full benefits of our society on those who suffer from mental disabilities.

Financing

It is clear that one of the primary reasons for the skewed economic distribution of clients treated in the community has been the inability of individuals in the lower socioeconomic groups to pay for psychiatric services. At the point at which such an individual develops a mental illness he is often forced to become a public charge, and publicly financed psychiatric services have, with few exceptions, been made available only in state or V.A. hospitals. It is difficult to conceive, therefore, of any community-based mental health program meeting the needs of blue collar and low income groups unless the services remain in large

part publicly financed. Without the guarantee of long-range public support, community facilities will have to look toward income derived from fees to sustain their programs. Inevitably, reliance on fees will impel them to give priority to those who can afford to pay and will tend to reinstate the present discriminatory situation.

PUBLIC SUPPORT

Since 1824, when the first state-supported mental institution was established in the United States, public funds have provided the major form of financing for psychiatric care programs. In the past, these funds were used to cover the rising costs of custodial care. Now, we stand on the threshold of an era in which community mental health centers will have the means to carry out effective programs of prevention, treatment, and rehabilitation, and funds invested in these programs will realize a great social gain. Nevertheless, in most discussions on the financing of the new programs, the outlook has been advanced that care for mental illness should now be financed on the same basis as care for physical illness. Unexpressed assumptions are that present methods of financing for physical illness have resulted in a satisfactory level of care, and that they are appropriate with few, if any, modifications for the treatment of mental illness. Since there can be no possibility of translating the unmet needs of blue collar workers and lower income groups for mental health services into "effective demand" for such services until the financial obstacles are removed, we should like to examine these assumptions and some of the proposals put forward.

The major proposals seem to be that needs of those unable to pay full costs from their own personal incomes can be met by "a reasonable volume" of free services and that they can be met by extension of voluntary prepaid insurance to cover mental illness.

FREE SERVICES

Assurance that "a reasonable volume of services will be made available to persons unable to pay" will not go far toward meeting the problem of utilization by blue collar and low income groups, as experience in the case of physical illness has plainly demonstrated. Medical indigency is not identical with poverty. It is well known that the bulk of the industrial working population would not qualify for psychiatric treatment programs that require "indigency" as a condition of eligibility while, on the other hand, even if they should entirely drain their family resources, they would still be unable to secure the kind and quality of treatment needed.

We cannot leave this point without noting that any attempt to impose a means test or to require an individual to demonstrate indigency as a condition of securing psychiatric services is a particularly noxious re-

quirement, since its effect is to add to the stigma which already attaches itself to mental illness in many sections of our society. The objective of creating treatment programs that will deal with the mentally ill on a new level of human dignity cannot be met unless it is possible for the individual to avail himself of care, relieved from overwhelming financial pressure, on the one hand, or the burden of being a recipient of charity, on the other.

VOLUNTARY HEALTH INSURANCE

In recognition of the scope of the problem, steps are being taken to press for the extension of voluntary health insurance protection to cover mental illness on the same basis as physical illness. It is true that the long overdue correction of the exclusion features of voluntary insurance plans would offer some relief to workers and their families, the great majority of whom are covered by negotiated insurance plans of either the service or indemnity type. However, the insurance mechanism has a number of serious limitations.

In spite of its rapid growth in recent years, health insurance still excludes millions from coverage, especially those in dire need—the retired and aged, the unemployed, the unorganized. Benefits are uneven and rarely meet the full needs of the low-cost policy holder. Criticism has been expressed in labor and other quarters that after two decades of experience in negotiating insurance benefits, results have been a great increase in cost of medical care without a concomitant increase in quality. There is reluctance, therefore, to push for extension of insurance programs which do not offer the consumer some control over quality and cost.

There are other problems in attempting to include psychiatric illness in negotiated insurance plans of the kind now common. For one thing, we have shown the importance of preserving a flexible and experimental approach to psychiatric treatment, but insurance programs tend to impose rigidity on medical care patterns. There is an incongruence between the kinds of services projected for the new community mental health centers and the typical insurance benefit schedules, which are based on strictly defined, "homogeneous" units of treatment such as office visit, home visit, days of hospitalization, and the like. Care is needed not to stifle new and promising treatment techniques—day care, visits from the public health nurse, sheltered workshop programs, and many others—in order to have them conform to what the insurance policies cover. The results of disguising and distorting diagnostic and treatment services now rendered for illnesses primarily psychogenic in nature so that they may be compensable as "physical illnesses" should be reason enough for caution.

We do not have a set solution to put forth but have gone into these questions at some length here since solving the problem of making psychiatric services financially possible for the majority is decisive

for the outcome of the new program. Government at all levels—federal, state and local—has an obligation to provide whatever resources are required to deal effectively with this question.

Education

It would be an oversimplification to consider inability to pay as the sole factor in the low rate of utilization. Investigations conducted by NILE Mental Health Program and others reveal that important obstacles to improvement of psychiatric services for workers lie in the area of values and attitudes.[6]

The social backgrounds and attitudes of many psychiatrists, psychologists, and social workers are such that they are frequently less inclined to accept blue collar and low income patients and more inclined, when they are accepted, to treat them by physical rather than psychological means. We have already indictated, too, that the ideas and attitudes many workers have on mental illness and psychiatry militate against their receiving early and effective treatment. Within these two areas lies a major job of education, which has to be undertaken if the new services are to be used effectively.

PROFESSIONAL TRAINING PROGRAMS

The need to help mental health professionals increase their understanding of the style of life, values, and attitudes of blue collar workers and their families should be taken into account in all formal and in-service training programs. Some medical schools have already indicated their sensitivity to this growing need by reorienting their psychiatric training programs to include the treatment methods and modalities discussed above. Apart from what can be done in training, the creation of opportunities for professional mental health planners and practitioners to meet with and, most importantly, to work with labor representatives offers one of the more effective means of accomplishing the mutual modification in attitudes necessary for the fullest development of mental health programs.

UNION EDUCATIONAL CHANNELS

The need to acquaint blue collar workers and their families with the nature and purpose of community mental health services can best be met, we believe, by making use of already existing educational channels of labor organizations representing the great bulk of industrial workers in the community. Labor organizations have the machinery for

reaching their membership on many questions and they have, in addition, thousands of union counselors and others trained to function as liaison representatives between the shop and various kinds of union and community services. They are thus a key, untapped resource for mental health education.

It is true that the use of union educational channels will not automatically result in full coverage of all families in lower socioeconomic groups; special measures will be needed to reach them through other organizations in the community which represent their needs and aspirations. But effective educational programs conducted through the union machinery can be a powerful impetus to such community-wide mental health education.

Labor's Participation

Our consideration of the needs that have to be met to provide more effective coverage for blue collar workers and lower socioeconomic groups leads to the conclusion that the national community mental health program could be vastly strengthened by involving organized labor from the very beginning in planning and programming the new services.

It has frequently been pointed out that one of the great assets of the community centers, as compared to the large isolated mental institutions, is that they will be able to make use of the already established resources of the community. The trade unions, which are the institutionalized expression of the aspirations of millions of workers, and of unorganized, economically underprivileged groups as well, are one of the important community resources too frequently overlooked. They have a vital part to play in a number of areas: Through their collective bargaining and legislative roles, unions can help to strengthen financial support of the program; labor's community services machinery and health center facilities can be important sources for case-finding and referral; collaboration with unions can make possible modifications in the work milieu which might be crucial to treatment and rehabilitation but otherwise inaccessible to intervention; union educational channels are an important means of disseminating mental health information.

In short, it is difficult to conceive of community mental health services achieving widespread support and acceptance and a higher rate of utilization by blue collar workers and lower socioeconomic groups without the active interest and participation of organized labor. Two practical measures which might be taken to increase labor's involvement are inclusion of labor representatives on the planning and advisory bodies being established under the new program, and utilization of unions and union health centers as settings for demonstration mental health programs.

It has long been a recognized public health principle that consumers of health services should be represented on planning and administrative bodies. This principle is carried out in the composition of the Federal Hospital Council which, under the terms of the new mental health legislation, is charged with the responsibility of serving as an advisory body to the Secretary of Health, Education, and Welfare. Organized labor is one of the largest consumers of health services in the country and from this standpoint alone is entitled to representation in program development and implementation.

That such representation is not ordinarily provided on state and community mental health bodies is a reflection of the past lack of cooperation between labor and the mental health movement, and the strongest indication of the need for special efforts to effect a change. Consideration should be given by the National Institute of Mental Health and State Mental Health Authorities to the means whereby labor representation on state and local planning committees becomes recognized, as a matter of sound public policy. Membership on those bodies would not only increase labor's support for the program but would set in motion the process of professional-labor interaction which we noted would be so helpful for the development of effective programs for working families.

DEMONSTRATION PROGRAMS

In addition to fostering labor participation in the planning of the program, national and state mental health agencies and authorities might give serious consideration to the development of demonstration mental health programs in a variety of union or union-sponsored settings, to test the kind of program needed to reach union membership, to stimulate the development of new techniques, and to provide a suitable setting for the training of mental health professionals who will be at home with the working class client. Labor-sponsored health centers and community health centers having labor participation are appropriate types of facilities for such demonstration programs.

Beyond this, consideration might be given to encouraging labor-supported health service organizations of this kind to become the sponsors of a community mental health center that would introduce into the national program those fresh and creative elements which sponsorship by consumer and labor groups could provide.

We have stated here the conclusions we have reached from our observation and study of the unique needs of labor in the field of mental health. It is our hope that this interim report can contribute to the understanding and cooperation necessary to make labor participation in the new national mental health program fruitful and productive.

Notes

1. Outstanding findings of studies investigating the relationship between the form of psychiatric treatment given and the socioeconomic status of the patient are summarized in "Mental Health Issues," April 1963, published by the NILE Mental Health Program. The classic study by Hollingshead and Redlich (*Social Class and Mental Illness,* New York, 1958) and the Midtown Study conducted some years later (Srole, Langner, et al., *Mental Health in the Metropolis,* New York, 1962), in spite of differences in communities studied and in methodology, both found that 90 per cent of the mentally ill individuals in the lower socioeconomic groups are institutionalized.

For the relative ineffectiveness of traditional outpatient mental health services in treating blue collar workers, see, among other discussions, Claire Rudolph, and John Cumming, "Where are Additional Psychiatric Services Most Needed?" *Social Work,* July 1962, a survey of the opinions of social agencies in one New York State community; Anita K. Bahn, Caroline A. Chandler, and Paul V. Lemkau, "Diagnostic Characteristics of Adult Outpatients of Psychiatric Clinics as Related to Type and Outcome of Service," *Milbank Memorial Fund Quarterly,* 1962, a study based on reports of services of outpatient psychiatric clinics in Maryland; and Jules V. Coleman, "Mental Health Consultation to Agencies Protecting Family Life," in Elements of a Community Mental Health Program," Milbank Memorial Fund, 1956. The last paper is a comparative study of the caseloads of a psychiatric clinic and a family service agency in New Haven.

2. Dr. Harris B. Peck, Associate Director of the Division of Social and Community Psychiatry of the Albert Einstein College of Medicine, reports that experiences with the Division's Psychiatric Day Hospital, which is operated on an experimental-research basis, indicate it may be utilized as an alternative to twenty-four hour total institutionalization for between two-thirds and three-fourths of all patients who would ordinarily be hospitalized for acute psychotic manifestations. See Harris B. Peck, "The Role of the Psychiatric Day Hospital in a Community Mental Health Program," *American Journal of Orthopsychiatry,* April, 1963.

The Director of the Fort Logan Mental Health Center in Denver, Colorado reports that the Center's broad spectrum of services will make it possible to provide all required treatment with a 400 bed hospital, although the national average for the ratio of State hospital beds to population would indicate the need for a 3,500 bed hospital. "Our initial experience with the use of the day hospital indicates that of all patients in treatment, only one in three requires twenty-four hour care." Alan M. Kraft, M.D., "Fort Logan Mental Health Center —Progress Report. Mimeographed. February, 1963.

3. Some of these techniques are described in Frank Riessman, "New Models for a Treatment Approach to Low-Income Clients," presented at American Orthopsychiatric Association Annual Meeting, March 1963. Small group processes are discussed in Harris Peck, *op. cit.*

4. Dr. Philip Wagner, head of the psychiatric care program of Retail Clerks Local 770 in Los Angeles (one of the few in the country serving exclusively union members and their families) reports that employees have been more ready to turn to the clinic for help for their children than for themselves. The retail clerks' program includes, in addition to adult psychiatric services, family counseling, adolescent counseling, marital counseling, and child services. "This service, though primarily in the form of individual psychotherapy interviews, is showing a sustained shift towards more family and marital joint counseling." "Insurance Coverage of Mental Illness, 1962," issued by the Joint Information Service of the American Psychiatric Association and the National Association for Mental Health.

5. The necessity for "a re-alignment of functions of (community) psychiatric and social agencies" as a result of the return of the return to or maintenance of an increasingly large number of mental patients in the community is stressed in Ernest M. Grueunberg and Matthew Huxley, "Implications of Rehabilitation," in *Rehabilitation of the Mentally Ill,* Washington, D.C., 1959.

6. Even when financial barriers to

treatment are minimized, there is a marked difference in utilization rates between blue collar groups and others. Helen Avnet, "Psychiatric Insurance," New York, 1962. This report draws attention to "popular misconceptions about mental illness and psychiatry" as a major factor influencing utilization.

The Retail Clerks Psychiatric Clinic, which was organized within the Southern California Permanent Medical Group, in 1961, to offer psychiatric services at low cost to union members and their families, was not swamped with referrals when it opened. Caseload built up gradually until it has levelled off to roughly one per thousand of the total eligible group. Success in building up utilization has been attributed to the setting of the clinic and to "the low cost and the educational program through the union newspaper (which) have served to remove realistic and emotional obstacles to using these services." Reported in "Insurance Coverage of Mental Illness, 1962," *op. cit.*

For commentary on how the disparity between the attitudes and values of psychotherapists and blue collar workers impairs effectiveness of treatment, see Paul Lowinger, and Shirley Dobie, "Studies of the Psychiatrist in the Initial Interview," mimeographed report on studies conducted at Lafayette Clinic, Detroit, 1963; and Betty Overall and H. Aronson, "Expectations of Psychotherapy in Patients of Lower Socioeconomic Class," 76–97.

Part 4

Rehabilitation of the Criminal, the Delinquent, and the Drug Addict

Introduction

While it is incontestable that prisons, training schools, and probation caseloads draw disproportionately from the economically disadvantaged, this fact has not been sufficiently appreciated in rehabilitating the offender. Too often programs that make sense by middle class standards are completely inappropriate for low income persons. For example, consider punishment of the offender. Without at this time entering into an evaluation of the effectiveness of punishment, it is pertinent to ascertain whether punishment by middle class standards is interpreted similarly by low income delinquent subcultures. Sentencing a delinquent to a training school may be preceived as punishment by the judge but may be regarded by the delinquent as recognition by society for significant accomplishment, and the sentence may be construed as an official ceremony for bestowal of status.[1] The problem is further complicated, for *not* sentencing the delinquent to a training school may also provide him with status. Now he may be acclaimed for his ability to "con the man."

The illustration is offered to indicate the current state of knowledge about every aspect of rehabilitation. Knowledge is needed in many different areas. The most fundamental need is for gross evaluation of programs that stem from appraisals of post-program response of the recipients of the treatment. J. Douglas Grant, in his article, "It is Time to Start Counting," cogently states the case for this type of research.

We must go further—we must know much more about the of-

fender, how he thinks, what he values, and how he becomes involved and reinvolved in illegal pursuits. We must know what is available to the offender in the form of legitimate activity. If there are blocks and barriers these must be discovered, and methods introduced to overcome or bypass them.

There is another body of knowledge that must be systematically obtained, and that is detailed information about what is actually being done in any given program. Accounts of treatment of the offender may be couched in glittering terms but practice often little resembles the announced program. More important, the program content is frequently general, and a great many different things may occur within the apparent boundlessness of treatment description. For example, group counseling encompasses a great variety of things: groups differ in focus, membership, settings, and leadership; yet programs are described merely as featuring group counselling without further elaboration or analysis of the process. Essential to the operation of any complex intervention is something akin to the "quality control" of industry, in which continual feedback is supplied the operating agency, verifying that the program is indeed meeting its aims. If amendment is necessary, it is done deliberately and consciously. Every program should have definable limits and whenever any aspect of the program exceeds its tolerances, notification should be given to those in charge so the program can be brought into control.[2]

In this part of the book, rehabilitaton is considered in the institution, in intermediate facilities, and in the community. In each section efforts are made to ascertain how appropriate the particular approach is for the offender coming from economically disadvantaged backgrounds, how generalizable are its effects, and what refinements and extensions seemed to be indicated.

Society is reexamining many of its traditional approaches to the treatment of the offender. In the past decade many exciting and promising innovations have been attempted. These are presented here and the comments that introduce them are intended to emphasize that while there has been much progress, much yet remains to be done.

The New Institution—The Highfields Model

If treatment of the offender occurs at all, the lion's share occurs in an institution. This is true because society is not at all clear

about what it wants to do with an offender, and the penal institution appears to satisfy all of its diverse desires. The institution is the place where deviants can be sent so that the rest of the community may be protected against outrage and criminality. It is a place where criminals may receive punishment for transgressions. The institution is a place where criminals go to be rehabilitated. The institution symbolizes a deterrent for those who are considering a criminal act. It is apparent from even superficial examination that these diverse functions are contradictory. As presently conceived the deterrent, punishment, and quarantine roles of the institution do not agree with the rehabilitative function. This is particularly true if the treatment posture is permissive and the other attitudes are restrictive.

Upon closer examination, the institution has few of the aspects necessary to assist the offender to adjust to free society. The offender must learn to live in free society—difficult for him to do even prior to his involvement with the law, much more difficult after he has been stigmatized as a criminal or delinquent. He must acquire the skills necessary to make an adequate adjustment in a complex society. Yet, while in an institution, none of the demands of free society are made of him. He is fed, clothed, and tucked in bed at night; yet after he is released from this protective environment there is some surprise that he returns to crime. In recent years institutions have been subjected to experimental modification. The basic ingredient of many of these approaches is to place some responsibility upon the offender for managing his existence while he is in the institution.

The Highfields experiment is the most celebrated example of this approach. Highfields, established in New Jersey as an adjunct to probation, has had a long history and has made impressive claims for rehabilitation of delinquents. C. Howland Shaw, in his brief commentary, "Factors in the Success of Highfields," outlines the hypothesized virtues of the program. In the Pearl article, the Highfields program is critically examined and its relevance to low income delinquents with a commitment to a delinquent subculture is questioned.

Adaptations of the Highfields model have been incorporated by the Division for Youth of the State of New York. The New York program has extensive commitment to research in which emphasis is on both evaluation of outcome and systematic study of process.

It is hoped that research conducted in New York State's modifications of the Highfields program will analyze the results more

particularly with respect to socioeconomic background of the youthful offender. Ultimately, society must design treatment programs
specifically geared to the needs of different types of delinquents. In
order to reach this point, experimental programs must invest their
primary effort in obtaining information necessary to refine and
particularize their effects.

Evidence that institutional treatment is not effective for all types
of delinquents is presented in the Grant and Grant article. The type
of supervision that was most effective for "high maturity" offenders
in the residential program at Camp Elliot was least effective with
the "low maturity" subjects. The low maturity subjects exhibited
characteristics generally held to be typical of low income subcultures, whereas the high maturity subjects manifested the presumed attributes of the middle class. It is unfortunate that no effort was made to report the relationship between social background
and maturity level of the subjects in the Grant article. However,
the most important feature of that program was a demonstration
that devising treatment for a particular type of offender can produce the most productive and efficient use of professional staff.

The other feature of the program at Camp Elliot that is worthy
of further attention is the utilization of nonprofessional staff as
part of a treatment team. The central role of the professional was
as consultant to the nonprofessional supervisor who shared a common background with the persons for whom he was responsible.
The use of nonprofessionals sharing common characteristics with
persons drawn from delinquent subcultures needs to be explored
further. Questions of recruitment, training, supervision, and utilization of nonprofessionals must play a paramount role in the
planning of residential rehabilitative programs for criminals and
delinquents.

In summary, it can be said that while institutions have become
more humanitarian there is no evidence that they have become more
effective rehabilitative agents. It must be further emphasized that
institutions are extremely expensive means of handling society's
problems. It costs approximately $10,000 to build one cell in a
maximum security institution and nearly $4,000 a year to keep an
inmate in that cell.

Funds to rehabilitate the delinquent are not unlimited. Correctional programs must be considered as part of a zero-sum game,
and money invested in institution programming comes at the expense of community programming. The correctional program will

be maximally effective when, at every level, integration of services is achieved and administrative structures are developed to permit continuity between the institution and in the community.

The Halfway House and Other
Intermediate Institutions

In recent years a number of programs have aimed at facilitating the integration of the inmate into a noncriminal society. These programs are designed to provide a continuity of services in the progress from custodial institutions to nonsupervised existence in free society.

The Justice Department has introduced, as a part of its rehabilitation program for youth committed to the Bureau of Prisons, three pre-release guidance centers. These centers, located in Brooklyn, Los Angeles, and Chicago, are designed to:

> provide a means for orderly reintroduction of the offender into the community through the use of all available community resources, together with a structured guidance and counselling program. The purpose of the project is to assist the youth in becoming gainfully employed and in gaining a sense of usefulness and self-worth. In addition, the program provides a social orientation for the youths by exposing them to a wide variety of constructive influences and activities in the community.[3]

It was clearly recognized in the conceptualization of this program that low-income youth presented special problems: "Most released offenders must return to the same sub-standard, economically depressed neighborhoods where opportunities for adjustment and social conformity are extremely limited." [4]

The California Department of Corrections has built a halfway house into its experimental Narcotic Treatment Control Program (this program is discussed further in the section on narcotic addiction, pp. 595–647).

New York State Division for Youth has introduced halfway house programs into its experimental START (modeled after Highfields) and camp programs. A variant of the halfway house is the home program of the New York State Division for Youth.[5] The home programs are for youth referred by courts or social agencies to remove them from intolerable family situations. They serve as halfway houses, in that they afford intermediate custody between

ordinary probation services and the residential centers operated by the Division for Youth. The home programs will operate within the local community while the other residential centers are open, but will be removed from the pressures and temptations of the community.

There are various halfway house programs operated under private auspices to aid in the rehabilitation of released inmates. Among the better known are Crenshaw House in Los Angeles, St. Leonard's in Chicago, and Dismas House in St. Louis. In the section on narcotics addiction, Synanon's distinctive approach and its claim to effectiveness are discussed by Rita Volkman and Donald Cressey.

The Pearl article argues that halfway houses—besides offering a logical continuity between institution and community—become the base for converting delinquents from criminal to noncriminal ways of life.

Treatment in the Community

A program specifically designed to alleviate the inadequacies of institutional programming has been inaugurated in Provo, Utah. This program is described in the article by LaMar Empey and Jerome Rabow, "The Provo Experiment in Delinquency Rehabilitation."

The program emanates from a rational base: if low-income, slum delinquents are attached to a delinquent subculture then the obvious intent of rehabilitation is to bring about a transfer from a delinquent subculture to a "conventional" subculture. The latter operates outside the institution; therefore, the logical place for investment of rehabilitative effort is in the community.

The Provo experiment is important because it attempts to develop a treatment program based on sociological theory that utilizes the current state of knowledge. The experiment truly exemplifies commitment to rigorous application of scientific methodology. Results of the Highfields experiment were considered inconclusive since no account was furnished of the response of youth comparable to Highfields and Annandale youth, who were given the alternative of probation supervision.[6] The Provo experiment cannot be criticized on this score; the program is contrasted with both traditional institution and probation efforts.

There are, however, some aspects of the Provo experiment that must be viewed critically. The boys involved in the program are assumed committed to a delinquent subculture, and while they undoubtedly share some characteristics with the delinquents of the major urban centers, it is also true that there are important dfferences between the delinquent in Utah County and for example, the youth of East Los Angeles or the Lower East Side of New York. What might work in Provo, Utah, might be singularly ineffective in Chicago, Illinois. This does not imply criticism of the Provo experiment; rather it is a call for replication of the program in areas where the urban afflictions are more acute. Another difficulty is that the Provo experiment expects too much from the delinquent. The program's emphasis is on reducing commitment to delinquent subculture and developing recognition that other ways are better; but the program is not designed to equip the delinquent to function in the conventional culture, nor does it imply that it is necessary to condition the conventional culture to permit the adjudicated delinquent access to its benefits.

Donald Cook's article, "Delinquency Programs in the Open Community," highlights many issues involved in rehabilitation in free society. He stresses the ambivalence of the community toward treatment and antagonisms of conflicting interests. He cautions that detached gang workers, rather than enticing the gang member from delinquency, may succumb to the blandishments of the delinquent subculture. He concludes that unless society finds a role for the ex-delinquent to play, it cannot realistically expect him to remain free from reinvolvement in delinquency.

Concrete evidence that a program which offers treatment within a context of job placement can have a powerful rehabilitative effect is presented by Massimo and Shore, in "A Vocational Psychotherapeutic Program for Delinquent Boys." Evidence for the beneficial effects of the program is extremely convincing, although the authors do not offer much detail about the actual program operation. It is not clear whether the delinquents were predominantly from low income slum areas. Nor do the authors divulge where the jobs were found for the youngsters. However, most importantly, Massimo and Shore provide solid support for the thesis that were employment opportunities made available, a therapeutic program that exploited these opportunities could aid in the rehabilitation of delinquents.

An effort to meet the delinquent on his terms and on his own "turf" has been made in a number of urban areas.[7] Walter Miller describes the nature of the detached gang worker program in the article entitled "The Impact of a Community Group Work Program on Delinquent Corner Groups." He presents a program drawing upon a theoretical focus [8] and set in the context of evaluative research. He offers evidence supporting the effectiveness of such interventions. He does not emphasize sufficiently the skills necessary for effective group work, nor does he appear to be cognizant of the danger that the worker may be subverted by the delinquent group referred to by Cook in his article.[9] Moreover, Miller does not appear to give central importance to employment as a way out of delinquency. His orientation, similar to that advocated by the Provo experiment,[10] is that redirecting the delinquent appears to have sufficient impetus. In this respect, the program differs significantly from those suggested by Pearl in his article on the halfway house.[11]

A gang worker who became discouraged with his impact upon delinquent youth published, in collaboration with a professional writer, his disillusionment with that type of work.[12] Paul Goodman's brief review of this book is presented here. The review places delinquency rehabilitation in the perspective of broader issues. The Goodman desire to attack society's most sacred beliefs permeates the review, but his concern with fundamental problems (if not his proposed solutions) must be considered if rehabilitation of delinquents is to be maximally effective.

A program which has as its primary emphasis enhancing opportunities for low income youth is New York City's demonstration program, Mobilization For Youth. This program, based on the theoretical formulations of Cloward and Ohlin,[13] is broadly outlined by one of its directors, George Brager, in the article, "Improving Services for Street Corner Youth." [14] The aims of the Mobilization program are ambitious and laudatory. This program departs dramatically from prior activities. It has emerged as the outgrowth of viable theory, and it is immersed in evaluative research.

The central thrust of the Mobilization For Youth program is to mount a massive integrated attack on the precipitants of delinquency. The program, if it is to accomplish its goals, must achieve effective coordination of a wide array of services and agencies. To the extent that Mobilization is able to accomplish efficient functioning systems it may represent a model to be implemented

elsewhere; to the extent that it fails, its research should provide the basis for development of more promising auspices and procedures.

Mobilization For Youth is designed to meet the problems of a community. It does not focus upon isolated individuals imputed to possess characteristics that make them likely to become delinquent. It has been suggested that programs designed to prevent delinquency fail because persons who are designated as "high risk" are singled out for special treatment and this identification leads to attachment of stigma and sabotage of the program.

> Regardless of the client problem that is being addressed through a special treatment program for predelinquents, that program must avoid the boomerang effects of early stigmatization. Perhaps boomerang effects are the major reason why not a single validated example exists of successful early identification and intensive treatment programs.[15]

While the Mobilization program protects the participant against stigmatization, the cost of this protection may be excessive. The program effort is being diffused and services may be wasted on those who do not need them. If those in need of service are not identified, services may be offered exclusively to those in least need. Another problem inherent in mass attack programs is that there is not sufficient recognition of the possibility that programs beneficial to some persons might be harmful to others.

Mobilization For Youth is designed primarily to overcome the devastation of poverty. It has at its disposal relatively large sums of money. Poverty is effectively attacked when the unemployed are offered meaningful long-term employment. Mobilization is in a position to employ a considerable number of indigenous persons in the performance of technical roles in the area of human service.[16] Some nonprofessional residents of the community have been employed but the majority of those on the staff of Mobilization For Youth are nonresident professionals. A rule of thumb by which programs designed to alter the opportunity structure can be gauged could be the proportion of the employees of the program who are indigenous to the community and possess few marketable skills that would permit them to readily enter the world of work.

While Mobilization For Youth's good features undoubtedly outweigh its bad, it cannot be considered the final word in coordinated mass attacks on delinquency. If a truly effective research effort emerges from the Mobilization program, if careful attention

is given to program process, if the effects of each program are evaluated separately, the gain from the Mobilization experience will be great even if it cannot demonstrate the desired impact upon delinquency.

The article by R. R. Schwitzgebel, "Delinquents with Tape Recorders," introduces the technique of paying an ex-offender to talk into the tape recorder. This innovation deserves comment. It has been continually emphasized in our account that a meaningful career must be created for the delinquent. In one sense, the programs developed by Charles Slack and the Schwitzgebel brothers constitute a variation of this theme. However, it is questionable that merely refraining from engagement in delinquent behavior offers much promise for recompensable life careers. In the Schwitzgebel article it was emphasized that the delinquent may generate insight into underlying problems, by talking into the tape recorder.

The article about the New York City Board of Education program, "Film Experiment with Delinquent Boys," presents evidence that motion pictures may be used to stimulate verbal and behavior reactions and aid a therapeutic resolution. Schwitzgebel's experiment and the New York City program share a number of important features. Both strive to meet the delinquent on a level and with a language he can undersatand. Both use apparatus that are in themselves intriguing and provide the opportunity for physical manipulation. Both add a touch of glamor and allure to otherwise drab proceedings. It is hardly likely that these features, in themselves, will lead to profound and long-range effects. It is equally unlikely that programs which do not include such elements will meet with much success.

Drug Addiction

Addiction is a special problem in the United States. Few social problems have engendered as much controversy and as little consensus for solution. Pearl, in his article "Narcotic Addiction Is A Special Problem," reviews the various aspects of narcotic addiction in the United States, focusing on a consolidated total treatment approach.

The article by Volkman and Cressey, "Differential Association and the Rehabilitation of Drug Addicts," vividly describes the Synanon experiment. Cressey and Volkman see in Synanon a vali-

dation of the Differential Association Theory. Synanon stresses quite pointedly the conversion of addicts to another way of life. The point must be made that the conversion is to a special, isolated existence, and while some former addicts may favor this new existence, a majority of addicts who turn to Synanon are unable to make this transition. Furthermore, only a small percentage of addicts have found Synanon appealing.

It is difficult to conceptualize the life of an addict. Romanticized, fictional accounts have given an unreal pictures of the addict's social existence. The addicts residing in Synanon may differ in many respects from the addicts who populate the prisons and jails of the United States. To give a picture of this lower class addict, his way of life, his language style, and his values, an interview with such a person is presented in the article entitled "An Addict Tells His Story." Each addict lives a unique life but he shares with many others a common socioeconomic history and a similar hopeless future unless given access to another way of life.

The concluding article by Freedman *et al.*, entitled "Response of Adult Heroin Addicts to a Total Therapeutic Program," presents still another experimental approach to dealing with the addict. Freedman and his colleagues attempt to bring professional treatment to bear in a community setting. Systematically, they study the failures of earlier attempts to treat the addict in order to increase the effectiveness of new programs. Both the measures advanced by Freedman and his associates and the Synanon experiment attempt to convert the addict to new ways of life. The programs differ in that the latter attempts to create a new life for the addict within the confines of the Synanon environment, whereas the former attempts to alter that life within the natural community. Synanon eschews the services of the professional as culturally foreign to the addict and lacking the appropriate skills to help him. Freedman and his associates accept these charges as essentially true, but view them as a challenge to instituting changes in attitude and approach that will make professional services more suitable to the addict's needs. It is hoped that in further refinements of program they can find a significant role for the indigenous nonprofessional to play in their treatment team.

During the past decade rehabilitation of the delinquent has been marked by a number of encouraging trends. There has been a great willingness to experiment with new approaches. It has become increasingly apparent that rehabilitation services must be solidly

grounded in knowledge. It has become increasingly recognized that rehabilitation is a total experience involving continuity between institution and community and coordination of all available resources. Employment of the ex-offender is a primary requirement for rehabilitation, and if employment resources are unavailable, then rehabilitative agencies must play a role in creating new opportunities. With growing knowledge and refinement and sophistication of theory, rehabilitation of even the most recalcitrant offender can become a reality.

Notes

1. As graphically stated by a delinquent describing a colleague to the author in an interview, "Man, he was a tough stud—he did a lotta time."

2. This type of research is amplified by Arthur Pearl, "Quality Control in Evaluation Research of Correctional Programs," paper given at the National Council on Crime and Delinquency Conference, Seattle, July 23, 1963.

3. Pre-Release Guidance Program, "First Impressions," *Progress Report*, 10:3 (July–September 1962), 3. Department of Justice, Bureau of Prisons, Washington, D.C.

4. Ibid, p. 2.

5. New York State Division for Youth, "The Opportunity and Rehabilitation Center Program." Mimeographed, New York, 1962.

6. This variation was part of the Highfields original research design, but for a great variety of reasons, was not implemented.

7. The most celebrated of these programs has been attempted in New York City. For information about that program see *Reaching the Fighting Gang* (New York City Youth Board, 1960).

8. Miller, Walter, *op. cit.*

9. Cook, Donald, *op. cit.*

10. Empey, LaMar, and Rabow, *op. cit.*

11. Pearl, *op. cit.*

12. Vincent Riccio, and Bill Slocum, *All the Way Down—the Violent Underworld of Street Gangs* (New York, Simon and Schuster), 1963.

13. Cloward, C. and Ohlin, *op. cit.*

14. A more detailed picture of the Mobilization program can be obtained in "Mobilization For Youth: A Proposal for the Prevention and Control of Delinquency by Expanding Opportunities" (New York: Mobilization For Youth, 1961).

15. Jackson, Toby, "Early Identification and Intensive Treatment of Predelinquents: A Negative View," *Social Work*, 6; 3 (July 1961), 13.

16. Technician roles are described in the Pearl article, "The Halfway House: The Focal Point of the Model Program for the Rehabilitation of Low Income Offenders," pp. 497–508.

It's Time to Start Counting

J. Douglas Grant

Any correctional agency not using a prediction procedure to study the effectiveness of its decisions and operations is perpetrating a crime against the taxpayer. This is no longer a merely theoretical argument. Studies support each of the following contentions:

1. Experience is not enough; systematic self-study is essential to correctional effectiveness.

2. Correctional agencies are spending millions collecting information and millions making decisions, although these functions have had little influence on each other.

3. Systematic study can develop prediction devices which will hold up for at least several years.

4. While correctional programs are rehabilitating some kinds of offenders, they are in fact increasing the criminal activity of other kinds of offenders.

5. Correctional agencies are spending public funds on "good risks" who do not need the program in order to perform satisfactorily. Furthermore, these "good risks" are receiving more than their share of the available program budget.

6. The fact that a correctional agency relies on subjective decisions rather than on statistical formulas in no way excuses it from accountability for the effectiveness of its decisions. A question that should be empirically determined is: Which combination of information and procedures (*including* use of subjective decisions) prove most effective?

Reprinted from *Crime and Delinquency*, Vol. 8, No. 3, July 1962, pp. 259–264.

Experience Is Not Enough

Not too long ago, medical men "knew from experience" that "bleeding" sick people was good for them. Medical men also "knew enough from experience" not to prescribe tomatoes for one's diet. Neither of these "knowns" had been obtained from systematic study; rather, they were the kinds of folklore "knowns" that had arisen from chance experience: physicians had seen sick people get well who had had their blood let; they had not fed tomatoes to many people who did not get sick.

Rightfully, present-day management training courses stress that experience is not enough. They teach that when someone says he has eighteen years' experience, you should ask him whether he means eighteen years' experience or one year's experience eighteen times.

At the turn of the century, a psychologist ran a series of experiments to test the premise that experience at a task necessarily brings improvement in performance.[1] Taking the game of darts, he drew a line fifteen feet from the target on the wall. The subjects were given darts and told to stand behind the line and try to hit the target. However, the psychologist added another condition to the game: he placed an opaque curtain, from the floor to above eye level, between the subject and the target. Subjects had to toss the dart over the curtain into a target they could not see. Perhaps even more important, they could not see how close they came to the target at each throw. No matter how many times they threw the darts, ignorance of results prevented them from improving their ability to hit the target.

Nonsensical, you say. Of course experience is useless if one does not know where the target (goal) is or how close are one's throws. Yet, much of our experience in the correctional field is exactly like this. How much do we agree on our correctional goals? How many of us receive feedback on how well we are doing in achieving our goals? Can we make explicit what we expect and then compare what actually happens with what we expected to happen?

That experience is not enough has been dramatically demonstrated by Hakeem.[2] He presented the case summaries of 200 former parolees to experienced professional parole agents and asked them to classify these summaries into successes and failures. He then asked a group of accountants to do the same. The agents did slightly worse than the accountants and neither did better than chance. In addition, there was a systematic bias. While the records had been evenly divided between successes and failures, the parole agents classified too many as failures, markedly reducing the possibility of accurate prediction.

An associate superintendent of the California Department of Corrections recently put some of *his* years of experience to the test.[3] (He should be commended. This is the only way to separate truth from fantasy.)

He interviewed 283 inmates just prior to their release on parole and made predictions concerning their likelihood of success. In addition, he reviewed psychiatric case histories and made further predictions on the basis of this material. The result was that his interview predictions correlated .20 with parole outcome; his predictions based on interview *plus* clinical information correlated .21. A base expectancy formula developed two years previously, however, correlated .48 with the parole outcome. Even when combined with the interview and clinical record judgments, the base expectancy formula was not markedly improved; the multiple correlation was still .48. Conclusion: This administrator's wealth of experience was much less effective in predicting parole performance than was systematic study of one year's experience. Further, with much more information, the expected professional was unable to add anything to improve the predictions derived from systematic study.

Too Much Money for Too Little Return

Thirty years ago Adolf Meyer suggested that social agencies could get closer to their clients by trying to understand the whole person.[4] He proposed case histories as a way of doing this. But, as with many good ideas, the case history method has become distorted. Often, workers in social agencies are so busy collecting, completing, and filing case histories that they have little time left for their clients. Further, the case history records often become so voluminous that they can be used only superficially, if at all, in making decisions affecting the clients.

Vinter and Janowitz conducted an organizational study of seven older-youth correctional institutions.[5] One of their major findings was that the institutions had far more information on their inmates than they were able to use. Many decisions concerning program changes and inmate management were constantly being made, but the voluminous information files seldom had any effect upon these decisions.

Correctional agencies, like other social agencies, have two main concerns: keeping case records and making decisions. Both represent tremendous expenditures of time and money, but the two activities have little influence on each other. The information-collectors are busy describing the whole person. The decision-makers are busy trying to cope with a multitude of pressures in a field where little systematic study or body of facts is available. This lack of integration does not imply that management is unconcerned with facts, but rather that no adequate means of bringing the two together has yet been devised.

Leslie Wilkins, however, has shown how prediction procedures can help management to state what it expects from known information and to study systematically the ways of bringing about variations from the expected.[6]

Prediction Devices Hold Up

A formula based on one year's releases to parole will predict parole success for subsequent years. The California Department of Corrections has tested this out by using various formulas in several studies over a number of years.

In a study of parole caseload size, a base expectancy formula predicted releases for 1957 and 1958 as well as it did for its original cross-validation sample in 1956.[7] The studies discussed previously, in which interview-derived predictions were compared with formula- derived predictions, showed that a formula predicted parole releases better than it predicted its original cross-validation sample. These validations held up when analyzed by quarter year, geographic region to which paroled, and institution from which released. In addition, they held up for both arrest and recommitment criteria.

Base expectancies developed for women parolees during the three years ending in June, 1958, also held up for women released to parole in 1959 and 1960.[8]

A very promising development is Gottfredson's effort to predict actual Parole Board decisions.[9] It appears that parole boards are more predictable than parolees. From intake information such as severity of offense, prior incarceration, minimum eligible parole date, and age, Gottfredson is able to predict the Parole Board's decisions in setting institution time and parole time. He found that correlations between predicted time and actual time set by the Board were greater than .60.

While cross-validations have yet to be made, these findings are most encouraging. They form the basis for a study, sponsored by the National Institute of Mental Health, of decisions made by the Adult Authority and California's Board of Trustees for Women.[10] Discrepancies between formula predictions and actual decisions will be studied for additional relevant information.

Gottfredson's data suggest that the Parole Board was not setting terms on the basis of case history information known to predict parole success. Even when the Parole Board's decisions were studied separately for each offense group, there was almost no relationship between an inmate's base expectancy score and the institution or parole time he actually served. Since this study, the base expectancy scores have been made available to the paroling authority.

Programs Help Some, May Harm Others

Intensive psychiatric casework was given institutionalized older wards of the California Youth Authority.[11] Before treatment, these wards had been divided into amenables and non-amenables. Both groups were

matched with controls who did not receive treatment. The first 100 amenables released from treatment and institutionalization had a total of only 206 months reconfinement, compared with the 480 months for the first 100 control amenables released. This difference was based on a 33-month follow-up. More important, perhaps, is the finding that the treated non-amenables had 550 months of reconfinement while the *control* non-amenables had only 481. These latter negative effects of treatment on particular types of inmates, though not statistically significant, are similar to the results of other studies.

The Navy has experimented with a therapeutic community type of program for its confines,[12] in which subjects were divided into high and low social maturity classifications and members of the community supervisory staff were judged according to their probable effectiveness in bringing about a reduction in the delinquency-prone attitudes of those confined. High-maturity confinees, it was found, performed better upon return to military duty when their therapeutic-community experience had been under effective rather than ineffective supervision. Low-maturity confinees, however, performed much worse upon restoration to duty when they had been under effective supervision than when they had been under supervision judged ineffective.

Recent California studies of parole,[13] group counseling,[14] and vocational training [15] reveal similar interactions. The programs show positive effects for some types of offenders, but no effect or negative effects for other types; the main positive effects took place within the second lowest quartile of the base expectancy distribution. While further replications are needed and are being conducted, present studies strongly suggest that agencies must systematically determine which clients should receive which programs. Further, prediction procedures are proving effective both in providing bases for evaluation and in developing relevant classifications.

Programs Wasted on "Good Risks"

To repeat, base expectancy tables can aid in identifying those who will benefit from specific correctional programs. Base expectancies also have identified offenders who will perform well with less than the regularly prescribed program. What is more, these "good risk" clients have been found to receive more than their share of available programing.

California's Department of Corrections experimentally placed good parole risks, as determined by base expectancy rates (best 15 per cent), under minimal supervision. The "good risks" performed as well as they were predicted to do under regular supervision.[16]

The California Women's Parole Division analyzed the frequency of interview contacts for three different base-expectancy-derived classifications and found that the top 15 per cent (good risks) were receiving more than their share of interviews.[17] Partly as a result of these analyses,

the Women's Parole Divison has developed a new classification and supervisory system. Good risks receive minimal attention. The supervisory time thus saved is redeployed in treatment-oriented supervision of amenable parolees and in surveillance of the nonamenable.

California's Adult Parole Division has developed "good risk" caseloads of male parolees and is using the saved supervisory time for more intensive supervision of "middle risk" parolees—a result of experiments in which a prediction procedure was used to study parole.[18]

Subjective Decisions Also Need Study

In defense of subjectively based as opposed to statistically based decisions, much has been written about the uniqueness of the individual.[19] Kluckhohn and Murray, however, suggest that the unique qualities of a client provide only one kind of information which can aid us in making decisions. "Every man is in certain respects (a) like all other men, (b) like some other men, (c) like no other man." [20] All three kinds of information are, and should be, subject to empirical study.

More needs to be known about human behavior. More needs to be known about prediction devices. Certainly, more needs to be known about predicting future behavior of a person on the basis of past behavior.

The point to emphasize, however, is that to refer to the uniqueness of an individual is to indicate an area for systematic study. It is no justification for making decisions about his future in a sloppy, unsystematic, and costly manner.

As discussed by several, it is not a question of subjective vs. statistical prediction.[21] Judgments can be used to improve prediction formulas as well as decisions, while statistical study of subjective judgment can improve the judgment.

Perhaps what I have said here can best be summarized by Kelvin's frequently quoted words: "When you can measure what you are speaking about and express it in numbers, you know something about it, but when you cannot measure it, when you cannot express it in numbers your knowledge is of a meagre and unsatisfactory kind." [22]

Notes

1. Edward L. Thorndike, *The Fundamentals of Learning* (New York: Columbia University Teachers College, 1932).

2. Michael Hakeem, "Prediction of Parole Outcome from Summaries of Case Histories," *Journal of Criminal Law, Criminology, and Police Science*, July–Aug., 1961, pp. 145–155.

3. E. Savides, "A Parole Success Prediction Study," and D. M. Gottfredson, "Comparing and Combining Subjective and Objective Parole Predictions," *The Research Newsletter*, Sept.–Dec., 1961, No. 3–4.

4. Adolf Meyer, "Thirty-five Years of Psychiatry in the United States and Our

Present Outlook," *American Journal of Psychiatry*, July, 1928.

5. Robert D. Vinter and Morris Janowitz, *Comparative Study of Juvenile Correctional Institutions: A Research Report*, Dec., 1961 (mimeo.), Ann Arbor, University of Michigan School of Social Work.

6. H. Mannheim and L. T. Wilkins, *Prediction Methods in Relation to Borstal Training* (London: Her Majesty's Stationery Office, 1955).

7. Joan Havel and Elaine Sulka, "Special Intensive Parole Unit, Phase III" *Research Report No. 3*, California Department of Corrections, March, 1962.

8. Paul F. C. Mueller, "Outcome Prediction for Women Parolees through CDC-BE-CIW 62A," *Research Report No. 6* (in preparation), California Department of Corrections.

9. D. M. Gottfredson, "Efforts to Predict Institutional Time," *Research Report No. 13* (in preparation), California Department of Corrections.

10. D. M. Gottfredson, "A Strategy for Study of Social Agency Effectiveness," *Social Agency Effectiveness Study*, NIMH Project OM 823.

11. Stuart Adams, "Interaction between Individual Interview Therapy and Treatment Amenability in Older Youth Authority Wards," Monograph No. 2, California Board of Corrections, July, 1961.

12. J. D. Grant and M. Q. Grant, "A Group Dynamics Approach to the Treatment of Nonconformists in the Navy," *Annals of the American Academy of Political and Social Science*, March, 1959, pp. 126–135.

13. Havel and Sulka, *op. cit.*

14. P. F. C. Mueller, "Clue-Hunting about Group Counseling and Parole Outcome," *Research Report No. 11* (in preparation), California Department of Corrections.

15. D. M. Gottfredson and P. F. C. Mueller, "The Utility of a Release Evaluation for Parole Outcome Prediction," *Research Report No. 12* (in preparation), California Department of Corrections.

16. Joan Havel, "Special Intensive Parole Unit, Phase IV," *Research Report No. 10* (in preparation), California Department of Corrections.

17. Isabel Betts, "Six Months Experience with a Parolee Classification System," *The Research Newsletter*, Sept.–Dec., 1961, No. 3–4.

18. Havel, *op. cit.* and Havel and Sulka, *op. cit.*

19. Elmer Reeves, "A Fresh Look at Prediction and Supervision," *Crime and Delinquency*, Jan., 1961, pp. 37–41.

20. Clyde Kluckhohn and Henry A. Murray. *Personality in Nature, Society, and Culture* (New York: Knopf, 1953), p. 53.

21. A. D. de Groot, "Statistical via Clinical Prediction," address to the Western Psychological Association, San Jose, Calif., April 1960; L. J. Cronbach and G. C. Gleser, *Psychological Tests and Personnel Decisions* (Urbana: University of Illinois Press, 1957); and D. M. Gottfredson, J. A. Bonds, and J. D. Grant, "Combining Clinical and Statistical Prediction for Correctional Decisions" (unpublished).

22. Lord Kelvin, quoted in *Tables for Statisticians and Biometricians* (London: Pearson, 1945).

The New Institution:

The Highfields Model

Factors in the Success of Highfields

G. Howland Shaw

For those willing to look realistically at the institutional treatment of juvenile delinquents the record is far from encouraging. Not that there are not institutions doing or striving to do constructive work in the light of the knowledge at our disposal, and not that there are not many individuals who do their utmost and more and are not frustrated because, through no fault of their own, they do not command the facilities essential to the task. Institutional names have changed over the years. Reform schools became industrial schools, then training schools, and at present we are hearing about residential treatment centers. But however the institutions are named, the percentage of former inmates who "graduate" from juvenile to adult correctional institutions is disconcertingly large. Our present inability to state in anywhere nearly specific terms just how large it is, and why, is a major handicap in securing public confidence and support.

The Highfields experiment—and I label it so advisedly, for, because of the gaps in our knowledge, any project of prevention and treatment of juvenile delinquency must be considered experimental—has had the courage and the wisdom to subject itself to the most rigorous possible evaluation in the light of existing research techniques; statistical, psychological, and sociological. That fact is in itself a most important achievement, one that, it is to be hoped, will be followed by others. The evaluation has shown a balance of results, quantitatively and qualitatively, in favor of Highfields as compared with that obtained under the more conventional correctional program of the Annandale Reformatory. The percentage of success following release appears significant, and the

Reprinted from *Youthful Offenders at Highfields*, H. Ashley Weeks, Ann Arbor: University of Michigan Press, 1958, pp. 145–148.

test responses of graduates from Highfields are appreciably less stereo-typed than those of releases from Annandale. To those familiar with the stereotyped responses of youngsters who have been in a correctional institution for any length of time, that seems no mean achievement.

Obviously, Highfields is not *the* answer to the problem of institutional treatment of juvenile delinquency: there is no one answer. But the Highfields project has demonstrated that, in the space of a few months and at relatively small cost, positive results can be obtained with the upper-teen-age delinquent who is reasonably intelligent, not too patterned in delinquency, and not too emotionally disturbed. Opinions may and do differ as to the size of this group, but that it is important numerically cannot be disputed. It is furthermore a group that tends, because of the present fashionable emphasis on the phychiatrically oriented institution, to be forgotten and relegated to state training schools with large and necessarily heterogeneous populations.

With this particular group in mind, Highfields has unquestionably added to our treatment resources. The following, I suggest, are some of the more important factors that have contributed to its success. They are in striking contrast to conditions in the average institution.

1. The group is small and reasonably homogeneous. The danger of bullying is therefore at a minimum, and the newcomer is not confronted with the immediate problem of finding a place for himself in a large group, with the traumatic experiences frequently involved. State training schools with as many as six hundred inmates are by no means unknown. In such schools at least some contact between delinquents of the less developed kind and those whose pattern of delinquency is well established cannot be avoided. Defective delinquents associate with those of normal intelligence. Under these conditions the application of any system of classification becomes difficult; rigidity is the rule, and rehabilitation is of necessity sacrificed to custody.

2. Because the Highfields group is small it is possible to establish with little delay and to maintain intimate contact between staff and boys. We have tended to attach too much importance to formal programs and buildings and not enough to the personality of the staff and particularly of those members who come into the closest and most continuous contact with inmates. We have even at times fallen into the superstition that academic degrees are a guarantee of an effective and mature personality. It is a truism, or at least it should be, that there is no rehabilitative force more powerful than the positive influence of somebody who cares and who, while retaining prestige, can suitably express his care for a youngster to whom nobody has shown interest, still less affection. In Europe, and especially in England's Borstal institutions, this truism has been recognized. In this country it has a certain force of novelty and needs constantly renewed emphasis.

3. Since the project is housed in a former private residence, the physical surroundings are noninstitutional, and maintaining an atmosphere of informality is greatly facilitated. Much has been said and written about "institutional atmosphere." That it can have a powerfully

depressing affect on both inmates and staff cannot be questioned. Especially in the older training schools efforts to escape this atmosphere and to make conditions more homelike are severely handicapped by the physical structure of the plant and the obviousness of the purpose for which it was built. Furthermore, an atmosphere of informality is next to impossible where the population is large and heterogeneous and where a more or less complicated type of organization is unavoidable.

4. There are few rules, and there is opportunity for initiative. One of the paradoxes of our traditional institutional treatment of delinquency is that we maintain a youngster under conditions that make the exercise of initiative difficult, often impossible, and where an elaborate set of rules is constantly and forcibly brought to his attention, and then project him into the outside world with the expectation that he will display a proper initiative and apply his own rules with a minimum of supervision.

5. The work program at Highfields is carried on outside the institution and under conditions normal in the world to which the boy will return. Since adjustment to these is a major problem for the delinquent youngster of the older group on his release, this feature of Highfields deserves special emphasis. In many institutions for delinquents, hours, standards of performance, and supervision do not approximate comparable conditions on the outside.

6. By means of the guided group interaction program the kind of negative talk characteristic of boys in an institutional setting is to an important degree replaced by talk that is deflating and at the same time socializing. A boy becomes aware of his problem, aware too that the boy sitting next to him has much the same problem. He can hardly escape the conclusion that he can help himself by helping the other boy. Since the delinquent is usually selfish and self-centered, such a conclusion has important therapeutic value.

The Highfields Program:
A Critique and Evaluation

Arthur Pearl

In 1950, Highfields was established by the State of New Jersey as an experimental innovation for the rehabilitaton of juvenile delinquents. The program developed at Highfields departed radically from those of traditional institutions for delinquent boys. The program had the following features: Offenders were referred by the court for a stay not to exceed four months in a completely open institution, with no more than twenty boys in the program. While at Highfields, the boys worked at meaningful jobs for which they received modest payment. The program provided a version of group counseling (in groups of ten) called guided group interaction—to indicate that the counselor was to play a somewhat active part in focusing the interchange of ideas and discussion.[1]

Evidence has been presented to indicate that youth from Highfields made a better adjustment on return to society than did a somewhat comparable group of youngsters who were sent to the New Jersey state reformatory, Annandale Farms. A report summarizing the evaluative research of the program concluded that, using recidivism as a criterion of success, "This research points out the fact that a higher proportion of Highfields than Annandale boys succeed and that this is true even when the background variables which are related to their success or failure are held constant."[2]

The research further indicated that Negro youth when compared with their reformatory counterparts had an even more favorable response than did white youth.

481

Of every hundred white boys, 64 Highfields and 59 Annandale boys completed their treatment and needed no further institutional care. The situation is quite different for the Negro boys: 59 of every hundred Highfields Negroes completed their treatment and got into no further difficulty severe enough to reinstitutionalize them, whereas this is true for only 33 of every hundred Annandale Negroes.[3]

The authors attempting to explain this extreme difference in the post-treatment adjustment of Negro youth explore whether the increment of gain attributed to Highfields could be the result of the characteristics of the persons sent to the two institutions. Although noting that the Highfields youth tended to possess more favorable attributes than did their Annandale "controls," the authors found that the disparity was not sufficient to account for differential success of the Highfields Negro youth.

From this analysis it would seem that differences in the total programs at the two facilities must account for the large differences between the proportions of Negroes at the respective facilities who complete their residence and do not get into further trouble." [4]

The fact that Negro youth do better at Highfields raises questions that are particularly pertinent to the treatment of the disadvantaged. In Highfields the Negro youth were drawn from economically disadvantaged backgrounds to a greater extent than was true for the white residents. None of the fathers of the Negro youth had white collar jobs, two-thirds of them had no more than grade school education, and the youth indicated, by responses to structured questionnaires, negative attitudes toward obeying the law and toward law enforcement.[5]

Jenkins, commenting on this finding, suggests that the Negro youth in a traditional institution comes under white authority but often constitutes a majority in the institution, which leads to displaced aggressiveness among other inmates. He adds:

A combination of motivation toward aggressive behavior and some status reward for aggressive behavior toward others of comparable status can hardly be expected to have a rehabilitative effect. By contrast the program at Highfields involves the acceptance of the Negro boy in a small, relatively informal group in which he shares his experience in fact and in discussion on a friendly and constructive basis with adolescents of the white race who have had many of the same experiences. This association may go far toward reducing a hostile antagonism toward authority and the law." [6]

The evidence is strong that Negroes enjoyed true integration in the Highfields experiment. Only 17 per cent of the total sample were Negro, which means that on the average, three Negro youths were living in close proximity with seventeen white youth. However, it is at best only suggestive that meaningful integration of racial and ethnic groups in institutions by itself will have a salubrious effect on post-institutional

adjustment for underprivileged minority groups. At present we do not know that Highfields was rehabilitative. It may merely have been less harmful for Negro youth than the Annandale experience.

There are other factors that must be considered before we arrive at the conclusion that the Highfields program had a rehabilitative effect. Highfields recruited the best available staff. The quality of staff alone might account for the demonstrated differences. So might the lack of prejudicial attitudes on the part of the Highfields staff (or conversely, the presence of prejudice among the staff at Annandale). Differences between attitudes of parole officers (who supervised the Annandale youth on return to the community) and probation officers (who were responsible for the Highfields youth) toward Negroes could also have produced the observed effect.

Other aspects of the Highfields experiment are troubling. The experience was intended to produce changes in the attitudes of the residents. And yet, there is no evidence that systematic change occurred in attitudes concerning family, law, general authority, self-confidence, and acceptance of others. It may be that the measures used were not sensitive enough or appropriate to measure change, but certainly a thorough study of the life processes of youth involved in a Highfields experience, as well as a precise statement of what actually occurred, is necessary if the value of Highfields is to be accurately assessed.

It is assumed that Highfields would be equally effective for youth from various economic backgrounds and there are some shreds of evidence, alluded to above which suggest that persons from deprived backgrounds might be most amenable to the treatment regime offered there. Yet, the treatment program features precisely those ingredients which low income people eschew in noncorrectional settings. The leader is relatively permissive, he offers little in concrete services, he suggests that the soution of the problem (an important part of the Highfields treatment is designation by the youth of a "problem") rests within the offender although he may obtain help from the group. While the program offers some opportunity to increase coping ability in work and language skills, the skills developed are general and there is no follow-through to insure that these skills are put into service. The problems faced at Highfields hardly relate to what disadvantaged youth must face in "free" society. Although from the available evidence it would appear that low income delinquents were involved in the Highfields program, it is not at all clear whether these were the "typical" low income delinquents with whom society has to deal. A rather choice group was selected for Highfields—youth with relatively high measured IQ's who were not too severely disturbed, and who were without a history of long-term institutionalization. These delinquents may be unrepresentative of the deprived delinquent universe. There is evidence that favorable background affected differentially Highfields and Annadale white youth. Some background variables were negatively correlated with post-program response. Youths who committed a number of delinquencies had little education, had few jobs and those of short duration, had crime partners, lived in

specific counties, moved frequently, and were less likely to succeed in free society. When Annandale youth with three or fewer adverse background attributes are compared with Highfields youth with the same number of adverse conditions, the Highfields youth attained 82 per cent successful outcomes, the Annandale group, 73 per cent. However, when youth with four or more adverse attributes were compared, 44 per cent Highfields group were adjudged successful whereas this was true for 55 per cent of the Annandale youth.[7] The adverse variables include measures of education, employment, and mobility, all characteristics generally used to differentiate, in demographic terms, relative social status. Inferentially, then, this data suggests that Highfields is much more appropriate for the relatively advantaged white delinquent than for the disadvantaged white delinquent.

The general applicability of Highfields is questioned further by Clarence Sherwood. Using responses to questionnaire items and establishing two types of failure, a failure to adjust to the situation in Highfields and a failure to adjust to the situation in free society he found: "those who got along best in the institution (Highfields) are those most likely to get into trouble in the post-release situation." [8]

Sherwood found that youth who responded to questionnaires in such a fashion that they were categorized as having hostile attitudes to authority and were *unaccepting* of others, tended to be unable to adjust to Highfields; whereas youth hostile to authority but *accepting* of others tended to make the most favorable adjustment to Highfields. Youth with precisely the latter characteristics fared the poorest in adjusting to free society. Youth regarded as having favorable attitudes to authority *but with little acceptance* of others had the best record in free society.[9]

Sherwood postulates that the youth hostile to authority but able to get along with other youth should have no trouble at Highfields. They will seek out others like themselves. They will in effect control the groups. The program demands interaction and they derive satisfaction from their status and power without the need to be hostile to the formal authority structure at Highfields.[10] He argues that this group will do poorly in free society because still seeking out others similar to themselves but now lacking the power and status that they had in the institution the natural response is to give vent to their hostile attitudes and therefore they will become embroiled in antisocial activities.

Sherwood's thesis has serious implications for programs designed to rehabilitate the low income gang member. He argues, in effect, that the Highfields program permits the gang member to be unreconstructed and yet give the appearance of great change. He is returned unprepared to grapple with life's problems "on the street."

The Highfields model represents a dramatic break with the past, and therefore the program has immense historical importance. But the inadequacies of Highfields also need to be clearly stated ánd universally understood. Highfields did not provide a reintroduction to society, nor was there sufficient emphasis on community programming. In recent years the Highfields model has been adapted in other settings. In New

Jersey, Essexfields, which incorporates many of the Highfields' features in a non-residential setting, has been established. The Divison for Youth of the State of New York has added after-care staff to facilitate integration of youth released from the variations of the Highfields programs, which are in operation in that state. The Divison for Youth has created another adaptation of the Highfields program in its Home program. These residential centers are located within the home community of the youth. The boys reside there and are able to maintain school and work responsibilities and relationships with "significant others" in the community. Each variation of the Highfields program that is systematically studied will add to this knowledge of the rehabilitation process and from such knowledge more effective institutional programs for delinquent youth will emerge.

Institutional emerging programs must recognize the importance of the background of the delinquent, must offer something more satisfying to him than a delinquent way of life, and must be prepared to follow through to make those adjustments in the community that are necessary if the delinquent is to enter an alternative style of existence.

Notes

1. For a complete description of the Highfields experiment see L. W. Mc-Corkle, A. Elias, and F. L. Bixby, *The Highfields Story: A Unique Experiment in the Treatment of Juvenile Delinquency* (New York: Holt, Rinehart & Winston, 1958).

2. H. A. Weeks, *et al.*, *Youthful Offenders at Highfields* (Ann Arbor: The University of Michigan Press, 1958), 127.

3. *Ibid.*, p. 42.

4. *Ibid.*, pp. 45–46.

5. *Ibid.*

6. Richard L. Jenkins, in *ibid.*, 155.

7. Data obtained from Weeks, *ibid.*, p. 60.

8. Clarence C. Sherwood, "A Dimensional Theory of Recidivism." Unpublished Ph.D. dissertation, New York University, June, 1955.

9. *Ibid.*, pp. 30–31.

10. *Ibid.*, p. 35.

A Group Dynamics Approach to the Treatment of Nonconformists in the Navy

J. Douglas Grant and Marguerite Q. Grant

Since 1952 the Navy has been conducting a research program [1] in the prediction and treatment of military delinquency. Three questions outline the aims of this program:

What are the personality characteristics of the recruit who will prove himself a nonconformist?

With men who demonstrate extreme nonconformity, what are the characteristics of those who will be able to modify their behavior sufficiently to adjust to the group aspects of military life?

What is the nature of the process that brings about attitudinal and behavioral change in the nonconformist so that he is able to meet the demands of military life?

This report deals with a study relevant to the second and third questions.

Camp Elliott, where the research was conducted, is a place of confinement and retraining for approximately 1000 sailors and marines who have been courtmartialed. They are confined for offenses ranging from asbence without leave (about 85 per cent) to murder. The average period of confinement is about four months. Between 55 and 60 per cent of the men are restored to military duty at the termination of their confinement.

It is often assumed that the man who has offended against a military law is not the same sort of person as the civilian delinquent. While it is true that the majority of military men are confined for absence offenses, which are not civilian crimes, there is considerable evidence that civilian and military delinquent groups of comparable age show similar attitudes and nonconformity patterns.[2]

Reprinted from *Annals of American Academy of Political and Social Science*, Vol. 322, March 1959, pp. 126–135.

Frame of Reference

The frame of reference for this research program is a theory of sequential levels of interpersonal maturity. The case for an interpersonal relations approach to delinquency has been steadily gaining ground. Donald Bloch [3] has described delinquent behavior as an effort to handle interpersonal anxiety. Croft and Grygier [4] have been able to show that the social relationships of truants and juvenile delinquents vary markedly from those of their nontruant and nondelinquent classmates. Gough and Peterson [5] and Sarbin [6] have stressed the delinquent's inability to visualize himself in the role of another person. In studying military delinquents, Osborn [7] found the main difference between repeated absence offenders and matched nonoffenders to be an inadequacy in childhood and adolescent interpersonal relationships for the offender group. The Camp Elliott Delinquency Potential Scale,[8] which at the recruit stage predicts later military delinquency, contains many interpersonal items. Most of these items relate to what has been called social imperturbability —a tendency to deny any involvement with the relationships between one's self and others.

Although this frame of reference suggests that delinquent behavior results from interactions between individuals, the emphasis has been put on delinquency proneness and what it is within the individual that he takes with him into interpersonal relationships. This approach has recently received new emphasis from the methodological work of Cronbach.[9] He has stated that we need to know much more about the "sets" that people bring with them into interpersonal situations. More needs to be understood about the nature of the delinquency proneness, in terms of interpersonal "sets," before we can study the effect of interpersonal interactions in determining delinquent behavior. The maturity levels theory maintains that these "sets" are extremely important. It further suggests that there are interpersonal problems laden with anxiety which form the core of the individual's social understanding in his efforts to integrate what is happening between himself and others as well as between others.

Maturity Levels

This theory of interpersonal maturity has been described in detail elsewhere.[10] Seven successive stages of interpersonal maturity characterize psychological development. They range from the least mature, which resembles the interpersonal interactions of a newborn infant, to an ideal of social maturity which is seldom or never reached in our present culture. Each of the seven stages or levels is defined by a crucial

interpersonal problem which must be solved before further progress toward maturity can occur. All persons do not necessarily work their way through each stage but may become fixed at a particular level. Not all who are described as immature along this scale will be delinquent, but it is contended that those who are immature are more likely to find themselves in difficulties and to be apprehended for delinquency than are others.

Almost all persons who have grown to adulthood and not progressed beyond the first maturity level are found in institutions where they have to be cared for much like infants. Such personalities have not been found in a military delinquent population. At the other end of the scale, maturity levels 6 and 7 are also not represented in the Camp Elliott population. The adjustive capacity inherent in these "stages" would almost preclude delinquent activity.

A brief description of the levels of interpersonal maturity which are found in the population of military delinquents follows:

Maturity Level 2: The individual whose interpersonal understanding and behavior are integrated at this level is primarily involved with demands that the world take care of him. He sees others solely as "givers" or "withholders" and has no conception of interpersonal refinement beyond this. He is unable to explain, understand, or predict the behavior or reactions of others. He is not interested in things outside himself except as a source of supply. He behaves impulsively, unaware of the effects of his behavior on others, and is apt to explode or run away when frustrated or thwarted.

Maturity Level 3: The individual who operates at this level is attempting to manipulate his environment in order to get what he wants. In contrast to level 2, he is at least aware that his own behavior has something to do with whether or not he gets what he wants. He still does not differentiate, however, among people except to the extent that they can or cannot be useful to him. He sees people only as objects to be manipulated in order to get what he wants. His manipulations may take the form either of conforming to the rules of whoever seems to have the power at the moment ("If you can't lick them, join them.") or of the type of maneuvering characteristic of a "confidence man" ("Make a sucker out of him before he makes a sucker out of you."). He tends to deny having any disturbing feelings or strong emotional involvement in his relationships with others.

Maturity Level 4: An individual whose understanding and behavior are integrated at this level has internalized a set of standards by which he judges his and others' behavior. He is aware of the influence of others on him and their expectations of him. To a certain extent, he is aware of the effects of his own behavior on others. He wants to be like the people he admires and may feel guilty about not measuring up to his internalized standards. The conflict produced by the feelings of inadequacy and guilt may be internalized with consequent neurotic symptoms or acted out in antisocial behavior. Because the individual at level 4 tends to be uncomfortable about himself and because he is able to in-

ternalize values, he appears more amenable to treatment than previously described maturity levels.

Maturity Level 5: A person who functions at this level is able to see patterns of behavior; he may see himself and others behaving in the same way in different situations or see a continuity in his past, present, and future. His perceptions of himself and others are more differentiated than before. He begins to see others as complex, flexible objects which cannot be dealt with on the basis of a few single rule-of-thumb procedures. He is aware of many points of view in the world around him and sees interwoven reasons for behavior. He is able to play different roles in different situations and is thus more flexible. He is more capable of establishing and carrying through long-range plans than persons at lower levels. Delinquency, for a person at this maturity level, is apt to be situationally determined.

Theory of Treatment

A good deal of pessimism has been expressed regarding the possibility of curing delinquents with our traditional methods of treatment or psychotherapy. Traditionally, psychotherapy was aimed at helping the neurotic whose conflicts are internalized, who carries his guilt and anxiety with him. This kind of neurotic tends to know that he is upset or uncomfortable. He may, for example, feel afraid, have bad dreams, or not be able to speak in groups. In contrast, the acting-out personality tends to dissipate his anxiety before he feels it by running away, striking out at someone, or having an affair. Since the acting-out person periodically resolves his uncomfortableness, he abates any felt need for personality change. Traditional psychotherapeutic methods then are not appropriate for this kind of personality, since he feels no need to change and since he most certainly would run away from any therapy relationship which made him feel anxious.

Since almost all delinquents are acting-out personalities, the task in treatment becomes one of putting the offender in a nonpanic-producing correctional situation, which keeps him concerned about and facing his problems, in an attempt to bring about personality change in him. Acceptance of a need to change or grow results from a challenging uncomfortableness. Since this prerequisite for personality change—this uncomfortableness—is absent or easily dissipated, it needs to be created or maintained for the acting-out person. However, intense anxiety leads to rigidifying panic where no personality change can occur. Therefore, the goal of the treatment program here described was an attempt to create in a correctional situation a program which would produce in the subjects a challenging uncomfortableness without rigidifying panic.

The Camp Elliott research subjects were placed for six or nine weeks in groups of twenty in small closed communities called Living Groups.[11] The twenty men, with three supervisors, lived together in the same

barracks, ate together, worked on a farm as a unit, held classes together, participated as a team in recreational activities. The group was "closed," not only in the sense that no new members were admitted nor old members dismissed, but also in the sense that great effort was made to eliminate interpersonal dealings with anyone outside the group. The attempt was made to establish close, continuing interpersonal relationships within the group—with no way out. Ordinarily in confinement institutions there is much opportunity for running away even while staying within the fence by getting transferred from job to job or one living unit to another or running from therapist to therapist. To as great an extent as possible, all chances for this kind of acting-out or running away from anxiety were eliminated.

Many members of this population have been running away from close relationships all their lives. They may have run away from home, left school, held jobs for very short periods—and, for our military population—85 per cent of them have run away from the military service and have absence or deserter charges against them. They may never in their lives have worked through a single interpersonal relationship. They tend to leave any relationship before it is obvious to them that they have interpersonal problems.

SUPERVISORS AND CONSULTANTS

The three supervisors assigned to each Living Group were Marine noncommissioned officers, all of whom had volunteered for the program. They were on a two day out of three duty schedule. Two of the three supervisors were with the men on the job for half of each day; they held discussion classes with the men for the other half day. During free time and evening hours, one of the three supervisors was in the barracks available to the men for individual or small group "bull sessions." A psychologist was assigned to each team of three supervisors to act as a consultant. The psychologist was available to the confinees and supervisors for individual conferences, although every effort was made to keep as much as possible of the interpersonal relationships for group discussion.

Each consultant's main function was to conduct 90 minute, 5 days a week group therapy sessions attended by the twenty men and the supervisors. These sessions were the heart of the attempt to encourage social maturing through "forced" working through of the anxiety provided by the close, continuing interpersonal relationships. The psychologist's job was to prevent the challenging uncomfortableness from turning into rigidifying panic, yet not to allow subjects to flee the group. The focus in the group discussions was the interpersonal interactions within the group. An attempt was made to create a self-study atmosphere in which group members were encouraged to notice some interpersonal dealing of self with others or among others—to notice this interaction and to bring it to the group for discussion.

For the reader familiar with methods of psychotherapy, six or nine weeks may seem an impossibly short time in which to bring about personality change. Without presenting these short periods as ideals, it is worth remembering that the "treatment" here was a twenty-four hour a day process, a much more intensive experience than is usual in psychotherapy.

The closed Living Groups may be seen as the primary family situation revisited. Group therapy has often been likened to a family constellation with the therapist representing a parent and other group members, the siblings. In the Camp Elliott Living Groups two additional factors were present which contribute to the analogy, the twenty-four hours a day together and the "closedness" of the group. One of the characteristics of the family situation for the young child is that it is a closed system— he is trapped in it—he has no other resources. In our closed Living Groups, the men also could not escape. There is the possibility that interpersonal problems which for some reason could not be worked out in the original closed group—the family—may be worked through on such a return trip, especially with a parent figure who is perhaps more able to be supportive.

Experimental Design

Over a two-year period, twenty-seven Living Groups were run. During most of that period three groups were running simultaneously, one handled by each of the three supervisory teams. Three aspects of the Living Group experience were systematically varied in order to measure the effect of each aspect on later success of subjects. First, the three supervisory teams were ranked in order of their predicted effectiveness in bringing about reduction in delinquency-prone attitude; this ranking of the teams was one of the variables in the experimental design.

A second aspect was the level of maturity of the group members. Six of the groups were composed only of individuals of maturity levels 4 and 5. For the discussion here, these subjects will be called high maturity subjects, keeping in mind that their maturity level is high only in relation to other confined men. Six of the groups included only maturity levels 2 and 3, here to be called the low maturity subjects. The remaining fifteen groups included maturity levels 2, 3, 4 and 5. Nine of these mixed maturity groups operated for six weeks rather than nine in order to handle scheduling difficulties.

A third aspect of the experimental design was the duration of the supervisor-group relationship. Eighteen of the groups had the same supervisory team for the entire research period, while the other nine changed supervisors and consultant every three weeks.

The Living Groups were described to all incoming offenders at Camp Elliott, and 98 per cent of all the eligible men volunteered. In order to be eligible, the subject had to have a good chance of being restored to duty

and have at least six months left on his enlistment time so that follow-up information would be available on him; and he had to have sufficient confinement time to be able to complete the research program. Eligible volunteers were tested on a battery of personality tests given routinely at Camp Elliott.[12] Two psychologists independently assessing the test profiles made estimates of each volunteer's maturity level.[13] If the two psychologists agreed that the subject appeared to fit the maturity level of the group currently being formed, the subject was given a one-hour recorded interview. On the basis of this interview, the subjects were put into the appropriate group. No attempt was made to equalize our selection of Navy and Marine subjects, nor to have them represent their proportion in the service or in confinement.

Many interpersonal rating scales were built into the Living Group design.[14] Early and late in the research group experience, peer evaluations, supervisor-confinee, consultant-confinee, and cosultant-supervisor evaluations were systematically obtained. In addition, at the completion of the research period, the subjects were again tested and interviewed to determine the effects of the program on them. This report, however, will discuss only the relationship of later duty success to (1) the individual subject's maturity level, (2) the maturity level characteristics of the group in which the subject was a member, (3) the duration of the supervisor-group relationship, (4) the predicted effectiveness of the supervisory team, and (5) the interaction of these variables.

Results

Tables 1 and 2 summarize these five relationships. (1) The high maturity subjects did significantly better ($P = .01$) on restoration to duty than low maturity subjects. (2) Success rate was not affected by the maturity characteristics of the group; that is, high or low maturity subjects did as well following mixed maturity group experience as they did following groups composed of only low or only high maturity subjects. (3) Totaling results for all subjects over all conditions, the duration of the supervisor-group relationship did not affect the success rate. (4) Again, totaling over-all experimental conditions, no significant differences were found which can be attributed to predicted supervisory effectiveness. (5) However, the interaction between the predicted supervisory effectiveness and the maturity of the subject significantly (Analysis of variance, $P = $ less than $.05$) affected restoration success. The relationship between the subject's maturity and restoration success varied markedly and consistently with the amount of exposure to the supervisory teams in the order of predicted effectiveness. For subjects spending time only with T company supervision, predicted most effective, the relationship between maturity of the subject and restoration success was high ($r_t = .45$; $N = 114$). For subjects supervised by R company only, predicted second most effective, the relationship was

Table 1—Percentage Restoration Success by Maturity Characteristics of the Living-Group and Supervisory Effectiveness

Supervisory Team	Predicted Supervisory Effectiveness	9-Week High Maturity Only		9-Week Low Maturity Only		9-Week High Maturity Mixed		9-Week Low Maturity Mixed		6-Week High Maturity Mixed		6-Week Low Maturity Mixed		Total High Maturity		Total Low Maturity		Total High and Low Maturity	
		No.	Per Cent	No.	Per Cent	No.	Per Cent	No.	Per Cent	No.	Per Cent	No.	Per Cent	No.	Per Cent	No.	Per Cent	No.	Per Cent
T Co.	First	19	68.0	18	39.0	9	78.0	9	56.0	42	69.0	17	35.0	70	70.0	44	41.0	114	59.0
R Co.	Second	19	68.0	17	41.0	8	88.0	12	67.0	38	71.0	18	61.0	65	72.0	47	55.0	112	65.0
S Co.	Third	18	67.0	13	77.0	10	50.0	10	40.0	33	61.0	25	60.0	61	61.0	48	60.0	109	61.0
Subtotal		56	68.0	48	50.0	27	70.0	31	55.0	113	67.0	60	53.0	196	68.0	139	53.0	335	61.0
RST Co's.	Fourth	20	65.0	20	70.0	10	60.0	10	60.0					30	63.0	30	67.0	60	65.0
STR Co's.	Fourth	16	69.0	33	51.0	10	60.0	7	86.0					26	65.0	40	58.0	66	61.0
TRS Co's.	Fourth	14	50.0	17	65.0	10	80.0	9	67.0					24	63.0	26	65.0	50	64.0
Subtotal		50	62.0	70	60.0	30	67.0	26	69.0					80	64.0	96	63.0	176	63.0
Totals		106	65.0	118	56.0	57	68.0	57	61.0	113	67.0	60	53.0	276	67.0	235	57.0	511	62.0

Table 2—Percentage Restoration Success of High Maturity Subjects Compared with Low Maturity Subjects Over Kinds of Supervision

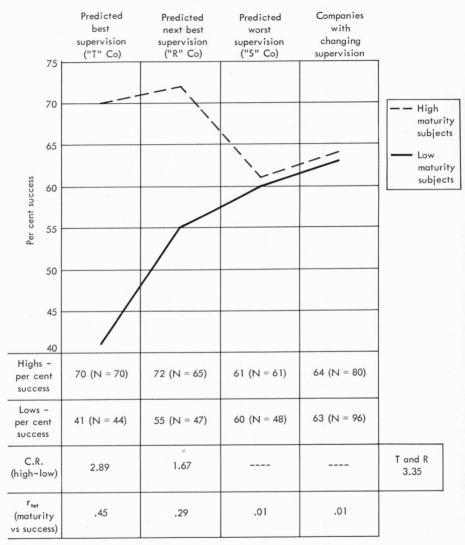

	Predicted best supervision ("T" Co)	Predicted next best supervision ("R" Co)	Predicted worst supervision ("S" Co)	Companies with changing supervision	
Highs – per cent success	70 (N = 70)	72 (N = 65)	61 (N = 61)	64 (N = 80)	
Lows – per cent success	41 (N = 44)	55 (N = 47)	60 (N = 48)	63 (N = 96)	
C.R. (high–low)	2.89	1.67	----	----	T and R 3.35
r_{tet} (maturity vs success)	.45	.29	.01	.01	

present but lower ($r_t = .29$; $N = 112$). For S company subjects, supervised by the predicted least effective team, the relationship vanished ($r_t = 0.1$; $N = 109$). If the Living Group experience was under supervision that changed every three weeks, there again was no relationship ($r_t = .01$; $N = 176$). Under conditions of changing supervision, only when the last six weeks were spent with the predicted most and next most effective teams did some relationship again emerge.

This interaction between the nature of supervision and the relationship between maturity and success was impressively consistent over several breakdowns of the data. The interaction holds for both Navy and Marine personnel, for both mixed and dichotomized maturity groups.

Another way of stating this interaction is that the over-all difference in success rate for high and low maturity subjects was found entirely under conditions of predicted effective supervision, T and R Company (C.R. = 3.35). The different success rate for high and lows failed to exist under predicted ineffective supervision (S Company) or under changing supervision. The maturity classification system appears valueless without an effectiveness of supervision classification, and an effectiveness of supervision classification appears valueless without a maturity classification.

Although further research needs to be done, these findings suggest that the cost of military recidivism could be reduced by installing a closed Living Group program with effective supervision for high maturity inmates. High maturity inmates have a high potential for improved restoration behavior but, unless subjected to an attitude-change program under effective supervision, this potential is not expressed in improved restoration behavior. This study does not support a closed Living Group program for low maturity inmates and, in fact, strongly suggests that at least aspects of an effective program for high maturity inmates can be detrimental to low maturity inmates.

Important as these applications are, the implications of these data for delinquency research in general are far greater. Correctional researchers have been finding it hard to demonstrate relationships between classification systems and postinstitutional behavior. They also have found it hard, if not impossible, to demonstrate relationships between treatment situations and postinstitutional behavior. As long as the data of the Camp Elliott research are viewed as a study of single variables, its findings are comparable to earlier correctional studies; that is, no demonstratable situational (supervisory effectiveness) effect and only a low, though significant classification (maturity) effect. It is when the interaction of the situation and classification variables is considered that one finds productive relationships with restoration behavior. It now appears likely that, in many of our correctional studies, the classification and situation effects have been masking each other. Future studies need to consider all three factors: kinds of subjects, kinds of supervisors, kinds of programming. This study has demonstrated for delinquency research the point that Cronbach [15, 16] has been emphasizing for social research in general.

Notes

1. The opinions expressed are those of the authors. They are not to be construed as reflecting the views or endorsement of the Department of the Navy.

Sponsored by, at the time of this writing: Neuropsychiatric Branch, BuMed; Corrective Services Branch, BuPers; ONR Group Psychology Branch, under ONR contract Nonr 1535(00) with Family Relations Center, Berkeley, California, J. Douglas Grant, Principal Investigator.

2. The following point to similiarities in the two populations: Offenders in both populations have similar juvenile records; norms on a delinquency potential test are very similar for prisoners in the State of California institutions and Camp Elliott; a delinquent high school population showed test scores much more similar to the Camp Elliott population than to the nondelinquent high school population.

3. D. A. Bloch, "The Delinquent Integration," *Psychiatry*, Vol. 15 (1952), pp. 297–303.

4. I. J. Croft and T. G. Grygier, "Social Relationships of Truants and Juvenile Delinquents," *Human Relations*, Vol. 9, No. 4 (1956).

5. H. G. Gough and D. R. Peterson, "The Identification and Measurement of Predispositional Factors in Crime and Delinquency," *Journal of Consulting Psychology* (1952), p. 16.

6. T. R. Sarbin, "A Preface to a Psychological Analysis of the Self," *Psychological Review* (1952), p. 59.

7. H. G. Osborn, "Situational and Personal Variables in AWOL Behavior." Presented at the Annual Meetings of the American Psychological Association in Cleveland, 1953.

8. E. K. Gunderson, K. B. Ballard, and P. S. Huge, "The Relationship of Delinquency Potential Scale Scores of Naval Recruits to Later Military Performance." Ninth Technical Report, Rehabilitation Research, U. S. Naval Retraining Command, Camp Elliott, San Diego, 1958. Available in mimeographed form at Rehabilitation Research, U. S. Naval Retraining Command, Camp Elliott, San Diego 44, California.

9. L. J. Cronbach, "Proposals Leading to Analytic Treatment of Social Perception Scores," in *Person, Perception and Interpersonal Behavior*, edited by R. Tagiuri and L. Petrullo (Stanford, Calif.: Stanford University Press, 1958), pp. 353–78.

10. C. E. Sullivan, M. Q. Grant, and J. D. Grant, "The Development of Interpersonal Maturity: Applications to Delinquency," *Psychiatry*, Vol. 20 (1957), pp. 373–85.

11. "A Group Dynamics Approach to Treating Acting-Out Personalities." Presented at the Eighth V.A. Clinical Research Conference in Berkeley, November, 1953.

12. E. K. Gunderson, *Group Testing Diagnostic Manual*, First Revision, U. S. Naval Retraining Command, Camp Elliott, San Diego, 1956.

13. Virginia Ives and M. Q. Grant, "Initial Steps in the Measurement of Interpersonal Maturity," Sixth Technical Report, Rehabilitation Research, U. S. Naval Retraining Command, Camp Elliott, San Diego, 1956.

14. R. W. Carey, *Research Companies Procedures Manual*. Rehabilitation Research, U. S. Naval Retraining Command, Camp Elliott, San Diego, 1954.

15. L. J. Cronbach, "Two Disciplines of Scientific Psychology," *The American Psychologist*, Vol. 12 (1957), pp. 671–84.

16. L. J. Cronbach and G. C. Gleser, *Psychological Tests and Personality Decisions* (Urbana: University of Illinois, 1957).

The Halfway House and Other Intermediate Institutions

The Halfway House: The Focal Point of a Model Program for the Rehabilitation of Low Income Offenders

There are two essential ingredients in a model program for the rehabilitation of delinquents and criminals from economically and socially disadvantaged backgrounds. There is a need for developing a continuity of service with a strategy for decreasing the nature and extent of supervision as the ability of the offender to function in free society increases. In addition, the correctional process must produce a conversion from a criminal to a noncriminal way of life.

If viewed in the light of these two basic purposes, the halfway house becomes the critical point for making a rehabilitation program effective. There is very little need to amplify the statement that continuity of treatment is essential for effective rehabilitation. Correctional institutions offer an increasing variety of therapeutic interventions. There has been marked increase in sophistication with the use of different types of group techniques, vocational and academic training, pastoral counseling, and experimentation with varying implementations of authority.

The problem is that these interventions are not readily transferable by the ex-inmate to life outside the institution. The halfway house becomes a base for extending and modifying the skills developed in an institution in a new context, and then logically extending the utilization of these adaptive devices to functioning in free society. However, while continuity of service is extremely important for the low income offender, this paper will stress the importance of the halfway house for meaningful conversion of the delinquent to stable nondelinquent life patterns.

Many current theories of delinquency stress the group character of

offenses. Low income delinquents tend to become involved in criminal activity through membership in gangs. The gang's influence on individual members is imputed to be pervasive and binding. Individual associations, values, identifications, and permissible behaviors are established and perpetuated by delinquent subculture.

Various theoretical explanations have been advanced to explain the development of delinquent subcultures. Among the most widely accepted have been those formulated by Cloward and Ohlin,[1] who argue that various types of gangs will emerge depending upon the opportunity for youth to enter legitimate (or organized illegitimate) enterprises and the intensity of their aspirations to succeed; Cohen,[2] who views delinquent subcultures as a reaction against dominant middle class standards and conventionality; Yablonsky,[3] who perceives violent gang behavior as a manifestation of the overwhelming social inadequacy felt by the economically and socially disadvantaged youth; and Miller,[4] who sees delinquency as logical behavior within the context of the codes and values of the lower class.

Although these theoretical formulations differ markedly, all argue that organized delinquency for low income persons represents a "way of life." Unfortunately, the correctional process to which the delinquent is subjected reinforces commitment to this way of life. All the theorists agree essentially in describing delinquent behavior. The delinquent is alienated from nondelinquent groups. He is estranged from school and other stabilizing social influences. By virtue of his eruptive behavior he has been expelled from youth groups, recreation programs, and character-building organizations. He has had, at best, sporadic employment and has shown neither the inclination nor the stability to function adequately in any job role.

The habitual adult criminal presents a somewhat different problem. His alienation from stable functioning society is more protracted and he manifests little of the hyperaggressivity of the juvenile. While the procedures used must be altered to fit the population, employment possibilities, use of education, and the social universes available for the ex-offender, in broad outline, the program described here is advocated for both adult and juvenile offenders with a history of commitment to a delinquent subculture.

An effective rehabilitation program must do more than discourage the delinquent from relapsing into an old behavior; the program must actively offer opportunity for a meaningful substitute pattern of existence. This substitute existence has to be all-encompassing, involving employment, social contacts, ways of using leisure time, and a change in attitudes, values, and identifications.

The Provo Experiment [5] attempts to confront the delinquency subculture in a nonresidential setting. However, Empey and Rabow do not perceive conversion of delinquents as necessary. It is their view that the ambivalence the delinquent feels about his status can be used to effect change.[6] A program resembling that of Highfields, but in a nonresidential setting, has been established in Provo. Through the use of the

"guided group interactions" and application of authority, it is hoped that the delinquent will learn to distinguish the differences between conventional and delinquent alternatives and will begin to recognize the greater utility of the conventional approach.

The main theme presented in this article is that recognition of the value of conventional paths is not enough. The delinquent must have the equipment to participate in conventional life. Neither experience in prison nor free society has provided him with the requisite skills. There must be a facility established to perform this function, and a logical place is the halfway house.

A commitment to a subculture involves a wide spectrum of human activity. A member of a subculture derives a set of values, a language, and a style that includes dress, deportment, and etiquette. His perception of the available social universe is limited. He feels adequate only with members of the same culture. Prestige and status are conferred for specific behaviors and postures. He is uncomfortable when removed from this culture. He sees very little in common with members of other cultures because he has different interests, is unfamiliar with their activities, and uses leisure time differently. For example, a member of a low income delinquent subculture sees very little recreational value in such middle class pursuits as bridge or golf. He has developed an entirely different taste in aesthetic and cultural pursuits.[7]

When conversion to another way of life is to be considered, certain aspects must be stressed. First, the new way of life must have some attractiveness, that is, it must form some link with the existing interests, desires, and skills of the delinquent subculture member. Second, there must be significant desire and readiness for the way of life to initiate the new member, and the conversion process must include changing and developing of coping skills and new interests on the part of the former member of the delinquent subculture. It must be quite clear that conversion is a gradual process, and that during the period of conversion the delinquent must be kept in a limbo status. He must be prevented, or at least discouraged, from returning to the old way of life. He must be encouraged to recognize the desirability of alternate ways of life. Without acceptance of the utility of other ways, conversion cannot take place—it is assumed that most delinquents and criminals eventually would like to relinquish their commitment to illegal roles. The delinquent must be provided the skills to enter another mode of existence and a time and place must be provided for these new adaptive mechanisms to mature and for him to gain confidence in his ability to function in a new pattern of existence.

The halfway house, which stands between the old and the new, provides a medium for gradual change. Central to a conversion process is recognition of a world open to the emigrant from delinquency.

The low income delinquent cannot be middle class-ized. There is no evidence that the middle class, with its strong academic, professional, and economic status orientation, will readily accept the low income deviant. The group most likely to accept him is that with

which he has had some contact and familiarity, the stable working class. Its interests, its concerns, its leisure time pursuits, occupations, and language styles are compatible with the experience of the low income deviant. His leisure time pursuits, musical interests, and social activities are consistent with those of the stable working class. He has some requisite skills for establishing himself in this subculture. He can, by means of previous contacts, enter the social universe; but he must develop the stable life patterns that characterize this subculture. He must be willing to work and have some pride in what he does. He must also develop a modicum of social responsibility, of trust, and of self-control.

In the course of conversion the delinquent must develop an economic base, that is, he must acquire the physical possessions that stabilize the working class. He must have a home or a car to provide a setting for his social existence. A car not only presents mobility, but can be the medium of contact with other members of the working class, for in the process of repair and embellishment the car becomes a catalyst for social intercourse.

A distinguishing feature of a delinquent subculture member upon release from an institution is his nearly total economic impoverishment. His relative deprivation compared to members of the employed lower class is great. Often the impetus to renew criminal activity is a desire to catch up quickly and to establish a basis for respect and status. It must be remembered that in an institution the delinquent is accorded his status by his peers. He can exercise leadership in an organized community. The only way he can re-establish status in free society is by returning to a delinquent subgroup. The halfway house provides a moratorium during which he can establish an economic base, develop a stable means of income, and begin to acquire those basic material possessions which serve as the initiation rites to a new way of life.

The Central Role of Employment

It is impossible to talk of rehabilitation without stressing the central role of employment. It is impossible to talk of employment without an analysis of the job market. A member of the delinquent subculture characteristically lacks the requirements to enter any but the most unskilled occupations. Even were he to acquire some specialist skill, his previous record as a delinquent or criminal would tend to bar him from professional or technical occupations. The work for which he is eligible currently has more applicants than jobs available.

A rehabilitation program must not only take cognizance of the lack of available employment, it must do something about it. The halfway house can facilitate entrance of the resident or delinquent into a stable job in several ways. First, it can survey and prospect work opportunities by meaningfully organizing information about the community's avail-

able resources. Jobs that normally become available can be sought out in an orderly fashion and made available to the halfway house resident.

The halfway house can become a base for meaningful work which is generally performed within the institution as a correctional industry. Correctional industries range from the manufacture of furniture and clothing to electronics repair. There is no reason why similar industries could not be adapted to halfway house operation and performed in a setting similar to that of a sheltered workshop.

A third form of work that may be organized through the halfway house is a program of contracted services. Such services might include yard work, cleaning, and hauling. The halfway house could constitute itself as the contracting agency and advertise these services for hire in the community.

It must be stressed, however, that these three devices only call for the performance of unskilled labor, a category of unemployment for which demand is declining and which therefore provides very limited opportunities. There are more jobs than people in the area of human service, e.g., recreation, education, social work, child care, and health services. The halfway house *must* be a center for training residents to occupy nonprofessional technician roles in these fields.

Structure, Staff, and Treatment in the Halfway House

In structure, halfway houses are open facilities located within an urban community (and thus are distinguished from a rural, "camp" setting), which provide room and board and a measure of supervision to residents. Halfway houses are generally made-over private residences with from eight to forty beds. Residents of halfway houses are encouraged to find gainful employment and to otherwise become integrated into the community's social structure. Halfway houses are not a new concept for dealing with social problems. Parolees, drug addicts, alcoholics, and unwed mothers have been exposed to such interventions. To date, most halfway houses have been operated under private auspices and, while there is favorable subjective opinion of their worth, there is no evidence obtained by means of rigorous research to prove that halfway houses have been an effective intervention. Privately run halfway houses must be evaluated, and if proven valuable, utilized to a greater extent in correctional systems.

The halfway house projected here is regarded as part of a continuity of state sponsored conventional services. The resident is assigned there after serving a sentence in a correctional institution.

The halfway house should be located close to the family and associates most likely to accept the ex-inmate. This implies establishing a facility in precisely the same area where delinquency is spawned. Juxtaposing the facility to the delinquent-saturated environment is at vari-

ance with the orientation of Synanon, a private residential program for former narcotic addicts. Synanon operates in total isolation from former associates and proposes continual association with the facility and conversion into a Synanon "way of life." The halfway house presented here emphasizes gradual disassociation with the facility as a community-based existence emerges.[8]

Having been assigned to the halfway house as a condition of parole, the resident will be informed about the nature of his responsibilities and the limitations on his rights. He will be told that the length of his stay will be contingent upon his development of stable employment and residence programs. At the time he will be oriented to a program devised to disengage him from further delinquency.

The "treatment" aspects of this program will consist of the following: diagnosis and assignment to a specific treatment plan; a modified therapeutic community program; group and family counseling on rare occasions; individual therapy, training, and remedial instruction; assignment to community-based programs, continuous testing, and a "phasing out" procedure.

Not all ex-inmates require identical treatment programs; in fact, there is good evidence that what is advocated for some is clearly harmful to others.[9] Each person entering the halfway house must be assessed for: (a) commitment to delinquent subculture, (b) nature and extent of nondelinquent relationships, (c) qualifications for immediate and long-range employment, (d) likelihood of return to criminal activity, and (e) relationship to staff which, considering personality structure and previous experience in the correctional system, should be positively developed. An individualized treatment program whose efficacy could be continuously tested and altered when necessary would be prescribed for each resident.

In general, the halfway house will constitue a therapeutic community, but in operation it will have to vary greatly from institutions. The residents would have the responsibility for management of the facility. They would be responsible for appraising the activity of group members and dealing with minor infractions. However, because the focus of the halfway house is to the outside community, significant members of the community, e.g., employers, family, social group members, would be encouraged to participate in halfway house functions. In keeping with therapeutic community enterprises, the vehicle for community concerns about individuals will be in meetings in which all staff and residents participate.[10] These meetings would occur once weekly, probably on Saturday morning. In addition to the large local government meetings, each resident would also be assigned to a small group. The smaller group would be patterned after the "guided group interaction" of the Highfields program and would be concerned with appraising and evaluating each member's adjustment to free society.

Role playing should constitute an important part of the treatment program. Role playing can, in a nonformal, non-threatening way, introduce concepts and cognitive change in a treatment process. Role play-

ing, further, becomes an instrumentality for the acquisition of skills needed for performance of various roles in nondelinquent subcultures. While the ex-offender is in the halfway house he should be introduced to simulated activity and experience of a wide array of existences. He should practice appropriate role behavior and be permitted to test his abilities in free society so that the areas where further practice is needed can be identified and the role playing situation adjusted accordingly. As confidence and competence in new roles are acquired, commitment to the old can be relinquished. The wider variety of nondelinquent roles the ex-offender can successfully perform, the less likely it is that he will have to resort to delinquent conduct. It must be emphasized that a better environment for treatment exists in the halfway house than is available through either prison or parole. The treatment program would also include training designed to enhance employability. Where marketable skills exist, the resident would be encouraged to develop these further. The resident without skills would be offered training in the new "technician" roles referred to briefly in the section on employment, above.

Space does not permit an elaborate discussion of this aspect of the treatment program, but a brief notation is necessary. In the realm of recreation for example, many duties do not require a professional status for performance. The professional is needed for overall direction, administration, program development, and use of recreation to aid in development of self, but nonprofessionals can carry out specific recreation tasks. The technician can supervise organized play, can instruct youngsters in rules of games, can help develop skill and accomplishment in sports, and can keep records. Most recreation centers already do use nonprofessionals in a limited way. It is necessary to increase markedly the environment of nonprofessionals, to make their participation an integral part of the structure, and to provide training to better qualify the technician.

It is not suggested that the halfway house be the only place where training for these new job roles be given. It should not be necessary that low income youth should have to go to prison before they would be eligible to enter the world of work. The point is that there will be a growing need for these jobs in the future and rehabilitation can take place best when the ex-offender is able to enter an occupation where he is truly needed.

Optimally, the training for new career roles would take place outside the halfway house residence and the training center could become a place where the ex-offender and the stable nondelinquent community could form a relationship.

As the inmate shows an ability to meet the responsibilities of society, the halfway house must release its hold upon him. To accomplish this phasing out, the halfway house must develop detached or extended services—more and more of the ex-offender's activities must be shifted to community-based activity. Group participation should be transferred from the halfway house to churches and neighborhood cen-

ters. Groups should include persons without previous legal entanglements. In the latter phase the groups no longer are manifestly therapeutic, but the group worker would be related to the halfway house operation and provide therapeutic orientation and guidance to the group function.

The role of the church is crucial in gradually replacing the halfway house program with community-based social support. The churches must not only influence values but, most importantly, must open the doors to new contacts. Other stabilizing groups in the community must also be encouraged to accept and integrate halfway house members.

The treatment program advocated, while tailored to individual need, permits a maximum of flexibility. While the purpose of the program is to phase persons into the community as quickly as possible, the program should permit reintroduction into the increased supervision of the halfway house when failure to adjust to the community is evident. In more extreme cases, the program should also allow for the necessity of short- or even long-term commitment for persons unable to adapt to the halfway house program.

The primary professional staff component of the halfway house is the parole agent. He has the major responsibility for discouraging relapse of the residents to delinquency subculture membership. It will be his responsibility to insure that the halfway house is truly a functioning unit. He must use his skills and training to facilitate meaningful group discussions. He must make the ultimate decision on whether a resident should be allowed further degrees of freedom or should be returned to a more confined setting.

It must, however, be recognized that the professional role is limited, at least with respect to being an effective agent of conversion. The professional, regardless of his origin, has ceased to have meaningful contact with the stable working class. He shares with the parolee one common attitude—neither the parole agent nor the parolee wants the other one in his home. To facilitate the conversion process other staff must be employed since the parole officer can only influence the community from the outside. The parole agent cannot forsake his authority role. To pretend to be permissive or nonjudgmental is a cruel hoax on his charges. Considering the attributes of the parolee, in most instances the parole officer's therapeutic role would be directive. He would supply information and he would indicate pleasure and displeasure about adjustment of the ex-offender. He would alert the resident to impending failure.

A category of staff capable of playing a major role in the conversion process are residents in the community retained to function in the halfway house. As previously indicated, there is need for a great variety of new occupational roles to supplement the activity of professionals. The primary requisite for a "new career" [11] in the halfway house would be a solid footing in the community. An applicant would have to exhibit values and identifications consistent with the rehabilitation goals of the

program. While educational accomplishment would not be considered in determining eligibility, the technician (as contrasted with the professional) would be required to take and successfully complete an intensive training course. The curriculum would include designation of responsibility of parole, probation, and parolee, the administrative structure of the correctional system, the extent and limitations of the technician role, group methods, record keeping, goals of a therapeutic program, and so forth.

The technician would have diverse responsibilities. He would provide information to the counseling groups about the behavior of individuals. He would facilitate introduction of residents to occupational and social opportunities. He would visit with family and friends of the resident. He would provide an independent interpretation of the resident's behavior.

The technician would constitute the detached force of the halfway house, assigned to neighborhood centers and fraternal, social, or religious organizations, and he would facilitate integration into these organizations. It would be his responsibility to report problems to the parole officer. He would, under the direction of the parole officer, play a role in group meetings. These new careers should not be confused with traditional custodial, clerical service duties currently performed in correctional institutions.

Successful graduates from the halfway house program are logical, but by no means exclusive, candidates for performing technician roles. Giving the former inmate a salaried, important role in the rehabilitation process provides a basis for commitment to a new way of life currently absent in most correctional programs.[12]

Psychiatrists, psychologists, programmed learning experts, and other specialists would serve as consultants to both professional and technician staff. Only in very special circumstances would the consultants be involved in a direct treatment relationship. They would use their expertise in the training and supervision of the halfway house staff.

Institutional programs fail miserably as agents of punishment. They are intended to be agents of punishment because noncriminals value their freedom greatly and perceive deprivation of liberty as excruciating, and noncriminals devise the formal punishment for criminals. But noncriminals know how to function in free society. The habitual criminal has proved his inability to do so. As an ex-felon he is stigmatized and ostracized, further limiting his function in free society. For the habitual criminal the prison (no matter how primitive) is a haven where he has no responsibilities. This is not to say that prisoners do not desire freedom while they are confined, but the freedom they desire is full of fantasied glories. The real world they return to provides few of the envisioned rewards. In many instances the failures of the correctional system stem from the fact that the prison is too comfortable for the prisoner and the free world too punishing.

The halfway house provides a situation where punishment takes the form of forcing the inmate to face some responsibility for his deci-

sions in the harsh reality of his renewed contact with society. This form of punishment is in a sense self-controlling, for it will diminish in proportion to the degree that the individual is able to meet the demands of the world at large.

The last of the demands made upon correction programs is to quarantine the offender for the protection of society. However, if rehabilitation fails, society is afforded only short term protection, since most inmates are eventually released. The alternative of eternal confinement is discounted as intolerable and extravagant.

If one regards residence in a halfway house as an adjunct of parole and as part of the parole process, then its protective value for society is evidenced in several ways. More complete supervision is available in the halfway house than on parole. A more accurate appraisal of how the felon will behave in society can be made from his performance in the halfway house than can be made from prison performance. More flexible control can be maintained in a halfway house than is possible in either prison or parole. The extent of supervision can be controlled for each resident and can be altered, depending on day-to-day performance of the parolee. If the parolee has a healthy and cooperative attitude, shows no tendency to return to criminal pursuits or to associate with suspect persons, and is gainfully employed, he may be permitted to absent himself from the halfway house for increasingly longer intervals until he is firmly established in the community, at which time he no longer will be required to reside in the halfway house. On the other hand, parolees who are unable to refrain from improper association or are unable to maintain adequate employment may be restricted to the confines of the halfway house for prolonged periods of time. If parolees are unable to maintain themselves in the halfway house, they can be returned to an institution for additional treatment.

But probably more important than the immediate advantages for both felon and community in the halfway house is its potential as a laboratory for the study of problem behavior. Our failure to come to grips with recidivism stems from a basic lack of knowledge of the etiology of crime. One of the difficulties in obtaining knowledge is that we are not in a position to observe an offender in an environment where criminal activity is possible. In prison settings there is maximum opportunity to observe the inmate but his decisions with respect to criminal activity are trivial and only analogous to what is possible in free society. In contrast with the prison setting, ordinary parole permits the parolee a wide array of behaviors, but opportunities for observation are few.

That the halfway house provides the residents with greater latitude in behavior than does an institution is a most disturbing quality for correction administrators. No person in public service enjoys administering a facility which may at any second attain negative publicity, as for example, "Parolees Engineer Bank Holdup from State Facility" or "Half Million Cache of Narcotics Found in State Halfway House." Yet if the halfway house does not provide the freedom which may

result in criminal activity, it ceases to be a halfway house. Nothing would be accomplished by creating a prison, with all its attendant security provisions, within a community. The risks are certainly present, but it is vital that they be taken if the factors in recidivism are ever to be met and dealt with effectively. The chance of analyzing such criminal relapses as may occur will at least provide far more comprehensive clues for preventing future lapses than will the unknowns of standard parole.

Certain measures to prevent relapse to criminal activity must be incorporated in the halfway house. These are: appropriate selection of residents, proper training and supervision, involvement of local law enforcement in an advisory capacity, and cooperation of the local community.

Appropriate selection of residents can be aided by knowledge obtained from research on predictions of parole success. Parole prediction studies are statistical and therefore allow for error. They are also relatively primitive but are continually being refined. As they mature, such studies will provide even better indices of probable success and appropriate placement.

The staffing of a halfway house provides a second line of defense. The halfway house provides a setting for the parole agent and technician to get to know their charges. If experienced, courageous, and sensitive persons are selected to serve in the halfway house, and given additional training to the end of becoming more effective and perceptive, remedial action may be instituted prior to the onset of criminal activity. If the halfway house is coordinated with short term custodial institutions, then a suspected parolee may be remanded to short term custody and additional treatment before he engages in activities which may lead to long term custody.

The rehabilitation program advanced here is complex; it assumes integration of a wide network of agencies. Different categories of staff are to be employed. It would be impossible for such a program to operate with maximum efficiency unless there was systematic and rigorous observation of the process. There must be research activity to ascertain precisely what is happening in the program. Whenever the program departs from its goals, this information must be forwarded quickly to the appropriate administrative officer in order for the program to be brought "under control."

No program can be advocated without consideration of cost. The program suggested would be more expensive than normal parole but would be far less costly than an institution program. If there is rehabilitative value in such a program, it would repay the cost to the taxpayer in the reduction of recidivism alone.

The role of the police is crucial in the operation of a halfway house. Law enforcement has knowledge of criminal acivity not available to ordinary correctional resources. Often the police are in a position to indicate to parole agents that their charges are in danger of criminal involvement.

A major value of a state-run halfway house is its relationship with other parts of the system—the institution and parole. This relationship provides for maximum flexibility and specialization of treatment. The major strength in privately run halfway houses is their freedom from bureaucratic control. There is need for both kinds of halfway houses, and both should be subjected to research and evaluation, from which could come not only better techniques but also better integration between state and private resources.

The halfway house is no panacea. For some inmates it is unnecessary, for others it would be inappropriate, but for many, if it can make possible meaningful employment and changed social relationships, it offers the hope of rehabilitation where otherwise the prospects would be exceedingly bleak.

Notes

1. Richard A. Cloward and Lloyd E. Ohlin, *Delinquency and Opportunity: A Theory of Delinquent Gangs* (New York: The Free Press of Glencoe, 1960).

2. Albert K. Cohen, *Delinquent Boys The Culture of the Gang* (New York: The Free Press of Glencoe, 1955).

3. Lewis Yablonsky, *The Violent Gang* (New York, The Macmillan Co., 1962).

4. Walter Miller, "Lower Class Culture as a Generating Milieu of Gang Delinquency," *Journal of Social Issues*, XV:5 (1958), 5–19.

5. LaMar T. Empey, and Jerome Rabow, "The Provo Experiment in Delinquency Rehabilitation," *American Sociological Review*, 26 (October 1961), 679–96.

6. *Ibid.*

7. A vivid fictional description of the inability of persons from different subcultures to communicate with each other is presented in Robert Gover's novel, *One Hundred Dollar Misunderstanding* (New York: Grove Press, 1961).

8. For further discussion of the Synanon approach see Rita Volkman and Donald R. Cressey, "Differential Association and the Rehabilitation of Drug Addicts," *American Journal of Sociology*, 64:2 (September 1963), 129–42.

9. For evidence to demonstrate differential response to treatment programs, see Stuart Adams, "Interaction Between Individual Therapy and Treatment Amiability in Older Youth Authority Wards" (*Monograph No 2*—California Board of Corrections, July, 1963). J. D. Grant, and M. Q. Grant, "A Group Dynamics Approach to the Treatment of Non-Conformist in the Navy," pp. 486–96.

10. For further discussion of therapeutic concept see Maxwell Jones, *The Therapeutic Community: a New Treatment Method in Psychiatry* (New York: Basic Books, 1953).

11. If these are truly to be considered as new careers, advancement must be permissible, i.e., ultimately civil service must recognize the duties and job specifications to be agreed upon and appropriate classification and compensation determined. Further, technicians should be encouraged to continue education and changes in grade be afforded on the basis of obtaining for example, an A.A. Degree (two years of college) and another differential with a B.A. Degree. In this manner incentive is given to those who are willing and able to obtain full professional status.

12. In limited ways the California State Department of Corrections and the New York State Division for Youth are experimenting with using the ex-offender in the rehabilitation process.

Treatment in the Community

The Provo Experiment in Delinquency Rehabilitation

LaMar T. Empey and Jerome Rabow

Despite the importance of sociological contributions to the understanding of delinquent behavior, relatively few of these contributions have been systematically utilized for purposes of rehabilitation.[1] The reason is at least partially inherent in the sociological tradition which views sociology primarily as a research discipline. As a consequence, the rehabilitation of delinquents has been left, by default, to people who have been relatively unaware of sociological theory and its implications for treatment.

This situation has produced or perpetuated problems along two dimensions. On one dimension are the problems engendered in reformatories where authorities find themselves bound, not only by the norms of their own official system, but by the inmate system as well. They are unable to work out an effective program: (1) because the goals of the two systems are incompatible; and (2) because no one knows much about the structure and function of the inmate system and how it might be dealt with for purposes of rehabilitation.[2] Furthermore, the crux of any treatment program has ultimately to do with the decision-making process utilized by delinquents in the community, *not* in the reformatory. Yet, the decisions which lead to success in "doing time" in the reformatory are not of the same type needed for successful community adjust-

Reprinted by permission of American Sociological Association, from *American Sociological Review*, Vol. 26, No. 5, October 1961, pp. 679–695.

The inception and continuation of this experiment were made possible through the co-operation of the Judge (Monroe Paxman) and staff of the Third District Juvenile Court, a voluntary group known as the Citizens Advisory Council, and Utah County Officials. Evaluation is supported by the Ford Foundation. Grateful acknowledgment is made to all involved.

ment. Existing conditions may actually be more effective in cementing ties to the delinquent system than in destroying them.[3]

The second dimension of the problem has to do with the traditional emphasis upon "individualized treatment." [4] This emphasis stems from two sources: (1) a humanistic concern for the importance of human dignity and the need for sympathetic understanding; [5] and (2) a widespread belief that delinquency is a psychological disease and the offender a *"sick"* person.[6] If, however, sociologists are even partially correct regarding the causes for delinquency, these two points of view overlook the possibility that most persistent delinquents do have the support of a meaningful reference group and are not, therefore, without the emotional support and normative orientation which such a group can provide. In fact, a complete dedication to an individualistic approach poses an impasse: How can an individual who acquired delinquency from a group with which he identifies strongly be treated individually without regard to the persons or norms of the system from whom he acquired it? [7]

A successful treatment program for such a person would require techniques not normally included in the individualized approach. It should no more be expected that dedicated delinquents can be converted to conventionality by such means than that devout Pentecostals can be converted to Catholicism by the same means. Instead, different techniques are required for dealing with the normative orientation of the delinquent's system, replacing it with new values, beliefs, and rationalizations and developing means by which he can realize conventional satisfactions, especially with respect to successful employment.

This does not suggest, of course, that such traditional means as probation for dealing with the first offender or psychotherapy for dealing with the disturbed offender can be discarded. But it does suggest the need for experimental programs more consistent with sociological theory, and more consistent with the sociological premise that most *persistent* and *habitual* offenders are active members of a delinquent social system.[8]

This paper presents the outlines of a program—the Provo Experiment in Delinquency Rehabilitation—which is derived from sociological theory and which seeks to apply sociological principles to rehabilitation. Because of its theoretical ties, the concern of the Experiment is as much with a systematic evaluation and reformulation of treatment consistent with findings as with the administration of treatment itself. For that reason, research and evaluation are an integral part of the program. Its theoretical orientation, major assumptions, treatment system, and research design are outlined below.

Theoretical Orientation

With regards to causation, the Provo Experiment turned to a growing body of evidence which suggests two important conclusions: (1) that

the greater part of delinquent behavior is not that of individuals engaging in highly secretive deviations, but is a group phenomenon—a shared deviation which is the product of differential group experience in a particular subculture,[9] and (2) that because most delinquents tend to be concentrated in slums or to be the children of lower class parents, their lives are characterized by learning situations which limit their access to success goals.[10]

Attention to these two conclusions does not mean that emotional problems,[11] or "bad" homes,[12] can be ignored. But only occasionally do these variables lead by themselves to delinquency. In most cases where older delinquents are involved other intervening variables must operate, the most important of which is the presence of a delinquent system—one which supplies status and recognition not normally obtainable elsewhere. Whether they are members of a tight knit gang or of the amorphous structure of the "parent" delinquent subculture,[13] habitual delinquents tend to look affectively both to their peers and to the norms of their system for meaning and orientation. Thus, although a "bad" home may have been instrumental at some early phase in the genesis of a boy's delinquency, it must be recognized that it is now other delinquent boys, not his parents, who are current sources of support and identification. Any attempts to change him, therefore, would have to view him as more than an unstable isolate without a meaningful reference group. And, instead of concentrating on changing his parental relationships, they would have to recognize the intrinsic nature of his membership in the delinquent system and direct treatment to him as a part of that system.

There is another theoretical problem. An emphasis on the importance of the delinquent system raises some question regarding the extent to which delinquents are without any positive feeling for conventional standards. Vold says that one approach to explaining delinquency ". . . operates from the basic, implicit assumption that in a delinquency area, delinquency is the normal response of the normal individual—that the non-delinquent is really the 'problem case,' the nonconformist whose behavior needs to be accounted for." [14] This is a deterministic point of view suggesting the possibility that delinquents view conventional people as "foreigners" and conventional norms and beliefs as anathema. It implies that delinquents have been socialized entirely in a criminal system and have never internalized or encountered the blandishments of conventional society.[15]

Actually, sociological literature suggests otherwise. It emphasizes, in general, that the sub-parts of complex society are intimately tied up with the whole,[16] and, specifically, that delinquents are very much aware of conventional standards; that they have been socialized in an environment dominated by middle-class morality; [17] that they have internalized the American success ideal to such a degree that they turn to illegitimate means in an effort to be successful [18] (or, failing in that, engage in malicious, or retreatist activities); [19] that they are profoundly ambivalent about their delinquent behavior; [20] and that in order to cope with the

claims of respectable norms upon them, they maintain a whole series of intricate rationalizations by which to "neutralize" their delinquent behavior.[21]

This suggests that delinquents are aware of conventional structure and its expectation. In many conventional settings they can, and usually do, behave conventionally. But it also suggests that, like other people, they are motivated by the normative expectations of their own subsystem. Consequently, when in the company of other delinquent boys, they may not only feel that they have to live up to minimal delinquent expectations but to appear more delinquent than they actually are, just as people in church often feel that they have to appear more holy than they actually are.

If this is the case, the problem of rehabilitation is probably not akin to converting delinquents to ways of behavior and points of view about which they are unaware and which they have never seriously considered as realistic alternatives. Instead, the feeling of ambivalence on their parts might be an element which could be used in rehabilitation.

An important sociological hypothesis based on this assumption would be that the ambivalence of most habitual delinquents is not primarily the result of personality conflicts developed in such social *microcosms* as the family but is inherent in the structure of the societal *macrocosm*. A delinquent subsystem simply represents an alternative means for acquiring, or attempting to acquire, social and economic goals idealized by the societal system which are acquired by other people through conventional means.

If this hypothesis is accurate, delinquent ambivalence might actually be used in effecting change. A rehabilitation program might seek: (1) to make conventional and delinquent alternatives clear; (2) to lead delinquents to question the ultimate utility of delinquent alternatives; and (3) to help conventional alternatives assume some positive valence for them. It might then reduce the affective identification which they feel for the delinquent subsystem and tip the scales in the opposite direction.

Major Assumptions for Treatment

In order to relate such theoretical premises to the specific needs of treatment, the Provo Experiment adopted a series of major assumptions. They are as follows:

1. Delinquent behavior is primarily a group product and demands an approach to treatment far different from that which sees it as characteristic of a "sick," or "well-meaning" but "misguided," person.

2. An effective program must recognize the intrinsic nature of a delinquent's membership in a delinquent system and, therefore, must direct treatment to him as a part of that system.

3. Most habitual delinquents are affectively and ideologically dedi-

cated to the delinquent system. Before they can be made amenable to change, they must be made anxious about the ultimate utility of that system for them.

4. Delinquents must be forced to deal with the conflicts which the demands of conventional and delinquent systems place upon them. The resolution of such conflicts, either for or against further law violations, must ultimately involve a community decision. For that reason, a treatment program, in order to force realistic decision-making, can be most effective if it permits continued participation in the community as well as in the treatment process.

5. Delinquent ambivalence for purposes of rehabilitation can only be utilized in a setting conducive to the free expression of feelings—both delinquent and conventional. This means that the protection and rewards provided by the treatment system for *candor* must exceed those provided either by delinquents for adherence to delinquent roles or by officials for adherence to custodial demands for "good behavior." Only in this way can delinquent individuals become aware of the extent to which other delinquents share conventional as well as delinquent aspirations and, only in this way, can they be encouraged to examine the ultimate utility of each.

6. An effective program must develop a unified and cohesive social system in which delinquents and authorities alike are devoted to one task—overcoming lawbreaking. In order to accomplish this the program must avoid two pitfalls: (a) it must avoid establishing authorities as "rejectors" and making inevitable the creation of two social systems within the program; and (b) it must avoid the institutionalization of means by which skilled offenders can evade norms and escape sanctions.[22] The occasional imposition of negative sanctions is as necessary in this system as in any other system.

7. A treatment system will be most effective if the delinquent peer group is used as the means of perpetuating the norms and imposing the sanctions of the system. The peer group should be seen by delinquents as the primary source of help and support. The traditional psychotherapeutic emphasis upon transference relationships is not viewed as the most vital factor in effective change.

8. A program based on sociological theory may tend to exclude lectures, sermons, films, individual counseling, analytic psychotherapy, organized athletics, academic education, and vocational training as primary treatment techniques. It will have to concentrate, instead, on matters of another variety: changing reference group and normative orientations, utilizing ambivalent feelings resulting from the conflict of conventional and delinquent standards, and providing opportunities for recognition and achievement in conventional pursuits.

9. An effective treatment system must include rewards which are realistically meaningful to delinquents. They would include such things as peer acceptance for lawabiding behavior or the opportunity for gainful employment rather than badges, movies or furlough privileges which are designed primarily to facilitate institutional control. Rewards, there-

fore, must only be given for realistic and lasting changes, not for conformance to norms which concentrate upon effective custody as an end in itself.

10. Finally, in summary, a successful program must be viewed by delinquents as possessing four important characteristics: (a) a social climate in which delinquents are given the opportunity to examine and experience alternatives related to a realistic choice between delinquent or non-delinquent behavior; (b) the opportunity to declare publicly to peers and authorities a belief or disbelief that they can benefit from a change in values; (c) a type of social structure which will permit them to examine the role and legitimacy (for their purposes) of authorities in the treatment system; and (d) a type of treatment interaction which, because it places major responsibilities upon peer-group decision-making, grants status and recognition to individuals, not only for their own successful participation in the treatment interaction, but for their willingness to involve others.

The Treatment System [23]

The Provo Program, consistent with these basic assumptions, resides in the community and does not involve permanent incarceration. Boys live at home and spend only a part of each day at Pinehills (the program center). Otherwise they are free in the community.[24]

History and Locale. The Provo Program was begun in 1956 as an "in-between" program designed specifically to help those habitual delinquents whose persistence made them candidates, in most cases, for a reformatory. It was instigated by a volunteer group of professional and lay people known as the *Citizens' Advisory Council to the Juvenile Court.* It has never had formal ties to government except through the Juvenile Court. This lack of ties has permitted considerable experimentation. Techniques have been modified to such a degree that the present program bears little resemblance to the original one. Legally, program officials are deputy probation officers appointed by the Juvenile Judge.

The cost of treatment is financed by county funds budgeted through the Juvenile Court. So near as we can estimate the cost per boy is approximately one-tenth of what it would cost if he were incarcerated in a reformatory. Research operations are financed by the Ford Foundation. Concentrated evaluation of the program is now in its second year of a six year operation. Because both the theoretical orientation and treatment techniques of the program were in developmental process until its outlines were given final form for research purposes, it is difficult to make an objective evaluation of the over-all program based on recidivism rates for previous years, especially in the absence of adequate control groups. Such an evaluation, however, is an integral part of the present research and is described below.

Relations with welfare agencies and the community, *per se*, are in-

formal but extremely co-operative. This is due to three things: the extreme good will and guiding influence of the Juvenile Court Judge, Monroe J. Paxman,[25] the unceasing efforts of the Citizens' Advisory Council to involve the entire county as a community, and the willingness of city and county officials, not only to overcome traditional fears regarding habitual offenders in the community, but to lend strong support to an experimental program of this type.

Community co-operation is probably enhanced by strong Mormon traditions. However, Utah County is in a period of rapid transition which began in the early days of World War II with the introduction of a large steel plant, allied industries, and an influx of non-Mormons. This trend, both in industry and population, has continued to the present time. The treatment program is located in the city of Provo but draws boys from all major communities in the county—from a string of small cities, many of which border on each other, ranging in size from four to forty thousand. The total population from which it draws its assignees is about 110,000.

Despite the fact that Utah County is not a highly urbanized area, when compared to large metropolitan centers, the concept of a "parent" delinquent subculture has real meaning for it. While there are no clear-cut gangs, *per se,* it is surprising to observe the *extent* to which delinquent boys from the entire county, who have never met, know each other by reputation, go with the same girls, use the same language, or can seek each other out when they change high schools. About half of them· are permanently out of school, do not participate in any regular institutional activities, and are reliant almost entirely upon the delinquent system for social acceptance and participation.

Assignees. Only habitual offenders, 15–17 years, are assigned to the program. In the absence of public facilities, they are transported to and from home each day in automobiles driven by university students. Their offenses run the usual gamut: vandalism, trouble in school, shoplifting, car theft, burglary, forgery, and so forth. Highly disturbed and psychotic boys are not assigned. The pre-sentence investigation is used to exclude these people. They constitute an extremely small minority.

Number in Attendance. No more than twenty boys are assigned to the program at any one time. A large number would make difficult any attempts to establish and maintain a unified, cohesive system. This group of twenty is broken into two smaller groups, each of which operates as a separate discussion unit. When an older boy is released from one of these units, a new boy is added. This is an important feature because it serves as the means by which the culture of the system is perpetuated.

Length of Attendance. No length of stay is specified. It is intimately tied to the group and its processes because a boy's release depends not only upon his own behavior, but upon the maturation processes through which his group goes. Release usually comes somewhere between four and seven months.

Nature of Program. The program does not utilize any testing, gathering of case histories, or clinical diagnosis. One of its key tools, peer group

interaction, is believed to provide a considerably richer source of information about boys and delinquency than do clinical methods.

The program, *per se,* is divided into two phases. Phase I is an intensive group program, utilizing work and the delinquent peer group as the principal instruments for change. During the winter, boys attend this phase three hours a day, five days a week, and all day on Saturdays. Activities include daily group discussions, hard work, and some unstructured activities in which boys are left entirely on their own. During the summer they attend an all-day program which involves work and group discussions. However, there are no practices without exceptions. For example, if a boy has a full-time job, he may be allowed to continue the job in lieu of working in the program. Other innovations occur repeatedly.

Phase II is designed to aid a boy after release from intensive treatment in Phase I. It involves two things: (1) an attempt to maintain some reference group support for a boy; and (2) community action to help him find employment. Both phases are described below.

Phase I: Intensive Treatment

Every attempt is made in Phase I to create a social system in which social structure, peer members, and authorities are oriented to the one task of instituting change. The more relevant to this task the system is, the greater will be its influence.

Social Structure. There is little formal structure in the Provo Program. Patterns are abhorred which might make boys think that their release depends upon *refraining* from swearing, engaging in open quarrels or doing such *"positive"* things as saying, "yes sir," or "no sir." Such criteria as these play into their hands. They learn to manipulate them in developing techniques for beating a system. Consequently, other than requiring boys to appear each day, and working hard on the job, there are no formal demands. The only other daily activities are the group discussions at which attendance is optional.

The absence of formal structure helps to do more than avoid artificial criteria for release. It has the positive effect of making boys more amenable to treatment. In the absence of formal structure they are uneasy and they are not quite sure of themselves. Thus, the lack of clear-cut definitions for behavior helps to accomplish three important things: (1) It produces anxiety and turns boys towards the group as a method of resolving their anxiety; (2) It leaves boys free to define situations for themselves: leaders begin to lead, followers begin to follow, and manipulators begin to manipulate. It is these types of behavior which must be seen and analyzed if change is to take place; (3) It binds neither authorities nor the peer group to prescribed courses of action. Each is free to do whatever is needed to suit the needs of particular boys, groups, or situations.

On the other hand, the absence of formal structure obviously does not mean that there is no structure. But, that which does exist is informal and emphasizes ways of thinking and behaving which are not traditional. Perhaps the greatest difference lies in the fact that a considerable amount of power is vested in the delinquent peer group. It is the instrument by which norms are perpetuated and through which many important decisions are made. It is the primary source of pressure for change.

The Peer Group. Attempts to involve a boy with the peer group begin the moment he arrives. Instead of meeting with and receiving an orientation lecture from authorities, he receives no formal instructions. He is always full of such questions as, "What do I have to do to get out of this place?" or "How long do I have to stay?", but such questions as these are never answered. They are turned aside with, "I don't know," or "Why don't you find out?" Adults will not orient him in the ways that he has grown to expect, nor will they answer any of his questions. He is forced to turn to his peers. Usually, he knows someone in the program, either personally or by reputation. As he begins to associate with other boys he discovers that important informal norms do exist, the most important of which makes *inconsistency* rather than *consistency* the rule. That which is appropriate for one situation, boy, or group may not be appropriate for another. Each merits a decision as it arises.

Other norms center most heavily about the daily group discussion session. These sessions are patterned after the technique of "Guided Group Interaction" which was developed at Fort Knox during World War II and at Highfields.[26] Guided Group Interaction emphasizes the idea that only through a group and its processes can a boy work out his problems. From a peer point of view it has three main goals: (1) to question the utility of a life devoted to delinquency; (2) to suggest alternative ways for behavior; and (3) to provide recognition for a boy's personal reformation and his willingness to reform others.[27]

Guided Group Interaction grants to the peer group a great deal of power, including that of helping to decide when each boy is ready to be released. This involves "retroflexive reformation." [28] If a delinquent is serious in his attempts to reform others he must automatically accept the common purpose of the reformation process, identify himself closely with others engaged in it, and grant prestige to those who succeed in it. In so doing, he becomes a genuine member of the reformation group and in the process may be alienated from his previous pro-delinquent groups.[29] Such is an ideal and long term goal. Before it can be realized for any individual he must become heavily involved with the treatment system. Such involvement does not come easy and the system must include techniques which will impel him to involvement. Efforts to avoid the development of formal structure have already been described as one technique. Group processes constitute a second technique.

Before a group will help a boy "solve his problems" it demands that he review his total delinquent history. This produces anxiety because, while he is still relatively free, it is almost inevitable that he has much more to reveal that is already known by the police or the court. In an

effort to avoid such involvement he may try subterfuge. But any reluctance on his part to be honest will not be taken lightly. Norms dictate that no one in the group can be released until everyone is honest and until every boy helps to solve problems. A refusal to come clean shows a lack of trust in the group and slows down the problem-solving process. Therefore, any recalcitrant boy is faced with a real dilemma. He can either choose involvement or relentless attack by his peers. Once a boy does involve himself, however, he learns that some of his fears were unwarranted. What goes on in the group meeting is sacred and is not revealed elsewhere.

A second process for involvement lies in the use of the peer group to perpetuate the norms of the treatment system. One of the most important norms suggests that most boys in the program are candidates for a reformatory. This is shocking because even habitual delinquents do not ordinarily see themselves as serious offenders.[30] Yet, the tradition is clear; most failures at Pinehills are sent to the Utah State Industrial School. Therefore, each boy has a major decision to make: either he makes serious attempts to change or he gets sent away.

The third process of involvement could only occur in a community program. Each boy has the tremendous problem of choosing between the demands of his delinquent peers outside the program and the demands of those within it. The usual reaction is to test the situation by continuing to identify with the former. Efforts to do this, however, and to keep out of serious trouble are usually unsuccessful. The group is a collective board on delinquency; it usually includes a member who knows the individual personally or by reputation; and it can rely on the meeting to discover many things. Thus, the group is able to use actual behavior in the community to judge the extent to which a boy is involved with the program and to judge his readiness for release. The crucial criterion for any treatment program is not what an individual does while in it, but what he does while he is *not* in it.

The fourth process involves a number of important sanctions which the group can impose if a boy refuses to become involved. It can employ familiar techniques such as ostracism or derision or it can deny him the status and recognition which come with change. Furthermore, it can use sanctions arising out of the treatment system. For example, while authorities may impose restrictions on boys in the form of extra work or incarceration in jail, the group is often permitted, and encouraged, to explore reasons for the action and to help decide what future actions should be taken. For example, a boy may be placed in jail over the week-end and told that he will be returned there each week-end thereafter until his group decides to release him. It is not uncommon for the group, after thorough discussion, to return him one or more week-ends despite his protestations. Such an occurrence would be less likely in an ordinary reformatory because of the need for inmates to maintain solidarity against the official system. However, in this setting it is possible because boys are granted the power to make important decisions affecting their entire lives. Rather than having other people do things to them, they are doing things to themselves.

The ultimate sanction possessed by the group is refusal to release a boy from the program. Such a sanction has great power because it is normative to expect that no individual will be tolerated in the program indefinitely. Pinehills is not a place where boys "do time."

Authorities. The third source of pressure towards change rests in the hands of authorities. The role of an authority in a treatment system of this type is a difficult one. On one hand, he cannot be seen as a person whom skillful delinquents or groups can manipulate. But, on the other hand, he cannot be perceived permanently as a "rejector." Everything possible, therefore, must be done by him to create an adult image which is new and different.

Initially, authorities are probably seen as "rejectors." It will be recalled that they do not go out of their way to engage in regular social amenities, to put boys at ease, or to establish one-to-one relationships with boys. Adult behavior of this type is consistent with the treatment philosophy. It attempts to have boys focus upon the peer group, not adults, as the vehicle by which questions and problems are resolved.

Second, boys learn that authorities will strongly uphold the norm which says that Pinehills is not a place for boys to "do time." If, therefore, a boy does not become involved and the group is unwilling or unable to take action, authorities will. Such action varies. It might involve requiring him to work all day without pay, placing him in jail, or putting him in a situation in which he has no role whatsoever. In the latter case he is free to wander around the Center all day but he is neither allowed to work nor given the satisfaction of answers to his questions regarding his future status.

Boys are seldom told why they are in trouble or, if they are told, solutions are not suggested. To do so would be to provide them structure by which to rationalize their behavior, hide other things they have been doing, and escape the need to change. Consequently, they are left on their own to figure out why authorities are doing what they are doing and what they must do to get out of trouble.

Situations of this type precipitate crises. Sometimes boys run away. But, whatever happens, the boy's status remains amorphous until he can come up with a solution to his dilemma. This dilemma, however, is not easily resolved.

There is no individual counseling since this would reflect heavily upon the integrity of the peer group. Consequently, he cannot resolve his problems by counseling with or pleasing adults. His only recourse is to the group. But since the group waits for him to bring up his troubles, he must involve himself with it or he cannot resolve them. Once he does, he must reveal why he is in trouble, what he has been doing to get into trouble or how he has been abusing the program. If he refuses to become involved he may be returned to court by authorities. This latter alternative occurs rarely, since adults have more time than boys. While they can afford to wait, boys find it very difficult to "sweat out" a situation. They feel the need to resolve it.

As a result of such experiences, boys are often confused and hostile. But where such feelings might be cause for alarm elsewhere, they are

welcomed at Pinehills. They are taken as a sign that a boy is not in command of the situation and is therefore amenable to change. Nevertheless, the treatment system does not leave him without an outlet for his feelings. The meeting is a place where his anger and hostility can be vented —not only against the program but against the adults who run it. But, in venting his confusion and hostility, it becomes possible for the group to analyze, not only his own behavior, but that of adults, and to determine to what end the behavior of all is leading. Initial perceptions of adults which were confusing and provoking can now be seen in a new way. The treatment system places responsibility upon a boy and his peers for changing delinquent behavior, not upon adults. Thus, adult behavior which was initially seen as rejecting can now be seen as consistent with this expectation. Boys have to look to their own resources for solutions of problems. In this way they are denied social-psychological support for "rejecting the rejectors," or for rejecting decisions demanded by the group. Furthermore, as a result of the new adult image which is pressed upon them, boys are led to examine their perceptions regarding other authorities. Boys may learn to see authorities with whom they had difficulties previously in a new, non-stereotyped fashion.

Work and Other Activities

Any use of athletics, handicrafts, or remedial schooling involves a definition of rehabilitation goals. Are these activities actually important in changing delinquents? In the Provo Experiment they are not viewed as having an inherent value in developing non-delinquent behavior. In fact, they are viewed as detrimental because participation in them often becomes criteria for release. On the other hand, work habits are viewed as vitally important. Previous research suggests that employment is one of the most important means of changing reference from delinquent to law-abiding groups.[31] But, such findings simply pose the important question: How can boys be best prepared to find and hold employment?

Sociologists have noted the lack of opportunity structure for delinquents, but attention to a modification of the structure (assuming that it can be modified) as the sole approach to rehabilitation overlooks the need to prepare delinquents to utilize employment possibilities. One alternative for doing this is an education program with all its complications. The other is an immediate attack on delinquent values and work habits. The Provo Experiment chose the latter alternative. It hypothesized that an immediate attack on delinquent values, previous careers, and nocturnal habits would be more effective than an educational program. Sophisticated delinquents, who are otherwise very skillful in convincing peers and authorities of their good intentions, are often unable to work consistently. They have too long believed that only suckers work. Thus concentration is upon work habits. Boys are employed by the city and county in parks, streets, and recreation areas. Their work habits are

one focus of group discussion and an important criterion for change. After release, they are encouraged to attend academic and vocational schools should they desire.

The Starter Mechanism: Putting the System in Motion

There are both theoretical and practical considerations relative to the purposeful creation of the social structure at Pinehills and the process by which it was developed. The foregoing discussion described some of the structural elements involved and, by inference, suggested the means by which they were introduced. However, the following is presented as a means of further clarification.

The first consideration involved the necessity of establishing structure which could pose realistically and clearly the alternatives open to habitually delinquent boys. What are these alternatives? Since in most cases delinquents are lower-class individuals who not only lack many of the social skills but who have been school failures as well, the alternatives are not great. Some may become professional criminals but this is a small minority. Therefore, most of them have two principal choices: (1) they can continue to be delinquent and expect, in most cases, to end up in prison; or (2) they can learn to live a rather marginal life in which they will be able to operate sufficiently within the law to avoid being locked up. Acceptance of the second alternative by delinquents would not mean that they would have to change their entire style of living, but it does mean that most would have to find employment and be willing to disregard delinquent behavior in favor of the drudgery of everyday living.

Until these alternatives are posed for them, and posed in a meaningful way, delinquents will not be able to make the necessary decisions regarding them. The need, therefore, was for the type of structure at Pinehills which could pose these alternatives initially without equivocation and thus force boys to consider involvement in the rehabilitative process as a realistic alternative for them.

By the time delinquents reach Pinehills they have been cajoled, threatened, lectured, and exhorted—all by a variety of people in a variety of settings: by parents, teachers, police, religious leaders, and court officials. As a consequence, most have developed a set of manipulative techniques which enable them to "neutralize" verbal admonitions by appearing to comply with them, yet refraining all the while from any real adherence. For that reason, it was concluded that *deeds,* not *words,* would be required as the chief means for posing clearly the structural alternatives open to them.

Upon arrival the first delinquents assigned to Pinehills had every reason to believe that this was another community agency for which they possessed the necessary "techniques of neutralization." It was

housed in an ordinary two-story home, and authorities spent little time giving instructions or posing threats. It must have seemed, therefore, that Pinehills would not constitute a serious obstacle for which they could not find some means to avoid involvement.

The following are examples of happenings which helped to establish norms contrary to this view. After attending only one day, a rather sophisticated boy was not at home to be picked up for his second day. Instead, he left a note on his front door saying he was at the hospital visiting a sick sister. Official reaction was immediate and almost entirely opposite to what he expected. No one made any efforts to contact him. Instead, a detention order was issued by the court to the police who arrested the boy later that evening and placed him in jail. He was left there for several days without the benefit of visits from anyone and then returned to Pinehills. Even then, no one said anything to him about his absence. No one had to; he did not miss again. Furthermore, he had been instrumental in initiating the norm which says that the principal alternative to Pinehills is incarceration.

A second occurrence established this norm even more clearly. After having been at Pinehills for two months and refusing to yield to the pressures of his group, a boy asked for a rehearing in court, apparently feeling that he could manipulate the judge more successfully than he could the people at Pinehills. His request was acted upon immediately. He was taken to jail that afternoon and a hearing arranged for the following morning. The judge committed him to the State Reformatory.[32] Since that time there has never been another request for a rehearing. In a similar way, especially during the first year, boys who continued to get in serious trouble while at Pinehills were recalled by the court for another hearing and assigned to the reformatory. These cases became legendary examples to later boys. However, adults have never had to call attention to them; they are passed on in the peer socialization process.

Once such traditions were established, they could yet be used in another way. They became devices by which to produce the type of uncertainty characteristic of social settings in which negative sanctions should be forthcoming but do not appear. The individual is left wondering why. For example, not all boys who miss a day or two at Pinehills now are sent to jail. In some cases, nothing is said to the individual in question. He is left, instead, to wonder when, and if, he will be sent. Likewise, other boys who have been in serious trouble in the community are not always sent to the State Reformatory but may be subjected to the same kind of waiting and uncertainty. Efforts are made, however, to make it impossible for boys to predict in advance what will happen in any particular case. Even adults cannot predict this, relying on the circumstances inherent in each case. Thus, both rigidity and inconsistency are present in the system at the same time.

The same sort of structural alternatives were posed regarding work. Boys who did not work consistently on their city jobs, where they were being paid, were returned to Pinehills to work for nothing. At Pinehills, they were usually alone and had to perform such onerous tasks as scrub-

bing the floor, washing windows, mowing the lawn or cutting weeds. They might be left on this job for hours or weeks. The problem of being returned to work with the other boys for pay was left to them for their own resolution, usually in the group. So long as they said nothing, nothing was said to them except to assign them more work.

This type of structure posed stark but, in our opinion, realistic alternatives. It was stark and realistic because boys were still living in the community, but for the first time could sense the omnipresence of permanent incarceration. However, another type of structure less stringent was needed by which boys could realistically resolve problems and make choices. Since, as has been mentioned, peer-group decision-making was chosen as the means for problem-resolution, attention was focussed upon the daily group meetings as the primary source of information. It became the focal point of the whole treatment system.

The first group, not having any standards to guide it (except those which suggested resistance to official pressures), spent great portions of entire meetings without speaking. However, consistent with the idea that deeds, not words, count, and that a group has to resolve its own problems, the group leader refused to break the silence except at the very end of each meeting. At that time, he began standardizing one common meeting practice: he summarized what had been accomplished. Of silent meetings he simply said that nothing had been accomplished. He did point out, however, that he would be back the next day—that, in fact, he would be there a year from that day. Where would they be, still there? The problem was theirs.

When some boys could stand the silence no longer, they asked the group leader what they might talk about. Rather than making it easy for them he suggested something that could only involve them further: he suggested that someone might recite all the things he had done to get in trouble. Not completely without resources, however, boys responded by reciting only those things they had been caught for. In his summary, the leader noted this fact and suggested that whoever spoke the next time might desire to be more honest by telling all. Boys were reluctant to do this but, partly because it was an opportunity to enhance reputations and partly because they did not know what else to do, some gave honest recitations. When no official action was taken against them, two new and important norms were introduced: (1) the idea that what is said in the meeting is sacred to the meeting; and (2) that boys can afford to be candid—that, in fact, candor pays.

The subsequent recitals of delinquent activities ultimately led to a growing awareness of the ambivalence which many delinquents feel regarding their activities. In the social climate provided by the meeting some boys began to express feelings and receive support for behavior which the delinquent system with its emphasis on ideal-typical role behavior could not permit.

Eventually, the meeting reached a stage where it began to discuss the plethora of happenings which occurred daily, both at Pinehills and elsewhere in the community. These happenings, rather than impersonal,

easily speculated-about material, were urged as the most productive subject matter. For example, many boys had reached the stage of trying devious rather than direct methods of missing sessions at Pinehills. They came with requests to be excused for normally laudatory activities: school functions, family outings, and even religious services. But, again adults refused to take the traditional course of assuming responsibility and making decisions for boys. Boys were directed to the meeting instead. This not only shifted the responsibility to them, but provided the opportunity to develop five important norms: (1) those having to do with absences; (2) the idea that the place for problem-solving is in the meeting; (3) that everyone, not just adults, should be involved in the process; (4) that if a boy wants the meeting to talk about his problems, he has to justify them as being more important than someone else's and (5) that any request or point of view has to be substantiated both by evidence and some relevance to the solution of delinquent problems.

It became obvious that even simple requests could be complicated. Boys found themselves using their own rationalizations on each other, often providing both humorous and eye-opening experiences. The climate became increasingly resistant to superficial requests and more conducive to the examination of pressing problems. Boys who chose to fight the system found themselves fighting peers. A stubborn boy could be a thorn in the side of the whole group.

The daily meeting summaries took on increased importance as the leader helped the group: (1) to examine what had happened each day; (2) to examine to what ends various efforts were leading—that is, to examine what various boys were doing, or not doing, and what relevance this had for themselves and the group; (3) to suggest areas of discussion which had been neglected, ignored, or purposely hidden by group members; and (4) to describe the goals of the treatment system in such a way that boys could come to recognize the meaning of group discussions as a realistic source of problem-resolution.

The structural lines associated with the meeting eventually began to define not only the type of subject matter most relevant to change, but the general means for dealing with this subject matter. However, such structure was extremely flexible, permitting a wide latitude of behavior. Great care was taken to avoid the institutionalization of clear-cut steps by which boys could escape Pinehills. Problem solving was, and still is, viewed as a process—a process not easily understood in advance, but something which develops uniquely for each new boy and each new group.

Finally, in summary, the Pinehills system, like many social systems, has some rigid prerequisites for continued membership. The broad structural outlines carefully define the limits beyond which members should no go. However, unlike most extreme authoritarian systems, there is an inner structure, associated with the meaning, which does not demand rigid conformity and which instead permits those deviations which are an honest expression of feelings.

The admission of deviations within the structural confines of the

meeting helps to lower the barriers which prevent a realistic examination of their implications for the broader authoritarian structure, either at Pinehills or in society at large. Boys are able to make more realistic decisions as to which roles, conventional or delinquent, would seem to have the most utility for them.

This brief attempt to describe a complex system may have been misleading. The complexities involved are multivariate and profound. However, one important aspect of the experiment has to do with the theoretical development of, and research on, the nature of the treatment system. Each discussion session is recorded and efforts are made to determine means by which treatment techniques might be improved, and ways in which group processes can be articulated. All would be very useful in testing theory which suggests that experience in a cohesive group is an important variable in directing or changing behavior.

Phase II: Community Adjustment

Phase II involves an effort to maintain reference group support and employment for a boy after intensive treatment in Phase I. After his release from Phase I he continues to meet periodically for discussions with his old group. The goal is to utilize this group in accomplishing three things: (1) acting as a check on a boy's current behavior; (2) serving as a law-abiding reference group; and (3) aiding in the solution of new problems. It seeks to continue treatment in a different and perhaps more intensive way than such traditional practices as probation or parole.

Efforts to find employment for boys are made by the Citizens' Advisory Council. If employment is found, a boy is simply informed that an employer needs someone. No efforts are taken by some well-meaning but pretentious adult to manipulate the boy's life.

These steps, along with the idea that delinquents should be permitted to make important decisions during the rehabilitative process, are consistent with structural-functional analysis which suggests that in order to eliminate existing structure, or identification with it, one must provide the necessary functional alternatives.[33]

Appropriateness of Techniques

Many persons express disfavor with what they consider a harsh and punitive system at Pinehills. If, however, alternatives are not great for habitual delinquents, a program which suggests otherwise is not being honest with them. Delinquents are aware that society seldom provides honors for *not* being delinquent; that, in fact, conventional alternatives for them have not always promised significantly more than delinquent

alternatives.[34] Therefore, expectations associated with the adoption of conventional alternatives should not be unrealistic.

On the other hand it should be remembered that in terms familiar to delinquents, every effort is made at Pinehills to include as many positive experiences as possible. The following are some which seem to function:

1. Peers examine problems which are common to all.

2. There is a recurring opportunity for each individual to be the focal point of attention among peers in which his behavior and problems become the most important concern of the moment.

3. Delinquent peers articulate in front of conventional adults without constraint with regard to topic, language, or feeling.

4. Delinquents have the opportunity, for the first time in an institutional setting, to make crucial decisions about their own lives. This in itself is a change in the opportunity structure and is a means of obligating them to the treatment system. In a reformatory a boy cannot help but see the official system as doing things to him in which he has no say: locking him up, testing him, feeding him, making his decisions. Why should he feel obligated? But when some important decision-making is turned over to him, he no longer has so many grounds for rejecting the system. Rejection in a reformatory might be functional in relating him to his peers, but in this system it is not so functional.

5. Delinquents participate in a treatment system that grants status in three ways: (a) for age and experience in the treatment process— old boys have the responsibility of teaching new boys the norms of the system; (b) for the exhibition of law-abiding behavior, not only in a minimal sense, but for actual qualitative changes in specific role behavior at Pinehills, home or with friends; and (c) for the willingness to confront other boys, in a group setting, with their delinquent behavior. (In a reformatory where he has to contend with the inmate system a boy can gain little and lose much for his willingness to be candid in front of adults about peers, but at Pinehills it is a primary source of prestige.) The ability to confront others often reflects more about the *confronter* than it does about the *confronted*. It is an indication of the extent to which he has accepted the reformation process and identified himself with it.[35]

6. Boys can find encouragement in a program which poses the possibility of relatively short restriction and the avoidance of incarceration.

7. The peer group is a potential source of reference group support for law-abiding behavior. Boys commonly refer to the fact that their group knows more about them than any other persons, parents or friends.

Research Design

An integral part of the Provo Experiment is an evaluation of treatment extending over a five year period. It includes means by which

offenders who receive treatment are compared to two control groups: (1) a similar group of offenders who at time of sentence are placed on probation and left in the community; and (2) a similar group who at time of sentence are incarcerated in the Utah State Industrial School. Since it is virtually impossible to match all three groups, random selection is used to minimize the effect of sample bias. All three groups are drawn from a population of habitual delinquents who reside in Utah County, Utah, and who come before the Juvenile Court. Actual selection is as follows:

The Judge of the Court has in his possession two series of numbered envelopes—one series for selecting individuals to be placed in the *probation* treatment and control groups and one series for selecting the *reformatory* treatment and control groups. These series of envelopes are supplied by the research team and contain randomly selected slips of paper on which are written either *Control Group* or *Treatment Group*.

In making an assignment to one of these groups the Judge takes the following steps: (1) After hearing a case he decides whether he would ordinarily place the offender on probation or in the reformatory. He makes this decision as though Pinehills did not exist. Then, (2) he brings the practice of random placement into play. He does so by opening an envelope from one of the two series supplied him (see Table 1). For

Table 1—Selection of Treatment and Control Groups

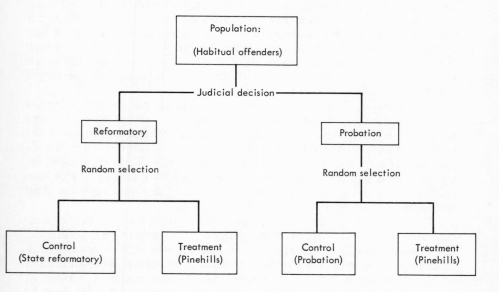

example, if he decides initially that he would ordinarily send the boy to the reformatory, he would select an envelope from the *reformatory* series and depend upon the designation therein as to whether the boy

would actually go to the reformatory, and become a member of the *control* group, or be sent to Pinehills as a member of the *treatment* group.

This technique does not interfere with the judicial decision regarding the alternatives previously available to the Judge, but it does intercede, after the decision, by posing another alternative. The Judge is willing to permit the use of this alternative on the premise that, in the long run, his contributions to research will enable judicial decisions to be based ultimately on a more realistic evaluation of treatment programs available.

In order to make the comparison of treatment and control groups more meaningful, additional research is being conducted on the treatment process. Efforts are made to examine the problems involved in relating causation theory to intervention strategy, the role of the therapist in Guided Group Interaction, and the types of group interaction that seem most beneficial. Finally, a detailed examination is being made of the ways in which boys handle "critical incidents" [36] after release from treatment as compared to the way they handled them prior to treatment.

Summary and Implications

This paper describes an attempt to apply sociological theory to the treatment of delinquents. It concentrates not only upon treatment techniques, *per se,* but the type of social system in which these techniques must operate. The over-all treatment system it describes is like all other social systems in the sense that it specifies generalized requirements for continued membership in the system. At the same time, however, it also legitimizes the existence of a subsystem within it—the meeting—which permits the discussion and evaluation of happenings and feelings which *may* or *may not* support the over-all normative structure of the larger system.

The purposeful creation of this subsystem simply recognized what seemed to be two obvious facts: (1) that the existence of contrary normative expectations among delinquent and official members of the over-all system would ultimately result in the creation of such a subsystem anyway; and (2) that such a system, not officially recognized, would pose a greater threat, and would inhibit to a greater degree, the realization of the over-all rehabilitative goals of the major system than would its use as a rehabilitative tool.

This subsystem receives not only official sanction but grants considerable power and freedom to delinquent members. By permitting open expressions of anger, frustration, and opposition, it removes social-psychological support for complete resistance to a realistic examination of the ultimate utility of delinquent versus conventional norms. At the same time, however, the freedom it grants is relative. So long as opposition to the demands of the larger system is contained in the meeting subsystem, such opposition is respected. But continued deviancy outside the meeting cannot be tolerated indefinitely. It must be

seen as dysfunctional because the requirements of the over-all treatment system are identified with those of the total society and these requirements will ultimately predominate.

At the same time, the over-all treatment system includes elements designed to encourage and support the adoption of conventional roles. The roles it encourages and the rewards it grants, however, are peer-group oriented and concentrate mainly upon the normative expectations of the social strata from which most delinquents come: working-rather than middle-class strata. This is done on the premise that a rehabilitation program is more realistic if it attempts to change normative orientations towards lawbreaking rather than attempting (or hoping) to change an individual's entire way of life. It suggests, for example, that a change in attitudes and values toward work *per se* is more important than attempting to create an interest in the educational, occupational, and recreational goals of the middle-class.

The differences posed by this treatment system, as contrasted to many existing approaches to rehabilitation, are great. Means should be sought, therefore, in addition to this project by which its techniques and orientation can be treated as hypotheses and verified, modified, or rejected.

Notes

1. Donald R. Cressey, "Changing Criminals: The Application of the Theory of Differential Association," *American Journal of Sociology*, 61 (July, 1955), p. 116.

2. Daniel Glaser maintains that the prison social system has not received the study it merits. Most writing about prisons, he says, is "impressionistic," "moralistic," "superficial," and "biased," rather than "systematic" and "objective." "The Sociological Approach to Crime and Correction," *Law and Contemporary Problems*, 23 (Autumn, 1958), p. 697; see also Gresham M. Sykes and Sheldon Messinger, "The Inmate Social System," in *Theoretical Studies in Social Organization of the Prison*, Social Science Research Council, March 1960, pp. 5–19; and Lloyd W. McCorkle and Richard Korn, "Resocialization Within Walls," *The Annals of the American Academy of Political and Social Science*, 293 (May, 1954), pp. 88–98.

3. Sykes and Messinger, *op. cit.*, pp. 12–13; Richard McCleery, "Policy Change in Prison Management," *Michigan State University Political Research Studies*, No. 5, 1957; Richard A. Cloward, "Social Control in the Prison," in *Theoretical Studies in Social Organiza-*

tion of the Prison, op. cit., pp. 20–48; and Stanton Wheeler, "Socialization in Correctional Communities," in this issue of the *Review*.

4. Cressey, *op. cit.*, p. 116.

5. For example, see John G. Milner, "Report on an Evaluated Study of the Citizenship Training Program, Island of Hawaii," Los Angeles: University of Southern California School of Social Work, 1959, p. IV. Irving E. Cohen implies that anything which interferes with the establishment of "confidence, sympathy and understanding" between adult and offender interferes with the effectiveness of the individualized approach. See "Twilight Zones in Probation," *Journal of Criminal Law and Criminology*, 37, No. 4, p. 291.

6. Michael Hakeem, "A Critique of the Psychiatric Approach to Juvenile Delinquency," in *Juvenile Delinquency*, edited by Joseph S. Roucek, New York: Philosophical Library, 1958. Hakeem provides a large bibliography to which attention can be directed if further information is desired. See also Daniel Glaser, "Criminality Theories and Behavioral Images," *American Journal of Sociology*, 61 (1956), p. 435.

7. Cressey, *op. cit.*, p. 117. LaMay

Adamson and H. Warren Dunham even
imply that the clinical approach cannot work successfully with habitual offenders. See "Clinical Treatment of Male
Delinquents: A Case Study in Effort and
Result," *American Sociological Review,*
21 (June, 1956), p. 320.

8. One program consistent with this
premise is the Highfields Residential
Group Center in New Jersey. Modern
penology is indebted to it for the development of many unique and important
aspects. See Lloyd W. McCorkle, Albert
Elias, and F. Lovell Bixby, *The Highfields Story: A Unique Experiment in the
Treatment of Juvenile Delinquency,*
New York: Henry Holt & Co., 1958; H.
Ashley Weeks, *Youthful Offenders at
Highfields,* Ann Arbor: University of
Michigan Press, 1958; and Albert Elias
and Jerome Rabow, Post-Release Adjustment of Highfields Boys, 1955–57, *The
Welfare Reporter,* January, 1960, pp.
7–11.

9. Richard A. Cloward and Lloyd E.
Ohlin, *Delinquency and Opportunity: A
Theory of Delinquent Gangs,* Glencoe,
Ill.: The Free Press, 1960; Albert K.
Cohen, *Delinquent Boys—The Culture
of the Gang,* Glencoe: The Free Press,
1955; Albert K. Cohen and James F.
Short, Jr., "Research in Delinquent Sub-
cultures," *The Journal of Social Issues,*
14 (1958), pp. 20–37; Solomon Kobrin,
"The Conflict of Values in Delinquency
Areas," *American Sociological Review,*
16 (October, 1951), pp. 653–661; Robert
K. Merton, *Social Theory and Social
Structure,* Glencoe: The Free Press, 1957,
Chapters IV–V; Walter B. Miller, "Lower
Calss Culture as a Generating Milieu of
Gang Delinquency," *The Journal of Social
Issues,* 14 (1958), pp. 5–19; Clifford R.
Shaw, *Delinquency Areas,* Chicago: Uni-
versity of Chicago Press, 1929; Clifford
R. Shaw, Henry D. McKay, *et al., Juve-
nile Delinquency and Urban Areas,*
Chicago: University of Chicago Press,
1931; Edwin H. Sutherland, *Principles
of Criminology,* 4th ed., Philadelphia:
Lippincott, 1947; Frank Tannenbaum,
Crime and the Community, Boston:
Ginn and Co., 1938; F. M. Thrasher, *The
Gang,* Chicago: University of Chicago
Press, 1936; William F. Whyte, *Street
Corner Society,* Chicago: University of
Chicago Press, 1943.

10. Richard A. Cloward, "Ilegitimate
Means, Anomie, and Deviant Behavior,"
American Sociological Review, 24 (April,
1959), pp. 164–176; Cloward and Ohlin,
op. cit.; Robert K. Merton, "Social Conformity, Deviation, and Opportunity-
Structures: A Comment on the Contributions of Dubin and Cloward," *American Sociological Review,* 24 (April,

1959), pp. 177–189; Robert K. Merton,
"The Social-Cultural Environment and
Anomie," *New Perspectives for Research
on Juvenile Delinquency,* edited by Helen
Kotinsky, U.S. Department of Health,
Education, and Welfare, 1955, pp. 24–
50; Merton, *Social Theory and Social
Structure, op. cit.*

11. Erik H. Erikson, "Ego Identity and
the Psycho-Social Moratorium," *New
Perspectives for Research on Juvenile
Delinquency, op. cit.* pp. 1–23.

12. Jackson Toby, "The Differential
Impact of Family Disorganization,"
American Sociological Review, 22 (October, 1957), pp. 505–511; and F. Ivan
Nye, *Family Relationships and Delinquent Behavior,* New York: John Wiley
and Sons, 1958.

13. Cohen and Short, Jr., *op. cit.,* p.
24.

14. George B. Vold, "Discussion of
Guided Group Interaction and Correctional Work," by F. Lovell Bixby and
Lloyd W. McCorkle, *American Sociological Review,* 16 (August, 1951), p.
460.

15. As Glaser points out, sociologists
have tended to be deterministic and to
ally themselves with psychiatrists in
the struggle against classical legalists
and religious leaders over the free will
versus determinism issue. He labels this
struggle as a "phony war," involving
polemics more than reality. However,
he says the war is losing its intensity
because of a declining interest in meta-
physical issues and a recognition of the
importance of voluntaristic rather than
reflexive conceptions of human behavior. Contrary to their protestations, the
determinists, for example, recognize
that humans are aware of alternative
possible courses of behavior and make
deliberate choices between them. See
"The Sociological Approach to Crime
and Correction," *op. cit.,* pp. 686–687.

16. Sutherland, it will be recalled,
maintained that "While criminal behavior is an expression of general needs
and values, it is not explained by those
general needs and values since noncriminal behavior is an expression of the
same needs and values." Op. cit., pp.
6–7, italics ours. The accuracy of the
statement would hinge on the definition
of "needs" and "values." See also David
J. Bordua, *Sociological Theories and
Their Implications for Juvenile Delinquency,* U.S. Department of Health, Education, and Welfare, 1960, p. 8, and
Robin M. Williams, Jr., *American Society,* New York: Alfred A. Knopf, 1955,
Chapter 11.

17. Cohen, *op. cit.,* p. 133.

18. Merton, *Social Theory and Social*

Structure, op. cit.

19. Cloward, *op. cit.*, and Cloward and Ohlin, *op. cit.* See also Robert Dubin, "Deviant Behavior and Social Structure: Continuities in Social Theory," *American Sociological Review,* 24 (April, 1959), pp. 147–164.

20. Cohen, *Delinquent Boys, op. cit.,* p. 133; Cohen and Short, *op. cit.,* p. 21. See also John I. Kitsuse and David C. Dietrick, "Delinquent Boys: A Critique," *American Sociological Review,* 24 (April, 1959), p. 211.

21. Gresham M. Sykes and David Matza, "Techniques of Neutralization: A Theory of Delinquency," *American Sociological Review,* 22 (December, 1957), pp. 664–670.

22. McKorkle and Korn, *op. cit.,* pp. 88–91.

23. Except for the community aspects, the above assumptions and the treatment system are similar to those pioneered at Highfields. See McCorkle, Elias, and Bixby, *op. cit.* The Provo Program is especially indebted to Albert Elias, the present director of Highfields, not only for his knowledge about treatment techniques, but for his criticisms of the Provo Experiment.

24. The idea of a community program is not new. The Boston Citizenship Training Group, Inc., a non-residential program, was begun in 1934–36. However, it is for younger boys and utilizes a different approach. A similar program, initiated by Professor Ray R. Canning, in Provo, was a forerunner to this experiment. See "A New Treatment Program for Juvenile Delinquents," *Journal of Criminal Law and Criminology,* 31 (March–April, 1941), pp. 712–719.

25. Judge Paxman is a member of the Advisory Council of Judges to the National Council On Crime and Delinquency and is a member of the symposium preparing a work entitled, *Justice for the Child,* University of Chicago (forthcoming).

26. See F. Lovell Bixby and Lloyd W. McCorkle, "Guided Group Interaction and Correctional Work," *American Sociological Review,* 16 (August, 1951), pp. 455–459; McCorkle, Elias, and Bixby, *The Highfields Story, op. cit.;* and Joseph Abrahams and Lloyd W. Mc-Corkle, "Group Psychotherapy on Military Offenders," *American Journal of Sociology,* 51 (March, 1946), pp. 455–464. These sources present a very limited account of techniques employed. An intimate knowledge would require attendance at group sessions.

27. Other goals relating to the emphasis upon group development, the role of the group therapist, and the nature of the therapeutic situations have been described briefly elsewhere. See *The Highfields Story, op. cit.,* pp. 72–80.

28. Cressey, *op. cit.,* p. 119.

29. Vold maintains that guided group interaction assumes that there is something wrong inside the individual and attempts to correct that. He is right in the sense that it emphasizes that an individual must accept responsibility for his own delinquencies and that no one can keep him out of prison unless he himself is ready to stay out. Vold, in our opinion, is incorrect if his remarks are taken to mean that the group does not discuss groups and group processes, what peers mean to a boy or how the orientations of delinquent groups differ from that of conventional society. *Op. cit.,* p. 360.

30. Delinquents are like other people: The worst can never happen to them. See also Mark R. Moran, "Inmate Concept of Self in a Reformatory Society," unpublished Ph.D. Dissertation, Ohio State University, 1953.

31. Glaser, "A Sociological Approach to Crime and Correction," *op. cit.,* pp. 690–691.

32. Co-operation of this type between the Juvenile Courts and rehabilitative agencies is not always forthcoming. Yet, it also reflects two things: (1) the fact that Judge Paxman sentences only those boys to Pinehills who are habitual offenders; and (2) the fact that it is his conviction that rehabilitation must inevitably involve the Court's participation, both in posing alternatives for boys and in determining the effectiveness of various approaches.

33. Edwin M. Schur, "Sociological Analysis in Confidence Swindling." *Journal of Criminal Law, Criminology and Police Science,* 48 (September–October, 1957), p. 304.

34. Gwynn Nettler has raised a question as to who perceives reality most accurately, deviants or "good" people. See "Good Men, Bad Men and the Perception of Reality," Paper delivered at the meetings of the American Sociological Association, Chicago: September, 1959.

35. Support for this idea can be found in a recently developed matrix designed to measure the impact of group interaction. See William and Ida Hill, *Interaction Martix for Group Psychotherapy,* mimeographed manuscript, Utah State Mental Hospital, Provo, Utah, 1960. This matrix has been many years in development.

36. John C. Flanagan, "The Critical Incident Technique," *Psychological Bulletin,* 51 (July, 1954), pp. 327–358.

Delinquency Programs in the Open Community

Donald A. Cook

In recent months I have studied accounts of a number of programs concerned with the problems of delinquency, and have enjoyed the opportunity to visit several current programs in large cities, and to talk with people active in them. The technical backgrounds of these people have ranged into corners as diverse as psychiatry, anthropology, and experimental psychology. To organize these impressions into a coherent account I shall bypass a discussion of the distinct theoretical views of the various approaches, and emphasize instead an almost political analysis of the relations between the major groups involved in any such program. For if these relations go badly, it does not matter what one's theory is; and if handled well, theory is often absorbed in the process.

Delinquency programs of the sort I refer to operate in the open community, and their target populations typically include both young people who have, and who have not, already been in trouble with the law. A community-based program, encountering as it must the existent social network in a "population at risk," must deal with both groups.

The population at risk (or target population) toward which such programs are typically directed is that of a subset of urban, lower-class males; more recently females have come in for increasing attention. Usually they are weighted with members of low-status ethnic groups— Negroes, Puerto Ricans, Irish, Italian—whose distinctive traditions, rural or European—have become dysfunctional in modern American city life; they live in disorganized and deteriorated areas of the city,

Reprinted by permission of Institute for Social Research, University of Michigan, from Document Series No. 3, Inter Center Program on Children, Youth and Family Life.

and are further beset with problems of poverty, discrimination, and crime. It is in such groups that the correlations between delinquency and other indices of social disorder—public assistance, venereal disease, and so on—are usually high.

Three major groups can be designated as involved in any delinquency program. First is the already mentioned target population of delinquents or potential delinquents. Their behavior offends the community of which they are a subset, and this larger community is the second group. If there were no delinquency threat, there would be no delinquency program in the sense here under discussion: the most effective "preventers" of delinquency, because of their very effectiveness, are never known as delinquency programs. The community responds to its disruption by differentiating out a third group which we shall call the specialist group, whose function is to set up a program. The full network of relations between these three groups may be very complex, and to describe it completely may well be to characterize any program in rather complete detail. This discussion, emphasizing *treatment* measures, will select those elements of the network which have strongest bearing on this operation.

To a psychologically trained audience, it may appear that the social network surrounding the treatment transaction may be—to be sure—a necessary support, but that treatment techniques and theory are essentially independent of this supporting context. It is perhaps the main point of this paper that this traditional view is inadequate, and that for delinquency programs especially this inadequacy has very immediate effects. This is so because the transaction between specialist and target entails an exchange of goods and services which in the long run can be and is controlled by agencies of the surrounding community in many ways, so that the specialist is governed finally by the total community situation, regardless of his own theory of strategy.

Let us examine the relation between specialist and target more closely by contrasting it with the more conventional relationship out of which available theories of psychotherapy have developed. The typical neurotic patient usually enters treatment voluntarily. The behavior regarded as symptomatic in neurotic treatment is so regarded by both patient and therapist—at least to start with: the surprises for the patient will come later. And this behavior is not so socially visible that large segments of the community are concerned about its alteration. Delinquents on the other hand do not present themselves voluntarily for treatment, nor regard their behavior as symptomatic; they feel, often rightly, that its social consequences are of more concern to the treatment enterprise than its meaning for them.

Conventional therapy begins with the participants accepting mutually the value of solicitude for fellow men. The therapist is specially trained so that he will not react in the usual ways to the patient's aberrant behavior; thus his technique is based upon his ability to present a non-punishing audience. But the behavior which he reacts to non-punitively (or does *not* react to punitively) is primarily *verbal* behavior, and an

ordinary office setting insures that its audience shall be restricted to the therapist.

The delinquent does not respect the solicitude of the therapist. And the therapist is faced with the problem of containing the behavior he is working with, both in and out of therapy. First, in the encounter itself, his values and possibly his person, are under threat of attack. Second, the patient's actions outside the therapy may bring in the law and cause the loss—or severe disruption—of the relationship. How has the therapeutic relation evolved to cope with these problems?

First, of course, is the problem of recruitment. Perhaps more developments have occurred in this phase of the transaction in recent years than in any other. With the recognition that referrals to clinics were not picking up the delinquency-prone population, the various programs of "reaching out" began to develop. There are several varieties of this technique, but perhaps the purest—because the most free from the mediation of clinical referral—the method of the detached street worker, or gang worker.[1] He recruits by "hanging around" his target in its natural social setting, often a "hangout" such as a candy store. Initially, he may be regarded with suspicion, since anyone interested in these youths before has been a "cop," a "queer," or perhaps a "social worker." In the initial phase some preliminary weakening of distrust may occur, as well as some establishment of the worker as a reinforcing agent: he buys cokes, plays the juke box for the crowd, and so on. *In other words, the therapist, not the patient, is the supplicant in recruitment.* This is a crucial point, and several things need to be said about it. First I shall mention one recent development of this situation; that is the technique developed by Charles Slack at Harvard for recruiting his target individuals: *he pays them.*[2] I want merely to point out that this step is a logical development of the "reaching out" trend, and to suggest that much of the furor which his work has brought forth—"It's not really therapy," "It's just a gimmick," etc.—springs from the clear reversal of the direction of the flow of money, and its implications for conventional professional status patterns. *For where referral reverses its direction and becomes recruitment, the norms of a private practice profession can no longer apply.*

The fact that the specialist seeks his target and recruits him through positive reinforcements (goods and services) has several implications. The first is that the specialist himself is either a private philanthropist or more typically, is dependent upon a source of capital. Therefore he is dependent upon the support of an organization, and this is usually a part of the larger community whose disturbance by delinquency gave rise to the program in the first place. Who pays the piper may eventually call the tune—unless, of course, he can be prevented from hearing what is being played. This relation of dependence of the specialist upon outside agencies of the community, together with the fact that he requires capital to relate to the target, is perhaps the prime element accounting for the control of therapy by the community at large.

But why should the community at large ever act to disrupt the

therapeutic relationship? There seem to be several sequences which may bring this about. One sequence arises when delinquency programs are set up jointly by two or more segments of the community which are antagonistic to each other; the delinquency program then serves as a sort of "good-will smoke screen" to display solidarity so long as no important vested interests are threatened.[3] But an active community delinquency program is likely sooner or later to touch upon these vested interests, and then its community support may be withdrawn. Examples have occurred in the areas of race relations, housing policy, and organized crime. In one instance, a program which was set up when school racial integration led to youth-group hostilities, eventually floundered when the same community which had backed the program faced the issue of racial restrictions in its housing policies.

There is, of course, a school of thought which holds that a successful delinquency program must be part of a total community enterprise, in which the whole spectrum of social issues which usually characterizes high delinquency areas is taken on. Saul Alinsky is one of the earliest, and still the most forthright, of the proponents of this view.[4] Alinsky's radicalism has kept him from being widely studied, for he can be read as suggesting that the delinquency-breeding community can be united only by setting it against a common enemy outside the community— usually the bureaucratic venality of absentee landlords who profit from chronic slums. In a recent discussion, his view was caricatured in the remark: "Eliminate the little rumbles by making one great big rumble." Still, his writings are most instructive to anyone concerned with practical delinquency programs.

Another sequence which may lead to the withdrawal of support by the community arises, not when community agencies are in conflict, but when the specialist fails to mediate the alienation between this community and its target population. A good example is given by an attempt on the part of a program in New Milford, N.J., to set up a special recreation center for a group of alienated youngsters who would not come to the regular teen center.[5] (This special attempt followed an incident in which a rumble involving the target group was narrowly averted.) The community behind the program at first stipulated that the center should be closely supervised. But under these circumstances the target group refused to attend. The prospect of an unsupervised center struck the backers as dangerous. Finally, an agreement was worked out whereby the center was unsupervised, except that a telephone was available to call for help from one of several members of the specialist group who would always be available on standby. Shown this degree of trust, the group accepted the plan. (As a matter of fact, such groups are often relieved to have provision made for help in case of trouble—provided loss of face is not entailed.) And yet, despite the fact that the arrangement worked—the group camé to enjoy the center, and no trouble occurred—the step was severely criticized at the following Citizen's Hearings.

The same problem may arise with a crisis in the opposite direction.

A program for delinquent-prone boys was tried out one summer by Fuld Neighborhood House in Newark.[6] When the House opened its regular program in the fall, this group appeared and claimed not only club membership but also the right to pass on all other members. When officials of the House denied the boys these prerogatives, a riot occurred in which chairs were thrown and the threat made that "new members trying to enter the House would be beaten."

In some of these disruptive sequences the concern of the wider community seems to be fear of destruction or violence. But in others the issue is less direct, and it appears that the community is reluctant to grant the target group full status as worthy youngsters whose needs are to be taken seriously. Specialist personnel have run into trouble justifying budget expenditures for leather jackets and insignia, a TV set for a recreation center, and other goods. The attitude of the community is "Clear yourself of stigma, *then* you can have good things." The attitude of the alienated group is: "Grant us citizenship in the community, *then* we will negotiate about being civilized." The specialist is in danger of being caught in the resulting crossfire. Maintaining effective relations with both sides in this crossfire is undoubtedly one of the most critical skills of the specialist.

I think there are several reasons why the greatest danger for the specialist in this "cold war" is that of too close identification with the delinquent side. First, such work is not highly regarded or highly paid, and it is very demanding of time (including nights and weekends), so that selection may favor workers with delinquent identifications to begin with. Second, the intensity of interaction engaged in by the specialist clearly favors intimacy with the target population relative to the larger community. Third, many demands and expectations of the conventional community are in fact inconsistent, hypocritical, unfair; and it is the special genius of delinquency to locate normative ambiguity and inconsistency in the surrounding adult world, and to sense rejection or status-degradation behind much talk of "readjustment," "healthful recreation," "service activities," and so on. Even if this attitude of estrangement has functions in rationalizing the pathology of the delinquent,[7] it nonetheless finds in our society plenty of objective support; and the specialist worker will have to come to terms with this fact as a personal problem for him in his work. For these reasons, then, it may be that the dialectic of intense work with the delinquent may be phrased thus: *"He who can reach them, may be tempted to join them."*

The problems discussed so far all illustrate the dependence of the therapeutic transaction upon the specialist's relation with the larger community. I want to indicate briefly, for the sake of completeness, some additional boundaries laid down by the fact that the target population has its own relations with members of this larger community. Four such groups of importance are: (1) friendly peers, such as members of the gang; (2) enemy peers, such as those in rival gangs; (3) parents; (4) the police and courts. Each group may complicate the specialist's problem. The entire gang as a unit for specialist work is an obvious conse-

quence of the importance of the first group. Walter Miller and others have discussed the problems of working with the whole group, such as its splitting into a more and a less "social" group when the worker tries to move the group as a whole in a more socialized direction.[8] Enemy groups are a complicated problem. Miller, once again, provides data showing the turning of groups without workers against those having workers.[9] (Such an effect is, of course, a good reason for a program to work with all potentially delinquent groups at once.) Variations in the roles of parents and police are too great to typify here. Two points must be made. One is that these multiple involvements of the young potential offender require great versatility on the part of the specialist. One account, written by a specialist who directed a recreation center in a severe high delinquency area, records the following activities developing in the course of a year: coaching and refereeing basketball, negotiating between gangs, negotiating between gang and police, throwing groups out of the center, calling the police for help, at other times slugging it out alone, holding firearms under some conditions and letting boys carry them at other times, finding doctors for narcotics users but *not* informing the police, arranging an audition for a singing group which got them a theater engagement, inviting a group to his home in the country, visiting members of his group in hospitals in jails, arranging analytic treatment for several boys. My informant in this instance showed me a scar which he had acquired in the course of his work, then proudly reported that he was invited to the wedding, five years later, of the youth who had inflicted the scar.

I have seen instances where delinquency programs have run afoul of the law. In one large American city, court-ajudicated delinquents are warned that participation in a certain delinquency program would constitute a violation of parole. It is unclear whether the objectionable feature of the program was its success in recruiting offenders who had hitherto been "unreachable," or lay in the fact that the replaying of taped interviews for the interviewee himself constituted pornography. In another large American city, an independent businessman of great genius with rough kids turned his cellar into a combined home and club for alienated youngsters. The police raided the establishment and held a hearing at which charges were nearly placed against this special-ist, for contributing to the delinquency of minors.

The social system may take steps to solve many of these problems by establishing "street club workers" as an official civil service role. In New York, which has pioneered in this enterprise, the Council of Social and Athletic Clubs has offices on Madison Avenue, where an organiza-tion chart on the wall shows the jurisdiction of the 90-odd workers.[10] In this case the organization of the social system begins to approximate, in its scope and complexity, that of the gangs themselves. Here the worker is protected, thanks to his ties with fellow-specialists, from being sucked too deeply into gang life, and guidelines and training help solve problems of conflict and identification. Under these circumstances the containment of destructive behavior can become a skilled enterprise.

When all else fails, the worker can negotiate "a fair one": a fight between members of rival gangs whose outcome is accepted as authoritative by both sides.

To some extent, of course, this solution transfers some of the community conflicts "upstairs," to take place between agencies of the city administration. The Youth Board keeps its own gang file, privy from the encroachments of the Police Department—which has *its* file too. At budget hearings and in the press, these interest groups speak out against each other.

The recruitment of personnel for this role still poses an interesting problem. New York City Youth Board workers are predominantly Negro, and a social work degree is required. Thus a new avenue of upward mobility has evolved, replacing that once provided by the grass-roots interplay of ward politics and rackets which served so well for the Irish and Italians.[11] In Washington, D.C., the five "roving leaders" are currently all Negroes (one is a woman). There were several whites initially, but these have left for greener pastures. For the four current openings for this job, there are many Negro applicants and no white applicants; and at present at least one Negro specialist is working with white gangs. The group hopes, by raising both requirements and salary, to redress the balance of staff. Thus it too is part of the larger community system, and incorporates the problems posed by its value system.

I would like finally to point out one special feature of our target populations relevant to their relations with the larger community: their youth. The young, like the old, are the first to feel the impact of a nation's inability to provide valued roles in the economic system for everyone, and this is especially true for the alienated groups which contribute so heavily to delinquency statistics.[12] Many delinquency programs, therefore, concentrate upon special training in employable skills or their precursors, or in outright job-finding. These actions take on a therapeutic tinge when the learning of new behavior is impeded by the defenses against such learning so typical of the delinquent. In "tutorial group therapy," for example,[13] children with reading problems tell their own stories; the tutor-therapist writes these down to provide the text for reading practice, which then goes hand in hand with group discussion of the stories' contents—which may be remarkably wild. We can look to the future for further developments in such work, in which therapy and new learning are integral parts of the same operation. Modifications of automated instruction by "teaching machines" for retarded, disturbed, correctional, and similar special populations may be expected soon.[14]

Psychology, through special methods of education, can contribute toward the maximizing of individual potential, but society must have roles for such well-prepared individuals to enter. Delinquency programs in New York reported this summer one job for every one hundred applicants. This is perhaps only one sense in which the problems of the delinquent may be a prophetic leading edge for those of society as a whole.

Where, in this network of social processes, is therapy for the delinquent? Does the sum total of all the conditions discussed here define the problems of therapy, or merely the preliminary conditions? Perhaps a bit of both, but I don't know for sure. I do believe that a therapeutic endeavor which cannot handle adequately the problems here raised, cannot succeed, because it cannot maintain itself in the community. The richest clinical literature on therapy with delinquents has come, not from the community, but from residential treatment and correctional settings. Such information is extremely valuable, but in such special settings the final issues of the larger community are not solved; they are merely held in abeyance and, in some instances, complicated. I have chosen to emphasize the conditions of therapeutic work in the open community setting, as the next great arena for the encounters of behavioral technology and issues of social policy.

Notes

1. The fullest account of street-work with gangs is given in "Reaching the Fighting Gang" (New York City Youth Board, 1960).

2. C. W. Slack, "Experimenter-Subject Psychotherapy: A New Method of Introducing Intensive Office Treatment for Unreachable Cases," *Mental Hygiene*, 44:2 (April 1960), 238–56.

3. A detailed analysis of an instance of this type is given in W. B. Miller, "Inter-Institutional Conflict as a Major Impediment to Delinquency Prevention," *Hum. Org.*, 17:3 (Fall 1958), 20–23.

4. S. Alinsky, *Reveille for Radicals* (Chicago: University of Chicago Press, 1946).

5. "New Ways to Reach Unreached Youth: a Challenge to New Jersey" (Third Annual Report and Recommendations of the State of New Jersey Youth Study Commission, June, 1958). The account of the center is given on pp. 93–99. Public reaction to the program is presented in the Twenty-Second Public Hearing before the New Jersey Youth Study Commision, held in Newark, N.J., March 19, 1958, pp. 43–67.

6. A. Fried, "A Work Camp Program for Potential Delinquents," *The Annals*, 322 (March 1959), 38–46.

7. An excellent account of the functions of estrangement for the delinquent is given in G. M. Sykes, and D. Matza, "Techniques of Neutralization: A Theory of Delinquency," *Am. Soc. Rev.*, 22 (Dec. 1957), 664–70.

8. W. B. Miller, "The Impact of a Community Group Work Program on Delinquent Corner Groups," *Soc. Serv. Rev.*, 31:4 (Dec. 1957), 390–406.

9. ———, "Preventive Work with Street-Corner Groups: Boston Delinquency Project," *The Annals*, 322 (March 1959), 97–106.

10. *Reaching the Fighting Gang, op. cit.*

11. W. F. Whyte, *Street Corner Society: The Social Structure of an Italian Slum* (Enl. Ed, Chicago: University of Chicago Press, 1955). This issue is also discussed in R. A. Cloward, and L. E. Ohlin, *Delinquency and Opportunity: a Theory of Delinquent Gangs* (New York: The Free Press of Glencoe, 1960).

12. A provocative discussion of youth groups as barometers of social change is given in P. Goodman, *Growing up Absurd: Problems of Youth in the Organized System* (New York: Random House, 1960).

13. J. B. Margolin, M. Roman, and C. Harari, "Reading Disability in the Delinquent Child: A Microcosm of Psychosocial Pathology," *Am. J. Orthopsychiat.*, 25:1 (Jan. 1955), 25–35.

14. A comprehensive anthology of papers in this new area is A. A. Lumsdaine and R. Glaser, *Teaching Machines and Programmed Learning: A Source Book* (Washington, D.C.: National Education Association of the United States, 1960).

The Effectiveness of a Comprehensive, Vocationally Oriented Psychotherapeutic Program for Adolescent Delinquent Boys

Joseph L. Massimo and Milton F. Shore

One of the most important recent developments in the treatment of juvenile delinquency is the growing recognition of the need to make vocational assistance available to the adolescent delinquent. Although there is general agreement about the value of work experience as a form of therapeutic intervention, specific knowledge regarding the role of employment in the treatment process has been limited.

Delinquents who are not attending school are technically considered members of the school dropout population. Many schools offer vocational services to those who leave prematurely, with the expectation that delinquents among this group will also benefit from them. Close examination of the structure of such programs reveals, however, that a large number of delinquents are unable to avail themselves of these services. In fact, even programs designed specifically for these adolescents are often inadequate. Usually they have involved many workers from various disciplines collaborating in a loosely integrated fashion.

Although seriously disturbed delinquents need psychological, educational, and vocational help, they often reject such assistance when it is offered by isolated professionals in a way that seems unrelated to the circumstances of their everyday existence. The unique problems facing antisocial adolescents isolate them from the remainder of the dropout

Reprinted from *American Journal of Orthopsychiatry*, Vol. 33, No. 4, July 1963, pp. 634–642. Copyright, the American Orthopsychiatric Association, Inc.

population and demand special vocational services more commensurate with their needs.

Since treatment within the usual clinical setting has not been uniformly successful, increased experimentation is needed to determine what types of therapeutic procedures are most effective. The purpose of this study was to devise and evaluate a multidimensional approach to the treatment of delinquency in adolescent boys. The program reported here made use of intensive psychotherapy for exploring personality conflicts, remedial education as a means of supporting the learning sector of ego functioning, and employment, which was not only therapeutic in itself but provided a focus in reality for the psychotherapy and the reeducative endeavors. Several studies have concerned individual treatment procedures, but no systematic research has previously been designed to investigate a flexible combined approach, offered by a single practitioner, with job placement as a matrix for other therapeutic efforts.

Nature of the Program

The major characteristics of the treatment program can be summarized as follows:

1. The service was initiated at a crisis point when the subject was expelled from school or dropped out for reasons of his own. It was believed that even though the delinquent overtly rejected school, leaving it was still a crisis to him and made him more amenable to help.

2. Original contact was established in terms of help in "getting a job." Other possibilities (assistance with personal problems, getting a license, and the like) were merely mentioned as being available if desired. This was based on the experience that delinquents reject any academic program or psychotherapy, but are motivated to some degree to find a job.

3. Pre-employment counseling focused on job readiness. To assist the delinquent in getting and keeping a job, his expectations and attitudes in regard to working were developed.

4. The self-initiating, individualized aspects of the service were stressed. No part of the program was compulsory. The boy was responsible for making the decisions. In this way dependency, which delinquents characteristically fear and which frequently is encouraged in the usual psychotherapeutic situation, was not fostered.

5. Flexibility of technique and service was maintained. There were few time restrictions on contact or activities with the therapist. Role rigidity was avoided. Techniques varied with the demands of the immediate situation. Thus the therapist spoke with or saw the boy any time of day or night, and as often as eight or ten times a week.

6. Mobility and action were emphasized. The therapist had no central office, and made frequent field trips when necessary. In essence, the

therapist entered all areas of the adolescent's life. Job finding, court appearances, pleasure trips, driving lessons when appropriate, locating and obtaining a car, arranging for a dentist appointment, going for glasses, shopping for clothes with a first pay check, opening a bank account and other activities require this maximum commitment.

7. The independence of the service from school, hospitals, court or authoritarian agencies was made evident. "Return to school" overtures were not made. Also the therapist was in no way involved in influencing the courts' decisions on these boys, or in influencing the decision of employers to keep or fire a boy.

8. The treatment focused on individual responsibility, not group activity or participation. Support was constantly available and was on a one-to-one basis.

9. The job was mutually selected in terms of the boy's interest, abilities and goals. Failures were thus minimized (fantasies of omnipotence frequently drive these boys toward jobs that are too difficult and in which they repeatedly experience failure).

10. After placement, the focus of psychotherapy shifted from job readiness to the problems encountered at work. The reality situation was used as the mode of communicating psychotherapeutic insights.

11. The remedial education program was tailored to individual needs and initially related to work performance. It was initiated when the delinquent was ready to seek such assistance to improve his skills on the job.

Hypotheses

General Hypothesis. The comprehensive psychotherapeutic approach will lead to positive changes in ego functioning evidenced by changes in the areas of academic learning, personality attitudes, and overt behavior.

Hypothesis I. The comprehensive psychotherapeutic approach will lead to positive changes in areas of academic learning.

Hypothesis II. The comprehensive psychotherapeutic approach will lead to positive changes in attitudes toward the self, toward authority and toward control of aggression.

Hypothesis III. The comprehensive psychotherapeutic approach will lead to positive changes in overt behavior as evidenced by a more favorable job history and a decline in antisocial behavior.

Procedure

SELECTION OF SUBJECTS

Twenty adolescent boys with records of antisocial activity were selected for the study through the co-operation of supervisors of attend-

ance, guidance personnel and other public school officials in three suburban areas of Boston. Each subject met the following criteria:

1. Age 15–17. (In Massachusetts delinquents over 17 are adult criminals; full-time employment is permitted only in special cases for children under the age of 15.)

2. An IQ in pretesting of 85–110 on either the WISC or WAIS.

3. A history of antisocial behavior with repeated truancy, longstanding problems in school adjustment and performance, overt aggression toward peers and authority and a reputation familiar to attendance officers, courts or police.

4. Suspension from school, or voluntary dropping out, attributable by the school to poor school performance combined with antisocial behavior.

5. No gross observable psychotic behavior. (Special treatment procedures would be required for such individuals.)

6. No previous psychotherapy for the boy or any members of his family.

The boys were randomly assigned to two groups of ten each. One group was treated, one was not. An analysis of age, IQ and socioeconomic differences between the two groups revealed no significant differences, indicating that the assignment was indeed random. All the boys approached agreed to try the service offered and none were lost after the program was initiated. Although there was some reluctance by those not treated to return for retesting, persuasion and encouragement succeeded in gaining their co-operation.

TESTING

All the boys were tested immediately following the termination of their formal education, and retested approximately ten months later, after the experimental group had been given the intensive treatment described above. No contact was maintained with the control group during the ten-month period. Pretesting was explained as a school exit procedure, follow-up testing as a method of gaining a better understanding of the boy's history since leaving school. All pre- and posttesting was done by an experienced psychologist who did not know the specific aims of the project or which boy was in which group.

To measure changes in performance in academic areas, the Metropolitan Achievement Tests in Reading, Vocabulary, Arithmetic Fundamentals and Arithmetic Problems were administered. Form R of the test was used for pretesting; Form U for posttesting.

To measure changes in attitude toward authority, control of aggression, and self-image, thematic stories were obtained from pictures individually administered by a trained clinical psychologist. Some of the cards were taken from the Standard Thematic Apperception Test battery, others from a special group of cards devised by Dr. Seymour Epstein of the University of Massachusetts. Five pictures were selected

for each of the three variables. These 15 were chosen from 35 pictures presented to three clinical psychologists who were asked to rate the stimulus value of the pictures with respect to their ability to elicit stories dealing with that variable. No single picture was used to measure more than one variable.

RATING PROCEDURE

To evaluate changes in the three personality variables, the stories were presented in pairs (a pre- and poststory) to a clinical psychologist who had had many years of clinical experience with delinquents. The pairs were randomized so that sometimes the prestory was presented first and sometimes second. The order of the 300 sets of stories from the 20 subjects was randomized so that no two successive pairs of stories came from the same boy. The psychologist who did the rating knew nothing about the design or aims of the project. He was asked to rate the second story as better or worse than the first or "no change." He was discouraged from rating "no change." (In statistical analysis the two stories that were rated "no change" were included under "worse" because of the directional nature of the hypotheses.) The criteria for judging the change in these stories were clearly delineated by a rating guide. This guide was derived from the aspects of form and content considered by W. C. Henry (*The Analysis of Fantasy*. John Wiley & Sons, New York, 1956) to be important in the analysis of thematic material. From the criteria, the rater was asked to arrive at one over-all clinical judgment on the basis of his evaluation of each pair of stories.

The reliability of the "improvement" rating procedure was established by pretesting the scale. This was accomplished by obtaining ten pairs of thematic stories unrelated to the experiment, from the files of the Judge Baker Guidance Center, and having them rated by three clinical psychologists. Perfect agreement was obtained on nine of the ten pairs.

No satisfactory way has yet been found to quantify changes in job history and legal status. Changes in these areas have therefore been handled descriptively.

Results

1. Hypothesis I stated that the comprehensive psychotherapeutic approach should lead to positive changes in areas of academic learning.

Standard scores were used to equate Intermediate and Advanced batteries of the two forms of the Metropolitan Achievement Test. Table 1 shows the results in the four academic areas of reading, vocabulary, arithmetic fundamentals and arithmetic problems. The t-tests are significant beyond the .01 level for all four areas. Note that the mean

Table 1—Means of Difference Scores, Standard Deviations, and T-Test Results of the Two Groups on Metropolitan Achievement Tests

		Mean of Difference Scores	S.D.	t	P
Reading	Experimental	5	1.153	4.47	<.01
	Control	−1.3	4.297		
Vocabulary	Experimental	4.6	1.264	7.88	<.01
	Control	−3.2	2.863		
Arithmetic fundamentals	Experimental	3.5	2.121	6.65	<.01
	Control	−2.8	2.224		
Arithmetic problems	Experimental	2.7	2.660	7.74	<.01
	Control	−4.5	2.268		

N = 20.

scores of the difference between the pre- and posttest of the controls all dropped, while the mean difference scores of the experimental group all rose. Hypothesis I was confirmed for all the academic areas measured.

2. Hypothesis II stated that the comprehensive psychotherapeutic approach should lead to positive changes in three personality variables —attitudes toward self-image, authority, and control of aggression.

Since five stories were rated for each variable, a majority of the stories from the second testing were classified either as "improved" or as "not improved." Chi squares were computed for the two groups, the dependent variable being the number in each group that had a majority of stories in the "improved" or "not improved" categories.

Table 2 shows the results of the chi squares for each of the three

Table 2—Chi Square Results on Ratings for Control of Aggression, Attitude Toward Authority, and Self-Image

Variable	X^2	P
Control of aggression	5.0	<.05
Attitude toward authority	3.28	.10 < .05
Self-image	7.27	<.01

N = 20; d.f. = 1.

personality variables. At the .05 level of significance, two of the variables (self-image and control of aggression) were significant. Self-image, in fact, was significant beyond the .01 level. The third variable, attitude toward authority, approached significance, being between .10 and .05. Hypothesis II was therefore confirmed.

These results suggest an interesting trend. Delinquents receiving vocationally oriented psychotherapy may improve first in self-image, next in control of aggression and lastly in their attitude toward authority. This trend is confirmed in an analysis of the individuals. One boy did

not improve in any of the three areas; a second who did not improve in attitude toward authority improved in self-image and control of aggression; a third improved in self-image but did not improve in control of aggression or attitude toward authority.

3. Hypothesis III stated that the comprehensive psychotherapeutic approach would lead to positive changes in overt behavior as evidenced by a more favorable job history and a decline in antisocial behavior.

Because no way to quantify changes in overt behavior has yet been found, these variables were evaluated descriptively by appraisal of the work history (Table 3) and the legal status (Table 4) of the two groups following the ten-month experimental period.

Members of the experimental group had a better employment record than those of the control group. At the end of the ten months, all but three of the experimental subjects were employed. The three not working had left their jobs to return to school. In the control group, three subjects were unemployed throughout the entire period and a fourth was without work at the time of final contact. On the average, the control group members who were working had held more jobs than the experimental group subjects. These positions had been held for shorter periods of time. Five of the treated adolescents were able to maintain a single job throughout the ten months, while no control subject succeeded in this.

Table 3 reveals some further interesting facts regarding the subjects' reasons for leaving their jobs. Employers fired five members of the control group but only two of the experimental subjects. Three experimental group members left a job on their own initiative for a better position. No boy in the control group did so.

Table 4 reveals that only three experimental subjects were on probation at the end of the ten-month period. One of these boys was awaiting a hearing for a traffic violation. In the control group, four of the ten were on probation and two others who had been were institutionalized awaiting hearings for rather serious offenses. Two more also had hearings pending. Despite the small number of subjects in this study, it seems highly probable that the trend suggested by these results would prove statistically significant.

Personal contact with attendance and probation officers indicated that they had observed a notable improvement in the behavioral patterns of the experimental delinquents. They were "picked up" less, and involved in fewer gang activities than were the control group subjects. The officers felt that nine of the ten treated adolescents had improved in their overt behavior. The one exception was considered to be extremely disturbed and unable to respond to any rehabilitative efforts. In contrast, control group delinquents had become increasingly troublesome since they left school. (It should be noted that community officials did not know which adolescents were participating in the program until after they were officially notified at the end of the treatment period.)

Hypothesis III, which stated that the comprehensive psychotherapeutic approach should lead to positive changes in overt behavior as

Table 3—Work Histories of the Two Groups During the Ten-Month Experimental Period

Group		Number of Jobs	Time Held (Mos.) (P = Present)	Reason for Leaving
Experimental subject	1	2	7, 3-P	Better position
	2	2	9, 1-P	Better position
	3	1	10	School
	4	2	2, 8-P	Fired
	5	1	10	School
	6	2	1, 9-P	Better position
	7	1	10-P	
	8	3	2, 4, 3	Fired, Quit, School
	9	1	10-P	
	10	1	10-P	
Control subject	1	2	3, 4-P	Fired
	2	Unemployed		
	3	3	1, 2, 4-P	Fired, Arrested
	4	1	7-P	
	5	Unemployed		
	6	2	1, 4-P	Fired
	7	3	2, 2, 1 (Not working)	Fired, Fired, Quit
	8	Unemployed		
	9	2	3, 4-P	Fired
	10	1	8	School

N = 20.

Table 4—Legal Status of the Two Groups Following the Ten-Month Experimental Period

Group		On Probation	Hearing Pending	Institutionalized
Experimental subject	1	*		
	2			
	3			
	4	*	* (Traffic)	
	5			
	6	*		
	7			
	8			
	9			
	10			
Control subject	1			
	2	(*)	* (Sullivan Act)	*
	3		* (Breaking and Entering)	
	4			
	5	(*)	* (Car Theft)	*
	6	*		
	7	*	* (Traffic)	
	8	*		
	9	*		
	10			

N = 20.

evidenced by a more favorable job history and decline in antisocial behavior, was confirmed.

Discussion of Results

It is clear from the results that the comprehensive treatment approach, combining remedial education and psychotherapy within the context of job placement, had positive results in all specified areas— academic learning, personality attitudes and overt behavior. The positive experimental results are particularly important in light of the fact that delinquents characteristically display marked resistance to any forms of educational activity. It is clear, too, that the positive changes were not superficial but were marked by modifications in such basic personality functions as attitudes toward self, authority and control of aggression. These were closely correlated with performance on the job and a decrease in antisocial behavior.

One important feature of the program was that all aspects of it were administered by a single practitioner. The importance of not subdividing the areas of help "by departments" in a clinic setting but of offering that assistance most necessary at a given time in the delinquent's life suggests that it may be necessary to train people in multiprofessional activities for work with delinquents. It is within the context of a relationship that can help him in any area of life at any time that the adolescent delinquent appears to be able to make his greatest gains.

The course of the treatment process is of interest in itself. The results indicate that the first area of change is in attitude toward self, while the last is in attitude toward authority. This is consistent with what one would expect in a vocationally oriented program where failure experiences are reduced and where the focus is on development of skills and abilities to perform on the job. As he becomes more successful, the delinquent has less need to use aggression as an adaptive technique for dealing with the world and its frustration. Of special interest is that the last area to change is attitude toward authority. Is this because the nature of the adolescent process itself involves a certain degree of rebellion against authority? Or is it that the community continues to reinforce the negative image these boys have made? (Although their behavior improved, some officials still saw them as "bad boys," potentially dangerous, and were on the look-out for them.)

In such a comprehensive program, the question always arises as to what specific factors brought about the change. Was it the fact that these adolescents were contacted at a crisis point, or that the techniques were flexible and individualized? Was it the informality of the total approach, the focus on the job, or the specific personality of the therapist? No doubt all these factors in combination were successful, but it is the task of future research to determine the importance of any single factor or various combinations of them.

The necessity of a flexible, informal approach focused on the personality dynamics and needs of each individual delinquent cannot be overemphasized. To meet the challenge of the greatest social problem of our day—juvenile delinquency—programs employing new approaches and techniques must be undertaken. Flexible but intensive programs of vocationally oriented psychotherapy and remedial education offer much promise with delinquents of working age.

Summary and Conclusions

A comprehensive, vocationally oriented psychotherapy program administered by a single practitioner was instituted for delinquent adolescent boys. The evaluation of the program indicated that there were major changes in areas of academic learning, personality attitudes and overt behavior. The necessity for a concrete, flexible, individually tailored program, incorporating intensive psychotherapeutic principles and remedial education within the context of employment, in helping this group of youngsters was stressed.

The Impact of a Community Group Work Program on Delinquent Corner Groups

Walter B. Miller

What happens when a group of professionally trained young social workers goes into an urban working-class community with the express intention of changing the customary behavior patterns of adolescent corner gangs? The "area worker" approach to troublesome adolescent groups—also called the "detached worker" or "corner-group worker" approach—is being tried out by a growing number of urban communities faced with increasingly severe problems in coping with gang delinquency.[1] In 1954, Helen Witmer stated that the area-worker approach "holds great promise of reducing delinquency" but went on to say that "little has been done to determine how effective this work is and under what circumstances it succeeds or fails." [2] This paper will report selected preliminary findings on the corner-group work efforts of one community delinquency control project—the Boston Special Youth Program.

The Special Youth Program Structure, Objectives, and Methods

Aroused public opinion was primarily responsible for setting into motion the forces that led to the establishment of the Program. The murder of a rabbi, allegedly by a gang of Negro boys, dramatically called attention to juvenile gang activity in the section of Boston where the

---

Reprinted from *Social Service Review*, Vol. 31, No. 4, December 1957, pp. 390–406.

murder occurred. After the murder, a series of newspaper articles entitled "Teenage Gangs Prowl Boston" heightened the sense of public apprehension over "gang delinquency," and a special committee was set up by United Community Services—Boston's central agency for planning, financing, and co-ordinating private health and welfare services—to take action in response to these events.[3]

After more than a year of preliminary discussion and planning, during which many diverse and often conflicting proposals about the most effective approach to the problem of juvenile delinquency were forwarded and debated, a decision was made to conduct a three-year experimental program in an effort to demonstrate the potential effectiveness of concentrating an intensive program of delinquency control measures in one limited geographical area.

After extended debate over whether the Program should be conducted within the framework of existing agencies or by a separate and relatively autonomous agency, the latter alternative was selected. It was also agreed that the locale of this experiment would be part of the district where the rabbi's murder took place—an area containing about 30,000 of the district's 112,000 population. The Special Youth Program began operations in June, 1954, and terminated in June, 1957, the date originally agreed upon. Although certain administrative functions were performed for the Program by facilities of United Community Services, the Program had its own board and operated out of its own offices in a city health unit.

In common with most community-based delinquency prevention programs currently in operation, the original plan of the Special Youth Program called for a multiple, co-ordinated approach to the problem of delinquency in the community rather than for primary reliance on any single technique or method.[4] This approach was to comprise four major efforts: (1) direct intensive group work with adolescent groups identified as troublesome or "delinquent"; (2) casework with a selected group of families presenting persistent, long-term problems for city welfare agencies; (3) a program of research to furnish information on the nature of community culture and social organization and to evaluate the effectiveness of the service efforts; and (4) a community organization effort, which had two major objectives; (a) to facilitate the formation of local citizens' organizations and strengthen existing ones in order to increase the capacity of the community for self-help and (b) to arrange a pattern of co-operation among existing community welfare agencies so that the services started by the Program could be continued under local auspices after Program termination.[5]

Of the three direct-service subprograms, the most intensive effort was devoted to the work with corner groups. During the three years of Program operations seven group workers worked in four neighborhoods for periods ranging from nine months to two and one-half years. All workers but one were graduates of schools of social work; five of the workers were men and two were women; ages ranged from twenty-five to forty. Seven corner-group units were the object of intensive attention,

and seven others received less intensive or sporadic attention. Workers went to their neighborhoods between three and five times a week to work directly with their groups or on their behalf.[6]

Of the seven units given intensive attention, three were Negro and four white—predominantly Irish. Of the seven workers, one was Negro, one Irish, one Italian, two Jewish, and two of English background. No attempt was made to match ethnic status of worker and group; the Negro worked with white groups; both Jews worked with Catholic groups; workers with Negro groups were of Italian and English background. In general, women worked with girls' groups and men with boys'.

The objective of work with groups was conceptualized as "redirecting the energies of group members into constructive channels." Methods used in attempting to achieve this end reflected attempts to accommodate group work methods—as outlined in textbooks and geared primarily to relatively well-behaved agency groups—to the realities of life in an open, complex working-class community.

Only one of the project groups could be characterized as severely delinquent either in the sense that the majority of group members had criminal records or that the commission of serious crimes constituted a significant proportion of their activities. The groups represented fairly typical working-class street-corner groups for whom occasional acts of theft, truancy, gang-fighting, and vandalism represent normal and expected behavior.[7]

Workers with boys' groups devoted considerable effort to encouraging and facilitating participation in organized athletics—primarily baseball, football, and basketball. In most instances an organized club was formed to facilitate team athletics. Workers with girls' groups found group-centered techniques of less utility, since the girls' groups were much less stable than the boys' and many of their basic interests could be pursued outside the context of organized group life. In consequence, the girls' workers became progressively less involved with groups as such and more involved with individuals and their families.

Assessing Program Effectiveness

Since the Special Youth Program was conceived as an experimental or "demonstration" project, original plans called for the inclusion of a research effort as an integral part of the Program. The actual nature of this research was vaguely conceived, but it was recognized that a program whose primary obligation was to "demonstrate effectiveness" should include some sort of systematic method for examining, evaluating, and reporting the results of the effort. Despite plans that research concerns be built into the initial formulation of Program operating procedures, the research effort did not begin until nine months after service

efforts were under way. This delay may be attributed in part to strong pressure for immediate action and in part to feelings by some that research represented a secondary priority.

The research program was directed by a cultural anthropologist as a full-time staff member with the aid of graduate student research assistants. A major task in formulating the research program was that of selecting areas of concentration from among the varied efforts of the Program. It was decided to focus research on the work with groups and within this area to develop two major efforts: first, the collection of background data on the nature of the community and its adolescent groups, and, second, an effort to answer the central question of the Program—"Just how effective is corner-group work in achieving its objectives?"

As is frequently the case in undertakings of this kind, there was wide divergence among the Program's various sponsoring groups as to what these objectives were or should be. In consequence, statements of Program goals which had to accommodate these diverse and frequently conflicting conceptions were for the most part highly generalized. This lack of specificity made a decision on the research focus contingent on two prior tasks. The first involved selecting from the various conceptions of the Program's proper objectives a goal or set of goals that would be so definite that it would be possible to see whether or not they were attained and at the same time would be sufficiently significant to be of recognizable value. For these purposes the central goal of the group work program was taken to be the limitation or reduction of illegal or delinquent behavior by members of Program groups. Second, it was necessary to rephrase this statement of purpose so that it would be "researchable," that is, would furnish guides to the collection of specific pertinent data. On the assumption that "delinquent" behavior could not be meaningfully treated in isolation from the over-all pattern of group behavior, the primary research question in reference to work with groups was formulated as follows: "To what extent did customary patterns of behavior of members of Program groups—including behavior defined as in violation of official norms—change in quality and frequency during the period when the worker was involved with the group?"

This particular formulation, as well as the research design derived from it, embodies several considerations arising from inadequacies characterizing much current research relating to group work. First, it defines the primary task of the worker as that of deliberately effecting changes in the group's customary ways of behaving, rather than in more nebulous terms such as "promoting group health" or "enhancing social adjustment." Second, it takes as its primary focus the behavior of the *group* rather than the activities and role of the worker. Much current study in the group work field devotes major attention to what the *worker* did and how he did it and treats only incidentally or unsystematically what happened to the group as the result of these efforts. Third, it conceives the primary object of efforts toward change to be the group as a whole—

considered as a collective entity with collective characteristics rather than as an aggregate of individuals with designated personality characteristics. Fourth, it calls for a descriptive examination of changes through time in a specific set of operationally defined behavior patterns, recorded in detail as they occurred, rather than utilizing more subjective estimates by a panel of raters as to what "movement" occurred in designated groups.

This formulation also rests on the assumption that currently available research techniques cannot demonstrate a clear-cut cause-and-effect relationship between group behavior changes and worker efforts when operations are carried out in so complex an arena as a modern urban community.[8] In addition to the efforts of the worker, the behavior of group members is also subject to influence by a wide range of interrelated forces—police activity, recreation programs, efforts of other community agencies, activities of outside corner groups, and many others. Thus, the more inclusive question, "Did the workers have a measurable impact on delinquency?" is broken down into two separate questions: "To what extent did observable changes occur in group behavior patterns?" and "To what extent can the workers' efforts be credited with observed changes?" Resolving the more general question into these two components makes it possible to provide much more accurate and reliable answers to the first and to approach the second with the caution demanded by its greater difficulty and complexity.[9]

RESEARCH METHOD

Research techniques for answering the question, "What changes occurred in the customary behavior patterns of group members?" are based primarily on the systematic analysis of a range of written records compiled both by the project and by outside agencies. Three indexes to behavior change are used: qualitative changes in general group behavior patterns, quantitative changes in officially recorded illegal behavior, and qualitative changes in "systemic" group relations. Each of these indexes utilizes research techniques geared to its particular approach.[10]

The first approach deals with changes in the total range of customary activities and behaviors engaged in by Program group members. Research techniques involve both qualitative and quantitative examination of about sixty kinds of observable group behavior patterns and how they changed through time. This information is obtained by the application of a uniform data-processing system to five sets of continuous records reporting events relating to Program corner groups.[11]

The second approach focuses on specifically illegal acts performed by group members coming to the official attention of legal and penal agencies and recorded by these agencies. Research procedure entails a statistical analysis of records kept by courts, police, and other non-Program agencies. Trends in the incidence of officially recorded illegal

acts as indicated by court action or arrests for theft, assault, vandalism, truancy, etc., and involving members of Program groups are compared with trends for non-Program "control" groups, and delinquency rates for the Program area are compared with rates in similar areas.[12]

The third approach takes as its field of examination the established system of intergroup relationships in the community. For this purpose the corner groups are seen as part of an interrelated system of groups and subgroups—a system whose component parts and interrelations are subject to change by a directed effort. The analysis of changes in this system of relationships—which may be called "systemic changes"—is perhaps the most difficult to subject to codifiable research techniques but is nonetheless an area of great importance.[13] The present account will limit itself to a discussion of this latter type of change and will describe "systemic" changes of four kinds: first, changes in community perception of a type of worker role; second, changes in customary relations between local neighborhood corner groups; third, changes in relations between subunits of these larger groups; and fourth, changes in relations within these subunits.[14]

The Influence of Program Workers on Adolescent Groups in the Community

To what extent did the efforts of Special Youth Program workers result in changes in the activities and behavior of adolescent street-corner groups in the community? A community is much more than a collection of individuals. It is composed of many different kinds of groups, systematically related to one another. A community includes groups of parents, of teachers, of policemen, of social agency workers, of recreation workers, of businessmen, and many others. The boys' or girls' adolescent street-corner group is one of the many different kinds of groups in a community; and these adolescent groups are related both to one another and to other local groups. A service project such as the Special Youth Program is bound to affect not only the individuals who are members of these groups but relations between the groups themselves and between the groups and other parts of the community.

Before describing changes in this system of relationships, it is important to emphasize that much of the following material is tentative and that further fact-finding and analysis are necessary before these conclusions can be considered as well established. Two further reservations should be added. First, much of the following material relates primarily to boys' groups; girls' groups are sufficiently different in structure and in appropriate service procedures to make some of these generalizations inapplicable. Second, some of the general statements included here will naturally apply more accurately and specifically to some of the seven Program groups than to others.

CREATING A NEW ROLE IN THE COMMUNITY

In any community residents recognize and are familiar with a specific set of roles or formally established positions. In a downtown urban community, roles familiar to adolescents include those of policeman, schoolteacher, social welfare worker, truant officer, numbers man, recreation department worker, priest or minister, and parole officer. Because adolescents are familiar with these roles, they manifest an established set of attitudes and ways of behaving toward those who fill them. When a stranger first comes into the community, adolescents feel uncomfortable until they are able to identify him as fitting one of the roles with which they are already familiar. Is he a plain-clothes cop, a welfare department investigator, a numbers man? Once the stranger has been identified as filling a familiar role, the adolescents feel on firm ground in knowing how to act and react toward him.

When the street-corner workers of the Special Youth Program first came into the community, they were faced with a difficult problem. There was no precedent in the community for the role of "street-corner worker," and therefore local adolescents were unable to fall back on known ways of acting and reacting. At first the youngsters attempted to tag the workers according to roles they were familiar with; one worker was asked during an early contact with the group, "Are you a cop or a welfare worker?" It became the task of the workers to make known to the community just what role they were to play, and they did this primarily by demonstrating in action just what a corner-group worker does do, a task requiring time and patience.

This process might best be illustrated through the experience of a local agency caseworker who was working with a member of a neighborhood group at the time a Program worker was first establishing contact. When asked by the caseworker to describe this new person, a group member, a girl, said, "Oh, she's the one who comes down to the corner and hangs out with us." A few months later the girl had changed her description of the worker to, "She's the one that helps us." Later still the girl began to refer to the worker as "our social worker." It is evident that a new role had been established in the community, the role of "social worker," which had a specific and distinctive meaning for the youngsters. A "social worker" was evidently someone who came down to the corner to hang out with you and who helped you. This conception of the role of social worker later became so firmly established in parts of the community that only a corner-group worker was identified as a "social worker," and other kinds of social workers were not recognized as filling this role.

It took between one and two years for the new role of "social worker" to become generally familiar and acceptable. A social worker came to be seen as someone who spends a great deal of time in the neighborhood, who helps youngsters to form clubs and find jobs, who serves as a

liaison between children and parents, teachers, and other authorities, and who can be turned to in times of trouble.[15]

The establishment of this new role has important implications for future service in the community. It means that a new worker who comes into the area and is identified as a social worker will be accepted and turned to without having to undergo the long and difficult initial period of antagonism, suspicion, and "testing" that persons filling an unfamiliar role must undergo. The activites of Program area workers resulted in establishing among the youth and many of the adults of the community the conception of a new role—that of "social worker"—which came to be almost as familiar and well understood as that of policeman or priest.

CHANGING RELATIONS BETWEEN

CORNER-GROUP AGGREGATES

When Special Youth Program workers first came into the district, they found a situation quite typical of most urban working-class communities.[16] Scattered throughout the area were a number of well-established corner gangs, or street-corner groups. These neighborhood corner groups usually included about fifty to seventy youngsters ranging in age from twelve to twenty. Each of the larger local corner groups contained a number of subdivisions or segments, based on age. In most instances the group as a whole shared a common name and set of traditions as to the reputation and place of their group in the community. The component subdivisions of these larger localized groupings can be referred to as "segments," and the group as a whole may be termed a corner-group "aggregate."

Corner-group aggregates in different neighborhoods maintained systematic mutual relationships. These relationships resembled those of some of the American Indian tribes or the small Balkan countries. One group defined a second group as its traditional enemy and a third as its traditional ally. Rivalry between different aggregates was expressed in various ways: in gang fights, in competition in athletic contests, in individual fights between members of rival groups, and in insults and derogatory references to rivals. Each group vied with the other for "rep" or reputation in the community—with "rep" based on how tough a group was, how effective in fighting, how many of its members had records of arrest or detention. Periodic gang fights were held to establish or maintain the "rep" of the group. Beneath their swagger, many corner-group members were afraid of fighting other gangs but were more afraid of not fighting them. "If you chicken out on a fight, they'll step all over you—your name will be mud in the neighborhood from then on" was a common sentiment. Thus, the various neighborhood corner groups could be seen as forming a network of fighting units, each of which was committed to defend its honor and maintain its "rep."

One of the earliest and most evident changes to occur in this situation

was that groups worked with directly by the Program relinquished active participation in this network of conflict groups. Once the worker had established good relations with a particular group, the group became actively and intensely involved in a series of activities centering primarily around organized athletics. Neither the time, the energy, nor the inclination to fight other groups was as available to the youngsters as before the advent of the worker.

In addition, as Program groups became more successful in fielding winning football, baseball, and basketball teams and in running dances and other club activities, the basis of their "rep" began to shift—both in their own eyes and in the eyes of the adult community; effectiveness in running legitimate group enterprises began to supplant "toughness" in fighting as the basis of prestige or "rep." Further, the corner-group workers devoted particular attention to providing an acceptable "out" for a group which felt under obligation to attack or retaliate, so that the group could save face and respond by "means short of war." Most corner-group members, beneath their tough exterior, are frightened of gang fights, and if the workers were able to arrange an acceptable way for the group to save face—possibly by providing assurance that the police would take measures against the rival group or that the group would demonstrate superior acumen by refusing to be baited—the groups in most cases refrained from fighting, while asserting at the same time, "Anyway, we coulda clobbered them guys."

It appears then that one of the most marked changes accompanying the corner-group workers' efforts in the initial phases of their work was a reduction in the incidence and severity of community gang fights, due to the fact that important fighting units had been removed from the network of available conflict groups.[17] During later phases of the Program, however, an upsurge in gang fights involving Program groups appeared to be related to Program efforts. These conflicts did not involve Program groups fighting one another but represented for the most part attacks on Program groups by corner groups in adjacent areas who did not have an area worker. There is good reason to believe that these attacks were an unintended product of Program efforts.

The groups worked with by the Program had become increasingly and visibly effective in producing winning teams and in staging successful group enterprises, such as dances and raffles. This success did not escape the attention of groups in adjacent areas, who became envious of the groups with social workers. They reasoned, and correctly, that the colorful jackets worn by members of Program groups, their winning ball teams, their periodic club dances, were quite directly related to the fact that they had a social worker. The attacks on Program groups by these outside groups were motivated by several related factors. First, because they were envious of Program groups, members of outside groups felt like lashing out against them to "cut them down to size." Second, the outside groups knew that Program groups were given a social worker in the first place because they were troublesome; so they reasoned. "They were bad, and they got a social worker; if we're bad enough now, we'll get a

social worker, too." One of the best ways to bring this "badness" inescapably to the attention of the Program was to attack Program groups.

This antagonistic behavior by outside groups represented a plea that they be given the same kind of advantages they perceived Program groups to enjoy. Groups without social workers came to be considered at a definite disadvantage in the total community situation. The plea, "We want a social worker, too," was expressed frequently by such groups. To have a social worker would enhance the group's "rep" in the community, rather than detract from it. These gang fights involving outside groups were controlled fairly effectively by Program workers, both because they were able to exert direct influence on the behavior of their own groups and because their familiarity with the local community made them aware of potential trouble spots. This knowledge enabled them to undertake preventive measures with hostile groups before local frictions developed into full-scale "gang wars." This type of development, however, would appear to present a problem for programs operating in areas where local groups maintain systematic relations with groups outside the area. The community group work effort of the Special Youth Program appears to have been effective in reducing gang conflict within its chosen area of concentration but at the same time to have created an ever widening need for its own progressive extension. The "saturation" approach employed by the New York City Youth Board (workers for all groups in an area) represents an attempt to meet this problem, but in a city such as Boston where each section of the metropolitan area merges into the next. the feasibility of such an approach is doubtful. A program aiming to "clean up" the gang situation in a single section of the city cannot count on limiting its influence to that section but must anticipate the fact that its very successes in its home district may increase difficulties in adjacent areas.[18]

CHANGING RELATIONS BETWEEN
CORNER-GROUP SEGMENTS

Although corner-group aggregates differ from one another in size and composition, most of them are composed of a number of subdivisions or segments which can be thought of as groups in their own right. The full or total corner group seldom assembles at the same time and in the same place, except for unusual occasions such as defense against a rival gang attack. Corner groups are subdivided on the basis of age. A fairly typical corner group, the "Outlaws," might include six segments: the Midget Outlaws—boys thirteen to fifteen; Junior Outlaws—boys fifteen to seventeen; Intermediate Outlaws—boys seventeen to nineteen; Senior Outlaws—boys nineteen and over; the Outlawettes—girls fourteen to sixteen; and the Little Outlawettes—girls twelve to fourteen. Members of different segments associate primarily with one another, although a few corner-group members divide their time among several segments.

Under ordinary circumstances, relations between the several seg-

ments of a corner group resemble those of siblings. Members of a boys' segment will tease and scuffle with girls in the slightly younger group. Girls will taunt boys and goad them into fights. Boys' segments, much like brothers, both compete and co-operate with one another. One of the most important relationships between male segments is that of younger to older groups. Younger groups look to older groups to learn what to do and how to do it—to learn "correct" standards of behavior, what is and what is not acceptable, what activities to pursue and how. If the older group is active in community-condoned activities such as athletics, there is a good change that the younger groups will seek to excel in similar areas. If, on the other hand, the older group prides itself on its toughness, its ability to "get away with" law violations, its "rep" for gang fighting, the younger group will want to emulate these ways of acting. There is a very strong motivation to "be like the big kids."

The older groups, for their part, keep a watchful eye on the "little kids" to make sure they follow in their footsteps and perpetuate the traditions of the corner group. They watch to see that the "little kids" toe the line in many kinds of behavior so that they will not bring disgrace to the "rep"—for toughness or for achievement—built up by the group. Members of older groups frequently serve as athletic coaches, managers, and general counselors and advisers for members of younger groups. Thus, they are in a most influential position to advise them on how to behave—how to act toward girls, what to do about cheating and fair play, whether to stay on the right or wrong side of the law, and many other things.

As Special Youth Program workers became more intimately involved in the lives of corner-group members, their presence and activities had an increasing impact on relations between segments. The worker took over many of the functions formerly assumed by older group members for younger. Serving at first in the roles of team manager, athletic coach, and club adviser, he later was turned to more and more frequently as guide, as teacher, and as moral adviser. He became the one to whom group members turned for advice on how to act, on the "correct" thing to do, on what is right and what is wrong. In important respects he took the place of the "older brother" group in setting the tone for group behavior. Since the worker evidently supported standards which place high value on legally and morally acceptable behavior, there was now a much higher probability that younger groups would be exposed to and would follow such standards than when older segments served as a primary model and source of guidance.

If the worker initially devoted most of his attention to a younger segment, the older group would begin to resent the fact that he was becoming a more important influence than they in the lives of younger group members. But, in addition, the growing influence of the worker also promoted the realization by the older group that the worker was a force to be reckoned with. They began to become envious of their "younger brothers," who were receiving so much attention and were becoming increasingly successful in group enterprises. These factors provided for the

worker a good entree for establishing relations with the older group. Once this relationship was solidified, the worker was in a more strategic position to influence behavior of both groups, since the standards of the older group, which now began to change in directions approved by the worker, continued to serve as a model for the younger group.

As the worker's activities became increasingly important to the groups he worked with, relational ties between the several age-level segments began to loosen. Since the worker assumed many of the functions formerly performed by older for younger segments, the natural dependency of younger on older was diminished. At the same time, as the older groups became progressively more solidary and self-contained, their need to exercise authority over and provide nurture for the younger groups lessened. Further, competition among the several segments for the lion's share of the worker's attention aroused some degree of hostility between groups. However, such hostility did not produce any appreciable increase in overt intersegment aggression; the most evident change observed was a progressive estrangement between segments as increasing dependence on the worker lessened needs for mutual dependence.

A similar phenomenon was observed in relations between the corner groups and local adults. Under ordinary circumstances, there are generally a number of adults in the community who play a part similar to that of older segment members in influencing the lives of younger group members. Included among such adults are owners of the stores where group members "hang out," local fathers who frequently act as team coaches, and local recreation workers. Since, by virtue of their job commitment, it was possible for Program workers to devote considerably more time and concerted attention to the youngsters than was possible for local adults, and since they were trained specialists in forming relations with groups and participating with them in varied activities, the workers assumed many of the functions formerly served by these adults. As in the case of relations with older segments, Program workers represented and supported a much more consistent and middle-class oriented set of standards than did local adults, whom they to a considerable extent supplanted. The ultimate results of this loosening of group moorings to the relational and cultural system of their local community are not known. One might conjecture, on the one hand, that an attempt might be made to resolidify these weakened ties after the workers' departure, or, on the other hand, that the relatively minor estrangement of the group from its local milieu might continue, resulting in a weakening of group solidarity or the alienation of group members from their local community. The results could be assessed only by follow-up studies.

CHANGING RELATIONS WITHIN CORNER-GROUP SEGMENTS

The primary focus of worker effort was the corner-group segment itself. When workers first came in contact with the groups, the main

ties binding members together were friendship ties. A male corner-group segment usually consisted of a number of friendship cliques of three or four boys each, who associated with one another to form a corner-group unit of fifteen to twenty boys. Each clique had its own "leader" or "most important" boy, and leadership for the whole unit was based primarily on special personal qualities and abilities of different boys. The most skilful baseball player might be the "leader" in baseball, the best organizer the "leader" in running a dance, the best fighter the "leader" in planning a gang fight. Leadership patterns varied both according to the nature of the activity and the presence or absence in the area of certain "key" youngsters.

One of the principal techniques used by Program workers involved changing group units from a set of informally related friendship cliques into a formally organized association or "club." The form of the "club," seen as a specialized device for arranging and ordering relations between individuals characteristic of middle-class American society, is quite different from that of the informal friendship group of the working-class community. A club involves a whole set of specialized forms and practices, such as regular meetings, a set of named offices (president, vice-president, secretary, etc), committees, a special set of procedural rules (nominations, voting, making motions, majority rule, etc.), the collection of dues, a schedule of planned activities, and a constitution that specifies the purposes of the organization and what kind of person may or may not be a member. All but one of the Program groups, at varying intervals following initial contact, became formal clubs possessing some of all of the features just mentioned.[19]

Once the club was formed, workers were in a much more strategic position to influence attitudes and behavior of group members. But the very process of changing from a corner group into a club was accompanied by important changes in the form and quality of intra-group relationships. In any urban working-class community, adolescents may choose from at least two important sets of standards or paths of life. One might be called the "law-abiding" path of life and the other the "law-violating" path. This does not mean that all who follow the law-abiding path never violate laws or that all who follow the law-violating path always violate laws. The law-abiding path represents, in general, an implicit resolution to make one's way in life primarily by staying on the right side of the law and adhering most of the time to formal standards of morality. The law-violating path, which frequently appears much more tempting and colorful to the adolescent, involves a willingness to reach for what one sees as the good things in life (cars, wealth, reputation as a lady-killer) through whatever means appear most available, be they legal or illegal.

Adolescence is a critical time for choice, and it is very often in the street-corner group that the youngster tests out various ways of acting that will lead to a choice of one of these ways of life. The natural street-corner group frequently includes some youngsters who have made some sort of commitment, however tentative or dimly perceived, to each of

these paths of life. This means that there is always the potentiality of a conflict in values between those who favor one path and those who favor the other. However, under ordinary circumstances this conflict does not come to the surface, because the boys seldom put themselves in a position which demands that they declare clearly which side they are on. Nor do the youngsters force one another to stand up and be counted, because such forcing, they realize unconsciously, might lead to a break-up of the group. The struggle goes on under the surface.

When Program corner groups assumed the form of organized clubs, the situation changed. Two things necessarily involved in setting up a club made it very difficult for members to keep under the surface a commitment as to which side they were on. One was the necessity of specifying in the constitution the purposes of the club, and the other, and more important, the necessity of setting up qualifications for membership. It was a striking experience for Program workers to watch the struggles of the newly forming clubs trying to come to a decision as to who should and who should not be a member. As names were proposed, one by one, the group would engage in a heated discussion as to whether or not this person was acceptable—and acceptability was decided primarily on the basis of which path of life the boy was known to favor, although this was not the way the group phrased it. The basic issue was forced to the surface: Will this club and those in it follow the law-abiding or law-violating path of life? In no case was this issue resolved at the outset, and the membership list usually included boys with inclinations toward both paths of life, but a conflict heretofore vaguely defined and hidden was now brought much more sharply into focus. As the clubs developed, the presence and activities of the workers constituted a subtle but persistent force in support of the law-abiding way of life. By promoting community-approved activities, by discouraging illegal behavior directly or indirectly, and by pointing out to the boys in many different situations the wisdom of the law-abiding choice and the likely consequences of the law-violating, the workers' activities and sentiments became an increasingly important factor in determining the groups' moral climate.

One important effect of these continuing pressures was that the groups began to split into two factions—one clearly supporting the law-abiding way of life and the other supporting it only half-heartedly or, in particular instances, opposing it. The conflict between the two factions was fought out over specific issues. Should we or should we not attack a rival gang? Should we or should we not allow drinking at our next dance? The club became a battleground of an intense struggle between two opposing sets of values, with the boys themselves aligned on both sides rather than, as in some situations, the boys supporting one side and the adult leader the other. In one instance, there was an extended debate over whether or not drinking should be permitted at a forthcoming dance. The law-abiding group won out, but one member of the opposing faction refused to accept the decision of the majority and defiantly came to the dance drunk. At the dance he was ignored by most group members,

but at the meeting following the dance he was subjected to intensive criticism by other group members, primarily in the form of sarcastic kidding—one of the most effective kinds of pressure used by corner groups. This criticism by members of his own group constituted a powerful and persuasive form of sanction, and the offending member clearly, though reluctantly, acknowledged that he had acted wrongly.[20]

The tendency of the group to split into factions posed a difficult problem for the worker, who had to use every device at his command in an attempt to re-unify the group and to bring the members of the law-opposing faction back into the formal club as fully participating members. This effort constituted a critical test of the corner-group worker method. To leave the resistant members outside the fold would be to abandon a most effective force for influencing their behavior—the direct example and persuasive pressures of the law-abiding members of their own club. These pressures, from peers whose esteem they valued highly and whose disapproval they feared, could constitute a powerful motivation for adhering to approved standards, provided the dissidents were enabled to remain within the sphere of influence of their law-abiding compeers. The workers, therefore, used many measures to keep the dissident members with the group. They talked to them personally, trying to learn from them the inner forces driving them to law-violating behavior; they spoke to their parents to learn what influences in the home background contributed to the boys' actions; and they continued to make the activities and achievements of the club group so evident and so attractive that those who moved away from the club would feel deprived and disadvantaged.

The effects of these measures varied from group to group. In one instance, the worker definitely succeeded in reincorporating the dissident faction into the club, with two of the leaders of the formerly law-violating group subsequently taking the lead in socially-approved club activities. For this group the sequence of events described here—the formation of the club, the development of the factions, and the reuniting of the factions—took about two years. As in any effort to bring about changes in deep-rooted patterns of behavior, developments were gradual.

Summary and Conclusions

This paper has described the corner-group work of the Boston Special Youth Program, an experimental effort in community delinquency control. The objectives and structure of the service program and the organization of the associated evaluative research program were described briefly. The main account discussed four kinds of changes in systemic community relationships of Program groups. These changes were: (1) The conception of a new role, that of "corner-group social worker," became established in the community. The creation of this role-definition enables individuals identified with it to relate to and gain initial accept-

ance by community groups without undergoing the long period of suspicion and "testing" necessary when this role is unknown. (2) Intergroup conflict diminished in frequency and intensity within the area of Program concentration during initial phases of Program operations; however, later phases were characterized by conflicts involving groups outside the Program service area. (3) As Program workers assumed for their groups an increasing range of responsibilities and functions formerly performed for the groups by one another and by local adults, relational ties between the included segments of corner-group aggregates and between the aggregate as a whole and its local community were weakened. (4) The activities and influence of the workers tended to precipitate factional splits within corner-group segments; attempts to reunite the more law-abiding and less law-abiding factions within the framework of a formally organized club were successful in some instances.

The examination of changes in the system of inter- and intra-group relations of Program corner groups gives evidence that the Program did have a definite impact on this relational system. If we consider the nature of these changes in reference to the goal of reducing community delinquency, it would appear that some changes were positive, some negative, and some neutral. The ultimate impact of these changes on the over-all pattern of community delinquency cannot as yet be predicted and will require further research on post-Program developments.

It is important to stress once more that the conclusions presented in this paper are based on a preliminary consideration of collected data, and that all general statements included here do not apply with equal accuracy to all Program groups. Changes or modifications of these conclusions may result from further analysis of collected data, from the collection of additional relevant material, or from both.

Appendix

The area-worker or detached-worker method of attempting to induce changes in delinquent or otherwise troublesome adolescent groups ("gangs") had its roots in the middle 1920's, largely as a result of the efforts of a group of Chicago researchers and social workers, particularly Frederick M. Thrasher and Clifford R. Shaw. In 1927, Thrasher stated:

> . . . there are really only two alternatives in . . . reforming the boy who has become delinquent through the influence of his gang: he must either be removed completely from the gang . . . or his gang must be reformed. . . . Official agencies have usually attempted the former alternative without success and have, for the most part, completely neglected the latter.[21]

Methods for implementing this theoretical position were developed by Clifford R. Shaw in Chicago during the thirties [22] and by the Los Angeles

Youth Project during the forties.[23] In both of these ventures, the gang-worker technique was only one of several methods being tried at the same time, with community organization efforts a dominant concern. A much more direct focus on this approach as a distinctive technique resulted from the upsurge in gang delinquency after World War II, with New York City taking the lead. The area-worker approach was the primary focus of the Central Harlem Street Clubs Project of the New York City Welfare Council, the first project to report extensively on methods and results. This project pioneered many features of this approach which are now becoming standardized and provided the basis for a subsequent series of similar projects in New York City, most of which were initiated or taken over by the New York City Youth Board "Street Clubs" Program.[24] By 1957 the corner-group worker method as a distinctive technique was being employed as a major feature of over twenty-five delinquency control programs in about a dozen large American cities. In May, 1957, a conference sponsored by the Children's Bureau brought together over two hundred persons either engaged in this type of work or interested in its application.[25]

Notes

1. For a brief summary of the development of this method, see the Appendix.

2. Helen L. Witmer and Edith Tufts, *The Effectiveness of Delinquency Prevention Programs* (Children's Bureau Publication No. 350 [Washington, D.C.: Government Printing Office, 1954]), pp. 31–34.

3. Plans that led to the setting up of the Special Youth Program were formulated in 1953 by members of the Greater Boston Council for Youth, a special committee of the Recreation, Informal Education, and Group Work Division of the United Community Services of Boston. See F. B. Taylor and A. Morris, "A Special Program for Youth" (Boston: United Community Services of Boston, August, 1953 [mimeographed]). The Council was composed of representatives of the major youth-concerned organized groupings of Metropolitan Boston and included representatives of the schools, courts, churches, correctional system, public recreation, and social agencies. The administrative structure of the Program as well as its financing was arranged by the Council. The primary source of finance was several local private trust funds, with additional funds provided by the United Community Services.

4. The person most responsible for

developing this conception and incorporating it into a functioning service program was David M. Austin, currently executive secretary of the Group Work Council of the Cleveland Welfare Federation. A fuller description of the philosophy underlying the Program is contained in his unpublished manuscript, "A Rationale for a Delinquency Prevention Program," a paper given at Harvard University, December, 1956.

5. Discussion of the nature and conduct of the community organization and family work aspects of the Special Youth Program lies beyond the scope of this paper. Initial plans to include a caseworker on the Program staff were not carried out, and direct service to families did not get under way until about six months before the end of the project. The "chronic-problem" family subproject of the Special Youth Program brought together caseworkers from several existing agencies to undertake a "reaching-out" effort in the Program district with consultative and co-ordinative functions provided for by the Program. At present, this effort is continuing, and financing and coordination will probably be arranged by United Community Services. The community organization aspect of the Program was conducted by one full-time community organization worker, but represented, for

about two years, a parallel rather than a joint effort with the group work program. During the last six months of the project some convergence between the group work and community organization efforts began. The district citizens' council, which was the primary focus of attention of the community organization effort, continued its existence after the termination of the Program. Material on the community organization program is contained in L. Houston and L. DiCicco, "Community Development in a Boston District" (1956 [mimeographed]). The family project is discussed in E. Faucett *et al.*, "The Boston Family Project: A Community-centered Approach to Delinquency Prevention" (submitted to United Community Services of Boston, June, 1957 [mimeographed]).

6. For a fuller description of the community group work aspect of the Special Youth Program, see David M. Austin, "What about 'Reaching-out'?—An Account of the Boston Youth Project," *Round Table* (published by National Federation of Settlements and Neighborhood Centers, Inc.), XIX (September–October, 1955), 1–7.

7. Selected social and cultural characteristics of the Program district are described in Walter B. Miller, "The Culture of a Lower-Class Community," reproduced and distributed by United Community Funds and Councils of America, Inc. Included in this account is material on the structure and culture of adolescent street-corner groups.

8. Several discussions of the problems involved in evaluative research are included in "Proceedings of the Conference on Research in the Children's Field," *Social Service Review*, XXX (September, 1956), 237–357. See especially papers by Vinter and Konopka.

9. A third set of questions concern the issues of the worth and feasibility of the Program's method. They are: "To what extent are observed changes in a desired direction?" and "If changes are those desired, is their magnitude commensurate with the cost of bringing them about?" These questions are, evidently, the questions of greatest signifiance to those conducting or considering such programs; however, questions that are primary in terms of general significance must frequently be secondary in terms of research procedure; that is, the question, "What observable changes have occurred?" must be answered before any attempt is made to answer the question, "Were these changes what we wanted, and are they worth it?"

10. A more detailed description of research aims and techniques is included in Walter B. Miller, "A Research Project on a Community-focused Method of Delinquency Control," prepared for the National Institute of Mental Health, May, 1956. The research program is supported primarily by the National Institutes of Health under National Institute of Mental Health Research Grant M-1414. Funds have also been made available locally through the Greater Boston Council for Youth.

11. These five sets of records are: (1) The process records kept by the group workers of daily contacts with their groups (ca. 6,000 pages). (2) The journal of the Program director containing accounts of conferences with the workers and other data on the groups (ca. 1,000 pages). (3) Interviews with workers by the research director (ca. 500 pages). (4) Direct observations of groups recorded by the research director. (5) Tape recordings of group meetings and other activities. The technique used to process these records is modeled after the content-analysis system used by the Yale Cross-Cultural Survey, modified extensively for use with social work materials. This system ("Manual for Processing Group Work Records" [75 pages], on file, Special Youth Program) uses as an analytic unit the "object-oriented behavior sequence," and analyzes reported group behavior patterns into some sixty kinds of "object-oriented" behavior, such as "verbal-evaluative orientation to Police Institutions" (attitudes to police); "actional orientation to inter-group assault" (engaging in gang fights), etc.

12. Two reports containing preliminary statistical findings on official delinquency trends have been compiled: "Juvenile Crime in the Special Youth Program Area in 1956 Compared to Other Areas" (January, 1957), and "Trends in Juvenile Crime between 1952 and 1956 in the Special Youth Program Area Compared with Trends in Similar Nearby Areas" (March, 1957), on file, Special Youth Program. One finding of the latter report indicates that the average yearly rate of commitment of male juveniles to state Youth Service facilities dropped 14 per cent between 1952–53 (pre-Program) and 1955–56 (during Program) in the area of Program operation, while rising 46 per cent in non-Program areas of the same district and 107 per cent in a contiguous district.

13. In contrast to the first two approaches which use isolatable units as the basis of analysis ("the object-oriented behavior sequence"; "the court appearance") and thus are amenable to quantitative treatment, trends involving systemic changes are determined by

deriving from a multiplicity of separate concrete events higher-level abstractions which relate to the nature of the system. This involves an analytical examination of the numerous relevant events recorded in the Program's five sets of documents and the abstracting of a series of higher-level descriptive generalizations from this examination.

14. Findings derived from all three analytic approaches to group-behavior change, as well as material on other aspects of Program operations, will be included in a comprehensive report on the Program, tentatively entitled "Social Workers and Corner Gangs: A Report on the Special Youth Program." This report is scheduled for completion in 1959.

15. No attempt is made in this paper to describe the many and varied activities undertaken by the corner-group workers in fulfilling their roles. The focus here is on the worker's role as perceived by the *community*, not as it is defined or elaborated by the professional social worker. A detailed treatment of the varied functions and services performed by the worker as well as the techniques he employs is being prepared by members of the Special Youth Program service staff. This material, dealing primarily with the practice techniques employed by the worker, will place primary emphasis on worker activity, whereas this and future research reports will focus primarily on group behavior.

16. Further data on the structure and culture of adolescent street-corner groups is contained in Walter B. Miller, "The Culture of a Lower-Class Community," *op. cit.*

17. Similar results have been reported by programs in New York City utilizing the corner-group worker method. See in particular Paul L. Crawford, James R. Dumpson, and Daniel J. Malamud, *Working with Teen-Age Gangs* (New York: Welfare Council of New York City, 1950), pp. 78, 147–48; and "Council of Social and Athletic Clubs" (New York: New York City Youth Board, May, 1952 [mimeographed]), p. 116. Statistical documentation of the reported decrease in gang fighting is cited in neither of these cases. The trend noted here toward an increase in gang fighting involving outside groups during later phases were not reported by these projects.

18. The original boundaries of the Program area of concentration were decided upon primarily on the basis of certain geographical features (main thoroughfares, census-tract boundaries) and statistics on income level, crime rates, etc., which appeared on the map to define a more or less "natural" community. This area did not, in fact, correspond to the actual social community of the corner groups—the area within which a specific set of aggregates maintained a fairly high interaction rate. In consequence, one large corner group which was intimately involved in the relational network of the Program groups was defined as being outside the "service" area of the Program. It was this group which played a major part in the series of conflicts occurring during later phases of the Program, and the Program was finally forced, shortly before it terminated, to undertake emergency work with this group so as to preserve the gains it had made with the other groups. It is possible that if pre-Program research had been undertaken to ascertain the actual network of groupings comprising the "natural" community relational system, plans could have been made to "serve" all important units of this system rather than omitting critical groupings.

19. For a more detailed account of how a corner group becomes a club, and the implications of this conversion for bringing about changes in behavior and values, see Walter B. Miller, "The Place of the Organized Club in Corner-Group Work Method" (December, 1956), on file, Special Youth Program.

20. A detailed study of the forms, patterning, and functions of aggressive behavior in the street-corner group is presented in W. Miller, H. Geertz, and H. Cutter, "Patterns of Aggressive Behavior of a Male Adolescent Street Corner Group," based on an intensive analysis of all aggressive acts observed during one year of contact with a boys' corner group. This study, financed under National Institute of Mental Health Grant M-1342, is in preparation.

21. *The Gang* (Chicago: University of Chicago Press, 1926), p. 501.

22. *Delinquency Areas* (Chicago: University of Chicago Press, 1929).

23. Duane Robinson, *Chance To Belong: Story of the Los Angeles Youth Project, 1943–49* (New York: National Board of YWCA, 1949).

24. See Paul L. Crawford, James R. Dumpson, and Daniel J. Malamud, *Working with Teen-Age Gangs* (New York: Welfare Council of New York City, 1950).

25. For a preliminary report, see *Social Legislation Information Service Bulletin*, No. 20, May 27, 1957.

Dead End Story

Paul Goodman

           This is the report of a spell with the Youth Board by an energetic and athletic man of average intelligence and sensibility, with a strong affection for kids, and for the kind of tough kids among whom he grew up in Brooklyn. It ends with his quitting street-work to become a high-school teacher and coach, largely because of disrespect for the bureaucracy of the Board and his judgment that the work does not offer enough advancement and money to support his growing family. His present feeling is regretful and despairing.

Vincent Riccio's work was important and exciting, but he accomplished little; the obstacles are overwhelming, and the conditions are deteriorating. He is concerned especially about the increase in drug-addiction, leading to ever longer prison terms and sudden death from overdose.

It is worthwhile to review the book because of the exemplary ordinariness of Riccio's values and motives and the journalistic reporting of the delicate texture of living (helped by Bill Slocum of The Daily Mirror). Riccio seems to be a good joe, unusually outspoken, fairly courageous and altogether unradical. In the upheaval of our urbanism, the baseness of our economy and politics and the breakdown of conventional morals, we are in a more revolutionary situation than this kind of values and style can cope with: they are too unpolitical, too unphilosophically real, the standard of excellence is too low.

Riccio's frankness is refreshing. He detests the New York police, who are no doubt a fine body of men but who, in his almost universal experi-

Review of *All the Way Down, the Violent Underworld of Street Gangs*, Vincent Riccio and Bill Slocum, New York: Simon & Schuster, 1962. Reprinted by permission from *The New York Times Book Review*, November 11, 1962. Copyright 1962, by The New York Times Company.

ence, are brutes and grafters. He has contempt for the Narcotics squad
and for Harry Anslinger (recently retired): "Mr. Anslinger has been
leading the war against addiction for over thirty years. Need I say more?"
He is impatient with the Youth Board brass for endangering its workers
and hurting kids just in order to allay public hysteria. (I do not follow
Bill Slocum in The Mirror, but I wonder how he copes with the fact that
his paper gleefully fans this hysteria. Why doesn't he explode and get
fired?)

But Riccio's lack of perception of the big enemies of the kids (and
himself) is painful. He has an inkling that the disruption of neighborhoods by our ghetto housing is a cause of bad trouble, but there is no
anger against Webb & Knapp or Robert Moses; how does he think the
buildings get there? In one passage he compares gang rumbles to wars
and points out that "only the psychopaths and some of the generals want
war," but he taught judo and combat hand-to-hand fighting in the Navy,
and we do not read that he led his kids into the Worldwide General Strike
for Peace. There is no criticism of the school system that has let his kids
down. He is realistic in most sexual matters, but is silent about the role
of his church in giving the kids a bad conscience and taking the innocent joy out of their lives.

Even more painful than the book's lack of philosophy is that Riccio
shares and reinforces many of the delinquent traits that stunt his kids'
growth. He naively boasts of conning the kids (for example, on their
boxing prowess), as if they could be cured without being taken seriously
as persons. He encourages them to act for reputation rather than for the
value of the activity itself. He even outdoes them in his contempt for
eggheads. He rails at city urchins' fear of the dark and wild animals, but
cannot make therapeutic use of the nerve of fright, hostility and instinct-
anxiety that they have thereby exposed. Indeed, often the dramatic tone
of his little scenes with them is of a contest of wills between stubborn
siblings. Naturally, then, the kids like Rick, because he is useful and
kindly; but they can hardly get out of themselves by means of him, for
what he offers is no wiser or more interesting than what they are already.

Riccio's chief positive proposal in this book is the adoption of the
English system of legalizing heroin under medical prescription and
treatment—as he puts it, "I think we must give dope-addicts dope." His
arguments for this are the standard one of the social-scientists (though
throughout he is disdainful of sociologists and psychologists) to destroy
the economic motive of the pushers and to integrate the addict into a
quiet and hopefully curative milieu. I wish he would learn to extrapolate
the same attitude to the kids' other hang-ups. The cure for their violent
sexuality is to allow them guiltless sex. The cure for their defiance is to
teach them their real enemies to fight. The cure for their foolish activism
is to provide them a world that has worthwhile tasks.

Improving Services for Street-Corner Youth [1]

George Brager

The factors to which an individual ascribes his emotional problems in large part determine the nature of his attempt to relieve them. Similarly, the solutions that one proposes for social problems depend to a large degree on one's assumptions regarding the causes of these problems.

Some persons, for example, attribute the frustration which produces pressures toward delinquent behavior to environmental factors, such as racial discrimination and other social injustices. Others look inward, attributing their difficulties to personal deficiencies, such as a lack of discipline, zeal, or intelligence. Whether the youngster blames the social order or himself is of central importance, for the former attribution leads to alienation from the social order and the latter to self-depreciation.

In the ideology of our society, success and failure are explained in essentially individualistic terms. Success is viewed as a result of ambition, perseverance, and talent; failure is said to stem from a lack of these traits. This tendency to equate success with individual merit and failure with individual inferiority helps to maintain existing inequalities by deflecting criticism from the institutional order. Those who attribute failure to their own shortcomings are accepting the prevailing ideology of the society. They see their adjustment problems as essentially personal.

Those who feel that they are victims of arbitrary institutional arrangements, however, are at odds with the social order. Their alienation from conventional society generates a great deal of tension in their dealings with the carriers of the dominant ideology, such as teachers, social workers, policemen, and judges; for those who have rejected con-

Reprinted from *National Conference on Social Welfare: Social Work Practice*, New York: Columbia University Press, 1962, pp. 27–40.

ventional roles are then free to experiment with illegitimate ways of achieving wealth or status. To some extent, the tension of these alienated persons is relieved if they gain support from others in the same position who share the view that their misfortunes are due to unjust social conditions. Collective support can provide reassurance, security, and validation for a frame of reference toward which the world at large is hostile and disapproving. Hence, many embittered youngsters join delinquent gangs.

Delinquency-prevention programs are based on certain assumptions, explicit or implicit, about why delinquency exists in the first place. The tendency of social workers is to explore the motivations underlying the individual's membership in a delinquent group, to assess the ways in which he has learned to satisfy his needs through antisocial behavior. The result, whether intended or not, is often to explain the existence of the gang on the basis of the maladjustment of its individual members, without acknowledging the influence of the social order. The projected remedies are thus of an exclusively individual nature, and the ideological and structural foundations of the social order are unchallenged.

This bias is true of most preventive programs, even those that are organized on a group basis and operate within the community milieu. For example, exponents of detached-worker programs have advanced two major rationales for their attempts to influence the behavior patterns of youth gangs.

One approach emphasizes the worker's relationships with individual youngsters. Through close personal ties, the worker attempts to convince them that they should relinquish delinquent activities. If a boy responds to, and identifies with, the worker, it is hoped that he then will begin to strive for the conventional, socially acceptable goals that the worker represents, gradually abandoning his ties to the deviant peer-group values. Another approach attempts to redirect the group's energies and interests into socially acceptable leisure-time pursuits. The worker gradually persuades the group to plan recreational and social events which offer satisfaction and recognition without illegitimate or conflict behavior. Thus, it is hoped that gang members will seek "rep" by running a local dance rather than by trying to take over another gang's "turf." Once the group is able to participate in legitimate forms of expression, it is anticipated that it may begin to be receptive to the program of community agencies and their value systems.

Detached-worker programs undoubtedly reduce conflict behavior, at least while the worker is assigned to the group. The intervention of a trusted adult who advises caution, settles disputes, and provides face-saving alternatives generally results in a diminution of conflict. Increased status as tough guys is gained by members of gangs to which a worker is assigned, and this too may lessen the need for "bopping." However, the long-range effectiveness of such programs may be questioned. A recent preliminary report on the impact of the Roxbury Youth Project in Boston, for example, indicates only negligible differences between gangs and control groups in the frequency of members' involve-

ment in criminal and socially disapproved behavior. This was so although there was little question regarding the competence of workers, the good relationships established, and the effectiveness of the project in increasing participation in organized recreation.[2]

Perhaps the major limitation of detached-worker programs is their exclusive concern with intervening in the motivation and value system of gang members, without attempting to provide the social resources that would make conformity more possible for these youngsters. Motivation is a prerequisite to conformity, but it hardly ensures conforming behavior. If the possibilities for a conventional adjustment are restricted or absent, the likelihood is that the delinquent, no matter how favorably motivated, will continue to engage in nouconforming behavior. To extend services for street-corner youth, we must provide genuine opportunities for different behavior.

One theoretical formulation regarding the sources of delinquency provides a significant framework for the development of service programs.[3] In this view, the single most important pressure toward delinquent behavior in lower-income groups arises from the discrepancies between the social and economic aspirations of youth in these groups and their opportunities to achieve their ambitions by legitimate means. These aspirations are the result of living in a society that places great emphasis on economic and occupational success and whose ideology stresses the possibility of achievement by all its members, irrespective of their ethnic or socioeconomic background. Members of low socioeconomic or minority groups, however, are subjected to discriminatory practices which have the effect of denying them the usual means by which one can rise in the social and occupational scale—adequate and suitable education. For these youth there seems to be no legitimate way out of poverty. They experience desperation born of the certainty that their economic position is relatively fixed—desperation made all the more poignant by their exposure to a cultural ideology in which failure to attain upward mobility is regarded as proof of moral defectiveness. In a society that did not encourage them to set their sights high, they might more easily adjust to their impoverished circumstances; but since social worth is so closely identified with social position, discontent and frustration pervade the lower reaches of the social order.

Services for the delinquency-prone youngster must then take into account the importance of the world of work. The scarcity of jobs for young people in general, and particularly for lower-class adolescents, requires radical intervention. Although sensitive vocational counseling and aggressive placement are important means of meeting this condition, they are futile without job opportunities about which to counsel youth and vacancies in which to place them. Given the enormity of the task, job-finding programs in private industry cannot be expected to fill the need.[4] In view of the persistent marginality of many lower-income youngsters, their lack of marketable skills, their underdeveloped academic abilities, and their social immaturity, it is not surprising that few employers are willing to hire them. Nor is it feasible or desirable to

attempt to place young people in jobs now held by older, more experienced workers. Men with families obviously have priority in the competition for scarce jobs, and the gap between the requirements of the labor force and the number of laborers is growing steadily wider. Therefore, jobs must be created for young people. These new employment opportunities must be designed to meet some of the many social needs that are now unsatisfied. The increase in leisure time, for example, creates a market for workers in such fields as recreation.

It is important to publicize employment opportunities and the means by which these young people can use their opportunities. Lower-income youngsters are at a special disadvantage because of their lack of contacts and the inadequacy of their role models. The youngster whose father knows the boss or high-placed workers who can give him advance information about job openings obviously has an important foothold in the competition for work. Furthermore, the vocational goals of youngsters are affected by the adults whom they know. Thus boys in deprived inner-city areas shun blue-collar jobs because the adults they know who work with their hands perform menial, unrewarding tasks. Their image of the blue-collar worker is of someone at the bottom of the ladder, an unskilled laborer rather than a highly paid craftsman.

Service programs must help to make jobs more accessible to young people; that is, they must make youth more employable. The factors that influence access to employment opportunities are of two kinds: achieved and ascribed. Achieved factors are acquired in the process of socialization; ascribed factors, such as ethnicity and age, are fixed biologically. Lower-class youngsters are disadvantaged on both counts.

The educationally deprived of our slum areas not only lack the skill and academic knowledge required for advancement, they are often so undereducated as to be unable to fulfill the simple requirements of an application process, from reaching the employment office to filling out the necessary forms. In addition, lower-class youngsters, because of their own distinctive socialization, often lack such middle-class graces as good speech, promptness, neatness, and politeness. This handicaps them in work settings which tend to be mechanized, routine, and formal. It is not surprising, therefore, that they are as often fired for poor work attitudes as for poor performance.

Negroes and Puerto Ricans, overwhelmingly members of the lower class, face the further barrier of discriminatory practices in regard to job training, referrals, hiring, and promotion. This reality discourages Negro and Puerto Rican youngsters from adequately preparing themselves, as it does teachers from helping them to do so, and vocational counselors from referring them to otherwise appropriate positions.

Both situations need attention. On the one hand, employment programs must contain a training component to improve work habits and upgrade job skills. On the other, militant attempts must be made to attack discriminatory practices, whether they are based upon color, "foreignness," language difficulty, or class mores.

The immensity of youth unemployment perhaps discourages some

group-service agencies from giving it appropriate attention. Indeed, the need for government intervention to expand employment opportunities for disadvantaged youth through a subsidized work program is implicit in what we have said thus far. Nevertheless, unless group-service agencies deal with the issue, programs may consist of palliatives rather than solutions, designed to "cool out" rather than to help the disadvantaged youngster.

The temptation to diagnose problems so as to fit remedies available to social work must be resisted. "Oversold" efforts often direct attention from more pressing needs. Group-serving agencies must recognize the appropriate priority of youth employment programs in the struggle for the public and private youth dollar. They can, furthermore, generate support for legislation that will promote youth employment and reduce job discrimination.

Detached-worker programs, as well as services within the agency, can contribute directly to a solution of the problem. One conceptualization of the role of the street-corner worker is as a mediator through whom the street gang can relate to the major institutional orders that impinge upon it. Thus the worker becomes a bridge between the group and school authorities, potential employers, and so forth. He makes young people aware of vocational and training resources and in some cases he provides "connections." He may introduce the youngsters to people who are "one rung up the ladder," so that routes to mobility become visible and are perceived as accessible. The effective fulfillment of these functions, however, requires a reorientation of professional focus. The worker as mediator performs significant tasks which require as much skill as is demanded of the worker whose major interest is the personality growth of gang members through group activity. The two roles are, of course, by no means mutually exclusive, although the former has not received as much professional attention or analysis.

Detached-worker programs may also be designed to provide work and training opportunities for youth. The Chicago YMCA street program, for example, has made cooperative arrangements with local businesses to employ and train youngsters, while YMCA staff members work closely with the foremen as well as with the boys themselves. A vocational counselor and remedial specialists provide additional services. The YMCA has also hired gang leaders as "consultants" to their staff.

The "Coffee Shop" project of Mobilization For Youth, a demonstration and research program in New York's Lower East Side, is another group-service program with employment components. The plan is to set up several store-front centers which resemble coffee houses. Each shop will have a distinctive artistic or cultural motif. One, for example, will be a folk jazz center, for instruction in, and sponsorship of, indigenous jazz groups. Neighborhood adolescents will be employed to help construct the facility, and those with "rep" will be hired to assist in policy-planning, decoration, and management. Each shop will be run as a cooperative undertaking. In the natural setting of the youth, professional staff, acting the role of "informed bartenders," can offer

counseling to youngsters in need of vocational, educational, or psychiatric assistance.

Education is the principle means by which young people achieve occupational mobility. Their fortunes in the world of work depend in large part on the adequacy of the educational experiences made available to them. Often, however, the clients of street-worker programs are so lacking in education that rehabilitation is well-nigh impossible. Obviously, then, preventive programs must place major emphasis upon preschool and elementary school children and their families.

The principal of equality of opportunity in American education has been taken to mean that all children have a right to a public school education. It has also been interpreted as meaning that discrimination imposed by racial or ethnic identification, lack of family connections, or inadequate income should be eliminated and that individual differences in ability to learn must be taken into account. Prolonged effort by many groups is gradually resulting in progress in achieving these goals.

Equality of opportunity also means that cultural and economic (social-class) differences among children need to be considered, and these factors are more likely to be overlooked. Unless the school can gear its program to the class and ethnic background of the child, unless it attempts to reverse the educational inequalities arising from particular forms of social and cultural conditioning, equality of opportunity is largely fiction.

The barriers facing the slum child in the slum school must be reduced. In the lower-income family, the necessity to concentrate upon bare economic survival severely limits the amount of attention that parents can allocate to such "nonessential" activities as stimulating their children's intellectual growth or planning their educational future. Further, the overcrowding, lack of privacy, and disorder characteristic of family life in many slums are poor preparation for the quiet, orderly classroom. The lower-income child is also handicapped educationally by the inexperience of his parents, by their shyness or suspicion in dealing with teachers, which limits their ability to help the youngster achieve academic success.

Rather than the special understanding and attention they need, lower-income youngsters often receive short shrift from the public schools. Teachers are middle-class in orientation, often alien to the community in which they work. The high turnover of the teaching staff in slum schools results in inexperienced instructors and reduced instructional time. Its effect is especially unfortunate when one considers the characteristic instability of a slum, the economic uncertainties of the youngsters' lives, and the frequent changes in the composition of their family. In addition, the typical school curriculum is middle-class-oriented. A study of one lower-class school in New York City, for example, charges that Negro children strongly question their own competencies because the larger society expects inferior performance from them; yet "the middle-class orientation of the school helps little in recognizing the reali-

ties of the problem, and contributes little toward the development of value systems and activities directed toward breaking this circular dynamic process." [5]

Our efforts must be directed to supporting the child in his attempt to bridge the two disparate adult worlds of home and school. We must use whatever influence we possess to move those worlds toward greater integration. Programs within the schools must go beyond special instruction to the basic orientation, values, and curriculum of the school system itself.

In our discussion of services to street-corner youth we have stressed the need to expand objective opportunities for conformity, especially in the spheres of employment and education. It does not follow, however, that these youngsters will seize opportunities simply because they suddenly become more available. Sometimes people who have been subjected to extreme deprivation for long periods of time lose the capacity to use opportunities when they are afforded. When groups are subjected to barriers to education, for example, their capacity to take advantage of educational opportunities gradually diminishes. Indeed, educational skills may come to be considered irrelevant precisely because they seem so remote from the circumstances of a life of poverty.

Such a response to the realistic unavailabiilty of opportunity generally becomes "functionally autonomous"; that is, once it comes into existence, it tends to persist independent of the forces to which it was initially a response. This adaptation, although self-defeating, becomes refined as a way of life into which people are directly socialized from birth.

Major objectives of casework for street-corner youth and their families have been to arrest these self-defeating modes of adaptation and to strengthen the capacities of individuals to cope with their problems. Lower-income persons are not likely to be drawn to clinical services, however, for they lack the skills in introspection, verbal facility, and the conduct of formalized relationships which are essential to the success of such services. Their focus on the present, desire for greater authority, and need for more structure also run counter to the requirements of traditional treatment processes.[6] Lower-income clients who participate in such clinical programs are usually those with a middle-class orientation, who are therefore unlikely to contribute to the delinquent-group census.

The parents of gang youth are drawn to programs which offer concrete services, because their income-maintenance and related problems are overwhelming. Unfortunately, there is a widespread tendency to separate systems designed to provide social services from those designed to give professional psychological help. This split is exemplified in the traditional division between government agencies, which disburse funds to help people maintain a minimal standard of living, and private agencies which provide primarily psychological services. The failure to integrate these two kinds of assistance may be a significant impediment to the provision of effective aid.

Furthermore, individual services for street-corner youth and their families must be organized in a way that is congenial to a lower-income clientele. Methodology must be refined to take into account that group's characteristic interests, definitions of problems, modes of interaction, and the like. We know, for example, that many lower-income people tend to seek informal advice from friends and family rather than professional help. This suggests a need to lessen the professional's social distance and impersonality, while preserving his understanding of people and his scientific attitude. If, as we assume, lower-class persons are less likely to make distinctions between personal and community-related problems, such distinctions by the service-giver may mitigate his attempt to offer help in an informal, friendly way and may even appear to be rejection. We must revise organization and techniques to suit the people whom we hope to serve rather than expect that we can change clients to fit predetermined structures and techniques.

It is not sufficient, however, to emphasize expanding opportunities and increasing capacity to make use of them. To the extent that pressures toward delinquency stem from discrepancies between aspirations and opportunities, the former are also targets for change. No discussion of what aspirations ought to be can avoid value biases and moral dilemmas. Service programs should nevertheless incorporate a skeletal view of "the good life" that includes an adequate standard of living, a stable home and family life, and meaningful relations with other people. It might also include a striving for realistic goals—objectives that are within an individual's ability to achieve. A program that strongly emphasizes the goal of social ascent, however, may lead to the repudiation of many worthwhile values inherent in the cultural traditions of various ethnic and nationality groups in the lower strata of society. The exclusive promulgation of middle-class values in a program to combat delinquency may have other unfortunate consequences; if, for example, we succeed in inculcating middle-class aspirations in working-class children who are unable to achieve them, we simply frustrate them all the more.

Group-service programs are in a unique position to emphasize the positive features in the youngsters' lives and to provide alternate satisfactions to deviant behavior, such as participation in leisure-time activities meaningfully related to contemporary lower-class youth style. Programs which feature the folksy ways of an earlier day are likely to be unattractive. Programs may also be made ineffective by the bureaucratization of service-giving, as, for example the "flight from the client" of the most highly regarded workers who quickly ascend the bureaucratic ladder; and by a tendency to emphasize process and ignore content.

If, as noted earlier, alienation from the social order is an important factor in the development of delinquent gangs, then the implication for prevention is clear. We must frankly recognize the barriers faced by lower-class people generally and by participants in delinquent gangs in particular. Angry youngsters (and adults) must be shown, not that their anger is without basis, but that there are conforming, if controversial,

ways to express such sentiments. Programs in which youngsters learn to come to grips with issues that affect their lives and develop skill in acting collectively to correct abuses should be emphasized. Persuading slum youth to join in efforts to expand legitimate opportunities for all people in their social category is a difficult task because of the alienation of the youngsters and the relationship of sponsoring group-service agencies to other special-interest groups. Group programs so oriented can, nevertheless, be developed. For example, a youth organization composed not only of the lower-class "elite"—youngsters on their way up and out of their class—but also of those for whom working-class life may be a more permanent expectation, an organization that treads the thin line between adult guidance and adolescent autonomy, that gives a hearing to the largely submerged point of view of adolescents, that visibly and dramatically provides an outlet for adolescent culture and capers, can open channels for the expression of grievances and the creation of hope.

For minority-group youngsters particularly, and for lower-income youth in general, there is value in the example of adults who handle social injustices through community action. Such an example demonstrates that there is another way to handle dissatisfaction with the social order and that it is not necessary to resort to delinquent activity. The spectacle of adult members of their social and ethnic group "fighting back" also is a source of identification and pride for these youth. Observing a sit-in demonstration can enhance the self-image of the Negro youngster, for example.

Furthermore, participation by adults in decision-making about matters that affect their interests increases their own sense of identification with the community and the larger social order. People who identify with their neighborhood and share common values are more likely to try to control juvenile misbehavior.[7] Strengthening indigenous institutions in the community, increasing the observance of adult prohibitions against extreme violence, and enhancing the community power to impose sanctions will be much more effective than simply repressing conflict behavior through harsh measures imposed by the police and other agencies. In the long run, the young will be far more responsive to an adult community which exhibits the capacity to organize itself, to manage its own problems, to impose informal sanctions, and to mobilize local resources for young people than they will be to a community which must have these functions performed by external agents.

Most efforts to organize lower-class people, however, attract individuals on their way up the social-class ladder. We tend to identify as leaders persons who are relatively responsible about participation, articulate, and successful at managing organizational "forms," rather than individuals who actually reflect the values of lower-class groups. Ordinarily, the slum's network of informal group associations is not reached. Thus, "the effective community" of street-corner youth [8]—that is, the individuals, families, and groups with whom these youth interact and identify—is not organized to exert more positive influence on them.

A community-organization program so structured as to attract lower-

income persons is thus a further component of an extended program for delinquent youth. If such a program is to be successful, it must be geared to the life-style and needs of those whom it hopes to attract. The successful involvement of the deprived urban population may require, for example, identification of the informal groupings within the community, establishment of communication between staff and this network of associations, and the stimulation of greater interaction among the clusters of informal associations. The structure of the organization itself needs to be sufficiently informal and fluid to provide a congenial field of operation for lower-income persons. As we have implied, the leadership of the organization must consist of persons actually representative of, and influential in affecting, the value systems of lower-class groups.

The tendency of social workers to emphasize the amelioration of conflict and the reduction of tension, while often appropriate and helpful, may discourage the participation of lower-income groups in such an organization. With issues smoothed over and differences minimized, there may be little to arouse the interest of a group that lacks the predisposition to participate. Matters sufficiently vital to engage the interest of slum residents are almost inevitably controversial, or challenging to some powerful community interest. If a community organization avoids these matters, it can be expected to be avoided in turn.

When lower-income persons are (or feel) dominated, they are likely to withdraw from collective activities. Sponsorship of such an organization must therefore be developed so as to maximize its independence.

The capacity of people to realize their aspirations depends, in great measure, upon the character of the network of relationships and experiences provided by their community. In this sense, the target of services to street-corner youth must be not the individual delinquent or even the delinquent gang but the community itself.

Notes

1. A considerable portion of this material is drawn from "Mobilization for Youth: a Proposal for the Prevention and Control of Delinquency by Expanding Opportunities," including parts from one of the chapters which was prepared primarily by Richard A. Cloward. The author wishes to acknowledge the assistance of Mrs. Gertrude Goldberg, Action Associate, and others of the Mobilization for Youth Staff.

2. Walter B. Miller, "Brief Summary of 'Impact' Findings of the Roxbury Youth Project" (1961; mimeographed).

3. Richard A. Cloward and Lloyd E. Ohlin, *Delinquency and Opportunity: a Theory of Delinquent Gangs* (New York: The Free Press of Glencoe, 1960).

4. Judge Justine Wise Polier, of the New York City Domestic Relations Court, reports that the Mayor's Committee on Industrial Leaders for Youth, consisting of top New York business executives, had produced only fifty jobs by July 5, 1960, after having pledged earlier that year to find work for large numbers of youngsters from deprived areas (New York *Times*, July 19, 1960).

5. Martin P. Deutsch, *Minority-Group and Class Status as Related to Social and Personality Factors in Scholastic Achievement* (New York: Society for Applied Anthropology, 1960), p. 11.

6. A more extensive discussion of this disparity is contained in an unpublished paper by Frank Riessman, "Some Suggestions concerning Psychotherapy with Blue-Collar Patients" (1962).

7. A study of two lower-class neighborhoods of similar socioeconomic levels found that in the more integrated neighborhood, persons knew their neighbors, perceived common interests, shared common viewpoints, and felt that they were a part of the community. See Eleanor E. Maccoby, Joseph P. Johnson, and Russell M. Church, "Community Integration and the Social Control of Delinquency," *Journal of Social Issues,* XIV, No. 3 (1958), 38–51.

8. Derek V. Roemer, "Focus in Programming for Delinquency Reduction" (1961; mimeographed).

Delinquents with Tape Recorders

R. R. Schwitzgebel

To Streetcorner Research, Farewell

When I first came to Boston over six months ago, I was down and out and I was a Juvenile Delinquent. I had did many things during my 17 years of life. Most of them were wrong things. I stole, cheated, lied and just about everything you can think of. I left home at the age of 15, but I always depended on other people no matter what the cost. My cost was friendship, now of which I have none. My cost was prison and the loss of the love of my parents. I was lucky when I met you.

. . . I know that a little while back I started leaning on you and the project as you would lean on a crutch. The crutch must fall but I must stand. It is time for me to go out on my own and make good and I will because though you and I know I can. I can think for myself and do not have to set at a tape recorder to do my thinking for me.

. . . I wish that there was a way to make people realize what has been inside of me for the last six months. The misery and the hell I have went through. To wake up in the morning knowing that you did not have a friend in the world, no money, no job—no nothing. I wish I could tell them how to pull out of that. You have to think for yourself and do as you feel. Follow your feeling as you would your big brother, your dog, or your best friend.

This letter was written by a 17 year old subject of a research project shortly before his return home on July 25, 1959. He was one of 20 male delinquents employed as research subjects on a part time basis for a period of approximately nine months. The primary job of the employees was to talk into a tape recorder for

Reprinted from *New Society*, Vol. 1, No. 18, January 1963, pp. 11–13.

two or three hours each week. Employees were encouraged to choose their own topics.

The project started in 1958 when Dr. Charles W. Slack, then an Assistant Professor of Clinical Psychology at Harvard, was conducting extensive tape-recorded interviews with undergraduate conscientious objectors and with adolescent delinquents referred to his office by community officials. The purpose of these interviews was to gather specific information regarding the repression of hostility. The delinquents, as well as the undergraduate college students, were paid the small customary honorarium for their services as research subjects.

It was observed that the delinquents began to enjoy the interview hours and that they soon, in fact, requested more work. Various forms of psychotherapy were begun. Still the attendance remained regular and dependable among this group of persons known to be openly hostile and resistant to most forms of psychological or psychiatric help.

Dr. Slack's work encouraged a couple of graduate students to try going into areas with a high crime rate and hiring delinquents directly without the usual procedure of referral. In addition, a "laboratory" was set up at the intersection of two busy city streets which would be easily accessible to a delinquent population. This storefront operation was the first "Streetcorner Research" laboratory. Since that time, so-called laboratories have been set up in a city hall, a church, a clubhouse on a garage roof. Each setting has offered the experimenters some interesting surprises. For example, the church which at first seemed to be a most unpromising meeting place proved to be quite acceptable. After the employees had assured themselves that there were no disguised police in the church spying on them, they wanted to make the basement into a gang headquarters—by tradition, arrests are not made inside a church.

The project, from its inception, has been a very small operation working on a limited budget. In some ways this has prohibited the exploration of certain ideas, but in other ways it has insured flexibility by avoiding the restrictions inherent in large investments in equipment, professional staff, or real estate.

Prospective employees were contacted through acquaintances or met casually on streetcorners, at poolhalls, or at similar locations where persons meeting the requirements of the research were known to spend leisure time. The employees ranged in age from 15 to 20; all had records of incarceration.

An experimenter would meet a prospective employee, introduce himself as a person doing research at the university, and offer the boy a job at a dollar an hour to talk into a tape recorder. The initial conversation would go something as follows:

We're from (*name of institution*) and doing research. We're interested in finding out what kids around here think about cops, and parents, and school and stuff like that. We decided that instead of reading a bunch of books, the best way would be just to go out and ask the kids themselves. If a guy's been in trouble we'll pay him a

dollar an hour just for talking into a tape recorder about anything he wants. We're straight and not cops. The guy doesn't have to tell us anything he doesn't want to—no names or anything like that. Maybe it sounds kinda crazy, but it's true. What do you think?

If the boy was hesitant, the experimenter would give him the name of a respected gang member who had already worked for the project and assure him that he could quit anytime he wished. The employee would also be allowed to keep the tapes if he was afraid that they would be turned over to the police. As soon as the boy seemed interested the experimenter asked if he had a record but did not press for any details.

Prospective employees who remained hesitant were told that they didn't have to make up their minds right then, that helping with the research was a good deal, that they could ask around about it (giving names when possible), and that maybe the experiments would come around some other time.

Once the delinquent had come to the laboratory to look over the situation and to give the job a try, the problem became one of gaining steady attendance. A typical pattern among the delinquents was to arrive at their own convenience rather than to adhere to a pre-arranged meeting time. They might arrive as much as three hours late or two hours early. To avoid this rather inconvenient fluctuation, an informal programme of bonuses and rewards was instituted. An employee would be variously rewarded for behaviour which approximated to the final goal. For example, a new employee who came to the laboratory for the first time and for any reason would be received with a warm welcome, and Cokes or some food would be shared with him. On subsequent occasions if he arrived late or not at all, he would not be punished; if, however, he arrived closer to the scheduled time than was customary for him to do, he would be immediately rewarded with a cash bonus.

The amount of the rewards and the frequency of the rewards for desirable behaviour constantly varied for each Streetcorner Research employee. In other words, reinforcements were given on a variable interval—variable ratio schedule. An employee did not come to expect any particular reward for any particular act; rather he came only to expect that it would be generally more rewarding to do certain types of things than to do others. This reinforcemet procedure is known as "shaping behaviour."

The reinforcements were always given in as natural a manner as possible in the first few contacts. The strangeness of the situation might already strain the boy's tolerance. It was soon learned that sharing a single candy bar was better than trying to give him three of them. Offering the boy a cigarette when having one yourself was another type of reward which could be easily accepted. The offering of a cigarette or the sharing of a candy bar was not seen as an act of "charity" since it is customary to offer the same to an acquaintance regardless of his ability to pay. The goal was to meet the delinquent on his own terms, and temporarily to accept those terms. We let the individual tell the

experimenter what was rewarding and painful for him. This is a matter of respect as well as of therapeutic effectiveness.

The most common activity involved in the work of Streetcorner Research was talking into a tape recorder. Taking motion pictures of their daily life or keeping behaviour graphs were supplementary tasks for several of the employees. The job looked unbelievably easy to the delinquents at first. They thought the employer was a "soft touch" or a "grape." On one occasion, a new employee finished his first tape, was paid in cash, and was asked to return the next day. He went along with the "game" until the experimenter showed him to the door and said goodbye. The delinquent, still suspecting that some illegal activity was to be required on his part, whispered, "OK. Now tell me what you want me to do." The experimenter explained that everything had already been done. The boy responded, "Don't kid me; nobody gets paid for just *talking!*"

The delinquents worked approximately one hour, two or three times a week for about nine months. After a few weeks, the delinquents came to discover that the job was perhaps not as easy at it first appeared. Even though they were free to talk about most any topic, it became difficult to fill up tapes with well rehearsed opinions or stories of their adventures. They were forced to draw upon deeper and more personal feelings, and serious work began.

In the course of the employment, the experimenters set a few clear limits. The experimenters, for example, did not participate in illegal activities, and the employees were not permitted purposefully to destroy project property. Within such broad limits, the experimenters remained as far as possible non-punitive, supportive, alert to possibilities of kindly surprise.

The behaviour-change system we are describing here requires that the rewards the *experimenter* gets from the work also be specified. The job offered to the delinquent must be, from the experimenter's viewpoint, an honest job—not "busy work" designed as therapy. The integrity of both the experimenter and the employee is at stake. Jobs focused on the delinquent's own behaviour may be the most effective in obtaining a reduction in crime, but almost any type of work may be used where a concrete and socially valued product is the end result (e.g. an apprentice programme in a skilled trade). Employers may get additional reward from, say, satisfying their curiosity about a person of a different orientation than their own. Employers need not be highly trained specialists; however, it is absolutely necessary that they have some understanding and ability to implement the basic rules of the behaviour-change system. Specifically, an employer should be able to (1) meet the delinquent on the boy's own terms in a natural setting, (2) provide a mutually rewarding and honest job, (3) maintain a spontaneous and non-punitive attitude, (4) adhere to a few broad but necessary limits, (5) apply a flexible reinforcement schedule.

The records of the 20 experimental employees were compared with the records of a control group of delinquents who had no actual contact

with the project. The control group consisted of 20 delinquents paired with experimental subjects on the basis of age of first recorded offence, type of offence, nationality, religion, months of incarceration. The average age of the experimental group for the first offence was 13.6 years, for the control 13.7 years. The number of months of incarceration for the experimental group was 15.0, for the control group 15.3. The offences of both groups included breaking and entering, larceny, auto theft, rape, assault and battery, violation of parole, truancy, drunkenness. In general, the groups may be considered to have had a relatively early and serious record of anti-social behaviour.

On the basis of a follow-up study three years after termination of employment, the table (which follows) was compiled. Seven members of the project were incarcerated compared to nine members of the control group. This was not a significant difference. (The significant difference would have to be less than $a = .05$.) However, when one considers the accumulative number of arrests in each group and the seriousness of the offences as measured by the number of months of incarceration, the experimental and the control groups did significantly differ. The mean number of months of incarceration for the experimental group was 3.5 while the control group averaged 6.9 months (significant below .05). The experimental group averaged 2.4 arrests as compared to 4.7 for the control group (significant below .025).

Comparison of Experimental and Control Groups for Three Years After Employment of the Experimental Group Has Ended

	INCARCERATION		ARRESTS
	No. People	No. Months	Average No.
E group	7	3.5	2.4
C group	9	6.9	4.7

The conclusion drawn from these data was that the procedure of employment was effective in reducing, by almost one half, the expected number of arrests and months of incarceration of male adolescents with extensive records of delinquent behaviour. These results have encouraged us to look more carefully at the procedure in terms of specifying the nature of reinforcement and to search for ways of increasing contact between experimenter and delinquent.

A development which may be of some promise in specifying what situations are reinforcing for an individual and in increasing experimenter-subject contact is the work of the Science Committee on Programmed Experimentation (SCOPE), an independent research organization which has designed a special electronic communications system. Briefly, the system works in the following manner.

An employed delinquent attaches a small unit called a "behaviour transmitter reinforcer" (BTR) to his belt and wears it wherever he happens to go. The BTR is capable of transmitting a tone signal which is received and recorded at the SCOPE project base station. Thus far, delinquents have readily volunteered to wear such transmitters. Just

as with the tape recording experiment, the research has been more limited by the amount of funds available than by resistance on the part of the delinquent subculture. Both projects have had to turn away applicants.

Under normal conditions, the delinquent may turn the set off whenever he wishes. He may also send and receive code messages to and from the base station. Being a tone system, it does not transmit voice signals and thus the privacy of third parties is guaranteed. Tone transmission has the additional advantage of providing less opportunity for employees to misuse the sets. Early trials with voice transmission showed that delinquents would, for example, answer taxi cab calls on their frequency.

Behaviour transmitter-reinforcers have at least three purposes:

1. Research. The transmitters permit the experimenter unobtrusively to record location of the employee. In this way one may objectively determine where the delinquent spends his time. Almost all information to date regarding how a particular delinquent spends his time, joins a gang or learns to change habit patterns is based on the reports of the delinquent himself. Theories of behaviour are, of course, dependent upon the reliability of the data to be organized. Data obtained by electronic means are not subject to the purposeful (or the unintentional but unavoidable) distortion of recall from memory.

2. Preventive parole. Often an employee will give the experimenter specific instructions long in advance that if he is ever found at a particular place at a particular time (say, in a high crime area in early morning) he should be taken home. A person on legal parole may be required to have the set on during certain hours. Persons on parole are often suspected of committing crimes of which they are, in fact, innocent. An objective record of their whereabouts may alleviate unnecessary suspicion.

It is also possible that an employee will signal for help while on his way to commit a crime. Many times a serious and compulsive act is preceded by conscious ambivalent feelings. A public telephone may not be available, or it may be in use, or the employee may not wish to spend the money. The "cry for help" may be quite weak and the smallest inconvenience can result in the person giving up. This is particularly true for adolescent delinquents where a depressive syndrome is rather common. The attempt of behaviour electronics is to make it as easy as possible for the person to get help when he feels he legitimately needs it. The best help, we believe, is given *before* a crime is committed.

3. Immediate reinforcement. A characteristic of almost all offenders is their inability to delay gratification. An experimenter may be relatively less handicapped by a delinquent's mode of operation if the electronic system can be used. A transmitting set would allow the experimenter to more immediately reinforce desirable behaviour. For example, a boy may have been warned by his school that one more incident of misbehaviour in a certain class will be punished by expulsion. His restraint is therefore presumably rewarded by his getting a diploma in

several months and by avoiding punishment. This is not likely to be as effective as more immediate positive reinforcements.

Using a transmitter it might be arranged to have the student signal the experimenter at the end of the class period or at a certain hour what has happened. It may be quite possible for the student to control troublesome impulses for forty minutes if he knows that he will be able to signal success at the end of the class. A short response from the experimenter may be enough to assure him that someone was concerned enough to wait for the result. In this way, reinforcement of small units of behaviour may be a clue to more effective development of social skills.

Film Experiment with Delinquent Boys:
Neighbors, Black Patch, Little Grey Neck

Celia M. Anderson and Carol C. Smith

The group selected was composed of fifteen eleven- and twelve-year-olds with a median IQ of 85. Under the leadership of the same teacher for seven (to eight) months this group had achieved a measure of· cohesion and had established a basis for interaction.

Since the basic philosophy of the "600" program is to redirect these boys toward constructive citizenship and to assist them in relating to others in behavior that is personally satisfactory as well as socially acceptable, it was hoped that the films presented to them would also contribute toward their rehabilitation. Furthermore, since the attention span ranged anywhere from two to twenty minutes, it was imperative to present film fare that would capture and sustain their interest and attention, for those boys are never a captive audience. They must be *captivated*. They repudiate the quasi-realistic, the phony, or the contrived situations so frequently presented in films.

We chose a short film, *Neighbors,* to initiate the series. This is a ten-minute film, in color, and was produced by Norman McLaren of the National Film Board of Canada. It is an experiment in the use of stop-motion, live-action techniques. There is no voice on the sound-track but the music is so intimately, subtly synchronized with the action that no narration is necessary. As one of the boys said, "The music talked. I heard it!" Two friendly neighbors, sitting comfortably over their newspapers in front of their paper maché houses, develop an argument over a flower which grows up between them on the boundary line between

Reprinted from a report on the Film Experiment with Delinquent Boys. Board of Education, New York City, December 1960.

their homes. The result is an increasingly savage battle which results in death for both, and the film ends with the phrase, "Love your Neighbor" in many languages.

The film was shown in the classroom, and the first few minutes were spent getting acquainted with Miss Anderson and in establishing an atmosphere of informal friendlines. Then a few statements were made about the film they were going to see. They were asked to listen to the music, to note that stop-motion was used, and that there was a fight in the film. We developed a brief discussion on the meaning of the word "neighbor." When the film went on there was amusement and, from the begining of the fight, rapt attention. The lively discussion that followed indicated their ability to identify with the characters and action:

> We fight over silly things, too—like when A— takes my pencils.
> Yeah, we fight over who wins the game.
> And who should be first on the lunch line or first to type.

Comments indicated that the boys realized that the reaction of the men in thè film was out of proportion to the provocation. One boy (who witnessed a real life drama when, in a family quarrel, the father used a gun) said, "These men acted like children. Grown-ups are often worse than kids!" Little stunted A— wailed, "They hit the womens and the babies! Why they want to do that?"

R— said, "Did you see how their faces changed? They didn't look like men any more." In the discussion following this remark the boys decided that the men became "savage." In the weeks that followed the showing of this film they adopted this word permanently, using it frequently.

In answer to the question as to what other means the men could have used to solve their problems, many suggestions were offered:

> They could have shared the flower like they shared the matches when they were friends in the beginning.
> They could have put up a little round circle fence so all the neighborhood could smell and see the flower.
> They could let it grow until it had seeds and then planted the seeds.
> They could cut it down so no one would own it.

The film was shown twice with unabated interest and attention. The boys expressed the idea that this was a "grudge" fight—that the two men could have had a "fair" fight, like a boxing bout, winner to own the flower.

During the weeks following, the material in *Neighbors* was used for oral discussion, art, word study, spelling, written reports (which were typed on the manuscript typewriter), letters, and so on. Each boy made drawings of the scenes which interested him most and these were displayed next to the reading chart on *Neighbors* which had evolved as a group project.

No comments were made indicating any traumatic effect as a result of the "horror" in the film. These children are so conditioned by their life in the streets where they spend so much of their time outside of school, that needless cruelty, physical violence, and degrading behavior are an accepted part of their daily lives. The film served to bring home to them that "in a grudge fight no one is really a winner." They expressed regret over the cruelty to the mothers and babies, deciding that these two men "deserved to die." Frequently during the days that followed the showing the boys themselves brought up the subject of lack of self-control. They seemed to have acquired a clear concept of what the term means and what it involves.

It is difficult to measure the total impact of this experience on these boys but it is quite obvious that they retained far more from the exposure to this film than from any regular class lesson on human relations, brotherhood, and the like.

It was demonstrated to our satisfaction that adults (teachers) are not able to predict positively the effect of a particular experience on children. Their "tolerance quotient" is evidently much higher than is generally believed. This is apparently true of these boys, conditioned as they have been by exposure to life's grimmest realities.

After a three-week interval we presented *Black Patch,* a documentary-style film, twenty minutes, black and white, which told the story of a herd of mountain goats and their struggle for survival against natural enemies, wolves, and a panther, and against men who hunted them for sport and for the zoo. There are two scenes of violence, one a fight between *Black Patch,* the leader of the herd and a competing male mountain goat, and another fight with wolves. The herd escapes capture for the zoo in an extraordinary scene where the goats, following their leader, jump from wall to wall of a narrow canyon, eluding their pursuers.

For this film the boys were prepared by a study of the habits of the mountain goat, by pictures, etc. In the discussion following the showing the boys brought out that in many ways the problems of existence facing the mountain goat resembled those of human beings. One boy noted how the mother went in search of her kid regardless of her own danger, "just like a real mother."

Another observed that the kid went in search of his "brothers" when the mother goat was killed.

At this point C__ remarked, "I wouldn't look for my brother. *I hate his guts!*" This hint of sibling rivalry led to a thorough investigation of the case history and revealed home conditions not heretofore recorded. This insight resulted in a new approach directed toward relieving some of the pressure on C__ at home.

H__ said the goats harmed no one, yet they had no friends, just got pushed around like some real kids get pushed around by everyone.

The out-of-season hunter who shot the mother was the butt of many nasty comments, this in spite of the fact that these boys are so innately cruel to their own weaker classmates. Why do they sympathize so readily

with the "underdog" in the film situation unless it may be assumed that the hunter is the grown-up in disguise, whom they consider their natural enemy?

V__ was excited over the manner in which Black Patch assumed leadership because "it would take the strongest, bravest, smartest leader to keep the herd out of danger."

Through discussion, fighting for existence as in *Black Patch* was distinguished from "grudge fights" as in *Neighbors*. Fighting was deemed right and proper in certain circumstances such as protecting one's self, family or country.

There was a great admiration for the goats who followed the leader so fearlessly and confidently, even to jumping over the edge of the precipice and richocheting from side to side of the canyon. These boys will also follow any strong leader into any activity, acceptable or not.

The film session began at 10:20, was repeated, and the second discussion ended at 12:05. This is an unheard of length of time for their uninterrupted application to a subject theme. They skipped their P. T. period and the regular recess period without raising a single protest, another history-making event! The dramatic quality of the material presented, the appeal to their keen interest in animals, in adventure, in dangerous situations, and the satisfaction in identifying with the "heroic leader" were sufficient to insure their prolonged attention.

In an attempt to discover if there might be any transfer of learning, the class was exposed to a film and a filmstrip on the life of a Navajo Indian boy who had charge of a herd of goats and sheep. The remarks made by the boys indicated a definite transfer of learning, i.e.:

The teacher observed a keener spotting of details such as noting a "black sheep" in the herd; the injury to the puppy; the shapes of the rocks; the designs on the silver jewelry and rugs; the fact that Indian men wore jewelry such as bracelets, necklaces and fancy belts.

Two weeks after the showing of *Black Patch* the class was invited to visit the New York University Film Library where we showed them *Little Grey Neck,* a twenty minute color cartoon. The story concerns itself with a little duck who, in an effort to save his friend, a rabbit, has his wing damaged by a fox and is saved in turn from the fox and protected during the cold winter by the rabbit. In the spring when his wing has healed *Little Grey Neck* deceptively leads the fox into disaster and is then himself reunited with his mother and family.

In spite of the fact that the boys were somewhat excited by the newness of their surroundings they gave this film the same attention given the other two. After the initial showing the boys applauded spontaneously and voted that this was the best film yet. When asked why this film was the best, the reasons given were indicative again of the amount of self-realization that had taken place:

The duck and rabbits were such good friends! They helped each other.
They did favors for each other.

Little Grey Neck risked his life for his friend. Then the rabbits risked their necks for him.

A good friend never rats on you.

Or leaves you when there's trouble and lets you take the rap.

Grey Neck didn't leave until he had gotten rid of the fox so the little rabbits would be safe, too.

The little duck was smart. He pretended he was still crippled and tricked the fox into following him right into the river so the fox drowned.

"I liked the part where the duck family all got together again," said J___, who had cried during the scene where Little Grey Neck had been left behind.

Remarks of another type indicated that the boys were becoming aware of details and were actually "seeing" and "hearing" better than ever before:

I liked the good music. It was soft.

It was nice hearing animals speak with voices of people.

Wasn't the mother's voice good?

Yeah, and the old woodcock kept saying, "Come a little closer. I can't hear you!" (The boys mimicked the various voices.)

It was a good cartoon because the animal drawings were so real-like.

I liked the pictures of the country and when spring was coming.

As a check on their awareness of detail and alertness to indirect learnings, we repeated the filmstrip *The Ugly Duckling,* used earlier in the year. An obviously greater concern with details and implications in the plot was noted. The boys now showed much greater insight in their discussion of the rejection and the pushing around experienced by the ugly duckling. For the first time, they indicated awareness of "stereotypes" as presented by the cat who asked, "Can you purr?" and the hen who asked, "Can you lay eggs?" In one scene the duckling said that he could swim, and was told, "You are very queer. We don't want you here. Go away!" The boys spent considerable time in identifying this behavior with their own, both in rejecting others and in being rejected.

General Conclusions

1. These three films elicited discussion in the course of which the boys indicated their own problems, difficulties, and confusions. The boys were stimulated to express themselves in writing reports and original stories, to do research in locating pictures which would be helpful in making their own illustrations, and in finding other stories about goats, ducks, rabbits, etc., to read.

The Language Arts program became a joy with the strong motivation provided by the film materials. Up to this point in the school year,

reports, letters and reading charts had been prepared as cooperative efforts by the entire class. Now, they actually demanded that each boy be permitted to write his own story or letter. They insisted that they be given opportunities to type their products which they read with considerable pride to all visitors.

2. More constructive use was made of all "free periods" (time left after assignments are completed) and the materials of the films were used in every conceivable way. Extra supplies of drawing paper, tracing peper, crayons, and typing papers were needed and this in itself could be considered a yardstick or measuring device in evaluating the appeal of these films.

3. It was observed that throughout the project the boys displayed keen interest in three specific areas, namely, that of the mother figure, as portrayed in each film, friendship, and in the specific conflicts (violence) presented.

4. It cannot be emphasized too strongly that in such an experiment the children themselves will teach us what *they need,* what material will so rivet their attention that the learning process may begin. With *Neighbors* we seemed to have achieved this goal with somewhat astonishing success. In *Black Patch,* the commentary proved too wordy, and somewhat pompous. It was obvious that they listened to it only when it was simple and direct. *Little Grey Neck* is a well-organized film, clear and simple, and was accepted whole-heartedly.

5. To learn from the children themselves the teacher must achieve a relationship with them which enables her to hear what they hear and see what they see as well as to observe what they do not hear or see. This means, in essence, that the children will indicate clearly to those trained in patient observation the material which touches them deeply and releases energies which may be directed into positive channels.

6. At the outset there was no quarrel with the hypothesis that films are teaching tools. This exploratory project served to reinforce the validity of this hypothesis, but it served also to focus attention on the need for greater selectivity in the implementation of any visual aids program for therapeutic purposes. Whatever may be considered proper film fare for "normal" children, it seems obvious that for children damaged by home and environmental influences dramatic conflict serves as a projective technique whereby their own conflicts may find expression. They ask for alleviation and resolution of such conflict so that they may be assured that alleviation and resolution are possible. They also demand that conflict and resolution be presented in terms which they can believe and accept.

The Drug Addict

Narcotic Addiction is a Special Problem

Arthur Pearl

Narcotic addiction is a special problem. It has become a special problem due to dissemination of conflicting information and misinformation, and because so much ambiguity and mystery surrounds it. There is confusion about the magnitude of the problem, the characteristics of those affected, and the extent to which the narcotic drug impedes normal human functioning. There is no clearly demonstrated program of effective treatment of drug addiction, and, in fact, there is even confusion over what the goal of treatment should be.

Narcotic addiction is a special example of deviant subculture. The addict is not only bound by the styles, customs, and values of the subculture, but he must also negotiate that subculture to obtain the drugs in which so much of his life is directly and indirectly invested.

It is on this last point that those persons who advocate furnishing drugs to addicts legally focus. In their emphasis on undermining the hold that the culture has on the individual, a much more important point is overlooked. That is, the addict, with or without drugs, has nowhere else to go. With few exceptions, his life is devoid of even a fingerhold in any nondelinquent world. He has a poor or nonexistent job history, no social contact with the world of the "squares," and has eroded his welcome with family and friends by irresponsible acts of all dimensions. He is untrusted and untrustworthy and all the drugs in the world will do nothing to change his status.

It has been stated here that narcotic addiction is a special problem for many reasons, but the primary reason is that men of science who otherwise are reasonable and restrained become irrational when discussing the problem and its solutions.

595

There can be no rational attack on the addiction problem until programs begin to have a solid basis in knowledge. Narcotic addiction should be considered a public health problem because, using this definition, the competencies of public health agencies can be brought to bear on the problem in a systematic fashion.

Once addiction is accorded the status of disease, public health has to assume certain responsibilities. The first task is appraising the magnitude of the problem. If a disease state is to be attacked intelligently, incidence and prevention must be determined, epidemic areas delineated, and etiologic factors isolated. At present, the only information about prevalence of addiction comes from law enforcement agencies. Law enforcement agencies consider (by definition) only the criminal addict who is also the heroin addict. Such measures of prevalence must be gross underestimations, for ignored are the barbiturate and amphetamine addicts who qualify on all counts as true addicts. These substances have high addictive liability, physiological dependence is developed, and gross withdrawal distress is noted when the drug is removed. On the basis of biased measurements of prevalence the belief that drug addiction flourishes among the economically deprived is fostered. There is growing evidence that heroin is a drug most often used by underprivileged minority groups, whereas the barbiturate is a drug of choice of the middle class Caucasian. From a public health point of view, both groups are equally affected with the disease, although a different course of treatment may be applicable for each.

It has been authoritatively stated that the drug addict spontaneously delivers himself from his problem after he reaches a certain age and, to buttress this claim, it is cited that there are very few known addicts over the age of forty-five. It may be that there is spontaneous regeneration of adicts, but other explanations may be equally sound. It may be that the addicts die young. Without a careful search of health department death records, such an alternative cannot be discounted. There is some evidence that the death rate of addicts is much higher than that of the general population. It may be that the addicts continue to be addicts but cease to be criminals, and therefore are not detected by law enforcement agencies. And, it may be that there are relatively few old addicts today because there were relatively few young addicts thirty years ago.

That public health has a role in clarifying these issues is manifestly clear. Public health has an additonal role in the realm of education. The misconceptions that people hold today about the nature of addiction stem from imprecise and often erroneous statements about the nature of the addiction process. No other disease is presented with such grotesque fascination, as is addiction. Education often is relegated to agencies that sensationalize rather than inform. I have yet to see a film on the problem of addiction that did not feature the drug addict's paraphernalia. Rather than discouraging youth from becoming addicts, these educative devices become training films on how to prepare a "fix."

Public health has a role in educating the physician about treatment

philosophies. In this light, if public health can only use its influence to reject panaceas or simple solutions, an important contribution will have been made. There is no simple solution to the narcotic addiction problem. It has now become generally accepted that addicts are difficult to treat, and many experts believe addiction to be incurable. Any views about addict's amenability to treatment have to be accepted on faith rather than knowledge, because little effort has been made to treat the addict. Treatment of addicts has been concentrated almost exclusively in institutions. It is not a difficult job to keep an addict off drugs in an institution; most supervisors of institutions frown upon drug use there. The problem is in keeping an addict off a drug while he is in the community. It is in the community that the addict has proven himself to be inadequate, as shown by his inability to adjust to the problems and conflicts of society. There is evidence that when addicts have the opportunity for successfully functioning in society there is a high rate of cure. The California Board of Medical Examiners reports 92 per cent of doctor addicts show no relapse to the use of drugs in five years, when placed under the special program of rehabilitation.[1] Some experts have taken the position that law enforcement agencies restrict effective treatment of the addict. I do not believe that there is inherent conflict between treatment of an addict and punishment of an illegal trafficker. There is no inconsistency in this position even though it is recognized that pusher and addict are likely to be one and the same person. Effective treatment should remove the need for pushing; effective treatment should limit the market for pushing. The answer to the illegal narcotic traffic is effective prevention and early detection of addiction, and rehabilitation of the addict. Rather than being concerned about supplying the addict with narcotics, the medical profession should be concerned with limiting the demand for narcotics. Without the current demand for drugs there would be no illegal narcotic traffic and heroin would be less costly than the milk sugar with which it is adulterated.

It has been stressed by many that alcoholism is generally considered a disease, whereas addiction is viewed as criminal behavior. Part of the distinction between alcoholism and addiction is temporal; not too many years ago alcoholism was greeted with the same opprobrium that faces addiction now. Public attitudes change with education and treatment programs. The fulfilling of public health responsibilities will go a long way to alter the public image of addiction. Partly, however, the difference between addiction and alcoholism is illusory. Often alcoholics are treated as criminals; more than 50 per cent of all arrests in California are of alcoholics arrested on internal possession of alcohol, "drunkenness," [2] and the illegal sale of alcoholic beverages is as energetically prosecuted as the illegal sale of narcotics. The essential difference between addiction and alcoholism is that with addiction there is a tendency by some medical practitioners to blame law enforcement for the failure of the medical profession to deal with the problem of treatment of the addict. The issue, apparently, is whether narcotics should be dispensed to addicts as part of the treatment process. There is general agreement

that treatment of the alcoholic should not include alcoholic beverages, although this is a legally available course to the doctor. From a treatment point of view, the same should hold true for the addict. From the little we know today, it appears that no cogent argument could be advanced for a course of treatment that would include providing narcotics to the addict.

It is a relatively simple procedure to detoxify an addict. It can be done in a fairly short period of time, it can be done humanely, and it is the least difficult feature in the treatment process. It is a generally accepted fact that treatment can begin only when the patient desires to be helped. Such desire must perforce be reflected in anxiety or guilt; the addict uses a narcotic to allay guilt or anxiety. Giving narcotics to addicts can hardly be justified, even on an experimental basis. Research should be inaugurated on some theoretical basis; research should be the culmination of knowledge. The argument stressed by doctors in defense of dispensing narcotics is that such a program would reduce crime against person and property committed by the addict to obtain his drugs. The argument is advanced although it is not in the area of competence of the physician. The concern over giving addicts drugs has been an unfortunate line for medicine to take. I think it would be readily agreed that most known addicts should not be given drugs. The known addict who can function in society and use drugs is a rare case. To raise such furor over the unusual at the expense of the general serves no useful purpose. To deal with the unusual, functioning drug user, it has been suggested that medical boards be established to rule on whether a particular addict should receive drugs.[3] Certainly such a procedure should satisfy that segment of the medical profession that views narcotics as having value in the treatment of some addicts.

It is also argued that treatment, to be effective, must be voluntary and nonpunitive. A criminal's treatment is mandatory and, if mandatory, has to be punitive. It is argued that the addict is too alien to society to accept mandatory treatment. I do not believe that there is any evidence to support this view. In fact, with the current state of knowledge, it would appear that a mandatory treatment approach has more chance to be effective than a permissive, voluntary program, with most addicts and alcoholics. I would concur that punishment without a treatment focus has been proven to be a totally ineffective antidote for addiction (or for any social problem), but mandatory treatment has not been proven ineffective.

The California Medical Examiner Program for doctor addicts, cited earlier, is a mandatory program. The Anti-Opium Law Program inaugurated in India many years ago [4] had success under mandatory conditions. The highly publicized Synanon Foundation,[5] a voluntary program of self-help run by former addicts, operates under extremely authoritarian principles in which all narcotic use is proscribed and addicts must cut off all ties with the outside world during the first phase of this program (from six to eighteen months).

The experimental Narcotic Treatment Control Program of the Cali-

fornia Department of Correction [6] features mandatory treatment and, while not presenting evidence of prolonged abstinence, has demonstrated conclusively the addicts' willingness, and, in fact, eagerness, to partici- pate fully in the treatment program. The challenge lies in translating this desire to effective community programming.

There are unlimited opportunities for use of imagination in providing new and more effective means of treating the detoxified addict in the community. There is need for creativity in education and detection of the addiction-prone. It is in these areas that the challenge of addiction lies and the responsibility of public health rests.

Notes

1. L. E. Jones, "How 92 Per Cent Beat the Dope Habit," *Bulletin of the Los Angeles County Medical Association* (April 3, 1956).

2. State of California Department of Public Health: *Alcoholism in California 1900–1956—Related Statistics, 1957.*

3. State of California, *Special Study Commisison on Narcotics,* Final Report (June, 1961).

4. R. N. Chopra and I. C. Chopra, "Treatment of Drug Addiction, Experi- ence in India," *Bulletin on Narcotics* (United Nations, Vol. IX, No. 4, Oct.– Dec., 1957).

5. For further discussion of the pro- gram see: Rita Volkman and Donald R. Cressey: "Differential Association and the Rehabilitation of Drug Addicts." *Amer. J. of Sociology,* 64:2 (September, 1963) 129–42.

6. A. Pearl, "The Narcotic Treatment Control Program in California." Board of Correction monograph No. 1, 1960.

Differential Association and the Rehabilitation of Drug Addicts

Rita Volkman and Donald R. Cressey

In 1955 Cressey listed five principles for applying Edwin Sutherland's theory of differential association to the rehabilitation of criminals.[1] While this article is now frequently cited in the sociological literature dealing with group therapy, "therapeutic communities," and "total institutions," we know of no program of rehabilitation that has been explicitly based on the principles. The major point of Cressey's article, which referred to criminals, not addicts, is similar to the following recommendation by the Chief of the United States Narcotics Division: "The community should restore the former addict to his proper place in society and help him avoid associations that would influence him to return to the use of drugs." [2]

Cressey gives five rules (to be reviewed below) for implementing this directive to "restore," "help," and "influence" the addict. These rules, derived from the sociological and social-psychological literature on social movements, crime prevention, group therapy, communications, personality change, and social change, were designed to show that sociology has distinctive, non-psychiatric, theory that can be used effectively by practitioners seeking to prevent crime and change criminals. Sutherland also had this as a principal objective when he formulated his theory of differential association.[3]

Assuming, as we do, that Cressey's principles are consistent with Sutherland's theory and that his theory, in turn, is consistent with more general sociological theory, a test of the principles would be a test of the

Reprinted by permission of University of Chicago Press, from *American Journal of Sociology*, Vol. 64, No. 2, September 1963, pp. 129–142.

more general formulations. Ideally, such a test would involve careful study of the results of a program rationally designed to utilize the principles to change criminals. To our knowledge, such a test has not been made.[4] As a "next best" test, we may study rehabilitation programs that use the principles, however unwittingly. Such a program has been in operation since 1958. Insofar as it is remarkably similar to any program that could have been designed to implement the principles, the results over the years can be viewed as at least a crude test of the principles. Since the principles are interrelated, the parts of any program implementing them must necessarily overlap.

"Synanon," an organization of former drug addicts, was founded in May, 1958, by a member of Alcoholics Anonymous with the assistance of an alcoholic and a drug addict. In December, 1958, Volkman (a non-addict) heard about the two dozen ex-addicts living together in an abandoned store, and she obtained permission of the Synanon Board of Directors [5] to visit the group daily and to live in during the weekends. In July, 1959, she moved into the girls' dormitory of the group's new, larger quarters and continued to reside at Synanon House until June, 1960. Cressey (also a non-addict) visited the House at Volkman's invitation in the spring of 1960; for one year, beginning in July, 1960, he visited the organization on the average of at least once a week. He deliberately refrained from trying to influence policy or program, and his theory about the effects of group relationships on rehabilitation were unknown to the group. Most of the interview material and statistical data reported below were collected by Volkman during her 1959–60 period of residence and were used in the thesis for her Master's degree, prepared under the direction of C. Wayne Gordon.[6] As both a full-fledged member of Synanon and as a participant observer, Volkman attended about three hundred group sessions, a few of which were recorded. She was accorded the same work responsibilities, rights, and privileges as any other member, and she was considered one of Synanon's first "graduates."

The Subjects

Background data were available on only the first fifty-two persons entering Synanon after July, 1958. These records were prepared by a resident who in July, 1959, took it upon himself to interview and compile the information. We have no way of determining whether these fifty-two persons are representative of all addicts. However, we believe they are similar to the 215 persons who have resided at Synanon for at least one month.

Age and sex distributions are shown in Table 1: 44 per cent of the fifty-two were Protestant, 35 per cent Catholic, 8 per cent Jewish.[7] Racially, 27 per cent were Negro, and there were no Orientals; 19 per cent of the Caucasians were of Mexican origin and 13 per cent were of Italian origin. Educational attainment is shown in Table 2. Although

Table 1—Age and Sex

Age (in Years)	MALES		FEMALES		TOTAL	
	No.	Per Cent	No.	Per Cent	No.	Per Cent
18–20	0	0	1	7	1	2
21–30	17	44	11	79	28	54
31–40	18	48	2	14	20	38
41–50	1	3	0	0	1	2
51–60	2	5	0	0	2	4
Total	38	100	14	100	52	100

Median ages: males, 31.0; females, 27.5.

Table 2—Educational Attainment

	No.	Per Cent
Part grade school	1	2
Completed grade school	3	6
Part high school	24	46
Completed high school	11	21
Part college	13	25
Completed college	0	0
Total	52	100

the data on early family life are poor because the resident simply asked "What was your family like?" it may be noted that only five of the fifty-two indicated satisfaction with the home. Words and phrases such as "tension," "arguing," "bickering," "violence," "lack of warmth," "went back and forth," and "nagged" were common.[8]

The sporadic and tenuous occupational ties held by the group are indicated in Table 3. This table supports the notion that addicts cannot

Table 3—Length and Continuity of Employment

No. of Years on One Job	Unsteady (Discontinuous or Sporadic)	Steady (Continuous)	Total
Under 1	36*	4	40
2–3	3	2	5
4–5	1	3	4
6 or over	2	1	3
Total	42	10	52

* Of this category 67 per cent defined their work as "for short periods only."

maintain steady jobs because their addiction interferes with the work routine; it suggests also that these members had few lasting peer group contacts or ties, at least so far as work associations go. In view of their poor employment records, it might be asked how the addicts supported their addictions, which cost from $30 to $50 a day and sometimes ran to $100 a day. Only four of the men reported that they obtained their incomes by legitimate work alone; thirty (79 per cent) were engaged in

illegitimate activities, with theft, burglary, armed robbery, shoplifting, and pimping leading the list. One man and seven women were supplied with either drugs or money by their mates or families, and five of these females supplemented this source by prostitution or other illegitimate work. Five of the fourteen women had no income except that from illegitimate activities, and none of the women supported themselves by legitimate work only.

Institutional histories and military service histories are consistent with the work and educational histories, indicating that the fifty-two members were not somehow inadvertently selected as "easy" rehabilitation cases. The fifty-two had been in and out of prisons, jails, and hospitals all over the United States. Table 4 shows that ten men and one

Table 4—Confinements in Institutions

No. of Confinements	Male	NO. Female	Total*
1–3	9	6	15
4–6	12	7	19
7–9	8	0	8
10–12	0	1	1
13–15	2	0	2
Total confinements	166	59	225

* Three males indicated "numerous arrests," and four supplied no information. These seven were not included in the tally.

woman had been confined seven or more times; the mean number of confinements for males was 5.5 and for females 3.9. The table seems to indicate that whatever value confinement in institutions might have had for this group, it clearly did not prevent further confinements.

In sum, the pre-Synanon experiences of the fifty-two residents seems to indicate non-identification with pro-legal activities and norms. Neither the home, the armed services, the occupational world, schools, prisons, nor hospitals served as links with the larger and more socially acceptable community. This, then, is the kind of "raw material" with which Synanon has been working.[9]

The Program

ADMISSION

Not every addict who knocks on the door of Synanon is given admission. Nevertheless, the only admission criterion we have been able to find is *expressed willingness* to submit one's self to a group that hates drug addiction. Use of this criterion has unwittingly implemented one of Cressey's principles:

If criminals are to be changed, they must be assimilated into groups which emphasize values conducive to law-abiding behavior and, con-

currently, alienated from groups emphasizing values conducive to criminality. Since our experience has been that the majority of criminals experience great difficulty in securing intimate contacts in ordinary groups, special groups whose major common goal is the reformation of criminals must be created.

This process of assimilation and alienation begins the moment an addict arrives at Synanon, and it continues throughout his stay. The following are two leaders' comments on admission interviews; they are consistent with our own observations of about twenty such interviews.

1. When a new guy comes in we want to find out whether a person has one inkling of seriousness. Everybody who comes here is what we call a psychopathic liar. We don't take them all, either. We work off the top spontaneously, in terms of feeling. We use a sort of intuitive faculty. You know he's lying, but you figure, "Well, maybe if you get a halfway positive feeling that he'll stay. . . ." We ask him things like "What do you want from us?" "Don't you think you're an idiot or insane?" "Doesn't it sound insane for you to be running around the alleys stealing money from others so's you can go and stick something up your arm?" "Does this sound sane to you?" "Have you got family and friends outside?" We might tell him to go do his business now and come back when he's ready to do business with us. We tell him, "We don't need you." "You need *us.*" And if we figure he's only halfway with us, we'll chop off his hair.

It's all in the *attitude.* It's got to be positive. We don't want their money. But we may just tell him to bring back some dough next week. If he pleads and begs—the money's not important. If he shows he really cares. If his attitude is good. It's all in the attitude.

2. Mostly, if people don't have a family outside, with no business to take care of, they're ready to stay. They ain't going to have much time to think about themselves otherwise. . . . Now, when he's got problems, when he's got things outside, if he's got mickey mouse objections, like when you ask him "How do you feel about staying here for a year?" and he's got to bargain with you, like he needs to stay with his wife or his sick mother—then we tell him to get lost. If he can't listen to a few harsh words thrown at him, he's not ready. Sometimes we yell at him, "You're a goddamned liar!" If he's serious he'll take it. He'll do anything if he's serious.

But each guy's different. If he sounds sincere, we're not so hard. If he's sick of running the rat race out there, or afraid of going to the penitentiary, he's ready to do anything. Then we let him right in. . . .

This admission process seems to have two principal functions. First, it forces the newcomer to admit, at least on a verbal level, that he is willing to try to conform to the norms of the group, whose members will not tolerate any liking for drugs or drug addicts. From the minute he enters the door, his expressed desire to join the group is tested by giving him difficult orders—to have his hair cut off, to give up all his money, to sever all family ties, to come back in ten days or even thirty days. He

is given expert help and explicit but simple criteria for separating the "good guys" from the "bad guys"—the latter shoot dope. Second, the admission process weeds out men and women who simply want to lie down for a few days to rest, to obtain free room and board, or to stay out of the hands of the police. In the terms used by Lindesmith, and also in the terms used at Synanon, the person must want to give up drug *addiction,* not just the drug *habit.*[10] This means that he must at least *say* that he wants to quit using drugs once and for all, in order to realize his potentials as an adult; he must not indicate that he merely wants a convenient place in which to go through withdrawal distress so that he can be rid of his habit for a short time because he has lost his connection, or for some other reason. He must be willing to give up all ambitions, desires, and social interactions that might prevent the group from assimilating him completely.

> If he says he just wants to kick, he's no good. Out with him. Now we know nine of out ten lie, but we don't care. We'd rather have him make an attempt and *lie* and then get him in here for thirty days or so—then he might stick. It takes months to decide to stay.
> Most fish [newcomers] don't take us seriously. We know what they want, out in front. A dope fiend wants dope, nothing else. All the rest is garbage. We've even taken that ugly thing called money. This shows that they're serious. Now this guy today was sincere. We told him we didn't want money. We could see he would at least give the place a try. We have to find out if he's sincere. Is he willing to have us cut off his curly locks? I imagine cutting his hair off makes him take us seriously. . . .

Although it is impossible to say whether Synanon's selective admission process inadvertently admits those addicts who are most amenable to change, no addict has been refused admission on the ground that his case is "hopeless" or "difficult" or that he is "unreachable." On the contrary, before coming to Synanon, twenty-nine of the fifty-two addicts had been on drugs for a least ten years. Two of these were addicted for over forty years, and had been in and out of institutions during that period. The average length of time on drugs for the fifty-two was eleven years, and 56 per cent reported less than one month as the longest period of time voluntarily free of drugs after addiction and prior to Synanon.

INDOCTRINATION

In the admission process, and throughout his residence, the addict discovers over and over again that the group to which he is submitting is antidrug, anticrime, and antialcohol. At least a dozen times a day he hears someone tell him that he can remain at Synanon only as long as he "stays clean," that is, stays away from crime, alcohol, and drugs. This emphasis is an unwitting implementation of Cressey's second principle:

*The more relevant the common purpose of the group to the refor-
mation of criminals, the greater will be its influence on the criminal
members' attitudes and values. Just as a labor union exerts strong
influence over its members' attitudes toward management but less
influence on their attitudes toward say, Negroes, so a group organized for recreation or welfare purposes will have less success in influencing criminalistic attitudes and values than will one whose
explicit purpose is to change criminals.*

Indoctrination makes clear the notion that Synanon exists in order
to keep addicts off drugs, not for purposes of recreation, vocational education, etc. Within a week after admission, each newcomer participates
in an indoctrination session by a spontaneous group made up of four or
five older members. Ordinarily, at least one member of the Board of
Directors is present, and he acts as leader. The following are excerpts
from one such session with a woman addict. The rules indicate the
extreme extent to which it is necessary for the individual to subvert
his personal desires and ambitions to the antidrug, anticrime group.

Remember, we told you not to go outside by yourself. Whenever
anybody leaves this building they have to check in and out at the
desk. For a while, stay in the living room. Don't take showers alone
or even go to the bathroom alone, see. While you're kicking, somebody will be with you all the time. And stay away from newcomers.
You got nothing to talk to them about, except street talk, and before
you know it you'll be splitting [leaving] to take a fix together. Stay
out of the streets, mentally and physically, or get lost now.
No phone calls or letters for a while—if you get one, you'll read
it in front of us. We'll be monitoring all your phone calls for a while.
You see, you got no ties, no business out there any more. You don't
need them. You never could handle them before, so don't start
thinking you can do it now. All you knew how to do was shoot
dope and go to prison.
You could never take care of your daughter before. You didn't
know how to be a mother. It's garbage. All a dope fiend knows how
to do is shoot dope. Forget it.

There are two obvious illustrations of the antidrug and anticrime
nature of the group's subculture. First, there is a strong taboo against
what is called "street talk." Discussion of how it feels to take a fix, who
one's connection was, where one took his shot, the crimes one has committed, or who one associated with is severely censured. One's best friend
and confidant at Synanon might well be the person that administers a
tongue lashing for street talk, and the person who calls your undesirable
behavior to the attention of the entire group during a general meeting.
Second, a member must never, in any circumstances, identify with
the "code of the streets," which says that a criminal is supposed to keep
quiet about the criminal activities of his peers. Even calling an ordinary
citizen "square" is likely to stimulate a spontaneous lecture, in heated
and colorful terms, on the notion that the people who are *really* square

are those that go around as bums sticking needles in their arms. A person who, as a criminal, learned to hate stool pigeons and finks with a passion must now turn even his closest friend over to the authorities, the older members of Synanon, if the friend shows any signs of nonconformity. If he should find that a member is considering "sneaking off to a fix somewhere," has kept pills, drugs, or an "outfit" with him when he joined the organization, or even has violated rules such as that prohibiting walking alone on the beach, he must by Synanon's code relinquish his emotional ties with the violator and expose the matter to another member or even to the total membership at a general meeting. If he does not do so, more pressure is put upon him than upon the violator, for he is expected to have "known better." Thus, for perhaps the first time in his life he will be censured for *not* "squealing" rather than for "squealing." [11] He must identify with the law and not with the criminal intent or act.

The sanctions enforcing this norm are severe, for its violation threatens the very existence of the group. "Guilt by association" is the rule. In several instances, during a general meeting the entire group spontaneously voted to "throw out" both a member who had used drugs and a member who had known of this use but had not informed the group. Banishment from the group is considered the worst possible punishment, for it is stressed over and over again that life in the streets "in your condition" can only mean imprisonment or death.

That the group's purpose is keeping addicts off drugs is given emphasis in formal and informal sessions—called "haircuts" or "pull ups"—as well as in spontaneous denunciations, and in denunciations at general meetings. The "synanon," discussed below, also serves this purpose. A "haircut" is a deliberately contrived device for minimizing the importance of the individual and maximizing the importance of the group, and for defining the group's basic purpose—keeping addicts off drugs and crime. The following is the response of a leader to the questions, "What's a haircut? What's its purpose?"

> When you are pointing out what a guy is doing. We do this through mechanisms of exaggeration. We blow up an incident so he can really get a look at it. The Coordinators [a coordinator resembles an officer of the day] and the Board members and sometimes an old timer may sit in on it. We do this when we see a person's attitude becoming negative in some area.
>
> For a *real* haircut, I'll give you myself. I was in a tender trap. My girl split. She called me on the job three days in a row. I made a date with her. We kept the date and I stayed out all night with her. Now, she was loaded [using drugs]. I neglected—or I refused—to call the house. By doing this I ranked everybody. You know doing something like that was no good. They were all concerned. They sent three or four autos looking for me because I didn't come back from work. You see, I was in Stage II.
>
> X found me and he made me feel real lousy, because I knew he worked and was concerned. Here he was out looking for me and he had to get up in the morning.

Well, I called the house the next morning and came back. I got called in for a haircut.

I sat down with three Board members in the office. They stopped everything to give the haircut. That impressed me. Both Y and Z, they pointed out my absurd and ridiculous behavior by saying things like this—though I did not get loaded, I associated with a broad I was emotionally involved with who was using junk. I jeopardized my *own* existence by doing this. So they told me, "Well, you fool, you might as well have shot dope by associating with a using addict." I was given an ultimatum. If I called her again or got in touch with her I would be thrown out.

("Why?")

Because continued correspondence with a using dope fiend is a crime against *me*—it hurts *me*. It was also pointed out how rank I was to people who are concerned with me. I didn't seem to care about people who were trying to help me. I'm inconsiderate to folks who've wiped my nose, fed me, clothed me. I'm like a child, I guess. I bite the hand that feeds me.

To top that off, I had to call a general meeting and I told everybody in the building what a jerk I was and I was sorry for acting like a little punk. I just sort of tore myself down. Told everyone what a phony I had been. And then the ridiculing questions began. Everybody started in. Like, "Where do you get off doing that to us?" That kind of stuff. When I was getting the treatment they asked me what I'd do—whether I would continue the relationship, whether I'd cut it off, or if I really wanted to stay at Synanon and do something about myself and my problem. But I made the decision before I even went in that I'd stay and cut the broad loose. I had enough time under my belt to know enough to make that decision before I even came back to the house. . . .

GROUP COHESION

The daily program at Synanon is consistent with Cressey's third principle, and appears to be an unwitting attempt to implement that principle:

> *The more cohesive the group, the greater the members' readiness to influence others and the more relevant the problem of conformity to group norms. The criminals who are to be reformed and the persons expected to effect the change must, then, have a strong sense of belonging to one group: between them there must be a genuine "we" feeling. The reformers, consequently, should not be identifiable as correctional workers, probation or parole officers, or social workers.*

Cohesion is maximized by a "family" analogy and by the fact that all but some "third-stage" members live and work together. The daily program has been deliberately designed to throw members into continuous mutual activity. In addition to the free, unrestricted interaction in small

groups called "synanons," the members meet as a group at least twice each day. After breakfast, someone is called upon to read the "Synanon Philosophy," which is a kind of declaration of principles, the day's work schedule is discussed, bits of gossip are publicly shared, the group or individual members are spontaneously praised or scolded by older members. Following a morning of work activities, members meet in the dining room after lunch to discuss some concept or quotation that has been written on a blackboard. Stress is on participation and expression; quotations are selected by Board members to provoke controversy and examination of the meaning, or lack of meaning, of words. Discussion sometimes continues informally during the afternoon work period and in "synanons," which are held after dinner (see below). In addition, lectures and classes, conducted by any member or outside speaker who will take on the responsibility, are held several times a week for all members who feel a need for them. Topics have included "semantics," "group dynamics," "meaning of truth," and "Oedipus complex."

There are weekend recreational activities, and holidays, wedding anniversaries, and birthdays are celebrated. Each member is urged: "Be yourself," "Speak the truth," "Be honest," and this kind of action in an atmosphere that is informal and open quickly gives participants a strong sense of "belonging." Since many of the members have been homeless drifters, it is not surprising to hear frequent repetition of some comment to the effect that "This is the first home I ever had."

Also of direct relevance to the third principle is the *voluntary* character of Synanon. Any member can walk out at any time; at night the doors are locked against persons who might want to enter, but not against persons who might want to leave. Many do leave.

Holding addicts in the house once they have been allowed to enter is a strong appeal to ideas such as "We have all been in the shape you are now in," or "Mike was on heroin for twenty years and *he's* off." It is significant, in this connection, that addicts who "kick" (go through withdrawal distress) at Synanon universally report that the sickness is not as severe as it is in involuntary organizations, such as jails and mental hospitals. One important variable here, we believe, is the practice of not giving "kicking dope fiends" special quarters. A newcomer kicks on a davenport in the center of the large living room, not in a special isolation room or quarantine room. Life goes on around him. Although a member will be assigned to watch him, he soon learns that his sickness is not important to men and women who have themselves kicked the habit. In the living room, one or two couples might be dancing, five or six people may be arguing, a man may be practicing the guitar, and a girl may be ironing. The kicking addict learns his lesson: These others have made it. This subtle device is supplemented by explicit comments from various members as they walk by or as they drop in to chat with him. We have heard the following comments, and many similar ones, made to new addicts lying sick from withdrawal. It should be noted that none of the comments could reasonably have been made by a rehabilitation official or a professional therapist.

It's OK boy. We've all been through it before.

For once you're with people like us. You've got everything to gain here and nothing to lose.

You think you're tough. Listen, we've got guys in here who could run circles around you, so quit your bull——.

You're one of us now, so keep your eyes open, your mouth shut and try to listen for a while. Maybe you'll learn a few things.

Hang tough, baby. We won't let you die.

STATUS ASCRIPTION

Cressey's fourth principle is:

Both reformers and those to be reformed must achieve status within the group by exhibition of "pro-reform" or anti-criminal values and behavior patterns. As a novitiate . . . he is a therapeutic parasite and not actually a member until he accepts the group's own system for assigning status.

This is the crucial point in Cressey's formula, and it is on this point that Synanon seems most effective. The house has an explicit program for distributing status symbols to members in return for staying off the drug and, later, for actually displaying antidrug attitudes. The resident, no longer restricted to the status of "inmate" or "patient" as in a prison or hospital, can achieve any staff position in the status hierarchy.

The Synanon experience is organized into a career of roles that represent stages of graded competence, at whose end are roles that might later be used in the broader community. Figure 1 shows the status system in terms of occupational roles, each box signifying a stratum. Such cliques as exist at Synanon tend to be among persons of the same stratum. Significantly, obtaining jobs of increased responsibility and status is almost completely dependent upon one's attitudes toward crime and the use of drugs. To obtain a job such as Senior Coordinator, for example, the member must have demonstrated that he can remain free of drugs, crime, and alcohol for at least three to six months. Equally important, he must show that he can function without drugs in situations where he might have used drugs before he came to Synanon. Since he is believed to have avoided positions of responsibility by taking drugs, he must gradually take on positions of responsibility without the use of drugs. Thus, he cannot go up the status ladder unless his "attitudes" are right, no matter what degree of skill he might have as a workman. Evaluation is rather casual, but it is evaluation nevertheless—he will not be given a decent job in the organization unless he relinquishes the role of the "con artist" and answers questions honestly, expresses emotions freely, co-operates in group activities, and demonstrates leadership. In a letter to a public official in May, 1960, the founder explained the system as follows:

Continued residence [at Synanon], which we feel to be necessary to work out the problem of interpersonal relationships which under-

lie the addiction symptom is based on adherence by the individual to standards of behavior, thinking, and feeling acceptable to our culture. There is much work to be done here, as we have no paid help, and each person must assume his share of the burden. Increased levels of responsibility are sought and the experience of self-satisfaction comes with seeking and assuming these higher levels and seems to be an extremely important part of emotional growth.[12]

An analogy with a family and the development of a child also is used. Officially, every member is expected to go through three "stages of growth," indicated by Roman numerals in Figure 1. State I has two phases, "infancy" and "adolescence." In the "infancy" phase (I-A) the member behaves like an infant and is treated as one; as he kicks the habit "cold turkey" (without the aid of drugs) in the living room, he is dependent on the others, and he is supervised and watched at all times. When he is physically and mentally able, he performs menial tasks such as dishwashing and sweeping in a kind of "preadolescent" stage (I-AB) and then takes on more responsible positions (I-B). In this "adolescence" phase he takes on responsibility for maintenance work, participates actively in group meetings, demonstrates a concern for "emotional growth," mingles with newcomers and visitors, and accepts responsibilities for dealing with them. In work activities, for example, he might drive the group's delivery truck alone, watch over a sick addict, supervise the dishwashing or cleanup crews, or meet strangers at the door.

Stage II is called the "young adult stage." Here, the member is in a position to choose between making Synanon a "career," attending school, or going to work at least part time. If he works for Synanon, his position is complex and involves enforcing policy over a wide range of members. In Stage III, "adult," he moves up to a policy-making position in the Board of Directors or moves out of Synanon but returns with his friends and family for occasional visits. He can apparently resist the urge to resort to drugs in times of crisis without the direct help of Synanon members. One man described this stage by saying, "They go out, get jobs, lose jobs, get married, get divorced, get married again, just like everyone else." However, the group does maintain a degree of control. Graduates are never supposed to cut off their ties with their Synanon "family," and they are expected to return frequently to display themselves as "a dope fiend made good."

From Table 5 it is apparent that seniority in the form of length of residence (equivalent to the number of "clean" days) is an important determinant of status. As time of residence increases, responsibilities to the group, in the forms of work and leadership, tend to increase. In June, 1962, twenty-seven of the 105 members of Synanon were in Stage II. It should be noted that while stage is associated with length of residence, advancement through the stages is not automatic. The longer one lives as Synanon, the "cleaner" he is, the more diffuse the roles he performs, and the higher his status.

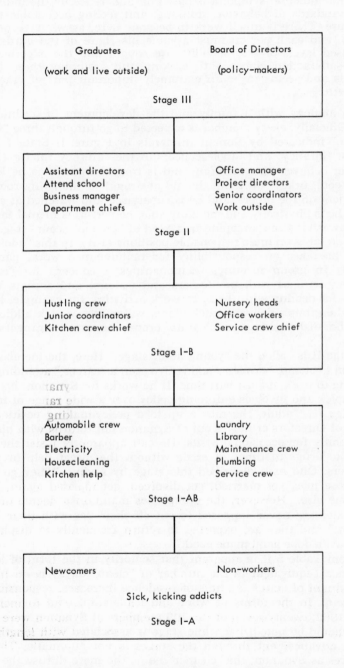

Figure 1—*Division of labor and stratification system, Synanon, June, 1962.*

Table 5—Length of Residence and "Stage" of Members, June, 1962

Length of Residence (in Months)	I	STAGES II	III	No.	Per Cent
1–3	20	0	0	20	19
4–6	15	0	0	15	14
7–9	7	3	0	10	9
10–12	2	0	0	2	2
13–15	3	4	0	7	7
16–18	3	0	2	5	5
19–21	4	1	0	5	5
22–24	0	4	1	5	5
25 and over	0	12	24	36	34
Total	54	24	27	105	100

It is also important to note that high status does not depend entirely upon one's conduct within the house. Before he graduates to Stage III a member must in some way be accorded an increase in status by the legitimate outside community. This is further insurance that status will be conferred for activities that are antidrug in character. In early 1960, the members began to take an active part in legitimate community activities, mostly in the form of lectures and discussion groups. Since Synanon's inception, more than 350 service groups, church groups, political groups, school and college classes, etc., have been addressed by speakers from Synanon. Such speeches and discussions gain community support for the organization, but they further function to give members a feeling of being important enough to be honored by an invitation to speak before community groups. Similarly, members are proud of those individuals who have "made good" in the outside community by becoming board members of the P.T.A., Sunday-school teachers, college students, and members of civic and service organizations. Over thirty-five Synanon members are now working full or part time in the community, holding a wide range of unskilled (janitor, parking attendant), skilled (truck driver, carpenter, electrician), white-collar (secretary, photographer), and executive (purchasing agent) posts.

Further, the legitimate status of the *group* has increasingly risen during the last two years. Since the summer of 1960, an average of 100–150 guests have attended open-house meetings, and the guests have included distinguished persons from all walks of legitimate life. Well-known psychiatrists, correctional workers, businessmen, newspapermen, and politicians have publicly praised the work of the group. There have been requests for Synanon houses and for Synanon groups from several communities, and Synanon projects are now being conducted at Terminal Island Federal Prison and the Nevada State Prison. Recently, the group has been featured in films, on television and radio shows, and in national magazines. At least two books and a movie are being written about it. Over five hundred citizens have formed an organization called "Sponsors of Synanon." Even strong attacks from some members of the local community and complicated legal battles about

zoning ordinances have served principally to unite the group and maximize the *esprit de corps*.

THE "SYNANON"

Synanon got its name from an addict who was trying to say "seminar." The term "Synanon" is used to refer to the entire organization, but when it is spelled with a lower-case *s* it refers only to the meetings occurring in the evenings among small groups of six to ten members. Each evening, all members are assigned to such groups, and membership in the groups is rotated so that one does not regularly interact with the same six or ten persons. The announced aim of these meetings is to "trigger feelings" and to allow what some members refer to as "a catharsis." The sessions are not "group therapy" in the usual sense, for no trained therapist is present. Moreover, the emphasis is on enforcing anticriminal and antidrug norms, as well as upon emotional adjustment.[13] These sessions, like the entire program, constitute a system for implementing Cressey's fifth principle, although they were not designed to do so.

> *The most effective mechanism for exerting group pressure on members will be found in groups so organized that criminals are induced to join with noncriminals for the purpose of changing other criminals. A group in which criminal A joins with some noncriminals to change criminal B is probably most effective in changing criminal A, not B; in order to change criminal B, criminal A must necessarily share the values of the anticriminal members.*

In the house, the behavior of all members is visible to all others. What a member is seen to do at the breakfast table, for example, might well be scrutinized and discussed at his synanon that evening. The synanon sessions differ from everyday honesty by virtue of the fact that in these discussions one is expected to *insist on* the truth as well as to tell the truth. Any weapon, such as ridicule, cross-examination, or hostile attack, is both permissible and expected. The sessions seem to provide an atmosphere of truth-seeking that is reflected in the rest of the social life within the household so that a simple question like "How are you?" is likely to be answered by a five-minute discourse in which the respondent searches for the truth. The following discussion is from a tape recording of a synanon session held in June, 1961. It should be noted that an "innocent" question about appearance, asked by an older member who has become a non-criminal and a non-addict, led to an opportunity to emphasize the importance of loyalty to the antidrug, anticrime group.

What are you doing about losing weight?
Why? Is that your business?

I asked you a question.

I don't intend to answer it. It's not your business.

Why do you want to lose weight?

I don't intend to answer it.

Why?

Because it's an irrelevant and meaningless question. You know I had a baby only three weeks ago, and you've been attacking me about my weight. It's none of your business.

Why did you call your doctor?

Why? Because I'm on a diet.

What did he prescribe for you?

I don't know. I didn't ask him.

What did you ask for?

I didn't. I don't know what he gave me.

Come on now. What kind of pills are they?

I don't know. I'm not a chemist. Look the doctor knows I'm an addict. He knows I live at Synanon. He knows a whole lot about me.

Yeah, well, I heard you also talking to him on the phone, and you sounded just like any other addict trying to con a doctor out of pills.

You're a goddamned liar!

Yeah, well X was sitting right there. Look, does the doctor know and does the Board know?

I spoke to Y [Board member]. It's all been verified.

What did Y say?

I was talking to . . .

What did Y say?

Well, will you wait just a minute?

What did Y say?

Well, let her talk.

I don't want to hear no stories.

I'm not telling stories.

What did Y say?

That it was harmless. The doctor said he'd give me nothing that would affect me. There's nothing in it. He knows it all. I told Y.

Oh, you're all like a pack of wolves. You don't need to yell and scream at her.

Look, I heard her on the phone and the way she talked she was trying to manipulate the doctor.

Do you resent the fact that she's still acting like a dope fiend and she still sounds like she's conning the doctor out of something? She's a dope fiend. Maybe she can't talk to a doctor any differently.

Look, I called the doctor today. He said I should call him if I need him. He gave me vitamins and lots of other things.

Now wait a minute. You called to find out if you could get some more pills.

Besides, it's the attitude they heard over the phone. That's the main thing.

Yeah, well they probably projected it onto me.

Then how come you don't like anyone listening to your phone calls?

Are you feeling guilty?

Who said?

Me. That's who. You even got sore when you found out X and me heard you on the phone, didn't you? You didn't like that at all, did you?

Is that so?

(*Silence.*)

I don't think her old man wants her back.

Well, who would? An old fat slob like that.

Sure, that's probably why she's thinking of leaving all the time and ordering pills.

Sure.

(*Silence.*)

My appearance is none of your business.

Everything here is our business.

Look, when a woman has a baby you can't understand she can't go back to normal weight in a day.

Now *you* look. We're really not interested in your weight problem now. Not really. We just want to know why you've got to have pills to solve the problem. We're going to talk about that if we want to. That's what we're here for.

Look, somethin's bugging you. We all know that. I even noticed it in your attitude toward me.

Yeah, I don't care about those pills. I want to know how you're feeling. What's behind all this? Something's wrong. What is it?

(*Silence.*)

Have you asked your old man if you could come home yet?

(*Softly.*) Yes.

What did he say?

(*Softly.*) He asked me how I felt. Wanted to know why I felt I was ready to come home. . . .

(*Silence.*)

(*Softly.*) I did it out of anger. I wasn't very happy. (*Pause.*) A day before I tried [telephoning him] and he wasn't there. (*Pause.*) Just this funny feeling about my husband being there and me here. My other kid's there and this one's here. (*Pause.*) A mixed-up family.

Why do you want to stay then? Do you want to be here?

No. I don't want to be here. That's exactly why I'm staying. I need to stay till I'm ready.

Look, you've got to cut them loose for a while. You may not be ready for the rest of your life. You may not ever be able to be with those people.

(*Tears.*)

I know. . . .

After the synanon sessions, the house is always noisy and lively. We have seen members sulk, cry, shout, and threaten to leave the group as a result of conversation in the synanon. The following comments, every one of which represents the expression of a pro-reform attitude by the speaker, were heard after one session. It is our hypothesis that such expressions are the important ones, for they indicate that the speaker has become a reformer and, thus, is reinforcing his own pro-reform attitudes every time he tries to comfort or reform another.

Were they hard on you?

I really let him have it tonight.

I couldn't get to her. She's so damned blocked she couldn't even hear what I was trying to tell her.

Hang tough, man; it gets easier.

One of these days he'll drop those defenses of his and start getting honest.

Don't leave. We all love you and want you to get well.

At Synanon, disassociating with former friends, avoiding street talk, and becoming disloyal to criminals are emphasized at the same time that loyalty to non-criminals, telling the truth to authority figures, and legitimate work are stressed. We have no direct evidence that haircuts, synanons, and both formal and spontaneous denunciations of street talk and the code of the streets have important rehabilitative effects on the actor, as well as (or, perhaps even "rather than") on the victim. It seems rather apparent, however, that an individual's own behavior must be dramatically influenced when he acts in the role of a moral policeman and "takes apart" another member. It is significant that older members of Synanon like to point out that the "real Synanon" began on "the night of the big cop out" (confession). In its earliest day, Synanon had neither the group cohesiveness nor the degree of control it now has. Some participants remained as addicts while proclaiming their loyalty to the principle of antiaddiction, and other participants knew of this condition. One evening in a general meeting a man spontaneously stood up and confessed ("copped out") that he had sneaked out for a shot. One by one, with no prompting, the others present rose to confess either their own violations or their knowledge of the relations of their friends. From that moment, the Board of Directors believe, the organization became a truly antidrug group; there has been no problem of drug use since.

The Results

Of the fifty-two residents described earlier, four are "graduates" of Synanon, are living in the community, and are not using alcohol or drugs. Twenty-three (44.2 per cent) are still in residence and are not using alcohol or drugs. Two of these are on the Board of Directors and eleven are working part or full time. The remaining twenty-five left Synanon against the advice of the Board and the older members.

Information regarding the longest period of voluntary abstinence from drugs after the onset of addiction but prior to entering Synanon was obtained on forty-eight of the fifty-two persons. Eleven reported that they were "never" clean, six said they were continuously clean for less than one week, ten were continuously clean for less than one month. Thirty-nine (81 per cent) said they had been continuously clean for less than six months, and only two had been clean for as long as a one-year period. Twenty-seven (52 per cent) of

the fifty-two residents have now abstained for at least six months; twelve of these have been clean for at least two years and two have been off drugs continually for over three years.

Between May, 1958 (when Synanon started), and May, 1961, 263 persons were admitted or readmitted to Synanon. Of these, 190 (72 per cent) left Synanon against the advice of the Board of Directors and the older members. Significantly, 59 per cent of all dropouts occurred within the first month of residence, 90 per cent within the first three months. Synanon is not adverse to giving a person a second chance, or even a third or fourth chance: of the 190 persons dropping out, eighty-three (44 per cent) were persons who had been readmitted. The drop-out behavior of persons who were readmitted was, in general, similar to first admissions; 64 per cent of their dropouts occurred within the first month, 93 per cent within the first three months after readmission.

Of all the Synanon enrollees up to August, 1962, 108 out of 372 (29 per cent) are known to be off drugs. More significantly, of the 215 persons who have remained at Synanon for at least one month, 103 (48 per cent) are still off drugs; of the 143 who have remained for at least three months, 95 (66 per cent) are still non-users; of the 87 who have remained at least seven months, 75 (86 per cent) are non-users. These statistics seems to us to be most relevant, for they indicate that once an addict actually becomes a member of the antidrug community (as indicated by three to six months of participation), the probability that he will leave and revert to the use of drugs is low.

Conclusions

Synanon's leaders do not claim to "cure" drug addicts. They are prone to measure success by pointing to the fact that the organization now includes the membership of forty-five persons who were heroin addicts for at least ten years. Two of these were addicted for more than thirty years and spent those thirty years going in and out of prisons, jails, the U.S. Public Service Hospital, and similar institutions. The leaders have rather inadvertently used a theory of rehabilitation that implies that it is as ridiculous to try to "cure" a man of drug addiction as it is to try to "cure" him of sexual intercourse. A man can be helped to stay away from drugs, however, and this seems to be the contribution Synanon is making. In this regard, its "success" rate is higher than that of those institutions officially designated by society as places for the confinement and "reform" of drug addicts. Such a comparison is not fair, however, both because it is not known whether the subjects in Synanon are comparable to those confined in institutions, and because many official institutions do not concentrate on trying to keep addicts off drugs, being content to withdraw the drug, build up the addicts physically, strengthen vocational skills, and eliminate gaps in educational backgrounds.[14]

We cannot be certain that it is the group relationships at Synanon, rather than something else, that is keeping addicts away from crime and drugs. However, both the times at which dropouts occur and the increasing antidrug attitudes displayed with increasing length of residence tend to substantiate Sutherland's theory of differential association and Cressey's notion that modifying social relationships is an effective supplement to the clinical handling of convicted criminals. Drug addiction is, in fact, a severe test of Sutherland's sociological theory and Cressey's sociological principles, for addicts have the double problem of criminality and the drug habit. The statistics on dropouts suggest that the group relations method of rehabilitation does not begin to have its effects until newcomers are truly integrated into the antidrug, anticrime group that is Synanon.

Notes

1. Donald R. Cressey, "Changing Criminals: The Application of the Theory of Differential Association," *American Journal of Sociology*, LXI (September, 1955), 116–20 (see also Cressey, "Contradictory Theories in Correctional Group Therapy Programs," *Federal Probation*, XVIII [June, 1954], 20–26).

2. Harry J. Anslinger, "Drug Addiction," *Encyclopaedia Britannica*, VII (1960), 677–79.

3. Edwin H. Sutherland and Donald R. Cressey, *Principles of Criminology* (6th ed.; Philadelphia: J. B. Lippincott Co., 1960), pp. 74–80.

4. See, however, Joseph A. Cook and Gilbert Geis, "Forum Anonymous: The Techniques of Alcoholics Anonymous Applied to Prison Therapy," *Journal of Social Therapy*, III (First Quarter, 1957), 9–13.

5. The Board at first was composed of the three original members. It is now made up of the founder (an ex-alcoholic but a non-addict) and seven long-term residents who have remained off drugs and who have demonstrated their strict loyalty to the group and its principles.

6. Rita Volkman, "A Descriptive Case Study of Synanon as a Primary Group Organization" (unpublished Master's thesis, Department of Education, University of California, Los Angeles, 1961).

7. In May, 1961, 20 per cent of the residents were Jewish.

8. Cf. Research Center for Human Relations, New York University, *Family Background as an Etiological Factor in Personality Predisposition to Heroin Addiction* (New York: the Author, 1956).

9. Of the fifty-two members 60 per cent first heard about Synanon from addicts on the street or in jails, prisons, or hospitals; about a fourth heard about it on television or read about it in a magazine; and the remainder were told of it by members or past members.

10. Alfred R. Lindesmith, *Opiate Addiction*, Bloomington: Principia Press, 1947), pp. 44–66.

11. See Lewis Yablonsky, "The Anti-Criminal Society: Synanon," *Federal Probation*, XXVI (September, 1962), 50–57; and Lewis Yablonsky, *The Violent Gang* (New York: Macmillan Co., 1962), pp. 252–63.

12. See Volkman, *op. cit.*, pp. 90–96.

13. See Cressey, "Contradictory Theories in Correctional Group Therapy Programs," *op. cit.*

14. Cf. Harrison M. Trice, "Alcoholism: Group Factors in Etiology and Therapy," *Human Organization*, XV (Summer, 1956), 33–40 (see also Donald R. Cressey, "The Nature and Effectiveness of Correctional Techniques," *Law and Contemporary Problems*, XXIII [Fall, 1958], 754–71).

An Addict Tells His Story

Well, it's kind of hard to start. Shall I go back to Albuquerque when I was a kid and when they sent my father to prison for burglary? He wasn't working. He used to work on the WPA—$24.00 a month, I think it was—every fifteen days. But I loved him very much. My father gave us more affection than my mother —she loved us but I guess in a different way—her actions were—and he gave me more affection, and therefore when they sent him to prison it really hurt me. I can't forget that.

He used to take off at night—used to take off for two or three hours and come back with things for us. We were poor, you know. Clean, but poor. And one time this came to my mind. It was Christmas Day and all of us woke up and we didn't have nothing, you know, for Christmas, so he left early in the morning. He used to go and take a walk down to my grandmother's in Albuquerque—they lived about two or three miles, and he used to go and bring us food or something like that. And that day, that Christmas, he left and he came with a box full of toys and things for us and he told us that the mailman or something was running and was going on a truck and they just dropped it and—well, the truck didn't come back or something. I don't know where he had it, and I thought a lot about him and things that come to my mind—he done that for us.

But going back to when he went to prison, my mother and my aunt come in from court and they said that they send your father to prison. I don't remember if I knew what prison was but at the time I just ran into a room—see we had that room there where people visit, you know

A tape recorded interview (slightly edited) obtained from a narcotic addict who was a participant in the Narcotic Treatment Control Program of the State of California, Department of Corrections. The respondent was interviewed in the state prison of Chino, California, where he had been retained for 90 days of intensive treatment of relapse to use of drugs while on parole. The interview was obtained as part of the research effort of the project. The interviewer, Arthur Pearl, was in charge of research of the project.

they must save it for people—and I went in there and cried and cried and cried. I thought the world had come to an end for me.

We had to separate. Two of my mother's children were from her first husband—he had died—and three of us were—there was four, but one my grandmother had raised (she was over there all the time) my sister, Sallie. That left Joe, Dolores, and I, and we had to get separated and I didn't understand why my grandfather and grandmother didn't want to take the other two kids because I always looked at them as my brother and sister. I didn't think they were half-brother and half-sister. They took us three and we went to live with my grandmother and grandfather, you know, and I kept hearing things about my mother—like other men involved and things like that. They never did care much for my mother. I went to school to second grade, until six months later my father got out and took us back.

It was politics there—and my grandfather—that's why I couldn't understand why my father couldn't make nothing of himself. My grandfather was a very intelligent man and he was in politics in his own small way but he had something. He used his head and he worked and I never could understand why my father was like that. My grandfather used to get him jobs and he would last a little while and quit then or get fired or something. But most of the time that I remember my father I can remember more times that he didn't work than he worked.

It was different with my mother, she always—she worked for $1.00 a day, I remember, that time. She used to go and clean houses out there in the Heights. That's a part of Albuquerque where people with a little money used to live and she used to take me with her and I used to clean the yard for the people and the lawn and all that, and they used to pay me. And she used to work for $1.00. Now it comes to me, my mother sure did work hard—four or five hours for just $1.00.

And I don't know what happened—all of a sudden my mother left to California so that left my father who was at home and my stepbrothers and sisters and the family—there was about six of us. I was a kid then, you know, and then my father left us and he said that he had arranged everything with my grandfather and grandmother for us to stay over there, but he hadn't. He just left us with my older sister—she was married then. But he left so I always stood it in my mind that he didn't love us very much. After all he showed us a lot of love but to leave us like that. I don't think I would ever leave my kids like that, you know.

My sister didn't know what to do so the thing actually we had to do was go back with my grandfather and grandmother, and when I asked them, "I remember my father had fixed everything with you," he said "No, he didn't tell us nothing."

I keep coming back to my sister—that was originally our house, where my sister stayed with my brother-in-law. I used to take her dresses and there was an old lady that had a store there that used to buy the dresses. I was around eleven or ten, you know, and I sold about three or four of her dresses, I don't know, for two cents or three cents, you

know, and then my brother-in-law he found out and he give me a beating. He didn't beat me like a—try to understand me—like a kid or nothing, you know. He just boom, boom, you know, like a man, kicked me. There was a lot of older guys than me there and my brother, my older brother, and none of them tried to stop him from hitting me. He just went to work on me, kicking me and hitting me, all the time I wasn't thinking of my brother-in-law hitting me. I was thinking of my father hitting my mother and that they had left us like that. I was mostly sorry for myself.

Then I remember when my grandfather brought us here (Los Angeles) on the train. My father and my mother sent him money over there. They decided that they were going to stay here and then sent some money, and I don't know the circumstances, but they sent some money over there to send us on the train, and my grandfather said, "No, I'm going to take them over and hand them to you. I won't send them by themselves." So they put us on the train and brought us here.

It was a rainy day, I remember, when we got in. We lived on Olive and First. They had one room—kitchen and one room and a bedroom. Let's see, there was about five then of us. Two beds. My sister slept with my father and mother—my youngest sister. She was small then and my brother and I slept in the other bed. And I cried a lot. I wanted to go back. I was real sad. I wanted to go back to Albuquerque. I told them I didn't want to stay here in Los Angeles. I used to cry a lot, you know. I guess I was a cry-baby—they used to call me the cry-baby. And then I remember telling them "O.K." I said to myself, I don't recall if I told this, to my mother or to myself, but I remember real clearly, I was going to get in trouble and do everything. If they wanted me to stay here I was going to be the worst kid there is.

I don't know if that had anything to do with it but I wasn't going to school. My mother sent me to a registered school, because she was very much for school. You see my mother was mostly—well, she was the brains. She was intelligent, working, and very clean and very pretty and my father just didn't give a damn if we go to school or not. So I used to go to the shows down on Main Street to the Jay Theatre where you could get in for a nickle and see four pictures and the truant officer caught me one night—day. I don't know how I handled that situation but all I know I found myself enrolled in Central Junior High.

I wasn't making any progress in school. I wanted to learn but I wasn't making any progress, you see, and I felt very self-conscious. I remember if anything pertained to me, if the teacher asked me for something, I used to get red in the face. If they asked me to read I used to get red in the face. I tried to learn but I couldn't and then they sent me to Fort Hill. That's a school where they send, you know, kids that mess up—fight or something like that. And I wanted to go to Fort Hill. Oh, I was a big shot then, see? I used to feel real important, walking along with the guys because I was coming from the all-boys school. The kids from the other side used to see me in there and I felt real important because I was going to that school, you know.

We used to take money, you know, off the kids to eat hot dogs and things like that. So I wanted to borrow from an Anglo kid, you know, Mexican-Anglo. He was a little taller than me and I asked him for a nickel. He didn't want to give me a nickel so I started fighting with him. So he told the principal, Mr. Smith. So they called me over and without a chance to explain myself sent me to Jackson High School. That's worser yet. Well, it's a trade school, but it's supposed to have the delinquent kids and all that.

The next day a teacher went out there for me and they felt that they had done the wrong thing in sending me over there so fast without giving me a chance to explain myself because I was doing good in my working at Fort Hill, as far as book learning is concerned. They said, "If you want to come back here it's all right," and I said, "No, I want to stay where I am at Jackson." Jackson was mostly gangs out there, see? I was a little scared going out there—there was nothing but rough kids, you know. Even if you tried to learn in your classroom, well, you was nothing if you went against the crowd. You had to go along with them, so I guess ever since then I've been hiding my feelings, you know. I wanted to do the other thing, you know, if I felt that some guy was doing wrong to a kid I wanted to tell him, "Don't do that" and all that. But if I did that I wouldn't belong or they would pick at me and I'd have to get in a fight and I didn't want to do that. So I went along with them—I just went along for the ride.

I didn't learn nothing. It was mostly grade school and I didn't learn nothing. So from there I told them that I was going to Albuquerque, and to give me a transfer. I don't know where my mother and father were all this time but I took it upon myself. So they gave me a transfer—they didn't put too much pressure on me or anything like that.

I don't recall if I actually left for Albuqueque but I found myself enrolled in Metropolitan High School—that's where you had to go four hours a week to school, you know, and work. When you wasn't working you had to go four hours a day and look for work in the afternoon, and if you was working you just had to go four hours every week. I remember I had it in the afternoon—I slept all day. My mother was working and my father was working—they gave me money. And I went to school—didn't learn anything, you know. Just going. All the teachers did was just pass you. I just got along the best I could, and I was about sixteen then.

That's the way it went for a while. Then I started working. I worked at Melody Lane—or, no, selling papers for a little while. I used to work four hours every day when I got out of school. (It's coming to me now, I'm going back.) I remember working at Melody Lane—that was a little before my mother died—and the money I used to get there. I used to make about $35.00 a week in tips. Melody Lane is a restaurant down on Eighth and Hill—I worked there as a bus boy. I was about seventeen then, in 1947. My mother died when I was working there. I used to get a lot of compliments from the manager. I used to be one of the best bus boys there, you know. Once I had fifteen tables. I'd clean the

dishes—oh, I was a good worker, you know. But I still felt it was beneath me to clean other people's garbage and dishes, you know. Some rich people used to come in there with women or girls, or some girl my age, and I tried to hide. And if I had to do it in front of them, oh, I felt embarrassed. I felt like they said, "Well, look at this guy—look what he is—he's nothing because he's got to clean the dishes." I felt self-conscious of myself for doing that for people but still I did it.

I used to have a lot of arguments with the waitress there. I was doing good but still I just got along with certain people and argued with other people. They had a hostess—she come to me and told me, "You know you're a nice worker and all that but how come you argue?" I think I took a tip from this waitress, you see. You're not supposed to take tips. They give you the tips—the money is on the table. You leave it there and the waitress takes it, and I think I took a half-dollar that time. In fact I'm sure I did. Well, you don't do that because the waitresses knew. Mostly the same people come to eat there and they knew how much they had on the table and all that. It was stupid of me, but I did it and I denied it but this waitress, she was crying for her money and all that, and I denied it all the way, you know, and then she went and told the hostess and I still denied it and then they told the manager, Mr. Moody. So Mr. Moody said, "Look, you have to straighten out," and all that, you know, "but you're a good bus boy. You work good, you look nice, you're presentable and all that." He gave me a lot of compliments, but "You have to straighten out, not to argue too much." "O.K.," I said, "Mr. Moody." So they transferred me to behind the counter—working behind the counter, see? Where they sell ice cream and all that. I was doing very good there and I was even helping the ice cream man there —I felt important then. He was teaching me how to be a soda jerk. To me that was really good because I was doing something then. I used to see girls come in and I used to act real proud of myself. But I wasn't. You know I was just mixing the ice cream—little things he let me do, see? And this accident I had once—that sort of got me away. You know molasses, it comes in great big cans and when you slide it in the counter there you have to easy it, you know. Well, I let it drop so I wouldn't catch my fingers and it just spilled all over some man and some women that was there—some office workers, you know. Spilled all over their clothes. I was so humiliated to the point that I think I got red and orange and all colors. So I ran downstairs and I don't know if it was the manager or the head waiter that come down and told me, "Well, it wasn't your fault, you didn't know. This soda jerk—he shouldn't have let you put that there because it is hard to go in there so don't feel bad." But I was embarrassed with myself—real embarrassed—like I couldn't go back up there and work again and this man wanted to get me fired and this woman, see, but Mr. Moody said, "No, all I can do is send your clothes to the cleaners and send us the bill." Nothing else was said about it. But I still had that on my mind.

And then my mother died. I remember the day that my brother came and told me that "she's dead—she died." They had taken her to the hos-

pital. I expected her to die—we all did—because the nurse and doctor told us she had a fifty-fifty chance. So when he got here my brother just looked at me and I said, "No, it didn't happen." I said, "No, no, no." So I told Mr. Moody about it and Mr. Moody was very nice about it and he said, "Do you need any money?" I said, "No, I don't need any money." So for the first time in my life someone offered me money and I refused it. At that time it was one of the only times that I ever refused money.

I remember it was close to Christmas because she died December 10, three days after her birthday—that's why I remember so clearly. So while she was getting arranged for the funeral and everything I got my check, $35.00, and I went and bought and spent it all on other kids— on my nephews and nieces and everybody, see? In fact my niece is about eighteen years old now and she still has the little kimono—she never forgot the little kimono. I went and bought things for everybody. I wanted to spend the whole check on everyone. I don't know why. I was happy because I was buying things for everyone.

I remember the wake—my mother—seeing my mother—she didn't look exactly like she was—she didn't look as pretty as she was. Of course she suffered a lot when she died. And I remember that I used to feel that people know about me—they know what kind of kid I was. I had no respect for my mother and all that and what's the use of crying because everyone say I don't feel nothing and that I'm putting on an act, and my sister—every time my sister looked my way I felt like "you killed her." I was the last one to leave that night. I remember I stood there—about twelve or one o'clock. I was the last one to leave. I stood by her coffin all the time, thinking how chicken I had been, you know. And I remember even telling the man that runs the mortuary, I said, "This is a nice business you got" or something about a business and he said, "This is no business, this is art," and he took me on a trip, you know. He told me a tale, told me a long story, you know it has to be in your heart—it has to be in you to want to work like that—not just any-one can do it. It made a lot of sense what he told me.

Then I left. I went home. I got to the room—just my father, my younger brother and sister and myself were there, and my aunt I think had come from Albuquerque. I saw my father crying and as much as I love my father and I still do I said, "You don't mean it!" I thought my father was putting on an act when he was crying out loud. I said, "You don't mean it—you don't love her that much" or something, you know, because he didn't work. But I didn't say it out loud, I just thought it and I got a guilty feeling for thinking that, you know, and I went to bed and cried in bed all night and then I dreamed of my mother, but I dreamed she was alive and ever since then I always dream of my mother living. I hate to remember how I saw her in the coffin because she wasn't the same woman.

Well, we buried that on behind and she left a little money—even to the day she died she had a little money. She had it in the bank—she wanted to buy a home—she was always planning for a home. She wanted to move out to the suburbs—to Whittier—and buy a home and

live because in Albuquerque we were poor like I told you but we were clean. That's one thing I learned from my mother, manners and cleanliness. She was a clean woman. We lived in that apartment and believe me it was dirty but our room and as poor as we were we were clean and she had it clean. And oh, that's one thing I like to brag about my mother, how clean, and manners she used to have. She used to brag about never stealing nothing, "Not even a safety pin have I stolen." She left that money—she was going to buy a home. She was working and she left social security benefit and insurance and even to her death she contributed something to the house and I thought that about my father, you know, but I never said it to anybody.

I thought, well, my mother went to work—and my father, he cleaned the house or something like that and then he cleaned himself and went out to the barn and then come back and had everything prepared for when we kids come from somewhere—I don't remember—my mother was alive, you see. And then about twelve o'clock go pick up my mother when she got out of work. She was working at the National Biscuit Company, she was the floor lady. She had even got a promotion. She worked there a long time. And that's all he did. I remember him telling —that's why there's a doubt in my mind—I remember him telling my mother something that to me I figure that he found out something somewhere I guess about my mother. I guess my mother had somebody love her, I don't remember. That's why I always try to find out and I tell my sister when my sister come out and said my father don't work. Oh, when my sister said something about my father—one time we were eating dinner one time when I got out of the joint (prison) or something and my sister said that my father was shiftless. They all love him and they like him—there's something about him that you can't help but like him, you know, he's very sweet and all that. But my sister said something about my father not working when my mother was alive and I said, "Well, look, Louise, one of these days you and I got to have a serious talk about when my father didn't work." I was getting to it that my father had found out something about my mother and that was why he didn't work, see, ever since that day. Because someone had planted that seed in my mind that my mother had a lover and my sister knew about it and she kept it to herself, see?

After my mother died the whole family spread out. My younger brother, Joe, a very nice guy, wanted to leave to the Army while my mother was alive but he was under age and my mother never would sign, but as soon as my mother died he went. I don't remember if my father signed, but he went. My sister and this guy she is married to now—I don't know if they were married then, I don't think they were, I think they were just shacking out together—they left and everyone left and then I left to Albuquerque.

I left for Albuquerque with the little clothes I had acquired and all that. And we all left from my father—we all went away and left him with that money he had. And I was having a good time in Albuquerque —playing the part, I was a big shot—like I always have, you know. But

still having them guilty feelings—inferiority complexes and all that, see? Oh, I had an inferiority complex about wearing a hat—I had to wear a hat all the time because of my hair. I never took my hat off, and if they asked me to go into a night club—guys were always inviting me and girls, you know—and I wouldn't go because of the reason being—I said everything except the truth—my hair. That was ridiculous, I laugh at it now and I remember girls used to say, "Well, take your hat off," you know.

I remember this Cecelia girl that I met in Albuquerque had a very nice background. We hit it off real good. She was from a wealthy family, you know. And she used to tell me, "Take your hat off" and I never did. I used to say, "No, I don't like nobody to touch that hair." It was my hair all the time. One day I took it off and went down to a restaurant, and I was self-conscious—I was conscious of my hair. So she said, "You know I thought you was bald."

A hat made me look different—I always had compliments—got compliments putting on a hat, you know. I don't know if it made me look like a gangster or pimp or something. A pimp—I wanted to be a pimp all my life. Oh I wanted to be a pimp real bad, you know. I didn't know then how hard it is. You have to be a cold—it's not easy at it seems, you know. But I still had that complex and I felt that Cecelia liked me but I felt that I couldn't do nothing with her because of my background. I said, well, her background is so nice—her people have money. I didn't know then how her people had got that money—where they come from —they just had it. She's educated, has gone to school, and her brother —her brother was one like me. But he had education on the piano but he was a weedhead (marijuana smoker) and he liked me very much.

I started using pot (marijuana) when I was thirteen years old. I remember hanging around with older guys than me all my life. I don't know how we got in that room but I found myself in the room with Big Louie—oh, I thought he was the greatest—and Lodi and Charlie and Tony. We used to call him "Tony, the reefer," and I always heard from my mother and people back home that when you smoke weed you go crazy and you kill. Because there was some other guy there in Albuquerque that used to be a weedhead, but he was a wino at the same time, so he drank wine and smoked weed but the wine made him act the way he did—you know, mean and wanted to fight. I remember that they used to say, "Here comes Tommy," and everybody used to run in their houses and close the door because that man was coming through and he was drunk and they say he was a weedhead—that you kill and all that, see? So they took out a joint (marijuana cigarette) in that room and everybody started blasting and I was scared, you know. I said, "Them guys are going to kill or something," and then Big Louie said, "Well give that kid some so he won't have nothing to say," you know. So I took it. I don't know if they forced me but I took it and I felt good and I laughed a lot but every time they started arguing I thought they were going to kill each other because I had that planted

in my mind and all that, that they would kill each other. I said, "Don't argue," and all like that. So we kept on and when we went to eat and I found out how hungry I was. We ate and we came back to that room. They were guys from Albuquerque—they were hoboing it here. You know, they left home—their home was over there—they didn't have no family.

This was at night. And they lived in the room. They were from Albuquerque so actually they just had a transient room, you know. And we went back to that room and I laughed all night. I slept there with them—I slept in the chair. I pulled the chair by the window and the next day I got up and I tell them, "Oh, what made me laugh so much— how come I was so happy last night?" They said it was the weed. So I came home that morning—I don't know what I told my mother and father but whatever I said they accepted, I guess. Don't get me wrong— my mother tried to give me all the supervision in the world but it was in one ear and out the other.

I went back the second day and asked for it. I wanted the weed. I wanted a blast and I did and ever since then I kept on blowing weed, blowing weed, and I used to come home from school or from wherever I come, and I come and ate. And my mother was there and she was always talking about the—they call them "marijuanos"—and they kill. And I used to look at my mother and think "Oh, how dumb she is. She don't know that they don't kill when you're on weed" and all that. "You just feel good and want to do good things, and you want to dress and look sharp and that's all, you know, but it's nothing like she used to say." I remember it, and I used to smile and keep on eating because you eat a lot, I do anyway, and feel real good—I used to. That's the way I started.

The way my family found out was this way. I was dealing I guess for someone, or someone gave me weed, you know, and out of that weed, I sold them for fifty cents and I got all the joints I could blast. But only I smoked them all. And I was going down Temple Street one time—going to the Cathedral. That's a club where you—they have dancing and parties around and all that, you know, and I had two joints in a Lucky Strike package and instead of going to Temple to get to Olive I went down and tried to cut through Grant Street. There was an alley behind this club—the Cathedral Club we called it, and there was two bulls there—policemen there—and they jumped me. I said, "I don't have nothing—how come you jumped me?" and all the time I was thinking about those two joints and they said, "If you don't have nothing what are you afraid of?" So boom, I took out. . . . He got me and he said (I remember this) he said, "My partner here is a witness. You were found on the safety code," and boom, they handcuffed me. So they're bringing me down to get a car and they took me down to Georgia Receiving Hospital where they take the juveniles.

I was around fifteen or sixteen at that time they took me to Georgia Receiving Juvenile and there they found out I had the gonorrhea. A girl had given me the gonorrhea and I had lasted all this time without

telling my mother and my father about it. I never told them. I thought
it was something you didn't discuss with your mother and father. So
they found out, so they threw me in the hold because they didn't want
to put me in with the rest of the guys. They give me a mattress and a
blanket and they threw me in the hold and the next morning my mother
comes because she was the one that was always there when I was in trouble. And they called me to the juvenile office there—the detective—and
he said that he didn't want to press charges but the narcotic boys did.
Possession of weed, you know, but it was going to be handled through
juvenile courts. But more important is this, "You got the gonorrhea. We
want to know how you got it." And my mother was there, and oh, man!,
I felt real embarrassed, you know. And she said, "Who's the girl?" I said
I didn't know. I knew who the girl was but I said I didn't know. I said
I just met her in the show—took her to the hills. They said, "Just like a
dog." I was saying that—I couldn't look straight at my mother, you
know, and my mother promised then that if they would release me to
her she would take me to a doctor. I guess penicillin was just coming
into its own then, or pills, and that she would pay and that she would
save the State or City all that money. You know, she would pay the
doctor bills. And there's where it comes in, the embarrassment to my
mother. I remember she took me out. The police officer said, "All right."
He was very nice about it, so they took me back to the cell but they
released me and we was walking out and I remember I kept walking
ahead of my mother—she was in the back and she kept calling me
and I'd go back and I don't know what I said but I actually found out
that I asked her for some money to get the street car and I said I'll meet
you somewhere and then we'll go to the doctor which she did. I guess
she understood me more than I did myself—I don't know if I was embarrassed of her or what. I guess I thought it was something sissy to
walk with his mother—or about the gonorrhea—I don't know. She took
me to the doctor but nothing else was said about it.

The story I had given the police about the weed was that I had found
them and I was taking them to the President of that Club—the Cathedral
Club—which wasn't true, of course. I was on probation then for something else, you know. I think it was running away from home and purse
snatching in Bakersfield. We went to court and the probation officer
was there and the judge, my mother, and my father, and my mother
had—she was always—she wasn't religious to extreme, but she was
religious—she had a rosary wrapped around her hand next by me. And
the judge was asking, you know, and I told him how I found it, and
he said, "You don't find that stuff, big boy." I said, "Yes, your Honor, but
I found it." He said, "You don't find that stuff." The probation officer said
that he didn't want to violate but it was up to the judge and then they
ask my mother and my father a few questions—it was mostly my mother
—and then I remember something that he said—the judge—I'll never
forget—I guess I remember compliments more than anything, you know,
because I never thought I was much. He said, "Your son has the makings
of a great man," because evidently I had because there's so many people

testifying. I thought I was using the people but now I realized they was trying to help me.

When we got outside and my probation officer told me that, "You're a very lucky boy. Usually they would send you to Preston or something like that, you know." But I didn't consider myself like that—I considered myself shrewd, you know. I just left and went out to the Cathedral Club and bragged about it to the guys—you know, big shot, me, "I didn't get time—I got more probation," and I kept on using weed.

This girl that caused the gonorrhea wasn't my girl friend. The first I ever had was a little older than me. I was ill. Like I told you—I was always after older people. I was ill. So we got introduced to another girl and another guy and I brought her home—I remember she was even taller than I was—and we grabbed hands and kissed and I brought her home. I remember—I'll never forget it—I was going to grammar school and she was going to junior high. I was in the sixth and I guess she was in the seventh and we used to get out first and I used to run— it was about three or four blocks to junior high—and I used to run to pick her up over there at junior high, see? I guess she was at least two years older than me, so I could take it just grabbing hands and that was my first girl friend. We just kissed—nothing ever—to me, when I was a kid, I always wondered how come kids now get girls thirteen, fourteen years old pregnant. At that time the biggest thing we did was kiss—and kissing was it. When I had my first relation—I can remember that. I had girls but not steady girls after after. I shied away from them. I always been fortunate that way, you know—I always let them make the first move but I never had trouble making girls.

My first relation was in Albuquerque also. It was the wrong girl. I had been in Los Angeles. I was back home—I called it vacation but I used to go over there. There was a bunch of us kids and girls that used to go to this restaurant to drink coffee or eat and there was a waitress there—oh, she was at least five years older than me—and I don't know how the conversation got to her but all of a sudden she was inviting me that night to her room. I never had had relations before with a woman and she called me over and I don't remember where the rest of the kids were when she called me and I said, "Yes." She told me where she lived and I said, "Yes, I'll go tonight." And I come out of there and I met another buddy of mine, and I told him about it but he was hepper than me—he knew what the score was—so he said, "I'll go with you and I'll have her first and then I'll show you what to do" and all that. So I kept going back to this girl. I used to go and knock on the door when she was asleep—I used to go in through the transom. She would wake up and she saw me and she'd say, "Oh, it's you. I was thinking of you." She used to tell me and I used to get in bed with her and do what I had to do and then get up. After that I—but I couldn't see her as —I get like that to a woman that once I had used her I couldn't see her. I thought because a woman took and you gave it that she was nothing.

Then I came back to Los Angeles. I told you all that story. Remem-

ber when I told you that my mother died and we left my father? I'll take it from there. I heard that he was sick and he was running out of money —we used to get letters from my grandmother that he wasn't doing any good here, he was just drunk, spending the money—so I wondered— maybe I could go over there. Him and I always been the closest so I thought maybe I can go over there and help him. So he sent me $13.00 and some rings—some rocks that we used to sell. He taught me how or I taught him—we used to pass them as diamonds and rubies. They would wreck it now but we did it when I was a kid. He sent me that and I sold them—I don't know if I passed them as diamonds or rubies. I don't know if I got $10.00 out of every one of the thirteen but I spent it. So he said, "I want my money," and I said, "No, I worked for that money to come over here." As a matter of fact that's all I had because I remember eating peanuts on the bus to get over here. I had just a pair of pants and an old hat. I had taken clothes but I had sold my clothes.

I spent the money running with crowds and running with girls. I had a girl friend there that I met and she wanted to get married. She was a virgin—and I wanted to get that virgin. I had had one virgin before and to me getting a virgin just for the sake of bragging about it was something that every man had to do. And that night I had gone around with this girl, Lollie, from El Paso, for a little while and we was getting to like each other. I told her if she loved me she would prove it and all that. So that night before I'm coming I want that cherry and she has a sister and another guy took her sister out, like I told you, and I'm working with her, you know. I'm getting her, and I'm working real hard and she said, "No, if you loved me you wouldn't really ask me for this," you know, and all that there, and I said, "No" so I had it my way. I told her, "We'll get married. I'll go to California and make a little money and I'll come back and we'll get married—I'll be here by Christmas." It was September, I guess. And I told her, "I'll come back for you," so I took her skirts off—you know they were real tight on her. And I'm getting to the panties when her sister come and she said, "Lollie, what are you doing?" and I felt disgusted with her—not with her but with the guy that had her sister. "Why can't you take care of your business— why did you let her walk over here," I felt like telling him, but I didn't say nothing. We changed the subject—put the coat on and we didn't do nothing, see? She's still a virgin. They took me to the bus and then they kissed me. They both kissed me—her sister too, and when her sister kissed me I got the feeling I was running around with the wrong sister. That was me—I wanted to make a play for everyone, you know. I wanted to stay over there. Well, anyway I got on the bus and came over here to L.A.—eating peanuts all the way.

When, I met this woman that I had discussed in the group about the prostitute, you know. Well, evidently this woman had seen me. She's older than me—she's thirty-six or thirty-seven. You can say "just like a Cadillac, it gets old but the class is there"—about six years older than me. She had seen me around there when I was a kid—I had talked to her—but she kept telling my father—asking for me all the time and

telling other guys, you know. When I came back I was around eighteen or nineteen and she was about twenty-four, twenty-six. And one morning I woke up and I find a picture of her in my wallet—because I have a habit when I take my pants off I took my wallet and put it next to me. I was living with my father and cousin. I look at the picture—she's a very attractive woman. I wonder what this is doing in here. My father had put it there. He didn't tell me, he just put it there. She gave it to him.

There was a friend of mine. He lived across the street. He was a friend of hers too. He came one time and he said, "Jean wants to meet you." They had sent her old man to the joint—she was by herself then. "And she wants to meet you," he said. I said, "Oh, I don't believe—a girl like that—what does she want with a kid like me?" She was glamorous, beautiful, fine looking. Guys in Cadillacs were going after her and everything, you know. So he said, "Well," you know I couldn't believe that I could get next to a girl like that. I still had that complex. I said, "How can I get next to her?" He said, "I'm going to go up there and I'm going to be up there looking out the window and then you pass across the street from her apartment and I'll pretend like you're just passing by and I'll go like—like that to you and there is where you enter." So we did it that way. I don't know what he told her, if she expected me to do that or what—I know I found myself waving at him and her and she had always told me since I was a kid that she wanted me, you know. And, well I was a kid—I didn't believe her. And to me a woman didn't want me—a woman couldn't have me—I had the woman. I was under that impression. So he called me up and I went upstairs and we met each other and we talked and she kept giving me compliments and compliments and compliments and naturally it was going to my head— that was one of my biggest faults—I didn't know how to go about making a broad like that. She talked to me and the deal was for me to get in her panties, see. She told me she was a prostitute and she had been around with other guys so actually the picture I had of a broad like that—a woman like that—was that she was nowhere. You know how a man thinks that she has been used and that she is nothing, but that night we were on the porch—Eddie and his girl and Jean and I—and she had a negligee, a black negligee, and she looked real pretty because she always dressed well and, I don't know how I got courage but I start feeling her all over and I said, "Well, this woman is not the way they talk about her." I had a picture of being, you know, just an old—she had a fine body, you know—I had had young girls but not too many of them. But this woman I was feeling all over and she felt like a woman to me—real warm and all her curves and all that, see? Well, I found out something that it wasn't like the talk that I heard about her, you know, and all that—it was mostly talk. So I got hot—I wanted to go to bed with her but she said "No. You want something to get over your hotness?" I said, "Yah, come over here." So she took me in the room and gave me some cold orange juice. I remember drinking it and I was mad but I was a young kid so all of a sudden she talked me out of it and I went down stairs and Eddie and I and his girl, and all of a sudden

I get a cramp. I don't know if it was from hotness and I fall down on the curb like that and I stay like that and I tell Eddie where it hurt and he explained why—I never had experienced that. He said I got too emotional or hot or something—I don't know what he said. So he took me home and I went out to the apartment and I remember falling in bed and I was sick—I never had gotten that way. I guess I got too hot and I just fell on the bed—I was sick and the next day I came down with a cold and everything and I didn't see this woman again for about a week or so, and she heard what happened to me and it was all a joke. See I was a young kid—it was all a joke—they had spread the story around. So I used to telephone her, but I didn't say who it was. I'd say it was a mysterious—which means a mysterious weedsmoker or something like that, and I used to talk to her and I had her interested in another guy. It was me that was doing the talking, but I felt that if I told her she would lose interest so I had her believing I was somebody else— oh, I gave her a line over the phone, and she used to get a kick and laugh and say, "Well, who is this?" I'd say, "I'm a great admirer of you" and all that. She didn't know it was me. Not realizing it was me she used to tell me about this mysterious guy who used to call her and it was me, you see?

Then I went up to her—the second time I went up to her apartment we talked and talked and talked and I wanted to get up—Eddie had put the seed in me. Before we got there the second time he said, "You got to lay her." I don't know what was his intention—"Don't let her talk you out of it." I said, "O.K., I'll work it." So I went up there again and she talked me out of it and I know she talked me out of and we left with Eddie and he—went downstairs and then they say, "You go back up there—don't you know that chick wants you real bad—and she's only acting this way because that's a woman's way of acting." I said, "Well, I'm going back there." About fifteen minutes later when I'm going back she's in bed—she's got pajamas. She says, "Who is it?" I said, "It's me" and she said, "Well, what do you want?" "Well, I want to get in—I want to talk to you." She said, "No, you better go on." I said, "Well, I want to get in." She said, "If I let you in will you promise to behave good?" I said, "Yes." She let me in. So the first thing I did was go over to where she was and try to. She said, "No, no." I said, "Well, you wanted me." She said, "Yah, but now I just want you as a friend— you're too young." And I kept on and finally I forced down her pajamas and I made it with her and to me I never had a woman that moved me that much. I used to hear stories about her—maybe that's why I treat her as bad as I do, you know, and all that—but to me that woman I'll never forget it, you know. She got up and I got up and she went to douche—she was in the bathroom, I remember, and I don't know, them words hit her. I said, "Don't forget that I had you now that you're smarter now, that you're wiser." I guess I was trying to tell that a lot of guys had had her before when she was a kid, you know, but I got her when she had wised up and nobody had used her.

I said she was a prostitute—she's not actually—she finds her sugar-

daddy. The fact that I had her I was real proud. She was real beautiful and I know a lot of guys were after her but it bothered me that some other guys were after her, you know. But then it bothered me that some other guys had had her and to me that was taboo for me to have another woman that somebody else had had and remember I had a cherry back home that I was going to marry—and to me that was it, for a guy to get you a virgin. I guess that was the style then. I kept on with this girl, you know, and she told me one time, "You bring in a dollar in here and I'll bring in two." But I guess at first she didn't love me or I don't know what, but we used to argue a lot. The only time I ever felt that I really owned her and she was a woman and I was a man was in bed—when we were having sexual relations. Outside of that I'm not sure of her. We kept on like that and I took her away from where she lived. Pretty soon she went to see her sugar-daddy and she used to come back to me and I would say, "You get in that bathroom and wash yourself." And while I didn't boss her around, well if another guy was there maybe he would be glad for her to go make some money like that—not me. I don't know, I let her go make the money because I guess she wanted to, but when she come back I didn't want her to sleep in the same bed with me. I let her sleep in the bed by herself and I used to go lay somewhere else—the couch or somewhere.

I started using heroin when I was living with her—her and I was living as man and wife. I was making good money hustling, after I stopped working. I stopped working because some other guy told her that I went out with another girl and I made the other girl and things like that. And she went and tears a lot of clothes I had—and messed up. I had a car—I had credit in different stores—I had the zoot suit—in fact I still owe. You know I had credit all over, I was working and she tears my clothes. I had a lot of clothes and a lot of things. We had furniture. And all on account of one guy that told her that I was trying to make another broad. She got drunk and messed my clothes up and everything. So ever since then I said, "What the hell do I build for," you know, "if you're going to destroy it just like that." So ever since then I don't work —I didn't give a damn. We sold that furniture and bought something else. Sold that furniture and moved into a furnished place and from there on I kept hustling. I didn't give a damn what she did to tell you the truth. All I wanted her to be home.

By hustling, I mean playing pool, here, middleman here, and every-thing, you know—not pimping. I had this woman, I loved her, pimping was something very cold to me now. I found out when I had this woman how much it hurt me for her to go and hustle, you know. I found a pimp has to go through a lot—you cannot love a woman and make her hustle, you know. I'm not cold enough to be a pimp. Lot of guys think that being a pimp is easy—you got to be chicken shit and cold and you don't have to have no self-respect.

So, I was making money . . . and living with this woman. And I met this—well, he said he was French, Creole French, but he was strictly, I think, colored guy—Negro. I never been prejudiced. So we

start going out together and he used to bring in money and give it to my old lady—I made a hundred or so—give it to her $25.00, $30.00 and I'd say, "Well, this is for the house," and I kept this for me. Every day, you know, or every two or three days—but out of $25.00 or $30.00, I'd expect her to buy food, pay bills and rent and everything. But I gave her more—about $100.00 a week. But when we started partying— I had too much time on my hands, I guess—that's what I call it. This guy told me something about sniffing snow—they call that white stuff. Colored guys use it a lot—real fine stuff. They bring it in from Germany, I think, not from Mexico. And I knew that would happen if I started using—I had seen all them pimps around Temple Street. They're real big—they start using and then go down. And I admired them—and then as soon as I grew up they were asking me for quarters. All trampy like, all dirty, and they don't give a damn about themselves. Turning and ratting on people—all that, see? I knew what was going to happen—I wasn't ignorant of the fact—so I went out and partied with them, sniffing (inhaling heroin), you know. We got the stuff, and I used it for three or four days straight and then I quit and I didn't see this guy for a little time, and I got sick and I don't know what it was all about. And I telephoned him and I said, "I'm sick." He said, "You're kicking." "I'm kicking? I got hooked so easy?" So he says, "Get some wine and seven-up and kick like that." so Jean she got suspicious of that—she had seen it around somewhere—she hates . . . she still does to this day. She got suspicious of me. I was sick, my bones were hurting, and I was drinking wine. If I had a cold I could have taken aspirin, not drink wine and seven-up, but she just hinted around. So I got over it but then I met this guy again and I found out that this stuff made me feel real good and gave me a lot of confidence, and I felt better when I was going around with my old lady. I could take her out and felt better not that somebody out there had her or that she was a prostitute—I was nothing. Didn't come to me when I was with stuff. I walked out on the street, you know, real big shot, you know. Kept on using then and sniffing. Then I found out that you can sniff a gram or something like that through the nose and it don't get you as high when you fix two caps. And you spend a lot of money, so I started using it in the veins. I fell in '54 for burglary. Oh, I was using quite a bit. I was using about a gram or gram and a half a day—something like that. I got involved in burglary to support my habit. I kicked a couple of times. In fact that time that I got caught I was kicking. But I'd go back each time.

One time this woman kept insisting that I was always loaded—I can remember that—maybe I was on bennies or wine or something, so she said I was loaded on stuff. So I said, "What the hell—she accuses me of it so I'm going to do it," and I came back or maybe I had fights with her and she told me I was nothing and she brought that education up at me and she told me I couldn't support her in the style which she was accustomed to, and she was right. I couldn't do nothing, for her, you know. And I went back to stuff. But one time I stood eight days without it. Kicked at home and she helped me so I said, "I'm going down town."

And she knew where I was going so I wanted to fool myself. I said, "No, I'm not going to use." So I went down town and I still had the sniffs I mean and I met this girl and she said, "Do you want a little one?" And I said, "No, I just got through kicking." After suffering eight days— three hours later I'm back.

I fell on burglary in '54. I didn't go to prison—I went to the county jail and did about ten or eleven months all together. When I came out I went back to this woman. I was back on stuff about three or four months after that. This woman and I weren't hitting it too good, I guess—feeling inadequate or feeling lonesome or rejected—I don't want to burglarize no more. I was idle. I wanted to be a big shot and I didn't want to work for it. I felt like washing dishes or construction work would bring me down if the people around my neighborhood saw me—that I was coming in dirty—so I started using junk and felt real good. You know that complex, you know false pride comes in there.

In '56 I hit this woman a lot—I hit her a lot—and they called the law and they laid me off of the job I had down there and I was hot, I guess, and they send me to prison for burglary in '56. I didn't want to burglarize before I used it—before I used stuff.

When I got out of the joint in '59 I stood out about six or five months without using. I couldn't get a job—the job I wanted, you know. I wanted a big job, and I started feeling the complex again, you know, I started using stuff again, shoplifting. They got me maybe about two months or a month. I went right back after that about four months and here I am.

Response of Adult Heroin Addicts to a Total Therapeutic Program

Alfred M. Freedman, M.D., Clifford J. Sager, M.D., Edwin L. Rabiner, M.D., and Richard E. Brotman, Ph.D.

Narcotic addiction in the United States has represented a challenge to the medical profession for the past half century. Until quite recently, however, that challenge was not accepted. After the passage of the Harrison Act in 1914 and the subsequent judicial interpretations of that act by the United States Supreme Court, the dangers of attempting to treat addicts outweighed for most physicians the possible satisfactions to be derived from treating this group of patients. As a result, narcotic addiction has been of greater concern as a criminal problem than as a medical one, and the law-enforcement official has taken precedence over the doctor in its management. For the individual, however, addiction is a chronic disease closely associated with alienation, rootlessness, institutionalization, and criminality. Perhaps its chief difference from other chronic diseases is the extent to which it meets certain social, psychological—and eventually physical— needs of the patient and is therefore preferred by him to a life free from addiction.

Those writers, including Nyswander (3) and others, who have dealt with the problems associated with the treatment of addicts have drawn a dismal picture of the record of results. Even more disheartening is the sparsity of systematic, scientifically evaluated studies of addiction as a disease and the outcome of treatment efforts. Furthermore, the studies that have been made have been made in prisons, hospital wards and, occasionally, the psychotherapist's office, but little attention- has been

Reprinted from *American Journal of Orthopsychiatry*, Vol. 33, No. 5, October 1963, pp. 890–899. Copyright, the American Orthopsychiatric Association, Inc.

paid to the addict in the social milieu in which he develops his disease, lives with it and retains it in spite of the efforts of psychiatrists, social workers or police to cure him.

The basic criteria of any study directed toward the treatment or elimination of chronic disease should be: selection and description of sample; uniformity of treatment program, in regard to the milieu and philosophy, as well as therapeutic modalities administered; and, lastly, a thorough follow-up of a substantial number of individuals to obtain a reliable picture of the results. These are basic features of any treatment study, coming even before a control group or other refinements of sophisticated, scientific investigation. Without such a basic approach, no one can profit from the work of others, or even from his own previous work; comparisons from center to center cannot be made; and we can gain no clues on the strength of which we can modify existing programs or establish new ones.

An opportunity for systematic study of addiction was afforded by the establishment, in 1959, of a new treatment center for male narcotic addicts in New York City. Although it was never assumed that setting up a new program, even a voluntary one in a general hospital, would lead to a high percentage of cures, the service was viewed as a laboratory for study and research in the treatment of the narcotic addict. Thus, by establishing the service as an action research program, one is able to modify and experiment by utilizing feedback from critical evaluation and follow-up of patients. The patient in treatment becomes an object of study.

The narcotic-addiction treatment unit established at New York Medical College-Metropolitan Hospital Center has three unique features: First, the addict is treated in a general hospital, as part of the psychiatric service. The care of the addict has been moved away from a special hospital, heavily guarded, or fenced in, or placed on an island.

Second, the service has been set up as a benign, voluntary program. As nearly as possible, the addict is treated as a sick patient, just as are other patients in the hospital with special needs (as there are special needs for the patient on cardiovascular surgery or rehabilitation). All the adult patients in the service are voluntary admissions; none who are under the jurisdiction of the court may be admitted.

Third, the department of psychiatry of a medical school is actively engaged in the treatment of addicts and in research into the etiology and therapy of narcotic addiction, utilizing all the resources of a large and active medical center.

The program is based at the Metropolitan Hospital, an 1100-bed, municipal general hospital in East Harlem, an area in which narcotic addiction is endemic. Two wards of 25 beds each are designated for the treatment of heroin addicts. The average anticipated period of hospitalization is 28 days, during which withdrawal by means of Methadone is carried out and the patient is introduced to the aftercare program. Outpatient facilities are available for individual and group psychotherapy. Psychotherapists are, in the main, board-eligible psychiatrists who have

completed or are undergoing psychoanalytic training. Ancillary staff includes social workers, psychologists, vocational counselors and recreation therapists. A social club for discharged patients was established early in the program.

Statement of Treatment Philosophy

The individual addict undergoes a Procrustean experience as he develops heroin addiction. He is brought to addiction by a variety of psychological factors within himself and social forces in the environment. Once addiction is established, his life pattern is shaped by the fact of addiction. Verily, he is cut down or stretched out to fit the "bed" of the addict subculture. No matter what differences exist among the personality structures and social experiences of individuals prior to addiction, the impact of addiction presses individual differences toward a common pattern. Irrespective of its determinants, drug use is taken over by the personality as the dominant mode of dealing with anxiety and producing gratification. The individual is impelled toward new associations and activities for the maintenance of his habit. He enters the addict subculture, which has its own argot, its own hierarchy, and its own value system. His movement between his prior milieu and the addict subculture becomes progressively limited as the social repercussions of his addiction cast him out of his own society. His psychological life line—his drug supply—is as much threatened by those who would medically impose abstinence on him as it is by those who would jail him.

Some seek treatment primarily to facilitate their addiction through reversal of tolerance or substitution of hospital-supplied drug for underworld-supplied drug, but, regardless of the reason for the addict's foray into the treatment world, when he is in it there is an opportunity to alter his motivation and to engage him in rehabilitative efforts. The therapeutic team must establish itself as truthworthy, benevolent, and understanding. It is of prime importance that therapists be available to assist in the crucial struggle against psychic dependency on narcotics when the patient indicates he is sincerely ready to engage in the struggle to end that dependency. Provision must be made for continuing care of the addict through whatever number of relapses he may have. Regardless of his level of readiness to participate, continuing service should be available to him during his times of crisis. If recidivism is related to the fact that addiction is endemic in the urban community, it is here, within the addict's own life space, that the major battle must be fought, not in the remotely placed hospital, work camp or even on the ward of the municipal hospital within the community.

While the operation of the Metropolitan Hospital service derives from this basic treatment philosophy, clinical experience has already led to major modifications in practice. The treatment program has passed through two major phases and is now entering a third.

First Treatment Phase

The first 22 months of operation, beginning in November 1959, were characterized by efforts to apply standard psychotherapeutic practice to the problems of drug addiction. Members of the part-time psychotherapy staff met the patient (who had numerous contacts involving personnel other than the therapists) as soon as possible after his admission for detoxification. It was hoped that the personal relationship established with the individual therapist would provide a bridge to participation in the after care program. To make the program attractive, every effort was made to free detoxification of as much discomfort as possible. Soporific and tranquilizer drugs were prescribed freely in the clinic, but prescriptions were written to carry the patient only up to his next clinic appointment, to reinforce motivation to attend.

Of 490 adults who comprised 683 admissions during the first 22 months, only 66 patients were attending the aftercare clinic in September of 1961. Another dozen or so were regularly attending the social club. In the absence of tests to determine whether these patients were currently using heroin, there were no reliable data on the percentage who had actually altered their pattern of drug use as a result of contact with the program. On the basis of aftercare clinic attendance as a crude and really questionable gauge of effectiveness, the program as it was then set up appeared meaningful to only about one-seventh of the patients.

The treatment continuum began with referral and extended through preadmission screening, admission for detoxification, a drug-free interval on the ward, discharge to aftercare psychotherapy, vocational referral (though not training or placement), the social club and readmission. There were dropouts at all points in the process. Patients referred by agencies often did not arrive at the hospital for screening. Screened patients often could not be located when beds became available. Some patients signed out during detoxification, some afterwards. Some remained on the ward for the suggested 28 days and failed their first clinic appointment. Some came to the clinic one or more times and then dropped out. Each dropout point provided a focus of inquiry upon the fruits of which procedural innovations could be based.

Preadmission dropouts The preadmission screening procedure required several visits to the clinic over an interval of one to two weeks. As the waiting list grew, it was often four to six weeks before actual ward admission could be arranged. During this interval an undetermined but presumably substantial number of applicants were picked up by the police. Some who desperately sought admission passed their point of crisis or moment of fleeting resolve to abandon addiction. Others, unable to wait, sought admission to a nearby proprietary hospital which, though it lacked an aftercare program, admitted far more promptly. The importance of providing more immediate service became increasingly clear to the staff.

How to test the notion that immediate response would minimize dropping out at this point was a difficult problem. This 50-bed unit serves a metropolis estimated to have anywhere from 23,000 to 100,000 addicts. The more attractive the program became, the longer was the preadmission interval, since the number of applications increased. Prompt readmission upon relapse was considered essential for maintaining the addict in treatment. Thus, aftercare patients competed with new applicants for beds. Choosing between providing token service to all comers or effective service to a limited group became inevitable. A definitive solution obviously must await the establishment of an adequate number of facilities offering a full range of care.

Detoxification dropouts At first glance, the least motivated and therefore prognostically most unfavorable group of addicts would seem most likely to drop out at this point; dropouts here, of course, include: (a) those who admit themselves simply to "free load" for a few days until the decreasing dosages of Methadone fail to provide the desired effect; (b) patients transiently motivated but frightened at the prospect of any further restriction of their psychological life line; and (c) those unable to tolerate the structure that ward routine imposes on their habitually anarchic life pattern.

Closer inspection has indicated yet another determinant that at this point forces patients with more favorable prognosis to drop out. This has to do with the tenuousness of the detoxified addict's hold on abstinence, which is discussed further on, since it led to a reorganization of our two wards in the second treatment phase.

Dropouts after discharge from the hospital and during aftercare Factors responsible for failure of engagement at this point can be grouped into two categories: deficiencies in approach prior to discharge, or predisposing factors and inadequacies in the treatment process itself subsequent to the point of discharge.

The first of these categories involves the actual intensity of contact between the ward patient and the therapist who would be following him in aftercare. Although provision had been made during his ward stay for each patient to be seen twice a week by his assigned therapist, in practice this was seldom carried out.

One problem area was the quality of patient-therapist interaction. The findings of Hollingshead and Redlich, (2) as well as others, have called attention to social-class determinants in therapist-patient transactions. The therapists in this program derived primarily from middle-class backgrounds and had been schooled in a technique that is essentially middle-class oriented. Patients were in the main from socially and economically deprived backgrounds, in two-thirds of the cases from Spanish-speaking or Negro subcultures whose values and projection systems were unfamiliar to the therapists. Serious communication and countertransference problems were inevitable. Little in the background or training of most of the staff equipped them to comprehend the realities of life in a socially deprived, urban community.

That interactional problems were present was apparent from the

oft-observed behavioral transformation of addict patients as they moved from an informal group setting on the ward into the one-to-one psychotherapeutic interview situation. Their spontaneity and animated conversation in the group of fellow users gave way to guardedness, reticence, and defensiveness in the one-to-one doctor-patient relationship. It was as if the addict found within the peer group a kind of acceptance and understanding he could not hope to find outside of it.

It is well known that drug addicts have been notoriously resistant to treatment by conventional psychotherapeutic methods. In addition, their way of life in the addict subculture differs markedly from that of the vast numbers of people around them who get up in the morning, go to work, come home, have meals at fairly regular hours and go to sleep for eight hours each night. This more or less universal pattern of living is characterized—even shaped—by a conformity to the exigencies of time, but for the addict time may have either no meaning or a totally different meaning. Consequently, an expectation that a two o'clock appointment in the clinic will find the addict waiting for his therapist may be naive. In addition to the fact that the addict's sense of time may be structured by the reality of his living from one shot of heroin to the next, there is reason to believe that he derives satisfaction from his difference from the world of "squares" around him. In contrast to the nonaddicted psychotic or neurotic individual who feels isolated and alienated from people and who yearns to be understood and accepted, the addict feels a kinship with fellow addicts and looks upon nonaddicts—therapists included—as uncomprehending or incomprehensible.

Differing expectations of each other on the part of addicts and therapists were identified as further contributors to tensions. The therapist expected his addicted patient to see his habit as ego alien, to be motivated for cure, to discuss his feelings about relationships, to achieve insight and movement. The patient, on the other hand, simply expected the therapist to understand how much he needed his drug, how painful and impossible it was to be weaned and how little anything else mattered. It was as though the doctor said, "If you come to my office, you must feel sick and wish me to use my skills to cure you," to which the patient invariably responded, "No, doc, I just came in here to get out of the rain."

A further knotty problem lay in the disparity between the reality principle implicit in the long-range goals of reconstructive psychotherapy and the addict's tendency to operate exclusively according to a pleasure principle, unable to endure temporary frustrations in the pursuit of more meaningful, long-range goals. Thus, when an addict asked his therapist, "What sould I write to my girl to keep her from leaving me?" the therapist would invite the patient to inquire into the history of his feelings about women, so that at some time in the future he could work out the answer for himself. In contrast, some of the nurses, volunteers and recreation workers, to whom the addicts often seemed to relate more meaningfully, were inclined to tell him specifically what to write to cope successfully with his immediate situation. For an analytically trained psychiatrist to respond in such a fashion would mean a difficult break

with his training and mental set. There is ample clinical evidence, however, to suggest that, with the addict, present needs must be directly gratified rather than deflected or analyzed, if an initial engagement is to occur. Most therapists are able to make the necessary adaptation in technique. However, many do not long remain motivated to work with patients on this presumably more superficial level.

If we held to the thesis that the major battle must be fought in proximity to the addict's actual life problems, then the primary tasks were clearly to engage him in his own treatment (a necessity with any psychiatric patient) and to build a bridge to the aftercare program. The factors enumerated above seemed clearly destructive of such efforts. In an attempt to obviate some of them, procedures were revised in the Fall of 1961.

The Second Treatment Phase

The staff was divided into four treatment teams, each led by a psychiatrist devoting a minimum of 20 hours a week to the program. The team leaders took personal responsibility for the recruitment and screening of new patients. Further, at least four times a week each team leader was to see each ward patient admitted by him to one of his 12 team beds. There on the ward, on the basis of their observations as well as those of other team personnel, team leaders would then refer appropriate patients for vocational counseling, social casework with family members, psychological testing and individual psychotherapy. To capitalize on the greater spontaneity of the addict within groups of fellow users, the team leader was to see his ward patients in groups of six at least four times per week for 45-minute group therapy sessions. It was hoped that the patients, through mutual reinforcement in the group therapy sessions, would neutralize the therapist's need to structure the situation along traditional lines.

To facilitate the team leaders' fuller appreciation of the realities of life in East Harlem, each leader spent two hours a week at a family neighborhood medical clinic, sometimes accompanying a youth worker into the streets where addicts abounded on every block, and seeing them as patients when they presented themselves at the neighborhood clinic. The co-operation and counsel of a leading clergyman who had been deeply involved in a neighborhood-based program for narcotic addicts over a ten-year period was sought and obtained. He began to send a single patient, known to him and his co-workers over an extended period of time, to each team leader during the leader's two-hour neighborhood clinic session, for screening and admission to the hospital on the following day. A full interagency sharing of information was inaugurated so that the follow-up potentialities of both staffs could complement each other. In addition, the staffs of both agencies together attended both professional meetings and meetings with groups of addicts. Admission

within 24 hours was offered to patients seen in the neighborhood clinic, utilizing the agency's knowledge of the life history and family history of the patients to facilitate screening. This was intended to decrease preadmission dropout for this group.

Another major change in the operation during this second phase grew out of increasing awareness of the tenuousness of the former addict's hold on abstinence, as mentioned above. In the hospital social club, it was observed that individuals who are using drugs present the severest kind of challenge to those actively fighting resumption of drug use. On the wards, many sign-outs seemed to be precipitated by restlessness engendered in the detoxified addict by patients still receiving Methadone. The addict who was off drugs was often pulled down by those not so far advanced in treatment. Accordingly, during the second phase, the two wards were changed from a parallel operation to that of a series, to avoid the stress upon detoxified patients of mingling with those still receiving Methadone. Thus, an admission ward was set up where detoxification would take place. After a two-week period of detoxification, the patient would be sent to an advanced ward where rehabilitation would begin.

It was at this point that the first opportunity arose to study and work with the addict who was not only off drugs himself, but also functioning in a drugfree environment. Since the structure and purpose of the advanced ward made clear that the addict would be unable to wrest more Methadone from the staff, an important contaminant of motivation was eliminated. The addict's willingness to stay in the hospital could no longer be attributed to the hope that, through dramatization of withdrawal symptoms or an assortment of power maneuvers, he could obtain more Methadone.

As the medication-seeking activity that had previously dominated the ward behavior of addicts on the mixed wards subsided, group-therapy sessions also became relatively free and patients began to focus on underlying feelings and problems.

The stated aims of the two-week stay on the advanced ward required for discharge with medical consent were:

1. To restore normal sleep patterns;

2. To provide sanctuary from the temptations of the streets during the difficult period imediately following detoxification;

3. To devise an aftercare treatment plan appropriate to the needs of each individual, including social-work intervention in the family situation prior to discharge, vocational counseling and placement, and pairing patients with individual psychotherapists if the team judged the patient could utilize individual psychotherapy profitably.

While the continuity of contact with the team leader and other team personnel, as well as with peers who had been coparticipants in group therapy sessions on the detoxification ward, seemed to sustain some patients through the ward transfer and the two-week stay, for a goodly number the *raison d'être* of further hospitalization clearly disappeared with their last Methadone shot. An intermediate group emerged that

seemed sincerely motivated toward rehabilitation, but lacked the necessary strength to stay away from the streets and the possibility of prompt resumption of drug use for the required two weeks. In this group, it was striking to observe how the sudden decision of one addict to sign out would weaken the resolve of others, so that at times premature discharges reached epidemic proportions. Accordingly, in an effort to deter sign-outs, it was made known that readmission priority would be denied to those leaving against medical advice. While there was little reason to have faith in the addict's ability to think this far ahead, there was a hope that the threatened loss of hospital contact would make some think twice about signing out.

During the five-month period of the second treatment phase, the average ward stay increased from 17 to 20 days. There has been a small but perceptible improvement in aftercare attendance. That part of a total therapeutic program for drug addicts that is provided appears to be operating more effectively. The range of aftercare services is not yet sufficient to motivate the majority of addicts to continue treatment at the termination of their hospitalization.

Discussion

The immensity of the task of treating the narcotic addict has been driven home time and time again during the past two years' experience. One is dealing here with a serious social deviation having numerous obstacles that prevent the addict from resuming (or assuming for the first time) a productive and useful life. The difficulties in treating an addict can be well illustrated by the following study of the 24 hours in the life of an addict following his discharge from Metropolitan Hospital. These observations were made by one of the research team members, who for the past several months has been living this first 24-hour period with selected patients, including eating and sleeping with them.

The patient was signed out at 10:30 A.M., but remained on the ward because he felt he might as well have lunch there. After lunch he got involved in a ping pong game and did not arrive on the street in front of the hospital until 4:30 P.M. At this point he seemed totally adrift; the researcher asked what he planned to do. The patient replied, "I don't know." The researcher asked him, "Why not go home?" The patient replied, "I guess I might as well."

They arrived at his home in East Harlem where his mother kissed him and his father shook his hand. After dinner at home, the researcher asked the patient what he planned to do that evening. "Maybe go to a movie," was the reply. After sitting through a grade C film, they returned home and went to bed. The patient stated that he would need pills to sleep. "How do you know you need them?" "I just know it." "Wouldn't it be just as helpful to you if I gave you a rap in the mouth and put you out? Please try to sleep without the

pills." Within five minutes the patient was snoring, although the field worker was awake most of the night. The next morning the patient, complaining that he hadn't slept, said he would have to get some pills for the night. They watched TV together and took a walk.

His first aftercare psychotherapy appointment was three days hence. The total picture is many respects seemed analogous to discharging an individual onto Yucca Flats with the understanding that a 45-minute appointment later would tide him over.

The aimlessness and lack of meaningful external attachments reflected in this thumbnail sketch seem to be characteristic of the addict although, to be sure, there are many variations in their manifest expression. Against such a background, the folly of assuming that the provision of detoxification beds and aftercare psychotherapy constitute a meaningful treatment program becomes starkly apparent.

Obviously the social rehabilitation of the narcotic addict must take place in the community. The ideal locus for such an effort would be a day-night hospital—a facility where the dischargees could spend their days or, alternatively, their nights. Thus, those with jobs or living with their families would have an island of security during the day or the night. A full range of services would be provided, including a street-work staff reaching out into the neighborhood and the precinct home, psychotherapy, drug therapy, vocational counseling, educational rehabilitation, selected vocational placement, sheltered workshop, family counseling and recreational therapy. It is this kind of broad effort that seems necessary for attacking the problem.

At the Metropolitan Hospital the start of a third treatment phase has begun with the establishment of a small day hospital as part of the aftercare program. It will be through such facilities that new methods and ideas will be brought to bear on the treatment of the narcotic addict.

The preceding description of the changing nature of this treatment effort make it clear that the response of the program to the addict is considered as important as the response of the addict to the program. Further, the simultaneous development of criteria for the judgment of response is essential since there is reason to believe that the normally accepted criteria for cure of a disease may not apply to drug addiction. For example, the notion that all dropouts are necessarily failures is only presumably true. Some addicts may have periods of abstinence—equivalent to remission in other chronic diseases—that they achieve without medical help. Many will succeed in overcoming their addiction when they grow older, in their thirties or forties, for reasons unknown to us. This is one more illustration of the lack of knowledge that characterizes the entire field of addiction, from etiology to therapy and prevention.

The full range of services that have been identified as helpful in the treatment of other social deviations will not easily apply to the problem of the narcotic addict. The failure of efforts to prevent the continued recruitment of large numbers of people into the ranks of the addicts, and the failure of hospital patient-care programs to extend their services deeply enough into the community to provide meaningful after-

care and rehabilitative experiences for addicts are the two fundamental deficiencies. The lack of community-based aftercare programs necessary for the development of a direct continuum of patient-care services does not involve the choice of a physical site for such implementation alone, but rather includes this as merely one phase in attempting to reach a more complex objective, which is to prevent the spread of addiction as a public health problem. In a previous paper (1) we have suggested some practical steps in a preventive program with adolescents. In keeping with this goal of prevention, the clinical treatment process we have described will be supplemented by, and closely interwoven with, an ongoing research program aimed at discovering how a range of patient-care services can be established that will bridge the gaps between hospital-based care and neighborhood-based care.

Among the problems that will be studied for their relevance to this end are: an assessment of the effects on the treatment process of the addict's alternation between the roles of "patient" and "criminal"; identifying those social and cultural elements in the East Harlem community that tend to support and those that tend to undermine the patient-care process; examining the types of motivations of patients for hospitalization for their relevance to admission and treatment procedures; examining the divergent expectations and values of patients, professional staff and nonprofessional staff as they affect the treatment process; investigating the effect of treatment failure, as presently understood, on hospital personnel and on patients; formulating realistic goals of treatment for the purpose of modification of present methods; and, finally, developing a methodology for the continuous collection and evaluation of data relevant to the goals of the program.

The methods to be used in the pursuit of this research will include: participant observation by research workers of addicts and dischargees both on the street and in neighborhood agencies, as well as patients on the wards; formal interviews with patients, ex-patients and family members; group discussions with patients on the wards and with addicts and dischargees in neighborhood agencies; and examination of the records of other social and health agencies, public and private, as well as of the City and State Departments of Correction.

It must be emphasized again and again that, because of the multiplicity of factors involved in the genesis of narcotic addiction and the small percentage of therapeutic success following present treatment efforts, a complex model of investigation is necessary. Furthermore, research should be done simultaneously on two levels—basic research and action research. There are areas in which new clues may emerge— the investigation of metabolic factors involved in addiction, for example—and those of us involved in programs of treatment and prevention must be prepared to be constantly evaluating and using new knowledge to modify ongoing programs. Experimentation and new methods of treatment should be attempted at various centers with common methods of evaluation that permit comparison of results. Only then can there be the application of the traditional, scientific processes

of investigation appropriate to the study of disease. Progress will require the collaborative effort of physicians, behavioral scientists, social workers, law enforcement agencies, sociologists, lawyers, judges, legislators and executives of governmental departments, but a genuinely creative and experimental approach may go far toward conquering the disease of narcotic addiction.

References

1. Freedman, A. M. 1962. Adolescent narcotic addiction. Am. Recreat. J. 2(4): 16–19.

2. Hollingshead, A. B. and F. K. Redlich. 1958. Social Class and Mental Illness. John Wiley and Sons, Inc. New York, N.Y.

3. Nyswander, M. 1956. The Drug Addict as a Patient. Grune & Stratton, Inc. New York, N.Y.

RIESSMAN + others, eds
Mental health of the poor